TABLES OF WEIGHTS AND MEASURES

METRIC UNITS	ENGLISH UNITS

LENGTH

10 millimeters (mm) = 1 centimeter (cm)	12 inches (in) = 1 foot (ft)
100 centimeters (cm) = 1 meter (m)	3 feet (ft) = 1 yard (yd)
1,000 millimeters (mm) = 1 meter (m)	1,760 yards (yd) = 1 mile (mi)
1,000 meters (m) = 1 kilometer (km)	5,280 feet (ft) = 1 mile (mi)

LIQUID VOLUME

1,000 milliliters (ml) = 1 liter (l)	16 ounces (oz) = 1 pint (pt)
1,000 liters (l) = 1 kiloliter (kl)	2 pints (pt) = 1 quart (qt)
	4 quarts (qt) = 1 gallon (gal)
	128 ounces (oz) = 1 gallon (gal)
	8 pints (pt) = 1 gallon (gal)

DRY VOLUME

1,000 cubic millimeters (mm³) = 1 cubic centimeter (cm³)	1,728 cubic inches (cu in) = 1 cubic foot (cu ft)
1,000,000 cubic centimeters (cm³) = 1 cubic meter (m³)	27 cubic feet (cu ft) = 1 cubic yard (cu yd)
	46,656 cubic inches (cu in) = 1 cubic yard (cu yd)

WEIGHT

1,000 milligrams (mg) = 1 gram (g)	16 ounces (oz) = 1 pound (lb)
1,000 grams (g) = 1 kilogram (kg)	2,000 pounds (lb) = 1 ton
1,000 kilograms (kg) = 1 metric ton	

METRIC PREFIX MEANINGS

kilo- = one thousand

deci- = one tenth

centi- = one hundredth

milli- = one thousandth

micro- = one millionth

SCIENCE *for the* ELEMENTARY SCHOOL

EDWARD VICTOR

Professor Emeritus, Northwestern University
Adjunct Professor, Arizona State University

SCIENCE

for the

ELEMENTARY SCHOOL

fourth edition

MACMILLAN PUBLISHING CO., INC.

New York

COLLIER MACMILLAN PUBLISHERS

London

To my wife Jeannette

MACMILLAN PUBLISHING CO., INC.
866 Third Avenue, New York, New York 10022

COLLIER-MACMILLAN CANADA, LTD.

Library of Congress Cataloging in Publication Data

Victor, Edward (date)
   Science for the elementary school.

   Includes bibliographies and index.
   1. Science—Study and teaching (Elementary)   I.   Title.
LB1585.V46   1980   372.3′5   78-24462
ISBN 0-02-422900-8

Printing: 1 2 3 4 5 6 7 8   Year: 8 9 0 1 2 3 4

PREFACE

This book continues to serve two purposes. First, it gives direction to both prospective and experienced teachers on how to organize and conduct successful science learning experiences in the elementary school. Second, it provides teachers who have an inadequate science background with (1) detailed outlines of science concepts for each area of science, and (2) appropriate science learning activities to teach the concepts in the outlines.

This revision retains the original format of two parts. Part One considers all the pertinent aspects of teaching and learning elementary school science. Part Two contains science content outlines, learning activities, and bibliography for use in the classroom.

Feedback from those who used the previous edition reveals that making the learning activities more behaviorally and process oriented has been helpful. Including illustrations of commonly used laboratory equipment in the appendix has been useful to teachers unfamiliar with such equipment. Finally, stating all the measurements in metric units, with the equivalent English units included in parentheses, has also been welcome. Putting tables of metric and English weights, measures, and equivalents in the front and back endpages has been convenient.

Several key changes have been made in Part One. First, an entire chapter is now devoted to the theories of Piaget, Bruner, and Gagné on child development and learning, including their implications for what should be taught in elementary science, how it should be taught, and the sequence in which it should be taught. The section on children's characteristics is also included here. This new chapter is now Chapter 2 in the present edition. The contents of former Chapter 2 have been moved to Chapter 1, now titled "Objectives of Elementary Science."

Second, the chapter on methods of teaching science now includes a new section on teaching science through inquiry and on discovery learning. The impact of this highly effective teaching strategy on other methods of teaching science is discussed throughout the chapter.

[v

Third, in Chapter 6A the Friction unit has been rewritten in the form of the current popular discovery unit with its single sequential column worksheets. The new unit lists (1) content objectives, and (2) process and behavioral objectives. The single sequential column consists of a series of investigations that contain directions on how to conduct the investigations, appropriate questions or problems to be raised, and the anticipated answers or results. Thus, Chapter 6A now has three different sample units: a teaching unit with multicolumn worksheets, a discovery unit with single sequential column worksheets, and a resource unit.

Fourth, descriptions of the large-scale elementary science curriculum programs and their materials have been updated. References to programs that are now extinct have been replaced with descriptions of newer ones that have appeared.

Part Two contains one major revision and many smaller ones. The major change involves the chapters on plants and animals. In earlier editions Chapter 13 included both plants and protists. However, in keeping with the latest thinking in the classification of the protists, it has become necessary at this time to divide Chapter 13 into two separate chapters: Chapter 13A and Chapter 13B. Chapter 13A is now concerned only with seed plants and seedless plants. Chapter 13B is devoted to protists, together with a new section on viruses and their appropriate learning activities and bibliography. The section on protozoans, formerly included in Chapter 14, has been relocated to Chapter 13B under the section on protists, where the protozoans rightfully belong.

Finally, in Part One the reference lists for obtaining science equipment, materials, and printed matter have been updated and expanded. In Part Two, out of date and obsolete publications in the bibliographies at the end of the chapters have been replaced by more recent publications.

Again, as has been done in previous editions, some learning activities in Part Two have been replaced by more appropriate ones. Others have been revised or reworded, wherever necessary.

E. V.

CONTENTS

PART ONE

Teaching Science *in the* Elementary School

PART TWO

Basic Science Information, Learning Activities, *and* Bibliography

EARTH AND THE UNIVERSE

LIVING THINGS

PART ONE

TEACHING SCIENCE

in the

ELEMENTARY SCHOOL

CHAPTER 1

OBJECTIVES *of* ELEMENTARY SCIENCE

TODAY an unprecedented amount of attention is being paid to elementary science. School communities have begun to think in terms of an overall K–12 science sequence, with the provision for a continuous and integrated science program from kindergarten through grade 6. As a result, committee meetings and workshops are being held everywhere, either to reorganize existing elementary science programs or to develop new ones. A number of elementary science curriculum projects have been developed by nationwide or regional groups. The exercises, units, and materials produced by these groups are now being used in many elementary schools throughout the country.

There is a trend among state departments of education to increase the science prerequisites for those persons planning to become elementary school teachers. Many teacher-training institutions have already raised the science requirements for their prospective elementary school teachers. The position of elementary science supervisor is becoming prevalent, both in state departments of education and in individual school systems.

More science materials have become available. New elementary science textbooks are appearing and existing series are being revised. A large variety of sourcebooks of experiments has been published, and the number of methods books for the teaching of elementary science has increased. School systems are beginning to make specific provisions for science materials in their elementary school budget.

There are at least three basic causes for this unusual attention to elementary science. First, an unprecedented explosion of science knowledge, beginning early in the twentieth century and continuing at an ever-increasing rate, created a need to examine and reorganize science programs at all school levels. Second, a marked interest in science education had been awakened in scientists, science professors, educators, administrators, teachers, and parents. Consequently, the kind and amount of science being taught and learned in our schools became a matter of concern on city, state, and national levels. Third, at first science curriculum projects were developed to reform high school and junior high school science. Upon the completion or near completion of these projects, it was logical that attention now be turned toward elementary school science.

History of Science in the Elementary School

SCIENCE was the last of the major subject areas to be included in the elementary school curriculum. Until 1875 practically no science was taught in the elementary school, the emphasis being upon reading, writing, spelling, and arithmetic. Shortly thereafter, *nature study* was introduced in a few scattered schools. Its purpose was to get the children to know their environment by observing everyday things around them. The emphasis was on getting the information about our environment from firsthand observations rather than from books. This idea became increasingly popular, and the nature study movement began to grow. By the end of the nineteenth century a large number of elementary schools in several states included nature study in their curriculum.

However, almost from the beginning this movement encountered obstacles and criticism that increased rather than decreased with time. At its start, nature study was introduced by people who were both specialists in science and master teachers. They were able to make the study of nature a dynamic and unforgettable learning experience for the children. However, once entrusted to teachers with little or no background in science and with varying degrees of teaching effectiveness, the study of nature in the elementary schools deteriorated badly.

Undue emphasis was placed upon incidental items. Identification and classification assumed increasing importance and eventually became the end, rather than the means to an end. Learning activities involving firsthand observation gave way to reading about nature in books, where much of the science content was often only partially correct, and where fable and fancy were usually interspersed with the science.

By 1920 it was obvious that nature study was not successful. Its popularity waned steadily and the movement died out. Yet, despite its faults, the nature study movement did make one important contribution. It directed attention to the need for teaching science in the elementary school.

In 1932 a landmark for elementary science education appeared. The National Society for the Study of Education (NSSE) published its Thirty-first Yearbook, dealing exclusively with the teaching of science in our schools. The yearbook recommended a continuous science program from kindergarten through the twelfth grade. It also proposed that the objectives of science teaching were to develop an understanding of (1) the major generalizations of science and (2) associated scientific attitudes.

In 1947 the NSSE devoted its Forty-sixth Yearbook again to the problems of science education. The yearbook recognized the impact that science was obviously having on society and reaffirmed its recommendations for a continuous K–12 science program in our schools. It stressed that the learning outcomes in science education be **functional,** and it proposed the following objectives for science education: (1) the functional understanding of facts, principles, and concepts; and (2) the development of functional scientific skills, attitudes, appreciations and interests.

The Third NSSE yearbook on science education (the Fifty-ninth Yearbook, published in 1960) expressed its awareness of the increasing dependence of society on science. It now took for granted that our schools would have a continuous K–12 science program. It repeated the objectives stated in the Forty-sixth Yearbook, but deleted the word "functional" from the statement. However, it added "problem-solving" and "critical thinking" to its list of objectives, and it stressed the importance of teaching science as a process of inquiry.

Meanwhile, in the mid 1950's the United States became concerned about its serious shortage of scientific manpower and its race with the rest of the world for technological supremacy. This concern was intensified late in 1957 when Russia sent its first satellite, Sputnik, into orbit. Sponsored largely by government agencies and by private foundations, a large number of programs were initiated for the purpose of improving the teaching and learning of science in our schools.

At first projects were developed that were designed to upgrade science education in the high school. The first high school science curriculum project was the Physical Science Study Committee Course (PSSC). This was followed by the Chemical Bond Approach Project (CBA), the Chemical Education Material Study (CHEM Study), the Biological Sciences Curriculum Study (BSCS), the Earth Science Curriculum Project (ESCP), the Harvard Project Physics (HPP), and the Engineering Concepts Curriculum Project (ECCP).

Meanwhile, projects were created for improving junior high school science. Three well-known junior high school science curriculum projects were the Introductory Physical Science Program (IPS) conducted by the Education Development Center at Newton, Massachusetts, the Secondary School Science Project (SSSP) conducted at Princeton University, and the Intermediate Science Curriculum Study (ISCS) conducted at Florida State University at Tallahassee.

Finally, attention was focused on elementary science, and a number of curriculum projects were developed. Some of the more well-known projects were the AAAS Commission on Science Education *Science—A Process Approach* (SAPA) conducted by the American Association for the Advancement of Science, the Elementary Science Study (ESS) conducted by the Education Development Center, the Science Curriculum

(William Means/Van Cleve)

Children should develop into scientifically literate citizens.

Improvement Study (SCIS) conducted at the University of California at Berkeley, the Minnesota Mathematics and Science Teaching Project (MINNEMAST) conducted at the University of Minnesota, the Elementary School Science Project (ESSP) conducted at the University of Illinois, and the Conceptually Oriented Program in Elementary Science (COPES) conducted at New York University. Because of all this activity, we have ushered in a new era in science education.

The Broad Goals for Elementary School Science

THE RECOMMENDATION of a continuous K–12 science sequence in our schools has met with wide acceptance. An ever-increasing number of elementary schools are either developing new science programs, reorganizing existing ones, or adopting programs of the elementary science curriculum projects. It is imperative, then, that all those concerned with such programs understand clearly the role of science in the elementary school. To fulfill this role there should be at least six broad goals for the elementary science program.

HELP OUR CHILDREN BECOME SCIENTIFICALLY LITERATE CITIZENS

The goal of all science education is to develop scientifically literate and personally concerned citizens who are able to think and act rationally. The elementary science program should play an important role in getting our children off to a good start in achieving this goal.

When the child develops into a scientifically literate person, he will have an understanding of the concepts, conceptual schemes, skills, attitudes, and values of science, and he will use all of them in making daily decisions as he interacts with other persons and with his environment. He will know the social implications of science and he will recognize the role that rational thinking can play in making value judgments and in solving social problems. He will learn how to learn, how to inquire, how to acquire knowledge, and how to attack new problems. He will continue to inquire and to increase his knowledge throughout his life, and he will utilize all he has learned to promote the development of man as a rational human being.

HELP OUR CHILDREN LEARN TO SOLVE PROBLEMS BY THINKING CRITICALLY AND CREATIVELY

Children are natural problem raisers and problem solvers. The elementary science program should help children learn the techniques and skills that scientists use to solve their problems. When children use these techniques and skills to solve problems in the classroom, they develop the ability to think more abstractly, more critically, and more creatively. However, the methods of problem solving should never be presented to the children so rigidly that the children are discouraged from trying to do things their own way. Children can and do learn from their own mistakes, and they sometimes even devise surprisingly interesting and satisfactory solutions.

A good science program will take advantage of the fact that children have inquiring minds, and it will encourage them to look for the cause and effect of things that are happening to them. It will raise problems that will encourage real learning, not rote memorization, to take place. It will also whet, not dull, the children's natural curiosity and enthusiasm. Each time a child uses a scientific approach to try to solve a problem that confronts him, that child has taken one step further toward becoming a scientifically literate citizen.

HELP OUR CHILDREN UNDERSTAND THEIR ENVIRONMENT AND THE PROBLEMS OF CONTROLLING IT

Children are tremendously interested in almost everything about them. They are interested in the same things that interest adults: the sky, the earth, matter and energy, and living things. As a result, the elementary science program should help the children learn science concepts and conceptual schemes that will enable them to understand and interpret their environment. These concepts and conceptual schemes

(George Cassidy/Van Cleve)

Children should understand the need to control our environment.

should be learned, not memorized. Facts should be utilized primarily for building concepts and conceptual schemes.

The program should be organized so that there is opportunity to reinforce the children's understanding of the concepts and their relationships. It should help children realize that science knowledge is cumulative and that it is usually necessary to use previous knowledge to acquire further knowledge. In the process the children will become familiar with many historical incidents in science, both experimental and biographical, and thus assimilate some of the historical flavor of science. Finally, while learning about their environment, the children will be developing a science vocabulary that will be useful to them in later years.

Today our environment is faced with a number of complex problems such as air and water pollution, disposal of solid wastes, depletion of resources, and ecological imbalance. It is obvious that science and technology will have to play an important role in solving these problems. The science program, then, must be vitally concerned with getting the children to learn both the nature of our environmental problems and the ways that are available for controlling these problems.

HELP OUR CHILDREN BECOME AWARE OF SOCIAL AND ECONOMIC ASPECTS AND VALUES OF SCIENCE AND TECHNOLOGY

The elementary science program should take into consideration the impact of science and technology on society. Science and technology are interrelated and interdependent, but they are not the same and their goals are different. Science is a process of inquiry whereby man attempts to explain satisfactorily the natural phenomena he observes. Technology, often called applied science, is the translation of science knowledge into the development of new products and processes. Science usually has a long-range effect on mankind and on the course of civilization, whereas technology has an immediate effect on the physical, economic, social, and cultural aspects of man's existence.

The achievements of science and technology often call for social and economic innovations if the achievements are to be utilized advantageously for the benefit of mankind. Consequently, the science program must be extended so that it not only includes the learning of science concepts and skills but also develops an awareness and understanding of the social and economic aspects and implications, the values of science and technology, and the values to be derived from them.

HELP OUR CHILDREN LIVE SUCCESSFULLY IN A CHANGING WORLD

We are living in a world of rapid change. Our science knowledge is changing, and our society is changing. The elementary science program should help children understand that science knowledge is tentative and will change as more evidence accumulates. However, the program

[9

should also play a role in helping children learn to expect and adjust to societal change. It can do this by giving children the science knowledge, skills, and associated values that they will need in later life so that they will react more intelligently and cope more successfully when trying to solve the problems of a rapidly changing society.

Because children feel more comfortable and secure with the known and the familiar, the program should help them understand that change is an inevitable part of their lives. However, it can also show that in science there is often a pattern and rhythm, even a definite periodic order, in change. The seasons, the phases of the moon, the water cycle, the wearing down and building up of the earth's surface are all examples of natural and periodic changes in science.

HELP OUR CHILDREN GROW ACCORDING TO THEIR INDIVIDUAL ABILITIES, INTERESTS, AND NEEDS

The elementary science program should provide for the individual growth of our children. Children vary widely in abilities, interests, and needs. Gifted children are quick to learn, read easily and rapidly, and remember concepts longer and with sharper detail than average children. They have a longer attention span, greater powers of concentration, and are more persistent in working with problems that confront them. They are intellectually curious, capable of a high degree of originality, and have much initiative. They usually grasp key concepts the first time, and they can think more abstractly and critically. They have a strong ability to deduce the science concepts that underlie observations and facts, and they can derive further concepts from these deduced concepts. They are extremely critical of their work and are constantly evaluating it. They have a wide range of interests and are usually versatile in many areas.

On the other hand, slow learners are poor readers, require much time to grasp a concept, and then tend to forget quickly or become hazy about what they have learned. They have a short attention span, cannot concentrate for any length of time, and give up easily when they encounter difficulties in solving problems. They require consistent guidance and encouragement from the teacher; they have little initiative, and would rather carry out than plan directions and instructions. They are slow to grasp abstract ideas and have great difficulty in arriving at key concepts on the basis of observation or reading. They need more concrete, first-hand experiences, with ample opportunity for needed repetition. They are unable to evaluate their work critically and, as a result, have difficulty in correcting their mistakes. They are much more limited in their interests, and often show large differences in capability when participating in various phases of the elementary school curriculum.

The science program can offer a wide range of learning activities for the children, thus making it possible for the school to provide for the varied abilities, interests, and needs that children have. A good science program lends itself well to individual learning, and therefore it is able to help each child grow in science to the utmost of his ability and capacity. This development is especially important for children who display keen interest and competence in science. Challenging experiences can consistently stimulate their interests and sharpen their competencies, thus providing a basic foundation for future continued study in science.

Objectives of Elementary Science

IT IS imperative that the teacher be completely familiar with the objectives of elementary science for real learning to take place. Objectives are vital to the science program. They help justify the selection of science content. They serve as a guide to decide which learning activities will be used and which skills will be developed. They become criteria for developing effective methods of evaluation.

Elementary science objectives are listed in various texts and bulletins. At first glance the lists of objectives may seem to differ slightly, or some lists may appear to be more complete than others. However, on closer scrutiny, all of the lists are found to be in close agreement, and they differ mainly in the way that the objectives are described.

The consensus is that the objectives of elementary science are to help the children (1) learn science concepts and conceptual schemes—the **content** of science, (2) become familiar with the key operations of science and the scientist—the **process** of science, and (3) develop such desirable behavioral outcomes as scientific skills, attitudes, apprecia-

(William Means/Van Cleve)

Help children learn concepts and conceptual schemes.

tions, and interests. Achieving these objectives will help the children grow in scientific literacy. It will help them become proficient in problem solving and in critical and creative thinking. It will also help them understand the differences and relationships between science and technology, and the impact of both these enterprises upon society.

THE CONTENT OF SCIENCE

One of the prime objectives of elementary science is to help the children learn science concepts and conceptual schemes that will help them understand and interpret their environment. Children who develop an adequate science background have a reservoir of reliable knowledge to draw from and use, and it will affect their thinking, their method of work, the conclusions they draw, and their future behavior.

The teacher must carefully select the science content that will be learned in the classroom. Provision should be made to include those concepts and conceptual schemes that have been accepted for a long time and will most likely be accepted for some time to come. New ones should be added as they appear. These concepts and conceptual schemes, then, become the high points around which the teacher's unit and daily lessons, and the children's learning, are organized.

Learning facts is also important because children must have a command of the more important facts in science if they are to acquire a firm understanding of concepts. The science content to be learned in the elementary school, therefore, should include facts as well as major concepts. But the facts should not be learned as isolated items of information. They should be related so that all together they contribute to the development of key concepts. In this way, that is, by making the science content all-inclusive and interrelated, the children will be better able to understand the nature of the universe.

When the children learn science content, they should use an inquiry and discovery approach so that they *learn*, not memorize.

This approach not only leads to real learning, as opposed to memorization, but also lends itself well to open-ended experimentation. In some open-ended experiments there are one or more conditions that may be changed in many ways. In other open-ended experiments the findings of one experiment may produce questions that require another experiment, those findings produce further questions that require still another experiment, and so on. Open-ended experiments involve real scientific investigation. The results are not given in advance by the teacher. The experiment does not necessarily have to arrive at well-known laws and principles. In all cases the experiment should reveal the need for further investigation.

THE PROCESS OF SCIENCE

Learning the key operations of science and the scientist is a vital objective of elementary science. As an objective it has more than one goal. When children learn the process of science, they gain insight and

(Carol Bales/Van Cleve)

Help children learn the process of science.

practice in the different methods that scientists use to solve problems. They also become familiar with effective ways of working, and they acquire experience in thinking critically and creatively. As a result, the children can develop valuable scientific behavioral outcomes.

Today both elementary science textbook series and curriculum projects are concerned with the teaching of science as a process of inquiry and discovery. The units and materials that they produce provide specifically for the learning of a number of key operations of science and the scientist, and for the development of desirable behavioral outcomes. For the first time, perhaps, the learning of the process of science and the development of scientific behaviors have been given the emphasis in elementary science that they have so long and so rightfully deserved.

The following are some of the operations that can be conducted in an elementary science program:

1. Abstracting key concepts from the science content in texts.
2. Analyzing (observations, findings, results, reading, etc.).
3. Applying previous knowledge to explain new situations.
4. Classifying (observations, ideas, findings, results, objects, etc.).
5. Communicating (speaking and writing clearly, etc.).
6. Conducting experiments.
7. Constructing and/or interpreting charts, tables, graphs, etc.
8. Making deductions.
9. Describing (observations, ideas, findings, properties, etc.).
10. Distinguishing between pertinent and irrelevant results.
11. Formulating and understanding operational definitions.
12. Formulating clear and intelligent questions.
13. Formulating hypotheses.
14. Formulating mental models.
15. Making inductions.
16. Making inferences.
17. Interpreting (observations, ideas, findings, reading, etc.).
18. Keeping records.
19. Making comparisons.
20. Manipulating science equipment.
21. Measuring.
22. Noting similarities and differences.
23. Observing.
24. Organizing effective oral or written reports.
25. Organizing and formulating plans to solve problems.
26. Participating in group discussion.
27. Planning or designing experiments.
28. Predicting.
29. Reasoning.
30. Recognizing and using number relations.
31. Recognizing and using space/time relations.
32. Using controls when experimenting.
33. Using numbers of experiments to obtain valid results.
34. Using table of contents, index, and glossary of science texts.
35. Working together in small or large groups.

Scientists constantly use these operations to solve problems. Furthermore, the key operations of science and the scientist can be used to solve problems in other content areas and even in daily life as well. By keeping this objective in mind at all times and by trying to inculcate it into the minds of the children whenever and wherever possible, the teacher is laying the groundwork for the eventual realization by the children that science is more than just a body of knowledge. Science is a process of inquiry that should govern our behavior at all times.

The children should be led to understand that scientists use different methods when solving problems. In addition, although there is a general sequence to the various methods, scientists do not always follow this sequence, nor do they necessarily use all of the key operations of science in the sequence. All the different methods employed by scientists, however, do have the same elements in common.

Although science in the elementary school is on a much simpler plane, many of the methods used by scientists can be used by children to solve their problems in the classroom. Of course, the children's problems will be much easier than those of scientists, and their methods of solving problems will be less complicated or rigid. The children may at times use only some of the methods. In all cases, however, the children should be given proper encouragement and guidance in using these scientific methods so that with practice they can become quite proficient in working with and solving problems.

Another reason why problem solving assumes such importance is that it can give children an opportunity to think critically and creatively. In the past, teachers have been too prone to do much of the thinking for the children, especially in science. Yet science is an area that lends itself well to the development of critical and creative thinking, particularly in problem solving.

The children can think critically when making discriminating observations, when organizing and analyzing facts and concepts, when giving reasons for expecting particular outcomes, when evaluating and interpreting the results of experiments, and when drawing justifiable conclusions.

The teacher can also tell whether children are beginning to learn to think critically when they can apply what they have learned to interpret a new situation. For example, when studying different methods of heat travel, the children have learned that conduction is a method of heat travel where the heat energy is passed along from molecule to molecule by collision within a substance. If the children understand this concept, they should be able to think critically and apply what they have learned by answering the following question asked by the teacher: "Why does the part of the spoon that is not submerged in hot water (or cocoa) become hot?"

Again, if the children are learning to think critically, they should be able to predict what will happen when the conditions of a phenomenon in nature are changed. For example, when studying the relationship between the sun and the earth, the children have learned the cause of day and night and of the seasons. If the teacher now asks the children to predict what would happen to the earth if the earth's axis were not tilted at an angle of 23½ degrees, the children will have been thinking critically if they predict that the length of day and night would always be the same, and that different parts of the earth would always have the

[15

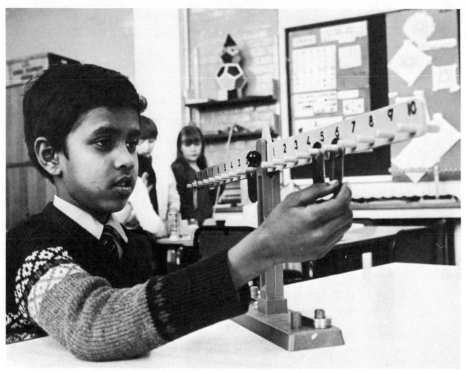

Help children develop desirable behavior.

same season (barring any minor variations caused by the effect of local conditions, of course).

There is also ample opportunity for the teacher to encourage creative thinking in the classroom. The children can formulate hypotheses and propose solutions to problems. They can devise original experiments or equipment to help solve problems. They can suggest reasons why experiments fail to work, then think of ways to test the validity of these reasons. It is evident, then, that critical and creative thinking can be an important adjunct when children are involved in solving problems.

BEHAVIORAL OUTCOMES

Some extremely valuable behavioral outcomes can be developed when children learn the product and process of science. These outcomes usually emerge from the learning activities and may be immediate or long-range. They include scientific skills, attitudes, appreciations and interests.

Skills • Scientific skills are developed when the children perform the key operations of science, and they are usually called process skills. An examination of the operations listed earlier will indicate the kinds of process skills that can be developed.

Skills are usually classified under two domains: the cognitive and the psychomotor domains. The cognitive domain includes problem-solving and critical-thinking skills. The psychomotor domain includes both motor and manipulative skills.

Attitudes • Scientific attitudes evolve most often when the children are learning the process of science. They have to do with behavior patterns and with mind sets. Some attitudes are intellectual by nature and are developed as a result of knowledge or understanding. Others are emotional and are based upon appreciations. The following are examples of both kinds of scientific attitudes:

1. Curiosity.
2. Going to reliable sources for evidence.
3. Open-mindedness.
4. Persistence.
5. Reluctance to let decisions be affected by personal emotions.
6. Reluctance to generalize on the basis of limited evidence.
7. Respect or tolerance for the ideas and opinions of others.
8. Suspended judgment until all available evidence is in.
9. Unwillingness to accept statements without sufficient proof.
10. Unwillingness to believe in superstitions.
11. Unwillingness to compromise with the truth.
12. Willingness to allow others to question one's ideas.
13. Willingness to change one's mind in the light of new evidence.
14. Willingness to cooperate when engaged in group activities.

Appreciations • Appreciations are often defined as satisfying emotional responses. They must have as a base some background in science. For example, children must first know some content and process of science before they can appreciate the part that science can play in our daily life. Appropriate appreciations should evolve while the children are engaged in a variety of learning activities. The following are examples of worthwhile science appreciations:

1. The role science plays in our daily lives.
2. The many ways that science can be used to explain the environment around us.
3. The impact of science and technology on our civilization.
4. The influence of science upon man's way of thinking, his relations with others, his religion, and his social responsibility.
5. The role that problem solving and critical and creative thinking can play in our personal habits, attitudes, and relationships.
6. The understanding that science is the result of human endeavor and flourishes best when there is intellectual freedom.
7. The constant striving of scientists to know more about the world.
8. The contributions of scientists to the world we live in.
9. The tools and techniques of science.

[17

10. The orderliness of nature and of natural laws.
11. The ever-changing nature of science.
12. The beauty in nature.

Interests • Interests may or may not have as a base some background in science. Interests are also based on positive emotions, which the teacher can try to evoke at the suitable occasion. There are two main kinds of science interests that can be developed. One kind of interest has to do with science as a vocation. An interest in science in the elementary school can often be a contributing factor in a young person's eventual decision to choose a vocation in the pure or applied sciences. The other kind of interest has to do with avocations. Science is a field that is rife with opportunities to interest young people in hobbies that many will pursue even in later life. Such hobbies include active interest and participation in astronomy, photography, and horticulture. Many persons become interested in tropical and other kinds of fish. Others collect rocks and minerals, seashells, and butterflies or other insects. These hobbies are often started while the children are learning science in the elementary school.

For Discussion

1. If you had to choose two of the six broad goals for the elementary science program as the most important, which two would you choose, and why?

2. What pollution problems could you take up in class in the area where you plan to teach or are now teaching?

3. What achievements of science and technology can you think of that have affected the social, economic, or cultural aspects of man's existence?

4. Which do you think is the more important objective: content or process? Why? Should one be taught without the other? Why?

5. What observable behaviors can you think of that would enable you to know whether a child was learning how to solve problems? to think critically? to think creatively?

6. What other skills, attitudes, appreciations, and interests can you suggest that might be desirable behavioral outcomes of elementary science?

(Barbara Van Cleve)

CHAPTER 2

LEARNING *and* CHILD DEVELOPMENT

AN UNDERSTANDING of how children develop intellectually, and also how children learn, is essential to teaching science effectively in the classroom. For guidance in this aspect, science educators have turned to the research and theories of developmental psychologists. Improvements and innovations in elementary science education often follow new discoveries of theories of learning in the field of child development.

Most theories of learning fall into two distinct categories, called behaviorist and cognitive theories. Behaviorist psychologists believe that learning consists of making strong connections (or forming strong links) between events called stimuli and appropriate behaviors called responses. This is why they are usually referred to as S–R (Stimulus-Response) psychologists. According to these psychologists the task of teaching is to establish strong connections, or associations, between stimuli and the appropriate response reactions of the learner. Thus, when children are presented with a series of questions (stimuli) and supply answers (responses), the correct answers should be reinforced because responses that are reinforced will be strengthened and are most likely to be retained.

Cognitive psychologists are concerned not only with S–R behavior, but also with the mental processes that cause behavior. They believe that learning also occurs through the development of new patterns of thought, called insights. Instead of seeing learning as the formation of connections or associations between stimuli and responses, these psychologists view learning as either the gaining of new insights or the changing of previous ideas and perceptions to lead to new insights. The task of teaching is to provide situations that encourage insight so that the children can discover ideas on their own.

There are three cognitive psychologists whose theories have made a tremendous impact on elementary science in recent years. Their theories have broad implications for what should be taught in elementary science, how it should be taught, and the sequence in which it should be taught. These three psychologists are Piaget, Bruner, and Gagné.

JEAN PIAGET

Perhaps no other person has made such a wide-ranging impact on the restructuring of the elementary school science program during the past two decades than the Swiss psychologist Jean Piaget. Although he began to publish his now extensive insights into the maturation and intellectual development of children in the 1920's, his works were not rediscovered by psychologists in the United States until the early 1960's.

Piaget has concentrated on describing the different kinds of internal representation which the child holds during his various stages of growth. Piaget's experiments have been largely of the clinical type, which means that he has worked with only one or a few children at a time, and talked extensively with them. Using careful questioning techniques, he has been able to gain valuable insights into what a child understands from the statements that the child makes. These experiments have encompassed interviews with thousands of children.

Piaget has developed a theory of intellectual development in chil-

dren. According to Piaget, children develop intellectually in a sequence of stages by age from infancy to post-adolescence. Each stage of learning is necessary for the development of the stages that follow. A child cannot skip a stage because each stage not only utilizes and integrates the one before it but also serves to pave the way for the one that follows it. Although the sequence of stages is the same for all children, the rate at which particular children pass through these stages will depend upon both the children's heredity and their socioeconomic environment.

There are three major stages in Piaget's theory of intellectual development: (1) the sensorimotor period, from birth to about two years of age, (2) the concrete operations period, from two to eleven or twelve years, and (3) the formal operations period, from eleven or twelve years on. During the second period, the development of operational (or logical) thought appears. Consequently, this period is usually divided into two major substages: the stage of preoperational (prelogical) thought, from two to seven years, and the stage of concrete logical operations, from seven to eleven or twelve years.

Sensori-Motor Stage (Birth to 2 Years) • In this stage, at first an object exists for the child only when he can see or feel it, and he locates hidden objects by random searching. Later he begins to understand that objects exist even when he cannot see or touch them. For the child there usually is no other time but the present, and no other space than what he now sees. He cannot imagine an act before he carries out the act. Through his senses and motor activities he learns about properties of things, and he begins to develop a practical basic knowledge that forms the foundation for learning in the next stage.

Preoperational Stage (2–7 Years) • This stage is given its name because the child does not yet use logical operations in his thinking. In this stage the child is egocentric, so his view of the world around him is subjective rather than objective. Because he is egocentric, the child is unable to take into account another person's point of view. Also, the child is perceptually oriented; that is, he makes judgments in terms of how things look to him. He does not think logically, and therefore cannot reason by implication. Instead he uses an intuitive approach and makes judgments in terms of how things look to him. He depends upon trial and error to make corrections.

He can observe and describe variables (properties of an object or aspects of a phenomenon), but he concentrates or "centers" on only one variable at a time, usually a variable that stands out visually. He cannot coordinate variables, so he has difficulty in realizing that an object has several properties. Consequently he lacks the ability to combine parts into a whole. He can make simple classifications according to one or two properties, but he finds it hard to realize that multiple classifications are possible. Also, he can arrange objects in simple series, but he has trou-

[21

(H. Armstrong Roberts)

Children develop intellectually in a series of stages.

ble in arranging them in a long series or in inserting a new object in its proper place in a series. To the child space is restricted to his neighborhood, and time is restricted to hours, days, and seasons.

He has not yet developed the concept of conservation. This means he does not understand that a number of objects can be rearranged and that the size or shape or volume of a solid or liquid can be changed, yet the number of objects and the amount of solid or liquid will be unchanged or conserved. For example, if two rows of ten objects are arranged so that they take up the same area, the child will state that the two rows are the same and there are the same number of objects in each row. But if the objects in one row are spread out so that the row is longer, the child is likely to maintain that the longer row now has more objects in it. Similarly, if the child is shown two identical balls of clay, he will agree that both balls contain the same amount of material. When, in full view of the child, one of the balls is stretched out into the shape of a sausage, the child is likely to say that the sausage has more clay because it is larger, or less clay because it is thinner. Either way, the child at this stage is "centering" his attention on just one particular property (here, length or thickness) to the neglect of the other properties.

The reason for the child's thinking in both these examples is that the child does not yet understand reversibility. His thinking can not yet reverse itself back to the point of origin. As a result, the child does not "see" that since nothing has been removed or added, the extended row of objects can be rearranged to its original length and the clay sausage can be made back into the original ball. The child does not yet comprehend that action and thought processes can be reversed.

Concrete Operations Stage (7–11 Years) • In this stage the child can now perform logical operations. He can observe, judge, and evaluate in less egocentric terms than in the preoperational stage, and he can formulate more objective explanations. As a result, he knows how to solve physical problems. Because his thinking is still concrete and not abstract, he is limited to problems dealing with actual concrete experiments. He can not generalize, deal with hypothetical situations, or weigh possibilities.

He is capable of decentration, which means that he no longer "centers" his thinking on just one property or aspect of an object, but can now "center" on two or more at one time. He can now understand multiple relationships and can combine parts into a whole. He acquires good motor skills and can move objects around to make them fit properly.

He can make multiple classifications, and he can arrange objects in long series and place new objects in their proper place in the series. He begins to comprehend geographical space and historical time. He develops the concepts of conservation according to their ease of learning: first, numbers of objects, then matter, length, area, weight, and volume, in that order. He also develops the concept of reversibility and can now reverse the physical and mental processes when numbers of objects are rearranged or when the size and shape of matter are changed.

Formal Operations Stage (11–15 Years) • In this stage the child's method of thinking shifts from the concrete to the more formal and abstract. He can now relate one abstraction to another, and he grows in ability to think conceptually. He can develop hypotheses, deduce all possible consequences from them, then test these hypotheses with controlled experiments in which all the variables are identical except the one to be tested. When approaching a new problem, the child begins by formulating all the possibilities and then determining which ones are substantiated through experimentation and logical analysis. After he has solved the problem, he can now reflect upon or rethink the thought processes he used.

JEROME S. BRUNER

Although it is often stated that Bruner has been a leading interpreter and promoter of Piaget's ideas in the United States, Bruner has made his own significant contributions on how children learn. He also has developed a theory of intellectual development in children. Like Piaget, he maintains that each child passes through stages that are age-related and biologically determined, and that learning will depend primarily on the developmental level that the child has attained.

Bruner's theory also encompasses three major sequential stages, but he calls them representations instead. These three representations are, as follows: *enactive representation, ikonic representation,* and *symbolic representation.* They correspond to the sensorimotor, concrete operations, and formal operations stages of Piaget. Bruner's general description of what happens during his three representations also corresponds to that of Piaget's stages, but he differs from Piaget in his interpretation of the role language plays in intellectual development. Piaget believes that although thought and language are related, they are basically different systems. He theorizes that the child's thinking is based on a system of inner logic that evolves as the child organizes and adapts to experiences. Bruner, however, maintains that thought is internalized language. The child translates experience into language, and then uses language as an instrument of thinking.

Bruner and Piaget differ in their attitude toward the child's readiness for learning. Piaget's experiments led him to conclude that the child's readiness for learning depends upon maturation and intellectual development. Bruner, however, believes that a child is always ready to learn a concept in some form or manner. He states that any subject can be taught effectively in some intellectually honest form to any child at any stage of development. He supports this already famous statement by noting that the basic ideas of science and mathematics are simple, and only when these ideas are formalized in terms of equations and complex verbal statements do they become incomprehensible to the young child.

According to Bruner, when a child learns science concepts, he can learn them only within the framework of whichever stage of intellectual development he is in at the time. In the teaching of science to children, it is essential that the child be helped to pass progressively from one stage of intellectual development to the next. The teacher can do this by providing challenging but usable opportunities and problems for the child that tempt him to forge ahead into the next stages of development.

As a result, the child acquires a deeper understanding of science concepts and conceptual schemes.

Bruner states that the act of learning involves three almost simultaneous processes. The first is the process of acquiring new knowledge. The second is the process of manipulating this knowledge to make it fit new tasks or situations. The third is the process of evaluating the acquisition and manipulation of this knowledge. A major objective of learning is to introduce the child at an early age to the ideas and styles that will make him an educated man. Consequently, the science program should be built around the major conceptual schemes, skills, and values that society considers to be of vital importance. These conceptual schemes, skills, and values should be taught as early as possible in a manner that is consistent with the child's stages of development and forms of thought.

Bruner has been the most articulate spokesman in the United States for **discovery learning,** a term with which all elementary and secondary school science teachers are now familiar. He advocates that, whenever possible, teaching and learning should be conducted in such a manner that children be given the opportunity to discover concepts for themselves. He claims that four major benefits are derived from learning by discovery. First, there is an increase in intellectual potency. Discovery learning helps children learn how to learn. It helps the child learn problem-solving and inquiry skills, enabling him to arrange and apply what he has learned to new situations, and thus learn new concepts. Second,

(William Means/Van Cleve)

Children learn through discovery.

there is a shift from extrinsic to intrinsic rewards. Discovery learning shifts motives for learning away from that of satisfying others to that of internal self-rewarding satisfaction, that is, satisfying oneself. Third, there is an opportunity to learn the working heuristics of discovery. By heuristics Bruner means the methods in which a person is trained to find out things for himself. Only through the exercise of problem solving and by the effort of discovery can the child find out things for himself. The more adept the child becomes in the working heuristics of discovery, the more effective the decisions he will make in problem solving, the decisions leading to a quicker solution than any trial-and-error approach would. Fourth, there is an aid to memory processing. Knowledge resulting from discovery learning is more easily remembered, and it is also more easily recalled when needed.

ROBERT M. GAGNÉ

Gagné is best known among American psychologists for his hierarchy of learning levels. According to Gagné, learning is the establishment of a capability to do something that the learner was not capable of doing previously. Gagné assumes, therefore, that there is a hierarchy of learning capabilities. Learning one particular capability usually depends upon having previously learned one or more simpler capabilities.

For Gagné, observable changes in behavior comprise the only criteria for inferring that learning has occurred. It follows, then, that the beginning, or lowest, level of a learning hierarchy would include very simple behaviors. These behaviors would form the basis for learning more complex behaviors in the next level of the hierarchy. At each higher level, learning would require that the appropriate simpler, or less complex, behaviors have been acquired in the lower learning levels.

Gagné identifies eight levels of learning in his hierarchy. Beginning with the simplest and progressing to the most complex, these levels are as follows:

Signal Learning • The individual learns to make a general conditioned response to a given signal. Examples of signal learning include fright induced by loud noises, pleasure produced by the sight of a favorite toy, and startled movement caused by a loud clap. Normally the response is diffuse, undefined, and emotional in nature.

Stimulus-Response Learning • Here, the individual acquires a precise physical response to a discriminated stimulus. Almost all examples of S–R learning involve voluntary motor behavior, including vocalization. The child's initial learning of words by repeating the sounds and words of adults, and the training of a dog to sit or lie down, are examples of S–R learning.

Chaining • Frequently called *skill learning*, it involves the linking together, or chaining, of two or more units of simple Stimulus-Response learning. Chaining is limited to physical, nonverbal sequences. The important prerequisite for establishing a chain is that each individual S–R link must be formed before the building of the chain. Examples of chaining include winding up a toy, unlocking a door, writing, running, catching, and throwing. All these examples involve a set of sequenced muscular responses. Often the strength of the learned chain depends on the variables usually known to be effective in such learning: practice, previous experience, and reinforcement.

Verbal Association • This is also a form of chaining, but the links are verbal units. Naming an object is the simplest verbal association. In this case the first S–R link is involved in observing the object, and the second S–R link is involved in enabling the child to name the object. A more complex example of verbal chaining would be the rote memorization of a poem, formula, or the letters of the alphabet in sequence. Considered alone, these learned behaviors are not usually seen as important goals of teaching. However, viewed as a level in a hierarchy, they may be important first steps in certain higher levels of learning.

Multiple Discrimination • Here, individual learned chains are linked to form multiple discriminations. Again, the necessary previous chains that are lower in the hierarchy have to be learned first. In this level of learning, the individual learns a number of different responses to as many different stimuli. As a result, the individual is able to identify something that might be confused with other similar things or phenomena. An example of multiple discrimination learning would be the identification of the names of children in a classroom. Here, the learner associates each individual child with his or her distinctive appearance and correct name, and with no other name. Another example of this learning level is making a distinction between solids, liquids, and gases.

Concept Learning • Learning a concept means learning to respond to stimuli in terms of their abstract characteristics (such as position, shape, color, and number), as opposed to concrete physical properties. A child may learn to call a two-inch cube a "block," and also to apply this name to other objects that differ from it somewhat in size and shape. Later, the child learns the concept *cube,* and by so doing is able to identify a class of objects that differ physically in many ways (e.g., by material, color, texture, and size). Many concepts are learned by children in a trial-and-error accidental fashion. The role of the teacher must be to carefully design efficient learning sequences that lead to the concept.

Principle Learning • In simplest terms, a principle is a chain of two or more concepts. In principle learning the individual is required to relate two or more concepts. An example of principle learning is the relation of a circle's circumference to its diameter. Three separate concepts (circumference, pi, and diameter) are linked or chained together.

Problem Solving • In problem solving, the individual applies principles he has learned to achieve a goal. While achieving this goal, however, he becomes capable of new performances by using his new knowledge. When a problem is solved, new knowledge has been acquired, and the individual's capacity moves ahead. The individual is now able to handle a wide class of problems similar to the one solved. What has been learned, according to Gagné, is a higher-order principle, which is the combined product of two or more lower-order principles.

Thus, whenever a child has acquired the capabilities and behaviors of a certain level of learning, we assume he has also acquired the capabilities and behaviors of all the learning levels below this level. Furthermore, if the child were having difficulty in demonstrating the capabilities and behaviors for a certain level, the teacher could simply test the child on the capabilities and behaviors of the lower levels to determine which one or ones were causing the difficulty.

Gagné and Bruner differ greatly in their emphasis upon learning. Gagné emphasizes primarily the product of learning, whereas Bruner's emphasis is on the process of learning. For Gagné the key question, "*What* do you want the child to know?" For Bruner it is, "*How* do you want the child to know?" For Gagné the emphasis is on learning itself, whether it is by discovery, review, or practice. For Bruner the emphasis is on learning by discovery; it is the method of learning that is important.

Gagné emphasizes problem solving as the highest level of learning,

(Wiiliam Means/Van Cleve)

Problem solving is one of the highest learning levels.

with the lower learning levels prerequisite to this highest level. For him, the appropriate sequence in learning (and teaching as well) is from these lower learning levels toward problem solving. The teacher begins with simple ideas, relates all of them, builds on them, and works toward the more complex levels of learning he seeks to attain. On the other hand, Bruner begins with problem solving, which in turn leads to the development of necessary skills. The teacher poses a question to be solved and then uses it as a catalyst to motivate children to develop the necessary prerequisite skills.

Piaget, Bruner, and Gagné differ in their attitude towards the child's readiness for learning. As has been stated earlier, Piaget believes that readiness depends upon the child's maturation and intellectual development. Bruner feels that the child is always ready to learn a concept in some form or manner. Gagné, however, feels that readiness is related to the successful preliminary development of subskills and subconcepts rather than to the child himself.

Like Bruner and Piaget, Gagné believes that elementary science should be taught and learned as a process of inquiry. Giving the child practice in inquiry involves giving him opportunities to carry out inductive thinking, to make hypotheses, and to test these hypotheses in a large variety of situations in the laboratory, in the classroom, and in individual study. However, Gagné claims there are two major prerequisites to successful practice in inquiry. First, the child must have a broad science background that can be applied to the solving of new problems. Second, the child must be able to discriminate between a good idea and a bad one, that is, between a probably successful course of action and a probably unsuccessful one.

Gagné believes that as the child progresses from kindergarten through college, he should go through four levels of science instruction. The first level should be conducted in the elementary school. At this level the child should be given instruction in certain kinds of skills or competencies that will stay with him for the rest of his life. These would include number computation, spatial and manipulative skills, and the skills of observing, describing, classifying, measuring, inferring, and model conceptualizing. While developing these skills, the child will acquire some knowledge of scientific principles.

The second level of science instruction should probably begin in about the sixth or seventh grade. At this level there would be an emphasis upon the student's acquiring a broad background of knowledge in all science areas. At the same time the student would be given an opportunity to engage in activities that use, in as wide a variety of contexts as possible, the skills he has learned at the first level.

The third level of science instruction should probably begin at the eleventh grade. At this level the emphasis would be upon the method of inquiry. Here the student would be able to use both his broad knowledge and his training in skills to form and test hypotheses, to solve problems by using inductive thinking, and to discriminate between good and bad ideas. At the same time the student would continue to acquire more science knowledge, perhaps with a somewhat greater degree of specialization.

If the schools could successfully inaugurate and teach the first three levels of instruction, the fourth level could be achieved at the third year of college instead of the second or third year of graduate school study. At this level the student learns to become an independent scientific investigator, making full use of his broad science background, his competency in science skills, and his thorough familiarity with the method of inquiry.

Implications for Elementary Science

THE THEORIES of Piaget, Bruner, and Gagné are primarily concerned with how children develop intellectually and learn. Consequently, all three theories have important implications for elementary science. These implications can help serve as guidelines in developing a science program. They also help give direction to the teaching and learning of science in the classroom. Although there are some differences in philosophy among the three theories, these differences are not great enough to constitute major contradictions. For the most part, the theories either reinforce or else supplement each other with respect to the implications they have for teaching and learning elementary science. The following are some of the more pertinent implications.

READINESS FOR LEARNING

Although Piaget, Bruner, and Gagné differ in their attitude towards the child's readiness for learning, the implications are both consistent and clear. The child's readiness must keep pace with, and proceed within the framework of, Piaget's and Bruner's stages of intellectual development. Bruner's belief that the child is always ready for a concept in some form or manner carries with it the implication that the teacher must be sure to bring the concept down to the child's level of understanding. Similarly, since Gagné relates readiness to the development of subconcepts and subskills, the teacher must make certain that the child has mastered the necessary subconcepts and subskills before the child can be ready for learning any higher level concepts and skills.

SEQUENCE OF LEARNING ACTIVITIES

Learning activities should be carefully planned so that they take into consideration the level of thinking attained by an individual or a group. Consequently, the concepts to be learned, the problems to be solved, and the skills to be developed should be arranged in a sequence that proceeds from the very simple to the most complex. It is imperative, then, that the teacher should carefully diagnose the proper sequence of complexity of all the concepts, problems, and skills, so that the teacher can then arrange the sequence of learning activities to insure maximum effectiveness of teaching and learning. The teacher must also determine how much the children know, so that he can decide where to begin in the sequence.

The effectiveness of learning activities often depends on how clearly the child understands what he is to do. At the same time, teaching will become more effective when the teacher knows explicitly the concepts and behaviors to be developed from the learning activities. Consequently, the objectives of the learning activities should be stated clearly in terms of desired behavioral outcomes.

DISCOVERY LEARNING

Discovery learning provides children with opportunities to learn on their own through activity and direct experience with science materials. This enables children to assume an active role, instead of a passive one, in the learning process. Discovery learning should not mean that each child must necessarily discover by himself something which others have discovered for him, because this can often be a futile and unrewarding enterprise. The whole point of discoveries is that once they are made, everyone can share in them without having the process of discovery repeated over and over again. Also, discovery learning should not be the only teaching strategy used in elementary science. Many concepts cannot be learned by discovery, and the teacher will have to use other appropriate strategies to accomplish the learning of these concepts.

There are two forms of discovery: free discovery and guided discovery. In free discovery the child is given an opportunity to explore at will, pacing himself, and making his own decisions regarding what to do. In this form of discovery the teacher becomes a resource person, to be used by the child as needed. In guided discovery the teacher assumes a more controlling role by helping the child to make "correct" decisions and by supplying pertinent information at appropriate moments. The nature of the learning activity will often help the teacher determine whether the discovery learning will be free or guided.

USE OF SCIENCE MATERIALS

Since children in most of the elementary grade levels are incapable of formal operations, and are more able to perform concrete operations, the science program should emphasize "hand-on" learning involving the use of a large variety of materials. Such learning will be more concrete and self-pacing. Psychologists agree that the basis of concept formation is through perceptual encounters. Consequently, the introduction of any new science content to the children will be helped immeasureably through the presentation of strong perceptual props. Apparatus that can be handled and manipulated, together with pictures and images that can be reacted to, will provide the kind of perceptual stimuli upon which concepts can be developed and learned.

INTEREST AND MOTIVATION

The interest and motivation of the child are intrinsically related to successful learning. The child is more likely to become interested and be motivated to learn when he is in a situation that is rich in "doing" activities where he can handle and manipulate things. Also, giving the child an opportunity to explore and find out for himself seems to have a built-in motivation for the child.

REWARDS

The rewards that the child receives for learning are closely related to the child's interest and motivation. Schools generally give rewards for work that has been performed as a result of some external demand on the child. He is asked to know something because the teacher requires it, or because there will be a test and a grade, or because his parents want him to succeed. However, rewards that result from the child's own interest in pursuing an area or topic are more potent motivators for learning in science. When the child's efforts can be shifted from external rewards, such as pleasing parents or teachers, to internal rewards of interest and self-accomplishment, the child's learning will be more efficient.

SOCIAL INTERACTION

The teacher should arrange for learning situations that permit social interaction among the children. This will provide the children with an opportunity to learn from each other. Also, during social interaction a child is confronted with the views and ideas of other children, and this serves as an important force in overcoming the child's tendency towards egocentrism by stimulating him to consider and possibly adopt the viewpoints of the other children.

Characteristics of the Child

IF THE science program in the elementary school is to be effective, the teacher must be aware of and utilize what research tells us about characteristics of the child. Knowing and understanding what psychology says about children will do much to make the teaching and learning of science a profitable and rewarding experience for both teacher and children.

The teacher should keep in mind the following characteristics of children when participating in the science program.

EGOCENTRICITY

Children are egocentric. Everything is important to children insofar as it relates to themselves. This egocentricity is only natural, because children find themselves in a strange yet wonderful world, filled with phenomena that are constantly affecting them. They tend to interpret the phenomena in the light of how the phenomena affect them, and to utilize everything they learn for the express purpose of adjusting to the world in which they live.

CONSTANT INTERPRETATION OF ENVIRONMENT

Children are constantly interpreting their environment. They are affected by all kinds of environmental phenomena, and they continually try to interpret these phenomena. Very often these interpretations are incomplete, or even incorrect, because of the complexity of the science principles involved. However, children will continue to make the effort to arrive at interpretations that satisfy them. In so doing, children show evidence of using their imaginations in developing hypotheses and in devising ways of verifying these hypotheses. At the same time the teacher must remember that the interpretations will change with different stages of maturity. Consequently, children will be engaged in a constant process of revising interpretations as they grow in ability to understand concepts and think abstractly.

CURIOSITY

Children are curious. The children's world is a world filled with wonder and excitement. They naturally are curious about things in every field of science. Their curiosity will vary, depending upon what catches their interest. They are more interested in things that move than in things that are still. They are more interested in an object that makes

(William Means/Van Cleve)

Children would rather do things than listen.

things happen than in an object to which things are happening. Their curiosity reaches a peak, however, with things that seem mysterious and magical. A good science program will take advantage of this curiosity to initiate effective learning in the classroom.

LOVE OF INVESTIGATION

Children are investigators. Children love to explore. If given an object with which to play, they invariably try to take it apart and then put it together again. They love to touch and feel things. When a boy asks to see another boy's baseball glove, the boy really wants to touch and feel the glove. The same behavior carries into adulthood. Children are always wondering "what will happen if . . . " and suggesting ideas for finding out. The words *what, why,* and *how* are common in their vocabulary. While investigating, children work and learn best when their experiences are firsthand. Therefore the teacher should provide a wide variety of science experiences that involve *doing* learning activities.

ENERGY

Children are very energetic. They cannot sit still for long periods of time. They would rather do things than listen. Even while listening, they move their bodies restlessly. This restlessness is especially true of boys. The difficulty in sitting still for any length of time has a direct bearing on the children's attention span. As a result, the science program should provide for many activities which give the children an opportunity to move about and do things.

PERSISTENCE

Children are persistent. Children like to achieve their objectives. They will often spend unusual lengths of time and effort to solve problems that are important to them. With the solving of the problem comes a feeling of satisfaction and a sense of accomplishment. The teacher can take advantage of the children's persistence and their desire to achieve their objectives by presenting the science learning to them in the form of problems, provided that the problems are really problems and not just questions posed in the form of problems.

SOCIABILITY

Children are social persons. They like to be with and be accepted by their peers. They like to work together in planning and carrying out their activities. If given proper encouragement, direction, and opportunity children will work very well together and engage in all phases of the democratic process. Furthermore, each child begins to form a self-concept for himself through his early experiences in school. He will consider himself to be adequate only if he receives assurance of his worth. Therefore, giving the child an opportunity to work with others, to offer his own ideas, and to work out peer relationships, is an important part of developing the child's sense of self-worth. A good science program will recognize these factors and provide for the children to plan and work together.

NEED FOR RECOGNITION

All children crave recognition and attention. They want the esteem of their teachers and peers. When children are frustrated in satisfying this need, their classroom behavior becomes affected. Some children tend to become aggressive and disrupt normal classroom proceedings, hoping in this way to obtain the recognition they want so badly. Others tend to become apathetic and end up by failing to participate in the class activities. The science program in the elementary school often calls for learning activities where experiments and demonstrations are performed in front of the class. These activities are conducted either by the children themselves or by the teacher with the assistance of the children. In such situations many teachers often call upon only those children who are bright, quick, and dextrous. These teachers neglect the slower-learning, awkward children. The wise teacher first evaluates the science activities with regard to ease or difficulty of performance. Then the teacher calls upon the appropriate children whom the teacher knows will be able to conduct these activities successfully. In this way all the children in the class are given an opportunity to perform, and thus they obtain the recognition and status they desire.

For Discussion

1. How would you conduct an experiment with a six-year old child, involving conservation of liquid volume, using a given amount of colored water and glass containers of different sizes and shapes? What questions would you ask the child? What answers might you expect?

2. Piaget, Bruner, and Gagné differ in their attitude toward the child's readiness for learning. Which attitude do you prefer? Why?

3. Bruner and Gagné differ in their emphasis on learning. Which emphasis do you prefer, and why?

4. Discovery learning may be free or guided. What situations can you think of where free discovery would be desirable? Where guided discovery may be preferable?

5. One criticism of discovery learning is that it is time consuming, hence inefficient. Do you think this criticism is a valid one? Why?

6. What other implications do you think the child psychologists' theories of learning will have for elementary science?

7. What other characteristics of children do you know that might have an effect on teaching and learning elementary science?

CHAPTER 3

The ELEMENTARY SCIENCE PROGRAM

WHEN a school system undertakes to develop its own elementary science program, either as a separate program or as part of a K–12 science sequence, the persons involved in planning begin with an unfortunate handicap. Although a sizable number of excellent science programs for the elementary school are emerging, the details of very few of these programs—if any—are readily available to other school systems for use as guides or examples. As a result, a school system that is involved or interested in developing a new science program is unable to take advantage of the thinking and efforts of those school systems that have already had this experience. Similarly, although prerequisites for an effective elementary science program can be found in many publications, accompanying suggestions for fulfilling the prerequisites are generally not included.

Consequently, the persons entrusted with the organization and development of the elementary science program are confronted with a wide variety of serious, thought-provoking questions. What science content should be included in the program? What guidelines are there for selecting the science content? What are the prerequisites of an effective program? What is the best way to organize and develop the program? How can a scope and sequence chart be developed that is a satisfactory part of a K–12 sequence and is acceptable to teachers, supervisors, science specialists, and administrators? Once the scope and sequence chart is created, what is a suitable procedure for developing a curriculum guide? All of these questions which are discussed in this chapter, must be carefully thought through and answered if the elementary science program is to be a successful one.

The Science Content

THE PROBLEM of selecting science content for an elementary science program is always difficult. Science encompasses such a wide body of knowledge that it would be impossible for anyone to learn it all, even in a lifetime. It seems obvious, then, that the task is to decide, not how much, but what science should be taught in the elementary school.

All science content can be classified into three general areas: the earth and the rest of the universe, living things, and matter and energy. These three areas encompass the five major fields of science: astronomy, biology, chemistry, geology, and physics. There is general agreement that the science program should select its content from all three areas, giving equal consideration to both the physical and the biological sciences.

When determining what science content should be selected for an elementary science program, there are some guides that can be used to help in making the final selection.

The Sciences • The sciences themselves will contain the important concepts and conceptual schemes, upon which their organization and development as sciences are based. They help indicate which science concepts are most pertinent and desirable. They also suggest ways of thinking and methods of working that will be helpful to children in learning science.

The Child • Research of psychologists provides many clues about the mental, emotional, and physical behavior of the child. When selecting science content, consideration must be given to the children's intellectual capacity, their capability for grasping abstract ideas, their curiosity about themselves and their environment, their aptitude for originality and creativity, and their persistence and attention span.

(William Means/Van Cleve)

The science program should provide an understanding of the community.

The Community • Science content should be selected that will help provide an understanding of the community in which the children live. Such content will vary, depending upon the location and nature of the community. The climate, for example, will play an important part in the selection of the living things to be studied and in learning what the effects of this climate will be upon the living things. Selection of content should also vary according to whether the community is industrial or rural and whether the local terrain is seashore, mountain, plain, or desert. Even though the content will vary among communities, the key concepts learned will still be constant.

The Elementary Curriculum • The science program should be correlated wherever possible with the rest of the elementary curriculum. Social studies, language arts, mathematics, music, and art all are concerned with understandings that are equally important to science. The science content, then, should both reinforce and be reinforced by the content of the other programs of the elementary school.

A final recommendation about the selection of science content is that the science program should also plan to include content involving the areas of health, safety, and conservation. Some schools prefer to teach these areas separately and independently of the science program. Others incorporate these areas into the science program, but take them up as separate topics. Still others prefer to correlate these areas with the relevant science content, based on the assumption that more effective learning will take place when there is a direct association between these areas and the science content as it is being learned. Thus, safety and safety rules are introduced when the children study such topics as machines, electricity, and fire and fuels. Conservation and the control of environmental pollution is brought up when the children learn about animals, plants, soil, air, water, and the earth's natural resources. Health and nutrition are studied when the children learn about the human body and its functions.

Prerequisites of an Effective Elementary Science Program

IN RECENT years an increasing number of local science programs for the elementary school have been emerging. These programs are the result of cooperative efforts of classroom teachers, supervisors, administrators, and science specialists.

These new programs are rich in content and process, and provide for an abundance of learning activities. These activities are directed specifically at giving the children an opportunity to investigate and explore so that effective learning takes place and desirable behavioral outcomes emerge. Provision is made for all kinds of learners: slow, average, and fast. Teachers are supplied with source materials and with necessary equipment. Competent supervisors or specialists are available for assistance.

Science programs may vary somewhat in their science content, learning activities, and teaching or unit format. However, all programs should meet the following prerequisites, if they are to be effective and successful.

PLANNING

A science program should be planned. When science was first taught in the elementary school, and for some time thereafter, there was no such thing as a planned science program. Science learning was organized around incidents that occurred in the classroom. If a child brought a magnet, whistle, unusual-looking rock, queer insect, or pretty leaf into class, a lesson or unit in science was developed around the incident. Often the lesson was quite brief and ended the same day. Usually this kind of lesson tended to stress identification, nomenclature, and the learning of facts rather than major science concepts. If there were no incidents, there were often no lessons in science.

There is no question that incidents arising in the classroom can be a tremendous motivating experience for the children. Under the direction of experienced and skillful teachers with a good science background, such incidents can be used to produce excellent teaching and learning. However, incidents alone are not sufficient to ensure an adequate science program for the elementary school. Nor would the teachers even think of teaching other areas in the elementary curriculum solely on this basis.

One of the most significant forward trends in science education today is the general agreement that the science program should be planned and structured, just as the programs in the other areas of the elementary school curriculum are planned and structured. A planned program not only provides a steady progression of science learning in all grades, but also gives the teacher a definite background and framework of basic science information with which to work in the classroom.

A properly organized program will not discourage incidents that occur, but rather will welcome them as an additional means for producing more effective learning in the classroom. In fact, a planned program now makes it possible for the teacher to create deliberately the kinds of incidents that will instill in the children a desire for exploration and investigation. And when unusual or important incidents do arise, such as sending a satellite or astronaut into space, the planned program can be flexible enough to provide time for these incidents to be taken up in detail.

A planned program should provide for and be guided by the interests of the children. An effective program takes into consideration the children's interests and uses them to motivate learning in science. At the same time it permits the children to help plan and carry out the daily and long-range work in science.

(Nancy Simmerman/Van Cleve)

A planned program takes advantage of children's interests.

A COORDINATED PART OF A K–12 SCIENCE PROGRAM

Science in the elementary school should be planned and coordinated so that it is part of an overall K–12 science program. In this way haphazard teaching, unnecessary repetition, overlap, and flagrant omissions are eliminated. Instead, a steady progression of learning takes place at each grade level, building upon knowledge from previous grades and leading to further knowledge in the following grades. The science content to be learned will proceed steadily from the very simple to the abstract, as the children grow in maturity. At the same time, the children will become progressively more proficient in the process of science, proceeding from the simpler to the more complex operations of science and the scientist. In addition, the children will gradually acquire experience in solving problems and in thinking critically and creatively.

CORRELATION WITH THE ELEMENTARY CURRICULUM

The elementary science program should correlate science, whenever possible, with other phases of the elementary school curriculum. The science program is only one part of the entire elementary school curriculum. However, learning can be more effective when all phases of the curriculum are integrated. The study of machines in science, for example, can be correlated very effectively with the study of transportation in social science. The study of light and sound can be correlated with the study of communications. The study of plants, animals, water, soil, air, and minerals can be correlated with the study of conservation and the control of environmental pollution. There are many opportunities in science to use measurements and other aspects of mathematics.

Arts and crafts are especially suited for correlation with science in the lower grades. One ingenious teacher had her children make an effective mobile when studying weather. The sun and moon were made of cardboard and then painted with appropriate colors. Stars were made or purchased in the stationery store. A jagged arrow, cut from cardboard and painted white, represented lightning. Models of snow flakes were drawn and cut out. For rain the children used strings of pearls and beads. Each pearl, representing a raindrop, was separated by a glass bead that was shaped like a narrow, hollow tube.

Finally, a constant correlation can be made between science and the language arts. Reading, writing, and talking are also involved in the learning of science. These are language arts activities. Thus science learning can help reinforce learning in the language arts.

Care should be taken, however, when correlating science with the rest of the curriculum, that the learning of science is not lost in the process. Real science learning cannot take place in a combined social studies-science unit on "Communications," when teachers take up the social aspects in great detail and merely talk about the science portion. Moreover, although it is good educational practice to correlate science

[41

when possible with the rest of the curriculum, it is also impractical and unwise to insist that all science be integrated with other areas. There are many phases of science that are learned best alone. Also, there are times where it is more logical to integrate the other areas with science rather than integrate science with the other areas.

SCOPE AND SEQUENCE

The science program should have scope and sequence. *Scope* refers to the content in the program, and *sequence* refers to the grade level or levels where the content will be allocated. The science program should be broad in scope so that the children will have ample opportunity to learn major concepts and basic principles that affect all the principal aspects of their environment. These broad understandings should be drawn from all areas of science, and their introduction should begin as early as kindergarten, then be developed and expanded through the elementary grades. This will help enable the children to acquire a greater understanding of their environment, of how man strives to use and control his environment, of how living things adapt and adjust to their environment, and of how living things are or may be interdependent and interrelated.

An examination of the current elementary science textbooks and science programs shows a fair amount of agreement on the scope of science content to be taught in the elementary school. However, this agreement is not true of sequence. Both textbooks and science programs vary widely and consistently in their grade placement of science topics. Some research is being conducted to determine the age levels or grades where selected science topics or understandings can be taught successfully. The findings generally tend to show that children at any grade level can learn something about all areas of science, provided the concepts are within the children's level of maturity and comprehension.

It is becoming more obvious that any attempt to develop one universal science program, with a rigid or fixed grade-placed sequence, is virtually impossible. Children can and do differ widely in ability between schools in the same community, and also between schools of different communities. It is not uncommon for a teacher to find that the children differ in ability from year to year even in the same grade.

Yet it is equally obvious that some kind of sequence is necessary. In every science topic the concepts range from the very simple to the more complex. Some topics involve concepts that are more abstract than others. Whatever topics are assigned to a lower grade level will contain concepts that cannot be developed fully, regardless of the children's ability. Further development of these concepts will be needed later on to ensure complete comprehension and learning.

Earlier science programs attempted to solve the problem of sequence by adopting a spiral pattern in which the same topic—such as Sound or Heat—was taken up periodically. This would provide for a steady spiral of concepts to be developed, progressing from the easily understandable to the more difficult ones. New and more difficult concepts would be built upon previously learned ones, and from this progression a major conceptual scheme would emerge. In each case, previous knowledge about the topic was to be reviewed briefly, and then this knowledge was to be extended further. Repetition thus would serve to reinforce learning and to associate the old concepts with the new. Some schools used a spiral pattern in which the same topic was taken up twice in grades K–6: once in grades K–3, and again in grades 4–6. Other schools preferred to take up the same topic three times: once in grades K–2, a second time in grades 3–4, and a third time in grades 5–6.

Today's programs reflect the current thinking that the elementary science programs should be organized around a unifying framework of conceptual schemes. Consequently, the present trend in sequence seems to be that each topic is taken up just once and the topics are incorporated under broader related content areas associated with these conceptual schemes. As a result, fewer topics are taken up in each grade, but each topic can now be explored in greater depth and in more satisfying detail. Not only is there a greater opportunity for more concepts to be learned at one time, but also the relationships between these concepts as part of a major conceptual scheme can now develop more easily, in a number of ways, and from more than one direction.

Provision for teaching science in the kindergarten varies. Some schools assign specific science units to the kindergarten. Others suggest only that the teacher scrutinize her daily program of activities closely for science implications, then plan accordingly for experiences in science. Still others provide for both planned science units and incidental activities arising from the questions that the children will ask.

Exact grade placement of science content in the science program is usually an individual concern, left to the decision of those working with the program. The grade placement may vary from school to school within the same community, or from community to community. Allocation of concepts will depend upon the children's intellectual development and their ability to understand cause-and-effect relationships, to recall and rationalize, and to grasp abstract ideas. Most concepts allocated for a specific grade level can be learned with equal success in one grade level immediately above or below the specified grade. However, difficulties are more likely to arise when the difference in allocation of concept involves two or more grade levels.

The following suggestions may be helpful in organizing the sequence of topics and concepts for a science program. To begin, many individual topics can be related and incorporated to form broader content areas. Magnetism, static electricity, and current electricity, for example, can be combined to constitute one content area. Similarly, machines can be combined with friction, heat with fire and fuels, water with weather and climate, soil with rocks and minerals, and air with planes and space travel.

Some science topics might be placed in the same grade because they are all concerned with a common conceptual scheme. For example, an understanding of the theory of molecular motion will explain many of the phenomena of heat, sound, and physical states of matter. If the molecular theory is allocated to a certain grade level, the placement of these topics in the same grade level may save needless repetition and at the same time ensure a greater understanding of the theory because it was approached from different directions. Also, when the atomic theory is allocated to a certain grade, magnetism, static electricity, and current electricity could also be profitably placed in the same grade.

Finally, the science program should evaluate its sequence continuously, not periodically. Only if the effects of a particular sequence on learning in the classroom are carefully observed, and the sequence constantly reshuffled whenever the grade placement appears to be unsuited, can a well-organized and effectively structured science program emerge.

BALANCE

The science program should have balance. A well-balanced program should provide opportunities for the children to explore regularly in each of the three major areas, which include the earth and the universe, living things, and matter and energy. Equal emphasis should be given to the physical and the biological sciences in the overall program. A

(William Means/Van Cleve)

Science is a process of inquiry and discovery.

balance in the length of units might be desirable so that some would be long and others would be shorter. There should also be balance in the number of units taught each year. The present trend is toward the adoption of a relatively small number of units per year, however, with provision for greater depth in science content.

EMPHASIS UPON CONCEPTS AND CONCEPTUAL SCHEMES

The science program should be concerned with more than technology. Too many science programs place undue emphasis upon how science helps us in our daily life, and not enough emphasis upon the underlying science concepts. The result is that the children, our future adult citizens, acquire a distorted image of science. They tend to view science primarily as an agent for developing useful gadgets and appliances, thus making their lives more pleasant and comfortable. The science program should provide children with ample opportunity to learn some of the key concepts and conceptual schemes that play such an important part in their daily lives, their environment, and the world in which they live.

EMPHASIS ON THE PROCESS OF SCIENCE

The science program should make children aware that science is a way of life—an exciting process of inquiry and discovery that man uses to explore, discuss, and explain the natural phenomena of the world in which he lives. Consequently, wherever possible, the children should be given an opportunity to learn and gain proficiency in the use of the key operations of science and the scientist. They should be given practice in learning how to solve problems and how to think critically and creatively. As they perform these operations they will learn concepts and conceptual schemes, and they will develop such desirable behavioral outcomes as scientific skills, attitudes, appreciations, and interests.

VARIETY OF ACTIVITIES

The children should have ample opportunity to use a large number of diversified activities when learning science. Some children seem to learn better or more easily from one kind of activity than another. They should have a chance to do experiments and demonstrations, read, give reports, participate in discussion, take field trips, listen to resource persons, use audio-visual materials, do research, and work on projects. There should also be activities that reinforce learning for the slow learner, and activities that challenge and extend the knowledge of the fast learner. At the same time, opportunities should be provided for children to investigate incidents or problems that arise and are not part of the planned program.

PROVISION FOR INDIVIDUAL DIFFERENCES

The science program should provide for the individual abilities, needs, and interests of the children. It should offer a wide range of

(William Means/Van Cleve)

Plan to use a variety of learning activities.

learning activities that will help the individual growth of children in science. The children should be given an opportunity to work in large groups, in small groups, and individually. It will allow slow learners to participate actively with the other children and to learn from them, yet permit them to work individually or in small groups for remedial purposes. It will enable fast learners to share their knowledge and ability with the other children, thus helping them, and yet it should permit the fast learners to extend their own knowledge and to explore further in areas which interest them.

Some schools have made changes in the organizational pattern of the classroom, claiming that one of the advantages of such changes is the greater opportunity to provide for individual differences in children.

One such organizational change is the nongraded classroom. Most schools have self-contained classrooms, where each classroom is under the direction of one teacher for one full year or grade. The nongraded classroom disregards single grade levels. Instead the children are placed in flexible groups on the basis of several related factors. They spend three years, and occasionally two or four years, in one group before moving on to the next group. Consequently, the children have a better opportunity to progress at their own individual rate and optimum speed at a time when maturation and growth in children is notoriously uneven and unpredictable.

Some schools have adopted team teaching, where two or more teachers are assigned to a group of pupils. This arrangement calls for different schedules, and different allocations of time and space for teaching and learning. Team teaching lends itself to differences in grouping, thus providing for large-group, small-group, and individual learning activities as needed.

Other schools have departmentalized their science (and other) programs, so that a teacher with a good science background and with expertise in the teaching of science is responsible for the learning of science by all the children in one or more grades. This background and expertise presumably enables the teacher to provide more and better learning activities that will take into consideration the individual differences of the children.

PROVISION FOR NECESSARY MATERIALS

It is useless for a science program to include "doing" learning activities unless the necessary supplies and equipment are made available. Thus an annual budget must be allotted to the elementary school for science materials so that the science program can function successfully. Moreover, each classroom should have its own science library, and the school library should have an adequate selection of science books. Provision must also be made for easy accessibility to films, filmstrips, and television programs.

HELP AND ENCOURAGEMENT FOR THE TEACHER

Giving the elementary teacher as much help as possible is an important facet of any planned science program. An examination of current elementary science textbooks shows that approximately 33 percent of the content is in the area of biology, 33 percent is in the area of physics, 20 percent is in the area of geology, 8 percent is in the area of astronomy, and 6 percent is in the area of chemistry. (Meteorology is incorporated into the area of geology.) Thus to teach science effectively in the elementary school, the teacher should have a certain measure of knowledge and proficiency in these five areas. Unfortunately, this knowledge and proficiency requires a greater science background than most elementary school teachers receive in their pre-service training. It is generally agreed, and is verified by the findings of research, that most elementary school teachers have inadequate science backgrounds. Consequently, many of these teachers are reluctant to teach science.

Therefore, if teachers with an inadequate science background are given units that do not contain the basic science information, the teachers will be reluctant to use the units. This situation is easily understandable because all teachers realize that, unless they are at least moderately qualified to teach any subject, they may eventually be put into the embarrassing position of appearing inept before the children. A teacher does not mind saying "I don't know" occasionally to the children. But, when she has to say "I don't know" repeatedly, she soon stops teaching the particular topic or subject that places her in this awkward position.

The teacher prefers to teach subjects in which she feels competent, comfortable, and secure.

If one of the objectives of science is to help the children understand and learn key concepts and conceptual schemes, it is imperative that the teacher be well informed about the science content and process that is being studied. Otherwise the teacher will not be able to guide the children's learning profitably.

Teachers can be given help in several ways. Providing them with science textbooks on both the junior and senior high school level can do much to upgrade their limited science background. A large number of reference books on individual science topics at the elementary school level are now available. The teachers can be provided with excellent professional books, sourcebooks, and curriculum materials on elementary science. In-service education in science content and process, in the form of workshops or courses, can be offered.

Many of the larger school systems are beginning to employ science supervisors or coordinators. These persons, proficient both in science and in working with children, can do much to strengthen the science program and the morale of the teachers. They can plan with the teachers, suggest additional learning activities, frequently do demonstration teaching, locate and order equipment, and conduct local workshops.

Some school systems employ full-time science supervisors or coordinators. They are given either a limited teaching schedule or none at all so that they can spend most of their time working on the program or with those teachers who need help. Other school systems may have supervisor or coordinator on a part-time basis. Sometimes school systems use a competent junior high school teacher, who is given only a half-time teaching load so that the rest of the time can be devoted to the elementary teachers. Sometimes they use a science-minded elementary school teacher, letting someone else take over her class part of the time while she works with the other teachers in her building. Some school systems have a science educator come periodically to furnish advice and assistance to the teachers. Planned science programs in the elementary school are still comparatively new, and the position of elementary science supervisor or coordinator is even newer. The trend, however, seems to be quite definitely toward the increased use of full-time supervisors or coordinators.

SUFFICIENT TIME

There is definite agreement that science should be a regular part of the daily program, and have adequate time within the program. Both interest and learning are lost if science is scheduled only once or twice a week. Opinions vary, however, as to how much time should be allotted to science, daily or weekly. The general feeling is that more time should be devoted to science in grades 4–6 than in K–3. Some schools require that a definite amount of time be devoted daily to science. One recommended time allotment is 20–30 minutes per day for K–3 and 30–40 minutes per day for grades 4–6. Some schools set aside three days a week for science, with an average of 40–60 minutes per day. Other schools merely stipulate a definite amount of time per week, usually 120–180 minutes, and let the teacher allocate the time as needed throughout the week. Still other schools require that science be taught, but leave the time allotment to the discretion of the individual teacher.

CONTINUOUS EVALUATION

To be effective the science program should be evaluated continually, with everyone involved in the program participating in the evaluation. The scope of science content must be examined for corrections, additions, or deletions. The sequence must be evaluated to ensure optimum grade placement. Activities should be scrutinized critically to see whether they are achieving maximum learning of content and process. Newer, more productive activities should be substituted as they appear in text, reference, and resource books. Initiating activities may be evaluated for greatest possible motivating and problem-raising potential. Even the evaluation techniques themselves should be examined regularly to see whether learning is taking place in the classroom.

Developing a Local Science Program

A WELL-DEVELOPED science program will make a large difference in the amount and kind of science being taught and learned in the elementary school. There are several factors that affect the successful development of an effective science program. The manner in which the science program is organized will influence its success or failure. A democratic and cooperative procedure, where the teachers all take an active part in creating the program, will greatly enhance the likelihood of the program's acceptance and widespread use. Furthermore, it is commonly acknowledged that no crash program has ever had a long or satisfactory life. There is a direct relationship between the success of a program and the time and effort that was spent in developing it.

Finally, leadership is absolutely necessary. Although the teachers are willing to work hard, spending many hours, on a science program, this work is not enough. Administrators must assume leadership in initiating the program. They must stimulate the teachers, encourage the emergence and growth of leadership from the ranks of the teachers themselves, guide the teachers in working cooperatively and effectively, obtain expert assistance and resource persons, and provide materials wherever and whenever needed.

The following is a description of one of the several ways that have proved to be highly successful in developing an effective local science program in the elementary school.

(H. Armstrong Roberts)

Teachers should take part in planning the science program.

DEVELOPING A SCOPE AND SEQUENCE CHART

The first step in setting up a science program is the development of a scope and sequence chart. This chart development requires a science curriculum committee, consisting of teachers who are experienced or interested in teaching science. An ideal committee for a K–6 program would consist of one or more representatives from each grade. These teachers would then meet regularly with the rest of the teachers in their grade, report on the work and progress of the committee, and present committee proposals for suggestions, recommendations, approval, or disapproval.

The committee should also have one or more representatives from the junior and senior high schools, especially if the program is to be part of an overall K–12 program. In this way the junior and senior high schools will be informed about what the elementary school is doing. They can learn what science content is being considered for the elementary program and utilize this information when organizing or reorganizing their own science programs. Besides, the junior and senior high school representatives can be of great help to the committee in selecting science content, suggesting suitable activities, and recommending needed materials.

The committee should also have guidance and leadership from a science supervisor, if one is available, or from a science educator. Either person can help in many essential ways, such as suggesting or obtaining professional literature, other scope and sequence charts, courses of study or curriculum guides, materials, and so forth. He will often perform a valuable service by acting as a moderator when the discussion becomes heated.

The committee should meet regularly; bimonthly meetings seem to work well. The progress of the committee will increase manyfold if the members are given released time from their teaching duties so that they can devote sufficient time and effort to the undertaking. Many committees have either failed or limped along slowly because meetings were held after school, when the teachers were tired from their long day's work, or else on Saturdays, when many teachers resent the infringement upon their own time.

The committee should work upon scope first. When doing so, the committee might think in terms of not only selecting topics, but also in terms of agreeing to the minimum amount of science content the children should know by the time they leave the sixth grade. In this way all the children from different elementary schools in a school system can enter the junior high school with a comparatively equal science background and an equal opportunity to succeed in the junior high school science program. Reasonably uniform preparation of elementary students will also help the junior high school teachers in conducting or planning their science program. It would be wise for the committee to

(Rohn Engh/Van Cleve)

The science coordinator can provide guidance and leadership.

[51

agree only on the *minimum* science content, which would include the concepts and conceptual schemes that all the children, regardless of ability, should know. Each teacher in each school may go as much further as she likes or can with the fast learners.

When selecting content the committee should consult every means available. It can go to the literature and recommendations of science educators, analyze the contents of elementary science textbooks, consult professional scope and sequence charts, and examine other courses of study. The science supervisor or consultant may be able to inform the committee of trends in the scope of other science programs throughout the country. In its selection of science content the committee should also consider the children's interests and the local scene or community.

The committee would now select the topics it thinks should be included in the program. Related topics would be combined to form broader content areas organized around a framework of major conceptual schemes, in the manner suggested earlier in this chapter when discussing scope and sequence as a prerequisite of the science program.

After the topics have been selected, the next step would be to make a simple outline of all the key concepts that should be included under each topic. It would be helpful to arrange the concepts so that they lend themselves to a logical sequence of learning. There are many such arrangements possible, all equally effective, so that arrangement can be a matter of personal preference by the committee. One way to facilitate the work of making outlines is to have the individual committee members assume the responsibility for constructing outlines for specific topics. These outlines can then be evaluated by the whole committee for additions, corrections, or omissions. When the committee has finally agreed on all the topics and their outlines, which will constitute the scope of the science program, the members can bring the plan to the teachers of their respective grades for examination, comments, and subsequent approval.

The committee should always keep in mind that when they are making an outline of the key concepts to be included under each topic, there should be a logical progression from simple to more complex concepts. For example, in an outline on the topic of machines, the children can first be introduced to the different ways that machines help make man's work easier. As the children study how each simple machine operates, they can progress from qualitative to quantitative operations. At the appropriate time, the concept of input and output can be developed, and the children can be led to an understanding of the principle of work. Then the concept of ideal mechanical advantage is introduced and, as the children learn how friction affects the efficiency of machines, is followed by actual mechanical advantage. Finally, the concept of power is developed and the relation between work and power investigated.

With the acceptance of the scope of the program, the task of grade placing the science content begins. It is really a task because so little research has been conducted in this area. Consequently, until sufficient valid and reliable findings become available, the committee will have to rely upon what child psychologists have to say about intellectual development and learning in children and also upon common sense, the previous experiences and recommendations of others, and trial and error.

The rest of the elementary curriculum should be taken into consideration when grade placing the science topics. For example, if the social studies program is teaching the topic of communications quite successfully in one or more grades, it would see desirable to see whether sound and light could be allocated successfully in the same grades. The choice of basic elementary science textbooks will also make a difference in grade placement, especially if the school system prefers using a single series. If, in this series, the topic of heat is taken up in the fifth-grade text, the committee should try to place the topic in this grade as well, so that the children can take full advantage of the science content and activities contained in the textbooks. For those school systems that use multiple textbooks, there will be much more freedom in coordinating the sequence of the program with that of the textbooks.

When the committee has completed the grade placement, in the form of a scope and sequence chart, the members should then go back again to the teachers in their own grades. This time the teachers in each grade will have to consider a list of topics for the grade, as well as the completed, overall plan. No further steps should be taken until there is general approval of the chart, both as to scope and sequence. It will be understood, of course, that the chart is tentative and can be revised

(Dave Logan/Van Cleve)

Printed materials should be an integral part of the program.

whenever necessary. Changes are usually made either when a comprehensive curriculum guide is being developed or after the new program has been tried out in the classroom and evaluated.

DEVELOPING A CURRICULUM GUIDE

Developing a curriculum guide is the next step in organizing a local science program. The nature of the guide will vary, depending upon the preference of the school system. It can be kept to a minimum or expanded in great detail. In either case the guide should never be so rigid that it discourages individual initiative in the teacher's work in the classroom. The more effective guides do include specific science content to be learned by the children, suggested activities for learning both content and process, necessary materials, and appropriate references. Many also include possible initiating activities, anticipated pupil questions or problems, additional activities for slow and fast learners, and suggestions for the evaluation of both science content and process.

Once the science curriculum committee has approved and accepted the format of the curriculum guide, the procedure would then be to involve as many teachers as possible in working on the guide itself. The ideal situation is to have all the teachers participate, because the guide will then be *theirs*—something that they have approved, worked on, and developed. However, the teachers must first become completely familiar with the format of the guide and the methods that can be used to prepare its contents. The supervisor or consultant can meet with the teachers for this purpose, either all at one time or in smaller groups if necessary. Sample curriculum guides and courses of study with formats similar to the one that has been adopted could be made available for study and discussion. The supervisor could also prepare a brochure on how the work could be planned and organized, containing the kind of instructions described in Chapter 5, "Planning for Science in the Classroom." As many meetings as necessary should be held with the teachers until they all are completely familiar with the method for developing the guide.

At this time a number of committees may be appointed which can be of great service. Several groups might work on individual science topics, selecting all the science concepts that will be included in each topic, then apportioning the concepts among the grades. Their results should be evaluated by the science curriculum committee, especially those members from the junior and senior high schools, for accuracy of content, omissions, and suitability of grade placement.

Now the teachers themselves can begin working on the guide. First-grade teachers could develop the guide for the first grade, second-grade teachers for the second grade, and so on. Smaller groups of teachers within each grade might be assigned to work on individual topics or units, so that the task for any one group would not be too great. As each topic or unit was completed, teachers in the same grade and also in other grades would examine it for gaps, overlap, and needless repetition. The science curriculum committee would then go over it for final approval. In this way active participation of all, or as many teachers as possible, would be obtained.

One final step is necessary to ensure successful use of the guide, and that is to familiarize all the teachers with the contents of the guide or at least the contents for their particular grade level. The reason is obvious. If a group of teachers from one grade worked on a single topic, these teachers will have become very familiar with the science content, activities, and materials for that topic. However, these teachers might be completely unfamiliar with the topics worked on by other teachers from the same grade. If the school system is very large, there may even be teachers who are unfamiliar with every topic for their grade.

To remedy this situation, it might be profitable to institute workshops in the form of teachers' meetings. For example, the third-grade teachers would meet periodically. At each meeting a group of teachers who had worked on a particular topic would explain the science concepts underlying the topic and demonstrate the learning activities, pointing out the process skills to be developed. The rest of the teachers could then ask questions, and afterward come up to try the experiments themselves. In this way all the teachers in all the grades would become familiar with the content of the curriculum guide, especially for their own grade level.

The only area that is somewhat rigid in a curriculum guide is the minimum amount of science content that has been mutually agreed to be included in the guide. This minimum standard seems to be essential if unnecessary repetition is to be avoided, if the children are to enter the junior high school with any degree of uniformity of science background, and if the junior high school is to be able to plan its own program with any degree of certainty.

The remaining areas in the guide should be flexible enough to allow a degree of freedom for the individual schools or teachers. There should be freedom for grade placement of science topics between schools. A science topic assigned to a third grade in one school can be allocated to a fourth grade in another school, if the teachers so desire. All teachers should have a choice in the selection of the learning activities they may use to teach for the science content to be learned. Teachers may also delve deeper into a unit, if they so prefer. There should be ample opportunity to provide for individual differences within the classroom. There should even be allowance for variation in the time of the year when the science topics are taken up. Some teachers prefer to study plants in the spring, whereas others prefer to study plants in the fall when the leaves are turning color. Many programs even provide some free time within the school year so that teachers and pupils can work or study on some science projects of their own choice.

Also, it is obvious that any curriculum guide should undergo continuous evaluation if it is to be permanent rather than ephemeral. Teachers must be encouraged to analyze critically the contents of the guide as they use it. These criticisms, together with suggestions and recommendations, should be forwarded to the science curriculum committee for consideration when the guide is eventually revised.

Programs of the Elementary Science Curriculum Projects

THE DECADE of the 1960's will be long remembered as that period when elementary science became such a major concern that it received national attention. This period was marked by the initiation and development of a large number of elementary science curriculum projects that were designed to revise and improve the science program in the elementary school.

These curriculum projects were the most exciting things that had happened to elementary science in a long time. They were extensively publicized because heavy financial support, for the most part by the

(William Means/Van Cleve)

Improving skills in performing the key operations of science.

National Science Foundation and to a lesser extent by the United States Office of Education, made possible the large-scale involvement of scientists, science educators, teachers, and children in these projects. This financial support also enabled the projects to print and disseminate a variety of bulletins and other descriptive literature that publicized the projects' objectives, characteristics, and progress.

All these projects were actively concerned with teaching science in the elementary school as a process of inquiry. This method is often called the inquiry or discovery approach to the teaching of science. Exercises, units, materials, and teacher's guides have been produced that stress this approach. For guidance and direction in developing their programs, the projects turned to the research and theories of child development psychologists, especially Piaget, Gagné, and Bruner, on how children develop intellectually and learn.

Although all the curriculum projects felt that elementary science should be taught as a process of inquiry, they did not agree on the role and emphasis, as well as the scope and sequence, of the science content in their programs. This difference in agreement ranged widely, from the belief that the science program should be designed primarily to develop the skills of science to the belief that the science program should be organized so as to have as its unifying principle the major conceptual schemes of science.

Regardless of this difference in agreement, the curriculum projects have served to bring sharply into focus the need for teaching process as well as content in elementary science. This need has existed for a long time and the projects have done much to ensure that process will now receive the emphasis it has so long deserved and that it will assume its rightful place in the elementary science program.

The following is a brief description of the purpose and characteristics of some of the well-known elementary science curriculum projects. Sample lessons from units developed by some of these projects are presented in Chapter 6B, "Sample Lessons from Curriculum Project Units."

ELEMENTARY SCIENCE STUDY (ESS)

The Elementary Science Study, a branch of the Education Development Center (EDC), was established in 1960 in Newton, Massachusetts. Its goal was to develop meaningful science materials for the children in grades K–9. The program consists of more than 50 units designed to make children curious about some part of their world and to encourage them to learn more about it.

Although science processes such as observing, measuring, classifying, inferring, predicting, and experimenting are an integral part of the program's units, the units do not aim solely at teaching individual skills and illustrating particular concepts or processes. Instead, the units provide the children with an opportunity to explore interesting problems that extend their knowledge, their insight, and their enjoyment of the physical and natural world.

The units do not make up a sequential science program. Instead, each unit is separate and, for the most part, unrelated to the others. Schools and school systems are invited to make up their own science programs, incorporating all or part of the Elementary Science Study units.

The program's units and materials are marketed by the Webster/McGraw-Hill Co., 1221 Avenue of the Americas, New York, N.Y. 10020

The following units, with suggested grade levels, are available:

Animal Activity (4–6)	Microgardening (4–7)
Attribute Games & Problems (K–8)	Mirror Cards (1–6)
Balloons & Gases (5–8)	Mobiles (K–4)
Batteries & Bulbs (4–9)	Mosquitoes (3–9)
Behavior of Mealworms (4–8)	Musical Instruments (K–9)
Bones (4–6)	Mystery Powders (3–4)
Brine Shrimp (1–4)	Optics (4–6)
Budding Twigs (4–6)	Pattern Blocks (K–6)
Butterflies (K–5)	Peas & Particles (4–6)
Changes (1–4)	Pendulums (4–6)
Clay Boats (2–8)	Pond Water (1–7)
Colored Solutions (3–8)	Primary Balancing (K–4)
Crayfish (4–6)	Printing Press (1–6)
Daytime Astonomy (5–8)	Rocks & Charts (3–6)
Drops, Streams & Containers (3–4)	Sand (2–3)
Earthworms (4–6)	Senior Balancing (4–8)
Eggs & Tadpoles (K–6)	Sink or Float (2–7)
Gases & "Airs" (5–8)	Small Things (4–6)
Geo Blocks (K–6)	Spinning Tables (1–2)
Growing Seeds (K–3)	Starting from Seeds (3–7)
Heating & Cooling (5–7)	Stream Tables (4–9)
Ice Cubes (3–5)	Structures (2–6)
Kitchen Physics (6–9)	Tangrams (K–8)
Life of Beans & Peas (K–4)	Tracks (4–6)
Light & Shadows (K–3)	Water Flow (5–6)
Mapping (5–7)	Where Is the Moon? (3–7)
Match & Measure (K–3)	Whistles & Strings (3–6)

SCIENCE CURRICULUM IMPROVEMENT STUDY (SCIS)

The Science Curriculum Improvement Study was established in 1962 at the University of California at Berkeley. Its goal was to develop scientific literacy. This involves (1) understanding basic concepts, (2) developing a free, inquisitive attitude, and (3) using rational procedures for decision making. A sequential series of units for grades K–6 uses common experiences of children to develop a real understanding of science concepts. The program has already been revised, and its acronym is now SCIIS.

The theories of Piaget and Bruner have been integrated into the program. There are two sequences, one in physical science and one in life science, each having six levels, as follows:

PHYSICAL SCIENCE SEQUENCE	LIFE SCIENCE SEQUENCE
Material Objects	Organisms
Interaction and Systems	Life Cycles
Subsystems and Variables	Populations
Relative Position and Motion	Environments
Energy Sources	Communities
Models: Electric and Magnetic Interaction	Ecosystems

The units in the physical science sequence are concerned with the fundamental concepts involving change and interaction. The units in the life science sequence are concerned with organism-environment interactions. The procedure in all the units involves free or guided preliminary exploration with the materials, "invention" lessons that introduce new concepts, and then "discovery" lessons that help the children develop applications of the concepts.

The program's units and materials are marketed by Rand McNally Company, P.O. Box 7600, Chicago, Ill. 60680

SCIENCE—A PROCESS APPROACH (SAPA)

The Commission on Science Education, sponsored by the American Association for the Advancement of Science (AAAS), was established in 1962 in Washington, D.C. Its goal was to improve science education at all levels. Its elementary science project has implemented the ideas of Gagné to develop a K–6 program that stresses teaching the processes of science. The program has already been revised, and its acronym is now SAPA-II.

The program breaks the complex set of skills used by the scientist when conducting an investigation down into a number of processes and has developed a number of units designed to improve the children's skill in using these processes. A total of thirteen processes, eight basic and five more complex, are identified. The basic processes are taught in the primary grades, the more complex ones in the intermediate grades. These processes are named, as follows:

PRIMARY GRADES	INTERMEDIATE GRADES
Observing	Formulating Hypotheses
Classifying	Controlling Variables
Measuring	Interpreting Data
Communicating	Defining Operationally
Inferring	Experimenting
Predicting	
Using Numbers	
Using Space/Time Relationships	

(Carol Ashton)

Encourage the development of an inquisitive attitude.

The program has also developed a hierarchy chart for each process. The charts identify the behaviors that the child is expected to acquire from the activities of the program. These behaviors are arranged in a sequential hierarchical order of increasing complexity. The charts show not only the relationships among the behaviors within a single process but also the relationships among behaviors of the other processes. The procedure for developing these behavioral hierarchies is based upon the findings of Gagné that there is a greater probability of learning a higher, more complex, behavior when the learner first masters behaviors that are subordinate to the higher behavior.

The program's units and materials are marketed by Ginn and Company, 191 Spring St., Lexington, Massachusetts, 02173.

CONCEPTUALLY ORIENTED PROGRAM
IN ELEMENTARY SCIENCE (COPES)

The Conceptually Oriented Program in Elementary Science was established in 1965 at New York University. Its goal was to develop a K–6 program using interrelated major schemes of science as unifying principles. Consequently, five conceptual schemes were selected, around which the program was developed. These conceptual schemes are, as follows:

The Structural Units of the Universe
Interaction and Change

The Conservation of Energy
The Degradation of Energy
The Statistical View of Nature

The program is structured so that all five conceptual schemes are interwoven in a logical hierarchy. All five schemes are developed concurrently and presented spirally by grades. The activities in grades K–2 are devoted primarily to introductory materials designed to provide children with the skills and conceptual framework needed for entering the main sequences, which start at grade 3. The concepts intended to develop the five conceptual schemes are spread through grades 3–6. To date the project has been unable to negotiate marketing by a commercial firm.

OTHER WELL-KNOWN CURRICULUM PROJECTS

The Elementary School Sciences Program (ESSP) was developed by the Biological Sciences Curriculum Study. Its goal was to develop an activity-oriented program for grades K–6. Its program was built around children's interests and their perception of self and environment. The emphasis was on "doing" activities, not on reading science.

The Minnesota Mathematics and Science Teaching Project (MINNE-MAST) was established 1961 at the University of Minnesota. Its goal was to produce a coordinated science and mathematics program for grades K–6 and to develop in-service teacher training materials to go along with the program. Its program was built around the following six processes of science: observation, measurement, experimentation, description, generalization, and deduction. (Unfortunately, curtailment of funds made it necessary to terminate the program after grade 3.)

The Oakleaf Individualized Elementary School Science Project (later called Individualized Science) was established in 1964 at the University of Pittsburgh. Its goal was to develop materials that would let children in grades K–6 work independently on individually prescribed laboratory activities.

SUGGESTIONS FOR SELECTING A CURRICULUM PROJECT
PROGRAM

Most school administrators and curriculum directors probably would prefer to develop an elementary science program specifically designed to meet the individual backgrounds, learning characteristics, abilities, and needs of the children in their schools. If it is to be done well, developing such a program can be long and arduous, involving a considerable amount of time, effort, and personnel. Consequently, if a decision is made to use a curriculum project instead, it is imperative to select a program that will coincide most closely with the school's philosophy and goals, that will most successfully promote and facilitate learning by the children, and that will put the teachers most at ease when conducting the lessons and units.

There are certain steps that school systems may take that will help them decide which program to select from the curriculum projects that are still currently available. The companies that market such programs can provide informational literature. Their units and materials can be purchased and tried out by individual teachers. Schools will often try out two or more different programs at the same time in different classrooms, then compare the reactions of teachers and children to the programs. The companies that market the programs will usually send representatives to demonstrate their materials to interested schools.

There are also certain guidelines that schools or school systems can follow that will help them in selecting a program. One such guideline has to do with the main focus of the program. This main focus varies for the different programs. SAPA focuses on the development of specific process skills, and evaluation is made in terms of the attainment of these skills. Concepts are a necessary part of the program, but the program does not focus on them, and the concepts have no control in how the objectives of the units in the program are sequenced. SCIS and COPES focus on conceptual schemes more than on the development of process skills. These projects believe that the conceptual schemes should be the basis for explaining a large number of natural phenomena and, in the process, help develop process skills. ESS focuses on environmental phenomena and uses nondirected exploration, first to raise questions about the causes and effects of these phenomena and then to find ways of obtaining answers to these questions. Although ESS doesn't provide for the development of process skills, it believes that its program can be used for this purpose, if desired.

A second guideline is the examination of the teaching strategy of the program. All the programs use an inquiry and discovery approach for teaching their individual units. They suggest procedures for introducing and conducting the lessons and for developing successful attainment of the objectives. In all the programs the role of the teacher is primarily a nondirective one, and the children are encouraged to inquire, discover, explain, and apply what they have learned on their own. However, the programs do vary in how closely the teacher should follow the suggested procedures and how uniform the approach should be for the lessons. SCIS specifies a single procedure of instruction for most of its units. SAPA, ESS, and COPES suggest different instructional procedures for different units and encourage the teachers to devise their own procedures if they are dissatisfied with the recommended ones. SAPA, however, does qualify its encouragement of alternative procedures by insisting that whatever procedure is selected, the outcome must be consistent with the behavioral objectives set for the unit.

A third guideline has to do with the sequencing of the lessons and units in the programs. The programs vary in the degree in which learning in one lesson of a unit depends upon successful completion of learning in a previous lesson. Also, programs vary in their degree of flexibility in allowing a teacher to determine or change the order in which the lessons and units will be taken up in class. These factors will also have an influence on how easily a program can be adapted to a school's existing program. SAPA and COPES specify clearly the sequencing of individual units. SCIS also specifies sequencing but recognizes and encourages the occasional need to resequence lessons as the need arises. ESS does not specify a sequence at all for any of its units, but it does indicate which units are appropriate for the primary grades and which ones are best suited for the middle grades.

A fourth guideline has to do with the possibility of being able to coordinate the programs with required existing science programs or textbooks. This is a factor in areas that have state-adopted textbooks or curriculum guides that must be followed. ESS seems to have the only program whose materials can be easily incorporated into an existing program or text. The programs of the other projects are sequenced in such a way that incorporation into existing programs or texts would be difficult.

For Discussion

1. Granted that all the prerequisites for an effective elementary science program are necessary, which prerequisites do you think are the most important? Justify your choice.

2. What other specific examples can you think of for correlating science with the rest of the areas in the elementary school curriculum?

3. Why is scope and sequence so important to a science program?

4. Can science really be taught effectively in the kindergarten? Why?

5. What kinds of in-service activities do you think would help the beginning teacher and the teacher with an inadequate science background?

6. What should the role of the supervisor be in the elementary science program? The curriculum director? The principal? The superintendent?

7. What effect do you think the curriculum projects have had on the kind and amount of science being taught in the elementary schools?

8. Do you think there should be a national curriculum for elementary science? Why?

CHAPTER 4

METHODS *of*
TEACHING SCIENCE

METHODS of teaching science—the *how* of teaching science—are the means whereby the children use inquiry and discovery to learn both the content and process of science, thereby achieving the objectives of science. In the process, desirable behavioral objectives and outcomes are attained.

Many teachers are interested almost exclusively in only the methods of teaching science. They feel that this is the really important phase of science teaching and learning. Consequently, when these teachers plan to teach a science topic, invariably their first action is to look for good experiments and demonstrations, which they can perform, or good films or filmstrips, which they can show. They assume that if their selections are good, the learning of content and process will automatically follow. Often these teachers are very disappointed when they are frustrated in achieving the desired results. The teachers then blame the activities they have selected, discard the activities, and continue their quest for better ones.

This procedure is a good example of putting the cart before the horse. It is true that the methods of teaching science are the means through which content and process are learned and the objectives of science are achieved. However, these results cannot be accomplished by selecting the methods first. We must first know what we want to teach and why we want to teach it before we can begin to think of how we want to teach it.

The most common methods of teaching science in the elementary school involve the use of experiments, reading, reporting, discussion, field trips, resource persons, and audio-visual materials.

Some methods lend themselves better to a learning situation than do others. Often the availability of supplies and equipment, textbooks and references, or films and filmstrips will help determine the method to be used. Also, the children like variety as well as a change of pace. This variety tends to promote better interest, especially since the children's attention span is not usually long. At the same time a variety of methods will provide different children with an opportunity to assume leadership roles while learning is in progress.

Learning Through Inquiry

THE PHILOSOPHY that science should be taught as a process of inquiry is now universally accepted. This means that learning activities involving the use of experiments, reading, reporting, discussion, field trips, and audio-visual materials should be conducted, wherever possible, in such a way that they all are highly activity-oriented.

Learning through inquiry is an integral part of discovery learning, in which the children are given the opportunity to discover for themselves the answers to problems. In the process, the children develop desirable behaviors and learn key concepts and conceptual schemes. When learning through inquiry, the children use their skills (both physical and mental) and previous science background to actively search for and collect information, using whatever methods of investigation that are available or can be devised, which will help them discover the solutions to problems they are attempting to solve.

Learning through inquiry follows a general pattern. First, a question (or series of questions) is raised, the answers to which the children do not know. Through discussion a problem is identified and narrowed until it seems likely that the children can investigate and possibly solve the problem. With the help of the teacher the children then propose ways of investigating the problem and of gathering the data, using their mental resources and whatever materials (laboratory, printed, audio-visual, etc.) that are available. Working either individually, in small groups, or as a class, the children now conduct investigations, gather data which they interpret and summarize, and come to conclusions which they evaluate. All this leads to new questions which raise new problems which require new investigations which produce new conclusions, and this procedure is then repeated over and over again.

Learning through inquiry takes time, but this is necessary if children are to discover for themselves the answers to problems. Discovering the answers for themselves is of prime importance in helping children learn how to learn. Consequently, in inquiry learning there is no urgency to finish the investigation of a problem in a specified length of time.

Since inquiry learning is centered around a series of problem-solving investigations that actively involve the children, there must be careful planning by the teacher. The teacher must plan problem situations that will initiate curiosity and questions. The teacher must become familiar with a variety of learning activities and methods that the children will have to use or choose from to answer the questions and thus solve their problems. The teacher must be knowledgeable about the concepts and conceptual schemes that will be learned when the problems are solved.

(Barbara Van Cleve)

Learning through inquiry.

The teacher must be familiar with the process skills that will be used or developed by the children when they seek answers to the questions. The teacher must have additional investigations and other kinds of activities available for slow and fast learners. Finally, plans must be made to evaluate investigation results and the learning that has taken place.

The teacher plays an equally important role while the children are in the process of learning through inquiry. The teacher provides a variety of thought-provoking questions that will start inquiry learning and keep it moving along. The teacher directs the learning activities so that the children can discover for themselves the answers to their questions and problems. This means that the teacher is a guide and a counselor, not a source or dispenser of knowledge. When inquiry learning bogs down, the teacher does not supply answers, but offers cues instead that will help the children continue with the investigation. The teacher is constantly on the alert to keep the children from jumping to hasty conclusions or getting side-tracked into other problems that are either barely related or unrelated to the original problem being investigated. Finally, the teacher participates actively in the enthusiasm that prevails during the investigations, and shows both excitement and delight when the children discover the answers to their problems.

There are several distinct benefits and advantages to be derived when children learn through inquiry. First, the child becomes a participant rather than a spectator. The focus of attention is on the child, not on the teacher. This eliminates boredom and encourages the children to rely more on their own resources. It also gives children a satisfying sense of accomplishment and promotes their self-confidence. Also, since this technique is highly activity-oriented, it tends to develop competency in the use of process skills, and it encourages the promotion of desirable scientific attitudes. Finally, learning through inquiry is in keeping with the theories of such educational psychologists as Piaget, Bruner, and Gagné on how children develop intellectually and learn.

Learning through inquiry also has its problems as well as advantages. Some psychologists and educators believe that learning through inquiry is very difficult for slow learners because such learners find it hard to persist in tasks that are not immediately fruitful. Others maintain that learning through inquiry is not appropriate for younger children, especially those below the age of nine, because these children do not have the high motivation to master intellectual tasks and because they tend to be impulsive, jump prematurely to conclusions, and fail.

Some psychologists and science educators feel that a prerequisite for learning through inquiry is a good science background. Because children in the elementary school rarely have such a background, learning through inquiry will often falter and fail. Others maintain there is a greater possibility of failure when learning through inquiry, and failure often dampens many children's interest in learning further in science.

Finally, many teachers who become enthusiastic about inquiry teaching tend to overemphasize the use of experimentation at the expense of other methods that are also effective and even necessary. Everything can not be learned by experimentation only. For example, a teacher explanation is sometimes absolutely necessary. Reading, which is an integral part of the elementary school curriculum, also is often needed. This is why those who try to teach inquiry only through experimentation often find themselves beset with problems that affect successful learning.

Experiments

EXPERIMENTS are the heart and soul of science teaching and learning. Of all the methods used to teach science, the use of experiments is the one that produces the most curiosity, interest, excitement, and satisfaction. It is the technique that is ideally suited for learning through inquiry. It is the means whereby the children can develop proficiency in a large number of process skills while they are discovering science concepts and conceptual schemes. Other methods and techniques are also valuable for teaching and learning science, but they are usually most effective when used either in conjunction with or as a result of the use of experiments.

Experiments can be used in many ways, all of which should be employed. They can arouse interest and raise questions or problems. They can be used to answer questions or solve problems. They can help the children learn how to think by having the children apply what they have learned to new, unfamiliar situations.

WAYS OF USING EXPERIMENTS

Arousing Interest and Raising Questions or Problems • Nothing does more to initiate a unit or daily lesson successfully than an experiment that arouses the interest of the class and raises questions or problems. On a cold, dry day in winter, rub an inflated rubber balloon briskly against a wool suit or with a piece of wool cloth, then place the balloon against the wall. This initiating activity may be done by the teacher or, if enough balloons are available, by the pupils as a class experiment. The children's interest will be aroused immediately when they see the balloon stick to the wall. Their interest should naturally provoke comment and much discussion. When questions are raised and problems stated, the class is well on its way to the study of static electricity.

When used as an initiating activity for a unit or daily lesson, the experiment also serves to give the children an orientation to the science topic. At the same time, by raising questions or problems, it often helps make the children aware that they must learn much more about the science topic before they can explain the experiment.

(Dave Logan/Van Cleve)

Experiments help children learn to solve problems.

Helping to Solve Problems • Experiments are ideal techniques for problem solving, which has already been described as one of the key objectives of science in the elementary school. Experiments are helpful in solving such problems as why eyeglasses fog in the winter when a person comes into the warm house from the cold outside, why airplanes fly, how plants get their food, and how heat travels. In the process of solving these problems the children are learning to think critically and creatively, and to develop proficency in the key operations of science and the scientist. The children learn how to define the problem and the terms involved, to make accurate observations and to classify them, to formulate and test hypotheses, to understand the nature of controls and

[69

the value of numbers of experiments to ensure reliability and validity, and to draw conclusions.

Applying What Has Been Learned to New Situations • In a sense this application serves as an evaluative technique. If the children have really learned the desired science understandings, they should be able to apply what they have learned to a new situation. Thus, if the children have acquired a thorough knowledge of electromagnets, they should be able to explain the operation of a simple telegraph set. If they are completely familiar with simple machines, they should be able to identify, classify, and explain the operation of many of the common tools and appliances used in the home.

This method of using experiments helps, at the same time, to relate what has been learned to the children's environment. Furthermore, the method is directed toward developing critical thinking, because the children must now review the aspects of the experiment, weigh and sift the evidence, call upon their store of science knowledge, make and suspend judgments, hypothesize, and finally come to a satisfactory conclusion.

Encouraging and Challenging Slow and Rapid Learners • The performance of experiments provides an excellent opportunity to help the slow learner. They help develop the ability to observe and report accurately. They help give slow learners needed confidence in organizing the data, in sensing problems, and in solving these problems scientifically. They provide the satisfying status involved in occasionally assisting the teacher and in having the opportunity to explain to the rest of the children the reasons or principles underlying the experiment.

Experiments are also an excellent way to challenge the rapid learner. There are several ways in which this challenge can be accomplished. The rapid learner can repeat experiments done by the teacher to gain new insights. He can do additional experiments by himself with the consent and supervision of the teacher. He can assist the teacher in doing experiments. In this situation the teacher should make sure that the rapid learner is a real assistant, and not a helper who fetches and carries materials and who then cleans up and stores the materials afterward.

The rapid learner can also be of great value in helping the slow learner. In many cases a child can explain or demonstrate things very satisfactorily to another child, even after the teacher has failed to do so. It often seems as if the children have their own special jargon, by which they communicate with each other very effectively. Besides, while helping the slow learner, the rapid learner is also helping himself. In the process of helping the slow learner, the science understandings involved in the experiment become quite firmly fixed in the mind of the rapid learner. It is a common axiom that a person really knows a subject when he is able to explain or demonstrate it effectively to another person.

SUGGESTIONS FOR DOING EXPERIMENTS

The Experiment Should Have a Purpose • Do not perform experiments without a specific purpose. Some teachers may think that as long as they conduct a large number of experiments, they are teaching much science and at the same time gaining a reputation as good science teachers. This impression is completely erroneous. Every experiment should have a definite purpose, either as a planned, integral part of a lesson or as a learning situation that has arisen extemporaneously.

Moreover, this purpose should be altogether clear, so that it is known and understood by all the children. In every experiment the children should know just what they are looking for. Otherwise the results may be ineffective and meaningless.

Planning Is Important • Experiments should be planned carefully and exactly. The necessary materials should be collected in advance and be ready for assembling or distributing so that there will be no delay or break in continuity of the learning situation. Also, the experiment should be tried out in advance. Even though the instructions in the text or reference book are usually clear, sometimes there are slight ambiguities or tricky manipulations. By doing the experiment in advance, the teacher can clear up these complications and revise or amplify the instructions so that successful performance will be assured.

(William Means/Van Cleve)

Planning is important.

It is also a good idea to follow instructions very carefully and exactly. Very often a person is tempted to heat a solution a little longer or add more than the called-for quantity of a chemical to make sure the experiment will go well. In such cases sometimes the result is likely to be quite unexpected, ineffective, or even disastrous.

Find Opportunities to Involve the Children • The children should help in defining the purpose of the experiment. Children can often state the purpose in a much more challenging way than the teacher. When this kind of statement is made, the experiment now becomes much more meaningful to the children. In a sense it has become their personal property and problem.

The children can help in planning experiments. This involves many worthwhile phases and methods of learning. For example, they may read and discuss the science principles involved. They may suggest different ways and means of doing the experiment. They may plan and work together. They may collect materials. They may gather and organize observations and data. They may plan to check their findings and conclusions. In this way it becomes their plan. And if something should go wrong with the experiment, they now have a personal stake in finding out why it did not work.

Whenever possible, let the children do the experiment themselves. If this procedure is not advisable, one or more children can assist the teacher. This privilege should be rotated so that all the children will have an opportunity to participate. In those cases where, for various reasons, the experiment is performed by just one or two persons, the teacher should always keep in mind that it is being given for the benefit of all the children. The teacher should check to make sure that the experiment is conducted in such a way that it is interesting, clearly presented, not too long or tedious, and capable of producing the desired outcomes.

Finally, the teacher should keep in mind that the children themselves can originate experiments. Very often an experiment will raise further questions and problems that call for original planning and investigation. The teacher should take advantage of the situation because it involves the children in all the elements of the problem-solving process. It also has the added advantage of offering a challenge to the children, especially the gifted.

Aim for Thinking and Discussion • Whenever possible, conduct the experiments in such a way as to arouse thinking and discussion. Do not tell the children the answer or have them read the answer in advance because, if you do, there is no point in doing the experiment. When the children are told in advance that the experiment they are to do will show them that the shorter the vibrating string the higher the musical note produced, this advance information will immediately take away the thrill of discovery and will destroy much of the interest.

Open-ended experiments lend themselves very well to thinking and discussion because they excite the children's curiosity and stimulate their imagination. Children respond instantly to the challenge of the question, "What will happen if . . . ?" Through thinking and discussion they can devise ways and means of attacking the problem, suggest experiments or other ways and means of solving the problem, even devise equipment at times, make careful observations and notations, and check their conclusions to see if they are correct.

Keep the Experiments Simple and Easily Visible • Use simple and familiar materials rather than complicated and specialized equipment. Although some of the simple apparatus used in the high schools may be most helpful and even necessary, there is no justification for a wholesale transfer of high school equipment and apparatus to the elementary school. Complicated and unfamiliar equipment will often distract the children's attention. They become much more interested in the way the equipment works than in the results of the experiment. In many cases the simpler and more familiar the materials, the more effective the experiment.

The experiment should be easily visible to all students. This is an aspect that many teachers forget or ignore. There is no reason to assume that, because the equipment is easily visible to the children in the front of the room, all the other children can see it just as well. Furthermore, there is often a tendency to keep the demonstration table so cluttered that either the children cannot see what is going on, or their attention is distracted by the other materials on the table. When one or two persons are doing the experiment, they usually should be in back of the counter or table. The table should be high enough so that all can see quite clearly. The lighting should be checked so that visibility is good for all. Use equipment and materials that are as large as possible. As it is they will look small enough to those children in the rear of the room. In some cases it may be helpful to have the experiment done in the middle of the room so that all the children can gather around to watch it.

Apply What Is Learned to the Children's Environment • Experiments should do more than answer the immediate questions and problems. If there is to be any real value gained, the experiment should also help answer questions about things that are happening in the children's daily environment. The results should be applied to corresponding situations that occur in everyday living. Thus, the children should learn not only that dark objects absorb more heat than do light objects, but also that this is one reason why light-colored clothing is preferable in the summer and dark-colored clothing is preferable in the winter.

Repeat the Experiment If Necessary • Sometimes the understandings or concepts involved in an experiment are quite complex or numerous, so that it is necessary to repeat the experiment if the learning is to

[73

be profitable to all the children. Teachers and children, when doing an experiment, often run through it quickly without giving the rest of the class an opportunity to grasp all the understandings and implications involved. They forget that what seem like simple ideas or relationships to them may be unfamiliar to the other children.

Use Controls and Numbers of Experiments Wherever Possible • The use of controls in experiments is one of the key operations of the scientist. Children are able to understand very easily the need for, as well as the nature of, a control experiment. In an experiment using a control, all the conditions are duplicated except one, and this single condition is the one that is being tested. For example, when studying the effect of heat upon the rate of evaporation, a control helps prove conclusively that heat makes liquids evaporate more quickly. The same measured quantity of water is poured into each of two identical pie tins. One tin is placed on the hot radiator, and the other tin is placed on a table on the other side of the room. The windows and door are kept closed so that any effect caused by the wind or air circulation will be eliminated. Now all the conditions are the same except one, namely, the temperature to which the water is exposed. Consequently, as a result of the control, the results of the experiment become clear-cut and obvious.

Teaching the nature of a control experiment to children today is much less complicated because the children have been exposed to television. The commercials widely use so-called "experiments" with controls to prove a product superior. It would be an interesting assignment for the

(William Means/Van Cleve)

Use controls and numbers of experiments wherever possible.

children to observe closely to see whether all the conditions but one are duplicated, and especially to look for unwarranted assumptions. This observation would create a learning situation that would be just as popular and profitable as the situation involving superstition versus science.

After the children have learned the nature and value of control, they should also be exposed to the necessity of sometimes having to use numbers of experiments to secure results that are valid or reliable. Children are quick to understand the need for using numbers of experiments. If a teacher were to suggest that the class should conduct an experiment to see which was the faster writer, a right-handed or left-handed child, the class would be quick to object to an experiment involving just one right-handed and one left-handed child. The need for using a number of children to make the experiment reliable would be obvious to all.

Similarly, when you are finding the dew point (the temperature at which water vapor in the air will condense back into water), it will be so difficult to note the exact temperature when the dew point is reached that the children will recognize the need to repeat the experiment a number of times and perhaps take an average to obtain satisfactory results. In this way, experiments requiring a number of repetitions will help prevent the children from making broad generalizations from just one experiment.

Aim for Quantitative as Well as Qualitative Results • Science in the elementary school has been primarily qualitative in nature; very little has been quantitative. Quantitative results should also be stressed. The children are constantly exposed to the "why" and "what" of science and rarely to the "how much." As a result a golden opportunity is being missed not only to show the child key relationships, but also to provide for practice in measurement, which is one of the key operations of science and the scientist.

Take, for example, the experiments designed to show how the strength of an electromagnet may be increased. It is customary to prove this either by increasing the number of turns of wire around the piece of iron or by using more dry cells.

However, consider how much more effective a learning situation this becomes if we make the experiments quantitative in nature. When first making the electromagnet, the children wrap 30 turns of wire around the iron nail or bolt. Then they count the number of tacks the electromagnet will pick up. Now when the children wrap 60 turns of wire around the iron nail, they find that the second electromagnet will pick up twice as many tacks. There should be little difficulty in realizing that, if we double the number of turns of wire, we double the number of tacks that will be picked up. Consequently, the electromagnet has been made twice as strong. If the experiment is repeated, however, this time using the same number of turns of wire in each case and using first one and then two dry cells (connected in series), the results will be the same

(William Means/Van Cleve)

Aim for quantitative as well as qualitative results.

as when the number of turns of wire was doubled. If we double the number of dry cells, using the same number of turns, we double the number of tacks that will be picked up, and again we have made the electromagnet twice as strong. The children could then be asked to find out what would happen if we doubled both the number of dry cells and the number of turns at the same time.

In this experiment the children not only learn science understandings and principles, but also are given an opportunity to discover mathematical ratios and relationships. There are many opportunities in the teaching of science to include the teaching of measurement, numbers, size, and simple ratio. This is a phase that has been neglected too long.

Aim for Quality Not Quantity • Because the elementary school curriculum is already so crowded and because such a small portion of the school day is usually devoted to teaching science, minutes become very precious. At the same time the teacher will often come upon several different experiments, all of which illustrate or develop the same science understandings or principles. Because all these experiments are quite effective or even spectacular, the teacher is often tempted to use all of them. The teacher may justify her decision by believing that the repetition will help secure the children's learning of the understandings involved. Although this justification may be true in some cases, it is likely that a teacher who follows this practice repeatedly will teach much less science than actually should and could have been taught during the school year. The primary loss, of course, will be to the children.

The teacher, then, should look for quality when selecting experiments and demonstrations, restricting herself to those that will teach the most and best in the shortest possible time. This emphasis of quality over quantity will vary somewhat in the lower and upper elementary grades. In the lower elementary grades the amount of science content to be taught is still relatively small, and the ability of the children to read and to think abstractly is low. Consequently, it would seem advisable to use a comparatively large number of experiments and demonstrations to ensure proper learning of content and process. In the upper elementary grades, however, the amount of content and process to be taught becomes progressively greater. Time is important, and quality of selection becomes increasingly more important than quantity.

It should be noted that this suggestion is not intended to minimize the use or value of doing experiments. It is meant as a recommendation not to use them wastefully. If the teacher has collected many experiments and then decides not to use them all, the excess need not be wasted. They should be set aside for both slow and rapid learners. When time is available the slow learners can do some of these experiments to reinforce their knowledge of the science understandings involved while the rapid learners can do the others to extend their knowledge further.

WHEN EXPERIMENTS FAIL TO WORK

Sometimes experiments fail to work. This can happen even if the teacher and children have followed the instructions carefully and accurately, measured out the exact amounts, checked the apparatus and equipment, and even tried out the experiment in advance. Many teachers are embarrassed when this happens, especially new and inexperienced teachers. They may become distressed because what they have worked so hard to accomplish seems to have fizzled miserably. They may even feel that they have lost face or prestige and as a result appear inept or incompetent before the children. If it happens often, these teachers may become reluctant to use experiments in class, or perhaps even to teach science.

Actually, failure of an experiment to work can become a valuable learning situation. The failure becomes a real problem for both teacher and children. The children now have been provided with an unexpected opportunity to help solve a common problem, to think critically and creatively, and to propose solutions. If the children have been involved in the experiment from the beginning, they will have a vested interest in the outcome and in any difficulties that may arise.

When an experiment fails to work, one approach would be first to analyze the situation, with the help of the children, and decide upon the possible reasons for the failure. Next, check each factor methodically and carefully. It is likely that the cause of the failure will become apparent, and a valuable learning experience will have been gained.

One elementary school teacher took advantage of the failure of an experiment when the class was studying expansion and contraction. To see what happens to gases when heated, an experiment was selected involving a rubber balloon and a soda bottle. The balloon was snapped over the neck of the bottle and the bottle was placed upon the radiator in the room. Ordinarily the balloon will fill up and grow larger as the air inside the bottle is heated and expands. This time nothing happened. The teacher was disconcerted because the same experiment had been used in other classes, always with successful results. However, the teacher immediately called upon the class for suggestions. After some discussion the children concluded that either the balloon was punctured, the bottle was cracked, or the radiator was not hot. Each reason was checked, and the cause of the failure, a radiator that had cooled down, was quickly found. Instead of being annoyed or frustrated, both the teacher and the children were pleased that they had solved this problem so quickly and scientifically.

It is important to remember that if every possible reason has been suggested and tried and the experiment still does not work, the fault may lie with the reference or textbook from which the instructions were obtained. Some books may suggest experiments that the authors have not tried themselves. In other cases ambiguous or incomplete directions are given, or the authors have failed to warn the reader of an especially tricky manipulation. Because more than one textbook will usually contain the experiment, it might be wise for the teacher to check a second source.

A final suggestion is that the teacher not spend too much time on an unsuccessful experiment. If, after every suggestion that has been offered has been tried and the cause of the failure still cannot be found, further investigation will only be a waste of time. Ask the children to think about it overnight and come in the next day with further recommendations. Meanwhile try to get in touch with an experienced science person, such as a junior or senior high school science teacher or a scientist, as soon as possible for suggestions and advice.

TEACHER OR PUPIL EXPERIMENT?

The elementary school teacher is consistently urged to involve the children when doing the experiments. The teacher is reminded constantly that science is a *doing* subject and that the children rather than the teacher should do the doing. This suggestion is obviously intended to discourage the teacher from dominating the lesson by doing all the experiments while the children become a passive audience.

There is no fixed rule about who shall do experiments. Sometimes the teacher should do them and other times the children should do them. In some cases it is advisable for the teacher, or one or two children, to do an experiment rather than the entire class. In some cases the teacher alone should do the experiment whereas in other cases the children should do it with the teacher acting as an assistant. There are several factors that should be considered whenever a teacher is trying to decide whether the teacher or children should do an experiment.

Safety • The safety factor is extremely important when deciding who shall do the experiment. The use of strong acids or bases, heat or flame, sharp tools, high voltage electricity, or any other procedure involving a hazard—especially in the lower grades—should make it advisable for the teacher to do the experiment. Accidents in the classroom usually produce awkward situations and should be avoided wherever possible.

Sufficient Equipment • Sometimes the availability of the equipment will easily solve the problem about who should do the experiment. If there is very little available equipment and no hazard, the logical decision would be for one or two children to do the experiment. If there is sufficient equipment, all the children should participate.

Expensive Apparatus • If the apparatus is quite expensive, it is likely that there is only one of its kind available. This fact would immediately limit the performance of the experiment to the teacher alone with the assistance of one or two children. If the teacher is willing to take the risk, however, the experiment may be conducted by one or two children with the teacher close by to assist or watch.

Time • Time is also an important factor because such a small portion of the daily program is usually allotted for teaching science. The beginning teacher sometimes does not realize how much time may be involved when the entire class is doing an experiment. Materials must be distributed; instructions must be given (and repeated); time must be used to see that everyone is doing the experiment properly; then the materials must be collected. There is not enough time available in the school for *all* the children to do *every* experiment. The teacher, therefore, should constantly evaluate each experiment. If the value to be derived by having all the children participate is worth the time, by all means have all the children do the experiment.

Learning Potential • Perhaps the most important factor in trying to decide who shall do the experiment is the amount or kind of learning that will take place in each case. If the class would learn just as much when one or two children do the experiment, this might warrant having just the one or two children do the experiment. Take, for example, the experiment to discover the law of magnets, that is, when like poles repel and unlike poles attract each other. The children would learn little more, if any, by doing the experiment themselves rather than by watching one or two of their classmates do it. There are no further understandings to be learned, or new skills to be gained, by having all the children do the experiment.

However, when studying open and closed electrical circuits or good and poor conductors of electricity, there are definite values to be gained by learning how to set up a simple electrical circuit. In this case, greater insights may be attained, and skills acquired, which would warrant having each child do the experiment.

Thus, if there is no difference in the amount and kind of learning that will take place, have one or two children perform the experiment rather than the entire class. But if there is a difference, and especially if the learning of skills is involved, let the entire class do the experiment.

Reading

LEARNING science through reading is and will continue to be an important method of teaching science in the elementary school. Not everything can be learned either directly by doing experiments and demonstrations or vicariously by taking field trips, bringing in resource persons, and using audio-visual materials. There is much that can, and must, be learned by reading the material contained in textbooks, supplementary books, magazines, bulletins or journals, and newspapers.

The ability to learn through reading is a reliable indication that, by being able to absorb abstract ideas successfully, the children are growing in mental maturity. The use of reading in science can also make a valuable contribution to the reading program in the elementary school. It can help develop the children's vocabulary, increase their enjoyment in reading, and stimulate their desire to read for information.

The use of reading as a method of teaching science has occasionally

(William Means/Van Cleve)

Reading is most effective when it has a purpose.

been criticized. This criticism has not been directed at the use of reading as a means of learning, but rather at its misuse. Too often the learning of science in the elementary school has been nothing more than reading about science. When this type of teaching occurs, the learning of science becomes quite sterile and unproductive, with the consequent loss of interest by the children. Little, if any, real and lasting values result. When properly handled, however, reading can make a vital contribution to learning.

Reading is most effective when it has a purpose. Nothing can make the children dislike or lose interest in science more quickly than an arbitrary reading assignment, followed by talking or discussion. On the other hand, when reading has a purpose, interest is easily aroused and enthusiasm is kindled.

Reading for a purpose can be used to motivate the study of science in all phases of the learning process. It can be used in planning or preparing for experiments, demonstrations, field trips, resource persons, films, and filmstrips. While these activities are going on, reading can be used to find answers to questions, solve problems, and obtain additional information. When finishing these activities, reading can be used to check findings and conclusions. It can also reinforce, supplement, and extend further what the children have learned.

SUGGESTIONS FOR USING READING

Aim for Helping the Children to Think and Learn • Reading can be used to encourage the children to think. After the children have read with a specific purpose in mind, reading should be followed by discussion, experiments, reports, or any other activities that will help the children think about and interpret what they have read and learned.

Teach the Children How to Use Reading Materials Effectively • As the children become sufficiently mature, teach them how to use the table of contents, index, and glossary. Give the children practice in how to find the information they are seeking. It would be helpful to familiarize them with the broad science areas and topics under which the more specific terms would be listed.

Make sure the children are aware of the different sources—supplementary books, encyclopedias, bulletins, journals, magazines, newspapers, and so forth—where they may obtain the information they want. Show them where all these materials are located in the library. If there is a card catalog, help the children learn how to use it.

Simple charts and graphs are new to the children. Show the children both how to construct and how to read them. The same should be done for line drawings and diagrams. The children should also learn how to take notes about what they are reading, especially if they are preparing reports.

Point Out the Difference in Purpose of the Various Reading Materials • Some books are written primarily for the reader's enjoyment.

Although attention may be paid to detail and accuracy, the prime purpose of the book is to give pleasure. Animals and plants may speak or are given human characteristics. Other books are written primarily for science information. Although both kinds of books are most acceptable, the children should learn to make a distinction between them and use each kind for the purpose it was intended.

Have Several Sources of Information Available, on Different Reading Levels • Although most textbooks and supplementary books contain approximately the same science information, they do vary both in style and content. Some present the material from a slightly different or simpler point of view. Some may be a little more complete or may have clearer and more detailed drawings and diagrams. Some may have more experiments and "things to do" in them. All of them, when made available to the children, supplement each other and help provide a rich background of material that the children can explore and utilize.

Because the reading ability of the children will vary in each class, it is wise to have reading materials on different levels. Most elementary textbook series do not agree on the grade placement of science topics. Consequently, it is not unusual to find a science topic in a fifth-grade textbook of one series, and in fourth- or even sixth-grade textbooks of other series. Thus, even if the class is committed to one textbook, it will be helpful to have a few copies from other series available.

Supplementary books have been written on many science topics, ranging in content and readability from lower elementary grade levels to junior high levels. If the teacher has a variety of such references available, she will provide reading materials suitable and appropriate for children of all levels of reading and learning ability.

Several weekly and monthly magazines often present material that is not only scientifically accurate but is written from a human interest point of view. These sources also contain beautifully colored illustrations, which ordinarily do not appear in textbooks and reference books.

Aim for Developing the Children's Science Vocabulary • The science program is just one part of the elementary school curriculum. It should be correlated, when possible, with the language arts, social studies, arithmetic, and other programs in the elementary school. It follows, then, that reading from a science book is no different from reading from any other book for developing vocabulary. Here the emphasis is on learning science words.

When new words appear while the children are learning science, the exact meaning of these words should be made evident to the children. Close attention should be paid to the correct spelling of such words. Give the children an opportunity to say the words out loud a few times to get the feel of the word on their tongues. Children are often delighted with the way a word sounds when spoken aloud. Take advantage of this delight to fix the word clearly in the children's minds.

Develop the understanding of science words through experiments, discussion, reports, and other activities. Encourage the children to use these words freely during their learning experiences. Look for opportunities to use the words later, when the children are learning about other science topics that are related to the topic where the words were originally introduced.

Reports

THE USE of oral and written reports in teaching science is fairly common in the elementary school. When properly presented, both oral and written reports will provide a valuable learning experience for the children giving the reports as well as for those children listening to the reports.

Very often, however, the children's reports can be disappointing to the teacher. The results are not those for which the teacher hoped or expected. Some oral reports seem to have no logical method of presentation, and they wander aimlessly. Some reports are long and drawn-out whereas others are absurdly brief. Many reports are not true oral reports, but rather written reports read orally. The result is that oral reports are often boring, confusing, or even mirth provoking.

Written reports also suffer from the same shortcomings. There is also

(William Means/Van Cleve)

Giving a report can be a valuable learning experience.

an additional hazard. Too often the contents of written reports have been copied literally from textbooks, supplementary books, and encyclopedias. Interestingly enough, the children as a rule are surprised that the teacher is able to spot a "copy job" so quickly. They apparently do not realize that the writing style in textbooks and supplementary books, and especially in encyclopedias, is unique, designed to give the maximum information in the shortest possible space, and consequently it is not difficult to recognize.

When teaching children how to report properly, point out that each report, oral or written, should have a beginning, a middle, and an end. The beginning of the report contains the title or purpose of the report, often stated to catch the listener's or reader's interest. The middle of the report contains the body of information to be communicated. The end of the report contains the summary and conclusions.

When oral reports are given, they should be quite short, lasting no more than about five minutes. They should be clear and explicit, and stated in the children's own words. The children may refer to notes, but there should be no wholesale reading from the notes. The children should be instructed to speak loudly and clearly. The children should put diagrams and new vocabulary words on the chalkboard in advance so that the continuity of the report will not be broken and the comprehension of the audience will be maintained at all times. Oral reports have greater value when afterward the class is requested to ask questions and discuss the report.

The content of the written reports should be simple and clear, and in the children's own words. Point out the evils of plagiarizing, and teach the children the use of quotes, when this becomes necessary. Encourage the children to express their own opinions and to reach their own deductions and conclusions. Help them learn how to give the sources from which they obtained their information for the report.

Discussion

THE USES and values of discussion are manifold. It is an excellent means of communication between teacher and children. Through discussion the teacher learns to know the children, and the children develop a closer bond with the teacher. Discussion can be extremely valuable in initiating a unit. When planning to involve the children in a unit, the teacher first begins with a thought-provoking experiment, demonstration, or question. Or the teacher may even begin with an eye-catching display, either of actual models and specimens, or of pictures and drawings on the bulletin board. These techniques invariably arouse interest. Questions or problems are raised, which are followed by much discussion as the children and teacher plan together to answer the questions or solve the problems.

While the unit is in progress, discussion helps in explaining or clarifying experiments, demonstrations, reading, reports, field trips, resource persons, films, filmstrips, and television programs. When solving problems discussion is one of the techniques that can be used to define the problem, suggest methods of solving the problem, and check results and conclusions. Discussion can also help the children learn how to think critically, as they become involved in the process of discovering science understandings and concepts, making interpretations and judgments, and trying to apply what they have learned either to their environment or to new situations. At the same time discussion tends to develop desirable scientific attitudes, such as respecting the opinions of others, rejecting unreliable or unqualified evidence, not jumping to hasty conclusions, listening intelligently, speaking effectively, and participating cooperatively and democratically.

Discussion can also serve as an evaluation technique. It can be used as a pretest to find out how much the children already know about the science topics to be studied. The teacher can determine through discussion whether the children have learned the science content or acquired scientific attitudes. Discussion also enables the teacher to find out which children are extroverts and which children are shy or withdrawn, and therefore have to be encouraged and drawn out of their shells. It helps the teacher to identify the slow and fast learners.

When holding a discussion, the teacher should remember certain things. First, the function of the teacher during a discussion is to be a combination question-raiser, guide, helper, leader, and director of learning. To keep a discussion going profitably, the teacher must curb the

(Rohn Engh/Van Cleve)

Discussion can help develop desirable scientific attitudes.

impulse to interrupt constantly. Otherwise the children will tend to turn constantly to the teacher as the person who makes the final decision. The teacher, of course, should interrupt when the discussion seems to be going off on a tangent or in the wrong direction. When the children begin to flounder, the teacher can then offer suggestions. However, the teacher should restrain herself from giving answers; rather, she should try to answer a question with another question that will point the way to the answer. Also, during the discussion the teacher should make sure that every child who so desires will have an opportunity to participate in the discussion. Otherwise a few children may monopolize the discussion and thus exclude shy or quiet children who may have much to offer.

Second, there is a strong temptation for the teacher, who already knows the answers, to insist upon a quick, rapid-fire discussion. This procedure is unwise because discussion can be something new to many children. They need time to recall previously learned science knowledge, to digest new ideas, to apply this knowledge to new situations, and to arrive at or propose solutions. By insisting that the children take enough time to formulate and express their thoughts clearly, the teacher will help discourage quick, superficial, and inaccurate thinking.

Finally, it is important to remember that discussion works best when the children have previous learning or experiences upon which to draw or call. This fact explains why discussion is usually used in conjunction with the other teaching techniques. While the unit is in progress, a discussion presents no problems because a sufficient number of activities have been carried out to provide the children with the necessary background or experience to participate freely in the discussion. However, to begin a unit with discussion alone is another matter. If the children have had no previous background or experience in the science topic, the discussion often becomes a teacher monologue or lecture, in which the teacher both asks and answers the questions. To ensure adequate discussion when initiating a unit, more-experienced teachers first begin with a thought-provoking experiment, demonstration, question related to the children's environment, or display. This procedure ensures a discussion in which the children can make intelligent and constructive contributions to the questions and problems raised by the original initiating activity.

Field Trips

FOR MANY teachers and school systems the term *field trip* is interpreted as a visit by the teacher and children to museums, aquariums, planetariums, or industrial plants within the community. Actually, the term has a broader and more inclusive meaning. The field trip should refer to any learning activity that is carried on by the children as a group outside the classroom. Other terms are used for this kind of learning activity, depending upon the various school systems and their locality. The most common alternate terms are *excursion* and *school journey.*

The field trip is a unique teaching technique in that, like experiments and demonstrations, it provides the children firsthand experiences with materials and phenomena. It goes further than experiments and demonstrations, however, by providing experiences that cannot usually be brought into the classroom. Often it enables the children to see the materials and phenomena in their true or natural relationships. It helps the children see more clearly how the science content they have learned applies to their environment. When visiting major industries in their community, museums containing indigenous materials, or geographical points of interest, the children can begin to understand and appreciate the contributions of their community to the state, area, or country. The field trip has the added advantage of being an activity that lends itself very easily to integration with the other phases of the elementary school curriculum.

WHERE TO VISIT

All communities, urban or rural, offer a wide variety of opportunities for the children to take field trips. These may vary in time or distance. A great many can take place in or close by the school. In the school building itself the children can, for example, visit the furnace and learn about fuels, heat, and how heat travels. In the school yard the children can explore plant and insect life, the teeter-totter (as a lever), the flagpole (as a pulley), weather, and different forms of precipitation, soil, and erosion. Within walking distance of the school there may be industrial plants, quarries, dairies, or other establishments. Many of these field trips will take comparatively little time and can be used to supplement rather than interfere with activities planned for other phases of the elementary school curriculum. These field trips are just as valuable and instructive as the occasional longer trips taken to museums, zoos, factories, and other places of interest.

To utilize fully the potentialities of the community for field trips, it is wise to make a survey of all possible sources for field trips. This survey should include not only the immediate vicinity but the surrounding areas as well. The preparation of a file of potential field trips can be most helpful to the teacher. Each card can include the place to be visited, where it is located, what it has to offer, and other pertinent information. In many school systems, groups of teachers have compiled comprehensive lists of places to visit. These lists have been put into booklet form and then distributed to all the teachers in the district.

The following are some of the places that can be visited in cities, towns, or rural areas with profitable results for the learning of science.

1. Airports.
2. Apiaries.
3. Aquariums.
4. Automobile service stations.
5. Backyards.

6. Bird sanctuaries.
7. Botanical gardens.
8. Buildings under construction.
9. Chemical plants.
10. Dairies.
11. Farms.
12. Fire departments.
13. Flower shows.
14. Forests and forest preserves.
15. Gardens.
16. Gas companies.
17. Gravel pits.
18. Greenhouses.
19. Health departments.
20. Industrial plants.
21. Mines.
22. Museums.
23. Newspaper plants.
24. Observatories.
25. Orchards.
26. Parks.
27. Photography establishments.
28. Planetariums.
29. Power plants.
30. Quarries.
31. Radio stations.
32. Sanitation departments.
33. Sawmills.
34. Scientific apparatus companies.
35. Shorelines (lake and ocean).
36. Telephone buildings.
37. Television stations.
38. Water purification plants.
39. Weather bureaus.
40. Zoological parks.

WAYS OF USING FIELD TRIPS

Introducing a Unit • This method is particularly effective when the children have had little or no background in the topic to be studied. The field trip then serves as a motivating factor to create specific interest in the science topic. In this way the children are able to get an overview of the topic and a desire to learn more about it. The teacher should keep in mind that, when using a field trip to initiate a unit, the main purpose is to arouse interest and raise questions or problems, and not to find answers.

Obtaining Information during the Unit • Probably the best time to take a field trip is while the class is obtaining information during the unit. In the middle of the unit sufficient questions or problems will have been raised to warrant taking a field trip. In this case the children can use the field trip to find the answers to their questions and problems, and also to check on previous experiments, reading, discussion, and conclusions. At the same time the field trip may raise further questions and problems and thus lead into the next phase of the unit.

Providing a Culminating Activity • When used as a culminating activity at the end of the unit, the field trip is an excellent technique for summarizing the highlights or important understandings of the science topic that the children have studied. This activity helps fix the learnings firmly in the children's minds. The field trip also gives the children an opportunity to really see many of the things they have read or talked about. When planning the field trip as a culminating activity, the teacher should take care not to try to recapitulate all the learnings in the entire unit. This procedure will tend to make the field trip tedious and boring. Try instead to select the key understandings to be reviewed, and then use the field trip to illustrate and consolidate these understandings for the children.

SUGGESTIONS FOR TAKING FIELD TRIPS

The Field Trip Should Have a Purpose • The field trip can be effective as a teaching technique only when it has a purpose. There must be a real reason for taking the field trip. The purpose may be to introduce or arouse interest in a new science unit, to find the answers to questions and problems raised during the unit, or to summarize the highlights and important understandings of the unit. Whatever the purpose, it should be understood by all the children. If there are special things to look for or if there are specific answers to questions or problems to be found, make sure the children have these items clearly in mind.

Do Some Preliminary Investigation and Planning • Before the children take the field trip some necessary investigation and planning must be done by the teacher. Exactly what does the field trip offer? Is the trip worth taking? How far away is it and how much traveling time is involved? Is it suitable for the grade level and ability of the children? If the visit is to certain establishments such as museums, industrial plants, public service departments, and so forth, how many children will be allowed to come at one time? What hours are these places open? Is there a fee involved? If there is a fee, will it be paid by the children or by the school?

Find out when would be the best time to take the field trip. Some establishments like to have sufficient notice, especially if visits to these places are quite popular. Others may prefer that the children come only in the morning or afternoon. Inquire whether there is a guide or suitable personnel member available so that this person's services may be reserved.

Check to see whether there are special arrangements to be made with the school authorities. Some school systems limit the number of full-day field trips that a teacher may make each year. This limitation requires that the best possible selection be made for the field trips in science. Do the children have to obtain written permission from their parents, especially if transportation is involved? Are there any interested parents who might like to join the trip as assistants or guides?

An important phase of preparing for a field trip is inquiring about and planning for transportation. Does the school provide a bus? Is there a fee involved? If there is a fee, is it paid by the children or the school? If the school does not supply transportation, find out what other kinds of transportation are available. Does the school have group accident insur-

(Lawrence Manning/Van Cleve)

Field trips provide children with first hand experiences.

ance for the children when they take field trips by school bus or private transportation? Some localities allow children to travel in private cars. If so, arrangements must be made for all the cars to meet at a certain place at an agreed time. The route to be taken should be worked out and well known to all the drivers. Give specific, and perhaps written, instructions about meeting places, starting time, route, and time of return. Have a driver who knows the way lead the procession. Find out about parking facilities. Also, check as to whether the children are covered by the owner's accident insurance when riding in private cars.

Make a Preliminary Trip • If possible a preliminary trip should be made; this trip can be made by the teacher alone or with a committee of children. One of the first things to determine at this time is how much the children should see during the trip. Some places offer so much that it is impossible for the children to see it all at one time. There is also the possibility of undue fatigue or loss of attention. In such cases it is necessary to decide which things the children should see that will best achieve the purpose of the field trip. A second trip can always be made later if additional information is necessary.

Look for any safety hazards that may exist. Safety is one of the prime factors to be considered when making any field trip. Many teachers take a small first-aid kit during the field trip. Make a list of precautions, which should be discussed in great detail when planning with the children for the trip.

Find out whether any special demonstrations will be performed or whether any films will be shown and, if so, at what time they will be offered. If free materials are available for distribution, make sure there will be sufficient copies for all the children. Some places offer materials for sale. Make a list of these materials and their cost so that the children may come prepared to buy them.

Have a conference with the guide or personnel member who will act as guide. This conference is very important. Tell the guide the purpose of the field trip and describe the science unit in progress. Suggest aspects that the guide should stress when the children come. Remind the guide of the grade level of the children and urge strongly that the talk be kept at the level of the children's understanding. Otherwise there will be no value in having a guide. If possible, the teacher should supply the guide with a list of anticipated questions the children will raise or want answered.

For the children's convenience, the teacher should find out where the rest rooms and drinking fountains are. If the field trip will take all day, there is the problem of lunch. Some industrial plants, museums, and zoos have lunchrooms. Other places may not have cafeterias but do provide a room where the children may eat lunches they can bring.

PLAN WITH THE CHILDREN FOR THE TRIP

Pupil participation in planning the trip is an essential part of the learning experience to be gained by taking the trip. The children will feel that it is their trip, and, because they have worked cooperatively and democratically in planning, the trip should proceed more smoothly. It is also likely that a greater amount of learning will take place.

The children can play an important part in planning the trip. Some of the children can accompany the teacher on the preliminary trip and help the teacher with the preliminary investigation and planning. Others, or even the entire class, can help compose and send a letter asking the owner of a private concern for permission to visit. The children can discuss and agree upon the proper conduct and behavior to be maintained while they are on the trip. Discipline is much easier to maintain when the children clearly understand the rules, and especially when they themselves have helped draw up these rules. This discussion should encompass proper behavior and courtesy not only for the time the children are traveling to and from the place to be visited, but also for the time they are at the place itself. This determination of rules of conduct helps in maintaining good relationships, and ensures continued permission to visit the establishment.

In all field trips the teacher must be constantly concerned with two things: preventing accidents and making sure that no one strays or gets lost. Discuss both factors with the children, especially potential hazards. Have the children select leaders or lieutenants to assist the teacher. These assistants can help take attendance when needed. Each may be put in charge of small groups during the trip, with instructions to watch out for accidents or lagging. One or two of the assistants may be in the rear while the teacher remains in front with the guide, or vice versa. The "buddy" system, as in swimming, may also be used to advantage.

Let the children help decide what they will see or do on the field trip. The children are quick to understand that not everything can be done in one day. Otherwise the trip will be hurried, and the value of taking the trip may be lost. Help the children draw up the list of questions they want answered and the items they want to see. They should try to make the questions as explicit as possible so that the answers will be definite and to the point.

Give Specific Assignments to Individuals or Small Groups • Giving specific assignments to individuals or small groups is one of the most effective ways of ensuring that the field trip will be successful as a learning experience. Most persons, after they have visited a museum, for example, usually leave with two impressions: first, that they have seen a great many things and, second, that they are fatigued. This reaction is common in adults as well as children. But, although they have seen many things, they are able to recall only a few items vividly. The rest is rather vague. This phenomenon explains why so many teachers are disappointed in field trips. The children may have seemed to learn a lot during the field trip, but they can recall comparatively little during the follow-up in class the next day.

The situation can be remedied substantially by assigning individuals or small groups to observe or listen to certain things, which they will report to the class the next day. This method is an excellent way of really involving the children in planning the field trip. After the children have made up a list of questions to be answered, specific questions can be allocated to each child, or to small groups if there are not enough questions to go around. Each child now has a definite responsibility. During the field trip the child will still observe everything closely, but he will pay special attention to the material that will provide the answer to the assigned questions. Actually, this method is better than giving each child a checklist of all the questions to be answered. Sometimes the children become so involved with the checklist that they do not have an opportunity to see what is going on or to get the whole picture.

Have a Follow-up • Follow-up should be provided as soon as possible after the field trip if the learning experience is to be worthwhile. When the children are in class the next day it would be wise to recall first the purpose of the trip and to talk about the highlights or unusual things the children saw or did. Then the list of questions to be answered would be reviewed, followed by oral reports from the individuals or small groups who were assigned to find the answers to specific questions. This procedure is an excellent way to establish understandings, bring out relationships, and arrive at conclusions.

During the follow-up the teacher should be prepared for new questions that may be raised as a result of the field trip. If these questions are related to the unit being studied, they will pave the way for further learning in the unit. If the questions are in areas that are unrelated to the present unit, they may provide excellent leads for the study of new units later. In either case these new questions will be helpful to the teacher for further learning by the children.

The follow-up is an excellent time for the teacher and class to prepare a letter thanking those persons who made the field trip possible. At the same time behavior on the trip can be evaluated, and future plans can be developed for avoiding any unpleasant situation that may have occurred. It is not advisable to make the follow-up a test. This procedure may spoil the field trip for the children and destroy interest in future trips.

Integrate the Field Trip with the Other Phases of the Elementary School Curriculum • When properly handled, the field trip should be an integral part of the daily program. Certainly the field trip will call for further reading. There will be oral and written reports, and letters to write. Most of the materials in field trips carry implications for social studies. In some cases there will be a need for problems in arithmetic. In the lower elementary grades particularly, there will be occasion for art and poster work.

LIMITATIONS OF FIELD TRIPS

Many teachers dislike taking field trips, especially the longer ones. Several disadvantages are offered, some of which are more valid than others. Occasionally, for instance, school administrators disapprove of field trips. Or teachers may find that they are unable to take the trip at the desired time during the unit because many establishments are so popular that reservations must be made weeks or months in advance. Some places are small and cannot handle large groups of class size. This limitation means that the class may have to be broken up into two or more groups, with the resulting lack of teacher supervision or control.

Some places encourage field trips but are not geared to give the children full or adequate learning experiences. They may use personnel who are either untrained or do not have the aptitude to be guides. Consequently, the guides are often unintelligible to the students. In some cases demonstrations may be given in rooms where it is impossible for all the children to gather around where they can see and hear what is going on. As a result, only those children in front can take full advantage of the experience, while the others become bored and restless.

One strong objection of teachers to field trips is based on their unwillingness to risk the possibility of accidents to the children. Even with the best supervision and precautions, when a large group is taken through the streets, on buses or in cars, a safety hazard is introduced.

[93

There is also the possibility of accidents in factories and other establishments. Many teachers who can handle large groups in the school building without any difficulty become quite distraught during field trips and dislike the emotional stress and strain involved.

Although many of these objections are valid, they should not discourage the teacher from taking any field trips at all. There are so many possibilities for field trips that the teacher can surely select those where the above disadvantages do not exist or are at a minimum. To provide for safety, careful planning with the children and all others concerned will help greatly in preventing accidents.

Resource Persons

EVERY community, large or small, urban or rural, has a large number of people whom the school can call upon to serve as resource persons when the children are learning science. These persons are able to bring a wide variety of special information, experiences, skills, and even hobbies into the classroom. Many teachers apparently have not yet learned to take advantage of this opportunity and thus are failing to utilize an excellent teaching technique.

When resource persons come to the classroom, it is much like taking a field trip, except that now the field trip is brought to the children. The use of resource persons as a teaching technique is also less complicated and more easily manageable than taking a trip. It does not disrupt the school schedule. No time is wasted in transportation. All the problems of transportation, together with the possibilities of accidents during transportation or at the site of the field trip, are eliminated. The resource persons can come at the exact time they are needed during the unit. All the children are able to see and hear clearly, without distractions, and can give the persons their undivided attention. A disadvantage of using resource persons, however, is that the children are likely to see less and listen more than when participating in field trips.

There are all kinds of persons that can be used for resource purposes. Examples of such persons include scientists, doctors, veterinarians, dentists, gardeners, representatives from industry, labor, and public utilities, members of local and state public works departments, and even artists and musicians. Science teachers and professors are excellent sources that can be used. Wherever possible, the teacher should try to get a resource person who is also a parent of one of the children in the class because using the parent in this way helps the parent realize and appreciate the learning that is going on in the classroom. No matter who is asked, the person is generally willing to come into the classroom to demonstrate, exhibit, talk, discuss, answer questions, and share what he knows with the children. Furthermore, the children will become quite

(Barbara Van Cleve)

Resource persons bring special information to the classroom.

excited at the prospect of having a real scientist, pilot, or engineer come to visit them.

Resource persons can be used in exactly the same ways as field trips. They may be used to introduce or arouse interest in a new science unit, supply answers to questions and problems raised during a unit, or provide a culminating activity at the end of a unit. In whatever way the persons are used, there should be a definite purpose for bringing them into the classroom, and this purpose should be clearly understood by all the children.

Before the children invite the resource person, the teacher should contact the person to find out whether the person will be available and what days and hours are suitable to come. Describe what is being learned in class and state what information will be desired. Give the person an idea of how long the visit should be and decide together how much material could be taken up during that time. Above all, be sure to tell the person the age level and maturity of the children, and urge that the person's vocabulary be geared to the level of the children.

There will be much planning for the children to do. They can help select the resource person, and then either send a committee to invite the person to the classroom or write a letter of invitation. One child may be elected to wait for the person in the principal's office, and another child may be given the privilege of introducing the person to the rest of the class. Conduct and courtesy while the person is speaking must be discussed and agreed upon. The children should draw up a list of questions that they would like answered. Just as with the field trip, the teacher can give individuals or small groups the responsibility of obtaining answers to specific questions, which they will report to the class either the same day or the next day. This is likely to give the resource person a pleasant surprise. So many persons offer stimulating demonstrations, talks, or discussions, but, when a question period follows, often there is little or no response from the audience. This reaction is always disappointing to the person, and the entire presentation diminishes and ends on a low note. When the children have specific questions to be answered, however, and either do not have all the information they need or do not understand something the speaker has said, the children will bombard the resource person with further questions after the person has finished speaking.

A follow-up should be conducted as soon as possible. The individuals or small groups who were assigned to find the answers to specific questions will now report their findings to the class. Important understandings should be listed, relationships established, and conclusions drawn. New questions that arose as a result of the visit by the resource person can be used as leads either for further learning in the unit or for introducing new units. Finally, a letter of thanks should be written and sent to the resource person.

Audio-Visual Materials

ANOTHER method of teaching science uses audio-visual materials. This term is very broad because it includes visual materials and audio materials, as well as a combination of the two. Actually, the term audio-visual materials refers to many media, all of which, when properly used, can be powerful teaching techniques. A list of potential audio-visual materials would include such materials as films, filmstrips, slides, transparencies, study prints, pictures, models, specimens, charts, graphs, posters, recordings, radio, and television.

Films

WHEN IT is not possible for the children to obtain firsthand experiences with materials and phenomena, the next best thing is to provide these experiences vicariously. The film is a teaching device that more than any of the other devices achieves closeness to reality. As a result, the film has become one of the most widely used teaching aids in our schools. Like the field trip, the film can provide experiences that cannot usually be brought into the classroom, show materials and phenomena in their true or natural relationships, and explain in greater detail how science concepts apply to the children's environment. Unlike the field trip, it does not disrupt the daily program, consume valuable time in transportation, or risk the possibility of accidents. It does, however, enable the children to see and hear everything clearly, many times if necessary, without distractions.

There are many films available to the teacher on all levels, produced by industrial concerns, public service organizations, museums, and state and federal departments. The quality of most of these films is good. Many publishing companies now provide films that accompany their textbooks. Usually a teacher's guide comes with the film, giving background material and suggestions for additional activities or reading. Most state departments of education and state universities or teachers' colleges have film libraries, and they will send films free or for a very nominal charge. These institutions, as well as those institutions described above, provide catalogs upon request. Many large cities have their own film libraries for distribution to the teachers in their school systems.

Most of the films produced for school use are the standard 16 millimeter sound films, either in black and white or color. Recently the major industries connected with photography have begun to recognize the market potentialities of the 8 millimeter film. They have developed 8 millimeter sound films which produce bright, sharp pictures and are run by less expensive projectors that are quite simple to operate.

Another innovation is the film loop. This consists of a continuous loop of film contained in a cartridge which protects it from dust and fingerprints. The film loop needs no rewinding and is always ready for showing. Simple, relatively inexpensive cartridge-loading projectors make it possible for almost any child to view these loops as needed. Most film loops are silent and run for only three or four minutes, so they are quite inexpensive. They are used to show experiments or phenomena, usually dealing with a single concept, which children would not ordinarily see in the classroom. The children can replay the short loop as often as they wish, thus giving them the opportunity to view the contents of the loop as often as is necessary. Longer (20–30 minute) sound film loops are also becoming available.

WAYS OF USING FILMS

Introducing a Unit • When used to introduce a science unit the main purpose of the film is to arouse interest in the science topic to be studied and raise questions to be answered or problems to be solved. Therefore, the film to be used for this purpose should be general in nature. If the films are specific rather than general, they are likely to furnish the answers to questions before the questions can be asked, or they may solve problems before there is an opportunity to raise them; therefore, the interest of the children would be stifled, and the purpose of using the film at this time would be defeated. The film would not create a learning situation, but it would become the learning situation itself, under conditions which would not be conducive to effective learning. Since most films contain both general and specific information, only the portion of the film that shows the general information should be shown to the children whenever the film is used to introduce a unit.

Obtaining Information during the Unit • Films can be used to obtain many kinds of information during the unit. They can help the children answer questions, solve problems, and check previous experiments, reading, discussion, and conclusions. If the class is unable to go on a field trip when required, a film may be used instead. Although the film does not really take the place of a field trip, it can approximate the trip. When teachers have limited supplies and equipment, or if the classroom facilities are inadequate, a film may be used for performing experiments and demonstrations. It can also show phenomena that cannot be seen under the ordinary magnifying glass or microscope. Here again, the teacher need not show the entire film, but only the portion that pertains to the experiment or demonstration. When a film is used as a field trip, experiment, or demonstration, the teacher should follow the same kind of planning, preparation, and suggestions that would be appropriate if the real activity were being performed by the children or teacher.

Culminating the Unit • When films are used as culminating activities, they help summarize and review the important understandings of the science topic the children have studied. This use of the film helps the children fix the understandings and their relationships to each other and the environment firmly in their minds. A film will often help the children get a clearer and more vivid picture of the things that they have learned and read about because it operates in real life situations in their proper proportion and environment.

Using Films to Evaluate • In certain situations films can be used as an evaluative technique. In this case the teacher merely turns off the sound portion of the film and asks the children to describe or explain what is happening. This operation can be done for specific portions of a film or, if the film is short, for the entire film.

SUGGESTIONS FOR USING FILMS

There Should Be a Real Purpose for Using the Film • Too many teachers show films either because the films are easily available or because it is considered good teaching to use films in the classroom. Just as with experiments, demonstrations, or field trips, there must be a purpose in showing the film. This purpose should be clearly understood by all the children. In this way the film becomes an integral part of the unit, designed to introduce the unit, obtain information during the unit, or serve as a culminating activity at the end of the unit.

Select the Film Carefully • Is the film designed for the children's grade level or ability? If it is not, the entire value of the film may be lost.

Does the content of the film bear directly upon the science topic being studied, and will it yield the desired information or produce the intended effect?

It is helpful to make a card file of all potentially useful films. Catalogs may be obtained from commercial film distributors, film companies, and state and federal departments that provide film services. From these catalogs the teacher can obtain the following information, which may be put on each card: the title of the film, the name of the producer, where the film may be obtained, whether there is a fee to be paid, the grade level for which the film is designed, how long it takes to run the film, and whether the film is in color or black and white. After the film has been used in class, the teacher can add to the file card a brief evaluation of the film for accuracy of content, clarity of explanation, appropriateness of grade level, and desirability for use another year.

Preview the Film • The film should be previewed whenever possible. Many times the brief description in the film catalog does not give a complete or true picture of the contents of the film. Sometimes the designated grade level of the film is questionable, and the film may be either too simple or too complicated. By previewing the film the teacher becomes completely familiar with its contents. The teacher can then decide whether all or a part of the film should be shown, and which parts may be complicated or important enough to warrant repeating. By previewing a film the teacher also can learn whether the film will answer the children's questions. At the same time the teacher can anticipate further questions that might be raised.

Plan with the Children for Viewing the Film • Just as the field trip or any of the other methods of teaching science are planned with the children, the viewing of the film should be planned with the children. When the children are not involved in the planning, they often look upon the film as a means of entertainment rather than as a learning situation. The reader may recall classroom situations where the teacher unexpectedly announced that a film was to be shown—and the announcement served as an immediate signal for everyone to sit back and relax. The film was an unexpected, and probably welcome, respite or vacation. While watching passively, in a darkened, warm room, the pupils became drowsy, especially if the film was long. When the lights were snapped on, the class was dull and sluggish, and not in a mood for discussion or review. Only a few persons could recall the important points of the film or answer the teacher's questions.

The results are very different when the children are involved in the planning. They can help select the film. They can draw up a list of questions to be answered or points to be noted. Here, too, the teacher should assign specific questions to individuals or small groups. While the film is being shown, these children will now have the responsibility of getting the answers to these questions, which they will report to the rest of the class after the film is over. The children can even help the teacher evaluate the film.

Have the Film Ready to Be Shown • If the teacher begins to set up the equipment for showing the film at the last minute, often the tempo of the whole lesson may be broken. Sometimes the teacher is ready to show the film at the appropriate time in the unit and finds that the equipment is not available or out of order. To avoid this the teacher should make sure the projector and screen are reserved for the desired time. The film can be threaded in advance, and the projector can be tested and focused properly. The screen and projector should be placed a suitable distance apart from each other so that the picture fills the screen. At the same time the screen should be placed at a height convenient for all the children to see comfortably and clearly. Place the speaker in the best possible position, facing the class, and adjust the volume of the sound. Then get the room ready for quick darkening.

Have a Follow-up • It is important that the follow-up take place as soon as the film has been shown. The answers to the questions assigned to individuals and small groups can be given and put on the chalkboard in a logical sequence. Discussion is an important part of the follow-up. Discussion is where understandings are established, relationships developed, and conclusions drawn. During the follow-up new questions may be raised, which will lead either to further study in the same science topic or exploration into a new science topic.

The Film May Be Shown More than Once • Repetition is often necessary or desirable when the film is either very long or highly appropriate. If the film is long, the children's attention span may determine whether the film should be shown a second time. To show a film twice, with discussion sandwiched in between, is often an excellent way of having the children fix the science understandings firmly in their minds. Sometimes only a portion of the film may be shown a second time, and even a third time if it seems necessary. Very often teachers will turn off the sound, when a film is shown a second time, and substitute their own narration. The teacher narration is often more effective than the original sound because it can be stated in simpler terms, directed specially at the children's questions, and show relationships and conclusions that are being sought.

DIFFICULTIES IN USING FILMS

Although the use of films is a valuable teaching technique, there are difficulties that have tended to discourage many teachers from using films as often as the teachers would like. The biggest and most frustrating problem is getting the film at the desired time. Because the demand for films is so great, it is usually necessary to order the films far in advance. In many cases teachers are required at the close of the school year to submit a list of the films they would like for the following year. This requirement means that the teachers must predict a year in advance exactly when and where the various teaching units will be in progress, which is something that is almost impossible to do. Even then there is no assurance that the teachers will get the films they ordered, owing to the heavy demand. This demand for films is also true of school systems that maintain their own film libraries. So many teachers want the same film for the same week. Since all orders for films are filled in order of receipt, many teachers must be disappointed, and therefore have to do without the films ordered.

Films are customarily loaned to a school for one week. Often several teachers would like to use the film during this time. When this crowding occurs, not only have the teachers had no opportunity to preview the films before ordering them, but also many teachers are pressed to find the time to preview the films before using them in class. The limitation of using the film for only one week prevents many teachers from using different parts of the film for special purposes as the unit progresses. Some teachers hope to use one part to introduce the unit, the second part to answer questions during the unit, and perhaps the entire film to review the unit as a culminating activity. Usually the teacher must return the film before it can be used for all three purposes.

Once the film starts, it must keep moving. The teacher cannot stop at a certain frame of the film for comment or discussion because the heat of the projector will cause the film to melt. If the teacher wants to show only one part of the film, and then show this part a second time, there is the problem of rewinding the film when it is only half run off. The children must wait until the entire film is shown before they can raise questions.

Filmstrips

FILMSTRIPS are particularly suited for use in the elementary school. They can be used in exactly the same ways as films, namely, to introduce or arouse interest in a science unit, obtain information during the unit, and serve as a culminating activity at the end of the unit. A filmstrip lends itself more easily than the film for use as a test. With filmstrips the teacher merely shows the desired frame to the children, using a strip of paper or cardboard to hide the caption at the bottom of the frame. There is also the added advantage of being able to show the frame to the children for as long as necessary.

Most of the filmstrips produced for school use consist of a roll of between 35 and 50 pictures which are commonly called frames. Science content is included on the frames as needed. Filmstrips are now available accompanied by sound recordings, thus eliminating the need for printed matter on the frames. A special combination projector-phono-graph is used which synchronizes the sound with the appropriate frames of the filmstrip.

The suggestions for using films are also applicable for using film-strips. There should be a real reason for using the filmstrip. It should be selected carefully and previewed. The children should be involved in planning to use the filmstrip. A follow-up is necessary, and the filmstrip or portions of it should be shown as often as necessary. When it is the proper time to show the filmstrip, everything should be set up and prepared.

Many elementary teachers prefer to use filmstrips rather than films because of the many advantages of filmstrips. Filmstrips are relatively inexpensive and therefore are purchased rather than rented by the schools. This purchase makes them the permanent property of the school and easily available at all times. As a result they can be used at the right time during the unit, and for as long as is necessary.

When using filmstrips that come without recordings, the teacher can stop at any frame and keep that frame on the screen while the teacher and the children speak, have discussions, and answer or raise questions. The teacher can skip back one or more frames without any trouble, or go forward in the same way. All the frames in the filmstrip are num-bered, and, by knowing what is in each frame, the teacher can select any combination of frames to be shown. Turning the knob of the film-strip projector quickly will blur the other frames enough so that the chil-dren will not learn some of the material too soon or out of context with the learning in progress. Even filmstrips designed for the junior or senior high schools can often be used to advantage in the elementary school. In this case the elementary teacher simply selects the frames that will be of use to the children and restates the captions underneath in simpler terms.

Filmstrip projectors are much less expensive than movie projectors. Consequently, there are usually several in the school instead of just one. They are easy to operate, and there is less chance of anything going wrong with the machine. Small filmstrips viewers, which do not need a screen, are now available, and they can be used by looking directly into an eyepiece. They are so inexpensive that one could be provided for each classroom. With such a viewer, filmstrips can be used by the chil-dren just like other supplementary textbooks or reference materials. The children could go to them to get the desired information whenever necessary.

Filmstrips do have a few disadvantages when compared with films. The chief disadvantage is the lack of motion, with the resulting loss of sense of immediacy and the inability to see the necessary motion or changes involved in many scientific phenomena. Sometimes the fixed sequence of the filmstrip is a disadvantage, especially if the sequence is not suitable. This factor can be partially compensated for, however, by showing the frames to the children in a sequence other than the original.

It may require some ingenuity and turning of the knob, but it can be done.

Transparencies, Study Prints, Slides, and Pictures

A LARGE variety of transparencies and study prints are now available for use in elementary science. The transparancies are about 8 × 10 inches large, so they project a good-sized picture on the screen when used with an overhead projector. Each transparency usually presents a single concept. Many contain one or more overlays, thus making possible a sequential development of the concept. Study guides offer suggestions for using the transparencies profitably in the classroom.

Study prints are large (about 13 × 18 inches), beautifully reproduced pictures of living things, objects, and phenomena from all areas of science. These pictures can help arouse interest when the teacher initiates a unit. They can also help raise questions or keep interest alive while the unit is in progress. Teachers often place them around the classroom just to beautify the room. On the back of each study print there usually is science content, discussion questions, and suggestions for further study which both teacher and children can use when learning about the object or phenomenon that is illustrated.

The use of slides in the classroom, especially the 2 × 2 slides, has been increasing steadily. Teachers can take pictures that have scientific value and interest. These pictures may be taken within and in the

(Barbara Van Cleve)

Audio-visual materials help when first hand experiences are not possible.

immediate vicinity of the community, or while the teachers are away on vacation during the summer. Many teachers who have very little experience with photography are able to get cooperative persons in the community to take such pictures for them. Commercial companies are now putting out 2 × 2 slides for classroom use. There are several advantages to using these small, individual slides. The slides can be arranged in any order the teacher prefers. Because the pictures have been taken by the teacher or children and often contain items and materials that are indigenous to the community, the slides have a personal touch that creates added interest in the classroom.

The use of pictures from magazines can also be of great value during the science lesson. These pictures should be selected carefully, with distinct purposes in mind. The pictures should be clear, accurate, and be able to arouse interest. Teachers should start building a collection of worthwhile pictures and keeping them in a file in the classroom, classified under appropriate titles or headings. A legal-size filing cabinet may be necessary because many of the pictures are large. If a cabinet is not available, wooden boxes or cardboard containers of suitable size may be used instead.

Models, Specimens, Charts, Graphs, and Posters

VISUAL materials such as models, specimens, charts, graphs, and posters are readily available from scientific supply houses. Although teachers should buy some of these, there is much to be gained when the children themselves collect or make most of them. For example, in preparing a display of specimens and homemade models, the children will have to do much reading, planning, and discussing. Measurements will have to be made to scale the models properly. The same holds true when the children make the charts, graphs, and posters. Setting up the display will involve arranging and labeling, which will help the children develop an understanding of classification and relationships. The best of the materials can be saved by the teacher for use when teaching future classes. In time an accumulation of such materials can form the nucleus for a small science museum in the school.

Television

TELEVISION has captured the imagination of everyone as a potential teaching device. The acceptance and support of television is bolstered by the unusually high appeal it has for the children. No other audiovisual aid has ever received as much recognition and attention in so short a time. Television sets are now found in schools throughout the country. Large sums of money have been spent for experimental programs in schools and colleges to explore all possible means of using television in education. Educational television stations are now found in almost all cities. Many school systems now have their own closed-circuit television. Industrial concerns sponsor programs of educational value on commercial stations at hours suitable for home viewing.

The advantages of using television as a teaching device are numerous. Television is the only medium that allows its viewers to see historical events, important happenings, and discoveries as they are made. It is also particularly appropriate for giving children and the public current information about progress in science. It is able to create the illusion that the viewer is sitting beside the scientist as he demonstrates and explains his findings. Children can watch a rocket sent into space and, with the help of the scientist, learn more about rockets and space travel than might be accomplished by hours of unguided reading and study. Furthermore, video tapes make it possible to show programs and events again and again, and at time periods suitable for classroom viewing.

Like the film, television can give the children a direct view of experiments and demonstrations. It can use equipment that is unavailable in many schools, and it has the added economic factor of using only one set of apparatus or equipment. Explanations are given by experts in science who at the same time understand children and know how to teach them. It can incorporate and use all the other audio-visual aids in its programs.

However, although a good film can be seen effectively by only one or two classes at a time, television can be seen by as many children as possible. This eliminates the frustration of teachers who have to order films well in advance, the disappointment of not being able to get the film, and the inconvenience of receiving films at unpropitious times. Television programs can also be geared to the textbooks and courses of study in the schools.

Television can be of great indirect benefit to the children by providing opportunities for in-service teacher education. This use may eventually be the most valuable contribution of television to education. Programs can be used to enrich the science background of the teachers and to keep them informed of the latest developments in science. Programs can also familiarize the teachers with the key operations of the scientist, and suggest ways and means of increasing their effectiveness as science teachers. Such programs can do much to overcome the reluctance of many elementary teachers to teach science because of an inadequate science background and an unfamiliarity with science equipment. Teachers, as adults who can think abstractly, are also better able than the children to cope with the difficulty of using a technique like television, which communicates only one way.

Television also has limitations. Most schools have television sets with picture tubes 21 to 25 inches in size. This size may be adequate for the children sitting in front, but the picture will be too small for those sitting in the back of the room. Experts generally agree that the minimum screen size acceptable for classroom use is 40 inches. Consequently, when children must view television in rooms containing just one standard set, they often become bored, inattentive, and restless. This problem can be solved by putting more television sets in the auditorium or classroom.

Another limitation is that a program may be given just once and must be used at the time it is presented, regardless of whether the children have the necessary background and preparation for seeing the program. This situation now has been greatly eased by the use of video tapes. Once the program starts, it cannot be stopped at any point for questions or discussion. Sometimes teachers are given no advance preparation or preview of a program to be shown. This lack of preparation creates an awkward situation for the teacher when the program is over, particularly if the program is in an area of science that is not very familiar to the teacher.

Television programs working successfully in school systems use a basic format. The program is geared to the textbook and course of study. Teachers' manuals or guides have been prepared and distributed to every teacher involved in the program. These guides contain background material for the teacher and children and a preview of each program. The teacher is thus able to prepare the children for seeing the program in much the same manner as for any other teaching technique. When the program is used to introduce a unit by raising thought-provoking questions and problems, suggestions are given in the guide for further experimentation, reading, discussing, reporting, or other suitable activities. The same is true when the program is used to supply information during the unit. As a culminating activity, the program reviews the highlights of the unit and provides leads for new units. Many school systems supply the children with leaflets containing notes, pictures and diagrams, questions, and things to do.

When programs are operated in this manner, they serve to strengthen the function of the classroom teacher. The teacher now becomes even more strongly the director of learning in the classroom. After the television program has been shown, the teacher takes over. The teacher asks pertinent questions, participates in raising problems, conducts discussions, suggests different ways of obtaining information, helps draw conclusions, and evaluates the work of the children. Thus, television does not and cannot replace the teacher, but it acts as a powerful teaching device to supplement the work of the teacher.

For Discussion

1. How does learning through inquiry coincide with the theories of Piaget, Bruner, and Gagné on how children develop intellectually and learn?

2. How do experiments help slow and fast learners? Can the same experiment help both kinds of learners at the same time? If yes, how?

3. Under which conditions will discussion be most effective as a learning technique?

4. If you had your choice of using either films or filmstrips, which would you select? Why? What are the advantages and disadvantages of the one you selected?

5. What other "do" and "don't" suggestions for field trips can you think of beside those already described?

6. Why and how do individual differences complicate the teaching of elementary science?

7. What are some of the ways that you could motivate the slow learner? the fast learner?

CHAPTER 5

PLANNING *for* SCIENCE *in the* CLASSROOM

PLANNING is a major prerequisite for successful teaching. This fact may not be immediately evident to many who observe an experienced and skillful teacher in action. The science lesson may seem to develop so extemporaneously, often without any visible evidence of lesson plans or unit plans, that the observer at first thinks that no special planning was involved. However, as the lesson progresses, the observer gradually becomes aware that learning is taking place in a logical, well-defined way. The problems that have been raised are being solved. The materials necessary for experiments or demonstrations appear or are available in the right place at the right time. When ref-

108]

erences are needed to find information or check conclusions, the books are ready.

The observer now realizes that this kind of teaching and learning occurs only as a result of intensive planning and preparation. And if there are no lesson plans or unit plans in evidence, it is not because these plans have not been carefully constructed. It is likely that, over a period of years, the teacher has devoted much time and effort to planning, and now she no longer needs the specific plans at her side when teaching. A brief review the night before, together with planning to provide the necessary materials and references, is all that is necessary to be prepared for the class the next day.

What kind of planning is necessary for successful science teaching? The teacher must plan to become completely familiar with the science content pertinent to the topic being studied. This familiarity with the content is absolutely necessary if the teacher is to be the guide and director of learning in the classroom. Only by acquiring a thorough understanding of the key concepts can the teacher know which concepts are relevant to the topic, which concepts the children can learn at a particular grade level, which concepts should be deferred for a later grade level, which concepts will evolve from each learning activity, what relationships exist between the concepts within the topic, and what interrelationships can be found with concepts in other science topics.

The teacher must look for a wide variety of appropriate learning activities, and then select those that will most effectively use inquiry and discovery to teach these science concepts, help the children learn the process of science, and develop desirable behavioral outcomes. These activities may include experiments, demonstrations, reading, discussion, reports, films, filmstrips, field trips, or speakers. If the experiment is unfamiliar, the teacher must try it in advance. If the film is new, it must be previewed. Supplies and materials must be collected or assembled. Textbooks and references must be readied for consultation.

Suitable activities must be found that will initiate pupil curiosity, interest, questions, or problems. These activities are the ones that get the children involved in the learning situation. Special attention must be given and provisions made for slow and fast learners. Time must be allowed for the slower pupils to absorb and completely understand the science concepts. Additional activities and projects must be made available for both slow and fast learners.

Provision must be made for evaluating the learning that is taking place and the behavioral outcomes that are being developed. The teacher must strive for the best possible means of communication with the children because communication, too, is a prerequisite for successful teaching. Finally, the teacher must plan, not for just one day's work at a time, but for a complete unit of work, with definite scope and sequence. In this way the teacher can review what has gone before, and plan for what will come in the future. At the same time it will ensure an even and uniform learning sequence, with no embarrassingly short or overly long science periods.

The Unit

CONCOMITANT with the need for planning is the need for organizing the elements of good planning into a suitable framework, through which the teaching-learning situation in the classroom has scope and sequence. A highly effective means of organizing such a framework is the unit.

The unit is a logical division of class work or activity. When constructed, the unit becomes an *anticipated* plan for using a wide variety of activities involving inquiry and discovery so that learning can take place. The objectives of the unit are to help the children learn content and process, and to develop such behavioral outcomes as scientific skills, attitudes, appreciations, and interests. Thus, the unit presents a plan for providing learning activities that will achieve the objectives of the unit.

Sometimes beginning teachers are told that a good teacher does not have to plan the unit carefully and rather should try to build from questions, conversations, arguments, or other sporadic incidents that occur in the classroom. This method is not as simple as it may sound. Definite

(Barbara Van Cleve)

The unit provides for a variety of learning activities.

readiness is required for this kind of emerging lesson or unit. First, the teacher must have a competent science background so that she is familiar with the topic under discussion. Then the teacher must be acquainted with a wide variety of experiments, demonstrations, and other learning activities suitable for teaching the understandings associated with the topic. Finally, the appropriate supplies, equipment, references, and other materials must be easily or already available. Once the teacher has this background of science knowledge, activities, and materials, she is in an excellent position to convert questions and incidents into worthwhile learning situations. The same readiness is also necessary for experienced teachers. A science lesson or unit can emerge from incidents in the classroom only when the teacher has the necessary knowledge and tools to take advantage of the situation.

Construction of a unit entails careful planning and preparation, but the rewards are great, namely, effective teaching and learning. When units bog down or collapse, the failure is generally due to a lack of adequate planning and preparation. A very hastily prepared or poorly constructed unit will create "dead spots" in a learning situation, which cannot ordinarily be remedied by the teacher's ingenuity or ability to think quickly. When this situation occurs often—and sometimes one unfortunate experience suffices—the teacher is likely to reject all unit construction as a "waste of valuable time," and thus discards what is generally considered a most valuable and effective teaching technique.

Initial attempts to construct units are often slow and time-consuming, as are other valid teaching techniques when planned and presented for the first time. The teacher may spend a lot of time in finding the best sources for collecting the science concepts and learning activities, and an equal amount of effort in coordinating all the unit components into an effective working plan. However, once the pattern becomes familiar, the time and effort involved lessens considerably, and the results become increasingly satisfying and rewarding.

When planning and constructing the unit, the teacher or curriculum committee selects the objectives, develops the means for arousing pupil interest and problems, anticipates a logical sequence of learning activities, provides for the necessary laboratory and reference materials, and even gives consideration to the possibilities for evaluating both the learning and the behavioral outcomes that the children will gain. The teacher or committee strives at all times to give the unit suitable scope and sequence.

The unit should never be rigid. It must be flexible enough to permit digression at any point, if necessary, without interrupting the broad pattern of learning anticipated by the unit. It is necessary to plan the day's work in advance, but the plan should be pliable enough to include and incorporate new situations and questions as they arise.

What to include in a unit is always a matter of discussion. Proponents of the various types of units differ somewhat about content and organization. However, it is generally agreed that a unit should contain most—if not all—of the following:

1. Overview.
2. Objectives.
3. Initiating activities.
4. Learning activities.
5. Materials.
6. Bibliography.
7. New science vocabulary.
8. Culminating activities.
9. Evaluation.
10. Work sheets.

A discussion of each of these components of a unit follows.

OVERVIEW

The purpose of the overview is to describe the nature and scope of the unit. Some teachers or school systems, when constructing units, omit the overview. However, the overview can serve a definite purpose. When a school system develops a science program and constructs units, it is likely that a science committee is given the responsibility of preparing the units for the rest of the teachers in the school system. This preparation will result whenever a school system is large and has so many elementary school teachers that it becomes impossible to involve all the teachers in constructing every unit for each grade level. Furthermore, with the consistent rapid turnover of elementary school teachers, there will always be new teachers or beginning teachers who have started teaching after the units have been constructed. In such cases, whenever units are presented to teachers who have had no part in constructing them it is always helpful to provide an overview with a brief description of the nature and scope of the unit. Even when the teacher makes her own unit, an overview can be of real service when shown to administrators, parents, or other teachers who visit her class and need a quick briefing on what is going on.

One highly effective way of presenting an overview is to give it in written form, consisting of two or three paragraphs. The overview might begin by describing the importance of the unit topic in our daily lives, for both child and adult. Then it might list the key concepts, and conclude by giving some general values and desirable behaviors that the children will derive from the unit.

An example of this kind of overview, for a unit on "Leaves," is as follows:

Leaves are important to the daily life of both children and adults because they are one of the primary sources of food for all living things. Leaves and grass contain chlorophyll and can manufacture food, and from green leaves and grass we get all our food—either directly or indirectly. Hence, the study of leaves can be basic to the understanding of life and how it exists on earth. In addition, leaves give us one of the several signs of the change of seasons in many parts of the country.

This unit hopes to teach (1) the kinds of leaves and how they differ from one another, (2) the parts of the leaf, including its external and internal structure, (3) the function of the leaf, with special emphasis on photosynthesis, and (4) the change in color of leaves in the fall.

From the learning activities in this unit the children may gain a better understanding of leaves and their function, and an appreciation of the beauty and the way leaves are constructed. The children will develop further their ability to observe carefully and accurately, to listen intelligently, and to read science books for information. They will be asked to draw conclusions from what they have learned, and to apply these conclusions to life situations. Finally, they will learn how to express themselves more effectively, to participate more ably in class discussion, and to work cooperatively with their peers.

TEACHER'S OBJECTIVES

In general, the teacher has two main objectives: (1) to help the children learn science content—the **product** of science, and (2) to help the children learn the key operations of science and the scientist—the **process** of science. Both objectives are vital, and one is meaningless without the other. Consequently, definite provision must be made to incorporate both objectives into the unit. Otherwise the unit will fail to accomplish its purpose.

Some school systems develop only a scope and sequence chart, leaving the construction of units to the individual teacher. Other school systems appoint a science curriculum committee, which, under the guidance of a science supervisor or consultant, constructs a comprehensive set of units for all the teachers. An analysis of science units which have proven to be highly successful, and which have enabled the teacher to achieve effective learning in the classroom, shows that they all have one factor in common. In all cases, the units contain an outline or list of the science concepts that the children are expected to learn while the units are in progress. And it seems that the more specifically the concepts are expressed in behavioral terms, the more successful are the units.

The preparation of an outline or list of concepts for inclusion in the unit helps the teacher in two ways. First, regardless of whether the unit is constructed by the teacher or by a committee, such an outline can be of great help as a guide when the learning activities are selected for the unit. Second, the outline serves as a check to make sure that the teacher will have the necessary science background for the topic being studied. If the teacher's school system has a detailed curriculum guide, she will have some indication of what science concepts to teach. If there is no such guide, the selection of concepts will have to be left to the judgment of the teacher. In this case she may have to simplify the wording of these concepts (without losing their scientific accuracy) to meet the vocabulary level of her class, and organize them into what she thinks will be a logical sequence of learning. The latter is very important because one set of understandings will lead easily into another set of understandings, and in this way learning can take place more quickly and efficiently.

The learning of science content, then, is one of the teacher's two major objectives. The second major objective is the learning of science process, accompanied by the development of desirable behaviors. These behaviors include scientific skills, attitudes, appreciations, and interests. They also involve how to think critically and creatively, and how to solve problems. These behaviors emerge from the learning activities that are conducted while the unit is in progress. The behaviors may be either immediate or long-range behaviors. Examples of these behaviors have already been described in Chapter 1, "Objectives of Elementary Science."

The learning of process and the development of behaviors will depend to a large extent upon the kinds of learning activities that will be selected. Each learning activity, as a rule, will call for the use of certain operations and the development of certain behaviors. Consequently, if process is to be taught effectively, the teacher must become completely familiar with all the key operations of science and the scientist and with all the desirable behavioral outcomes. The teacher can then examine each learning activity closely to determine which operations and behaviors are associated with that activity. Provision for the inclusion of a wide variety of learning activities in the units will ensure ample opportunity for the children to develop proficiency in any or all of the desired operations and behaviors.

Many units include a list of those key operations and behaviors that will constitute one of the objectives for the unit. These operations and behaviors should be incorporated with the science concepts and expressed in specific behavioral terms that lend themselves to proper observation and evaluation. In most units the behavioral objectives are written in the form of statements. In some units they are written as questions.

PUPIL OBJECTIVES

Units often include pupil objectives. These objectives are the anticipated pupil questions or problems that will emerge from the initiating activities. The questions and problems are stated as the children might raise them in the children's own vocabulary. Pupil objectives thus also remind us that the children's aims may be quite different from those of the teacher. The teacher may want the children to learn about heat expansion. The children, however, will want to know why cracks are intentionally put into concrete sidewalks. The teacher is interested in electrical circuits; the children want to learn how to connect a dry cell, wires, and a porcelain socket containing a bulb so that the bulb will light up. The teacher is interested in the laws governing vibrating strings; the children want to know what can be done to make the musical note from a violin or guitar higher or lower. The teacher is primarily concerned with the learning of basic science information and the development of desirable behaviors. The children want to know "why," "what," "how," "when," "what will happen if," and so forth.

If the initiating activities are properly selected, the pupil objectives will emerge easily. However, because the pupil questions and problems in the planned unit are anticipated, if the children should fail to raise them, the teacher may ask them instead. Actually, the children often raise better or more questions and problems than those anticipated by the teacher. The wise teacher incorporates these questions and problems into the unit.

INITIATING ACTIVITIES

The purpose of initiating activities is to involve the children in the unit; these activities are the means whereby pupil interest and curiosity are aroused. In the process, questions and problems are raised that, when answered or solved, will help achieve the teacher's objectives. The main purpose of initiating activities is to raise questions or problems, the answers to which the children do not know but will find out as they proceed with the learning activities in the unit. Because the children do not know the answers, their curiosity is piqued and their interest in finding out the answers is aroused.

General or Overall Initiating Activity • Usually a general or overall initiating activity is used to introduce or "initiate" the entire unit to the children. There are several ways of initiating the entire unit. Sometimes a previous unit will lead the children quite naturally into a new unit. If the class has just finished a study of magnets, for example, it will require very little effort to motivate the children for the study of electromagnets. Units can also be initiated by books and stories. Sometimes, merely the announcement of the next topic or problem may be sufficient to arouse pupil interest and problems.

Another way to initiate a unit is to set the stage for the unit. A good example is an attractive bulletin-board display, accompanied by thought-provoking questions. To initiate a unit on "Evaporation and Condensation," a teacher may plan to put on the bulletin board a series of pictures showing evaporation and condensation taking place. This display can include pictures of a puddle of water on a concrete sidewalk under the warm sun, sheets or towels drying on the clothesline, droplets of water on a bottle of soda pop or on the sides of a pitcher of lemonade, fogged-up windows, a person's breath visible on a cold, wintry day, and so on. Under the pictures can be questions such as "How does the water get into the air?" "How does water come out of the air?" "How can we make water go into or come out of the air more quickly or more slowly?"

Another way to set the stage for a unit is to have a display of materials on a table with accompanying questions. Materials for display can include pictures, books, models, or specimens. When initiating a unit on leaves, it will be natural to have a variety of leaves on display, especially in the fall. Typical questions that can be asked would be "Are these leaves alike?" "How are they different?" "How many parts does each leaf have?" "What do leaves do?" "Why do leaves change color in the fall?"

A thought-provoking demonstration is an excellent way to initiate a unit. A teacher can initiate a unit on "How Does Heat Travel" by simply placing a spoon in a cup of hot water. Pupil interest and curiosity will be raised about why the part of the spoon that is out of the water also becomes hot.

Even a thought-provoking discussion can initiate a unit. In temperate climates most children are quite familiar with the effects caused by static electricity, especially on a cold, dry day. The teacher can initiate a unit on such a day by first asking the children to describe personal experiences with static electricity and then leading into an on-going discussion about the characteristics of and reasons for this phenomenon.

Initiating Activities during the Unit • There are some who believe that one good general or overall initiating activity is sufficient to sustain

(William Means/Van Cleve)

Initiating activities arouse interest and curiosity.

pupil interest and motivation for the entire unit. They feel that the one activity will raise enough questions and problems to ensure the learning of all the science content and process in the unit. On the other hand, there are many who think that additional initiating activities are necessary as the unit progresses. These additional activities may be necessary, especially when a unit extends over two, three, or even more weeks. Interest and motivation may flag over a period of time for even the most enthusiastic children.

Also, in those units which include an outline or list of science concepts, the concepts seem to arrange themselves into related groups. These groups differ sufficiently among themselves to have their own initiating activities. Thus, the unit will need enough initiating activities to raise pupil questions or problems involving all the understandings involved in the outline or list of science concepts. Usually one initiating activity is needed for each group of related concepts.

Thus, additional initiating activities—other than the general or over-all initiating activity—may be used at various intervals as the unit progresses. The most effective activities are thought-provoking experiments and demonstrations, questions or series of questions, and discussions. Occasionally, one or more frames of a filmstrip can be used as an initiating activity. Often the general or overall activity can also be used as the initiating activity for the first group of related understandings in the outline or list of concepts.

Films, field trips, and speakers should rarely be used as initiating activities. The purpose of initiating activities is to raise questions or problems, the answers to which the children do not know, which then necessitates special learning activities to find the answers. Films, field trips, and speakers as a rule not only raise questions, but also usually provide the answers to the questions immediately afterward. This procedure defeats the purpose of the initiating activity.

Similarly, because the initiating activity raises questions instead of giving answers, the initiating activity is almost never used as the first learning activity. The purpose of the learning activity is to obtain answers whereas the initiating activity is designed only to raise questions. However, the initiating activity can be used to advantage as an evaluative technique later in the unit. If the children have really learned the science understandings in the subsequent learning activities, they should now be able to answer the questions or solve the problems raised by the initiating activity.

The selection of good initiating activities is perhaps the most difficult phase of unit construction. Very often, many pupils are able to explain what were intended to be thought-provoking experiments or demonstrations. Thus, the initiating activities have not fulfilled their purpose and are valueless. The curriculum committee or teacher should not become discouraged, but must discard the unsuccessful initiating activities and continue to search for new and better ones.

LEARNING ACTIVITIES

Learning activities are the means by which the children learn both the content and process of science. Using inquiry and discovery, the children acquire understandings that enable them to answer the questions or problems raised by the initiating activities, gain proficiency in doing the processes of science, and develop desirable behavioral outcomes. The teacher uses a wide variety of learning activities to accomplish this purpose. All the techniques suggested in Chapter 4, "Methods of Teaching Science," are utilized. These include experiments, demonstrations, observation, reading and study, discussion, oral and written reports, films, filmstrips, speakers, models, charts, posters, planning, and so forth.

Many teachers have a tendency to use many more learning activities than are necessary to ensure satisfactory learning. This excessive use

(H. Armstrong Roberts)

A unit provides for learning both content and process.

tends to prolong the unit unneccessarily, slow down learning, and dull pupil interest. The experienced teacher employs her learning activities wisely and economically, especially when teaching for science understandings. She realizes that sometimes one activity is enough for an understanding to be learned. Occasionally one good learning activity will suffice to produce the learning of more than one understanding, especially if the understandings are simple or are related to each other. Other times, when an understanding is difficult or abstract, more than one activity may be necessary to obtain adequate learning. Slow learners usually learn better when more than one activity is used.

The grade level may also influence the number of learning activities needed. In the lower grades, where the children's attention span is small and their ability to think abstractly is not well developed, more than one activity is often necessary to obtain satisfactory learning of an understanding. However, in the upper grades one well-chosen activity is usually sufficient.

In all cases the best procedure is for the teacher to use as many—but *only* as many—activities as are necessary to ensure satisfactory learning. And if the teacher finds that there is a surplus of activities, they can always be used as additional activities for slow and fast learners.

MATERIALS, BIBLIOGRAPHY, NEW SCIENCE VOCABULARY

Units usually list all the materials that will be needed for the learning activities. This list includes supplies, equipment, textbooks, reference materials, films, filmstrips, and other learning aids. In this way the teacher can begin to accumulate the necessary materials and have them ready and available as the activities require them.

Most units contain a bibliography of the textbooks and other reference materials that will be used during the unit. This bibliography includes materials for both the children and the teacher. The pupil list contains those references that the children will use to answer questions, solve problems, learn how to do an experiment, check conclusions, and find additional information for reports, and so forth. Wherever possible, the pupil list should include duplicate references on the same topic, but on different grade (reading) levels. Thus, there will be available reading materials for slow and rapid learners. The teacher list should contain those references that will provide the teacher with more detailed information about the science topic or about the experiments and demonstrations the teacher plans to conduct.

For clarity, the pupil and teacher references should be listed separately. Each reference should include the title, author(s), publisher, place and date of publication, and grade level (if it is part of an elementary science textbook series). Films and filmstrips should be included in the bibliography, usually under a separate listing. Besides listing the title and the producer, it may be helpful to include such information as the running time, whether it is in black and white or color, and so forth.

The unit anticipates needed materials.

With the development of concepts and understandings, the children regularly will encounter new words and terms. This new vocabulary must be thoroughly explained and understood for maximum learning to take place. Many units include a vocabulary list of the new science terms that will be learned and used during the unit. This list reminds the teacher to give full attention to the learning of the terms when they appear for the first time.

CULMINATING ACTIVITIES

A culminating activity is an activity that concludes the unit. It should be a logical part of the unit and a natural outgrowth of the work in the unit. It should appear when the objectives of the unit have been achieved. The culminating activity helps summarize the learnings and brings the high points of the unit into focus.

Culminating activities can be many things. They can be films, filmstrips, field trips, or speakers. They can be exhibits, science fairs, news letters, or reports. They can even be discussions, programs, assemblies, or dramatizations. However, the teacher should always keep in mind that culminating activities are primarily for the benefit of the children, even though others may profit from them as well.

Certain precautions should be noted about the use of culminating activities. They should not try to summarize every science understanding in the unit because this procedure would make the activity much too long, with the resulting loss of interest and educational value. Not every unit needs a culminating activity. Some units do not lend themselves well to such activity, and to have one arbitrarily would make the activity highly contrived and artificial. Also, sometimes a culminating activity can actually hinder the children from continuing quite naturally to another unit. Finally, tests and other evaluative techniques are not culminating activities and should not be used as such.

EVALUATION

Evaluation should be continuous while the unit is in progress. The teacher must determine how well the children have learned science content and process and have developed desirable behavioral outcomes. Since evaluation is an ongoing continuous process, it is impossible to complete the evaluation section of a pre-planned unit. However, the unit can indicate the kinds of evaluation techniques that may be used while the unit is in progress. It can also indicate specific places in the unit outline where the learning activities lend themselves particularly to the development of certain behaviors.

The children themselves can—and should—participate in much of the evaluation. They can evaluate their work, their daily progress, and their learnings and behaviors as well. The various techniques for evaluation that can be used by both teacher and children are described in Chapter 8, "Evaluation of Science Learning in the Classroom."

WORK SHEETS

When units are constructed, careful consideration must be given to how the work of the children and teacher will proceed. Once the unit is in progress all the components of the unit must be coordinated and uti-

(William Means/Van Cleve)

The working period is a vital part of the unit.

lized to achieve maximum learning. At the same time provision must be made for evaluation of the work that is being done. Consequently, the working period is the vital part of the unit and, as such, must be thoroughly integrated. For in the working period lies the success—or failure—of the unit.

There are several forms in which the working period can be presented. Of these forms, two are most commonly used and both involve work sheets. One form makes use of a single running column. This single column contains in varying order of sequence the initiating activities, discussion questions, science concepts, behavioral outcomes, needed materials, bibliography for teacher and children, learning activities or investigations, and additional activities for slow and fast learners.

In the other form all the unit components are placed in a varying number of parallel columns. In these parallel columns the corresponding science concepts, anticipated pupil questions, learning and culminating activities, materials, teacher and pupil bibliography, process skills to be developed, and evaluative techniques are all placed side by side. By using adequate spacing in the parallel columns, the work sheets provide the teacher with a horizontal row of related components, all clearly delineated.

KINDS OF UNITS

When looking for guides or models for constructing units, the local curriculum committee or teacher will encounter in the literature what seems to be a large variety of units. Curriculum experts, all interested in good teaching and learning, have proposed or described units with the following names: teaching units, experience units, resource units, problem units, activity units, textbook units, center of interest units, topical units, survey units, and so forth. To add to the confusion, the term *unit* has become so popular that teachers use it very loosely to describe almost any kind of teaching-learning situation.

However, a closer examination of these units will reveal that many are quite similar, differing in varying degrees with regard to style or format. Accordingly, all these units can be classified into one of three basic kinds of units: **resource units, teaching units,** and **textbook units.**

Resource Units

A RESOURCE unit usually consists of an extensive collection of objectives, activities, and materials dealing with a science topic. The resource unit contains many more suggestions for study than any single classroom can pursue. The idea is to provide the teacher with the opportunity to select from the resource unit the learning activities that will best fit the needs, abilities, and interests of the children, yet still achieve the objectives of the unit. This is why the resource unit is organized in such a broad and flexible fashion.

The contents of the resource unit may be arranged in a number of different formats. One very common format divides the contents of the unit into four broad sections, as follows:

I. OBJECTIVES
    A. Key Science Concepts and Understandings
    B. Behavioral Outcomes
    C. Anticipated Pupil Objectives or Problems

II. ACTIVITIES
    A. Initiating Activities
    B. Learning Activities
    C. Enrichment Activities
    D. Culminating Activities
    E. Evaluating Activities

III. BIBLIOGRAPHY
    A. Teacher Bibliography
    B. Pupil Bibliography

IV. MATERIALS
    A. Science Supplies and Equipment
    B. Audio-Visual and Other Materials

Resource units found in school system curriculum guides often begin with an overview of the unit. In some curriculum guides the suggested learning activities are placed under or beside the pertinent science concepts. Almost all the curriculum guides urge the teacher not to use all the suggested learning activities, but rather to select only as many as are needed to achieve the objectives of the unit. Otherwise the unit will become overly long and repetitious. The teacher is also urged to take full advantage of the suggested teacher bibliography to become thoroughly familiar with the concepts, experiments, and demonstrations listed in the unit.

A sample resource unit is presented in Chapter 6A, "Sample Teaching and Resource Units."

Teaching Units

A TEACHING unit differs from a resource unit in that the teaching unit contains only those objectives, activities, materials, and bibliography that the teacher and children will actually use during the unit. It is a highly developed detailed plan for teaching and learning in the classroom. Curriculum guides that contain resource units usually suggest that the teacher use these resource units to prepare teaching units. Some curriculum guides bypass resource units and instead contain teaching units that have been constructed cooperatively by all or part of the teachers in the school system.

In a teaching unit the teacher carefully selects the science concepts to be learned, then organizes them into a logical learning sequence. Specific learning activities are chosen that will enable the children to learn these concepts. At the same time these learning activities are carefully examined to determine which key operations of science and the scientist will be involved, and also which behaviors can be developed, when the children do the activities during the unit. Provision is made for evaluating the learning of science content and process, and for evaluating the development of the behaviors. Additional activities are selected and included for slow and fast learners. Then the science and audio-visual materials that will be needed for all the activities are listed.

A general or overall initiating activity is selected to stimulate interest in the unit as a whole. Additional initiating activities which will raise pupil questions or problems are added, and these anticipated questions or problems are also incorporated into the unit.

The teaching unit contains a bibliography of only those pupil and reading materials that will be used during the unit. Some teaching units also add a supplementary bibliography to be used for enrichment purposes as needed. Many teaching units even include a vocabulary list of the new science words and terms that will be learned during the unit. Finally, an overview is often included, especially in those units that appear in curriculum guides.

One of the predominant characteristics of most teaching units is the work sheets. These sheets indicate how the teacher anticipates the learning will proceed in the unit. To accomplish this, the unit components are usually placed either in a single running column or in a number of parallel columns. Using parallel columns involves much more work, but it helps greatly by providing the teacher with a comprehensive view of all the unit components, placed side by side and delineated clearly.

Work sheets that have parallel columns will vary in the number of columns used and in the order the columns appear in the work sheets. One format, using six columns, is described here in detail, as follows:

INITIATING ACTIVITIES AND PUPIL OBJECTIVES	BASIC SCIENCE INFORMATION	LEARNING ACTIVITIES	SUPPLIES AND EQUIPMENT	TEXTS AND REFERENCES	EVALUATION

A. Column 1: Initiating Activities and Pupil Objectives • The "Initiating Activities and Pupil Objectives" column contains any subsequent initiating activities needed to raise pupil questions or problems. There should be enough initiating activities to assure the teacher that questions or problems will be raised about every group of related understandings in the outline of concepts.

Usually one initiating activity is needed for each group of understandings in the outline. Sometimes more than one activity may be considered necessary for one group of understandings. Conversely, one activity can be used for two or more groups of understandings. And occasionally the general or overall initiating activity can also serve as the initiating activity for the first group of understandings. Each initiating activity should be described briefly but adequately, using one or more sentences as needed.

The column also contains the pupil objectives, namely, the anticipated pupil questions and problems that will arise from the initiating activities. These questions can be placed beside the appropriate science understandings, which appear in the second column. Only logically anticipated or real questions and problems should be listed. Some teachers feel that they must have a pupil objective for each science understanding; it is not necessary, however.

B. Column 2: Basic Science Information • Column 2 contains the list of science concepts, which usually appear in outline form with related groups of understandings. Teachers often begin the outline in this column a short distance below the initiating activity in the previous column. They organize the material in this way to remind themselves that the initiating activity should be carried out first.

C. Column 3: Learning Activities • Learning activities include experiments, demonstrations, observation, reading and study, discussion, oral and written reports, films, filmstrips, field trips, speakers, individual and group planning, and so forth. These activities are the means by which the children learn science content that enables them to answer the questions or problems raised by the initiating activities, and in the process to develop desirable behaviors.

The teacher should almost never use an initiating activity as the first learning activity as well because the initiating activity raises questions rather than gives answers. It is the purpose of the learning activities to answer the questions raised by the initiating activity. The initiating activity, however, can be used as an evaluation technique later in the unit. If the children have really learned the science understandings, they should now be able to answer the questions or solve the problem raised by the initiating activity.

The learning activities need not be described in detail in the column. A sentence, or even a phrase, is usually adequate. It should be just long enough for the teacher to recognize the activity now as well as in the future. If the activity is an experiment or demonstration and the teacher would like to review the entire procedure, she can look at the reference for the experiment or demonstration, located in the column for textbooks and references.

The learning activity should be located beside the corresponding science understanding or understandings. Sometimes one activity is sufficient to produce satisfactory learning of an understanding and/or development of a desirable behavior. Sometimes one activity is sufficient to produce learning of more than one understanding. Often, however, more than one activity is needed to produce satisfactory learning of one understanding. In this case the activities should be listed in logical sequence of presentation. Also, when this happens, the spacing in the column for basic science information must be adjusted. Adequate blank space should be left between understandings so that the teacher can recognize immediately that all the learning activities apply to only one understanding.

The culminating activity appears in this column, usually on the last work sheet if there is only one culminating activity. If there are several short culminating activities in the unit, they should be located at appropriate positions in the column and labeled "Culminating Activity" before the description of each activity.

Some teaching units incorporate activities for slow and fast learners in this column of the work sheets. Others prefer to include a separate list of extra activities for slow and fast learners at the end of the unit. Usually two separate lists are made, one for each kind of learner. Each list has two columns. In one column the activity is described briefly. The other column contains the necessary materials and/or references for the corresponding activity.

D. Column 4: Supplies and Equipment • Column 4 lists all the special materials the teacher and children will need to conduct an experiment, demonstration, or other working activity. It also contains any materials that might be used for the initiating activities or the culminating activity.

The materials should be listed beside the corresponding learning activity that will require these materials. If the list of materials needed for a particular learning activity is quite long, adequate blank space should be left in the column for the learning activities so that the teacher can see immediately which materials are needed for which activity. Thus, by allowing adequate space in each column, the teacher should be able to identify quickly which materials belong to which activity for which understanding, and for which pupil objective.

E. Column 5: Texts and References • Column 5 contains all the textbooks and references used for reading, discussion, reports, locating and doing experiments, checking observations and conclusions, and so forth.

(Ron Larsen/Van Cleve)

The unit provides opportunity for individualized learning.

It also includes films and filmstrips as well as any references that might be needed for the initiating activities or the culminating activity.

Some teaching units contain a separate listing of the bibliography before the references appear in the work sheets. Here each reference is presented completely, with the title, author(s), publisher, and date and place of publication. By assigning a code number to each reference, when references are required in the work sheets, only the code number and the page numbers have to be written in the work sheets. Many units place a P or T beside the code number in the worksheets, thus making it possible to distinguish between pupil and teacher references, respectively. Similarly, the units use the letters F and FS to distinguish between films and filmstrips, respectively.

The textbooks and references should appear beside the corresponding learning activity. Incidentally, the nature of the activity will determine whether it is necessary to list supplies and equipment, textbooks and references, or both. Usually an activity involving reading does not require supplies and equipment. However, an experiment or demonstration may require both a list of materials and a reference for the teacher or pupils.

F. Column 6: Evaluation • Column 6 contains the skills and behaviors that the children will develop from the learning activities, and also the various methods that will be used to determine whether learning of science content has taken place.

The skills and behaviors can be stated as phrases or as questions, and should be listed beside the corresponding learning activities. Only those that will really develop from the activities should be included.

The methods for determining whether learning has taken place should appear either beside the corresponding learning activities or at the end of a set of understandings. Some teachers just indicate briefly what technique will be used, such as oral or written report, question and answer, short objective test, and so forth. Other teachers prefer to describe in greater detail how they will evaluate to find out whether learning and changed behaviors have occurred.

This column can also be used to check whether the children can now answer the questions, or solve the problems, raised by the initiating activities.

G. Additional Suggestions • Allow sufficient space when filling in the columns of the work sheets. This space is necessary if the teacher is to see at a glance which pupil objective belongs to which understanding, which understanding requires which learning activity, and which activity calls for which materials or references or desirable behavior or evaluation technique. In other words, all the related materials in the six columns should be easily identified by being side by side in the columns. Sufficient space also enables the teacher to incorporate additions or make changes in the unit and work sheets without having to rewrite the unit or work sheets each year.

All of the columns do not have to be the same width. Obviously, the columns for the basic science information and the learning activities need more space than the others. However, to compensate for this extra width, the columns for the supplies and equipment and for the textbooks and references can be much narrower.

Finally, it will help the teacher if the six columns are spread out over two sheets of paper. This spacing makes it easy to incorporate the sheets into a folder or a loose-leaf notebook. The work sheets will then look like the pages of a book, with the first two columns on the left-hand page and the remaining columns on the right-hand page.

Sample teaching units are presented in Chapter 6A, "Sample Teaching and Resource Units." One unit has its components in a number of parallel columns. The other unit makes use of a single running column.

Textbook Units

WHEN properly utilized, the elementary science textbook can become the basis for an effective teaching unit. Most elementary science textbook series today are quite well organized. They are developed around a nucleus of key concepts and conceptual schemes. Each textbook in the series contains a comparatively small number of chapters, permitting a science topic or area to be treated with some degree of depth and detail. The science content has been organized into a logical learning sequence. Consideration has been given to the children's levels of understanding and reading ability. A variety of activities are presented, and an effort is made to teach process and content through inquiry and discovery. The teacher's edition often provides additional science background for the teacher and suggests additional activities for the children.

When preparing a textbook unit, the first step is to construct an outline of science concepts for the unit. The science content for a topic in the textbook should be examined closely, and a list made of all the concepts already taken up in the topic. Some elementary science textbook series may have already prepared such an outline and included it in the teacher's manual. This list of concepts must be carefully checked to see whether it is inclusive enough, and whatever additional concepts that seem to be pertinent and necessary, should be added. Then all the concepts should be rearranged, if necessary, and organized into a logical learning sequence.

The next step is to look for and select a wide variety of additional learning activities. These activities will be needed not only for the new concepts that have been added to the outline, but also for many of those concepts that were originally in the textbook and for which there were either inadequate activities or no activities at all. Provision should be made in the unit to present these additional activities in such a way that the children also learn the process of science and develop desirable behavioral outcomes. Finding additional activities will be no problem because today there are a goodly number of sourcebooks of science experiments and other activities for the elementary school on the market. These books are described and listed in Chapter 7, "Materials for Teaching Science." Additional reading materials for the children may also be provided.

To complete the unit, a number of initiating activities should be selected that will arouse interest in the unit and also raise pupil questions or problems. Then a list must be made of all the science materials and audio-visual aids that will be needed for these additional learning and initiating activities. When completed, the textbook unit becomes quite similar to the teaching unit.

Daily Lesson Plans

THERE are so many different kinds of daily lesson plans currently being used in the elementary school today that it would be virtually impossible to describe all of them. They vary especially in format and in the amount of detail required. Some school systems leave the decision as to format and quantity of detail up to the individual teachers. Others have adopted a standard format, requiring all teachers to follow this format quite rigidly. Some school systems give their teachers commercially prepared lesson plan books that enable the teachers to describe their daily plans in outline form for all subject areas in the elementary school curriculum. Others require the teachers to keep a continuous and often rather detailed descriptive log of what does or will go on in the classroom.

Regardless of the kinds of lesson plans that are required, there is general agreement that specific planning for the daily lesson is necessary if effective teaching and learning in the classroom is to be achieved. The daily lesson is that period of time when all the preliminary planning for the unit comes to fruition. There is also general agreement that all lesson plans should consist of three integral parts: a beginning, a middle, and an end.

The beginning of the lesson is that part which "sets the stage" for learning to take place. The teacher uses appropriate initiating activities selected from the unit that will raise questions or problems. In the beginning of the lesson the teacher and children also plan what they will do to answer the questions or solve the problems.

The middle of the lesson is that part where actual learning takes place. Here the children conduct experiments, watch demonstrations, read books, and view films or filmstrips. The children can also work on special projects or reports at this time, and present them to the rest of the class when the projects or reports are completed. The children will work in large groups, small groups, or individually when they engage in these learning activities.

The end of the lesson is that part where summary and evaluation takes place. Here the children summarize what they have learned and draw conclusions. Questions and other evaluating activities are used to determine whether the children have learned content and process and have developed desirable behaviors. Opportunities are provided to see whether the children can apply what they have learned to new situations. The end of the lesson is also used to plan with the children for the next day's lesson. Planning may be needed for experiments to be done the next day, or materials may have to be collected in advance. Individual and group assignments may also be given at this time.

It is interesting to note that the detailed work sheets with parallel columns of the teaching unit can also be used quite effectively as daily lesson plans. The teacher merely has to anticipate how much can or should be taken up in one day, then draw a dotted line all the way across the work sheets to indicate a break or stopping point. This section of the work sheets now has all the necessary components of a good daily lesson as described above. Furthermore, there is enough empty space in the parallel columns for the teacher to write in additional activities and materials as needed.

When using the work sheets of a teaching unit as a lesson plan, there are two guidelines for determining how much will constitute a day's lesson. One guideline would be to examine the learning activities, estimate the time involved in doing these activities, then decide how many of these activities can be done in one day. The second guideline would be to examine the outline of concepts and then select a group of related understandings that could be conveniently learned in one day.

The teacher, especially the beginning teacher, should keep in mind that this is only an estimate of what will constitute a day's lesson. No harm will be done if the lesson turns out to be too long or too short. All the teacher has to do is to erase the original dotted line and put in a new line at the appropriate place.

For Discussion

1. What are the basic differences between a teaching unit, resource unit, and textbook unit? Which kind do you prefer, and why?

2. How useful is the overview in a science unit? the culminating activities?

3. Does the detailed structure of a science teaching unit deter exploration, investigation, and creativity from taking place in the classroom? Justify your answer.

4. Can the teaching unit, resource unit, and textbook unit make adequate provision for teaching process?

5. What role should poems, dramatizations, and songs play in a science unit?

6. Administrators often tell their teachers, "Remember! You are not teaching science. You are teaching children!" Why do you think the administrators make this statement? Do you agree with this statement? Would you modify it?

CHAPTER 6A

SAMPLE TEACHING *and* RESOURCE UNITS

NO MATTER how precise and explicit the description of units and instructions for constructing them may be, as given in Chapter 5, "Planning for Science in the Classroom," nothing helps as much as one or two representative models of units to clarify the directions and to illustrate the techniques involved in unit construction.

Accordingly, three inquiry-oriented science units are presented in this chapter as examples. Two are teaching units, and one is a resource unit. In one teaching unit the worksheets have a number of parallel columns. In the other, the worksheets have a single running column.

Teaching units were selected because they are quite structured, and such structure is often necessary for the beginning teacher and the teacher whose science background needs strengthening. These teachers are not yet thoroughly familiar with science content, process skills, learning activities, materials, and bibliography. Consequently, detailed planning must be made to ensure that the concepts to be learned and the questions or problems to be answered are stated within the framework of the children's level of understanding and are then organized into a logical sequence of learning.

Learning activities involving inquiry and discovery must be selected which will enable the children to learn these concepts and become familiar with the key operations of science. This is why the teaching unit specifically lists the skills and attitudes that the children will develop when the activities are in progress. To provide for individual differences, additional activities are planned for slow and fast learners.

In the teaching unit with the multi-columned worksheets there are dotted lines across the worksheets. These lines indicate a tentative estimate by the teacher of the end of each day's activities. If in actual practice the estimate is too long or too short, the teacher can delete these dotted lines and insert new ones in more appropriate places.

The sample lessons of both teaching units should be compared with the units in Chapter 6B, to see how the philosophy of the science curriculum projects has affected unit and lesson plan construction today.

Because of the simpler structure of the resource unit, the impression may arise that the resource unit is less time-consuming to construct than the teaching unit. This impression is false. Much more time and effort is required to compile the extensive list of objectives, activities, materials, and bibliography that comprise the resource unit. The same high degree of planning is required to ensure that successful teaching and learning takes place.

Teaching units often evolve from resource units. When the teacher selects from a resource unit everything she plans to use, then organizes the materials into a logical teaching and learning sequence, the resource unit becomes a teaching unit.

NOTE: Teachers who plan to make use of the sample teaching units in this chapter may find that the page numbers of some texts listed in the work sheet column on "Texts and References" will not coincide with the page numbers of these texts they already have in their classrooms. This discrepancy will be due to a difference in publication dates of editions, with a corresponding difference in page numbers. Because these sample units are intended primarily as guides, the page numbers are relatively unimportant.

CARE OF PLANTS AND
WAYS OF GROWING THEM
A Teaching Unit for Grade 2

OVERVIEW

WHAT WOULD the earth be like without any plants? Let us see how important they are to everyday life. Plants are good for the soil because they help prevent erosion. When they die, plants become fertilizer for the soil. Plants purify the air by taking out the carbon dioxide and producing oxygen. They are also important in industry. Perfume is made from the flowers of certain plants; paper is made from trees; and cloth such as cotton and linen also comes from plants. Many homes are built with lumber, and are heated with coal that came from dead plants. People work in their gardens to grow beautiful flowers. But most important, plants are the source of food for all living things. Without plants there would be no life!

In this unit the children will learn the conditions necessary for plant growth, how soil affects their growth, and some of the different ways in which plants are grown. They will also learn that different plants grow in different parts of the country, and that plants grow during certain seasons of the year.

At the completion of this unit, the children should have a greater awareness and interest in plants around them. They should learn how to plan experiments carefully and accurately, and realize the need for a control. They should be able to abstract the main ideas from their reading and report them effectively to the class. They should develop competence in observing accurately and drawing satisfactory conclusions.

BASIC SCIENCE INFORMATION

I. CONDITIONS NECESSARY FOR GROWTH.
    A. All plants need air to grow.
        1. Air is used to make food.

(M.G. Reid/Van Cleve)

A unit on the care of plants and ways of growing them.

B. Plants also need water.
1. Plants need water to make their food.
2. Plants get the water from the ground.
3. Some plants need more water than others.
C. Plants cannot grow without light.
1. Green plants need light to make food.
2. Usually plants get light from the sun.
3. Light is needed to keep a plant green.
D. Plants need the right warmth to grow.
1. If the temperature becomes too hot or too cold, a plant will stop growing; often it will die.

II. EFFECT OF SOIL.
A. Plants need good earth, or soil, to grow.
1. Good earth has water and chemicals (called minerals) in it.
2. Good earth contains sand, clay, and humus—small bits of dead plants and animals.
B. If the soil has too much sand in it, most plants will not grow.
1. Sandy soil dries out quickly.
2. Sandy soil does not have enough minerals for most plants.
C. Earth that has too much clay will not have many plants growing in it.
1. Clay soil holds water, but it gets sticky and gummy and does not let the water get into the plant.

[135

2. When clay soil becomes dry, it gets as hard as rock.
    3. Dry clay will crush a plant.
D. Good earth, or loam, is the best soil for growing plants.
    1. It holds water well, and also has enough minerals.

III. EFFECT OF CLIMATE, SEASONS, AND WEATHER.
    A. Plants grow differently in warm and cold weather.
        1. Some plants grow better where the weather is very hot.
            a. They grow better in the South, where it stays warmer longer.
            b. They do not grow as well where the summers are short.
            c. A palm tree is a plant that needs warm weather.
        2. Other plants grow better where the weather is cooler.
            a. In Alaska there is a small red plant that grows in the snow.
        3. A maple tree is a plant that grows best where it is neither very hot nor very cold.
        4. When the weather gets too cold, some plants will die.
    B. Most plants cannot stand the large changes in weather between summer and winter.
        1. During the spring, summer, and fall, plants grow beautifully.
        2. Many plants live for only one year and then die when the winter cold comes.
        3. Most trees lose their leaves when the weather gets cold.
            a. Trees do not die, but they rest during the cold months.
            b. They get new leaves in the spring.
            c. Evergreens have leaves that look like needles, and they stay green all winter.

IV. WAYS OF GROWING PLANTS.
    A. Seeds.
        1. Most plants grow from seeds.
        2. When a seed is planted, roots, stems, and leaves grow.
        3. Beans and radishes are seeds that will grow into new plants.
    B. Stems.
        1. Sometimes a new plant can be grown from a cutting of another plant.
            a. A cutting is usually a piece of the stem with the leaves.
            b. Philodendron and coleus can be grown from cuttings.
        2. Many plants grow from bulbs.
            a. A bulb is a stem that grows underground.
            b. Onions, tulips, narcissus, and lilies are all grown from bulbs.
        3. A new plant can be grown from a white potato.
            a. A white potato is another kind of underground stem.
            b. The "eye" of a potato is really a small bud.

C. Roots.
  1. Some roots will grow into new plants.
  2. Carrots, radishes, beets, and sweet potatoes are roots that will grow into new plants.
D. Leaves.
  1. Some plants can be grown from leaves.
  2. African violets, sedum, and begonias can be grown from leaves.

GENERAL INITIATING ACTIVITY

IF POSSIBLE, this unit should be started during the end of April or the beginning of May, when trees are showing their leaves and flowers are beginning to appear. The teacher will ask the children if they would like to grow some plants for the classroom, and possibly a plant of their own to take home.

With the children's interest and curiosity awakened, the following questions should arise, or be asked by the teacher, during the planning period:

1. What shall we plant?
2. How do we start growing the plants?
3. What must we do when taking care of the plants?

These questions will be put on the chalkboard, and referred to during the unit.

Note: Because a long time is required to test the effect of different conditions on plant growth and to grow new plants, this unit will most likely have to be taught in conjunction with another unit.

NEW SCIENCE VOCABULARY

soil	loam	bulb
minerals	cutting	"eye"
humus		

TEACHER BIBLIOGRAPHY

T–1 BLANC, SAM S., ABRAHAM S. FISCHLER, and OLCOTT GARDNER. *Modern Science: Earth, Space, and Environment.* New York: Holt, Rinehart and Winston.

T–2 HONE, ELIZABETH B., ALEXANDER JOSEPH, and EDWARD VICTOR. *A Sourcebook for Elementary Science.* New York: Harcourt Brace Jovanovich.

T–3 OTTO, JAMES H., and ALBERT TOWLE. *Modern Biology.* New York: Holt, Rinehart and Winston.

T–4 NELSON, LESLIE W., and GEORGE C. LORBEER. *Science Activities for Elementary Children.* Dubuque, Iowa: William C. Brown.

T–5 PARKER, BERTHA M. *Garden Indoors.* New York: Harper & Row.

T–6 THURBER, WALTER A., and MARY C. DURKEE. *Exploring Science.* Rockleigh, N.J.: Allyn & Bacon. (Grade 5)

T–7 UNESCO *Source Book for Science Teaching.* New York: UNESCO Publications Center.

T–8 VICTOR, EDWARD. *Science for the Elementary School.* New York: Macmillan.

T = Teacher reference.

PUPIL BIBLIOGRAPHY

P–1 MARSHALL, J. STANLEY, and WILBUR L. BEAUCHAMP. *The Basic Science Program.* Chicago: Scott, Foresman. (Grade 2)

P–2 BLOUGH, GLENN O. *Plants Round the Year.* New York: Harper & Row.

P–3 JACOBSON, WILLARD J., EDWARD VICTOR, et al. *Science: Comparing Ideas.* New York: American Book. (Grade 2)

*P–4 NAVARRA, JOHN G., and JOSEPH ZAFFARONI. *The Young Scientist: Exploring His World.* New York: Harper & Row. (Grade 2)

†P–5 BRANDWEIN, PAUL F., et al. *Concepts in Science.* New York: Harcourt Brace Jovanovich. (Grade 1)

†P–6 SCHNEIDER, HERMAN, and NINA SCHNEIDER. *Science for Work and Play.* Boston: D. C. Heath. (Grade 1)

‡P–7 SELSAM, MILLICENT E. *Play with Plants.* New York: William Morrow.

†P–8 FRASIER, GEORGE W., HELEN D. MACCRAHEN, and DONALD G. DECKER. *Science for You.* Syracuse, N.Y.: L. W. Singer. (Grade 1)

‡P–9 SCHNEIDER, HERMAN, and NINA SCHNEIDER. *Plants in the City.* New York: John Day.

P = Pupil reference.   * = Basic classroom text.
† = Slow reading level. ‡ = Slow reading level.

FILMS

F–1 *What Plants Need for Growth.* Chicago, Ill.: Encyclopaedia Britannica Films. 11 minutes, color.

F = Film.

SUPPLEMENTARY BIBLIOGRAPHY

FENTEN, D. X. *Indoor Gardening*. New York: Franklin Watts.

FOSTER, LAURA L. *Keeping the Plants You Pick*. New York: Thomas Y. Crowell.

GALE, FRANK, and CLARICE GALE. *Experiences with Plants for Young Children*. Palo Alto: Pacific Books.

GAMBINO, ROBERT. *Easy to Grow Vegetables*. New York: Harvey House.

HOLMES, ANITA S. *Plant Fun: Ten Easy Plants to Grow Indoors*. New York: Four Winds.

MILLARD, ADELE. *Plants for Kids to Grow Indoors*. New York: Sterling.

RAHN, JOAN. *Seeing What Plants Do*. New York: Atheneum Press.

SULLIVAN, GEORGE. *Understanding Hydroponics: Growing Plants Without Soil*. New York: Frederic Warne.

WARNER, MATT. *Flowers, Trees, and Gardening*. New York: Western.

**TEACHING
SCIENCE IN
THE
ELEMENTARY
SCHOOL**

W O R K

INITIATING ACTIVITIES AND PUPIL OBJECTIVES	BASIC SCIENCE INFORMATION
Initiating Activity: The children should be shown two plants, one that is healthy and growing, and one that is dead. Why is one plant still growing while the other has died? What do plants need to be healthy and grow?	
	I. CONDITIONS NECESSARY FOR GROWTH.
Do plants need air?	A. All plants need air to grow. 1. Air is used to make food.
Should we water plants?	B. Plants also need water.
	1. Plants need water to make their food 2. Plants get the water from the ground 3. Some plants need more water than others.
Why do we plant flowers in the sun?	C. Plants cannot grow without light.
	1. Green plants need light to make food 2. Usually plants get light from the sun 3. Light is needed to keep a plant green.

Learning Activities	Supplies and Equipment	Texts and References	Evaluation
	Two plants: one growing and one dead.		
...at leaf of plant with vase-...ne. Observe for one week. ...llow with class discus-...on.	Leafy plant. Vaseline.	T1–8 p. 460	Skill in distinguishing between pertinent and irrelevant observations.
...few pupils will water one ...ant and not water the other ...r four days. They will ...port to the class what they ...d, and will show the rest of ...e class the results.	Two growing plants.	P–4 p. 58	Skill in using controls.
...iscussion, followed by ...acher explanation, if neces-...ry.		T–8 p. 452–453	Skill in participating actively in group discussion.
...et a small group experi-...ent by growing one plant ...the light and the other in ...rkness. The group will ...ow the class the results in ...out five days, and will ...port what they observed.	Grass seed. Two small flower pots. Soil.	P–4 pp. 56–57	Skill in describing observations.
...iscussion, followed by ...acher explanation, if neces-...ry.		T–5 pp. 273–283	Skill in inferring.
...he group will complete the ...ove experiment (putting ...e grass back in the sun), ...d then will proceed to ...ass discussion.	Grass that has been grown in the dark.	P–4 pp. 56–57	Skill in communicating.

INITIATING ACTIVITIES AND PUPIL OBJECTIVES	BASIC SCIENCE INFORMATION
Do plants have to be warm?	D. Plants need the right warmth grow.
	1. If the temperature becomes t hot or too °cold, a plant will st growing; often it will die.

- -

Initiating Activity: Take the children on a walk around the school. Have the children observe the places where they find plants growing; also have them look at the places where plants are not growing.

II. EFFECT OF SOIL.

In what do plants grow, wherever they are found?	A. Plants need good earth, or soil, to gro
What does good earth, or soil, have in it?	1. Good earth has water and chemic; (called minerals) in it.
	2. Good earth contains sand, clay, a humus—small bits of dead plants a animals.

- -

Learning Activities	Supplies and Equipment	Texts and References	Evaluation
ave a small group keep one nt hot, one plant cold, and e plant at room tempera- e (warm). Explain to the ss what was done. Follow th class discussion.	Three healthy plants.	T–4 p. 69 P–3 p. 45	Skill in using controls.
al review of the conditions cessary for plants to grow d be healthy.			
			Test: Short objective test on the conditions necessary for plant growth.
ng-range pupil experi- ent: Have each child plant me seeds in soil, and some stones. The children will scuss what they observe at e end of the first, second, d third weeks. They will aw their conclusions at the d of the third week.	Jar. Pan. Soil. Stones. Seeds.	P–1 pp. 110– 111	Attitude of willing- ness to change one's mind in the light of new evidence.
ass discussion, followed reading.		P–4 pp. 150– 154	Skill in abstracting key concepts from the reading.

Initiating Activity: Place three flower pots, containing garden soil, clay, and sand, on the science table. Have the children see and feel the difference. Ask: In which pot will seeds grow the best?

What happens if there is a lot of sand?

B. If the soil has too much sand in it, m[ ] plants will not grow.

1. Sandy soil dries out quickly.

2. Sandy soil does not have enou[ ] minerals for most plants.

Will plants grow if there is a lot of clay?

C. Earth that has too much clay will n[ ] have many plants growing in it.

1. Clay soil holds water, but it ge[ ] sticky and gummy, and does not l[ ] the water get into the plant.

2. When clay soil becomes dry, it gets hard as rock.

3. Dry clay will crush a plant.

Learning Activities	Supplies and Equipment	Texts and References	Evaluation	
	Three flower pots. Garden soil. Clay. Sand.			**SAMPLE TEACHING AND RESOURCE UNITS**
vide the class into three ups. One group will plant e radish seeds in sandy l, another group will plant e seeds in clay soil, and third group will plant e seeds in loam. Water ch pot with the same ount of water and keep all er conditions the same. ep a record of the results.	Radish seeds. Three flower pots. Sand, clay, and loam.	T–4 p. 72	Skill in keeping records.	
nduct experiment to show w sand, clay, and loam ld water.	Three small jars. Three juice cans. Masking tape. Clay, sand, and loam.	T–2 p. 79	Skill in observing.	
scussion followed by teach- explanation, if necessary.		T–8 p. 307	Skill in reasoning.	
bserve and discuss the sults of the three-group periment described above.			Skill in interpreting results.	
scussion of experiment show- g how soils hold water.				
ave class design experi- ent to show how hard clay il becomes when it gets y. Follow with class dis- ssion.	Glass jar or beaker. Clay soil. Water.		Skill in designing an experiment.	

[145

INITIATING ACTIVITIES AND PUPIL OBJECTIVES	BASIC SCIENCE INFORMATION
What is the best dirt for plants?	D. Good earth, or loam, is the best soil growing plants.
	1. It holds water well, and also enough minerals.

Initiating Activity: Put up a bulletin board display. The display should be divided into two parts. One side should have pictures of one area and scene in each of the four seasons. The other half of the bulletin board should have pictures of different kinds of plants growing in different parts of the country.

III. EFFECT OF CLIMATE, SEASONS, AN THE WEATHER.

Why do not all plants grow where we live?

A. Plants grow differently in warm a cold weather.
    1. Some plants grow better where t weather is very hot.
        a. They grow better in the Sou where it stays warmer long
        b. They do not grow as w where the summers are sho
        c. A palm tree is a plant th needs warm weather.

LEARNING ACTIVITIES	SUPPLIES AND EQUIPMENT	TEXTS AND REFERENCES	EVALUATION
›serve and discuss the ›ults of the three-group ›periment described above.			Skill in induction.
›scussion, followed by teach- explanation, if necessary.		T–8 pp. 307– 308	
			Test: "Who am I?" Have each child describe one charac- teristic of a soil. The child who knows what soil is being described must tell why it is important. The child who has the right answer gets to go next.
	Four pictures of the same area and scene taken in fall, winter, summer, and spring. Pictures of plants growing in different parts of the country.		
›iscussion, followed by ›acher explanation, if nec- ›sary. Pictures should be ›ed for illustration when- ›er possible.		T–1 pp. 312– 322	Skill in deduction.

INITIATING ACTIVITIES AND PUPIL OBJECTIVES	BASIC SCIENCE INFORMATION
Do all plants have to grow where the weather is hot?	2. Other plants grow better where t weather is cooler. a. In Alaska there is a small r plant that grows in the snow. 3. A maple tree is a plant that gro best where it is neither very hot n very cold. 4. When the weather gets too co some plants will die.

Why do some plants die in winter?	B. Most plants cannot stand the lar changes in weather between summ and winter.
	  1. During the spring, summer, and fa plants grow beautifully.
	
	  2. Many plants live for only one ye and then die when the winter come

Why do trees not die?	3. Most trees lose their leaves whe the weather gets cold.
	  a. Trees do not die, but they re during the cold months.
	  b. They get new leaves in the sprir
	
	  c. Evergreens have leaves that lo like needles, and they stay gree all winter.

Initiating Acitivity: Recall experiments where plants were grown from grass and radish seeds. Ask: Is this the only way to grow plants (by seed), or are there other ways of growing plants?	
	IV. WAYS OF GROWING PLANTS.
Are many plants grown from seeds?	A. Seeds. 1. Most plants grow from seeds.

Learning Activities	Supplies and Equipment	Texts and References	Evaluation
cussion, followed by cher explanation, if necary.		T–1 pp. 312–322	Skill in participating actively in group discussion.
iew of experiment of wing plant in refrigerator.			Skill in applying the knowledge learned from a previous experiment to explain a new situation.
oil reading about plants in different seasons.		P–2 pp. 17–18, 29–30, 4–5	Skill in abstracting key concepts from the reading.
ss discussion.			Skill in communicating.
oil reading followed by cher explanation, if necary, and class discussion.		P–2 pp. 15–16	Skill in arriving at logical conclusions from the reading and discussion.
ss discussion.			Skill in describing characteristics.
ss discussion, followed a demonstration of differt varieties of seeds. Ask ldren to suggest other ds that produce plants.	Variety of seeds.		Skill in describing similar situations.

INITIATING ACTIVITIES AND PUPIL OBJECTIVES	BASIC SCIENCE INFORMATION
	2. When a seed is planted, roots, ste~~m~~ and leaves grow.
	3. Beans and radishes are seeds t~~hat~~ will grow into new plants.
Can plants be grown from stems?	B. Stems.
	1. Sometimes a new plant can be gro~~wn~~ from a cutting of another plant. a. A cutting is usually a piece of t~~he~~ stem with leaves.
	b. Philodendron and coleus can ~~be~~ grown from cuttings.
Can plants be grown from bulbs?	2. Many plants grow from bulbs. a. A bulb is a stem that grows und~~er~~ ground.
	b. Onions, tulips, narcissus, and lil~~ies~~ are all grown from bulbs.
Will a plant grow from a white potato?	3. A new plant can be grown from ~~a~~ white potato.
	a. A white potato is another kind ~~of~~ underground stem. b. The "eye" of a potato is reall~~y a~~ small bud.

Learning Activities	Supplies and Equipment	Texts and References	Evaluation
g up a newly grown plant l observe the parts of the ınt.	Radish plant.		Skill in observing.
ıss experiment growing ın seeds.	Bean seeds. Flower pots or jars.		Skill in planning and conducting an experiment.
pil reading to be followed class discussion.		P–4 p. 65	Skill in abstracting key concepts from the science content in the textbook.
ve two pupils make a cut- g from a coleus plant, and ›w roots from the cutting. llow with discussion.	Glass jar. Coleus cutting.	P–4 p. 65	Skill in interpreting results.
ıcher explanation and ss discussion. ing in bulbs (not growing) the children to look at l feel.	Bulbs.	T–8 p. 455	Attitude of suspended judgment until all available evidence has been collected.
ıve some children prepare uitable container for grow- ؛ a narcissus bulb, and ؛n have the children plant	Narcissus bulbs. Bowl. Pebbles or pearl chips. Small pieces of charcoal.	P–4 p. 64	Skill in observing and describing results.
؛ve the class grow a white ؛tato in the classroom.	White potato. Flower pot. Soil.	T–8 p. 469	Attitude of curiosity.
ıcher explanation fol- ved by class discussion.		T–3 pp. 334– 335	Skill in interpreting observations and ideas.

Initiating Activities and Pupil Objectives	Basic Science Information
Can plants be grown from roots?	C. Roots.

1. Some roots will grow into new plan
2. Carrots, radishes, beets, and swe potatoes are roots that will grow ir new plants.

Is it possible to grow a new plant from a leaf?

D. Leaves.

1. Some plants can be grown fro leaves.
2. African violets, sedum, and begon can be grown from leaves.

Learning Activities	Supplies and Equipment	Texts and References	Evaluation
ass discussion. ave a small group grow a ot garden. The garden will ow the tops of carrots, ets, and radishes. After o weeks the children will scuss the new plants.	Box. Soil. Tops of beets, radishes, and carrots.	T–7 p. 42	Skill in analyzing and interpreting results.
lass discussion. emonstration of a rex egonia leaf that has been arted at least two weeks fore.	Rex begonia leaves. Shallow box. Sand. Knife. Piece of glass. Four small pieces of wood.	T–5 pp. 16–17	Attitude of willing-ness to change one's mind in the light of new evidence.
ulminating Activity: ow film, *What Plants ed for Growth*. Follow ith a display of all the ants grown in different ays, with each plant beled appropriately. onclude with a question-d-answer period, where the main concepts in the it are reviewed.	Projector. Screen.	F–1	

ADDITIONAL LEARNING ACTIVITIES FOR SLOW LEARNERS

LEARNING ACTIVITIES	MATERIALS
1. Experiment to show that plants need light.	P–8 pp. 108–109. Seeds. Two cans. Soil.
2. Experiment to show that plants need good soil.	P–8 pp. 100–107. Pan. Jar. Can. Sand. Soil. Seeds.
3. Reading about the effect of the seasons on plants. The children can make a small notebook, drawing the trees in the various seasons.	P–6 pp. 92–95. Colored paper. Crayons.
4. Have the children place a board over a small portion of grass for a week or two to show that plants need sunlight.	T–2 p. 93.
5. Have the children grow a tumbler garden.	P–5 p. 63. Lima beans. Jar or tumbler. Blotting paper.

ADDITIONAL LEARNING ACTIVITIES
FOR FAST LEARNERS

SAMPLE
TEACHING
AND
RESOURCE
UNITS

LEARNING ACTIVITIES	MATERIALS
1. Additional experiment on where plants will grow. The children can also make a chart of the plants that grow in the area in which they live.	P–3 p. 42.
2. Experiment to show why cactus plant will hold so much water.	P–9 pp. 28–29. Two sheets of paper.
3. Make a water garden.	P–9 pp. 64–66. Aquarium tank or glass bowl. Sand. Water plants. Pebbles or pearl chips.
4. Experiment growing bird seed.	P–9 p. 60. Sponge. Bird seed.
5. Experiment growing an avocado seed.	P–7 p. 28. Avocado pit. Tall jar.
6. Experiment growing pussy willow stems.	P–7 p. 17. Pussy willow stems. Jar or glass.
7. Help slow learners.	
8. Make short oral reports on the effect of the seasons on plants.	

FRICTION
A Teaching Unit for Grade 4

OVERVIEW

CONCEPT OBJECTIVES
1. Friction occurs whenever objects rub against each other.
2. Certain factors will affect the amount of friction produced.
3. Friction can be reduced or increased.
4. Friction can be harmful or helpful.
5. Friction is necessary in many everyday activities.

BEHAVIORAL AND PROCESS OBJECTIVES
1. Observe and describe friction, and infer what causes friction.
2. Conduct experiments to determine factors that affect friction.
3. Investigate and describe ways to reduce and increase friction.
4. Describe and compare the harmful and useful effects of friction.

BIBLIOGRAPHY

1. HONE, ELIZABETH, ALEXANDER JOSEPH, and EDWARD VICTOR. *A Sourcebook for Elementary Science.* New York: Harcourt Brace Jovanovich Pub. Co. (Teacher)
2. PINE, TILLIE, and JOSEPH LEVINE. *Friction All Around.* New York: McGraw-Hill Book Co. (Pupil)
3. VICTOR, EDWARD. *Friction.* Chicago: Follett Pub. Co. (Pupil)

GENERAL INITIATING ACTIVITY

PREPARE a poster in advance and display it at the beginning of the unit. The poster will have two rows of six drawings. In each drawing a child will be smiling or frowning, depending on whether friction is a

(Barbara Van Cleve)

A unit on friction.

help or a hindrance. Call attention to each set of matching drawings, have the children observe and describe what is going on in each set, then start a discussion about the cause of the conditions in each set.

Why This?	Why Not This?
1. Picture of a girl in a car with wheels.	1. Picture of the same girl in the same car without wheels.
2. Picture of a gleeful boy sledding in the snow.	2. Picture of a sad boy on a sled on bare ground.
3. Picture of a smiling girl pushing a small, light stack of books to a friend who is at the other end of a table.	3. Picture of the same girl frowning as she pushes a large, heavy stack of books to the same friend at the other end of the table.
4. Picture of a boy playing on his knees with his blue jeans rolled up over his knees.	4. Picture of the boy, jeans rolled down, playing on one knee with a hole in the jeans at the knee.
5. Picture of a wagon with the word "squeak." The boy watching is sad.	5. Picture of the same wagon, but the boy is smiling as he stands with an oil can in his hand.
6. Picture of a girl walking forward on the sidewalk.	6. Picture of a girl losing balance as she walks on the ice.

WHAT CAUSES FRICTION?*

INITIATING ACTIVITY AND DISCUSSION QUESTIONS

Obtain a large cardboard carton and place a child in it. Have another child push the carton across the floor.

What makes the carton bump and stick as it moves?
How can this happen if the carton and the floor are smooth?

CONCEPT OBJECTIVES

1. Friction occurs whenever objects rub against each other.
2. Friction is the force that resists the movement of one object over another object.
3. Friction is caused by irregularities in the surfaces of objects.

BEHAVIORAL AND PROCESS OBJECTIVES

1. Observe, feel, and describe the force of friction.
2. Infer and state the cause of friction.

MATERIALS

two small rough boards   coping saw
one small smooth board   coarse sandpaper
magnifying glass   fine sandpaper
block of balsa wood

PUPIL INVESTIGATION #1

1. Rub two pieces of wood with rough surfaces back and forth. Does one piece of wood move easily over the other?
2. Examine the surface of one piece of wood under a magnifying glass. What does this surface look like? (There are bumps and hollows.) Can you feel the bumps and hollows with your fingers?

PUPIL INVESTIGATION #2

1. Obtain a block of balsa wood about 15 centimeters (6 in) long, 7½ centimeters (3 in) wide, and 4 centimeters (1½ in) thick. With a coping saw cut the balsa wood horizontally in half, doing it in such a way that you create large-sized bumps and hollows.
2. Now reverse the position of the top half of the balsa wood and rub the bumps and hollows of the top half against the bumps and hollows of the bottom half. What do the bumps and hollows of each half do? (They bump and catch against each other.)

* A more detailed description of the concepts and learning activities, together with appropriate diagrams, can be found in Chapter 17 on "Friction and Machines," pp. 638, 650.

INQUIRING FURTHER

1. Examine the surface of a smooth piece of wood under a magnifying glass. Does this surface have bumps and hollows? Are the bumps and hollows as big as those in the rough piece of wood?

2. Observe the surface of a sheet of coarse sandpaper closely. Rub your finger over the sandpaper. Can you see and feel the bumps and hollows in the sandpaper? How do the bumps and hollows look when you examine the sandpaper with a magnifying glass? Repeat the experiment, using a sheet of fine sandpaper instead. Could you see the bumps and hollows with just your eye? Could you see them with a magnifying glass?

3. Use the magnifying glass to examine the surfaces of other objects. Do the surfaces have bumps and hollows?

4. Metal machine parts usually feel very smooth to the touch. You can not feel any bumps and hollows, nor can you see them under a magnifying glass. Yet there is friction between the metal parts as they slide over each other. What do you think you would see if you examined the surface of a smooth metal under a powerful microscope? (You would see very tiny bumps and hollows.)

5. Why did the carton with the child in it bump and stick as it was pushed? (There was friction between the carton and the floor.)

WHAT FACTORS AFFECT FRICTION?*

INITIATING ACTIVITY AND DISCUSSION QUESTIONS

Review the discovery that friction is caused by irregularities in the surfaces of objects. Ask the children what conditions they think may have an effect on the amount of friction produced.

Will the nature of the materials have an effect on friction?
Will the nature of the surfaces have an effect on friction?
Will the amount of pressure between two surfaces affect friction?
Will the amount of area between two surfaces affect friction?

CONCEPT OBJECTIVES

1. Hard materials produce less friction than soft materials.
2. Smooth surfaces produce less friction than rough surfaces.
3. The greater the force pressing two surfaces against each other, the greater the friction will be.
4. The friction between the narrow surfaces of two objects will be the same as the friction between the wide surfaces.

BEHAVIORAL AND PROCESS OBJECTIVES

1. Describe and compare friction produced by hard and soft materials.
2. Describe and compare friction produced by rough and smooth surfaces.
3. Measure and compare the effect of pressure between two surfaces on the amount of friction produced.
4. Measure and compare the effect of difference in the area between two surfaces on the amount of friction produced.

MATERIALS

two small rough boards	spring balance
two small smooth boards	coarse sandpaper
two slices of bread	rough sandpaper
rectangular block of wood	mirror
screw eye	absorbent cotton
string	magnifying glass

PUPIL INVESTIGATION #1

1. Rub two rough pieces of wood back and forth. Note the amount of friction produced.
2. Now rub two slices of soft bread back and forth, and again note the amount of friction produced.

---

* A more detailed description of the concepts and learning activities, together with appropriate diagrams, can be found in Chapter 17 on "Friction and Machines," pp. 638, 650–651.

3. Which materials produced more friction: the hard or soft materials? Why? (The bumps and hollows of the soft materials bump and catch into each other more easily.)

PUPIL INVESTIGATION #2

1. Rub two rough pieces of wood back and forth. Note the amount of friction produced.
2. Now rub two smooth pieces of wood back and forth, and again note the amount of friction produced.
3. Which kind of surfaces produced more friction: the smooth or rough surfaces? Why? (Rough surfaces have bigger bumps and deeper hollows, so they bump and catch more against each other.)

PUPIL INVESTIGATION #3

1. Get a rectangular block of wood and put a screw eye into one end.
2. Place the block of wood, wide surface down, on the table and put a book on top of the block.
3. Use a loop of string to connect the screw eye to a spring balance. While holding the balance horizontally, pull the block across the table. Note on the spring balance how much force is needed to pull the block across the table. Write it down.
4. Put two more books of the same kind as the first book on top of the first book. There will now be three books on the block of wood. Again, holding the balance horizontally, pull the block across the table, and note the amount of force needed to do this. Write it down. Is this force greater or smaller than the force needed to pull the block when just one book is on it?
5. What effect on the pressure between the surface of the block and the table did the three books have as compared to the one book? (The three books made the block push harder against the table top.) Why does an increase in the pressure between two surfaces increase the amount of friction produced? (The increase in pressure makes the bumps and hollows of the two surfaces bump and catch against each other more strongly.)

PUPIL INVESTIGATION #4

1. Place the rectangular block of wood, with the screw eye in one end, wide surface down on the table and put a book on top of the block.
2. Using a loop of string to connect the screw eye to a spring balance, hold the balance horizontally and pull the block of wood across the table. How much force is needed to pull the block. Write it down.
3. Now repeat the experiment, but this time use the narrower surface of the block of wood. How much force is needed to pull the

block of wood across the table? Write it down. Is this force greater or smaller than the force needed to pull the wider surface? (The forces are the same.)

4. What effect does the amount of area between two surfaces have on the amount of friction? Why? (There is no difference in the pressure between the surfaces, regardless of the area.)

INQUIRING FURTHER

1. Feel the texture of a rough piece of wood. Look at the bumps and hollows in the wood. Can you see them with just your eye? Can you see them under a magnifying glass? Now do the same thing with a smooth piece of wood. What is the difference between the bumps and hollows in the rough and the smooth pieces of wood? (The bumps are smaller and the hollows are not as deep in the smooth piece.)

2. Rub a ball of absorbent cotton across the surface of a rough piece of wood, a sheet of coarse sandpaper, a sheet of fine sandpaper, and a mirror. On which materials do bits of cotton catch and stick the most? The least? What effect does the kind of surface of a material have on friction? (The rougher the surface of the material, the greater the friction will be.)

HOW CAN FRICTION BE REDUCED?*

INITIATING ACTIVITY AND DISCUSSION QUESTIONS

Have the children rub two rough pieces of wood back and forth, and note the amount of friction produced. Start a discussion on how the friction might be reduced.

How can we reduce the friction between the pieces of wood?
Is there more than one way of reducing this friction?
Have things at home ever been hard to move or turn due to friction?
What did you or your parents do to reduce the friction?

CONCEPT OBJECTIVES

1. Making the surfaces smoother will reduce friction.
2. Smoothing a surface makes bumps and hollows in the surface smaller.
3. Lubricants will reduce friction.
4. A lubricant covers the bumps and fills in the hollows, so that the surfaces slide over the lubricant.
5. Rollers and wheels will reduce friction.
6. Rollers and wheels roll instead of slide over bumps and hollows.

BEHAVIORAL AND PROCESS OBJECTIVES

1. Observe and describe how smoothing the surfaces reduces friction.
2. Investigate and describe how lubricants reduce friction.
3. Measure and compare sliding friction and rolling friction.

MATERIALS

two small rough boards	spring balance
sandpaper	12 round pencils
two pieces of dry toast	large cardboard carton
jam	play wagon
magnifying glass	bicycle
lubricating oil	stopwatch
soap	glass jar screw cap
candle	large marbles
silicone spray, gel, stick	beginner's roller skate
string	ball-bearing roller skate

PUPIL INVESTIGATION #1

1. Rub two pieces of wood with rough surfaces back and forth, and note the friction produced.
2. Now sand one surface of each piece of wood until it is smooth.

* A more detailed description of the concepts and learning activities, together with appropriate diagrams, can be found in Chapter 17 on "Friction and Machines," pp. 639, 652.

3. Rub these smooth surfaces back and forth, and again note the friction produced. Which produced less friction: the rough surfaces or the smooth surfaces? Why? (The bumps and hollows are smaller in smooth surfaces, so they don't bump and catch as much.)

PUPIL INVESTIGATION #2

1. Rub two pieces of cold, dry toast back and forth. Note the friction produced.
2. Now spread some jam thickly over each piece of toast, and rub the pieces back and forth again. Note the friction produced. What did the jam do to the toast? (It covered the bumps and filled in the hollows.) How did this affect the friction between the pieces of toast? (The pieces of toast slide smoothly over the jam instead of roughly over each other.)

INVESTIGATION #3

1. Look at the tips of your forefinger and thumb under a magnifying glass. What do you see? (There are bumps and hollows.)
2. Rub the tips of your thumb and forefinger back and forth. Note the friction produced.
3. Place a drop of lubricating oil on the tip of your forefinger. Rub your thumb and forefinger back and forth again. Is the friction between your fingers greater or smaller now? Why? (The oil covers the bumps and fills in the hollows, so that the finger tips now move easily over each other.)

INVESTIGATION #4

1. Find a wood desk or bureau where the drawers stick and do not move in and out easily. Remove one drawer and turn it upside down. Locate the runners on the drawer and inside the desk or bureau, along which the drawer moves in and out.
2. Will putting lubricating oil on the runners help the drawer move in and out more easily? Why? (Wood is porous and absorbs most of the oil, so friction will not be reduced much.)
3. Rub soap or candle wax on the runners of the drawer and the desk or bureau, and try moving the drawer in and out. What happens? (The soap or wax covers the bumps and fills in the hollows of the wood runners, so the drawer moves in and out more easily.)
4. Try using a silicone spray, gel, or stick on another drawer that is hard to move. Read the labels and find out what other objects the silicone will lubricate. Try it for yourself.

INVESTIGATION #5

1. Slip a loop of string inside a book and set the book on the table.
2. Attach the string to a spring balance. Holding the balance hori-

zontally, pull the book across the table. Note on the balance how much force is needed to pull the book. Write it down.

3. Now put 4 round pencils underneath the book. Put 8 round pencils about 5 centimeters (2 in) apart, beside the book and facing the direction that you will pull the book. Again, holding the balance horizontally, pull the book across the table and note the amount of force needed to do this. Write it down. Which was less: the force needed to pull the book along the surface of the table or along the pencils? Why? (The round pencils roll rather than slide over the bumps and hollows.)

PUPIL INVESTIGATION #6

1. Get a large cardboard carton about the same size as the body of a child's play wagon.
2. Put a child in the carton and push the carton across the floor. Note the force needed to push the carton.
3. Now have the child in the carton climb into a play wagon. Push the wagon across the floor. Note the force needed to push the wagon. Did you have to use more force or less force now? Which is greater: sliding friction or rolling friction? Why? (In sliding friction the bumps and hollows of each surface bump and catch against each other. In rolling friction the rollers or wheels roll over the bumps and hollows of the surfaces.)

INQUIRING FURTHER

1. Have a child bring in a bicycle whose wheels do not spin very easily because they need oil or are rusty. Set the bicycle upside down, and get a stopwatch from the physical education teacher. Now make one wheel spin, and use the stopwatch to see how long it takes for the wheel to stop spinning. Apply lubricating oil to the wheel and the axle. Again make the wheel spin, being sure to apply the same force as you did the first time. Use the stopwatch again to see how long the wheel spins after lubrication. Compare the length of time the wheel spins before and after oiling.
2. Look for a door whose hinges squeak when the door opens or closes. Apply oil to the hinges. What happens to the squeak? Why?
3. Visit an auto service station and ask the service man to show you what parts of an auto he lubricates and what kinds of lubricants he uses for the different parts.
4. Visit a locksmith and find out what special lubricant he uses for locks that stick and are hard to turn. (He uses powdered graphite.) Why doesn't he use lubricating oil? (The oil would get thick and gummy after a while, making the lock even harder to turn.)
5. Put the screw cap from a large glass jar, lip down, on the table. Put a heavy book on the screw cap and try to spin the book.

What happens? (The book makes only one or two turns, then stops because of friction.) Take away the book. Put as many marbles as you can under the screw cap, making sure you use large enough marbles so that the lip of the cap does not touch the table. Now put the book back on the cap and try to spin the book again. What happens this time? (The book spins easily.) Why? (The round marbles roll over the bumps and hollows.)

6. Bring a beginner's roller skate and a ball-bearing skate to class. Examine the wheels of both skates closely. Note the ring of small steel balls around the axle of the ball-bearing skate. What do you think is the purpose of these balls? (They make it possible for the surfaces to roll rather than slide.) Turn both skates upside down. Use the same amount of force on one wheel of each skate to set them turning. Which wheel turns the longest? Why?

IS FRICTION HELPFUL OR HARMFUL?*

INITIATING ACTIVITY AND DISCUSSION QUESTIONS

Review the different ways of reducing friction. Start a discussion on whether friction is good or bad.

Can friction be harmful? How?
Can friction be helpful? How?
What would happen if there were no friction?

CONCEPT OBJECTIVES

1. Friction can be both harmful and helpful.
2. Friction can be harmful by wearing away things.
3. Friction makes sliding parts stick and move more slowly.
4. Friction makes work harder because extra force must be used to overcome the friction.
5. Some of the mechanical energy needed to overcome friction is changed into heat energy which may be harmful.
6. Friction is helpful in making things smoother.
7. Friction is helpful in making things slow down and stop.
8. Friction is necessary in many of our everyday activities.

BEHAVIORAL AND PROCESS OBJECTIVES

1. Conduct investigations to determine and describe the harmful and the useful effects of friction.
2. Infer or predict what would happen if there were no friction in our daily life.

MATERIALS

piece of rough wood	block of wood
piece of smooth wood	long nail
sandpaper	hammer
jar with screw cap	nylon cloth

PUPIL INVESTIGATION #1

1. Rub sandpaper back and forth over a piece of smooth wood, then over rough wood. Which surface is easier to sand? Why? (The rougher the surface, the more force is needed to overcome friction.)
2. Rub the sandpaper hard over the rough piece of wood. Keep rubbing. What do you feel after a while? (You feel heat.) Where does this heat come from? (Some of the mechanical energy used to overcome friction is changed into heat energy.)
3. Keep sanding the rough piece of wood. What happens to the sandpaper after a while? (It wears out because of friction.)

* A more detailed description of the concepts and learning activities, together with appropriate diagrams, can be found in Chapter 17 on "Friction and Machines," pp. 639–640, 652.

PUPIL INVESTIGATION #2

1. Get a new piece of chalk and measure its length carefully.
2. Write with the chalk a while. Measure the chalk length again. What happened to the chalk? (It is worn away because of friction.)

PUPIL INVESTIGATION #3

1. Rub the eraser part of a pencil briskly back and forth on a table. Quickly put the eraser on your upper lip. What do you feel? Why?
2. Rub your hands briskly back and forth. What do you feel? Why?

PUPIL INVESTIGATION #4

1. Visit an auto service station. Ask the service man to show you a new and a used tire. Why does the used one have a smoother surface or smaller grooves? (The rubber is worn away by friction.)
2. Ask the service man to show or tell you how brakes use friction to slow down or stop a moving auto. What happens to the brakes after they have been used a long time? (They wear out.)

PUPIL INVESTIGATION # 5

1. How does sandpaper help a carpenter? (The friction between the sandpaper and wood helps make the wood smooth.)
2. Visit an optician. Ask him to show you how he uses friction to grind and polish his eye glass lenses.

PUPIL INVESTIGATION #6

1. Get a glass jar with a screw cap. Screw the cap on tightly. Now wet your hands and soap them well. Try to unscrew the cap with your soapy hands. What happens? (There is little or no friction between your hands and the cap, so you can't unscrew the cap.)
2. Dry your hands, then try again to unscrew the cap. What happens this time? Why?

INQUIRING FURTHER

1. Get a piece of nylon cloth and rub it back and forth on a sheet of coarse sandpaper. What happens to the cloth? Why?
2. Hammer a long nail half-way into a block of wood. Try to pull the nail out with your fingers. What happens? (The friction between the nail and the wood holds the nail firmly in the wood.) If there were no friction, what would happen when you pulled on the nail? (The nail would pull out easily.) What other unusual situations would happen if there were no friction on earth?
3. Is it easy to walk on ice? Why? (There is little friction between

your shoes and ice.) How would spreading sand on ice help? (The sand would help increase the friction between the shoes and ice.)

CULMINATING ACTIVITIES

1. Display or call attention to the poster board used for the General Initiating Activity. Go over all the drawings, asking the children to answer in each case the questions "Why This" and "Why Not This." If necessary, make up additional sets of drawings to include those concepts not provided for in the poster board.
2. Draw two columns on the chalkboard. Have the children list in one column the harmful effects of friction, and in the other column the useful effects. For each effect have the children tell what causes the friction, what factors could affect the friction, and how the friction might be reduced or increased, as needed.

ELECTROMAGNETS
A Resource Unit for Grades 5–6

I. OBJECTIVES

A. *Key Science Concepts and Understandings*

1. When electric current passes through a wire, there is a magnetic field with lines of force around the wire.
2. When the wire carrying an electric current is wound into a coil, the coil acts just like a bar magnet, with a north-seeking and a south-seeking pole.
3. Placing a bar of soft iron inside the coil greatly increases the strength of this magnet, which is called an electromagnet.
4. An electromagnet is a temporary magnet, its magnetism continuing only as long as electric current flows through the wire.
5. Soft iron is almost always used as the core of an electromagnet because it magnetizes easily and loses its magnetism just as easily.
6. When the connections of the wire to the source of electric current are reversed, the electromagnet's poles will also be reversed.
7. Increasing the number of turns of wire in the coil will make the electromagnet stronger.
8. Increasing the strength of the electric current flowing through the wire will make the electromagnet stronger.
9. An electromagnet is like a permanent magnet in that it has a magnetic field and two poles, it will attract only magnetic materials, and its magnetic force will pass through nonmagnetic materials.
10. An electromagnet is different than a permanent magnet in that its magnetism can be turned on or off, its poles can be reversed, it can be made stronger or weaker, and its core is made of soft iron whereas the magnet is usually made of steel.
11. Electromagnets are used in such communication devices as the telegraph, telephone, radio, and television.
12. Electromagnets are used in industry in such devices as the motor, generator, transformer, and crane.
13. Electromagnets are found in the home in bells, buzzers,

A unit on electromagnets.

(Luth Rohr/Van Cleve)

chimes, circuit breakers, some electrical appliances, and many electric toys.

B. Behavioral Outcomes

1. Skill in analyzing.
2. Skill in applying previous knowledge to new situations.
3. Skill in communicating.
4. Skill in deduction.
5. Skill in experimenting.
6. Skill in formulating hypotheses.
7. Skill in induction.
8. Skill in keeping records.
9. Skill in making comparisons.
10. Skill in measuring.
11. Skill in noting similarities and differences.
12. Skill in observing and describing.
13. Skill in predicting.
14. Skill in using controls.
15. Skill in using numbers and experiments.
16. Attitude of curiosity.
17. Attitude of open-mindedness.
18. Attitude of reluctance to generalize on the basis of one experiment.
19. Attitude of suspended judgment.
20. Attitude of willingness to change one's mind in the light of new evidence.

C. Anticipated Pupil Objectives or Problems

1. Why does a wire carrying an electric current act like a magnet?
2. What do the lines of force around the wire look like?
3. What will happen if we put the wire over a compass? Under a compass?
4. What will happen if we arrange the wire into a coil?
5. What do the lines of force around the coil look like?
6. What will happen if we put an iron nail inside the coil?
7. Why do we use soft iron instead of steel inside the coil?
8. What will happen if we use a

[171

steel core in an electromagnet?

9. What will happen if we disconnect one wire from the dry cell?
10. How can we tell which end of an electromagnet is the north-seeking pole?
11. What will happen if we reverse the connections of the wires to the dry cell?
12. How can we make an electromagnet stronger?
13. How are electromagnets like permanent magnets?
14. How are electromagnets different from permanent magnets?
15. How are electromagnets used in industry? In the home?

II. ACTIVITIES

A. Initiating Activities

1. Set up a bulletin board displaying an electromagnet, devices that use electromagnets, and so forth, with appropriate materials on a nearby table.
2. Show a film, or parts of it, on electromagnets with the sound turned off.
3. Show selected frames from a filmstrip on electromagnets.
4. Spread books, pictures, and other printed materials about electromagnets on the library table.
5. Make an electromagnet and use it to pick up magnetic materials. Ask, "What kind of magnet is this?"
6. Use a wire carrying an electric current to pick up iron filings. Ask, "Why does the wire act like a magnet?" Repeat, arranging the wire into a coil.

7. Stop the flow of electricity through an electromagnet. Ask, "Why did the electromagnet lose its magnetism?"
8. Ask the class to suggest ways to find out how it can tell which end of an electromagnet is a north-seeking pole.
9. Reverse the connections of an electromagnet's wires to a dry cell. Ask, "What effect will this have on the electromagnet?"
10. Ask the class to suggest ways to make an electromagnet stronger.
11. Ask the class how electromagnets are similar to and different from permanent magnets.
12. Bring in devices like the bell, buzzer, telegraph, motor, etc. Ask class to locate the electromagnet in each device. Ask, "How does the electromagnet work in this device?"

B. Learning Activities

1. Connect the bare ends of a length of copper bell wire to the terminals of a dry cell and pick up iron filings with the middle part of the wire. Disconnect one end of the wire from the dry cell and try again to pick up the filings.
2. Bring a compass near a wire carrying an electric current. Place the wire over, then under, the compass. Observe the deflection of the needle.
3. Run a piece of bell wire through a hole in a square of white cardboard. Place four compasses on the cardboard, arranging them into north, east, south, and west positions about two inches from the wire. Connect the bare ends of the wire to the terminals of

a dry cell. Observe the new positions of the needles.

4. Remove the compasses and instead place iron filings on the cardboard. Connect the bare ends of the wire to the terminals of the dry cell, then tap the edge of the cardboard lightly. Note the pattern made by the filings.

5. Wind about 2 feet of bell wire around a pencil to make a coil. Remove the pencil and attach the bare ends of the wire to the terminals of a dry cell. Try to pick up iron filings and tacks with each end of the coil.

6. Bring a compass near one end of a coil of wire carrying an electric current. Note the position of the needle. Bring the compass near both ends of the coil and determine which is the north-seeking and south-seeking pole of the coil.

7. Sprinkle some iron filings on a piece of white cardboard. Rest a coil of wire carrying an electric current on the cardboard and tap the edge of the cardboard.

8. Wind some bell wire in a coil around a large iron nail. Connect the bare ends of the wire to the terminals of a dry cell. Try to pick up iron filings and tacks with one end of the nail. Observe any difference in strength now that the coil has a core of iron in it. Repeat activities #6 and #7 with this electromagnet.

9. Make an electromagnet, using a large iron bolt instead of a nail.

10. Make a horseshoe electromagnet. Compare the strength of this electromagnet with a straight one.

11. Make an electromagnet having 30 turns of wire and count how many tacks it will pick up. Now make an electromagnet with 60 turns of wire and note the number of tacks this electromagnet will pick up. Relate the number of tacks to the number of turns.

12. Compare the number of tacks an electromagnet will pick up, using first one dry cell and then two dry cells which are connected in series.

13. Wrap about 100 turns of thin insulated copper wire around a hollow cardboard mailing tube. Place a steel knitting needle inside the tube. Attach the bare ends of the wire to the terminals of two dry cells connected in series. After a few seconds disconnect the wire from the dry cells and remove the needle. Test the needle for magnetism over a period of days. Note the permanence of this knitting needle magnet.

14. Make a simple telegraph set.

15. Set up a two-way telegraph system.

C. *Enrichment Activities*

1. Show how an electric buzzer works. Make an electric buzzer.

2. Show how a bell works. Make a simple electric bell.

3. Show how electric chimes work.

4. Show how a circuit breaker works.

5. Show how a telephone transmitter and receiver work.

6. Show how a St. Louis motor works. Make a simple motor.

7. Show how a generator works. Make a simple generator.

8. Read and report on Hans Christian Oersted and his early experiments on electromagnetism.
9. Read and report on Samuel Morse and the invention of the telegraph and Morse code.
10. Read and report on the laying of the first telegraph cable across the Atlantic Ocean.
11. Read and report on Guglielmo Marconi and the invention of the wireless telegraph.

D. Culminating Activities

1. Show films or filmstrips on electromagnetism.
2. Have a classroom "science fair" of experiments, demonstrations, and models that the pupils made during the unit.
3. Have fast learners give reports, accompanied by demonstrations or experiments.
4. Have pupils make a list of appliances and other devices in the home or in industry that make use of electromagnets.
5. Visit a museum of science and industry that has a display on electromagnets.
6. Visit a telephone or telegraph company.

E. Evaluating Activities

1. Observation by the teacher for indications of pupil development of scientific skills, attitudes, appreciations, and interests.
2. Objective-type tests.
3. "Thought" questions, such as:
   a. What would happen if you used a steel core in an electromagnet?
   b. What advantages does an electromagnet have over a permanent magnet?
   c. What advantages does a permanent magnet have over an electromagnet?
   d. When a telegraph key is connected to an electric bell or buzzer circuit and pressed like a pushbutton, why is there only one sound instead of repeated sounds as with the bell or buzzer?

III. BIBLIOGRAPHY

A. Teacher Bibliography

1. BLOUGH, GLENN. O., and JULIUS SCHWARTZ. *Elementary School Science and How to Teach It.* New York: Holt, Rinehart and Winston.
2. CARIN, ARTHUR, and ROBERT SUND. *Teaching Science Through Discovery.* Columbus, Ohio: Charles E. Merrill.
3. CRAIG, GERALD S. *Science for the Elementary School Teacher.* New York: Ginn.
4. GEGA, PETER C. *Science in Elementary Education.* New York: John Wiley.
5. HENNESEY, DAVID E. *Elementary Teacher's Classroom Science Demonstrations and Activities.* Englewood Cliffs, N.J.: Prentice-Hall.
6. HONE, ELIZABETH, ALEXANDER JOSEPH, and EDWARD VICTOR. *A Sourcebook for Elementary Science.* New York: Harcourt Brace Jovanovich.
7. JACOBSON, WILLARD J. *The New Elementary School Science.* New York: Van Nostrand Reinhold.
8. LEWIS, JUNE E., and IRENE C. POTTER. *The Teaching of Science in the Elementary School.* Englewood Cliffs, N.J.: Prentice-Hall.

9. SUND, ROBERT et al. *Elementary Science Teaching Activities.* Columbus, Ohio: Charles E. Merrill.
10. UNESCO. *Source Book for Science Teachers.* New York: Unesco Publications Center.
11. VICTOR, EDWARD. *Science for the Elementary School.* New York: Macmillan.

B. *Pupil Bibliography*

1. COLBY, CARROL B. *Communications.* New York: Coward-McCann.
2. FREEMAN, IRA M. *All About Electricity.* New York: Random House.
3. FERAVOLO, ROCCO. *Junior Science Book of Electricity.* New York: Grosset & Dunlap.
4. HOLDEN, RAYMOND. *Magnetism.* New York: Golden Press.
5. PARKER, BERTHA M. *Electricity.* New York: Harper & Row.
6. SCHNEIDER, HERMAN, and NINA SCHNEIDER. *Your Telephone and How It Works.* New York: Whittlesey House.
7. SEEMAN, BERNARD. *The Story of Electricity and Magnetism.* Irvington-on-Hudson, New York: Harvey House.
8. VICTOR, EDWARD. *Exploring and Understanding Magnets and Electromagnets.* Westchester, Ill.: Benefic Press.
9. YATES, RAYMOND F. *The Boy's Book of Magnetism.* New York: Harper & Row.

IV. MATERIALS

A. *Science Supplies and Equipment*

dry cells
insulated bell wire (#18)
thin insulated wire (#28)
iron filings
compasses
white cardboard square
iron tacks
paper clips
large iron nails
roofing nails
large iron bolts
screws
screw eyes
metal washers
pins
cardboard mailing tube
steel knitting needle
wood boards
metal strips
buzzer
bell
chimes
circuit breaker
telephone transmitter and receiver
St. Louis motor
simple generator

B. *Films*

1. *Electromagnets.* McGraw-Hill, Text-Film Div. 11 min.
2. *Electromagnets: How They Work.* Encyclopaedia Britannica Films. 11 min.
3. *How an Electric Motor Works.* McGraw-Hill, Text-Film Div. 11 minutes.
4. *Magnetic, Electric, and Gravitational Fields.* Encyclopaedia Britannica Films. 11 min.
5. *Magnetism.* Coronet. 11 min.

C. *Filmstrips*

1. *Electric Magnets.* Harper & Row.
2. *Electromagnetism at Work.* Charles Scribner's Sons.
3. *Electromagnets.* McGraw-Hill, Text-Film Div.
4. *Magnetism and Electricity.* Society for Visual Education.

(United Press International)

CHAPTER 6B

SAMPLE LESSONS *from* CURRICULUM PROJECT UNITS

THE ELEMENTARY science curriculum projects, which began in the 1960's, are now completed. They all were slowly and carefully developed, utilizing the intellectual manpower and experience of scientists, child psychologists, science educators, supervisors, and experienced elementary school teachers. At first, trial editions were developed and tried out in selected schools throughout the country. Then appropriate revisions were made, as needed and recommended. Now final editions are available, produced commercially by publishing houses.

These projects use an inquiry and discovery approach to teaching science and involve the use of a wide variety of materials. Because many elementary school teachers were unfamiliar at first with the approach and materials, and others had an inadequate science background, they experienced some difficulty in teaching the units and using the materials of the projects effectively. Consequently, many colleges and universities had to conduct a variety of institutes, seminars, and courses on one or more programs of these curriculum projects. Today this assistance is no longer offered.

For those teachers who wish to know more about the curriculum projects and their materials, one approach would be to ask the superintendent of schools, the principal, or the science supervisor to contact the publishing houses that supply the programs of the projects. These publishing houses will be glad to send representatives who will speak to interested groups of teachers and demonstrate how the materials can be used. Another approach would be for the teachers to visit schools that are using these programs, discuss the programs with the teachers who are involved, and see the programs in action in the classroom.

It is extremely difficult to arrive at an adequate evaluation of the effectiveness of all these projects. It suffices to say that each project set its own goals and produced science units and materials that presumably achieved these goals. Although the projects differed with regard to the role and emphasis, as well as the scope and sequence, of the science content in their programs, they all agreed that science in the elementary school should be taught using an inquiry or discovery approach.

Unfortunately, space does not permit the inclusion of more than just a few sample lessons from units of the more well-known curriculum projects. However, the ones included in this chapter are sufficient to give some indication of how the programs of these projects differ in rationale and content.

It would be profitable to compare the sample lessons in this chapter with the sample lessons in the previous chapter and note the impact the curriculum projects have had on the kinds of units now being developed by schools not using the projects. This would explain why the teaching units with the worksheets arranged in a single running column have become so popular today.

The names and addresses of the companies that market the materials of the various curriculum projects are listed in Chapter 3 in the section on "Programs of the Elementary Science Curriculum Projects."

AAAS Commission on Science Education
Science—A Process Approach

AT PRESENT the AAAS Commission on Science Education curriculum project, called *Science—A Process Approach* (SAPA), consists of seven Teacher's Guides, one for each grade level (K–6). The lessons in each Guide contain a list of objectives for the lesson, an underlying rationale, a list of science vocabulary, a list of materials needed, an initiating activity, several learning activities, a culminating generalizing experience, an appraisal for measuring pupil achievement in terms of the stated objectives, and an evaluating competency measure. Equipment needed for the lessons is available as a kit. There are no written materials provided for the children.

SAMPLE LESSON[1]

The AAAS Commission on Science Education has granted permission to include just one unit from *Science—A Process Approach*. This unit, taken from Part C, is usually taught in grade 2 and is designed to develop the process of **communicating.**

COMMUNICATING 8: DESCRIBING GROWTH FROM PARTS OF PLANTS

OBJECTIVES

At the end of this exercise the child should be able to

1. *DISTINGUISH* between new plant growth and the part of the plant it is growing from.
2. *DESCRIBE* vegetative growth qualitatively.
3. *DESCRIBE* the techniques used to produce new plant growth from plant parts other than seeds in terms precise enough that other people will be able to follow the procedure.

RATIONALE

At some time children should have the opportunity to observe that some plants can start growth by other means than seeds. Plants have two forms of reproduction. The most common and most obvious is the sexual form, which results in seed production.

Many of the children will have observed and can report upon an example of vegetative reproduction at school or home. Many times in classrooms the teacher grows a sweet potato vine from the potato itself, and not from the seed. The children may also have seen their mothers start a "new" philodendron, geranium, or coleus plant from a stem. Children in rural communities may have seen their parents start white potatoes from a piece of a potato that contains an "eye" of the tuber of the potato.

Not only potatoes start growth vegetatively, but also sugar cane, grapes, and a great many ornamental plants

[1] From *Science—A Process Approach*, Part C. New York: Xerox Education Division, 1967. Reprinted by permission. SAPA is now marketed by Ginn and Company.

and shrubs. Children will learn in this exercise that only certain parts of particular plants can be used to grow a new plant. The degree to which root, stem, or leaf cuttings develop into mature plants varies with the type of plant. This exercise will also show that many plants will almost certainly not be started vegetatively. Corn is a good example of the latter type.

The child's ability to communicate depends partly upon his ability to observe precisely. But he also needs experience in organizing and reporting his observations in a fashion appropriate to his level of maturity. During this exercise, you should plan so that each child has at least one opportunity to give an oral report.

(**Note:** The *Appraisal* requires an African violet leaf that has rooted in water. This takes about three weeks. Be sure the container is properly identified and labeled as to the variety of plant and the date of the cutting.)

VOCABULARY

cutting
tuber
bulb

MATERIALS

(Materials not with those provided for this exercise are with the general materials.)
*A plant, such as a philodendron or geranium
*Several shallow, wide-mouthed jars, or aluminum pie pans
*Several slender glass bottles (olive bottles—about 1 decimeter tall)
*Several paring knives
*A box of toothpicks
*Several white potatoes (preferably not chemically treated)
*Several sweet potatoes (preferably not chemically treated)
*Several carrots
*Several large onions

*Ivy, philodendron, coleus, and/or geranium plants (more than one of these, if possible)
*Two wide, flat flowerpots, with soil and saucers
Thirty-six small containers to be used as flowerpots
*Potting soil
Thirty-six tongue depressors (for plant identification)
*An African violet plant
*An African violet leaf that has been in water and has developed roots
A picture of a daffodil plant, showing a bulb with roots, leaves, flowers, and small bulb or bulbs on the side of the large bulb
*A begonia plant

---

*Not Supplied

INSTRUCTIONAL PROCEDURE

Introduction

Show the children a plant (a philodendron or a geranium) and say that you did not plant a seed to produce it. Ask whether anyone can suggest a way the plant may have been developed. Some children may say that you bought it; others, that it was given to you; and still others, that you found it. Someone may say that you planted a stem to get the plant. If not, suggest this yourself.

Ask the children if they have ever observed anything like this before. For example, **Do you have any plants at home that were started without seeds? Have you ever planted potatoes? Have you ever taken strawberry plants on the end of a runner and set them out? Have you ever seen asparagus planted?** Some in the class may be able to relate such an experience. If not, you may want to tell them about one.

(**Note:** In the following activities, a knife must be used to cut parts of the plants. If the children are sufficiently mature, you can let them do the cutting. If not, do this yourself.)

Activity 1

Arrange several of each of the following on a table near the front of the room:

> Shallow, wide-mouthed jars, or aluminum pie pans
> Slender glass bottles (olive bottles—about 1 decimeter tall)
> Paring knives
> Toothpicks
> White potatoes
> Sweet potatoes
> Carrots
> Large onions
> Ivy, philodendron, coleus, and/or geranium plants (include more than one if you can)

Divide the class into as many groups as there are different kinds of plants on the table. Invite one of the groups to come to the front of the room to observe carefully what you do. Select a carrot, and ask whether anyone has any ideas about how to make it grow into a green plant. Accept a general statement that a member of the group may suggest, such as "Cut the carrot and put it in water." If no one says this, you should.

Since most of the class members cannot observe what is being done, tell the small group at the front of the room that when you have finished, they will have to report to the others on what they have seen.

Select an aluminum pan or wide-mouthed jar, and put water in it to a height of about 2 cm. Remove any leaves from the carrot, and cut off the top 4 or 5 cm. Put this top piece in the water with the cut surface on the bottom of the container. Then put the cutting where there is as much daylight as possible.

Ask one member of the group to report the procedure precisely to the rest of the class. Ask other members of

the group to add any information that the first child omitted. Insist upon accurate reporting of such details as the depth of the water (2 cm), the place the carrot is cut (4 to 5 cm from the top), the way the carrot is placed in the container, and where the container is located. Refer to the original statement about how to make the carrot grow into a green plant, and ask whether it was a sufficiently good one. Review what needed to be added to it.

Invite each of the other groups in turn to be the observers and reporters as you do the following:

a. Select a sweet potato and a pan, or wide-mouthed jar, and repeat the procedure you used for the carrot. If the sweet potato is large, it may be wise to make the cut 6 or 7 cm from the leaf end.

b. Put a whole white potato in a jar or pan with water 2 cm deep.

c. Select a large onion, three toothpicks, and a jar; mount the onion as in Figure 1 so that 1 to 2 cm of the bottom of the onion dips into the water.

d. Select a branch from a coleus or geranium plant with two or more leaves, and make a sharp cut below the leaves. Put the stem (cut end) in a slender glass jar that has been filled with water.

e. Make similar cuttings from philodendron and ivy plants. A leaf and small stem area will constitute a cutting.

Activity 2

Divide the class into groups of two or three children, and tell each group to choose as a project observation of one of the cuttings they *heard* described in *Activity 1*. (This should not be the one that the group itself observed and described.) Suggest to the children that they review the procedure and list the materials they need. When they have done this, tell them to get the materials and make the cuttings. Encourage them to make additional observations.

Have a child from each group report to the rest of the class on the kind of cutting his group made, the procedure the group followed, and any additional observations.

Every few days, have a child from each group report any new observations to the class. **What changes have occurred in the plants? Are there any signs of new growth? Where does the new growth occur? How big is it? How fast is it growing? What shape is it? Are there any changes in the appearance of the parent plant material?** Then, **What conclusions can you draw from these results? Do the results indicate that all plants will be able to grow new plants from part of the old one? Do they indicate that some parts of some plants can do this?** Tell the children to plan carefully before giving their reports.

Activity 3

This activity could begin before *Activity 2* is completed, but it should not come before each group has seen some evidence of growth from the parts of plants it is working with in *Activity 2.* The question to be answered in this activity is: Can any fragment of a plant grow and give rise to a new plant?

Show the children a white potato and ask, **Can we make a test with the potato to find out if any plant fragment will be able to grow another plant?** A child may suggest that they plant a section of potato that contains "eyes" and a section that does not contain "eyes." If not, you should suggest this possibility.

As a class activity, plant five or six pieces of potato, each with two or three eyes, in 6 to 8 cm of soil in a wide, flat flowerpot. Using the same potatoes, plant the same number of pieces that do not have eyes in a similar pot in the same amount of soil.

Label each of the pots properly with tongue depressors. Strongly emphasize placing the pots close enough together so that they will have the same growing conditions and giving each pot the same amount of water each day. Put a saucer under each pot to hold temporarily any water that drains out of the bottom. Appoint a committee of children to note and record all observations daily.

After several days, ask, **Have you noticed any difference in the growth between sections with "eyes" and those without "eyes"?** If the children have noted such differences, ask, **What factor was responsible for the difference? What can we conclude from this activity?** (Growth of a new potato plant requires planting a piece with "eyes.")

You may want to make the point that successful growth of fragments may vary from one potato to another. It is likely that not all of the pieces with "eyes" will grow equally well. The experience should help the children discover that not all fragments may grow, although they may appear similar in many ways to those fragments that do grow.

(**Note:** You can start *Activity 4* soon after you have set up *Activity 3*.)

Activity 4

Ask the children whether they can think of other parts of plants that they might use to find an answer to this question: Will any part of a plant produce a new plant? Give each group of children parts of onions, ivy plants, philodendron, carrots, geraniums, or coleus. Suggest that they select one kind of plant and conduct their own investigation in a manner similar to that in *Activity 3,* except that they will use a different part of the plant. For example, one group may try planting (or putting in water) the bottom half of a carrot instead of the top half.

Ask each group to report orally to

the rest of the class. This report should include the following:

What they want to find out.

The plan they are using to find the answer to the question.

The observations made to date.

GENERALIZING EXPERIENCE

Let the children find out whether other kinds of plants can produce new plants in this way. Groups of two or three children might try to grow kinds of plants that are different from those they have already studied. For example, they might try a celery stalk instead of an onion bulb, or an apple instead of a potato, and so on. Let the children use whatever plants and parts of plants they suggest and can bring from home.

In all of these investigations, encourage each child to observe carefully and to record what he did and what he observed and concluded. Have the children report their findings to the class in a well-planned way. Help them to generalize from their observations when appropriate.

APPRAISAL

Bring an African violet plant to the classroom, and ask the children to describe it. Then tell them that you are about to do something important that you want them to watch carefully. Tell them that when you are finished, you will ask someone to report in detail what you did and what you might be trying to find out.

Cut one of the leaves from the African violet plant. Put the cut end of the leaf in water to a depth of a few centimeters. Label it with its name and the cutting date, and set it aside. Ask several of the children to tell you what they think your question and plan are.

Now put in front of the class a container of water that has an African violet leaf that has been in water for some time and has developed roots.

Ask one child to look at it closely and to describe what he sees to the rest of the class. Ask other children to look at it closely too and to add any other observations. Help the children to keep their comments descriptive by asking whether their contribution is really what they see or what they think was done earlier.

COMPETENCY MEASURE

(Individual score sheets for each pupil are with the general materials.)

Give the child a picture of a daffodil plant showing a bulb with roots, leaves, flowers, and a small bulb or bulbs on the side of the large bulb.

TASK 1 (OBJECTIVE 2): Ask, **How might new growth occur in this plant?** Put one check in the acceptable column if the child makes some statement that he observes small bulbs alongside the big one, and new plants might develop from these.

TASK 2 (OBJECTIVE 1): Say, **Show me the part of the plant that new growth might come from.** Put one check in the acceptable column if he points to the small bulb.

Now show the child a begonia plant.

TASK 3 (OBJECTIVE 3): Say, **Describe how you might start a new plant from this one without using seeds.** Put one check in the acceptable column if the child's description includes the following:

a. Take a cutting from the plant so that there is a piece of the stem with two or three leaves.

b. Make the cut below a leaf joint.

c. Put the cutting into a container of water.

d. When roots have developed on the piece of stem, plant the cutting in soil.

TASK 4 (OBJECTIVE 3): Put one check in the acceptable column if the child's suggested procedure in response to Task 3 is in logical sequential order.

SAMPLE
LESSONS
FROM
CURRICULUM
PROJECT
UNITS

Elementary Science Study

THE Elementary Science Study (ESS) offers a goodly number of individual units, and there is a Teacher's Guide for each unit. The lessons in the Teacher's Guide contain a list of materials needed for the lesson, directions for getting ready for the lesson, and suggestions for procedure. These suggestions include the kinds of questions the teacher should ask the children, probable questions that the children may raise, and different techniques the teacher may use to encourage inquiry. A pupil kit containing needed equipment for the experiments comes for each unit. Worksheets, pictures, film loops, and supplementary pupil booklets accompany some units. There are no written manuals for the children.

SAMPLE LESSONS[2]

Three lessons from the unit on *Growing Seeds*, which is recommended for grades K–3, are included here. They are taken from *Part 1: What Are Seeds? What Do They Do?*, and are concerned with identifying seeds, planting seeds, and finding out what is inside a seed.

WHAT ARE SEEDS? WHAT DO THEY DO?

Part One begins by having the children bring in anything that they think might be a seed. The teacher contributes some seeds and some other things which resemble seeds. Soon the children are asking their own questions:

What are these?

How can we tell which ones are seeds and which are not?

These questions lead to discussion, and eventually to planting of the objects to find out what happens.

Will they change?

Will they grow?

The children examine the planted objects from day to day. They look inside the seeds. Gradually they build a definition of what a seed is in terms of what a seed does.

GETTING READY

WHAT ARE THESE?

Materials

From the kit:

envelopes

paper plates

"seeds": morning glory seeds, popping corn, beet seeds, radish seeds, yellow-eyed beans, dried peas, red kidney beans, gravel, charcoal granules, vermiculite, cinnamon candy drops, mung beans, grass seed, corn seeds. Do not use the ear of corn in Part One.

You could add or substitute other "seeds":

acorns, lima beans, poppy seeds, grapefruit seeds, candy bits, pea shooter peas, Cocoa Puffs, birdseed, cloves, lentils

---

[2] From Teacher's Guide for *Growing Seeds*. New York: Webster/McGraw-Hill, 1967, pp. 9–19. Reprinted by permission.

Preparation

Fill one envelope for each child with one of each kind of "seed." At the same time you may wish to prepare the envelopes for the second lesson, "Planting Day."

Procedure

One or two days before you plan to begin, ask the children to bring to school anything which they think might be a seed. What they bring will depend a great deal on their experience. Some children bring packages of seeds sold for gardens. Some bring apple seeds, prune pits, nuts. Some bring seeds from trees, bushes, and weeds in their neighborhood. As they bring in their "seeds," the children tend to have no doubts at all about the fact that these *are* seeds they are bringing. Occasionally this will be because they have already planted seeds like them, and have grown plants. More often it is because they have been told that these are seeds.

When they have started to bring in their seeds, you can make your contribution to the collection by giving each child the small envelope containing a variety of seeds you have prepared for them, to compare with their own.

The children usually recognize one or two of these little objects—the candy for instance—and they may think you are trying to fool them. This raises just enough question in their minds that they may start wondering about some of the other objects and about some of the things they have brought themselves. *How can you tell whether something is a seed or not?* You will hear a strange variety of ideas expressed.

Welcome all responses whether they are questions or statements about differences, likenesses, color, or texture or whether they are ideas about what makes a seed a seed. Some of their criteria for claiming that an object is or is not a seed may be dubious ones:

This can't be a seed; it's too hard.
This is a seed because it's bumpy.
Seeds aren't round.
Seeds aren't flaky. This can't be a seed.

On the other hand, some child may point out more helpful criteria such as, *There's a little mark,* as he notices the scar on a kidney bean.

The children themselves will be highly critical of one another's reasons. Try to promote such critical interplay among them whenever possible. From time to time, you will need to take part in their discussions yourself. Try to point out inconsistencies in their arguments. If a child says that an object is a seed because it's bumpy, you could point to a bumpy object in his pile of things that he thinks are *not* seeds; if he says that something can't be a seed because it's too shiny, show him a shiny object in his "seed" pile.

Hold back on definitive responses such as, *You are right* or, *You are wrong.* It won't be difficult if you remember that during the coming weeks you will have a chance to watch the children do many things to their "seeds." On their own they are going to discover the need to change some of their earlier notions.

Twenty or twenty-five minutes of these preliminary comparisons and discussions will lead to some thinking and many good observations. The class as a whole will then be ready to consider better ways to find out whether their objects are seeds. Before long, many will be eager to try planting them in soil, to see if any of them grow.

As one of the ideas about what to do to the little objects, someone may suggest: *Open them up.* If this is not volunteered, it might be wise to interject this idea yourself, because it raises the important question: *What is inside a seed?* Since most of the seeds are hard, opening them will be a difficult operation at this point. But let the children attempt anything reasonable. They can take their envelopes home and follow up on the problem, since you can supply more of these objects for the children to plant at school.

Encourage them to bring to school anything else they think might be a seed.

SAMPLE
LESSONS
FROM
CURRICULUM
PROJECT
UNITS

SECOND DAY

Planting Day

Materials

From the kit:
the "seeds"
one envelope of each kind of "seed"
1 clear plastic container for each pair
  of children
1 plastic sheet
You will need to supply:
large cardboard box
cellophane tape
soil
watering pitchers
newspapers or paper towels (to keep
  desks clean)

Preparation

Line one cardboard box with a sheet of plastic, as shown in the photographs. Put soil in it to a depth of about three inches.

Put 10 or 15 of the same kind of "seed" into an envelope. Use as many envelopes as you have varieties of "seeds."

Plant several extra small boxes (clear plastic containers) with red kidney beans for the children to dig up and examine.

Procedure

By drawing lines in the soil, divide the large box into small plots—one for each kind of "seed." Assign two or three children to each of the envelopes, and let them take turns planting the contents of their envelopes in one of the plots.

How will the children remember which kind of "seed" they have planted in each plot? One of our trial classes came up with a neat solution, they attached a "seed" to a stick with transparent tape and stood the stick in the plot.

While the children are taking turns planting in the big box, distribute the small plastic boxes to pairs of children. In these boxes each pair of children can plant whatever they wish— seeds they have brought, seeds left over from the first class, more seeds from the class supply.

As long as the children include soil, seeds, and some water, let them do the planting without too much formal instruction. They will make mistakes, but they will learn a great deal from them.

THREE OR FOUR DAYS AFTER PLANTING

What Is Inside a Seed?

Materials

You will need to supply:
paper towels or newspapers for each
  child

soaked beans and peas—six or eight per child

Preparation

Twenty-four hours before the class meets, put dried peas and beans into

[185

a container; cover with water, and let them soak. If you soak them much longer than this, they will start to rot. Schedule at least 30 minutes for this lesson.

Procedure

As you give each child six or eight soaked peas and beans, suggest that he look at them carefully.

Questions such as these will guide the examination.

What are they like now?

Are they larger than they were before?

Can you open them?

What do you see inside the pea when it comes apart?

Encourage the children to comment on what they see and to pose further questions. You will begin to hear remarks like these:

The outside skin pops off.

There are two pieces inside.

Sustain their interest in looking and in talking about what they see. They will be impressed by the differences between the peas and beans and excited over the size of the little plant in the beans. They may want to dig up some more of the planted things and compare them.

SAMPLE
LESSONS
FROM
CURRICULUM
PROJECT
UNITS

Science Curriculum Improvement Study

THE Science Curriculum Improvement Study (SCIS) has produced a number of units, some of which introduce concepts that are new to elementary science. There is a Teacher's Guide for each unit. Each Guide has a general introduction which explains the underlying concepts in the unit and offers suggestions for teaching the unit. The unit is divided into parts, with one or more lessons to each part. The objectives for each part are listed, and essential background information for the teacher is given. Each lesson contains a list of materials needed and suggestions for teaching the lesson. Often there are optional activities at the end of the lesson. There is a Student's Manual which is designed to help the children organize their observations and ideas after they have had some firsthand experiences with the topics in the unit. There is also a pupil kit of equipment needed for each unit.

SAMPLE LESSONS[3]

Two lessons from the unit on *Interaction* (now called *Interaction and Systems*), which is recommended for grade 2, are included here. They are taken from *Part One: Objects Interact,* and introduce the concept that objects interact when they do something to each other.

OBJECTS INTERACT

OBJECTIVES

To isolate and manipulate groups of objects.

To make a record of objects used for an experiment.

To recognize changes that occur during an experiment.

To understand and use the word interact.

To identify interacting objects in demonstrations and photographs.

BACKGROUND INFORMATION

The interaction concept has been explained on pages 11–14 of this guide. In Part One you introduce the concept to the children through the invention lesson in Chapter 3. The invention is based on the paraphrase that interacting objects are objects which do something to each other.

Prior to the invention lesson, the children engage in preliminary explorations with a boxful of assorted objects. During this work you focus the children's attention on the objects they choose for an experiment and on the changes that occur during the experiment. The changes are important because they lead to the conclusion that the objects did something to each other. The objects are important because they must be found again if the experiment is to be repeated in order to verify its outcome.

We have found that many children report experiments in terms of what they do, rather than in terms of the

[3] From Teacher's Guide for *Interaction.* Boston: D. C. Heath, 1967, pp. 27–29, 31–34. Reprinted by permission. SCIS is now published by Rand McNally, Chicago.

objects they used and the changes that occurred. This is part of children's egocentric thinking patterns during the primary grades. Your patient and tactful guidance will frequently be needed to help them overcome their limitation.

A second source of difficulty is some children's inability to recognize the time during which the objects interact. They tend to think of a phenomenon as a single entity and have difficulty thinking of it as having a beginning, a middle, and an end. In some of the demonstrations, therefore, you will call special attention to the fact that objects may interact at one instant (as when you clap your hands) or during a certain time (as when you and a friend shake hands), but not before or afterward.

Part One lays the groundwork for the remainder of the unit in five ways. First, the interaction concept is at the heart of all the experiments, of course, and will be strengthened and broad-ened as the unit progresses. Second, attention to the objects that interact in an experiment leads to the selection and mental isolation of systems in Part Two. Third, changes that are observed and described will later be interpreted as evidence of interaction. Fourth, making simple records by marking pictures of objects, which is done in Chapter 2, leads naturally to making written reports of more complicated experiments. Fifth, the experimental materials are related to those used in later activities. Thus, the candy spheres dissolve, as does the copper chloride in Part Four, the magnet will be used to illustrate interaction-at-a-distance in Part Five, and the battery-bulb-wire system is an example of the electric circuits studied in Part Six. Since all these aspects of Part One are developed further in subsequent chapters of the unit, you should leave extensive review, clarification, and reinforcement for later on in the unit.

EXPERIMENTING WITH COMMON OBJECTS

TEACHING MATERIALS

For each pair of children:
  1 box containing:
    capped vial with water
    colored candy spheres
    scissors*
    paper clips*
    rubber band*
    3″ × 5″ card*
    plastic clay
    small magnet (Part Five)
    battery*
    flashlight bulb (Part Six)
    aluminum wire
    2 "mystery pictures"
    sharpened pencil with steel
      eraser band
    *(to be provided by teacher)

TEACHING SUGGESTIONS

Pairs of children carry out experiments of their own choice with a few objects at a time. It is wise to limit the children in the number of objects they use at a time, because their attention will then be directed toward the changes that they observe and not toward trying to build something very complicated.

Advance Preparation

Each set of objects is to include some items that are among the usual school supplies and a battery that must be purchased; you should first collect these items. The other items are packed in the kit in sufficient quantity to complement sixteen sets. The "mystery pictures" are printed six to a sheet and must be cut apart. The end of the aluminum wire has to be twisted once around the base of the bulb. One set of objects, pictured on page 2 of the student manual, should be prepared for each pair of children. You will be able to save your time by having two or three interested children assemble the sets. Plan to have the boxes emptied and the permanent equipment items returned to their storage space after you teach Chapter 4. The batteries may be stored in the drawer for Part Six or in the utility compartment.

Children's Experiments

Distribute the sets and ask the children to experiment with the objects from the box. They may include objects from their pockets and desks but should not take more than three or four objects out of the box at one time. Walk among the groups to observe and admire their work, but try not to interrupt their progress. Encourage the children to use as many combinations of objects as they wish, but ask them to keep unused objects in the box so that these will not distract the children's attention from the objects they are actually using. The children will find that the "mystery pictures"

are made visible by rubbing the tip of the pencil lightly over the paper. They will also find that they can make the flashlight bulb light up by connecting the objects as shown in the illustration.

After individual children have manipulated the objects, they may want to show you their experiments. To guide these children to talk about just the objects they are using, make comments such as, "I see you are doing an experiment with the magnet, the paper clip and the pencil. Tell me what happened in your experiment." Your interest as you listen to the child will encourage him to talk about the changes he observed. You might also suggest that he try another experiment with the same objects. If he can't think of one, you might make a specific suggestion such as, "Rub the magnet back and forth across the paper clip, and then tease parts of the pencil with the paper clip."

When the children have had enough time to try out their ideas, ask them to return the objects to the boxes. Collect the boxes, as they will be used in later chapters. No organized discussion is suggested at this time. Postpone it until the end of Chapter 2, after the children have been able to make records of their experiments.

INVENTION OF INTERACTION CONCEPT

TEACHING MATERIALS

For demonstration purposes:
spring
steel ring
support stand (Part Five)
2 steel roller skates (Utility)
large magnet (Part Five)
vinegar in squeeze bottle
concentrated bromothymol blue

solution in squeeze bottle
3 clear plastic tumblers (Utility)
pitcher of water (Utility)
plastic pail for waste liquid (Utility)
1 box of objects (from Chapter 1)

TEACHING SUGGESTIONS

In this chapter, you review the experiments of Chapter 1 and demonstrate several new experiments to introduce the idea that objects *interact* when they do something to each other.

Advance Preparation

Setting up all the materials before class will allow for a smooth-flowing demonstration.

The first demonstration makes use of the spring and one roller skate. To prepare the experiment, set up the tripod support stand and suspend the spring through the hole, using the steel ring to keep the spring from falling through. Test the support by hanging the roller skate from the spring; then remove the skate again.

The second demonstration employs the large magnet and the second roller skate. Practice attracting the skate with the magnet by holding the magnet above and in front of the skate. As the skate rolls forward, keep withdrawing the magnet so the skate does not catch up with it. You may also pick it up.

The last experiment, which is used after the invention of the interaction concept, involves a dilute solution of bromothymol blue dye in one tumbler and a dilute solution of vinegar in another tumbler. When these are poured together into the third tumbler, the dye turns yellow. You may prepare the two dilute solutions either beforehand or in class. Squeeze three drops of the concentrated liquids into tumblers about one-third full of water. These liquids should be set out of the way until needed. See the Background Information for Part Three for more information about bromothymol blue.

Preliminary Activities

To open the session, gather the children around the demonstration table and use a group of objects from the activities in Chapter 1 to demonstrate an experiment. Ask about the changes that took place. For instance, you might use the battery and wire to light the bulb. Hold up the objects and ask the children what changes occurred and are occurring in this system during the experiment. If they do not seem to understand the question, explain that the bulb is now lit. Demonstrate one or two other experiments, such as rubbing a pencil over a "mystery picture," dropping a candy into water in the vial, or cutting a paper card with scissors, and ask about the changes that occurred.

Next you turn to the two demonstrations that lead to the invention of the interaction concept. First, identify the roller skate and the spring as the objects to which the children should pay special attention. Ask the children to watch closely as you hang the roller skate from the spring. Remove and reattach the roller skate two or three times to give everyone a chance to notice the stretching of the spring. Briefly discuss the changes that occur and then set the objects aside with the roller skate and the spring unattached.

Second, select the magnet and the other roller skate, and use the magnet to attract the skate several times as described above. Again ask the children what changes they notice.

Invention

At this point you and the class have observed and discussed the changes which took place during several experiments. Tell the children, while indicating one set of objects with your hands, that you will use the word *interact* whenever objects do something to each other, as in the case of the battery and the bulb, the skate and the spring, and so on. Write *interact* on the chalkboard and let the children pronounce it several times.

Illustrate the meaning of the word *interact* by hanging the roller skate on the spring and saying, "Now the skate and the spring interact." Remove the skate and say, "Now the skate and the spring do not interact." Repeat the experiment with the skate and the magnet and at various stages of the experiment ask the children, "Do the objects interact now?" "What is your evidence?" As another example of objects that interact, firmly hold the roller skate and the magnet so close to one another that you can feel the attraction even though you do not let them come together. Let the children see you "straining" to keep them apart and ask them the same questions. (This example illustrates interaction-at-a-distance, which will be introduced by name in Part Five.)

After this explanation, and perhaps after answering some of the children's questions about your experiments, tell the children that you will show them another system of objects that can interact. Display the three tumblers on a paper towel, and identify by name the liquids in two of them (prepared either ahead of time or now by filling two tumblers one-third full of water and squeezing three drops of vinegar into one, bromothymol blue into the other). Ask the children to watch carefully as you mix the liquids by pouring them together into the third tumbler. Let them describe the changes which mean that the liquids interacted while you were pouring them together.

Optional Activities

Follow-up Experiments

Encourage all the children to use the support stand, the spring, the empty pail, the magnet, and the roller skates, by leaving these on the science table. We have found that it is best not to leave the materials on the table for more than a few days, however, unless you suggest specific projects or experiments, such as placing various objects in the pail and observing how far the spring is stretched when the pail plus content is attached.

Bromothymol Blue Interaction with Vinegar

The children will probably want to know more about the liquids. Show them the squeeze bottles and let them smell the vinegar. Repeat the experiments with variations suggested by the children and with their participation. Pour waste solutions into the plastic pail. The children may want to use much or little vinegar, water with no vinegar, and so forth. Note: A very small amount of vinegar will change the color of the blue dye. Mix the dye with water, therefore, in tumblers that have never contained vinegar or have been washed carefully. Perhaps you should put a label or mark on the tumbler that you reserve for the bromothymol blue. If the blue color turns to green or yellow when you do not expect it, the change is evidence that the container was not clean. You can stage such a "surprise" purposely and challenge the children to explain it.

Testing with Bromothymol Blue

Have the children bring samples of materials from home to test how they affect the bromothymol blue. Salt, sugar, baking powder, lemon juice, milk, pickle juice, dishwasher detergent, liquid fertilizer, ammonia, and other materials can be grouped or listed according to how they interact with the dye. The dye should always be used in dilute solution form, a few drops in half a tumbler of water. If you need it, you may be able to obtain additional dye from a local high school chemistry teacher or from a swimming pool supply dealer.

CAUTION: Supervise these experiments to insure safe handling of the substances, and be sure to dispense the concentrated bromothymol blue yourself.

Conceptually Oriented Program in Elementary Science

THE Conceptually Oriented Program in Elementary Science (COPES) has produced a Teacher's Guide consisting of a volume of units. The Guide is divided into sections, or units, with several lessons to each section. The sections have been developed in such a way that they all make up a sequence of concepts which will be learned in grades K–6. Accordingly, the sections become progressively more advanced, and each section is recommended for a certain grade level. The sections furnish the rationale for a particular sequence of concepts, and show the relationship of these concepts with other concepts and with the major conceptual scheme. The sections also provide the teacher with the background needed to explain these concepts. Each lesson contains a list of needed materials, directions for advance preparations, suggestions for teaching, and questions for generating discussion. Kits of special equipment needed for the experiments are available.

SAMPLE LESSONS[4]

Two lessons from the unit on *Conservation of Energy* are included here. They are taken from *Section C: Matter and Heat Energy,* which is recommended for grades K–2, and are concerned with classifying materials into solids and liquids.

STATES OF MATTER: TRANSITIONS AND INTERACTIONS

INTRODUCTION

The purpose of this section of the Presequence is to prepare children for the thermal energy segment of the main sequence. The thermal energy segment is introduced with activities that lead to an awareness of the conservation of thermal energy when water systems are mixed. Later more sophisticated activities are developed by which children are helped to understand the role of thermal energy in the "work" of melting, dissolving, and simple chemical changes.

In this section of the Presequence, the concepts of solid, liquid, and gaseous states of matter are introduced.

This is followed by an introduction to the role of heat energy in change of state.

In the early part of this section, the addition of thermal energy is introduced as the cause of a change of state (melting). In a later part the interaction between heat energy and liquid water is pursued. Skills in the correct use of the thermometer are developed, and further experience with bar graphing is provided. Children learn about different sources of heat energy. They find out that when heat energy is added to water its temperature will rise. They discover that the amount of temperature rise depends upon the

[4] From Teacher's Guide for a *Conservation of Energy Sequence.* New York: Conceptually Oriented Program in Elementary Science, 1967, pp. 80–86. Reprinted by permission.

quantity of water heated and on the source of the heat energy.

The term *system* is used in many of the activities of this section. A *system* is defined as a selected group of objects forming a unit that is mentally isolated from its surroundings for purposes of careful observation. In general, one looks for relationships between objects within the system unit. No special effort is made to define a system formally, but merely to acquaint the children with the term in its appropriate context. For example, water in a cup may be thought of as a system. The water is one object, the cup another, and they are related in that the cup contains the water. When a thermometer is put in the water to determine its temperature, the cup, the water, and the thermometer become a new system. If an ice cube is put in the water to cool it, then the cup, the water, the ice cube, and the thermometer become still another system. The use of the term is emphasized because we have found that the concept of *system* helps children to think about the principal components of whatever they are observing or manipulating

ACTIVITY C-1. CLASSIFYING MATERIALS INTO SOLIDS AND LIQUIDS

This activity is designed to give children experience in classifying selected materials as solids or liquids.

Materials

1 rock
1 marble
1 pencil
3 beans or other seeds
3 pieces of rock candy in a transparent jar
1 candle
1 ruler
1 small bottle of syrup
1 small bottle of milk
1 small bottle of soda water
1 small bottle of vegetable oil
2 trays, lunchroom or equivalent, one marked System A, the other System B
1 box, cardboard, approximately $20'' \times 20'' \times 12''$

Preparation for Teaching

Put all materials, except the two trays, in the box before the lesson begins. Keep it covered and out of sight so that a study of its contents can be used as a game with the children. Label one tray System A and the other one System B.

Suggestions for Teaching

Place the two empty trays on the table where all the children can see them. Remove the rock from the covered box. Feel it, press it, and put it into System A, while keeping the rest of the materials out of sight. Remove the bottle of vegetable oil. While holding the bottle, move it around so that the children can see the oil flow in the bottle and put it into System B. Repeat the process with the marble and with the bottle of milk. Next remove the pencil, holding it up as you feel it and press on it. Ask the children into which system it should be placed.

Ask the children to play the "Which System?" game with you. As you work with them in classifying each of the remaining objects as belonging to System A or System B, emphasize the use of the term *system*. Since the term is to be used throughout the conservation of energy sequence to indicate groups of objects, practice in its use at this early stage should prove valuable in the future.

After the solids have been placed into System A and the liquids into System B, ask children why the materials were put into the different systems. They should have no difficulty in identifying the materials in System

B as liquids. They may be inclined to use a different vocabulary in describing liquids, such as "they are runny." Whatever characteristics the children are able to identify, have them concentrate on the sameness of these characteristics as you go from liquid to liquid.

There may be difficulty in identifying the materials in System A as solids. If so, discuss ways in which the liquid materials are different from the materials in the other system. Solids do not need containers; they keep their same shape even when they are moved around. If no one mentions the term *solid,* introduce it and review how a solid is different from a liquid. Have the children name other things that are solids. Also have them name other liquids that are familiar to them.

A difficulty may arise in classifying the solids and liquids. All of the liquids are in containers while only one of the solids, the rock candy, is in a container. Because of the container, some very young children may want to put the rock candy into System B. If this occurs, take the rock candy out of the container and direct attention to the rock candy alone. Let the children see that the container is just a convenience and that the key to classification is the nature of the substance.

Activity C-2. A Fluid Solid

This activity is intended to expand the experiences that children have had earlier with Activity C-1. The children will find that one substance that appears to be "runny" like a liquid is actually a solid.

Materials

  1 rock
  1 marble
  1 pencil
  3 beans or other seeds
  1 candle
  1 ruler

  3 pieces of rock candy in a transparent jar
  1 small bottle of syrup
  1 small bottle of milk
  1 small bottle of soda water
  1 small bottle of vegetable oil
  2 trays, lunchroom or equivalent, one marked System A, the other System B
  1 box, cardboard, approximately $20'' \times 20'' \times 12''$
  1 cup of sand
30 magnifiers, hand lens

Preparation for Teaching

Put all materials except the two trays in the box before the lesson begins. Keep it covered and out of sight so that a study of its contents can be used as a game with the children. Label one tray System A and the other one System B. Distribute hand lenses.

Suggestions for Teaching

Repeat Activity C-1 spending no more time than is needed to review it. However, when you display the sand and ask to which system it belongs, show that it can be poured as a liquid, that it is "runny."

A closer examination of the sand particles will give the children the evidence they need to make a more adequate classification. They can feel the individual particles of sand, which they cannot do in the case of liquids.

Distribute the hand lenses and show the children how to use them to examine small objects. Give them a few minutes to investigate the lenses. Then give each one a small sample of sand on a sheet of paper and ask him to examine it with his hand lens. The fact that the individual granules have their own shape and do not need a container should convince children that sand is a solid. Ask them to suggest other materals that look like sand. Granular sugar and salt are examples of such materials that they can examine with a hand lens.

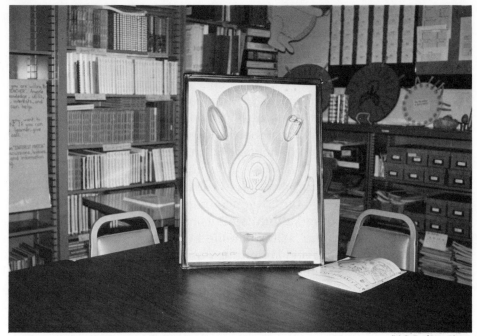

(M.G. Reid/Van Cleve)

CHAPTER 7

MATERIALS *for* TEACHING SCIENCE

ALL PLANNED elementary science programs, whether newly organized or well established, must have an adequate supply of materials available. Quantity alone is not enough. The success of any science program largely depends upon both the quantity and quality of the materials that can be utilized when needed. The need for all kinds of materials is obvious. When developing or evaluating the science program, the teachers should have ample opportunity to consult professional and scientific literature, and to examine existing courses of study. In the classroom the children must have easy access to supplies and equipment, textbooks and other printed materials, films, filmstrips, models, specimens, and charts. Teachers and children both need adequate facilities so that they can work and explore effectively in science.

Even today, many school systems have made little, if any, provision for supplying their schools with science materials. There are several reasons that may be offered to account for this condition. First, when science programs in the elementary school are fragmentary or nonexistent, there is little need for science materials. Second, many teachers with an adequate science background are reluctant to teach science because they are unfamiliar with the science content and equipment. These teachers, therefore, rarely request that the schools furnish them with science materials. Third, to encourage the teaching of elementary science, both teachers and administrators have been told repeatedly that science in the elementary school should be kept simple, and that, when possible, the materials used should be equally simple. This recommendation is sound. To many teachers, however, it has been transformed into a fixed impression that all science materials should be homemade or improvised and that consequently there is no need to allocate or furnish funds for science materials. Fourth, it is assumed that, if there should be an occasional unprecedented need for specific equipment, the equipment can be borrowed without trouble from the junior or senior high school.

These attitudes have created a hardship on many science-minded teachers who are interested in and anxious to teach science to the children. It is often very time-consuming to construct or look for needed equipment. Many worthwhile learning activities call for materials that cannot be found at hand or be homemade. Often teachers have had to wheedle money from the school petty cash fund, or else pay for the needed equipment themselves. It can often be dissatisfying or fruitless to try to borrow equipment from the junior or senior high school. These schools usually run on a tight budget, and are often hard pressed to meet their own needs, let alone the needs of others. Even when they do have equipment that can be loaned, the request from the elementary teacher may be made while the equipment is being used or is reserved for use in the near future, and is therefore unavailable. When equipment is loaned to the elementary teacher, such a short time may be imposed upon the loan that the teacher is pressed to make full and satisfactory use of the equipment in the time allotted. There is also the problem of contacting the secondary school teacher to make suitable arrangements for getting together. Both elementary and secondary school teachers are confined to their schools during the day, and the equipment must be picked up and returned after school hours. Finally, if the equipment should be returned damaged or broken, the possibility of further borrowing becomes quite remote. For all of these reasons science learning in the elementary school has been consistently hampered.

The strong emphasis upon science during the past few years has resulted in a trend toward the growth of highly active and effective ele-

(William Means/Van Cleve)

Commercial materials are essential to the science program.

mentary science programs. Both the public and the government consider such programs advisable, and have expressed their willingness to support them. All of these newly developed programs call for a wide variety of materials, without which the programs will be ineffective. Consequently, it has become quite evident that the schools must now establish a definite policy about furnishing funds for science materials. Annual budgets should be created, providing for both the purchase of new equipment and the replacement of worn-out or used-up equipment.

Fortunately, an increasing number of school boards are now beginning to make provisions in their school budget for funds that are specifically allotted for elementary science. These funds make possible the purchase of necessary laboratory equipment and other supplementary instructional materials. Curriculum directors and supervisors are given responsibility for administering the funds and for encouraging teachers to make requests for the purchase of needed materials.

The schools should also make a small petty cash fund available throughout the year so that incidental needs and emergency replacements can be met without having to wait for the annual order. Furthermore, administrative procedures should be created to help in the ordering of supplies and equipment. These procedures involve helping the teachers make their orders correctly, collecting and pooling the orders from each school, sending the orders to the various supply houses, and distributing the materials when they arrive.

It should be stressed that the materials should be built around the program, rather than the program around the materials. The decision about what should be taught in the program, and the kinds of learning activities that will be used, should determine what science materials will be needed.

Obtaining Supplies and Equipment

OF ALL the areas in the elementary school curriculum, science holds a unique position. Science alone offers the children a multitude of opportunities to do experiments and demonstrations. When the children work with a wide variety of materials learning experiences become real and not vicarious. Manipulative skills are developed in the process. By handling and operating some of the same kinds of materials that scientists use, the children can acquire a little of the flavor of science and at the same time gain greater insight into the different ways that scientists work.

USING SIMPLE MATERIALS WHEN POSSIBLE

In general it is best to use simple supplies and equipment in the elementary school. When simple materials can be as effective as the more complicated materials in evolving or illustrating a science concept, it is preferable to use the simple materials. Complex equipment often tends to confuse the children and distract their attention from the experiment itself, thus interfering with the process of learning. Also, principles learned by using complex equipment may often become isolated in the children's minds so that the children do not see the connection between the principles and the phenomena in their daily environment. Simple materials are inexpensive and, when damaged or broken, can be replaced much more easily than complicated, more expensive materials.

Many materials that are extremely useful in teaching and learning science may be found in the school itself. The pencil sharpener, door knob, door latch, and curtain or window pulley are excellent examples of machines. Some of the newer schools have ramps instead of stairways, and they can be used to teach the principles of the inclined plane. The school's piano, other musical instruments, bells, and the public address system are available for studying sound, music, and communications. The thermometer and thermostat can introduce learning about heat, temperature, and expansion and contraction of materials. The school's heating, lighting, and electrical systems are conveniently near for observation and study. When its front lens is removed, the filmstrip or slide projector becomes an excellent source for a beam of light. A globe of the earth enables the children to learn the reason for day and night, the seasons, solar and lunar eclipses, and air masses. A gooseneck lamp, with the shade removed, serves as the sun. Maps help in the study of climate, kinds of terrain, and location of natural resources.

On the school grounds, there are many evidences of erosion, although on a smaller scale. The children can observe small gullies formed by rain water, roots of trees that are exposed, dust spatters on basement windows, and rock that has been weathered. There are trees, plants, flowers, seeds, and all kinds of insects to be studied. Weather phenomena can be observed throughout the year. Teeter-totters, slides, and swings are present for experiments. Several specimens of rock can be collected and examined.

At home there are a wide variety of tools that can be used in the study of machines. In the workshop there are hammers, pliers, wire cutters, screw drivers, chisels, saws, and drills. In the kitchen there are knives, scissors, egg beaters, can openers, corkscrews, mops, and brooms. In the garden there are garden shears, wheel barrows, axes, shovels, hoes, and rakes. Toys are wonderful materials for teaching science. There are carts, wagons, bicycles, balls, bats, fishing poles, roller skates, electric trains, Tinker Toys, Erector sets, and chemical sets.

HOMEMADE OR IMPROVISED EQUIPMENT

In the past, when little or no funds were available for commercial supplies and equipment, many of the learning materials were homemade or improvised. Many of these materials proved to be valuable teaching devices and are still extremely popular today. There will always be a place for this kind of equipment, provided that the learnings that result are worthwhile and the teachers or pupils do not have to spend undue time and effort in either finding the materials or making the equipment.

All kinds of useful homemade equipment are used constantly in science programs throughout the country. Several examples of these kinds of equipment and how they may be constructed are described in detail later in this textbook. They include such equipment as an electric switch, telegraph set, simple electric motor, galvanometer, convection box, ball-and-ring expansion apparatus, unequal expansion bar, light-ray box, sonometer, constellation box, wooden stands and supports, balance, animal cage, insect cage, bird feeder, aquarium, and terrarium.

Improvised materials are found in every elementary school classroom where science is taught. Tin cans, glass jars, bottles, pots and pans, cookie and pie tins—of all sizes and shapes—are common. Plastic straws are used instead of glass tubing. Pyrex pots and pans are substitutes for beakers. Pyrex baby bottles have served as test tubes on occasion. Often, when litmus paper is unavailable for detecting if solutions are acid or alkaline, the juice from boiled red cabbage has been used.

A constant difficulty for most elementary school teachers is the problem of obtaining a source of heat because heating is required in many experiments. There are various ways of overcoming this problem. The simplest source of heat, naturally, is a candle. A candle is not very good, however, where steady or much heat is required. Also, the flame tends

(William Means/Van Cleve)

Homemade materials can be effective substitutes.

to deposit soot. Canned heat is much better. It gives a colorless flame that is quite hot. There are small stoves available for use with canned heat, upon which metal and Pyrex vessels can be rested.

An alcohol burner is a good source of heat. It can be purchased commercially or, if the teacher wishes, can be homemade. A homemade alcohol burner uses a small glass jar with a metal screw-on cap as the container. A kerosene lamp wick can be obtained from the hardware store. To provide an opening for the wick, unscrew the metal cap and place it upside down on a piece of scrap wood. Punch a rectangular slit from the inside of the cap, using a screw driver or chisel, so that the slit flares outward. This will make it easier to pull the wick up as needed, without catching on the jagged edges of the slit. The slit should be long enough and wide enough so that the kerosene wick can be pulled through the slit easily. Now one end of the wick should be slid through the slit, the jar filled with alcohol, the cap pulled onto the jar, and the homemade burner will be ready for use. Wood or grain alcohol can be used as the fuel. When the burner is not being used, the alcohol will continue to rise up the wick and evaporate unless steps are taken to prevent this evaporation. There are several ways of doing this. One way is to pour the alcohol out of the jar and into a stoppered bottle when the burner is not being used. Another way is to wrap the wick tightly with aluminum foil. A glass jar about the same size or smaller than the original jar, but with a larger mouth, when placed over the homemade alcohol burner, will also prevent evaporation.

Another common source of heat used in the classroom is the electric hot plate. One of the problems in using a hot plate is that the intensity of the heat usually cannot be controlled. There are some hot plates where the heat intensity can be controlled by a dial, but these hot plates are more expensive. As a safety measure the hot plate should be placed on an asbestos pad when being used.

Recently, scientific supply houses, and also stores like Sears and Montgomery Ward, have begun to sell a comparatively inexpensive portable Bunsen burner. This burner consists of a small tank of propane or butane gas and a piece of metal shaped like a Bunsen burner that is screwed onto the tank. The tank rests upon a stand, which makes the burner quite stable. The heat produced by the burning gas is very intense, and a tank will produce a flame that lasts for several hours. After the complete outfit is purchased, the only additional minor expense required is periodic replacement of the tank when the supply of gas in it is used up.

COMMERCIAL SUPPLIES AND EQUIPMENT

Teachers and science educators have developed great resourcefulness in improvising and constructing all kinds of materials to provide for science experiences in the classroom. There are many commercial materials, however, that will still have to be purchased if the science program is to be effective. Dry cells, wire, porcelain sockets, lamps, assorted magnets, compasses, lenses, prisms, Petri dishes, rubber stoppers with and without holes, glass rods, glass tubing, and various chemicals are only a few of the many items needed when teaching science in the elementary school.

Furthermore, even when substitutes can be improvised, it is often essential to purchase the commercial equivalents. Although the children can construct a homemade barometer, it is equally important to have a commercial barometer in the classroom so that they can learn how to read and use barometers accurately. This fact also is true for the study of temperature and thermometers. If the children can see and use Celsius (Centigrade) and Fahrenheit thermometers, it is much different from constructing reasonable facsimiles. A homemade electric switch is fine, but children will get a clearer picture of how a switch actually operates in the home when a push-button buzzer or bell is also available for examination. The construction of a simple motor will help the children better understand the science concepts involved in the construction and operation of the motor and, as such, is a perfectly warranted activity. But a simple commercial St. Louis motor will enable the children to gain a greater insight into the operation and purpose of the motor, and at the same time provide for further exploration and additional activities of an advanced nature.

Most of the commercial supplies and equipment recommended for use in elementary science are relatively inexpensive. However, if a

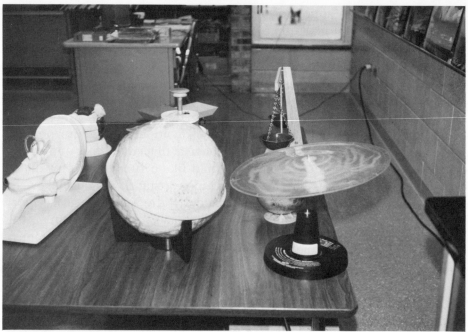

(M.G. Reid/Van Cleve)

Some specialized equipment is often highly desirable.

school system is organizing a planned science program, complete with materials, the initial outlay required to obtain basic materials for the program will be rather large. It would be understandable, then, that at first only the most essential items would be produced, and that the numbers of each kind of item available for use in the classroom might necessarily be limited. But as long as a definite science budget is provided each year, even though modest, teachers can plan and order cooperatively and build up a good-sized inventory of needed materials in a comparatively short time. In this way a wide variety of materials can be made available to the children, and in sufficient quantities so that they all can have an opportunity to work with the materials.

Some of the more specialized pieces of equipment are also highly desirable in the elementary school. These items include the microscope, microprojector, barometer, planetarium, and telescope. To plan for the purchase of such equipment needs careful consideration because the items are expensive and should be bought only if there is definite provision for the equipment's use in the classroom. Although most budgets are not large enough to accommodate the purchase of such equipment, the teachers should nevertheless try to acquire these items, even if it is done gradually and with a great deal of planning. Incidentally, this case is an example where the Parent-Teachers Association can be very helpful. When they are made aware of the need for such equipment and the learning values the children will accrue from its use, contributions will often be made for the purchase of the needed items.

SELECTING AND ORDERING SUPPLIES AND EQUIPMENT

Most elementary schools have a budget each year for ordering general supplies and equipment. Very seldom, however, do these schools have a separate science budget. Requests for science materials are usually given equal consideration with requests for other materials, and then a proportion of the general budget is allocated for science. The usual policy is for the school to prepare requisitions for supplies and equipment in the early spring to be available for the succeeding year. Teachers are given, or asked to prepare, order forms for needed materials. The teachers may work either individually or in groups as committees when preparing the forms. The forms are then given to the principal, who goes over the lists and determines how much of the material can be purchased, depending upon the budget. The principal sends a total list for the school to the superintendent's office, where the lists from all the schools are compiled into a master list. Orders for materials are sent to various supply houses, and, when the materials arrive, they are separated so that each school receives the materials that it ordered. This procedure is the same when a school has a definite science budget, except that in this case the teachers now know exactly how much money they can spend. Also, when there is a specific budget for science materials, there is a greater likelihood that more money will be allocated for science and that it will be increased when necessary.

By knowing that the order will be due in the spring, it might be helpful for the teacher to keep a record during the year of materials to be replaced and of additional materials needed or wished. When preparing the list in the spring, the teacher should consult the catalogs of the scientific supply houses. Careful attention is necessary to avoid mistakes in ordering. Each catalog lists different sizes and qualities of the same article. Also, it is necessary to know the exact use for which the article is intended. If the teacher is in doubt, she should ask the science consultant or a high school science teacher to check the list. For clarity in ordering, the teacher must include the name of the item, together with any special characteristics such as size, dimensions, and so forth, the quantity desired, the catalog number of the item, and the cost.

When a school system has a planned and structured science program, a committee for ordering materials would be very helpful. There could be small committees for each school, and possibly a central committee for the school system. The committee could take inventory, receive requests from the teachers, prepare the school science order, and work with the principal in determining what materials could be obtained within the means of the budget. It would be wise for the committee to consist of members with a fairly good science background and knowledge of science materials. The science consultant or supervisor, if there is one, could be of very great service and should assume a leadership role with the committee. If there is no supervisor available, a high school science teacher can be consulted instead.

[203

Purchasing materials from local sources has advantages and drawbacks. On one hand, the service is quick, and it is a good policy to patronize local merchants. On the other hand, there is the possible risk that much time and effort will be required to locate the items. Many small orders may have to be prepared rather than one uncomplicated, large order. To please all the merchants, purchases would either have to be rotated periodically or bids requested. The question of whether to make local purchases is usually decided individually by the school systems. Many use local sources during the year when drawing from petty cash to buy small items that are needed in an emergency or that must be purchased only at the last minute.

SUGGESTED LIST OF SUPPLIES AND EQUIPMENT

Any suggested list of supplies and equipment is usually arbitrary. As stated previously, the materials needed by a school system will depend upon the kind of science program the school system has. If the science program is built around a single textbook series, a list of materials needed for the experiments and other activities described in the books will be the materials list for the program. Actually, many publishers of such textbooks have already prepared such lists and will mail them to schools upon request.

When the science course is structured and has a specific course of study, the materials needed will depend upon the activities suggested in the course of study. In such cases the list can become quite extensive. It might be profitable to divide the materials into more than one category. For example, there might be one list of materials considered basic or essential to the course. A second list might contain materials that would help to enrich further the children's learning. The materials in the second list could be purchased whenever sufficient funds were available.

A list of supplies and equipment usually needed in active, on-going science programs is given in Table 7-1. For convenience, the supplies and equipment are combined and appear alphabetically under an alphabetical listing of separate science topics or general equipment categories. A list of miscellaneous materials commonly found in the home is also included. The supplies and equipment can be ordered from any general scientific supply house. Many items can also be obtained locally from hardware stores, drug stores, variety stores, groceries and supermarkets, and toy shops.

TABLE 7–1. Supplies and Equipment for Elementary Science

AIR AND WEATHER	
Anemometer	Rain gauge
Barometer, aneroid	Tubes, barometer
Fan, electric	Weather forecast indicator
Hygrometer, wet and dry	

ANIMALS

Animal cages	Insect nets
Aquarium	Wire mesh, ½ inch
Dip nets	Wire screen
Insect cages	

ASTRONOMY

Balls, assorted	Lamp, gooseneck
Flashlight	Planetarium, inexpensive
Globe, terrestrial	Telescope and tripod

CHEMICALS

Alcohol, denatured or wood	Manganese dioxide
Ammonia	Mercury, metal
Ammonium dichromate	Nitric acid, dilute
Baking soda (sodium bicarbonate)	Paraffin
Carbon tetrachloride	Plaster of Paris
Copper sulfate, crystals	Salt, table
Food coloring, assorted	Splints, wood
Hydrochloric acid, dilute	Starch
Hydrogen peroxide, 3 percent	Sulfur, powdered
Iodine, tincture	Sulfuric acid, dilute
Limewater (calcium hydroxide)	Vinegar
Litmus paper, red and blue	Washing soda (sodium carbonate)

CORK AND RUBBER

Balloons, rubber	Stoppers, rubber, one-hole
Dam, rubber	Stoppers, rubber, two-hole
Stoppers, cork, assorted	Tubing, plastic, assorted
Stoppers, rubber, solid	Tubing, rubber, assorted

ELECTRICITY

Bell, electric	Generator, electric, hand powered
Buzzer, electric	Motor, St. Louis type
Copper strips, 1 inch × 4 inches	Porcelain sockets, screw base, for
Copper wire, insulated, #18 or #20,	flashlight bulb
Copper wire, insulated, #28	Switches, knife

ELECTRICITY, CONTINUED

Dry cells, #6	Fuses
Flashlight and batteries	Switches, push button
Flashlight bulbs, screw base, 1½ and	Telegraph set
3 volt	Zinc strips, 1 inch × 4 inches

GLASSWARE

Beakers, Pyrex, assorted	Funnels, short stem
Cylinders, graduated, assorted	Jars, battery
Droppers, medicine	Rods, assorted thicknesses
Evaporating dishes, porcelain	Test tubes, Pyrex, assorted
Flasks, Erlenmeyer, assorted	Thistle tube
Flasks, Florence, assorted	Tubing, assorted widths

HEAT, FIRE, AND FUELS

Alcohol burner	Hot plate, electric
Asbestos mat	Matches, safety
Ball-and-ring apparatus	Tea kettle
Boiler, double	Thermometer, clinical
Candles	Thermometers, Celsius (Centigrade)
Canned heat	Thermometers, Fahrenheit
Chimneys, lamp	Thermometer, outdoor
Compound bar apparatus	Wire, copper
Convection box	Wire, iron
Gas burner, portable	

IRONWARE AND GENERAL SUPPLIES

Filter paper, assorted sizes	Test tube holders
Forceps	Test tube rack
Ring stand and rings	Tongs, crucible
Spatula, stainless steel	Tripod
Test tube clamps	Wire gauze, plain and asbestos center

LIGHT

Blueprint paper	Lenses, concave and convex
Cellophane, assorted colors	Mirror, concave and convex
Color top	Mirrors, plane
Flashlight	Prism, equilateral
Lamp, gooseneck	

MACHINES AND FRICTION

Balance, platform, and weights	Rope, clothesline and cord
Balances, spring, assorted	Rulers
Gyroscope	Scale, bathroom
Meter sticks	Wood boards, assorted lengths
Pulleys, single and double	Yardsticks

MAGNETISM

Blueprint paper	Magnets, cylindrical, Alnico
Compasses, magnetic	Magnetic needle, mounted
Iron filings, fine	Nails, large, assorted
Lodestone	Steel needles, knitting
Magnets, bar	Steel needles, sewing
Magnets, horseshoe	Tacks, iron
Magnets, U-shaped	

MISCELLANEOUS

Aluminum foil	Cotton, absorbent
Baby bottles, Pyrex	Funnels, metal and plastic
Bags, paper and plastic	Glue and paste
Bottles, assorted	Hose, garden
Boxes, cigar and wood	Jars, glass, assorted
Cans, assorted	Marbles
Cardboard	Nails, assorted
Cement, household	Nuts and bolts
Clothespins, spring type	Paints and paint brushes
Clay, modeling	Paper clips
Coat hangers, thin wire	Ping-Pong balls

Pins
Pots and pans, aluminum and Pyrex
Potholders
Razor Blades
Rubber bands, assorted
Screws, assorted
Sealing wax
Soda straws

Sponges, assorted
Steel wool
String, assorted
Tacks, assorted
Thread, assorted
Utensils (forks, knives, spoons)
Wood, strips and boxes

PLANTS

Bouillon cubes
Bulbs, assorted
Gelatin
Germinating boxes
Lens paper, microscope
Microscope
Nutrient agar
Petri dishes

Plants, assorted
Seeds, assorted
Slides, microscope
Soil, fertile
Soil-testing kit
Sprinkling can
Terrarium
Trowel

SOUND

Musical instruments, toy
Telephone receiver and transmitter

Tuning forks, set
Wire, music or fine steel

STATIC ELECTRICITY

Balloons
Cat fur
Electroscope
Glass rods
Pith balls

Polyethylene bags
Rubber rods, hard
Silk cloth
Thread
Wool cloth

TOOLS

Cork borer
Drill
File, flat
File, round
File, triangular
Hacksaw and blades
Hammer, claw
Hammer, geological
Jackknife
Knife (not folding)

Pliers, with cutters
Sandpaper
Saw
Scissors
Screw drivers
Soldering iron and solder
Tin snips
Vise
Wrench

SOURCES OF GENERAL SUPPLIES AND EQUIPMENT

The following are some companies that provide general supplies and equipment for all areas of science. This list includes companies who provide apparatus, instruments, ironware, glassware, rubber and plastic materials, chemicals, models, live and preserved specimens, charts, and so forth. Some of these companies also provide more specialized materials as well.

1. Turtox/Cambosco-Macmillan Science Co., 8200 S. Hoyne Ave., Chicago, Ill., 60620
2. Central Scientific Co., 2600 S. Kostner Ave., Chicago, Ill., 60623

3. Fisher Scientific Co., Educational Materials Division, 1259 N. Wood St., Chicago, Ill., 60622
4. Sargent-Welch Scientific Co., 7300 N. Linder, Skokie, Ill. 60076

SOURCES OF SPECIALIZED SUPPLIES
AND EQUIPMENT

The following are only a few of the companies that provide specialized supplies and equipment; the specialties of each company follow its address. There are usually local companies in each city or town that also offer specialized materials. All of the listed companies will send the school a catalog upon request.

1. American Optical Co. Eggert and Sugar Roads Buffalo, N.Y., 14215	Microscopes.
2. Bausch & Lomb, Inc. 1400 N. Goodman St. Rochester, N.Y., 14602	Microscopes.
3. Carolina Biological Supply Company 2700 York Road Burlington, N.C., 27215	Biological supplies and equipment, living and preserved specimens, charts, models, and so forth.
4. Denoyer-Geppert Co. 5235 N. Ravenswood Ave. Chicago, Ill., 60640	Biological charts, models, and so forth, general science transparencies, teaching aids.
5. Edmund Scientific Corp. Barrington, N.J., 08007	Teaching aids in astronomy, optics, magnets, weather.
6. Hach Chemical Co. Box 907 Ames, Iowa 50010	Water analysis test kits; equipment for teaching ecology, and soil nutrient kits.
7. Hubbard Scientific Co. 1946 Raymond Drive Northbrook, Ill., 60062	Models, globes, transparencies.
8. Jewel Industries 5005 W. Armitage Ave. Chicago, Ill., 60639	Salt water aquariums, animal cages, plant study materials.
9. Ken-A-Vision Manufacturing Company 5615 Raytown Road Raytown, Mo., 64133	Microprojectors, microscopes, and science supplies.

10. Lamotte Chemical
    Products
    Box 329 Chestertown, Md.,
    21620

    Test kits for environmental science studies.

11. NASCO
    901 Janesville Ave.
    Ft. Atkinson, Wis., 53538

    Anatomical models, kits on nature study and water-air pollution.

12. Nalgene Labware Division
    Nalge Company
    75 Panorama Creek Drive
    Rochester, N.Y., 14602

    Transparent and translucent plastic graduated cylinders, beakers, flasks, funnels, and so forth.

13. Nystrom Division
    Carnation Company
    3333 Elston Ave.
    Chicago, Ill., 60618

    Biological, earth science, and space science models, charts, maps, and globes.

14. Ohaus Scale Corp.
    29 Hanover Road
    Florham Park, N.J., 07932

    Balances, weights, and science educational equipment.

15. Science Kit, Inc.
    777 E. Park Drive
    Tonowanda, N.Y., 14150

    Science kits, laboratory equipment and supplies.

16. Swift Instruments, Inc.
    P.O. Box 562
    San Jose, Calif. 95106

    Microscopes and microtomes for all grade levels.

17. Ward's Natural Science
    Establishment
    Box 1712
    Rochester, N.Y., 14603

    Earth science and life science materials.

SCIENCE KITS

Commercical science kits are boxes or chests of science materials assembled and sold by various scientific supply houses. The kits are especially designed for the elementary school for use in any grade. They are extremely popular with the busy principal or superintendent, who does not have time to order a wide variety of items from different catalogs. Instead he can merely purchase one item from one supply house. The kits are usually found in schools with no planned or structured science program, where the administrator would like to encourage the teachers to conduct science learning in the classroom. The kits are also welcomed by teachers who have a weak background in science and science materials.

The boxes or chests are specially built, are quite sturdy, and have handles so that they can be carried easily from room to room; they pose no storage problem. They contain a variety of materials, often almost exclusively in the area of physics or physical science. These materials are useful in teaching science, and are materials that the teacher could not ordinarily obtain, make, or improvise. Included in the kit is a booklet of suggested experiments and demonstrations that either the teacher or the children can do.

There has been much discussion about the value of commercial science kits. There are definite advantages in using these kits, but there are strong disadvantages as well. The favorable factors include those factors already listed above. Also, replacements, and even additions, to the kit can be purchased from the company manufacturing it. Where there is no planned or structured program, and little or no provision is made for science materials, the kit can be very helpful to the teacher.

On the other hand, such kits cannot take the place of a well-defined science program with suggested activities, and with materials selected specifically to conduct these activities. Furthermore, although the kits can be used wisely and well, many teachers tend to become overdependent upon the kits, and they confine their activities only to those activities suggested in the accompanying booklet. Some teachers follow the booklet so rigidly and do the experiments in such a stereotyped fashion that the result is often a "cookbook" type of science teaching. Because the supplies in the kit are predominantly in the area of physics or physical science, the teachers are likely to neglect other important areas of science. In some kits the cost of the items is more than the cost would be if the items were purchased separately. Finally, although replacements can be ordered, often the teachers fail to do this ordering. Unless the principal or a designated teacher makes a periodic inventory of the contents of the kit, the broken or missing parts are not replaced, thus making the kit ineffective. After a certain point it is impossible to use the kit, and the kit is either neglected or discarded.

Many schools with well-organized science programs make their own kits. These kits differ from the commercial kits in that there are many homemade kits, each containing a variety of materials designed to teach concepts in only one topic or area in science. In this way there would be kits on sound, light, color, expansion and contraction, magnets, electromagnets, electricity, weather, the earth and the sun, earth science, and so forth. Often suggested activities, together with instructions, are included in the kit. Sometimes, for those teachers who are inexperienced in science, a list of the equipment is also enclosed, accompanied by drawings or pictures of special equipment with which the teacher might be unfamiliar.

So many of these homemade kits use shoe boxes to hold the materials that they are usually called "shoe-box kits." Another common name is "science-concept boxes." Some schools have sturdier boxes made, either by local carpenters or by school personnel. All the homemade kits are uniform, easy to pick up and return, and easy to store. This method is one way of supplying materials to the teachers, either when the budget is limited or the storage facilities in the classroom are minimal. The chief advantage of these homemade kits is that their contents can be geared to the objectives of the school science program and to the suggested activities that are a part of the program.

ACQUAINTING TEACHERS WITH UNFAMILIAR EQUIPMENT

As the schools purchase and accumulate science materials, it is essential that all the teachers become thoroughly familiar with the purpose, use, and care of these materials. Many teachers are reluctant to conduct experiments or demonstrations when they are unfamiliar with the equipment. In such cases an orientation program can be very helpful. This program may be part of an in-service workshop designed to acquaint the teachers with the basic science information selected for the science program and with the activities that can be used to achieve the purposes of the program. It may also consist of a short series of group meetings, where the materials are displayed, their purpose and use explained, and the teachers given an opportunity to handle the materials and become adept at working with them.

At the same time the teachers should be informed of the precautions to be taken when using certain equipment. Instructions can be given about how to handle and store glassware, work with glass tubing, pour acids, and manipulate fragile apparatus. The teachers can be forewarned of certain measures they can take to prevent damage to materials. For

(Barbara Van Cleve)

Printed materials are also necessary for science learning.

example, when creating a short circuit by placing a piece of metal across two bared parts of the wires in an electric circuit, or by touching the bared parts together, it should be pointed out that the teacher or children must "short" the circuit for a very few seconds only. Otherwise the dry cell will quickly burn out. When storing chemicals, ammonia water should be placed as far away as possible from acids, especially hydrochloric acid. If not, a fine white salt will be formed (with hydrochloric acid the product is ammonium chloride) that will cover and possibly affect ironware, contaminate loosely sealed chemicals, coat bottles, and cause the labels to disintegrate.

The teachers should also be warned about the care they must take to avoid accidents, both to themselves and the children, when working with science materials. Many times schools have banned certain materials or activities because accidents that could have been prevented happened in the classrooms. In some cases, when children have received burns, the use of open flames—even from candles—has been prohibited in the classroom. Bites or scratches by animals have resulted in the banning of all animals from the school.

The teacher must thoroughly inculcate in the children good safety habits until these habits become automatic. The children should be taught to avoid careless handling of tools, sharp or pointed objects, all kinds of glassware, and sources of heat. The teacher must be extremely careful whenever electrical appliances, such as lamps or hot plates, are used. Wiring should be examined for frayed or cracked insulation. Children should be warned never to touch an electric switch, cord, or appliance with wet hands. When electric appliances are not being used, they should be disconnected. Definite rules must be established about the handling and treatment of pets in the classroom. As a safety measure, a bucket of sand or water should be nearby for emergencies, and a fire extinguisher and first-aid kit should be easily accessible.

STORING SUPPLIES AND EQUIPMENT

All teachers should have in their classrooms certain essential supplies and equipment, especially those items used regularly throughout the year. In an on-going, active science program, however, there will be many items that are used only periodically. Special pieces of equipment and a wide variety of chemicals are also included. All these materials must be stored. Ideally, each school should have its own central supply room for science materials. If it is not possible to have such a room, perhaps some space from an already existing supply room can be utilized. In an emergency, storage cabinets could be purchased and placed in a convenient location.

It might be helpful to store the equipment by science topics or areas. Thus, one shelf might have materials for the study of machines, another one for electricity, and so on. The shelves should be labeled for easy identification and also to keep the materials arranged in an orderly manner. Sometimes a list of the materials is attached to each shelf, together with drawings or pictures of items that are likely to be unfamiliar to the teachers. Glassware should be kept separately from ironware. Chemicals must be stored separately from apparatus; they are usually arranged alphabetically. The chemicals should be kept in tightly closed containers and labeled clearly and correctly. If children are allowed to obtain materials from the supply room, it would be wise to place strong acids and bases, and other chemicals that are poisonous or harmful, high on the shelves.

A science-minded teacher should be placed in charge of the supply room or storage cabinets. This person can keep an inventory of all the materials, listing in each case the name of the item, the quantity, the size, where it was purchased, the catalog number, and the price. The materials would be checked periodically for needed repairs or replacement. Moreover, provision should be made for checking materials in and out. This checking is always a problem because much time can be wasted in trying to locate materials that some teacher is either using or has forgotten to return to the supply room. An effective method is to have a notebook in the supply room. Each teacher could write down the items that were borrowed, the teacher's name, the date the items were borrowed, and the date returned. If a piece of equipment is broken or a chemical is used up, it would be helpful if the person in charge of the supply room were informed immediately.

Science Facilities in the Classroom

IF SCIENCE is to achieve its proper place in the elementary school curriculum, with effective teaching and learning of science going on in the classroom, adequate facilities are needed. Each classroom must be self-contained, with sufficient materials and facilities available for both the teacher and children to perform satisfactorily the science learning activities.

All elementary school classrooms need a table where experiments and demonstrations can be conducted. Many teachers have learned—to their distress when mishaps occur—that the teacher's desk does not make a suitable demonstration table. It would be ideal to have a small, permanent laboratory table in some, if not all, of the rooms, equipped with gas, hot and cold running water, and electrical outlets. Several scientific supply houses now sell movable laboratory tables. These tables are on rollers and can be moved within the room, or from room to room. They have chemical resistant tops, small stainless steel sinks with a pump faucet, a supply of fresh water, and provision for drainage of waste water into special containers. An electrical receptacle with more than one outlet, and with an extra long cord, is attached to the desk. Inside the table are adjustable shelves. The tables can be purchased with or without equipment and/or science kits.

These movable tables are becoming more popular in the elementary school. They are rather expensive, however, and it is not easy to acquire them, especially as most budgets for elementary school science are still quite limited or nonexistent. Consequently, most elementary schools have one, or very few, of this kind of table. Although the tables can be rolled from room to room, they often are found only in the rooms of the science-minded teachers, remaining there the entire year. These tables are quite heavy and are rather difficult to lift or carry. In older, two-story elementary school buildings the tables usually are confined to the level on which they are originally placed.

Many schools are using improvised, movable laboratory tables, constructed by local or school personnel. The tables are made of wood with rollers attached to the bottom. One end is open, without the sliding doors found in commercial tables, and there is usually one fixed shelf. Inlaid linoleum is used instead of a chemically resistant top. There is no sink or pump faucet with a supply of water. A hole bored through the top, to one side, allows a funnel to be inserted, and a rubber or plastic hose attached to the end of the funnel connects to a pail inside the desk. Fresh water must be brought into the classroom with a bucket or another container. An electrical receptacle is attached to the table. These tables are obviously much less ornate and do not have some of the desirable features of the commercial tables, but they are equally useful. Furthermore, for the same amount of money as required to purchase one commercial table, several classrooms can be equipped with improvised tables. It is interesting to note that many enterprising teach-

(William Means/Van Cleve)

A science center in the classroom is desirable.

ers have been using tables of this kind for some time; they are made from old desks, dressers, and bureaus.

Every classroom should also have a Science Center where the children can do experiments, work on projects, or display materials. Also, there should be facilities for storing supplies and equipment. Teachers seriously need storage space for bottles, beakers, flasks, ring stands, supports, clamps, tongs, wire, flower pots, tools, simple chemicals, and other materials. There are several ways in which storage space can be provided. Cabinets or cases are a possibility. Wall counters, with storage space and shelves below, installed along the window side of the room are another possibility. The tops of the counters can be used to hold plants, germinating beds, aquariums, or terrariums. They may also serve to display models, specimens, and completed projects. Where school funds are limited, open shelves can be constructed, and the tops covered with inlaid linoleum.

Free and Inexpensive Materials

A LARGE number of industrial organizations supply excellent free or inexpensive science materials for use in the elementary classroom. Many of the firms either have special personnel or employ the services of scientists and educators to develop these materials. The materials include charts, maps, pictures, leaflets, booklets, films, filmstrips, phonograph records, and sometimes small quantities of materials. Most of the printed materials are well written, geared for the elementary school, and contain a minimum of advertising. These materials can be obtained by writing directly to the organizations that supply them. Because almost all the materials contain some advertising, it might be advisable for the teacher to check with the school administration about policy in allowing materials containing advertising to be given to the children.

REFERENCES

To list all the organizations that provide free and inexpensive materials would be impossible. However, the following are some organizations that have consistently made available such materials. Also included are some publications that tell where these materials may be obtained. Prices of these publications, where listed, are subject to change.

1. Aluminum Assn., *Teaching Aids*. Aluminum Assn., 750 Third Ave., New York, N.Y., 10017
2. American Gas Assn., *Educational Aids*. American Gas Assn., Educational Services Div., 1515 Wilson Blvd., Arlington, Va., 22209
3. Conservation Foundation, *Aids to Educators*. Conservation

Foundation, 1717 Massachusetts Ave., N.W. Washington, D.C. 20036

4. Educator's Progress Service. *Educator's Guide to Free Films* $12.75, *Educator's Guide to Free Filmstrips* $11, *Educator's Guide to Free Science Materials* $11.25, *Educator's Guide to Free Tapes, Scripts, and Transcriptions* $10.75, *Elementary Teacher's Guide to Free Curriculum Materials* $11.25. Educator's Progress Service, Dept. AYL, 214 Center St., Randolph, Wisconsin 53956

5. Field Enterprises, World Book and Childcraft, Encyclopedia Division. *Teaching Aids.* 510 Merchandise Mart Plaza, Chicago, Ill. 60654

6. General Motors Corp., School Service. *Aids to Educators.* General Motors Corp., General Motors Bldg., Detroit, Mich., 48202

7. Manufacturing Chemists Assn., *Aids to Educators.* 1825 Connecticut Ave., N.W., Washington, D.C. 20009

8. National Dairy Council, *Educational Aids.* National Dairy Council, 111 North Canal St., Chicago, Ill. 60606

9. National Science Teachers Assn., *Elementary Science Packets.* National Science Teachers Assn., 1742 Connecticut Ave., N.W., Washington, D.C. 20009 $3 per packet. (Available free to elementary members and to life members.)

10. Science Service. *Science Service Aids to Youth.* Science Service, 1719 N St., N.W., Washington, D.C. 20036

11. Soil Conservation Society of America, *Teaching Aids.* Soil Conservation Society of America, 7515 N.E. Ankeny Rd., Ankeny, Iowa. 50021

12. United Fresh Fruit and Vegetable Assn., *Educational Aids.* United Fresh Fruit and Vegetable Assn., Educational Services Div., 1019 Nineteenth St. N.W., Washington, D.C. 20036

13. U.S. Department of Health, Education and Welfare. *Sources of Free and Low-Cost Materials.* Superintendent of Documents, Government Printing Office, Washington, D.C. 20402

14. United States Steel Corp. *Teaching Aids.* United States Steel Corp., School Service, 71 Broadway, New York, N.Y. 10004

15. Westinghouse Electrical Corp., School Service. *Teaching Aids.* Gateway Center, 401 Liberty Ave., Pittsburgh, Pa. 15222

Printed Materials

MANY kinds of printed materials are necessary for the successful operation of an elementary science program. Teachers must avail themselves of the large number of professional publications that will help them develop or reorganize the program, and guide them in teaching science more effectively in the classroom. They should be able to consult a wide variety of source books that describe experiments, demonstrations, and other science activities. Children need textbooks, trade books, and reference books. There are also a number of bulletins and pamphlets that are specifically printed to help both teachers and children.

Sources of printed materials fall into several categories. There are sources on the teaching of science, sources of experiments and demonstrations, sources of science textbook series, sources of supplementary science series, and sources of science tradebooks and reference books.

SOURCES ON THE TEACHING OF SCIENCE

All of the following materials are designed to help the elementary school teacher in developing science programs, planning daily work, and increasing teaching effectiveness in science. For convenience, these materials have been listed under three separate classifications: (1) books, (2) bulletins, and (3) journals and magazines. Latest names and addresses are given, in cases in which the original publisher has merged with another.

Books on the Teaching of Elementary Science

1. BLOUGH, GLENN O., and JULIUS SCHWARTZ. *Elementary School Science and How to Teach It.* New York: Holt, Rinehart and Winston, 1974. 768 pp.
2. BUTTS, DAVID P. *Teaching Science in the Elementary School.* New York: Free Press, 1973. 199 pp.
   ———. and GENE E. HALL. *Children and Science: The Process of Teaching and Learning.* Englewood Cliffs, N.J.: Prentice-Hall, 1975. 284 pp.
3. CARIN, ARTHUR, and ROBERT B. SUND. *Teaching Science Through Discovery.* Columbus, Ohio: Charles Merrill, 1975. 640 pp.
   ——— and ———. *Teaching Modern Science.* Columbus, Ohio: Charles Merrill, 1975. 416 pp.
4. DeVITO, ALFRED, and GERALD CROCKOVER. *Creative Sciencing: A Practical Approach.* New York: Little, Brown, 1976. 184 pp.
5. EDWARDS, CLIFFORD H., and ROBERT L. FISHER. *Teaching Elementary School Science: A Competency-Based Approach.* New York: Praeger, 1977. 464 pp.
6. ESLER, WILLIAM K. *Teaching Elementary Science.* Belmont, Calif.: Wadsworth, 1977. 584 pp.
7. GEGA, PETER C. *Science in Elementary Education.* New York: John Wiley, 1977. 284 pp.

8. GEORGE, KENNETH, and others. *Elementary School Science—Why and How*. Lexington, Mass.: D.C. Heath, 1974. 242 pp.

9. GOOD, RONALD G. *How Children Learn Science*. New York: Macmillan, 1977. 352 pp.

10. HUBLER, H. CLARK. *Science for Children*. New York: Random House, 1974. 676 pp.

11. IVANY, J.W. GEORGE. *Today's Science: A Professional Approach to Teaching Elementary School Science*. Palo Alto, Calif.: Science Research Associates, 1975. 341 pp.

12. JACOBSON, WILLARD. *The New Elementary School Science*. New York: Van Nostrand Reinhold, 1970. 579 pp.

13. KUSLAN, LOUIS I., and A. HARRIS STONE. *A New Look at Elementary School Science*. Chicago: Rand McNally, 1972. 544 pp.

14. LANSDOWN, BRENDA, PAUL E. BLACKWOOD, and PAUL F. BRANDWEIN. *Teaching Elementary Science Through Investigation and Colloquium*. New York: Harcourt Brace Jovanovich, 1971. 433 pp.

15. NAVARRA, JOHN, and J. ZAFFARONI. *Science in the Elementary School*. Columbus, Ohio: Charles Merrill, 1975. 640 pp.

16. PILTZ, ALBERT, and ROBERT SUND. *Creative Teaching of Science in the Elementary School*. Rockleigh, N.J.: Allyn & Bacon, 1974. 320 pp.

17. RENNER, JOHN W., DON G. STAFFORD, and WILLIAM B. RAGAN. *Teaching Science in the Elementary School*. New York: Harper & Row, 1973. 408 pp.

18. ROWE, MARY B. *Teaching Science as Continuous Theory*. New York: McGraw-Hill, 1978. 608 pp.

19. WASHTON, NATHAN. *Teaching Science in Elementary and Middle Schools*. New York: David McKay, 1974. 482 pp.

Science Education Bulletins

1. BROWN, BILLYE W., and WALTER R. BROWN. *Science Teaching and the Law*. National Science Teachers Association, 1742 Connecticut Ave., N.W., Washington, D.C. 20009, 1969. 80 pp.

2. BUTTS, DAVID P. (ed.). *Designs for Progress in Science Education*. National Science Teachers Association, 1742 Connecticut Ave., N.W., Washington, D.C., 20009, 1969. 105 pp.

3. BYBEE, RODGER W. *Personalized Science Teaching*. National Science Teachers Association, 1742 Connecticut Ave., N.W., Washington, D.C. 20009, 1974. 40 pp.

4. Educational Policies Commission. *Education and the Spirit of Science*. National Education Association, 1201 Sixteenth St., N.W., Washington, D.C., 20036, 1966. 27 pp.

5. EISS, ALBERT F., and MARY B. HARBECK (ed.). *Behavioral*

Objectives in the Affective Domain. National Science Supervisors Association, an affiliation of National Science Teachers Association, 1742 Connecticut Ave., N.W., Washington, D.C., 20009, 1969. 42 pp.

6. *Elementary Science Packets.* (Teaching aids from industry and government.) National Science Teachers Assn., 1742 Connecticut Ave., N.W., Washington, D.C. 20009

7. GARAGLIANO, L., and B. KNAPE (ed.). *Environmental Education in the Elementary School.* National Science Teachers Assn., 1742 Connecticut Ave., N.W., Washington, D.C. 20009, 1977. 142 pp.

8. HARBECK, MARY B. (ed.). *The 2nd Sourcebook for Science Supervisors.* National Science Supervisors Association, an affiliation of National Science Teachers Association, 1742 Connecticut Ave., N.W., Washington, D.C., 20009, 1976. 264 pp.

9. *How To Do It Series.* National Science Teachers Association, 1742 Connecticut Ave., N.W., Washington, D.C. 20009

10. JENKINS, EDWARD S., GOSSIE H. HUDSON, SHERMAN JACKSON, and EXYIE RYDER. *American Black Scientists and Inventors.* National Science Teachers Association, 1742 Connecticut Avenue, N.W., Washington D.C. 20009, 1971. 256 pp.

11. MATTHEWS, WILLIAM H. (ed.). *Helping Children Learn Earth-Space Science.* National Science Teachers Association, 1742 Connecticut Ave., N.W., Washington, D.C. 20009, 1971. 256 pp.

12. *Pre-Service Science Education of Elementary School Teachers.* American Association for the Advancement of Science, 1515 Massachusetts Avenue, N.W., Washington, D.C., 20005, 1970. 73 pp.

13. SULLIVAN, JOHN J., and CALVIN W. TAYLOR. *Learning and Creativity in Science.* National Science Teachers Association, 1742 Connecticut Ave., N.W., Washington, D.C., 20009, 1967. 51 pp.

14. TRIEZENBERG, HENRY J. (ed.). *Individualized Science—Like It is.* National Science Teachers Association, 1742 Connecticut Ave., N.W., Washington, D.C., 20009, 1972. 99 pp.

Science Education Journals and Magazines

1. *American Biology Teacher.* National Association of Biology Teachers, 1420 N Street, N.W., Washington, D.C. 20005. Monthly, 9 times a year.

2. *Arizona Highways.* Arizona Highway Dept., 2039 W. Lewis Ave., Phoenix, Arizona 85009. Monthly.

3. *Audubon.* National Audubon Society, 950 Third Ave., New York 10022. N.Y. Bimonthly.

4. *The Conservation Foundation Letter.* Conservation Foundation 1717 Mass. Ave., N.W. Washington, D.C. 20036. Monthly.
5. *Environmental Science and Technology.* American Chemical Soc., 1155 16th St., N.W., Washington, D.C. 20036. Monthly.
6. *International Wildlife.* National Wildlife Federation, 1412 16th St., N.W., Washington, D.C. 20036. Monthly.
7. *Journal of Chemical Education.* American Chemical Society, 1155 16th St., N.W., Washington, D.C. 20036. Monthly.
8. *Journal of College Science Teaching.* National Science Teachers Association, 1742 Connecticut Avenue, N.W., Washington, D.C. 20009. Monthly, 5 times a year.
9. *Journal of Geological Education.* The National Association of Geology Teachers, 2201 M Street, N.W., Washington, D.C. 20037. 5 times a year.
10. *Journal of Research in Science Teaching.* Wiley-Interscience, John Wiley, 605 Third Ave., New York, N.Y. 10016. Quarterly.
11. *National Geographic School Bulletin.* National Geographic Soc., Seventeenth and M Streets, N.W., Washington, D.C. 20036. Weekly, Sept. to May.
12. *National Parks and Conservation Magazine: The Environmental Journal.* National Parks and Conservation Association, 1701 18th St., N.W., Washington, D.C. 20009. Monthly.
13. *National Wildlife.* National Wildlife Federation, 1412 16th St., N.W., Washington, D.C. 20036. Bimonthly.
14. *Natural History.* Museum of Natural History, 79th St. & Central Park West, New York, N.Y. 10024. Monthly, 10 times a year.
15. *Physics Teacher.* American Assn. of Physics Teachers, 335 East 45th St., New York, N.Y 10017. Monthly, 9 times a year.
16. *School Science and Mathematics.* School Science and Mathematics Assn., Lewis House, P.O. Box 1614, Indiana Univ. of Pennsylvania, Indiana, Pennsylvania 15701. Monthly, 9 times a year.
17. *Science.* American Association for the Advancement of Science. 1776 Mass. Ave., N.W., Washington, D.C. 20036. Monthly.
18. *Science and Children.* National Science Teachers Assn., 1742 Connecticut Ave., N.W., Washington, D.C. 20009. Monthly, 8 times a year.
19. *Science Education.* Wiley-Interscience, John Wiley & Sons, 605 Third Ave., New York, N.Y. 10016. Quarterly.
20. *Science News.* Science Service, 1719 N. St., N.W., Washington, D.C. 20036. Weekly.
21. *The Science Teacher.* National Science Teachers Association, 1742 Connecticut Ave., N.W., Washington, D.C. 20009. Monthly, 9 times a year.

22. *Scientific American.* Scientific American Publisher, 415 Madison Ave., New York, N.Y. 10017. Monthly.
23. *Sky and Telescope.* Sky Publishing Corp., Harvard College Observatory, 49 Bay State Rd., Cambridge, Mass. 02136. Monthly.
24. *Weatherwise.* American Meteorological Society, 45 Beacon St., Boston, Mass. 02108. Monthly.

GENERAL SOURCEBOOKS OF EXPERIMENTS
AND DEMONSTRATIONS

There are already a tremendous number of books that can be used as sources for experiments and demonstrations in elementary science. More books are being printed daily, as the present interest in science continues to grow. Some books are general and suggest activities in several or all areas of science. Other books are restricted to individual science topics. Some are designed primarily for the teacher whereas others are written for the children on their level.

The following are some of the general sourcebooks of experiments and demonstrations, intended primarily for teacher use. Books on specific topics, for teachers and children, are listed at the end of each science chapter later on in this textbook.

1. BENDICK, JEANNE. *Science Experiences: Adaptation.* New York: Franklin Watts, 1971. 72 pp.
2. ———. *Science Experiences: Motion and Gravity.* New York: Franklin Watts, 1970. 72 pp.
3. BROWN, BOB. *200 Illustrated Science Experiments for Boys and Girls.* New York: William Collins & World, 1973. 114 pp.
4. COBB, VICKI. *Science Experiments You Can Eat.* Philadelphia: J. B. Lippincott, 1972. 128 pp.
5. DAVIS, HOWARD T. *Projects in Biology.* Normal, Illinois: Science Publications, 1970. 174 pp.
6. DeVITO, ALFRED, and GERALD H. CROCKOVER. *Creative Sciencing: Ideas and Activities for Teachers and Children.* New York: Little, Brown, 1976. 272 pp.
7. FISHER, S. H. *Tabletop Science: Physics Experiments for Everyone.* New York: Natural History Press, 1972. 124 pp.
8. FRIEDL, ALFRED E. *Teaching Science to Children: The Inquiry Approach Applied.* New York: Random House, 1972. 337 pp.
9. GALE FRANK, and CLARICE GALE. *Experiences for Young Children.* Palo Alto, Calif.: Pacific Books, 1975. 118 pp.
10. GEORGE, KENNETH, et al. *Science Investigations for Elementary School Teachers.* Lexington, Mass.: D.C. Heath, 1974. 124 pp.

[221

11. HILL, KATHERINE. *Exploring the Natural World with Children*. New York: Harcourt Brace Jovanovich, 1976. 154 pp.

12. HONE, ELIZABETH, ALEXANDER JOSEPH, and EDWARD VICTOR. *A Sourcebook for Elementary Science*. New York: Harcourt Brace Jovanovich, 1971. 475 pp.

13. HOUNSELL, PAUL B., and IRA TROLLINGER. *Games for the Science Classroom*. Washington, D.C.: National Science Teachers Association, 1977. 246 pp.

14. HYER, JAMES E., and MILDRED D. HYER. *Science Fun*. New York: Henry Z. Walck, 1973. 166 pp.

15. LOWERY, LAWRENCE F. *The Everyday Science Sourcebook: Ideas for Teaching in the Elementary and Middle School*. New York: Allyn & Bacon, 1978. 300 pp.

16. MILGROM, HARRY. *ABC Science Experiments*. New York: Crowell-Collier, 1970. Unnumbered.

17. MUSSELMAN, VIRGINIA. *Learning About Nature Through Crafts*. Harrisburg, Pa.: Stackpole, 1970. 128 pp.

18. NELSON, LESLIE W., and GEORGE C. LORBEER. *Science Activities for Elementary Children*. Dubuque, Iowa: William C. Brown, 1976. 320 pp.

19. NELSON, PEARL A. *Elementary School Science Activities*. Englewood Cliffs, N.J.: Prentice-Hall, 1968. 210 pp.

20. PRIME, C.T., and AARON KLEIN. *Seedlings and Soil: Botany for Young Experimenters*. New York: Doubleday, 1973. 168 pp.

21. SCHMIDT, VICTOR, and VERNE ROCKCASTLE. *Teaching Science with Everyday Things*. New York: McGraw-Hill, 1968. 168 pp.

22. SCHNEIDER, HERMAN, and NINA SCHNEIDER. *Science Fun with a Flashlight*. New York: McGraw-Hill, 1975. 42 pp.

23. —— and ——. *Science Fun for a Minute or Two*. New York: McGraw-Hill, 1975. 64 pp.

24. SIMON, SEYMOUR. *How Science Is at Work*. New York: Franklin Watts, 1972. 88 pp.

25. ——. *Science Projects in Ecology*. New York: Holiday House, 1972. 128 pp.

26. ——. *Science Projects in Pollution*. New York: Holiday House, 1972. 118 pp.

27. ——. *Science Projects with Air*. New York: Franklin Watts, 1975. 96 pp.

28. SOOTIN, HARRY. *Experiments with Electric Currents*. New York: Norton, 1970. 88 pp.

29. STONE A. HARRIS. *Science Project Puzzlers: Starting Ideas for Those Who Are Curious About Science*. Englewood Cliffs, N.J.: Prentice-Hall, 1970. 64 pp.

30. STRONGIN, HERB. *Science on a Shoestring*. Menlo Park, Calif.: Addison-Wesley, 1976. 200 pp.

31. SUND, ROBERT, WILLIAM TILLERY, and LESLIE TROW-BRIDGE. *Investigate and Discover: Elementary Science Lessons.* Rockleigh, N.J.: Allyn & Bacon, 1975. 400 pp.

32. SWEZEY, KENNETH M. *Science Shows You How.* New York: McGraw-Hill, 1964. 164 pp.

33. UNESCO. *The New Unesco Sourcebook for Science Teaching.* New York: Uni Publishing, Inc., 1975. 270 pp.

34. VERMEER, JACKIE. *The Little Kid's Craft Book.* New York: Taplinger, 1973. 128 pp.

35. VIVIAN, EUGENE. *Sourcebook for Environmental Education.* St. Louis, Mo.: C.V. Mosby, 1973. 206 pp.

36. WEBSTER, DAVID. *How to Do a Science Project.* New York: Franklin Watts, 1974. 72 pp.

37. WHITE, LAURENCE B. *Investigating Science with Nails.* Palo Alto, Calif.: Addison-Wesley, 1970. 108 pp.

38. ———. *Investigating Science with Rubber Bands.* Palo Alto, Calif.: Addison-Wesley, 1970. 96 pp.

39. WYLER, ROSE. *The First Book of Science Experiments.* New York: Franklin Watts, 1971. 70 pp.

40. ———. *What Happens If? Science Experiments You Can Do by Yourself.* New York: Walker, 1974. 32 pp.

SELECTING ELEMENTARY SCIENCE TEXTBOOKS

Textbooks play an important role in the elementary science program. As such, they should be used in the many ways suggested in Chapter 4, "Methods of Teaching Science," and not just for reading and discussion. Some school systems use only one science textbook series and develop the course of study around it. Other systems have a certain number of copies, ranging from two, three, or even four textbook series, in each grade. Their reason for using this method is that the grade placement of science topics varies among the various series and some topics are taken up in greater detail in one series than in another. The school systems find it easier to incorporate the use of textbooks in their science programs when multiple series are used.

When selecting textbooks, the teachers or committee should examine each series carefully. Several guides and checklists are available that will help in determining the final selection. The books should be attractive, of convenient size for handling, and with a durable cover and binding. They should have a table of contents, glossary, and index that the children can use quickly and easily.

The illustrations should be clear-cut and attractive. They should teach as well as illustrate, and their captions should include questions that stimulate thinking or the desire to read further. The experiments should be clear with directions that are easily understood; they should be the kind of experiments for children to do rather than for teachers to demonstrate. They should involve the use of simple materials so that the experiment can be repeated in the classroom if desired. The diagrams should be simple, accurate, easily understood, and labeled. The results of the experiment should not always be given immediately after the experiment is described.

The science content should be stated clearly and in an interesting manner, with the type large enough for convenient reading. The sentences should not be too long, and the content should be at the proper reading level. The material must be accurate and up-to-date, and related to the daily life and environment of the child. All the content should be part of a scope and sequence plan, with balance between the physical, earth, and biological sciences. The books should, under no circumstances, ascribe to plants and animals human traits and personalities, or attribute to them a conscious purpose in changing their behavior when conditions change. Each book should contain a relatively short number of well-developed units rather than a large number of scattered, fragmented topics. The units should be flexible enough to allow the exploration of situations that arise while the unit is in progress.

The books should stress the learning of content and process, using technology to illustrate concepts. They should show the relationship of science to social studies, and include, where applicable, the areas of health, safety, and conservation. The experiments should be left open-ended, if possible, and be directed toward the promotion of problem solving and critical thinking, the development of scientific attitudes, and the inculcation of process skills. There should be provision for review for slow learners and opportunities for going further for fast learners. Finally, the books should have been tested during and after their preparation.

The series should provide teachers' guides or manuals. These guides should list key science concepts for the teacher. They should suggest initiating activities and show how to coordinate the learning activities with the science content. They should include additional activities for slow and fast learners, and make recommendations for evaluation. They should append a bibliography of books, films, and filmstrips.

The following publishers offer elementary science textbook series, including teachers' guides, scope and sequence charts, and other aids.

1. Addison-Wesley, 2725 Sand Hill Rd., Menlo Park, Cal. 94025
2. Benziger Bruce Glencoe, 17337 Ventura Blvd., Encino, Cal. 91316
3. Cambridge Book Co., 448 Madison Ave., New York, N.Y. 10022
4. Ginn & Co., 191 Spring St., Lexington, Mass. 02173
5. Harcourt Brace Jovanovich, 757 Third Ave., N.Y., N.Y. 10017
6. D. C. Heath & Co., 125 Spring St., Lexington, Mass. 02173
7. Holt, Rinehart and Winston, 383 Madison Avenue, New York, N.Y. 10017
8. Houghton Mifflin Co., 1 Beacon St., Boston, Mass. 02107
9. Laidlaw Bros., Thatcher & Madison, River Forest, Ill. 60305

10. J.B. Lippincott, E. Washington Square, Philadelphia, Pa. 19105
11. Rand McNally & Co., P.O. Box 7600, Chicago, Ill. 60680
12. Silver Burdett Co., 250 James St., Morristown, N.J. 07960
13. Steck-Vaughn Co., P.O. Box 2028, Austin, Texas 78767
14. Webster/McGraw-Hill Book Co., 1221 Avenue of the Americas, New York, N.Y. 10020

SUPPLEMENTARY ELEMENTARY SCIENCE SERIES

There is also a growing trend to publish supplementary science textbooks for the elementary school. As such, these books can be used as auxiliary textbooks and reference books in the classroom. The following are some of the series now being published.

1. *A First Look at Science Books.* Walker and Co., 720 Fifth Ave., New York, N.Y. 10019
2. *ABC's of Science Books.* Walker and Co., 720 Fifth Ave., New York, N.Y. 10019
3. *Exploring and Understanding Science Books.* Benefic Press, 10300 W. Roosevelt Road, Westchester, Ill. 60153
4. *Finding Out Books.* Parents Magazine Press, 52 Vanderbilt Ave., New York, N.Y. 10017
5. *Follett Beginning Science Books.* Follett Publishing Co., 1010 W. Washington Blvd., Chicago, Ill. 60607
6. *Golden Science Books.* Western Publishing Co., 850 Third Avenue, New York, N.Y. 10022
7. *How Did We Find Out Books.* Walker and Co., 720 Fifth Ave., New York, N.Y. 10019
8. *Let's Find Out Books.* Franklin Watts, Inc., 730 Fifth Ave., New York, N.Y. 10019
9. *Let's Read and Find Out Books.* Thomas Y. Crowell, 666 Fifth Ave., New York, N.Y. 10019
10. *Science I Can Read Books.* Harper & Row, 10 E. Fifty-third St., New York, N.Y. 10022

SOURCES OF SCIENCE TRADE BOOKS AND REFERENCE BOOKS

The following are some publications that contain bibliographies of science trade and reference books for use by teachers and children. Specific title references are listed at the end of each science chapter later in this textbook.

1. *A Bibliography of Books for Children.* Association for Childhood Education International, 3615 Wisconsin Ave., N.W., Washington, D.C. 20016
2. *A Bibliography of Science Courses of Study and Textbooks, K-12.* National Science Teachers Association, 1742 Connecticut Avenue, N.W., Washington, D.C. 20009

3. *The Science Book List for Children.* American Association for the Advancement of Science, 1776 Massachusetts Ave., N.W., Washington, D.C. 20036

SOURCES OF FILMS AND FILMSTRIPS

Many companies produce excellent films and filmstrips for elementary science. Although some large school systems buy films and have their own film library, usually films are rented. Many museums and state universities have their own rental libraries, and will send catalogs upon request. The catalogs include a short summary of the contents of each film to help in making the appropriate selection. A number of industrial firms also produce excellent films that can be rented at a very nominal cost. Filmstrips, which are much less expensive than films, are usually bought.

The following are some of the companies that produce or distribute films and filmstrips. They will all send catalogs upon request.

1. ACI Films, 35 West 45th St., New York, N.Y. 10036
2. AIMS Instructional Media Services, Inc., P.O. Box 1010, Hollywood, Calif. 90028
3. Association Films, Inc., 866 Third Ave., New York, N.Y. 10022
4. Audio-Visual Associates, 180 East California Boulevard, Pasadena, Calif. 91105
5. Bailey Films, 6509 DeLongpre Ave., Hollywood, Calif. 90028
6. Barr Productions, P.O. Box 7-C, Pasadena, Calif. 91104
7. Bell Telephone, Film Library (see local business office)
8. Churchill Films, 662 N. Robertson Blvd., Los Angeles, Calif. 90069
9. Coronet Films, 65 E. South Water St., Chicago, Ill. 60601
10. Denoyer-Geppert Audiovisuals, 5235 Ravenswood Ave., Chicago, Ill. 60640
11. Walt Disney Productions, Educational Media Co., 800 Sonora Ave., Glendale, Calif. 91201
12. Educational Dimensions Group, Box 126, Stamford, Conn. 06904
13. Educational Film Library, 43 W. 61st St., New York, N.Y. 10023
14. Encyclopedia Britannica Educational Corp., 425 N. Michigan Ave., Chicago, Ill. 60611
15. Eye Gate House, Inc., 146-01 Archer Ave., Jamaica, N.Y. 11435
16. Family Films, 5823 Santa Monica Boulevard, Hollywood, Calif. 90038
17. Film Associates of California, 11559 Santa Monica Blvd., Los Angeles, Calif. 90025
18. Filmstrip House, 432 Park Ave. South, New York, N.Y. 10016
19. Gateway Productions, 1859 Powell, San Francisco, Calif. 94111

20. Heritage Filmstrips, 89-11 63rd Dr., Rego Park, N.Y. 11374
21. International Film, 332 S. Michigan Ave., Chicago, Ill. 60604
22. Journal Films, 909 W. Diversey Pkway, Chicago, Ill. 60614
23. Learning Corporation of America, 1350 Avenue of the Americas, New York, N.Y. 10019
24. Library Filmstrip Center, 3033 Aloma, Wichita, Kansas 67211
25. McGraw-Hill Book Co., Text-Film Dept., 1221 Avenue of the Americas, New York, N.Y. 10020
26. National Geographic Society, Film Dept., Seventeenth & M Sts., N.W., Washington, D.C. 20036
27. Parents' Magazine Films, Inc., 52 Vanderbilt Avenue, New York, N.Y. 10017
28. Shell Oil Co., Film Library, 1433 Sadlier Circle West Drive, Indianapolis, Ind. 46239
29. Society for Visual Education, Inc., 1345 W. Diversey Parkway, Chicago, Ill. 60614
30. Sterling Films, 241 East 34th St., New York, N.Y. 10016
31. Time-Life Films, Multimedia Div., Time-Life Bldg., New York, N.Y. 10020

For Discussion

1. What are some of the more important criteria to use in choosing an elementary science textbook series?

2. What arguments would you use in trying to get your school to adopt multiple texts in elementary science?

3. What kinds of materials do you think would be available in the school, home, drug store, dime store, hardware store, supermarket, and so forth, that could be useful in teaching elementary science?

4. What provisions should be made for the storage, care, and distribution of science equipment in the elementary school?

5. Construct a floor plan for a room to be used as a Science Center. Include provisions for experimenting, storage, conferences, library materials, display shelves, chalkboards, and bulletin boards.

6. What are the advantages and disadvantages of using science kits?

(Fred Leavitt/Van Cleve)

CHAPTER 8

EVALUATION *of* SCIENCE LEARNING

EVALUATION is the *how well* of science teaching and learning. Earlier chapters discuss the *why, what,* and *how* of science teaching. These factors are the three components considered essential for the effective teaching and learning of science in the elementary school. The term *why* refers to the objectives of elementary science, the term *what* to the science content and process, and the term *how* to the methods of teaching science.

228]

Evaluation, then, refers to how well the children have learned the science concepts and conceptual schemes, become proficient in the key operations of science and the scientist, and developed desirable behavioral outcomes. Evaluation also refers to how well the teacher has used appropriate learning techniques in the classroom. It should be quite obvious, therefore, that evaluation is vital to teaching and learning, and must be an integral part of the science program in the elementary school if the program is to be effective.

Prerequisites for Effective Evaluation

ALTHOUGH there are several excellent textbooks on evaluation and testing techniques available to the elementary school teacher, the role of evaluation in elementary science should be discussed briefly now. Science is still comparatively new in the elementary school. The transition from incidental and unstructured science programs to planned programs with definite scope and sequence is taking place slowly. There is general agreement about the objectives of elementary science, and there is also a trend toward consistency in content, methods, and grade placement.

If evaluation of science in the elementary school is to be effective and successful, a number of prerequisites must be met.

APPRAISAL OF ALL THE OBJECTIVES

Evaluation requires more than testing for simple recall or factual knowledge. Evaluation should attempt to appraise all the objectives of elementary science. These objectives include both the learning of science content and process, and the development of desirable behaviors. Consequently, it is imperative that the elementary school teacher become thoroughly familiar with the objectives of elementary science.

To evaluate effectively the children's growth in knowledge and understanding of science content, the teacher must know the key science concepts and conceptual schemes, together with the facts, laws, and principles that make up these concepts and conceptual schemes. To evaluate effectively the development of process and desirable behaviors, the teacher must first know exactly what behaviors are entailed in solving problems, in thinking critically and creatively, and in developing scientific skills, attitudes, appreciations, and interests. These behaviors must then be stated simply and clearly, in *specific behavioral terms,* so that they can be easily tested or observed.

CONTINUOUS EVALUATION

Usually, teachers tend to do most of their evaluation toward the end of a unit. However, good teaching and learning call for continuous evaluation by both the teacher and children. For the teacher it should be apparent that objectives, content and process, and methods in elemen-

(Barbara Van Cleve)

Evaluation should appraise the learning of content.

tary science are interrelated and interdependent. As a result, the teacher
should constantly evaluate the objectives of the science program, the
content and process being learned, and the methods and materials being
used to see whether the children are achieving the objectives of the
program. The teacher should also constantly evaluate the evaluation
techniques themselves. On the other hand, the children should constantly evaluate their growth in science learning and in behaviors, their
strengths and their weaknesses, and their progress both with relation to
their individual abilities and with the abilities of their classmates.

VARIETY OF PURPOSES

Most of the purposes for which evaluation may be used can be classified under three main categories. First, evaluaton can be used to
appraise achievement. Here the teacher tries to determine how well the
children have learned the science content and developed desirable
behaviors.

Second, evaluation can be used for diagnostic purposes. As such, evaluation can help identify children's strengths and weaknesses. The
teacher can then redirect the learning activities and work toward correcting the weaknesses. Evaluation can determine how well the children can work individually and in groups. This evaluation can be carried on by both the teacher and children. Evaluation can also be used
as a pretest to explore and plan for future instruction. Finally, the
teacher can use evaluation to diagnose the effectiveness of the teaching
methods being used. This technique enables the teacher not only to

learn whether other methods should be used when planning future learning activities, but also to learn which methods are most effective for a particular group of children.

Third, evaluation can be used for predictive purposes. In this case the teacher tries to predict the children's behavior and achievement in the future or under different conditions. This kind of evaluation is becoming more important as a guide for placement in team teaching, tracks, or other forms of homogeneous grouping.

VALIDITY

During the school year the teacher will have ample opportunity to use a variety of techniques to evaluate progress in elementary science. When using these techniques the teacher should clearly know what each technique can and cannot do. No matter which technique the teacher selects and uses, the teacher should always be concerned about two characteristics that determine how effective the technique really is

One characteristic is the validity of the technique. Validity is the degree with which a technique measures what it intends to measure. In other words, when the teacher uses an evaluative technique, is the technique really testing what the teacher wants to test? For example, if the teacher wants to find out if the children have learned how the position of the fulcrum in a first-class lever will make a difference in the amount of effort exerted, the teacher should carefully select a test question or situation that will clearly indicate that this is what the teacher is evaluating. One way this evaluation could be done would be to make a line drawing of a first-class lever, showing a weight at one end of the lever, an effort at the other end, and a fulcrum at a certain position between them. The children would then be asked to predict the effect of the fulcrum's position on the effort exerted.

RELIABILITY

Reliability is the second characteristic the teacher should consider when deciding how effective an evaluative technique is. Reliability is the accuracy and consistency with which a technique measures what it is measuring. In other words, when the teacher uses an evaluative technique, how well does the technique measure what the teacher wants to test? No technique can have real validity unless it also has reliability.

The need for reliability can be shown quite clearly with the example just described, that of the effect of the fulcrum's position on the effort exerted in a first-class lever. If the teacher asks the children to predict this effect on the basis of just one position of the fulcrum, the answer will give the teacher no real assurance that the children really know what will happen. It is necessary to use several positions of the fulcrum and have the children successfully predict what will happen in each case for the teacher to be confident that the children definitely know how the fulcrum's position affects the effort exerted. Thus, the greater the number of test questions or situations is, the higher the reliability will be. And the higher the reliability is, the more consistent the children's scores will be.

USE OF APPROPRIATE TECHNIQUES

In science, as in other areas of the elementary school curriculum, there is no one evaluative device that can be used exclusively for appraising the teaching and learning process. All kinds of techniques are necessary to measure the children's progress in learning science content and process, their growth in solving problems and thinking critically, and their development of desirable behaviors. Even though some

(Barbara Van Cleve)

Evaluation should appraise the learning process.

of our existing techniques may need refining, the teacher is still more likely to obtain a fairly adequate and complete picture of each child by using a variety of devices rather than by relying upon just one form or instrument.

There are many different methods of evaluation available to the elementary school teacher. These methods may be classified under three broad groups, namely, oral methods, written methods, and observation methods. Within each group there are a variety of instruments that can be used. Teachers vary in their preference of instruments. However, regardless of which instrument is preferred, there are certain points the teacher should keep in mind when selecting or constructing an evaluative device.

First, the teacher should remember that the objectives to be evaluated are more important than the kind of instrument to be used. Actually, the desired objectives or outcomes will play an important part in the kind of instrument selected. For example, evaluation of the skill in manipulating apparatus might require an appropriate experiment or demonstration, accompanied by observation. A problem situation could be used to test the ability to reason and interpret, form hypotheses, and draw conclusions. Evaluation of knowledge or identification might require an objective test.

Second, good test questions are difficult and time-consuming to prepare, and they should be constructed with much thought and care. Third, all tests contain an element of subjectivity, some tests more than others. The subjectivity can be largely restricted by checking the findings from one technique with those findings obtained from other techniques.

Oral Methods of Evaluation

ALTHOUGH objective tests are quite popular in the elementary school, there is still a great reliance upon oral methods of evaluation. Such methods are especially necessary in the lower elementary grades. The most commonly used oral techniques seem to be question and answer, discussion, and oral reports.

The question-and-answer method, also known as the recitation method is widely used, although it has serious drawbacks as an evaluative technique. It can reach only a limited number of children, and therefore it is quite likely to have a low reliability. Not only is it unreliable because of inadequate sampling, but also because the questions will usually vary in difficulty. Moreover, there is a tendency for teachers to test for recall or memorization of facts when using this technique.

Discussion is much more effective. It can involve a larger number of children at one time. When properly conducted, discussion can be useful in appraising the children's knowledge of science content, in determining scientific attitudes and other behaviors, and in diagnosing the children's strengths and weaknesses. Some teachers combine question and answer skillfully with discussion to obtain a highly effective evaluative instrument.

Oral reports can be another useful means of evaluation. Suggestions for using this technique successfully in the classroom have been described in detail in Chapter 4, "Methods of Teaching Science."

Written Methods of Evaluation

WRITTEN methods of evaluation have a definite place in the elementary science program. These methods include the use of essay tests, objective tests, and written reports. Usually, there is a tendency for elementary teachers to ignore the use of essay tests or questions, confining themselves primarily to simple objective tests, especially true-false tests, and written reports. This failure to use essay questions is a mistake because essay questions have unique functions, lending themselves well to effective evaluation.

Because essay questions involve more abstract thinking and because the technique of written expression is still comparatively new for the children, it may be wise to use essay questions mostly in the upper elementary grades. The best arrangement seems to be a combination of objectives and essay questions, with approximately one essay question offered per test.

Discussion of written methods of evaluation in this chapter will be limited only to essay and objective tests. Written reports have already been discussed in Chapter 4, "Methods of Teaching Science."

ESSAY QUESTIONS

Essay questions have distinct advantages. They can be constructed quickly. They can be used to measure how well children can analyze problems, think critically, recall and select previous knowledge, organize and present thoughts or ideas, arrive at conclusions, and show creativity and originality. They can also be quite helpful to the teacher in diagnosing partially understood science concepts or incorrect interpretations.

Essay questions have definite disadvantages as well. They do not allow for adequate sampling because only a few questions can be asked at one time. As a result they tend to have low validity and reliability. They take much time to correct. They are often worded so that they are vague and ambiguous. They can be scored in a highly subjective manner. The teacher often will either have a rudimentary scoring key or no key at all. As a result the children's marks on essay questions may be affected by such extraneous factors as neatness, grammar, spelling, or the children's previous performances (halo effect).

With a little care, some of these disadvantages can be eliminated, especially vagueness, ambiguity, and unreliable scoring. In such cases the chief difficulty seems to be the way in which the essay question is constructed. So many teachers do not spend enough time or effort to word the questions carefully and completely. Instead they tend to ask broad, almost meaningless, "discussion" questions. Typical examples are as follows:

1. Discuss tides and their effects.
2. Discuss friction and how it affects us.

Such questions can be very difficult for children to answer. They give the children no direction so that the children do not have a clear idea of what the teacher wants or expects of them. At the elementary school level the children are not particularly adept at organizing and presenting their thoughts or understandings. When left to their own devices, the children are likely to turn in a wide variety of responses. Some answers may be short and incomplete. Other answers may be quite detailed, rambling, and lengthy, perhaps with much extraneous material. These kinds of answers are hard to grade because they are so highly disorganized.

The difficulty may be greatly alleviated if the teacher takes time to give the children some direction. One method, which has proved to be quite helpful, is for the teacher to divide the essay question into a number of parts. Each part is worded clearly and carefully, asking for specific information pertaining to the major concepts called for in the essay question. The difference in approach is immediately obvious when the same two essay questions listed above are now written as follows:

1. Every day the waters of the ocean rise and fall to give us high tides and low tides.
   a. What causes these high tides and low tides?
   b. Why do we get two high and two low tides a day?
   c. Why are some high tides higher than others at certain times?
2. Friction is a common occurrence in our daily life.
   a. What causes friction?
   b. How can friction be increased?
   c. How can we reduce friction?
   d. What are some of the useful effects of friction?
   e. What are some of the harmful effects of friction?

Notice how much easier it will now be for the children to attack these questions. They know exactly what the teacher wants of them, yet the teacher has given them no clues or answers, only directions. Furthermore, the parts of the essay question are presented so that the children's answers will provide a logically organized sequence of concepts. This method may set up a habit pattern that will be helpful to the teacher when showing the children how to organize their thinking and writing. Finally, this improved type of essay question is much easier to grade. The teacher can examine each part of the question, determining how many key ideas are involved and what they are worth. From this examination the teacher can arrive at a much more objective scoring key, thus reducing subjectivity.

PROBLEM-SITUATION QUESTIONS

The essay questions described above usually call for explanation, description, or identification. Problem-situation questions are also essay questions, but are more concerned with attempting to measure the behaviors involved in solving problems and thinking critically. Such questions have already become popular in the high school and junior high school, and are now beginning to be found in the elementary school.

Perhaps the simplest form of the problem-situation question is a picture or a diagram drawn on poster board and shown to the class. Each picture contradicts a science concept or principle, and the children are asked what is wrong with the picture. In order to know what is wrong, the children must have a clear understanding of the science concept or concepts involved. Examples of this type of question would be to ask the children what is wrong with a picture showing a magnet holding a wooden pencil, a picture showing a compass with the needle pointing to the west, and a picture showing the sun shining on a plant with the leaves and stem turned away from the sun.

A very popular form of the problem-situation question is more commonly known by many teachers as a "thought" question. Here the children are asked either to explain familiar and new phenomena around them, or to make predictions on the basis of changed conditions. This procedure is excellent for finding out if the children have really learned science principles rather than just memorized them. At the same time the children are required to think critically by observing closely the elements involved in the phenomenon, recognizing the science area to which it belongs, mentally reviewing concepts that seem to be pertinent, and then selecting the concept that explains the phenomenon satisfactorily.

The following are examples of such thought questions:

1. During the summer why does a swimmer feel cooler when coming out of the water on a windy day than on a calm day, even though the temperature is the same during both days?
2. In the summer why do we get a breeze that blows in from the land in the morning and from the ocean in the afternoon?
3. When your mother cannot unscrew the metal cover from a bottle, even after tapping it, why will pouring hot water over the cover often succeed in loosening it?
4. What would happen to conditions on earth if the earth did not turn on its axis?
5. What would happen to conditions on earth if the earth's axis were not tilted?

(Lawrence Manning/Van Cleve)

Problem situations lend themselves to effective evaluation.

A more complicated form of problem-situation question describes a situation in varying detail. Several reasons, all apparently logical, are offered to explain the situation. The children are asked to consider the reasons carefully, select the correct one, and explain why each of the other reasons could not be correct.

The following has often been used as an example of this kind of question:

> One evening, during a thunderstorm, a boy walks into his room and sees that his table lamp has fallen over. He sets the lamp upright again and flips the switch to see if the lamp is all right. Just then there is a violent flash of lightning. The lamp does not light up, but now the overhead light in his room goes out. The boy flips the lamp switch back and forth. The switch clicks, but the lamp does not light up. The boy looks out the window and notices that the lights are still on in his friend's house next door.
>
> Which one of the reasons given below is the most likely to explain why the table lamp did not light up? Explain why the other reasons could not be correct.
>
> 1. The filament inside the bulb was broken.
> 2. The light switch did not work.
> 3. There was a short circuit in the wires connected to the lamp.
> 4. The flash of lightning put out the lights in the neighborhood.

Questions of this type can be extremely effective evaluative devices. They help determine how well the children can classify and interpret the data properly, weigh the evidence, recall science concepts, formulate hypotheses, check both the interpretations and the hypotheses against the data, and arrive at conclusions that can be justified. However, very few, if any, ready-made questions of this type are available. They are difficult to prepare, and their construction taxes the ingenuity of the teacher. Yet their value can be so great that they are worth the time and effort expended.

OBJECTIVE TESTS

Objective tests are short-answer tests. There are four types of items generally associated with such tests, namely, true-false, completion, multiple-choice, and matching items. An objective test may consist exclusively of items of one type only, or it may include items of two, three, or even all four kinds. These tests are used more commonly in elementary science than all other tests.

The advantages of using objective tests are numerous. They can be designed to evaluate specific outcomes, and still be scored very objectively. Also, many questions can be asked in a relatively short testing time. As a result, the objective test tends to have high validity and reliability. Because of its objectivity, the test can be scored very quickly

and easily. Extraneous factors, such as grammar and neatness, do not
interfere with the scoring; and subjectivity—with its partiality or halo
effect—is reduced. Finally, the objective test can be used for a wide
variety of purposes. These include the evaluation of achievement in
learning science content, the identification of strengths and weaknesses
in science knowledge, and the prediction of behavior and achievement
in the future or under different conditions.

On the other hand, objective tests have drawbacks. Unless they are
carefully thought out and worded, the test items may be obvious, mis-
leading, or ambiguous. An even more serious limitation is the strong
tendency of teachers to construct the tests so that they are primarily
directed toward the evaluation of isolated bits of knowledge and memorization or cheap recall, all of which constitute superficial learning. It
may be hard work to prepare good objective test items, but, after they
are prepared, they can be used over and over again.

A good objective test has several characteristics. Some of the more
pertinent ones are as follows:

1. It should be constructed as carefully as possible, keeping in
   mind the objectives to be evaluated.
2. It should bring out the best thinking and efforts of the children,
   rather than encourage guessing or bluffing.
3. It should be as objective as possible.
4. It should have adequate sampling.
5. It should have a high validity and reliability.
6. It should contain items that are brief and easy to read, to avoid
   ambiguity and confusion.
7. It should contain carefully worded items, to avoid questions
   that mislead, are obvious, give cues to answers for other questions, or provide clues because of transparent grammar, word
   form, or phrasing.
8. It should include items of varying difficulty so that the teacher
   can measure individual learning differences in the children.
9. It should give directions that are simple, clear, and complete.
10. It should be easy and quick to score.

TRUE-FALSE ITEMS

With items of this type the children indicate by a T and F (or + and
o) whether the sentence is true or false. Examples of true-false items are
as follows:

DIRECTIONS: The following sentences are either true or false. If a
sentence is true, put a T on the blank line. If a sentence is false, put an F on the line instead.

_____ 1. A cirrus cloud looks like a large puff ball of cotton.
_____ 2. A dry cell changes chemical energy into electrical
energy.

[239

True-false items are the most widely used objective test items. They are extremely popular because they are easy to construct and very objective, many can be put on a single page, and the scoring is very quick and easy. However, the true-false test is the objective test most criticized because of its decided drawbacks. Most true-false items call for rote memory or cheap recall, rather than broad understandings. They encourage guessing. The questions are often obvious, vague, or tricky. Sometimes the items are worded so that they supply clues. Sentences containing such words as "all," "none," "always," or "never" are usually false. Those sentences that contain "some," "generally," "may," or "should" are usually true.

The quality of true-false items can be improved if the teacher devotes much care in preparing the test sentences, trying to relate them as much as possible to significant science concepts rather than to unrelated facts. Also, guessing may be discouraged by modifying the directions so that, if the sentence is false, the children must replace an underlined word with another word that will make the sentence true. The following shows how the two true-false items described above can be modified in this manner:

> DIRECTIONS: The following sentences are either true or false. If a sentence is true, put a T on the blank. If a sentence is false, on the blank line put another word that will take the place of the underlined word in the sentence and will now make the sentence true.
>
> _____ 1. A cirrus cloud looks like a large puff of cotton.
> _____ 2. A dry cell changes chemical energy into electrical energy.

COMPLETION ITEMS

In this type of item the children are required to fill in a blank line, which will complete the sentence. The following are examples of completion items:

> DIRECTIONS: Complete each sentence by writing the word or words that make the sentence correct.
>
> _____ 1. The layer of atmosphere closest to the earth is called the _____.
> _____ 2. When the moon passes between the sun and earth, the kind of eclipse we get is called _____.
> _____ 3. The point around which a lever turns is called a _____.

Completion items are also very widely used and quite popular. They are easy to construct and can be highly objective. They are also easy and quick to score. Unfortunately, most of these items also call for memorization and recall. When constructing completion items, the teacher should avoid making indefinite and ambiguous statements. Moreover, the blank line in the sentence should call for only one word or at most a very short phrase. Otherwise the item will be very difficult to score, especially if the answer is partially correct. Most teachers find these items easier to score if the omitted word or phrase is placed at the end of the sentence.

MULTIPLE-CHOICE (SELECT-THE-BEST-ANSWER) ITEMS

These items usually consist of either an incomplete sentence followed by several possible completions or a direct question followed by several possible answers. As a rule, four possible completions or answers are offered, all equally plausible and appropriate, and the children are required to select the one that is most appropriate. Examples of multiple-choice items are as follows:

DIRECTIONS: Choose the word or words that will best complete the sentence. Put the letter of the best answer on the blank line beside the sentence.
_____ 1. A flame is a mass of burning
(a) heat;   (b) gas;   (c) liquid;   (d) solid.
_____ 2. If all four strings were equally tight, the one that would make the lowest-pitched sound would be
(a) short and thick;   (c) long and thick;
(b) short and thin;   (d) long and thin.

Multiple-choice items are generally considered the best type of objective test items. Although they are more difficult to prepare, they can be much more valid and reliable than true-false or completion items. When properly designed, the items can evaluate understanding of major concepts, reasoning and judgment, the ability to see relationships, and the ability to apply science principles to explain familiar or new phenomena. Multiple-choice tests are well liked by the children, can be very objective, and are easy and quick to score.

Some forms of problem-situation questions are really multiple-choice items, with the additional requirement that the children justify their selection of the correct answer.

MATCHING ITEMS

A matching item is essentially a group of multiple-choice items arranged in two columns; the children are asked to associate the items. The following is an example of a matching item.

DIRECTIONS: In the blank space next to each word in the first column put the letter of the best answer from the second column.

[241

_____ 1. nutcracker
_____ 2. block and tackle
_____ 3. knife
_____ 4. door handle
_____ 5. ramp
_____ 6. tweezers

a. first-class lever
b. inclined plane
c. second-class lever
d. screw
e. pulley
f. wedge
g. wheel and axle
h. third-class lever

Matching items are well suited for determining if the children can associate science principles with examples of the principles, materials with their uses or function, and persons with discoveries or events. These items are very compact so that many can be put on one page. However, they often tend to test primarily memory or recall, and they are tedious and time-consuming to prepare.

It is usually wise to have more items in one column than in the other, for two reasons. First, if there are five items in each column and a child matches the first four correctly, the child gets the fifth answer without having to work. Second, if both columns have the same number of items and a child matches one pair of items incorrectly, the child must automatically get a second pair incorrect.

A variation of the matching item is to have a diagram or picture with numbered or lettered parts. The children are asked to identify each part and/or describe its function. Although this kind of item is aimed primarily toward recall, it does serve to inform both the teacher and children how much the children know and have yet to learn.

Standardized Science Tests

A NUMBER of standardized elementary science tests are now available. These tests have been prepared by test specialists for nationwide use. Norms for each grade level have been developed so that teachers using the test can compare the achievement of their pupils with the achievement of other groups of children.

These tests have a high reliability, so that the scores are consistent from one administration of a test to another. The tests also enable teachers to find out how their children stand as compared to the national norm. When a test is given in a large school system, it is possible to find out how the children in one district compare with those of another district. Some of the tests make it possible for the teacher to identify specific areas of strength and weakness of individual children.

However, there are some limitations to the use of these standardized tests. Many tests are concerned primarily with the remembering of facts rather than with concepts. The tests may not be valid with respect to the relevance of their contents to the objectives of a particular school system's science program. The tests usually cannot be used to evaluate the teacher's effectiveness or the success of a particular unit of study.

The best source of information about elementary science and other standardized tests can be found in *The Mental Measurements Yearbook* (Oscar K. Buros, ed.), which is published periodically by the Gryphon Press, Highland Park, New Jersey. The following are some of the more widely used standardized science tests:

Coordinated Scales of Attainment: Science Test. Educational Test Bureau, Minneapolis, Minn.

Every Pupil Test: Elementary Science and Health. Ohio Scholarship Tests, State Department of Education, Columbus, Ohio.

Every Pupil Scholarship Test: Elementary Science. Bureau of Educational Measurements, Kansas State Teachers College, Emporia, Kansas.

Metropolitan Achievement Tests: Intermediate Science Test. Harcourt Brace Jovanovich, New York, N.Y.

National Achievement Tests: Elementary Science, Forms A and B. Psychometric Affiliates, Chicago, Ill.

Standardized Science Tests: A Descriptive Listing. National Science Teachers Assn., Washington, D.C. (Describes almost all standardized tests available and gives sources for them.)

Sequential Tests of Educational Progress: Science, Forms 4A and 4B. Educational Testing Service, Cooperative Test Division, Princeton, New Jersey.

SRA Science Achievement Test: Elementary Science. Science Research Associates, Chicago, Ill.

Stanford Achievement Test: Intermediate Science Test. Harcourt Brace Jovanovich, New York, N.Y.

Methods for Observation of Behavior

OBSERVATION of behavior is a valuable method of evaluation because it supplies evidence that cannot usually be obtained by the other evaluative methods, and thus it helps give the teacher a more complete appraisal of the child. As a result, it plays a vital role in the evaluation of the children's growth in understanding science concepts, in performing the key operations of science and the scientist, and in acquiring desirable behavioral outcomes. It can also be of great value in determining the effectiveness of the teaching-learning process, and in ensuring the successful administration of the entire science program.

The use of observation of behavior is often ignored by teachers who either are not aware of its potentialities or are reluctant to accept it as a valid evaluative device. Teachers are constantly observing children and drawing conclusions about the children's changes in behavior. Yet many of the same teachers, by being concerned about the apparently high degree of subjectivity of these observations, are inclined to think that the observations lack both validity and reliability. Consequently, the belief has become widespread that observation of behavior is an unreliable method of evaluation.

The element of subjectivity, when making observations can be greatly reduced, or even eliminated, if the teacher will take certain precautions. First, the teacher should be familiar with objectives and behavioral outcomes described in Chapter 1, "Objectives of Elementary Science." These behaviors must be expressed in *specific terms* so that they can be easily observed and identified. This procedure will enable the teacher to gather evidence that is objective and concrete. Second, the teacher should give every child an equal number of opportunities to show whether growth in desirable behaviors has taken place.

Third, if the teacher is aware of the subjectivity in this kind of evaluation and conscientiously tries to avoid it, there will be less possibility of bias in the observations. Fourth, the teacher should keep in mind that quality of behavior will vary greatly among children at different grade levels in the elementary school. Standards must be different, then, for children of different age groups. For example, first-graders cannot manipulate materials or follow instructions as well as third-graders, and the third-graders will not perform as well as sixth-graders. Consequently, the teacher should not look for perfection as much as for steady growth.

There are several techniques available for observing and recording behaviors. Some of the more common techniques include descriptive records, checklists, and rating scales. Regardless of which technique is used, in all cases the teacher should keep a permanent record of each child's growth in behavior. These records should be consulted periodically to give the teacher some indication of how well the children are doing and what can be done to help them. At appropriate intervals the teacher should have a conference with each child to make him aware of his progress and his strengths and weaknesses.

ANECDOTAL RECORDS

In this technique the teacher records a short statement or two, describing a particular remark or action by a child that showed evidence of changed behavior. The statement should be recorded as soon as possible after the observation was made. In time the teacher will have accumulated enough material about each child to furnish pertinent and significant information about the child's growth in desirable behaviors.

RECORDING REMARKS VERBATIM

This technique is better than the technique of using anecdotal records because it tells precisely what the children said. But there is one drawback. It is difficult for the teacher to write down remarks verbatim while discussion is going on, and it is time-consuming as well. This problem can be somewhat alleviated by either using tape recordings at periodic intervals or by remembering the most pertinent remarks and adding them verbatim to the anecdotes as soon as possible.

CHECKLISTS AND RATING SCALES

These techniques are essentially similar, and they are quite popular with teachers. They can be used to evaluate both individual and group behavior when children are conducting experiments, giving reports, solving problems, and participating in discussion or other classroom activities. The results can be used to evaluate each child's progress over a period of time, and also to compare the progress of one child with that of the rest of the class.

For each activity the teacher makes a list of desirable behaviors involved in the activity. In a checklist the teacher then checks off whether or not the behaviors were manifested by the children. Some teachers prefer to assign a code number or letter to each behavior. As each child demonstrates evidence of one of the behaviors, the teacher enters the appropriate number on a sheet containing a list of all the children's names. The procedure enables the teacher to gather evidence quickly and as often as is considered feasible. In time the teacher will have a sizable cumulative record of changes in behavior.

Rating scales are like checklists, except that they introduce the factor of quality. The same behaviors can be rated on a scale ranging from excellent to poor. The teacher thus has the added advantage of being able to evaluate the degree with which the children are developing desirable behaviors. Rating scales, like checklists, can also be used to evaluate individual and group behavior.

For Discussion

1. Why is the present trend in evaluation in science education for the elementary school shifting away from the emphasis upon evaluation for just knowledge of science content?

2. How is it possible to do an adequate job of evaluation by observation of behavior (anecdotal records, recording statements verbatim, and so forth) with all that an elementary school teacher has to do in one day?

3. Do you believe that a teacher's evaluation of her pupils should be based upon their performances according to individual abilities or upon their performances compared to the rest of the children? Why?

4. Which techniques would be most effective for evaluating the learning of content and process in grades K–3? In grades 4–6?

5. What other advantages and disadvantages, beside those already described, are there in using standardized elementary science tests?

PART TWO

BASIC
SCIENCE INFORMATION,
LEARNING ACTIVITIES,
and BIBLIOGRAPHY

EARTH *and the* UNIVERSE

CHAPTER 9

The UNIVERSE

THE SUN

I. THE NATURE OF THE SUN

  A. The sun is a star.
    1. It is only one of the billions of stars that make up the universe.
    2. It is not a large star, but it looks larger than the other stars because it is so much closer to us on earth.
  B. The sun is much larger than the earth.
    1. The diameter of the sun at its equator is about 1,380,000 kilometers (860,000 mi), which is about 109 times larger than the diameter of the earth.
    2. If the sun were a hollow ball, we could place more than a million earths into it.
  C. The sun is about 150,000,000 kilometers (93,000,000 mi) from the earth.

II. THE SUN GIVES OFF ENERGY

  A. Like all other stars, the sun gives off a vast amount of radiant energy, including light.
  B. This energy does not come from ordinary burning.
  C. The energy comes from a nuclear reaction that takes place inside the sun.
    1. Astronomers believe that hydrogen atoms in the sun keep combining to form helium atoms.
    2. While the helium is being formed, some of the hydrogen is converted into tremendous amounts of energy.
  D. The energy from a hydrogen bomb is produced the same way except that the reaction in a hydrogen bomb lasts for a moment, and the reaction in the sun goes on all the time.
  E. This reaction makes the sun very hot.
    1. Its surface temperature is about 6000° Celsius (10,800° Fahrenheit).
    2. Its temperature at the center is estimated to be about 15,000,000° Celsius (27,000,000° Fahrenheit).

III. THE PARTS OF THE SUN

  A. The sun is not a solid body like the earth, but it is a huge ball of very hot gases.
  B. Three layers of gases, which are often called the sun's atmosphere, surround the main body of the sun.
  C. The first layer is called the **photosphere.**
    1. The photosphere glows brilliantly and is the source of most of the sun's light.
    2. The photosphere goes up 160 to 320 kilometers (100 to 200 mi).
  D. Beyond the photosphere is a second layer of gas called the **chromosphere.**
    1. This layer of gas is bright red, and it can only be seen when the sun is blotted out in total eclipse.

2. It rises about 16,000 kilometers (10,000 mi) above the photosphere.

E. A silvery halo of gases, called the **corona,** surrounds the chromosphere.

1. The corona also can only be seen when there is a total eclipse of the sun.

2. The corona reaches out very far in all directions.

3. The corona is very thin and glows with a weak light.

IV. SOLAR STORMS

A. The sun seems to have violent storms on its surface.

B. These storms are tied up with the presence of **sunspots** on the sun's surface.

C. Sunspots are dark spots that seem to move slowly from east to west across the sun's surface.

1. Actually, the sunspots stand still while the sun turns on its axis.

2. The spots look dark because they are a little cooler than the surrounding, glowing gases.

3. The spots usually appear in the photosphere near the sun's equator.

4. Their size can range from 800 kilometers (500 mi) to more than 80,000 kilometers (50,000 mi).

5. They often form in pairs, and sometimes they form in large groups.

D. Astronomers think sunspots are caused by magnetic storms within the sun.

E. These magnetic storms often affect the earth.

1. The storms send out electrified particles from the sun's surface.

2. When these electrified particles strike the earth's ionosphere, they interfere with radio, television, and long-distance telephone communication.

3. These particles also strike the earth's lower atmosphere and produce the brilliant show of colored lights near the north and south poles.

4. These colored lights are called the north-ern lights (Aurora Borealis) and the southern lights (Aurora Australis).

F. Sunspots usually appear in 11-year cycles, in which the sunspots reach their greatest number every 11 years.

G. Very often a **solar flare** accompanies a sunspot.

1. The solar flare is a bright cloud of gas that leaps up from the sun's surface.

2. The flare may cover an area of a billion square kilometers and shoot up as high as 480,000 kilometers (300,000 mi).

3. The flare becomes 20 to 30 times brighter than the other areas of the sun, and then it fades away in about an hour.

H. When the sun's rotation carries a sunspot to the edge of the sun, **solar prominences** are sometimes formed.

1. These prominences send great streamers of bright gas far out into the sun's atmosphere.

2. These prominences are not as violent as flares, but they move more gracefully.

3. Some prominences suddenly rush back to the sun, whereas, others seem to be blown off the sun.

I. Although it seems fairly obvious that a big disturbance is going on inside the sun, scientists do not yet know the exact reason for the appearance of sunspots, followed by solar flares and prominences.

V. THE FUTURE OF THE SUN

A. Astronomers think that the sun has been producing energy for about five billion years.

B. They also think that the sun will continue to produce energy for many billions of years more.

C. When about 15 percent of its hydrogen atoms have been used up, the nuclear reaction inside the sun will speed up, slowly at first, then faster and faster.

D. The inside of the sun will get hotter, and the sun will expand to about 100 times its size.

E. Meanwhile the surface of the sun will become cooler, and its color will change to orange and then red.

F. When enough of the hydrogen has been used up, the sun will suddenly collapse and become so small that both its size and its light will be only a small amount of what they originally were.

G. The sun will become cooler and cooler, and fainter and fainter, until it finally becomes completely dark and cannot be seen at all.

THE SOLAR SYSTEM

I. THE MEMBERS OF THE SOLAR SYSTEM

A. The solar system is made up of a group of heavenly bodies that move around the sun.
  1. These heavenly bodies are called **satellites.**
  2. A satellite is any heavenly body that travels around another heavenly body.
B. The principal members of the solar system are nine large bodies called **planets.**
  1. The word *planet* means "wanderer."
  2. The planets were given this name because they seemed to wander over the sky instead of appearing to stay in a fixed position like the stars.
  3. The names of the planets, in order of their increasing distance from the sun, are—Mercury, Venus, Earth, Mars, Jupiter, Saturn, Uranus, Neptune, and Pluto.
  4. Between Mars and Jupiter there is a belt of several thousand bodies of different sizes, called **asteroids** or **planetoids,** which also move around the sun.
C. Planets are not stars.
  1. Stars shine because they give off light, but planets shine because they reflect the light of the sun or other stars.
  2. Planets are much smaller than the sun and most of the other stars.
D. The planets travel in an elliptical (oval) path, called an **orbit,** around the sun.
  1. All the planets move or revolve in a counterclockwise direction (from west to east) around the sun.
  2. The time needed for a planet to make one complete turn, or revolution, around the sun is called the planet's **year.**
E. The planets spin like a top, or rotate, as they travel around the sun.
  1. They rotate around an imaginary line, called an **axis,** which runs through the north and south poles of the planet.
  2. The time needed for a planet to make one complete rotation on its axis is called the planet's **day.**
F. Many of the planets have their own smaller satellites that revolve around them.
  1. The satellites of the planets are called **moons.**
  2. Astronomers have discovered 35 moons: one for Earth, two for Mars, fourteen for Jupiter, ten for Saturn, five for Uranus, two for Neptune, and one for Pluto.
G. The planets are all alike in certain ways.
  1. They are all satellites of the sun.
  2. They all revolve in a counterclockwise direction (from west to east).
  3. They all rotate on their axis.
  4. They all obtain their energy from the sun.
  5. They all contain the same basic chemicals, although the proportions are different.
H. The planets are also different in many ways.
  1. They differ in their distance from the sun.
  2. They differ in size and heaviness.
  3. They differ in the kind and amount of atmosphere they have.

4. They differ in the time it takes them to revolve around the sun.
5. They differ in the time it takes them to rotate once on their axis.
6. They differ in the number of moons they have.

I. In the solar system there are also bodies, called **comets,** which have long oval-shaped orbits that bring the comets very close to the sun and then far out into the solar system.

J. In the solar system there are also billions of fast-moving rocks of all sizes, called **meteors.**

II. How the Solar System Was Formed

A. Many theories have been proposed to explain how the solar system was formed.

B. All these theories fall into two general classes.
1. One class claims the solar system was formed quickly and violently.
2. Another class claims the solar system was formed slowly and moderately.

C. The older **planetismal theory** proposes that long ago the sun and another star collided.
1. Large amounts of matter were thrown out of the sun.
2. This hot material then cooled to form the planets.

D. The newer **planetismal theory** proposes that the two stars did not collide, but only came very close to one another.
1. The pull of gravity of one star upon the other raised great tides on the sun.
2. The materials that were lifted from the sun remained as large spiral arms.
3. As these spiral arms cooled, they broke away from the sun, shrank, and became the planets.

E. All the different versions of the planetismal theory have one serious weakness.
1. Astronomers believe that the material taken or raised from the sun or any other star would be millions of degrees hot.

2. This hot material would quickly spread out into space as a gas before it could cool to form the planets.

F. The **exploding star theory** proposes that long ago the sun had a companion star beside it.
1. The companion star exploded and most of the material was thrown into space.
2. However, a cloud of gas was left behind, held by the sun's pull of gravity.
3. From this cloud the planets were formed.

G. The **nebular theory** proposes that the sun and planets were formed from a large, whirling cloud of hot gas and dust.
1. As the cloud cooled and grew smaller, it began to spin faster, causing rings of matter to break away from the outer edge of the cloud.
2. The main part of the cloud eventually became our sun, and the rings became the planets.

H. The major weakness of the nebular theory is that mathematicians do not believe it is possible for rings of material to collect into balls of matter large enough to form the planets.

I. The **dust cloud theory** is the theory that seems to be most in agreement with the facts, and is the most widely accepted theory today.
1. According to this theory the solar system was formed from huge clouds of gases and dust.
2. The atoms in these gases and dust were pushed toward one another by the light from the stars, and they formed larger particles.
3. These larger particles were attracted to each other by the pull of gravity on one another, and they began to crowd together.
4. Large numbers of these particles came together, shrank, and grew heavier.
5. Eventually a huge ball of material was formed, with its particles all packed closely together.
6. The hydrogen atoms in the center of the ball began to collide with each other,

and gradually a nuclear reaction took place, with the formation of helium and the release of radiant energy, including light.

7. In this way the star, our sun, was formed.

8. Part of the cloud of dust and gases, from which the sun was formed, stayed all around this new star and slowly rotated.

9. Later, huge whirlpools formed in this rotating cloud, causing smaller globes of gases and dust.

10. Each globe eventually cooled into a planet that still revolves around the sun because of the original motion of the rotating cloud of gases and dust.

11. The satellites of the planets were formed the same way from this rotating cloud.

J. The dust cloud theory is very popular because it explains satisfactorily not only the formation of the sun and the solar system, but also the formation of all the stars and their satellites.

III. WHY THE PLANETS REVOLVE AROUND THE SUN

A. There are two conditions, affecting each planet at the same time, that keep the planets revolving around the sun.

B. One condition is the **inertia** of the moving planet.

1. According to Newton's first law of motion, a body that is at rest will stay at rest unless some force starts it moving, and a body that is moving will continue to move in the same direction and at the same speed unless some force makes it change direction or speed.

2. Because the planet is already moving, if no force were acting on it, the planet would continue straight into space and far away from the sun.

C. The second condition is the sun's **pull of gravity** on the planet.

1. According to Newton's law of gravitation, every body in the universe attracts or pulls on every other body.

2. The heavier a body, the greater is its pull on another body.

3. Because the sun is heavier than any of its planets, the sun's pull of gravity on any given planet is very much more powerful than the planet's pull of gravity on the sun.

4. If only gravity were acting on the sun and each planet, the more powerful pull of the sun's gravity would make the planet rush quickly to the sun and burn up.

D. However, both inertia and gravity affect each planet at the same time and in such a way that the planet travels neither straight into space nor toward the sun, but instead it travels around the sun.

IV. MERCURY

A. Mercury is the planet nearest the sun, and it is about 58 million kilometers (36 million mi) away from the sun.

B. It is the smallest planet, with a diameter of about 4800 kilometers (3000 mi).

C. It can be seen near the horizon shortly after sunset or just before sunrise.

D. It is sometimes called an "evening" or "morning" star, even though it is really a planet.

E. It revolves around the sun once every 88 days, so its year is much shorter than Earth's year.

F. It rotates on its axis once in 59 days, so it has very long days and nights.

G. The side that faces the sun is very hot, and the temperature can be as high as 700° Celsius (1300° Fahrenheit).

H. The side that faces away from the sun is not as cold as would be expected.

1. The temperature of this dark side is about 20° Celsius (68° Fahrenheit).

2. The dark side does not completely cool off after being in the sun's heat for the long period of daylight.

I. Neither side of Mercury has any air or water.

V. VENUS

A. Venus is the next closest planet to the sun, and it is about 107 million kilometers (67 million mi) from the sun.

B. It is about as big as Earth, with a diameter of about 12,200 kilometers (7600 mi).

C. It also can be seen near the horizon as an "evening" star just after sunset and as a "morning" star just before sunrise.

D. It revolves around the sun once every 225 days, so it has a short year.

E. It rotates on its axis only once in about 250 days.

F. The hottest part of the sunlit side is about 600° Celsius (1100° Fahrenheit).

G. The dark side that faces away from the sun is not as cold as expected.

  1. On this side the coolest part is about 200° Celsius (360° Fahrenheit).

  2. Apparently strong winds transfer heat from the sunlit to the dark side.

H. Venus is surrounded by thick clouds that hide most of its characteristics.

  1. The clouds trap the sun's heat to give Venus its high surface temperature.

  2. Scientists think that the clouds contain 10 percent carbon dioxide gas and a small amount of water vapor.

I. Venus is the brightest body in the sky next to the sun and moon because its thick clouds reflect so much sunlight.

VI. EARTH

A. Earth is the next planet after Venus, and it is about 150 million kilometers (93 million mi) from the sun.

B. It has a diameter of about 1260 kilometers (7900 mi).

C. It revolves around the sun once every 365¼ days, and it rotates on its axis once every 24 hours.

  1. At its equator Earth rotates at a speed of about 1600 kilometers (1000 mi) an hour.

  2. This speed becomes smaller and smaller as we move from the equator toward the poles.

D. Earth has one moon.

E. Earth is the only planet where the temperature of its surface is usually between the boiling and freezing points of water, so most of the water on Earth is found in the liquid state.

VII. MARS

A. Mars is the next planet after Earth, and it is about 225 million kilometers (140 million mi) away from the sun.

  1. It is the next closest planet to Earth.

  2. Every 15 years the paths of Mars and Earth come closer, and there are only about 56 million kilometers (35 million mi) between them.

B. It is a small planet, with a diameter of about 6700 kilometers (4200 mi).

C. It revolves around the sun once every 687 days, so its year is almost twice the length of Earth's year.

D. It rotates on its axis once every 24½ hours, so its day is about the same as Earth's day.

E. It has two small moons.

F. It has seasons just like Earth.

  1. An ice cap at its poles grows smaller in summer and larger in winter.

  2. The surface also changes color with the seasons, growing darker in the summer and lighter in the winter.

G. About three fourths of Mars' surface is covered with bright reddish or yellowish patches, which astronomers think may be deserts.

H. Mars has an atmosphere, but its air is much thinner than that on Earth, so there must be very little oxygen and water vapor in its air.

I. The average temperature on Mars is about 50° below zero Celsius (−68° Fahrenheit), as compared to an average of about 15° Celsius (59° Fahrenheit) on Earth.

  1. During the day the temperature at the equator of Mars may be as warm as 20° Celsius (68° Fahrenheit).

  2. At night, however, the temperature drops

to about 70° below zero Celsius (−94° Fahrenheit).

VIII. THE ASTEROIDS OR PLANETOIDS

A. The asteroids or planetoids are a belt of about 25,000 bodies that circle the sun between Mars and the next planet Jupiter.

B. They are called *asteroids* because they look like stars, and *planetoids* because they are really "little planets."

C. All the asteroids revolve around the sun in the same direction as the larger planets.

D. The asteroids are irregular lumps of rock, perhaps mixed with metal, that differ in size and brightness.
1. Only a few are larger than 160 kilometers (100 mi) in diameter.
2. A few hundred are 16 to 160 kilometers (10 to 100 mi) in diameter.
3. The rest are less than 16 kilometers (10 mi) in diameter, with some perhaps only as large as basketballs.

E. Scientists do not know how the asteroids were formed.
1. Some think they are part of a planet that exploded.
2. Others think that they are the parts of two planets that collided and exploded.
3. Still others think that they are part of the solar system that never grew large enough to form an ordinary planet.

IX. JUPITER

A. Jupiter is the next planet after Mars, and it is about 776 million kilometers (485 million mi) from the sun.

B. It is the largest planet, with a diameter of about 139,000 kilometers (87,000 mi), about eleven times that of Earth.

C. It appears as a very large "star" in the sky.

D. It revolves around the sun once in about 12 years.

E. It rotates on its axis once in about 10 hours, so it has a very short day.
1. Its speed of rotation is very fast, that is, about 40,000 kilometers (25,000 mi) an hour at its equator, or about twenty-five times faster than Earth's speed of rotation at the equator.
2. This rapid rotation makes Jupiter flatten at its poles and bulge at its equator even more than Earth does.

F. It has 14 moons.

G. Through the telescope Jupiter does not show a solid surface, but it does show shifting belts of clouds.
1. These belts run parallel with its equator.
2. These clouds are spread out in colored bands, which keep changing their patterns and colors.

H. Scientists think that Jupiter has a solid core of rock and metal that is about 64,000 kilometers (40,000 mi) in diameter.
1. This core is surrounded by a layer of compressed ice.
2. Next are the thick layers of different gases, one on top of the other, which make up Jupiter's atmosphere.

I. Jupiter has a red spot on it that changes in brightness from time to time.

J. A very thin, flat, faintly visible ring of what seems to be boulder-sized debris is encircling Jupiter.

X. SATURN

A. Saturn is the next planet after Jupiter, and it is about 1430 million kilometers (890 million mi) from the sun.

B. It has a diameter of about 120,000 kilometers (75,000 mi).

C. It revolves once around the sun in about 29½ years.

D. It rotates on its axis once in about 10 hours.

E. It has ten moons.

F. It is a planet of unusual interest because it is surrounded by seven broad but thin rings that revolve at different speeds around its equator.
1. Most scientists think that the rings are made of pieces of rock like that of the asteroids.
2. These rocks may be as small as grains of sand or as large as small islands.

XI. Uranus

A. Uranus is the next planet after Saturn, and it is about 2900 million kilometers (1800 million mi) from the sun.

B. It has a diameter of about 50,000 kilometers (31,000 mi).

C. It revolves once around the sun in about 84 years.

D. It rotates on its axis once in about 10 hours.

E. It has five moons.

F. Eight rings surround it, but unlike Saturn the rings are narrow and quite faint.

G. Like Jupiter, Uranus seems to have a solid core, surrounded by an icy layer and a thick atmosphere of gases.

H. Uranus rotates in a different position from all other planets.

   1. All the other planets rotate on an almost vertical axis, like a top that is spinning the regular way.

   2. Uranus rotates on an almost horizontal axis, like a top spinning on its side.

XII. Neptune

A. Neptune is the next planet after Uranus, and it is about 4500 million kilometers (2800 million mi) away.

B. It has a diameter of about 53,000 kilometers (33,000 mi).

C. It revolves once around the sun in about 165 years.

D. It rotates on its axis once in about 16 hours.

E. It has two moons.

F. Scientists call Uranus and Neptune the twin planets.

   1. They both are about the same size.

   2. They both are made up of a solid core, surrounded by an icy layer and an atmosphere of the same kinds of gases.

XIII. Pluto

A. Pluto is the last, and most recently discovered, planet in the solar system.

B. It is about 5900 million kilometers (3700 million mi) from the sun.

C. Astronomers are not quite certain of its diameter, but they think it is about 2900 kilometers (1800 mi).

D. It revolves once around the sun in about 248 years.

E. It has one moon.

F. Astronomers do not yet know how long it takes Pluto to rotate once on its axis.

XIV. Comets

A. Comets are bodies that revolve around the sun in long, oval-shaped orbits.

   1. The sun is at one far end of the comet's orbit.

   2. The comet's orbit cuts across the paths of the planets' orbits.

B. The comet has a head and a tail.

C. The comet's head is made up of small rocks and dust, mixed with frozen gases.

D. The comet does not have a tail until it nears the sun.

   1. As the comet nears the sun, the frozen gases in the comet's head melt and are changed into vapor.

   2. The comet's tail is actually this very thin stream of melted gases.

   3. The tail may be millions of kilometers long and so thin that stars can be seen through it.

   4. When the comet travels away from the sun, the gases freeze again and the tail disappears.

E. The head and tail of the comet reflect the light of the sun.

F. The pressure of the light from the sun makes the tail point away from the sun when the comet both approaches and leaves the sun.

G. The comet gains speed as it nears the sun and the sun's pull of gravity on it becomes stronger, then it slows down again as it travels away from the sun and the sun's pull of gravity on it becomes weaker.

H. Some comets return rather quickly, but others take much longer to return.
1. Encke's comet returns every 3½ years.
2. Halley's comet returns every 76 years.
I. Some comets never return because they either waste away as material is forced out of the head into the tail or they are destroyed as they come near a larger body.
J. Scientists do not know exactly how comets were formed.

XV. METEORS AND METEORITES

A. **Meteors** are rocks in the space through which the earth passes as it travels around the sun.
1. These rocks may be tiny grains of sand or they may be vary large.
2. Some meteors are metallic and have iron and nickel in them.
3. Other meteors are stony and have silicates in them.
B. Billions of meteors enter the earth's atmosphere each year, traveling about 160,000 kilometers (100,000 mi) an hour.
C. About 80 kilometers (50 mi) above the earth the friction of the air rubbing against the meteors makes them white hot, and they begin to burn.
1. The burning meteors make a bright streak of light as they travel through the air.

2. These bright streaks are called "shooting stars."
D. Most meteors burn up before they reach the earth's surface.
E. Those meteors that strike the earth's surface before they burn up are called **meteorites.**
F. If meteorites are large enough, they can form a large crater when they strike the earth.
1. Meteor Crater in Arizona and Chubb Crater in Canada were probably made by meteorites.
2. One meteor, weighing about 55,000 kilograms (60 tons), has been found in Africa and is still in the original spot where it struck the earth.
3. Another meteor, weighing about 32,000 kilograms (35 tons), is in the American Museum of Natural History in New York City, and was found by Admiral Peary in Greenland in 1894.
G. The meteors that reach Earth seem to come from two different sources.
1. Most of them are probably small bits of rocks, like those in the belt of asteroids between Mars and Jupiter, that are traveling through space.
2. Some also seem to come from comets because swarms of meteors called **meteor showers** are seen every time the earth crosses the path of a comet.

THE EFFECTS OF THE SUN ON THE EARTH

I. THE SUN CAUSES THE YEAR ON EARTH

A. The earth travels in an elliptical (oval) path, called an **orbit,** around the sun.
B. It moves around, or revolves, in this orbit in a counterclockwise direction (from west to east).
C. The time needed for the earth to make one complete turn, or revolution, around the sun is called the earth's **year.**

D. The earth's year is 365¼ days.

II. THE SUN CAUSES DAY AND NIGHT ON EARTH

A. The earth also spins like a top, or rotates, as it travels around the sun.
1. It spins around an imaginary line, called an **axis,** which runs through the earth's north and south poles.
2. It rotates on its axis in a counterclock-

wise direction (from west to east).

3. The time needed for the earth to make one complete turn on its axis is called the earth's **day**.

4. The earth's day is 24 hours.

B. At the equator the earth rotates at a speed of about 1600 kilometers (1000 mi) an hour.

1. This speed becomes smaller and smaller as we move farther away from the equator toward the north and south poles.

2. Halfway between the equator and the North pole the speed is about 1280 kilometers (800 mi) an hour.

C. The earth gets its light from the sun.

1. Because the earth is shaped like a ball, only one half can be lighted at one time.

2. When one half is lighted by the sun, the other half is in darkness.

3. The half that is turned toward the sun has daylight, or daytime.

4. The half that is turned away from the sun is in darkness, or has nighttime.

5. Every 24 hours, as the earth rotates once on its axis, one part of the earth will have had one period of daytime and one period of nighttime.

D. Because the earth turns from west to east, the sun seems to move across the sky from east to west.

E. Therefore, the sun seems to rise in the east and set in the west.

F. The sun looks bigger when it is just rising or setting.

1. When it is seen against buildings or other objects on the horizon, it looks bigger by comparison.

2. When it is by itself high in the sky, it looks smaller.

G. Also, when the sun is rising or setting, it looks orange or reddish.

1. This phenomenon happens because rays of red light can pass through the thicker part of the earth's atmosphere much more easily than rays of blue light.

2. When the sun is low on the horizon, the light from the sun must travel a much greater distance through the thicker part

of the earth's atmosphere than when the sun is overhead.

3. The blue rays in sunlight cannot get through this greater distance of air, and they are reflected and scattered by the dust particles in the air.

4. The reflection and scattering of the blue light by the dust particles is what makes the sky appear blue.

5. However, the red rays in sunlight can still pass through.

6. The sunlight now has less blue in it, so the sun looks orange or reddish.

7. When the sun is high in the sky, all the rays of light can get through this shorter distance of air so the sun looks white.

III. The Sun Causes the Seasons on Earth

A. The earth's axis is tilted at an angle of 23½ degrees, and it is always pointed toward Polaris, the North Star.

B. Because of this tilt and because of the earth's revolution around the sun, the earth has different seasons of the year.

C. When the northern hemisphere is tilted toward the sun, the northern hemisphere has summer.

1. Summer begins on June 21, which is called the **summer solstice.**

2. In the summer the sun's rays are shining directly upon the northern hemisphere.

3. The stronger, direct rays cover a smaller amount of the earth's surface, and the surface becomes quite hot.

4. Because of the tilt of the earth's axis, the northern hemisphere also gets more daylight than darkness in the summer, so the days are longer than the nights.

5. More daylight means that the northern hemisphere gets the stronger, direct rays of the sun for a longer time, which also helps the northern hemisphere become warmer in the summer.

6. When it is summer in the northern hemisphere, the north pole has daylight all 24 hours.

D. When the northern hemisphere is tilted

away from the sun, the northern hemisphere has winter.

1. Winter begins on December 22, which is called the **winter solstice.**
2. In the winter the sun's rays are shining at a slant upon the northern hemisphere.
3. The weaker, slanted rays now cover a large amount of the earth's surface, and the surface is not heated as much.
4. Because of the tilt of the earth's axis, the northern hemisphere gets more darkness than daylight in the winter, so the nights are longer than the days.
5. Longer nights mean that the northern hemisphere gets the sun's rays for a shorter time, which also helps the northern hemisphere become much colder in the winter.
6. When it is winter in the northern hemisphere, the north pole is in darkness all 24 hours.

E. When it is summer in the northern hemisphere, the southern hemisphere is tilted away from the sun and the southern hemisphere has winter.

F. When it is winter in the northern hemisphere, the southern hemisphere is tilted toward the sun and the southern hemisphere has summer.

G. In the spring and fall, the earth is tilted neither toward nor away from the sun.

1. Neither hemisphere receives strong rays of sunlight, and it is not summer or winter in both hemispheres, but rather somewhere between.
2. At the same time, the days and nights are just as long.
3. The northern hemisphere spring begins March 21, the **vernal equinox;** fall begins September 23, the **autumnal equinox.**

IV. The Sun Is a Source of Energy
 for the Earth

A. The sun sends out radiant energy in all directions.

B. Only a very small part of the sun's energy travels to the earth.

C. This small part heats the earth and gives it light.

D. The sun's energy also makes it possible for green plants to make food.

1. These plants make food by a process called **photosynthesis.**
2. In this process the leaves of the plant take carbon dioxide from the air and water from the soil and change these materials into carbohydrates and oxygen.
3. The energy of sunlight and the green coloring of the leaves, called **chlorophyll,** cause the chemical reaction of photosynthesis to take place.
4. Photosynthesis is important because animals eat plants, and human beings eat both animals and plants.
5. The food we eat gives us energy and makes us grow.

E. Without the energy of sunlight, the earth would be frozen and lifeless.

F. The sun's energy is stored in natural fuels such as wood, coal, oil, and gas.

1. Coal is the remains of fernlike plants that died, were buried under masses of soil and rock, and then subjected to tremendous heat and pressure.
2. Oil and gas are the remains of tiny animals and plants that died, were buried under layers of mud and sand, and then subjected to tremendous heat and pressure.
3. When natural fuels are burned, they give off energy in the form of heat and light—the same energy that originally came from the sun and was stored in the plants by photosynthesis.

V. The Sun Causes the Weather

A. The sun does not heat every part of the earth equally.

1. The parts of the earth near the equator are heated more than the parts of the earth away from the equator because the rays of light become more slanted farther away from the equator.
2. Because the sun's rays heat only one half

of the earth at one time, a regular heating and cooling cycle is produced each day.

3. The land on earth is heated and cooled more quickly than water.

4. Dark-colored bodies of land absorb more heat than light-colored bodies.

B. This unequal heating causes movements of great masses of air.

1. Some air masses are cold, and others are warm.

2. The cold air masses come from the polar regions, and the warm air masses come from the tropical regions.

3. The warmer, lighter air from the equator rises and moves toward the poles, and the colder, heavier air from the poles moves down toward the equator.

4. The colder, heavier air masses have greater pressure than the warmer, lighter air masses.

C. At the same time the heat of the sun causes some of the water on earth to evaporate into the air and become a gas called water vapor.

1. The warmer the air masses, the more it expands, and the more water vapor it can hold.

2. The colder the air mass, the more it will contract, and the less water vapor it can hold.

D. When warm air masses meet cold air masses, the warm air masses are cooled, and some of the water vapor comes out of the air, or condenses, in different forms, called **precipitation.**

E. The combination of moving air masses, differences in air pressure, and changing amounts of water vapor in the air—all caused by the sun—are responsible for the different kinds and changes in weather throughout the earth.

THE MOON

I. THE NATURE OF THE MOON

A. The moon is a very large ball of rocky material that revolves around the earth.

B. It is about 3500 kilometers (2160 mi) in diameter.

1. Its size is about one fourth of the diameter of the earth.

2. In volume, the moon is about one fiftieth of the size of the earth.

C. It weighs about one eightieth as much as the earth.

D. Its pull of gravity is about one sixth of that of the earth.

1. A broad jumper who can jump 7 meters (23 ft) on earth will jump 42 meters (138 ft) on the moon.

2. A high jumper who can jump 2 meters (6½ ft) on earth will jump 12 meters (39 ft) on the moon.

3. The high jumper would not fall any harder from the greater height because he would weigh only one sixth as much on the moon as he did on earth.

E. The moon has no atmosphere.

1. Without air there is no wind on the moon.

2. Without air sounds cannot travel, so no sounds can be heard on the moon.

F. The moon has no water or water vapor.

1. There can be no brooks, rivers, lakes, or oceans on the moon.

2. There can be no clouds or weather.

G. The temperature on the surface of the moon varies greatly, depending upon whether it is day or night.

1. During the day the temperature is very hot, and it may be as high as 104° Celsius (220° Fahrenheit).

2. At night the temperature is very cold, and it may be as low as 70° below zero Celsius (−94° Fahrenheit).

H. The surface of the moon is made up of smooth plains, jagged mountains, and craters.

I. There are about 30 plains on the side of the moon that we can see.
1. These plains cover about half the surface of this side, and they are shaped like rough circles.
2. The plains appear dark because they do not reflect as much sunlight as the mountains.
3. Early astronomers thought the dark areas were seas and the light areas were continents.

J. The surface of the moon is covered with a layer of dust particles, and possibly small rocks, that have fallen from space.
1. A man who walked on the moon would kick up a cloud of loose dust.
2. The dust would fall back to the surface just as quickly as heavy pieces of stone or iron because there would be no air to slow down the falling dust.

K. There are many mountain ranges on the moon.
1. Most of these ranges are concentrated in the moon's southern hemisphere.
2. Some of the mountains are more than 7500 meters (25,000 ft) high.
3. Astronomers have measured the height of these mountains by the length of the shadows they throw on the moon's surface.
4. The mountains are very jagged because there are no forces of wind and water to wear them down to smoother and gentler forms.

L. There are also many rounded depressions, called craters, spread throughout the plains of the moon's surface.
1. More than 30,000 craters have been counted on photographs taken of the moon.
2. The largest craters are as much as 240 kilometers (150 mi) in diameter.
3. In most craters the floor of the crater is much lower than the plains surrounding them.

4. In some craters the floor of the crater is above the level of the surrounding plain.
5. Some craters have smooth floors, but others have very rough floors, often with smaller craters in them.
6. All the craters look much like the volcanic craters that are found on earth.

M. Some craters have a number of light-colored streaks, called rays, that radiate in all directions.
1. The most conspicuous rays come from the crater called Tycho.
2. Because the rays throw no shadow, they must be made by a material spread out over the moon's surface.

N. There are two common theories about how the craters were formed.
1. The volcanic theory proposes that they are the craters of extinct volcanoes that were active a long time ago.
2. The meteorite theory proposes that they were formed by large meteorites that struck the moon's surface.

O. The meteorite theory is weakened by the fact that no new craters have been formed since the moon has been observed by telescope, even though the moon is being continually bombarded by meteorites.

P. The moon's surface is also covered with many cracks, called rills.
1. They are usually about 1 kilometer (⅝ mi) wide and of unknown depth.
2. Some rills are crooked, but others run in a straight line.

II. THE MOTION OF THE MOON AROUND THE EARTH

A. The moon travels around the earth in a path, or orbit, that is shaped like an ellipse.
B. The moon moves or revolves around the earth in a counterclockwise direction (from west to east), which is the same direction as the earth revolves around the sun.
C. Because the moon's orbit is elliptical, the moon comes a little closer to the earth on one side of its orbit than on the other side.

1. The point of its orbit nearest the earth is called its **perigee,** and the point of its orbit farthest away from the earth is called its **apogee.**
2. At perigee the moon is about 350,000 kilometers (220,000 mi) from earth.
3. At apogee the moon is about 400,000 kilometers (250,000 mi) from earth.
4. Its average distance from earth is 384,000 kilometers (240,000 mi).

D. The moon keeps revolving around the earth because two conditions are affecting the moon at the same time.
1. The two conditions are the same ones that keep the planets revolving around the sun.
2. One condition is earth's **pull of gravity** on the moon, which would make the moon rush to the earth if this were the only condition affecting the moon.
3. The other condition is that of **inertia,** which would make the moving moon travel away from the earth if there were no earth's pull of gravity on it.
4. However, both inertia and gravity affect the moon at the same time and in such a way that the moon travels neither straight into space nor toward the earth, but around the earth instead.

E. The moon revolves around the earth at a speed of about 3500 kilometers (2200 mi) an hour.
F. The time needed for the moon to revolve once around the earth is called the **lunar month.**
1. It actually takes the moon 27¼ days to revolve once around the earth.
2. However, because the earth is revolving around the sun at the same time, the moon seems to take a longer time to revolve once around the earth.
3. It takes 29½ days for the moon to go from one full moon to the next.
4. Calendars use 29½ days as the time for one lunar month.

G. The moon rises about 50 minutes later each day.
1. This difference in rising time happens because the moon moves in its orbit in the same direction (counterclockwise) as the earth rotates.
2. Therefore, it takes the earth a little longer each day to turn around so that the moon can be seen farther in its orbit.

H. The moon rotates on its axis in a counterclockwise direction (from west to east).
1. It takes the moon just as long to rotate once on its axis as it does to revolve once around the earth.
2. This rotation time means that the moon's day is just as long as its month.
3. Thus, the moon has about two weeks of daylight at one time, followed by about two weeks of nighttime at one time.

I. Because the earth rotates in a counterclockwise direction (from west to east), the moon seems to rise in the east, move across the sky, and set in the west.
J. Like the sun, the moon looks bigger when it is rising or setting.
1. The moon also looks bigger when seen against buildings or other objects on the horizon.
2. It then looks smaller when seen by itself high in the sky.

K. When the moon is rising and setting, it looks yellow or even orange.
1. This phenomenon, as with the sun, happens because rays of red light can pass through the thicker part of the earth's atmosphere much more easily than rays of blue light.
2. When the moon is low on the horizon, the light from the moon must travel a greater distance through the thicker part of the earth's atmosphere than when the moon is overhead.
3. The blue rays in moonlight cannot get through this greater distance of air, and they are reflected and scattered by the dust particles in the air.
4. However, the red rays in moonlight can still get through.
5. The moonlight now has less blue in it, and thus the moon looks yellow or orange.

6. When the moon is high in the sky, all the rays of light can get through this shorter distance of air, and thus the moon looks white.

L. Because of the moon's rotation on its axis only once in a lunar month, all we see is one half of the moon's surface.

1. Actually we see a little more than one half (about 59 percent) of the moon's surface.

2. Because the moon's orbit is slightly tilted, we can look a little over the moon's top and under its side as it travels around.

3. We can also see a little more of each side of the moon because the moon moves faster at perigee than at apogee.

4. At perigee, when the moon increases its speed, the earth lags behind and we see a little more of one side of the moon.

5. At apogee, when the moon decreases its speed, the earth moves ahead and we see a little more of the other side of the moon.

M. Moon flights and earth satellite pictures taken of the other side of the moon seem to show that it is not much different from the side that we can see.

III. PHASES OF THE MOON

A. The moon does not give off light, but it shines because it reflects the light of the sun.

B. Because the moon is so close to the earth, it is the second brightest heavenly body in the sky.

C. The side of the moon that faces the sun is always brightly lighted, but the side that is turned away from the sun is in darkness.

D. The lighted side of the moon cannot be seen in the daylight, except in early morning and late afternoon, because the sun's light is very bright and because the earth's atmosphere scatters the sunlight in all directions.

E. As the moon travels in its orbit around the earth, we see different amounts of the moon's lighted surface.

F. These changes in the amount of lighted surface that we see are called the **phases of the moon.**

G. During the calendar lunar month, when the moon makes one complete revolution around the earth in 29½ days, the moon passes through all its phases, going from completely dark to completely bright, and then back to completely dark again.

H. When the moon is between the earth and the sun, the dark side of the moon is turned toward the earth and we cannot see the moon at all.

1. This phase is called the **new moon.**

2. Sometimes the new moon can be seen faintly because it is lighted by earthshine, which is sunlight reflected from the earth onto the moon.

3. The new moon rises at sunrise and sets at sunset.

I. About one or two days later, as the moon continues to revolve from west to east around the earth, a little of the lighted side of the moon can be seen on earth.

1. The part of the moon that can now be seen is shaped like a thin **crescent.**

2. The rest of the dark part of the moon can be seen faintly because of the earthshine.

J. About one week after the new moon, one half of the lighted side of the moon can be seen on earth.

1. This phase is called the **first quarter,** or **half moon.**

2. The first quarter rises at noon and sets at midnight.

K. A few days later almost all of the moon's lighted side can be seen on earth, and this phase is called the **gibbous moon.**

L. About two weeks after the new moon, all of the lighted side of the moon can be seen.

1. This phase is called the **full moon.**

2. Now the earth is between the moon and the sun.

3. At full moon, the moon has made one

half of one complete revolution around the earth.

4. The full moon rises at sunset and sets at sunrise.

M. When the moon goes from new moon to full moon and the amount of lighted surface that we see grows larger, we say the moon is **waxing**.

N. When the moon goes from full moon to new moon and the amount of lighted surface that we see grows smaller, we say that the moon is **waning**.

O. About one or two days after the full moon, the amount of the lighted side that we can see grows smaller, or wanes, and we see a gibbous moon again on earth.

P. About one week after the full moon, only one half of the moon's lighted side can be seen on earth.

1. This phase is called the **last quarter**, or **half moon**.

2. The last quarter rises at midnight and sets at noon.

Q. After the last quarter the moon wanes even more until it is shaped like a crescent again.

R. About one week after the last quarter, the moon has completed one revolution around the earth and is back in its original position as a new moon.

S. The phases of the moon then start again, with the moon waxing until it becomes a full moon and then waning until it is a new moon again.

IV. THE MOON CAUSES TIDES

A. **Tides** are the rise and fall of the oceans caused by the moon's pull of gravity on earth.

1. The earth has a pull of gravity on the moon, and at the same time the moon has a pull of gravity on the earth.

2. Because the earth is larger and heavier than the moon, its pull of gravity on the moon is greater than the moon's pull of gravity on the earth.

3. The earth's stronger pull of gravity helps keep the moon revolving around the earth.

4. The moon's weaker pull of gravity affects the earth in the form of tides.

B. Tides are formed because the moon's pull of gravity on the side of the earth facing the moon makes the easily movable waters of the earth on that side bulge out toward the moon.

1. This watery bulge is called a **high tide**, or **flood tide**.

2. Because this tide is on the side of the earth facing the moon, it is also called the **direct tide**.

C. At the same time another high tide is formed on the opposite side of the earth.

1. This tide is formed because the moon not only pulls on the earth's waters nearest it, but also pulls hard on the solid part of the earth.

2. This pull leaves the water on the opposite and farthest side, where the moon's pull of gravity is weakest, bulging out behind to form another high tide.

3. Because this tide is on the opposite side of the earth, away from the moon, it is called the **opposite** tide.

D. The water that is drawn in to make bulges at these two points on earth comes from the remaining water at the opposite two points on earth.

1. The water at the opposite two points now flattens out and forms lower levels.

2. These lower levels are called **low tides**.

E. Because the earth rotates on its axis once every 24 hours, the earth has two high tides and two low tides every 24 hours at different points of the earth.

F. The tide rises for about 6 hours; then it falls or ebbs for about 6 hours.

G. Because the moon rises about 50 minutes later each day, high tide and low tide also are about 50 minutes later each day.

H. At its perigee, about 48,000 kilometers (30,000 mi) closer to the earth than at apogee, the moon's pull of gravity on the earth becomes greater, so the tides are higher and lower than usual.

I. The sun's pull of gravity on the earth also causes tides on earth.

  1. However, because the sun is so much farther away from the earth, the sun's tides are weaker than the moon's tides.
  2. The sun produces tides that are a little less than half as big as the tides produced by the moon.

J. When the sun is in line with the moon, very high and very low tides are formed.

  1. These tides occur because the sun and the moon combine their pull of gravity on the earth.
  2. The sun and moon are in line with each other twice a month, at new moon and at full moon.
  3. These very high and very low tides are called **spring tides.**

K. When the sun and moon are at right angles to each other, tides that are not as high or as low as usual are formed.

  1. These tides occur because the sun's pull of gravity and the moon's pull of gravity are now working against each other.
  2. The sun and the moon are at right angles to each other twice a month, at first quarter and at last quarter.
  3. These smaller high and low tides are called **neap tides.**

L. The rise in tides differs at different parts of the earth, depending upon the kind of shoreline and ocean floor found at each part.

  1. On the open sea the rise in tides is only about 1 meter (3 ft).
  2. At Cape Cod Bay the rise in tides may be 3 meters (10 ft) at times.
  3. At the Bay of Fundy the narrow bay can produce tides that rise more than 15 meters (49 ft).

M. If man knows when the tides will be high and low, this knowledge can be useful to him.

  1. For some channels, ships arrive and leave only at high tide when the channel is deep enough to allow the ships to come and go safely.
  2. Ships like to leave port when the tide is going out so that they do not have to fight a tide that is coming in.
  3. People like to go swimming at high tide rather than at low tide.

V. ECLIPSES

A. As the sun shines on the earth and the moon, both throw a long shadow into space.

  1. The earth's shadow is about 1,400,000 kilometers (866,000 mi) long.
  2. The moon's shadow is about 384,000 kilometers (240,000 mi) long.

B. We have night on earth because we are carried around by the earth's rotation into the earth's own shadow.

C. At certain times the moon passes between the earth and the sun in such a way that people on earth cannot see the sun.

  1. This phenomenon is called an **eclipse** of the sun, or a **solar eclipse.**
  2. An eclipse of the sun happens only when there is a new moon, where the moon is between the earth and the sun.

D. In a solar eclipse the moon's shadow falls on the earth.

E. The shadow of the moon on the earth has two parts.

  1. There is a cone-shaped inner part, called the **umbra,** which is completely dark.
  2. There is also a broader outer part, called the **penumbra,** in which the light is only partially blocked.

F. The tip of the umbra only covers a very small part of the earth's surface so that only this small part of the earth's surface is in complete shadow or darkness.

  1. People who are inside the umbra see the sun become completely covered and blotted out from view.
  2. When the sun's light is completely cut off, we say that a **total eclipse** of the sun has taken place.
  3. At any given spot on earth, a total eclipse lasts about 8 minutes.
  4. During a total eclipse, the sun's corona can be seen.

G. The penumbra covers a much larger part of the earth's surface.
   1. People who are inside the penumbra see only part of the sun covered and blotted out from view.
   2. When the sun's light is only partially cut off, we say a **partial eclipse** of the sun has taken place.
H. Sometimes, especially if the moon is near apogee and the moon is in the right position to produce a solar eclipse, the moon's umbra may be too short to reach the earth's surface.
   1. When this phenomenon happens, the sun is still eclipsed, but not completely; it shows a thin ring of light around the edges.
   2. This kind of solar eclipse is called an **annular** or **ring** eclipse.
I. Total eclipses of the sun do not happen very often.
   1. For a total eclipse of the sun, the moon must be in an exact line between the sun and the earth when the moon reaches the new moon phase.

   2. This position is not reached very often, because the moon's orbit is tilted a little; consequently the moon usually passes between the earth and the sun either too high or too low for its shadow to fall on the earth.
J. Sometimes the earth passes between the sun and the moon in such a way that the earth cuts off the sunlight that the moon reflects, and the moon cannot be seen.
   1. This phenomenon is called an **eclipse of the moon**, or a **lunar eclipse.**
   2. An eclipse of the moon occurs only when there is a full moon, where the earth is between the moon and the sun.
K. In a lunar eclipse the earth's shadow falls on the moon.
   1. The moon passes quite often through the earth's rather large penumbra so that a partial eclipse of the moon happens quite often.
   2. However, because the moon's orbit is tilted, the moon does not pass through the earth's umbra very often so that a total eclipse of the moon is quite rare.

BEYOND THE SOLAR SYSTEM

I. THE STARS

A. Stars are suns in space, and they produce their own light.
B. There are countless stars in the sky, and about 3000 can be seen with the naked eye.
C. Stars are not in a fixed position, but they are moving rapidly through space in all directions.
D. Stars differ in size.
   1. Small stars, like the sun, are called **dwarfs.**
   2. Large stars, like Aldebaran and Pegasi, are called **giants.**
   3. Tremendously large stars, like Antares and Betelgeuse, are called **supergiants.**

E. Stars differ in color, depending upon their age and temperature.
   1. As the stars become older, their surfaces become cooler so that the stars change color.
   2. The youngest stars are blue-white or white, and their surface temperatures are about 7500° to 30,000° Celsius (13,500° to 54,000° Fahrenheit).
   3. Yellow star surfaces are about 6,000° Celsius (10,800° Fahrenheit).
   4. Orange star surfaces are about 4000° Celsius (7200° Fahrenheit).
   5. Red stars are the oldest stars, and have surface temperatures of about 3000° Celsius (5400° Fahrenheit).

6. Our sun is classified as a yellow star.

F. The brightness of a star depends upon its temperature, size, and distance from the earth.

1. Astronomers call the brightness of a star its **magnitude.**

2. The brighter the star, the smaller the magnitude number it will have.

3. **First-magnitude** stars are the brightest stars.

4. A first-magnitude star is two and one-half times as bright as a second-magnitude star.

5. A **second-magnitude** star is two and one-half times as bright as a third-magnitude star, and so on.

6. The faintest stars that the eye can see are **sixth-magnitude** stars.

7. Stars with a **twenty-third magnitude** have been seen with the telescope.

G. **Variable** stars are stars that flare up and become brighter, and then grow dimmer again.

1. For some stars this happens because the star has exploded.

2. For other stars this change in brightness happens because they grow larger and shrink regularly.

H. A **nova,** or "new star," is a dim star that suddenly becomes thousands of times more brilliant than it was before.

1. A nova is not really a new star, but it only seems to be new because it has suddenly become so conspicuously bright.

2. Occasionally, an unusually bright nova, in this case called a **supernova,** will appear in the sky.

3. Astronomers do not know the exact cause of a nova.

I. **Double** stars, also called **binary** stars, are two stars that are held very closely together by their pull of gravity on one another.

J. In some cases whole groups of stars, called **star clusters,** are held together by their pull of gravity on one another.

1. Some star clusters are made up of a few stars that are moving in parallel paths.

2. Other star clusters are loose collections of stars, and they are called **open clusters.**

3. **Globular clusters** are shaped like a ball or globe, and they have as many as 100,000 stars in them.

4. Clusters that are so large and thick with stars that they look like shining clouds are called **star clouds.**

K. Although stars seem to twinkle, they really do not.

1. The stars are so far away that they are only small dots of light when we look up at them.

2. Movements of the earth's air make the thin rays of light from these distant stars move back and forth, or twinkle.

L. Planets do not twinkle.

1. The planets are nearer the earth and their rays of light are thicker.

2. Movements of the earth's air do not affect these thicker rays of light.

II. CONSTELLATIONS

A. Long ago, astronomers divided the stars into groups, which made it easier to describe where a heavenly body was.

B. These groupings of stars are called **constellations.**

C. The constellations were named after gods, legendary heroes and heroines, animals, and objects.

D. Most of the constellations do not look like the persons, animals, or objects after which they were named.

E. The movement of the earth as it turns on its axis makes the constellations seem to move through the sky as if they were on a transparent globe surrounding the earth.

1. If the earth's axis were extended into space, it would also become the axis for this imaginary globe.

2. In the earth's northern hemisphere all the constellations seem to move around a point, called the **celestial north pole,**

that is directly above the earth's north pole.

3. In the southern hemisphere all the constellations seem to move around a point, called the **celestial south pole,** that is directly above the earth's south pole.

4. A star located directly on the celestial north or south pole would not seem to move.

5. The North Star, called **Polaris,** is so close to the celestial north pole that it does not seem to move at all.

6. Polaris is the last star in the handle of the Little Dipper, which is part of the constellation called the **Little Bear.**

7. All the constellations in the northern hemisphere seem to revolve around Polaris.

F. Because the earth is in different positions as it revolves around the sun, different constellations are seen at different times of the year.

G. Also, persons living in the northern hemisphere see constellations that are different from those seen by persons living in the southern hemisphere.

III. THE ZODIAC

A. The sun's path among the stars during 1 earth-year is called the **ecliptic.**

B. A strip of sky a little above and below the sun's path or ecliptic is called the **zodiac.**

C. Special names have been given to 12 star formations, one for each month of the year, in the zodiac.

1. These special star formations are known as the "signs of the zodiac."

2. In any month, an observer on earth can look toward the sun and see one particular sign of the zodiac facing him.

IV. GALAXIES

A. A **galaxy** is a large collection of stars, dust, and gas, all held together in a group by the pull of gravity.

B. The sun and the solar system are part of a galaxy called the **Galaxy.**

C. Part of the Galaxy, called the **Milky Way,** can be seen each night.

1. The Milky Way is a broad band of light stretching across the sky.

2. There are millions of stars in the Milky Way, and their light makes a milky band in the sky.

D. The Galaxy has billions of stars in it, and it has a shape that is somewhat like a flattened, circular wheel.

1. The distance across the wheel is about 100,000 light years, which is the distance light would travel for 100,000 years.

2. There are three spiral arms that curve out from the center of the Galaxy.

E. The whole Galaxy is rotating around its center at a tremendous speed.

1. All the stars in the Galaxy rotate in the same direction, but at different speeds.

2. The sun and the solar system are about 26,000 light-years from the center, or about halfway between the center and the rim of the Galaxy.

3. The sun and the solar system are moving at a speed of about 225 kilometers (140 mi) a second in a circular orbit around the center of the Galaxy.

4. The stars at the rim of the Galaxy are moving about four times as fast.

5. It takes the Galaxy about 200 million years to rotate once around its center.

F. A **nebula** is a great cloud of dust in a galaxy.

1. There are many nebulae in each galaxy.

2. Nebulae do not give off any light of their own.

3. Some nebulae are easily seen because they reflect the light of nearby stars.

4. Other nebulae are dark because they either cut off the light from stars behind them or because there are no stars nearby to light them up.

G. There are more than a billion galaxies beyond the Galaxy, all rotating at tremendous speeds.

H. Galaxies are usually found in three shapes: **irregular, spiral,** and **elliptical.**

I. Irregular galaxies have many blue-white giant stars in them and are probably young galaxies.

J. Spiral galaxies have a number of spiral arms extending from their centers.
  1. There are blue-white giant stars in the arms and red stars toward the center.
  2. Many astronomers think that a spiral galaxy forms from an irregular galaxy.
  3. As the galaxy rotates, spiral arms form and direct the younger blue-white stars toward the center of the galaxy.

K. Elliptical galaxies are shaped like an oval or ellipse and are smaller than spiral galaxies.
  1. Most of their stars are the older yellow and red stars.
  2. Many astronomers think that an elliptical galaxy forms from a spiral galaxy, where all the stars in the spiral arms have been gathered into the main body of the galaxy.

V. THE UNIVERSE IS EXPANDING

A. To astronomers the universe seems to be a tremendous expanse of space that is at least 10 billion light-years across.

B. Scattered over this space are millions of galaxies.

C. Most galaxies are separated from their neighbors by millions of light-years of space.

D. Astronomers believe that the galaxies are all moving away from each other at high speed.
  1. The galaxies that are farther away from us seem to be traveling faster than those nearer to us.
  2. Some of these galaxies are moving at a speed of more than 48,000 kilometers (30,000 mi) a second.

E. This high speed means that the space between the galaxies is steadily increasing, but the galaxies themselves remain the same size.

VI. HOW DISTANCES IN THE UNIVERSE ARE MEASURED

A. Until recently, astronomers measured the vast distances in the universe by using a unit of measurement called the **light-year.**
  1. Light travels through space at a speed of about 300,000 kilometers (186,000 mi) a second.
  2. A light-year is the distance that light travels for 1 year.
  3. A light-year is about 9600 billion kilometers (6000 billion mi).

B. Now astronomers use another unit of measurement, called the **parsec.**

C. A parsec is about 3¼ light-years, or 31,000 billion kilometers (19 billion mi).

VII. HOW THE UNIVERSE IS STUDIED

A. Scientists use different kinds of instruments to study the heavenly bodies.

B. The oldest types of instruments used have been the **telescopes.**

C. Two kinds of telescopes are used: the **refracting telescope** and the **reflecting telescope.**

D. The refracting telescope is a hollow tube with convex lenses at each end.
  1. Rays of light from a planet or a star enter one lens of the telescope and then are bent to form a small image of the planet or star.
  2. This image is then magnified by the other lens in the telescope.
  3. The largest refracting telescope, having lenses 1 meter (39 in) in diameter and weighing 225 kilograms (500 lb), is at Yerkes Observatory in Wisconsin.
  4. Refracting telescopes cannot be made with lenses larger than 1 meter (39 in) in diameter because the lenses must be supported at the rims, and larger lenses are so heavy that they sag out of shape from their own weight.

E. The reflecting telescope uses a large, curved mirror instead of a lens to collect the rays of light from a planet or star and produce an image.

1. The large curved mirror collects rays of light from a planet or star to form a small image of the planet or star.
2. This small image is then magnified by a convex lens in another part of the telescope.
3. The largest reflecting telescope, having a diameter of 5 meters (200 in) and weighing 13,150 kilograms (14½ tons), is the Hale telescope on Mount Palomar in California.
4. A reflecting telescope can be made much larger than a refracting telescope because the mirror can be supported from behind.
5. The very large mirror of a reflecting telescope helps gather and focus more light than the smaller lens of the refracting telescope.
6. With a reflecting telescope, stars more than two billion light-years away can be seen.

F. Astronomers rarely look through a telescope with their eyes; instead they use a camera that is attached to the telescope.
1. The human eye tires after a while, is not sensitive to colors when the light is dim, and cannot build images into stronger or larger ones.
2. On the other hand, the camera always works well and can use film that is very sensitive to colors and dim light.
3. The camera can also take pictures over a period of several minutes or even hours, and in this way it builds up weak images into stronger ones.
4. At the same time the photograph becomes a permanent record of the observation that was made, and it can be studied again and again.

G. Telescopes are mounted on a platform so that astronomers can take a picture of a star over a long period of time.
1. The platform always rotates at the same rate as the earth, but in the opposite direction.
2. This rotation makes the star seem to stay in the same position so that a strong, clear picture can be produced instead of a streak of light.

H. The air above the earth presents a problem to astronomers when they use telescopes.
1. The rays of light from the stars must pass through the air above the earth before they reach the telescope.
2. The air is always moving, which makes these rays bend back and forth, so that the stars seem to twinkle and cannot be seen sharply and clearly.
3. The air also has dust and water vapor, which dims the light rays from the stars.
4. If the telescopes are built high on a mountain, this location helps very much because the air higher up is thinner and has less dust and water vapor in it.

I. Temperature is also a problem to astronomers using telescopes.
1. Changes in temperature make the mirrors, lenses, and other parts of the telescope expand and contract.
2. The expansion and contraction makes the telescope operate differently from one time to another.
3. The astronomers have to adjust the telescope all the time and make corrections in their observation.

J. The **radio telescope** is able to study objects too far away to be seen with ordinary telescopes by detecting the radio waves these objects give off.
1. Radio telescopes have very sensitive receivers with very large antennas that can be pointed to any spot in the sky.
2. The antennas usually have large metal "mirrors," shaped like a bowl, that gather and focus the radio waves in the same way as the curved mirrors in reflecting telescopes gather and focus light rays.
3. The largest radio telescope, built by the United States Navy in Sugar Grove, West Virginia, is about 185 meters (600 ft) across.

K. Another important instrument that astronomers use is the **spectroscope**, which finds out what chemical elements there are in the planets and stars.

1. Light rays that enter the spectroscope pass through a prism, which breaks the light up into the colors of the spectrum.
2. Bright and dark lines can be seen in the different colored bands of the spectrum.
3. These lines always appear when certain chemicals are present in glowing gases that give off light.
4. The position and width of the lines in the different colored bands tell us what elements are present.
5. By comparing the position and width of the lines in a spectrum produced from the light of a star with those produced from the glowing gases of chemical elements that we already know, astronomers can tell what chemical elements are in the particular star.
6. Astronomers have found that the sun, planets, and most of the stars have the same kinds of elements as those found on earth.
7. Helium was first discovered in the sun by a spectroscope before it was found on earth.

LEARNING ACTIVITIES FOR "THE UNIVERSE"

THE SUN

1. *Compare the size of the sun and the earth* · Draw two circles, one with a diameter of 54½ centimeters (21⅜ in) and the other with a diameter of ½ centimeter (⅛ in). The larger circle, labeled *sun,* will be 109 times larger than the smaller circle, labeled *earth.* Place the circles 150 centimeters (93 in) apart. By letting 1 centimeter equal 1 million kilometers (or 1 inch equal 1 million miles), then the 150 centimeters (or 93 in) would indicate the distance from the sun. If the sun were a hollow ball, more than one million earths would fit inside it.

2. *Explore the source of the sun's energy* · Describe the nuclear reaction that is continually taking place inside the sun. Compare this reaction with that of a hydrogen bomb, which lasts only for a moment. Point out the difference in temperature at the surface and at the center of the sun.

3. *Investigate the parts of the sun* · Discuss its parts: the hot gases that make up the body of the sun, the layer of the photosphere, the red chromosphere above it, and the silvery corona surrounding the chromosphere. Look for a photograph of a solar eclipse that shows the corona quite clearly. Also, look for photographs showing sunspots and solar prominences.

4. *Observe sunspots* · Arrange a telescope or binoculars (at least six-power) so that it is pointing directly at the sun (Figure 9–1). This arrangement can be made by getting a long, rectangular cardboard carton from the supermarket. One side of the carton should be open to

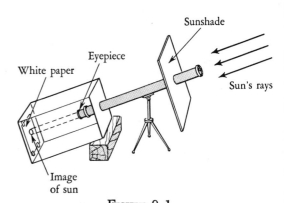

FIGURE 9–1.

ARRANGEMENT FOR OBSERVING SUNSPOTS.

allow the sunspots to be easily seen. Prop the carton on a box or other carton in such a way that the rear end is facing the sun's rays directly. In the front end of the carton make a hole large enough for the eyepiece end of the telescope or binoculars to be inserted.

If a telescope is used, make just one hole, and also make a large cardboard sunshade for the barrel of the telescope. If binoculars are used, make two holes and fasten the binoculars securely with tape to the box. Cover one of the outer binocular lenses with dark paper so that only one image of the sun will be produced inside the carton. A sunshade is not necessary when binoculars are used.

Now adjust the eyepiece of the telescope or binoculars until there is a sharp, clear image of the sun on the inside rear end of the carton. A sheet of white paper that is taped on the rear end will make the image more easily visible. The sunspots will appear on the sun's image as small, dark marks near the equator. Observe the sunspots every day at the same time. They will slowly move across the sun as the sun rotates. Note that they appear only on or near the sun's equator and never at the poles. If the sunspots seem to be moving from west to east (instead of east to west), this is because of the way the astronomical telescope operates. Also, the sunspots will be upside down.

(*Note: Do not look directly at the sun through the telescope or binoculars! You can permanently damage your vision in this way!*)

THE SOLAR SYSTEM

1. *Make diagrammatic models of the sun and the planets* · Compare the size of the planets with each other and with the sun, and also show their relative distances from the sun. To get the correct relative sizes and distances, use a model of the sun that is 27 inches in diameter, and let 1 inch represent 20 million miles. On this basis, Table 9–1 shows the proper size and distance for each planet.

TABLE 9–1. Dimensions and Distances for a Chalkboard Diagram of the Sun and Planets.

BODY	DIAMETER	DISTANCE
Sun	27″	—
Mercury	⅛″	1¾″
Venus	¼″	3¼″
Earth	¼″	4¾″
Mars	⅛″	7″
Jupiter	2¾″	2′
Saturn	2⅜″	3′ 8″
Uranus	1″	7′ 5″
Neptune	⅞″	11′ 8″
Pluto	⅛″	15′ 3″

Cut out a large cardboard or paper circle, 27 inches in diameter, and write the word *sun* in large letters across its surface. Tape this circle to one end of the chalkboard. Now draw circles on the chalkboard, each circle representing a planet. Give each circle its proper size and place it at the proper distance from the sun, as shown in Table 9–1. If the chalkboard is not wide enough, cut out paper circles and tape them on the wall beside the chalkboard. Be sure to insert a large number of dots between Mars and Jupiter to show the presence of the asteroids. Write on the chalkboard, as close to the planets as possible, such pertinent information as the name of the planet, its actual size, its distance from the sun, and the number of moons it has.

2. *Draw the elliptical shape of a planet's orbit* · Place a sheet of white paper on a flat piece of wood. Hammer two long tacks or small nails, placed 5 centimeters (2 in) apart, half-

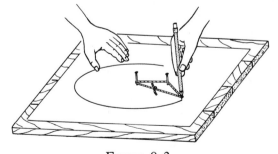

FIGURE 9–2.
DRAWING AN ELLIPSE.

way into the paper and wood (Figure 9–2). Tie a string about 25 centimeters (10 in) long into a loop. Put the loop around both nails, place a pencil inside the loop, and stretch the loop as far as possible with the pencil. Now, while keeping the string as tight as possible and the pencil point vertical, move the pencil point all the way around the loop. The pencil will draw an ellipse. This ellipse will almost be a circle, and it will be very much like the orbit of the earth around the sun. Repeat, either using a shorter loop of string or moving the tacks farther apart, and the ellipse will be more oval in shape.

3. *Investigate how we see planets by reflected light* · Let a rubber ball represent a planet. The "planet" can barely be seen in a darkened room. In a closet or room that can be completely darkened, the "planet" cannot be seen at all. Let a lighted flashlight represent the sun. When the "sunlight" of the flashlight shines on the "planet," the "planet" can now be seen because the light is reflected to the eye. Planets do not give off their own light. They can be seen because they reflect the light given off by the sun, which is a star.

4. *Discover why planets revolve around the sun* · Attach a string that is 1 meter (3 ft) long to a ball or a chalkboard eraser. Hold one end of the string in your hand and whirl the ball around your head. Then let go of the string suddenly and note how the ball travels out in a straight line as it obeys Newton's first law of motion. Whirl the ball around your head again. Note how your hand must pull inward on the string so that the ball will travel around in a circle and not fly out. This pull on the string corresponds to the pull or force of gravity, whereas the tendency of the ball to fly out and travel in a straight line corresponds to the movement due to inertia.

Both conditions affect a planet's motion so it neither falls toward the sun nor flies straight out into space, but travels around the sun instead. Draw a diagram on the chalkboard to illustrate this action (Figure 9–3). Be sure to

make the arrow showing the direction due to gravity small (because of the planet's great distance from the sun), and the arrow representing direction due to inertia long. This diagram will show why the sun's pull of gravity on a planet, although not very big, is still big enough to affect the tendency of the planet to move straight out into space. As a result, the direction of the planet's motion due to inertia changes just enough so that it falls around the sun. By drawing a number of tiny circles to represent the planet, and arrows to show the continual action of gravity and inertia, it becomes quite clear why a planet moves in an orbit around the sun.

5. *Observe the effects of gravity* · Let a ball drop. Earth's gravity pulls it to the ground. Jump into the air. Earth's gravity pulls you down. Both you and the ball have a pull of gravity on the earth, but the earth's pull of gravity is greater. Have a child stand with his hand stretched out, palm up. Place a heavy

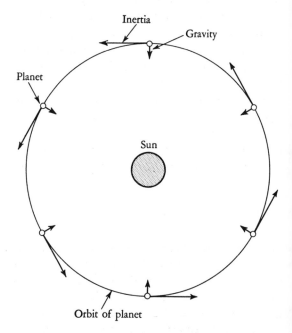

FIGURE 9–3.

GRAVITY AND INERTIA TOGETHER ACT ON A PLANET IN SUCH A WAY THAT THE PLANET REVOLVES AROUND THE SUN.

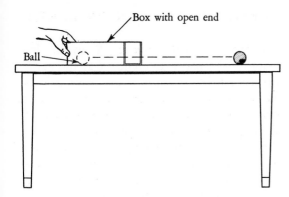

FIGURE 9–4.

INERTIA WILL CAUSE THE BALL TO CONTINUE
TO TRAVEL IN A STRAIGHT LINE.

book on the child's palm. He will soon feel the earth's pull of gravity on the book as his muscles work to keep the book in this position.

6. *Observe the effects of inertia* · Remove one end of a shoe box and put a ball in it. Move the box, open end forward, along a table and then stop the box suddenly after it has traveled about one third of the distance of the table top (Figure 9–4). The inertia of the ball will make it continue to travel in a straight line on the table top.

Place a small-size index card over the mouth of a glass tumbler. Put a coin on top of the card, positioning the coin so that it is at the center of the tumbler's mouth (Figure 9–5). Now snap the card quickly and suddenly with your finger, and the coin will fall into the

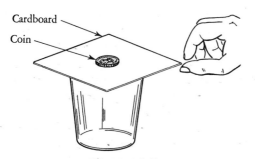

FIGURE 9–5.

INERTIA WILL KEEP THE COIN FROM MOVING
WITH THE CARD.

tumbler. Because of its inertia, the coin will stay at rest and not move with the card.

Have the children recall what happened when a car, in which they were riding, stopped suddenly. Their bodies snapped forward because their bodies, which were in motion, tended to stay in motion even though the car had stopped. When the car started again suddenly, their bodies snapped backward because their bodies were at rest and tended to stay at rest even though the car had begun to move.

7. *Observe morning and evening stars* · The morning and evening stars are really planets. Planets, such as Venus and Jupiter, are called morning stars when they are just above the horizon at sunrise and evening stars when they are just above the horizon at sunset. These planets can be easily identified because they are brighter than the real stars at that time. An almanac will indicate which morning and evening stars are visible at any time. Observe these planets each day for a few weeks. Note the time of their appearance and their position.

8. *Make a chalkboard model of a comet's orbit* · Draw a sketch of the orbits of the planets around the sun. Then show the long, oval orbit of Halley's comet, with the sun at one end of the orbit (Figure 9–6). Note how the comet's orbit cuts across the orbits of the planets.

9. *Look for "shooting stars"* · Meteors are very easily seen in the summer, especially in the suburbs and in the country where a comparatively dark and a broad expanse of sky is visible. Also, there are meteor showers that visit the earth annually. These meteor showers are named after the constellations from whose direction the meteors seem to come. Look for the Perseid shower about August 10–14, the Orionid shower about October 20–24, the Leonid shower about November 15–19, and the Geminid shower about December 10–14.

10. *Examine meteorites* · Sometimes it is possible to borrow small meteorites from college, public, or private museums. Have the

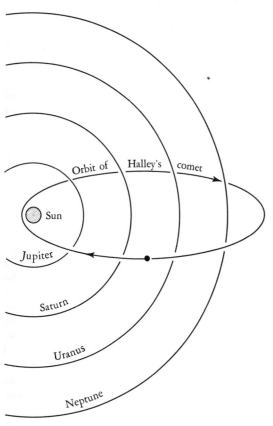

FIGURE 9–6.
ORBIT OF HALLEY'S COMET.

children hold and examine these meteorites that actually came from outer space. Visit museums to look at and find information about larger meteorites. If possible, obtain and show pictures of the Meteor Crater in Arizona or the Chubb Crater in Canada.

11. *Discuss how the solar system was formed* · Have the children read the theories proposed about the formation of the solar system. Promote a discussion of the merits and drawbacks of each theory.

12. *Explore the possibility of life on other planets* · Read about conditions, such as temperature, atmosphere, and water, on other planets and discuss the possibility of life, as it exists on earth, on these planets.

EFFECT OF THE SUN ON EARTH

1. *Infer the earth is round* · Show the class a globe of the earth. Inference that the earth is curved can be drawn in many ways. A person on land who watches a ship disappear sees the hull disappear first and the smokestacks last. During a lunar eclipse, the earth's shadow on the moon is curved. Photographs taken by astronauts in outer space, and on or near the moon, clearly show that the earth is round. Satellites have already gone around the earth.

2. *Investigate the earth's orbit around the sun* · Repeat Learning Activity 2 of "The Solar System" (p. 273), keeping the nails about 5 centimeters (2 in) apart. Let a lamp with the shade removed represent the sun. Move a globe of the earth counterclockwise in a complete orbit around the "sun," pointing out that it takes 365¼ days or 1 year to make this orbit.

3. *Observe how the earth rotates on its axis* · Push a knitting needle through a grapefruit. The knitting needle represents the axis, or imaginary line, running through the earth's north and south poles. Tilt the needle slightly and make the orange, which represents the earth, spin or rotate. An excellent analogy of the earth rotating on its axis is the merry-go-round. It turns around and around, and it has a center pole that acts as its axis.

4. *Account for day and night* · Get a globe that rotates. This globe will represent the planet Earth. Find out exactly where on the globe you live, then either put a mark or tape a small cutout figure on this spot. Let a source of light represent the sun. You can use a gooseneck or table lamp with the shade removed. Alternate sources of light could be a slide projector or a flashlight.

Now darken the room. Shine the lamp on the globe so that the globe is illuminated evenly by the light (which represents the sunlight). To achieve an even lighting effect, the bulb should be at the same height as the middle of the globe, and the globe should be moved back and forth until it is in the proper position (Figure 9–7).

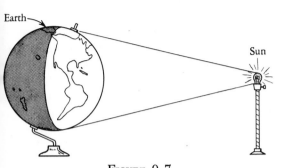

FIGURE 9–7.
THE SUN CAUSES DAY AND NIGHT.

Half the globe will be lighted (daytime) and half the globe will be in darkness (nighttime). Now spin the globe slowly from west to east (counterclockwise when looking down on the north pole from above). The part of the earth where you live will go from day to night and back to day again. Also, the east will receive the light before the west so that, when it is dawn in New York City, it is still dark in Chicago and Los Angeles.

5. *Discover why the sun is red at sunrise and sunset* · Draw a diagram of the sun and the earth at noon and sunset (Figure 9–8). The sun's rays must travel a greater distance through the thicker part of the atmosphere when the sun is low on the horizon than when the sun is overhead. The red rays in the sunlight travel through the atmosphere in either case, but the blue rays are scattered, making the sun appear to be orange or reddish.

6. *Observe that the earth's axis is tilted* · A globe of the earth is tilted at an angle of 23½ degrees. Push a knitting needle through an orange or grapefruit. First hold the knitting needle (which represents the earth's axis) vertically, then tilt it about 23½ degrees to show how the earth (represented by the orange or grapefruit) rotates and revolves in this position.

7. *Compare the effect of direct and slanted rays* · Shine a flashlight on the inside of the

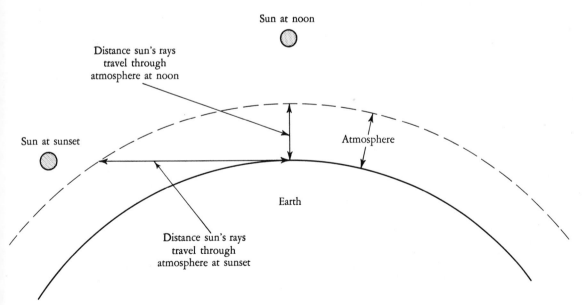

FIGURE 9–8. WHY THE SUN APPEARS RED OR ORANGE AT SUNRISE AND SUNSET.

[277

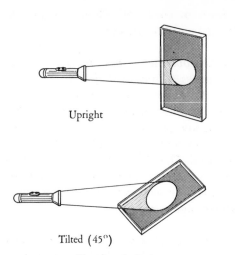

Upright

Tilted (45°)

FIGURE 9–9.

DIRECT RAYS ARE MORE CONCENTRATED THAN SLANTED RAYS.

cover of a shoe box that is held vertically upright (Figure 9–9). A small intense circle of light will be produced as the rays shine directly on the cardboard. Now tilt the cardboard cover away from you at an angle of 45 degrees. The same amount of light will be spread out over a larger area and it will not be as bright. By reading a light meter in the morning and at noon, it will also show that the slanted morning rays of the sun are not as intense as the more direct rays of the sun at noon.

8. *Account for the seasons* · Darken the room. Set up a globe and a gooseneck lamp, and position them as described in Activity 4 above. The globe should be to the left of the lamp with the axis tilted toward the sun (Figure 9–10). This position is the position of the earth when it is summer in the northern hemisphere. The light rays will strike the northern hemisphere vertically and the southern hemisphere at a slant. The north pole will be lighted completely while the south pole will be dark. Spin the globe slowly. The days will be longer than the nights in the northern hemisphere while the nights are longer than the days in the southern hemisphere.

Now move the globe to the other side of the lamp. Conditions will be reversed for both hemispheres. Move the globe to the spring and fall positions. Days and nights are just as long, and the sun's rays strike both hemispheres at the same angle or slant.

9. *Observe the sun seem to change its position during the year* · Note where the sun rises and sets each day, using a building or a tree to fix the position. The sun will rise and set farther to the north during the first half of the year, and farther to the south during the second half. As a result the sun seems to be higher in the sky during the summer. The sun will also strike different parts of the room during the year. This change in position is caused by the earth's movement around the sun.

10. *Measure and compare shadows* · Have the children stand with their backs to the sun and observe the shadows formed. Measure and compare these shadows in the morning, noon, and late afternoon and note the different lengths, depending upon whether the rays strike the body at a slant or vertically.

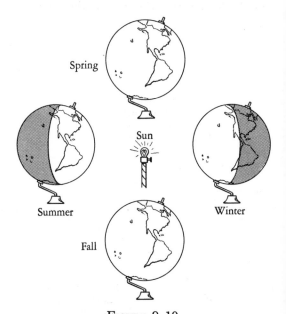

Spring

Sun

Summer

Winter

Fall

FIGURE 9–10.

THE TILT OF THE EARTH'S AXIS AND THE REVOLUTION OF THE EARTH AROUND THE SUN TOGETHER CAUSE SEASONS ON EARTH.

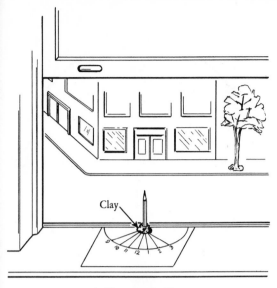

FIGURE 9–11.

A SUNDIAL.

11. *Make a sundial* · Place a short pencil upright in a lump of clay and set the pencil on a piece of blank paper located on a window-sill that gets sunlight all day (Figure 9–11). Draw a semicircle around the pencil, using the length of the pencil as the radius and the position of the clay as the center of the circle. The pencil will cast a shadow on the paper. Mark the position of this shadow every hour, drawing a line along the shadow and extending the line until it reaches the semicircle. At the points where the lines reach the semicircle, write down the hour when this shadow occurred. Use this sundial to tell the time on the next sunny day.

12. *Discover why only a small amount of the sun's energy reaches the earth* · Set up a table lamp, without a shade, at one end of a long table and a marble at the other end. Point out that the bulb (which represents the sun) sends out its light in all directions, and the marble (which represents the earth) receives only a very small part of the sun's energy.

13. *Discuss the sun as a source of energy* · Select appropriate activities from Chapter 11

"Water, Weather, and Climate"), Chapter 13A ("Plants"), and Chapter 18 ("Heat, Fire, and Fuels") to show that the sun's energy heats the earth, causes weather, makes it possible for plants to manufacture food, and is stored in fuels.

THE MOON

1. *Compare the size and distance of the moon and earth* · Make two balls of clay, one 10 centimeters (4 in) in diameter and the other 2½ centimeters (1 in) in diameter. Place these two balls either 384 centimeters or 240 in. apart. This will give a relative idea of the size of the moon and its distance from the earth. If 1 centimeter equals 1000 kilometers (or 1 inch equals 1000 miles), then the 384 centimeters (or 240 in) will indicate the distance of the moon from the earth. Point out that the moon seems so small to us, even though it is one fourth the diameter of the earth, because it is so far away from the earth.

2. *Observe the nature of the moon* · When the moon is full, have the children observe the moon through a telescope or powerful field glasses. Let them try to find the more important craters, plains or "seas," and mountains, and then identify them by consulting a map of the moon.

3. *Explore the characteristics of the moon* · Discuss its prominent features—its pull of gravity, its temperature, and its lack of atmosphere and water, resulting in the absence of sound and weather.

4. *Illustrate how the moon revolves around the earth* · Repeat Learning Activities 4, 5, and 6 of "The Solar System" (p. 274). The moon's orbit is almost a circle. Let a tennis ball represent the moon, and move it around a globe of the earth to show the moon's orbit. Be sure to tilt the moon's orbit a little so that the moon passes a little above and below the earth in its travels.

5. *Discover how the same side of the moon always faces us* · Make an "X" with chalk on a large ball, such as a volley ball, that represents the moon. Let one child, representing the earth, sit in the center of the room. Have a second child hold the ball and walk counterclockwise around the first child in a large circle, always keeping the "X" facing the first child's head. It should be obvious to the rest of the children that the moon rotates just once as it makes one revolution around the earth. Therefore the moon shows only one side to the earth at all times.

6. *Discover why the rising and setting moon seems larger* · Though comparison with nearby objects on the horizon makes the rising or setting moon appear to be larger, this phenomenon can be shown to be an optical illusion. Bend a paper clip so that it fits a yardstick snugly, as shown in Figure 9–12. When there is a full moon on the horizon, sight the moon so that it fits exactly within the two ends of the paper clip, pinching or widening the ends if necessary. Look at the moon again through the paper clip later when the moon is higher in the sky. Its size will not have changed at all.

7. *Discover that the moon shines by reflected light* · Let a tennis ball represent the moon and a flashlight represent sunlight. Place the ball on a table and darken the room com-

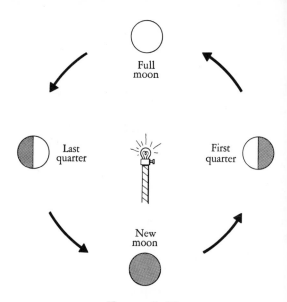

FIGURE 9–13.
PHASES OF THE MOON.

pletely. The ball cannot be seen. Then shine the flashlight on the ball. The ball can now be seen because the light from the flashlight strikes the ball and is reflected to the eye. If the room cannot be darkened completely, have the children do the experiment individually at home, using a closet.

8. *Observe and compare phases of the moon* · Get a styrofoam ball about the size of an orange or grapefruit. These balls are sold as decorations, and they have small stems. Remove the shade from a gooseneck or table lamp and turn on the lamp. Have a child kneel in front of the lighted bulb so that the child's head is level with the bulb. Let the rest of the class sit or stand directly in front of the child.

Darken the room. Now, holding the styrofoam ball by its stem, have the child move the ball slowly in a counterclockwise direction around her head (Figure 9-13). If the ball does not have a stem, insert the sharp end of a pencil or long thick nail into the ball.

The ball will represent the moon, the child's head the earth, and the bulb the sun. When the ball moves around the child's head, the class

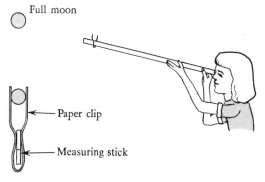

Full moon

Paper clip

Measuring stick

FIGURE 9–12.
THE APPARENT CHANGE IN THE MOON'S SIZE WHEN IT IS RISING OR SETTING IS AN OPTICAL ILLUSION.

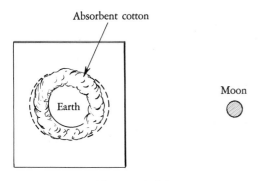

FIGURE 9–14.
THE MOON CAUSES TIDES ON EARTH.

will be able to see a continual complete cycle of all the phases of the moon.

9. *Make a model that shows tides* · Obtain a large piece of white poster board, a roll of absorbent cotton, a bottle of blue ink, and some glue. On the poster board draw a circle 15 centimeters (6 in) in diameter, and paint the word *earth* inside it. Roll and shape some absorbent cotton until it looks like a doughnut 5 centimeters (2 in) wide, which will fit around the circle, then glue the cotton to the poster board (Figure 9–14). After the glue has set, pour the ink on the cotton to give the effect of blue waters. Tape the poster board securely to the chalkboard.

Cut a paper circle 5 centimeters (2 in) in diameter and write the word *moon* on it. Tape the "moon" to the chalkboard to the right of the "earth." Gently pull the cotton on the side of the "earth" nearest the "moon." A bulge

that shows the formation of a high tide will form. Gently pull the cotton on the side farthest from the "moon" to produce a second high tide. The top and bottom of the cotton circle will flatten out to form two low tides.

If you want to show how spring tides and neap tides are formed, cut out another circle and write the word *sun* on it. Place the "sun" to the right of the "moon" and create a spring tide effect with the cotton. Then place the "sun" above the "earth," at right angles to the "moon," and create a neap tide effect with the cotton.

10. *Compare solar and lunar eclipses* · Let a light represent the sun. This source can be a gooseneck or table lamp (with the shade removed), a slide projector, or a powerful flashlight. Get a globe of the earth, and position the globe and light source so that the light falls evenly on the globe when the room is darkened. Let a tennis ball represent the moon. Hold the tennis ball between the "sun" and the "earth" so that a shadow falls on the "earth" (Figure 9–15). The ball may have to be moved back and forth until a sharp shadow forms on the globe. Observers on earth in this shadow would see a solar eclipse.

To show a lunar eclipse hold the tennis ball or "moon" on the far side of the "earth" so that the "earth" is between the "sun" and the "moon." Move the ball back and forth until the "moon" is completely within the earth's shadow, forming a lunar eclipse. Move the ball around the globe in a slightly tilted orbit to show that

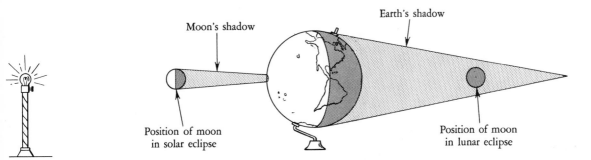

FIGURE 9–15. SOLAR AND LUNAR ECLIPSE.

most of the time the shadows of the moon and earth are either too high or too low to produce an eclipse.

11. *How to watch a solar eclipse* · Get a long, rectangular cardboard carton from the supermarket. Cut a hole a little larger than the size of your head on one long side of the carton. Tape white paper to one end of the carton. At the other end of the carton cut a small hole 2½ centimeters (1 in) square, as high as possible and near the long side opposite the side where you cut a hole for your head to enter. Tape aluminum foil over the hole, then make a pinhole in the center of the aluminum foil. Close all four sides of the cardboard carton and tape them securely together to keep out the light.

Now stand with your back to the sun, put your head into the carton, and bend forward until light from the sun enters the pinhole and forms an image on the white paper (Figure 9–16). *At no time should you look directly at the sun because it will damage your eyesight permanently.*

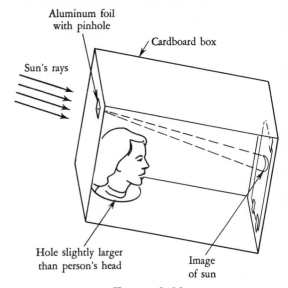

FIGURE 9–16.
ARRANGEMENT FOR OBSERVING A SOLAR ECLIPSE.

BEYOND THE SOLAR SYSTEM

1. *See how stars differ in color* · Heat a wire until it glows. It will glow orange at first. Then, as it becomes hotter, it will glow yellow. Turn on a table or gooseneck lamp, with the shade removed, that has a light bulb of clear glass so that the wire inside can be seen. The extremely hot wire will glow a yellowish white. Point out that our hottest stars are blue-white and white, and, as they become cooler, they turn yellow, orange, and then red.

2. *Discover why stars seem to twinkle* · Form an image of a light source on a screen. This image can be formed by placing a small porcelain socket containing a lighted flashlight bulb on a pile of books. Place the handle of a magnifying glass (convex lens) in a tall lump of clay so that the magnifying glass remains upright in a fixed position. Adjust the height of the magnifying glass so that the center of the lens is the same height as the flashlight bulb in the porcelain socket (Figure 9–17). Place

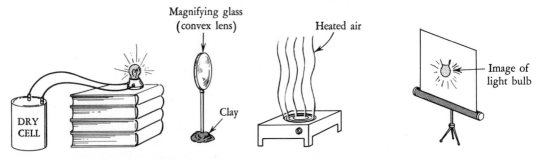

FIGURE 9–17.   MOVING AIR MAKES LIGHT RAYS SHIMMER AND TWINKLE.

the magnifying glass in front of the bulb, between the bulb and the screen, and adjust the position of the glass and screen until a clear image of the bulb appears on the screen. Darken the room. Note that the image is fixed, and it does not move or twinkle.

Now place a hot plate close to the lens and below it. Turn on the hot plate; the image will tremble or twinkle, just as a star does, because heat energy from the hot plate makes the air above the hot plate move back and forth. This movement makes the light rays shift back and forth, or twinkle, as well.

3. *Find the North Star* · Find the Big Dipper in the sky. The two outside stars of the bowl of the Big Dipper are called the "pointer" stars because they point to the North Star. If a line is drawn through these two stars that continues away from the bottom of the Dipper it will lead you to the North Star (Figure 9–18). The North Star is about five times as far from the "pointer" stars as the distance between the two "pointer" stars. The North Star is at the end of the handle of the Little Dipper. The Big and Little Dippers are always positioned so that, when one is right side up, the other is upside down. Do not expect the North Star to be very bright. It is only moderately bright.

Another way to find the North Star is to find north with a compass. Face north and look

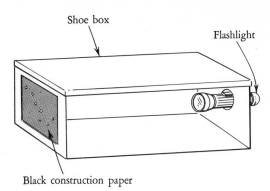

Shoe box

Flashlight

Black construction paper

FIGURE 9–19.
A CONSTELLATION BOX.

halfway up. Stretch your arm and finger to a point halfway between the horizon and straight up (at an angle of 45 degrees). The star you will point to, or the nearest star to where you are pointing, will be the North Star.

4. *Make a bulletin-board exhibit of constellations* · Cover the bulletin board with dark blue paper or cloth, then paste silver stars to show the constellation patterns. White ink can be used, if desired, to draw the figures represented by the constellations. In many popular books on astronomy these constellations are well illustrated. Put up the summer constellations in the early fall, and the winter constellations later in the year. Also, let the children become familiar with the constellations of the zodiac.

5. *Make a constellation box* · Get a shoe box and cut out a large rectangle at one end. Cut up several rectangular sheets from black construction paper, making the sheets slightly larger than the rectangle that was cut out of the box. On each black sheet make pin pricks to form the pattern of one of the common constellations. Tape one of the black sheets over the rectangular hole in the box. At the other end of the box cut out a circular hole large enough to insert the head of a flashlight. Now darken the room and turn on the flashlight (Figure 9–19). The constellation will glow brightly in the "night sky." If the dots of light

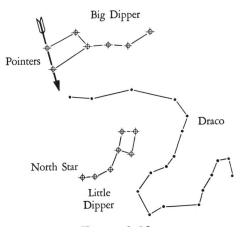

Big Dipper

Pointers

Draco

North Star

Little Dipper

FIGURE 9–18.
FINDING THE NORTH STAR.

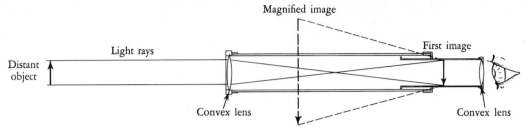

FIGURE 9–20.   HOW THE REFRACTING TELESCOPE WORKS.

cannot be seen clearly, make the holes larger with a large sewing needle or a small knitting needle. Replace this constellation with sheets containing other constellation patterns.

6. *Observe how the constellations seem to change their position* · Observe the position of constellations, such as the Big and Little Dippers or Orion, early in the evening and then later in the evening. Their positions will have changed. This apparent change is caused by the earth's rotation. Observe their position 1 night each week for 4 weeks at the same time each night. Again their positions will have changed. This apparent change is caused by the earth's revolution around the sun.

An excellent star chart, called the "Star Explorer," can be obtained inexpensively by writing to Star Explorer, Hayden Planetarium, New York, N.Y. 10024. It has excellent instructions and can be adjusted for different times of the year. Use this star chart to locate the constellations in the sky.

7. *Collect pictures of the stars* · Look for and collect pictures of stars, double stars, different varieties of star clusters, nebulae, and galaxies.

8. *Observe the Galaxy* · Locate the Milky Way on a clear moonless night as far away from the lights of the city as possible. Binoculars or a small telescope will help. Look for a picture of the Galaxy. Show the position of the sun and the solar system in the Galaxy. Point out the three spiral arms and discuss the differences in the speed of the stars in the Galaxy.

9. *Calculate the distance traveled in a light-year* · The speed of light is about 300,000 kilometers (186,000 mi) per second. The distance that light travels in 1 year can be found by

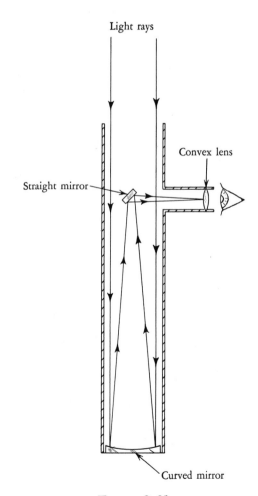

FIGURE 9–21.

HOW THE REFLECTING TELESCOPE WORKS.

284]

multiplying 300,000 kilometers (186,000 mi) by 60 seconds, then by 60 minutes, then by 24 hours, and then by 365¼ days. By multiplying this answer by 3⅓, the distance traveled in a parsec will also be obtained.

10. *Study the refracting telescope* • Draw a diagram of the refracting telescope (Figure 9–20). Trace the rays of light as they come from a distant object, enter the lens, and are bent to form a small image, which is then magnified by the other lens.

11. *Study the reflecting telescope* • Draw a diagram of the reflecting telescope (Figure 9–21). Trace the rays of light as they come from a distant object, are collected by the curved mirror, and travel to a straight mirror, where they are reflected and form a small image, which is magnified by the convex lens.

BIBLIOGRAPHY FOR "THE UNIVERSE"

ASIMOV, ISAAC. *Alpha Centauri: The Nearest Star*. New York: Lothrop, Lee & Shepherd, 1976. 190 pp.
———. *Comets and Meteors*. Chicago: Follett, 1972. 32 pp.
———. *Galaxies*. Chicago: Follett, 1968. 32 pp.
———. *How Did We Find Out About Comets?* New York: Walker, 1974. 64 pp.
———. *How Did We Find Out the Earth Is Round?* New York: Walker, 1972. 64 pp.
———. *Mars*. Chicago: Follett, 1966. 32 pp.
———. *The Moon*. Chicago: Follett, 1967. 32 pp.
———. *The Solar System*. Chicago: Follett, 1975. 32 pp.
———. *Stars*. Chicago: Follett, 1968. 32 pp.
———. *The Sun*. Chicago: Follett, 1975. 32 pp.
BERGAUST, ERIK. *Mars—Planet for Conquest*. New York: G. P. Putnam's Sons, 1968. 96 pp.
BRANLEY, FRANKLIN M. *A Book of Mars for You*. New York: Thomas Y. Crowell, 1968. 96 pp.
———. *A Book of Planet Earth for You*. New York: Thomas Y. Crowell, 1973. 34 pp.
———. *A Book of Venus for You*. New York: Thomas Y. Crowell, 1970. 72 pp.
———. *Eclipse—Darkness in Daytime*. New York: Thomas Y. Crowell, 1973. 34 pp.
———. *Gravity Is a Mystery*. New York: Thomas Y. Crowell, 1971. 34 pp.
———. *The Nine Planets*. New York: Thomas Y. Crowell, 1971. 86 pp.
———. *Sunshine Makes the Seasons*. New York: Thomas Y. Crowell, 1974. 40 pp.
CHESTER, MICHAEL. *Let's Go to the Moon*. New York: G. P. Putnam's Sons, 1974. 48 pp.
COLLINS, LORENCE, and BARBARA COLLINS. *Exploring and Understanding the Solar System*. Westchester, Ill: Benefic Press, 1970. 96 pp.

FODOR, R. V. *Meteorites.* New York: Dodd, Mead, 1976. 48 pp.

FREEMAN, MAE B. *Do You Know About Stars?* New York: Random House, 1970. 26 pp.

IRVINS, ANN. *Stars and Constellations.* New York: Crowell-Collier, 1969. 28 pp.

KNIGHT, DAVID C. *The First Book of Mars.* New York: Franklin Watts, 1973. 82 pp.

———. *32 Moons: Natural Satellites of Our Solar System.* New York: William Morrow, 1974. 96 pp.

KYSELKA, WILL, and RAY LANTERMAN. *North Star to Southern Cross.* Honolulu: Univ. Press of Hawaii, 1976. 152 pp.

LYON, JENE. *Astronomy: Our Sun and Its Neighbors.* New York: Western Pub., 1974. 48 pp.

MAYALL, R. NEWTON, MARGARET MAYALL, and JEROME WYCOFF. *The Sky Observer's Guide.* New York: Golden Press, 1965. 125 pp.

MOCHE, DINAH. *What's Up There? Questions and Answers About Stars and Space.* New York: Arrow, 1975. 64 pp.

MOORE, PATRICK. *Comets.* New York: Charles Scribner's Sons, 1976. 150 pp.

MOTZ, LLOYD. *On the Path of Venus.* New York: Pantheon, 1977. 206 pp.

NOURSE, ALAN. *The Giant Planets.* New York: Franklin Watts, 1974. 96 pp.

POLGREEN, JOHN, and CATHLEEN POLGREEN. *The Earth in Space.* New York: Random House, 1965. 80 pp.

——— and ———. *The Stars Tonight.* New York: Harper & Row, 1967. 88 pp.

POSIN, DANIEL Q. *Exploring and Understanding the Solar System.* Westchester, Ill.: Benefic Press, 1968. 96 pp.

SHAPP, MARTHA, and CHARLES SHAPP. *Let's Find Out About the Moon.* New York: Franklin Watts, 1975. 48 pp.

——— and ———. *Let's Find Out About the Sun.* New York: Franklin Watts, 1975. 48 pp.

ZIM, HERBERT S., and ROBERT H. BAKER. *Stars.* New York: Golden Press, 1965. 160 pp.

CHAPTER 10

The EARTH

THE COMPOSITION OF THE EARTH

I. How the Earth Was Formed

A. Scientists believe that the earth was formed in the same way as the sun, planets, and other heavenly bodies in the universe were formed.

B. They also believe that the earth must have been formed from the same materials as those that are in the sun.

C. At first the earth was a huge ball of white-hot gases with a temperature of many millions of degrees Celsius.

1. This heat was not produced because of a nuclear reaction that took place inside the earth, as is the case with the sun, but because of the attraction of the particles of gases for each other.

2. As these particles were attracted to each other, they moved closer and closer together until they were pressed together tightly, or compressed.

3. When particles of gases are squeezed together, or compressed, heat is given off.

D. After a long while the earth began to cool.

1. The color of the spinning ball of gas changed slowly from white to yellow to red, until finally the earth gave off no light at all.

2. As the earth cooled, it grew smaller, or contracted, and most of the material changed from a gas to a liquid.

3. The heavier liquid materials settled toward the center of the earth, and the lighter liquid materials floated on top.

4. The lighter liquid materials combined to form molten, or liquid, rock.

5. The rest of the earth's material remained as hot gases above the surface of the liquid.

E. As the earth continued to cool, a solid crust that floated on top of the liquid material was formed.

1. As this crust continued to cool, it contracted, wrinkled, and burst open in many places.

2. More molten rock flowed out through these openings; then it cooled to form solid rock.

F. At this time there was no water on earth.

1. Some water was in the hot gases above the earth in the form of water vapor.

2. Most of the water was under the crust, combined with other materials.

G. As the earth's crust continued to cool and contract, great cracks appeared, and the trapped water was able to escape into the atmosphere as water vapor.

H. When the top of the earth's atmosphere became cool enough, the water vapor condensed into tiny droplets to form thick layers of clouds that covered the earth and shut out the sun.

I. After a while the droplets of water in the

upper layers of clouds combined to form larger droplets, and then some rain began to fall.

1. This rain immediately evaporated into water vapor when it fell into the hot, lower layers of clouds.
2. However, these lower layers of clouds were cooled, after a long time, both by the rain and by the loss of heat energy from the lower cloud layers as they evaporated the rain into water vapor.
3. Eventually the rain reached the earth's surface, but it quickly boiled away when it touched the earth's hot rocks.
4. As more rain fell, it made the earth's crust much cooler, causing the crust to contract and crack even more, so that more of the water trapped inside the earth was squeezed out and evaporated.

J. Finally, the earth's surface became cool enough for water to be able to stay on the earth.

1. The water trickled down the rocks to form small pools.
2. This water was the beginning of the earth's lakes and oceans.

K. For a long time it rained constantly, filling the earth's surface with bodies of water.

L. At this point all of the waters of the earth were fresh, becoming salty only after they had sufficient time to dissolve some of the chemicals in the earth's crust.

M. After thousands of years the thick clouds thinned out as they cooled and gave up their water.

N. At the same time many of the other gases above the earth's surface disappeared.

1. Some of the lighter gases escaped into space.
2. Other gases turned into liquids, and even solids, as they became cooler.

O. The gases that were left behind became our earth's atmosphere.

P. Eventually the sun shone through to the earth, lighting up a bare, bleak earth that only had rocky land masses and bodies of water.

II. THE LAYERS OF THE EARTH

A. The earth is made up of three separate layers: the **crust**, the **mantle**, and the **core**.

B. The crust is a very thin outer layer of rock, which is mostly granite and basalt.

1. The raised parts of the rock form the earth's continents and the low parts form the ocean floors.
2. The crust is thickest underneath the continents, and it can be as much as 48 kilometers (30 mi) thick.
3. The crust is thinnest underneath the oceans, and it can be as little as 11 kilometers (7 mi) thick.

C. Tremendous forces inside the earth are constantly acting on the crust, causing it to bend and crack, and producing mountains, earthquakes, and volcanoes.

D. In the earth's crust are found the soil, water, coal, oil, gas, and minerals that we use.

E. Although there are at least 90 chemical elements found in the earth's crust, only 5 of these elements make up about 92 percent of the crust's weight.

1. Oxygen makes up about 47 percent of the crust's weight, and it is found in air, water, sand, quartz, limestone, clay, and other materials.
2. Silicon makes up about 28 percent of the crust's weight, and it is found in sand, quartz, clay, and other materials.
3. Aluminum is the earth's most abundant metal, making up 8 percent of the crust's weight, and it is found in clay and other materials.
4. Iron makes up about 5 percent of the crust's weight, and it is usually found combined with oxygen and sulfur.
5. Calcium makes up about 4 percent of the crust's weight, and it is found in limestone, and other materials.

F. Beneath the earth's crust is the mantle, or middle layer.

1. There is a boundary or zone, commonly called the **Moho**, between the crust and the mantle.

2. The mantle goes down to a depth of about 2900 kilometers (1800 mi).

3. The mantle is made up of rock, called peridotite, which is heavier than the basalt and granite in the earth's crust.

4. The mantle is very hot, but the rock in it is solid rather than liquid because of the great pressures exerted on it.

5. Geologists believe that when deep cracks are formed in the earth's crust, the pressure on the mantle is reduced, and the solid rock then turns into liquid rock.

G. Beneath the earth's mantle is the core, or third layer.

1. The core goes down about 3500 kilometers (2200 mi) to the center of the earth.

2. The core is a mixture of about 90 percent iron and 10 percent nickel.

H. The presence of metals in the core seems to confirm the theory that, as the earth cooled, the heavier materials settled toward the center, and the lighter materials floated up toward the surface.

I. There are two parts to the core: the **outer** and the **inner** core.

1. The inner core extends about 1280 kilometers (800 mi) from the center of the earth, and seems to be solid.

2. The outer core is about 2160 kilometers (1350 mi) thick, and seems to be in a plastic form.

J. The inside of the earth is very hot.

1. Geologists have found that the temperature rises as they go deeper into the earth's crust.

2. Although the outside of the earth has cooled, the inside has lost little of the heat it had when it first formed.

3. Also, much heat is generated by radioactive materials in the earth's crust.

4. In mines and oil wells the temperature rises about 1° Celsius (2° Fahrenheit) for every 36 meters (120 ft) of depth.

5. Geologists think the temperature of the mantle may be as high as 1,600° Celsius (2,880° Fahrenheit), and the temperature of the core may be as high as 4,500° Celsius (8,100° Fahrenheit).

III. ROCKS

A. The solid part of the earth's crust is made up of great masses of hard material called **rock.**

1. The smaller rocks and boulders, with which we are familiar, are just differently sized pieces that were broken off from these large masses.

2. Some large masses may be several miles thick.

3. Most of the rock on the earth's surface is covered with soil.

B. Although there seems to be many different kinds of rocks, they can all be divided into three main groups, according to the way in which they were formed.

C. The three kinds of rocks are—**igneous, sedimentary,** and **metamorphic** rocks.

D. Igneous rocks are rocks formed from molten material in or below the earth's crust.

1. Igneous means "formed from fire."

2. The hot molten material is called **magma.**

E. Magma forms when the pressure below the earth's crust changes.

1. When the pressure is reduced, the solid material in the earth's mantle becomes liquid magma.

2. The magma may then work its way upward through layers of rock lying above it.

3. The heat and pressure of the flowing magma may also cause the rock above it to move, break up, or even melt, which makes room for the magma to rise.

4. The hot magma may then break through cracks in the earth's surface and flow out, covering wide areas of the land.

F. Rock formed from magma that reached the earth's surface and then cooled is called **extrusive** rock.

1. Liquid magma that reaches the earth's surface is also called **lava.**

2. Extrusive rocks are either glassy or made up of very fine crystals.

3. The magma or lava cools so quickly that

large crystals do not have an opportunity to form.

G. Rocks formed from magma that could not reach the earth's surface because of the rocks lying above the magma, and therefore cooled below the surface, are called **intrusive** rocks.
1. Intrusive rocks are coarser than extrusive rocks.
2. They have large crystals because the magma cooled slowly.
3. When the rocks lying above the intrusive rock are worn away, or eroded, the intrusive rock becomes exposed to view on the earth's surface.

H. Granite is the most common igneous intrusive rock.
1. It is easily recognized by its speckled appearance which is caused by the presence of three minerals—quartz, feldspar, and mica.
2. Quartz has glasslike crystals that are usually colorless or milky.
3. Feldspar can be most any color, but is usually white.
4. Mica also can be any color, but usually is a shiny brown or black.
5. Granite is used in road construction, buildings, and monuments.

I. Basalt is a common igneous extrusive rock.
1. It is dark colored, and a heavier rock than granite.
2. Geologists believe that the continents are huge masses of lighter granite that are resting on a foundation of heavier basalt.

J. Pumice and obsidian are examples of igneous extrusive rocks formed from magma or lava given off by erupting volcanoes.
1. Pumice comes from lava that had many hot gases in it. The lava cooled so quickly that the gases did not have time to escape and they were trapped inside the cooled lava, thus forming a light-colored spongy rock.
2. Some samples of pumice are so light, because of the many gas bubbles trapped in them, that they can float in water.

3. Obsidian is another form of lava that cooled very quickly.
4. Obsidian is black and glassy, and it has a chemical composition similar to that of commercial glass.

K. The second group of rocks, called sedimentary rocks, were formed from different sediments that accumulated for several thousand years and then were cemented tightly together.

L. One kind of sediment that forms sedimentary rock includes such materials as sand, clay, silt, pebbles, and gravel.
1. Streams and rivers carry these sedimentary materials to lakes or oceans, where they settle to the bottom.
2. As the sediment accumulates, layers are formed, which then slowly change into solid rock.
3. This change happens because the weight of the top layers presses the sediment in the bottom layers tightly together.
4. At the same time, chemicals that are already dissolved in the water now begin to deposit out again on and between the particles of sediment, fill the tiny spaces between the particles, and then cement them firmly together.

M. Conglomerate, sandstone, and shale are examples of sedimentary rock formed this way.
1. Conglomerate is made of pebbles and gravel that are cemented together.
2. Sandstone is made of grains of sand that are cemented together.
3. Some sandstones are sharp and jagged, but others are worn smooth by the action of water and wind on the sand grains.
4. The material that cements the sand together determines the color and hardness of the sandstone.
5. Sandstone may be red, brown, yellow, or very light colored; it can be very soft or it can be hard enough to use as a building material.
6. Shale is clay or mud that has become sedimentary rock.
7. Because clay is made of fine, flaky mate-

rials, shale usually can be split easily into flat, thin pieces.

8. The color of shale is usually gray or green, but it may be red, blue, purple, or even black.

N. A second kind of sediment that forms sedimentary rock includes the remains of many plants and animals that live in the ocean and take calcium carbonate from the water to form shells or skeletons.

1. As these plants and animals die, their shells and skeletons accumulate and then harden to form great beds of calcium carbonate, which is more commonly called limestone.

2. The limestone formed from corals and from tiny plants that live in clear, warm, shallow water is very fine and is almost pure calcium carbonate.

3. The limestone formed from the remains of the other tiny sea animals, as well as the shells of such larger animals as clams, oysters, and mussels, is much coarser and will have pieces of shell in it.

4. This kind of limestone may also have sand and clay, in small or large amounts, mixed in it.

5. Chalk is a soft porous form of limestone, made from the shells of tiny animals that lived milllions of years ago.

O. A third kind of material that forms sedimentary rock includes such chemicals as salt and calcium carbonate, which are dissolved in the seawater.

1. Conditions in the oceans often change so that the water in certain parts of the ocean can no longer hold these chemicals that are dissolved in it.

2. These chemicals then deposit out, forming accumulations that later harden into rock.

3. Rock salt is formed from salt that once was dissolved in seawater.

4. A very pure and fine form of limestone is formed from calcium carbonate that deposited out of seawater.

P. Sedimentary rocks often contain the re-mains of early animals and plants, called fossils, embedded in them.

Q. Iron ores and other metal ores sometimes accumulate as sediment and are then found in sedimentary rock.

R. Soft coal is sedimentary rock formed from the remains of plants that died long ago, accumulated in a swamp, and were covered by other sediment to form layers that were then changed by heat and pressure into a rocky material.

S. The third group of rocks, called metamorphic rocks, are igneous and sedimentary rocks that were changed by heat and pressure.

1. Metamorphic means "changed in form."

2. Some changes are physical in nature, where the original materials in the rock were only rearranged.

3. Other changes are chemical in nature, where new minerals were formed.

T. Common metamorphic rocks are gneiss, quartzite, slate, marble, and hard coal.

1. Gneiss is a coarse rock that has parallel streaks or bands of minerals in it, and it is commonly formed from igneous granite and from many other kinds of igneous or sedimentary rocks.

2. Quartzite is a very hard rock formed from sedimentary sandstone.

3. Slate is a fine-grained rock that splits very easily into thin sheets, and it is formed from sedimentary shale.

4. Marble is a large-crystal rock, formed from sedimentary limestone.

5. Hard coal is formed from soft coal, and it has much more carbon in it.

6. Hard coal is also changed by further heat and pressure to graphite, which is pure carbon, now no longer useful as a fuel, but useful for making pencils, as a lubricant, and for other purposes.

IV. MINERALS

A. Rocks are made up of one or more minerals.

B. **Minerals** are chemical elements or compounds that are found naturally in the earth's crust.

C. Minerals are solid materials, having an orderly arrangement of atoms and therefore a definite crystal structure.

D. They are not made, or do not come, from living things.

   1. For this reason, a pearl, even though it is a chemical compound, is not considered a mineral, because a living thing—the oyster—produced it.

   2. For the same reason coal is not considered a true mineral, because it was formed from plant materials.

E. Most rocks are made up of more than one mineral.

F. Geologists classify minerals into groups, depending upon the kinds of chemicals in them and also upon the structure of the crystals they form.

G. Accordingly, minerals have been classified into four broad groups.

H. The first broad group of minerals includes those that contain the chemical element silicon.

   1. The members of this group are called the **silicate** minerals.

   2. Well-known examples of this group are quartz, feldspar, mica, hornblende, augite, garnet, olivine, and talc.

   3. This group of minerals includes about 40 percent of the commonly known minerals on earth.

   4. The minerals in granite, which makes up 90 percent of the earth's crust, are found in this group.

I. The second broad group of minerals are those that are considered to be nonmetallic by nature.

   1. The members of this group are called the **nonmetallic** minerals, although some of the members contain chemical elements, such as calcium or magnesium, which chemists call metals.

   2. Well-known examples of this group are calcite, dolomite, sulfur, rock salt, gypsum, apatite, fluorite, and graphite.

J. The third broad group of minerals are those that contain the common metal ores.

   1. The members of this group are called the **metal ore** minerals.

   2. Such metals as gold, silver, iron, copper, lead, zinc, tin, aluminum, mercury, titanium, and uranium are found in the minerals of this group.

K. The fourth broad group of minerals are those that are made into precious and semiprecious stones.

   1. The members of this group are called the **gem** minerals.

   2. Well-known examples of this group are the opal, jade, garnet, topaz, tourmaline, emerald, aquamarine, ruby, amethyst, sapphire, zircon, and diamond.

V. THE IDENTIFICATION OF MINERALS

A. Only rarely can a mineral be identified by applying a single test to it.

B. Geologists usually apply many tests to a mineral before they are absolutely sure they have identified the mineral.

C. Geologists identify minerals by testing the properties, or characteristics, that the minerals have.

D. One test is the **color** test.

   1. Experienced geologists always look at the color of a fresh surface of the mineral.

   2. This fresh surface shows the true color of the mineral, rather than the dull or tarnished color of a surface that has been exposed to air or been in contact with particles of soil for a long time.

   3. Sometimes amateur geologists are confused by small amounts of impurities in the minerals, which change the true color of the minerals.

E. Another color test is the **streak** test.

   1. The streak is the color produced when the mineral is rubbed against a piece of unglazed porcelain tile, which is called a **streak plate**.

   2. Nonmetallic minerals usually produce a

colorless or a light-colored streak, but metallic minerals often produce a dark streak that may differ from the original color of the mineral.

F. Another test has to do with the **luster** of the mineral.

1. Luster is the shine that the mineral has when light strikes it.

2. Such terms as dull, pearly, silky, metallic, glassy, and brilliant or diamondlike are used to describe the luster of a mineral.

G. Another way to identify minerals is by observing the **crystal form** of the mineral.

1. Most minerals are made up of crystals, showing that the atoms in the minerals are arranged in definite patterns.

2. These crystals have distinct forms, such as a square, double triangle, pyramid, or cube.

H. Geologists also identify some minerals by the way they split or break when struck.

I. A very widely used test for minerals is the **hardness** test.

1. Minerals differ very much in hardness; consequently, if the hardness of a mineral is known, it is a great help in identifying it.

2. Because there is so much difference in hardness, certain minerals are used as standards of hardness, and all the other minerals are compared with these special minerals.

3. These standard minerals are arranged in a scale, in which the minerals are listed in the order of their hardness, with the softest mineral listed first.

J. The commonly used scale of hardness is called **Mohs'** scale.

1. Mohs' scale has ten minerals in it, arranged in the order of their hardness, with each mineral being harder than the ones above it in the scale.

2. Talc, which is one of the softest minerals, is first in the scale, and the diamond, which is the hardest of all minerals, is last in the scale.

K. Ten minerals make up Mohs' scale, as follows.

1. Talc. 6. Orthoclase.
2. Gypsum. 7. Quartz.
3. Calcite. 8. Topaz.
4. Fluorite. 9. Corundum.
5. Apatite. 10. Diamond.

L. The hardness of a mineral is found by using it to make scratches on the minerals in Mohs' scale.

1. The geologist finds out which minerals in the scale the unknown mineral can and cannot scratch, and then the geologist determines the hardness of the mineral.

2. For example, apatite, 5, is harder than fluorite, 4, but softer than orthoclase, 6.

3. Any mineral that scatches apatite, but not orthoclase, is said to have a hardness on Mohs' scale of between 5 and 6.

4. This mineral will also scratch all the minerals below apatite and will scratch none of the minerals above orthoclase in the scale.

M. The following simple materials also help determine the hardness of a mineral on Mohs' scale.

1. A fingernail has a hardness of about 2.5, and it will scratch gypsum, 2, but not calcite, 3.

2. A penny has a hardness of 3, and it will just about scratch calcite, 3, but not fluorite, 4.

3. The sharp point of a piece of glass or the blade of a jackknife has a hardness of 5.5; it will scratch apatite, 5, but not orthoclase, 6.

4. A steel (tool) file has a hardness of 6.5.

N. Another way to identify minerals is to find the specific gravity, or heaviness, of the mineral.

O. Geologists also use special tests for certain groups of minerals.

1. Some minerals, such as lodestone or magnetite, are magnetic and will be attracted by a magnet.

2. Some minerals, such as sulfur, will be-

come electrically charged when rubbed or squeezed.

3. Some minerals, when exposed to invisible ultraviolet light, become fluorescent and give off light.

4. Many of these fluorescent minerals are also phosphorescent, and they will give off light after the ultraviolet light has been turned off.

5. Some minerals, such as uranium, are radioactive.

6. When a drop of dilute hydrochloric acid is placed on a mineral containing calcium carbonate, a chemical reaction takes place and bubbles of carbon dioxide gas are given off.

7. Some minerals give a special color to a flame when a bit of the powdered mineral, which has first been moistened with hydrochloric acid, is placed on one end of a clean platinum wire and thrust into the flame.

8. Certain minerals will give a special color to powdered borax that has been put on one end of a clean platinum wire and heated to form a small glassy bead; the color changes when some of the powdered mineral is put on the bead and the bead is thrust into a flame that has been made hotter with a blowpipe.

VI. CONSERVATION OF OUR MINERALS

A. Economists classify our mineral resources into three main groups: **metals, nonmetals,** and **fuels.**

1. Metals include such materials as iron, aluminum, lead, zinc, copper, and silver.

2. Nonmetals include such materials as limestone, marble, quartz, slate, and phosphates.

3. Fuels include such materials as coal, petroleum, and natural gas.

B. Our mineral resources are sometimes called **fixed resources,** or nonrenewable resources.

1. Our plant and animal life can be used over again many times, or replaced, so

that with careful management they can last indefinitely.

2. But most minerals, after they have been taken from the ground, are gone forever.

C. Because minerals cannot be replaced and because we use more minerals each year, the problem of conserving our mineral resources is important.

1. We must use our metals wisely and efficiently.

2. We must find ways to extract metals from low-grade ores.

3. We must locate and develop fresh sources of minerals.

4. We must develop substitutes for minerals that are being used up quickly.

D. Although we use a large amount of coal each year, there is still enough coal available to last for several generations.

E. However, our petroleum and natural gas supplies are being used so quickly that we shall soon face the problem of having to do without them.

F. Scientists are constantly looking for ways to extend our fuel supplies.

1. They have developed improved methods of mining coal and using low-grade sources.

2. They are developing better techniques of drilling and pumping petroleum so that we get more petroleum from each oil well.

3. They have improved the methods of refining petroleum to give us more gasoline and Diesel oil.

4. They are experimenting to find an inexpensive way of preparing gasoline from natural gas and from coal.

G. We can do much to help scientists and fuel experts in conserving fuel.

1. Insulation of homes will cut the use of fuel.

2. Many home owners waste fuel by keeping the temperature too high inside during the winter.

3. Many automobile engines waste gasoline because their carburetors are not adjusted properly.

FORCES THAT SHAPE
AND CHANGE THE EARTH'S SURFACE

I. THE SOLID PARTS OF THE EARTH CAN MOVE

A. Geologists have discovered that the solid parts of the earth can move and have moved, both a long time ago and fairly recently.

B. In some cases, parts of the earth's crust have been lifted.
1. Islands have risen from the deep Pacific Ocean.
2. Parts of continents, as in Sweden and Finland, have been raised.
3. Long ago the basins of the Great Lakes were tilted and lifted to a higher position than they were originally.

C. In some cases, parts of the earth's crust have sunk.
1. Occasionally, islands in the Pacific Ocean have disappeared beneath the water.
2. Parts of continents have been lowered, allowing shallow seas to cover them.

D. Sometimes there has been horizontal motion of the earth's crust, where large layers of rock move in wavelike folds, or slide over one another, and take up new positions.

E. Geologists are not sure why these movements of the earth take place, but there are four theories that are common today, which try to explain this movement.

F. According to the **theory of isostasy** (which means "equal standing"), the continents, ocean basins, mountains, and plains are all in a state of balance.
1. These land forms keep this balance by slowly adjusting their positions.
2. As rock from a higher region is worn down and carried away to a lower region, the higher region becomes lighter and rises slowly while the lower region becomes heavier and slowly sinks.
3. This theory helps explain why the wearing down of mountains and the filling

up of ocean basins have not produced a level surface all over the earth.
4. The theory also explains why thick beds of sediment can be found in ocean basins without filling up the oceans.
5. However, the theory does not explain why the rock layers in the earth's crust will move in wavelike folds to form mountains, or move against each other to cause earthquakes.

G. According to the **contraction theory** the earth is gradually shrinking, either because it is cooling or because great pressures are squeezing parts of it into a smaller volume.
1. Because of this shrinking, the inside of the earth is always becoming a little too small for the outside crust.
2. To adjust this condition, the stronger and heavier parts of the crust sink, crowding and squeezing the lighter parts, which are then pushed upward.
3. This theory does explain why the layers of rock in the earth's crust move to form mountains and cause earthquakes.

H. According to the **convection theory**, a convection current takes place inside the earth's core, so that the warmer, lighter parts of the earth rise while the colder, heavier parts fall.
1. Convection currents take place only with liquids, plastics, and gases, but not with solids.
2. However, although the rock inside the earth is solid, the rock is very hot and under great pressure, and with such conditions the rock will move just as if it were liquid.

I. Most scientists now accept the **continental drift theory** that there was only one large continent when the earth cooled.
1. The continent split up and the parts moved away to eventually form the con-

tinents and major islands we now know.

2. When the different parts pushed hard against the ocean floor, mountain ranges were formed, and there were earthquakes and volcanoes.

3. The continents are still moving, and some parts will eventually break away or come together, causing disturbances and changes in the earth's surface.

II. FOLDING AND FAULTING

A. Because of great temperature and pressure, tremendous sideward forces will often act on horizontal layers of rock, making them bend and wrinkle into wavelike **folds.**

1. These wavelike folds can have a crest and a trough, just like ocean waves.

2. The crest of a rock fold is called an **anticline,** and the trough a **syncline.**

3. Often the rock fold will have a crest but not a trough.

B. Some rock folds may be very small, but others are so large that they produce great mountain ranges.

C. Sometimes, in the process of folding, the rock may crack or break rather than bend.

D. Under great stress, very large masses or blocks of rock may move along this crack or break.

E. The crack or break in the rock is called a **fault** and the movement of the rock itself is called **faulting.**

F. Both folding and faulting play an important part in shaping and changing the earth's surface.

III. EARTHQUAKES

A. **Earthquakes** happen when faulting, and sometimes folding, takes place.

1. The great blocks of rock that lie next to a fault are pressed tightly together.

2. These blocks are under very great stress because one block is usually being pushed in one direction, while the other is pushed in the opposite direction.

3. After many years of increasing strain there is a sudden movement as the blocks slide and then come to rest in a new position that eases the pressure.

4. The blocks may move up and down, sideways, up and over each other, or they may even pull away from each other.

5. With this sudden movement a series of violent vibrations occurs that can shake large land masses for many seconds.

6. The movement may be very slight, but it may set up earthquake vibrations that can destroy a whole city.

B. Sometimes the earthquakes take place just below the surface, and sometimes they take place deep inside the earth.

C. Although earthquakes may take place all over the earth, they happen most often along two large areas of the earth, called **earthquake belts.**

1. These earthquake belts are usually areas where high mountain ranges are next to deep ocean floors.

2. It seems as if these areas are weak parts of the earth's crust.

3. One earthquake belt circles the Pacific Ocean, starting with Chile and going northward to Peru, Central America, Mexico, California, and Puget Sound, then to the Aleutian Islands and Japan, and southward to the Philippines, Indonesia, and New Zealand.

4. The second earthquake belt includes the mountainous areas next to the Mediterranean Sea, a section of Northern Africa, and Asia Minor and southern Asia.

D. Earthquakes that begin under the ocean set up huge sea waves, called **tsunamis.**

1. Tsunamis are mistakenly called "tidal waves."

2. Tsunamis may travel as fast as 800 kilometers (500 mi) an hour and may be more than 30 meters (100 ft) high when they reach the seacoast.

E. Earthquakes are detected by an instrument called a **seismograph.**

1. When an earthquake occurs, the vibrations that are produced will travel as waves through the earth.

2. The seismograph detects and records these vibrations, and from it we can tell where the earthquake took place and how strong the vibrations are.

3. Scientists use the **Richter Scale,** based on the amount of seismographic movement, to measure the strength of earthquakes at their source.

4. The scale is numbered 1–10, each higher number showing an earthquake 10 times stronger than the one before it.

5. An earthquake with a number of 2 is just strong enough to be felt; a number of 5 can cause much damage; and a number of 7 or more is a major earthquake.

IV. MOUNTAINS

A. **Mountains** are great masses of rock pushed high into the air by forces inside the earth.

B. Mountains are formed in four different ways, in which the masses of rock have been folded, tilted, shaped into domes, or built up from volcanic materials.

C. Mountains are also formed when the earth around a great mass of rock is worn away.

D. **Folded** mountains are formed when layers of rock are pushed into a series of wavelike folds by tremendous sideward forces that are produced by great pressure within the earth.

1. The **anticlines,** or crests of these waves, become mountain peaks.

2. The **synclines,** or troughs of these waves, become valleys.

3. Folded rocks can be uplifted many times over a long period of time, producing a whole region of long ridges that curve back and forth on each other.

4. Part of the Appalachian Mountains are folded mountains.

E. **Fault-block** mountains are formed when folded layers of rock break or crack, producing a fault.

1. Eventually faulting takes place, and the layers of rock on one side are pushed

up higher than those on the other side.

2. The layers of rock often tilt to one side after they have been pushed up.

3. Mountains formed in this way are called block mountains because they look like huge blocks.

4. In some areas these mountains are called "hogbacks" because one side of the mountain is steep and almost vertical, and the other side has a gentle slope.

5. The Sierra Nevadas are an example of fault-block mountains.

F. **Domed** mountains are formed either by folding or when magma in the earth flows up and between two layers of rock.

1. As the molten rock accumulates, it pushes up the layers of rock above it to form a large dome.

2. The Black Hills of South Dakota and the Adirondack Mountains of New York are examples of domed mountains.

G. **Volcanic** mountains are formed by the building up of lava and other materials that are thrown up when a volcano erupts.

1. These mountains build up gradually as they accumulate the material from erupting volcanoes.

2. Mount Lassen and Mount Rainier in the United States, Mount Popocatopetl in Mexico, Mount Vesuvius in Italy, and Mount Fujiyama in Japan are all examples of volcanic mountains.

3. Volcanic activity, going on in the ocean floor near the Aleutian Islands and the Hawaiian Islands, is building up a series of volcanic mountains at the bottom of the ocean around both of these areas.

H. Mountains are usually grouped together to form a **mountain range,** with a series of peaks of different heights.

I. Many ranges that are side by side, or parallel, are called a **chain** of mountains.

J. The Rocky Mountains are really a chain of many parallel mountain ranges.

K. Mountains have a life history, passing from youth to maturity to old age.

L. During their youth the mountains are still growing.

1. Young mountains are high and rugged, with steep slopes, rushing streams, and narrow valleys.

2. Many young mountains have snow all the time on their tops, and snowslides and avalanches are quite common.

3. The Rocky Mountains, Andes Mountains, Alps, and Himalaya Mountains are examples of young mountains.

M. At maturity the mountains have stopped growing.

1. The action of water, ice, wind, and other elements of the weather wears away the mountains, lowering their peaks and making the slopes more gentle.

2. Sometimes the mountains become so much lower that trees grow to the very top of the mountains.

3. The streams now flow more slowly and the valleys become much wider.

4. The Appalachian Mountains, the Adirondack Mountains, and the White Mountains are mature mountains.

N. At old age the mountains have been worn down until they are almost level.

1. The flat surface that is left is called a **peneplane,** which means "almost a plane level."

2. Southern New England and the areas of Manhattan and Westchester County of New York are peneplanes.

3. Sometimes a peneplane has low, rolling hills with an occasional high hill, called a **monadnock,** which is made of hard igneous rock that resisted wearing away and so remained behind.

4. Monadnock Mountain in New Hampshire and Pikes Peak in Colorado are examples of monadnocks.

5. The rivers of old mountain areas move very slowly and have low banks.

O. After mountains have passed through their life history and have been worn away, the process of mountain building eventually starts again.

V. PLAINS AND PLATEAUS

A. Plains and plateaus are different from mountains because they are made up of rock layers that are in the very same horizontal position in which the layers were originally formed.

B. **Plains** are low-level flat surfaces and **plateaus** are high-level flat surfaces, compared to the land around them.

C. **Coastal** plains are made up of pieces of rock that either were worn away from rocks along the seashore by ocean waves or were carried by rivers to the ocean.

1. The wave motion of the ocean spread out the pieces of rock until a smooth, flat surface was formed.

2. A coastal plain extends into the ocean, sometimes for great distances, forming what is called the **continental shelf.**

3. Sometimes forces inside the earth lift up all or part of the continental shelf so that it too becomes a coastal plain.

4. Some coastal plains are very narrow, and others are quite broad.

D. **Interior** plains were formed from large, shallow inland seas.

1. Sediments filled up these shallow seas until the water disappeared and flat plains were formed.

2. The Great Plains of the United States and the Argentine pampas are examples of interior marine plains.

E. **Lake** plains were formed from the bottom of large lakes.

1. Some lake plains were formed when forces inside the earth's surface caused the lake floor to be lifted.

2. Other lake plains were formed when conditions caused all the water in the lakes to drain away.

3. The largest lake plain in North America includes a large part of Minnesota, North Dakota, and the provinces of Saskatchewan and Manitoba in Canada.

F. Most plateaus were formed by forces beneath the earth's surface that raised horizontal layers of rock straight up, high in the air.

G. Some plateaus were also formed by lava flowing out of cracks in the earth, spreading out over a large area and forming a level region of layers of volcanic rock.

H. Plateaus, like mountains, also have a life history, passing from youth to maturity to old age.

I. Young plateaus are very high and flat, and they have not been worn away much by rivers flowing through them.

J. Mature plains are often called mountains, even though they are not mountains.
  1. They are mistakenly called mountains because many rivers and streams have cut wide valleys through the broad surfaces of the original plateau, giving the effect of a series of mountains.
  2. The tops of these "mountains" are usually flat.
  3. The Catskill Mountains are an example of a mature plateau.

K. At old age, plateaus are worn almost level, with only a few parts of the original plateau standing here and there.
  1. In dry areas the parts that remain have high walls and flat tops.
  2. The large plateaus with broad tops are called **mesas,** and smaller plateaus with more rounded tops are called **buttes.**
  3. Both mesas and buttes are found in New Mexico and Arizona, but mostly buttes are found in North Dakota, South Dakota, Montana, and Wyoming.
  4. In humid areas the remaining parts of a plateau are more rounded, and they look more like hills.

VI. VOLCANOES

A. A **volcano** is a mountain or a hill formed around a crack in the earth's crust, through which molten rock and other hot materials are thrown out.
  1. The rock inside the earth's mantle is very hot, but it is solid because of the great pressures upon it.
  2. When the pressure upon some of this solid rock is reduced, such as when a crack or fault forms in the earth's crust, the rock becomes a liquid, called **magma.**
  3. The molten rock, or magma, flows upward to the earth's surface, either through the crack that was formed or through a weak spot in the earth's crust.
  4. At the same time steam and other very hot gases, some of which are poisonous, are given off.

B. Some volcanoes, like those in Iceland and the Hawaiian Islands, erupt quietly.

C. Others, like those in the East Indies and the Mediterranean, erupt violently because of tremendous pressures inside them.

D. Some, like Stromboli in Italy, alternate between being quiet and explosive.

E. When molten rock, or magma, reaches the earth's surface, it is called **lava.**
  1. Sometimes lava hardens to form a rough and jagged surface, and other times it hardens to form a smooth, ropy surface.
  2. The tiniest drops of lava spray form fine **volcanic dust** which spreads out far and high into the atmosphere.
  3. The larger drops of lava become **volcanic cinders** (coarse) and **volcanic ash** (fine), which fall fairly close to the volcano.
  4. **Obsidian** is a dark glassy rock formed from lava that cooled quickly.
  5. **Pumice** and **scoria** are very light rocks, with holes in them, that formed from lava that hardened while steam and other gases were still bubbling from it.
  6. **Tuff** is volcanic ash that became cemented to form a rock.

F. There are three main types of volcanoes: **shield, cinder cone,** and **composite.**

G. Shield volcanoes are usually formed from quiet eruptions.
  1. The lava spreads out to form a broad base and gentle slopes.
  2. Mauna Loa and Kilauea in Hawaii are examples of shield volcanoes.

H. Cinder cone volcanoes are usually formed from explosive eruptions.
  1. They have a fairly narrow base and steep slopes.
  2. Paricutin in Mexico is an example of a

cinder cone volcano formation.

I. Composite volcanoes are usually formed from eruptions that have had alternate quiet and explosive periods.

1. As a result, they have alternate layers of lava and cinders or ash.

2. They are steeper than shield volcanoes, but gentler than cinder cone volcanoes.

3. Fujiyama in Japan and Rainier in the United States are examples of composite volcanoes.

J. The opening at the top of the volcano is called the **crater.**

1. Usually the crater is rather narrow, but sometimes the upper part of the crater will blow apart or collapse, forming a very wide basinlike hollow, called a **caldera.**

2. These calderas often fill with water and become a lake, such as Crater Lake in Oregon.

K. Volcanoes are also classified as **active, dormant,** and **extinct.**

1. Active volcanoes are those that are erupting or have recently erupted.

2. Dormant volcanoes are those that have not erupted for some time, but still show signs of some activity.

3. Extinct volcanoes are those that have not erupted for a long time, with no signs of activity.

L. Almost all of the volcanoes on earth are found in the same place as the two earthquake belts.

1. One belt circles the Pacific Ocean, and the other belt extends from the Mediterranean area eastward across Asia Minor and the southern part of Asia.

2. There are also volcanic areas in Iceland, the Azores, and some islands in the West Indies.

M. In the area around the Aleutian Islands and the Hawaiian Islands large volcanic mountain chains are being built up at the bottom of the ocean.

N. Most of the islands in the South Pacific are really the tops of submerged extinct volcanoes.

VII. HOT SPRINGS AND GEYSERS

A. Hot springs and geysers are common where hot rock is present below the surface of the earth.

B. **Hot springs** are formed when underground water is heated by hot rock or gases below the earth's surface and then flows to the surface before cooling off.

1. The passageway along which the water travels is wide and open, so the water reaches the surface quickly and easily.

2. The temperature of the water may range from just warm to boiling.

3. On its way to the surface the water dissolves large amounts of minerals.

4. These minerals are deposited around the mouth of the hot spring when the water evaporates, and they tend to build up colored layers or terraces.

C. A **geyser** is a hot spring that throws its water high into the air from time to time.

1. This eruption of water occurs because the geyser has to travel up a narrow, twisted passageway to reach the earth's surface.

2. Heated water is often trapped in this passageway, where it continues to be heated far above its boiling point of 100° Celsius (212° Fehrenheit) without being changed into steam.

3. This happens because the water on top presses down on the water below, and this water under pressure can be superheated without boiling.

4. The superheated water expands and causes some of the water above it to overflow onto the earth's surface.

5. This loss of water on top eases the pressure on the superheated water on the bottom so that some of it is suddenly changed to steam, which blows all the water above it high into the air.

6. After the geyser erupts, some of the water flows back into the passageway, where it meets more underground water coming up, and the process starts again.

7. Some geysers, like Old Faithful in Yel-

lowstone National Park, erupt at regular intervals; others erupt at very irregular intervals.

8. Almost all the geysers in the world are found in only three places: Yellowstone National Park, Iceland, and New Zealand.

FORCES THAT WEAR AWAY THE EARTH'S SURFACE

I. THE EARTH'S SURFACE IS ALWAYS CHANGING

A. Although the surface of the earth appears to be quite solid and permanent, it is always changing.
B. The rocks that make up the earth's surface are always being broken up and carried away.
C. This process of breaking down rocks is called **weathering.**
  1. Weathering is caused by the action of the sun, air, and water.
  2. There are two kinds of weathering: **mechanical** or **physical weathering,** and **chemical weathering.**
D. The process of taking away the products of weathering is called **erosion,** and it is carried on by water, ice, and wind.
E. The forces of weathering and erosion are constantly at work on the earth's surfaces, but forces inside the earth keep building these surfaces up again.

II. MECHANICAL OR PHYSICAL WEATHERING

A. Mechanical weathering is the breaking down of rock into small pieces without any chemical changes in the rock itself.
B. One way that mechanical weathering takes place is water seeping into cracks and pores of rocks and then freezing.
  1. When water freezes it expands and exerts much pressure, which causes pieces of rock to break off.
  2. This kind of weathering takes place when the days are above freezing and the nights are below freezing.
C. Another way that mechanical weathering takes place is rock being heated by day

and cooled by night, with the temperature above freezing in both cases.
  1. This kind of weathering happens more often in humid places.
  2. When rocks are heated during the day, the minerals in them expand.
  3. Water that seeps into the rocks combines with these minerals, causing them to swell and form cracks in the rocks.
  4. At night the rocks cool and contract, causing the outside of the rocks to peel off in thin layers or sheets.
  5. This process, where layers are peeled off rock, is called **exfoliation.**
D. Plants can cause mechanical weathering because, as shrubs and trees grow, their roots work into small cracks in the rock, making the rock split and crumble.
E. Animals also play a part in mechanical weathering.
  1. Burrowing animals, like gophers and prairie dogs, dig constantly and expose new rock surfaces for weathering.
  2. Earthworms bring fine particles of rock to the surface, and they also make tiny passageways in the earth, which let air and water enter the soil easily.
F. A wind which carries fine rock particles can rub away solid rock.

III. CHEMICAL WEATHERING

A. In chemical weathering chemical changes take place in the rock, forming new products that can be carried away more easily than the original rock.
B. Chemical weathering is more likely to take place in areas where the air is humid or where water is present.

C. The carbon dioxide gas in the air can produce chemical weathering in certain rocks.
   1. When carbon dioxide from the air dissolves in water, it forms a weak acid called **carbonic acid.**
   2. Carbonic acid attacks rocks such as limestone, forming materials that dissolve easily in water and are carried away.
   3. Many rocks have at least one mineral that is affected by carbonic acid, and, when this mineral is removed, the rest of the minerals are exposed, making it easier for other forms of weathering to break them up.
D. The oxygen in the air combines directly with many minerals in rocks, forming materials that crumble easily.
E. Water, either in the air or on the ground, combines with many minerals, causing them to swell and form cracks in the rock, making it easier for mechanical weathering to take place.
F. Small plants, called **lichens,** grow on rocks and produce chemical weathering.
   1. The lichens use the minerals from the rock to live and grow.
   2. The lichens obtain these minerals by giving off an acid that attacks the rock and breaks it up.
G. When plants and animals die and decay, acids that attack the rock and make it crumble are formed.

IV. EROSION BY WATER

A. Water is the greatest of all the forces that produce erosion.
   1. Each year great quantities of water fall on the earth's land surface.
   2. Some of this water seeps into the earth and stays there as ground water.
   3. Some water evaporates back into the air.
   4. The rest of the water flows over the earth's surface in a huge number of streams and rivers.
   5. This running water carries with it the materials formed by weathering, and it carries them to lakes and oceans, where they are deposited.
B. Ground water causes erosion below the earth's surface.
   1. The carbon dioxide in the air combines with water to form weak carbonic acid, which attacks limestone and forms materials that dissolve in water and are carried away.
   2. Where much limestone is present, large caves are formed because of the action of carbonic acid upon the limestone.
   3. Sometimes the underground water, which has limestone dissolved in it, will form solid deposits inside these caves.
   4. The underground water forms these deposits by dripping so slowly through the roof of these caves that some of the water evaporates, and the limestone in the water deposits out again.
   5. Over a long time limestone "icicles," called **stalactites,** will hang from the ceiling of the caves, and columns of limestone, called **stalagmites,** will form on the floor.
   6. The Carlsbad Caverns in New Mexico and Mammoth Cave in Kentucky are examples of caves with stalactites and stalagmites in them.
C. Running water causes erosion on the earth's surface.
   1. As rainwater runs off to join streams and rivers, it carries particles of soil and rock with it.
   2. As the water flows in the streams and rivers, it wears away the beds and causes the sides to cave, making the streams and rivers wider.
   3. The particles of rock in the water also act as weathering forces to wear away more of the earth's rock.
   4. The running water in streams and rivers continues to carry these pieces of rock with it to oceans and lakes.
   5. Many large rivers move very slowly as they near the mouth of an ocean or lake,

and they then drop the materials they are carrying, forming deposits called **deltas.**

D. The oceans both erode and build up the earth's surface.

1. The waves, pounding against the rocks and land along the shore, wear them away and carry off the rock particles.

2. At Cape Cod 1 to 2 meters (3 to 6 ft) of shoreline are worn away by the ocean each year.

3. The currents and waves will also carry materials, such as sand and pebbles, to the shore and make sandy beaches.

4. However, storms and strong undertows will often carry beach materials away faster than the waves can deposit them.

5. Some waves will deposit materials just off the shore, forming sandbars and sandy islands.

V. Erosion by Ice

A. **Glaciers** are huge masses of ice formed where the climate and weather are very cold.

1. In these places much snow falls each year, and more snow falls than can melt or evaporate.

2. The snow stays from one year to the next, accumulating layers that pile up into deep masses.

3. The great weight of the snow presses on the layers underneath, causing these layers of snow to melt and refreeze again as ice grains or pellets, called **neve.**

4. In the lowest layers the pressure is so great that the neve is recrystallized again to form one solid mass of ice.

5. Each winter more layers are added to the top, forming more ice below.

6. Eventually the weight of this huge mass of snow and ice becomes so great that the whole mass begins to move slowly.

7. This moving mass of ice is called a **glacier.**

B. **Valley** glaciers are glaciers formed in mountain valleys where snow remains the whole year.

1. Some valley glaciers are quite small, but, others are very large.

2. As the valley glacier begins to move to lower levels, it gouges out the rock beneath it and carries the broken pieces with it.

3. As the valley glacier moves, it also picks up more rock that it has worn away from the sides of the valley.

4. These rocks, embedded in the ice, act as a huge file to wear away the earth over which the glacier passes.

5. This movement of the valley glacier tends to smooth out the valley floor.

6. At the same time, the glacier grinds away the valley walls and straightens sharp bends, changing the V-shape of the valley to a broader U-shape.

7. As the valley glacier moves, big cracks, called **crevasses** form at the top and sides of the glacier.

8. When the glacier meets warmer temperatures, it begins to melt, and then it **drops** the material that it has been carrying.

9. The material that has been dropped is called a **moraine.**

C. **Continental** glaciers are found only at the polar regions today.

1. In the polar regions the average temperature is below freezing, and most of the snow that falls stays from one year to the next.

2. As a result, a glacier is formed that covers a tremendous amount of land surface, which is why it is called a continental glacier.

3. The continental glacier at the North Pole, which also covers most of Greenland, is more than 2440 meters (8000 ft) thick.

4. The glacier that covers Antarctica at the South Pole is more than 4270 meters (14,000 ft) thick.

5. These continental glaciers, covering

Greenland and Antarctica, move outward toward the seacoast.

6. The rise and fall of the tides snap off large pieces of the glaciers, which then float away as icebergs.

7. Because of their huge size and weight, continental glaciers tend to smooth the surfaces over which they pass by grinding down the higher parts of the land and filling in the valleys.

8. Where parts of the earth's surface are softer than other parts, the glacier may often gouge out huge depressions or basins.

9. When the climate becomes warmer and the glacier retreats, these basins often remain, fill with melted ice from the glaciers, and become lakes.

D. The earth has gone through glacial periods in which large parts of the earth were covered by glaciers.

1. All of these glacial periods followed a regular cycle.

2. First the climate became much colder, and huge glaciers formed at the poles.

3. The glaciers moved out in all directions tions from the poles and covered large parts of the earth.

4. Then the climate became warmer, whereupon the glaciers melted and retreated back to the poles.

5. The retreating glaciers left behind the rocky materials and the moraines they brought with them, and also the grinding changes they made on the earth's surface.

E. The earth has had four of these glacial periods.

1. The first period occurred about 800 million years ago, and it was followed by a warm period of roughly 3 million years.

2. The second period came about 500 million years ago, and it was again followed by a warm period of about 300 million years.

3. The third period came about 200 million years ago, and the fourth period about one million years ago.

4. At present we seem to be in a period where the glaciers are retreating.

VI. EROSION BY WIND

A. The chief work of wind is to carry away loose bits of soil and rock.

1. This erosion is quite common in dry areas where there are few plants, shrubs, or trees to cover the ground and protect it.

2. Even mild winds constantly move fine particles of dust and rock, but strong winds can create tremendous dust storms.

3. Over a long time, wind can blow away all the loose material from a desert floor, leaving only a floor of bare rock behind.

B. The wind can also deposit materials, especially when it slows down.

C. The most common wind deposits are hills of sand, called **dunes.**

1. Dunes are formed when something is in the way of the wind, slowing the wind down and causing it to deposit the particles it has been carrying.

2. As the mound of deposited material grows, it helps to slow down the wind even more, so that more material is deposited.

3. In this way the dune grows until it is quite high.

4. Winds will often move sand dunes from one place to another unless grass or shrubs are planted, which cover the sand sufficiently to hold it in place.

5. Sometimes fences are put into dunes to prevent the dunes from moving and covering highways, railroads, or even buildings.

D. Another kind of wind deposit is a fine sediment called **loess.**

1. This material is sometimes deposited over large areas of land, and the deposits are quite thick.

2. If water is available, loess makes very fertile soil.

E. The wind also serves as a weathering agent as well as an erosion agent.

1. As the wind blows against solid rock, the particles of rock that the wind is carrying often rub against solid rock and wear it away.

2. Beach cliffs and rocks are often made smooth this way.
3. Rocks and boulders in deserts are also made smooth this way.

SOIL

I. How Soil Is Formed

A. Although the forces of mechanical and chemical weathering act on rock very slowly, over millions of years these forces have broken up almost all the rock on or near the earth's surface.
1. This is the reason why the earth's surface has a layer of pieces of rock on it.
2. These pieces of rock are all sizes, ranging from tiny pieces to large boulders.
3. This layer of pieces of rock is called **mantle rock.**
B. The forces of weathering continue to act on this mantle rock until a layer of **soil** is formed.
1. Soil is made up of tiny grains of rock and minerals.
2. Soil that has not moved from the original mantle rock that formed it is called **residual** soil.
3. Soil that is carried by erosion from one place to another is called **transported** soil.
C. Soil becomes fertile when **humus,** the remains of dead animals and plants, is added to it.
D. Because humus is added only to the top portion of the layer of soil, there is a difference in the quality of the soil layer.
E. The first 20 centimeters (8 in) of soil is called the **topsoil** or **A-horizon.**
1. This layer of topsoil is rich in humus.
2. The topsoil also has air spaces in it, which are filled with either air or water.
3. The topsoil is fertile, and it is the soil that helps crops grow.
4. About 2½ centimeters (1 in) of topsoil

is formed in about 500 years.
F. The soil underneath the topsoil is called the **subsoil** or **B-horizon.**
1. The subsoil is a much thicker layer than the topsoil.
2. It has little or no humus in it.
3. It also has a lot of pebbles in it.
G. Beneath the subsoil is partly weathered bedrock (**C-horizon**), then solid bedrock.

II. Kinds of Soil

A. Soil contains different sizes and kinds of rocks and minerals.
1. These different rocks and minerals usually include large pebbles or gravel, smaller particles of sand, and tiny particles of clay.
2. Soil may also contain particles of silt, which is smaller than sand but larger than clay.
B. Soil is classified according to the predominant kind of material within it.
C. **Sandy** soil has mostly sand in it, together with a little clay, and it contains almost no humus.
1. Sandy soil does not hold water very well, and the water drains off quickly.
2. There are very few minerals in sandy soil that plants can use.
D. **Clay** soil has mostly clay in it, together with a little sand and humus.
1. Clay soil holds water very well, and it dries very slowly.
2. However, clay soil is sticky when wet, and it becomes almost as hard as rock when dry.
E. **Loam** is soil that has proper amounts of

gravel, sand, and clay in it, together with lots of humus.

1. It is usually dark brown, or even black, in color.
2. Loam is the best soil for most crops.

F. The best way to use soil for growing crops is to cultivate it.

1. When soil is cultivated, the large clumps are broken up and the earth around the plant roots is loosened.
2. This loosening makes it easier for plant roots to go down into the soil, and it also lets air and water get to the roots.
3. Cultivation of the soil is done by a spade, hoe, rake, plow, and harrow.

III. Soil Erosion

A. In areas that have not been troubled by man, erosion of the soil is a slow process.

1. Shrubs and trees above the ground, and their roots below the ground, help prevent the soil from being washed away by running water.
2. The little soil that is carried away is replaced by new soil formed over the years.

B. When man uses the soil to grow crops, erosion can take place very quickly.

1. Almost all the shrubs and trees that protected the soil have been removed.
2. This removal makes it easy for the forces of erosion to work on the soil.

C. The most powerful force of soil erosion is running water.

D. Erosion of the soil starts when the rain begins to fall.

1. The raindrops strike the earth and loosen the soil.
2. Particles of soil may then be splashed away.
3. This kind of erosion is called **splash** erosion.

E. When the rain falls steadily, the soil absorbs the water until it can hold no more.

1. When this absorption takes place, the water runs off in broad sheets, carrying soil with it.

2. This kind of erosion is called **sheet** erosion.
3. Sheet erosion can take away all of the topsoil, leaving the subsoil—or even bare bedrock—behind.

F. As the water runs off, it eventually collects into small streams that flow down to lower ground.

1. As a stream travels, it may wash out some of the ground and form a small channel, called a **rill.**
2. A rill is often formed when crops have been planted in rows that run up and down a field that slopes.
3. A rill can become deeper and wider with each rainfall, as the running water carries more soil away each time, forming a larger channel, called a **gully.**
4. This kind of erosion is called **rill** or **gully** erosion.

G. The small streams flow into larger streams, each taking away soil from the bottom and sides of the bed upon which the stream flows.

IV. Methods of Preventing Soil Erosion

A. Unless something is done to stop soil erosion, the soil will soon become completely worthless for growing crops.

B. There are many ways to slow down soil erosion, especially where the land slopes downward.

C. In **contour plowing** the rows of crops follow the contours of the land.

1. This form of cultivation means that on hills the rows run sideways rather than up and down.
2. Rows that run sideways slow down the water as it flows down the hill.
3. These rows catch the soil and stop it from being carried away.

D. **Terracing** is used when the slope or hill is rather steep.

1. Steplike ridges, called **terraces,** are built, which follow the contours of the hill and run sideways.
2. These terraces either hold or slow down

the water sufficiently for it to soak into the soil so that the soil is not washed down the hill and carried away.

E. **Strip cropping** is used on milder slopes.
  1. In strip cropping different crops are grown on the same piece of land.
  2. First there is a plot of row crops, such as corn, where the plants are grown in rows.
  3. Next there is a plot of cover crops, such as alfalfa or hay, where the plants cover the ground.
  4. The cover crops catch and hold any soil that may be washed away from the rows.
  5. The next year the cover crops are grown where the row crops were grown, and the row crops are grown where the cover crops were grown.
F. Bare land, unsuitable for growing crops, is planted with trees and grass to help replace the soil that was washed away.
G. In dry parts of the country as well as those parts where it has not rained for a long time, the wind can erode the soil.
  1. When the land has become really dry and bare and there are no crops on it, the wind can produce large dust storms.
  2. Erosion of this kind will often occur when the grasslands in rather dry areas are plowed up and crops are planted.
  3. When there is very little rainfall and no grass to hold the soil, the wind blows away the soil easily.
H. Sometimes trees are planted close together in rows to form a **shelter belt** for the farms.
  1. When the wind travels across the land, it is forced upward by one shelter belt after another.
  2. This forcing of the wind upward stops the wind from staying close to the ground and blowing the soil away.

V. Enriching the Soil

A. There are many minerals in the soil that growing plants need to make food.
B. The most important of these minerals are those that have nitrogen, phosphorus, potassium, calcium, and magnesium in them.
C. The plants take away large amounts of these minerals from the soil each year, which must be replaced if the soil is to stay fertile.
D. One of the best ways to replace these minerals is to use a natural fertilizer, such as animal manure, which adds both minerals and humus to the soil.
E. Another way is to use commercial fertilizers, which contain the minerals that plants need to grow.
F. A third way is to change crops every few years.
  1. Certain crops need different kinds and amounts of minerals from other crops.
  2. If the same crops are grown year after year, all of these minerals are taken from the soil, and only by using large amounts of fertilizer can the farmer continue to grow these crops.
  3. By growing different crops every few years, which need different kinds and amounts of minerals, the soil can get back the minerals it has lost.
G. When the soil becomes low in nitrogen, the farmer can grow such crops as clover, alfalfa, beans, or peas.
  1. These plants have little, round bumps attached to their roots.
  2. In the bumps there live certain bacteria, called **nitrogen-fixing bacteria.**
  3. Although 78 percent of the air is nitrogen, plants cannot use this nitrogen in the gaseous form in which it is found in the air.
  4. However, the nitrogen-fixing bacteria take the nitrogen from the air and change it into materials that plants can use.

VI. Testing the Soil

A. Soil is often tested to see what must be done to it to grow better crops.
B. Soil is tested to find out what minerals are

needed and what kinds of plants or crops will grow best in the soil.

C. Soil is also tested to find out whether it is too acid or alkaline.
   1. Some plants or crops grow better when the soil is slightly alkaline, and other plants or crops grow better when the soil is slightly acid.
   2. If the soil is too alkaline, an acid material is added to it.
   3. If the soil is too acid, an alkaline material is added to it.
   4. One alkaline material used to cut down the acidity of the soil, or "sweeten" it, is lime.

D. The amount of humus in a soil is found by heating a sample of the soil.
   1. Only the humus in the soil will burn away.
   2. By weighing the soil before and after it was heated, the loss in weight will indicate how much humus there was in the soil.

E. Tests can also be made to see how quickly water can go into or leave the soil, and how much water the soil can hold.

THE HISTORY OF THE EARTH

I. How Geologists Learn About the Earth

A. The history of the earth is recorded in the rocks.

B. This is the reason why geologists spend much time patiently studying rocks over the earth, looking for clues that will help them learn the complete history of the earth.
   1. They examine the rocks carefully for information about changes in the earth's surface.
   2. They look for evidence of change in climate.
   3. They also look for signs and traces of living things that lived long ago.

C. Although there are still a few gaps, geologists have managed to fit together the pieces of information they have collected and obtain a fairly complete history of the earth.

D. The following three areas of geology have helped geologists obtain this history: **stratigraphy, petrology,** and **paleontology.**

E. Stratigraphy is the study of rock layers.
   1. The order in which layers of rock are found is a very important clue to the earth's past.
   2. These layers are usually formed hori-

zontally, with the oldest rocks on the bottom and the youngest rocks on top.
   3. If these layers are not disturbed, geologists can tell by the position of these layers how and when they were formed.
   4. Even when the layers are folded and faulted, or the rocks in the layers have been changed to metamorphic rock, geologists can still identify them, knowing that one layer of rock is older than the layer above it.
   5. These layers tell geologists where earlier oceans, mountains, plains, and plateaus were located.
   6. They also show the kinds of changes that took place on the earth's surface long ago.
   7. By matching layers of the same age that are located in different parts of the earth, geologists have been able to learn about the entire earth, rather than just one part of the earth.

F. Petrology is the study of the rocks themselves.
   1. Geologists study the rocks to learn how they were formed, what happened to them, and what kinds of minerals are in them.
   2. Every rock tells a story through its

structure, texture, physical and chemical makeup, and traces of former plants and animals embedded in it.

3. A piece of old sandstone may have ripple or wave marks on it, or there may be seashells in it, showing that the sandstone was formed in the ocean.

4. A conglomerate rock may show that it was made by a swiftly moving stream or by heavy ocean waves.

5. The earlier existence of shallow seas, lakes, deserts, glaciers, and other forms of the earth's surface can all be learned from the sediments they left behind.

6. These sediments can also tell us what kinds of rocks there were a long time ago, the climate at that time, and other conditions on earth a long time ago.

G. Paleontology is the study of fossils, which are the remains or traces in rock of earlier plants and animals.

1. The remains may be skeletons, or they may be the complete plants and animals themselves.

2. The traces may be footprints or body and tail marks.

3. Fossils are rarely found in igneous rock.

4. Fossils can be found in sedimentary rocks that were changed to metamorphic rocks, but most fossils were usually destroyed or greatly damaged when the sedimentary rocks were changed.

5. From the sedimentary rocks the geologist can learn such things about living things of long ago as their development, body structure, nature habits, and the climate in which they lived.

6. If coral is found in the Arctic region, geologists know that at one time the climate was warm in this region.

7. If seashells are found on mountain tops, geologists know that at one time this land was under the ocean.

H. Fossils have been formed in many different ways.

I. Some animal fossils were formed when animals were covered by sediment.

1. Animals that lived in or near bodies of water sometimes were buried by the mud, dirt, and gravel.

2. This sediment then hardened into rock.

3. The hard parts of the body, such as the skeleton and teeth, were preserved in their original form in the rock.

J. Some animals fell into tar pits, swamps, or quicksand, which later hardened, and their bones and teeth were preserved.

K. Some fossils were formed when animals were frozen in ice and mud, and they were preserved whole.

L. Some insects became fossils when they were trapped by the sticky sap flowing from trees.

1. The insects became completely buried inside the sap, which then hardened.

2. Later on, oceans and their sediments covered the trees.

3. Eventually the sap was changed to the material we call **amber.**

4. The insects inside the amber dried out to almost nothing, but their bristles, wing scales, and thin outer skeleton were preserved as fossils.

M. Some plants and animals formed fossils by leaving a cast of their remains.

1. When the plants and animals were covered with sediment and died, their hard parts were left behind.

2. The water inside the sediment dissolved these hard parts, leaving a hollow space in the sediment that surrounded these parts.

3. The space then filled with minerals, which hardened to form a cast.

N. Many plants and animals have been preserved in great detail as fossils when they were petrified, or "turned into stone."

1. This petrification does not mean that the original material in the plant or animal was really changed into stone.

2. What actually happened was that, when the plant or animal was buried, the original material in the plant or animal was replaced, particle by particle, with minerals in such a way that an exact duplicate of the material was formed.

3. This substitution of minerals for the original materials has been so perfect in some cases that exceptionally clear and complete fossil specimens have been formed.

O. Animals without hard parts, such as jelly-fish and worms, and also plants without woody parts often left fossil prints.

1. When these soft, living things were covered with sediment and the sediment hardened, their parts were chemically changed into carbon.

2. This carbon formed an outline of the living things.

3. Even the delicate outlines of fish scales and leaf veins can often be seen in these prints.

P. Fossils of footprints, body and tail marks, outline and vein pattern of leaves, and imprints of stem and flowers have been formed.

1. These marks were first made in soft mud.

2. Later, soil or silt may have been gently blown or washed into these prints.

3. More layers of sediment were added, and eventually the mud and sediment hardened into rock, preserving at the same time the marks and imprints in the original mud.

Q. Fossils are often found in coal, especially soft coal.

1. Coal itself is the fossil remains of plants and trees that lived long ago in swampy land.

2. These plants and trees were buried under layers of sediment.

3. Under heat and pressure, the plant and tree materials were changed and hardened into coal.

4. Some of the original plant material can still be found as fossils in the coal.

II. How Geologists Calculate the Age of the Earth

A. Geologists have tried many methods to find out the age of the earth and the rocks in it.

B. One method to determine the age of rock is to use the rate of erosion of soil.

1. Careful scientific observations show that, on the average, erosion of rock and soil takes place at a rate of 30 centimeters (1 ft) in about 5000 years.

2. If we know this rate, we can estimate the age of the Grand Canyon.

3. In some places the Grand Canyon is about 180 meters (600 ft) deep.

4. With erosion taking place at 30 centimeters (1 ft) in about 5000 years, it would take about 30 million years for the Colorado River to erode 180 meters (600 ft) of the Grand Canyon.

C. Another method to find the age of rock is to use the rate at which sediment is deposited and changed into sedimentary rock.

1. Geologists think that it takes between 500 and 10,000 years for a layer of sedimentary rock 30 centimeters (1 ft) thick to be formed.

2. This method is not as accurate as the method of using the rate of soil erosion.

D. Some geologists have tried to estimate the age of the oceans by the amount of salt in the oceans.

1. First, the geologists find out how much salt there now is in the oceans.

2. Next, they find out how much salt is being carried by rivers into the oceans each year.

3. By comparing how much salt the oceans now have with how much salt they are getting each year, it is possible to estimate how many years the oceans have been receiving salt.

4. This method is not very accurate because the oceans most likely received less salt in the beginning than they do today.

E. The older methods described above are not too accurate, and they are of little use in finding the age of the earth itself.

F. Geologists now use the newer method of radioactivity to calculate both the age of rocks and the age of the earth.

G. One radioactive method involves the

study of the uranium found in igneous and metamorphic rocks.

1. Uranium is a radioactive chemical element that breaks down very slowly to form other elements.

2. It breaks down to form radium, which in turn breaks down into a number of other elements, and finally it becomes lead.

3. Uranium breaks up at a very slow and steady rate, which cannot be changed by temperature or pressure.

4. Scientists have calculated that it takes 5 billion years for half a piece of uranium to be changed into lead.

5. By examining a piece of rock that has uranium in it and comparing the amount of uranium still present with the amount of lead that has been formed from the uranium, geologists can calculate the age of the rock—and even the earth—quite accurately.

H. By using this radioactive method, geologists estimate that the earth is at least 4 billion, and most likely 5 billion, years old.

I. Another radioactive method involves the study of radioactive carbon-14, which is found in sedimentary rocks.

1. All living things have carbon-14 in them.

2. When living things die, no more carbon-14 is produced.

3. Instead, the carbon-14 begins to break down at a very slow and steady rate, just as uranium does.

4. Scientists have calculated that it takes about 5600 years for half a piece of carbon-14 to break down.

5. The fossil remains of living things, which once had carbon-14 in them, are found in sedimentary rocks.

6. By examining a piece of rock that has fossil remains and comparing the amount of carbon-14 in it with the amount of other elements that have been formed from the carbon-14, geologists can calculate the age of the rock.

J. The carbon-14 method is used to find the age of rocks to 15,000 years old, and the uranium method is used to find the age of older rocks.

III. The Geologic Timetable

A. Because the history of the earth involves such a long period of time, geologists find it convenient to use a special calendar, called a geologic timetable, when discussing what happened to the earth during that time.

B. The longest division of time in the geologic timetable is called an era.

C. Eras are broken down into smaller time units called periods, which are broken down still further into smaller units called epochs.

D. There are six major eras in the life of the earth; they are listed as follows.

1. Cenozoic era.

2. Mesozoic era.

3. Paleozoic era.

4. Proterozoic era.

5. Archeozoic era.

6. Azoic era.

E. The earliest era is the Azoic era, and the most recent era is the Cenozoic era.

F. Each era had its own periods and its own epochs.

G. During each era geologic changes took place.

1. New mountain ranges were formed.

2. Shapes of continents were changed, and shallow seas within the continents were either formed or drained off.

3. The circulation of the oceans and the atmosphere changed.

4. These new conditions produced changes in climate, which in turn caused changes in the kinds of living things that lived on earth.

5. New forms of living things developed, which were better able to live in the new and different climate.

6. At the same time, older forms of living things, which could not adjust to the new climate, died.

7. As a result, each era usually had its own

special kinds of plant life (flora) and animal life (fauna).

H. There were also geologic changes during periods and epochs, but these changes were not as great as those changes during the eras.

IV. THE AZOIC ERA

A. The **Azoic** era began between 4 and 5 billion years ago, and it lasted for roughly 2 to 3 billion years.

B. This era is the time when the earth was formed.

C. At the end of the Azoic era there was nothing on earth but rocks, water, and air.

V. THE ARCHEOZOIC ERA

A. The **Archeozoic** era began about 2 billion years ago, and it lasted for about 1 billion years.

B. During this era there was volcanic action, great mountain ranges were formed, and the oceans took turns covering the land areas and then withdrawing.

C. Some Archeozoic rocks contain much graphite, the form of carbon that is used in pencils and as a lubricant.

D. Very simple forms of life, such as the tiny, one-celled plants called bacteria and algae, may have existed during this era.

VI. THE PROTEROZOIC ERA

A. The **Proterozoic** era began roughly 1 billion years ago, and it lasted for about 450 million years.

B. During this era the basic shapes of the earth's continents developed, vast masses of igneous rock were formed, and there is evidence that glaciers may have been present.

C. Also, during this era most of the simpler animals without backbones, called **invertebrates**, made their appearance.

1. These included protozoa, sponges, jelly-

fish, coral, and animals that had a worm-like appearance.

2. There were also the beginnings of more advanced invertebrates, such as crabs, spiders, and insects.

D. There was not much plant life during this era.

1. Most of the plants belonged to the simplest group of plants, called **thallophytes.**

2. These included bacteria, blue-green algae, and the brown algae or seaweed.

E. Almost all of the living things in this era were found in the ocean.

VII. THE PALEOZOIC ERA

A. The **Paleozoic** era began about 550 million years ago, and it lasted for about 350 million years.

B. This era is called the **Age of Invertebrates, Fishes, and Amphibians.**

C. During this era many geological developments took place.

1. At the beginning of the era large parts of the North American continent were covered by shallow seas.

2. Then mountains were formed in Vermont, and also in northern Maine and eastern Canada.

3. Thick beds of salt were formed in New York, Pennsylvania, West Virginia, Ohio, and Michigan.

4. The Appalachian Mountains appeared, and all the shallow inland seas which covered eastern North America drained off.

5. During this era there also occurred a great ice age in South America, South Africa, India, and Australia.

D. Invertebrate life flourished in the early part of the Paleozoic era.

1. These animals included sponges, corals, worms, snails, starfish, and crabs.

2. Most of these invertebrates looked different from the kinds we see today.

E. Common invertebrates during this era

were the trilobites, often considered to be early ancestors of our present-day crabs and lobsters.

1. The trilobite had a shell that was divided lengthwise into three clearly notched lobes or sections.
2. They had jointed legs that they used for walking on the ocean floor.
3. They had eyes and feelers that helped them find food, although some trilobites had no eyes.
4. Most trilobites were less than 7½ centimeters (3 in) long, but some were more than 60 centimeters (2 ft) long and may have weighed as much as 7 kilograms (15 lb).
5. They ate small organisms and decaying plants and animals.
6. Trilobites died out and became extinct at the end of the Paleozoic era.

F. During the middle of this era a large number of fishes of different kinds began to appear.

1. These fishes were the first animals with backbones, which are called **vertebrates**.
2. These fishes included armored fish, the ancestors of sharks, and fish with lungs called lungfish.

G. At the same time, plants began to appear on land.

1. Mosses, ferns, and seed plants grew, first beside oceans and lakes and then further inland.
2. Some fernlike trees grew to heights of 12 meters (40 ft).

H. With the appearance of plants on land, animals began to live on land too.

1. These animals included scorpions, snails, spiders, and many kinds of insects.
2. There were hundreds of different kinds of cockroaches, some of them 10 centimeters (4 in) long.
3. There were also dragonflies with a wingspread of 60 centimeters (2 ft).

I. Coal was formed during this era, especially in the Pennsylvania area.

1. At this time there were large swampy forests, where land plants grew.

2. These plants included scale trees, horsetails, huge mosses and ferns, seed ferns, and plants that produced a primitive kind of cone.
3. The land in some of these forest areas sank very slowly and gradually so that huge piles of dead plants accumulated.
4. These piles of plants were slowly covered with water, which helped preserve them.
5. These areas of land kept sinking until they were far below sea level and were covered with deep, thick layers of sediment.
6. The weight of these layers produced much pressure and heat, which changed the plant material into coal.
7. This coal was soft coal, and some of it was later changed to hard coal by more heat and pressure caused by forces acting inside the earth.

J. Amphibians that were the ancestors of our frogs and toads appeared toward the middle and end of this era.

K. The beginnings of reptile life also appeared toward the end of this era.

L. Two important lines of reptiles developed at this time.

1. The root reptiles were probably the ancestors of our reptiles today.
2. The mammal-like reptiles had teeth and skulls very much like those of mammals, and most likely they were the ancestors of the mammals.

VIII. THE MESOZOIC ERA

A. The **Mesozoic** era began about 200 million years ago, and it lasted for about 140 million years.

B. This era is called the **Age of Reptiles**.

C. Many land and water changes took place in this era.

1. The shape of North America was very much like it is today, and the land for the most part was high and dry.
2. The Palisades were formed along the Hudson River, and they were really

mountains, which gradually have been worn down.

3. The Sierra Nevadas and the Rocky Mountains in North America and the Andes Mountains in South America were formed.

4. The Appalachian Mountains were worn down until they had become a fairly level peneplane, but toward the end of the era they were lifted up again, although not as high as they had been originally lifted.

D. Marked changes in plants took place.

1. In the beginning of this era the land was covered with cycads, which were palmlike seed plants that produced flowers that were not true flowers.

2. Conifers, which include pine, cedar, spruce, juniper, and cypress trees, were common in this era.

3. There were also ginkgo trees, which grew seeds but not flowers.

4. The giant mosses and ferns died out and were replaced by the flowering plants, such as oak, elm, maple, birch, and beech trees.

5. The grasses and grain plants also made their appearance at this time.

E. During this time the reptiles flourished and became highly specialized.

F. The most well-known of these reptiles were the huge dinosaurs.

1. The word dinosaur means "terrible lizard."

2. They left many bones and teeth behind as fossils, which explains why we know so much about them.

G. There were all kinds of reptiles, and they lived on land, in the oceans, and in the air.

1. Some were very large, and others were quite small.

2. Some ate only plants, and others ate flesh.

H. The **Brontosaurus** was about 20 meters (65 ft) long and weighed about 27,000 kilograms (30 tons).

1. It had a long, thin neck and a tiny head.

2. Its legs were the size of thick tree trunks, and it had a very long tail.

3. It had a very small brain.

4. It was amphibious, living both on land and in water.

5. It walked on all four feet, and it ate plants.

I. The **Diplodocus** looked like the Brontosaurus, but it was even longer.

J. The **Stegosaurus** had a double row of triangular bony plates that ran from its small head almost to the end of its tail.

1. Near the end of its tail there were two pairs of large, sharp, bony spikes.

2. It had a heavy body with short, thick front legs, and it ate plants.

K. The **Triceratops** was protected in a different way.

1. There were two sharp horns on top of its head and a third on its nose.

2. Over its neck there was a strong frill of bony plates connected to its head.

L. The **Tyrannosaurus** was about 15 meters (49 ft) long from head to tail and about 6 meters (20 ft) tall when it stood on its hind legs.

1. It had small front legs, and it could stand erect, using its tail to balance it.

2. It had a large head that was roughly 4 feet long, filled with sharp teeth that were 15 centimeters (6 in) long.

3. It was a meat-eating reptile.

M. In the sea there were crocodiles, turtles, and other kinds of reptiles.

1. The **Ichthyosaurs** were long, fishlike reptiles that used their feet and tails as paddles for swimming.

2. The **Plesiosaurs** were long, slender reptiles with necks that looked like snakes.

N. The **Pterodactyls** were one kind of reptile that flew in the air.

1. They had a wide piece of skin connected from the very long joints of their fourth finger of each front leg to their body near the hip.

2. The Pterodactyls were not true birds, and they glided rather than flew.

3. They were all different sizes, some as large as a sparrow, and others with a wingspread of 6 meters (20 ft).

4. They all ate flesh.

O. The first birds appeared during this era.

1. The birds developed from a different branch of reptiles than the Pterodactyls.

2. These birds were about the size of a pigeon.

3. Although their skeleton and teeth were like that of a reptile, their wings and body were partly covered with feathers.

4. These birds had fingers with claws at the end of each wing, jaws without bills, and teeth.

P. Toward the end of this era mammals began to appear.

1. They were small animals about the size of rats.

2. Although they looked like reptiles, they were real mammals because they were warm-blooded, covered with hair, and suckled their young.

Q. At the end of the Mesozoic era all the dinosaurs died out and became extinct.

1. Many theories have been proposed to explain why the dinosaurs died out.

2. One theory claims that their tiny brains, with resulting low intelligence, was responsible.

3. Another theory claims that the drying up of the swamps and the change in plant life made the dinosaur starve to death.

4. Another theory suggests that perhaps the growing number of mammals stole and ate all the dinosaur eggs.

5. Another theory proposes that, when the climate became very cold at the end of this era, the dinosaurs could not live in this new climate.

IX. THE CENOZOIC ERA

A. The **Cenozoic** era began about 60 million years ago, and it has lasted until today.

B. This era is called the **Age of Mammals.**

C. Final land changes took place in this era.

1. The fourth and final glacial period carried over into this era.

2. During this glacial period there were four separate ice ages, where glaciers at the poles moved down and covered large parts of the earth's surface and then returned to the poles.

3. In this era the areas along the Atlantic coast, the Gulf of Mexico, and parts of the Pacific coast, which had been still under water, gradually became dry land.

4. Much volcanic activity took place in North America.

5. The Colorado plateau was lifted, and the Colorado River began cutting through it to form the Grand Canyon.

6. The Rocky Mountains and the Appalachian mountains were lifted, and the forces of erosion began working on them.

7. As erosion continued, great amounts of sediment were formed and deposited.

8. The remains of many plants and animals were embedded in these sedimentary layers and became fossils.

D. The plants slowly continued to develop until all the kinds we see today were formed.

E. There was a tremendous increase in the number and kinds of insects on earth.

F. The fishes developed into the fishes we see today.

G. The only reptiles left from the Mesozoic era included mostly crocodiles, alligators, turtles, lizards, and snakes.

H. Modern toothless birds with beaks appeared, and they grew in number and kind.

I. The mammals became larger, and they flourished until they covered the earth.

J. At first there were two kinds of mammals: those that laid eggs from which their young were born, and those that give birth to their young alive.

1. Today almost all mammals give live birth to their young.

2. Only a few, such as the duckbill and the spiny anteater, still lay eggs.

K. Some mammals, called **marsupials**, developed pouches for their young.
1. The young of marsupials are always born prematurely.
2. These premature young stay in the pouch, where they get warmth, shelter, and milk.
3. The kangaroo and opossum are marsupial mammals.

L. One group of mammals went back to the sea and spent all their time in the water.
1. This group includes whales, porpoises, and dolphins.
2. They have no hind legs, their forelegs are shaped like paddles, and their tail is like that of a fish.
3. Their young are born alive and are fed by their mother's milk, just like the young of mammals that live on land.
4. Some mammals like the seal and sea lion spend most of their time in the water.

M. Mammals like the bat developed flaps between their very long finger bones, and they were able to fly.

N. Many of the earlier mammals in the Cenozoic era died out and became extinct.
1. The **Smilodon** or saber-tooth tiger had two large teeth, or fangs, in its upper jaw.
2. The **Megatherium** was a giant sloth that stood about 6 meters (20 ft) high on its hind legs.
3. The **Mastodon** looked like a large elephant, with hair that was coarse and wooly, and with very large tusks.
4. The **Mammoth** also looked like an elephant, but it had such big teeth that there were never more than eight teeth in its mouth at one time.
5. The **Canis Diris** looked like a wolf, and it was about 2 meters (6 ft) long.

O. Many of the earlier mammals gradually developed into the mammals we know today.

P. The horse is an example of a present-day mammal that developed from an earlier mammal in the Cenozoic era.

Q. The first horse was called **Eohippus**, and it appeared early in the Cenozoic era.
1. It was very small, being about the size of a small dog.
2. It had a short neck, a few stiff hairs instead of a mane, and a short tail.
3. Its teeth were not suited for eating grass, and it ate leaves and shrubs instead.
4. It had four toes on each front foot and three toes on each back foot.

R. The Eohippus was followed by the **Mesohippus**.
1. The Mesohippus was larger, being about the size of a large dog.
2. It had a slightly longer neck, the beginning of a mane, and a longer tail.
3. It now had just three toes on each foot, and the middle toe was much larger than the other two.
4. When it walked or ran, all three toes touched the ground.

S. The **Meryohippus** came after the Mesohippus.
1. It was larger, and it had a longer neck, mane, and tail.
2. It still had three toes, but only the middle toe now touched the ground when it walked or ran.

T. Eventually the **Pliohippus** developed.
1. It was quite tall, with a good-sized mane and a long, flowing tail.
2. Its teeth had become specialized for biting and grinding the tough grass it now ate.
3. It had just one very large toe on each foot, and this toe helped it run more swiftly than its ancestors.
4. The other two toes had become very small, and they could not be seen because they were now inside the foot.
5. The nail of this very large toe became the hoof.

U. The present-day horse, **Equus**, followed not long after the Pliohippus.

X. THE AGE OF MAN

A. Some geologists include the history of man in the Cenozoic era.

B. Other geologists prefer to put man in a new era, called the **Psychozoic** era.

C. The **Age of Man** began about a million years ago.
1. Crude tools made of flint have been found, which date back to this time.
2. These sharp-edged stones are called eoliths, and they were shaped to fit the hand.

D. Very few fossils of early man have been found, and these fossils are mostly skulls and bones of arms or legs.

E. From these fossils geologists have gained some idea of what early men must have looked like.

F. The first remains of earliest man were found in Java in 1891.
1. Only the top of the skull, three teeth, bits of nose bones, and a thigh bone were found.
2. However, from these pieces scientists were able to picture what this early Java man looked like.
3. He had apelike features, such as a low, flat forehead, a thick skull, and brow ridges or thick ridges of bone that jutted above the eyesockets.
4. Yet he was a primitive man because he stood upright and his brain case was much larger than that of an ape.
5. Scientists estimate that the **Java man** lived about 500,000 years ago.

G. The remains of the **Peking man** were found about 1927 in a cave near Peking (or Peiping), China.
1. The Peking man was very much like the Java man, but he had a bigger brain case.
2. He knew how to use fire, and he is called the early Stone Age man because he used a wide variety of stone tools that were fairly well shaped.
3. He made these tools by chipping away at pieces of stone, and he used them for chopping or scraping.

H. The remains of the **Neanderthal man** were found about 1858 in Neander Valley in Germany.

1. He lived in Western Europe, North Africa, and parts of Asia about 200,000 years ago.
2. Scientists believe that the Neanderthal man did not originate in Europe but came over from Asia, where he had developed from the Java man.
3. He looked like the Java man, but he had a much larger brain case.
4. He was the first man to be classified by scientists as a man, rather than an ape-man.
5. He lived in a cave, hunted animals, used fire for cooking, and made much better stone spear points, hand axes, scrapers for animal skins, and other such tools.
6. After the Neanderthal man lived for about 100,000 years, he became extinct, and no one knows how or why this happened.

I. The **Cro-Magnon man** is believed to be the ancestor of modern man.
1. Five skeletons of the Cro-Magnon man were discovered about 1868 in the Cro-Magnon Cave in Southern France.
2. Since then, many more fossils have been found in caves in France, Spain, Italy, and other parts of southern Europe.
3. The Cro-Magnon man appeared about 50,000 years ago, and he lived in different parts of Europe, Africa, and Asia.
4. He did not look like an ape at all, for he did not have the low brow, thick brow ridges, protruding chin, and receding jaw that the great apes have.
5. He was tall, stood perfectly upright, and had a brain as large as modern man.
6. He made excellent stone weapons and tools, hunted with a bow and arrow, and used animal skins for clothing.

J. The **Neolithic man**, also called the **Recent Stone Age man,** followed the Cro-Magnon man.
1. He knew how to grind and polish stone and bone to make smooth, sharp tools.
2. He tamed wild animals and kept them in herds to be used for work, food, and clothing.

3. He built his own shelter rather than look for a cave or other place to live in.

4. He joined with other men and lived in villages so that they could now protect themselves from enemies and from wild animals.

LEARNING ACTIVITIES FOR "THE EARTH"

THE COMPOSITION OF THE EARTH

1. *Discuss the origin of the earth* · Have the children read and then discuss the different theories about the origin of the earth. Observe a baked apple as it cools, dries up, and wrinkles, and note the "mountains" and "valleys" that form on the apple's surface.

2. *Make a model of the earth's layers* · Get a styrofoam ball 15 centimeters (6 in) or more in diameter. These balls are sold as decorations for Christmas trees. With a knife cut a good-sized wedge out of the ball so that the inside can be seen to the center (Figure 10–1). By using a soft pencil, draw lines on the inside of the ball to show the relative thickness of the earth's layers. Color these thicknesses with different colored wax crayons.

Without removing the shell, cut a hard-boiled egg in half. Have the children look at the cross-section of the egg and compare its layers with those of the earth. The yolk corresponds to the core, the white to the mantle, and the shell to the earth's crust.

3. *Collect, observe, and classify rocks* · Collect samples of different rocks in your community. Good sources of rocks are river banks, farmers' rock piles, road cuts, excavations for large buildings, beaches, gravel pits, quarries, and mine dumps. Such equipment as a knapsack, old newspapers for wrapping up specimens, a geologist's hammer or a bricklayer's adz (which is much less expensive than the hammer), a large chisel, and a small chisel will be helpful. When breaking up rocks, first put them in a paper or cloth bag, or wrap them in newspaper, so that chips will not fly and cause cuts or damage to the eyes.

After the rocks have been collected, classify them in groups according to similarities in color, shape, material, and other characteristics. Observe the rocks individually and try to deduce as much as you can about them. Smooth, round rocks have most likely been acted upon by running water. Flat rocks are usually pieces of sedimentary rock. Pebbles and smaller rocks embedded or cemented in the rock will probably mean that the rock is a conglomerate. Crystals in the rock usually mean that the rock is igneous.

4. *Examine igneous rocks* · Obtain samples of such igneous rocks as granite, basalt, obsidian, and pumice. Examine them carefully with and without a magnifying glass. Igneous rocks are usually light colored or dark colored. Light-colored igneous rocks, like granite, are

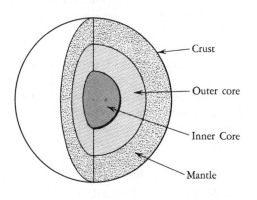

FIGURE 10–1.

MODEL OF THE EARTH'S LAYERS.

Crust

Outer core

Inner Core

Mantle

made up mostly of such light minerals as quartz and feldspar, together with small amounts of dark minerals such as mica or hornblende. Dark-colored rocks, like basalt, are made up of such dark-colored minerals as hornblende, biotite, mica, or augite. Note the smooth, glassy appearance of obsidian. Its black color is because of the tiny specks of magnetite scattered through it. Observe how pumice is spongy and full of air holes. See if the pumice will float in water. It will float if there are enough air holes in it.

5. *Examine sand* · Examine sand closely through a strong magnifying glass. Note the presence of different minerals, with differences in color, shape, and size. The colorless glassy crystals are quartz. Red crystals are usually garnet. Flaky black crystals may be mica or biotite. Rectangular black crystals are probably hornblende. If there are black crystals that are attracted to a magnet, they are most likely magnetite. Green crystals may be olivine, and purple crystals may be amethyst.

6. *Examine sedimentary rocks* · Obtain samples of such sedimentary rocks as conglomerate, sandstone, limestone, shale, and rock salt. Examine them carefully with and without a magnifying glass. Look for grains of sand, silt, or clay. Find out how each of these rocks was formed.

7. *Test for limestone* · By using a medicine dropper, allow some vinegar or lemon juice to fall on a piece of limestone. Bubbling will take place. The limestone is made of calcium carbonate, which reacts with the acid vinegar or lemon juice to form carbon dioxide gas.

8. *Identify the cementing material of sandstone* · Pour a few drops of vinegar or lemon juice on the sandstone. If the material between the grains of sand bubbles, the cementing material is limestone. If the rock is yellow, brown, or red, the cementing material is most likely to be iron oxide (a compound made from iron and oxygen). If the sandstone is colorless,

very hard, and does not bubble when vinegar is added, the cementing material is probably silica (quartz).

9. *Observe how sediments settle in water to form layers* · In a large glass jar add small stones, sand, and fine earth or silt until the jar is filled one third to one half. Add water until the jar is almost full, screw the cap on tightly, and then shake the jar and its contents. Put the jar down and allow the materials to settle. The heavier, coarser materials will settle to the bottom first, and the lighter finer particles will form a layer on top (Figure 10–2). If you wish, add a new layer of gravel (without water this time), then a layer of sand, then a layer of fine soil, and continue making layers until the jar is filled.

10. *Make artificial sedimentary rock* · Put some sand in a small cardboard container. Add a little powdered cement or plaster of Paris, and mix well. Now add a little water, stir, and allow the mixture to dry. An artificial sandstone will be formed, with cement or plaster of Paris as the cementing material.

Press wet clay together hard and allow it to dry. A rocklike material, similar to shale, will be formed.

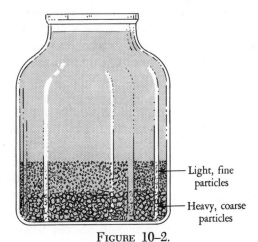

Light, fine particles

Heavy, coarse particles

FIGURE 10–2.

HOW LAYERS OF SEDIMENT ARE FORMED IN WATER.

11. *Examine metamorphic rocks* · Obtain samples of metamorphic rocks, such as gneiss, quartzite, slate, and marble. Examine them carefully with and without a magnifying glass to help determine the composition of the rock. Test the rocks with vinegar or lemon juice to see if any were formed from limestone and, therefore, will bubble. Find out how each of the rocks was formed.

12. *Test minerals for hardness* · Use a fingernail, cent, jackknife, steel file, and piece of glass to test minerals for hardness through number 7 on Mohs' scale. The scale shown in Table 10–1 can be used to classify minerals according to hardness.

TABLE 10–1. Classifying Minerals by Hardness

TEST	HARDNESS NUMBER
Mineral is scratched easily by fingernail	1
Mineral is scratched by fingernail	2
Mineral is scratched by a penny	3
Mineral is scratched easily by a knife blade	4
Mineral is scratched by a knife blade	5
Mineral is scratched by a steel file	6
Mineral will scratch glass	7

13. *Test minerals for their streaks* · Rub different minerals on a piece of unglazed porcelain tile, such as the back of a ceramic tile. Observe the streaks that are produced. Note that the streak is often a different color from the mineral. Consult some geology books for charts of streaks, and use the streaks as one of the clues in helping to identify the different minerals.

14. *Test minerals for cleavage* · By using a hammer, strike minerals until they break, and examine the pieces. Some minerals will split easily along one or more planes and form flat, smooth surfaces in one or more directions. Other minerals do not have this cleavage property, and, when they break, they form either rough, splintery surfaces or smooth, curved surfaces.

15. *Examine minerals for luster* · Examine minerals, noting their luster, which is the way they will reflect the light that strikes them. Some minerals have a metallic luster while other minerals have a nonmetallic luster and may look waxy, glassy, pearly, greasy, silky, earthy, or dull.

16. *Conduct flame and borax heat tests* · The tests are clearly described in chemistry textbooks or laboratory manuals as well as in books on minerals. The children may be interested in using them to help identify some of the minerals.

17. *Examine minerals for crystal structure* · Break open rocks and examine them with a magnifying glass, looking for crystals of minerals in the rocks. Mineral crystals will be different in color, shape, and size.

18. *Form crystals* · Dissolve as much sugar as possible in a tumbler half-filled with hot water, stirring vigorously. Pour the sugar solution into a small, deep saucer and put a string into the solution, allowing the string to hang over the edge of the saucer (Figure 10–3). Place the saucer in a quiet corner and allow it to evaporate for a day or two. Crystals will form on the string and at the bottom of the saucer. Pour off any solution that remains, allow the crystals to dry, and examine the crystal structure with a magnifying glass or through the low-powered lens of a microscope. Repeat the experiment, using salt, borax, or alum, and compare the crystal structure in each case.

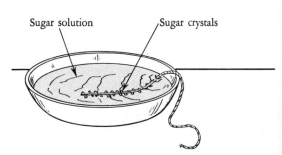

FIGURE 10–3.
FORMING SUGAR CRYSTALS.

19. *Form and compare extrusive and intrusive rock crystals* · Obtain some alum in the drugstore. Dissolve as much alum as possible in each of two beakers almost full of hot water. Place one beaker in the refrigerator or surround it with ice so that the solution cools as quickly as possible. Place the other beaker in a quiet corner and allow it to stand overnight. Examine the crystals from both solutions the next day. The crystals from the alum solution that was cooled quickly are rather fine and small, like extrusive crystals, because the solution was cooled so quickly that large crystals were not able to form. The crystals from the alum solution that was allowed to cool slowly are much coarser and larger, like intrusive crystals, because the solution cooled gradually and allowed large crystals to form.

20. *Examine the original color of rock* · Because the surface of rocks and minerals becomes weathered, their color often becomes dull. Break up some rocks and minerals, first wrapping them in paper or cloth. Compare the color of the freshly broken surface inside the rock or mineral with that of the weatherbeaten outside.

21. *Study samples from mineral groups* · Excellent sets of minerals may be purchased from scientific supply houses and natural history museums. Obtain sets containing representative examples of silicious, nonmetallic, and metallic ore, and gem minerals. Have the children examine them and make a list of the properties of each group as well as the well-known members in each group. Note and compare similarities and differences.

22. *Display a rock collection* · Display local rocks that have been collected and identified. Cigar or shoe boxes, with a layer of cotton on the bottom, make excellent containers. The children can also use a block of styrofoam and press the rocks firmly into the styrofoam so they fit snugly and will stay by themselves. Even egg containers made of pressed cardboard can be used.

Number each rock permanently by painting numbers with bright red fingernail polish directly on each specimen. Some collectors prefer to put a small round coat of white shellac on each specimen and then write numbers on this coat with black India ink. Put a label with the number of the rock and an adequate description of the rock next to the rock in the container (or on a master sheet if there is no room). The description should include the name of the rock, the place and date of collection, and the name of the collector.

23. *Make artificial rocks* · Place a small portion of plaster of Paris, powdered cement, and plasterer's lime in three paper cups. Add just a little water to each cup, stir, and set the cups aside for the materials to harden. After a few days tear the paper away and examine the artificial rocks that have been made. Concrete can be made by using three parts of sand to one part of powdered cement and adding enough water to form a thick, creamy mixture. Pour the mixture into a waxed milk carton, let it set for a few days, and then tear the cardboard away.

24. *Discuss uses of rocks* · Examine buildings (including your own school) and places where natural rocks have been used for construction purposes. You should find such natural rocks as marble, granite, limestone, lannon stone, and slate.

25. *Discuss uses of minerals* · Read about the different uses in the United States for mineral ores. Obtain or draw a map of the United States and label the location of important mineral deposits. Discuss the need for and importance of the conservation of our mineral resources.

FORCES THAT SHAPE AND CHANGE THE EARTH'S SURFACE

1. *Illustrate the theory of isostasy* · Obtain two large, spiral notebooks the same size and

thickness, and place one on each pan of a platform balance so that the notebooks are almost touching (Figure 10–4). The notebooks will

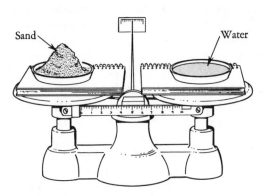

FIGURE 10–4.
HOW THE THEORY OF ISOSTASY EXPLAINS MOVEMENTS OF THE EARTH'S CRUST.

represent the earth's crust, and the pages the layers that make up the earth's crust. Place a pie tin on each notebook. In one tin put some water, which represents the oceans. Make a "mountain" of sand in the other tin, adding just enough sand to balance the water. Now take a teaspoon of sand away from the "mountain" and add it to the "ocean" to show that the mountain rock is worn away and carried down to the ocean. The higher "mountainous" region now becomes lighter and rises slowly while the lower "oceanic" region becomes heavier and slowly sinks.

2. *Illustrate the contraction theory of earth surface movement* · Let a hot baked apple cool or a fresh plum dry up. The fruit will contract and produce wrinkles and folds, which would correspond to the formation of mountains and valleys as the earth continues to contract.

3. *Illustrate the convection theory of earth surface movement* · Fill a Pyrex pot with water and add shredded blotting paper to the water. Muddle and stir the blotting paper until most of it settles to the bottom. Place the pot on a hot plate in such a position that only one side is in contact with the heating element (Figure 10–5). Now heat the pot of water. As the water heats up and boils, a convection current will be set up and the blotting paper will trace the route of this convection current. The hotter, lighter water rises, and the colder, heavier water falls. Inside the earth the rock is under great pressure and can move just like a liquid. Convection currents may also take place inside the earth and in this way affect the earth's crust.

4. *Discuss the continental drift theory of earth surface movement* · Observe a globe of the earth or a world geologic map. Note how, if North and South America were moved eastward against Europe and Africa, the shapes of the continents would match quite well. Madagascar would fit well against the east coast of Africa. Point out that if the earth were one continent that broke up, the drifting parts could push against the ocean basins, as they came to rest, and form mountain ranges.

5. *Illustrate folding* · Fold three differently colored towels until they are long, and then place one on top of the other to represent layers of rock. Now place one hand near each end of the pile of towels and push sideways

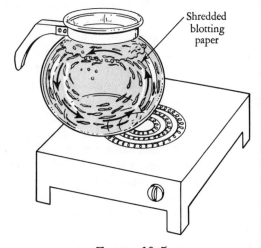

Shredded
blotting
paper

FIGURE 10–5.
A CONVECTION CURRENT.

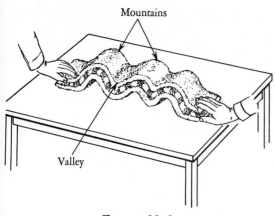

FIGURE 10–6.

HOW FOLDING PRODUCES MOUNTAINS AND VALLEYS.

toward the middle (Figure 10–6). Wavelike folds will form with a crest (anticline) and a trough (syncline), producing mountains and valleys.

6. *Illustrate faulting and earthquakes* · Put one palm of your hand on the other, as shown in Figure 10–7, with the heel of one

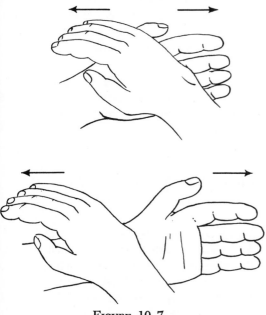

FIGURE 10–7.

HOW FAULTING PRODUCES EARTHQUAKES.

palm pressed hard against the other. Both palms will represent a layer of rock pushing against the other in opposite directions. Now push both palms hard in opposite directions. There will be a sudden movement as the "layers of rock" slide over one another, producing an earthquake.

7. *Locate earthquake belts* · Obtain a geologic map or globe of the world and trace the two large earthquake belts. Note the countries that are included in these belts. Read about or recall earthquakes that took place in these countries recently. Point out that volcanoes usually occur within the earthquake belts.

8. *Discuss tsunamis* · Have the children read about tsunamis that happened in the past. Point out that tsunamis are not tidal waves, but they are huge waves caused by earthquakes that began under the ocean.

9. *Make and compare models of mountains* · Make models showing the four common ways that mountains are formed. Place a card in front of each model, explaining the kind of mountain it is and where it can be found in the United States. Repeat Learning Activity 1 on Isostasy (p. 321) and Learning Activity 5 on Folding (p. 322) to show how block and folded mountains are formed.

10. *Make valley models* · Make models showing the life cycle of a valley.

11. *Compare plains and plateaus* · Read about and discuss the difference in formation between coastal plains, lake plains, and plateaus. Trace the life cycle of a plateau, and show pictures of mesas and buttes.

12. *Make a "volcano"* · Invert a flower pot and cover it with modeling clay to make a volcanic cone (Figure 10–8). Use green or brown clay to represent the earth, and red clay "rivulets" to represent the flow of lava. Have the crater extend above the pot so that the crater

[323

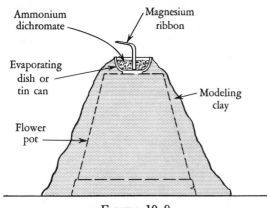

FIGURE 10–8.
A SIMULATED ERUPTING VOLCANO.

is 7½ centimeters (3 in) across and about 5 centimeters (2 in) deep. In the crater insert a small porcelain evaporation dish or a small frozen fruit-juice can, whose sides have been cut down with tinsnips so that the can is only 5 centimeters (2 in) high. Surround the can completely with the modeling clay.

Pour 1 tablespoon of ammonium dichromate into the crater. Cut a strip of magnesium ribbon 5 centimeters (2 in) long and place it in the ammonium dichromate so one end is in the chemical and the other end extends above the crater. Now apply lighted wooden matches repeatedly (and patiently) until the magnesium ribbon catches on fire. If magnesium ribbon is unavailable, put 10 drops of lighter fluid or alcohol on the ammonium dichromate crystals and apply a lighted match. The magnesium burns with a hot, white flame and sets off a rapid chemical reaction in which the ammonium dichromate decomposes. The "volcano" erupts, sparks shoot up into the air, and a green fluffy material (representing lava) is formed. If the room is shaded or in semidarkness, the effect will be more pronounced. Let the "volcano" cool for half an hour before cleaning it. Be sure to point out that in a real volcano the eruption takes place because of pressures inside the earth, which force magma upward and out through a crack or weak spot in the earth's crust.

13. *Discover why volcanoes erupt* · Let toothpaste in a tube represent magma. Squeeze the tube hard and insert a pin into the metal (which represents the earth's crust). This fault in the "earth's crust" allows the "magma," which is under pressure, to flow up and out.

14. *Examine volcanic rock* · Show samples of rock, such as lava, obsidian, and pumice. Point out that where lava cooled quickly, there was no time for crystals to form, and a glassy rock resulted. Where lava could cool slowly, large crystals were formed. The holes in pumice are caused by the presence of hot gases in the lava that did not have time to escape and were trapped inside the lava.

15. *Compare kinds of volcanoes* · Read about and list the well-known shield, cinder cone, composite, active, dormant, and extinct volcanoes throughout the world.

16. *Illustrate how geysers erupt* · Put a funnel in a Pyrex beaker and add water until the bowl of the funnel is covered and the water is level with the beginning of the stem (Figure 10–9). Heat the beaker on a hot plate. When the water begins to boil, the bubbles of steam expand and rise, pushing the water up the stem and making it spout like a geyser.

17. *Take a field trip* · Visit geological exhibits in natural history museums and college museums to observe and study rocks, models of land forms, and fossils.

FORCES THAT WEAR AWAY
THE EARTH'S SURFACE

1. *Observe how rocks wear away other rocks* · Get a rock that breaks rather easily and, while holding it over a sheet of white paper, rub it against a larger, harder rock. Note the rock dust that is worn off and falls on the paper. See how this dust compares with a pinch of soil.

mentary rock that is dry. Hold one end of the rock with forceps and heat the other end strongly in a Bunsen burner flame (Figure 10–10). After the end of the rock has been heated for some time, plunge this end quickly into a beaker or wide-mouthed jar full of cold water. As the rock contracts because of the sudden change in temperature, bits of the rock will break off and settle to the bottom.

5. *Test rocks for porousness* · Dip a piece of sandstone or limestone into water for a few moments and then lift the rock out and wipe it with a soft, absorbent cloth. The rock will still look wet. Weigh a piece of dry sandstone and then immerse it in a jar of water overnight. Remove the sandstone, wipe it dry, and weigh it again. The porous sandstone will be heavier because of the water it has absorbed.

6. *Discover that freezing water can crack rocks* · Fill a glass bottle, which has a metal screw cap, full of water. Put it in a plastic bag and leave it overnight in the freezer of a refrigerator. The next day examine the bottle. The freezing water expanded and broke the glass. Repeat the experiment, using water-soaked sandstone, limestone, or brick. The freezing water will crumble some of the rock.

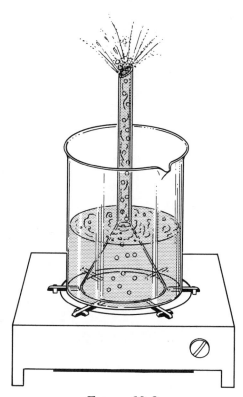

FIGURE 10–9.
A FUNNEL GEYSER.

2. *Observe how running water helps rocks wear away other rocks* · Get a large rock that breaks easily, and break it up into pieces. Note the rough appearance of the pieces, especially at the edges. Place some pieces into a glass jar, add water until the jar is about half-filled, and screw the cap tightly on the jar. Have the children take turns shaking the jar until their arms become tired. Now remove the pieces of rock from the jar, but leave the water in the jar. Note how much smoother the sharp edges of the rocks have become. Also note the sediment that settles to the bottom of the jar.

3. *Observe how roots crack rocks* · Look for sidewalks that have been pushed up, cracked, or broken by the roots of nearby trees.

4. *Discover how changes in temperature crack rocks* · Get a piece of shale or other sedi-

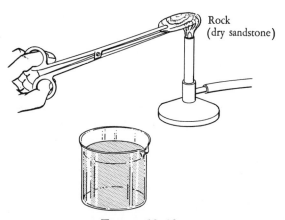

Rock
(dry sandstone)

FIGURE 10–10.
HEATING, FOLLOWED BY SUDDEN COOLING, BREAKS
UP ROCK.

7. *Observe how wind wears away rocks* · Many large rocks in the desert show the effects of wind-borne sand, which has worn away their surfaces. Point out that man uses sandblasting to clean stone buildings.

8. *Discover how air will affect rocks* · Place a wad of steel wool outdoors for a few days and note how rusty it becomes. Many rocks contain chemicals that react with the oxygen in the air and make them crumble.

9. *Combine carbon dioxide with water to form an acid* · Obtain some distilled water or fresh rainwater. Test the pure water with litmus paper for acidity. Now blow for quite some time through a straw into a glass of this water. Test again with litmus paper. This time the litmus paper will turn red, showing the presence of carbonic acid that was formed when the carbon dioxide from the air in your lungs dissolved in the water.

10. *Observe how germinating seeds can break up rocks* · Pack as many lima beans as possible in a glass jar. Fill the jar with water, screw the cap on tightly, put the jar in a plastic box, and let it stand overnight or longer. As the beans take in water and expand, the pressure should be great enough to break the jar.

Soak some lima beans overnight and plant them in a wax carton, half filled with damp soil. Pour a thin layer of plaster of Paris, mixed with water, all over the soil. As the beans germinate, they push up with enough force to crack the dried plaster.

11. *Observe how lichens crumble rock* · Find a rock with lichen on it. Scrape off some lichen and examine the rock underneath it. This part of the rock is softer and more crumbly than the rest of the rock because the lichen gives off an acid that attacks the rock.

12. *Examine weathered rock* · Compare the surfaces of new and old buildings that have been constructed with the same kind of rock. Headstones in cemeteries show the results of

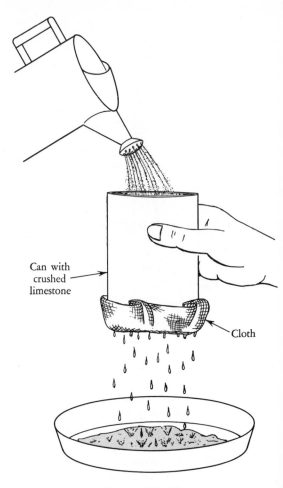

Can with crushed limestone

Cloth

FIGURE 10–11.
WATER DISSOLVES LIMESTONE.

weathering. Break open a weathered rock, wrapping it in cloth or paper first, and note how weathering has dulled or changed the color of the outside of the rock.

13. *Observe how ground water dissolves limestone* · Remove the top and bottom of a can. Cover one end of the can with cotton cloth or several layers of cheesecloth, and fasten the cloth securely to the sides of the can. Fill the can with crushed limestone and, while holding the can over a saucer, pour distilled water or freshly collected rainwater into the can (Figure 10–11). Collect a sizable quantity of the water

that has passed through the can. Place the saucer, together with another saucer of the same size and containing an equivalent amount of distilled water or rainwater, in a quiet place and allow the water in both saucers to evaporate. The water that passed through the limestone will leave behind a coating of limestone when it evaporates.

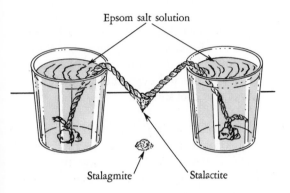

Epsom salt solution

Stalagmite   Stalactite

FIGURE 10–12.
FORMING A STALACTITE AND STALAGMITE.

14. *Make stalactites and stalagmites* · Obtain epsom salt or alum and dissolve as much of the salt as possible in each of two glasses of water resting on a piece of cardboard. Place a soft, thick piece of cotton cord into and between the glasses of saturated salt solution, as shown in Figure 10–12. Tie each end of the cord around a small stone or iron washer to prevent the ends of the string from floating on top of the water. In a day or so a "stalactite" and "stalagmite" will form as the water drops from the string, evaporates, and leaves the salt behind. Real stalactites and stalagmites are formed from calcium carbonate that had been dissolved in groundwater containing carbon dioxide.

15. *Observe how water erodes the earth's surface* · After a heavy rain examine the rivulets of water on the school grounds, carrying away the soil that has been worn away. Streams and rivers will show the same effect, but on a larger scale.

16. *Observe how snow changes to ice under pressure* · When it is below freezing, make a snowball from snow by compressing it firmly with your hands and then set the snowball aside for a few minutes. The pressure will change the snow from fluffy, flaky crystals to grains of ice, just as the pressure of huge piles of snow change the snow at the bottom to granular neve.

17. *Show how glaciers wear away the earth's surface* · Put pebbles and small rocks into a pie tin, barely cover them with water, and place the tin overnight in the freezer of a refrigerator. Remove the frozen mixture the next day and push it across the bare ground. The rocks in the mixture will scratch and gouge the ground carrying some earth with it. Let the ice melt on the gouged earth. Note how "lakes" are formed as the melted water fills up some of the hollows in the earth.

18. *Collect evidence of wind erosion* · Cut a piece of white paper so that it just fits the bottom of a deep cake tin. Place the paper in the tin and weigh it down with two or three metal washers, and then put the tin outside on the windowsill. After a day or so note the sediment that the wind has carried and deposited on the paper. An electric fan blowing against a pile of sand will show how the wind originally obtained the sediment.

SOIL

1. *Discover how soil is formed* · Repeat as many pertinent activities listed in the previous section, "Forces That Wear Away the Earth's Surface," as you consider necessary to show how weathering forms soil.

2. *Examine topsoil and subsoil* · Collect a sample of topsoil from a flower or vegetable bed. At the same time collect subsoil after you have dug 50 centimeters (20 in) into the earth. Compare both kinds of soil for quantities of

humus and pebbles or stones. While keeping all other conditions the same, plant a seed in topsoil and in subsoil, and see which kind of soil produces the sturdier plant.

3. *Examine bedrock* · Look for areas where the soil has been completely worn away and the solid bedrock can be seen.

4. *Compare the kinds of soil* · Have the children bring in samples of gravel soil, clay soil, sandy soil, and loam. Examine small amounts of the different kinds of soil carefully with and without a magnifying glass.

5. *Investigate the composition of soil* · Obtain a tall, cylindrical jar, and fill half of it with some garden soil. Add water until the jar is amost full and screw the cap on tightly. Shake the jar vigorously for a minute and then set the jar down. The soil will begin to settle in layers. The fine gravel sinks to the bottom immediately, followed by sand, and then by clay and silt. Particles of humus may float on top of the water. The muddy water may take days to become clear because it takes time for the very fine particles of silt and clay to settle.

6. *Test how fast water goes into the soil* · Cut out both ends of a juice can. Push one end of the can 13 millimeters (½ in) into the soil (Figure 10–13). Fill the can with water and see how long it takes the can to become completely empty. Do this with sandy, clay, and garden

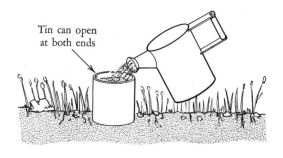

Tin can open at both ends

FIGURE 10–13.
MEASURING HOW FAST WATER RUNS INTO THE SOIL.

soils, packing all three soils to the same consistency.

7. *Test soil for air* · Put some soil into a glass tumbler and slowly pour water over it. Bubbles of air will leave the soil and appear in the water.

8. *Test soil for water* · Place a layer of soil on the bottom of a Pyrex pot. Put the cover on the pot and heat the pot gently on a hot plate. A thin film of water will condense on the sides of the pot and on the underside of the cover as the water in the soil evaporates and then condenses on the cool surfaces.

9. *Discover how soil is eroded* · Repeat as many pertinent activities listed in the previous section, "Forces That Wear Away the Earth's Surface," as you consider necessary to show how soil is eroded.

10. *Illustrate splash erosion* · Fill the cap of a jar with soil and tamp down the soil until it is exactly level with the edge of the cap (Figure 10–14). Place the cap of soil in the middle of a large sheet of white paper. Fill a medicine dropper with water and let a few drops of water fall on the soil from a height of 1 meter (3 ft). The soil will splash on the paper. If you put a flower or a small branch, or even a pencil, in the path of the falling drops, the force of the falling water will be broken and the amount of splash erosion will be greatly reduced.

After a rainfall or shower look for splash erosion on the sides of the school buildings or on cellar windows close to the ground. Compare the amount of splash erosion that took place on bare soil areas next to the building and on grassy areas next to the building.

11. *Look for rill, sheet, and gully erosion* · After a heavy rain look for rill, sheet, and gully erosion on the school grounds or on other areas in your community. Discuss the factors that caused the erosion and the action that could have been taken to prevent the erosion.

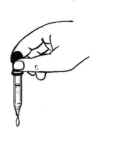

13. *Compare the erosion of loose soil and packed soil* · Obtain two long, sturdy rectangular aluminum cake pans. Use tin snips to cut away the middle part of one end of each pan. Place some fine wire mesh or screen, almost the same width as the end of the pan, inside each pan against the cut-out openings. Fill both pans with soil, one loosely packed and the other firmly packed. By using pieces of lumber, tilt the pans so that they both slope at the same angle (Figure 10–16). The lower ends of the pans should overhang so that runoff water from each pan can fall freely into a large, shallow cake tin below the pan. (It is advisable to conduct this learning activity outdoors, if possible.) Make two watering cans from glass jars with metal screw caps, as described in Learning Activity 12 above. Now pour the same amount of water in each watering can, and water each pan at the same time. The pan with the loose soil will lose its soil more quickly, and in greater amounts.

14. *Test the effect of slope on soil erosion* · By using the same pans and same materials described in Learning Activity 13, fill both pans with loose soil. Adjust one pan with additional lumber so that it tilts more sharply than the other pan. Water both pans with equal amounts of water. The pan with the

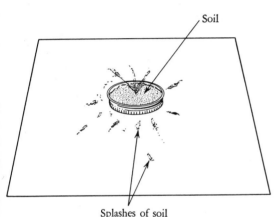

Soil

Splashes of soil

FIGURE 10–14.

SHOWING SPLASH EROSION.

12. *Compare the effects of light and heavy rain on soil* · Fill a flower pot with soil and press the soil down until it is level with the edge of the pot. Push three bottle caps into the soil so that only their heads show (Figure 10–15). Place the pot in a large basin and sprinkle the soil with water from a watering can. An excellent watering can may be made by punching holes in the metal screw cap of a glass jar. First sprinkle lightly to represent a light rain. Some of the soil will be splashed or washed away, leaving part of the bottle caps exposed. Now sprinkle for some time to represent a heavy rain. Enough unprotected soil will be splashed or washed away to leave the bottle caps completely exposed, with columns of soil remaining under the protecting bottle caps.

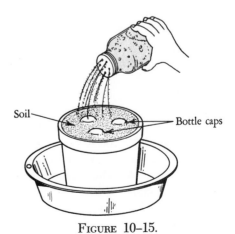

Soil — — Bottle caps

FIGURE 10–15.

HOW LIGHT AND HEAVY RAIN AFFECT EROSION OF THE SOIL.

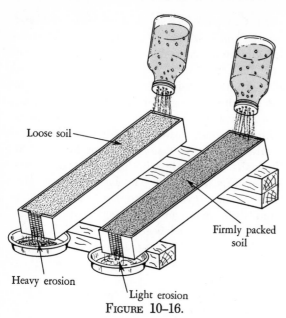

FIGURE 10–16.

SOIL ERODES MORE QUICKLY WHEN LOOSE THAN
WHEN FIRMLY PACKED.

steeper slope will lose its soil more quickly, and in greater amounts.

15. *Test the effect of contour plowing on soil erosion* · By using the same materials in Learning Activity 13 above, fill both pans with loose soil and have them slope at the same angle. With the blunt end of a pencil make long, vertical furrows in the soil of one pan and semicircular furrows in the soil of the other pan (Figure 10–17). Water both pans with equal amounts of water. The soil that has been contoured will be washed away more slowly, and in smaller amounts.

16. *Test the effect of terracing on erosion* · Repeat Learning Activity 13 above, but work the soil in one pan until you have made a series of terraces. When you water both pans with equal amounts of water, the terraced soil will be washed away more slowly, and in smaller amounts.

17. *Test the effect of vegetation on erosion* · Repeat Learning Activity 13 above, but now re-

place some soil in one pan with soil that has grass growing in it. When you water both pans with equal amounts of water, the soil with the vegetation will be washed away more slowly, and in smaller amounts.

18. *Discuss the effect of strip cropping and shelter belts on erosion* · Show pictures of strip cropping and shelter belts. Discuss the conditions under which each of these methods operates best and how each condition serves to prevent or slow down erosion.

19. *Collect samples of fertilizers* · Collect small amounts of natural and synthetic fertilizers in small bottles with screw caps. Find out what necessary elements or minerals are contained in each fertilizer and then label each botte, giving the name of the fertilizer, its constituents, and the percentage if possible.

20. *Investigate crop rotation* · Find out the different kinds of crops farmers grow in a crop rotation program, together with the sequence of the crops and the reason for using this sequence.

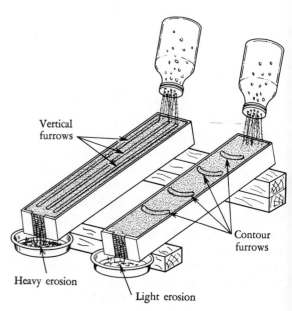

FIGURE 10–17.

CONTOURING THE SOIL REDUCES EROSION.

21. *Examine the roots of legumes* · Dig up a leguminous plant, such as clover, cow peas, soy beans, or alfalfa. Try to collect the roots as intact as possible. Wash the soil carefully and gently from the roots. Examine the nodules, or little white bumps, on the roots. These nodules contain nitrogen-fixing bacteria.

22. *Test soil for acidity and alkalinity* · Moisten the soil and press a pinch of it against litmus paper. Acid soil will turn blue litmus paper red, and alkaline soil will turn red litmus paper blue. If strongly acid or alkaline soil is unavailable, soil can be made acid by adding a few drops of vinegar or made alkaline by adding a few drops of limewater. This procedure also illustrates how soil may either be "sweetened" or made more acid.

HISTORY OF THE EARTH

1. *Collect and observe fossils* · If your school is in an area where fossil rocks are quite common, go fossil hunting. You will need a knapsack, old newspapers for wrapping up specimens, a geologist's hammer or a bricklayer's adz (which is much less expensive than the hammer), a large chisel, and a small chisel. Examine the specimens carefully and consult a good handbook on fossils for identifying them.

If you live in an area where fossils are not available, buy a collection from a natural history museum or scientific supply house. You may want to take the children to a natural history museum or show them pictures of fossils instead.

2. *Examine soft coal for fossils* · Imprints of fern leaves are quite common in soft coal. Collect pieces of soft coal, tap them with a hammer to separate them into layers, and examine the surfaces for leaf imprints and other signs of plants. Discuss how the imprints were formed.

3. *Examine petrified wood* · Many children collect or obtain specimens of petrified wood when they are away on vacation. These speci-

mens are usually well polished. Have the class examine the petrified wood and learn how it was formed.

4. *Make a leaf or a shell imprint* · Obtain a pie tin and coat the bottom and sides with a thin layer of Vaseline. Cover a leaf with Vaseline and place it on the bottom of the pie tin (Figure 10–18). Prepare a mixture of plaster of

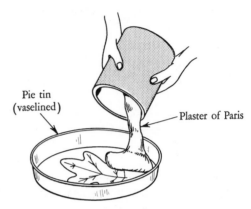

FIGURE 10–18.
A PLASTER OF PARIS LEAF IMPRINT.

Paris in a large tin can by adding water to the plaster of Paris according to instructions on the package. Stir the mixture gently with a flat stick until it is smooth and has the consistency of pancake batter. Now pour the plaster of Paris slowly into the pie tin over the leaf until you have a layer 13 millimeters (½ in) thick. Let the plaster of Paris set for 30 minutes and then remove the cast carefully. Wash the Vaseline off with soap and warm water the next day after the cast has become very hard. Dry the cast with a soft cloth.

Repeat this activity, using a small seashell such as a clam or oyster shell. The cast you obtain will be a negative cast with a hollow imprint of the shell. To make a positive cast with a raised imprint, cover the negative cast with a thin coat of Vaseline. Coat one side of a strip of cardboard, 7½ centimeters (3 in) high, with Vaseline, and wrap the cardboard around the cast, holding it firmly in place with a

[331

rubber band (Figure 10–19). Pour more plaster of Paris over the negative cast until you have a layer at least 2½ centimeters (1 in) thick. Let it set for 1 hour. Now remove the cardboard and, inserting a knife gently between the posi-

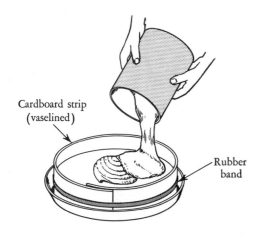

Cardboard strip
(vaselined)

Rubber
band

FIGURE 10–19.

MAKING A NEGATIVE AND POSITIVE CAST OF AN IMPRINT.

tive and negative cast, separate the two casts. Smooth the sides of the positive cast with sandpaper. The next day wash off the Vaseline with soap and warm water. Preserve the cast by giving it a coat of shellac.

5. *Make a carbon imprint of a leaf* · Coat a leaf with a very thin layer of Vaseline, making sure to coat the side of the leaf where the veins are raised. Place the leaf, vaselined side up, on some newspaper. Place a sheet of carbon paper, carbon side down, on the leaf. Cover the carbon paper with a sheet of white paper and rub the side of a round pencil or dowel back and forth many times on the white paper. The leaf will now be coated with carbon. Now place the leaf, carbon side down, between two fresh pieces of white paper, and rub the pencil or dowel back and forth on the top sheet several times. Re-

move the top sheet and the leaf. The bottom sheet will have a carbon imprint of the leaf, showing the size, shape, and vein formation. Draw in any gaps in the leaf's shape and vein pattern. Point out that you made an artificial coating of carbon on the leaf. What actually happens in nature is that the leaf itself carbonizes and forms an imprint on the top and underside of the rock.

6. *Preserve flowers or short plants* · Get some very fine sand. If sand is unavailable, borax or baking soda may be used. Cover the bottom of a small, deep cardboard box with a layer of 5 centimeters (2 in) of sand. Place a fresh flower or plant on the sand, then very gently sprinkle more sand over it until you have covered it with a layer of sand 7½ centimeters (3 in) thick. Let the box stand for a month and then carefully remove the flower or plant from the sand, brushing off the parts with a fine brush, if necessary, to remove any sand grains that cling to it. The flower or plant will look as if it has just been cut. Note that in nature living things are often buried in sand or volcanic ash and thus preserved.

7. *Have a fossil exhibit* · Show actual fossils, with identification labels or cards, accompanied by drawings or pictures of what the living plants and animals actually looked like.

8. *Set up a dinosaur display* · Models of dinosaurs may be purchased from the New York and Chicago Museums of Natural History, and also from certain scientific supply houses. Place cards in front of each dinosaur, giving pertinent information about the dinosaur.

9. *Make models of life in the geologic eras* · Make dioramas or murals of plants and animals that lived in the different geologic eras. Pictures may be substituted instead.

BIBLIOGRAPHY FOR ''THE EARTH''

ADAMS, GEORGE F., and JEROME WYCOFF. *Landforms.* New York: Golden Press, 1971. 160 pp.

ASIMOV, ISAAC. *How Did We Find Out About Dinosaurs?* New York: Walker, 1973. 64 pp.

———. *How Did We Find Out the Earth Is Round?* New York: Walker, 1973. 64 pp.

BRANLEY, FRANKLYN M. *The Beginning of the Earth.* New York: Thomas Y. Crowell, 1973. 40 pp.

———. *Shakes, Quakes, and Shifts: Earth Tectonics.* New York: Thomas Y. Crowell, 1974. 33 pp.

CAZEAU, CHARLES. *Earthquakes.* Chicago: Follett, 1975. 32 pp.

COLE, JOANNA. *Dinosaur Story.* New York: William Morrow, 1974. 26 pp.

DAVIDSON, ROSALIE. *When the Dinosaurs Disappeared—Mammals of Long Ago.* Chicago: Childrens Press, 1973. 28 pp.

ELLIOTT, SARAH. *Our Dirty Land.* New York: Julian Messner, 1976. 64 pp.

GANS, ROMA. *Caves.* New York: Thomas Y. Crowell, 1977. 40 pp.

GOETZ, DELIA. *Valleys.* New York: William Morrow, 1976. 24 pp.

GREEN, CARLA. *How Man Began.* New York: Bobbs-Merrill, 1972. 80 pp.

GUTNIK, MARTIN. *Ecology and Pollution: Land.* Chicago: Childrens Press, 1973. 44 pp.

HEADY, ELEANOR. *The Soil That Feeds Us.* New York: Parents' Magazine Press, 1972. 64 pp.

HEINTZE, CARL. *The Bottom of the Sea and Beyond.* New York: Thomas Nelson, 1975. 144 pp.

HELFMAN, ELIZABETH. *Our Fragile Earth.* New York: Lothrop, Lee & Shepard, 1972. 160 pp.

HUNGERFORD, HAROLD, and CLIFFORD KNAPP. *Exploring and Understanding Our Changing Earth.* Westchester, Ill.: Benefic Press, 1970. 96 pp.

HUSSY, LOIS, and CATHERINE PESSINO. *Collecting Small Fossils.* New York: Thomas Y. Crowell, 1972. 57 pp.

KAUFFMANN, JOHN. *Flying Reptiles in the Age of Dinosaurs.* New York: William Morrow, 1976. 40 pp.

———. *Little Dinosaurs and Early Birds.* New York: Thomas Y. Crowell, 1977. 40 pp.

KEEN, MARTIN. *The World Between Our Feet: The Story of Soil.* New York: Julian Messner, 1974. 96 pp.

KLAITS, BARRIE. *When You Find a Rock.* New York: Macmillan, 1976. 58 pp.

KNIGHT, DAVID. *Let's Find Out About the Earth.* New York: Franklin Watts, 1975. 48 pp.

LADYMAN, PHYLLIS. *Inside the Earth.* New York: William Scott, 1969. 32 pp.

LAYCOCK, GEORGE. *Caves.* New York: Four Winds, 1976. 102 pp.

LEE, ROBERT. *The Dinosaur Book.* New York: Western Pub., 1971. 24 pp.

MAHER, RAMONA. *Shifting Sands: The Story of Sand Dunes.* New York: John Day, 1968. 128 pp.

MAJOR, ALAN. *Collecting Fossils.* New York: St. Martin's Press, 1974. 210 pp.

MARTIN, ALICE, and BERTHA PARKER. *Dinosaurs.* New York: Western Pub., 1973. 48 pp.

——— and ———. *Rocks and Minerals.* New York: Western Pub., 1974. 48 pp.

MATTHEWS, WILLIAM. *The Story of the Earth.* Irvington-on-the-Hudson, N.Y.: Harvey House, 1968. 124 pp.

———. *The Story of Earthquakes and Volcanoes.* Irvington-on-the-Hudson, N.Y.: Harvey House, 1969. 126 pp.

———. *The Story of Glaciers and the Ice Age.* Irvington-on-the-Hudson, N.Y.: Harvey House, 1974. 142 pp.

McGOWAN, TOM. *Album of Dinosaurs.* Chicago: Rand McNally, 1972. 60 pp.

———. *Album of Prehistoric Animals.* Chicago: Rand McNally, 1974. 60 pp.

MIKLOWITZ, GLORIA. *Earthquake.* New York: Julian Messner, 1977. 96 pp.

PARISH, PEGGY. *Dinosaur Time.* New York: Harper & Row, 1974. 30 pp.

PITT, VALERIE, and DAVID COOK. *A Closer Look at Deserts.* New York: Franklin Watts, 1975. 32 pp.

RINKOFF, BARBARA. *Guess What Rocks Do.* New York: Lothrop, Lee & Shepard, 1975. 32 pp.

RHODES, FRANK. *Geology.* New York: Golden Press, 1972. 160 pp.

———, HERBERT S. ZIM, and PAUL R. SHAFFER. *Fossils.* New York: Golden Press, 1965. 160 pp.

ROBINSON, ROGER. *Exploring and Understanding Rocks and Minerals.* Westchester, Ill.: Benefic Press, 1970. 96 pp.

SORRELL, CHARLES. *Minerals of the World.* New York: Western Pub., 1973. 280 pp.

WATERS, JOHN. *Continental Shelves.* New York: Abelard-Schuman, 1974. 142 pp.

WATSON, JANE. *Dinosaurs.* New York: Western Pub., 1974. 24 pp.

WATTS, CHRISTOPHER. *Prehistoric Life.* New York: Franklin Watts, 1976. 48 pp.

WEISS, MALCOLM. *Lands Adrift.* New York: Parents' Magazine, 1975. 64 pp.

WILLIS, WILMA. *Sand and Man.* Chicago: Childrens Press, 1973. 64 pp.

ZIM, HERBERT S., and PAUL R. SHAFFER. *Rocks and Minerals.* New York: Golden Press, 1970. 160 pp.

CHAPTER 11

WATER, WEATHER,
and CLIMATE

WATER

I. THE WATER TABLE

A. When water falls to the earth as rain or other forms of precipitation, some of the water sinks into the earth.

B. The water sinks deeper into the earth until it reaches the solid rock underneath the soil.

C. This solid rock may be porous or nonporous.

  1. Porous rock, usually called **permeable** rock, is either loose (like gravel) or has spaces in it (like sandstone), and it allows the water to enter and pass through it.

  2. Nonporous rock, usually called **impermeable** rock, is firm and solid (like granite) so that it stops the water from sinking any deeper.

D. The water will continue to sink deeper into the earth until it is stopped by a layer of nonporous or impermeable rock.

E. The soil and rock above this nonporous layer then become soaked or saturated with water, which is called **ground water.**

F. The upper level of the ground water in the soaked soil and rock is called the **water table.**

G. The height of this water table depends upon how much rain has fallen recently, how porous the soil and rock are, and how far down the porous layer goes until it meets a layer of nonporous rock that will not let the water sink any deeper.

H. Also, during dry weather the level of the water table sinks, and during rainy weather the level rises.

I. As a rule, the level of the water table follows the general contour of the land, sloping where the surface of the land slopes, and rising where the surface rises.

J. The ground water can flow through a porous layer of soil and rock, and thus makes it possible for water to enter the ground at one place and to appear in another place later.

K. Whenever the land surface dips below the water table, the ground water flows out to the surface of the land, forming a spring, joining with a river, or helping to feed a pond or lake.

II. WELLS

A. A **well** is a hole that is dug or drilled deep enough into the ground to reach the water table.

  1. Water then flows into the hole, filling

it with water and forming a well.

2. When water is taken out of the well, it is replaced by the water that is flowing underground.

B. A well must be dug deep enough so that, when the level of the water table drops during dry weather, the well will not run dry.

C. An **artesian** well is a well that is sunk deep into the earth's surface.

1. In artesian wells the water is obtained from a layer of porous rock, called an **aquifer,** which is sandwiched between two layers of nonporous rock.

2. This layer of porous rock originally began at the earth's surface and then slanted downward into the earth.

3. Water entering this layer of porous rock can only travel through this porous layer, and it cannot move up or down through the nonporous layers of rock above and below it.

4. When a well is drilled deep enough to reach this porous layer, the water in it rises up again, either to the land surface or to just below the surface, depending upon the contour of the land.

5. The water rises because the water at the beginning of the aquifer is higher, and exerts pressure on water below it.

6. The water in the artesian well is under pressure in exactly the same way as the water at the bottom of a long, slanting pipe would be under pressure.

7. The water from artesian wells is usually very pure because it comes straight up the walls of the well and does not dissolve any minerals in other layers of rocks on its way up.

III. Springs

A. When the water table meets the earth's surface, a **spring** is formed.

B. Springs may also form on hillsides where the water table cuts across the earth's surface.

C. Spring water usually has minerals dissolved in it.

D. Spring water that comes from deep below the earth's surface may often have so many minerals dissolved in it that the water is not suitable for drinking.

E. Hot springs form when the ground water is heated because of volcanic activity going on below the earth's surface.

1. The water is either heated by contact with the hot, melted rock, called **magma,** or by mixing with steam and hot gases that are escaping from the magma.

2. Hot springs are common in regions where volcanic activity is going on because the heated rocks are very near the earth's surface in these areas.

3. Because hot water dissolves minerals better than cold water, most hot springs have a high mineral content.

IV. Lakes

A. **Lakes** are large bodies of water found on many parts of the earth's surface.

B. Lakes usually are made up of a depression, called a **basin,** that is filled with water.

1. Some lake basins were formed by **faulting,** in which layers of rock inside the earth slipped over other layers of rock and were pushed up to form a hollow in the earth's surface.

2. Some basins were formed when forces within the earth that were sideways acted on layers of rock and pushed them into wavelike folds with a crest and a hollow trough.

3. Glaciers often gouged out deep hollows as they moved across the earth's surface, leaving these hollows to fill with water as the glaciers later retreated.

4. Some basins were formed when lava from a volcano built a dam across a valley.

5. Lakes were often formed from rivers when trees, brush, and other debris

clogged up the river, making the river back up to form a lake.

C. Lakes obtain their water in many ways.
1. Rain and other forms of precipitation fall directly into the lake.
2. Rain that falls on land around the lake runs off into the lake.
3. Rivers flow into the lake.
4. When the water table is above the surface of the lake basin, ground water flows into the lake in the form of a spring.

D. Lakes do not stay on earth as long as hills or mountains do.
1. Some lakes become filled up with sediment carried by streams that fill the lake.
2. Sometimes plants growing at the edge of the lake advance farther and farther into the lake until the lake becomes filled up and disappears.
3. Some lakes disappear because the springs in their basins, or the rivers that feed the lakes, dry up and disappear.

E. A swamp is a lake basin that is partly or completely filled with live plants, dead plants, sediment, and water.
1. Some swamps are just beginning to become lakes, whereas others are slowly becoming dry land.
2. When swamps are drained, they make very fertile farm land.

V. IMPURITIES IN WATER

A. As rain begins to fall, it is quite pure.
B. However, as it falls through the air, it dissolves some of the gases in the air and also picks up bits of dust and bacteria that are floating in the air.
C. As soon as the rain reaches the ground, it begins to pick up many impurities.
1. Many kinds of minerals dissolve in the water.
2. Some sand, silt, mud, and other sediments are not dissolved, but they remain suspended in the water as very fine particles.
3. The water also comes in contact with all

kinds of bacteria that are found in plant and animal wastes.

D. Some of the impurities in water are harmless, whereas others can be very harmful.
1. Small amounts of minerals and gases in water make the water taste better because the water would taste "flat" without them.
2. Many bacteria are very harmful, and they must be removed or killed before the water is suitable for drinking.

VI. PURIFICATION OF WATER

A. In the home, harmful bacteria in the water can be killed by boiling, and suspended material and gases that give the water a bad taste can be removed by passing the water through charcoal.
B. In the laboratory, water can be purified by **distillation.**
1. In distillation the water is boiled, and the water vapor that forms is led through a tube that is surrounded by cold water, which condenses the water vapor back into water again.
2. The heat drives off the gases dissolved in the water before the water begins to boil and is changed into water vapor.
3. The hot, boiling water kills the bacteria, which are left behind when the water is changed into water vapor.
4. Minerals and suspended materials are also left behind when the water is changed into water vapor.
C. Cities go through several steps when they purify water for use in the home.
D. First, the water is run into large basins, where the suspended particles of sediment are allowed to settle to the bottom.
1. Because the very tiny particles settle very slowly, two chemicals—alum and lime—are added to the water.
2. In the water these chemicals form a jellylike material, to which the very fine particles of sediment stick.
3. The jellylike material becomes heavier

when the tiny particles are stuck to it, and it settles to the bottom.

4. Some of the bacteria in the water are also trapped by the material, and they are removed when the material settles.

E. The water is then passed to another basin that has layers of sand and gravel in it.

1. The water passes through these layers, which remove the rest of the suspended particles together with more of the bacteria.

2. Sometimes a layer of charcoal is placed between the sand and gravel to remove coloring matter and bad-tasting gases in the water.

F. Now the water is treated to remove the remaining bacteria.

1. One way to remove the bacteria is to spray the water into the air, which allows the oxygen in the air to kill the bacteria and at the same time puts air into the water to give it a better taste.

2. If there is a large amount of bacteria present, the water may also be treated with chlorine, which kills all the bacteria but gives the water a bad taste.

G. Some cities now add fluorides to the water because fluorides help prevent or reduce tooth decay.

VII. HARD WATER

A. Water that has certain minerals dissolved in it, in the form of calcium and magnesium salts, is called **hard** water.

B. Hard water is difficult to use for washing purposes because it will not form a lather with soap; instead, it forms a scum.

1. The scum is the product formed when the dissolved calcium and magnesium salts react with the soap.

2. We call it hard water because it is "hard" to make a lather or wash with this water.

C. Hard water is also objectionable because it leaves mineral deposits inside steam furnaces, hot-water heaters, hot-water pipes, and tea and coffee pots.

D. Hard water can be "softened" in different ways.

E. One way to soften hard water is to add such chemicals as ammonia, washing soda, borax, or trisodium phosphate, which remove the calcium and magnesium from the water.

1. A second way is to use a chemical called **zeolite.**

2. Zeolite removes the calcium and magnesium when hard water is passed through it, and it replaces these minerals with sodium, which does not affect soap.

3. When zeolite is used up and does not work any longer, it can be restored by soaking it overnight in a strong salt-water solution.

F. A third way to soften hard water is to use certain resins, which are able to remove calcium and magnesium from the water.

G. Rainwater that has not touched the ground is very soft water, and it is excellent for washing purposes.

H. Today, **detergents** are often used instead of soap.

1. Detergents are not soaps, but they are made up of chemicals that have a cleaning action just like soap.

2. The chemicals in detergents are not affected by the calcium and magnesium in hard water so that they lather easily in hard water and do not form a scum.

3. Detergents come either in solid or in liquid form.

VIII. WATER EXERTS PRESSURE

A. Water has weight, and it exerts a pressure because of its weight.

B. At any given point in the water, the water will exert a downward, upward, and sideways pressure.

1. At this particular point the pressure is the same in all directions.

2. At a deeper point in the water, the pressure will be greater, but this new and greater pressure will again be the same in all directions.

C. When water is placed in a container, its pressure is greatest at the bottom.
   1. The shape of the container does not affect the water pressure on the bottom, but the height of the container does.
   2. The higher the container, the deeper the water, and the greater the water pressure will be at the bottom.
   3. The pressure of the water on the bottom is greater than the pressure of the water on the sides of the container.
D. When water is in a closed container, any pressure on the water will be sent or transmitted in all directions through the container.
   1. This pressure occurs because the molecules of water are so close together that the pressure is passed unchanged from molecule to molecule.
   2. Special machines, called **hydraulic machines,** make use of this special behavior of water in a closed container, being able to send a small force elsewhere and, at the same time, change the small force into a much larger force.
   3. Common hydraulic machines include the **hydraulic press** for baling cotton, the **hydraulic lift** for raising automobiles, and the **hydraulic brakes** in a car or truck.

IX. MOVING WATER CAN DO WORK

A. When water moves from a higher level to a lower level, because of the earth's pull of gravity on the water, it has a great deal of energy.
   1. This energy of motion, which moving water has, is called **kinetic energy.**
   2. Because of kinetic energy, the water can exert a great deal of pressure and force.
   3. The faster the water moves, the greater kinetic energy it will have.
B. Moving water can be used to turn water wheels.
   1. Some water wheels are used to grind grain or run machines in factories.
   2. Other special water wheels, called **tur-**

bines, are used to run large electric generators that produce electricity.

X. STEAM CAN DO WORK

A. When water is heated to a high enough temperature, it will boil, changing from a liquid into a gas called steam.
B. When water changes into steam, it expands tremendously and can exert a great deal of pressure and force.
C. Steam can be used to run machines and engines.
D. Steam can also be used to turn large turbines, which will then run giant electric generators.

XI. SINKING AND FLOATING

A. When a body is placed in water, two forces act on the body.
B. One force is the earth's pull of gravity, which pulls downward on the body.
   1. The weight of the body determines the amount of downward force acting on the body.
   2. The heavier the body, the greater the earth's pull of gravity on it, and the larger the downward force will be.
C. The second force is the upward force of the water that has been displaced, or pushed out of the way.
   1. The size of the body determines the amount of upward force the displaced water can have.
   2. The larger the body, the more water it can displace, and the greater the upward force will be.
D. A small, heavy body will usually sink in water.
   1. Because it is small, the body will displace a small amount of water, and a small, upward force will act on the body.
   2. Because the body is heavy, the downward force due to the pull of gravity will be great.
   3. Because the downward force acting on the body is greater than the upward

[339

force acting on the body, the body will sink.

E. A large, light body will usually float in water.

1. Because it is large, the body will displace a large amount of water, and a large, upward force will act on the body.

2. Because the body is light, the downward force due to the pull of gravity will be small.

3. Because the upward force acting on the body is greater than the downward force acting on the body, the body will float.

F. Although steel is quite heavy, a steel ship can float.

1. The steel is spread out over a large area to form a hollow shell so that it will displace a large amount of water and a large, upward force will act on the steel.

2. The downward force, caused by the combined weight of steel, air, equipment, passengers, and cargo, is still less than the upward force caused by the displaced water, so the steel ship floats.

3. When a steel ship is set afloat, it sinks until it displaces just enough water to create an upward force greater than the downward force produced by the ship's weight.

4. When the ship is loaded, it sinks deeper until enough water is displaced to produce an additional upward force to support the weight of the cargo.

G. A submarine floats for the same reason that a steel ship floats.

1. The submarine is able to sink because it has tanks that let in water and make the submarine heavy enough (or increase the downward force enough) to sink.

2. When the water is pumped out of the tanks, the submarine becomes lighter and rises to the surface.

H. A body floats easier in salt water than in fresh water.

1. The same downward force of gravity acts on the body, whether the body is in salt water or fresh water.

2. However, salt water is heavier than fresh water because it has more minerals dissolved in it.

3. As a result, displaced salt water has a greater upward force than displaced fresh water.

4. If a ship sails from fresh water into salt water, it rises further out of the water because the salt water has a greater upward force than the fresh water.

5. If a ship sails from salt water into fresh water, it sinks further into the water because the fresh water has a smaller upward force than the salt water.

XII. CONSERVATION OF WATER

A. Every year there is a greater need for more water.

1. Today, each person in the United States uses about 58,000 liters (15,000 gal) of water a year for drinking, washing, laundry, cooking, heating, and air-conditioning purposes.

2. Scientists estimate that industry uses 606,000 liters (160,000 gal) of water a year for each person living in the United States.

3. Agriculture also uses large amounts of water to irrigate the land.

B. As the population in the United States grows, the need for water will soon become greater than the supply.

C. We must take steps to conserve all water that is available.

1. We should avoid needless use and waste of water.

2. Soil and forest conservation helps prevent water from running off quickly before it can be used.

3. The building of dams holds back river water that is rushing to the sea.

4. Scientists are looking for a way to change seawater into usable fresh water.

D. Our water is also being polluted.

1. Factories are pouring into rivers large amounts of waste materials that pollute the water.

2. Wastes and sewage from homes in many cities are also dumped into rivers without being treated first so that the water will not be polluted.

3. This pollution of water means that other cities and factories, which are located downstream, must purify the water before they can use it.

4. Sometimes the waste materials accumulate or are so strong that, even after all regular methods of purifying water are used, the water is still unfit to use.

E. This pollution of the water cuts down even more the amount of usable water that we need.

F. Pollution of water can be prevented.

1. Cities and factories should treat wastes and sewage instead of sending them downstream.

2. Modern sewage disposal plants should be established, which separate the waste materials from the water and thus make it possible for the water to be used again.

THE OCEANS

I. THE OCEANS OF THE EARTH

A. Although we usually think of the oceans as separate bodies of water, we should keep in mind that all the oceans are part of one great sea.

1. This sea covers almost 75 percent of the earth.

2. It is the deepest ocean, with an average depth of about 4250 meters (14,000 ft).

B. There are five great oceans on earth: the Pacific, Atlantic, Indian, Arctic, and Antarctic Oceans.

C. The Pacific Ocean is the largest ocean.

1. It includes about three eighths of the total area of the sea.

2. It is the deepest ocean, with an average depth of about 14,000 feet.

D. The Atlantic Ocean is the next largest ocean.

1. Its area is about one fourth of the total area of the sea.

2. Its average depth is about 4000 meters (13,000 ft).

E. The Indian Ocean has an area about one eighth of the total area of the sea.

F. The Arctic Ocean is really a northern extension of the Atlantic Ocean.

1. It is a small ocean, with about one thirtieth of the sea's area.

2. It is almost completely covered with ice to a depth of 3 meters (10 ft).

G. The Antarctic Ocean is at the south in the region that surrounds the antarctic continent.

II. THE OCEAN FLOOR

A. The lower parts of the earth's surface, where the oceans are located, are called **ocean basins.**

B. These ocean basins are the true surface of the earth whereas the continents are really huge islands that were raised above the ocean basins by forces acting inside the earth.

C. The depth of the ocean varies.

1. Over the **continental shelf,** which is really the edge of a continent under water, the ocean is shallow and rarely more than 180 meters (590 ft) deep.

2. Beyond the continental shelf, however, the ocean becomes much deeper very quickly, as the edge of the continent drops off sharply to the bottom of the ocean, forming a slope called the **continental slope.**

3. The deep **ocean floor** begins at the end of the continental slope.

4. The average depth of the ocean floor is

4 kilometers (2½ mi), although in some places the ocean is roughly 11 kilometers (7 mi) deep.

D. The ocean floor is not smooth, but it is made up of many mountains and valleys.

E. In the Atlantic Ocean there is a tremendous mountain chain, called the **Mid-Atlantic Ridge,** on the ocean floor.

1. This mountain chain is about 320 kilometers (200 mi) wide, 3050 meters (10,-000 ft) high, and stretches along the entire Atlantic Ocean to the southern tip of Africa.

2. Here the mountain chain joins with a similar mountain chain that runs through the Indian Ocean.

3. This Indian Ocean chain then joins with many chains of mountains that stretch across the Pacific Ocean.

4. The tops of these Mid-Atlantic mountains are higher than those found on the continents; yet most of them are at least a mile below the surface of the ocean.

5. The Azores in the North Atlantic and Ascension Island in the South Atlantic are tops of the very high mountains in this chain.

F. These mountains are believed to be formed from volcanic activity that took place long ago.

G. Volcanic activity has also been responsible for forming mountains in other parts of the ocean floor.

1. The islands in the oceans are the tops of these mountains extending above the surface of the ocean.

2. The Aleutian Islands, West Indies, and South Sea Islands are tops of mountains on the ocean floor.

H. Near these islands are huge **trenches** and **troughs,** which are very deep.

1. These trenches and troughs may be as long as 1600 kilometers (1000 mi) and as wide as 160 kilometers (100 mi).

2. They have been formed by cracks in the earth's crust, called **faults,** where the volcanic action that formed these islands took place.

3. The deepest parts of the ocean are found in these trenches and troughs.

I. In the continental slopes are deep **canyons,** some of which are larger than the Grand Canyon, which are believed to have been carved out of the slope by underwater ocean currents.

J. The entire ocean floor is covered with a large layer of sediment.

1. The continental shelf is covered with gravel, sand, clay, and shells.

2. The ocean floor itself is covered with a soft, fine ooze or mud, made up of volcanic dust and the remains of tiny sea plants and animals.

III. Exploring the Ocean

A. The science of the study of the oceans is called **oceanography.**

B. Oceanographers use many devices and instruments to study the ocean.

C. The **water-sampling bottle** is a device that collects water at different depths.

D. The deep-sea **thermometer** measures the temperature at different depths.

E. The **bottom sampler** is a device that collects samples of material at the bottom of the ocean.

F. The **current meter** is an instrument that measures the speed and direction of the ocean currents.

G. The **deep-sea camera** can take pictures of sea life in the deep parts of the ocean and of the materials on the ocean floor.

H. The **sonic-depth recorder** measures the depth of the ocean.

1. On the ship the recorder sends sound waves toward the bottom of the ocean.

2. The sound waves strike the bottom of the ocean and are reflected back to the ship.

3. The recorder records the time required for the sound to travel to the bottom of the ocean and to be reflected back to the ship.

4. By knowing the time, as well as the speed of sound in water, we can easily

calculate the distance to the bottom of the ocean.

I. Oceanographers also use a small underwater vessel, called a **bathyscaphe,** which allows men to explore the ocean and its bottom.

IV. SEAWATER

A. The composition of the seawater today is not the same as the water in the oceans long ago.
1. At first the waters of the oceans were fresh, and they had no salts in them.
2. As rain fell on the land, many minerals were dissolved and carried to the oceans by the rivers and streams.
3. Each year the oceans become more and more salty.

B. Today, every 45 kilograms (100 lb) of seawater contains about 1½ kilograms (3⅓ lb) of dissolved minerals.
1. About three fourths of this mineral material is common salt, or sodium chloride.
2. The rest of the minerals are salts of magnesium, calcium, and potassium.

C. Some of the dissolved minerals can be very valuable to man.
1. Each cubic kilometer of seawater has 1 million tons of magnesium, which is used in planes and for other purposes, and almost all the world's supply of magnesium is obtained from seawater.
2. Bromine is also obtained from seawater, and it is used in making high-test gasoline and photographic film.
3. Common salt, or sodium chloride, is obtained from seawater.
4. Although a cubic kilometer of seawater has about 50 million dollars worth of gold in it, scientists say that it would cost more than 50 million dollars to recover this amount of gold.

D. The temperature of the seawater varies.
1. Seawater is warmest at its surface.
2. The warmest surface water is found in oceans near the equator.
3. In the tropics, surface water is about 21° Celsius (70° Fahrenheit), although in the Persian Gulf it has been as high as 35° Celsius (95° Fahrenheit).
4. In the polar regions, the average temperature of the surface water is about −2¼° Celsius (28° Fahrenheit), which is the freezing point of salt water.
5. Most parts of the sea have surface temperatures between those of the tropical oceans and the polar oceans, depending upon their location and upon weather conditions.
6. Deeper down in the ocean, the temperature of the water becomes colder, and even at the equator, the temperature of the ocean may be 2° to 4° Celsius (35° to 40° Fahrenheit).

E. There are two kinds of ice found floating in the sea: **icebergs** and **floes.**

F. Icebergs are large blocks of glaciers that break off and float in the sea.
1. Icebergs are freshwater ice.
2. Icebergs are dangerous to ships because about nine tenths of an iceberg is below the surface of the water, and the part below the surface is often spread out far in all directions.
3. The larger icebergs in the northern hemisphere may be 1⅗ kilometers (1 mi) long, with 90 meters (295 ft) of ice showing above the water.
4. The icebergs that break off the Antarctic glaciers are huge and they may be more than 64 kilometers (40 mi) long.

G. Floes are large pieces of frozen seawater that come down from the Arctic Ocean.
1. In the Arctic Ocean, the temperature is cold enough for the surface water to freeze so that the Arctic Ocean is always covered with an ice pack about 4 meters (13 ft) thick.
2. During the summer, some of this ice pack melts and breaks up, sending large pieces of ice floating southward.
3. These floes are different from icebergs in that they are smaller, have a flat shape, and are saltwater ice.

V. WAVES

A. Ocean waves are made by winds.
   1. As the wind blows across the water, there is friction between the moving air and the surface of the water.
   2. This friction makes the water rise and fall in a regular rhythmic movement, called a **wave.**
B. A wave has two parts.
   1. The highest point to which the water rises is called the **crest** of the wave.
   2. The lowest point to which the water falls is called the **trough** of the wave.
C. The height of a wave is the vertical distance between its crest and its trough.
D. The length of a wave is the horizontal distance from one crest to another, or from one trough to another.
E. The stronger the wind and the greater the distance over which the wind blows, the greater the waves will be.
F. During a storm, waves may be more than 20 meters (65 ft) high and 150 meters (490 ft) long, and they may travel through the water at speeds as high as 96 kilometers (60 mi) an hour.
G. On very windy days, waves may have a foamy white top, called **white caps.**
   1. White caps occur when the strong winds push the water off the tops of the waves.
   2. White caps can be formed close to shore or far out at sea.
H. When waves reach the shore, **breakers** are formed.
   1. A wave approaching the shore travels smoothly until its trough hits the bottom of the seashore.
   2. The trough of the wave is slowed down as it rubs against the bottom of the seashore.
   3. At the same time the water in the wave piles up, and the wave becomes higher and higher.
   4. Finally, the wave crest falls forward, and the wave breaks to form a breaker.
   5. At beaches where the seashore is steep, breakers form very close to shore, and they do not last very long.
   6. At beaches where the seashore is very shallow, breakers form far out, and they can last for as long as a mile.
I. When a wave strikes the beach, the water immediately begins to move back along the ocean bottom as an **undertow.**
   1. The returning undertow moves underneath the waves that are coming in.
   2. The stronger the waves, the more water they throw up on the beach, and the stronger the returning undertows become.
   3. Undertows carry away sand from the beach to the deeper sea.
J. Giant waves, called **tsunamis,** are produced by earthquakes or volcanic explosions at the bottom of the ocean.
   1. Tsunamis are often mistakenly called "tidal" waves.
   2. Tsunamis are different from regular waves because they can be more than 160 kilometers (100 mi) long and can travel at speeds as high as 800 kilometers (500 mi) an hour.
   3. In midocean they are only a few meters or feet high, but close to shore they may be more than 30 meters (100 ft) high and cause great damage.

VI. SURFACE OCEAN CURRENTS

A. The surface waters of the oceans are constantly moving in the form of currents.
B. The movement of these surface waters is mainly caused by the force of the winds blowing on the water.
C. If the earth were completely covered with water and the winds always blew with the same force and from the same direction, the surface currents of the sea would move in a great circle around the earth.
D. However, there are many factors that affect the direction these currents follow.
   1. The winds on earth actually blow with different force and from different directions.

2. Because the earth rotates, the waters in the northern hemisphere move to their right and the waters in the southern hemisphere move to their left.

3. The outlines of the earth's continents make the currents turn and change direction.

4. The depth and shape of the ocean floor may also affect the direction of the currents.

E. Currents that flow away from the equator are warm currents, and currents that flow toward the equator are cold currents.

VII. THE EQUATORIAL CURRENTS

A. In the oceans that lie along the equator, there are powerful currents just above and below the equator.

B. These currents move toward the west, driven by the steady winds that are present in these regions.

C. If there were no continents, these currents would move in a continuous circle around the earth.

D. However, the continents make these currents turn to the north or the south, and they even make the currents turn back on themselves as well.

E. The current flowing just above the equator is called the **North Equatorial Current,** and the current flowing just below the equator is called the **South Equatorial Current.**

VIII. THE NORTH ATLANTIC CURRENTS

A. The North Equatorial Current moves westward to the West Indies.

B. At the West Indies this current branches.

1. One branch moves north along the east coast of the United States as the **Gulf Stream.**

2. The other branch goes into and around the Gulf of Mexico, where it becomes enlarged and warmer, and then it passes through the Straits of Florida and flows

north, rejoining the first branch at Cape Hatteras and becoming part of the Gulf Stream.

C. The Gulf Stream is one of the strongest water currents on earth, moving about 6½ kilometers (4 mi) an hour in a path that is about 160 kilometers (100 mi) wide.

D. Because of the earth's rotation, the Gulf Stream moves to the right, northeast toward Europe.

E. When the Gulf Stream reaches the North Atlantic Ocean, it branches into two weaker currents.

1. The first branch moves directly on to Europe, where it warms the shores of Iceland, the British Isles, Norway, and Sweden.

2. The second branch turns south, as the **Canary Current,** and returns to the North Equatorial Current.

F. In this way there is a complete circle of current in the north Atlantic Ocean.

G. In the center of this circle is a very large, quiet area of water, called the **Sargasso Sea,** where great masses of sargassum seaweed accumulate.

H. The **Labrador Current** flows out of the Arctic Ocean into the North Atlantic, carrying very cold water southward to the northeast coast of the United States as far as Cape Cod, where it then sinks below the surface.

IX. THE SOUTH ATLANTIC CURRENTS

A. The South Atlantic Currents are just like the North Atlantic Currents, but they flow in the opposite direction.

B. The South Equatorial Current moves westward, to the northern part of South America, where it turns south.

C. It then moves along the South American coast as the **Brazil Current.**

D. Then it moves east as the **South Atlantic Current** to Africa, where it moves north as the **Benguela Current,** and finally it returns to the South Equatorial Current.

X. THE NORTH PACIFIC CURRENTS

A. In the Pacific Area, the North Equatorial Current moves westward to the Philippines, where most of it turns northward as the **Japan Current** (the equivalent of the Atlantic Ocean's Gulf Stream).
B. The warm Japan Current then turns to the northeast as the **North Pacific Current.**
C. The North Pacific Current approaches the Pacific coast, and it divides into two branches.
   1. One branch, the **Alaska Current,** flows northward and warms the southern coast of Alaska.
   2. The other branch, the **California Current,** flows southward, carrying cooler waters down the west coast of the United States, and it rejoins the North Equatorial Current off the coast of Mexico.

XI. THE SOUTH PACIFIC CURRENTS

A. The South Equatorial Current of the Pacific moves westward across the Pacific Ocean.
B. Because of the many islands in the South Pacific, it is rather difficult to follow the direction of this current as it nears Asia and is turned to the south.
C. These islands weaken the current by dividing it into a number of smaller currents that go off in different directions.
D. The only strong current in the South Pacific is the **Peru Current,** which carries cold water from the south polar region to the coast of South America and then rejoins the South Equatorial Current of the Pacific.

XII. THE ANTARCTIC CURRENT

A. The **Antarctic Current** is formed in the southernmost parts of the Atlantic and the Pacific Oceans.
B. Winds that are blowing to the west produce this Antarctic Current.
C. Because there are no land masses in this area, this current completely circles the Antarctic region of the earth.

XIII. DEEP-SEA CURRENTS

A. In addition to surface currents that are driven by the wind, there are also powerful currents that flow deep below the surface of the sea.
B. Some deep currents are caused by the slow movement of cold water from the polar regions to the equator.
   1. Since cold water is heavier than warm water, the cold waters around the polar regions sink and travel along the ocean bottom to the equator.
   2. In 1959, which was the International Geophysical Year (IGY), scientists found a deep current 2750 meters (9000 ft) below the Gulf Stream, going in the opposite direction with a speed of about 13 kilometers (8 mi) a day.
   3. Other deep currents, also traveling in opposite directions from the surface currents, have been discovered in the South Atlantic Ocean and the Pacific Ocean.
C. Some deep currents are caused by a difference in the amount of salt in the seawater.
   1. The more salt in the seawater, the heavier the water will be.
   2. Since the Mediterranean Sea is shallow compared to the large oceans, a large amount of its water is exposed at its surface.
   3. As a result, the waters of the Mediterranean Sea evaporate more quickly than the waters of the larger Atlantic Ocean; consequently, its waters become more salty and heavier.
   4. At Gibraltar, where the Atlantic Ocean and Mediterranean Sea meet, there is a strong, deep current of saltier and heavier water that runs along the sea bottom past Gibraltar and into the Atlantic Ocean.
D. Scientists still know very little about deep-sea currents because the currents are so

deep and circulate so slowly that they are hard to follow and study.

XIV. LIFE IN THE OCEAN

A. The ocean water has all the necessary conditions to support a wide variety of plant and animal life.
   1. It has a tremendous amount of minerals and other chemicals dissolved in it.
   2. It also has a large amount of air dissolved in it.
B. Most plants and animals that live in the ocean are found either near the shore or in the surface waters.
C. At the bottom there can be found such living things as seaweeds, grasses, sponges, oysters, clams, crabs, and lobsters.
D. The ocean also has in it very tiny plants and animals, called **plankton,** which are the basic food for sea life.
   1. Plankton grow in tremendous numbers in the upper layers of the ocean, where the sun can reach them.
   2. All forms of sea life either feed directly on plankton or eat animals that feed upon plankton.
E. In the middle and bottom parts of the ocean there are also living things, but they do not look at all like the living things found near the surface.
F. Tiny sea animals, called **corals,** affect shorelines in warm waters.
   1. These sea animals live in colonies in warm, shallow water that must be 20° Celsius (68° Fahrenheit) or higher.
   2. The animals swim around freely when they are young, but, when they become older, they become fastened to the rocky sea floor.

3. Now the corals depend upon the waves and currents to bring food to them.
4. The corals also take lime from the sea-water to make the shells in which they live.
5. When the corals die, they leave their shells behind, and new colonies of corals grow on top of these shells.
6. Eventually, the shells accumulate until they form a **coral reef,** which is separated from the mainland by a broad lagoon of calm water.
7. Sometimes, when there is a sunken volcanic cone not too far below the surface of the water, the corals form in a narrow, circular ring, called an **atoll.**

XV. ECONOMIC IMPORTANCE OF OCEANS

A. Oceans are like huge highways, which ships use to bring food and supplies to all parts of the world.
B. The ocean supplies a large amount of the food we eat.
C. The ocean has chemicals in it, which industries take out and use.
D. The ocean makes it possible for us to grow things on land.
   1. Water evaporates in tremendous amounts from the surface of the oceans, forming water vapor that goes into the air.
   2. The air then moves across the land, and eventually the water vapor condenses out as rain and other forms of precipitation, providing water for the soil.
E. Because our demand for water eventually will become greater than the supply, scientists are already looking for inexpensive ways of changing salt seawater into the fresh water that we can use.

WINDS

I. THE EARTH AND ITS ATMOSPHERE ARE HEATED BY THE SUN

A. The radiant energy from the sun passes through the air without heating it very much.
B. Most of the sun's radiant energy strikes the earth's surface, which absorbs this energy and changes it into heat.
C. The heated earth's surface then warms the air above it in two ways.
  1. The warm earth radiates some of its heat energy back into the air, which absorbs much of this heat energy and becomes warmer.
  2. Although air is a poor conductor of heat, some of the earth's heat is conducted into the air just above the earth.
D. At the same time, as the sun's radiant energy passes through the air, a small amount of this energy will be absorbed by the air nearest the earth and be changed into heat.
E. Every day the air goes through a cycle of heating and cooling.
  1. When the sun shines upon the earth, the air becomes warmer as the heated earth radiates heat energy.
  2. At night the earth cools off, and the air becomes cooler.
  3. The air becomes much warmer in the summer, when the days are longer, than in the winter, when the nights are longer.
  4. Cloudy nights will be warmer than clear nights because the clouds act as a blanket to reflect and absorb the radiant energy given off by the earth, and in this way they keep the heat within the air next to the earth.

II. THE EARTH IS HEATED UNEQUALLY

A. The shape of the earth produces unequal heating.

1. The earth's surface is curved so that the sun's rays strike different parts of the earth at different angles.
2. At the equator, the sun's rays strike the earth's surface directly or at right angles.
3. Away from the equator, the sun's rays strike the earth's surface at a slant.
4. The closer we get to the polar regions, the more the earth is curved, and the greater is the slant of the sun's rays striking the earth's surface.
5. Direct rays are warmer than slanted rays because with direct rays the sun's energy is concentrated over a smaller area of the earth's surface, whereas with slanted rays the same amount of energy is now spread out over a large area, making the energy less concentrated.
6. Because the earth's surface that receives direct rays of the sun becomes warmer than the surface that receives slanted rays, the air above this warmer surface becomes warmer as well.
7. When one part of the earth has summer, this part is tilted so that the sun's rays shine directly on its surface, and this part of the earth becomes warmer.
8. When the same part of the earth has winter, this part is now tilted so that the sun's rays shine at a slant on its surface, and this part of the earth now becomes cooler.
B. The different surfaces of the earth are heated unequally.
  1. Some surfaces of the earth absorb and radiate heat faster than others.
  2. Dark and rough land surfaces, such as rocks and soil, absorb heat quickly and radiate it just as quickly.
  3. On the other hand, bodies of water have clear, smooth surfaces, and they absorb and radiate heat more slowly.
  4. As a result, when the sun shines directly upon land and water surfaces, the land surfaces become warmer than water sur-

faces, and the air above the land surfaces becomes warmer as well.

III. The Unequal Heating of the Earth Produces Winds

A. **Wind** is the movement of air set up by the unequal heating of the earth's surface by the sun.
B. This movement of air is in the form of a **convection current.**
  1. When air next to the earth is heated, it expands and becomes lighter.
  2. This warmer, lighter air is pushed up by the colder, heavier air that surrounds it.
  3. The colder, heavier air now is heated and becomes lighter, being pushed up in turn by more cold, heavy air that surrounds it.
  4. This process continues until there is a steady flow of air, called a convection current, with warm air rising and cold air falling.
C. Cold air is heavier than warm air, and so it exerts a greater pressure than warm air.
D. Winds are formed when cold air from high-pressure areas moves to low-pressure areas where the air is warmer.

IV. Wind Belts of the Earth

A. There is a constant movement of air over the entire earth in the form of **wind belts.**
B. If the earth did not rotate on its axis, the movement of the air over the earth would be quite simple.
  1. At the equator the heated air would rise and flow toward the north and south poles.
  2. At the north and south poles the colder air would move toward the equator.
C. However, because the earth does rotate, the movement of air over the earth becomes more complicated.
  1. The winds in the northern hemisphere are deflected to their right, and the winds in the southern hemisphere are deflected to their left.

  2. As a result, a series of wind belts is produced around the earth, with the winds in each belt moving in a definite direction.
D. Because the sun's rays shine differently on the northern and southern hemispheres in the summer and winter, the wind belts shift with the seasons.

V. The Doldrums

A. The **doldrums** is an area of low pressure at the equator.
B. Most of the air movement in the doldrums is upward, as the heated air rises.
C. As a result, there are mostly calms in the doldrums, with occasional light breezes.

VI. The Horse Latitudes

A. The heated air above the equator rises and moves toward the north and south poles, cooling as it moves high into the air.
B. At about one third of the distance from the equator to the poles (30 degrees latitude), the air has cooled enough to sink down toward the earth's surface again.
C. This belt of descending, high-pressure air is called the **horse latitudes.**
D. The air is still warm, but not as warm as the air in the doldrums.
E. There are also mostly calms in the horse latitudes, with occasional light, changeable winds.

VII. The Trade Winds

A. The air sinking down at the horse latitudes forms two wind belts: one flowing back to the equator and the other flowing toward the poles.
B. The winds flowing back to the equator are called the **trade winds.**
C. Because of the earth's rotation, in the northern hemisphere the trade winds are deflected or turned to their right and become the **northeast trade winds.**

[349

D. In the southern hemisphere the trade winds are deflected to their left and become the **southeast trade winds.**

E. The trade winds blow very steadily with respect to direction and speed.

VIII. The Prevailing Westerlies

A. The winds that flow from the horse latitudes toward the poles are called the **prevailing westerlies.**

B. Because of the earth's rotation, in the northern hemisphere the prevailing westerlies are deflected to their right and become the **southwesterlies.**

C. In the southern hemisphere the prevailing westerlies are deflected to their left and become the **northwesterlies.**

D. The prevailing westerlies are not as steady as the trade winds, and they will vary both in direction and speed.

IX. The Subpolar Lows

A. At a little more than two thirds of the distance from the equator to the poles (65 degrees latitude), there is a second belt of low-pressure area, called the **subpolar lows.**

B. At this point, the warmer air that is still moving toward the poles is pushed up by the cold air moving down from the poles toward the equator.

C. The upward movement of this warm air produces an area of low pressure.

X. The Polar Easterlies

A. At the poles, masses of cold air move down toward the equator.

B. They move to their right in the northern hemisphere to become the **polar northeasterlies,** and to their left in the southern hemisphere to become the **polar southeasterlies.**

C. These winds have the same direction as the trade winds, but they are very cold and violent.

XI. The Jet Stream

A. In the northern hemisphere, there is a narrow band of high-speed winds, called the **jet stream.**

1. These winds are located in the prevailing westerlies, but they are 8 to 16 kilometers (5 to 10 mi) above the surface of the earth and travel at speeds as high as 640 kilometers (400 mi) an hour.

2. They move eastward around the earth, but their direction often varies.

B. The position and speed of the jet stream varies with the seasons.

1. It moves closer to the north pole in the summer, and it shifts farther south in the winter.

2. It is about 13 to 16 kilometers (8 to 10 mi) high in the summer, and 8 to 11 kilometers (5 to 7 mi) high in the winter.

3. Its winds move faster in the summer.

C. In 1959, during the International Geophysical Year (IGY), scientists discovered three more jet streams.

1. There is one in the southern hemisphere that is exactly like the stream in the northern hemisphere.

2. There is one in the lower stratosphere of the Arctic Circle.

3. There is one in the lower stratosphere of the Antarctic Circle.

D. In the winter, jet planes take advantage of the jet stream, using it as a strong tailwind to cut down flying time.

XII. Monsoons

A. A **monsoon** is a seasonal wind that changes its direction in the summer and in the winter.

B. This wind is produced by the difference in heating between continents and oceans during the summer and winter.

1. In the summer, the land is heated more than the ocean so that the cooler air over the ocean moves in across the land.

2. In the winter, the land becomes colder than the ocean so that the cooler air

over the land moves out toward the ocean.

C. The best example of a monsoon is found in India.

D. In the summer, the Indian Ocean is cooler than the hot land.

    1. The air above the hot land becomes hot and light, forming a low-pressure area, and the cooler, moist air from the Indian Ocean blows across the land.

    2. This **summer monsoon,** also called a **wet monsoon,** brings India its rainy season from May through October.

E. In the winter, northern India becomes much colder than the Indian Ocean.

    1. The air above the cold land becomes cold and heavy, forming a high-pressure area, and the cold, dry air blows from the land to the Indian Ocean.

    2. This **winter monsoon,** also called a **dry monsoon,** brings dry weather to India from November through April.

F. Australia, Spain, and Portugal also have monsoons.

XIII. Land and Sea Breezes

A. Land and sea breezes are rather like daily monsoons.

B. They are winds at the seashore that blow in one direction in the daytime and in the opposite direction at night.

C. During the day, the land and sea receive the same amount of heat from the sun, but the land heats up more quickly and becomes hotter than the sea.

    1. The air over the land becomes warmer and lighter than the air over the sea.

    2. The warmer air over the land is forced upward by the colder air coming in from over the sea to produce a **sea breeze.**

    3. At the seashore a sea breeze usually begins before noon and dies down at sunset.

D. At night the land cools more quickly than the water, and the air over the land becomes colder and heavier than the air over the water.

    1. The colder, heavier land air moves out to sea, forming a **land breeze.**

    2. Land breezes blow during the night and die down at sunrise.

    3. Land breezes are weaker than sea breezes.

E. Land and sea breezes can also be formed at large lakes.

XIV. Mountain and Valley Breezes

A. Mountain and valley breezes are also a kind of daily monsoon.

B. During the day, the sunny, exposed mountain heats up more quickly than the sheltered, shady valley.

    1. The air over the mountain becomes warmer and lighter than the air in the valley.

    2. A cool **valley breeze** then blows up the mountain, as it pushes the warmer, lighter mountain air up and away.

C. At night the mountain cools more quickly than the valley.

    1. The air over the mountain now becomes colder than the air in the valley.

    2. A cool **mountain breeze** then blows down the mountain into the valley, pushing the warmer, lighter valley air up and away.

D. The narrower the valley, the stronger the mountain and valley breezes will be.

E. Because a valley breeze has to travel uphill, its speed is not as great as a mountain breeze.

WATER IN THE AIR

I. EVAPORATION

A. When water changes from a liquid into an invisible gas, called **water vapor,** this change is called **evaporation.**

B. Evaporation always takes place at the surface of the water.

C. Evaporation takes place because of molecular motion within the water.
1. Water is made up of tiny molecules that are constantly moving.
2. Some of these molecules have more energy and move faster than others.
3. The faster moving molecules near the surface of the water leave the surface and go off into the air, becoming molecules of water vapor.

D. Some solids, like moth balls, can evaporate directly as a solid without first becoming a liquid.

II. FACTORS AFFECTING EVAPORATION

A. There are several factors that affect the speed of evaporation.

B. Heat will make water evaporate more quickly.
1. Heat makes the molecules move faster.
2. As a result, more molecules can leave the water at one time.

C. The larger the surface, the more quickly evaporation will take place because more molecules can leave the water at one time.

D. The amount of water already in the air affects the speed of evaporation.
1. If the air already contains a lot of water vapor, there is less room in the air for more molecules of water vapor to enter, and the speed of evaporation is slow.
2. If the air contains only a little water vapor, there is plenty of room in the air for more molecules to enter, and evaporation takes place more quickly.

E. Wind helps water evaporate more quickly.
1. As the molecules leave the water and become water vapor, the air above the water eventually becomes filled, or saturated, with water vapor.
2. This saturation slows down evaporation because there is no more room in the air for more molecules of water vapor to enter.
3. Wind blows away the air that is saturated with water vapor, and provides fresh air that can hold a fresh supply of water vapor.

F. The lower the air pressure above the surface of the water, the faster evaporation takes place.
1. Lower air pressure means that the air is not pressing down as hard on the surface of the water.
2. This lower air pressure makes it easier for the molecules to leave the water and go into the air as water vapor.

G. Warm, dry air can hold more water vapor than cold, moist air; consequently, the warmer and drier the air above the water, the faster the water evaporates.

H. Liquids other than water also evaporate, and some liquids evaporate faster than others because their molecules are moving faster, from the beginning, at the same temperature.

III. EVAPORATION IS A COOLING PROCESS

A. When a liquid evaporates, it takes in, or absorbs, heat.

B. The liquid gets this heat from materials around it.

C. When a drop of liquid is placed on a person's skin, the liquid begins to evaporate.
1. In this case the evaporating liquid gets its heat from the skin, leaving the skin cooler.
2. The quicker the liquid evaporates, the more heat it needs, and the cooler the skin becomes.
3. This is the reason why the evaporation

of perspiration, or water, on the skin cools the body.

D. When a liquid evaporates, the liquid itself becomes cooler.

1. The faster moving molecules in the liquid have a higher temperature than the slower moving molecules.

2. When the faster moving molecules leave a liquid and become a vapor, the cooler, slower moving molecules are left behind, making the liquid cooler.

IV. HUMIDITY

A. **Humidity** refers to the water vapor in the air.

B. The **absolute humidity** is the actual amount of water vapor present in the air at a certain temperature.

C. The **relative humidity** is the ratio between the actual amount of water vapor in the air (absolute humidity) at a certain temperature and the maximum amount of water vapor the air can hold at that temperature.

D. The relative humidity is usually multiplied by 100 to give the result in percentages.

E. When the air contains as much water vapor as it can hold at a certain temperature, the air is said to be **saturated,** and the relative humidity is 100 percent.

V. CONDENSATION

A. When water vapor changes into a liquid, the change is called **condensation.**

B. Condensation takes place because of a change in molecular motion of the molecules of water vapor in the air.

1. When air containing water vapor is cooled, the water-vapor molecules move more slowly and come closer together.

2. If the air is cooled enough, the water-vapor molecules come close enough together to become water again.

C. Condensation also takes place because air contracts, or becomes smaller, when cooled.

1. As air containing water vapor is cooled, the air will keep on contracting until it is saturated with water vapor and can hold no more.

2. Any further cooling will make the air contract even more, and cause some of the water vapor to condense from the air.

D. The temperature below which air must be cooled for condensation to take place is called the **dew point.**

E. The same factors that affect the speed of evaporation also affect the speed of condensation, but in reverse, so that a condition that speeds up evaporation slows down condensation, and vice-versa.

VI. DEW AND FROST

A. Dew and frost are forms of condensation that take place on surfaces at or near the earth at night.

B. During the night, the earth's surface and solid objects on it give up their heat rather quickly and become cool.

C. The air coming in contact with these surfaces also is cooled.

D. If the air is cooled below its dew point, the water vapor in the air condenses on these surfaces as water droplets, called **dew.**

E. If the dew point is below freezing (which is 0° Celsius or 32° Fahrenheit), the water vapor condenses directly as crystals of ice, called **frost.**

F. Frost is not frozen dew.

G. Dew and frost condense on any surface that has a temperature lower than the dew point of the air that touches this surface.

H. Dew and frost form more easily on a clear night, when the surfaces can radiate their heat away more quickly through the air, whereas clouds act like a blanket to prevent the heat from radiating away.

I. Dew and frost form more easily on a calm

[353

night because winds blow the air around and prevent the air next to the earth from getting cold enough to cause condensation.

VII. Fog

A. When a sizable layer of air next to the earth's surface is cooled below its dew point, the water vapor in this layer condenses into tiny water droplets to form a **fog.**
   1. The water droplets are heavier than air, but they are so small and fall so slowly that the slightest air movement is enough to keep them floating in the air.
   2. A fog is really a cloud on the ground.
B. A **ground fog** is formed under exactly the same conditions as dew and frost are formed.
   1. Ground fogs often form in valleys, which fill with cold, heavy air.
   2. In the morning the sun warms the air, which expands and can now hold more water vapor, and the water droplets in the fog evaporate and the fog disappears.
C. An **advection fog** is formed when warm, moist air from one region blows over a cool surface.
   1. In the Grand Banks of Newfoundland, fogs are very common because the warm, moist air from the Gulf Stream blows constantly over the cold Labrador Current.
   2. Advection fogs are quite common along the seacoast when warm, moist air from the sea blows over the cooler land.

VIII. Clouds

A. Clouds, like fogs, are formed when a mass of air is cooled.
   1. When warm air containing water vapor rises high in the air, it becomes colder.
   2. The warm, rising air reaches levels where the air pressure is less, and the air expands.
   3. When air expands by itself, it uses up some of its heat energy to make it expand, and the air becomes colder.
   4. If the air is cooled below its dew point, the water vapor in the air condenses as tiny droplets of water to form a **cloud.**
   5. The water vapor usually condenses around tiny bits of dust or other particles in the air.
   6. If the air is below freezing 0° Celsius or 32° Fahrenheit), the water vapor condenses directly as tiny ice crystals.
   7. Just as with the fog, the droplets of water or ice crystals in the cloud are heavier than air, but they are so small and fall so slowly that the slightest air movement is enough to keep them floating in the air.
B. A cloud on earth would look like a fog, and a fog high in the air would look like a cloud.
C. The shapes of the clouds are determined by how they are formed.
   1. If the movement of the cooling air is vertical, the clouds form in large, billowy masses.
   2. If the movement of the cooling air is horizontal, the clouds form in layers.
D. There are three basic types of clouds: **cirrus, cumulus,** and **stratus** clouds.
E. Cirrus (meaning "curl") clouds are the highest clouds in the sky.
   1. They look like thin wisps of curls or like thin feathers.
   2. They can be from 6½ to 13 kilometers (4 to 8 mi) up in the sky.
   3. Because they are so high in the sky, they are always made up of tiny ice crystals.
F. Cumulus (meaning "heap") clouds look like large fluffs of cotton or wool.
   1. They are flat on the bottom, but they can pile up very high.
   2. They most often form in the afternoon, and they usually disappear toward evening.
   3. They are usually associated with fair weather.
   4. On hot summer days, cumulus clouds may grow very large and black, causing

thunderstorms with heavy rain and sometimes hail.

G. Stratus (meaning "layer") clouds are made up of low layers of clouds.

1. They are the nearest clouds to the earth.
2. They usually cover the whole sky and blot out the sun.
3. They are usually associated with stormy weather.

H. Sometimes a cloud is given two names because it has the characteristics of two different clouds.

1. **Cirrostratus clouds** are high, thin, feathery layers of ice-crystal clouds that often produce a halo or "ring" around the moon or sun, indicating the coming rain or snow.
2. **Stratocumulus clouds** are layers of cumulus clouds that cover the whole sky, especially in winter.
3. **Cirrocumulus clouds** are a large group of small, round, fluffy clouds that are made up of ice crystals.

I. Scientists also add prefixes to clouds, which help them describe the clouds more accurately.

1. Such prefixes include *alto* (meaning "high"), *nimbus* or *nimbo* (meaning "rain"), and *fracto* (meaning "broken").
2. **Altostratus clouds** are high stratus clouds.
3. **Nimbostratus clouds** are rain clouds.
4. **Cumulonimbus clouds** are thundershower clouds, also called **thunderheads.**
5. **Fractocumulus clouds** are cumulus clouds that have been broken up into smaller masses.

IX. PRECIPITATION

A. **Precipitation** refers to all forms of moisture that fall from the atmosphere.

1. **Rain, drizzle, sleet, snow,** and **hail** are forms of precipitation because they fall from the atmosphere.
2. Dew, frost, fog, and clouds are not forms of precipitation, according to scientists that study the weather, but are considered forms of condensation instead.

B. Rain is the water that falls from a cloud.

1. The droplets of water in a cloud are so small that the slightest air movement is enough to keep them floating in the air.
2. These droplets come together and form larger drops, which in turn come together to form even larger drops.
3. When the drops of water are large and heavy enough, they fall to the earth as rain.

C. Drizzle is the only other form of precipitation that falls as a liquid.

1. Drizzle is made up of very fine cloud (or fog) droplets that fall very slowly.
2. Ordinarily, these water droplets would stay in the cloud or fog, but sometimes the air is so still that they fall to earth.

D. Snow is the most common form of solid precipitation.

1. Snow forms from water vapor that condenses when the temperature of the air is below freezing.
2. The water vapor condenses directly into ice crystals, or snow.
3. Snow, therefore, is frozen water vapor, and not frozen rain.
4. Every snow crystal has six sides to it, but no two snowflakes are exactly alike.
5. When the air near the ground is cold, the snowflakes fall separately.
6. When the air near the ground is warmer, the snowflakes melt together to form large clots of wet, sticky snow.

E. Sleet is frozen rain, and it is usually formed during the winter when raindrops fall through a below-freezing layer of air that is near the ground.

F. Glaze is a coating of ice that forms when rain freezes after it reaches the ground.

1. The rain forms a thick coating of ice on streets, trees, telephone and electric wires, and other objects.
2. When this phenomenon occurs, it is called an ice storm.
3. The coating of ice often becomes so heavy that it makes bushes and tree branches collapse, breaks telephone and electric

wires, and makes traveling on highways dangerous or impossible.

G. Hail is formed mostly in the summer during a thunderstorm, when there are strong upward currents of air within the thundercloud.

1. These currents carry the raindrops high into a layer of below-freezing air.
2. The raindrops freeze and become pellets of ice.
3. These pellets of ice then fall into warmer air, where they pick up another coating of water.
4. Then the pellets, now coated with water, are blown up again into the colder air, where the coating of water freezes to form a second layer of ice.
5. This process is repeated until the pellets of ice, now called **hailstones,** become too heavy for the upward air currents to lift, and the hailstones fall to earth.
6. The hailstone is formed somewhat like an onion, with an ice pellet as its center and many layers of ice around this center.
7. Each layer shows one complete movement up into cold air and back down again into warmer air.
8. The more violent the thunderstorm, the more times the hailstones move up and down between the layers of cold and warm air, and the larger the hailstones become.
9. When hailstones are large, they can cause great damage to crops and can even hurt small animals.

X. The Water, or Hydrologic, Cycle

A. All the water on earth is constantly evaporating to form water vapor.

1. This evaporation takes place from the surfaces of the oceans, lakes, ponds, reservoirs, and rivers.
2. Water also evaporates from the soil, and plants give off water vapor during transpiration.

B. This water vapor is constantly condensing back into water again.

1. On or near the ground the water vapor condenses as dew, frost, and fog.
2. High in the air the water vapor condenses as clouds, rain, and snow.

C. This process of evaporation and condensation goes on in a continuous cycle, called the **water cycle** or **hydrologic cycle.**

D. The oceans are the basic source of all the water that the land surfaces receive because practically all the water that falls on the land surfaces eventually goes back to the oceans in some way.

1. Some of the water runs off into rivers and streams, and it is carried to the oceans.
2. Some of the water sinks into the ground, where it flows underground through roundabout paths either directly to the sea or to streams and lakes on the earth's surface.
3. Most of the water that falls on land surfaces evaporates directly into the air from bodies of water on land, and from the soil.
4. This evaporated water is carried by air currents to the oceans, where it falls as rain or snow.
5. The water then evaporates from the surfaces of the oceans, and the moist air is carried by air currents across the land, where it meets conditions that make the water vapor condense back to water again.

WEATHER CHANGES

I. Causes of Weather

A. When describing the weather at a certain time and place, the weatherman usually lists the conditions of the air at that time and place.

B. These conditions include the temperature of the air, the air pressure, the amount of moisture in the air (humidity), and the direction and speed of the wind.

C. When predicting the weather, the weatherman looks at the kinds of air masses that are moving across the earth.

D. These air masses are responsible for changes in the weather.

II. Air Masses

A. An **air mass** is a huge body of air that may cover a vast portion of the earth's surface and may be very wide and quite high.

B. In any air mass the temperature and the humidity are about the same throughout.

C. Air masses differ greatly from each other, and the weather that an air mass will bring depends mostly on the particular temperature and humidity that it has.

D. An air mass is formed when the atmosphere stays quietly over a certain part of the earth's surface until it picks up the temperature and humidity of that part of the earth's surface.

1. An air mass formed over Canada will be cold and dry.

2. An air mass formed over the Gulf of Mexico will be warm and moist.

E. Air masses are named according to the part of the earth's surface in which they are formed.

1. Those that are formed in the tropics are called **tropical** (T), and are warm.

2. Those that are formed in the polar regions are called **polar** (P), and are cold.

3. Besides the tropical and the polar regions, the air masses come from continents or oceans.

4. Air masses from continents are called **continental** (c), and are dry.

5. Air masses from oceans are called **maritime** (m), and are moist or humid.

F. As a result, there are four possible kinds of air masses.

1. The **continental tropical** (cT) air mass is dry and warm.

2. The **maritime tropical** (mT) air mass is moist and warm.

3. The **continental polar** (cP) air mass is dry and cold.

4. The **maritime polar** (mP) air mass is moist and cold.

G. Once an air mass is formed, it is usually carried to another place by the general movements of the atmosphere.

H. Air masses often change their conditions when they move from one place to another place.

1. A dry air mass can move out over the ocean and become moist.

2. When a cold air mass moves over a warmer surface, the lower part of the air mass becomes warmer and rises, producing clouds and possibly precipitation.

3. A warm air mass can become a cold air mass automatically, just by moving over a part of the earth's surface that is warmer than the air mass.

4. In the same way, a cold air mass can become a warm air mass if it moves over a colder part of the earth's surface.

III. North American Air Masses

A. The air masses that affect the weather in North America come from six different areas.

B. **Polar Canadian** (cP) air masses are formed over north-central Canada.

1. These air masses move in a southeasterly

direction across Canada and northern United States.

2. They are cold and dry.

3. In the winter they bring the cold waves that sweep across the United States and sometimes move as far south as the Gulf coast.

4. In the summer they bring cool, dry weather.

C. **Polar Atlantic** (mP) air masses are formed over the northern Atlantic Ocean.

1. Although they generally move eastward toward Europe, they can also move southward to affect the northeastern part of the United States.

2. They are cold and moist.

3. In the winter they bring cold, cloudy weather and some form of light precipitation.

4. In the summer they bring cool weather with clouds and fogs.

D. **Polar Pacific** (mP) air masses are formed over the northern Pacific Ocean.

1. They usually travel southward along the Pacific coast, but sometimes they move eastward across the United States.

2. They are cool rather than cold, and are very moist.

3. In the winter they bring rain and snow, and in the summer they bring cool, foggy weather.

E. **Tropical Continental** (cT) air masses are formed over Mexico and southwest United States.

1. They usually move in a northeasterly direction over the central part of the United States.

2. They are warm and dry.

3. They affect North America only in the summer, and they bring dry, clear, and very hot weather.

F. **Tropical Atlantic** (mT) air masses are formed over the tropical part of the Atlantic Ocean and the Gulf of Mexico.

1. They usually move in a northeast direction over the eastern part of the United States.

2. They are warm and moist.

3. In the winter they bring mild weather, and in the summer they bring hot, humid weather and thunderstorms.

G. **Tropical Pacific** (mT) air masses are formed over the tropical part of the Pacific Ocean.

1. They usually move in a northeasterly direction across the Pacific coast.

2. They are warm and moist.

3. They affect the Pacific coast only in the winter, and they bring cool, foggy weather.

IV. WEATHER FRONTS

A. When two air masses meet, the boundary between them is called a **front**.

1. Along the front there is almost always some form of precipitation.

2. This precipitation occurs because a very large amount of warm, moist air is rising to great heights along the front, and rising, moist air means precipitation.

B. There are two common kinds of fronts.

1. If warm air is pushing colder air ahead of it, the front is called a **warm front**.

2. Because masses of warm tropical air usually come from the southwest, warm fronts in the United States generally move toward the northeast.

3. If cold air is pushing warmer air ahead of it, the front is called a **cold front**.

4. Since masses of cold polar air usually come from the northwest, cold fronts in the United States generally move toward the southeast.

C. In the Temperate Zones of both North and South America, the principal changes in weather are brought about by the passage of warm and cold fronts.

D. When a warm front advances, warm air moves up over the retreating cold air.

1. The slope of the warm front is very gradual, and the warm air may have to travel as much as 1600 kilometers (1000 mi) to rise 8 kilometers (5 mi).

2 When the warm air rises, it becomes cool, and the water vapor in the air

condenses to form large masses of clouds along the entire warm front.

3. Where the level of the warm air is highest, cirrus clouds form.
4. Behind the cirrus clouds are different forms of stratus clouds, each kind floating lower and lower, with nimbostratus or "rain" clouds last and nearest the ground.
5. The rains produced by a warm front cover a wide area, are usually steady, and last until the warm front passes.

E. When a cold front advances, the cold air pushes under the warm air that is retreating, and lifts up this warm air.
1. The cold front moves more quickly than a warm front because the air in the cold front is colder and heavier.
2. Heavy, cold air can push light, warm air out of the way more quickly than light, warm air can push heavy, cold air.
3. As the warm air is lifted up very quickly, it cools, and the water vapor in the air condenses to form different kinds of clouds, especially cumulonimbus (or thundershower) clouds.
4. The rains produced by a cold front cover a smaller area, are rather violent, and last only a short time.
5. Cold front rains continue for a short time after the front passes.

F. A **stationary front** is the boundary line between a cold air mass and a warm air mass when both air masses stop and do not move for several days.
1. When this stoppage occurs, the boundary between the two air masses becomes a slope that is as gentle as that of a warm front.
2. As a result, the weather produced by a stationary front is about the same as that produced by a warm front.

G. Sometimes an **occluded front** is formed when a warm air mass, which lies between two cold air masses, is lifted up by the cold air mass behind it.
1. To create an occluded front, both cold air masses and the warm air mass be-

tween them must all be moving in the same direction.
2. Because cold fronts move faster than warm fronts, sometimes the second cold air mass at the rear catches up with the first cold air mass in front, and at the same time lifts the warm air mass completely off the ground.
3. This condition, called an occluded front, brings a combination of warm and cold front weather.
4. Also, as the occluded front passes, there is no change in the temperature of the air because there is only a change from one mass of cold air to another.

V. Lows and Highs

A. The air masses that move across earth differ in air pressure.
1. Cold air masses have higher pressures than warm air masses.
2. This difference occurs because cold air is heavier than warm air, and it can exert more pressure than warm air.

B. An area of low pressure is called a **low**, or a **cyclone**.
1. The lowest air pressure in a low is at its center.
2. As a result, air of higher pressure blows inward toward the center of the low.
3. Because of the earth's rotation, the air in the northern hemisphere is deflected to the right.
4. This deflection makes the air blowing toward the center of the low travel in a circular, counterclockwise direction.
5. Tornadoes, which are small, violent, whirling storms, are often wrongly called cyclones.

C. An area of high pressure is called a **high**, or an **anticyclone**.
1. The highest air pressure in a high is at its center.
2. As a result, air blows outward from the center of the high.
3. Because of the earth's rotation, the air blowing outward from the center of a

high travels in a circular, clockwise direction in the northern hemisphere.

D. Lows, or cyclones, usually bring bad weather.

1. This weather occurs because the warmer, lighter air in a low-pressure area is pushed up by the colder, heavier air around it.

2. The warmer, lighter air rises and becomes colder so that clouds and precipitation are formed.

3. The bad weather caused by lows usually covers a wide area.

E. The lows in the United States start in the northwest, southwest, and southeast.

1. They move toward the northeast and end in New England, bringing all kinds of weather changes.

2. They travel about 1100 kilometers (700 mi) a day in winter and 800 kilometers (500 mi) a day in summer.

F. Highs, or anticyclones, usually bring good weather.

1. This weather occurs because the colder, heavier air in a high-pressure area is falling toward the earth.

2. As the air falls, it becomes warmer.

3. Because warm air can hold more moisture, or water vapor, than cold air, no precipitation takes place and the weather is bright and clear.

G. Highs in the United States can start either in polar or tropical regions.

1. They also travel eastward across the United States, but more slowly than lows do.

2. Highs from the polar regions bring extreme cold waves in the winter, and cool, clear weather in the summer.

3. Highs from the tropical regions bring mild weather in the winter, and hot, dry spells in the summer.

VI. HURRICANES

A. **Hurricanes** are lows, or cyclones, that form in the tropics over the oceans.

1. They usually form between June and November.

2. During these months the tropics receive a tremendous amount of heat energy from the sun.

3. This heat energy causes vast amounts of ocean water to evaporate, and warm, moist air forms above the surface of the ocean.

4. Huge amounts of colder, heavier air move in on the warmer, lighter air and push the warmer, lighter air upward.

5. As a result, a violent, whirling storm is formed.

B. In some ways the hurricane is very much like a low.

1. The hurricane is also a low-pressure area, but its air pressure is much lower than the low.

2. The winds in both the hurricane and the low spiral in a counterclockwise direction in the northern hemisphere, and in a counterclockwise direction in the southern hemisphere.

3. Both the hurricane and the low cause heavy precipitation, but the precipitation is much heavier in the hurricane.

4. Near the center of the hurricane the rain comes down in torrents.

C. In other ways the hurricane is different from a low.

1. A hurricane is more intense and covers a smaller area, usually 320 to 640 kilometers (200 to 400 mi) in diameter.

2. The hurricane has no fronts.

3. In its exact center there is a calm area, called the "eye," about 19 to 24 kilometers (12 to 15 mi) in diameter, where the sun shines, the sky is clear, and there are almost no winds.

4. Around the "eye" the winds may whirl at a speed of more than 240 kilometers (150 mi) an hour.

D. Although the winds in a hurricane blow at a great speed, the hurricane itself moves rather slowly.

1. In the tropics the hurricane moves

slowly, with a speed of about 16 kilometers (10 mi) an hour.

2. As the hurricane moves away from the tropics into the area where the prevailing westerlies blow, it moves faster and can reach a speed of 80 kilometers (50 mi) an hour.
cane continues to move in a northeasterly direction, and eventually it moves out to sea and blows itself out.

E. The biggest damage produced by a hurricane is caused by the waves it produces.
1. Along the coast the winds form great waves that cause flooding, especially if the waves come at the same time as the high tides.
2. The force of the winds also causes damage to homes and property.

F. These lows or cyclones have different names in different parts of the earth.
1. In the West Indies they are called **hurricanes.**
2. In the western Pacific Ocean they are called **typhoons.**
3. In the Indian Ocean they are called **cyclones.**
4. In Australia they are called **willy-willies.**
5. In the Philippine Islands they are called **baguios.**

VII. TORNADOES

A. **Tornadoes** are the smallest, most violent, and most short-lived of all storms.
B. They occur almost exclusively in the United States, chiefly in the Mississippi Valley and the eastern half of the Great Plains.
1. The states where tornadoes commonly form are Iowa, Kansas, Texas, Arkansas, Oklahoma, Mississippi, Illinois, Indiana, and Missouri.
2. However, tornadoes may also occur in any level land area.
3. They are most frequent during the spring and early summer, and they usually occur during the afternoon.

4. There are about 200 tornadoes a year in the United States.

C. Tornadoes are formed under special conditions.
1. Ordinarily cold, heavy air moves under warm, light air.
2. When a tornado is formed, a layer of cold, dry air is pushed over a layer of warm, moist air.
3. The warm, moist air then quickly forces its way in a spiral movement through the layer of cold air.
4. Strong, whirling winds are formed around a center of low pressure, producing a tornado.
5. Tornadoes are also called **twisters.**

D. The tornado looks like a narrow, funnel-shaped, whirling cloud that is very thick and black.
1. The funnel reaches down toward the earth, and its tip touches the earth as it moves along.
2. Sometimes the funnel rises for a while, and then it comes down again a short distance away.
3. The tornado varies in size but can be as much as 1⅗ kilometers (1 mi) wide.
4. Although the tornado itself moves in a wandering path at a speed of about 40 to 64 kilometers (25 to 40 mi) an hour, the winds spin around like a top and can reach a speed of 800 kilometers (500 mi) an hour.
5. When a tornado passes a particular point, there is a deafening roar.
6. Usually a tornado is accompanied by lighhtning, thunder, and heavy rain.
7. The tornado lasts about 8 minutes and travels about 24 kilometers (15 mi).

E. A tornado that passes over a body of water is called a **waterspout.**
1. In a waterspout the bottom part of the funnel is made of spray instead of the dust and other materials found in a tornado over land.
2. The waterspout has very little water in it.
3. Most of the bottom part is a fine mist or

spray with perhaps a few feet of water at the bottom.

F. A tornado can cause a tremendous amount of damage.

1. The strong winds blow away almost everything in their path.

2. The center of the tornado is also very destructive because the air pressure within the funnel is very low.

3. Buildings within the center of the funnel often explode because the normal air pressure inside the building becomes so much greater than the suddenly reduced air pressure outside.

4. For the same reason cars, houses, trees, people, and animals are pushed or "sucked" into this funnel of very low pressure.

VIII. THUNDERSTORMS

A. **Thunderstorms** are strong, local storms that are formed from cumulonimbus clouds.

1. They are accompanied by lightning, thunder, heavy rain, and strong gusts of wind.

2. Sometimes hail falls at the beginning of a thunderstorm.

3. A thunderstorm is short, rarely lasting more than 2 hours, but it is possible to have many thunderstorms in a day.

B. Thunderstorms are formed whenever warm, moist air is pushed upward rapidly, accompanied by equally rapid downdrafts of cool air.

C. An **air-mass thunderstorm,** usually called a **summer thunderstorm,** is formed within an air mass during hot, summer afternoons.

1. It happens when hot, moist air above the earth's surface rises, forming first cumulus and then cumulonimbus clouds.

2. Summer thunderstorms are local storms, and they will form over scattered areas.

D. A **frontal thunderstorm** is formed when a cold front arrives, pushing warmer air ahead of it.

1. This air movement forms a series or long line of thunderstorms, which may be hundreds of miles long and up to 80 kilometers (50 mi) wide.

2. Frontal thunderstorms can happen at any time of the day or year.

E. **Lightning** is a huge electrical spark produced during thunderstorms.

1. The fast-rising air rubs against the water droplets in the cloud and charges them electrically.

2. The top of the cloud becomes positively charged while the bottom of the cloud becomes negatively charged.

3. Sometimes the fast-rising air is strong enough to rip the cloud in two so that each half has a different electrical charge.

4. When the force of attraction between the positively and negatively charged parts of a cloud becomes great enough, a huge spark of electricity, called lightning, flows from the negatively charged to the positively charged part.

5. Lightning can flow between the bottom and top of the same cloud, between two clouds of different charges, from a cloud to the earth, and sometimes even from the earth to a cloud.

F. **Thunder** is the sound produced by the rapid heating and expansion of the air through which the lightning passes.

1. The rumbling of thunder is a series of echoes produced when thunder is reflected many times by the clouds.

2. Lightning is seen first and the thunder is heard next.

3. This order happens because lightning travels with the speed of light, which is about 300,000 kilometers (186,000 mi) a second, whereas thunder travels with the speed of sound, which is about ⅓ kilometer (⅕ mi) a second.

4. Because it takes thunder about 3 seconds to travel 1 kilometer (5 seconds to travel 1 mile) whereas lightning is seen almost instantaneously, we can easily calculate how far away we are from the lightning

of a thunderstorm.

5. If a person counts the number of seconds that pass from the time he sees the lightning and hears the thunder, and divides this number by 3, the answer will be the number of kilometers the person is away from the lightning. (If he divides the number of seconds by 5, the answer will be the number of miles away from the lightning.)

G. **Heat lightning** is the lightning from a thunderstorm too far away to be heard.

H. **Sheet lightning** is lightning that takes place within the same cloud.
   1. The lightning cannot be seen, but part or all of the cloud lights up instead.
   2. Sheet lightning is often called heat lightning as well.

PREDICTING THE WEATHER

I. METEOROLOGY

A. **Meteorology** is the science that deals with the study of the weather, which is the condition of the atmosphere at a particular time and place.

B. A **meteorologist** is a person who studies and forecasts the weather.

C. Meteorologists can make fairly accurate weather forecasts by collecting the following information.
   1. The temperature.
   2. The air pressure.
   3. The direction and speed of the wind.
   4. The humidity.
   5. The kind and amount of precipitation.
   6. The condition of the sky.

D. To collect this information, the meteorologist uses a wide variety of weather instruments.

II. MEASURING THE TEMPERATURE OF THE AIR

A. A **thermometer** is used to measure the temperature of the air.

B. One kind of thermometer that meteorologists use is the **liquid thermometer.**
   1. This thermometer is very much like the household thermometer.
   2. It has a hollow, glass tube with a liquid, usually mercury, in it.
   3. The mercury expands and rises when heated, and it contracts and falls when cooled.
   4. The temperature scale on the weather thermometer is either the Fahrenheit (F) scale, or the Celsius (C) scale, which is the scale used in all science laboratories.
   5. The United States still uses the Fahrenheit scale, but the rest of the world uses the Celsius scale.

C. Meteorologists also use a **metal thermometer.**
   1. This thermometer does not have a liquid in it, but it uses a strip of metal made up of two different heat-sensitive metals that have been welded together.
   2. The metals expand and contract differently when heated and cooled, and this unequal expansion and contraction make the metal strip bend or twist.
   3. The metal strip is wound into a coil, and a pointer is attached to the outside free end of the coil.
   4. When the metal strip bends or twists, the pointer moves across a temperature scale and shows the temperature.

D. A **thermograph** is a metal thermometer that records the temperature continuously all day.
   1. In the thermograph there is a sheet of paper marked with the temperature scale, and this paper turns on a cylinder.

2. A little pen at the end of the pointer makes it possible for the pointer to draw a line on the paper and produce a permanent record of the temperature all day.

3. This permanent record will also show the maximum, or highest, temperature and minimum, or lowest, temperature for that day.

E. Because metal thermometers are not as accurate as liquid thermometers, a special liquid **maximum and minimum thermometer** is used to record the highest and lowest temperatures during a day.

1. Like a regular liquid thermometer, this special thermometer shows the temperature of the air at any particular time.

2. However, it also has special indicators in it, which stay at the highest and lowest temperatures for that day.

III. Measuring Air Pressure

A. The **barometer** is used to measure air pressure.

B. Two kinds of barometers are commonly used: the **mercury barometer** and the **aneroid barometer.**

C. The mercury barometer is a narrow, glass tube about 92 centimeters (36 in) long, sealed at one end, that has been filled with mercury and then turned upside down into a dish of mercury.

1. Some of the mercury runs out of the tube until the pressure of the air on the mercury in the dish just supports a column of about 76 centimeters (30 in) of mercury in the tube.

2. When the air pressure becomes greater, or increases, the air now pushes harder on the mercury in the dish, making the mercury in the tube rise.

3. The mercury moves easily up the tube because there is no air in the space above the level of the mercury, so there is nothing to slow down or stop the upward movement of the mercury.

4. When the air pressure becomes smaller,

or decreases, the mercury moves down the tube.

5. The height of the mercury in the tube is a measure of the pressure of the air at that time.

D. The aneroid (meaning "without liquid") barometer does not use mercury at all.

1. It has a thin, hollow disc from which some of the air has been removed.

2. This removal of air makes the disc very sensitive to changes in air pressure.

3. When the air pressure increases, the disc is squeezed in a little.

4. When the air pressure decreases, the disc expands a little.

5. This change in thickness of the disc is passed on to a pointer that moves across an air-pressure scale.

6. The aneroid barometer is sturdier and less awkward to use than the mercury barometer.

E. A **barograph** is an aneroid barometer that has a pen at the end of the pointer and uses a revolving sheet of paper with an air-pressure scale on it so that there is a continuous record of the changes in air pressure during the day.

F. Air pressure can be expressed in two ways.

1. It can be expressed in **inches** or **millimeters** of mercury, showing the height of a column of mercury that could be supported by a particular air pressure.

2. It can be expressed in **millibars**, which are international air pressure units used by physicists.

G. On the weather map, air pressure is shown by **isobars**, which are solid lines that join points throughout the United States where the air pressure is the same.

H. Falling air pressure means a low is coming, bringing bad weather with it.

I. Rising air pressure means a high is coming, bringing good weather with it.

IV. Measuring Wind Direction and Speed

A. A **wind vane** is used to measure the wind direction.

1. The wind vane that is commonly used looks like an arrow.
2. This arrow is mounted on a pole in such a way that it can swing freely when the wind blows on it.
3. The arrow has a broad tail, and the wind strikes this tail, making the arrow swing so that the head points to the direction from which the wind comes.
4. Winds are always named according to the direction from which they come, so that a south wind is one that comes from the south.
5. The south wind strikes the tail of the wind vane and makes the head point toward the south.
6. At airports, wind socks are used instead of weather vanes to show wind direction.

B. An **anemometer** is used to measure wind speed, or velocity.
1. The most common type of anemometer has three hollow cups, all facing the same way.
2. The hollow parts of the cup catch the wind and begin to move.
3. The stronger the wind, the faster the cups move.
4. The anemometer expresses wind speed in kilometers or miles per hour.

C. Sometimes the weather vane and anemometer are combined into one small instrument.

V. MEASURING THE RELATIVE HUMIDITY

A. The relative humidity can be found by dividing the actual amount of water vapor in the air (absolute humidity) by the maximum amount of water vapor the air can hold at that temperature, and multiplying the result by 100 to express the relative humidity in percentages.

B. A **hygrometer** is used to measure relative humidity.

C. One common form of hygrometer is the **psychrometer, or wet-and-dry-bulb thermometer.**

1. The psychrometer has two thermometers that are exactly the same, except that one of the thermometers has a water-soaked cotton cloth or wick wrapped around its bulb.
2. Air is made to pass across both thermometer bulbs, either by whirling the thermometers around or by fanning them with an electric fan.
3. The moving air does not affect the dry thermometer bulb, and the thermometer shows the temperature of the air around it.
4. However, the water in the wet cloth evaporates, taking from the thermometer bulb inside the cloth the heat it needs to evaporate.
5. This evaporation cools the thermometer bulb and makes the temperature fall.
6. The drier the air, the faster the water in the cloth evaporates, the cooler the bulb becomes, and the lower the reading of the "wet" thermometer.
7. When the temperature of the "wet" thermometer has reached its lowest point, the meteorologist finds the difference in temperature between the "wet" thermometer and "dry" thermometer.
8. The meteorologist then uses this difference in temperature to find the relative humidity by consulting a carefully worked out relative humidity table.

D. The **hair hygrometer** uses a bundle of human hairs to find the relative humidity.
1. Human hair is very sensitive to moisture, becoming longer when the air is humid and shorter when the air is dry.
2. This change in the length of the bundle of human hairs makes a pointer move across a scale, from which the relative humidity can be read directly in percentages.

E. The **hygrograph** is a hair hygrometer that uses a pen instead of a pointer and a revolving sheet of paper with the relative humidity scale on it to give a continuous record of the relative humidity.

VI. MEASURING RAINFALL AND SNOWFALL

A. The **rain gauge** measures the amount of rainfall.

B. The most common form of rain gauge is a narrow cylinder with a funnel on top.

1. The area of the mouth of the funnel is exactly ten times larger than the area of the mouth of the cylinder.

2. Therefore, the cylinder receives ten times as much water when the funnel is in it than it would receive alone.

3. This larger amount of water is easier to measure, but the amount must be divided by 10 to find the correct amount of rainfall.

4. To measure the amount of rain collected in the cylinder, a marked stick is dipped into the cylinder.

5. Rainfall is measured in centimeters or inches, and in tenths or hundredths of a centimeter or inch.

C. Snowfall can be measured with a rain gauge, or by measuring an open location.

1. A measuring stick is used to find the height of the snow.

2. Snowfall is usually measured in centimeters or inches and tenths of a centimeter or inch.

D. Meteorologists also find out how much rain the snowfall might have produced.

1. To determine this amount they melt and weigh a certain number of centimeters or inches of snow.

2. Because snow can be light and fluffy, or heavy and wet, the amount of rainfall that snow might have produced varies.

3. A light, fluffy snow may produce 2½ centimeters (1 in) of rain for every 50 centimeters (20 in) of snow, but a heavy, wet snow may produce 2½ centimeters (1 in) for every 15 centimeters (6 in) of snow.

4. As an average, 25 centimeters (10 in) of snow will make 2½ centimeters (1 in) of rain.

VII. MEASURING WEATHER CONDITIONS AT HIGH ALTITUDES

A. The **radiosonde** is an instrument used to measure weather conditions at upper levels of the air.

1. It contains a small thermometer, barometer, and hygrometer.

2. It also has a small radio transmitter that automatically sends out signals showing the temperature, pressure, and relative humidity of the air through which the radiosonde is passing.

3. The 1-kilogram (2-lb) radiosonde is attached to a 2-meter (6-ft) balloon filled with helium.

4. This balloon can travel 16 to 24 kilometers (10 to 15 mi) into the stratosphere before the balloon bursts.

5. A parachute opens when the balloon bursts, and it allows the radiosonde to return undamaged to earth.

B. **Radar** is also used to measure and predict the weather.

1. Cloud droplets and raindrops reflect the radar waves and show up on the radar screen.

2. Radar can also locate storms and tell how much area they are covering.

3. It can watch how a storm forms and moves across the earth.

4. It can measure the speed of high-altitude winds by tracking a balloon as it moves through the air at high levels.

5. It can track hurricanes, locate the "eye" of the hurricane, follow the movement of the hurricane, and predict its path.

VIII. THE UNITED STATES WEATHER SERVICE

A. The United States Weather Service in Asheville, North Carolina, provides weather information and services for the entire United States.

B. To get this information, observations are made at about 600 official Weather Service stations in the United States.

1. Information is also sent from stations in Canada, Mexico, Cuba, northern South America, Europe, northern Africa, and Asia.
2. Observers on ships also send information daily.
3. Observations are made four times a day, every 6 hours, and all the information is sent to the central office in Asheville, North Carolina.

C. The central office then draws a weather map and sends the information on it by radio, teletype, or wirephoto to all the forecast centers in the country.

D. To draw a weather map, the Weather Service needs the following information from its observers.

1. The temperature of the air.
2. The air pressure and changes in the air pressure in the past 3 hours.
3. The relative humidity and dew point.
4. The wind direction and speed.
5. The condition of the sky and the present weather.
6. The kind, height, and amount of clouds.
7. The visibility.
8. The weather in the past 6 hours.
9. The kind and amount of precipitation in the past 6 hours.
10. The time the precipitation began and the time it ended.

E. The Weather Service puts this information in the map, using symbols to fit all of it on the map.

F. The Weather Service also provides other services.

1. It makes detailed 24-hour weather forecasts, changing them twice a day if necessary.
2. It makes general 5-day forecasts, which are published in newspapers or announced over radio and television stations.
3. It provides weather and crop bulletins for farmers.
4. It gives hurricane, tornado, and severe storm warnings.
5. It gives frost warnings for fruit and crop farmers.
6. It forecasts floods.
7. It offers special information and forecasts for planes, sending this information to 17 aviation centers every 6 hours by teletype.
8. It has special forecasts for ships.

G. Almost every person in the United States is helped by the work of the Weather Service.

1. The daily forecast helps us decide what to wear.
2. It helps railroads, trucks, and ships protect shipments of perishable foods.
3. It gives gas, light, and power companies the chance to be ready for extra service when a cold spell or storm is coming.
4. It gives cities a chance to prepare their snow removal equipment for a coming snow storm.
5. It gives farmers a chance to save their crops from being killed by frost.
6. It helps save lives by warning persons of hurricanes, tornadoes, and floods.

IX. MAN-MADE WEATHER

A. Man is constantly trying to control the weather.

B. In some cases man has been able to get supercooled clouds high in the sky to give up their moisture.

1. By dropping small particles of dry ice, silver iodide, or other crystals into these clouds, man has caused some of the cloud droplets to become ice crystals.
2. These ice crystals grow larger as the water vapor in the cloud condenses on them.
3. When the ice crystals are large enough, they fall as snow.
4. This snow turns to rain when it falls into lower, warmer air.

C. Man has also invented devices that are able to reduce or eliminate fog on airport landing fields.

CLIMATE

I. WEATHER AND CLIMATE

A. **Weather** is the condition of the atmosphere at a particular time and place.
B. **Climate** is the average weather of a place over a period of years.
C. A scientist who studies the climate is called a **climatologist.**
D. Climatologists have discovered many factors that affect the kind of climate found in different parts of the earth.
E. These factors of climate can be divided into two classes.
  1. The first class consists of those factors that control the yearly temperature of a particular place.
  2. The second class consists of those factors that control the yearly rainfall of that place.

II. FACTORS THAT CONTROL THE YEARLY TEMPERATURE

A. **Latitude** influences temperature more than any other factor.
  1. The latitude of a region or place is its distance from the equator.
  2. A region near the equator is said to have a low latitude, and a region near the poles is said to have a high latitude.
  3. The higher the latitude of a place, the colder its climate will be.
  4. Near the equator, where the sun's rays are direct almost all year and the days and nights are equally long, there is the same hot climate throughout the year.
  5. Halfway between the equator and the north pole, the sun's rays are direct during the summer and the days are much longer than the nights so that the summers are hot.
  6. However, during the winter the sun's rays are slanted and the nights are longer than the days so that the winters are cold.
  7. Near the poles, the sun's rays are always slanted.
  8. During the summer near the poles, the sun shines all 24 hours of the day for months, and the weather is still cold, but it is mild in comparison with the winter.
  9. During the winter near the poles, the sun does not shine for months, and the weather is bitterly cold.
B. The higher the **altitude** of a place, the colder its climate will be.
  1. Altitude is the height above sea level.
  2. Even near the equator, if a city is located at a high altitude, its weather and climate will be much cooler than a city located at sea level.
C. Land and water masses affect the climate of a place.
  1. Land masses heat up and cool down more quickly than water masses.
  2. As a result, land regions are more likely to have hot summers and cold winters, and sea regions in the same latitude are more likely to have cooler summers and milder winters.
D. The direction of the prevailing winds affects the climate of a continent's seacoasts.
  1. On the northwest coast of the United States the prevailing westerlies blow in from the warm Pacific Ocean so that the northwest coast has a cool summer and mild winter.
  2. On the northeast coast of the United States the prevailing westerlies blow from the land out to the ocean so that the northeast coast has a hot summer and cold winter.
E. Mountain ranges and plains decide how much far-away winds affect a region's climate.
  1. The high Rocky Mountains stop the mild west-coast climate from extending any further into the Great Plains.

2. At the same time, the level Great Plains allow very cold winds to speed from the poles all the way to the Gulf of Mexico, and allow hot winds from the south to move north.

3. As a result, the Great Plains have hot summers and cold winters.

F. Ocean currents can make the climate of a region much warmer or colder than normal for the region's latitude.

1. The prevailing westerlies, blowing from the warm Gulf Stream, give the British Isles and northwestern Europe climates just as warm as those of regions that are nearer the equator.

2. At the same time, winds from the cold Labrador Current give northern Labrador a climate much colder than that of a region, such as southern Sweden, which has the same latitude.

II. FACTORS THAT CONTROL THE YEARLY RAINFALL

A. Latitude also affects the amount of rainfall a region receives.

1. The latitude decides in which wind belt a region will be located during the year.

2. Places where warm, moist wind is rising will have rainy weather, and places where cool, dry air is falling will have dry weather.

3. Places in the doldrums will have heavy rains all through the year.

4. Places in the trade winds and horse latitudes will be mostly dry during the year.

5. Places in the prevailing westerlies will have moderate rainfall all year.

6. Places in the polar easterlies will have light snow all year.

B. Because wind belts shift during the year, as the earth revolves around the sun, some places may be in a rainy belt for part of the year and in a dry belt for the other part of the year.

C. Sometimes seasonal wind changes give a region a dry season and a wet season.

1. The seasonal winds, or monsoons, of India produce wet and dry seasons.

2. In the summer the Indian Ocean is cooler than the hot land so that a warm, moist monsoon blows from the ocean over the land, bringing rainy weather from May through October.

3. In the winter the land is cooler than the Indian Ocean so that a cold, dry monsoon blows across the land out to the sea, bringing dry weather from November through April.

D. Mountains affect the amount of rainfall a region will receive.

1. When warm, moist wind strikes the windward side of the mountain and rises, there is much rainfall on this side.

2. However, the leeward or protected side will now have very little rain because most of the water vapor will have already condensed from the air before the air passed over the mountain to the leeward side.

E. When winds blow in from the ocean, the regions nearest the ocean get the most rainfall.

1. This distribution occurs because the moisture condenses out of the ocean air as it blows across the land.

2. The warmer the ocean, the heavier the rainfall will be.

F. When ocean currents are much warmer or colder than the land or water around them, much fog is formed.

1. The warm Gulf Stream air striking the cold British Isles causes a lot of fog.

2. In the summer New England has a lot of fog when the warm winds coming up from the south are cooled by the cold waters of the New England coast.

3. When the warm Gulf Stream air blows over the cold Labrador Current in the Grand Banks, thick fogs are formed.

IV. CLASSIFICATION OF CLIMATES

A. Climatologists no longer classify climates according to torrid, temperate, and frigid zones.

[369

B. Today they divide the earth into **tropical, middle latitude,** and **polar** climates.

C. Each of these climates is subdivided into different types of climates, depending upon the temperature and rainfall they have.

V. THE TROPICAL CLIMATES

A. Three different types of climates are included under the classification of tropical climates: the **tropical rain forest,** the **savanna,** and the **desert** climates.

1. These climates are all located within 30 degrees latitude above and below the equator.

2. They all have an average yearly temperature of at least 20° Celsius (68° Fahrenheit), but they differ in the amount of rainfall they get.

B. The tropical rain forest climate is found in regions at or close to the equator.

1. The regions in this climate have heavy rainfall all year, and the temperature is always high.

2. Because of these two conditions, there is a heavy growth of plants, forming a jungle.

3. The relative humidity is always high, and there is usually a thundershower every afternoon.

4. The African Congo, Amazon Valley, east coast of Central America, Madagascar, and Indonesia have this climate.

C. The savanna climate is found farther away from the equator.

1. The regions in this climate have wet and dry seasons as the wind belts shift during the year.

2. When these regions are in the doldrums, there is heavy rainfall.

3. When the wind belts shift, the regions now lie in the trade winds and have little or no rain.

4. Mostly coarse grasses, spiny plants, and a few trees grow in these regions, which are called **savannas.**

5. The Sudan of north Africa, the veldt of south Africa, campos of Brazil, llanos of Venezuela, downes of Australia, and parts of India and Burma all have this climate.

D. The desert climate is even farther away from the equator.

1. The regions in this climate are always in the wind belt of the trade winds so that they get practically no rainfall at all.

2. As a result, few plants grow in these regions.

3. When the rain does come, it falls as a thundershower or cloudburst.

4. Sand deserts are found in this climate.

5. Because there is very little moisture in the air, the days are very warm and the nights are quite cool.

6. The Sahara, Arabian, American, Kalahari (south Africa), Australian, and Peruvian Deserts are found in this climate.

VI. THE MIDDLE LATITUDE CLIMATES

A. Six different types of climate are included under this classification of middle latitude climates: the **Mediterranean, humid subtropical, marine west coast, humid continental, dry continental,** and **subarctic** climates.

1. These climates are all located between 30 degrees and 65 degrees latitude.

2. Although there is a wide range of temperature in these climates, they all have at least 1 month where the average temperature is 10° Celsius (50° Fahrenheit) or higher.

3. The regions in these climates lie mostly in the wind belt of the prevailing westerlies, which produces all kinds of weather.

B. The regions in the Mediterranean climate lie between 30 degrees and 40 degrees latitude in both the northern and southern hemispheres.

1. These regions are all found on the western side of the continents.

2. They lie in the trade winds or horse latitudes in the summer, and in the prevailing westerlies in the winter.

3. Their summers are warm or hot and almost completely dry, and their winters are mild and have some rainy months.
4. Fruits, olives, grapes, and nuts grow well in this climate.
5. Because the rainfall is only about 40 to 65 centimeters (16 to 26 in) a year, this climate is also called the **dry subtropical climate.**
6. Southern California, southern Australia, central Chile, and the lands around the Mediterranean Sea have this climate.

C. The regions in the humid subtropical climate also lie between 30 degrees and 40 degrees latitude, but on the eastern side of the continents.
1. They do not have a dry season, and the rainfall is greater, about 90 to 150 centimeters (36 to 60 in) annually.
2. The summers are warm and the winters are mild, but there are often cold waves and frosts during the winter.
3. The humidity is very high in the summer and can become uncomfortable.
4. Tall grasses and pine forests grow in this climate.
5. Southeastern United States, eastern and southern Asia, northern Argentina, and southern Brazil have this climate.

D. The regions in the marine west coast climate lie between 40 degrees latitude and the edges of the polar regions.
1. These regions are all on the western side of the continents.
2. They lie mostly in the prevailing westerlies all year so that they get a good supply of rain all year.
3. Where mountains block the movement of the winds, the rainfall is heavy on the windward side of the mountains.
4. Because the westerlies blow in from the ocean, the summers are cool and the winters are mild in these regions.
5. They get more rain and fog in the winter than in the summer.
6. Hardwood and evergreen trees grow in these regions.
7. The northwest coast of the United States, the British Isles, Norway, western Australia, New Zealand, and southern Chile have this climate.

E. The regions in the humid continental climate are in the same latitude as those of the marine west coast climate, but they are all on the east side of the continents.
1. These regions have hot summers and cold winters.
2. The weather changes are sharp so that the regions get blizzards, very cold spells, heat waves, high humidity, thunderstorms, and tornadoes.
3. More rain falls in the summer than in the winter, and the rainfall is heavier at the coast.
4. Where the rainfall is more than 76 centimeters (30 in) a year, leafy and evergreen trees grow.
5. Where the rainfall is less than 76 centimeters (30 in) a year, tall grasses grow, forming prairies.
6. Eastern United States from the Great Plains to the coast, eastern Europe, and eastern Asia have this climate.

F. The regions in the dry continental climate are also in the same latitude as the humid continental and marine west coast climates, but they are located in the interior of the continents.
1. These regions have hot summers and very cold winters.
2. Rainfall is light, and more rain usually falls in the summer than in the winter.
3. Those regions where the rainfall is 25 to 50 centimeters (10 to 20 in) a year are called **steppes.**
4. Those regions where the rainfall is under 25 centimeters (10 in) a year are called **middle latitude deserts.**
5. Low grasses and sagebrush grow in the steppes, and only sagebrush and cactus grow in the middle latitude deserts.
6. Steppes are found in the midwestern states of the United States, in Argentina, and in Russia.
7. Middle latitude deserts are found in the western United States, western

[371

Argentina, and the interior of Asia.

G. Most of the regions in the subarctic climate lie between 50 degrees and 65 degrees latitude.

1. These regions have very long, cold winters and short, mildly warm summers.

2. They have less than 40 centimeters (15 in) of precipitation a year, and most of it falls in the summer.

3. In the summer the days are very long, and in the winter the nights are very long.

4. Mostly small evergreen trees grow in this climate.

5. Most of northern Canada, most of Europe north of 60 degrees latitude, and almost all of Siberia have this climate.

VII. POLAR CLIMATES

A. Two different types are included under this classification of polar climates: the **tundra** and the **icecap** climates.

1. These climates start where the middle latitude climates end and extend to the poles.

2. These climates have no summer at all because the sun's rays are so slanted that they give very little heat.

3. There is very little precipitation because the air is too cold to hold much water vapor.

B. The tundra climate is a cold climate, beginning where the subarctic climate ends.

1. The average temperature of the warmest month is between 0° and 10° Celsius (32° and 50° Fahrenheit), and the average temperature of the coldest month is −40° Celsius (−40° Fahrenheit).

2. The light summer rains permit mosses and lichens to grow.

3. The tundra climate exists only in the northern hemisphere because there are no land areas in this latitude at the Antarctic.

C. The icecap climate is found near the poles, and the temperature never rises above 0° Celsius (32° Fahrenheit).

1. The average yearly temperature is between −24° and −35° Celsius (−11° and −31° Fahrenheit), and the lowest temperature ever recorded in this climate was −87° Celsius (−125° Fahrenheit) on the Antarctic icecap.

2. There are always either icecaps or glaciers in this climate.

3. Precipitation falls only as light snow, and there is very little precipitation.

LEARNING ACTIVITIES FOR "WATER, WEATHER, AND CLIMATE"

WATER

1. *Illustrate the water table* · Fill a wide-mouthed glass jar three-quarters full of a mixture of sand and gravel. Pour water down the side of the glass jar until the water level rises to about half the level of the mixture of sand and gravel (Figure 11–1). This water level will represent the level of the water table. Mark this level on the glass jar, using a wax crayon or marking pencil. Add more water, and the water table will rise.

2. *Test permeable and impermeable rock* · Weigh a piece of granite and a sandstone or a limestone separately. Soak both stones in a jar of water overnight. The next day remove the stones, wipe their surfaces with a dry cloth, and weigh the stones separately again. The permeable sandstone or limestone will have

FIGURE 11–1.
HOW THE WATER TABLE IS FORMED.

Sand and gravel

Level of water table

absorbed water and gained weight. The impermeable granite will not have absorbed any water, and its weight will not have changed.

3. *Diagram swamps, streams, and lakes* · On the chalkboard show that, wherever the land surface dips below the water table, ground-water flows out to the surface, forming springs or contributing to the water in swamps and lakes (Figure 11–2). Point out that during dry periods the level of the water table sinks, and some streams and swamps may dry up.

If possible, visit a swampy area in early spring, when the water table is nearer the land surface than at any other time of the year. Sometimes it is possible to reach the water table just by digging a small hole with a shovel.

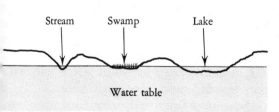

Stream   Swamp   Lake

Water table

FIGURE 11–2.
SWAMPS, STREAMS, AND LAKES ARE FORMED WHEN THE LAND SURFACE DIPS BELOW THE WATER TABLE.

4. *Investigate lakes* · Find out about the lake or lakes located in or near the area where you live. Learn how the basin was formed, and contrast this method of formation with the other ways that lake basins can be formed. Find out how your lakes get their water. Discuss the different ways that lakes can be destroyed, and suggest some measures that could be taken to prevent this from happening.

5. *Purify water by distillation* · Fill a glass jar one-half full with water. To the water add some food coloring, a tablespoon of salt, and some soil. Shake the mixture well, and then pour it into a tea kettle. Obtain a long piece of rubber tubing. Place one end of the rubber tubing inside the spout of the tea kettle and use modeling clay in and around the spout to hold the rubber tubing in place and to make sure that the steam will pass out only through the tubing (Figure 11–3). Place the other end of the rubber tubing into a glass tumbler that has been placed in a pan filled with ice cubes. Now place the tea kettle on a hot plate. When the water boils, drops of water will condense in the tumbler or drip from the hose into the tumbler. This water will be clear and pure, and it will not taste salty. When the water in the tea kettle boiled and changed into water vapor or steam, the impurities were left in the tea kettle. Only pure, clean water condensed

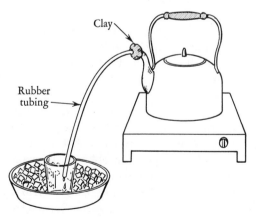

Clay

Rubber tubing

FIGURE 11–3.
DISTILLATION PURIFIES WATER.

as the steam was cooled in the tumbler.

6. *Purify water by settling* · Fill a glass jar about three-quarters full of water. Add a mixture of coarse and fine soil to the jar, shake the contents thoroughly, and then set the jar down and allow the soil to settle. The coarse soil will quickly settle to the bottom, but it may take many days for the fine soil to settle completely.

7. *Use chemicals to help settle muddy water* · Get two glass jars the same size, and fill each jar about three-quarters full of water. To each jar add a small amount of fine soil, shake the jars thoroughly, and then set the jars down. The finely divided bits of soil will be suspended in the water. Now add a teaspoon of alum crystals and a teaspoon of ammonia to a glass tumbler that is about one-quarter full of clear water. Stir the water well in the glass tumbler, and then pour the contents into one of the glass jars. The particles of fine soil will stick to the jellylike material that is formed, and will be carried to the bottom as the material settles. Compare the appearance of the chemically treated water with that of the untreated water in the jar that serves as a control.

8. *Purify water by filtering* · To a large plastic or glass funnel add a layer of small pebbles, then a layer of gravel or coarse sand, and finally a layer of fine sand (Figure 11–4). First pour some clean water through the funnel to allow the layers to settle and pack together. Then place the funnel in a narrow-mouth glass jar and pour some muddy water into the funnel. The layers will filter the mud, and clear water will pass into the jar.

9. *Destroy bacteria in water* · If your local water supply is chlorinated, fill a pan with cold water and heat the pan on a hot plate. You will be able to smell the chlorine by sniffing close to the top of the pan. If your local water supply is very lightly or not at all chlorinated, add a few drops of a chlorine bleach to a tumbler of water, and have the children smell the chlorine, which acts as a germicide.

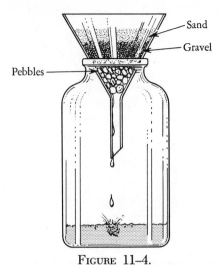

FIGURE 11–4.
FILTERING HELPS PURIFY WATER.

10. *Discuss use of fluorides* · If your water supply has fluorides added, find out the amount used. Discuss the value of adding fluorides to water, and collect information about the results of using fluorides in water for a period of years to prevent tooth decay.

11. *Make and soften temporary hard water* · Obtain some limewater from the drugstore. Pour limewater into a test tube until it is half full and, using a soda straw, bubble carbon dioxide from your breath through the limewater. At first the limewater will become milky, but continue the bubbling until the milkiness disappears. Pour an equal amount of distilled water or rainwater into a second test tube. Make a soap solution by dissolving soap shavings in warm water. Now add an equal number of drops of soap solution to each of the test tubes and, while holding a thumb over the mouth of each test tube, shake the test tubes vigorously. The soft water will make lots of suds, but the temporary hard water will make very few suds and form curds instead.

Make some more temporary hard water and boil it for a few minutes to remove the hardness. Add the same amount of soap solution as you did to the other two test tubes, and note how the boiled water now makes lots of suds

12. *Make and soften permanent hard water* ·
To a test tube half full of water add a small
amount of Epsom salts (magnesium sulfate),
shaking the test tube until the salt dissolves.
Pour the same number of drops of soap solution
(as prepared in Learning Activity 11 above)
into the test tube containing the freshly prepared permanent hard water and into a test
tube containing an equal amount of distilled
water or rainwater. Shake both test tubes
vigorously and note the difference in amount
of suds produced.

Soften the permanent hard water by adding
some washing soda, borax, or ammonia. Now
add the same number of drops of soap solution
as you did to the other test tubes, and compare
the increased amount of suds formed.

13. *Investigate the action of detergents* ·
Obtain some high-sudsing detergent. Prepare
samples of temporary and permanent hard
water (described in Activities 11 and 12
above). Obtain three test tubes. Pour some
temporary hard water into one test tube, an
equal amount of permanent hard water into
the second test tube, and an equal amount of
distilled water or rainwater into the third test
tube. Now add the same amount of detergent
to each test tube and shake the test tubes
vigorously. Note that all three test tubes have
lots of suds, showing that the sudsing (and
cleaning) action of detergents is not affected
by water hardness.

14. *Investigate water pressure* · Obtain a
tall can. Place a piece of two-by-four wood,
or any other wood of suitable thickness, in
the can. Use a hammer and large nail to punch
a hole in one side of the can near the bottom
(Figure 11–5). Now bring the can to the sink
and, while keeping one finger over the hole,
fill the can with water. Release your finger and
a stream of water will shoot out some distance
from the hole, showing that water exerts pressure.

15. *Observe that water pressure is the same
in all directions* · Use a hammer and large nail

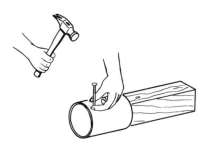

FIGURE 11–5.

USING A PIECE OF WOOD TO PUNCH A HOLE
IN ONE SIDE OF A CAN.

to punch holes around the sides of a tall can
near the bottom (Figure 11–6). It may help to
use a block of wood (as described in Learning
Activity 14) when making the holes. Bring the
can to the sink and run water into the can
rapidly so that it stays full while the water is
escaping through the holes. Note how the water
shoots out exactly the same distance from all
the holes.

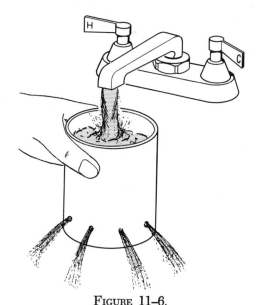

FIGURE 11–6.

WATER EXERTS THE SAME PRESSURE IN ALL
DIRECTIONS.

[375

16. *Observe the effect of depth on water pressure* · Use a hammer and large nail to punch three holes in one side of a tall can, using a block of wood (as described in Activity 14) if necessary. One hole should be near the top of the can, another hole in the middle, and the third hole near the bottom (Figure 11–7). Bring the can to the sink and run water into the can rapidly so that it stays full while the water is escaping through the holes. The greater the depth of the water, the farther it will shoot out of the hole.

17. *Visit a hydraulic lift* · Have the children visit a gas station, where the attendant can demonstrate the hydraulic lift and explain how it is used to raise a car. Have the children find examples of other hydraulic machines and their uses.

18. *Observe how moving water can do work* · Make a water turbine from the round top of a large can. Use a hammer and nail to punch a hole in the center of the top. With a pencil divide the top into eight equal sections extending from the center. Use tin snips to cut along the pencil lines of each section to about 13 millimeters (½ in) from the hole in the center. Then

twist each segment with pliers to form blades that are almost at right angles to the flat part of the tin (Figure 11–8). Obtain a knitting needle that has a head at one end, and pass the pointed end through the hole in the top. The

FIGURE 11–7.
THE DEEPER THE WATER, THE GREATER THE WATER PRESSURE WILL BE.

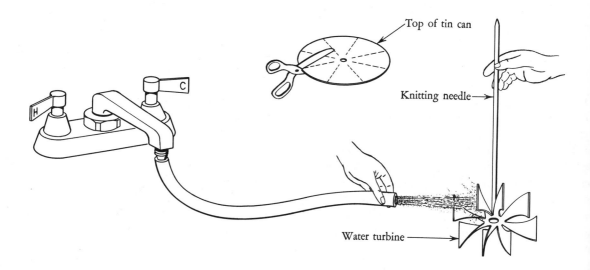

FIGURE 11–8. A WATER TURBINE.

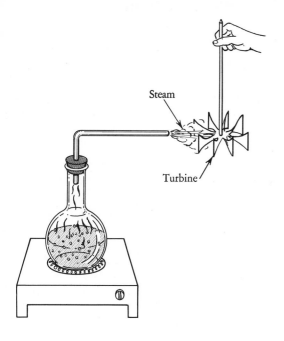

FIGURE 11–9.

A STEAM TURBINE.

flat part of the top should be next to the head of the needle. Attach the rubber tubing from a portable bath spray to a faucet. Turn on the faucet and pinch the end of the tubing so that a narrow but fast stream of water comes out of the tubing. Direct this stream against the blades of the water turbine, making it spin rapidly.

19. *Observe how steam can do work* · Make a steam generator (Figure 11–9), using a large Pyrex flask, a one-hole rubber stopper, and a piece of glass or plastic tubing bent at right angles. The stopper should not be pressed too tightly into the neck of the flask so that, if steam should form too quickly and build up pressure, the steam would be able to blow the stopper quite easily from the flask. Add water to the flask and heat the flask on a hot plate until the water boils and steam is escaping freely from the tubing. Make a turbine as described in Learning Activity 18 above. Hold the turbine in the path of the steam so that the

steam strikes the blades directly, making the turbine spin rapidly.

20. *Investigate the downward pull of gravity* · Repeat Learning Activity 5 of "The Solar System," (p. 274). This time put objects of different sizes and weights on the child's palm. The downward pull of gravity of small, heavy objects (like stones) will be greater than that of large, light objects (like balsa wood). The heavier the object, the greater the downward pull will be.

21. *Observe that water exerts an upward buoyant force* · Have the children try pushing a volleyball into a tub of water. The upward buoyant force exerted by the water will be felt quite noticeably.

22. *Measure a body's apparent loss of weight in water* · Tie a string around a stone, connect it to a spring balance, and note the weight of the stone in air (Figure 11–10). Now lower the stone in a large, wide-mouthed jar half filled with water. Observe the loss in weight caused by the upward buoyant force of the displaced water.

23. *Discover that a floating body displaces its own weight of water* · Make an overflow cup.

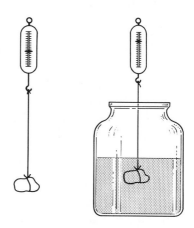

FIGURE 11–10.

WHEN LOWERED INTO WATER, THE ROCK SEEMS
TO LOSE WEIGHT.

Obtain a large styrofoam cup. Use a hole puncher to punch a hole near the top of the cup. Get a plastic soda straw with a diameter slightly larger than the hole, cut off a 5-centimeter (2-in) piece of straw, and insert it in the hole (Figure 11–11). Seal the outside spot

FIGURE 11–11.
AN OVERFLOW CUP.

where the straw enters the cup with glue or chewing gum. Coat the underside of the end of the straw lightly with Vaseline. Pour water into the cup until the water is just level with the straw. Get a block of wood that will fit inside the cup. Weigh the block. Get a small can and weigh it. Now place the can so that its center is underneath the end of the straw. Lower the block of wood gently into the cup of water. The displaced water will overflow into the empty can. When the water stops overflowing, weigh the can again. Subtract the weight of the can from the combined weight of the overflow water and the can. The difference will be the weight of the overflow water. Compare the weight of the overflow water with the weight of the block of wood. The weights should be just about the same.

24. *Discover why a steel ship floats* · Cut out two pieces of aluminum foil 15 centimeters (6 in) long and 10 centimeters (4 in) wide. Fold one piece in half again and again, flattening the foil each time with your fingers to remove any trapped air, until you have a small, flat wad. Drop this wad in a pie tin full of water, and it

will sink to the bottom because it displaces very little water to produce a small upward force. Shape the second piece of foil with your fingers until you have a figure similar to a rectangular boat. Place this boat in the water. It will float because it displaces a large amount of water to produce a large upward buoyant force.

25. *Observe the effect of more cargo on a ship* · Place a small rectangular cake pan in a rectangular glass aquarium almost full of water. Measure how much the sides of the pan sink below the level of the water. Now spread a few stones evenly along the bottom of the pan. Again measure how much the sides of the pan sink. The pan sinks more deeply in the water, displacing enough water to support the added weight of the stones.

26. *Compare the buoyancy of salt and fresh water* · Fill two identical large wide-mouthed jars about three-quarters full of water. Add salt to the water in one jar, a tablespoon at a time and stirring vigorously, until no more salt will dissolve. Now place an egg first in the fresh water and then in the salt water (Figure 11–12). The egg will float in the heavier, more buoyant, salt water. Get two large ice cubes the same size, put one into each jar, and note which ice cube protrudes the most from the water.

27. *Measure needless waste of water* · Adjust a faucet so that there is a steady drip of water. See how much water will drip into a

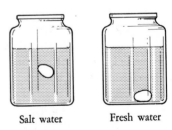

Salt water   Fresh water

FIGURE 11–12.
AN EGG WILL SINK IN FRESH WATER AND FLOAT
IN SALT WATER.

measuring cup in 1 hour. Calculate the amount of water that would be wasted in 1 day. Multiply this by the probable number of water users in your community. List other ways in which water is wasted needlessly.

28. *Observe water pollution* · Look for water pollution in nearby rivers and streams. Note the effect on plant and animal life. Make a large amount of suds in the sink, using a high-sudsing detergent. Note how difficult it is to wash these suds quickly down the drain. Collect information about the difficulty bacteria have in disposing of detergent suds in rivers, and the effect of these suds on plant and animal life in streams.

THE OCEANS

1. *Investigate ocean instruments* · Have the children read about the function of the different kinds of instruments used to study the ocean, and report some of the more pertinent findings made with these instruments. The reports of studies made during the most recent International Geophysical Year will supply interesting information about the topography of the ocean.

2. *Recover salts from seawater* · Pour seawater in a saucer and let the water evaporate completely. Have the children taste the white crystals that were deposited in the bottom of the saucer. If seawater is unavailable, use salt water instead.

3. *Make a "model" iceberg* · Place a square ice cube in a tumbler of water. Note how much (about nine tenths) of the ice cube is below the surface of the water. Collect and display pictures of icebergs. Point out that although the icebergs are huge, only about one tenth of the whole iceberg can be seen above the surface of the water.

4. *See how wind causes waves* · Pour some water into a soup plate. Blow hard at one end of the plate across the water (Figure 11–13). The water will ripple and form waves. The stronger you blow, the larger the waves will be. Discuss the parts of a wave, and show how white caps, breakers, undertows, and tsunamis are formed.

5. *Locate the major ocean currents* · Obtain a map of the world and locate the major ocean currents. Trace their movements for both hemispheres.

6. *Investigate the effect of the earth's rotation on ocean currents* · Obtain a globe that can spin. Spin the globe very slowly in a counterclockwise direction (from west to east). At the same time pour a small amount of fairly thick blue washable paint in a thin stream onto the north pole. As the stream flows down the northern hemisphere, it is deflected to its right (to the west) by the earth's rotation. When the stream crosses the equator and enters the southern hemisphere, it is now deflected to its left (to the east). It can be made equally obvious that ocean currents moving to the north pole are deflected to their right, and currents moving to the south pole are deflected to their left. This demonstration will help to show the children why the ocean currents have a clockwise circulation in the northern hemisphere and a counterclockwise circulation in the southern hemisphere.

FIGURE 11–13.
MAKING WAVES.

[379

7. See how winds help cause deep sea currents · Repeat Learning Activity 4 above, blowing across one end of a large soup plate of water. Point out that the water moved away on the surface by the wind may be replaced by water from below. This displacement helps create movement of water below the surface, producing a deep sea current.

8. Investigate the economic importance of the oceans · Learn about the extraction of magnesium, bromine, and other chemicals from the ocean, and the uses of these chemicals in our daily life. Give reports of the commercial fishing industry and locate the important fishing areas of the world.

WINDS

1. Observe that the earth is heated unequally by the sun · Repeat Learning Activity 7 of "The Effect of the Sun on Earth" (p. 277). Put the same amount of soil into two boxes. On a sunny morning or afternoon place both boxes in the sunlight. Let one box lie flat so that it receives rays slanted, and prop up the other box so that the sun's rays strike it directly

(Figure 11–14). Place thermometers that have the same reading into each box, inserting both thermometers into the same depth of soil. Take temperature readings every 10 minutes. The soil that receives the direct rays will become warmer. Point out that the earth's equator receives direct rays whereas the rays become more and more slanted in the northerly and southerly latitudes. Also point out that the air above the earth will be heated unequally as well.

2. Discover whether dark or light surfaces absorb radiant energy more quickly · Obtain two cans exactly the same size. Paint the outside of one can with flat, black paint, and paint the outside of the other can with white paint. Now add equal amounts of water into each can so that the cans are about one-half to three-quarters full. Place a thermometer in each can (the thermometers must have the same reading) and place both cans in the sunlight (Figure 11–15). Record the temperature read-

FIGURE 11–15.

A BLACK SURFACE ABSORBS RADIANT ENERGY MORE QUICKLY THAN A WHITE SURFACE.

ing every 15 minutes for 1 hour. The water in the black can will become warmer than the water in the white can.

3. Observe how unequal heating produces winds · Obtain a large shoe box. Cut a large rectangular hole in one side of the box and cover it with clear plastic wrap, pressing the wrap securely to the rest of the box. Cut two

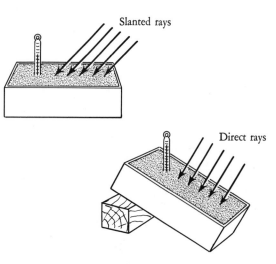

FIGURE 11–14.

DIRECT RAYS HEAT THE EARTH MORE THAN SLANTED RAYS.

holes about 4 centimeters (1½ in) in diameter, one near each end of the box. Place the box, open end down, over a lighted candle so that the candle is directly under one of the cutout holes (Figure 11–16). Now put a lamp chimney over each hole.

(A rectangular aquarium, covered by a piece of cardboard with two holes in it, can be substituted for the shoe box.) Produce smoke by lighting a cigarette, a thick rope, or a tightly rolled piece of paper towel. Hold the smoking material directly over the chimney that does not have the candle under it. The smoke will be carried down the chimney, across the box, and up the other chimney. This movement occurs because the air above the candle is heated, expands, and becomes lighter. The warmer, lighter air is pushed up by the cooler, heavier air around it, causing a convection current. Winds on earth are formed in a very similar way.

4. Infer that wind is moving air · Turn on a fan and have the children feel the "wind" blowing on their faces. Put a plant near the fan and let the children note the rustling of the leaves.

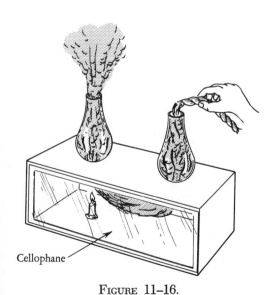

Cellophane

FIGURE 11–16.
WINDS ARE CAUSED BY CONVECTION CURRENTS OF AIR.

5. Investigate the effect of the earth's rotation on the movement of winds · Repeat Learning Activity 6 of "The Oceans" (p. 379). The winds moving north or south in the northern hemisphere are deflected to their right, and winds moving either north or south in the southern hemisphere are deflected to their left. Have the children discuss the kind of wind movements the earth would have if it did not rotate.

6. Locate the major wind belts · Draw on the board a round globe of the earth and mark in the major wind belts (Figure 11–17, p. 382). Discuss how the belts are formed, accounting for the motion and direction of the winds in each belt.

7. Trace jet streams · Read about the path of the jet stream in the northern hemisphere. Trace it on a globe of the world, during the winter and during the summer, and discuss the effects of this change in position on the earth's climate and weather. Consult the reports on studies made during the recent International Geophysical Year, announcing the discovery of new jet streams in the atmosphere of the earth.

8. Investigate monsoons · Consult a map and show why monsoons are found in India. Have the children explain why monsoons are found in such countries as Spain, Portugal, or Australia.

9. Discover the cause of land and sea breezes · Place soil in a tumbler until it is half full. To another tumbler add water until it is the same level as the soil. Place a thermometer in each tumbler and keep the tumblers in a shady place until both thermometers read the same (Figure 11–18, p. 382). Now place both beakers in direct sunlight, and read the thermometers every 15 minutes for 1 hour. The temperature of the soil will be higher than the temperature of the water. Relate this difference in temperature to the formation of sea breezes and land breezes.

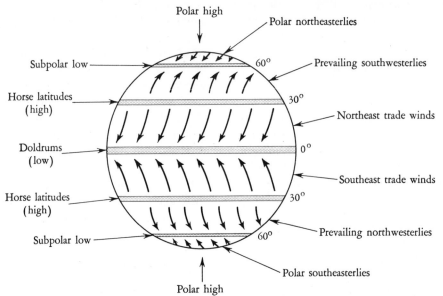

FIGURE 11–17. DIAGRAM OF THE MAJOR WIND BELTS ON EARTH.

WATER IN THE AIR

1. *Observe water evaporate* · Put some water in a dish and allow it to evaporate. Have the children make a list of phenomena they have seen that involve evaporation.

2. *Investigate the effect of heat on evaporation* · Put 10 drops of water in two pie tins the same size. Put one on the window sill where the sun can shine on it. Put the other tin in the coolest place in the classroom. The water will exaporate more quickly in the heated tin because the water molecules move faster, and thus more molecules can leave the water at one time.

3. *Investigate the effect of surface area on evaporation* · Using a measuring cup, put equal amounts of water in a pie tin, water tumbler, and bottle. Set all three containers on a table, where conditions such as temperature and air currents will be the same for each container. The next day pour any water remaining in the containers back into the measuring cup, one at a time for each container. In each case measure the amount of water that remains.

The most water will have exaporated from the pie tin, which has the largest surface area, because more water molecules were able to leave the water at one time.

4. *Investigate the effect of wind on evaporation* · Get two sponges the same size, and wet them. Make two spots of equal wetness on the chalkboard. Fan one of the spots vigorously with a cardboard. The moisture on the fanned spot will evaporate more quickly because the

Soil   Water

FIGURE 11–18.

SOIL HEATS UP MORE QUICKLY THAN WATER.

fanning blows away the saturated air above the spot and provides a fresh supply of unsaturated air.

5. *Investigate the effect of humidity on evaporation* · Compare the time it will take for water in a wet cloth (or in a pie tin) to evaporate on a dry day when the humidity is low and on a damp or rainy day when the humidity is high. The greater the humidity, the more water vapor there will be in the air, and the less opportunity there will be for more molecules of water to go off into the air.

6. *Discover the cooling effect of evaporation* · Dip your forefinger into a tumbler of water. Keeping the wet forefinger and dry middle finger a slight distance apart, blow on both fingers at the same time. As the water evaporates from the forefinger, the heat needed for evaporation is taken from the finger, leaving the finger cooler. The middle finger, which serves as a control, does not become cooler.

7. *Compare the rate of evaporation of different liquids* · Have a child hold out both hands palm down. Put one drop of rubbing alcohol or duplicating fluid on the back of one hand and a drop of water on the back of the other hand. The alcohol will evaporate more quickly because its molecules are moving faster from the beginning at the same temperature. In addition, because the rubbing alcohol evaporates more quickly, it takes heat away from the hand more quickly, and the spot with the alcohol on it will feel cooler as well.

8. *Observe water vapor condense* · Add water to a shiny can until the can is half filled. Add ice cubes and stir. Soon a thin film of tiny droplets of water will form on the sides of the can, as the air containing water vapor is cooled and the molecules of water vapor move more slowly and come close enough together to become water again. The thin film will gradually form large droplets. In the summer the humidity may be so high that the water vapor will condense without ice cubes having to be added. In the winter the humidity may be so low that salt will have to be added to the cold water and ice cubes to get the water vapor to condense.

9. *Investigate the factors affecting condensation* · The same factors affecting the speed of evaporation will also affect the speed of condensation, but in reverse. Repeat Learning Activity 8 above in (1) a cold and warm location, (2) a windy and calm location, and (3) a dry and humid location.

10. *Find the dew point* · Repeat Learning Activity 8 and relate the results to the formation of dew and rain. Find the dew point by slowly adding small pieces of ice to a tin can half-filled with water, stirring regularly with a thermometer. Measure the temperature at which a thin film of water appears on the sides of the can. Be careful not to breathe on the sides of the can when watching for dew to form. Otherwise the water vapor in your breath will condense on the cold sides of the can and produce inaccurate results.

11. *Make a fog* · Fill a clean, dry soda bottle (or any narrow-neck bottle) with very hot water, adding the water slowly to prevent the glass from cracking. Now pour out most of the water, leaving about 5 centimeters (2 in) at the bottom. Put an ice cube on the mouth of the bottle (Figure 11–19) and hold the bottle between you and the sunlight or the light of a lamp. A fog will form in the bottle as the warm, humid air is cooled by the ice cube and the cool air below the ice cube, and the water vapor condenses in tiny droplets that float in the air.

12. *Discover how clouds are formed* · Obtain a gallon jug and a one-hole rubber to fit the mouth of the jug tightly. Insert a short piece of glass or plastic tubing into the hole of the stopper. Pour in enough water at room temperature to cover the bottom of the jug. Allow the water to stay in the jug for about 20 minutes to let some of the water evaporate into

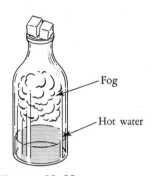

FIGURE 11–19.

CONDENSATION PRODUCES A FOG IN A BOTTLE.

the air inside the jug. Shake a little chalk dust into the jug. Now fit the stopper tightly into the jug and connect the rubber tubing of a bicycle pump securely to the glass tubing (Figure 11–20). Pump air into the jug for *no more than five or six strokes,* then remove the stopper quickly. A cloud will form in the jug, which can best be seen by holding the jug between you and the sunlight or the light of a lamp. If the cloud does not form, repeat the experiment, but add a little rubbing alcohol to the water this time.

When more air is pumped into the jug, the air inside the jug is compressed. When the stopper is removed, the air will then expand. When a gas expands it becomes cooler. The air is cooled below the dew point by the sud-

den expansion, and the water vapor in the air condenses on the particles of chalk dust, forming a cloud. Real clouds are formed the same way, being cooled because of the expansion of the warm, rising air.

13. *Observe different kinds of clouds* · Examine the sky daily and note the different kinds of clouds. Draw relationships between the clouds and the kinds of weather they forecast. Collect pictures of the different clouds. Below each picture place an index card, telling how the clouds are formed, their characteristics, and the kind of weather they bring.

14. *Make frost, snow, sleet, and glaze* · Fill a tall can with alternate layers of cracked ice and table salt. Make each ice layer twice as thick as the salt layer. Pack the mixture down firmly. Put some drops of water on a piece of wax paper, and set the can on top of the water (Figure 11–21). Use enough water to make one large drop high enough to touch the bottom of the can. Some dew may form on the sides of the can and then freeze, but frost will also form as the temperature of the air beside the can falls to below freezing.

After the sides of the can are well covered with frost, remove the can from the wax paper. The large drop of water will have frozen into ice. Point out that frost and snow are formed when water vapor condenses directly into ice crystals whereas sleet and glaze are formed when raindrops freeze.

15. *Examine snow crystals* · When it is snowing outside, catch some snowflakes on a soft,

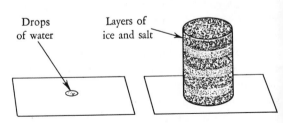

Drops of water   Layers of ice and salt

FIGURE 11–21.

FROST, SNOW, SLEET, AND GLAZE ARE FORMED AT TEMPERATURES THAT ARE BELOW FREEZING.

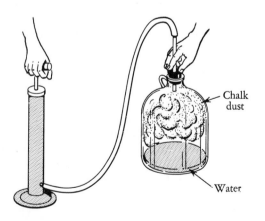

Chalk dust

Water

FIGURE 11–20.

CONDENSATION PRODUCES A CLOUD IN A JUG.

dark wool cloth. Try to capture small snow-flakes because they are individual flakes while the larger snowflakes are usually clusters of smaller flakes. Examine the snowflakes with a magnifying glass. Note that all snowflakes have six sides, yet no two snowflakes are ever exactly the same.

16. *Examine hailstones* · During a hailstorm, collect some hailstones and quickly cut them in half. Note the layers of ice that have been formed. Each layer represents one complete movement up into cold air and back again into warmer air.

17. *Make a model of the rain cycle* · Fill a Pyrex pot with water and heat it on a hot plate until the water is boiling. Fill a frying pan with

ice cubes and hold the pan about 10 centimeters (4 in) above the pot (Figure 11–22). A minia-

FIGURE 11–22.
A MINIATURE WATER CYCLE.

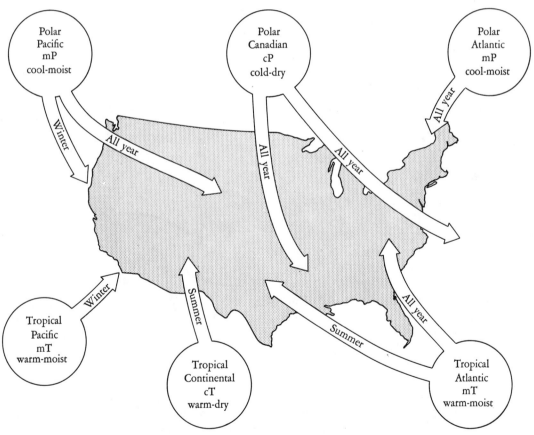

FIGURE 11–23. DIAGRAM OF THE MAJOR NORTH AMERICAN AIR MASSES.

[385

ture water cycle will be produced as the water vapor from the boiling water is cooled by the cold bottom of the frying pan, causing droplets of water to condense on the bottom of the pan and then drop back into the water.

WEATHER CHANGES

1. *Identify the six North American air masses* · Draw a relief map of North America, delineating the United States clearly. Chalk in the six air masses that affect the weather in the United States (Figure 11–23, p. 385). Identify these air masses as continental polar, maritime polar, continental tropical, and maritime tropical. Indicate whether the air masses are dry, moist, warm, or cold. Use arrows to indicate the paths of these air masses, and note whether they affect the United States all year or just during certain seasons.

2. *Observe cold and warm fronts* · Watch for the appearance of fronts, using the forecast as a guide. When a front begins to move in, keep a record of the weather conditions. Continue this record until the front has passed.

Draw on the chalkboard diagrams of the movement of a cold front and a warm front, showing the kinds of clouds and precipitation that are formed in each case (Figure 11–24).

3. *Investigate the rotation of highs and lows* · Repeat Learning Activity 5 of "Winds" (p. 381), showing why air in the northern hemisphere is deflected. Draw diagrams, using arrows, showing why highs travel in a clockwise direction and lows in a counterclockwise direction in the northern hemisphere (Figure 11–25). Be sure to draw the arrows moving outward from the center and toward the right for the highs, and moving inward toward the center and to the right for the lows.

4. *Examine weather maps* · Have the children cut out weather maps from the newspaper for a period of 2 weeks. You can also obtain official weather maps by consulting your local

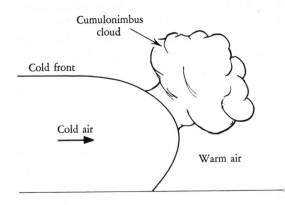

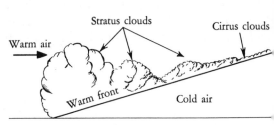

FIGURE 11–24.

DIAGRAM OF A COLD FRONT AND A WARM FRONT

weather station or by writing to the United States Weather Service at Asheville, North Carolina. Examine the weather maps closely. Note the

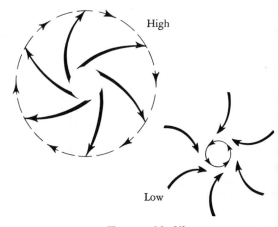

FIGURE 11–25.

HIGHS TRAVEL IN A CLOCKWISE DIRECTION, AND LOWS TRAVEL IN A COUNTERCLOCKWISE DIRECTION.

presence and movement of cold and warm fronts across the country. List the kinds of weather changes the appearance of each front might bring, and check your list with the actual weather conditions that took place in your locality. Note the location of highs and lows on the weather map. Compare the kinds of weather found in those parts of the country that had highs with those that had lows.

5. *Investigate hurricanes and tornadoes* · Have the children report how hurricanes are formed, trace their general path in the northern hemisphere, list the most destructive ones, compare their forward and circular speed, and describe the work of "hurricane hunters" in locating and charting the hurricanes.

Distinguish between hurricanes that form in the East in the late summer and fall, and tornadoes that form in the Midwest in the spring. Describe their similarities and differences, discuss the destruction and dangers each storm may cause, and list some safety precautions that should be taken.

6. *List unusual weather conditions* · Have the children bring in or make a collection of pictures of unusual weather conditions or unusual happenings that were influenced by the weather. Let the children try to trace the causes and events that produced these weather conditions.

PREDICTING THE WEATHER

1. *Make a barometer* · Obtain a milk bottle or a glass jar with a medium to narrow mouth. Cut out the dome-shaped end of a rubber balloon and stretch the rubber tightly across the mouth of the balloon, fastening the rubber sheet securely with a rubber band (Figure 11–26). Flatten both ends of a soda straw and cut one of the ends to a sharp point. Place rubber cement or glue on the flattened end of the straw and attach the flattened end to the middle of the rubber sheet. Cut a tiny piece of wood from a match and glue it at the

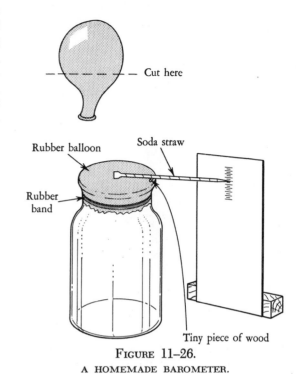

FIGURE 11–26.
A HOMEMADE BAROMETER.

edge of the rubber sheet so that the straw rests on top of the wood.

When the air pressure in the room increases, the rubber sheet is pushed down, making the straw move up. When the air pressure in the room decreases, the greater air pressure inside the bottle now pushes the rubber sheet up, making the straw move down. A cardboard scale will help the children see the change in air pressure. Calibrate the marks on the cardboard scale with the readings on a standard barometer. Keep the barometer in a place as free from temperature changes as possible. Otherwise the air inside the bottle will expand and contract, pushing the rubber sheet in and out. Have the children take barometer readings each day for two weeks or a month and predict the weather on the basis of rising or falling air pressure.

2. *Make a thermometer* · Pour water that has been colored dark red with food coloring into a Pyrex flask until the flask is almost full.

[387

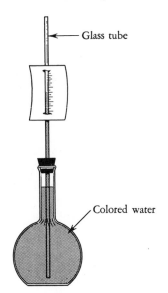

FIGURE 11–27.
A HOMEMADE THERMOMETER.

in) thick. Place one piece on top of the other so that they form four right angles. At the center, where both pieces meet, bore a hole just large enough for the glass part of a medicine dropper to pass through so that both pieces of wood will rest on the lip of the medicine dropper (Figure 11–28). Now use small screws or nails to fasten the two pieces of wood together, leaving the hole free. Obtain four paper cups, paint one cup red, and tack a cup horizontally to each end of the pieces of wood.

Hold the medicine dropper by the rubber bulb and place the tip of the dropper in the edge of a gas flame or the flame of an alcohol lamp. Rotate the dropper slowly but steadily as you heat it, and continue heating until the tip of the dropper melts and the opening is closed. Make sure that the tip is completely closed before you remove it from the flame. Set the tip to one side and allow it to cool for at least 5 minutes.

Insert a long glass or plastic tube in a one-hole rubber stopper and fit the stopper tightly into the mouth of the flask (Figure 11–27). The amount of water in the flask will have to be adjusted so that, when the stopper is inserted, the colored water will rise about one third to one half of the distance of the part of the tube above the stopper. Make two slits in an unlined index card and slide the card over the tube. Mark the original height of the water in the tube.

When the temperature of the room becomes warmer, the water is heated, expands, and rises up the tube. When the temperature drops, the water is cooled, contracts, and falls down the tube. Calibrate the marks on the scale of the index card with the readings on a standard thermometer. Have the children take daily readings outdoors on a standard thermometer (placed away from direct sunlight) for an extended period of time. Keep a record of these readings and make a chart showing the changes in temperature during the year.

3. *Make an anemometer* · Obtain two pieces of wood about 40 centimeters (16 in) long, 2 centimeters (¾ in) wide, and 7 millimeters (¼

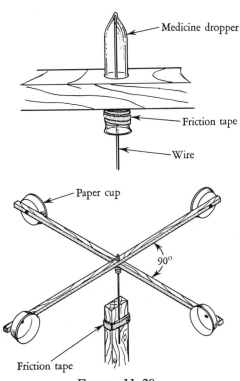

FIGURE 11–28.
A HOMEMADE ANEMOMETER.

Use wire cutters to cut a straight piece of wire from a coat hanger. File one end of the wire to a sharp point. Fasten the wire upright with friction tape to a sturdy piece of wood. Now remove the rubber bulb from the medicine dropper and insert the dropper into the center hole of the two fastened pieces of wood. Use friction tape above and below the hole, if necessary, to prevent the pieces of wood from slipping off the medicine dropper. Place the medicine dropper over the sharp point of the wire; the anemometer is now ready to operate with a minimum of friction.

To calibrate the anemometer, hold it outside the window of a moving car on a calm day when there is no traffic and the road is smooth and level. With the car moving at a steady speed of 8 kilometers (5 mi) an hour, use a watch with a second hand to count the number of turns the anemometer makes in 1 minute. The colored cup will make it easier to count the number of turns. Repeat the count at 16 kilometers (10 mi) an hour and also at 24 kilometers (15 mi) an hour. From these three counts you can make a graph that will enable you to calculate the wind speed at any time. (A quick but rough method for finding the wind speed is to count the number of turns in 1 minute and then divide by 10. The result will be the wind speed in miles per hour.)

4. *Make a weather vane* · Cut two large, identical arrows from a piece of heavy cardboard, making sure the tail is much larger than the head. Staple or paper clip the two arrows together at the edges of the head and the tail (Figure 11–29). Seal the tip of a medicine dropper, as described in Learning Activity 3 above. Place the arrow across the edge of a ruler and find the point where it best balances. Insert the medicine dropper between the two pieces of cardboard at this balancing point, and staple together the edges of the body of the arrow.

Use wire cutters to cut a straight piece of wire from a coat hanger, and file one end of the wire to a sharp point. Fasten the wire upright with friction tape to a sturdy piece of

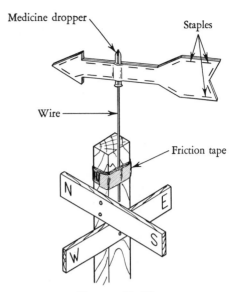

FIGURE 11–29.
A HOMEMADE WEATHER VANE.

wood, and place the medicine dropper over the sharp point of the wire. Use a compass when mounting the wind vane to fix the direction of the wind vane properly. If small strips of wood with the compass directions on them are nailed onto the vane, the children will be able to determine the wind direction more quickly and easily.

Because the tail is larger than the head, it will catch more wind. As a result, when the wind blows, the vane will swing around until it points into the wind toward the direction from which the wind is blowing.

5. *Make a wet-and-dry-bulb thermometer* · Obtain two chemical thermometers that have Fahrenheit scales on them and suspend them so that they hang side by side a few inches apart. If chemical thermometers are not available, use two identical wall thermometers, either suspended or strapped to a cardboard box with rubber bands.

Obtain a white, woven cotton shoelace or a piece of soft cotton cloth. Fit a section of the shoelace snugly around one of the thermometer bulbs and insert the end of the shoelace into

[389

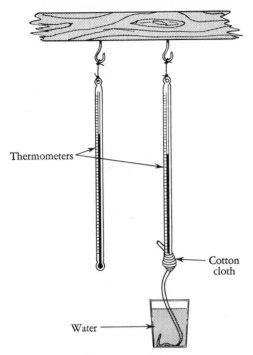

Thermometers

Cotton cloth

Water

FIGURE 11–30.
A WET-AND-DRY-BULB THERMOMETER.

Obtain a long, narrow nail, put it through the piece of soda straw, and drive it into the center of the two-by-four lumber near one end. Fasten one end of the hair to a piece of cellophane tape 5 centimeters (2 in) long, and glue the other end of the hair to the soda straw. When the glue has dried, turn the soda straw a few times to wrap the hair around the soda straw. Now attach the cellophane tape to the two-by-four lumber so that the hair is tight

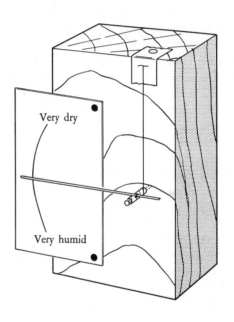

Very dry

Very humid

a tumbler of water (Figure 11–30). Now fan both thermometers, either by hand or with an electric fan, for a few minutes to blow away the air next to the cloth and keep it from being surrounded by a layer of saturated air.

To find the relative humidity, read both thermometers and find the difference between the two temperatures. Use this temperature difference and the temperature of the dry-bulb thermometer to find the relative humidity (in percentages) in Table 11–1.

6. *Make a hair hygrometer* · Obtain a blond human hair about 20 centimeters (8 in) long. Wash it in hot, soapy water, rinse in cold water, and let it dry. Obtain a piece of two-by-four lumber about 30 centimeters (12 in) long. Use a razor blade to cut a piece about 2½ centimeters (1 in) long from a soda straw, making sure to preserve its round form. Obtain a broomstraw 10 centimeters (4 in) long, and glue one end to the piece of soda straw (Figure 11–31).

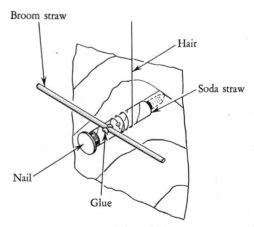

Broom straw

Hair

Soda straw

Nail

Glue

FIGURE 11–31.
A HOMEMADE HAIR HYGROMETER.

TABLE 11–1. Relative Humidity Index

DIFFERENCE BETWEEN WET- AND DRY-BULB READINGS

DRY-BULB READING ↓	1	2	3	4	5	6	7	8	9	10	11	12	13	14	15	16	17	18	19	20	21	22	23	24	25	26	27			
65	95	90	85	80	75	70	66	62	57	53	48	44	40	36	32	28	25	21	17	13	10	7	3							
66	95	90	85	80	76	71	66	62	58	53	49	45	41	37	33	29	26	22	18	15	11	8	5	1						
67	95	90	85	80	76	71	67	62	58	54	50	46	42	38	34	30	27	23	20	16	13	9	6	3						
68	95	90	85	81	76	72	67	63	59	55	51	47	43	39	35	31	28	24	21	17	14	11	8	4	1					
69	95	90	86	81	77	72	68	64	59	55	51	47	44	40	36	32	29	25	22	19	15	12	9	6	3					
70	95	90	86	81	77	72	68	64	60	56	52	48	44	40	37	33	30	26	23	20	17	13	10	7	4	1				
71	95	90	86	82	77	73	69	64	60	56	53	49	45	41	38	34	31	27	24	21	18	15	11	8	5	3				
72	95	91	86	82	78	73	69	65	61	57	53	49	46	42	39	35	32	28	25	22	19	16	13	10	7	4	1			
73	95	91	86	82	78	73	69	65	61	58	54	50	46	43	40	36	33	29	26	23	20	17	14	11	8	5	2			
74	95	91	86	82	78	74	70	66	62	58	54	51	47	44	40	37	34	30	27	24	21	18	15	12	9	7	4			
75	96	91	87	82	78	74	70	66	63	59	55	51	48	44	41	38	34	31	28	25	22	19	16	13	11	8	5			
76	96	91	87	83	78	74	70	67	63	59	55	52	48	45	42	38	35	32	29	26	23	20	17	14	12	9	6			
77	96	91	87	83	79	75	71	67	63	60	56	52	49	46	42	39	36	33	30	27	24	21	18	15	13	10	7			
78	96	91	87	83	79	75	71	67	64	60	57	53	50	46	43	40	37	34	31	28	25	22	19	16	14	11	9			
79	96	91	87	83	79	75	71	68	64	60	57	54	50	47	44	41	37	34	31	29	26	23	20	17	15	12	10			
80	96	81	87	83	79	76	72	68	64	61	57	54	51	47	44	42	38	35	32	29	27	24	21	18	16	13	11			
82	96	92	88	84	80	76	72	69	65	62	58	55	52	49	46	43	40	37	34	31	28	25	23	20	18	15	13	10		
84	96	92	88	84	80	77	73	70	66	63	59	56	53	50	47	44	41	38	35	32	30	27	25	22	20	17	15	12		
86	96	92	88	85	81	77	74	70	67	63	60	57	54	51	48	45	42	39	37	34	31	29	26	24	21	19	17	14		
88	96	92	88	85	81	78	74	71	67	64	61	58	55	52	49	46	43	41	38	35	33	30	28	25	23	21	18	16		
90	96	92	89	85	81	78	75	71	68	65	62	59	56	53	50	47	44	42	39	37	34	32	29	27	24	22	20	18		
92	96	92	89	85	82	78	75	72	69	65	62	59	57	54	51	48	45	43	40	38	35	33	30	28	26	24	22	19		
94	96	93	89	86	82	79	75	72	69	66	63	60	57	54	52	49	46	44	41	39	36	34	32	29	27	25	23	21	19	17
96	96	93	89	86	82	79	76	73	70	67	64	61	58	55	53	50	47	45	42	40	37	35	33	31	29	26	24	22	20	18
98	96	93	89	86	83	79	76	73	70	67	64	61	59	56	53	51	48	46	43	41	39	36	34	32	30	28	26	24	22	20
100	96	93	90	86	83	80	77	74	71	68	65	62	59	57	54	52	49	47	44	42	40	37	35	33	31	29	27	25	23	21

and the broomstraw is in a horizontal position. Press the cellophane tape down firmly on top of the two-by-four lumber, inserting thumb tacks to prevent the tape from loosening. However, let the rest of the cellophane dangle loosely over the side to keep the hair from rubbing against the wood. Tack an index card to the two-by-four lumber on the side nearer to the broomstraw.

When the air is dry, the hair contracts and the broomstraw moves up. When the air is humid, the hair becomes moist and expands, making the broomstraw move down. Calibrate the hygrometer by putting it into a pail and covering the pail with a towel that has been soaked in very hot water. The relative humidity in the pail will quickly reach 100 percent, and the broomstraw will move down as the hair stretches. After 15 minutes remove the hygrometer and mark the position of the broom straw as 100 percent relative humidity. Allow some time for the pointer to move back to a normal position, and then calibrate other positions on the index card by using either a commercial hygrometer or a wet-and-dry-bulb thermometer.

7. *Make a rain gauge* · Obtain a large kitchen funnel and a glass jar whose mouth has exactly the same diameter as the rim of the funnel. Pour exactly 1 centimeter or 1 inch of water into the jar, using a ruler to get the exact depth (Figure 11–32). Pour this water into a narrow bottle, such as an olive jar. Place a strip of paper about 12 millimeters or ½ inch wide against the side of the narrow bottle, using strips of cellophane tape to hold the paper in place. With India ink, make a mark on the strip

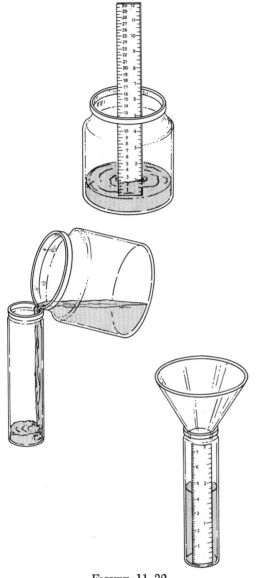

FIGURE 11–32.
A HOMEMADE RAIN GAUGE.

centimeter or $\frac{1}{10}$ inch of water. Empty the narrow bottle.

Put the narrow bottle in a large can so that the wind will not blow the bottle over during a rainstorm. Put the funnel in the neck of the narrow bottle, and place the can in an open area. The funnel will collect the rain and send it into the narrow bottle, where the amount of rainfall can be measured.

8. *Measure the amount of snowfall* · Immediately after a snowfall, select a spot where drifting of the snow has not taken place. Push a meter or yard stick into the snow until it touches the ground, and read the number of centimeters or inches of snow that fell. Divide this value by 10 to get a rough estimate of the number of centimeters or inches of rain that would have fallen instead.

To convert snowfall into exact equivalent rainfall, collect falling snow in a tall can and measure the depth. Bring the can indoors, cover the top with a cardboard, and let the snow melt slowly to cut the amount of evaporation down to a minimum. Measure the melted snow to get the equivalent number of centimeters or inches of rainfall.

9. *Set up a weather station* · Have the children set up their own weather station. Many instruments can be built by the children. You can obtain weather maps from the nearest local weather station or from the Superintendent of Documents, Washington, D.C. 20025. The children can post their own forecasts on the bulletin board for everyone to see. They might also post a chart comparing the accuracy of their predictions with those of the official weather forecasts.

10. *Keep a record of the weather* · Have the children keep a daily weather chart for a month. Make seven columns on a sheet of paper. In the first column put down the date and time the weather observations were made. The weather should be observed about the same time each day. In the other columns put down the following information: temperature out-

of paper to indicate the centimeter or inch of water, and label this mark "1 centimeter" or "1 inch." Measure the distance from this mark to the bottom of the water in the jar, and use this distance to make additional marks on the paper, each mark accounting for another centimeter or inch of water. Now divide the space between each mark into 10 smaller marks so that each smaller mark represents $\frac{1}{10}$

doors, air pressure, humidity, direction and speed of the wind, condition of the sky, and kind and amount of precipitation, if any. In the column describing the condition of the sky, make a small circle. Show how much of the sky is covered with clouds by blacking all, part, or none of the circle. While the children are keeping this chart, have them clip the weather forecast from the newspaper each day of the month. Then have the children compare the actual weather for each day with the weather predicted for that day, and see how often the weatherman was correct.

11. *Learn about the services of the United States Weather Service* · Find out about the services of the United States Weather Service. Information can be obtained from encyclopedias, science books, and the weather service itself. Many teachers combine a field trip to the local weather station with the trip to the airport.

12. *Investigate man-made weather* · Have the children find out about "seeding" clouds to produce rain, and report upon the technique and effectiveness of this method. Do the same for devices that eliminate fog in airports.

13. *Make a list of weather sayings* · Many

science books on weather have weather sayings. Have the children collect a list of these sayings and decide which sayings have any scientific basis.

CLIMATE

1. *Discuss factors controlling yearly temperature* · See maps of the United States and discuss what factors are involved in determining the yearly temperature of the city or town in which you live.

2. *Discuss factors controlling yearly rainfall* · See maps of the United States and discuss what factors are involved in determining the yearly rainfall of the city or town in which you live.

3. *Compare climates in the United States* · Consult encyclopedias and other sources for information about the different climates in the United States. Choose a representative selection of well-known cities, towns, or locations that illustrate the different kinds of climate. Compare the average rainfall, kinds of seasons, average yearly temperature, average summer and winter temperatures, and kinds of vegetation in these locations.

BIBLIOGRAPHY FOR "WATER, WEATHER, AND CLIMATE"

ANDERSON, MADELYN. *Iceberg Alley*. New York: Julian Messner, 1976. 64 pp.

ARNOV, BORIS. *Homes Beneath the Sea: An Introduction to Ocean Ecology.* Boston: Little, Brown, 1969. 132 pp.

BARLOWE, SY. *Oceans*. Chicago: Follett, 1969. 32 pp.

BERGER, MELVIN. *The National Weather Service*. New York: Thomas Y. Crowell, 1973. 128 pp.

———. *The New Water Book*. New York: Thomas Y. Crowell, 1973. 108 pp.

———. *Oceanography Lab*. New York: Thomas Y. Crowell, 1974. 128 pp.

BOESEN, VICTOR. *Doing Something About the Weather*. New York: G. B. Putnam's Sons, 1974. 120 pp.

BRANLEY, FRANKLIN M. *Floating and Sinking*. New York: Thomas Y. Crowell, 1967. 38 pp.

BRINDZE, RUTH. *Hurricanes—Monster Storms from the Sea*. New York: Atheneum, 1973. 106 pp.

BROWN, JOSEPH. *The Sea's Harvest*. New York: Dodd, Mead, 1975. 94 pp.

BUEHR, WALTER. *Storm Warning: The Story of Hurricanes and Tornadoes*. New York: William Morrow, 1972. 64 pp.

CARONA, PHILIP. *Water*. Chicago: Follett, 1966. 32 pp.

CARR, MARION. *Oceanography*. New York: Western Pub., 1973. 48 pp.

CARTWRIGHT, SALLY. *Water Is Wet*. New York: Coward, McCann & Geoghegan, 1973. 32 pp.

CORBETT, SCOTT. *What Makes a Boat Float?* Boston: Little, Brown, 1970. 42 pp.

CRAIG, M. JEAN. *Questions and Answers About Weather*. New York: Four Winds Press, 1973. 80 pp.

DEAN, AMABEL. *Exploring and Understanding Oceanography*. Westchester, Ill.: Benefic Press, 1968. 96 pp.

———. *Submerge! The Story of Divers and Their Crafts*. Philadelphia: Westminster, 1976. 112 pp.

DePAOLA, TOMIE. *The Cloud Book*. New York: Holiday House, 1975. 32 pp.

DOCKINGTON, WALLENE. *Weather or Not*. Nashville, Tenn.: Abingdon Press, 1976. 32 pp.

ELLIOT, SARAH. *Our Dirty Water*. New York: Julian Messner, 1973. 64 pp.

FELLGER, MERRILL. *Exploring and Understanding Water*. Westchester, Ill.: Benefic Press, 1968. 96 pp.

FISHER, JAMES. *The Wonderful World of the Sea*. New York: Doubleday, 1971. 96 pp.

GOETZ, DELIA. *Lakes*. New York: Morrow Jr. Books, 1973. 64 pp.

GUTNIK, MARTIN. *Ecology and Pollution: Water*. Chicago: Childrens Press, 1973. 48 pp.

HALL, JAMES P. *Exploring and Understanding Weather and Climate*. Westchester, Ill.: Benefic Press, 1970. 96 pp.

HAMBERGER, JOHN. *Birth of a Pond*. New York: Coward, McCann & Geoghegan, 1975. 24 pp.

HARVEY, FRAN. *Why Does It Rain?* New York: Harvey House, 1969. 46 pp.

JACOBS, FRANCINE. *The Sargasso Sea*. New York: William Morrow, 1975. 196 pp.

KAUFMANN, JOHN. *Winds and Weather*. New York: William Morrow, 1971. 64 pp.

KEEN, MARTIN. *Lightning and Thunder*. New York: Julian Messner, 1969. 94 pp.

KOVALIK, VLADIMIR, and NADA KOVALIK. *Undersea World of Tomorrow*. Englewood Cliffs, N.J.: Prentice-Hall, 1969. 52 pp.

LEFKOWITZ, R. J. *Water for Today and Tomorrow*. New York: Parents' Magazine, 1973. 64 pp.

LIMBURG, PETER, and JAMES SWEENEY. *102 Questions and Answers About the Sea*. New York: Julian Messner, 1975. 128 pp.

MAY, JULIAN. *Climate*. Chicago: Follett, 1969. 32 pp.

———. *Weather*. Chicago: Follett, 1966. 32 pp.

MCFALL, CHRISTIE. *Wonders of Snow and Ice*. New York: Dodd, Mead, 1965. 64 pp.

MICHELSON, DAVID. *The Oceans in Tomorrow's World*. New York: Julian Messner, 1972. 192 pp.

NELSON, CLIFFORD. *From One Drop of Water*. New York: Julian Messner, 1970. 32 pp.

PRINGLE, LAURENCE. *This Is a River*. New York: Macmillan, 1972. 56 pp.

RUSSELL, HELEN. *Water: A Field Trip Guide*. Boston: Little, Brown, 1973. 32 pp.

SIMON, SEYMOUR. *Water on Your Street*. New York: Holiday House, 1974. 48 pp.

———. *Weather and Climate*. New York: Random House, 1969. 128 pp.

SOULE, GARDNER. *New Discoveries in Oceanography*. New York: G. P. Putnam's Sons, 1974. 128 pp.

STAMBLER, IRWIN. *Weather Instruments: How They Work*. New York: G. P. Putnam's Sons, 1968. 96 pp.

VOSS, GILBERT. *Oceanography*. New York: Western Pub., 1972. 160 pp.

WEISS, MALCOLM. *Man Explores the Sea*. New York: Julian Messner, 1970. 128 pp.

———. *Storms—From the Inside Out*. New York: Julian Messner, 1973, 96 pp.

WINCHESTER, JAMES. *Hurricanes, Storms, Tornadoes*. New York: G. P. Putnam's Sons, 1968. 128 pp.

WOLFF, BARBARA. *Evening Gray, Morning Red*. New York: Macmillan, 1976. 64 pp.

CHAPTER 12

AIR, PLANES, *and* SPACE TRAVEL

AIR

I. WHERE AIR IS FOUND

  A. Air is all around us.
    1. We live at the bottom of an ocean of air.
    2. Air occupies the space all around the earth.
  B. Air is also found in all the tiny spaces between particles of materials.
    1. Air is found in soil.
    2. Air is found in water.
    3. Air is found in such porous materials as sponges, bricks, wood, and bread.

II. THE COMPOSITION OF AIR

  A. Air is a mixture of many gases.
  B. The two principal gases in the air are oxygen and nitrogen.
  C. About one fifth of the air is oxygen (21 percent).
    1. Animals and plants need oxygen for breathing and digesting their food.
    2. Homes and factories need oxygen to burn their fuels.
    3. Oxygen is a very active gas and combines easily with many materials.
  D. About four fifths of the air is nitrogen (78 percent).

    1. Nitrogen is the most abundant gas in the air.
    2. Nitrogen is not an active gas and will not help things burn or combine with materials easily, as oxygen does.
    3. If there were only oxygen in the air, without nitrogen, all burning would be very rapid and impossible to control.
    4. Nitrogen helps dilute the oxygen in the air and in this way controls burning.
    5. Nitrogen is needed by plants and animals as food, but they cannot use the nitrogen directly from the air.
    6. Man, and also certain plants, are able to change the nitrogen in the air into materials that plants and animals can use as food.
  E. Together, oxygen and nitrogen make up almost 99 percent of the air.
  F. The remaining 1 percent of the air is made up of carbon dioxide gas, hydrogen gas, and a group of rare and inactive gases known as helium, neon, argon, krypton, and xenon.
  G. Although carbon dioxide is present in the air in very small quantities, it is a very important gas.
    1. Plants use carbon dioxide to make food,

which is used not only by the plants themselves but by animals as well.

2. Carbon dioxide is used in making "soda water" and "dry ice."

3. The action of the yeast or baking powder in bread or cake dough releases bubbles of carbon dioxide gas, which expand and make the bread and cake rise.

H. Air also contains water in the form of an invisible gas, called **water vapor.**

1. The water vapor becomes part of the air by the evaporation of water from the waters on the earth's surface.

2. The amount of water vapor in the air differs from day to day and from place to place.

I. Air also carries changing amounts of dust, pollen, plant spores, and waste gases given off by factories.

J. The amount of oxygen and carbon dioxide in the air remains the same because of the **carbon dioxide-oxygen cycle.**

1. Green plants constantly take in carbon dioxide from the air to make food, and give off oxygen as a waste product.

2. Man and animals breathe in oxygen to digest their food, and give off carbon dioxide as a waste product.

K. The amount of nitrogen in the air remains the same because of the **nitrogen cycle.**

1. Bacteria, called **nitrogen-fixing bacteria,** live in the soil and in the roots of certain leguminous plants like beans, peas, and clover, changing the nitrogen of the air, which plants cannot use, into nitrogen materials that plants can use to live and grow.

2. Animals eat plants and give off waste materials containing nitrogen.

3. **Decay bacteria** in the soil act on these materials and also on dead plants and animals, break them down, and return the nitrogen in them to the soil.

4. Special bacteria, called **nitrifying bacteria,** then change the nitrogen from these waste materials and from the dead plants and animals into nitrogen materials which plants can use.

5. At the same time other bacteria, called **denitrifying bacteria,** change some of the nitrogen materials to free nitrogen, which returns to the air to continue the nitrogen cycle.

L. The present composition of the air is much different from what it was when the earth was first formed.

1. At first there were large amounts of hydrogen gas and helium gas, but these gases were very light and went off into space.

2. When the earth was cooling, there most likely was just nitrogen, carbon dioxide, and water vapor in the air at first.

3. As the earth continued to cool, most of the water vapor condensed, leaving just nitrogen and carbon dioxide in the air.

4. When green land plants began to appear, the plants took in the carbon dioxide to make food and gave off oxygen as a waste product.

5. Over billions of years the plants reduced the amount of carbon dioxide in the air and increased the amount of oxygen until the present composition of these gases in the air was reached.

6. A certain amount of carbon dioxide was also removed as it dissolved in the waters of the earth and as it formed minerals called carbonates.

III. Air Pollution

A. Every day our air is being polluted by large quantities of gases and solids.

1. These materials are given off by smokestacks, chimneys, and car exhaust pipes.

2. Some of these materials can be annoying, and even dangerous to our health.

3. Continuous exposure to polluted air can cause lung diseases or aggravate existing ones.

B. Atom and hydrogen bomb tests add dangerous radioactive particles to the air.

1. The harmfulness of these particles, when in air, has not been fully established.

2. However, if these tests increase, enough

radioactive particles may accumulate to become highly dangerous.

C. Air pollution becomes a very serious problem when weather conditions in which the polluted air cannot be blown away are formed.

    1. These conditions occur when there is a layer of cold air next to the ground, and a layer of warm air lies on top of the cold air.

    2. The upper layer of warm air acts as a cover, and it stops the cold air from being carried away.

    3. This condition is called a **temperature inversion.**

D. In many parts of the United States, attempts are being made to control air pollution.

    1. In some communities factories are being made to install equipment that will remove the poisonous gases and smoke particles from their exhaust gases before these gases can escape into the air.

    2. In Los Angeles, California, all automobiles must install anti-smog devices, which trap or burn up the irritating gases that the exhaust pipes normally give off.

E. We must do everything we can to learn how to control air pollution.

    1. We must first identify which of the materials in the air are dangerous.

    2. Then we must find out exactly how these materials get into the air.

    3. Finally, we must do everything we can to stop these materials from getting into the air.

IV. THE EARTH'S ATMOSPHERE

A. The ocean of air around the earth is called the **atmosphere.**

    1. The earth's pull of gravity holds the atmosphere to the earth's surface.

    2. The atmosphere is important because all animals and most plants need air to live.

    3. The atmosphere also acts as a protective blanket to cut down the sun's heat and to shield us from harmful rays that come from the sun and outer space.

B. Scientists divide the atmosphere into five principal layers: the **troposphere,** the **stratosphere,** the **mesosphere,** the **ionosphere,** and the **exosphere.**

C. The troposphere is the lowest layer of the atmosphere.

    1. It extends upward to a height of 8 kilometers (5 mi) at the equator and 16 kilometers (10 mi) at the poles, with an average of about 11 kilometers (7 mi) in the areas between these two.

    2. Because almost all the water vapor in the air is in this layer, almost all weather conditions such as clouds and storms are found in the troposphere.

D. The stratosphere is the layer above the troposphere, and it extends upward from the top of the troposphere to a height of about 32 kilometers (20 mi).

    1. The air is much thinner in the stratosphere.

    2. The stratosphere is clear and cloudless, and has little or no weather conditions.

E. The mesosphere, above the stratosphere, extends to a height of about 80 kilometers (50 mi).

    1. A special form of oxygen, called **ozone,** is found in the mesosphere.

    2. Ozone absorbs most of the ultraviolet rays coming from the sun, protecting people on earth from severe burns.

F. The fourth layer of the atmosphere, the ionosphere, extends upward from the top of the mesosphere to a height of about 640 to 800 kilometers (400 to 500 mi).

    1. This layer is different from the other two layers.

    2. Powerful ultraviolet rays from the sun strike the particles of air in this layer and make the particles become electrically charged.

    3. These electrically charged particles of air are called **ions.**

    4. Man has found the ionosphere useful because it makes radio reception around the earth possible.

5. When radio waves travel out into space and reach the ionosphere, the waves bounce off the ions and are reflected back to a different part of the earth.

6. The Northern Lights (Aurora Borealis) come from the ionosphere.

G. The fifth layer, the exosphere, begins at the outer limit of the ionosphere and extends far upward until it cannot be distinguished from outer space.

1. There is almost no air at all in the exosphere.

2. Man-made satellites have discovered an area of very intense radiation, called a **radiation belt,** in the exosphere.

3. This radiation belt is known as the **Van Allen radiation belt,** and it is thought to be shaped like a doughnut within a doughnut.

4. The inner belt begins about 1280 kilometers (800 mi) above the earth and extends to about 4800 kilometers (3000 mi).

5. The outer belt begins about 12,800 kilometers (8000 mi) above the earth and extends to about 64,000 kilometers (40,000 mi).

V. The Properties of Air

A. The gases that make up air are colorless, odorless, and tasteless.

B. Like all gases, air has no shape of its own, but it takes the shape of the container it fills.

C. Although air is invisible, it is real and takes up space.

D. Air has weight, and 1 liter of air weighs about 1⅓ grams (1 cu ft weighs about 1¼ oz).

VI. Air Pressure

A. Air has pressure.

1. Air has weight, and anything that has weight pushes or presses against things.

2. We live at the bottom of an ocean of air hundreds of kilometers or miles high.

3. This air presses down on the earth's surface and creates a pressure on it.

4. This pressure on the earth's surface is called **air pressure,** or **atmospheric pressure.**

B. As we go higher into the air, there is less air pressing down on us, and thus the air pressure becomes less.

C. Air presses in all directions—downward, upward, and sideways—on any exposed surface.

D. Air presses just as hard upward and sideways as it does downward.

1. Air presses on every square inch of surface of our bodies.

2. We do not feel this pressure because there is air inside our bodies that is pushing outward just as hard as the air outside our bodies is pushing inward.

3. The air pressure inside and outside our bodies is just the same.

E. Moving air exerts pressure.

1. When air moves, it pushes harder against things.

2. Wind is moving air.

3. The harder the wind blows, the greater pressure it will have.

VII. Measuring Air Pressure

A. At sea level the weight of the air pressing on 1 square centimeter of the earth's surface is about 1 kilogram (on 1 square inch it is about 15 pounds).

B. Scientists state this fact in another way, namely, that the pressure of the air at sea level is about 1 kilogram per square centimeter (15 lb per sq in).

C. The air pressure changes from day to day.

D. An instrument called a **barometer** is used to measure air pressure.

E. There are two kinds of barometers that are commonly used.

1. One contains a liquid, usually mercury, and is called a **mercury barometer.**

2. The other has no liquid in it, and is called an **aneroid barometer.**

F. The mercury barometer measures air pressure in terms of the number of inches of mercury standing in a glass tube.

1. The mercury barometer consists of a glass tube about 92 centimeters (36 in) long and closed at one end.
2. The tube is first filled with mercury, then it is turned upside down in a dish that contains more mercury.
3. The mercury falls a few centimeters or inches, but about 76 centimeters (30 in) remains standing in the tube.
4. The pressure of the air on the mercury in the dish holds the mercury up in the glass tube.
5. So, air pressure of about 1 kilogram per square centimeter (15 lb per sq in) holds up a column of mercury about 76 centimeters (30 in) high.
6. When the air pressure becomes greater, the air pushes harder on the mercury in the dish and forces the mercury in the tube to rise.
7. When the air pressure becomes smaller, the air does not push as hard on the mercury in the dish, which allows the mercury in the tube to fall.
8. Measuring the height of the mercury in the tube will give us the air pressure.

G. The aneroid barometer also measures air pressure in centimeters or inches of mercury, but it does not use mercury at all.
1. The aneroid barometer has a metal box in it with a thin, springy cover.
2. Most of the air inside the metal box has been taken out, which makes the cover very sensitive to changes in air pressure.
3. When the air pressure becomes greater, the air pushes harder on the cover, so the cover moves inward.
4. When the air pressure becomes smaller, the air does not push as hard on the cover, so the cover moves outward.
5. This movement of the cover is carried by levers to a pointer that moves across a dial marked in centimeters or inches.
6. In this way the air pressure may be read directly in centimeters or inches of mercury.

H. An **altimeter** is an aneroid barometer that measures the height above sea level.

1. The higher up in the air we go, the less air pressure there is, and the lower the barometer will read.
2. Scientists have found that for every 305 meters (1000 ft) we go up into the air, the air pressure will fall about 2½ centimeters (1 in).
3. The markings on the dial in an altimeter are changed so that, instead of giving the air pressure in centimeters or inches of mercury, they give the number of meters or feet above sea level.

VIII. Air Pressure Inside a Container

A. The air inside a container pushes, or exerts pressure, on the walls of the container.
1. The gases in the air are made up of tiny particles called molecules, which are moving rapidly.
2. When the fast-moving molecules hit the walls of a container, the molecules push against the walls and exert a pressure on them.

B. The air pressure in a closed container can be changed by adding or taking away more air.
1. If more air is added to the container, the air pressure inside becomes greater because more molecules of air are now striking and pushing against the walls of the container.
2. If air is taken away from the container, the air pressure inside becomes smaller because fewer molecules of air are now striking and pushing against the walls of the container.
3. If all the air is removed from a container, there will be no air pressure at all inside the container because there are no molecules of air inside to strike the walls.
4. An absence of all air inside a container is called a **vacuum.**
5. When only part of the air is removed from the container, there is only a partial vacuum present.

C. The air pressure inside a closed container

can be changed by making the size of the container larger or smaller.

1. If the size of the container is made larger, the air pressure inside becomes smaller because the air has spread out into a larger space so there are fewer molecules striking and pushing against each part of the container.

2. If the size of the container is made smaller, the air pressure inside becomes greater because the molecules of air have been squeezed into a smaller space, so there are more of them striking and pushing against each part of the container.

D. The air pressure inside a container can be changed by heating or cooling the container.

1. If the container is heated, the air pressure inside becomes greater because the molecules of air inside the container gain more energy and move faster, so they strike and push harder against the walls of the container.

2. If the container is cooled, the air pressure inside the container becomes smaller because the molecules of air inside the container loose energy and move more slowly, so they strike and push less strongly against the walls of the container.

IX. Some Effects of Decreasing the Air Pressure

A. Use of a soda straw depends upon decreasing the air pressure inside the straw.

1. When a straw is placed in a tumbler of soda, the soda rises up the straw to the level of the soda in the tumbler.

2. The soda in the straw does not rise any higher because the air pressure on the soda inside the straw and the air pressure on the soda outside the straw are equal.

3. When the movement of the cheek muscles sucks some air out of the straw, there is a partial vacuum inside the straw, and

the air pressure inside the straw is smaller.

4. Normal or regular air pressure on the soda outside the straw is now greater than the air pressure on the soda inside the straw.

5. The outside air pressure, because it is greater, forces the soda up the straw and into the mouth.

B. To fill a medicine dropper depends upon decreasing the air pressure inside the dropper.

1. When the bulb is pressed, some of the air is forced out of the dropper, forming a partial vacuum and smaller air pressure inside the dropper.

2. The regular air pressure on the liquid outside the dropper is now greater than the air pressure on the liquid inside the dropper.

3. The outside air pressure, because it is greater, forces the liquid up the dropper.

C. Use of a suction cup depends upon decreasing the air pressure inside the cup.

1. When the suction cup is pressed against a surface, some of the air will be forced out of the cup, forming a partial vacuum and smaller air pressure inside the cup.

2. The outside air pressure is now greater and holds the cup firmly in place.

3. If the cup is moistened first, this moistening will make a tighter seal so that outside air cannot get inside the cup and remove the partial vacuum.

D. The operation of a vacuum cleaner depends upon decreasing the air pressure inside the cleaner.

1. An electrically driven fan drives air out of a compartment in the machine, forming a partial vacuum and smaller air pressure inside the compartment.

2. The outside air pressure is now greater than the air pressure inside the compartment, and the air rushes in through the nozzle, carrying dirt and lint with it.

3. The dirt and lint are caught by a bag or screen while the air passes out of the machine.

[401

X. SOME EFFECTS OF INCREASING THE AIR
PRESSURE

A. When a great deal of air is pumped into
a container, the air is compressed and the
air pressure inside the container is increased.
1. The molecules of air are squeezed, or
compressed, very close together so that
there are many more of them striking
and pushing against the walls of the
container.
2. The molecules are now striking with
more force against the walls of the container so that the air pressure inside the
container becomes greater.
B. Many appliances make use of the increased
pressure of compressed air.
C. The air brake uses compressed air to stop
trains, street cars, buses, and heavy trucks.
1. A motor-driven pump in the vehicle
compresses the air, which is stored in a
tank.
2. When the brakes are applied, the compressed air passes into a cylinder, where
the compressed air exerts pressure
against a piston.
3. The piston then forces the brake shoes
tightly against a drum that is connected
to the wheels, making the vehicle come
to a stop.
D. The following items also make use of
compressed air.
1. The caisson makes it possible for men
to work under water.
2. The deep sea diver uses compressed air
in his diving suit to go down hundreds
of feet into water.
3. The submarine sinks when tanks let in
seawater, and rises when compressed air
forces the water out of the tanks.
4. Pneumatic drills and riveters operate by
compressed air.
5. Automobile tires, footballs, basket balls,
and volley balls have compressed air in
them.
6. Many paint and garden sprays are
operated by compressed air.

PLANES AND ROCKETS

I. THE FORCES INVOLVED IN FLYING A PLANE

A. When a plane is flying, there are four
forces acting on it: **gravity, lift, thrust,** and
drag.
1. The pull of the earth's gravity on the
plane, which becomes the weight of the
plane, is a downward force.
2. Lift is an upward force that acts against
gravity, because of the action of the air
on the wings, lifting the plane into the
air and keeping the plane there while it
is flying.
3. Thrust is the force that pulls the plane
forward, and it is produced by a propeller or by a jet engine.
4. Drag is the resistance that the air offers
because of friction when the plane moves
through it, and it is a backward force
that works against the thrust.
B. For a plane to take off, the lift must be
greater than the force of gravity, and the
thrust must be greater than the drag.

II. PRODUCING LIFT

A. The plane is lifted chiefly because of the
flow of air passing **over** the wing.
B. A scientific principle, called **Bernoulli's
principle,** explains why this lifting effect
takes place.
C. Bernoulli's principle states that, when air
moves faster across the top surface of a
material than across the bottom surface,
the pressure of the air pushing down on
the top surface is smaller than the pressure

of the air pushing up on the bottom surface.

D. The shape of the wing is designed to make use of Bernoulli's principle.

1. The front edge of the wing is thicker than the back edge, and the upper surface of the wing is curved whereas the under surface is straight.

2. When the wing moves through the air, some of the air flows over the wing and some flows under the wing.

3. Because the upper surface of the wing is curved, the air that flows over the upper surface must travel a longer distance than the air that flows along the bottom surface.

4. However, scientific tests show that all of the air flowing over and under the wing reaches the end of the wing at the same time.

5. Consequently, the air flowing over the curved, top surface of the wing must move faster than the air flowing along the shorter, bottom surface to reach the end of the wing at the same time.

6. According to Bernoulli's principle, because the air is moving faster across the top surface of the wing than across the bottom surface, the air pressure pushing down on the top surface is smaller than the air pressure pushing up on the bottom surface.

7. The greater air pressure underneath the wing pushes up on the wing and produces lift.

E. The greater the wingspread, the more air passes over and under the wing, and the greater the lift will be.

F. The faster the plane moves, the faster the air will flow over the wing, the smaller the air pressure pushing down on top of the wing will be, and the greater the lift will become.

G. The wing's angle of attack also helps lift the plane.

1. The wing is set so that it tilts a little, and meets the air at a small slant, or angle.

2. This slant, or angle, is called the **angle of attack.**

3. Because the wing is slanted, the air strikes the underside of the wing and pushes up on it.

4. When greater lift is needed, the wing can be made to slant even more, so the air will push up harder on the wing.

III. PRODUCING THRUST

A. Thrust is the force that pulls the plane forward and, at the same time, makes air flow above and below the wings.

B. A scientific principle, called **Newton's third law of motion,** makes thrust possible.

C. Newton's third law of motion states that, for every action, there is an equal but opposite reaction.

D. Some planes use a propeller to produce thrust.

1. The propeller is made to turn at a very high speed by an engine that uses gasoline as fuel.

2. The propeller bores into the air somewhat like a screw going into wood or a boat propeller going through water.

3. The whirling blades of the propeller are adjusted so that they will strike as much air as possible, in order to produce the greatest thrust.

4. The faster the propeller is turned by the engine, the greater the forward thrust will be.

E. Jet planes get their thrust from jet engines.

1. Jet engines are simpler than the engines in propeller-driven planes.

2. The jet engine is a hollow cylinder that is open at both ends.

3. Air that enters the front end of the cylinder is compressed, and then a fuel such as kerosene is sprayed into the cylinder.

4. The mixture of kerosene and compressed air burns with intense heat, giving off hot gases that expand and shoot out of the rear of the cylinder with great force and speed.

[403

5. As the hot gases shoot out with a backward force, we get an equal but opposite force, or thrust, that moves the plane forward at great speed.

6. The faster the fuel burns, the greater the backward push of the hot escaping gases, and the greater will be the forward push on the plane.

F. The three most common types of jet engines used in recent years are the **ramjet** engine, the **turbojet** engine, and the **turboprop** engine.

G. The ramjet engine is the simplest type of jet engine and has no moving parts.

1. It is a hollow tube, with nozzles inside to spray the fuel.

2. When the ramjet travels forward at great speed, air is packed or "rammed" into the front of the engine.

3. The "ramming" of the air into the engine helps to compress it.

4. Fuel is sprayed into the compressed air by the nozzles, and burns.

5. The hot gases expand and rush out through the rear of the engine with great speed.

6. These hot gases, escaping from the rear of the engine, produce the forward thrust needed to move the plane.

7. The ramjet plane cannot start from the ground, but it must be moving at high speed to "ram" air into the engine.

8. Usually a ramjet plane is carried into the air under another plane, which cuts the ramjet loose when the speed is high enough.

H. The turbojet engine is the engine used most often by commercial and military planes.

1. The turbojet engine has three main parts: a compressor, a combustion chamber, and a turbine.

2. The compressor compresses the air that enters the engine, and feeds the compressed air to the combustion chamber.

3. In the combustion chamber a fuel such as kerosene is sprayed into the compressed air.

4. The mixture of kerosene and compressed air burns, giving off hot gases that expand and shoot out of the rear of the engine.

5. Before the gases can leave the engine, they must first turn the blades of the turbine.

6. A shaft connects the turbine to the compressor so that the escaping gases turn the turbine, which then operates the compressor.

7. When the turbojet plane is on the ground, a small engine starts the shaft turning and operates the compressor.

8. After the plane has reached a high enough speed, the jet engine itself takes over and operates the turbine and the compressor.

I. The turboprop engine is just like a turbojet engine except that it has a propeller in front of it.

1. The propeller is attached to the same shaft that connects the turbine and compressor.

2. In this way both the propeller and the escaping gases from the rear of the engine produce the thrust that moves the turboprop plane forward.

3. The turboprop plane operates very well at low speeds or low altitudes because of the added thrust from the propeller, but the turbojet plane does not.

IV. Reducing Drag

A. The friction of the air rubbing against the moving plane causes the air to resist the plane's forward motion, and slows down the plane.

B. At high speeds this air resistance, or drag, can become very great and slow down the plane.

C. To overcome drag, the plane is streamlined.

1. Streamlining means that the plane is designed in such a way that the air flows past the plane smoothly.

2. Scientists copy the streamlined shapes of

fish, birds, and tear drops when designing planes.

3. Cars and trains are also streamlined.

V. The Parts of the Plane and Their Functions

A. The **fuselage** is the body of the plane, and it carries the cargo, passengers, crew, and fuel.

B. The **engine** provides the power or thrust to move the plane forward by turning a propeller or, if it is a jet plane, by the action of the jet engine itself.

C. The **wings** are attached to the sides of the fuselage and provide the lift for the plane.

D. The **ailerons** are long, narrow movable flaps located near the wing tips at the rear of the wings.
1. The ailerons move up and down, but, when one aileron moves up, the other must move down.
2. The ailerons are used to steer the plane to the right or left.

E. There are also movable flaps at the rear of the wings, between the ailerons and fuselage, that help the plane take off and land.

F. The **tail** of the plane has many parts to it.
1. The **fin**, or **vertical stabilizer**, does not move, and it helps keep the plane flying straight.
2. A movable **rudder** is connected to the back of the fin, and it helps turn the plane to the right or left.
3. The **horizontal stabilizers** on each side of the fin keep the plane from rising and falling while the plane is flying level.
4. The **elevators** are movable flaps connected to the horizontal stabilizers, and both elevators move up or down at the same time to make the plane climb or dive.

G. The **landing gear** is underneath the plane, and it is used for taking off and landing.
1. **Wheels** are used for planes that take off or land on hard surfaces.
2. In most planes the wheels fold up into the body of the plane after the plane is off the ground, to cut down the drag while the plane is flying.
3. Long, hollow floats, called **pontoons,** are used for planes that take off or land in water.
4. **Skis** are used for planes that take off or land in snow.

VI. Airplane Instruments

A. The **radio altimeter** measures how high the plane is above the ground.
1. It sends out a radio beam that hits the ground and bounces back.
2. The time it takes for the beam to reach the ground and return to the plane is changed by the radio altimeter into feet above the ground.

B. The **compass** helps the pilot keep the plane flying in the right direction.
1. Many small planes use a magnetic compass, and the pilots have to make corrections constantly because of irregularities in the earth's magnetic field.
2. Large planes use a **gyrocompass,** with a spinning gyroscope wheel inside it, that always points to the desired direction throughout the flight.

C. The **air-speed indicator** shows the flying speed of the plane, but the actual speed will be smaller if the plane is heading into the wind, or greater if the wind is at the plane's tail.

D. The **bank indicator** lets the pilot know if the plane is tilting, or banking, properly when making a turn.

E. The **turn indicator** lets the pilot know if the plane is turning properly and how fast the turn is being made.

F. The **fuel gauge** shows the amount of fuel in the tank.

G. **Pressure gauges** show the oil pressure, fuel pressure, and cabin pressure.

H. **Temperature gauges** show the temperatures in different parts of the engines.

I. The **tachometer** shows how fast the shaft in each engine is turning.

J. A **two-way radio** helps the pilot stay on course when the plane is flying, and gives him instructions for taking off or landing.

K. An **automatic pilot,** which uses spinning gyroscope wheels, takes over the controls and keeps the plane on the course set by the pilot.

VII. CONTROLLING THE PLANE IN FLIGHT

A. *The takeoff*
1. To take off, a plane must be going fast enough to rise in the air.
2. Planes take off into the wind because the wind will make the air flow faster over the surface of the wings and help make the lift greater.
3. This kind of takeoff means that the plane will not have to travel as far down the runway before taking off.
4. The plane goes faster and faster until it reaches its take-off speed, where the lift is great enough to make the plane rise.
5. The pilot then pulls the control wheel toward him just a little, which makes the elevators in the tail tilt up a little.
6. The rushing air strikes these elevators, which forces the tail down.
7. This action swings the nose of the plane up, and the plane takes off into the air.
8. As the plane rises, the landing gear is pulled back into the plane.
9. The plane climbs until it reaches the height the pilot wants to fly.
10. The elevators are then lowered until they are even again, and the plane flies level.

B. *Climbing and diving*
1. To climb, the pilot pushes the control wheels toward him, making the elevators in the tail tilt up.
2. The air strikes these elevators and forces the tail down, which swings the nose of the plane up so that the plane climbs.
3. The plane needs more power when it is climbing and moving against gravity so that the engines are given more fuel and consequently speed up.

4. To dive, the pilot pushes the control wheel away from him, making the elevators tilt down.
5. The air striking the elevators forces the tail up, which swings the nose down so that the plane dives.
6. The plane needs less power when it is diving, because gravity helps pull the plane down, so the engines are given less fuel and consequently slow down.

C. *Turning to the right and left*
1. To make a turn the pilot must tilt, or bank, the plane's wings in the direction he wants to turn, in much the same way that we tilt a bicycle when going around a curve.
2. To turn to the right, the pilot turns the control wheel to the right.
3. This turning of the wheel makes the right aileron in the wing go up, and the left aileron go down.
4. When the rushing air strikes the ailerons, it makes the right wing fall and the left wing rise.
5. This action makes the plane roll on its side and turn, or bank, to the right.
6. At the same time, the pilot pushes the right foot pedal and makes the rudder in the tail swing to the right.
7. The air strikes the rudder, making the tail swing to the left and the nose of the plane move to the right.
8. This action helps the plane turn to the right and also helps prevent the plane from yawing, or skidding sidewise, in the turn.
9. To make a left turn, the pilot turns the control wheel to the left, making the right aileron go down and the left aileron go up.
10. Air strikes the ailerons, making the right wing rise and the left wing fall, and the plane turns, or banks, to the left.
11. At the same time, the pilot pushes the left foot pedal, making the rudder swing to the left.
12. Air strikes the rudder, pushing the tail to the right and the nose to the left

D. *Landing*
1. To land, the pilot dives by making the elevators tilt down.
2. As the plane dives, the pilot lowers the landing gear.
3. The plane moves into the wind so that the resistance of the air striking the plane will cut down the landing speed.
4. When the plane nears the runway, the pilot moves the elevators up to make a level landing.
5. When the plane is ready to land, the pilot lowers the flaps in the wings between the ailerons and the fuselage.
6. These flaps act as air brakes.

VIII. THE SOUND BARRIER

A. The speed of sound is about 336 meters (1100 ft) per second, or about 1220 kilometers (760 mi) per hour.
B. As the plane moves through the air, it produces sound, which travels out in waves.
C. These sound waves are compressed, and then expanded, as they travel.
D. When a plane travels slower than the speed of sound, the sound waves travel away from the plane faster than the plane is moving.
E. But, when a plane travels at the speed of sound, these compressed sound waves cannot travel away from the plane because both the plane and the waves are now traveling at the same speed.
F. The sound waves then pile up in front of the plane and form a huge wall of air, called the **sound barrier.**
G. This wall of piled-up, compressed air pushes along at the speed of sound and becomes a shock wave.
1. The pressure of this shock wave is so great that it can rip the wings off an ordinary plane.
2. At the same time the shock wave produces a loud noise, like a giant clap of thunder, so strong that it can rattle— even break—dishes and windows.

H. When the plane breaks the sound barrier and travels faster than the speed of sound, the sound waves no longer affect the plane because they are now left behind.
I. Planes that fly through, or break, the sound barrier are designed in a special way.
1. The nose of the plane is made longer and more needlelike.
2. The wings are thin, with sharp edges in front.
3. The wings also sweep back at an angle so that they look like large triangles.
4. Wings shaped in this manner make it easier for the plane to break through the sound barrier.

IX. THE HEAT BARRIER

A. The friction of the air as it moves across the plane produces heat.
B. The faster the plane moves, the greater the air friction, and the more heat is produced.
C. The temperature at which the heat weakens and melts the parts of the plane is called the **heat barrier.**
D. The kinds of materials that make up the plane are more important in overcoming the heat barrier than the speed of the plane itself.
E. Scientists are trying to discover new materials, to be used in building planes and rockets, that will help them break the heat barrier.

X. THE HELICOPTER

A. The helicopter has a large wing or rotor that spins above the plane.
B. As the rotor spins rapidly, it provides both the lift to raise the helicopter in the air and the thrust to move the helicopter forward.
C. By changing the tilt of the rotor, the helicopter can go straight up or down, forward or backward, sideways, or just hover in the air.

D. As the rotor spins, it tends to twist the rest of the helicopter.
   1. To stop this twisting effect, a smaller propeller or rotor is placed on the helicopter's tail and spins in the opposite direction to that of the large rotor.
   2. The smaller rotor also is used to steer the helicopter.
E. The helicopter does not travel very fast, but it has many valuable uses.
   1. It can be used to rescue persons at sea or remove injured persons from spots that are hard to reach.
   2. It can carry mail or persons for short distances to airports.
   3. It can patrol the waterfront or supervise automobile traffic on highways.
   4. It can be used to spot forest fires or persons lost in a forest.

XI. ROCKETS

A. Rocket engines, like jet engines, make use of Newton's third law of motion that is concerned with action and reaction.
B. Like the jet engine, burning fuels in the rocket produce hot, expanding gases that blast from the tail of the rocket and give it the thrust required to go up into space.
C. The main difference between the rocket and the jet is in the source of oxygen needed to burn the fuel.
   1. A jet gets its oxygen from the air.
   2. A rocket carries its own oxygen supply, called the **oxidizer,** either as liquid oxygen (LOX) or as a chemical that contains oxygen and gives it up readily.
   3. The chemical that contains oxygen may be a liquid or a solid.
   4. The fuel and oxidizer together are called the **propellant.**
D. Because a rocket carries its own oxygen, it can travel in space where there is little or no air.
E. The simplest rockets are the **solid fuel,** or **solid propellant,** rockets.
   1. The solid fuel is really a mixture of a fuel and a chemical that contains oxygen.

2. These rockets are used to help launch planes, and they are also used in fireworks and as signal rockets.
F. High altitude rockets are **liquid fuel,** or **liquid propellant,** rockets.
   1. These rockets use both a liquid fuel and liquid oxygen.
   2. These two liquids are stored in separate tanks in the rocket, and are pumped into the combustion or burning chamber at the same time.
G. High altitude rockets do not have wings because they travel where there is no air to provide lift for the wings.
H. The **intercontinental ballistic missile** is a high altitude rocket.
   1. In the head of the rocket there is an atomic or hydrogen bomb.
   2. The missile can travel far out into outer space, and then go back to earth a great distance away from the point where it was launched.
I. Scientists have found that they can get rockets to travel faster and farther when they connect more than one rocket together, to form a **multistage rocket.**
J. A **three-stage rocket** has three rockets, one mounted on top of the other, each with its own fuel and combustion chamber.
   1. The first stage is the largest rocket, at the bottom.
   2. When the first stage is fired, it pushes up all three rockets.
   3. The three-stage rocket climbs until all the fuel in the first stage is used up.
   4. Then the first stage drops off, and the second stage is fired.
   5. The second and third stage together climb faster and higher until all the fuel in the second stage is used up.
   6. Then the second stage falls off, and the third stage is fired.
   7. The third stage holds the instruments, and even men, in it.
   8. The third stage climbs even higher and faster, and then either falls back to earth or goes into orbit around the earth as a satellite.

SPACE TRAVEL

I. Early Space Exploration with Rockets

A. During World War II and afterward, scientists made great advances in the study of rockets.

B. They improved the rocket design and were able to send rockets up to greater heights than had ever before been reached.

C. Rockets containing instruments, cameras, and recording devices were sent up as high as 400 kilometers (250 mi).

D. However, these rockets were fired almost straight up, reached their greatest height in minutes, and then fell back to earth.

    1. These rockets were at different levels of the air for only a very short time, and very little could be found out about space during that time.

    2. Also, because the rockets went straight up, only the space above just one part of the earth's surface could be explored.

II. Man-Made Satellites

A. After scientists had experimented with rockets that went straight up, they decided to try something different.

B. They tried the idea of a rocket going high above the earth's surface and staying there for some time.

C. The only way this could be done was to make the rocket travel around the earth in an orbit, just as the moon makes an orbit around the earth.

D. Because the moon is called a **satellite** (a heavenly body revolving around a planet), this orbiting rocket was called a satellite too.

E. On October 4, 1957, the Soviet Union sent up Sputnik I, the first earth satellite around the earth.

F. A month later the Russians sent up Sputnik II, with a dog in it.

G. On January 31, 1958, the United States sent up its first satellite, the Explorer I.

III. Orbiting and Escaping the Earth

A. Very high speeds and powerful thrusts are necessary to get a satellite or a space ship high into the air and then either send the satellite sideways in an orbit around the earth or else let the space ship escape the earth's pull of gravity.

B. To accomplish this, three or even more rockets are put together, one on top of the other, with the biggest rocket at the bottom, to form a **multistage rocket.**

    1. Each rocket is called a **stage,** and each stage has its own fuel and combustion chamber.

    2. The stages do not all go off together, but they are fired one after the other.

    3. When one stage uses up its fuel, it drops off, and the next stage takes over.

C. The satellite or space ship is on top of the last rocket, and it contains the instruments and astronauts.

    1. The satellite or space ship is the smallest part of the rocket.

    2. It has a nose cone over it to protect it from the heat produced by friction as the rocket moves through the air.

    3. It is often called the "**pay load**" of the rocket.

D. When the first stage of a three-stage rocket is fired, the rocket goes straight into the air.

    1. The rocket goes up slowly at first because it must overcome the pull of gravity, and also because the heavier air in the lower atmosphere would batter the rocket into pieces if the rocket were traveling at high speed.

    2. The rocket begins to pick up speed and then is made to tilt so that it travels at an angle.

    3. By the time the rocket is in the outer limits of the stratosphere, the fuel in the first stage burns out, and the stage drops off.

E. The second stage takes over and lifts the rocket higher and faster into space.
1. The rocket keeps tilting until its path is more in a line with the direction the space ship or satellite wants to go.
2. The fuel in the second stage burns out, and the stage drops off.
F. The third stage then either sends the space ship beyond the earth's pull of gravity or puts the satellite into orbit.
1. To put the satellite into orbit, the third stage fires at the proper height and tilts the satellite to as close a path parallel to the earth's surface as the instruments will allow.
2. The third stage then drops off, leaving the satellite in orbit.
3. The protective nose cone drops off the satellite at the same time.
G. Rockets are often launched toward the east because the east is the direction of the earth's rotation.
1. The earth rotates at a speed of about 1600 kilometers (1000 mi) per hour.
2. The earth's speed gives the rocket an extra push which helps the rocket reach the speed it needs to go into orbit.

IV. KEEPING THE SATELLITE IN ORBIT

A. The speeding satellite stays in orbit around the earth because there are two conditions affecting it.
B. One condition is earth's **pull of gravity** on the satellite, which tries to pull the satellite down to earth.
C. The second condition is that of **inertia,** which tends to make the satellite move in a straight line out into space.
1. The action of inertia is based upon a scientific principle, called Newton's first law of motion.
2. This law states that a body at rest tends to stay at rest and a body in motion tends to continue in motion **in a straight line** at the same speed, unless some outside force acts on the body to change this condition.

D. Both conditions act against each other.
1. If only gravity were affecting the satellite, the satellite would fall to the earth.
2. If only inertia were affecting the satellite, the satellite would fly off into space in a straight line.
E. The third stage of the rocket gives the satellite exactly the proper sideways speed, called the **orbital velocity,** so that the force of gravity and the effect of inertia balance each other.
F. As a result, the satellite neither falls to earth nor flies off into space, but instead it moves in an orbit **around** the earth.

V. THE PATH OF THE SATELLITE

A. Most man-made satellites travel in an elliptical, or oval-shaped, orbit rather than a circular orbit.
B. This kind of orbit is most common because it is very hard to launch a satellite at just the right angle and speed to get a perfect, circular orbit.
C. Some satellites are purposely made to travel in an elliptical orbit so that they can give information about conditions in space near the earth and much farther away.
D. In an elliptical orbit the satellite comes closer to the earth at one part of its trip and then goes farther away at another part of its trip.
1. The point in the orbit where the satellite is nearest the earth is called the **perigee.**
2. The point where the satellite is farthest away from the earth is called the **apogee.**
E. The satellite needs a sideways speed, called **orbital velocity,** to stay in orbit around the earth.
1. The farther the orbit is away from the earth, the smaller the earth's pull of gravity on the satellite becomes, and the less sideways speed the satellite needs.
2. To travel in an orbit at a height of 480 kilometers (300 mi), a satellite needs an orbital velocity of about 29,000 kilometers (18,000 mi) per hour.

3. At 3200 kilometers (2000 mi) the orbital velocity must be about 23,000 kilometers (14,400 mi) per hour.

4. At 16,000 kilometers (10,000 mi) the orbital velocity must be about 11,500 kilometers (7200 mi) per hour.

5. At 35,000 kilometers (22,000 mi) the orbital velocity must be about 10,900 kilometers (6800 mi) per hour, and the satellite would travel around the earth once every 24 hours.

6. At 35,000 kilometers (22,000 mi) such a satellite would seem to be stationary in the sky, if it traveled in the same direction as the earth (west to east).

F. Eventually, most satellites orbiting the earth fall back to earth.

1. At the perigee of its orbit, the heavier air slows the satellite a little, especially if the satellite started with a perigee fairly close to earth.

2. Each time the satellite enters its perigee, it is slowed down more so that its orbit gets rounder and smaller, and the earth's gravity pulls harder and harder on it.

3. When the satellite is slowed to the point where it cannot keep its orbit any more, the satellite falls.

4. The falling satellite gets very hot because of the friction of the air rubbing against it, and it will burn up unless it is protected from the heat.

G. Some satellites have stayed up as little as 3 months, but one satellite is expected to stay in orbit for about 200 years.

VI. TRACKING THE SATELLITE

A. Scientists follow the path, or track, of the satellite by radar and by telescope.

B. Direction-finding antennas, set up at special receiving stations, and radar are used to fix the position of the satellite.

C. Satellites are seen best by telescope at early dawn or at twilight.

1. In the daytime the satellite cannot be seen against the bright, sunlit sky.

2. At night the satellite is often in the shadow of the earth.

3. At early dawn and twilight, the satellite is in sunshine while on earth we still have a dark sky, and thus we are able to see the satellite.

D. The satellite is filled with automatic instruments and recording devices.

E. These instruments get the electrical energy needed to operate them from any one of three sources, listed as follows:

1. **Chemical** batteries, which change chemical energy into electrical energy.

2. **Solar energy** batteries, which change solar energy into electrical energy.

3. **Nuclear energy** batteries, which use radioactive isotopes to change nuclear energy into electrical energy.

F. These instruments have already discovered, studied, and measured many things.

1. They have measured cosmic, X-ray, ultraviolet, and infrared radiation.

2. They have measured how strongly the earth is being bombarded by tiny meteors coming into the atmosphere from outer space.

3. They have studied the size and shape of the earth's magnetic field.

4. They have studied the earth's force of gravity at high altitudes.

5. They have discovered that the earth is not round like an orange, but is more pear-shaped or egg-shaped.

6. They have studied the height of the earth's atmosphere, and the atmosphere's temperature, pressure, and composition at high altitudes.

7. They have taken pictures of cloud patterns to be used in predicting the weather.

8. They have measured the magnetic field, temperature, and pressure near the moon, and have taken pictures of the side of the moon that we cannot see.

9. They have reflected radio, radar, and television signals back to earth.

VII. UNITED STATES SPACE PROGRAMS

A. The National Aeronautics and Space Administration (NASA) describes its spacecraft by groups, or series, depending upon their design and what they are supposed to do or find out.

B. **Scientific satellites** like the Explorer, Vanguard, Discoverer, Orbiting Astronomical Observatory, Orbiting Solar Observatory, and Orbiting Geophysical Observatory, all built and launched by the United States, carry a large variety of instruments that supply information about radiation, the earth's magnetic field, the earth's shape, temperatures in space, micrometeoroids, and other conditions in the upper parts of the atmosphere and in outer space.

   1. There are also joint projects between the United States and other countries.

   2. Examples of such projects include the Ariel with England, the Alouette with Canada, the San Marco with Italy, the French-U.S. project, and the international Isis project.

C. **Weather satellites** like the Tiros and the Nimbus series make weather observations, help scientists forecast the weather more accurately, and contribute a better understanding of what causes weather.

D. **Communications satellites** like the Score, Echo, Courier, Telstar, Relay, Syncom, and West Ford are being used to send and reflect radio signals, telecasts, telephone calls, teleprints, and telephotos to other parts of the world.

E. **Navigation satellites** like the Transit series help guide aircraft and ships at sea during any weather by broadcasting special radio signals.

F. **Lunar** and **Interplanetary spacecraft** are being used to explore the moon and certain planets.

   1. The Pioneer series investigates interplanetary space to learn more about solar radiation, interplanetary magnetic fields, and micrometeoroids.

   2. The Ranger series gathers information about the moon to help pave the way for landing on the moon.

   3. The Surveyor series is designed to land gently on the moon, send television pictures back to earth, find suitable landing sites, analyze the moon's crust, check the moon's surface for strength and stability, and measure the bombardment of the moon by meteorites.

   4. The Lunar Orbiter series is designed to photograph suitable landing sites on the moon and to learn more about the moon's gravitational pull.

   5. The Mariner series is designed to fly near Venus and Mars, and to send back information about these planets.

G. There are also special projects for launching man into space and then bringing him safely back to earth.

   1. The purpose of **Project Mercury** is to investigate man's reactions and abilities during space flight, and to recover both man and spacecraft safely.

   2. The purpose of **Project Gemini** is to determine man's performance and behavior during prolonged space flight, develop techniques that will enable two or more spacecraft to rendezvous and couple together while in orbit, carry out space investigations that need the presence of man in the spacecraft, and demonstrate both controlled re-entry into the atmosphere and controlled landing at a specific site.

   3. The purpose of **Project Apollo** is to land men on the moon and then return them to earth.

VIII. PROBLEMS OF SPACE FLIGHT

A. *Getting enough thrust*

   1. The earth pulls on all bodies with the force called gravity.

   2. At the surface of the earth, the earth's pull of gravity on a body is the weight of that body.

   3. A rocket is very heavy and needs a huge thrust merely to lift its own weight.

4. The rocket then needs an even greater thrust to travel many thousands of miles per hour so that it can rise high above or beyond the earth.

5. To send up bigger space ships, more powerful rockets must be used in order to give greater thrust.

6. Today most rockets are driven by a mixture of liquid fuel and liquid oxygen (LOX).

7. However, scientists are looking for fuels that will burn faster and hotter, thus producing more thrust.

8. Investigations are being made to see if nuclear energy or solar energy can be used to drive rockets.

B. *Escaping the earth's pull of gravity*

1. The farther away a body is from the earth, the smaller the earth's pull of gravity is.

2. The body now weighs less, even though it still has the same amount of material.

3. If the body travels high enough, it reaches a point where it is no longer affected by the pull of the earth's gravity.

4. At this point the body has no weight.

5. To reach this point the body must be launched from the earth's surface at a speed of 11 kilometers (7 mi) per second, or about 40,000 kilometers (25,000 mi) per hour.

6. This speed is called the **escape velocity** of the body.

7. Space ships launched at less than this speed are affected by the earth's pull of gravity, and eventually fall back to the earth's surface.

8. However, space ships launched at the speed of 40,000 kilometers (25,000 mi) per hour overcome the earth's pull of gravity and are free to travel out to other parts of the solar system.

9. Also, as space ships become bigger, more powerful rockets must be used to give a thrust great enough to reach escape velocity.

C. *Coming back to earth and landing*

1. The return to earth and landing is a problem.

2. To dive quickly into the atmosphere would produce so much heat, because of the friction of the air rubbing against the satellite, that the space ship would burn up.

3. One way of returning and landing safely is for the space ship to turn around and back down.

4. Rockets at the back of the space ship can be fired to produce a reverse thrust that makes it possible for the ship to return and land slowly and safely.

5. A second way of returning and landing safely is to have the returning ship go part way into the atmosphere, and then pull up again.

6. The ship can go through this procedure again and again, slowing down more and more as it goes deeper and deeper each time into the earth's atmosphere, until it is able to land safely without being burned up by friction.

7. A third way is to put a protective ceramic shield over the space ship's nose.

8. The shield absorbs the heat produced by air friction and burns up slowly while the nose itself is not affected.

IX. PROBLEMS OF THE ASTRONAUT DURING SPACE TRAVEL

A. *The force of acceleration*

1. The astronaut must be able to endure the tremendous force acting upon him as the rocket speeds up, or accelerates, quickly.

2. This force is the same kind of force you feel when you go up quickly in an elevator.

3. You feel heavier, and it seems as if you are being pushed downward to the floor of the elevator car.

4. This force of acceleration really does make you heavier when you are speeding faster and faster, and going against gravity.

5. At the surface of the earth, the earth's pull of gravity on you is the weight of your body.
6. This pull, which is your weight, is called 1 g.
7. At a point during the first part of the flight, the astronaut feels a force of about 6 g's on him.
8. At this point, his weight is six times what it is on the ground.
9. At 3 g's a person cannot walk, and it is very hard to even move.
10. When seated, a person "blacks out" at 6 g's because his heart cannot pump blood to his brain against this great force of acceleration.
11. Tests show, however, that a person can endure this force without too much trouble if he is lying down on his back.
12. The astronaut must be able to endure the same force again when the rocket slows down, or decelerates, quickly.

B. *Weightlessness*
1. When the speeding up, or acceleration, stops and the space ship is in space, the astronaut and all the materials inside the ship have no weight.
2. The earth's gravity has been left behind, and everything is weightless.
3. The astronaut loses his feeling of what is "up" and what is "down."
4. He must use suction cups on his shoes, or else he would float rather than walk across the space ship.
5. If the things inside the rocket were not nailed down, they would float about in the ship, too.

C. *Food and water*
1. Because of weightlessness, food and water can be a problem.
2. It is impossible to pour water from a bottle.
3. If the astronaut lifted food toward his mouth, the food would continue moving to the roof of the ship.
4. The astronaut must use food and water stored in tubes, like toothpaste tubes.
5. A large amount of dehydrated food can be stored in tubes or as compressed wafers.
6. The water problem can only be solved by recovering, purifying, and reusing all water over and over again.

D. *Air*
1. The astronaut needs a steady supply of oxygen, or he will die.
2. At the same time the carbon dioxide that he exhales must be removed.
3. One way of supplying oxygen is to use tanks of liquid oxygen, which can be mixed with helium gas also in tanks, to give the astronaut the right proportion of oxygen for breathing.
4. At the same time, chemicals can remove the carbon dioxide that the astronaut exhales.
5. Scientists are also experimenting with the use of tiny, green water plants, called **algae.**
6. These algae can produce large amounts of oxygen by photosynthesis and use the carbon dioxide that is given off by the astronauts.
7. The algae can also be used as food on very long trips.

E. *Heat and cold*
1. The chief problem in the airtight space ship is to keep cool, or to keep warm.
2. Most of the space ship's travel is in direct sunlight, and the sun's rays strike at least one side of the ship all the time.
3. As a result, the ship could become so hot inside that the astronaut would die.
4. One way to keep the ship cool is to have the outside of the ship smooth and silvery so that the sun's rays are reflected.
5. If the space ship travels far from the sun, where it is very cold, the outside of the ship can be painted black to absorb the sun's rays and warm the ship.
6. Another way of controlling the temperature inside the space ship is to paint one side of the ship silver, and the other side black.
7. The ship can then be turned to adjust the temperature whenever necessary.

F. *Radiation*
1. Cosmic rays can pass directly through the metal walls into the space ship.
2. Short exposure to these rays shows no harmful effects.
3. However, it may be that the astronaut will have to be protected from long exposure to cosmic rays.

G. *Meteors*
1. Meteors of all sizes are always traveling through space.
2. If a meteor should strike a space ship and puncture a hole in it, the air in the space ship would quickly rush out and the astronaut would die.
3. Double walls can protect the ship from small meteors.
4. Most meteors are very small, so it is not likely that the ship would be struck by a large meteor.

X. SPACE STATIONS

A. A large satellite spinning around the earth can be a space station.
B. The orbit of the satellite can be almost circular, and the satellite can be well outside the earth's atmosphere.
C. Because there is no air resistance at this altitude, the station can stay in orbit for hundreds of years.
D. Supplies can be sent to the station by rockets acting as freight cars.
E. A space station can have many valuable uses.
1. It can collect a vast amount of knowledge about the earth, its atmosphere, its weather, and its fields of gravity and magnetism.
2. It can be used to reflect and send back radio, radar, and television signals all over the earth.
3. During war it can watch for enemy troops and planes, and discover industrial targets.
4. It can be used to launch rockets easily

into outer space because the rockets will not have to overcome the earth's pull of gravity to take off.

XI. FLIGHT TO THE MOON

A. The first body in space that man has visited is the moon.
1. It is the nearest body to us.
2. We have always been curious about our earth's only natural satellite.
B. It was very difficult to build a space ship large and powerful enough to reach the moon.
C. Scientists had to plan very carefully and skillfully to have the ship hit the moon.
D. When planning the flight, they had to consider the following factors.
1. The gravity of the earth, the moon, and the sun.
2. The rotation of the earth and the position of the moon in its orbit around the earth.
3. The tilt of the earth's axis and the tilt of the moon's orbit.
E. Landing on the moon is very tricky and very dangerous.
1. For most of the trip there is very little pull of gravity on the space ship.
2. But, about 38,500 kilometers (24,000 mi) from the moon, the moon's gravity pulls on the ship.
3. The ship falls faster and faster toward the moon.
4. To stop from crashing into the moon, the ship has to land tail first, and does this by using rockets at its tail to produce a reverse thrust that acts as a brake and helps the ship land safely.
F. To take off from the moon is easier than it is to take off from earth.
1. The moon's gravity is only one sixth that of the earth.
2. Also, the moon has no atmosphere.
3. Thus, much less thrust is needed on the moon to put the ship up into space again.

LEARNING ACTIVITIES FOR "AIR, PLANES, AND SPACE TRAVEL"

AIR

1. *Observe the presence of air in the soil* · Put some loose soil in a tumbler until it is half-full. Pour water in the tumbler until the tumbler is almost full. Bubbes of air will escape from the soil, showing the presence of air in soil.

2. *Observe the presence of air in water* · Fill a tumbler with cold water, and then set it aside for a few hours. Tiny bubbles of air will appear on the sides of the glass. Air is dissolved in the cold water. When the water becomes warmer, it cannot hold as much air so some of the dissolved air comes out of the water and forms bubbles on the side of the glass.

3. *Observe the presence of air in porous materials* · Drop a piece of brick into a wide-mouthed jar that is three-quarters full of water. Bubbles of air will escape from the tiny pores in the brick.

4. *Determine the percentage of oxygen in air* · Obtain two test tubes the same size. Insert a wad of steel wool down to the bottom of one of the test tubes. Pour some water into each test tube, shake well, and then pour off the water. Put each test tube, mouth down, into a wide-mouthed jar or beaker of water and fasten each test tube with a clamp (Figure 12–1). Have the mouth of each test tube the same distance (about 13 millimeters or ½ inch) below the surface of the water. Let the test tubes stand this way for 24 hours.

Water will have risen up the test tube containing the steel wool. Nothing will have happened in the empty test tube, which serves as a control. Measure the length of the test tube above the surface of the water, and then measure how high the water rose in the test tube. Compare both lengths and you will find that the water has risen about one fifth, or 20 percent of the way up the test tube. Note the rusty appearance of the steel wool. The steel combined with the oxygen in the air inside the test tube to form iron oxide (rust). Since the water rose one fifth of the way up the tube to replace the oxygen, this rising means that about one fifth, or 20 percent, of the air in the tube was oxygen. The rest of the air is mostly nitrogen, with small amounts of inert gases, carbon dioxide, and water vapor.

5. *Observe the presence of carbon dioxide in air* · Obtain some limewater from the drugstore. You can make limewater by obtaining some slaked lime from a hardware store. Place some slaked lime in a bottle, and then fill with water and shake well. Allow the mixture to settle overnight. The clear liquid above the settled material is limewater. Place some lime-

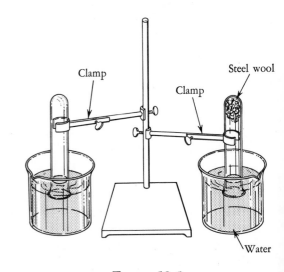

FIGURE 12–1.

ABOUT 20 PERCENT OF THE AIR IN THE TEST TUBE IS OXYGEN.

water in a small glass custard cup and leave the cup exposed to the air for a few hours. The limewater will become milky, showing the presence of carbon dioxide. The carbon dioxide combines with the limewater (which is calcium hydroxide) to form white, chalky calcium carbonate, which is suspended in the solution.

6. *Draw a chalkboard model of the nitrogen cycle* · Draw a diagram of the nitrogen cycle (Figure 12–2). Trace the conversion of free

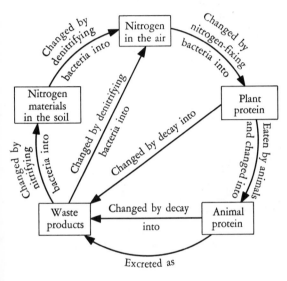

FIGURE 12–2.

DIAGRAM OF THE NITROGEN CYCLE.

nitrogen in the air into nitrogen materials that plants and animals can use, and then trace the conversion of the different nitrogen materials back into free nitrogen again.

7. *Observe the presence of water vapor in air* · Repeat Learning Activity 8 of "Water in the Air," Chapter 11 (p. 383), showing the condensation of water vapor from the air.

8. *Observe the presence of dust in air* · Cut out a piece of white paper to fit the bottom of a pie tin. Coat the paper with Vaseline, put it in the tin, and weight it down with one or two rocks. Put the tin outside on the window-

sill and, after a day or so, note the dust that has been deposited on the paper.

9. *Investigate air pollution* · Have the children list the ways that air is being polluted in your community. Find out what measures your community has taken to control air pollution. Discuss the causes of smog, its effects, and methods of reducing or eliminating it. Read about and report on radioactive fallout and the dangers that may result from an excess of this kind of air pollution.

10. *Draw the layers of the atmosphere* · Make a chart or draw a chalkboard diagram of the five layers of the atmosphere. Include the height of each layer, and show the relative densities of the layers by using different shades of the same colored chalk or crayon.

Turn on the radio late at night and note how much easier it is to tune in distant radio stations than during the day. The sun affects the thickness of the ionosphere. The ionized layers of air that reflects radio broadcasts becomes wider after sunset and narrower when the sun rises.

11. *Observe that air occupies space* · Crumple a dry paper napkin and stuff it into a tumbler so that it will not fall out when the tumbler is held upside down. Now, while holding the tumbler upside down, push the tumbler straight down to the bottom of an aquarium or large glass jar that is filled with water (Figure 12–3). Note that the water does not fill the tumbler. The space in the tumbler is occupied by air. Tilt the tumbler slightly, and you will be able to see air as it escapes from the tumbler in the form of bubbles. Now lift the tumbler straight out of the water. Remove the paper napkin and note that it is still dry.

12. *Observe that air has weight* · Place a pile of books at the edge of a table. Insert a flat stick about 30 centimeters (12 in) long between the books and the table top. Tie one end of a string about 25 centimeters (10 in) long to the stick, tie the other end to

[417

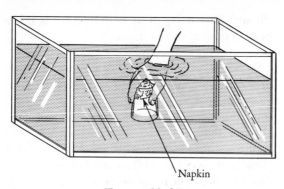

Napkin

FIGURE 12–3.

BECAUSE AIR OCCUPIES SPACE, THE NAPKIN DOES
NOT GET WET.

the middle of a meterstick or yardstick, and slide the meterstick back and forth until it balances (Figure 12–4). Obtain two large, round balloons the same size, and blow them up so they are also the same size when inflated. Tie a string about 15 centimeters (6 in) long around each balloon and hang each balloon near one end of the meterstick at the same distance from the ends. Slide the balloons back and forth until the meterstick balances evenly. Puncture one balloon with a pin. The deflated balloon will not weigh as much as the ballooon that still has air in it, and the meterstick will become unbalanced. (Note: When the balloon bursts, a piece or two of the rubber may be

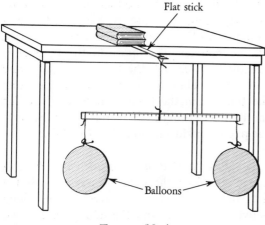

Flat stick

Balloons

FIGURE 12–4.

AIR HAS WEIGHT.

blown off. Be sure to collect these pieces and drape them around the balloon. Otherwise the results will be inaccurate.)

If a sensitive balance is available, weigh a basketball when deflated. Fill the ball with air and weigh it again. The difference in weights is the weight of the air in the ball.

13. *Observe that air exerts pressure* · Fill a tumbler with water. Put a piece of cardboard on top of the tumbler and hold it firmly against the tumbler with the palm of one hand. Grasp the base of the tumbler with the other hand and quickly turn the tumbler upside down (Figure 12–5). Remove the palm of

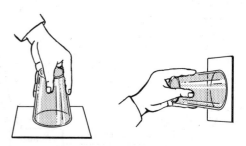

FIGURE 12–5.

AIR EXERTS PRESSURE IN ALL DIRECTIONS.

your hand carefully from below the cardboard, being careful not to jar the cardboard or the tumbler. The cardboard and the water will remain in place. Point out that the water stays in the tumbler because air is exerting a pressure on the cardboard. The pressure of the air against the cardboard is greater than the pressure of the water against the cardboard.

Turn the tumbler sideways and in many other positions. The water will still stay in the tumbler, showing that air exerts pressure in all directions. Point out that the perfect sphere of soap bubbles shows that the air in the bubbles is exerting pressure equally in all directions.

14. *Make a mercury barometer* · Obtain a thick-walled glass tube about 92 centimeters (36 in) long and closed at one end. Place a small funnel in the open end and slowly add

mercury, avoiding the formation of air bubbles, until the tube is filled to the top. Place your finger over the open end of the tube, invert the tube, and place it in a beaker that has about 2½ centimeters (1 in) of mercury in it (Figure 12–6). Do not remove your finger until the open

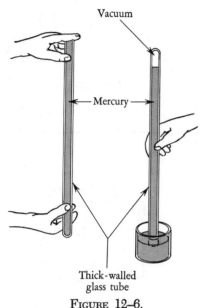

Vacuum

Mercury

Thick-walled
glass tube

FIGURE 12–6.

A HOMEMADE MERCURY BAROMETER.

end of the tube is below the surface of the mercury. When the finger is removed, the mercury will drop until the column of mercury in the tube is about 76 centimeters (30 in) high. This column of mercury is supported by the pressure of the air on the surface of the mercury in the beaker. When the air pressure increases, the mercury is forced higher up the tube. When the air pressure decreases, the mercury in the tube will drop. If properly supported, and if there is a meterstick or yardstick behind or beside it, the tube can be used as an accurate mercury barometer.

15. *Make an aneroid barometer* · Repeat Learning Activity 1 of "Predicting the "Weather," Chapter 11 (p. 387), showing how to make a milk bottle aneroid barometer.

16. *Investigate the effect of altitude on air pressure* · Take an aneroid barometer up and down a steep hill. The higher you go, the lower the air pressure on the surface of the barometer, and the more the pointer will move down. The lower you go, the greater the air pressure, and the more the pointer will move up. The same effect can be produced in an elevator in a tall building.

17. *Observe that air exerts pressure against the sides of a container* · Blow up a sturdy plastic bag and twist its mouth several times. The air exerts pressure against the sides of the bag and inflates it. Squeeze the sides of the bag. Note the pressure of the bag, and of the air inside it, against your fingers.

18. *Observe the effect of adding or removing air on the pressure inside a container* · Blow up a sturdy plastic bag and twist its mouth several times. Note the amount of pressure when you squeeze the sides of the bag. Blow more air into the bag and note the increase in pressure. Now deflate the bag by letting out some of the air. Note the decrease in pressure against the sides of the bag.

19. *Observe the effect of change in size of a container on the air pressure inside it* · Hold a sturdy plastic bag halfway down its sides, blow up the bottom half of the bag, and twist the middle of the bag several times. Let a child squeeze the sides of the bag and note the pressure. Now first twist the mouth of the bag several times, and then untwist the middle. The air inside will spread out through the increased space in the bag. Again note the pressure of the air inside the bag. The air pressure decreases as the size of the container increases.

Blow a little air into the bag and note the small air pressure inside. Now hold the mouth with one hand and use your other hand to push the air inside toward the bottom of the bag. Note how, as the size of the part of the container that holds the air decreases, the air pressure increases.

[419

20. *Observe the effect of heating and cooling on the air pressure in a container* · Snap a balloon over a Pyrex flask or bottle. Place the flask on a hot plate and heat it for 1 minute (Figure 12–7). The air inside the flask and balloon will expand when heated. This expanded air will exert pressure against the sides of the balloon and begin to inflate it. Now place the Pyrex flask into a pan of cold water containing ice cubes. The air inside the flask and balloon will contract when cooled and exert less pressure. As a result, the ballooon will deflate, and it may even be drawn inside the flask because the decreased pressure inside the

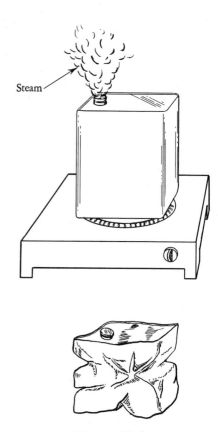

FIGURE 12–8.

WHEN THE AIR PRESSURE INSIDE THE CAN IS DECREASED, THE CAN COLLAPSES.

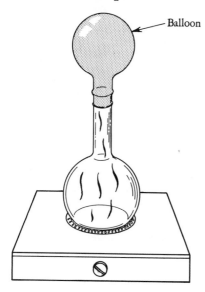

Balloon

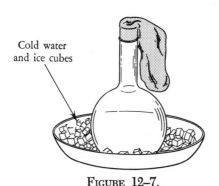

Cold water and ice cubes

FIGURE 12–7.

AIR EXPANDS WHEN HEATED AND CONTRACTS WHEN COOLED.

balloon is now so much less than the normal pressure of the air around the balloon.

21. *Infer that wind is moving air* · Have the children fan themselves with a cardboard and feel the "wind" against their faces. An electric fan will produce an even stronger wind.

22. *Observe how decreasing the air pressure causes a can to collapse* · Obtain a large can that has a metal screw cap. A duplicator fluid can will do. Rinse out the can thoroughly and pour in a cup of water. Place the can on a hot plate (Figure 12–8) and heat the can, with the cap removed, until the water boils and steam comes out of the can for a minute or two. Remove the can, using a pot holder, and quickly

screw the cap tightly on the can. As the can cools, it collapses. Pouring cold water on the can will hasten the collapse. Now put the can to your lips and try to blow it up to its original form.

Note that the steam from the boiling water fills the can, driving out most of the air. When the can was cooled, the steam in the can cooled and condensed, leaving a partial vacuum and decreased air pressure inside. The greater air pressure outside the can pushed inward on the can, making it collapse. Blowing into the can increased the air pressure inside, making the can inflate.

23. *Discover how decreased air pressure operates a soda straw* · Fill a drinking glass with milk and sip the milk with the straw. Observe that sucking on the straw removes some of the air in the straw, producing a partial vacuum inside the straw. The air pressure on the surface of the milk outside the straw is now greater than the air pressure on the milk inside the straw. The air pressure outside the straw, which is now greater, pushes the milk up the straw (Figure 12–9).

24. *Discover how decreased and increased air pressure operates a medicine dropper* · Place a medicine dropper in a tumbler of water and squeeze the bulb. Note the air bubbles leaving the medicine dropper, producing a partial vacuum inside the dropper. Now release the bulb, and water will be forced up the dropper. The air pressure on the surface of the water is now greater than the air pressure inside the dropper, and forces water up into the dropper. Remove the dropper from the tumbler and squeeze the bulb. The squeezing of the bulb compresses the air inside the dropper, and the increased pressure of the compressed air forces the water out of the dropper.

25. *Investigate the effects of increased air pressure* · Place a paper bag on the table so that its mouth extends beyond the table's edge. Put a book on top of at least half the paper bag. Now hold the mouth of the bag closely against your mouth without letting in any air and blow hard into the bag (Figure 12–10).

Paper bag

FIGURE 12–10.

USING INCREASED AIR PRESSURE TO LIFT A BOOK.

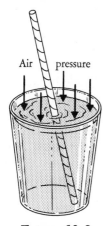

Air pressure

FIGURE 12–9.

USING DECREASED AIR PRESSURE TO SIP SODA FROM A STRAW.

The increased air pressure will lift the book easily. Repeat the experiment, this time using two books.

Roll up a sheet of paper so that it forms a tube. Crumple a piece of paper into a round ball, whose size is such that it just fits inside the tube. Place the ball into one end of the tube and blow hard into this end (Figure 12–11). The ball will be shot out of the tube by the compressed air you created. Point out that air

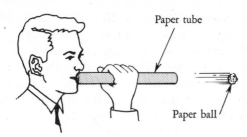

Paper tube

Paper ball

FIGURE 12–11.
HOW AN AIR GUN WORKS.

guns and air hammers are common examples of this method of using compressed air.

Press the pin in the valve of a bicycle or automobile tire and feel the force of the compressed air that is released. Use an air pump to inflate a tire, football, or basketball.

PLANES AND ROCKETS

1. *Investigate Bernoulli's principle* · Place one end of a sheet of paper inside a book so the paper hangs downward. Now hold the top of the book level with your lips and blow over the top of the paper (Figure 12–12). The sheet of paper will rise because the fast-moving stream of air across the top of the paper causes the air pressure on the top surface of the paper to be less than the air pressure underneath the paper.

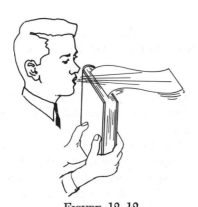

FIGURE 12–12.
USING BERNOULLI'S PRINCIPLE TO MAKE THE PAPER RISE.

2. *Observe the effect of a curved wing on lift* · Obtain a large index card and cut a strip lengthwise about 5 centimeters (2 in) wide. Bend and staple one end of the strip about 2½ centimeters (1 in) away from the

FIGURE 12–13.
A CURVED SURFACE PRODUCES LIFT.

other end (Figure 12–13). Gently pinch the rounded end of the strip until the upper surface is curved and the lower surface is straight. Slip a round pencil through the loop and blow across both the upper and lower surfaces at the same time. A lift will be produced on the wing because the air moves faster across the upper surface than the lower surface, so the air pressure on top of the wing is less than the air pressure underneath.

3. *Observe the effect of wingspread on lift* · Fly two model planes, one with a larger wingspread than the other. The greater the wingspread, the more air passes over and under the wings, and the greater the lift will be.

4. *Investigate angle of attack* · Demonstrate with a model plane that the wing is tilted at a slant so the air can strike the underside of the wing as well. Repeat Learning Activity 2 above, but this time blow against the bottom surface of the wing. The air striking the underside of the wing pushes up on the wing and adds to the lift.

5. *Discover how the propeller produces a thrust* · Examine the propeller of a model plane and observe that the blades are curved in

such a way that they strike as much air as possible, in order to produce the greatest possible thrust. Place a series of round pencils underneath a flat board. Then put a small electric fan (with a long extension cord) on top of the board (Figure 12–14). Turn on the fan. The spinning blades of the fan produce a thrust that makes the fan move.

6. *Investigate Newton's law of action and reaction* · Obtain a plastic bottle, preferably a flat one, and a cork to fit the bottle. Fill the bottle about one-third full of vinegar. Place a teaspoon of baking soda on a small piece of cleansing tissue, wrap the tissue into a roll, and twist the ends. Drop the roll into the bottle, give the bottle one good shake to break up the roll, and push the cork into the bottle firmly, but not too firmly. Immediately place the bottle on three or four round pencils, in the position shown in Figure 12–15. In a very short time the cork will blow out of the bottle, and the bottle itself will move in the direction opposite to that of the cork.

The baking soda reacts with the vinegar to form carbon dioxide gas, which pushes in all directions. When the force is strong enough, the gas blows the cork out of the bottle. As the gas shoots out of the bottle in one direction,

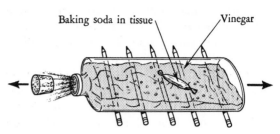

FIGURE 12–15.
ACTION AND REACTION IN A CORKED BOTTLE.

we get an equal but opposite force that moves the bottle in the opposite direction. The bottle moves a shorter distance than the cork because it is heavier than the cork.

The same effect of action and reaction can be seen when a boy on roller skates or seated in a wagon throws an object like a stone. The boy will move in a direction opposite to the stone that is thrown.

7. *Draw models of jet engines* · Draw or make models of the ramjet, turbojet, and turboprop engines, and explain their operation. Show how the jet engines get their thrust from hot gases that, escaping with a great backward force, produce an equal but opposite forward force or thrust.

8. *Make a jet-propelled balloon* · Inflate a narrow balloon and tie a string in a bow around the neck of the balloon. Attach the balloon to a soda straw, using cellophane tape, as shown in Figure 12–16. Run a long wire through the soda straw and attach both ends of

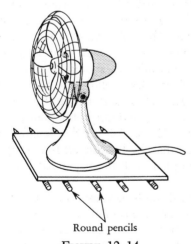

Round pencils
FIGURE 12–14.
THE CURVED BLADES OF THE FAN PRODUCE A THRUST.

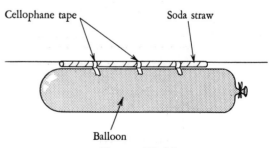

FIGURE 12–16.
MAKING A BALLOON ACT LIKE A JET PLANE.

the wire to opposite parts of the room, keeping the wire horizontal. Now untie the string so that the air can escape. The balloon will be "jet-propelled" across the room.

When the balloon is filled with air and the string is tied around its neck, the balloon does not move because the air pressure inside the balloon is equal in all directions. When the string is untied and air begins to escape from the balloon, the air pressure inside the balloon becomes unequal. The air pressure is now greater on the surface opposite the neck of the balloon because the air pressure on the neck decreases as the air escapes. Therefore the balloon moves in a direction opposite to that of the escaping air.

9. *Observe the effect of drag* · Have a child hold a large cardboard in front of him and run into the wind. The resistance of the air against the cardboard will cause drag and slow down the child's forward motion.

10. *Observe the effect of streamlining* · Bend one end of a large index card all the way over to the other end, and staple the two ends together. The card will have a teardrop shape. Set the card on edge and put a burning candle in front of the pointed end (Figure 12–17). Blow against the rounded end. When the air hits the streamlined card, the air stream divides

Index card

FIGURE 12–17.

STREAMLINING HELPS BLOW OUT THE CANDLE FLAME.

in two, each one traveling smoothly around the card and meeting at the end to blow out the flame. See what happens when you use an unbent card instead.

Tape ribbons to the rear edges of a model plane's wings and hold the plane in front of an electric fan. Now tape ribbons to the top rear of a wood block and hold the block in front of the fan. Compare the way the ribbons flutter in each case.

11. *Examine the parts of a plane* · Have a child bring in a model plane and point out the parts of the plane and their functions. Conduct a field trip to a nearby airport. This trip will give the children an opportunity to observe and study firsthand the different kinds of planes, their parts and functions, the plane instruments and their functions, the way the runways are arranged, the safety devices on the landing field, the control tower, directions for takeoff and landing, the refueling of planes, the loading and unloading of cargo and passengers, and the different kinds of weather instruments.

12. *Discover how a plane takes off and climbs* · Obtain a model of a plane that has movable elevators, rudder, and ailerons. If a plane with such parts is not available, make the parts out of cardboard and attach them firmly with cellophane tape to the tail and wings of the model plane. The rudder part should be able to move to the right and left, and the elevators and ailerons should be able to move up and down. Use cellophane tape to attach four lengths of strong cotton thread to the nose, each wing, and tail of the plane, as shown in Figure 12–18. Adjust the lengths of the threads so that, by holding all four ends in one hand, the plane will be suspended horizontally in the air.

Now push both elevators up, hold the plane in front of an electric fan, and turn on the fan. The air stream will strike the elevators and force the tail down, which swings the nose of the plane up, making it possible for the plane to take off or climb.

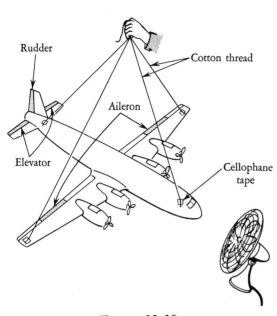

Rudder

Cotton thread

Aileron

Elevator

Cellophane tape

FIGURE 12–18.
SHOWING HOW THE PARTS OF A PLANE WORK.

13. *Discover how a plane dives and lands* · Repeat Activity 12 above, but this time make the elevators tilt down. The air stream will strike the elevators and force the tail up, which swings the nose of the plane down, making it possible for the plane to dive or land.

14. *Discover how a plane turns to the right and to the left* · Repeat Activity 12 above, but this time make the right aileron go up, the left aileron go down, and swing the rudder to the right. The air stream strikes the ailerons and makes the right wing fall and the left wing rise. This action makes the plane roll on its side and turn, or bank, to the right. The air stream also strikes the rudder and makes the nose of the plane turn to the right. Point out that the function of the rudder is to help prevent the plane from yawing, or skidding sideways, when the plane makes its turn.

Repeat the experiment, but this time make the right aileron go down, the left aileron go up, and swing the rudder to the left. The plane will now turn, or bank, to the left.

15. *Illustrate the sound barrier* · Blow up a paper bag. Strike it, causing the bag to burst with a loud noise. Point out that a shock wave was produced that is similar to that of the sound barrier.

16. *Illustrate the heat barrier* · Show how heat can melt a metal by holding a piece of lead (use forceps) in the flame of a Bunsen burner or alcohol lamp. Point out that the tremendous heat produced by the friction of the air moving across the metal parts of the plane may cause the parts to melt.

17. *Observe the action of the helicopter* · Get a model of a helicopter. The spinning pro-

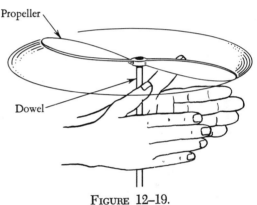

Propeller

Dowel

FIGURE 12–19.
HOW A HELICOPTER PROPELLER WORKS.

peller pushes air downward, producing a reaction or thrust that forces the helicopter upward. Make your own helicopter by gluing a wooden or plastic propeller firmly to the top of a small, round stick or dowel (Figure 12–19). Twirl the stick very rapidly between your hands and then let go. The stick will rise into the air.

SPACE TRAVEL

1. *Discuss early space travel* · Have the children read about and discuss the early space exploration with rockets.

[425

2. Make a model of a multistage rocket · Draw or make a model of a multistage rocket and explain the function of each stage in getting the rocket into space and orbit.

3. Discover why rockets are launched toward the east · Use cellophane tape to attach a small cutout of a rocket to a globe of the earth. Spin the globe from west to east, in the direction of the earth's rotation, and show how the earth's speed of rotation gives the rocket an extra push of about 1600 kilometers (1000 mi) per hour which helps the rocket reach the speed it needs to go into orbit.

4. Discover why a satellite stays in orbit · Repeat Activities 4, 5, and 6 of "The Solar System," Chapter 9 (p. 274). At the same time, explain how a satellite can overcome the earth's gravity and go off into space.

5. Draw satellite orbits · Repeat Learning Activity 2 of "The Solar System," Chapter 9 (p. 273). Draw orbits that vary from almost perfect circles to long, narrow ovals. Locate the apogee and perigee of each orbit.

6. Discuss ways of tracking the satellite · Have the children read about and discuss uses of the telescope and radar to track satellites. Have them also report on the instruments inside the satellites and their function.

7. Collect information about kinds of spacecraft · Have the children write to the Educational Publications Distribution Center, AFEE-1, National Aeronautics and Space Administration (NASA), Washington, D.C. 20546. They will receive *NASA Facts,* which is a periodic bulletin that contains detailed information on the different kinds of spacecraft, their function, what they have studied and measured, and what they have learned. Have the children look for articles on spacecraft published in weekly magazines and in newspapers.

8. Discuss problems of space flight · Have children read about and discuss such problems of space flight as getting enough thrust, escaping the earth's pull of gravity, landing on and leaving the moon or another planet, and returning to and landing on the earth.

9. Discuss problems of astronauts · Have children read about and discuss the problems of survival the astronauts have encountered in space travel. These problems will include the tremendous force of acceleration and deceleration, weightlessness, food and water, sufficient oxygen, disposal of carbon dioxide and of body wastes, heat and cold, bombardment by cosmic rays and other deadly radiations, bombardment by meteors, and mental problems caused by prolonged isolation.

Repeat Learning Activity 2 of "Winds," Chapter 11 (p. 380) to show how making one side of the space ship black will keep the ship warm whereas making the other side of the space ship white or silvery will keep the ship cool.

BIBLIOGRAPHY FOR "AIR, PLANES, AND SPACE TRAVEL"

BERGER, MELVIN. *The New Air Book.* New York: Thomas Y. Crowell, 1974. 130 pp.

BRANLEY, FRANKLYN M. *A Book of Flying Saucers for You.* New York: Thomas Y. Crowell, 1973. 74 pp.

———. *Gravity Is a Mystery.* New York: Thomas Y. Crowell, 1970. 34 pp.

————. *Man in Space to the Moon.* New York: Thomas Y. Crowell, 1970. 38 pp.

BREWER, A. C., and NELL GARLAND. *Exploring and Understanding Air.* Westchester, Ill.: Benefic Press, 1970. 96 pp.

CARLISLE, NORMAN. *Satellites, Servants of Man.* Philadelphia: J. B. Lippincott, 1971. 96 pp.

CHESTER, MICHAEL. *Let's Go on a Space Shuttle.* New York: G. P. Putnam's Sons, 1976. 48 pp.

————. *Let's Stop Air Pollution.* New York: G. P. Putnam's Sons, 1968. 48 pp.

CHROMIE, WILLIAM. *Skylab: The Story of Man's First Space Station.* New York: McKay, 1976. 146 pp.

COLBY, C. B. *Space Age Spinoffs.* New York: Coward, McGann & Geoghegan, 1972. 48 pp.

CORBETT, SCOTT. *What Makes a Plane Fly?* Boston: Little, Brown, 1967. 58 pp.

DEVERE, NICHOLAS. *The Book of Fantastic Planes.* New York: Western Pub., 1974. 32 pp.

DWIGGINS, DON. *Riders of the Winds—The Story of Ballooning.* New York: Hawthorne Books, 1973. 180 pp.

————. *The Sky Is Yours—You and the World of Flight.* Chicago: Childrens Press, 1973. 80 pp.

————. *Why Kites Fly: The Story of the Wind at Work.* Chicago: Childrens Press, 1976. 32 pp.

ELLIOT, SARAH. *Our Dirty Air.* New York: Julian Messner, 1971. 64 pp.

ELTING, MARY, and JUDITH STEIGLER. *Helicopters at Work.* Irvington-on-the-Hudson, New York: Harvey House, 1972. 96 pp.

ENGLE, ELOISE. *Parachutes: How They Work.* New York: G. P. Putnam's Sons, 1972. 92 pp.

FERAVOLO, ROCCO. *Around the World in Ninety Minutes.* New York: Lothrop, Lee & Shepard, 1968. 48 pp.

FRANCHERE, RUTH. *The Wright Brothers.* New York: Thomas Y. Crowell, 1974. 40 pp.

FREEMAN, IRA M. *The Look-It-Up Book of Space.* New York: Random House, 1969. 130 pp.

FREEMAN, MAE. *When Air Moves.* New York: McGraw-Hill, 1968. 46 pp.

GUTNIK, MARTIN. *Ecology and Pollution: Air.* Chicago: Childrens Press, 1973. 48 pp.

HENDRICKSON, WALTER. *Manned Spacecraft to Mars and Venus.* New York: G. P. Putnam's Sons, 1975. 128 pp.

————. *What's Going on in Space?* Irvington-on-the-Hudson, N.Y.: Harvey House, 1968. 48 pp.

KALINA, SIGMUND. *Air, the Invisible Ocean.* New York: Lothrop, Lee & Shepard, 1973. 64 pp.

KETTLEKAMP, LARRY. *Investigating UFO's.* New York: William Morrow, 1971. 96 pp.

KNIGHT, DAVID. *Those Mysterious UFO's.* New York: Parents' Magazine, 1975. 64 pp.

LANDT, DENNIS. *Catch the Wind: A Book of Windmills and Windpower.* New York: Four Winds Press, 1976. 114 pp.

LAYCOCK, GEORGE. *Air Pollution.* New York: Grossett & Dunlap, 1972. 73 pp.

LUKASHOK, ALVIN. *Communication Satellites: How They Work.* New York: G. P. Putnam's Sons, 1967. 160 pp.

MAY, JULIAN. *Astronautics.* Chicago: Follett, 1968. 32 pp.

——. *Rockets.* Chicago: Follett, 1967. 32 pp.

McGONAGLE, BOB, and MARQUITE McGONAGLE. *Careers in Aviation in the Sky and on the Ground.* New York: Lothrop, Lee & Shepard, 1975. 128 pp.

PERERA, THOMAS, and WALLACE ORLOWSKY. *Who Will Clean the Air?* New York: Coward, McCann and Geoghegan, 1971. 46 pp.

POSIN, DANIEL Q. *Exploring and Understanding Rockets and Satellites.* Westchester, Ill.: Benefic Press, 1967. 96 pp.

ROSS, FRANK. *Flying Paper Airplane Models.* New York: Lothrop, Lee & Shepard, 1975. 128 pp.

RYAN, PETER. *UFO's and Other Worlds.* New York: Puffin, 1975. 48 pp.

SCHIFF, BARRY. *Flying: A Guide to Principles and Practice.* New York: Western Pub., 1971. 160 pp.

SHEPHERD, WALTER. *How Airplanes Fly.* New York: Thomas Y. Crowell, 1974. 48 pp.

SMITH, NORMAN. *The Atmosphere.* New York: Four Winds Press, 1975. 42 pp.

URQUHART, DAVID. *The Airplane and How It Works.* New York: Henry Z. Walck, 1973. 48 pp.

VICTOR, EDWARD. *Planes and Rockets.* Chicago: Follett, 1965. 32 pp.

WEISS, HARVEY. *Model Airplanes and How to Build Them.* New York: Thomas Y. Crowell, 1975. 90 pp.

LIVING THINGS

CHAPTER 13A

PLANTS

CLASSIFICATION OF PLANTS

I. CLASSIFYING LIVING THINGS

A. All living things are grouped into main divisions, called **kingdoms.**
B. These kingdoms are subdivided into major groups called **phyla.**
  1. Phyla are very large groups of living things.
  2. All the members of a phylum have certain broad similarities in structure and in other characteristics.
C. The phyla are subdivided into smaller groups called **classes,** the classes into **orders,** the orders into **families,** the families into **genera,** the genera into **species,** and the species into **varieties.**
  1. A class is a finer subdivision of a phylum.
  2. An order is one of several groups within a class.
  3. A family is a group within an order.
  4. A genus is a smaller group within a family.
  5. A species is a group of very closely related living things.
  6. A variety is an individual of a species that varies slightly from other individuals in the same species, but not enough to be considered a separate species.
D. The further the phyla are subdivided into smaller groups, the greater the similarity there is among the members that make up each group.

E. When classifying living things, scientists give each phylum and its subgroups a scientific name made up of Latin words or words that have been Latinized.
  1. This scientific naming makes the classification of each living thing definite, so that there can be no duplication.
  2. The scientific name also describes the living thing well enough so that it can be readily identified.
  3. The scientific name also helps show relationships between the different living things.
  4. Latin is a universal language, so the names have the same meaning to scientists all over the world.
F. Until recently, scientists put all living things into just two kingdoms: the **plant kingdom** and the **animal kingdom.**
G. Today they feel that this classification is too broad and confusing.
  1. Many living things, especially the very tiny ones, do not fit very well into either kingdom.
  2. Some are like plants, some are like animals, some have the characteristics of plants and animals, and some seem to be neither plants nor animals.
  3. Scientists now put all these hard-to-classify living things into a separate kingdom, called the **protista kingdom.**
  4. Some scientists think this third kingdom

[431

is too much of a catch-all and break it up into the **protista kingdom** and the **monera kingdom.**

H. The new classification makes it easier to define each kingdom sharply and to distinguish one clearly from the others.

II. THE PLANT KINGDOM

A. The plant kingdom, scientifically called the **plantae kingdom** or **metaphyta kingdom,** is divided into just 2 major phyla: the **byrophytes** and the **tracheophytes.**

B. The plant kingdom is also commonly divided into two broad groups: plants that produce seeds, and plants that do not produce seeds.

C. Plants are the living things that can make their own food.

D. To make its own food, a plant needs a green material called **chlorophyll.**

III. THE BRYOPHYTES

A. The bryophytes are members of the plant phylum called **Bryophyta.**

B. The bryophytes are very simple plants.
1. They have simple leaves, but no true roots and stems.
2. However, they do have rootlike and stemlike parts.
3. They do not produce flowers, fruits, and seeds.

C. They have chlorophyll, are colored green, and can make their own food.

D. They are small plants, but they are found all over the world.

E. They live mostly on land.

F. Mosses and liverworts belong to this phylum.

IV. THE TRACHEOPHYTES

A. The tracheophytes are members of the plant phylum called **Tracheophyta.**

B. They have chlorophyll, are colored green, and can make their own food.

C. There are very basic differences between the tracheophytes and the bryophytes.

1. Tracheophytes have true roots, stems, and leaves.
2. Tracheophytes have a continuous system of tubes running through their roots, stems, and leaves.
3. The tubes let water and food move from one place in the plant to another.

D. Ferns, horsetails, and club mosses belong to this phylum.
1. They have roots, stems, and leaves, but not flowers, fruits, and seeds.
2. They range from small mosslike plants to plants the size of small trees.

E. All the seed plants are also included in this phylum.
1. Seed plants produce flowers, fruits, and seeds.
2. All trees, shrubs, crop plants and vegetables, garden and wild flowers, weeds, and grasses are seed plants.
3. They grow in soil and in fresh water.
4. The smallest seed plants are floating duckweeds, which are about 1 centimeter (¼ in) across.
5. The largest are the giant sequoias and the redwoods of California, which can be over 90 meters (300 ft) tall.

F. Scientists divide seed plants into two groups: **angiosperms** and **gymnosperms.**
1. The seeds of angiosperms are enclosed in a protective coat, called a **fruit.**
2. Gymnosperm seeds are unprotected.

V. GYMNOSPERMS

A. Gymnosperms are older seed plants than the angiosperms.

B. They are also called **conifers** because they produce woody cones.
1. The cone is the "fruit" of the conifers, and is made up of scales.
2. The unprotected seed lies on the scales.

C. Examples of conifers include pine, spruce, fir, cedar, bald cypress, redwood, hemlock, yew, and larch trees.

D. Conifer leaves are either in the form of needles or flat scales.
1. Conifers keep their leaves for two to five years, except the bald cypress and larch

trees, which lose their needles each autumn.

2. Because their leaves stay green all winter, conifers are also called evergreen trees.

3. When new leaves grow, they appear in the spring.

E. The trunk of the conifers does not divide, but grows tall and straight, and most of the branches are usually found nearer the top of the trunk.

F. Conifers give off a sticky substance, called **resin,** and this resin is characteristic of conifers only.

G. The wood of conifers is usually soft, and is widely used for lumber and making paper.

H. Conifers are also used to stop the force of the wind around farms, and as decorative trees in parks and yards.

VI. ANGIOSPERMS

A. Angiosperms are seed plants, producing flowers that form fruits with seeds inside them.

B. This group includes all garden and wild flowers, weeds, plants that produce crops and vegetables, grasses, cereal grains, and all trees and shrubs that lose their leaves in the autumn.

C. They have broad, flat leaves, which they lose each year.

1. This is the reason why they are called **deciduous** plants.

2. The word deciduous comes from the Latin word "to fall."

D. Angiosperm trees have a trunk that may divide into two, and their branches begin rather low on the trunk.

E. The angiosperms, or flowering plants, are divided into two large groups: the **monocotyledons** or **monocots,** and the **dicotyledons** or **dicots.**

1. A **cotyledon** is a special kind of leaf found in the seed.

2. The cotyledon has food stored in it, which feeds and nourishes the tiny plant inside the seed when the seed sprouts and grows into a new plant.

3. Monocotyledon plants produce seeds that have just one of these seed leaves, and dicotyledon plants produce seeds with two seed leaves in them.

4. Most of the monocotyledons are small, and include such plants as the lily, tulip, iris, onion, the cereal grains, and the coconut and date palms.

5. The dicotyledons include most of our flowers, vegetables, shrubs, and flowering trees.

VII. HERBACEOUS AND WOODY PLANTS

A. Scientists also divide plants into two broad groups: **herbaceous** and **woody** plants.

B. A herbaceous plant is any plant with a soft stem, which may or may not be green.

1. This soft stem lasts for only one growing season, and then dies to the ground.

2. Flowers, common weeds, garden vegetables, and the cereal grains are all herbaceous plants.

C. A woody plant has a hard stem, and is usually colored brown.

1. This hard stem does not die, but continues to grow year after year.

2. The stem grows both longer and wider each year.

3. Examples of woody plants include trees, shrubs, and such vines as the wild grape and poison ivy.

VIII. PARTS OF A FLOWERING SEED PLANT

A. Every part of a flowering seed plant has special functions.

B. The roots, stems, and leaves of flowering seed plants carry out all the processes the plants need to live, except that of producing seeds.

C. The root has the following functions.

1. It holds the plant firmly in the ground.

2. It takes in water and minerals from the soil and conducts them to the stem for delivery to the leaves.

[433

3. Many roots store food for the plant.

D. The stem has the following functions.

1. It produces the leaves and holds them up to the sunlight.
2. It conducts water and minerals from the roots to the leaves.
3. It also carries the food, which the leaves make, down to the roots.
4. Some stems store food for the plant.

E. The leaf, which is one of the most important parts of the plant, has the following functions.

1. It makes the food that the plant needs to live.

2. It lets gases in the air, such as carbon dioxide and oxygen, enter and leave the plant.
3. It allows water in the plant to escape into the air.

F. The flower is the special part of the plant that produces seeds from which new plants can grow.

1. Flowers produce fruits with seeds inside them.
2. The fruit is the protective covering for the seed.
3. The seed is the part of the plant that can grow into a new plant.

ROOTS

I. DEFINITION AND KINDS OF ROOTS

A. The roots are the part of the plant that grows downward into the ground.

1. When a seed first begins to grow, a root grows rapidly and pushes its way into the soil.
2. This root is called the **primary root.**
3. After a while, **secondary roots** branch out from the primary root, first near the top of the primary root, and then farther down.
4. The roots keep branching and rebranching until a complete root system is formed.

B. There are two main kinds of root systems: the **taproot system** and the **diffuse root system.**

C. In the taproot system, the primary root grows until it is the largest root in the root system.

1. This large root is called the **taproot.**
2. Much smaller secondary roots grow from this large taproot.
3. Dandelions and carrots have taproots.

D. In the diffuse root system, the primary root lives only for a short time.

1. The secondary roots then continue to grow as a cluster at the base of the stem.

2. These secondary roots are all thin, have the same size, and are called **fibrous roots.**
3. Beans, corn, and grasses have fibrous roots.

E. Some taproots and fibrous roots store food for the plant and become large.

1. These large roots are called **fleshy roots.**
2. Beets, carrots, and radishes are examples of fleshy taproots.
3. Dahlias and sweet potatoes are examples of fleshy fibrous roots.

F. In some plants, roots grow from the stems or leaves of the plant.

1. These kinds of roots are called **adventitious roots.**
2. The tomato, cucumber, and squash plants form adventitious roots when their stems touch the ground.
3. The leaves of the begonia, sedum, and sansevieria plants form adventitious roots when placed in the soil.

G. Some plants send out roots from their stems just above the ground.

1. These roots are a special kind of adventitious root, called **prop roots** or **brace roots.**
2. They grow into the ground and help hold the plant upright.

3. The corn plant is an example of a plant with prop or brace roots.

H. Climbing plants, such as English ivy, poison ivy, and tropical orchids, send out roots from their stems.
   1. These roots are also a special kind of adventitious root, called **aerial roots.**
   2. The aerial roots grow in the air, clinging to a wall or tree and holding the stem firmly in place.

II. THE STRUCTURE OF THE ROOT

A. A short distance behind the tip of each root are many tiny, fuzzy **root hairs.**
   1. These root hairs take in, or absorb, water and dissolved minerals from the soil.
   2. As the root moves downward into the soil, new root hairs form near the tip, and the older root hairs wither and die.
B. At the tip of the root is the **root cap,** which protects the delicate end of the root.
C. The length of the root varies, according to the needs of the plant and conditions of the environment.
   1. The taproot of the mesquite plant can grow 12 meters (40 ft) down into the desert to reach a water supply.
   2. The diffuse roots of a cactus plant cover large areas just below the surface of the ground to absorb quickly the water from infrequent rains.
   3. The eggplant and squash roots grow downward about 2 meters (7 ft) and spread sideways from 1 to 6 meters (3 to 20 ft).

III. THE FUNCTIONS OF ROOTS

A. The roots absorb, or take in, water and dissolved minerals from the soil, and send them to the stem and up into the leaves.
   1. The water and dissolved minerals are absorbed by the root hairs.
   2. The root hairs give off an acid that helps dissolve the minerals in the soil.
B. The roots also help hold the plant firmly in place.
C. Some roots, such as the beet, carrot, sweet potato, and dahlia, help store food for the plant.
D. Some roots, such as the sweet potato and dahlia, can produce new plants.
E. Roots adapt to the needs of the plant and conditions of the environment.

IV. USE OF ROOTS

A. Some roots, such as the carrot, turnip, parsnip, radish, beet, and sweet potato, are used for food.
B. Some roots, such as the horseradish, are used for seasoning foods.
C. Some roots, such as sassafras, ginger, licorice, and mandrake, are used for medicines.
D. Some roots, such as licorice and ginger, are used in making candy.
E. The roots of the madder and yellowwood trees are used to make dyes.

STEMS

I. DEFINITION AND KINDS OF STEMS

A. The stem of a plant is the part of the plant between the roots and the leaves.
B. Stems may be found above the ground, below the ground, or both above and below the ground.
C. There are two basic kinds of stems: **monocotyledon stems** and **dicotyledon stems.**

D. A plant with a monocotyledon stem grows from a seed with only one **cotyledon** or **seed leaf** in it.
   1. Monocotyledon plants, or monocots, can usually be recognized by their narrow, smooth-edged, parallel-veined leaves.
   2. The iris, orchids, lilies, corn, grasses, and palms are examples of monocotyledon plants.

[435

E. A plant with a dicotyledon stem grows from a seed with two cotyledons or seed leaves in it.
 1. Dicotyledon plants, or dicots, can usually be recognized by their broad, irregularly shaped, spread-veined leaves.
 2. The tomato, geranium, buttercup, bean, rose, and all woody trees and shrubs are examples of dicotyledon plants.

F. The trunk of a tree is actually the stem of the plant.
 1. The trunk of the palm tree is an example of a giant monocotyledon stem.
 2. The trunk of the oak or the elm tree is an example of a giant dicotyledon stem.

G. Scientists also classify stems as **herbaceous stems** and **woody stems.**

H. Herbaceous stems are usually soft and green, and have no woody tissue in them.
 1. They grow longer, but not thicker, and live only one season.
 2. The stems of tomatoes, beans, peas, corn, grasses, and most annual flowers are herbaceous stems.

I. Woody stems are brown and stiff, and have woody tissue in them.
 1. They grow both longer and thicker, form branches, and live season after season.
 2. The stems of trees and most shrubs are woody stems.

J. A stem that grows above the ground is called an **aerial stem.**
 1. Aerial stems vary in length, ranging from less than 2½ centimeters (1 in) to more than 30 meters (98 ft).
 2. There are four main groups of aerial stems: **shortened stems, creeping stems, climbing stems,** and **erect stems.**

K. Shortened stems are very small stems.
 1. Sometimes they are so short that they seem to be missing from the plant.
 2. The dandelion, primrose, and carrot all have shortened stems.
 3. Their very short, flat, circular stems can be seen growing just above the roots.
 4. Plants with shortened stems need open places to grow, where they can get lots of light.

L. Creeping stems are long and slender, and stay close to the ground.
 1. These stems do not have woody tissues and are weak, so they grow along the surface of the ground.
 2. The stems are also called **runners** or **stolons.**
 3. The strawberry plant and creeping bent grass have creeping stems.
 4. Plants with creeping stems also need open places to grow, where they can get lots of light.

M. Climbing stems are thin and very long.
 1. They do not have woody tissues and are weak, so they grow by wrapping themselves around and around a tall object.
 2. The ivy, morning glory, and sweet potato all have climbing stems.

N. Erect stems stand above the ground by themselves.
 1. They may be either a few centimeters or inches tall or very many meters or feet high.
 2. They may be either herbaceous or woody.
 3. Trees, shrubs, and most garden flowers have erect stems.

O. A stem that grows below the ground is called an **underground stem.**
 1. Because they are located underground, most persons do not usually think of them as stems.
 2. There are four main groups of underground stems: **rhizomes, tubers, bulbs,** and **corms.**

P. Rhizomes are long, underground stems that grow horizontally close to the surface of the ground.
 1. Some rhizomes are thick and fleshy, and filled with food; examples are the rhizomes of the iris, the lily of the valley, and the trillium.
 2. Other rhizomes are thin, such as those of quack grass and other grasses.

Q. Tubers are the enlarged tips of rhizomes with food stored in them.
 1. The white potato is an example of a tuber.

2. The "eyes" of the potato are really buds from which new growth begins.

R. A bulb is made up of a stem shortened to the size of a disk, surrounded by thick, fleshy, scalelike leaves.

1. The leaves have food stored in them.

2. The hyacinth, tulip, daffodil, and onion are examples of bulbs.

S. A corm is different from a bulb only in that most of it is stem.

1. This stem is surrounded by thin, scalelike leaves.

2. The crocus and gladiolus are examples of corms.

II. EXTERNAL STRUCTURE OF A WOODY (DICOTYLEDON) STEM

A. The bare, winter twig of a tree is an excellent example of a woody stem.

B. The twig has **buds** on it.

1. Each bud is a place on the twig where a new stem, leaves, and flowers can grow.

2. In cold climates the delicate buds are protected by overlapping **bud scales.**

C. Most twigs have a **terminal bud** at their tip.

D. Along the sides of the twig are **lateral buds,** from which branches may grow.

E. Along the twig there are also oval, circular, or shield-shaped **leaf scars,** which mark the spots where leaf stalks were attached during previous seasons.

F. The **node** is a point on the leaf scar where leaves or branches were produced by the stem.

G. Also along the twig there are rings circling the twig, called **bud-scale scars.**

1. These bud-scale scars show the exact locations of the terminal buds during previous seasons.

2. By starting at the present terminal bud and counting the number of bud-scale scars along the twig, one can find out the exact age of the twig.

H. Some twigs have thorns, which help in identifying the plant.

1. Some thorns are short and broad, others

are long and pointed, and still others are branched.

2. The thorns help protect the twigs.

I. Stems grow in length by forming new growth at their tips, or, in some cases, at their nodes or sides.

III. INTERNAL STRUCTURE OF A WOODY (DICOTYLEDON) PLANT

A. There are three distinct regions inside the branch or trunk of a woody tree: the **bark,** the **wood,** and the **pith** in the center.

B. The bark is the outer covering of the stem.

1. The bark has two parts: the outer and the inner part.

2. The outer bark protects the stem from injury, from disease, and from losing water.

3. The inner part of the bark conducts the food made by the leaves downward to the roots.

C. Sometimes bark-chewing animals, such as beavers, porcupines, deer, and horses, remove a circular section of the bark all the way around a tree.

1. The removal of bark in this way is called **girdling.**

2. Girdling will kill a tree because food cannot get down to the roots.

D. The wood of the stem is made up of hollow tubes, which conduct water and dissolved minerals upward from the roots to the leaves.

1. In an old stem there are often two kinds of wood: the **sapwood** and the **hardwood.**

2. The sapwood is live wood, and conducts water and dissolved minerals up from the roots to the leaves.

3. The sapwood contains the liquid sap of the tree.

4. The hardwood is dead wood, and its only use is to support the tree.

5. The hardwood is the part of the tree that man uses to make furniture and other articles.

E. The pith is in the center of the stem.

1. In an old, woody stem the pith is hardly

[437

noticeable, but in a young stem, because there is still little wood in it, the pith seems to be quite large and serves as a place to store food.

2. However, the size of the pith is the same in both cases because the pith never grows larger.

3. Regardless of how large a tree becomes, the pith never grows larger than the size it was during the first year of the stem's growth.

F. Between the bark and the wood of a stem there is a fourth region, called the **cambium,** which is made up of a very thin layer of delicate tissue.

1. Each spring and summer the cambium forms new wood and new inner bark for the stem.

2. As a result, each year a new layer of wood is added to the stem.

3. This new layer of wood forms a circle or ring, called an **annual ring,** inside the stem.

4. This formation of layers makes it possible to estimate the age of a tree by counting the number of annual rings in a cross section of a tree trunk or stem.

IV. THE STRUCTURE OF A HERBACEOUS STEM

A. A monocotyledon herbaceous stem has a hard, outer covering called a **rind,** and a dicotyledon herbaceous stem has a thin skin called an **epidermis.**

B. The monocotyledon herbaceous stem does not have a cambium, but the dicotyledon herbaceous stem has a cambium.

C. Because both stems live only one year, the stems are usually long and thin.

D. The bundles of hollow tubes inside a monocotyledon herbaceous stem are scattered at random inside the stem; however, in a dicotyledon herbaceous stem, the bundles of hollow tubes are arranged regularly in a circle inside the stem.

V. THE FUNCTIONS OF STEMS

A. Stems conduct water and dissolved minerals upward from the roots to the leaves.

B. Stems also conduct food from the leaves downward to the roots.

C. The stem produces and displays the leaves so that they receive the sunlight they need.

D. Most stems support the plant and hold it erect.

E. Green herbaceous stems can make food for the plant.

F. Some stems, like the potato, store food for the plant.

G. Some aerial stems, such as the coleus, philodendron, strawberry, and black raspberry, can grow new plants.

H. Most underground stems can grow new plants.

VI. USES OF STEMS

A. The potato, asparagus, and celery are used for food.

B. The sap of the maple tree and the juice of the sugar cane produce sugar.

C. Cinnamon bark is used to make spice for flavoring.

D. Rubber is made from the sap of the rubber tree.

E. The stem of the flax plant is used to make linen.

F. The cinchona bark produces quinine, which is used to treat malaria.

G. The bark of the cherry tree is used for cough syrups.

H. Camphor comes from the laurel tree, and witch hazel comes from the witch hazel shrub.

I. Ropes and all kinds of string are made from the fibers of hemp and other plants.

J. The bark of many trees is used to make dyes.

K. Turpentine from the pine tree is used in paint and varnish.

L. The wood of trees is used for making lumber, furniture, paper, telegraph and telephone poles, piles for piers, parts of machines, and wooden boxes, baskets, and barrels. Some people use wood for heating their houses and cooking their food.

LEAVES

I. PARTS OF A LEAF

  A. A leaf has two main parts: the **blade** and the **petiole.**
    1. The blade is the flat, thin, green part of the leaf.
    2. The petiole is the stalk of the leaf, and is attached to the stem of the plant at a node.
    3. Some leaves do not have a petiole, but are fastened directly to the plant stem.
  B. The blade of the leaf has **veins** in it.
    1. The veins are tiny, hollow tubes that carry water, dissolved minerals, and food between the leaf and the stem.
    2. The veins also help strengthen the leaf and make it firm.
    3. Leaves that do not have a petiole (stalk) are fastened directly to the stem by the veins.
  C. There are three main patterns in which the veins of a leaf are arranged: **palmate, pinnate,** and **parallel** patterns.
  D. In the palmate vein pattern, there are a few large veins that start at the tip of the petiole and spread out very much like the outstretched fingers of your hand.
    1. Smaller veins, called **veinlets,** then branch out from these large veins to all parts of the leaf.
    2. The geranium, maple, and sycamore leaves have palmate vein patterns.
  E. In the pinnate vein pattern, there is just one large vein, called a **midrib.**
    1. Smaller veins (veinlets) branch out on each side of the midrib, giving the same effect or appearance as the arrangement in a feather.
    2. The elm and willow leaves have pinnate vein patterns.
  F. In the parallel vein pattern, there are many large veins running parallel, or side by side, from the bottom of the leaf to its tip.
    1. Parallel vein patterns are found in the leaves of the lily, iris, and the grasses.

    2. Parallel veins are found mostly in the leaves of monocotyledon plants, whose seeds have only one seed leaf (cotyledon).

II. KINDS AND SHAPES OF LEAVES

  A. The size and shape of a leaf is tied up with the arrangement of the veins in the leaf.
    1. Leaves with parallel veins are long and thin.
    2. Leaves with pinnate veins are shorter and wider than those with parallel veins.
    3. Leaves with palmate veins are usually broad.
  B. Leaves have different kinds of edges.
    1. Some edges are smooth, like the leaves of the willow, redbud, and magnolia.
    2. Some edges are toothed, like the leaves of the elm.
    3. Some leaves have lobes, or fingerlike projections, like the leaves of the maple.
  C. If the blade of a leaf is all in one piece, it is called a **simple leaf.**
    1. It is still a simple leaf, even if the leaf is lobed or greatly indented.
    2. Maple, oak, elm, and apple leaves are simple leaves.
  D. If the blade of the leaf is divided into three or more separate parts, called **leaflets,** the leaf is called a **compound leaf.**
    1. Clover, horse chestnut, locust, ash, and strawberry leaves are compound leaves.
    2. When the leaflets spread out or radiate from a single common point, as in the horse chestnut and the clover, the leaf is called a **palmately compound leaf.**
    3. When the leaflets are arranged on each side of the midrib, or opposite each other, as in the ash and the pea, the leaf is called a **pinnately compound leaf.**
  E. The leaves of the evergreen trees are different from other leaves.
    1. In evergreens, such as the pine and the spruce, the leaves are very thin and like needles.

2. In evergreens, such as the cedar, the leaves are like scales.

III. THE LEAF AND PHOTOSYNTHESIS

A. The main function of the leaf is to make food for the plant.
B. Only green plants are able to make their own food.
  1. Green plants have a green material in the leaf, called **chlorophyll.**
  2. Chlorophyll gives the leaf its green color.
  3. Chlorophyll also makes it possible for the leaf to make food for the plant.
C. The leaf uses two materials to make food: **water** and **carbon dioxide.**
D. The water comes from the ground, together with dissolved minerals, passing into the roots, up the stem, and into the leaf.
E. Carbon dioxide is a gas in the air.
  1. There are many tiny openings, called **stomata,** in the leaf, especially in the underside of the leaf.
  2. The carbon dioxide gas in the air passes through these openings (stomata) into the leaf.
F. By using the energy of sunlight, the chlorophyll in the leaf makes it possible for the carbon dioxide and water to combine and form a sugar, called **glucose,** and **oxygen gas.**
G. This food-making process in the plant is called **photosynthesis.**
  1. "Photo" means "light."
  2. "Synthesis" means "putting together."
H. The leaf changes the sugar (glucose) to starch, either immediately or soon afterward.
I. The leaf also changes some of the sugar into fats and proteins.
J. The food made by the leaf then is carried to the stem and the roots for use or for storage.
K. Oxygen gas is a waste product of photosynthesis, and is given off into the air through the stomata of the leaf.

L. Green stems that have chlorophyll in them can also make food for the plant.

IV. THE LEAF AND TRANSPIRATION

A. Although the plant needs water to make food and for other uses, the plant usually takes in more water than it needs.
B. The excess water passes through the stomata into air as water vapor.
  1. This evaporation of water from the plant is called **transpiration.**
  2. The amount of water that a plant gives off by transpiration is very great.
  3. A sunflower gives off 1 liter (1 qt) of water a day.
  4. An average-sized tree can give off as much as 47 liters (50 qt) of water a day during the summer.
C. Tiny cells, called **guard cells,** control the amount of water that passes out of the leaf.
  1. Each one of the stomata is surrounded by two of these guard cells.
  2. Usually the guard cells keep the stomata wide open, allowing water to leave the plant freely.
  3. But, when the plant does not have enough water and is wilting, the guard cells make the stomata smaller, which slows down the evaporation of water from the leaf.
D. Although transpiration takes place mostly in the leaves, other parts of the plant can allow transpiration to take place as well.

V. OTHER FUNCTIONS OF THE LEAF

A. The leaf helps the plant digest the food and change the food into the energy it needs to live and grow.
B. The leaf helps the plant remove waste materials.
C. Some leaves, such as the sedum, sansevieria, and African violet, can grow new plants.

VI. SOME LEAVES CHANGE COLOR IN THE FALL

A. During the late spring and summer the

leaves keep making chlorophyll and stay green.

B. In the fall, when it becomes cold enough, the leaves stop making chlorophyll, and the green color in the leaves disappears.

C. The hidden yellow and orange colors in some of the leaves now begin to appear.

D. The cool weather and the increase in the amount of moisture in the air also produce red colors in other leaves.

E. When the weather becomes still colder, the leaves die and turn brown, and then fall to the ground.

VII. Uses of Leaves

A. Some leaves are used for food.
1. The leaves of the lettuce, cabbage, spinach, endive, parsley, and kale are eaten by man.
2. Tea leaves are used to make a beverage.
3. The leaves of spearmint, peppermint, sage, and thyme are used for spices and flavoring.

B. Tobacco leaves are used for smoking.

C. Leaves, such as palm and grass, are used to cover the roofs of the homes of natives in the tropics.

FLOWERS

I. Definition and Parts of a Flower

A. The flower is a special part of a plant that produces new plants of the same kind.
1. The flower lives for a short time only, and then parts of the flower become a fruit.
2. The fruit has seeds in it, and the seeds produce the new plants.

B. The large, flattened part of the stalk that holds the flower is called the **receptacle.**

C. Most flowers have four parts: **sepals, petals, stamens,** and **pistil.**

D. Sepals are the thin, green, leaflike parts on the outside of the flower.
1. They cover and protect the flower bud.
2. When the bud opens, the sepals separate and fold back.
3. They then support and protect the open flower.
4. All together the sepals are called the **calyx** of the flower.

E. Inside the sepals (calyx) are the petals of the flower.
1. The petals are usually larger than the sepals, and are brightly colored.
2. All together the petals are called the **corolla** of the flower.
3. At the base of the petals there are usually little pockets or cups of a sweet liquid, called **nectar,** which is attractive to bees and other insects.

F. In some flowers, like the tulip and the lily, both the sepals and the petals are the same color.

G. Inside the petals, and usually grouped in a ring around the center of the flower, are the stamens.
1. The stamens are the male part of the flower.
2. There are two parts to a stamen: the **filament** and the **anther.**
3. The filament is the thin stalk or stem of the stamen.
4. The anther is on top of the filament, and is usually knobby or boxlike.
5. The anther produces a yellow or reddish powder called **pollen.**

H. In the center of the flower, usually surrounded by the stamens, is the pistil.
1. The pistil is the female part of the flower.
2. There are three parts to a pistil: the **stigma,** the **style,** and the **ovary.**
3. The stigma is the sticky top of the pistil.
4. The style is the thin stalk or stem of the pistil.
5. The ovary is the large or swollen bottom of the pistil.

6. Inside the ovary are one or more **ovules,** which will later become seeds.

I. A flower, such as the rose or the lily, that has all four parts (sepals, petals, stamens, and pistil) is called a **complete flower.**

J. A flower, such as the willow or the oat, that has one or more of its parts missing is called an **incomplete flower.**

K. If a flower, such as the oat or wild ginger, has both stamens and pistil, even if its sepals and petals are missing, it is called a **perfect flower.**

L. If a flower, such as the pussy willow or cottonwood, has either the stamens or the pistil missing, it is called an **imperfect flower.**

M. Some flowers are not really a single flower but are a whole cluster of individual flowers.

1. Such flowers are called **composite flowers.**
2. Examples of composite flowers include the zinnia, aster, daisy, chrysanthemum, marigold, and dandelion.

N. The flowers of monocotyledon plants are different from the flowers of dicotyledon plants.

1. Monocotyledon plants have seeds with only one seed leaf (cotyledon), and dicotyledon plants have seeds with two seed leaves.
2. Monocotyledon flowers, such as the tulip and the lily, have their flower parts in threes or in multiples of three, such as six or nine.
3. The tulip has three sepals and three petals (both the same color), six stamens, and a pistil with three parts to its ovary.
4. Dicotyledon flowers, such as the rose, buttercup, and columbine, usually have their flower parts in fours or fives, or in multiples of fours or fives.

II. POLLINATION AND FERTILIZATION

A. For seeds to be formed, the pollen from the anther of a stamen must be carried to the sticky stigma of the pistil.

1. This transfer of pollen is called **pollination.**
2. When the pollen is carried from the anther to the stigma in the same flower, or to the stigma of another flower on the same plant, it is called **self-pollination.**
3. When the pollen is carried from the anther of one flower on one plant to the stigma of a flower on another plant, it is called **cross-pollination.**

B. Pollination can take place in many ways.

1. The pollen may just fall from the anther to the stigma.
2. The wind may blow pollen from flower to flower.
3. Water may carry pollen from flower to flower of plants that live in the water.
4. As insects, like the bee, crawl into flowers to look for nectar, they pick up pollen on their hairy bodies and carry the pollen from flower to flower.
5. Hummingbirds, looking for nectar, also carry pollen on their beaks and long tongues from flower to flower.
6. Man occasionally carries on pollination, called **artificial pollination,** when he wants to develop new kinds of flowers, fruits, vegetables, corn, and wheat.

C. The process of self-pollination does not occur often.

1. In some flowers the stamens are too short for the pollen to fall on the pistil.
2. In some flowers the stamens lose their pollen before the pistil is grown enough and ready to receive the pollen.
3. Some flowers, called **imperfect flowers,** do not have stamens or a pistil.

D. When a grain of pollen from the right kind of flower falls on the stigma, it starts to form a **pollen tube,** which grows down the stigma and the style into the ovary.

1. In the ovary, the pollen grain enters an ovule through a tiny opening, called a **micropyle,** and joins with the egg that is in the ovule.
2. The joining of the pollen grain with the egg in an ovule is called **fertilization.**
3. For fertilization to take place, a flower's

stigma must receive pollen that comes from the same kind of flower.

4. When fertilization does take place, the ovule develops into a seed.

5. Seeds are formed only if fertilization takes place, and, if an ovule is not fertilized, a seed will not be formed in that ovule.

III. THE SELECTIVE BREEDING OF FLOWERS

A. Very often man tries to produce certain kinds of flowers.

B. He produces these new flowers by controlling the pollination of flowers.

1. This controlled pollination is called **artificial pollination.**

2. In artificial pollination, pollen from one flower is transferred carefully by hand to the stigma of another flower of the same kind.

3. Usually, the flower with the stigma has had its stamens removed before the pollen was ripe to make sure that no other pollen could be transferred to that stigma.

4. After the flower has been artificially pollinated, it must be protected from visits by insects, which may have pollen on their hairy bodies.

C. This control of pollination by man is also called **selective breeding.**

D. In selective breeding, man tries to combine different qualities of two varieties of the same flower into the one new variety of the same flower.

1. For example, man may try to combine a large flower with little fragrance with a small, but fragrant flower to produce a large, fragrant flower.

2. Many new varieties of flowers, especially roses, have been produced by selective breeding.

3. A new variety of flower is called a **hybrid.**

IV. USES OF FLOWERS

A. Because of their beauty, flowers are used everywhere for decorative purposes.

B. The buds of the cauliflower are used for food.

C. Cloves are the dried flower buds of the myrtle tree, which grows in the tropics.

1. The buds are used as a seasoning or spice.

2. The buds also produce an oil that is used in medicines.

D. Saffron, a yellow dye, comes from the stigmas of the saffron crocus.

E. Flowers are used in making perfumes.

FRUITS

I. DEFINITION AND FUNCTION OF FRUITS

A. After the ovule in the ovary of a flower has been fertilized, seeds form and the ovary becomes large.

B. A **fruit** is the ripened ovary of the flower, with or without other parts of the flower.

C. The fruit is the part of the plant that contains the seeds that are formed.

D. To many persons the word "fruit" means only tree fruits, such as the apple, pear, peach, orange, grape, and banana.

E. To a scientist, however, the word "fruit" means the ripened ovary from any flowering plant.

1. Garden flowers, wild flowers, shrubs, and flowering trees produce fruits.

2. Cereal grains, such as corn, oats, and wheat, are fruits.

3. Nuts are fruits.

4. Many "vegetables," like the pea, bean, tomato, cucumber, pumpkin, and squash, are really fruits.

F. A fruit has two main functions.

1. One function is to protect the seeds inside it.
2. The other is to help scatter the seeds.

G. Fruits are classified into two main groups: **fleshy fruits** and **dry fruits.**
   1. Fleshy fruits are soft and fleshy when ripe.
   2. Dry fruits are dry when ripe.

II. FLESHY FRUITS

A. Fleshy fruits are classified into three main groups: **pomes, drupes,** and **berries.**
B. In the pome, the fleshy part is formed by the sepals (calyx) and the large, flattened end of the flower stalk, which is called the **receptacle.**
   1. The papery core of the pome is really the ovary, and has the seeds in it.
   2. The apple, pear, and quince are examples of such pomes.
   3. The strawberry is a pome in which many tiny, hard fruits (ripened ovaries) are embedded in one fleshy receptacle (flower stalk).
   4. The strawberry was formed this way because its flower had many pistils inside it.
   5. Pomes usually have many seeds in them.
C. In the drupe, the ovary wall ripens into two layers.
   1. The outer layer becomes soft and fleshy.
   2. The inner layer becomes very hard.
   3. There are usually one or two seeds in this hard, inner layer.
   4. The plum, peach, apricot, cherry, and olive are examples of drupes.
   5. The almond comes from a drupe; however, here we throw away the fleshy, outer part and eat the seed of the hard, inner part.
   6. The raspberry and blackberry are really collections of many tiny drupes clustered on one receptacle.
   7. The raspberry and blackberry were formed this way because their flowers had many pistils inside them.
D. In the berry, the whole ovary becomes fleshy.

1. Some berries, such as the tomato, grape, and gooseberry, have rather soft, thin skins.
2. Some berries, such as the canteloupe, watermelon, and cucumber, have hard skins.
3. Some berries, such as the orange, lemon, and grapefruit, have leathery skins.
4. Berries usually have many seeds in them.

E. The pineaple is a fleshy fruit that is really made up of many fruits joined together.
   1. This kind of fruit is called a **multiple fruit.**
   2. A multiple fruit forms from many flowers that are clustered together.
   3. The mulberry is another example of a multiple fruit.

III. DRY FRUITS

A. Dry fruits are classified into two main groups: **dehiscent** and **indehiscent** fruits.
B. Dehiscent fruits are further divided into **pod** fruits and **capsule** fruits.
   1. Pod fruits, such as the bean, pea, and milkweed, split open along definite seams when ripe.
   2. Capsule fruits, such as the poppy, iris, and lily, crack open when they are ripe.
   3. Both pod and capsule fruits have many seeds in them.
C. Indehiscent fruits do not split open along definite seams and do not open when they are ripe.
   1. Indehiscent fruits usually have just one or two seeds inside them.
   2. Some indehiscent fruits, such as the acorn, hazel nut, and chestnut, have a hard ovary wall covering the seed.
   3. Some indehiscent fruits, such as the corn, wheat, and oat, have a thin ovary wall fastened to the seed.
   4. In some indehiscent fruits, such as the sunflower, buttercup, and dandelion, the seed is not fastened to the ovary wall, but is separated from the ovary wall.
   5. In some indehiscent fruits, such as the elm, maple, and ash, the seed is also separated from the wall, but there are

winglike growths attached to the ovary wall.

IV. Some Fruits Do Not Have Seeds

A. Some fruits develop from the flower without forming seeds.
B. The banana is a seedless fruit.
1. Banana trees do not ordinarily produce seeds.
2. Instead, new sprouts grow from the roots each season, and their flowers produce more bananas without being fertilized.
3. What looks like seeds in the banana are really unfertilized ovules.
C. Seedless oranges, grapefruits, and grapes are produced by joining (or **grafting**) parts of seedless trees onto the roots and stems of ordinary trees that produce these fruits with seeds in them.

V. Selective Breeding

A. Man is always trying to improve the kinds of fruit we eat.
B. For example, he may try to make fruit larger, give the fruit more flavor, make the skin smooth instead of hairy, get more seeds in the fruit, eliminate seeds from a fruit, make fruit mature earlier, and make fruit sturdier and more resistant to disease.

C. Man improves the fruit by **selective breeding.**
1. In selective breeding man controls the pollination of the flower that produces the fruit.
2. To control this pollination he carefully transfers by hand the pollen from one flower to the stigma of another flower of another kind.
3. In this way he tries to combine different qualities of two varieties of the same fruit into one new variety of the same fruit.
4. To make sure that no other pollen will touch that stigma, usually the stamens of the flower with the stigma are removed before their pollen is ripe.
5. Also, after the flower has been artificially pollinated, it is protected from visits by insects, which might have pollen on their hairy bodies.
6. This new variety of fruit is called a **hybrid.**
D. Sometimes man creates new fruits.
1. He creates new fruits by transferring the pollen from a flower that produces one kind of fruit to the stigma of a flower that produces another kind of fruit.
2. The tangelo is a new fruit that is produced by crossing a tangerine with a grapefruit.
3. The plumcot is a new fruit produced by crossing a plum with an apricot.

SEEDS

I. Definition and Parts of a Seed

A. A seed is the part of a plant that grows into a new plant of the same kind.
1. The seed is a ripened ovule that has been fertilized by a grain of pollen.
2. The ovule is in the ovary of a flower's pistil.
B. All seeds have three parts: a seed coat, stored food, and a tiny young plant, called the **embryo.**
C. The seed coat is the covering of the seed.
1. The seed coat protects the seed.
2. Most seeds have two seed coats, but some seeds have only one seed coat.
3. The outer coat is usually thick and tough and the inner coat is much thinner.

D. The stored food helps the young plant grow until it can make its own food by photosynthesis.
1. Some seeds store their food in thick **seed leaves,** called **cotyledons.**
2. These seed leaves (cotyledons) are not true leaves, but part of the seed.
3. Monocotyledon plants, such as the corn plant, have only one seed leaf (cotyledon) in their seeds.
4. Dicotyledon plants, such as the bean plant, have two seed leaves (cotyledons) in their seeds.
E. The embryo is a tiny, young plant inside the seed.
1. The embryo has tiny roots, a stem, and leaves that will become the new plant.
2. When the embryo begins to grow, it lives on the stored food inside the seed until its leaves are able to make their own food for the plant.

II. CONDITIONS NECESSARY FOR SEEDS TO GROW

A. Seeds need water to grow.
1. The water makes the seed swell.
2. It also softens the seed coat.
B. Seeds need the right temperature to grow.
1. Most seeds grow best when the temperature ranges between 60 and 80 degrees Fahrenheit.
2. Some seeds grow better in higher temperatures.
C. Seeds need air to grow, and this is the reason why the soil in the garden must be loose and the seeds must be planted close to the surface of the soil.
D. Seeds need room to grow, and they grow best when they are scattered away from the plant that produced them.
E. Seeds do not need sunlight when they first begin to grow.
1. At first they live off the stored food in each seed.
2. When the new plant grows leaves, it needs sunlight to make its own food.

III. HOW SEEDS GROW

A. When a seed begins to grow, we say that it **sprouts** or **germinates.**
B. First, the seed takes in, or absorbs, water.
1. The water makes the seed swell and softens the seed coat.
2. This softening of the seed coat allows the tiny plant (embryo) inside the seed to grow out through the seed coat.
C. In most seeds, the roots are the first part to grow.
D. Then the stem grows up into the air.
E. The tiny leaves unfold, forming the first true leaves of the plant.
F. While the roots, stem, and true leaves are forming, the young plant lives off the stored food inside the seed.
1. As long as the young plant depends upon the stored food to live, it is called a **seedling.**
2. In the bean seed, which is a dicotyledon plant, the two cotyledons (seed leaves) grow with the stem above the ground.
3. In the corn seed, which is a monocotyledon plant, the one cotyledon (seed leaf) stays below the ground.
4. When the young plant is able to make its own food and no longer needs any of the stored food in the cotyledons, the cotyledons shrivel up and drop off.
5. The true leaves of the plant then continue to supply food for the plant by photosynthesis.

IV. HOW SEEDS TRAVEL

A. Seeds grow best when they are scattered far away from the plant that produced them.
1. If seeds only fell to the ground beside the plant, there would be too many seedlings together, all struggling to live and grow.
2. Some seedlings would choke each other.
3. The large number of seedlings would use up most of the minerals in the soil and make the soil poor for growing.
4. If there should be a condition that was

unfavorable for growing, all the seed-lings would be killed.

B. Some fruits scatter their own seeds.

  1. Some fruits that grow in pods, like the bean and the pea, twist when they ripen so that the pods break open and scatter the seeds.

  2. Some pods, like the balsam or touch-me-not, burst open at the slightest touch and throw their seeds some distance away.

  3. Tiny holes open in the fruit of the poppy, and, as the poppy stem moves back and forth in the wind, the seeds fly out through the holes.

  4. The witch hazel, pansy, and violet plants also scatter their own seeds.

C. The wind scatters many seeds.

  1. Some seeds, like the milkweed, cotton-wood, and dandelion, have fine hairs or tufts that act like parachutes and are carried far away by the wind.

  2. Some seeds, like the maple, ash, elm, and pine, have wings that act like tiny propellers or sails and are also carried away by the wind.

  3. The tumbleweed scatters its seeds as the wind rolls it across the ground.

D. Some seeds, like the coconut, are carried away by water.

E. Birds help scatter seeds.

  1. Mud on the bird's feet may have seeds in it.

  2. Seeds may stick to the bird's bill or feathers and be carried far away.

  3. Some birds eat fleshy fruits, like the cherry, and then drop the seeds to the ground.

  4. Sometimes the birds eat the whole fruit, but pass the seeds through them as waste products and fall to the ground.

F. Animals help scatter seeds.

  1. Squirrels bury nuts, such as the hickory and acorn, in the ground and forget to dig them up.

  2. Many plants, such as the thistle and burdock, produce fruits with stickers that cling to the fur of animals.

G. Man helps seeds travel.

  1. If a wagon or automobile passes through mud that has seeds in it, some of the mud may stick to the wheels and be carried away.

  2. Burrs of the thistle and cocklebur also cling to man's clothes and are carried away.

  3. Seed companies ship seeds to all parts of the world by plane, boat, train, and auto.

V. USES OF SEEDS

A. Seeds are used for food.

  1. The most valuable source of food in the world comes from the fruits and seeds of the grasses, such as wheat, corn, oats, rice, and barley.

  2. Peas and beans are used throughout the world for food.

  3. The peanut is used as food, and its oil is used for cooking.

  4. Chocolate and cocoa are made from the cacao bean, and coffee is made from the coffee bean.

  5. The seeds of pepper, mustard, nutmeg, and celery are used as spices.

B. Cotton seeds are used to make cooking oil, and the fibers that stick to the seed are used to make cotton cloth.

C. Oil from the seeds of the coconut tree is used to make soap, candles, and butter substitutes.

D. Seeds from the flax plant produce linseed oil, which is used to make paint, varnish, and other materials.

E. The soybean is used for food in China, but in the United States it has many uses in industry.

PLANTS AS LIVING THINGS

I. PLANTS ARE LIVING THINGS

A. Plants are living things, just as animals and protists are.

B. All living things are made up of one or more **cells.**
1. Cells are the smallest living parts of living things.
2. Many protists, such as algae, are made up of just one cell.
3. Small plants and animals can be made up of thousands of cells.
4. Large plants and animals can be made up of billions of cells.

C. Each cell is filled with a living material, called **protoplasm.**
1. Protoplasm is a jellylike material that often feels and looks like the white of an egg.
2. Protoplasm is usually clear, but it can also have tiny bubbles, threads, or grains in it.
3. It is usually colorless, but some protoplasm may appear grey, blue, or brown.

D. Inside the cell, there is a ball-shaped body of heavier protoplasm, called the **nucleus.**
1. The nucleus can be found in the center or at one end of the cell.
2. The nucleus controls and directs the activities of the cell.

E. Each cell is surrounded by a thin covering called the **cell membrane.**

F. Plant cells are different from animal cells in one way.
1. A plant cell also has a **cell wall,** which surrounds the cell membrane.
2. The cell wall is made up of a nonliving material, called **cellulose.**
3. The cell wall protects the plant cell and makes it stronger.
4. The woody part of a tree is a mass of old, empty cell walls.

G. Not all cells are alike.
1. Many cells have special work to do, so they differ in size and shape, and they may even have special parts.

2. This difference makes it possible for the cell to carry on its special kind of activity or work.
3. For example, the guard cells in a leaf control the opening and closing of the stomata.
4. The bones in an animal are made up of special bone cells.

H. A group of the same kind of cells that carry on the same activity or work is called a **tissue.**
1. The skin of an onion, the pith of a stem, and the bark of a tree are examples of plant tissue.
2. Animals have skin tissue, bone tissue, muscle tissue, nerve tissue, and even liquid tissue such as blood.

I. A group of tissues working together is called an **organ.**
1. The root, stem, leaf, and flower of a plant are all examples of plant organs.
2. The stomach, brain, heart, liver, and kidneys are all examples of animal organs.

J. All the organs together make up the whole plant or animal.

K. A group of organs that work together in a special activity is called a **system.**
1. Only higher animals have systems.
2. Examples of systems include the digestive and the circulatory systems.

L. Cells, then, carry on all the activities that plants and animals must carry on in order to live.
1. These activities are usually called the **life processes** of plants and animals.
2. The more important life processes of plants include photosynthesis, transpiration, respiration, digestion, circulation, assimilation, growth, excretion, reproduction, and tropisms.

II. PHOTOSYNTHESIS

A. Green plants are especially different from animals in that green plants can make their own food.

B. This making of food takes place mostly in the leaf of the plant, but it can also take place in green stems.

C. The leaf uses two materials to make food: water from the soil and a gas in the air, called **carbon dioxide.**

1. The water, together with dissolved minerals, passes from the soil into the roots, up the stem, and into the leaf.

2. The carbon dioxide in the air enters the leaf through tiny openings, called **stomata,** which are found mostly on the underside of the leaf.

D. In the leaf a green-colored material, called **chlorophyll,** makes it possible for the plant to produce its food.

1. By using the energy of sunlight, the chlorophyll helps the carbon dioxide and water combine to form a sugar, called **glucose,** and a gas, called **oxygen.**

2. Making of food by the plant is called **photosynthesis.**

E. The leaf changes the sugar (glucose) to starch, either immediately or soon afterward.

1. The leaf also changes some of the sugar into fats and proteins.

2. These kinds of food then pass to the stem and roots for use or storage.

F. The oxygen gas is a waste product of photosynthesis, and it passes off into the air through the stomata of the leaf.

III. TRANSPIRATION

A. A plant usually takes in more water than it needs.

B. This excess water passes through the leaf's stomata into the air as water vapor.

C. This evaporation of excess water from the plant is called **transpiration.**

D. Two tiny **guard cells** on each side of the stomata control the amount of water that leaves the plant.

1. Usually the guard cells keep the stomata wide open so that water can leave the plant freely.

2. But, when the plant is wilting because it does not have enough water, the guard cells make the stomata smaller, slowing down the evaporation of water from the leaf.

IV. RESPIRATION

A. Plants, as well as animals, need energy to live.

B. They get this energy by using oxygen from the air to burn the food they have made and stored.

1. The air enters the plants chiefly through the small openings (stomata) in the leaves.

2. The oxygen combines with the food to form carbon dioxide and water, and at the same time energy is set free.

3. The carbon dioxide and water are waste products and pass off into the air through the stomata.

C. This energy-freeing process is called **respiration.**

1. Some of the oxygen that is given off in photosynthesis may be used for respiration.

2. Some of the carbon dioxide given off in respiration may be used for photosynthesis.

D. Photosynthesis and respiration are quite different from each other.

1. Photosynthesis is a food-making process; respiration is a food-using process.

2. Photosynthesis stores energy; respiration sets energy free.

3. Photosynthesis uses carbon dioxide from the air and gives off oxygen; respiration uses oxygen from the air and gives off carbon dioxide.

4. Photosynthesis takes place only in cells that have chlorophyll in them; respiration takes place in all cells.

5. Photosynthesis goes on only in sunlight; respiration goes on day and night.

V. DIGESTION

A. Plants, like animals, prepare their food so that it can be taken in, or absorbed, by the cells.

[449

B. This process is called **digestion.**
  1. In plant digestion the food is broken up into very small pieces and then dissolved in the plant fluid, which is called **sap.**
  2. After it has been broken up and dissolved, the food is now able to pass through the cell membranes into the cell, where the food can be used.
C. Digestion takes place mostly in the leaf, but it can also take place in other parts of the plant.

VI. Circulation, Assimilation, and Growth

A. Just as with animals, the digested food of plants is carried through tubes to the cells in all parts of the plant.
  1. This movement of digested food is called **circulation.**
  2. The plant liquid that has the dissolved food in it is called **sap.**
B. Each part of the plant then takes from the sap the food it needs.
  1. The food passes through the cell membranes into the cells and is changed into protoplasm (the living material of the cell).
  2. The new protoplasm is used to repair worn cells and to grow new ones.
  3. This process of changing food into protoplasm is called **assimilation.**
C. Plants also use the process of assimilation to grow in size.

VII. Excretion

A. Like animals, plants get rid of their waste products.
  1. In photosynthesis the waste product is oxygen.
  2. In respiration the waste product is carbon dioxide.
B. These waste products leave through the stomata of the leaf.
C. This getting rid of waste products is called **excretion.**

VIII. Reproduction

A. Like animals, plants are able to produce new plants of the same kind.
B. This process is called **reproduction.**

IX. Tropisms

A. Although plants cannot move from place to place, as animals do, they can and do move.
B. When the plant is affected by such things as light, water, heat, or gravity, the plant responds by moving either toward or away from the thing affecting it.
  1. This plant movement is called a **tropism.**
  2. If the plant moves toward the thing that is affecting it, the movement is called a **positive tropism.**
  3. If the plant moves away from the thing that is affecting it, the movement is called a **negative tropism.**
C. The response of plants to light is called **phototropism.**
  1. Leaves and stems move toward the light.
  2. This movement is a positive tropism.
D. The response of plants to gravity is called **geotropism.**
  1. Roots grow downward because of the pull of gravity, and this movement is called a **positive geotropism.**
  2. Stems grow upward against the pull of gravity, and this movement is called a **negative geotropism.**
E. The response of plants to water is called **hydrotropism.**
  1. Roots turn in any direction to grow toward water.
  2. They even grow upward against the force of gravity because of this strong hydrotropism.
F. The response of plants to touch is called **thigmatropism.**
  1. The Venus's-flytrap has a leaf that quickly folds in half when touched by a fly or other insect.
  2. The leaves of the mimosa plant turn away from whatever touches them.

3. Vines, peas, and other climbing plants curl around any firm support.

G. The response of plants to heat is called **thermotropism,** and the leaves of certain plants, like the mimosa, turn away from strong heat.

H. The response of plants to chemicals is called **chemotropism,** and most roots turn toward soil that has a good supply of the chemicals that the plant needs.

X. ANNUALS, BIENNIALS, AND PERENNIALS

A. Plants are divided into three groups, depending upon how long they can live.

B. These three groups are **annuals, biennials,** and **perennials.**

C. Annuals live for only one season.
1. They sprout or germinate in the spring, grow, produce flowers and seeds, and then die, all in one season.
2. Annuals usually produce a large number of seeds so that there will be enough seeds to make sure that more annuals will grow the next season.
3. Examples of annuals include the zinnia, marigold, corn, wheat, bean, and pea.

D. Biennials live for two seasons.
1. During the first season the biennials grow only roots, stems, and leaves.
2. The second season they produce flowers and seeds, and then die.
3. Examples of biennials include the beet, carrot, turnip, hollyhock, and sweet clover.

E. Perennials live for more than two seasons.
1. Herbaceous perennials, like the daisy, violet, lily, and columbine, die to the ground each year, but their roots stay alive all winter and grow new plants in the spring.
2. Woody perennials, like trees and shrubs, do not die to the ground, although they usually lose their leaves in the fall and are not active all winter.
3. The giant sequoia tree is a perennial that can live for hundreds of years.

CARE OF PLANTS AND WAYS OF GROWING THEM

I. CONDITIONS NECESSARY FOR PLANT GROWTH

A. Plants need air to grow.
1. They use carbon dioxide from the air to make food by the process of photosynthesis.
2. They use oxygen from the air to burn their food and set energy free by the process of respiration.

B. Plants need water to grow.
1. They use water to make food by the process of photosynthesis.
2. The water also contains dissolved minerals that plants need for making new plant parts and for growing taller.

C. Plants need the proper temperature to grow.
1. Each kind of plant has a certain temperature at which it grows best.
2. Plants have temperature limits beyond which they cannot live.
3. Plants may die if the temperature rises and falls too quickly.

D. Plants need the energy of sunlight to make food and grow.

E. Land plants need soil to grow.
1. Most plants grow best in loam, which is a mixture of sand, clay, and humus (decayed animal and vegetable matter).
2. Some plants grow better in sandy soil and others grow better in clay soil.

F. Plants need chemicals in the soil to grow well.
1. Plants need nitrogen, phosphorus, potassium, calcium, magnesium, and other chemical elements.
2. Some plants grow better when the soil

[451

is acid, but most plants grow best when the soil is neutral or slightly alkaline.

G. The cutting or trimming of dead or dying branches from trees and shrubs will help keep the trees and shrubs healthy.
  1. This cutting and trimming is called **pruning.**
  2. Live branches are often pruned to give the trees a certain shape or to make the tree produce more fruit and less leaves.

II. Effect of Climate on Plants

A. The climate has a great deal to do with the kinds and amounts of plants that will grow in a certain region.
B. In the tropics there is an abundance of plants because of the high heat and large amount of rainfall.
  1. The foliage is dense, and the leaves are broad.
  2. Plants grow continuously the whole year around.
  3. Such plants as banana trees, date palms, bamboo, orchids, and large ferns grow in the tropics.
  4. A greater number and variety of plants grow in the tropics than anywhere else on earth.
C. Very few plants grow in the cold Arctic and Antarctic regions.
  1. There are no trees in these regions although a few dwarf willow trees can sometimes be found.
  2. Ferns, mosses, lichens, some flowering plants, and grass grow in the very short summer that these regions have.
  3. Many of the plants are covered with a sort of hair, and the plants have thick seed coats.
D. A wide variety of plants grow in the temperate climate regions.
  1. Oranges, lemons, limes, grapefruit, and cotton grow in regions where the climate is mild and there is little or no frost.
  2. All kinds of trees, shrubs, fruits, flowers, and cereal grasses grow in the moderate temperate regions.
  3. Evergreens and hardy trees, shrubs, flowers, and grasses grow in cold temperate regions.
E. Not many plants grow in warm desert regions because there is so little rainfall.
  1. Desert plants have less leaves, and, consequently, the loss of water from the plant is cut down.
  2. The leaves have a thick covering and are often narrower, which also helps cut down water loss from the plant.
  3. The mesquite plant sends long roots down to the water table many feet below the surface.
  4. The cactus plant has roots that cover a wide area just below the surface, and these roots can quickly take up any rain that falls.
  5. Desert plants bloom very quickly, and their flowers have brilliant colors, which immediately attract insects for pollination before the flowers die soon after in the hot sun.

III. Effect of Seasons on Plants

A. Because it is warm all year in the tropics, plants grow through all four seasons.
B. Most plants in the temperate regions grow only in the warm weather of the spring, summer, and fall.
  1. Leafy trees, like the oak and the maple, lose their leaves in the fall and stay inactive during the winter.
  2. Evergreen trees, like the pine and the spruce, do not lose their leaves in the fall and stay green all winter, but most of the activity in the tree stops.
  3. Some nonwoody plants, like the peony and chrysanthemum, die to the ground in the winter, but their roots stay alive and produce new growth in the spring.
  4. Other nonwoody plants, like the balsam and zinnia, die completely in the winter, but the seeds they produce will grow new plants in the spring.
C. Plants in the polar regions have a very short growing season because there may be no more than 10 weeks when the temperature is above freezing.

IV. CONSERVATION OF TREES

A. The United States has already lost three fourths of its original forests.
B. Early settlers cut down trees to clear the land and farm it.
C. Lumbering companies used the forests unwisely at first.
  1. Trees were cut down and allowed to fall on young trees and break them.
  2. Brush and branches were left on the ground, where they became dry and burned easily, helping to spread forest fires.
  3. Whole forests were cut down without planting new trees to replace those cut down.
D. Forest fires destroy much of our forests.
  1. These fires are set in many ways.
  2. Some persons set fire to forests deliberately.
  3. Persons who burn debris often let the fire get out of control.
  4. Smokers sometimes throw lighted cigarettes and matches from automobiles into the forest.
  5. Campers leave campfires burning or glowing.
  6. Lightning often starts a forest fire.
E. Fungi and insects destroy certain trees in our forests.
  1. A fungus has destroyed almost all the chestnut trees in the United States.
  2. A fungus carried by a beetle is destroying our elm trees.
  3. Another fungus is beginning to kill our oak trees.
F. Grazing and gnawing animals can also destroy our trees.
  1. When animals, such as cattle, sheep, hogs, or horses, are pastured in wood lots, the trees eventually disappear.
  2. The animals eat or trample young trees and destroy them.
  3. They eat the leaves from lower branches, and harm the trunk and roots.
G. Many efforts are now being made to conserve our forests.

H. Lumbering companies are now cutting trees more wisely.
  1. They are removing weed trees, crowded trees, crooked trees, damaged trees, and diseased trees so that the trees to be used for timber can grow bigger and healthier.
  2. They are cutting down only part of the forest, and then planting new trees that will eventually take the place of those cut down.
I. Spraying diseased trees will stop, or at least check, the spread of the disease.
J. The United States Forest Service, established in 1905, fights and prevents forest fires, develops and recommends better lumbering habits, and finds ways of controlling harmful fungi and insects.
K. Education programs have been developed to lessen man's carelessness in starting forest fires.

V. CONSERVATION OF WILD FLOWERS

A. Our wild flowers are disappearing as more homes and suburbs are built.
B. Persons often destroy wild flowers by picking them carelessly.
  1. Some persons destroy the trailing arbutus by pulling up the long trailing stem.
  2. Others pull up the whole plant instead of just picking the wild flower.
C. Some states are trying to protect their wild flowers by passing laws that forbid the picking of these flowers.
D. Many states establish forest preserves, to let wild flowers grow unmolested.

VI. WAYS OF GROWING PLANTS

A. There are many ways of growing plants.
B. All plants can be grown from the seeds they produce.
C. Some plants can be grown from roots.
  1. Such roots have food stored in them.
  2. The sweet potato, carrot, radish, parsnip, and turnip are roots that can grow new plants.
D. Some stems can grow new plants.
  1. When the stem of a climbing rose plant is laid flat on the ground and covered

with soil, roots will develop at the joints of the stem and grow new plants.

2. Stems of raspberry bushes can also grow new plants, but, because the roots usually form at the tip of the stem, only the tip is pushed into the ground.

3. The stems of strawberry plants grow along the surface of the ground, and will form roots at their joints, producing new plants.

E. Plants can be grown from rhizomes.

1. Rhizomes are long underground stems that grow horizontally close to the surface of the ground.

2. The iris, lily of the valley, and trillium have rhizomes that can grow new plants.

F. Plants can be grown from tubers.

1. Tubers are the enlarged tips of rhizomes, in which food is stored.

2. The white potato is a tuber that can grow a new plant.

3. The "eyes" of the potato are really buds, from which new growth begins.

G. Plants can be grown from bulbs.

1. A bulb is a very short underground stem that is surrounded by thick, fleshy, scalelike leaves.

2. Tulip, daffodil, and onion bulbs can grow into new plants.

3. A bulb in the ground will form new bulbs around it, and the new bulbs can be separated to grow new plants.

H. Plants can be grown from corms.

1. A corm and a bulb look very much alike, but most of the corm is stem, surrounded by thin, scalelike leaves.

2. The crocus and gladiolus have corms that grow into new plants.

I. Plants can be grown from **cuttings** or **slips**.

1. A cutting or slip is a piece of stem with leaves on it.

2. The cutting forms roots when placed in water, wet sand, or wet vermiculite.

3. The cutting is then transplanted into soil and grows into a new plant.

4. The geranium, philodendron, coleus, and pussy willow can grow new plants from cuttings.

J. Some plants like the African violet, sedum, and sansevieria can be grown from leaves.

K. Some plants, like phlox, chrysanthemums, and peonies, grow in clumps that can be divided, and the divisions can then be grown in other parts of the garden.

L. Sometimes new plants can be grown by **grafting.**

1. In grafting, the twig from one tree is joined to another tree of the same kind.

2. Grafting is done most often with fruit trees when a grower wants to grow a different variety of the fruit on a tree.

3. The grower can also save time in growing a certain variety of fruit by grafting twigs of that fruit tree onto a tree that is already growing.

4. Grafting is used to grow such seedless plants as seedless oranges and grapes.

M. Sometimes, new plants can be grown by **budding**.

1. Budding is like grafting except that a bud is used instead of a twig.

2. Budding is used only when a fruit tree is very young.

3. The bud is joined to the tree, and then all the rest of the tree is cut off.

4. The tree now produces only the kind of fruit that the bud would produce.

MOSSES AND LIVERWORTS

I. What Mosses and Liverworts Are

A. Mosses and liverworts are members of a large group, or **phylum,** of plants called **Bryophyta.**

B. They are found all over the world.

1. They are found on plains and on mountains.

2. They are found in the tropics and in the polar regions.

C. Most of them live on land.

D. They are all rather small plants.

E. They have chlorophyll, are colored green, and can make their own food.

F. They are very simple plants.
1. They have simple leaves, but no true roots and stems.
2. However, they do have rootlike and stemlike parts.
3. They do not produce flowers, fruits, and seeds.

II. Mosses

A. Moss plants are small and tend to grow crowded together.

B. They tend to form a thick velvety carpet on moist ground under trees in the deep woods, on damp creek banks, on decaying logs, and on wet rocks.

C. They have a very simple structure.
1. Each moss plant has tiny leaves and a slender stalk, but these leaves and stalks do not have tubes that conduct water and food, as real stems and leaves do.
2. The moss plant has no roots, but instead it has hairlike threads, called **rhizoids.**
3. These rhizoids anchor the plant to the ground and absorb moisture and dissolved minerals from the soil for the plant to use.

D. The moss plant has a very interesting method of reproduction.
1. Male reproductive organs form on some plants, and female reproductive organs form on other plants.
2. In some kinds of moss plants, both the male and female reproductive organs are formed on the same plant.
3. The male organ is club-shaped and has sexual cells (gametes), called **sperm,** in it.
4. The female organ is shaped like a narrow-neck bottle and has a single sexual cell (gamete), called an **egg,** in its swollen base.
5. When the male organ is fully grown, it opens and allows the sperm to escape.

6. The sperm cells have two threads, called **cilia,** at one end, and use these cilia to swim to the female organ after a rain or when the moss is covered with dew.

7. A sperm cell enters the female organ and unites with the egg to form a fertilized egg, called a **zygote.**

8. The zygote (fertilized egg) stays in the female organ and begins to grow, producing a long, thin stalk that rises above the top of the plant.

9. The top of the stalk then swells and becomes a spore case, which is covered by a little hood.

10. There are many tiny spores in the spore case.

11. When the spores become ripe, the hood falls off and the spore case bursts open, allowing the spores to escape.

12. The spores are carried away by the wind and eventually fall to the ground.

13. If conditions are right, the spore produces a mass of threads, which sends up leafy buds that develop into tiny moss plants.

14. These moss plants grow, develop sex organs, and start the whole process of reproduction all over again.

15. Moss plants thus go through a reproductive cycle in which there is a spore stage followed by a sexual stage, which forms a spore stage again.

E. Mosses are important because they help make soil.
1. Their rootlike parts (rhizoids) grow in cracks of rocks and make the rock crumble.
2. These rootlike parts also give off acids, which break up the rock and form more soil.

F. One kind of moss, called **sphagnum** or **peat moss,** is widely used by man.
1. It grows in small lakes and ponds, forming floating masses.
2. These masses become bigger and thicker each year, and eventually cover all the water and form a bog.
3. This bog may thicken, as grass, shrubs, and small trees grow in it, so that the bog

becomes solid land over a long period of time.

4. Dried peat moss is used as a packing material for dishes, glassware, and plants that are to be shipped to different parts of the country.

5. The gardener works peat moss into the soil because it helps loosen thickly packed soil and because it holds water in the soil during the dry summer months.

III. LIVERWORTS

A. Liverworts are small plants that grow in wet places, such as along the banks of a stream.

B. They look like thin, ribbonlike leaves that grow flat along the ground; they are attached to the ground with rhizoids.

C. Like mosses, liverworts also go through a reproductive cycle, having both a spore stage and a sexual stage.

FERNS, HORSETAILS, AND CLUB MOSSES

I. WHAT FERNS, HORSETAILS, AND CLUB MOSSES ARE

A. Ferns are members of the phylum called **Tracheophyta.**

B. Horsetails and club mosses are relatives of the fern.

C. They all have true roots, stems, and leaves, but they do not produce flowers, fruits, and seeds.

D. They are mostly land plants, and grow best in cool, damp, shaded places where the soil is rich.

E. Some grow in the cracks of rocks and cliffs, and others grow in fields and open woods.

F. They range in size from small mosslike plants to plants the size of a good-sized tree.

G. They all have chlorophyll, are colored green, and make their own food.

II. FERNS

A. Ferns were very numerous millions of years ago, forming large forests in the wet and marshy land that was common at that time.

1. Giant ferns as large as trees were quite common.

2. Smaller ferns, much like those found today, also lived during that period.

B. Today tree ferns are found only in the tropics, where they can be as much as 15 meters (49 ft) tall with leaves 4 meters (13 ft) long.

C. Ferns are much smaller in the temperate zones.

D. The stems of these small ferns are underground, growing horizontally just below the surface.

1. Such underground stems are called **rhizomes.**

2. Each year these stems put up new leaves.

3. Fine roots also grow from these stems.

E. Fern leaves are usually called **fronds,** and in most ferns these are the only parts of the plant that appear above the ground.

1. They are **compound leaves** because they have many tiny leaflets arranged along one main vein, called the **midrib.**

2. The veins of fern leaves are forked, and this forking is a characteristic of ferns.

3. When the leaves appear in the spring, they are rolled up tight and they are covered with a hairy growth at their base.

4. When the leaves unroll, they lose this hairy covering.

F. Ferns go through a reproductive cycle, having both a spore stage and a sexual stage.

1. When the fern leaves are fully grown, spore cases form on their underside.

2. There are many tiny spores in each spore case.
3. When the spores become ripe, the spore case bursts open, and the spores are carried away by the wind.
4. When a spore falls on a moist place where conditions are right for growth, the spore forms a threadlike chain or filament of cells.
5. This chain or filament thickens and then broadens at the tip, which becomes a flat, heart-shaped green body, called a **prothallus,** that is notched on its upper side.
6. The prothallus has hairlike threads, called **rhizoids,** on its underside.
7. The rhizoids hold the prothallus to the ground and absorb moisture from the soil.
8. Male sexual organs, each containing several **sperm** cells, develop among the rhizoids.
9. Female sexual organs, each containing one **egg** cell, develop on the underside of the prothallus near the notch.
10. When the male organ is fully grown, it opens up and allows the sperm cells to escape.
11. The sperm cells swim to the female organs after a rain or when the plant is covered with dew.
12. A sperm cell enters a female organ and unites with the egg to form a fertilized egg, called a zygote.
13. The zygote then grows into a fern plant, as we know it, with roots, stem, and leaves.

G. The leaves of some ferns form tiny buds, which break off and form new ferns.
H. Some ferns can form new ferns from their leaves, if the leaves bend down and touch the ground.
1. When the tip of the leaf touches the ground, roots form at the tip.
2. These roots then develop stems and leaves to become a new fern plant.
3. The tip of the leaf dies, which separates the new plant from the parent plant.

I. Many ferns are used to make Christmas wreaths.
J. Coal comes from the ferns that lived and died millions of years ago.
1. Large masses of dead ferns accumulated in layers in the swampy areas where they grew.
2. These layers turned into coal under the influence of great heat and pressure that were produced by strong upheavals and movements of the earth's crust.

III. HORSETAILS AND CLUB MOSSES

A. Horsetails and club mosses are like ferns, especially in the way they reproduce.
B. Like the ferns they were very numerous millions of years ago.
1. At that time they were the size of trees.
2. Most of them are now extinct, and their remains can be seen as leaf and stem imprints.
C. They have horizontal stems, underground for horsetails, and just above or below the ground for club mosses, but upright branches grow from these stems.
D. There is only one living group of horsetails today, but they can be found everywhere.
1. They are usually found in wet places and at the edges of lakes and bogs.
2. Some of their upright branches have bushy side branches.
3. Other upright branches produce spores in cones that develop at their tips.
4. There are small scalelike leaves in a circular pattern farther down the branches below the cones.
E. Club mosses are small, low-growing evergreen plants.
1. They grow on the ground in temperate regions, and they grow on tree trunks in tropical regions.
2. They grow best in damp places.
3. Their upright branches look like the leaves of fir and spruce trees.
4. They produce spores in cones (some of which are club-shaped) that grow at the tip of some of their branches.

5. Some club mosses are dainty and beautiful, and are very commonly used in making Christmas decorations and other ornamental arrangements.

LEARNING ACTIVITIES FOR "PLANTS"

CLASSIFICATION OF PLANTS

1. *Discover how scientists classify plants* · Show how the "red delicious" apple tree is classified, going step by step from the phylum to the variety itself, as shown in Table 13–1.

TABLE 13–1 Classification of Red Delicious
Apple Tree
KINGDOM: Plantae (metaphyta)
   PHYLUM: Tracheophyta (have system of tubes)
      CLASS: Angiospermae (flowering plants with seeds inside the fruits)
         SUBCLASS: Dicotyledoneae (seeds have two cotyledons)
            ORDER: Rosales (roses and their relatives)
               FAMILY: Rosaceae (produce roselike flowers)
                  GENUS: Pyrus (produce apple fruits)
                     SPECIES: malus (cultivated apple trees)
                        VARIETY: red delicious

2. *Compare gymnosperms and angiosperms* · Have the children compare a conifer tree and a deciduous tree. Note their characteristics and list their similarities and differences.

3. *Compare herbaceous and woody plants* · Have the children compare the stems of herbaceous and woody plants, note their special characteristics, and make a list of their similarities and differences.

ROOTS

1. *Observe the growth of primary and secondary roots* · Soak some radish seeds overnight. Put a darkcolored blotter on the bottom of a large saucer. Wet the blotter thoroughly with water, but do not have any excess water on the blotter. Scatter the seeds on the wet blotter and cover the saucer with a glass square. Place the saucer in a darkened part of the room. The radish seeds will germinate in 2 or 3 days. Keep the blotter moist constantly. Examine the seeds each day. Note the primary root that grows directly from the seed, and the secondary roots that branch out from the primary root.

2. *Observe root hairs* · Use a magnifying glass to examine the roots grown in Learning Activity 1 above. Look closely at the fuzzy outgrowths at the tips of the primary and secondary roots. These are the root hairs, which absorb water and dissolved minerals from the soil.

3. *Compare taproots and diffuse roots* · Dig up a dandelion, trying to get the complete root. Also, dig up a small clump of grass. Obtain both the dandelion and grass from a vacant lot, if possible. Note the long taproot of the dandelion and the many shorter diffuse roots of the clump of grass.

4. *Classify roots* · Make a collection of actual samples (or pictures wherever the actual examples are unavailable) of fleshy roots, adventitious roots, prop or brace roots, and aerial roots. Label and classify each example, using an index card.

5. *Discover that roots absorb water and dissolved minerals* · Dig up a complete dandelion

plant with its roots, and gently wash the soil from its roots. If dandelions are unavailable, use plants grown from bean, radish, or tomato seeds instead. Place the roots in a glass jar containing water that has been colored a very deep red with food coloring. In a few hours, or by the next day, the veins of the dandelion leaves will be colored red, because the water and dissolved food coloring will have been absorbed by the roots and then have traveled up to the leaves.

6. *Classify roots by their use* · Collect actual roots, using pictures wherever actual roots are unavailable, showing the different uses of roots. Classify the roots according to their uses, and label each root, describing the purpose for which the root is used.

STEMS

1. *Examine the external structure of a woody dicotyledon stem* · In the late fall or early winter take a field trip to examine a bare twig. Point out the presence of bark, terminal and lateral buds, bud scales, leaf scars, nodes, and bud-scale scars. Find the exact age of the twig by starting at the present terminal bud and counting the number of bud-scale scars along the twig.

2. *Examine the internal structure of a dicotyledon stem* · With a sharp razor blade obtain a slice of the stem from a herbaceous dicotyledon plant, such as the geranium. Observe the stem under a magnifying glass. Note the presence of the cambium between the outer skin and the central, or woody part, of the stem. Also note how the bundles of hollow tubes are arranged regularly in a circle inside the stem.

Obtain a slice of a good-sized log from a sawmill or a lumber dealer. Note the outer and inner part of the bark, the thin cambium between the bark and the wood, and the sapwood and hardwood. Estimate the age of the tree by counting the number of annual rings.

Sand the surface of the log slice until it is smooth, then coat the entire slice two or three times with shellac or varnish, and save it for your science museum.

3. *Examine the internal structure of a monocotyledon stem* · With a sharp razor blade obtain a slice of the stem from a herbaceous monocotyledon plant, such as the lily, tulip, iris, corn, or sugar cane. Observe the presence of only an outer covering and the pith inside the stem. Use a magnifying glass to show how the bundles of hollow tubes are scattered at random throughout the pith.

4. *Classify stems* · Make a collection of actual examples (or pictures wherever the actual examples are available) of stems that grow above and below the ground. Label and classify each example.

5. *Observe how stems support a plant* · Take a field trip to see how stems support the rest of the plant and how the trunk and branches of a tree hold the leaves up to the light.

6. *Discover that the stem carries water to all parts of the plant* · Obtain a stalk of celery with some leaves still on it, and put it in a glass of water that has been colored a deep red with food coloring (Figure 13A–1). With a sharp knife cut 2½ centimeters (1 in) off the bottom of the stalk while the stalk is under the colored water. Allow the celery stalk to stand overnight. Note that the colored water has moved up the stalk and into the leaves. Remove the stalk from the colored water and cut off a section of stalk from the bottom. Note the red color of the hollow tubes in the stem.

7. *Make a two-colored carnation* · Obtain a carnation with a long, thick stem. Split the stem in two parts for a distance of about 3 inches. Place one part in a test tube or glass of water that has been colored with red food coloring, and the other part in a test tube that has been colored with blue or green food coloring (Figure 13A–2). Allow the carnation to stand overnight. The flower will have two col-

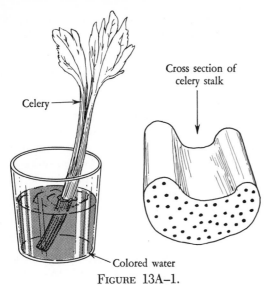

FIGURE 13A–1.

COLORED WATER RISES UP THE CELERY STALK.

ors, the color of the various petals depending upon which colored liquid reached them.

8. *Classify stems by their use* · Make a collection of actual stems and pictures of stems. Classify the stems according to their uses, and

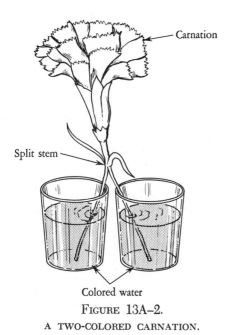

FIGURE 13A–2.

A TWO-COLORED CARNATION.

label each stem, describing the purpose for which the stem is used.

LEAVES

1. *Examine and classify leaves* · Collect a large variety of leaves to examine their parts, structure, and similarities and differences. Compare their sizes, shapes, edges, and different kinds of vein formation. Also, distinguish between simple and compound leaves. Representative leaves may be preserved by placing the leaves on a large piece of blotting paper, arranging the leaves so that they do not touch. Cover the leaves with another piece of blotting paper, and then place a board on top of the blotting paper. Weight the board down with heavy books or stones, and let the leaves stay this way until they have dried out thoroughly. The leaves may now be removed and either placed in albums or taped to pieces of construction paper.

2. *Make leaf prints* · Repeat Learning Activity 5 of "History of the Earth," Chapter 10 (p. 332) to make a carbon imprint showing a leaf's shape and vein pattern.

Make blueprints of leaves. Cut a piece of blueprint paper larger than the leaf and put the paper, sensitive side up, on a cardboard. Put the leaf on the blueprint paper and cover it with a pane of glass. Expose the leaf to sunlight for a few minutes until the paper darkens and turns blue. Dip the paper in a pan of cold water, rinse it well, then set it on a flat surface to dry. The paper will show a white print of the leaf's shape against a blue background.

3. *Discover that air enters a plant through the leaf* · Fit a flask or jar with a two-hole rubber stopper. In one hole insert a leaf with a long stem, such as the leaf of an African violet. In the other hole insert a piece of glass tubing bent at a right angle or a plastic soda straw bent at an angle (Figure 13A–3). Add enough water to the flask so that the stem of the leaf is below the level of the water when the cork is inserted. Now fit the stopper very

460]

tightly into the neck of the flask. Use drops of melted paraffin from a burning candle to seal the holes of the stopper containing the glass tubing and stem of the leaf. Suck air from the glass tubing. Air bubbles will come from the end of the leaf stem, showing that air entered the leaf and traveled down the leaf stem.

4. *Observe stomata and guard cells* · Select a leaf from a plant that has soft, tender leaves. Roll the leaf between your hands several times to loosen the bottom epidermis. By using a razor blade or sharp knife, slice or scrape a small piece of epidermis from the underside of the leaf. Place this piece of leaf on a microscope slide, add a drop of water, and cover with a cover glass.

Observe the piece of leaf under a microscope and look for stomata and the surrounding guard cells.

5. *Collect chlorophyll from leaves* · Obtain the water plant elodea from a store that sells aquarium supplies. Examine a leaf of elodea under the microscope and note the green chlorophyll bodies that are present.

You can extract chlorophyll from any green leaf by first boiling the leaf in water for several minutes to break down the plant cell walls. In the winter, a spinach leaf from the grocer can be used. Prepare a double boiler with water in the bottom section and rubbing alcohol in the upper section. Place the leaf in the alcohol and heat the double boiler until the water boils, and then continue to boil for 10 to 15 minutes. The hot alcohol will extract the chlorophyll from the leaf and become dark green.

6. *Discover that leaves need carbon dioxide for photosynthesis* · Obtain a geranium plant. Coat the top and bottom surfaces of one leaf with a thin layer of Vaseline. Keep the plant in a sunny location. In a few days the Vaseline-coated leaf will begin to turn yellow. Point out that the Vaseline prevented carbon dioxide in the air from entering the leaf's stomata, and this lack of carbon dioxide

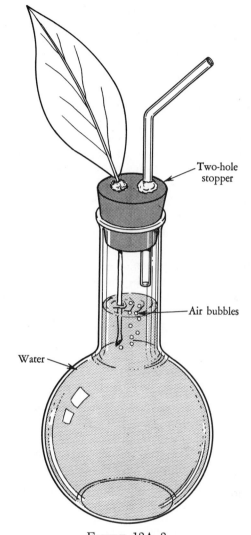

Two-hole stopper

Air bubbles

Water

FIGURE 13A–3.

AIR BUBBLES SHOW THAT AIR ENTERS THE LEAF AND TRAVELS DOWN THE STEM.

stopped the process of photosynthesis in the leaf.

7. *Discover that leaves need sunlight for photosynthesis* · Repeat Learning Activity 6 above, but now cover one leaf completely with aluminum foil. The leaf will turn yellow because the aluminum foil prevents sunlight from reaching the leaf, and this failure to receive sunlight stops the process of photosynthesis.

[461

8. *Discover that leaves produce starch during photosynthesis* · Put a plant, such as a geranium, in the sun for several hours so that photosynthesis can take place. Pluck one of the leaves and boil it in water for several minutes to break down the cell walls in the leaf. Prepare a double boiler with water in the bottom section and rubbing alcohol in the top section. Place the leaf in the alcohol, heat the double boiler until the water boils, and continue to boil for 10 to 15 minutes (or longer if necessary) until the alcohol extracts most of the chlorophyll from the leaf.

Remove the leaf and rinse it in hot water. Place the leaf in a large, shallow saucer and dry it by blotting gently with cleansing tissue. Place a few drops of tincture of iodine on the leaf. A dark blue or purple color will form after a few minutes, indicating the presence of starch in the leaf. Show that the blue color is a test for starch by adding a few drops of iodine to corn starch or to a slice of potato. If you use a coleus leaf, only the green sections will test for starch.

9. *Discover that leaves give off oxygen during photosynthesis* · Get a water plant such as elodea or sagittaria, from an aquarium supply store. Put the plant in an aquarium filled with water, and set a short-stemmed transparent funnel over the plant. Fill a test tube with water, making sure there are no air bubbles in the water, then invert the test tube, still full of water, over the stem of the funnel (Figure 13A–4). Now put the aquarium in a sunny place for several days. The plant will give off bubbles of oxygen, which will displace the water in the test tube. After most of the water is displaced, remove the test tube and hold it mouth upward. Blow out a burning wood splint and quickly put the glowing splint inside the test tube. The oxygen in the test tube makes the splint either glow more brightly or burst into flame.

10. *Discover that leaves give off water* · Obtain a geranium plant and a wooden stick about the same length as the flower pot and plant combined. Place the stick in the soil so

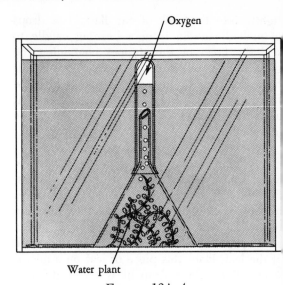

Oxygen

Water plant

FIGURE 13A–4.

THE WATER PLANT GIVES OFF BUBBLES OF OXYGEN DURING PHOTOSYNTHESIS.

that the top of the stick extends slightly above the plant. Cover the soil and the sides of the flower pot with aluminum foil. Now place a plastic bag over the plant and tie the mouth of the bag securely around the stem (Figure 13A–5). Prepare a control by duplicating every condition except the presence of the geranium plant. Such a control involves having the same size flower pot, same amount of soil and moisture in the soil, same size wooden stick, aluminum foil over the soil and sides of the pot, and the same size plastic bag over the stick and tied around the stick.

Now place both flower pots in the sun for a few hours. A large amount of water droplets will appear on the inside of the plastic bag covering the geranium plant. Point out that covering the soil and sides of the flower pot eliminated the possibility of the water coming from the soil or through the porous pot. Because no water droplets appeared in the control, the water could not have come from the air, which usually contains water vapor. Therefore, the water droplets could only have come from the plant itself.

11. *Discover why leaves change color in the fall* · Observe the changes in color of leaves in

462]

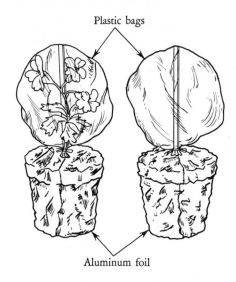

Plastic bags

Aluminum foil

FIGURE 13A–5.

A CONTROLLED EXPERIMENT TO SHOW THAT LEAVES GIVE OFF WATER.

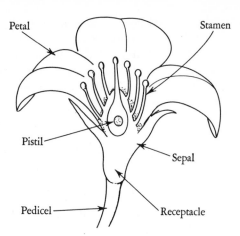

FIGURE 13A–6.

DIAGRAM OF THE PARTS OF A FLOWER.

the fall, and associate the change in color with the kind of tree. The colors appear when the leaves stop making chlorophyll. Get two plants the same kind and size. Allow one plant to stay in the sunlight all day. Keep the other plant in a dark closet for half the day. After a few days note the yellowish appearance of the leaves that had less sunlight. These leaves now have less chlorophyll in them as well, and the yellow pigment in the leaves has begun to show.

Have the children collect autumn leaves, then classify them by color and other ways.

12. *Classify leaves by their use* · Make a collection of actual leaves, using pictures wherever actual leaves are not available, that are used by man. Classify the leaves according to their uses, and label each leaf, describing the purpose for which it is used.

FLOWERS

1. *Examine parts of a flower* · Obtain a large simple flower, such as a tulip, lily, gladiolus, petunia, or sweet pea. Examine the flower closely (Figure 13A–6). Observe the flower stalk and its upper larger part, the receptacle. At the base of the receptacle note the sepals that surround the petals. In the tulip and the lily the sepals are the same color as the petals. Use tweezers to remove the sepals and petals and place them on separate pieces of paper, appropriately labeled. Count the number of sepals and petals.

Observe the stamens surrounding the pistil in the center of the flower. Count the number of stamens, remove them with the tweezers, and place them on a labeled piece of paper. Examine the stamens with a magnifying glass. Locate the filament and anther, and observe the pollen that may be present on the anther. Remove the pistil and observe the stigma, style, and ovary under the magnifying glass. With a razor blade or sharp knife cut through the ovary lengthwise. Observe the ovules with the magnifying glass and try to count the number present.

Have the children make a large drawing or diagram of the whole flower and its individual parts. Label the parts of the flower and also the parts of the pistil and stamen.

2. *Observe and compare kinds of flowers* · Have the children observe examples of different kinds of flowers. Note the basic difference between complete and incomplete flowers, per-

[463

fect and imperfect flowers, and monocotyledon and dicotyledon flowers. Point out that the flower parts of monocotyledon plants are in threes or multiples of three whereas the flower parts of dicotyledon plants are in fours and fives or their multiples. Also, the sepals and petals of monocotyledon flowers are often the same color.

Obtain a composite flower such as a daisy, dandelion, chrysanthemum, zinnia, marigold, sunflower, or aster. Pull out a ray flower (petal) and a disk flower (little tube in the center, and examine them with a magnifying glass. Do the ray flower and disk flower have all the parts of a perfect flower? What parts if any, are missing?

3. *Observe pollen grains* · Place a drop of water on a microscope slide. Shake pollen from a flower on the drop and cover with a cover glass. Examine the pollen under a microscope.

4. *Germinate pollen grains* · Pollen will germinate in a solution containing the right proportions of sugar in water. Fill three cups with boiled water. Add 1 teaspoon of sugar to one cup, 2 teaspoons of sugar to the second cup, and 3 teaspoons of sugar to the third cup. Stir the water in each cup until all the sugar is dissolved. Now pour a portion of the sugar solutions into shallow saucers. Shake pollen for different kinds of flowers on the surfaces of the sugar solutions. Cover each saucer with a piece of glass and let the solutions stand at room temperature for several hours. Examine the pollen grains with a magnifying glass to see if tubes are growing from them. If nothing is visible, place a drop of the sugar solution on a microscope, cover with a cover glass, and examine under a microscope.

5. *Discover how flowers are pollinated* · Obtain flowers that have a good amount of pollen on their anthers. Blow on the anthers, creating a "wind" that blows the pollen away. Have the children observe or recall how bees and insects travel from flower to flower looking for nectar. Observe the shapes of flowers that are visited by bees and other insects. Point out

that the stamens and pistils of the flower are positioned so that, when the insect obtains the nectar, it must pick up some of the pollen from the stamens and at the same time rub against the pistil. When the insect travels to other flowers, it touches the pistil again, and in this way it deposits some of the pollen that clings to its hairy body.

6. *Investigate fertilization and development of flowers into fruit* · Collect flowers at different stages in their growth, ranging from freshly opened buds to those where all the petals have fallen off. Cut open the ovary of each and observe what changes have taken place. Two excellent flowers to observe are the iris, which has hundreds of ovules in its ovary, and the rose, which forms a sizable fruit after it has been fertilized.

Obtain a quantity of fresh string beans or peas, and open some of the pods that do not seem to be completely filled. The tiny, seed-like parts are the remains of ovules that were not fertilized by pollen, and so did not develop into beans or peas.

7. *Investigate selective breeding* · Have the children read about how the selective breeding of flowers is conducted. The work of Luther Burbank should be of interest to many children.

FRUITS

1. *Discuss the definition of a fruit* · List well-known fleshy and dry fruits on the chalkboard. Point out that to a scientist the word "fruit" means the ripened ovary from any flowering plant. Thus, cereal grains, nuts, and many vegetables are really fruits. Flowers, shrubs, and flowering trees also produce fruits.

2. *Classify fruits* · Give the children a list of foods and ask them to tell you if, when eating these foods, they eat the whole fruit, just the fleshy part, or just the seed. Include such common items as the apple, peach, grape, pineapple, raspberry, strawberry, banana, to-

mato, cucumber, squash, hickory nut, pumpkin, pea, green bean, lima bean, and string bean. Have the children classify each of these fruits.

3. *Compare kinds of fruits* · Display or show pictures of examples of pomes, drupes, berries, dehiscent pod fruits, dehiscent capsule fruits, and indehiscent fruits. Describe how each fruit was formed, its parts, and the number and kind of seeds inside.

4. *Compare a peach seed and an almond* · Obtain a peach stone and an almond in the shell. Compare the appearance of the two stones. Break open the peach stone with a hammer, and crack open the almond. Compare the size, shape, and taste of both seeds. Point out that the almond is also the hard stone of a fleshy fruit, but in this case the flesh is thrown away, without being eaten and the stone is saved.

5. *Investigate selective breeding of fruits* · Take a field trip to an experimental farm and have the horticulturist show how cross-pollination and grafting are used to produce tastier, larger, and hardier fruits. If a field trip is not feasible, invite the horticulturist to visit the children instead.

Consult the yearbooks of the United States Department of Agriculture for articles on hybrid corn. Seed-corn companies also produce literature on hybrid corn and how it is grown. Your county agricultural agent will give you a list of the names and addresses of such companies.

SEEDS

1. *Examine the parts of a seed* · Soak a lima bean in water overnight. Remove and examine the seed coat. Separate the two seed leaves. Examine the tiny embryo that is attached to one of the seed leaves, using a magnifying glass. Repeat the learning activity, this time using a kernel of corn. Note the presence of only one seed leaf.

2. *Test seeds for food used during germination* · Soak lima beans, peas, and kernels of corn in water overnight, remove the seed coats, and mash the seeds thoroughly. If you like, you may grind the dried seeds, and then add a little water to the flour and stir to form a paste.

Add a few drops of tincture of iodine to some of the ground seeds. The seeds will turn a deep purple, showing the presence of starch.

Put some of the mashed seeds in a test tube. Add a small amount of nitric acid, boil for a few seconds, and then add enough ammonia to neutralize the nitric acid. If protein is present, the nitric acid will turn the solution a bright yellow, and the ammonia will change the yellow color to orange.

Rub a piece of walnut meat vigorously on a piece of white or brown paper. Warm the paper over a hot plate, but do not set the paper on fire. Then hold the paper up to the light and note the grease spot, showing the presence of fat.

When seeds sprout, the starch is changed to sugar. Mash some sprouting seeds, add a small amount of water, stir, and transfer to a test tube. Obtain some Benedict's solution from the drugstore, pour a small amount into the test tube, and heat. If sugar is present, the solution will turn a greenish-yellow and then a deep orange or brick red color.

3. *Observe seeds germinating* · Obtain lima beans and kernels of corn from the seed store. Do not use grocery store seeds because they may be immature or heat-treated, and so may not germinate. Line a water tumbler with a rectangular piece of dark-colored blotter, and stuff absorbent cotton or peat moss into the tumbler to keep the blotter tight against the sides of the tumbler (Figure 13A–7). Soak the lima beans and corn kernels overnight and slip a few of each between the blotter and the sides of the tumbler. Moisten the cotton and keep it moist throughout the experiment to make sure the blotter is always moist. Place the tumbler in a warm place away from direct sunlight. Observe the tumbler each day and note the way the seeds germinate. Con-

[465

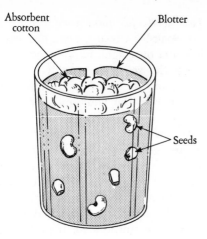

Absorbent cotton   Blotter

Seeds

FIGURE 13A–7.
A TUMBLER SEED GERMINATOR.

tinue the germination until the seeds are well sprouted.

4. *Investigate conditions necessary for germination* · Prepare eight tumbler germinators described in Learning Activity 3. Put one tumbler in the dark and one in the light (but not in direct sunlight). The seeds will germinate just as well in the dark as in the light. Point out that light is not necessary for germination and, in some cases, may even be harmful. However, once the plant has germinated and forms leaves, it needs light to grow.

Keep one tumbler watered regularly, and refrain from giving the other tumbler any water at all. The seeds in the dry tumbler will not germinate.

Cover one tumbler tightly with plastic wrap, or Saran Wrap, and keep the other tumbler continually exposed to the air. The seeds in the covered tumbler will not sprout because they need air to germinate.

Place one tumbler in the refrigerator and keep the other tumbler at room temperature. The seeds in the cold tumbler will not germinate because they need warmth to germinate.

Obtain three flower pots of the same size. Fill one pot with sand, the second with clay, and the third with rich soil containing humus. Soak some lima beans or radish seeds overnight, and

then plant two or three seeds in each pot. Keep all three pots at the same temperature and give all of them the same amount of water. Although the seeds in all three pots may germinate, the plants in the pot containing the rich soil will eventually be taller and sturdier.

5. *Test seeds for percentage of germination* · Get radish seeds from the seed store. Soak 50 of them overnight, and obtain a piece of cotton flannel 30 centimeters (12 in) square. Moisten the flannel cloth and place the radish seeds on the flannel. Roll the flannel into a loose roll and place it in a shallow pan. Keep the flannel moist and warm for a week, and then unroll the flannel carefully and count the number of seeds that have germinated. The number of germinated seeds divided by the total number of seeds (50), multiplied by 100, will give you the percentage of germination. Repeat the experiment using bean, corn, and tomato seeds.

6. *Discover that germinating seeds give off carbon dioxide gas* · Obtain 20 or 30 lima beans from the seed store and soak them overnight. Put the seeds in a flask or jar and add enough water to cover about half the seeds. Fit the flask with a two-hole rubber stopper. In one hole insert a thistle tube and let the tube extend to just above the bottom of the flask. In the other hole insert a glass tube that leads to a water tumbler (Figure 13A–8). Allow the beans to stay in the flask for a day or two. Then pour fresh limewater, which can be obtained from the drugstore, into the tumbler. Pour water slowly into the thistle tube until the flask is half-filled. The water will force the carbon dioxide, which is now above the seeds, through the glass tubing and into the limewater, making the limewater turn milky. You can first show that carbon dioxide turns limewater milky by bubbling air from your lungs into limewater through a soda straw.

7. *Measure the rate of seed growth* · Obtain some radish seeds from a seed store, soak them overnight, and then plant them in a flower pot filled with soil. Water the pot regularly and

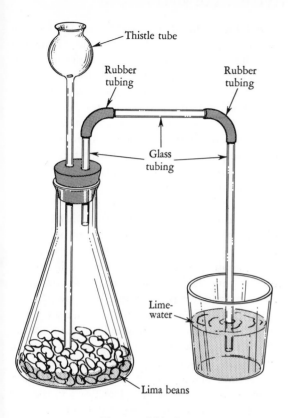

FIGURE 13A–8.

WHEN SEEDS GERMINATE, THE CARBON DIOXIDE GAS THEY GIVE OFF CAUSES LIMEWATER TO BE-COME MILKY.

wait until the tiny plants begin to appear above the soil. Obtain two pieces of glass about 30 centimeters (12 in) square, and insert a wet piece of dark-colored blotter between them. Each day, for 10 to 14 days, carefully remove one entire radish plant from the soil and place it on the moist blotter. You can keep the panes of glass together with string or rubber bands. Keep the blotter moist at all times. At the end of 2 weeks you will have a clear-cut record of the daily growth of the radish seeds.

8. *Investigate how seeds travel* · Collect seeds (or pictures, if seeds are unavailable) that will show some ways that seeds travel. Discuss methods of seed travel, and list on the chalkboard all the possible ways that seeds travel.

9. *Classify seeds by use* · Make a display of seeds, using pictures when actual seeds are not available, that are used by man. Classify the seeds according to their uses, and label each seed, describing the purpose for which it is used.

PLANTS ARE LIVING THINGS

1. *Examine plant cells* · Slice an onion into rings. Discard the first two outer layers. Tear off the thinnest possible piece of skin from the third layer. Place a portion of this skin on a microscope slide, add a drop of water and a drop of tincture of iodine, and cover with a cover glass. Soak up any excess liquid by placing the tip of a blotter against the edges of the cover glass. The iodine stains the onion cells and makes them stand out very clearly. Examine the onion cells under the microscope. The tip of the aquarium plant elodea also can be used to observe plant cells.

2. *Observe photosynthesis* · Repeat Learning Activities 3–9 of "Leaves" (pp. 460–462) to show that photosynthesis is a life process.

3. *Observe transpiration* · Repeat Learning Activity 10 of "Leaves" (p. 462) to show that transpiration is a life process.

4. *Discover that plants give off carbon dioxide* · Place a gallon-size, wide-mouthed glass jar over a small potted plant (Figure 13A–9) and keep the plant in darkness for a day. Remove the glass jar, quickly add a cup of limewater (which can be obtained from the drugstore) to the jar, cover the jar, and shake well. The limewater will turn milky, showing the presence of carbon dioxide. The carbon dioxide was formed during the process of respiration that took place in the plant during the period of darkness.

5. *Observe circulation in plants* · Repeat Learning Activity 5 of "Roots" (p. 458) and Learning Activity 6 of "Stems" (p. 459) to show that circulation is a life process.

[467

FIGURE 13A–9.

PLANTS GIVE OFF CARBON DIOXIDE DURING
RESPIRATION.

6. *Observe and measure growth of plants* •
Repeat Learning Activity 3 of "Seeds" (p. 465)
to show that growth is a life process.

Note that a plant grows taller at its tip, not
at the bottom. Plant some zinnia seeds. When
the plants are about 5 centimeters (2 in) high,
mark the stems with nail polish 2½ centimeters
(1 in) from the soil. Check the height of the
marks periodically.

7. *Observe plant excretions* • Repeat Learning Activities 9 and 10 of "Leaves" (p. 462) and
Learning Activity 4 above to show that excretion is a life process.

8. *Observe plants responding to light* • Obtain a geranium plant whose leaves already face
the sunlight. Turn the pot around so the leaves
now face away from the window. In a few days
the leaves will again turn toward the light.
Fast-growing plants, such as radish plants, will
turn toward light very quickly.

9. *Observe plants respond to gravity* • Grow
a "seed germinator" by repeating Learning
Activity 3 of "Seeds" (p. 465). However, after
the seeds have germinated and produced roots,
give one or two of the seeds a half turn so
that the roots face up and the stem faces
down. Note how the roots and stem change
the direction of their growth accordingly. The
roots respond positively toward the pull of
gravity, and the stems respond negatively away
from the pull of gravity.

10. *Observe plants respond to water* • Cut
off one side of a waxed carton, such as a milk
carton, to make a trough for holding soil. Cut
a rectangular hole from another side of the
carton and tape a piece of glass or some
clear plastic wrap over the hole on the inside of the carton to produce a window (Figure 13A–10). Punch a few holes in the bottom
of the carton for drainage, cover the holes with
flat rocks, and fill the carton with soil. Get
some lima beans from a seed store and place
them 2½ or 5 centimeters (1 or 2 in) in the soil
beside the plastic wrap so that their germination and root growth will be visible. Place the
carton in a shallow pan and water the soil

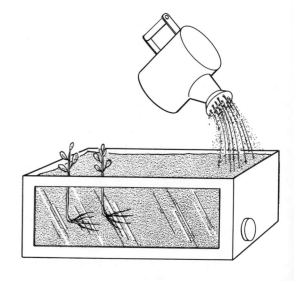

FIGURE 13A–10.

ROOTS TURN TOWARD WATER.

regularly until the beans have germinated into growing plants. Now water the soil at one end of the carton only. In a week or two you will see the roots turned toward the direction of the water.

11. *Observe climbing plants twist in a counterclockwise direction* · Grow two twining plants, such as a morning glory or a pole bean plant. Insert a long, thin, round stick or dowel into each of the pots for the plants to twine around. Allow only one tendril in each plant to twine around the stick. The tendrils will twine in a counterclockwise direction. Try twining one of the tendrils around the stick in a clockwise direction. In a few hours the tendril will unwind itself.

12. *Observe plants sensitive to touch and heat* · Obtain some mimosa seeds from a seed order house, a scientific supply house, or from someone that teaches in the South. Plant the seeds and cultivate them until they grow 15 centimeters (6 in) high. Now pinch one of the top leaves, or stroke it gently a few times. The leaf will droop, and will not regain its original shape for several hours.

Next, strike a match and let it burn for a second or two. Blow out the match and touch one of the leaves with the warm tip of the match. The leaf will droop, and will not regain its original shape for several hours.

13. *Make a woodland or desert terrarium* · A terrarium is a place where plants and animals may live under conditions similar to nature. Obtain a large rectangular aquarium. Cover the bottom with 2½ centimeters (1 in) of gravel. On top of the gravel spread 5 centimeters (2 in) of a mixture of three parts of humus to one part of sand, and water thoroughly. Bury small pieces of charcoal into the gravel and humus. If you like, add more soil to one part of the aquarium to simulate a small hill. Embed a pie tin into another part of the soil, and fill the tin with clear pond water or with tap water that has been allowed to stand for 24 to 48 hours. Add a rock or two and some pieces of bark. Now plant small ferns and mosses in the soil. You can place a tree frog, turtle, newt, and chameleon in the terrarium. If you have a chameleon or tree frog, insert a piece of branched wood for climbing. Now cover the terrarium with a glass plate that is slightly raised with rubber or cork pads to allow free circulation of air. Do not overwater the terrarium because the air inside will be quite moist, and water will condense on the inside of the glass. Keep the temperature of the terrarium constantly between 18° and 22° Celsius (64° and 72° Fahrenheit). A pet shop will provide the right food for each animal.

To make a desert terrarium, cover the bottom of the aquarium with about 5 centimeters (2 in) of a mixture of equal parts of sand and humus. Cover this mixture with about 13 millimeters (½ in) of fine sand. Add a few rocks, and embed a shallow saucer containing water until its top edge is level with the surface of the sand. Plant small cacti or yuccas in the soil, moistening the roots before planting and sprinkling the surface with water after planting. You can place a horned toad, collared lizard, and small desert snake in the terrarium. Cover the top of the desert terrarium with a fine wire screen rather than a glass plate. Water lightly just once a week, but keep the saucer of water full at all times. Keep the temperature of the desert terrarium constantly between 20° and 29° Celsius (68° and 84° Fahrenheit). The horned toad, lizard, and snake will eat insects, worms, and small live animals such as toads and frogs.

CARE OF PLANTS AND WAYS OF GROWING THEM

1. *Investigate conditions necessary for plant growth* · Get five potted plants, all the same kind and same size. Place one in a dark closet and another in the refrigerator. Cover the leaves of the third plant with a thin layer of Vaseline to keep air from entering the plant. Do not water the fourth plant, and use the fifth plant as a control. Water all plants regularly, except the one that has been designated to receive no water. After a few days, note the

effect of darkness, cold, no air, and no water on the growth of the plants.

Plant two or three seeds in separate pots containing sand, clay, and soil rich with humus. Water all three pots regularly and equally. Although the seeds in all three pots may germinate, the plants containing the rich soil will eventually be taller and sturdier.

2. *Discuss the effect of climate on plants* · Have children read about and discuss the kinds and amounts of plants that will grow in tropical, temperate, and arctic regions.

3. *Discuss the effect of seasons on plants* · Have the children observe, recall, or read about what happens to plants during the different seasons of the year.

4. *Explore the conservation of trees* · Have the children read about and discuss how forest fires, unwise lumbering practices, insects, and grazing and gnawing mammals can destroy our trees. Write to United States Forest Service, Washington, D.C. 20025, for materials on conservation of plants and trees. Make a list of good and bad practices for the use of fire in forests and wooded areas. Collect and display pictures showing forest fires and other kinds of destruction of trees.

5. *Discuss conservation of wild flowers* · Show pictures of wild flowers protected by state conservation laws. Because so many wild flowers grow very slowly, point out that overpicking these flowers will make them very rare or even extinct.

6. *Grow a plant from a seed* · Have the children grow plants from a variety of seeds, including radish, lima bean, corn, grapefruit, and orange seeds. Although most tree seeds are small and germinate slowly, the avocado seed is an exception. Place the avocado seed, pointed end up, into a tumbler of water so that one third of the seed is submerged. Insert three sturdy toothpicks horizontally into the seed at different positions, and let the toothpicks rest on the lip of the tumbler so that they hold the

seed in position. Put the tumbler in a warm, dark place, and add water as needed. Eventually white roots will appear, followed by a tall shoot. Put the plant near a window. After 6 weeks it may be transplanted in sandy soil.

7. *Grow a plant from a root* · Place a large sweet potato, narrow end downward, into a large, wide-mouthed glass jar of water so that the lower third is submerged. Hold the sweet potato in position by inserting three wooden meat skewers or pointed sticks horizontally into the sides of the sweet potato, and resting the skewers on the lip of the jar (Figure 13A–11). Put in a dark, warm place. When roots and stems appear, move the plant to sunlight. Add water as needed, and change the water weekly. A small lump of charcoal in the water will keep it "sweet" and avoid rotting.

Plants will also grow from the tops of carrots, beets, turnips, and pineapples that still have foliage on them. Cut off the top 2½ to 5 centimeters (1 to 2 in), and place this top portion in a shallow dish of water.

FIGURE 13A–11.
GROWING A PLANT FROM A SWEET POTATO.

8. *Grow a plant from a stem cutting* · Cut off a stem from a philodendron, coleus, or English ivy plant. Remove all but the top three or four leaves, and place the base of the stem in a tumbler of water. Keep the plant away from direct sunlight until a good root system has developed. Then transplant the stem into soil.

Repeat the process, using a geranium or begonia stem, but this time place the stem in moist sand. When roots are formed, transplant the stems into soil. The same procedure can be conducted with an African violet, using just one leaf and its stem.

9. *Grow a plant from a rhizome* · Obtain an iris from a greenhouse or select one from an old clump that has been dug up and divided. Plant the iris in soil, with the rhizome about 2½ centimeters (1 in) below the level of the soil. Water regularly, but do not overwater.

10. *Grow a plant from a tuber* · Obtain a white potato, preferably one that has begun to sprout, and submerge it halfway into a glass jar of water. Hold the potato in position with wood meat skewers or toothpicks, as described in Learning Activity 7 above. Put in a dark, warm place. When roots and leaves appear (in 2 or 3 weeks), move the plant to sunlight.

11. *Grow a plant from a bulb* · Place pebbles in a shallow saucer and add water. Insert a narcissus bulb, pointed end up, into the pebbles so that only the thickest part of the bulb is covered. Keep the saucer in a cool, dark place until roots form, and then move it to a bright or sunny area. Water as often as is necessary to keep the bulb moist. (Most bulbs need a cooling period before they can bloom, so first refrigerate them for several weeks.)

12. *Grow a plant from a leaf* · Fill a large flower pot with sand, and then water until the sand is quite moist. Select a good-sized begonia or African violet leaf and make several large cuts across the large veins on the veiny side of the leaves, using a razor blade or a sharp knife. Place the leaf, veiny side down, on the sand and carefully press down so that the cut edges of the veins are in close contact with the sand. Place a few small pebbles on the leaf to hold it down. Cover the pot with a piece of glass to prevent the water from evaporating too quickly, and water regularly as needed to keep the sand moist. In 2 or 3 weeks small roots will grow from the cuts in the veins. Soon after, a stem will begin to grow. Remove the glass cover, water regularly until the roots and stem are well developed, and then transplant into rich soil.

Sansevieria ("mother-in-law's tongue") and sedum leaves produce new plants very easily. Just cut a leaf into sections 15 centimeters (6 in) long, and place them in well-drained soil. The sections will root and grow.

13. *Investigate grafting and budding* · Read about and discuss how new plants can be grown by grafting and budding. Wherever possible, use actual demonstrations, films, or pictures showing these processes. Discuss the purpose and value of using these techniques.

MOSSES AND LIVERWORTS

1. *Collect and examine moss* · Mosses are easy to find in swampy areas and forests. However, they can also be found in cracks at the north side of buildings, in cracks of shaded sidewalks, on old paths, and on trees. Collect the mosses with a little of the soil in which they are growing and wrap them in damp newspaper. Cut out a few moss plants and place them in shallow water. Examine these plants with a magnifying glass and under the microscope. Note the tiny leaves, slender stalk, and hairlike rhizoids. Look for male and female reproductive organs, and for spore cases.

2. *Grow moss* · Place a mixture of rich soil and humus into a flower pot and water well. Shake some spore cases from growing moss on the soil, and place the pot in a place that has medium light. Cover the pot with a piece of glass to prevent the water in the soil from

evaporating too quickly, and water as often as is necessary to keep the soil constantly moist. Mosses will grow in a few weeks. Draw diagrams to show the life cycle of the moss.

3. *Examine peat moss* • Obtain some dry peat moss and place it in a dish. Add water, and note how much water the peat moss will absorb. Feel how soft and spongy the wet peat moss is. Show how peat moss may cover a pond or small lake, converting it into a bog so that eventually it becomes dry land.

4. *Collect and examine liverworts* • If you live near wooded areas where mosses and ferns can be found, you should be able to collect some liverworts. Be sure to collect them with a little of the same soil in which they are growing, and wrap them in damp newspaper. Examine the liverworts under the magnifying glass. Note the hairlike processes on the underside of the plant body. These processes attach the liverwort to the soil on which it grows.

FERNS, HORSETAILS, CLUB MOSSES

1. *Collect and examine ferns* • Make a collection of ferns that grow in your locality. They are usually found in shady places near streams and in moist, wooded areas. When collecting ferns, be sure to dig up their rhizomes and fine roots together with the soil in which they are growing. Wrap the ferns carefully in damp newspapers so that the soil is packed around the rhizomes and roots. Examine one of the ferns with a magnifying glass. Look for spore cases on the underside of mature fern fronds. If these spore cases cannot be seen with the magnifying glass, look for them under the low power of a microscope.

2. *Transplant ferns* • Place a layer of coarse gravel in a pot, and cover it with 2½ centimeters (1 in) of rich soil. Carefully place the rhizome and roots of the fern into the pot and, while holding the fern in one hand, slowly add a soil mixture made up of equal parts of rich soil, peat moss, and sand. Add this mixture until the rhizome is covered and the soil mixture is just as high around the fern as it was where the fern originally grew. Place the pot in a shallow pan of water, and keep in a place that has medium light. Do not water the soil on top of the pot, but keep water constantly in the pan instead.

3. *Grow ferns from spores* • Select a mature fern frond that has prominent spore cases on its underside, and place the frond on a piece of paper so that the spore cases touch the paper. Leave the frond on the paper for several days, and allow the spores to fall out on the paper. Tapping the frond occasionally will help the spores to fall out of their cases.

Place a layer of coarse gravel in a flower pot, and then add a soil mixture made up of equal parts of rich soil, peat moss, and sand. Slowly pour boiling water over the soil in the pot to kill any molds or bacteria in the soil that might damage the growth of the fern plants. When the soil is cool again, sprinkle the spores from the paper onto the soil in the pot. Set the pot in a shallow pan of water, and cover the pot with a small pane of glass to keep the air above the spores warm and moist. In about 4 weeks tiny, heart-shaped green plants will sprout. If too many plants sprout, pull some out to relieve the crowded condition. In about 10 weeks these green plants will be mature and produce eggs and sperm. The sperm will fertilize the eggs, and in 4 to 6 months the fertilized eggs will grow into the plants we call ferns. Ferns and mosses are good plants for a terrarium (see Activity 13, p. 469).

BIBLIOGRAPHY FOR ''PLANTS''

ALEXANDER, TAYLOR, R. WILL BURNETT, and HERBERT S. ZIM. *Botany.* New York: Golden Press, 1970. 160 pp.

ANDERSON, MARGARET. *Exploring City Trees and the Need for Urban Forests.* New York: McGraw-Hill, 1976. 102 pp.

BRANLEY, FRANKLIN M. *Roots Are Food Finders.* New York: Thomas Y. Crowell, 1975. 34 pp.

BROCKMAN, FRANK. *Trees of North America.* New York: Golden Press, 1968. 280 pp.

BROWN, DOUGLAS G. *Exploring and Understanding Plant Functions.* Westchester, Ill.: Benefic Press, 1970. 96 pp.

———. *Exploring and Understanding Plant Structure.* Westchester, Ill.: Benefic Press, 1968. 96 pp.

COOPER, ELIZABETH, and PADRAIC COOPER. *Sweet and Delicious—Fruits of Tree, Bush, and Vine.* Chicago: Childrens Press, 1973. 128 pp.

——— and ———. *A Tree Is Something Wonderful.* New York: Golden Gate, 1972. 48 pp.

DAVIS, BETTE. *Winter Buds.* New York: Lothrop, Lee & Shepard, 1973. 96 pp.

EARL, OLIVE, and MICHAEL CANTOR. *Nuts.* New York: William Morrow, 1975. 64 pp.

DOWDEN, ANNE. *The Blossom in the Bough: A Book of Trees.* New York: Thomas Y. Crowell, 1975. 72 pp.

———. *Wild Green Things in the City: A Book of Weeds.* New York: Thomas Y. Crowell, 1972. 64 pp.

EDWARDS, JOAN. *Caring for Trees on City Streets.* New York: Charles Scribner's Sons, 1975. 64 pp.

FENTON, CARROLL, and HERMINIE KITCHEN. *Plants We Live On: The Story of Grains and Vegetables.* New York: Thomas Y. Crowell, 1972. 128 pp.

FENTEN, D. X. *Indoor Gardening.* New York: Franklin Watts, 1974. 62 pp.

GALE, FRANK, and CLARICE GALE. *Experiences with Plants for Young Children.* Palo Alto: Pacific Books, 1975. 118 pp.

GALLOB, HENRY. *City Leaves—City Trees.* New York: Charles Scribner's Sons, 1972. 64 pp.

GAMBINO, ROBERT. *Easy to Grow Vegetables.* New York: Harvey House, 1975. 48 pp.

GRAHAM, ADA, and FRANK GRAHAM. *Let's Discover the Floor of the Forest.* New York: Western Pub., 1974. 48 pp.

——— and ———. *Let's Discover Winter Woods.* New York: Western Pub., 1974. 48 pp.

GUTNIK, MARTIN. *How Plants Are Made.* Chicago: Childrens Press, 1976. 46 pp.

———. *How Plants Make Food.* Chicago: Childrens Press, 1976. 46 pp.

———. *How Plants Reproduce.* Chicago: Childrens Press, 1976. 46 pp.

HEADY, ELEANOR. *Plants on the Go: A Book About Seed Dispersal.* New York: Parents' Magazine, 1975. 64 pp.

HOLL, ADELAIDE. *The Wonderful Tree.* New York: Western Pub., 1974. 34 pp.

HOLMES, ANITA. *Plant Fun: Ten Easy Plants to Grow Indoors.* New York: Four Winds Press, 1974. 126 pp.

KENWORTHY, LEONARD, and LAURENCE JAEGER. *Soybeans: The Wonder Bean.* New York: Julian Messner, 1976. 64 pp.

KNOBLER, SUSAN. *Dandelion Year.* New York: Harvey House, 1975. 28 pp.

LAUBER, PATRICIA. *Life on a Giant Cactus.* Champaign, Ill.: Garrard, 1974. 64 pp.

LAVINE, SIGMUND. *Wonders of the Cactus World.* New York: Dodd, Mead, 1974. 78 pp.

———. *Wonders of Herbs.* New York: Dodd, Mead, 1976. 64 pp.

LIMBURGH, PETER. *Poisonous Plants.* New York: Julian Messner, 1976. 96 pp.

———. *What's in the Name of Flowers?* New York: Coward, McCann & Geoghegan, 1974. 190 pp.

LIST, ALBERT, and ILKA LIST. *A Walk in the Forest: The Woodlands of North America.* New York: Thomas Y. Crowell, 1977. 224 pp.

MEYER, CAROLYN. *Coconut: The Tree of Life.* New York: William Morrow, 1976. 96 pp.

MILLARD, ADELE. *Plants for Kids to Grow Indoors.* New York: Sterling, 1975. 124 pp.

MONCURE, JANE. *Plants Give Us Many Kinds of Foods.* Chicago: Childrens Press, 1975. 26 pp.

MORTON, JULIA. *Exotic Plants.* New York: Western Pub., 1972. 160 pp.

PAGE, NANCY, and RICHARD WEAVER. *Wild Plants in the City.* New York: Quadrangle/N.Y. Times Book Co., 1975. 118 pp.

PRINGLE, LAURENCE. *Into the Woods: Exploring the Forest Ecosystem.* New York: Macmillan, 1973. 54 pp.

———. *Water Plants.* New York: Thomas Y. Crowell, 1975. 34 pp.

RAHN, JOAN. *Grocery Store Botany.* New York: Atheneum, 1973. 58 pp.

———. *How Plants Are Pollinated.* New York: Atheneum, 1975. 136 pp.

———. *How Plants Travel.* New York: Atheneum, 1973. 58 pp.

———. *More About What Plants Do.* New York: Atheneum, 1975. 74 pp.

———. *Seeing What Plants Do.* New York: Atheneum, 1974. 74 pp.

SELSAM, MILLICENT. *Bulbs, Corms, and Such.* New York: William Morrow, 1974. 48 pp.

———. *Vegetables from Stems and Leaves.* New York: William Morrow, 1972. 48 pp.

——— and JOYCE HUNT. *A First Look at Leaves.* New York: Walker, 1972. 32 pp.

SHEEHAN, ANGELA. *The Doubleday Nature Encyclopedia.* New York: Doubleday, 1973. 174 pp.

SHUTTLESWORTH, FLOYD S., and HERBERT S. ZIM. *Non-Flowering Plants.* New York: Golden Press, 1967. 160 pp.

SILVERSTEIN, ALVIN, and VIRGINIA SILVERSTEIN. *Apples: All About Them.* Englewood Cliffs, N.J.: Prentice-Hall, 1976. 112 pp.

——— and ———. *Potatoes: All About Them.* Englewood Cliffs, N.J.: Prentice-Hall, 1976. 118 pp.

SIMON, SEYMOUR. *A Tree on Your Street.* New York: Holiday House, 1973. 44 pp.

SULLIVAN, GEORGE. *Understanding Hydroponics: Growing Plants Without Soil.* New York: Frederick Warne, 1976. 96 pp.

VENNING, FRANK. *Cacti.* New York: Western Pub., 1974. 160 pp.

WARNER, MATT. *Flowers, Trees, and Gardening.* New York: Western Pub., 1975. 48 pp.

WATERS, JOHN. *Carnivorous Plants.* New York: Franklin Watts, 1974. 72 pp.

WEINER, MICHAEL. *Man's Useful Plants.* New York: Macmillan, 1976. 146 pp.

WOHLRABE, RAYMOND. *Exploring the World of Leaves.* New York: Thomas Y. Crowell, 1976. 150 pp.

ZIM, HERBERT S., and ALEXANDER C. MARTIN. *Flowers: A Guide to Familiar American Wildflowers.* New York: Golden Press, 1970. 157 pp.

—— and ——. *Trees: A Guide to Familiar American Trees.* New York: Golden Press, 1970. 160 pp.

CHAPTER 13B

PROTISTS *and* VIRUSES

Protists

CLASSIFICATION OF PROTISTS

I. CLASSIFYING LIVING THINGS

A. All living things are grouped into main divisions, called **kingdoms.**

B. These kingdoms are subdivided into major groups called **phyla.**
1. Phyla are very large groups of living things.
2. All the members of a phylum have certain broad similarities in structure and in other characteristics.

C. The phyla are subdivided into smaller groups called **classes,** the classes into **orders,** the orders into **families,** the families into **genera,** the genera into **species,** and the species into **varieties.**

D. Until recently, scientists put all living things into just two kingdoms: the **plant kingdom** and the **animal kingdom.**

E. Today they feel that this classification is too broad and confusing.
1. Many living things, especially the very tiny ones, do not fit very well into either kingdom.
2. Some are like plants, some are like animals, some have the characteristics of plants and animals, and some seem to be neither plants nor animals.
3. Scientists now put all these hard-to-

classify living things into a separate kingdom, called the **protista kingdom.**
4. Some scientists think this third kingdom is too much of a catch-all and break it up into the **protista kingdom** and the **monera kingdom.**

F. The study of viruses has raised even more classification problems.
1. Viruses seem to be both living and nonliving things.
2. When viruses are all by themselves, they do not seem to be alive at all.
3. When they are inside the cells of living things, they seem to be quite alive.
4. This is why viruses are at present not put into any kingdom.

II. THE PROTIST KINGDOM

A. The protist kingdom, scientifically called the **protista kingdom,** is divided into from nine to thirteen phyla.

B. These phyla include the following groups: **algae, bacteria, fungi, slime molds,** and **protozoans.**

C. The bacteria and one group of algae, called the blue-green algae, are often classified into a separate kingdom, which is called the **monera kingdom.**

ALGAE

I. WHAT ALGAE ARE

A. Algae are all members of the **protista kingdom.**
B. The cells of all algae contain chlorophyll, so the algae are able to make their own food by photosynthesis, just as plants do.
C. Although all algae contain green-colored chlorophyll, many algae also have other pigments that hide the green color.
D. There are five large groups, or **phyla,** of algae: **blue-green, green, golden-brown, brown,** and **red** algae.

II. STRUCTURE OF ALGAE

A. Some algae have only one cell, and others have many cells.
  1. Some seem to swim about like animals.
  2. Others float in the water or settle to the bottom.
B. Many algae form colonies, which are made up of many one-celled algae.
  1. All the algae that make up a colony are attached to each other.
  2. Yet each lives independently and does not have to depend on other algae for anything.
C. Many algae look like threads, called **filaments,** which are also attached to each other to form colonies.
D. Many kinds of algae have a jellylike cell covering.
  1. This covering protects the cell from losing water and from unfavorable conditions.
  2. These coverings make the algae feel slimy, and the algae are hard to grasp when in the water.

III. HOW ALGAE REPRODUCE

A. Algae can reproduce in many ways.
B. All of them can reproduce by **fission,** in which a cell divides into two parts.
  1. When a one-celled algae divides, two new algae are formed.
  2. When the algae in a colony reproduce by fission, the colony becomes larger because all the new algae are connected to the older ones and to each other.
C. Many algae reproduce by forming small bodies, called **spores.**
  1. At first the spores swim around freely like tiny animals.
  2. Later, they settle against some object.
  3. Some spores form new algae immediately.
  4. Other spores remain quiet for weeks or months until conditions are right, and then they form new algae.
D. Some algae produce sexual cells, called **gametes.**
  1. The male cell is called a **sperm.**
  2. The female cell is called an **egg.**
  3. The male and female cell unite to form a mass, called a **zygote.**
  4. Some zygotes form new algae immediately.
  5. Other zygotes remain quiet for a time, and then form new algae.

IV. THE BLUE-GREEN ALGAE

A. The one-celled blue-green algae are found in fresh and salt water.
B. They can be found in almost every stream, pond, or ditch.
C. They are usually found in colonies.
D. Most of them are blue-green in color, although some look almost black, and one kind is even reddish-brown.
E. They usually reproduce by fission.
F. They grow best in the summer.
  1. Some of them color the water.
  2. Others give the water a fishy odor and taste.
G. They belong to the phylum **Cyanophyta.**
H. Blue-green algae and bacteria are often classified in a separate kingdom, called the **monera kingdom.**

[477

1. One reason for this is that there is a striking difference between them and the other protists.
2. They do not have a distinct nucleus in their cells.

V. The Green Algae

A. The green algae are found in fresh water, in salt water, and on land.
B. Some green algae are one-celled, whereas others form large colonies.
C. Their color ranges from bluish-green to yellowish-green.
D. Some reproduce by fission, others by spores, and still others by sexual cells (gametes).
E. They belong to the phylum **Chlorophyta.**

VI. Diatoms: The Golden-Brown Algae

A. Diatoms are tiny, one-celled algae that are usually golden-brown in color, although some are yellow-green.
B. They have all kinds of shapes, and can be round, oval, triangular, rectangular, spindle-shaped, or boat-shaped.
C. Their cell walls are filled with a glasslike material, called **silica.**
  1. The cell wall is in two parts, which fit together, one over the other, like the halves of a little box.
  2. The cell walls have beautiful designs.
D. The diatoms reproduce by fission.
E. When diatoms die, their shell-like walls fall to the bottom of the ocean or pond and pile up into masses.
  1. These masses are scooped up, cleaned, and refined.
  2. They are then used in toothpastes and powders, scouring powders, blackboard chalk, and other materials.
F. They belong to the phylum **Chrysophyta.**

VII. The Brown Algae

A. The brown algae are found in salt water, usually near the seashore.

B. Some are very small, but others can be as long as 46 meters (150 ft).
C. Some of the larger brown algae are attached to rocks along the seacoast, and are commonly called **kelp** or **seaweed.**
  1. They have air bladders with air in them, which help keep them afloat.
  2. A cuplike part, called a **hold-fast,** holds them fast to the rock.
  3. They are used as packing around lobsters, crabs, oysters, and clams when these seafoods are shipped to different parts of the country.
D. Some of the larger brown algae float freely in water.
  1. These algae also have air bladders that keep the plants afloat.
  2. Sometimes these algae cover vast areas of water, as in the Sargasso Sea in the North Atlantic Ocean.
E. The smaller forms of brown algae usually reproduce by fission or by spores, but the larger forms usually reproduce by sexual cells (gametes).
F. They belong to the phylum **Phaeophyta.**

VIII. The Red Algae

A. The red algae are found mostly in salt water, and most of them are small.
B. They always grow attached to a solid object.
C. Some grow in shallow water, and others grow in deeper water.
D. Some reproduce by fission, others by spores, and still others by sexual cells (gametes).
E. They belong to the phylum **Rhodophyta.**

IX. Uses of Algae

A. Algae are the chief source of food for many of the animals that live in the water.
B. Because algae have chlorophyll and carry on photosynthesis, they give off oxygen, which water animals need to live.
C. Seaweeds are used by man for fertilizing the soil.

D. Algae are used in some parts of the world to make soups, gelatins, and a variety of other foods.

E. Algae are used in ice cream to make it smooth, and in salad dressings as a thickener.

F. One kind of algae is used to make agar-agar, which forms a jellylike material good for growing bacteria in hospitals and laboratories.

G. Algae may eventually be used in space flights.

1. Because algae carry on photosynthesis, they are able to use the carbon dioxide that the passengers give off, and produce fresh oxygen.

2. Because they grow so rapidly, there can always be a fresh supply to be strained, dried, and then prepared for use as flour in baking or for use in soups.

BACTERIA

I. WHAT BACTERIA ARE

A. Bacteria are the tiniest members of the **protista kingdom.**

B. They do not have any chlorophyll, so they cannot make their own food.

1. Bacteria that gets its food from living plants or animals are called **parasites.**

2. Bacteria that get their food from dead plants and animals, or from materials made from plants and animals, such as food products, are called **saprophytes.**

C. Because bacteria do not have chlorophyll, they were once thought to be animals.

D. They are usually colorless, but some are brightly colored.

E. They belong to the phylum called **Schizomycophyta.**

F. Bacteria and the blue-green algae are often classified in a separate kingdom, called the **monera kingdom.**

1. There is a striking difference between them and the other protists.

2. They do not have a distinct nucleus in their cells.

II. STRUCTURE AND KINDS OF BACTERIA

A. All bacteria are made up of just one cell.

B. They are so tiny that it is hard to see them even with a powerful microscope.

1. Their size ranges from 1/25,000 to 1/250,000 centimeter (1/10,000 to 1/100,000 in) in width

2. They are so small that hundreds of thousands of them can be placed on the period at the end of this sentence.

C. Bacteria cells are surrounded by a jellylike coating, called a **slime layer,** that differs in thickness.

1. This slime layer helps protect the cell whenever conditions for growth are not favorable.

2. It also helps the cell stick to the surface of its food supply.

3. If the slime layer is very thick, it is called a **capsule.**

D. Biologists classify bacteria into three main groups, according to their shapes.

1. The round, ball-shaped forms of bacteria are called **cocci.**

2. The rod-shaped forms of bacteria are called **bacilli.**

3. The curved, twisted, spiral-shaped forms of bacteria are called **spirilla.**

E. Many cocci and bacilli live together in groups, called colonies.

1. Some cocci live in pairs, and the two cocci are always together.

2. Some cocci colonies are in clumps, but other colonies form chains that look like a string of beads under the microscope.

3. The most common grouping of bacilli colonies is also in chains.

F. Many bacilli and spirilla have tiny, thread-like hairs, called **flagella,** growing out of their cells.
  1. Some have these hairs only at one or both ends of the cell, but others have these hairs all around the cell.
  2. These hairs have a whiplike movement, which makes it possible for the bacteria to move about in water, blood, and other liquids.
  3. Because these bacteria move, they were once thought to be tiny animals.

III. WHERE BACTERIA ARE FOUND

  A. Bacteria can be found everywhere.
  B. They are in the air.
  C. They are in the waters of streams, ponds, lakes, and oceans.
  D. They are found in ice on the surface of ponds and lakes.
  E. They are in the soil.
  F. They are found in living things (plants, animals, and man).
  G. They can be found in dead plants and animals, and in garbage.

IV. WHAT BACTERIA NEED TO GROW

  A. Bacteria need a suitable temperature for growth.
  1. This suitable temperature varies for different bacteria.
  2. Some bacteria grow well in high temperatures, and others grow well in low temperatures.
  3. Most bacteria grow best at temperatures ranging from 27° to 38° Celsius (80° to 100° Fahrenheit).
  4. Very high temperatures kill most bacteria.
  5. Cold temperatures do not usually kill bacteria, but they either stop or slow down their activity and growth.
  B. Bacteria need water or moisture for growth.
  1. Lack of water does not kill most bacteria, but it does stop or slow down their activity and growth.

  2. This is the reason why dehydrated foods can be stored for long periods of time without spoiling.
  C. Bacteria need darkness for growth.
  1. Sunlight slows down the growth of bacteria.
  2. The ultraviolet rays of the sun and of ultraviolet lamps can kill bacteria.
  D. Bacteria need a suitable food supply for growth.
  1. Parasitic bacteria get their food from living plants and animals.
  2. Saprophytic bacteria get their food from dead plants and animals, or from materials made from plants and animals, such as food products.
  3. Most bacteria can live on a wide variety of food materials.
  4. Some bacteria can live only on special food materials.
  5. Pneumonia bacteria prefer only lung tissues, and typhoid bacteria prefer intestine tissues.
  E. Some bacteria, called **aerobic bacteria,** must have free oxygen from the air to live, and will die in the absence of air.
  F. Some bacteria, called **anaerobic bacteria,** cannot live in free oxygen.
  1. They get their oxygen by breaking down chemicals in foods containing oxygen.
  2. Anaerobic bacteria in tightly sealed cans of food are responsible for food poisoning, which is called **botulism.**
  3. **Tetanus,** or lockjaw, is produced by anaerobic bacteria that live in the soil or on objects and become active in deep cuts or punctures where the air cannot reach them.

V. HOW BACTERIA REPRODUCE

  A. Bacteria reproduce by **fission,** in which the cell divides to form two new cells.
  1. The cell separates into two cells simply by forming a wall through its middle.
  2. In some cases the two new cells break apart, and in other cases they stay connected to form a colony.
  B. When conditions for growth are just right,

the new cells can reach full size in 20 to 30 minutes and be ready to split in two again.

1. This ability to grow and reproduce quickly is what makes bacteria so important and dangerous.
2. When conditions are right, a few hundred bacteria can become millions in a very short time.

C. When conditions are unfavorable for growth, bacteria protect themselves by having each cell shrink into a small round body, called a **spore.**

1. These spores develop thick protective covers or walls, which help the spores live through extreme conditions of cold, heat, dryness, and lack of food.
2. The spores can be carried in all directions for long distances by the wind and other means.
3. When bacteria are spores, they remain quiet and do not grow or reproduce.
4. But, when conditions are favorable again, the spores become bacteria cells once more, grow quickly, and then reproduce by fission.
5. Spore formation is especially common with bacilli, the rod-shaped bacteria.

VI. Helpful and Harmful Bacteria

A. Most bacteria are harmless, and live in the air, soil, water, and even in our bodies without seeming to do any harm.
B. Many bacteria are quite helpful to man in many ways.

1. One group of bacteria sours milk, which is important in the making of butter and cheese.
2. Certain kinds of cheeses, such as Swiss cheese, get their flavor from the action of bacteria.
3. One group of bacteria changes alcohol into vinegar.
4. The action of bacteria on the stems of the flax plant loosens the plant fibers, which are then stripped and woven into linen.
5. Bacteria are used in curing tobacco, giving the tobacco a special flavor.

6. Bacteria help separate the flesh from animal skins and, in a process called **tanning,** change the skin into soft leather.
7. Bacteria are used in septic tanks to get rid of sewage, by changing the solid wastes into easily removable liquids.
8. Bacteria act quickly on dead plant and animal matter, changing it into **humus,** which enriches the soil.

C. Certain bacteria, called **nitrogen-fixing bacteria,** take nitrogen gas from the air and change it into nitrogen materials that plants need to grow.

1. Although plants need nitrogen, they cannot use the free nitrogen in the air.
2. The nitrogen-fixing bacteria in the soil gather and form little knobs on the roots of leguminous plants, such as beans, peas, and clover.
3. These bacteria then take the free nitrogen from the air and change it into the kind of nitrogen materials that the plants can use.
4. When the plants die, they leave the soil richer in nitrogen materials, which can be used by other plants.

D. Some bacteria are harmful to man.

1. Some bacteria make food spoil, producing poisonous materials, called **toxins,** which can cause illness and even death.
2. Some bacteria cause disease, such as pneumonia, typhoid fever, tuberculosis, and scarlet fever.

VII. How Harmful Bacteria May Be Controlled

A. Ultraviolet rays can kill bacteria.
B. Chemicals, called **antibiotics,** can destroy many kinds of bacteria inside the body.
C. Chemicals, called **disinfectants** or **germicides,** can kill bacteria outside the body.
D. Heat kills many bacteria.

1. Harmful bacteria in raw milk are killed by heating the milk at 60° Celsius (140° Fahrenheit) 20 to 30 minutes.
2. Milk treated this way is said to be **pasteurized.**

3. When food is canned, it is first heated to kill any harmful bacteria in the food, and then sealed in airtight containers to prevent any other harmful bacteria from getting into the containers.
E. When it is difficult or inconvenient to kill bacteria, they can be controlled by stopping them from growing.
 1. Certain chemicals, called **antiseptics,** can stop bacteria from growing.
 2. Cold temperatures and quick-freezing

can slow down or stop the growth of bacteria.
3. The removal of water, called **dehydration,** from foods stops bacteria from growing.
4. Salting, sugar curing, and pickling all preserve foods because both the salt and sugar remove moisture from the bacteria cells and stop them from growing.
5. Smoking foods also removes moisture from bacteria and stops their growth.

FUNGI

I. WHAT FUNGI ARE

A. Fungi are tiny plantlike members of the **protista kingdom.**
B. They belong to the phylum **Eumycophyta.**
C. Fungi do not have chlorophyll and cannot make their own food.
D. The fungi include molds, mildews, yeasts, rusts, smuts, and mushrooms.

II. GENERAL CHARACTERISTICS OF FUNGI

A. There are almost 100,000 different kinds of fungi.
B. Fungi vary in size, some being so tiny that they can only be seen under the microscope, and others combining to form the large masses that make up mushrooms and puffballs.
C. Most fungi are made up of threads or filaments, called **hyphae.**
 1. Each hypha is made up of many cells, some with cell walls and some without cell walls.
 2. The whole mass of hyphae that make up the fungus is called the **mycelium.**
 3. The hyphae themselves are white or gray, but many fungi have red, orange, yellow, green, blue, or black pigments that give the fungi a special color.
D. Fungi grow best in darkness when there is moisture present and when the temperature is warm.

E. Since fungi have no chlorophyll, they must get their food from other sources.
 1. Some fungi are **parasites,** getting their food from living plants and animals.
 2. Other fungi are **saprophytes,** getting their food from dead plants and animals, or from materials made from plants and animals, such as food products.
F. Nearly all fungi are **aerobic,** being able to use the free oxygen in the air to live.
G. All fungi can reproduce by forming tiny round bodies, called spores.
 1. The fungi produce tremendous numbers of spores.
 2. These spores have a protective cover or wall around them.
 3. The spores are carried off in all directions by the wind and other means.
 4. When they land on objects, if conditions are favorable for growth (moisture, warm temperature, darkness, suitable food supply), the spores become fungi.
 5. When conditions are unfavorable, the spores can live quietly without growing for long periods of time until conditions become favorable for growth again.
H. Some fungi can reproduce by forming sexual cells, called **gametes.**
 1. The male cell is called a **sperm,** and the female cell is called an **egg.**
 2. The male and female cell unit to form a mass, called a **zygote.**
 3. The zygotes form new fungi, which can

then reproduce either by forming spores or by forming gametes and zygotes.

III. Molds

A. The word **mold** is a common name for many different kinds of fungi.
B. Molds grow best in places that are dark and damp.
C. Although most molds grow best in warm temperatures, some grow well at temperatures near freezing.
D. Molds can grow on most foods, and also on paper, leather, and wood.
E. Most molds are made up of tubular threads or filaments, called **hyphae.**
F. Some molds, such as bread mold, have three kinds of hyphae.
   1. Tiny, rootlike hyphae, called **rhizoids,** grow downward into the bread, digest the food materials, and then take in, or absorb, the digested food.
   2. Other hyphae, called **stolons,** spread out horizontally over the surface of the bread, and then grow downward to form more rhizoids.
   3. Some hyphae grow upright, and their purpose is to form spores.
   4. After a few days, round bodies or knobs appear on the ends of these hyphae.
   5. Each knob is a spore case, called a **sporangium,** with thousands of spores in it.
   6. These spores are colored, and give the molds their characteristic color.
   7. When the spore cases (sporangia) are ripe, they split open and the spores float away in the air.
   8. Each spore can form a new hypha, which will soon become a complete mold made up of many hyphae.
G. All molds reproduce by forming spores, but some can also reproduce by forming sexual cells (gametes).
   1. Sometimes two hyphae of the same mold develop connecting branches, which join together.
   2. Where the branches join together, a cell

from each branch acts as a sexual cell, and these cells unite to form a zygote.
   3. The zygote then begins to form a new mold.
H. Some molds are parasitic, and others are saprophytic.
I. Molds may be harmful.
   1. Many molds spoil foods.
   2. Molds growing on fruit trees damage the fruit.
   3. Some parasitic water molds kill fish and other sea animals.
J. Molds can be helpful.
   1. Molds are used in making such cheeses as roquefort, camembert, and limburger.
   2. The antibiotics, such as penicillin, streptomycin, and aureomycin, are obtained from molds.

IV. Mildews

A. Mildews are fungi that are closely related to molds.
B. Most mildews are parasites.
C. Some mildews are downy, and attack such plants as radishes, potatoes, cereal grains, sugar cane, and tobacco.
D. Some mildews are powdery, and attack such plants as lilacs, roses, phlox, clover, grapes, and apples.
E. Mildews are either whitish or dark colored.
F. Black mildew is often found on clothes exposed to dampness for a long time.
G. Mildews reproduce by spores.

V. Yeasts

A. Yeasts are tiny, one-celled fungi, usually oval in shape.
B. They usually reproduce in a special way, called **budding.**
   1. When conditions are favorable, a little knob or bud pushes out from one side of the yeast cell.
   2. This bud grows quickly and later breaks away to form a new yeast cell.
   3. Sometimes many buds stay attached to the same yeast cell and form a chain.

[483

C. When conditions are unfavorable, a yeast cell may produce a spore case, usually with four spores in the case.

D. Yeast is important to man because of its action on sugar.
1. It breaks down sugar to alcohol and carbon dioxide gas.
2. This action is called **fermentation.**

E. Yeast is used in making bread.
1. Bubbles of carbon dioxide gas are formed, which swell and make the dough rise.
2. This bubbling leaves many small spaces and makes the bread light and fluffy.
3. As the bread is baked, the heat drives off the carbon dioxide and the alcohol that have been formed.

F. When making alcohol by using yeast, the carbon dioxide is allowed to escape and the alcohol is saved.

G. Fruits, such as grapes and apples, ferment when they are crushed.
1. Their skins usually have wild yeast on them.
2. When the skin of these fruits is broken, the yeasts act on the sugar in the fruit, and turn the juice into wine and cider.

H. Yeasts are also helpful to man because they produce vitamin B_2 in their cells.

VI. RUSTS AND SMUTS

A. Rusts and smuts are parasitic fungi.

B. Rusts produce reddish-brown spores that look like rust, and destroy such plants as wheat, apple trees, white pine trees, roses, oranges, and melons.

C. Smuts produce blackish spores, and destroy cereal grains, such as corn, oats, barley, and wheat.

VII. MUSHROOMS

A. Mushrooms are the largest fungi.

B. They are saprophytes, living on dead plant and animal matter in the soil.

C. They may grow underground for years, producing a large mass of tangled threads (hyphae), which eventually come together just below the surface of the ground to form a small cap.

D. When the weather is damp, especially in the spring or the fall, this closely packed mass pushes its way above the ground and the cap opens to form a mushroom.
1. The mushroom stalk is called the **stipe.**
2. The umbrella-shaped top of the mushroom is called the **cap** or **pileus.**
3. On the underside of the cap are fleshy plates, called **gills,** which contain the spores of the mushroom.

E. Some mushrooms have a ring around their stalk (stipe) that is the point where the cap was attached to the stalk before the mushroom moved above the ground and the cap spread open.

F. Each fleshy gill contains hundreds of spore cases.
1. Each spore case contains four spores.
2. The spores may be colored black, white, pink, yellow, or brown.

G. Some mushrooms are good to eat, but others may be very poisonous.

H. Puffballs are like mushrooms, except that they are not umbrella-shaped.
1. They are either round or pear-shaped balls, usually white in color.
2. When the puffballs are fully grown, they dry up and split open, sending all their spores out into the air.
3. Puffballs can be as large as ⅔ meter (2 ft) across when fully grown.
4. They can be eaten when they are young and before their spores have ripened.

VIII. SLIME MOLDS

A. **Slime molds** are different than the fungi molds.

B. They belong to a separate protist phylum called **Myxomycophyta.**

C. They usually grow on damp, decaying leaves and other dead plant material.

D. During the slime mold's life cycle it is both animal-like and plant-like.
1. They are produced from spores.

2. At first they are one-celled, have thread-like hairs (**flagella**), and move as they feed and grow.

3. Then they join to form a very large colony that also moves as it feeds on bacteria, other protists, and dead plant or animal matter.

4. Later the colony moves to a drier place, stops moving, becomes plant-like, and produces spore cases.

E. Their colonies can be orange, yellow, white, or colorless.

IX. LICHENS

A. Lichens are often grouped with fungi.

B. Actually, a lichen is made up of an alga and a fungus that are living together.
1. The alga and the fungus both help each other.
2. The fungus gets its food from the alga, which has chlorophyll and makes food by photosynthesis.
3. In return, the fungus protects the alga with its hyphae (threads), and supplies the alga with the moisture it needs for photosynthesis.

4. This arrangement, where two living things live together and help each other, is called **symbiosis.**

C. Lichens are usually green because of the green algae in them, but some have other pigments too, which make the lichens appear red, orange, yellow, or brown.

D. Lichens grow on the bark of trees and on the ground.

E. Lichens growing on rocks make the rock crumble and turn into soil.
1. The lichen gives off carbon dioxide gas, which combines with water to form carbonic acid.
2. The acid causes the rock to become soft and crumbly, changing it eventually into soil.

F. Lichens can grow anywhere, some even growing in desert regions and others near the north and south poles.

G. One kind of lichen is used by reindeer as food.

H. Lichens have been used in making dyes, in tanning hides for leather, and in making perfumes. Litmus paper, used to test acidity, is made with a lichen dye. In China, Japan, and Iceland, people eat lichens.

PROTOZOANS

I. WHAT PROTOZOANS ARE

A. Protozoans are all very tiny, simple one-celled, animal-like protists.

B. They are so small that most of them can be seen only with a microscope.

C. Because they can eat, breathe, move, and reproduce, just as animals do, they used to be put in the animal kingdom.

D. Although most protozoans live separately, some live together in colonies; however, usually each member in a colony lives independently of the other members.

E. Protozoans live either in water or where conditions are moist.

1. Some live in fresh water, and others live in the ocean.
2. Some live in damp soil, and others live in decaying animal or plant matter.

F. Examples of protozoans include the **ameba, paramecium,** and **euglena.**

II. THE AMEBA

A. The ameba is the simplest protozoan.

B. It belongs to the phylum **Sarcodina.**

C. It can be found in the slime found on the bottom of ponds and rivers, and on the surface of the leaves of water plants.

D. Under the microscope it looks like a blob of grayish jelly with no definite shape.

E. The shape of the ameba keeps changing as it moves.
  1. The ameba sends out fingerlike projections that are called **false feet,** or **pseudopodia.**
  2. The rest of the ameba's body then flows into the false feet.
F. The ameba eats protists, such as algae or bacteria.
  1. When it touches food, the ameba sends out pseudopodia (false feet) that surround the food completely and take it into the cell.
G. There are tiny spaces or cavities, called **vacuoles,** in the ameba.
  1. Some vacuoles have food in them.
  2. One vacuole collects and gets rid of excess water, and possibly waste products as well, inside the ameba.
H. Oxygen in the water enters the ameba through the cell membrane (covering), and carbon dioxide produced by the digestion of food leaves the same way.
I. The ameba moves toward food, but away from bright light and chemicals, and it moves faster when the temperature becomes warmer.
J. The ameba reproduces by dividing into two equal parts, forming two new cells.
  1. This method of reproduction is called **fission.**
  2. First the nucleus divides, and the halves move to opposite ends of the cell.
  3. Then the cell narrows in the middle and pulls apart so that two new cells are formed.

III. THE PARAMECIUM

A. The paramecium is a larger protozoan than the ameba.
B. It belongs to the phylum **Ciliophora.**
C. It can be found in quiet ponds where a scum has formed on the surface.
D. It has a definite shape, and looks like a slipper or the sole of a shoe.

E. It is completely covered with fine, hair-like threads of protoplasm, called **cilia.**
  1. These cilia constantly move back and forth in the water like tiny oars, making the paramecium move.
  2. The paramecium can move forward or backward, and can also spin from side to side like a top.
F. The paramecium eats algae, bacteria, yeast, and other protists.
  1. The action of the cilia forces the food into a small opening that acts as a mouth.
  2. The food then passes into a narrow tube, called the **gullet,** which leads into the protoplasm of the cell.
  3. The food is then held in vacuoles (cavities) for digestion.
  4. The paramecium also has two vacuoles, one at each end of the cell, that get rid of excess water and some of the waste products.
G. Oxygen from the water enters through the cell membrane, and carbon dioxide produced by digestion of food leaves the same way.
H. There are two kinds of nuclei in the paramecium: large and small.
  1. The large nucleus controls and directs the regular activities of the cell.
  2. The small nucleus operates when reproduction takes place.
I. The paramecium reproduces like the ameba, that is, by splitting in two (fission).
  1. First the small nucleus splits, and each half moves to an end of the cell.
  2. Then the large nucleus splits in the same way.
  3. The cell narrows in the middle and separates, forming two new paramecia.
J. Occasionally, two paramecia come together and exchange nuclear material.
  1. This process is called **conjugation.**
  2. In conjugation no new paramecia are formed, but the original paramecia are given new vitality so that they can continue reproducing by fission.

IV. The Euglena

A. The euglena is especially interesting to scientists because it behaves both like a plant and a protozoan.
B. It belongs to the phylum **Mastigophora.**
C. It lives in freshwater ponds and streams.
D. It has a shape like a pear, with one end rounded and the other end pointed.
E. At the rounded end is a single, long, whip-like lash, called the **flagellum,** which turns in a spiral motion and drives the euglena through the water.
F. The euglena has chlorophyll in it and carries on photosynthesis when in the presence of sunlight.
G. However, when there is no light or the light is very weak, the euglena behaves like a protozoan.
  1. It then eats bacteria and other tiny bits of plants and animals.
  2. The food materials pass into the euglena and are digested in exactly the same way as in the other protozoans.
H. The euglena has a bright red spot, called an **eyespot,** which is sensitive to light and may help direct the euglena toward sunlight.
I. The euglena reproduces by fission, splitting lengthwise into two, with one half receiving the flagellum and the other half growing a new one.
J. When conditions become unfavorable, the euglena (and many other protozoans as well) forms a protective covering, called a **cyst,** around its cell and loses its flagellum.
  1. Inside this cyst the euglena can live through periods of hot or cold weather and through dryness.
  2. When conditions become favorable again, the cyst breaks open and the euglena becomes an active protozoan once more.

V. Spore-Forming Protozoans

A. Some protozoans reproduce by forming tiny, round bodies, called **spores.**
  1. The nucleus of the cell divides into many small nuclei.
  2. Parts of the protoplasm around the nucleus (cytoplasm) then surround each of the new nuclei to form spores.
  3. Finally, the whole protozoan breaks up and releases these spores.
  4. The spores then become new protozoans.
B. They belong to the phylum **Sporozoa.**
C. All spore-forming protozoans are parasites.
D. They have no organs for moving, but are carried along in water or in the blood.
E. Malaria is caused by a spore-forming protozoan.

VI. Protozoans Can Be Both Helpful and Harmful

A. Protozoans serve as food for fish and other water animals.
B. Protozoans help man because they eat large amounts of bacteria that may be harmful to man.
C. Some protozoans live in the intestines of termites and digest the food that the termites eat.
D. Some protozoans that live in the ocean have shells made of lime around their bodies.
  1. When they die, the shells fall to the bottom of the ocean, accumulate, and eventually may harden into a form of limestone called **chalk.**
  2. Chalk is white, and is used in making toothpowder, putty, and blackboard crayons.
E. Some protozoans cause serious diseases, such as malaria, African sleeping sickness, and amebic dysentery.

Viruses

I. What Viruses Are

A. Before viruses were discovered, it was easy to classify objects into living things and non-living things.

B. When scientists began to explore viruses, they found that viruses seem to be both living and non-living things.
   1. When viruses are all by themselves, they do not seem to be alive at all.
   2. When they are inside the cells of living things, they seem to be very alive.

C. This is why viruses are not put into any kingdom (plant, animal, or protist).

D. We usually think of a virus as something that has to do with a disease.
   1. The word "virus" comes from the Latin word meaning "poison."
   2. There are at least 300 viruses that can produce diseases in different kinds of living things.
   3. But there are also many viruses that seem to be quite harmless.

E. Scientists classify viruses into three groups, according to where they live.
   1. **Bacterial viruses** live in bacteria cells.
   2. **Plant viruses** live in the cells of seed plants, especially flowering plants.
   3. **Human** and **animal viruses** live in the cells of humans and animals.

II. Characteristics of Viruses

A. Viruses are very tiny.
   1. They are even smaller than bacteria.
   2. They can only be seen under an electron microscope.

B. Unlike plants, animals, and protists, the viruses are not made up of cells.
   1. They are very simple in structure.
   2. They are particles with an outer coat made of protein.
   3. Inside there is an acid, which is called **nucleic acid.**

C. Viruses have a great number of shapes.
   1. Some are round and look like tiny golf balls.
   2. Some are shaped like bricks or cubes.
   3. Some are shaped like needle-like rods.
   4. Some have a thin tail and an oval or many-sided head, and they look somewhat like tadpoles.

D. Viruses can live and grow only inside living cells.
   1. This means that a virus is a **parasite.**
   2. A parasite lives in or on a living thing, which is called the **host.**
   3. Scientists have tried to get viruses to live and grow outside living cells, but they have failed.

E. When viruses are outside living cells, they do not seem to be alive.
   1. Scientists have been able to separate some viruses from living cells and get them in the form of crystals, just like salt or sugar crystals.
   2. These virus crystals can be stored in a jar for long periods of time.
   3. But when the virus crystals are rubbed against or put inside living cells, the virus begins to live and grow.

F. Each virus will enter only certain kinds of living cells.
   1. A bacterial virus enters only a certain kind of bacterial cell.
   2. A plant virus may enter only the cells of the flowers or leaves or stem of a certain plant.
   3. A human or animal virus may enter the cells of the nervous system or skin or lungs of a human or animal.
   4. A human or animal virus may enter the cells of just one kind of nerve in the nervous system.

III. Bacterial Viruses

A. Much of what we know about viruses comes from the study of bacterial viruses.

B. These viruses are the ones that look like

tadpoles, having a thin tail and an oval or many-sided head.

C. They are also called **bacteriophages** or **phage viruses.**

D. From the study of how these viruses act on bacteria, scientists have learned how viruses reproduce to make new viruses.

1. When a virus meets a bacteria cell, part of the virus enters the cell.

2. The virus quickly takes over the activity and material of the bacteria cell.

3. The virus then makes the bacteria cell produce more virus material than its own bacteria material.

4. Soon the bacteria cell produces only new viruses.

5. In a short time the bacteria cell falls apart or bursts, allowing 200–300 newly-formed viruses to escape.

6. The new viruses are now free to enter and destroy other bacteria cells.

IV. PLANT VIRUSES

A. Plant viruses are often named after the plant they enter, the special part of the plant they damage, or the appearance they produce in the plant.

B. Many plant viruses will often damage and even kill plants, especially flowering plants, when they enter the plant cells.

C. Plant viruses will cause diseases in the tomato, lettuce, potato, bean, cucumber, beet, tulip, and aster plants.

D. They also cause diseases in the American Elm and the peach tree.

E. Plant viruses can be spread in many ways.

1. Most plant viruses are spread by insects, like the aphid and the leaf-hopper, that suck juices from leaves.

2. Some viruses are spread when one leaf of a plant rubs against the other.

3. Some are spread when the roots of an infected plant grow and touch the roots of a healthy plant.

4. Sometimes they are spread when gardeners handle diseased plants.

V. HUMAN AND ANIMAL VIRUSES

A. Viruses cause many diseases in humans and animals.

B. Some well-known virus diseases are the common cold, influenza, virus pneumonia, polio, smallpox, cowpox, chicken pox, measles, German measles, warts, cold sores and fever blisters, shingles, mumps, rabies, infectious mononucleosis, infectious hepatitis, yellow fever, and parrot fever.

C. Scientists think that cancer may be tied up with viruses, but they have not yet been able to prove it.

D. Human and animal virus diseases are spread in a number of ways.

1. Diseases that infect the breathing system, like the cold and influenza, are spread by coughing and sneezing.

2. Diseases with sores on the skin, like chicken pox and cold sores, are spread by touching the sores.

3. Viruses from diseases like polio and infectious hepatitis are passed out in the feces, which then may be touched by flies and carried to food and water.

E. Humans and animals often become **immune** to many diseases after they have had the disease.

1. Becoming immune to a disease means never getting that disease again.

2. When a person gets a virus disease, his body starts to make special chemicals, called **antibodies.**

3. Antibodies help destroy the viruses that have entered the body.

4. Scientists think that the antibodies do this by covering the viruses and making the viruses harmless.

5. The body will make a different kind of antibody for each virus.

6. The body makes more antibodies than it needs, and these extra antibodies float around in the blood.

7. Some antibodies stay in the blood for the rest of a person's life.

8. This means that the antibodies will de-

stroy a certain virus if it should ever enter the body again.

F. Humans and animals do not become immune to the common cold and influenza.

VI. How Harmful Virus Diseases May Be Controlled

A. Antibiotics like penicillin cannot be used to stop virus infections, because they only work against bacterial infections.

B. Some virus diseases can be controlled by using a **vaccine.**
  1. A vaccine has a small amount of weak or dead viruses in it.
  2. Some vaccines, like smallpox vaccine, are either scratched or injected into the arm or other part of the body.
  3. Giving a vaccine this way is called a **vaccination.**

4. Other vaccines, like the polio vaccine, are given by mouth.

C. When a person is vaccinated, the body begins to make antibodies immediately.
  1. The body makes many more antibodies than it needs, and the antibodies stay in the blood for a long time.
  2. Now the person becomes immune to the virus disease.
  3. If new disease viruses should get into the body, the antibodies will destroy the viruses.

D. We can stop virus diseases from spreading by covering our mouths when coughing or sneezing, by not touching virus sores, by disinfecting or burning things that have been touched by persons who are sick with the disease, and by being very careful when getting rid of body wastes from persons who have the disease.

LEARNING ACTIVITIES FOR "PROTISTS AND VIRUSES"

ALGAE

1. *Collect and examine algae* · Algae are easiest to collect during the spring and summer. They may be found as a greenish scum in shallow or stagnant pools and lakes, and also as a greenish coating on moist stones or on the damp bark of the shaded side of a tree. Collect the algae from pools and lakes in large wide-mouthed jars, taking along a good amount of the water in which the algae were found. Do not put too many algae in one jar. Collect algae from bark by prying off a few small pieces of the bark and soaking the bark in tap water that has been allowed to stand for 24 hours in a large, wide-mouthed, open jar (to allow any chlorine in the water to escape). Algae from stones may be scraped off and placed in jars containing tap water that also has been allowed to stand for 24 hours.

Because the algae kept in containers die rather quickly, they should be examined as soon as possible. Keep the containers in strong light, but not in direct sunlight. Place a drop of the green material on a microscope slide, cover with a cover glass, and examine the algae under both the low and high powers of a microscope. Note the tiny bodies containing chlorophyll. See if you can find examples of algae in different stages of reproduction. Find pictures of the common algae and use these to try to identify the specimens you have collected.

2. *Investigate conditions for growth of algae* · Place samples of algae in darkness, in medium to strong light, and in sunlight.

Also, keep samples of algae in the refrigerator, on or near a heated radiator, and at room temperature. This variation of conditions will help the children learn the optimum conditions of light and heat for the growth of algae.

3. *Examine seaweed or kelp* · Look for rockweed, seaweed, or kelp along the seashore. If you live inland, obtain some from the fish store. Ask for the kind of seaweed or kelp that is used to pack lobsters, clams, or oysters that are flown or shipped from the seacoast to your city or town. Examine and cut open the air bladders. Look for and examine the cuplike holdfast. The larger specimens will have divisions that look like stems and leaves.

Have the pupils read about and report on the Sargasso Sea and the sargassum floating in it.

BACTERIA

1. *Collect or grow bacteria* · Boil a pint of water and add 4 tablespoons of nutrient agar. If nutrient agar is unavailable, use 4 tablespoons of gelatin, one beef bouillon cube, a teaspoon of sugar, and a pinch of baking soda. Boil the mixture for about 15 minutes. Let the culture liquid cool a few minutes until it is quite warm, but not hot. An alternate and much simpler culture material may be prepared by boiling a potato in water to which a pinch of baking soda has been added. Slices of the boiled potato will also grow bacteria, but not as well as the nutrient solutions.

Obtain four or five Petri dishes that have been sterilized in an oven for 1 hour at 107° to 121° Celsius (225° to 250° Fahrenheit). If Petri dishes are unavailable, use saucers instead. Place one saucer on top of another and hold them in place by taping their edges at two or three places (Figure 13B–1). Stack four or five pairs of saucers in the oven and heat as directed. After 1 hour, remove the Petri dishes or saucers and allow them to cool to room temperature, keeping them covered at all times. These containers will be used to hold the

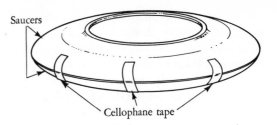

Saucers

Cellophane tape

FIGURE 13B–1.
A HOMEMADE PETRI DISH.

nutrient solution for collecting and growing bacteria.

Pour about 6 millimeters (¼ in) of nutrient agar or gelatin mixture into each dish and cover the dishes. If a boiled potato is used as a culture material, cut off thin slices with a sterilized knife and transfer them to the culture dishes with sterilized forceps or tweezers.

Collect and grow bacteria in several different ways. Expose the culture material by lifting the top of a culture dish quickly, and then have a child cough over the culture materials. Another child can stroke a dirty finger across the culture material or drop some dirt that has collected under his fingernails. Expose the culture material to the air in the classroom or street for about 15 minutes. Keep one dish sterile and closed at all times so that it will serve as a control. Keep the dishes in a warm, dark place. In a few days different colored spots will appear in the exposed dishes, showing the presence of colonies of bacteria.

2. *Examine bacteria under a microscope* · Make a transfer needle by pushing the sharp point of a needle well into a small cork stopper. Use the cork stopper as a handle and sterilize the eye of the needle in a flame. Use the eye of the needle to transfer the bacteria to a microscope slide. Add a coloring agent, such as methylene blue or eosin, which can be obtained from the drugstore. The coloring agent should be very dilute, and the proper dilution can be prepared for you by the pharmacist. Although bacteria are very small, some of the larger ones can be seen by focusing the microscope very carefully and by experiment-

[491

ing with the angle and amount of light entering the microscope. Look for examples of the
three different kinds of bacteria, and draw
diagrams of them on the chalkboard.

If the variety of bacteria is limited, try growing others by placing a handful of dead or
decaying grass and leaves in a large, wide-
mouthed jar of water. First expose the jar to
the air for 1 or 2 days, and then cover the jar
and let it stand for a few days more. The water should now have a good supply of bacteria.
Place a drop of the water on a microscope
slide, and a drop of the coloring agent described above, cover with a cover glass, blot
up the excess liquid around the edges of the
cover glass with the tip of a blotter, and examine the bacteria under the high power of a
microscope.

3. *Investigate conditions for growth of bacteria* · Prepare six sterile culture dishes of nutrient culture material, as described in Learning
Activity 1 above. Grow bacteria in each dish by
touching a sterile needle, prepared as described
in Learning Activity 2 above, to a bacteria
colony growing in another dish, and by smear-
ing the bacteria on the needle across the culture material in the dishes.

Place one dish in a dark, warm place and
another in the refrigerator, where it is dark
and cold, and examine the dishes after a few
days. Repeat the experiment, using a dark,
warm place and a bright, sunny, warm place.
Repeat the experiment, using a dark, warm,
moist place and a dark, warm, dry place. Create a dark, warm, dry place by placing the dish
on a radiator or a hot plate set at low heat,
and then covering the dish with a tin can
over it. The experiments will show that bacteria grow best under dark, warm, moist conditions.

4. *Predict bacteria reproduction* · Draw
diagrams showing how bacteria reproduce.
Assuming that reproduction takes place every
30 minutes, and that all the bacteria also live
and reproduce, have the children calculate how
many bacteria will be formed in 24 hours, starting with just one set of the bacteria.

5. *Compare helpful and harmful bacteria* ·
Have the children read about and discuss the
different ways that bacteria can be helpful and
harmful to man.

6. *Test ways of controlling harmful bacteria*
· Prepare and inoculate five sterile dishes containing nutrient culture, as described in Learning Activity 3. Place one dish in direct sunlight, and a second dish in the oven, where it
is both hot and dry. To the third dish add
some disinfectant, such as Lysol or Creosol. To
the fourth dish add some antiseptic, such as
tincture of iodine or Metaphen. To the fifth
dish add an antibiotic, such as a tablet or capsule of penicillin, which has been dissolved or
mixed in water. The antibiotic can be obtained
from the drugstore or a doctor. Note that bacteria colonies fail to grow in each dish.

Have the children read about the work of
such men as Pasteur, Koch, and Lister in controlling harmful bacteria.

FUNGI

1. *Collect or grow molds* · Rub a piece of
bread across a dusty surface, and then moisten
the bread. Place the bread in a closed container and place it in a warm, dark place.
After a few days a white, cotton-like mold will
form. Then black spots, which are spore cases,
will also appear. Molds can also be formed
by placing cheese, jam, or a wet orange in a
closed container and keeping the container in
a warm, dark place for several days.

New or more of the same items can now
be inoculated if some of the mold is transferred
to the items. An orange or apple can be inoculated simply by picking up some mold from
one fruit with a sterilized pin or needle, plung-
ing the mold into a fresh fruit, and then keeping the fruit in a warm, moist place.

2. *Examine molds* · A magnifying glass will
show the threads and black spore cases of
molds quite clearly. To see the spores themselves, place a bit of the mold on a microscope
slide, and then add a drop of water and a

drop of coloring agent, such as methylene blue, prepared and properly diluted by a pharmacist. Cover with a cover glass and examine under the high power of a microscope. Move the slide until a spore case can be clearly seen, and then examine the spores inside.

3. *Investigate conditions for control of molds* · Have the children try growing molds, as described in Learning Activity 1 above, under moist and dry, warm and cold, and light and dark conditions. Then have the children draw conclusions as to what are the most favorable conditions for growing and for controlling molds.

4. *Look for and examine mildew* · Mildew will often form when old shoes, pieces of leather, or books are placed in a dark, moist, warm place. This mildew is usually colored black. A white mildew will often form on the leaves of flowering plants when the air is hot and humid, and the weather has been rainy. Examine the mildew both under a magnifying glass and a microscope, as described in Learning Activity 2 above.

5. *Grow and examine yeast cells* · Dissolve 1 teaspoon of sugar in a tumbler of warm (not hot) water. Add a quarter of a yeast cake or a package of dried yeast, and let the tumbler stand for 24 hours in a warm place. Place a drop of the yeast culture, which is formed, on a microscope slide, cover with a cover glass, and observe the yeast plants under both the low and high power of a microscope. Look for cell shapes, special features of yeast cells, and evidence of budding.

6. *Observe the action of yeast on dough* · Mix flour, water, and sugar in the proper proportions to make bread dough. Divide the dough into two equal parts, and mix one part with half a yeast cake or package of dry yeast that has been stirred in some water. Place each dough sample in a pan and set in a warm place for a few hours. The dough with the yeast will rise as the action of the yeast produces bubbles of carbon dioxide that expand in the dough.

7. *Investigate the effect of temperature on yeast* · Prepare a batch of bread dough and yeast, as described in Learning Activity 6 above. Divide the dough into three equal parts and place each part in a pan. Put one pan in the refrigerator, another sample in a warm place, and the third sample in a hot place. Examine all three batches of dough after a few hours. The dough in the warm place will show the best action of the yeast.

8. *Discover that yeast causes fermentation* · Dissolve a full tablespoon of sugar in a tumbler of warm water. Add a quarter of a yeast cake or package of dried yeast, and let the tumbler stand for several days in a warm place. Smell the yeast culture, and note the odor of ethyl alcohol. Point out that the yeast causes the sugar solution to ferment, producing ethyl alcohol and carbon dioxide.

9. *Discover that fermentation produces carbon dioxide* · Prepare a yeast and sugar solution, as described in Learning Activity 8 above. Pour some solution into a test tube or narrow-necked glass jar and fit tightly with a one-hole rubber stopper or modeling clay. Insert a small glass or plastic tube into the hole of the stopper and connect this tube to another tube with rubber tubing (Figure 13B–2). Insert the second tube into a test tube or jar containing clear limewater, which can be obtained from the drugstore. Place the apparatus in a warm place. In a few hours the limewater will turn milky, showing the presence of carbon dioxide. Show that limewater is a test for carbon dioxide by bubbling your breath through a straw into a test tube containing a little limewater.

10. *Examine rusts and smuts* · If available, examine rusts and smuts under the microscope and look for special features. Have the children read about wheat rust, apple rust, white-pine blister rust, chestnut blight, Dutch elm disease, and corn smut. In each case they might like

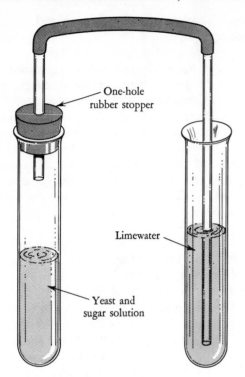

FIGURE 13B–2.

WHEN YEAST FERMENTS, THE CARBON DIOXIDE IT GIVES OFF CAUSES LIMEWATER TO BECOME MILKY.

to tell the type of fungus that causes the disease, the plants that are affected, and how the diseases are spread.

11. *Examine mushrooms and make spore prints* · Collect full-grown mushrooms and examine the stalk, cap, and gills. Carefully and gently cut away the stalk of the mushroom. Coat a piece of smooth or shiny cardboard with egg white. If the gills of the mushroom are covered with light-colored spores, use dark cardboard. If the spores are dark, use light cardboard. Push three toothpicks vertically into the sides of the mushroom cap so that they hold the cap 13 millimeters (½ in) above the cardboard (Figure 13B–3). Place the cap on the cardboard and cover it with a wide-mouthed glass jar to prevent air currents from disturbing the spores. After 24 hours remove the jar carefully, and then remove the cap. The gills

of the mushroom will be permanently outlined on the cardboard by the spores that have fallen upon it.

12. *Collect and examine puffballs* · Look for and examine puffballs that have not yet split open. Squeeze or crush the puffball over a piece of paper and observe the spores that drop on the paper. Examine the inside of the puffball.

13. *Collect and examine lichens* · Collect samples of lichens, which are found as gray-green patches on rocks and the bark of trees. Examine the lichens under a magnifying glass and a microscope. Note the network of gray fungus fibers that surrounds the green algae cells. Discuss the symbiotic arrangement whereby the fungus and algae live together and help each other.

Scrape a patch of lichen from a rock, and note the softer and more crumbly condition of the rock under the patch. The lichen gives off carbon dioxide gas, which combines with

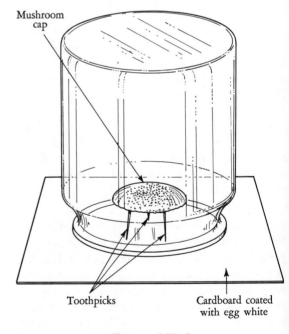

FIGURE 13B–3.

OBTAINING SPORE PRINTS FROM MUSHROOMS.

water to form carbonic acid. The acid causes the rock to crumble, and eventually turns the rock into soil.

PROTOZOANS

1. *Collect common protozoans* · There are several ways of collecting one-celled protozoans for classroom study. Very often protozoans can be found in the classroom aquarium. A second, almost infallible, source is the ponds and streams of parks and forests. To ensure adequate collection, take two or three glass jars. Fill each jar half full of water from different parts of the edge of the pond or stream. If the pond water has green scum on it, put a mixture of water and scum into one of the jars. Also put some small water plants into each jar. Bring the jars back to the classroom and leave them uncovered in bright light, but not in direct sunlight.

Another way of collecting protozoans is by making a grass or hay infusion. Place a handful of dry grass, weeds, or hay in a large glass jar. Fill the jar with tap water that has been left standing for 2 or 3 days (to allow all the chlorine in the water to escape). Cover the jar and place it in a bright part of the room, but not in direct sunlight. Let the jar stand for 2 or 3 days, and then examine drops of the mixture under the microscope each day for the presence of protozoans. Usually the mixture will teem with different kinds of tiny animals by the end of the week.

The simplest way of transferring protozoans to a microscope slide is by using a medicine dropper. One drop on a slide is sufficient. Because protozoans cluster near the food they eat, try to include a little of the plant material in the drop.

The most common protozoan found in all of these sources is the paramecium. Representative samples of protozoans can be obtained from most scientific supply houses.

2. *Observe protozoans* · Examine drops of ameba, paramecium, and euglena cultures under the microscope. Be sure to cover each drop with a cover glass (Figure 13B–4). These protozoans can usually be seen quite well under low power, but the high power may be quite helpful for observing fine details.

Have the children observe the form and parts of each protozoan. They can check their observations against pictures or drawings of the protozoan. Observe how each protozoan moves and obtains its food. Touch each gently with a pin and note its reaction to contact. Place a drop of culture first on a cooled slide and then on a heated slide and note the reac-

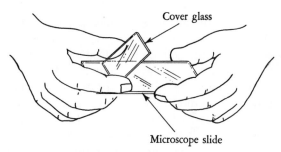

FIGURE 13B–4.
COVERING A DROP OF CULTURE WITH A COVER GLASS.

tion to changes in temperature. Observe the reaction to strong light. Follow the movements of a large, well-formed protozoan. Perhaps you will be able to see how it reproduces by fission.

3. *Investigate disease-producing protozoans* · Have the children read about and discuss such diseases as malaria, amebic dysentery, and African sleeping sickness.

VIRUSES

1. *Investigate the early identification and treatment of virus diseases* · Let the children read about and discuss how Edward Jenner performed the first vaccination for smallpox, and how Louis Pasteur developed a successful vaccine for rabies.

Explore how the Russian biologist Iwanowski first isolated the tobacco mosaic virus, the Dutch botanist Beijerinck invented the name

[495

"virus," and the American scientist Stanley first crystallized the tobacco mosaic virus.

2. *Compare healthy plants with those that have a virus disease* · Collect specimens of plants that are healthy and the same plants with a virus disease. When actual specimens are not available, augment the collection with pictures instead. Compare the appearance of the healthy and diseased plants. Classify plant virus diseases according to the parts of the plant that are affected, and also by the appearance of their symptoms.

3. *Classify human virus diseases* · Let the children classify these diseases in different ways. One method of classification might be by similarity of disease symptoms. A second method might be to group those diseases that produce a natural immunity and those that do not. A third method might be to list those diseases for which successful vaccines have already been developed and those for which there are as yet no vaccines.

4. *List ways of controlling the spread of virus diseases* · First classify the diseases according to which part or parts of the body the viruses attack. Then list the ways of controlling the spread of these viruses.

5. *Trace the victory of scientists over polio* · Have the children investigate and discuss the symptoms of polio, its crippling effects, the early treatments of the disease, and the final breakthrough in developing an oral vaccine.

6. *Investigate warts* · Have the children explore the early beliefs about what causes warts, and the various treatments that were used for getting rid of them. Find out how warts are treated today. Point out that when the belief that frogs and toads cause warts finally seemed to be discredited, scientists have recently found that a secretion from the skin of certain toads will cause warts.

7. *Explore the treatment of rabies* · Find out what other animals beside the dog can get rabies. Have the children learn what to do if a person is bitten by an animal with rabies. Learn what treatment is given to this person, and also what is done to the animal.

8. *Compare viruses and bacteria* · Compare the structure and method of reproduction of bacteria and viruses. How are the organisms alike? How do they differ? Which one is the more complex? What properties do the viruses have that would lead beginning investigators to believe they are living things?

9. *Investigate the possible association of viruses with cancer* · Explore what scientists have discovered about a possible relationship between the viruses and some forms of cancer. To date no virus has been definitely linked to human cancer, but one form of leukemia has already been induced in mice by injecting them with an extract that contains virus particles. Also, extracts containing virus particles have induced over twenty kinds of malignant tumors in mice, guinea pigs, and hamsters.

BIBLIOGRAPHY FOR "PROTISTS AND VIRUSES"

Asimov, Isaac. *How Did We Find Out About Germs?* New York: Walker, 1974. 64 pp.

Aylesworth, Thomas G. *The World of Microbes.* New York: Franklin Watts, 1975. 128 pp.

COHEN, DANIEL. *Vaccination and You.* New York: Julian Messner, 1970. 96 pp.

CONKLIN, GLADYS. *Fairy Rings and Other Mushrooms.* New York: Holiday House, 1973. 32 pp.

DONAHUE, PARNELL, and HELEN CAPELLARO. *Germs Make Me Sick.* New York: Alfred A. Knopf, 1975. 96 pp.

FROMAN, ROBERT. *Mushrooms and Molds.* New York: Thomas Y. Crowell, 1974. 40 pp.

GOLDSTEIN, PHILLIP, and MARGARET GOLDSTEIN. *How Parasites Live.* New York: Holiday House, 1976. 160 pp.

KAVALER, LUCY. *The Wonders of Algae.* New York: John Day, 1965. 96 pp.

KOHN, BERNICE. *Our Tiny Servants: Molds and Yeasts.* Englewood Cliffs, N.J.: Prentice-Hall, 1966. 62 pp.

LEITZ, GERALD S. *Junior Science Book of Bacteria.* Champaign, Ill.: Garrand, 1968. 68 pp.

LEWIS, LUCIA. *The First Book of Microbes.* New York: Franklin Watts, 1972. 84 pp.

MAY, JULIAN. *Plankton.* New York: Holiday House, 1972. 36 pp.

NOURSE, ALAN E. *Viruses: A First Book.* New York: Franklin Watts, 1976. 72 pp.

PATENT, DOROTHY. *Microscopic Plants and Animals.* New York: Holiday House, 1974. 160 pp.

PERRY, PHYLLIS. *Let's Learn About Mushrooms.* New York: Harvey House, 1974. 48 pp.

SILVERSTEIN, ALVIN, and VIRGINIA SILVERSTEIN. *Cancer.* New York: Thomas Y. Crowell, 1977. 96 pp.

SLATON, WILLIAM, and NELLIE SLATON. *Bacteria and Viruses: Friends or Foes?* Englewood Cliffs, N.J.: Prentice-Hall, 1969. 72 pp.

STERLING, DOROTHY. *The Story of Mosses, Ferns, and Mushrooms.* Garden City, N.Y.: Doubleday, 1965. 159 pp.

VILLIARD, PAUL. *The Hidden World: The Story of Microscopic Life.* New York: Four Winds Press, 1975. 90 pp.

CHAPTER 14

ANIMALS

COMPOSITION AND CLASSIFICATION OF ANIMALS

I. THE CELL

A. Cells are the smallest living parts of all living things.
B. Each cell is filled with a living material, called **protoplasm.**
  1. Protoplasm is a jellylike material that often feels and looks like egg white.
  2. It is usually clear, but it can also have tiny bubbles, threads, or grains in it.
  3. It is usually colorless, but some protoplasm may appear gray, blue, or brown.
C. Inside the cell there is a ball-shaped body of heavier protoplasm, called the **nucleus.**
  1. The nucleus can be found in the center or at one end of the cell.
  2. The nucleus is surrounded by a thin covering, called the **nuclear membrane.**
  3. The nucleus controls and directs the activities of the cell.
D. The rest of the protoplasm around the nucleus is called **cytoplasm.**
  1. There are often tiny grains or threads in the cytoplasm.
  2. The cytoplasm may also have spaces or cavities, called **vacuoles,** in it.
  3. Some vacuoles store food, and others have water or waste products in them.
  4. Many important life activities take place in the cytoplasm.
E. Each cell is surrounded by a thin covering, called the **cell membrane.**

  1. The cell membrane controls what enters and leaves the cell just as the nuclear membrane controls what enters and leaves the nucleus.
  2. Things like food and oxygen enter the cell through the cell membrane.
  3. Wastes like carbon dioxide leave the cell through the cell membrane.
F. Not all cells are alike.
  1. Many cells have special work to do so they differ in size and shape, and they may even have special materials.
  2. This difference makes it possible for the cells to do their special kind of work.
  3. Examples of special cells include bone, muscle, skin, nerve, and blood cells.
G. A group of the same kind of cells that do the same work is called a **tissue.**
  1. Examples of tissue include bone, muscle, skin, and nerve tissue.
  2. Even blood, which is a liquid, is a tissue.
H. A group of tissues working together is called an **organ.**
  1. Examples of organs include the heart, liver, stomach, kidneys, and brain.
  2. Organs carry out much more difficult tasks than tissues.
I. A group of organs that work together to carry out a special activity is called a **system.**
  1. The digestive system includes such organs as the esophagus, stomach, liver,

and intestines.

2. The circulatory system includes such organs as the heart, arteries, and veins.
3. The respiratory system includes such organs as the windpipe, lungs, and bronchial tubes.

J. Cells, then, carry out all the activities that living things do in order to live.
1. These activities are usually called **life processes.**
2. Some of the more important life processes include respiration, circulation, digestion, assimilation, excretion, growth, motion, and reproduction.

II. CLASSIFYING LIVING THINGS

A. All living things are grouped into main divisions, called **kingdoms.**
B. These kingdoms are subdivided into major groups called **phyla.**
1. Phyla are very large groups of living things.
2. All the members of a phylum have certain broad similarities in structure and in other characteristics.
C. The phyla are subdivided into smaller groups called **classes,** the classes into **orders,** the orders into **families,** the families into **genera,** the genera into **species,** and the species into **varieties.**
1. A class is a finer subdivision of a phylum.
2. An order is one of several groups within a class.
3. A family is a group within an order.
4. A genus is a smaller group within a family.
5. A species is a group of very closely related living things.
6. A variety is an individual of a species that differs slightly from other individuals in the same species, but not enough to be considered a separate species.
D. The further the phyla are subdivided, the greater the similarity there is among the members that make up each group.
E. When classifying living things, scientists give each phylum and its subgroups a sci-entific name made up of Latin words or words that have been Latinized.

1. This scientific naming makes the classification of each living thing definite, so that there can be no duplication.
2. The scientific name also describes the living thing well enough so that it can be readily identified.
3. It also helps show relationships between different living things.
4. Latin is a universal language, so the names have the same meaning to scientists all over the world.

F. Until recently, scientists put all living things into just two kingdoms: the **plant kingdom** and the **animal kingdom.**
G. Today they feel that this classification is too broad and confusing.
1. Many living things, especially the very tiny ones, do not fit very well into either kingdom.
2. Some are like plants, some are like animals, some have the characteristics of plants and animals, and some seem to be neither plants nor animals.
3. Scientists now put all these hard-to-classify living things into a separate kingdom, called the **protista kingdom.**
4. Some scientists think this third kingdom is too much of a catch-all and break it up into the **protista kingdom** and the **monera kingdom.**
H. The new classification makes it easier to define each kingdom sharply and to distinguish one clearly from the others.

III. THE ANIMAL KINGDOM

A. The animal kingdom, scientifically called the **animalia kingdom** or **metazoa kingdom,** is divided into from 9 to 18 phyla.
B. These phyla include the following groups: **poriferans, coelenterates, platyhelminths, aschelminths, annelids, echinoderms, mollusks, arthropods,** and **chordates.**
C. The animal kingdom is also commonly divided into two broad groups: animals with backbones and animals without back-

bones.

1. Animals with backbones are called **vertebrates,** and animals without backbones are called **invertebrates.**
2. Only the members of the chordate phylum are vertebrates.
3. Vertebrates include the fish, amphibians, reptiles, birds, and mammals.
4. The members of all the other phyla are invertebrates.

D. The cells of members of the animal kingdom are slightly different from the cells of the members of the plant kingdom.

1. Animal cells do not have chlorophyll.
2. Also, animal cells do not have a cell wall, made of cellulose, around them.

IV. THE PORIFERANS

A. Poriferans are the simplest of the many-celled animals.
B. The body is a hollow tube with many pores or openings in it.
C. Water flows into and out of the hollow tube, bringing in food and oxygen for the poriferan, and taking away carbon dioxide and other waste products.
D. The wall of the body is made up of two layers of cells.
E. Saltwater and freshwater **sponges** belong to this phylum.

V. THE COELENTERATES

A. The coelenterates, also called cnidarians, are also made up of two layers of cells.
B. They have tentacles that surround their mouths, radiating out regularly like the spokes of a wheel.
C. Some coelenterates have as little as six tentacles, but others have as many as hundreds of tentacles.
D. Circulation and digestion take place in their hollow bodies.
E. Their bodies have an opening at one end only.
F. The **jellyfish, hydra, coral,** and **sea anemone** are members of this phylum.

VI. THE PLATYHELMINTHS

A. The platyhelminths are flattened, ribbon-like worms, with bodies that are smooth and have no rings or body divisions, commonly called **segments.**
B. Their digestive tube has an opening at one end only.
C. Their bodies are made up of only three layers of cells.
D. They have very simple digestive and nervous systems.
E. Many of them are parasites.

1. Any living thing that lives on or in a plant or animal and gets its food from that plant or animal is called a **parasite.**
2. The plant or animal from which a parasite gets its food is called a **host.**

F. The **tapeworm, planarian,** and **fluke** belong to this phylum.

VII. THE ASCHELMINTHS

A. The aschelminths, also called nematodes, are worms with thin, round bodies having no rings or body divisions (which are called segments).
B. Sometimes the bodies are threadlike.
C. They have definite digestive systems, and their digestive tube runs the length of the body with an opening at each end.
D. Many of these worms are parasites in animals and plants.
E. The **hookworm, pinworm,** and **trichinella** belong to this phylum.

VIII. THE ANNELIDS

A. The annelids are worms with round bodies that are divided into rings or body divisions, called **segments.**
B. They have many well-developed organ systems, which include a digestive system, a circulatory system, an excretory system, a reproductive system, and a nervous system.
C. The **earthworm, sandworm,** and **leech** belong to this phylum.

IX. THE ECHINODERMS

A. The echinoderms are animals with spines on their bodies.
B. They have a hard, shell-like kind of skeleton, which is on the outside of their body.
C. The parts of their body usually radiate out regularly from the center like the spokes of a wheel.
D. The **starfish, sea urchin, sand dollar,** and **sea cucumber** are members of this phylum.

X. THE MOLLUSKS

A. The mollusks have soft, fleshy bodies with no segments.
B. Most mollusks have a protective shell made of lime.
  1. Because of this shell, mollusks are often called **shellfish.**
  2. They have a muscular foot and a special sheet of tissue, called the **mantle,** which produces the shell.
C. The **clam, oyster, scallop, snail, octopus,** and **squid** are members of this phylum.

XI. THE ARTHROPODS

A. The arthropods have skeletons on the outside of their bodies.
B. Their bodies are segmented and there are distinct body regions.
C. Their legs, and all other parts attached to the body, are jointed and can bend.
D. All their body parts are paired, and arranged on the right and left sides of the body in such a way that one side of the body is a mirror image of the other side.
E. The **lobster, crayfish, crab, shrimp, spider, tick, centipede, millipede,** and all **insects** are members of this phylum.

XII. THE CHORDATES

A. All chordates had a central nerve cord, called the **notochord,** before they were born.
B. Most chordates have a backbone, which replaced the notochord, and these chordates are called vertebrates.
C. Their skeletons are inside their bodies.
D. They all have two pairs of limbs attached to their body.
E. There are five important classes of chordates: **fish, amphibians, reptiles, birds,** and **mammals.**
F. Fish are cold-blooded animals.
  1. They have bony skeletons, and their bodies are covered with scales.
  2. They breathe by gills, and they have an air bladder that helps them rise or sink in the water.
G. Amphibians are cold-blooded animals.
  1. When they are young, they live under water and breathe by gills.
  2. Later, they change and develop lungs for breathing.
  3. They have a smooth skin without scales.
  4. Examples of amphibians include the frog, toad, and salamander.
H. Reptiles are cold-blooded animals.
  1. They breathe by lungs, and usually have a rough, dry, thick, scaly skin.
  2. Examples of reptiles include the snake, lizard, alligator, crocodile, and turtle.
I. Birds are warm-blooded animals.
  1. They breathe by lungs.
  2. Their front limbs are called wings, and they are covered with feathers.
  3. Their legs are scaly.
  4. Their skeleton is light, hollow, and streamlined for flying.
J. Mammals are warm-blooded animals.
  1. They breathe by lungs.
  2. They usually give birth to living young, and suckle their young with milk from glands, called **mammary glands.**
  3. All mammals have hair on their bodies even though there may be just a few bristles, as is the case with the whale.
  4. All mammals have seven neck bones, but these bones are not the same size for all mammals.

SIMPLE ANIMALS

I. What Simple Animals Are

A. All animals are made up of a great many cells.

B. The cells are not all alike, but are different and have special functions.

C. Some very simple animals have their cells arranged in just two layers.

D. Examples of such simple animals include the **sponge, hydra, jellyfish, sea anemone,** and **coral.**

II. The Sponges

A. A long time ago sponges were thought to be plants.
  1. This happened because the sponges looked like plants.
  2. They were attached to rocks and other objects in the water, and did not move from place to place.

B. Now we know that sponges are members of the animal phylum called **Porifera.**

C. Most sponges are found in the ocean, but there are also some freshwater sponges.

D. Sponges may be colored white, red, orange, yellow, brown, purple, black, and green.

E. They can live singly or in colonies.

F. A sponge's body is a hollow tube with many pores or openings in it.
  1. Water is always flowing into and out of the hollow tube.
  2. The water carries in food and oxygen for the sponge, and takes away carbon dioxide and other waste products.

G. Sponges eat tiny plants and animals.

H. Sponges have skeletons made of different kinds of materials.
  1. Some skeletons are made of lime.
  2. Some skeletons are made of silicon and look glassy.
  3. Some skeletons are made of a soft and flexible material, called **spongin.**

I. The natural sponges that we use are the spongin skeletons of large sponges that live in warm parts of the oceans.
  1. In deep waters the sponges are collected by divers.
  2. In shallow waters they are collected by men using hooks that are attached to the ends of long poles.
  3. The sponges are hung on the boats or piled on the shore and left there until the living cells die.
  4. The spongin skeleton parts that are left behind are then washed, dried, and sorted by size.
  5. The best places for collecting sponges are in the Mediterranean Sea, the Red Sea, the waters around the West Indies, and parts of the Gulf Coast of Florida.

J. Sponges can reproduce from sexual cells, called **gametes.**
  1. These special cells produce male cells, called **sperm,** and female cells, called **eggs.**
  2. A male cell (sperm) unites with, or fertilizes a female cell (egg).
  3. This fertilized egg (called a **zygote**) develops into a young sponge that can swim around in the water by means of long, whiplike threads, called **flagella.**
  4. As the young sponges become older, they settle to the bottom of the ocean and become attached to a rock or other object.

K. Sponges can also reproduce by a process called **budding.**
  1. A bud develops near the base of the sponge and grows into a new sponge.
  2. Some grown buds stay attached to the parent sponge, but others break off and live independently.

L. When a live sponge is cut up into many pieces, each piece can grow into a new sponge.

M. Some sponges look green because they are living together with tiny green plants, called **algae.**
  1. The algae have chlorophyll and make

[503

their food by photosynthesis, giving off oxygen which the sponges use.

2. The sponges give off carbon dioxide when they digest their food, and the algae use the carbon dioxide for photosynthesis.

3. This arrangement, where two living things live together and help each other, is called **symbiosis.**

III. THE HYDRA

A. The hydra is a member of the animal phylum that is called **Coelenterata** and also **Cnidaria.**

B. It is found only in fresh water, and is 3 to 6 millimeters (⅛ to ¼ in) long.

C. Some hydras are white whereas others may be brown or green.

D. The hydra has a round, tubular body with an open mouth at one end.

E. Surrounding the mouth are six to ten tentacles, which radiate out like wheel spokes.

1. The tentacles have stinging cells in them.

2. When tiny animals touch the tentacles, the stinging cells shoot out tiny threads with poison in them and paralyze or kill the animals.

3. Then the tentacles bend inward and push these animals through the hydra's mouth and into the hollow body.

4. Cells inside the hollow body digest the animals, and any waste products pass out through the mouth.

F. The hydra attaches itself to rocks or water plants at its closed end.

1. The hydra can move by leaving the point where it is attached, floating in the water, and then attaching itself at another point.

2. It can also move by turning "handsprings," in which the body bends over, the tentacles touch the ground, and then the body swings up and over.

G. When the hydra is disturbed or irritated, the tentacles and body quickly contract.

H. The hydra can reproduce by budding.

1. A bud grows from the side of the body and grows into a new hydra.

2. The new hydra then separates from its parent and lives independently.

I. The hydra can also reproduce sexually, usually in the autumn.

1. The hydra develops a swelling, called a **testis,** with many sperm in it.

2. Another hydra, or sometimes the same hydra, produces a swelling, called an **ovary,** with an egg in it.

3. The sperm leave the testis and swim to the ovary.

4. When a sperm unites with, or fertilizes, the egg in an ovary, the fertilized egg grows into a new hydra.

J. Like the sponge, when a hydra is cut up into little pieces, each piece will grow into a new hydra.

K. Also like the sponges, some hydras look green because they are living in symbiosis with green algae.

IV. THE JELLYFISH

A. The jellyfish is also a member of the Coelenterata (Cnidaria) phylum.

B. They live only in seawater.

C. Most of them are transparent and are hard to see in the water.

D. Some jellyfish are tiny, whereas others can be as wide as 2 meters (6½ ft) across.

E. The body of the jellyfish is shaped like an open umbrella or parachute.

1. Between the two cells of the body there is a jellylike material, which gives the jellyfish its name.

2. The mouth of the jellyfish is on the underside of the body, and is usually surrounded by tentacles.

3. The tentacles in very large jellyfish can be more than 15 meters (49 ft) long.

4. The tentacles have thousands of stinging cells in them.

5. When the tentacles of a jellyfish touch a swimmer's skin, the stinging cells can produce painful blisters.

6. The cells can kill small sea animals.

F. The jellyfish either floats or swims near the surface of the water.

1. It swims by taking some water into its

504]

umbrella-like body, then forcing the water out again.

2. As the water is forced out, it makes the jellyfish move with a jerk.

G. It eats small fish and other sea animals, which swim into its tentacles and are stung.

V. SEA ANEMONES

A. The sea anemone is also a coelenterate (cnidarian).

B. Sea anemones look like king-sized hydras, but have hundreds of short tentacles around their mouths.

C. Many are brightly colored and look like the anemone flowers found on land.

D. They can often be seen along some seacoasts at low tide.

VI. CORAL

A. The coral is a coelenterate (cnidarian) that lives in large colonies.

B. Corals live in seawater, and are most common where the water is warm and shallow.

C. A coral looks like a hydra, but it is just a little larger.

D. Each coral builds a skeleton of limestone around it, taking the limestone from the seawater.

1. Each skeleton is connected firmly to the skeletons around it, making one big mass.

2. The coral's body and tentacles usually extend beyond the skeleton.

3. When the coral is disturbed, it can withdraw its tentacles and shorten its body so that the entire body can be contained inside its skeleton.

4. When the coral dies, its skeleton remains.

E. Corals can reproduce by budding, and the new corals stay connected to the original ones.

F. Because of reproduction by budding, the mass of skeletons can become higher and wider until it forms a rocky ridge called a **reef.**

1. Reefs are usually under water, but some protrude above the water, either temporarily at low tide or permanently when changes take place inside the earth that make the sea level lower.

2. Coral reefs are commonly formed near islands, where the water is rather shallow.

3. Some reefs even circle a small island.

4. Sometimes a circular reef with open water in the center is formed, and this kind of reef is called an **atoll.**

G. Corals can also reproduce sexually.

H. A young coral can swim about freely, but when it gets older, it becomes attached to the sea bottom or to some object and does not move around any more.

I. Coral is made into jewelry, and is also used for decoration in homes and stores.

J. Crushed coral is sometimes used in building roads and highways.

WORMS

I. KINDS OF WORMS

A. To many persons that word "worm" means something that is long, has a soft, ringed body, and wiggles.

B. However, not all worms are the same.

C. Scientists divide worms into three large groups: **flatworms, roundworms,** and **segmented worms.**

D. These three groups of worms are members of separate phyla, and are completely different from one another.

[505

II. FLATWORMS

A. Flatworms are members of the animal phylum called **Platyhelminthes.**
B. They are the simplest of all the worms.
   1. Their bodies are flat and ribbonlike, with none of the rings or body divisions that are commonly called **segments.**
   2. The bodies are made up of only three layers of cells.
C. Some flatworms move about freely in water and get their food from the water.
D. Other flatworms live as **parasites** in larger animals, getting their food from the animal, which is called the **host.**
E. The **planarian** is a flatworm that is free-living (not parasitic).
   1. It is usually found under stones in ponds and streams.
   2. It is 3 to 13 millimeters (⅛ to ½ in) long, and colored brown, black, or white.
   3. The planarian's head is shaped like a spear, and there are two **eyespots** on the head, making the planarian appear to be cross-eyed.
   4. These eyespots are sensitive to light, and the planarian moves away from bright light.
   5. The planarian's mouth is in the middle of its body, on the underside, attached to a tube that sometimes sticks out of the body when the planarian is looking for or is feeding on food.
   6. The planarian has a simple digestive system that is open only at one end; thus food enters and waste materials pass out from the same end.
   7. The planarian lives on tiny water animals and also on dead plant and animal matter.
   8. It also has a simple nervous system.
   9. It moves by means of two layers of muscles under its skin, and also by many tiny hairs, called **cilia,** on its underside.
   10. The planarian can reproduce by fission (splitting in two).
   11. It can also reproduce sexually, with each planarian having both male cells (sperm) and female cells (eggs) in it.
   12. When a planarian is cut up into many pieces, each piece will form a new planarian.
F. The **tapeworm** is perhaps the most well-known parasitic flatworm.
   1. As a parasite, it lives in and gets its food from an animal, which is called the **host.**
   2. Man sometimes has a tapeworm because he has eaten meat that has not been cooked thoroughly.
   3. A tapeworm has a knob-shaped head with suckers, and sometimes hooks as well, on it.
   4. The suckers and hooks help the tapeworm clamp itself to the wall of a human's intestine.
   5. The parasite has no mouth or intestine, and the digested food from the human's intestine passes directly into the tapeworm's head.
   6. The tapeworm has no eyes, and it does not move.
   7. Sections keep forming just back of the tapeworm's head.
   8. As more new sections form, the older sections are pushed farther and farther back.
   9. As a result, the worm gets to look like a long piece of tape.
   10. Sometimes there are more than 200 sections to a tapeworm's body, and the tapeworm can be more than 50 feet long.
   11. The end sections of the tapeworm's body grow larger and older, and then drop off and pass out of the human's body.
   12. The sections that drop off are filled with egg cells that have already been fertilized because each section of the tapeworm is able to produce both male cells (sperm) and female cells (eggs).
   13. The sections that drop off soon decay, but the fertilized eggs stay alive.
   14. When these eggs are eaten by an animal, such as the cow or pig, with its

food, the eggs grow into tiny young tapeworms.

15. These young tapeworms cannot grow any larger and become adults until they enter the body of a human again.

16. They worm their way into some tissue, such as the muscle or liver, of the animal.

17. Inside the tissue each young tapeworm forms a capsule, called a **cyst,** around itself.

18. Inside the cyst the tiny tapeworm forms a head (with suckers) and a few sections, and then stops and rests or waits until the meat of the animal is eaten by a human.

19. If the animal's meat is not thoroughly cooked, a young tapeworm that is still alive can come out of its cyst, clamp onto the human's intestine, and grow into an adult tapeworm.

20. When segments from the new tapeworm drop off and pass out of the human's body, the whole life cycle of the tapeworm starts again.

21. During its life cycle the tapeworm has two hosts.

22. The host for the adult tapeworm is called the **primary host,** and the host for the young tapeworm is called the **secondary host.**

G. The **fluke** is another well-known parasitic flatworm.

1. Flukes are very dangerous to many animals and also to man.

2. They live in such organs as the stomach, intestine, liver, or lung, where they damage or destroy the lining tissues of these organs and cause loss of blood and ulcers.

3. Many of the flukes look somewhat like the planaria.

4. Almost all of the flukes have more than one host during their life cycle, and one of the fluke's secondary hosts is always a snail.

5. Fluke infections are most common in Africa and Asia.

III. ROUNDWORMS

A. Roundworms are members of the animal phylum called **Aschelminthes** by some scientists and **Nematoda** by others.

B. They have thin, round, smooth bodies that are not divided into rings or segments.

C. They have a complete digestive system, with a mouth at the front end and an opening, called the **anus,** at the rear end.

D. Some roundworms are free-living (nonparasitic).

1. They live in the soil, fresh water, or salt water.

2. Free-living roundworms are very tiny, and are harmless.

E. Some roundworms are parasitic, and live in animals or plants.

1. They can be 1¼ meters (4 ft) long.

2. Different kinds of parasitic roundworms have already infected about one third of the human race.

F. The most common parasitic roundworm is the **ascaris.**

1. It is a large worm, and lives in the intestine of larger animals, such as the pig and horse, and sometimes in man.

2. It feeds on the partly digested food in the intestine.

3. Ascaris worms lay millions of eggs, which pass out of the body with the waste products.

4. In regions where there is no modern sanitary sewage disposal, these eggs are deposited in water, soil, and food grown on that soil.

5. The eggs then enter and infect other animal and human bodies through the contaminated food or water.

6. Most infections caused by ascaris worms are not serious.

7. However, sometimes such large masses of these worms form that they block the intestine and death results.

8. Sometimes the adult worms bore through the intestine, travel through the body, and go into vital organs, such as the liver, causing death.

G. The **hookworm** is a parasitic roundworm that is a serious health menace to man.

1. It is found in all tropical and semi-tropical regions, as well as in the southeastern United States, wherever there are unsanitary sewage disposal conditions.

2. Hookworms are quite small, less than ½ inch, and thousands can live in the intestine at one time.

3. The adult hookworms attach themselves to the wall of the intestine by their hooklike teeth and suck the blood from the intestine wall.

4. This steady loss of blood makes the hosts tired and anemic.

5. In the intestines the worms reproduce and lay eggs, which pass out of the body with the waste products.

6. The eggs hatch in the soil and grow into young hookworms.

7. These young hookworms enter the body of animals and humans by boring through the skin, usually at the feet.

8. Once they enter the body, they travel in the blood to the lungs.

9. In the lungs they pass through the air passages and move up the windpipe into the throat.

10. In the throat they are swallowed and pass through the stomach into the intestine, where they attach themselves and grow into adult hookworms, producing more eggs for possible future infection.

H. The **trichinella** is a parasitic roundworm that can cripple and even kill a human.

1. It lives in the intestine of its host, which can be an animal or a human.

2. Each trichinella can produce as many as 2000 eggs.

3. These eggs hatch into young worms, which travel in the blood to muscles all over the body.

4. The young worms bore into the muscles and form tiny capsules, called **cysts,** around themselves.

5. The young worms stay inside these cysts and cannot grow into adults until the flesh of the host is eaten by another animal or by a human.

6. When another animal or man eats this infected meat, the young worms come out of their cysts, become adult worms, and start producing their own young worms.

7. These young worms find their way to the muscles of their hosts and form cysts there.

8. Man becomes infected by the trichinella from eating undercooked meat of an animal that is a host to the trichinella.

9. Usually this animal is the pig, and the meat is pork.

10. The pig gets the trichinella by eating garbage that has scraps of raw meat with trichinella worm cysts in them.

11. When a human is infected with the trichinella, the muscles become inflamed and painful as the young worms are boring their way into the muscles and forming cysts.

12. If too many worms find their way into the muscles, the person may become crippled or may even die.

13. Once the worms find their way into the muscles there is no way to remove them because they are very tiny.

14. The disease caused by the trichinella is called **trichinosis.**

IV. SEGMENTED WORMS

A. Segmented worms are members of the animal phylum called **Annelida.**

B. Annelids are the most highly developed group of worms.

1. Their bodies are divided into many rings or sections, called **segments.**

2. They have many well-developed organ systems, which include a digestive system, a circulatory system with blood and blood vessels, an excretory system for getting rid of waste matter, a nervous system, and a reproductive system.

C. Segmented worms can be found in salt

water, in fresh water, and in the soil.

D. The **earthworm** is a common segmented worm that lives in the soil.

1. Its front end is darker and more pointed than its tail.

2. Four bristles, called **setae,** stick out from the sides and underside of each body segment, except the first and the last segments.

3. These bristles help the earthworm move.

4. The earthworm is able to move because it has two sets of muscles: one set that can make the earthworm long and thin, and another set that can make the earthworm short and thick.

5. The earthworm has no respiratory system, but absorbs oxygen and gives off carbon dioxide through its thin skin, which must be kept moist.

6. Each earthworm forms both sperm and eggs, but the eggs of one worm can only be fertilized by the sperm of another worm.

7. As a result, two earthworms come together and exchange sperm so that the eggs in each earthworm can be fertilized.

8. The earthworm lays a batch of fertilized eggs in the soil, which eventually hatch and become young earthworms.

9. The earthworm eats dirt, digesting the decayed plant and animal matter from the dirt and eliminating the rest.

10. Earthworms are valuable to man because they bore holes and loosen the soil so that air and water can enter the soil and help plant roots grow.

11. Many scientists believe that the waste matter that passes out of the earthworm's body makes a good fertilizer.

E. The **sandworm** is a segmented worm that lives in the ocean near the shore.

1. It is more active than the earthworm.

2. It has four eyespots that are sensitive to light, and a group of tentacles on its head.

3. Sometimes the sandworm burrows into the sand, with only its head exposed to the water.

4. The sandworm can also swim about in the water, helped by little projections on each side of its body.

5. The sandworm eats tiny saltwater animals.

F. The **leech** is a parasitic segmented worm.

1. Most leeches are found in fresh water, but a few live in the ocean.

2. They are commonly called "bloodsuckers" because they live by sucking the blood of larger water animals, such as fish and turtles.

3. A leech has two suckers, one at each end of its body, for clinging to these water animals.

4. It uses the rear sucker to attach itself to the animal's body.

5. Then it attaches the front sucker to another part of the animal's body, and breaks the skin of the animal with sharp little jaws in its mouth.

6. A substance in the saliva of the leech prevents the animal's blood from clotting while the leech is sucking the blood of its victim.

SPINY ANIMALS

I. WHAT SPINY ANIMALS ARE

A. Spiny animals are members of the animal phylum called **Echinodermata.**

B. All the echinoderms live only in the ocean.

C. They all have a hard, shell-like kind of skeleton, which is on the outside of their bodies.

D. Almost all of them have some kind of spines on their bodies.

E. The parts of their bodies usually radiate out regularly, like the spokes of a wheel.

F. Members of this phylum include the star-fish, sea urchin, sand dollar, and sea cucumber.

II. THE STARFISH

A. The starfish is not a fish at all.

B. It has no head, but is made up of a circle of arms that come together at the center of its body, forming a star shape.
   1. Most starfish have five arms, but some have six or more arms.
   2. There are spines all over the body and arms.
   3. The stomach of the starfish is at the center of the body, and its mouth is on the underside.

C. A starfish eats clams and oysters.
   1. On the underside of each arm there are hundreds of little tubes, called **tube feet.**
   2. Each tube foot acts as a vacuum or suction cup and can stick firmly to any object on which it is pressed.
   3. The starfish crawls over the top of a clam and presses its tube feet firmly on both sides of the shell.
   4. The starfish pulls on the clam until the clam becomes tired and opens its shell.
   5. Then the starfish turns its stomach inside out so that the stomach extends through the mouth, and it digests the clam's body.

D. The starfish can crawl in any direction.
   1. An eyespot at the end of each arm is sensitive to light.
   2. The starfish moves about mostly at night.

E. Starfish are either male or female.
   1. They discharge their sperm and eggs into the water, where fertilization of the eggs takes place.
   2. A female starfish may lay more than 100 million eggs in one season.

F. Starfish can grow new parts.
   1. If a starfish loses an arm, it can grow a new one.
   2. If a starfish is chopped into three or four pieces, and if each piece has at least one arm and also part of the center of the body, each piece may grow into a new starfish.

III. OTHER ECHINODERMS

A. The **sea urchin** is a globe-shaped echinoderm with very long spines.

B. The **sand dollar** is very much like the sea urchin, but it is very flat and its spines are very short.

C. The **sea cucumber** is long and soft, and really looks like a cucumber growing under water.

SHELLFISH

I. WHAT SHELLFISH ARE

A. Shellfish are members of the animal phylum called **Mollusca.**

B. The word "shellfish" is a poor name for the mollusks.
   1. Mollusks are not fish.
   2. Not all of them have shells.
   3. Many live on land.

C. All mollusks have thick, soft, fleshy bodies.

D. Mollusks are divided into three large groups, which are commonly called **hatchet-footed, belly-footed,** and **head-footed** mollusks.
   1. The hatchet-footed mollusks live inside two shells that are connected by a muscular hinge which can open and close the shells.
   2. The belly-footed mollusks have just one spiral shell and seem to be moving on

their bellies, carrying their shells on their backs.

3. The head-footed mollusks have a definite head, surrounded by many arms called **tentacles.**

II. THE HATCHET-FOOTED OR BIVALVE MOLLUSKS

A. The hatchet-footed mollusks all have two shells, called **valves,** which are connected by a muscular hinge.
1. Because of these two shells or valves, they are usually called **bivalve** mollusks.
2. The muscular hinge opens and closes these shells.
3. Bivalves never shed their shells, and the shells become larger as the bivalve grows.
4. Lines on the outside of the shell tell roughly the age of the bivalve, each line representing a year's growth.
B. Bivalve mollusks include the **clam, oyster, scallop,** and **mussel.**
C. They all live in the ocean, but the clam can be found both in salt water and fresh water.
D. They all have a tough muscular foot, shaped somewhat like a hatchet, which sticks out from the shells and is used for digging.
E. The inside of their shells are lined with a special sheet of tissue, called the **mantle,** which produces the shell.
F. They have two tubes, called **siphons.**
1. Water carrying oxygen and food flows into one siphon.
2. Water carrying carbon dioxide and waste products flows out of the other siphon.
G. They have respiratory or breathing organs, called **gills,** which allow oxygen to enter the body and carbon dioxide to leave.
H. They have a well-developed digestive system, excretory system for getting rid of wastes, nervous system for controlling their movements, reproductive system, and a circulatory system with a heart, blood, and blood vessels.

I. Bivalve mollusks are either male or female, and reproduce sexually.
J. In the ocean the oyster and many kinds of clams do not move at all, but are attached to a rock or some other object.
K. In the South Pacific Ocean there are clams as large as 2 meters (6½ ft) across.

III. THE BELLY-FOOTED OR UNIVALVE MOLLUSKS

A. The belly-footed mollusks have one shell or valve, which is usually shaped in a spiral.
B. Because of the one shell or valve, they are usually called **univalve** mollusks.
C. Univalves include the **snail, slug, periwinkle, conch,** and **abalone.**
D. The conch and abalone live in the ocean whereas the slug lives on land, and there are both land snails and water snails.
E. Univalves all have the same vital body organs as the bivalves, except that some snails have lungs instead of gills for breathing.
F. Univalves also have a much larger foot than bivalves.
1. This large foot looks like part of the univalve's body to most people, and, therefore, they think the univalve is crawling on its belly and carrying its shell on its back.
2. When the univalve is attacked, it pulls its foot and head up inside its body.
G. The snail has two tentacles on its head.
1. Some snails have an eye on the tip of each tentacle.
2. When the snail is touched, it draws in its tentacles.
H. The slug does not have a shell and looks like a snail that has lost its shell.
I. The foot of land snails and slugs gives off a kind of slime, and the snails and slugs move only on this slime.
J. Snails and slugs also have a tonguelike structure that is very rough.
1. This "tongue" moves in and out, and acts very much like a file to scrape off bits of food.

2. Land snails and slugs use this tongue to eat plants.
3. Water snails help keep an aquarium clean by using their scraping tongue to eat algae, bacteria, and dead or decaying materials that collect on the glass sides of the aquarium.

IV. THE HEAD-FOOTED MOLLUSKS

A. The head-footed mollusks include the **octopus** and the **squid**.
B. They have the same parts as the other mollusks, but arranged differently.
C. Both the squid and the octopus live in the ocean.
D. The squid has a long, narrow, torpedo-like body.
   1. It has no shell on the outside.
   2. Its foot is divided into two long and eight short tentacles, which have double rows of suction cups on them for grasping objects firmly.
   3. It has a large eye on each side of its head.
   4. It also has a sharp beak, which it uses to bite off pieces of food.
   5. Most squids are no more than 1 meter (3 ft) long, but there are some giant squids that are at least 18 meters (59 ft) long.
E. The octopus is built much like the squid, but its body is short and rounded.
   1. It has only eight tentacles, all the same size.
   2. It has a shell, but the shell is inside its body.
   3. It has eyes and a sharp beak, just like the squid.
   4. Some octopuses have tentacles 15 centi-

meters (6 in) long, but others may have tentacles 4 meters (13 ft) long.
F. When attacking or being attacked, the squid and octopus can shoot out an inky material that makes the water cloudy.

V. IMPORTANCE OF MOLLUSKS

A. Clams, oysters, scallops, snails, and abalones are all eaten by man.
B. Octopuses and squids are eaten by man in some parts of the world, and very often they are cut up and used as bait by fishermen.
C. The inner surface of clam and oyster shells are used to make buttons and mother-of-pearl.
D. Shells are also ground up and sold to farmers for chicken feed because the lime in the shells is needed by the chickens for making egg shells.
E. Certain oysters make pearls.
   1. A pearl is formed when an irritating object, such as a parasitic worm, gets inside the flesh of the oyster and forms a tiny round capsule, called a **cyst**.
   2. The mantle (shell-producing tissue) forms layers of shell material around the cyst, producing the pearl.
F. The Japanese have discovered a way of making the oyster form a pearl.
   1. They take a small round bead made from shell, cover the bead with living mantle cells, and push the bead inside the oyster.
   2. The oyster is then put into the ocean for a few years and a pearl forms around the head.
   3. This pearl, which is called a **cultured pearl,** looks just like a natural pearl.

CRAYFISH, LOBSTERS, CRABS, AND SHRIMPS

I. What Crayfish, Lobsters, Crabs, and Shrimps Are

A. The **crayfish, lobster, crab, shrimp,** the tiny **water flea, sow bug,** and **pill bug** are all members of the very large animal phylum called **Arthropoda.**

B. Together they form a special class of arthropods called **Crustacea.**

C. All arthropods have the following similar characteristics.

1. They have an outside skeleton, made of a tough material, called **chitin,** which covers their bodies and has joints that can bend.

2. The muscles of the body are attached to the inside of the skeleton.

3. Their legs and the other parts that are attached to the body, all of which are called **appendages,** are also jointed and can bend.

4. Their bodies are segmented, and there are distinct body regions.

5. They have **bilateral symmetry,** which means that all the parts of their bodies are paired, being arranged on the right and left side of the body in such a way that one side of the body is a mirror image of the other side.

D. In addition to having the characteristics of all arthropods, the crustaceans have their own special characteristics.

1. They have two pairs of feelers, called **antennae.**

2. Their outer skeleton has a chemical called lime in it.

3. They all have two very distinct body regions.

4. Almost all of them live in saltwater or freshwater.

5. Many of them have special breathing organs, called **gills,** which allow oxygen to enter their bodies and carbon dioxide to leave.

II. The Crayfish

A. The crayfish is a good example of a typical crustacean.

B. It has a dark outer skeleton with lime in it.

C. It has two distinct body regions: the **cephalothorax** and the **abdomen.**

1. The cephalothorax is really made up of two regions: the head and the chest, or **thorax,** both grown together so that they look like one region.

2. The abdomen, commonly called the tail, is made up of seven movable segments.

D. The cephalothorax is covered by a hard shell, called the **carapace,** which gives the crayfish extra protection.

E. The crayfish has two eyes, one on each side of the front part of the cephalothorax.

1. The eyes are set on the ends of short, movable stalks.

2. Each eye is made up of many lenses, and for this reason it is called a **compound eye.**

F. The crayfish has two pairs of long feelers, called **antennae,** and several smaller feelers, called **antennules.**

G. It has six pairs of mouth parts.

1. Three pairs are connected to the head, and three pairs are connected to the chest, or thorax.

2. These mouth parts are used for holding food, cutting and grinding it, and pushing it into the mouth.

H. It has five pairs of legs, all connected to its chest, or thorax.

1. The first pair, called the **chelipeds,** is much larger than the other four pairs, and one cheliped is always larger than the other.

2. The chelipeds have large pincers, which are used for grabbing and holding food.

3. The remaining four pairs of legs are used mostly for walking.

4. Two pairs of these walking legs end in

tiny pincers, and two pairs end in tiny claws.

I. It has six parts of appendages, called **swimmerets,** on its abdomen.

1. Each segment of the abdomen has a pair of swimmerets, except for the last segment, which has nothing.

2. The first five pairs of swimmerets are quite small, being used by the female for carrying her eggs until they are hatched, and by both the male and female for slow, forward swimming.

3. The sixth pair of swimmerets is large and paddlelike; these swimmerets are called **uropods.**

4. The uropods and the seventh segment of the abdomen, called the **telson,** together make up the tail of the crayfish.

J. The crayfish usually moves backward, using its sixth and seventh abdomen segments and its four walking legs.

1. These appendages make it possible for the crayfish to move backward easily and swiftly.

2. The crayfish also uses its four walking legs to travel forward and sideways.

K. The crayfish breathes through special feathery organs, called **gills.**

1. These gills are attached to the five pairs of legs and the three pairs of mouth parts that are connected to the thorax.

2. The gills allow oxygen in the water to enter the body of the crayfish and carbon dioxide to leave.

L. The crayfish is a freshwater animal, living at the bottom of lakes, ponds, and streams.

M. It eats plants and any live or dead animal material it can grasp.

N. The crayfish breeds just once a year.

1. The female mates with the male in the autumn.

2. In the spring the female lays about 100 eggs, which are attached to the first five pairs of spinnerets on her abdomen.

3. The female carries these eggs until they hatch.

4. The young crayfish stay attached to the swimmerets for about 2 weeks, holding the hairs of the swimmerets with their pincers.

5. During this time the young crayfish feed on the yolk that was in the eggs.

6. After 2 weeks the young crayfish let go of the swimmerets and are now independent, growing up to be adult crayfish.

O. When a crayfish grows larger, it sheds its skeleton.

1. This process is called **molting.**

2. Because the shell is rigid and cannot stretch, the crayfish cannot grow larger unless it gets rid of its skeleton.

3. Most crayfish molt about seven times the first year, and once or twice a year thereafter.

4. While a crayfish is molting, it is quite defenseless, so it usually goes into hiding until the new skeleton is formed.

P. If the crayfish should lose one or more of its appendages during molting or in a battle, it can regenerate or grow new appendages to replace the lost ones.

III. THE LOBSTER

A. The lobster is built like the crayfish, except that the lobster lives in saltwater and is much larger.

B. One kind of lobster is exactly like the crayfish, and is found in the North Atlantic Ocean.

C. Another kind of lobster does not have the first pair of large legs (chelipeds), and is found along the coast of Florida, California, and the West Indies.

IV. THE CRAB

A. The body of a crab is wide and round rather than long and narrow like the crayfish and the lobster.

B. The crab's abdomen is very small and folds under the broad shell (cephalothorax).

C. Crabs move by walking sideways.

D. "Soft-shell" crabs are crabs that were caught just after they had molted.

V. THE SHRIMP

A. The shrimp is like the crayfish, lobster, and crab.
B. However, it has five pairs of walking legs and a large, muscular abdomen.
C. The shrimp can swim very fast, moving backward like the crayfish and lobster.
D. When the shrimp is frightened, it buries itself in the sand, with only its antennae and eyes exposed.

VI. ECONOMIC IMPORTANCE

A. Crayfish, lobsters, crabs, and shrimps are widely used as food.
B. They are also useful as scavengers because they eat dead animals.

INSECTS

I. WHAT INSECTS ARE

A. Insects are members of the very large animal phylum called **Arthropoda.**
B. All the insects together form a special class of arthropods called **Insecta.**
C. Insects have the characteristics common to all arthropods.
   1. They have an outside skeleton made of a tough material, called **chitin.**
   2. Their legs and other parts attached to the body, all of which are called **appendages,** are jointed and can bend.
   3. Their bodies are segmented, and there are distinct body regions.
   4. They have **bilateral symmetry,** which means that all the parts of their body are paired, being arranged on the right and left side of the body in such a way that one side of the body is a mirror image of the other side.
D. In addition to having the characteristics of all arthropods, insects have their own special characteristics.
   1. They all have three separate body regions: the **head, thorax,** and **abdomen.**
   2. They have one pair of feelers, called **antennae,** attached to their heads.
   3. They have three pairs of legs, all attached to the thorax.
   4. Most insects have one or two pairs of wings, also attached to the thorax.
   5. Most adult insects have both **simple eyes,** which are made up of just one lens, and **compound eyes,** which are made up of many single lenses.
   6. Almost all of the insects live on land.
   7. They breathe through branching tubes, called **tracheae,** which are connected to tiny outside openings, called **spiracles,** on each side of the abdomen and thorax.
E. Insects make up the largest class in the animal kingdom.
   1. There are about 700,000 different kinds (species) of insects that have already been classified, and scientists believe that this is less than half the total number on earth.
   2. Each kind produces thousands of young insects.
F. Insects are more highly specialized than man.
   1. Because of the way they are built, insects are able to adjust to their environment very well.
   2. As a result, they have been very successful in their struggle for existence, and have lived on earth much longer than man.

II. METAMORPHOSIS IN INSECTS

A. All insects develop from eggs.
B. However, from the time the eggs hatch until the young insects become fully grown adults, most insects pass through a series

of forms or stages, called **metamorphosis.**

C. There are two kinds of metamorphosis: **incomplete metamorphosis** and **complete metamorphosis.**

D. Insects like the grasshopper, cricket, dragonfly, true bug, aphid, and termite undergo incomplete metamorphosis.

1. Incomplete metamorphosis has three forms or stages: **egg, nymph,** and **adult.**

2. The nymph hatches from the egg and looks just like the adult except that it does not have wings and mature sex organs.

3. When it is first hatched, the nymph is only as large as the egg, and its head is much larger than its body.

4. The nymph eats and grows, but its outside skeleton does not grow as fast as the nymph itself.

5. As a result, from time to time the nymph rests, splits and sheds its skeleton, and then continues to grow a new, larger skeleton.

6. The shedding of the skeleton is called **molting,** and usually takes place about five times before the nymph becomes an adult insect.

7. After each molting the nymph looks and becomes more like the adult insect.

8. After the final molting the nymph becomes a fully grown adult.

E. Insects like the butterfly, moth, bee, ant, beetle, fly, and mosquito undergo complete metamorphosis.

1. Complete metamorphosis has four stages: **egg, larva, pupa,** and **adult.**

2. The larva hatches from the egg and looks like a segmented worm.

3. The larva eats and grows, and then stops from time to time to shed its skin (molt).

4. After each molting the larva does not change, but continues to eat and become larger.

5. After several moltings the larva goes into the pupa stage, which is commonly called the resting stage.

6. However, although there is no movement during the pupa stage, a remarkable change takes place.

7. In the pupa stage all the tissues of the larva are changed into those of an adult insect.

8. When the pupa stage is completed, a fully grown adult insect has been formed.

III. KINDS OF INSECTS

A. Biologists divide all insects into about 25 different groups, called **orders.**

B. The division of insects into orders is based, for the most part, on the kind of mouth parts, wings, and metamorphosis the insects have.

C. The following eight insect orders are quite common in the United States: the **grasshopper** order, the **dragonfly** order, the **beetle** order, the **true bug** order, the **aphid** order, the **butterfly** and **moth** order, the **fly** and **mosquito** order, and the **bee** and **ant** order.

IV. THE GRASSHOPPER ORDER

A. The grasshopper, cricket, praying mantis, katydid, walking stick, locust, and cockroach belong to this order.

B. They have mouth parts that are designed for chewing with hard jaws that move from side to side instead of up and down.

C. They have two pairs of wings.

1. The front wings are long, narrow, and like stiff paper.

2. The back wings look like cellophane and are wide, thin, and veined.

3. When not in use, the back wings fold up lengthwise like a fan under the front wings.

D. In some of these insects, like the grasshopper, the rear legs are large and highly developed for jumping.

E. The grasshopper makes sounds by rubbing a row of spines on its rear leg against a wing vein.

F. All the insects of the grasshopper order undergo incomplete metamorphosis.

G. The grasshopper and cricket are very destructive insects, eating pasture and grain crops.

H. The praying mantis is the only insect in this group that is useful to man; it eats other insects, many of which are harmful to man.

V. The Dragonfly Order

A. The dragonfly and damselfly belong to this order.

B. They have long, thin bodies and are often called "needles."

C. They have chewing mouth parts.

D. They have two pairs of wings.
1. The wings are thin, like cellophane.
2. They do not fold but stick straight out from the body, one pair below the other.

E. They undergo incomplete metamorphosis.

F. The larva form of these insects lives in the water and eats the larvae of other insects.

G. The adult dragonfly and damselfly eat mosquitoes, gnats and other insects.

VI. The Beetle Order

A. The Japanese beetle, potato beetle, wood-boring beetle, boll weevil, ladybug, and carrion beetle belong to this order.

B. They have chewing mouth parts.

C. They have two pairs of wings.
1. The front wings are very hard and meet in a straight line down the back.
2. The front wings fit closely over the body and look very much like a shell.
3. The back wings are thin and fold under the front wings.
4. Because of the hard front wings, these insects make a whirring noise when flying.

D. They undergo complete metamorphosis, and their larvae are commonly called **grubs.**

E. The potato bug destroys potato plants, the boll weevil destroys grain and cotton, and the Japanese beetle destroys the fruit and leaves of trees, shrubs, and grasses.

F. The ladybug eats many harmful insects, and the carrion beetle acts as a scavenger by feeding on dead animals.

VII. The True Bug Order

A. Many persons use the word *bug* for most insects, but to scientists the word *bug* refers to a special order of insects.

B. The bedbug, stinkbug, squash bug, and water bug belong to this order.

C. They have sucking mouth parts.
1. They feed by sticking these parts into plants and sucking the plant juices.
2. The bedbug sucks the blood of man, and is a carrier of disease as well.

D. Although one or two kinds of bugs have no wings, the rest have two pairs of wings.
1. Both the front and back wings are thin.
2. The edges of the wings overlap, and one half of the wing is thicker than the other.

E. They undergo incomplete metamorphosis.

F. Many of them are troublesome pests.

VIII. The Aphid Order

A. The aphid or plant louse, scale insect, mealy bug, leaf hopper, and cicada belong to this order.

B. They have sucking mouth parts, and feed on the juice of plants.

C. Some have two pairs of wings, but others are wingless.
1. Those that have wings hold the wings over their body like an upside down **V** so that the wings look like the roof of a house.
2. Both pairs of wings are thin.

D. They undergo incomplete metamorphosis.

E. Most of them do great damage to wild and garden plants.

F. The lac insect, however, gives us shellac, which is used in lacquers and wood finishes.

IX. THE BUTTERFLY AND MOTH ORDER

A. Butterflies and moths have sucking mouth parts.
  1. Some moths have no mouths at all.
  2. Other moths and all butterflies have a long, coiled tube, which they use to sip the sweet liquid, called **nectar,** inside the flowers.
B. They have two pairs of wings that are covered with tiny scales.
  1. These scales produce the brilliant and beautiful colors in their wings.
  2. Most butterflies and some moths have pretty wings, but many moths have single-colored, unattractive wings.
C. Butterflies and moths undergo complete metamorphosis, and their larvae are called caterpillars or worms.
  1. The moth larva usually spins a strong silk case, called a **cocoon,** when it goes into the pupa (resting) stage.
  2. The butterfly pupa, however, rests in a hardened case, called a **chrysalis.**
D. Many persons find it hard to distinguish between butterflies and moths, especially when they both have colored wings, but there are definite differences between them.
  1. The butterfly usually has a thin abdomen; the moth usually has a fat abdomen.
  2. The butterfly's antennae usually have knobs at their ends; the moth's antennae are usually feathery.
  3. The butterfly usually flies during the day; the moth usually flies at night.
  4. The butterfly's wings are usually vertical when at rest; the moth usually holds its wings horizontally when at rest.
  5. The pupa of the butterfly rests in a chrysalis; the pupa of the moth usually rests in a cocoon.
E. Some butterflies and moths migrate, traveling to different parts of the country or world during different seasons of the year.
  1. The monarch butterfly lives in northern United States during the summer.
  2. In late summer they fly away in very large groups, some going to the Gulf states, and others going to the Pacific Coast.
  3. They stay quietly in these places until the winter is over.
  4. In the spring they all fly northward again.
F. The larvae of butterflies and especially moths are very destructive to man.
  1. The apple worm, tomato worm, corn borer, cabbage worm, cotton boll weevil, and tobacco worm all eat and destroy vegetables and crops.
  2. The larvae of the gypsy moth and brown-tail moth eat the leaves of forest and orchard trees, destroying them.
  3. The larvae of the clothes moth feed on clothing, especially wool.
G. The silkworm moth is helpful because its larva spins a cocoon of silk threads, which we use to make silk cloth.
H. All butterflies and many moths help in the cross-pollination of flowers as they travel from flower to flower to obtain nectar.

X. THE FLY AND MOSQUITO ORDER

A. The housefly, tsetse fly, stable fly, and mosquito belong to this order.
B. They have sucking mouth parts.
C. They only have one pair of wings, which are thin and veined.
D. They undergo complete metamorphosis.
E. The housefly has large eyes, short antennae, and a bat-shaped sucking tube.
  1. It does not bite, although other flies like the stable fly, or horsefly, and the tsetse fly bite both animals and man.
  2. Its wings are highly developed and it can fly swiftly.
  3. Its feet have claws and sticky hairs, which help it stay securely on walls and ceilings.
  4. These sticky hairs only work well if they are free from dust; the fly is always cleaning its feet by rubbing one foot against the other.
  5. The female fly lays its eggs in stable

manure or other similar matter, and the larvae that hatch are commonly called **maggots.**

6. The fly picks up all kinds of bacteria on its hairy feet and body.

7. When the fly lands on food that humans eat, some of the bacteria that cause typhoid fever, dysentery, and cholera can be left on the food.

F. The female mosquito lays its eggs in water, and the larvae that hatch are commonly called **wigglers.**

1. The pupa stage of the mosquito is different from most insect pupa stages because the mosquito pupa can move.

2. The adult mosquito has mouth parts that are designed for piercing and sucking.

3. The mosquito usually feeds on human and animal blood.

4. To make the sucking of blood easier and to prevent the blood from clotting, the mosquito injects a little of its saliva in the blood, causing the irritation and swelling that we call a "mosquito bite."

5. Some mosquitoes carry disease germs, such as malaria and yellow fever, in their bodies and spread these germs from person to person as they bite and suck up the blood.

XI. THE BEE ORDER

A. Although most insects live alone, certain kinds of insects live together in large groups or communities, called **colonies.**

B. Such insects are called **social insects** because different members of the colony have special jobs that help the entire colony.

C. Bees, ants, and wasps are members of an order of insects of which many kinds live in colonies as social insects.

D. Members of this order have the following characteristics.

1. Most of them have two pairs of thin, veined wings, with the front pair much larger than the back pair.

2. They have biting, sucking, or lapping mouth parts.

3. They undergo complete metamorphosis.

4. There is a definite narrowing, or constriction, between the thorax and the abdomen.

E. There are three kinds of bees in a bee colony: the **queen,** the **drones,** and the **workers.**

F. The queen is the egg-laying bee.

1. She is the largest bee in the colony, and has a long, pointed abdomen with an egg-laying organ at the tip of the last abdominal segment.

2. Her function is to lay eggs so that the colony can continue to exist.

3. She can lay both fertilized and unfertilized eggs.

4. Fertilized eggs develop into non-egg-laying females, which become the workers.

5. Unfertilized eggs develop into males, which are the drones.

6. The queen is fertilized just once by a drone (male bee), receiving several million sperm cells, which she keeps in a pouch in her body and uses the rest of her life.

7. There is usually just one queen bee to a bee colony.

G. The drones are male bees, developed from unfertilized eggs.

1. They are smaller than the queen bee, but larger than the female workers.

2. They have fat bodies, very large eyes, and powerful wings.

3. Their mouth parts are not long enough to suck up nectar so they must be fed by the workers.

4. During the summer there are usually a few hundred drones around a bee hive, but only one of them will mate with the queen.

5. In the fall, when the supply of honey is low, the workers refuse to feed the drones, and sting them to death.

H. The workers are female bees, developed from fertilized eggs.

1. They are the smallest bees in the colony, but most of the colony is made up of workers.

2. They cannot lay eggs, but they carry on all the other duties of the colony.
3. They bring in the nectar and pollen from flowers.
4. They prepare the materials that make up the hive, and they build the hive as well.
5. They prepare the food for the members of the colony.
6. Some feed the queen, others feed the drones, and still others feed the larvae that hatch from the eggs.
7. Some bees keep the hive clean, and others fan the hive to keep it airy and cool, or to help the watery nectar evaporate more quickly.

I. Workers have a "sting" at the tip of their last abdominal segment.
1. The "sting" is connected to a gland that gives off a poison, which is why a bee sting is so painful.
2. When a bee stings a person or animal, the "sting" and parts of the bee's internal organs are pulled out, and the bee dies.
3. Drones do not have a "sting."

J. Workers collect pollen and nectar from flowers.
1. Their mouth parts form a long tube, or tongue, which makes it possible for the bee to suck up nectar from the flowers.
2. The nectar is sucked into the bee's **honey stomach** or **crop**, where the nectar stays until it is brought to the hive and used as food.
3. Although pollen collects on all parts of the bee's hairy body and legs, much of it is deposited in a hairy cavity, called a **pollen basket**, located on each hind leg, and the pollen is brought back to the hive to be made into food.

K. The workers make three kinds of material for use in the hive: **wax, honey,** and **propolis.**

L. The wax oozes out of the segments of a worker's abdomen.
1. It usually is produced after the worker has eaten a lot of honey.

2. Other workers remove the wax that forms, chew it to make it soft, and then bring it to still other workers who use the wax to make the **honeycomb** in the hive.
3. The honeycomb is a structure in the hive that is made up of six-sided cells.
4. The honeycomb is used for storing honey and a special food, called beebread, which is made from pollen and bee saliva.
5. Eggs are also put in the honeycomb, one to a cell, by the queen, where they hatch, and the larvae are cared for by the workers.

M. Honey is made from the nectar of flowers, which the bees have collected in their honey stomachs or crops.
1. Here the sugars in the nectar are changed into honey, which is then emptied into the cells of the honeycomb.
2. The honey is watery at first, but becomes thick as the water in the honey is allowed to evaporate.
3. Workers, by fanning their wings, help the water evaporate more quickly from the honey.
4. When the honey in a cell is thick enough, the cell is sealed.

N. Propolis is a kind of bee glue.
1. It is a brown material collected from the sticky leaf buds of certain plants.
2. The workers use propolis to hold the honeycomb together, patch up holes and cracks, make the inside of the honeycomb smooth, and sometimes even to cover the body of a small, dead animal inside the hive.

O. Scientists have discovered that bees communicate with each other by doing different kinds of "dances," and in this way are able to tell other bees where they have found pollen and nectar for the colony.

P. The length of a bee's life varies.
1. Queen bees usually live for 5 or 6 years, although some have been known to live for 10 years.

2. Drones are usually killed by the workers at the end of their first season.

3. Workers live for only 3 or 4 weeks in the summer, which is the working season, but may live as long as 6 months in the fall or winter.

Q. Occasionally, during the early spring or summer, a large group of bees may **swarm,** or leave the hive, and look for a new home.

1. The bees may leave if the colony becomes too big or if food becomes scarce.

2. Sometimes they may leave if another queen is developed in the colony.

3. A queen is developed when the workers give a fertilized egg special treatment.

4. The workers make one cell of the honeycomb larger, and, when the egg hatches, the workers feed the larva a substance called **royal jelly,** which is a mixture of honey and pollen.

5. The larva is fed this royal jelly until it spins a cocoon and goes into the pupa stage.

6. When the pupa becomes an adult bee, it is a queen bee.

7. This new queen bee tries to kill the old one, but, if the workers prevent it, the new queen bee leaves the hive together with many workers and some drones.

8. After the new colony is established, the queen bee flies up into the air, and is followed by the drones.

9. One of the drones mates with the queen bee, giving her several million sperm cells, then dies soon after.

10. The queen bee then returns to the hive and lays eggs for the rest of her life.

XII. The Ant

A. Ants are also social insects.

B. They belong to the same order of insects as the bee and the wasp.

C. There are many different kinds of ants.

1. Some are quite large, and others are very small.

2. Some kinds live in tunnels in the ground.

3. Some kinds build large mounds, called **anthills.**

4. Some kinds live in decaying trees.

D. Ants, like bees and wasps, have a definite narrowing, or constriction, between their thorax and abdomen.

E. Ants cannot sting like bees, but they have a strong bite because of their powerful jaws.

F. An ant colony has many workers, and a much smaller number of queens and males.

1. Both the queens and males have wings, but the workers do not.

2. During the mating season the females fly high into the air, followed by the males.

3. The males mate with the females, depositing a huge number of sperm cells.

4. When the females come back to earth, they bite off their wings and start laying eggs.

5. The males die soon after they mate with the females.

6. An ant colony usually has many queens, all living peacefully together.

G. Many kinds of ants also have soldiers in their colony.

1. These soldiers do the fighting for the colony.

2. They have larger heads and powerful biting jaws.

3. These soldier ants often attack another ant colony.

4. If they defeat the other colony, they carry away the larvae and pupae of the conquered ants.

5. When these larvae and pupae become ants, these ants become slave workers for the colony.

H. All ants undergo complete metamorphosis.

1. Their eggs are tiny, and usually can only be seen under a magnifying glass or microscope.

2. Their larvae are usually white and have no legs.

3. When the larvae go into the pupa, or resting, stage, they usually spin a white cocoon.

4. These white cocoons are often mistakenly called "ant eggs."

I. The workers in an ant colony have many duties.
 1. Some workers take care of and protect the larvae and pupae.
 2. Some workers gather food for the colony.
 3. Some workers build the anthill, and others keep the colony clean.

J. Many kinds of ants keep their own "cows."
 1. These "cows" are aphids, which are also called plant lice.
 2. During the winter the ants carry these aphids into their colony and care for them.
 3. In the spring the ants set the aphids on plants, where the aphids feed.
 4. The ants then stroke the bodies of the aphids with their antennae.
 5. This stroking causes the aphids to give off a sweet liquid, which the ants drink.

XIII. PROTECTIVE COLORATION OF INSECTS

A. Many insects have colors or appearances that protect them from their enemies.

B. Some insects have colors that make them look like their surroundings.
 1. The grasshopper's wings and upper parts are green and blend with the grass so that the grasshopper cannot be seen.
 2. The praying mantis has the same color as a green leaf and cannot be seen.

C. Some insects look like the object on which they are resting.
 1. The walking stick, a relative of the grasshopper, looks like a small twig.
 2. The walking-leaf butterfly looks like a large green leaf.
 3. The dead-leaf butterfly looks like a dead leaf.

D. Some insects look like other, more annoying insects.
 1. The robber fly looks like a bumble bee.
 2. The viceroy butterfly looks almost exactly like the monarch butterfly, which tastes bad to birds.

XIV. INSECTS CAN BE HELPFUL AND HARMFUL

A. Although there are more than three quarters of a million different kinds of insects on earth, most of them are neither helpful nor harmful to man.

B. Some insects are helpful to man.
 1. Many insects, such as bees, wasps, butterflies, moths, beetles, bugs, and certain kinds of flies, play an important part in the pollination of plants.
 2. Bees produce honey and beeswax.
 3. The silk moth gives us silk.
 4. The lac insect gives us shellac.
 5. The bodies of some insects, like the cochineal insect, are ground up to produce dyes.
 6. Some insects, like the dragonfly, praying mantis, and ladybug, eat harmful insects.
 7. Some insects, like the carrion beetle, are scavengers and feed on the dead bodies of animals.

C. Some insects are harmful to man.
 1. Many insects, like the grasshopper, cricket, boll weevil, and Japanese beetle, destroy grain crops, vegetables, and fruits.
 2. Some insects, especially certain kinds of moths, destroy trees.
 3. Some insects, such as the termite, destroy wooden buildings and foundations.
 4. Certain moths and beetles destroy clothes and carpets.
 5. Some insects, like the mosquito, flea, louse, and fly, carry disease germs to man and animals.
 6. Some insects, like the flea, louse, and bedbug, are parasites on man and pet animals.
 7. Some insects, like the cockroach and fly, contaminate food.
 8. Some insects, like the bee, wasp, mosquito, and gnat, annoy man and animals by stinging or biting.

D. Man uses many different methods for controlling harmful insects.

E. One method of controlling harmful insects

is to destroy the environment in which the insects live.

1. The draining of ditches and ponds, where mosquitoes breed, will break up the life cycle of the mosquitoes.
2. Changing or rotating the crops that harmful insects use for food will take away their food supply.

F. A second method of controlling harmful insects is to use quarantine laws to prevent the importing of insects into a country.

1. Sometimes the eggs or larvae of insects are brought into a country unknowingly because they are hidden on plants or fruit.
2. These insects often destroy the "balance of nature" in that country because the country has no natural enemies of the insects to hold them in check, and the insects quickly become very numerous and highly destructive.
3. Inspectors at seaports and airline terminals inspect any plants and fruit coming into the country, and take away and destroy those suspected of carrying harmful insects.

G. A third method of controlling harmful insects is to use chemicals.

1. Stomach poisons are sprayed on plants that are attacked by chewing insects.
2. Contact poisons are sprayed on plants that are attacked by sucking insects, which do not chew leaves, and these poisons kill as they come in contact with the insect's body.
3. Poison gases, which enter the insect's body through the tiny openings (spiracles) on each side of the thorax and abdomen, kill insects instantly, but the gas must be sprayed in a closed or confined area.

4. Some gases do not kill adult insects, but do destroy the larvae.
5. Many persons and scientists are very concerned about the use of chemicals to kill insects because the chemicals may enter the plants and be eaten by man, may pollute streams and kill the animal life in the streams, and may kill valuable birds, animals, and insects.
6. Also, many insects build up a resistance to chemical poisons, and their offspring inherit this resistance, making the poisons ineffective.

H. A fourth method of controlling harmful insects is to import natural enemies of the insects, or to make use of local natural enemies.

1. Birds are the best natural enemies of insects.
2. Other good natural enemies are spiders, frogs, toads, and snakes.
3. Importing a natural enemy may often become a problem because sometimes the "balance of nature" is upset, and the natural enemy becomes very numerous and equally destructive.

I. A fifth method of controlling harmful insects is to sterilize the male insects.

1. A large number of male insects are exposed to X-rays or radioactive materials.
2. This radiation makes the male insects sterile so that they cannot fertilize the female insect's eggs.
3. The sterile male flies are then released, and they mate with the female insects.
4. However, because the eggs are not fertilized by the sterile males, no new insects develop.
5. As a result, the number of harmful insects is greatly reduced, and, with repeated treatments, the harmful insects may even be wiped out completely.

SPIDERS, CENTIPEDES, AND MILIPEDES

I. WHAT SPIDERS ARE

A. Spiders are members of the very large animal phylum called **Arthropoda.**
B. Together with scorpions, mites, and ticks, they form a special class of arthropods called **Arachnida.**
C. Spiders have the characteristics common to all arthropods.
   1. They have an outside skeleton made of a tough material, called **chitin.**
   2. The parts attached to their bodies, called **appendages,** are jointed and can bend.
   3. Their bodies are segmented, and there are distinct body regions.
   4. They have **bilateral symmetry,** which means that all the parts of their body are paired, being arranged on the right and left side of the body in such a way that one side of the body is a mirror image of the other side.
D. Spiders are often thought to be insects, but they are not, having special characteristics different from those of insects.
   1. Spiders have eight legs; insects have six.
   2. Spiders do not have antennae; most insects do have antennae.
   3. The spider has its head and thorax joined together; the insect has its head and thorax separate from each other.
   4. Spiders have only simple eyes, made up of just one lens; nearly all insects have compound eyes, made up of many lenses.
E. Spiders have two pairs of appendages attached to their heads.
   1. One pair is hollow and has small openings in the tip, through which poison from glands in the spider's head can be injected into the spider's victim.
   2. The other pair is used as feelers, and is also used by the male spider to hold sperm cells during reproduction.
F. Spiders usually have eight eyes, arranged in a definite pattern on their heads.
   1. This arrangement pattern of the eyes is different for different kinds of spiders.
   2. Scientists use this special pattern to classify the different kinds of spiders.
G. The breathing organs of spiders are called **book lungs** because they have folds that look like the pages of a book.
   1. Spiders usually have either two or four of these book lungs.
   2. Air enters these book lungs from a slit in the spider's abdomen.
H. Many spiders have three pairs of appendages, called **spinnerets,** on the tip of the underside of their abdomen.
   1. Each spinneret has hundreds of tubes.
   2. Liquid silk from the spider's silk glands flows through these tubes out into the air, where it hardens to form a thread.
   3. This thread is used to spin its web and to build cocoons or nests for eggs.
   4. In the fall the young of some spiders spin long threads, and the wind carries the young far away.
I. Spiders do not sting, but bite instead.
   1. When they bite, they inject small amounts of poison into the wound.
   2. This poison causes pain and swelling.
J. Spiders usually mate in the late summer or early fall.
   1. The female spider is usually larger than the male, and she often eats the male after the mating has taken place.
   2. The female lays a large batch of eggs, around which she spins a cocoon or nest; soon afterward some females die.
   3. The eggs hatch in the winter, and stay inside the cocoon or nest.
   4. The young spiders that develop usually eat each other.
   5. In the spring the spiders that are still alive leave the cocoon or nest.
K. Spiders feed mostly on other insects.
   1. They do not eat the insects, but suck the juices from them instead.
   2. Spiders are helpful to man because many of the insects they kill are pests.

II. Some Unusual Spiders

A. The **tarantula,** or **banana spider,** is very large, and can measure as much as 15 to 20 centimeters (6 to 8 in) across when its legs are spread.
1. It lives in the tropics, but is sometimes brought to the United States in shipments of bananas.
2. It eats insects, but sometimes it attacks small birds.
3. Its bite is painful, but is not deadly.
B. The **black widow spider** is found mostly in warm climates, but can occasionally be seen in temperate climates.
1. It has a round, black abdomen, with a red spot, shaped like an hour glass, on the underside of its abdomen.
2. The female is vicious, and kills the male after she has mated with him.
3. Its bite is very painful and poisonous and sometimes can cause death.
4. Its thread is so fine that it has been used in marking lenses of gunsights, bombsights, and surveying instruments.
C. **Trapdoor spiders** are found in the southeastern United States.
1. Instead of spinning webs to catch insects, they build a kind of trapdoor.
2. They dig a tubelike hole in the ground, line it with silk, and fasten a hinged "door" over the hole.
3. When an insect comes into the hole, the open door is shut tight.

III. Relatives of Spiders

A. The **scorpion** is an arachnid found in all tropical countries and in southern and southwestern United States.
1. In addition to its four pairs of walking legs, it has a large pair of appendages attached to its head, with a large pincer at the end of each appendage.
2. It has a long, segmented abdomen that forms a tail at the end.
3. At the tip of the tail is a poisonous stinger, which the scorpion uses to kill insects and spiders.
4. The scorpion's sting is very painful, but it rarely is fatal to man.
B. The **harvestman,** or **daddy longlegs,** looks very much like a long-legged spider.
1. It is very useful to gardeners because it feeds mostly on plant lice.
2. It is found in gardens, fields, and woods.
C. **Mites** and **ticks** are very small arachnids that look like lice.
1. They live mostly as parasites on the bodies of man, chickens, cattle, dogs, and other animals.
2. They are dangerous because they carry germs from one animal to another.
3. Mites carry such diseases as sheep scab and dog mange.
4. Ticks carry Rocky Mountain spotted fever and Texas cattle fever.
5. **Chiggers** are mites that bore into the skin, causing itchiness and pain.
6. The "red" spider that harms apple leaves and fruit is really a mite.

IV. Centipedes and Millipedes

A. Centipedes and millipedes are arthropods that are often grouped together into a special class called **myriapods,** which means "many feet."
B. They both have bodies composed of many segments.
C. The centipede's head has its antennae and mouth parts.
1. Its first body segment has a pair of poison claws.
2. All the other segments, except the last two, have one pair of legs each.
3. It moves fast and is hard to capture.
D. The millipede's head also has its antennae and mouth parts.
1. All its body segments, except the last two, have two pairs of legs each.
2. It moves slowly and may roll into a ball when disturbed.

FISH

I. WHAT FISH ARE

A. Fish are members of the animal phylum called **Chordata.**

B. Together with amphibians, reptiles, birds, and mammals, they make up a special group of animals called **vertebrates.**

C. Most vertebrates have the following characteristics.
1. They have backbones.
2. Their skeletons are inside their bodies.
3. They usually have two pairs of limbs, or appendages (legs, legs and wings, or fins), attached to their bodies at the shoulder and hip.

D. Fish are grouped into three broad classes: the **bony fish,** the **lampreys,** and the **sharks** and **rays.**
1. The skeletons of the bony fish are made of bone, but the skeletons of the other two groups of fish are made of a tough tissue, called **cartilage.**
2. The bony fish make up the most important group, both on the basis of numbers and of economic importance.

II. WHERE THEY ARE FOUND

A. Fish live only in water.
1. Most fish are found in the ocean, but there are also many fish in lakes, ponds, rivers, and brooks.
2. Some live near the surface of the water; others live closer to the bottom.

B. Some fish live alone whereas others travel in large groups, called **schools.**

C. Although some fish are less than 2½ centimeters (1 in) long and others are as much as 15 meters (49 ft) long, most fish are less than 1 meter (3 ft) long.

III. PHYSICAL CHARACTERISTICS

A. There are three parts to the body of a fish: a head, trunk, and tail.
1. The head has no neck and is attached directly to the trunk.
2. The trunk is the largest part of the body.
3. The tail is the narrower part of the body behind the trunk, and is often confused with the tail fin.

B. The body of a fish is streamlined and tapers at both ends.

C. The bodies of most fish are covered with scales, which grow from pockets in the skin and overlap one another just like the shingles on the roof of a house.

D. The skin of a fish gives off a slime, which oozes between the scales and covers the body.
1. This slime makes it easier for the fish to swim.
2. The slime also protects the fish from being attacked by tiny parasites in the water.

E. Some fish are brightly colored, either partially or completely, with the colors often arranged in spots, lines, or bars.

F. Many fish are dark colored on top and light colored underneath, which helps prevent them from being seen by their enemies.

G. Most fish have eyes that are large and slightly movable.
1. The pupil of the eye is large, as compared with other vertebrates, and can admit a great deal of light.
2. A fish has no eyelids.

H. The trunk of a fish has a number of appendages, called **fins.**
1. Each fin is made up of many bony spines, called **rays,** which are covered by a thin fold of skin.
2. A pair of fins, called the **pectoral fins,** is located near the head, and corresponds to the front legs of land vertebrates.
3. In back of the pectoral fins is a second pair of fins, called the **pelvic fins,** which corresponds to the rear legs of land vertebrates.

4. Along the top of the trunk there can be found one or two **dorsal fins.**
5. Along the bottom of the trunk, toward the rear, there is an **anal fin.**

I. The tail of a fish ends in a fin, called the **tail fin** or **caudal fin.**

J. Fish are called **cold-blooded** animals because the temperature of their blood is the same as that of the surrounding water, and this temperature changes with the seasons.

IV. How Fish Breathe

A. Fish breathe through respiratory organs, called **gills,** located on each side of the head.
1. The gills are made up of many small, threadlike filaments, which give the gills a feathery appearance.
2. Each filament has tiny, thin-walled blood vessels in it.

B. Most fish breathe by opening and closing their mouths.
1. When a fish opens its mouth, water rushes in.
2. When the fish closes its mouth, the water is forced out through two openings on each side of the back of the head.
3. There are four or five gills in each opening.
4. As the water is forced out over the gills, dissolved oxygen in the water passes through the thin walls of the blood vessels and is picked up by the blood.
5. The blood gets rid of its carbon dioxide as it picks up fresh oxygen.

V. How Fish Swim

A. A fish swims forward rapidly by moving its tail and tail fin from side to side.

B. The dorsal and anal fins are used mostly for balance, and help keep the fish from tipping over.

C. The paired pectoral and pelvic fins have several functions.
1. They help a fish keep its balance when the fish is resting.

2. They act as oars when the fish is swimming slowly.
3. They help the fish steer to the right or left.
4. When spread out at right angles, they act as brakes to help the fish come to a stop.
5. The fish also uses them to swim backward.

D. Most fish have an **air bladder** inside their bodies.
1. Gases from the body can enter or leave the air bladder, making it inflate or deflate.
2. The air bladder makes it possible for the fish to rise, sink, or stay at a particular depth without rising or sinking.

VI. What Fish Eat

A. Some fish eat only algae and other water plants.

B. Some fish eat animals, such as insects, worms, crayfish, snails, and other fish.

C. Fish that eat other animals have many sharp teeth.
1. These teeth slant backward toward the throat, making it easy for a fish to swallow the animal, but making it hard for the animal to escape.
2. Fish can use their teeth to seize, tear, and hold food, but cannot use them for chewing.

VII. How Fish Reproduce

A. Most fish develop from eggs that the female lays outside her body.

B. At a certain time of the year a female fish lays a very large number of eggs.

C. This process of laying eggs is called **spawning.**

D. Shortly after the female lays her eggs, the male swims over the eggs and gives off a liquid, called **milt,** which contains large numbers of sperm cells.

E. The sperm cells swim to the eggs and fertilize the eggs by uniting with them.

F. The fertilized eggs hatch into tiny fish, usually from 10 to 40 days later, depending on the kind of fish and the temperature of the water.

1. While the fish are developing from the egg, they are fed by the yolk of the egg.
2. A part of the yolk, called the **yolk sac**, remains attached to the newborn fish for some time after they hatch, and supplies them with the food they need during this time.

G. The young of some freshwater tropical fish, like the guppy, molly, and swordtail, develop inside the female's body and are born alive.

1. The female keeps her eggs inside her body and receives the sperm of the male when he mates with her.
2. The sperm fertilize the eggs, which develop inside the female's body and then are brought forth alive.

H. As a rule, most freshwater fish either spawn where they live or travel a short distance to shallower water for spawning.

I. The eel, however, has a very unusual spawning habit.

1. The eel lives in rivers and streams that flow into the ocean.
2. At spawning time the eels that live in rivers flowing into the Atlantic Ocean and Gulf of Mexico swim far out into the Atlantic Ocean.
3. The female lays her eggs and the male deposits his sperm on the eggs; then both male and female eels die.
4. When the young eels that hatch are about 5 centimeters (2 in) long, they return to the rivers and streams from which their parents came.
5. After 3 to 8 years the adult eels return again to the same part of the Atlantic Ocean for spawning.
6. Although both American and European eels spawn in the same part of the Atlantic Ocean, the young eels never make a mistake and go to the wrong continent.

J. The Pacific salmon also has unusual spawning habits.

1. The adult fish live in the ocean along the north Pacific coast.
2. At spawning time they all swim up the Columbia River to the same streams where they had hatched 3 or 4 years earlier.
3. The females spawn and the males deposit their sperm, fertilizing the eggs; then both males and females die.
4. The young salmon that hatch from the eggs then return to the ocean and live there for 3 or 4 years until it is time for them to spawn.

VIII. THE ECONOMIC IMPORTANCE OF FISH

A. Fish are very valuable to man as food.

1. Common saltwater food fish include the tuna, herring, sardine, swordfish, halibut, mackerel, haddock, sole, flounder, cod, and sea perch.
2. Common freshwater food fish include the trout, salmon, pike, whitefish, perch, buffalo carp, and catfish.

B. Many persons catch fish for sport and recreation, as well as for food.

C. The eggs of the sturgeon, commonly called "caviar," and the shad are eaten as food.

D. The oil from the liver of the codfish, halibut, and shark is rich in vitamins A and D.

E. Fish oil is used in making certain paints.

F. Ground fish, called **fish meal**, is used in making foods for cats, dogs, and chickens.

G. The bones and waste parts of fish are used to make glue.

IX. THE CONSERVATION OF FISH

A. Many lakes, ponds, and streams lose their fish for many reasons.

1. Lakes may become lower during hot, dry spells or because of unwise treatment of the land around the lake, and this lowering of the water level may destroy spawning areas or areas where the food supply is rich.
2. Sometimes man straightens river channels, which discourages the breeding of

fish because fish live better in rivers that have bends, rapids, and quiet pools.

3. Dams across rivers stop fish from traveling upstream to spawn.

4. Many lakes and streams are contaminated by sewage and chemical wastes, which can poison and kill the fish.

5. Sometimes too many adult fish are caught during the spawning season, or too many young fish are caught before they can become adult and have the opportunity to breed new fish.

B. To protect and conserve the fish, the states have passed many protective laws with the following restrictions.

1. Fish under a certain length must not be kept, but must be thrown back.

2. Only a certain number of fish may be caught in one day.

3. Certain fish may not be caught during their spawning season.

4. Fish must not be caught by using explosives in the water.

5. Sewage and chemical wastes cannot be dumped in certain lakes and streams that have been set aside for fishing.

6. Dams that interfere with the travel of fish upstream to spawn must have beside them **fish ladders,** which are a series of small pools, one higher than the other, connected by small waterfalls that can be leaped by the fish.

C. Both the federal government and the states have established fish hatcheries to breed and raise fish for lakes and streams.

1. In the hatchery the eggs are taken from the female and put into a tank, and then milt, containing the sperm of the male, is poured over the eggs.

2. In this way almost all the eggs are fertilized, and hatch.

3. When the young fish are old enough to take care of themselves, they are taken to the lakes and streams.

D. Scientists are constantly investigating diseases, fungus infections, and natural enemies of fish, in an effort to keep the balance in nature constant.

X. RELATIVES OF THE BONY FISH

A. The **lamprey** is a very simple or primitive kind of fish.

1. Some kinds of lampreys live in saltwater, and other kinds live in freshwater.

2. The lamprey has a long, thin body and looks very much like an eel.

3. Its skeleton is made of cartilage instead of bone.

4. It has a soft, slimy skin.

5. The only fins it has are two fins along its back and a tail fin.

6. It has no jaws at all, but it has a round, sucking mouth lined with sharp teeth.

7. Its tongue is hard and rough, with teeth on it, so that it can act like a coarse file.

8. The lamprey is a parasite, living on the blood of other fish.

9. Its sucking mouth clamps onto the side of a fish, and it uses its teeth and tongue to rip through the scales and flesh of the fish.

10. The lamprey then sucks out the blood, and sometimes even the internal organs.

B. Although the **shark** is very much like a bony fish, it has certain characteristics that place it in its own group or class.

1. Sharks live only in saltwater.

2. Some sharks are about ⅔ meter (2 ft) long, but others can be 15 meters (49 ft) long or more.

3. The shark's skeleton is made of cartilage instead of bone.

4. A shark's scales do not overlap, like those of the bony fish, but instead lie side by side.

5. Its fins are very much like those of a bony fish, but the upper part of its tail fin is longer than the lower part.

6. Its mouth is on the lower side of its head, and is lined with many rows of very sharp teeth.

7. Sharks live on other fish.

C. The **ray** belongs to the same group of fish as the shark.

1. The ray is also called the **devilfish, sting ray,** or **blanket fish.**

2. It has a large, flat body that looks like a blanket.
3. When it swims, the sides of its body look somewhat like moving wings.
4. It has a long, whiplike tail with a sharp, poisonous stinger on the tip.

5. It uses this stinger to wound and kill the fish and other sea animals that it attacks and eats.
6. The ray lives only in saltwater, and often lies half-buried in the sand, looking somewhat like a blanket.

AMPHIBIANS

I. What Amphibians Are

A. Amphibians are members of the animal phylum called **Chordata.**
B. Together with fish, reptiles, birds, and mammals, they make up a special group of animals called **vertebrates.**
C. As vertebrates, amphibians have the following general characteristics.
   1. They have backbones.
   2. Their skeletons are inside their bodies.
   3. They have two pairs of appendages attached to their bodies at the shoulder and hip.
D. Amphibians also have their own special characteristics.
   1. Their bodies are covered with a thin, loose skin that is usually moist.
   2. Their feet are often webbed, and they have no claws on their toes.
   3. Their eggs are fertilized outside the female's body.
   4. Young amphibians live in the water, but adult amphibians live mostly on land (the term *amphibia* means "two lives").
   5. Young amphibians look different from adult amphibians, which means that a change, or **metamorphosis,** takes place when the young amphibian becomes an adult.
   6. They are cold-blooded, and their body temperature is always the same as that of the air or water around them.
E. Common amphibians include frogs, toads, and salamanders.
   1. They are all rather small vertebrates.

2. Most frogs and toads are from 5 to 15 centimeters (2 to 6 in) long, although the African frog is about 30 centimeters 12 in) long.
3. Salamanders are 5 centimeters (2 in) to ⅔ meter (2 ft) long, and there is a giant salamander in Japan that is 1½ meters (5 ft) long.

II. The Frog

A. The frog has a short, broad body.
   1. The body is covered by a thin, loose, moist skin that is colored very much like the surroundings the frog lives in.
   2. Glands in the skin give off a slimy mucus, which makes the skin slippery.
B. The frog has large bulging eyes, which have upper and lower eyelids.
   1. There is also a third eyelid, called the **nictitating membrane,** joined to the lower eyelid.
   2. This extra eyelid protects the eye when the frog is under water and keeps the eye moist when the frog is on land.
C. The frog has a very large mouth with a long, sticky tongue attached to the bottom in front.
   1. When a frog catches an insect, the mouth opens up wide and the tongue shoots out.
   2. The insect is caught on the sticky tongue, which throws the insect against the roof of the mouth.
D. The frog has two short, weak front legs.
   1. Each leg has four toes.

2. The front legs are used to support the frog and to break the force of the frog's fall after it has made a leap.

E. The frog has two highly developed rear legs, which are used for swimming and leaping.

1. Each leg has five long toes with webbing between them.

2. When the frog is resting on land, the rear legs fold together along the body in a position that makes it possible for the frog to make a quick leap at any time.

F. On land the adult frog breathes through its lungs.

G. In the water the frog breathes through its skin.

1. Oxygen dissolved in the water passes directly through the skin into the blood while carbon dioxide leaves the blood and passes out through the skin.

2. This breathing through the skin makes it possible for the frog to stay under water or bury itself in the mud for long periods of time.

H. In the early part of spring the female frogs lay their eggs in ponds.

1. The eggs are surrounded by a jellylike material that holds them together.

2. As the eggs pass out of the female, the male immediately spreads sperm over them.

3. The sperm enter the eggs and fertilize them.

I. The eggs of a frog are black and white.

1. The white part is the yolk, which contains stored food for the young frog when it first hatches from the egg.

2. The black part is the living protoplasm, which will produce the young frog.

J. The young frog that hatches from the egg is called a **tadpole.**

1. At first the tadpole is a tiny animal with a short body.

2. It immediately attaches itself to water plants and feeds on the yolk part of the egg and also on the jellylike material that surrounded the egg.

3. A mouth and horny jaws soon develop,

and the tadpole begins to feed on tiny plants.

4. The body begins to lengthen, gills form at the sides of the head, and the tail becomes longer.

5. The tadpole is now a fishlike animal and swims about freely in the water.

K. The tadpole eventually grows into an adult frog and lives on land.

1. First the hind legs appear, and then the front legs form.

2. As the legs develop, the tail is absorbed or taken into the body and disappears.

3. Changes take place inside the body, and lungs form.

4. The tadpole is now completely changed, or has undergone **metamorphosis,** into a frog.

L. Frogs are **cold-blooded** animals, which means that their body temperature is always the same as the surrounding air or water.

1. When winter comes the body temperature of the frog becomes so low that the frog cannot be active any more.

2. The frog buries itself in the mud at the bottom of a pond and stays quiet or inactive all winter.

3. This period of winter inactivity is called **hibernation.**

4. In the spring the days become warmer, and the frog becomes active again.

5. When it is very hot in the summer the frog may bury itself again in the cool mud and become inactive once more.

6. This period of summer inactivity is called **estivation.**

M. The **leopard frog** is the most common frog in the United States.

1. It lives in damp places near ponds, marshes, and ditches.

2. Its back is covered with dark spots surrounded by white or yellow rings, and it looks very much like the grass and rocks among which it lives.

3. Its underside is a creamy white.

4. The tadpoles of leopard frogs become adults in a single summer.

5. The leopard frog lives on insects, worms, and crayfish.
6. The leopard frog is often used by fishermen as bait, and it is also used for dissection in the laboratory.

N. The **bullfrog** lives mostly in water.
1. It is a large frog with legs as much as 25 centimeters (10 in) long.
2. Most bullfrogs are a greenish-brown, although their color may range from green to yellow.
3. Their undersides are a greyish-white mixed with dark splotches.
4. It takes two summers for the tadpole of a bullfrog to become an adult.
5. Bullfrogs feed on insects, worms, crayfish, and small fish.
6. The large legs of the bullfrog are eaten as food.

O. The **tree frog** is a very small frog, no more than an inch long, that climbs trees.
1. Its body looks very much like the bark of a tree.
2. Its toes have sticky pads on them that make it possible for it to climb trees easily.
3. It makes a very loud noise for its size.

III. THE TOAD

A. The toad is very much like the frog in many ways.
B. However, the frog's skin is moist and slippery, whereas the toad's skin is dry and covered with warts.
C. The toad has shorter legs than the frog.
D. The toad lives on land all the time, and returns to the water only to lay eggs.
E. The life cycle of the toad is very similar to that of the frog.
1. However, the toad's eggs are laid in strings instead of masses like the frog's eggs.
2. Also, the tadpole stage is very short, and the tadpoles become toads very quickly.

F. The toad has no teeth, but the frog does have teeth.
G. The toad cannot swim in water.
H. The rounded warts on its back, sides, and legs have poison glands, which help protect the toad from some of its enemies.
I. The toad sleeps most of the day under rocks and logs, and becomes active at night.
J. It feeds on insects and slugs that destroy garden plants.

IV. THE SALAMANDER

A. The salamander looks more like a lizard than a frog or toad.
1. It has a long body, long tail, and short legs, all about the same size.
2. Its skin is soft and moist, and its legs have no claws.
3. Some salamanders do not have legs at all.
B. Some salamanders live in water, and others live on land in damp places.
C. The **mudpuppy** or **necturus,** which is common in the Midwest, has a pair of red gills around its head just above its front legs, and keeps these gills all its life.
D. The **tiger salamander** has yellow bars on a brown body, whereas the **spotted salamander** has yellow spots on a black body.
1. The tiger salamander has a flat tail, and the spotted salamander has a round tail.
2. They both live in water the first three months of their lives, then on land the rest of the time.
E. The **newt** is a salamander that has a "triple life."
1. The first two months of its life it lives in the water and breathes only through its gills.
2. The next year or two it lives on land and breathes through lungs.
3. Then it goes back to the water for the rest of its life, breathing through its lungs on the surface of the water and through its skin when under water.

REPTILES

I. What Reptiles Are

A. Reptiles are members of the animal phylum called **Chordata.**

B. Together with fish, amphibians, birds, and mammals, they make up a special group of animals called **vertebrates.**

C. As vertebrates, reptiles have a backbone, their skeletons are inside their bodies, and most of them have two pairs of appendages attached to their bodies at the shoulder and hip.

D. Reptiles also have their own special characteristics.
1. They have a rough, thick, dry skin covered with scales.
2. Those reptiles with feet have claws on their toes.
3. Both young and adult reptiles breathe only through lungs.
4. Reptiles have a breastbone, called the **sternum,** which protects the heart and lungs.
5. The female's eggs are fertilized by the male's sperm inside her body.
6. The eggs that are laid have a protective shell or membrane around them.
7. Reptiles are **cold-blooded,** which means that their body temperature is always the same as that of the air or water about them.

E. At one time the reptiles were the most numerous and most powerful animals on earth.

F. Today there are only a few different kinds of reptiles that exist.

G. Common reptiles include the turtle, lizard, snake, alligator, and crocodile.

II. The Turtle

A. Some turtles live in salt water, others live in fresh water, and still others live on land.
1. Land turtles are often called **tortoises.**

2. Some kinds of freshwater turtles are also called **terrapins.**

B. Some turtles are quite small, but others, especially the sea turtles, can be 2½ meters (8 ft) long and weigh 450 kilograms (1000 lb).

C. All turtles have an upper and lower shell with the body between these shells.
1. The shells protect the turtle because most turtles can withdraw all of their body parts into the shells.
2. Some turtles can even close their shells tightly.
3. The shells have plates that are different in color and marking, and this difference helps biologists identify all the turtles.

D. A turtle has either a pointed or triangular head.

E. It has no teeth, but it does have horny jaws that form a sharp beak, which the turtle uses to bite off pieces of food.

F. It has well-developed eyes and good eyesight.
1. The eyes have an upper and a lower eyelid.
2. There is also a third eyelid, called the **nictitating membrane,** which is transparent and moves from the front corner of the eye to cover the eyeball.

G. The turtle's legs are quite short, and the turtle walks very slowly.
1. The skin on a turtle's legs is scaly and tough.
2. Most turtles have five toes on each leg, and the toes have claws on them.
3. Some turtles have completely webbed toes, but others have very little webbing between the toes.
4. Water turtles use their webbed feet for swimming.

H. Some turtles have good-sized tails, but others have little or no tails.

I. All turtles, even sea turtles, lay their eggs on land.

1. They lay their eggs in shallow holes and cover them with sand or earth.
2. The heat of the sun helps the eggs hatch.

J. Land turtles eat insects, earthworms, and plants; water turtles eat fish, frogs, and birds that live near the water.

III. THE LIZARD

A. Most lizards live in the tropics.
B. Some lizards, like the **skink** or **swift,** are very tiny, but the **Komodo dragon lizard** of the Dutch East Indies is 4½ meters (15 ft) long and weighs almost 115 kilograms (250 lb).
C. Most lizards have four legs, and some lizards can run very quickly.
D. A few lizards, like the **glass snake,** have no legs and are often mistaken for snakes.
E. The **chameleon** is the best-known lizard in the United States.
   1. It has a body that is about 5 centimeters (2 in) long and a tail about 7½ centimeters (3 in) long.
   2. The chameleon can change its color, not just once but many times.
F. The **horned toad** is really a lizard, and it can be found in western United States.
   1. It has scales of different lengths, which give it a horny appearance.
   2. Some horned toads lay their eggs, but others keep the eggs inside their bodies and the young are born alive.
G. The **Gila monster** is a poisonous lizard ⅔ meter (2 ft) long, found in Arizona and New Mexico.
   1. Its skin is brown or black and is covered with blotches of orange or pink.
   2. It has poison glands at the rear of its lower jaw.
   3. It bites very hard, twisting its head from side to side.
   4. Its poison affects the heart and can often kill a man.
H. The **iguana,** a lizard that lives in the tropics, looks like a dragon.
I. Some lizards, like the glass snake, can have their tails broken off, then grow new ones.

IV. THE SNAKE

A. Many biologists believe that snakes developed from lizards a long time ago.
B. Snakes have long, round bodies that are covered with scales, many of which are beautifully colored.
C. Snakes shed their outer layer of scales many times during a single season.
   1. This process is called **molting.**
   2. When the thin layer becomes loose, the snake hooks a loose part over a twig or stone edge, and then works its way out of this old layer of "skin."
D. The snake has no legs, and moves by using the broad scales, called **scutes,** on the underside of its body and by using a large number of muscles.
   1. Snakes commonly move by winding from side to side and forming curves.
   2. Some snakes move up and down slowly in a straight line, like a caterpillar.
   3. Some snakes that live in the desert have a side-winding movement, where the body is raised and twisted into S-shaped loops, touching the ground only at two or three points, with the snake moving across the ground only at these points.
   4. Most snakes move quite slowly, and even the fastest cannot travel faster than 5 kilometers (3 mi) an hour.
E. The snake has a large mouth with a double row of teeth on each side of its upper jaw and a single row of teeth on its lower jaw.
   1. The teeth all slant backward toward the throat.
   2. The snake swallows its food whole, and uses its teeth only to hold and pull the food while it is swallowing.
   3. The snake's jaws are flexible and can stretch very much, so that the snake can even swallow animals thicker than its own body.
   4. There is a long, forked tongue in the snake's mouth, which the snake thrusts out and uses for smelling.
F. The snake has no eyelids, which makes it different from other reptiles.

534]

1. There is a transparent scale, however, that covers the eye.
2. Some snakes have round eye pupils, and others have oval or elliptical eye pupils.

G. All snakes eat only animals, and they use different methods for getting their food.

H. Most snakes just grab the animal by their mouths and swallow it alive.
   1. These snakes eat insects, frogs, toads, lizards, rats, mice, squirrels, and other small animals.
   2. Examples of snakes that use this method of getting food include the **garter snake, hog-nosed snake,** and **milk snake.**

I. Some snakes first wrap their bodies around an animal's chest and squeeze hard so that the animal cannot breathe and dies.
   1. Usually these snakes are quite long and have fairly thick bodies.
   2. Examples of snakes that kill by this squeezing method include the **boa, python, king snake,** and **bull snake.**
   3. The king snake eats other snakes, even the poisonous ones.

J. Some snakes first poison the animal quickly, and then swallow it after it dies.
   1. These snakes have poison fangs in their mouths.
   2. These fangs are hollow, and, when the snake strikes the animal with these fangs, poison from poison glands flows through the fangs into the animal and kills it.
   3. Examples of snakes that kill by poisoning include the **rattlesnake, water moccasin, copperhead, coral snake,** and **cobra.**

K. Most snakes lay eggs that have a tough, white shell.
   1. Each egg has stored food in it for the young snake that is developing inside.
   2. The heat of the sun helps the egg hatch.

L. A few snakes, like the garter snake and copperhead, keep the eggs inside their bodies and the young snakes are born alive.

V. THE ALLIGATOR AND THE CROCODILE

A. The alligator and crocodile are large reptiles that live mostly in tropical and semi-tropical climates.
   1. Alligators are found mostly in the southern United States.
   2. Crocodiles are found largely in Africa and India, but there are also some crocodiles in the southern United States and in South America.

B. They are covered with large, bony scales, and their legs have toes that are partly webbed.

C. Most of them live in swamps and along the banks of a river.

D. The crocodile spends more time in the water than the alligator does.

E. Both the alligator and the crocodile look alike, but there are definite differences between them.
   1. The crocodile has a narrower and more triangular head, and its snout is more pointed.
   2. The alligator is a brown color, whereas the crocodile is a kind of grayish-green color.
   3. The alligator is rather sluggish, whereas the crocodile is more active.

F. The alligator and crocodile will eat fish and any land animals that may come near them.
   1. Some alligators and crocodiles eat man.
   2. The crocodile, especially the African crocodile, is more likely to attack man than the alligator.

G. Alligator hide is used to make fine shoes, handbags, and luggage.

BIRDS

I. CHARACTERISTICS OF BIRDS

A. Birds are members of the animal phylum called **Chordata.**

B. Together with fish, amphibians, reptiles, and mammals, they make up a special group of animals called **vertebrates.**

C. As vertebrates, birds have the following general characteristics.
1. They have backbones.
2. Their skeletons are inside their bodies.
3. They have two pairs of limbs, or appendages, attached to their bodies at the shoulder and hip.

D. Birds also have their own special characteristics.
1. Their bodies are covered with feathers.
2. They have a very light, compact skeleton with porous or hollow bones filled with air, and this kind of skeleton makes it easier for birds to fly.
3. Instead of front legs, birds have wings, which they use only for flying.
4. They stand and perch on two legs.
5. They have a horny beak and no teeth in their mouths.
6. The female's eggs are fertilized by the male's sperm inside her body.
7. The females lay eggs that have a protective shell.
8. Birds are **warm-blooded,** which means that their body temperature is always the same, regardless of the temperature of the air about them.

E. Birds are all different sizes.
1. The smallest bird is the hummingbird, which is a little more than 5 centimeters (2 in) long and weighs about 3 grams (1/10 oz).
2. The largest bird is the ostrich, which can be as much as 2 meters (6½ ft) tall and weigh more than 115 kilograms (250 lb).

F. The feathers of birds are really scales, whose form has been changed.

1. The feathers grow from little pits in the skin.
2. They grow only on certain **parts** of the skin, but they spread out to cover those parts that are featherless.

G. There are four kinds of feathers.
1. The soft **down feathers,** which are plainly seen on young birds, are close to the skin and help keep both young and adult birds warm.
2. The **filoplumes** are thin, almost hairlike feathers with a tuft on their ends.
3. The **contour feathers** cover and protect the body and also give the bird its characteristic color.
4. The large, strong **quill feathers** are in the wings and tails, and are used mostly for flying.

H. Baby birds have mostly down feathers, which makes them look slightly different from their parents.

I. As the baby birds become older, they grow the other kinds of feathers and begin to look more like their parents.

J. The feathers of birds are widely different in color.
1. Some kinds of birds have males that are brilliantly colored and females with little color.
2. In other kinds of birds both the males and females are colored the same.
3. Usually, young birds are colored a little differently from adults.

K. Birds shed, or **molt,** their feathers at least once a year, and new feathers replace those that have fallen out or been broken.

L. Birds have large eyes that not only give them sharp eyesight, but also make it possible for them to judge distances well.

M. Birds also possess a very keen sense of hearing.

N. Most birds have a small, horny tongue, which they use to touch things.

O. Most birds have a voice, and some birds can sing beautifully.

II. Where Birds Live

A. Birds live in all parts of the world, from the polar regions to the tropics.
B. All kinds of birds live in the woodlands and in the open fields.
C. Many kinds of birds live near oceans, lakes, swamps, and marshes.
D. Some birds, like the pigeon and starling, live in the city.
E. Many birds **migrate,** or move from one home to another, during the spring and fall of the year.
   1. Scientists offer different reasons to explain why birds migrate.
   2. Birds may migrate because the climate changes, because their food supply is gone, or because they are accustomed to breed in certain parts of the world.
   3. Most birds that live in the north fly south for the winter.
   4. The bobolink spends its winter in Argentina, the wood thrush in southern Mexico, and the house wren in Florida.
   5. Some birds make very long migration flights.
   6. The golden plover summers in northern Canada and winters in Brazil and Argentina.
   7. The arctic tern summers in the Arctic regions and winters in the Antarctic regions.
   8. The ruddy turnstone summers in Alaska and winters in Hawaii.

III. What Birds Eat

A. Birds are so active that they need large amounts of food, and they seem to be eating all the time.
B. The two main foods of birds are insects and seeds.
C. Some birds, like the crow, bluejay, and red-winged blackbird, also eat corn, grain, rice, and peas.
D. Some birds, like the bluebird, robin, cedar waxwing, and wren, also eat fruit and berries.
E. Some large birds, like the owl and hawk, eat small animals, such as the rat, field mouse, and rabbit.
F. Some birds, like the pelican, kingfisher, and loon, eat mostly fish.
G. Some birds, like the vulture and buzzard, eat dead animals.
H. Most birds drink by taking a beakful of water, tilting their heads back, and letting the water run down their throats.

IV. How Birds Reproduce

A. When birds mate, the male deposits sperm inside the female so that the female's egg cells are fertilized internally.
B. Soon after, the female lays a number of eggs with hard shells around them.
   1. Each egg has a tiny fertilized egg cell in it.
   2. The egg also contains yolk, a substance which serves as stored-up food while the young bird is gradually developing inside the egg.
   3. Some birds, like the owl and hawk, may lay just one egg, but other birds, like the chicken, duck, goose, and turkey, may lay two or more eggs at one time.
C. As soon as the female bird lays her eggs, she sits on them to keep them warm so that the eggs will develop into birds.
   1. This process of sitting on the eggs and keeping them warm until they hatch is called **incubation.**
   2. The time needed to incubate the eggs varies from about 10 days for smaller birds to as much as 50 days for larger birds.
   3. Usually the female sits on the eggs while the male gets food.
   4. For some birds, like the ostrich, the male bird will take turns with the female bird in sitting on the eggs.
D. When the egg is ready to hatch, the baby bird pecks the shell until it splits open, and then the baby bird works its way out of the shell.
E. Baby birds, like the robin and cardinal,

which hatch in 10 days to 2 weeks, are quite helpless.

  1. They are weak, almost blind, and covered with very few down feathers.

  2. They must be fed and cared for many days before they become feathered, are able to fly, and can get food for themselves.

F. Baby birds, like the chicken and the quail, which hatch in 3 to 6 weeks, are well formed and can run around and look for food within a few hours after they have hatched.

V. The Nesting Habits of Birds

A. Birds build nests to provide a place for incubating and hatching their eggs and for protecting the young birds when they are newly born.

B. Birds choose sites for their nests where they can get the greatest protection possible from their enemies and from such weather conditions as heavy rains or strong winds.

C. Nests differ greatly in size and shape, in the materials used to make them, and in how well they are made.

  1. Different kinds of birds build their nests in their own way, with the same kinds of materials, and in the same kind of location.

  2. Some birds build large nests, and the materials are put together very loosely.

  3. Other birds build small nests that are beautifully constructed with different materials, and the nests are then lined with soft materials.

  4. Birds use such materials as earth, clay, twigs, grass, stems, leaves, bark, hair, feathers, and even string to build their nests.

D. Shore birds, like the penguin and the arctic tern, lay their eggs on rocks or pebbles that have been arranged on the ground in such a way as to keep the eggs from rolling.

E. The whippoorwill lays its eggs on dead leaves in a small hole in the ground.

F. The kingfisher lays its eggs in a hole that has been dug in a clay bank, and the eggs rest either on the bare ground or on feathers.

G. The duck builds a very simple grass nest.

H. The oriole builds a long, baglike nest, made of grass, string, and hair, on the branch of a tree.

I. The owl and woodpecker live in holes that have been cut out of hollow or dead trees.

J. The bluejay builds a bulky, rough nest on a tree branch, and the nest is made of twigs, leaves, grass, and string.

K. The robin builds a heavy, bulky nest on a tree branch or in the crotch of a tree, and the nest is made of twigs and mud, and then lined with grass.

L. The meadowlark and quail build grassy nests in underbrush.

M. The barn swallow builds its nest in hollow trees or in the eaves of a house, using straw and mud, and it lines the nest with hay or feathers.

N. The hummingbird builds a tiny, basket-like nest on the high branches of a tree.

O. Some hawks and eagles build their nests in very tall trees.

P. Screech owls often build their nests in barns.

VI. Birds Have Different Beaks, Feet, Wings, and Tails

A. The feet, beaks, wings, and tails of birds are different in form and structure so that they are fitted for special functions, such as perching, swimming, catching food, eating, and flying.

B. These special forms, structures, and functions are called **adaptations.**

C. Birds have different kinds of feet, depending upon whether they are fitted or adapted for perching, climbing, swimming, wading, or grasping.

  1. Seed-eating birds, like the robin and bluebird, have three toes in front and

one behind, which are used for perching on branches.

2. Birds, like the duck and the goose, have long, webbed toes for swimming.
3. Birds, like the crane and the heron, have long legs and separate toes for wading.
4. Birds, like the duck and the loon, have short legs set far back for diving.
5. Birds, like the woodpecker, have two toes in front and two toes in back, and this arrangement helps them when climbing tree trunks.
6. Birds, like the owl, hawk, and eagle, have powerful claws, called **talons,** on their toes, which are used for grabbing and holding small animals.

D. Birds have beaks that are specially fitted or adapted for gathering their food and eating.
1. The duck has a wide, flat, and notched beak, which is used for scooping up and straining food.
2. The owl, hawk, and eagle have their upper jaw curved over the lower jaw, making the beak hooked, so that it is easy to tear flesh.
3. The heron and snipe have a long, pointed beak for searching food in the mud.
4. The sparrow and finch have a short, straight, stout beak for crushing seeds and other hard foods.
5. The hummingbird has a long, thin beak, which is curved in some cases, for reaching into the bottoms of deep flowers and obtaining nectar.

E. The shape of the bird's wing is fitted or adapted for the kind of flying that a bird does.
1. Soaring birds, like the hawk, have long, broad wings.
2. Sailing or gliding birds, like the gull, have long, slender wings.
3. Birds that maneuver quickly, like the robin, have short, broad wings.
4. Ground birds, like the pheasant and the partridge have short wings that can furnish only short, quick flights.

5. Chickens do not fly much, and have underdeveloped wings.
6. The penguin has wings that are paddle-shaped for swimming.

F. The bird's tail acts as a rudder in flying and as a balance in perching.
1. The woodpecker has a stiff tail, which supports the woodpecker when it is climbing a tree trunk.
2. The bluejay has a long tail for balancing itself on tree branches.
3. The pigeon has a broad tail, which helps it stop suddenly.
4. The duck and goose have small tails.

VII. BIRDS CAN BE HELPFUL AND HARMFUL

A. Most birds are quite helpful to man.
1. The crow, red-winged blackbird, bluebird, bluejay, quail, and pheasant eat grasshoppers.
2. The flicker eats ants, and the cuckoo eats caterpillars.
3. The sparrow, pheasant, and quail eat weed seed.
4. Some owls and hawks eat mice, moles, shrews, woodchucks, prairie dogs, and rabbits.
5. The buzzard and vulture are scavengers, eating dead animals.
6. The heron and crow eat dead fish.
7. The gull eats garbage that is thrown upon the water.
8. Game birds, such as the quail, pheasant, grouse, wild duck, wild goose, and wild turkey, are used for food.
9. Tame birds, such as the chicken, duck, goose, and turkey, are used for food.
10. The eggs of chickens and ducks are used for food.
11. The canary, parakeet, and parrot are kept as pets.

B. Some birds can be harmful to man.
1. Some birds, like the robin, bluebird, cedar waxwing, and wren, eat fruit and berries.
2. Some birds, like the crow, bluejay, and red-winged blackbird, eat grain.

[539

3. Some hawks eat small insect-eating birds, young chickens, and young ducks.

VIII. THE CONSERVATION AND PROTECTION OF BIRDS

A. Large numbers of song birds and game birds have been destroyed since the United States was established.
B. The destruction of nesting sites cannot be avoided when forests are cut, underbrush cleared, and fields burned.
C. However, much bird destruction is unnecessary and could be avoided.
  1. The unnecessary drainage of marshes and the lowering of the water level in lakes and ponds take away the food supply and nesting sites of both water birds and wading birds.
  2. In earlier times thousands of birds were killed for their feathers.
  3. Vast numbers of birds are killed for fun or for food.
D. Both the states and the federal government have passed laws to help protect and conserve our birds.
  1. Song birds cannot be killed at any time, nor can their eggs be collected.
  2. Game birds can only be killed at certain times of the year.
  3. However, birds, such as the starling, raven, crow, English sparrow, and certain harmful owls and hawks, can be killed at any time.
  4. Feathers of wild birds cannot be brought into the United States except for educational purposes.
  5. Agreements have been made between Canada, the United States, and Mexico to protect migrating birds.
E. The United States Department of the Interior controls the **Fish and Wildlife Bureau,** which has charge of conserving birds and animals, controls national wildlife reservations, and publishes educational bulletins about wildlife.
F. The **National Audubon Society,** together with its state and local chapters, publishes educational literature, pictures, slides, and films on birds and their habits, promotes laws to protect birds, and takes a yearly census of the bird population.

MAMMALS

I. CHARACTERISTICS OF MAMMALS

A. Mammals are members of the animal phylum called **Chordata.**
B. Together with fish, amphibians, reptiles, and birds, they make up a special group of animals called **vertebrates.**
C. As vertebrates, mammals have the following general characteristics.
  1. They have backbones.
  2. Their skeletons are inside their bodies.
  3. They usually have two pairs of limbs, or appendages, attached to their bodies at the shoulder and hip.
D. Mammals also have their own special characteristics
E. All mammals have hair on their bodies, the hair growing from tiny pits in the skin.
  1. Most mammals have much hair on their bodies.
  2. The whale has almost no body hair, but it does have a few bristles.
  3. Some mammals, like the mink, seal, beaver, and muskrat, grow thick coats of hair in the winter.
F. The hair of some mammals, like the weasel, arctic fox, and snowshoe rabbit, changes color in different seasons of the year.
  1. In late spring, summer, and early fall their hair is brown.
  2. In late fall they shed their brown hair

and grow white hair, which stays white all winter until the spring.

G. Some animals have hair that has been changed in form and structure.
   1. The porcupine's hair is in the form of quills.
   2. The armadillo's hair has been changed into horny plates that overlap and act like a coat of armor.
   3. The horns of the rhinocerous are made of masses of hair that have changed in form and structure.
H. Many mammals have fingernails and toe-nails growing from their skin.
I. All mammals have lungs for breathing.
J. All mammals are **warm-blooded,** which means that their body temperature is always the same, regardless of the temperature of the air or water around them.
K. All mammals have seven neck bones, but these bones are not the same size for all mammals.
L. Most mammals have two pairs of limbs.
   1. The whale and the manatee have lost their hind limbs, and their front limbs look like fins.
   2. The seal and the walrus have limbs in the form of flippers.
   3. The front limbs of the bat have very long finger bones with webbed skin between them, which the bat uses for flying.
M. Mammals have different numbers of toes on their legs, but there are rarely more than five toes on one leg.
   1. The horse walks and runs on one toe that has been changed into a hoof.
   2. The cow walks on a hoof that has been formed from two toes.
   3. Most of the smaller animals have separate toes, which help them walk and run.
   4. Some animals, like the lion and tiger, have powerful nails or claws on their toes, which are used for catching and ripping smaller animals.
   5. Animals, like the squirrel and raccoon, have claws that can bend, which are used for climbing trees.

N. The young of mammals are, with a very few exceptions, born alive.
   1. When mammals mate, the male deposits sperm inside the female, fertilizing the female's eggs.
   2. The female's eggs are very small and do not have enough yolk to feed the baby mammals while they are developing from the eggs.
   3. As a result, each egg becomes attached to the wall of an organ, called the **uterus,** in the female reproductive system.
   4. In the uterus the developing mammal receives food and oxygen from the mother's blood until it is born alive.
   5. It takes different periods of time for different mammals to develop from a fertilized egg into a live baby.
   6. It takes about 21 days for a mouse, 30 days for a rabbit, 63 days for a cat or dog, 40 weeks for a human, 48 weeks for a horse, and 20 to 22 months for an elephant to be born after the female's egg has been fertilized.
O. All mammals care for their young after birth, and nurse them by giving them milk that comes from special glands, called **mammary glands.**
P. Mammals differ in size.
   1. Some mice and shrews are about 5 centimeters (2 in) long and weigh less than 28 grams (1 oz).
   2. The largest mammal is the blue whale, which can be more than 30½ meters (100 ft) long and weigh more than 136,000 kilograms (150 tons).
Q. Mammals live in different places all over the world.
   1. Most mammals live on land.
   2. The whale and porpoise live in the ocean.
   3. The seal and walrus live in salt water and on land.
   4. The beaver, muskrat, and hippopotamus live in fresh water and on land.
   5. The mole and shrew live mostly underground.
   6. The monkey and squirrel live in trees.

[541

7. The mountain sheep and mountain goat live on high mountains.
8. Bats live in caves.
9. The polar bear and reindeer live in very cold climates.
10. The lion and tiger live in very hot climates.
11. A large number of mammals live in the temperate climates.

R. Mammals eat plants and other animals.
1. Mammals, like the cow and the horse, that eat only plants are called **herbivorous** mammals.
2. Mammals, like the lion and the tiger, that eat only animals are called **carnivorous** mammals.
3. Mammals, like the bear and the raccoon, that eat both plants and animals are called **omnivorous** animals.

S. Some animals will move to different parts of the country, or **migrate**, at different seasons of the year.
1. Seals spend the winter in the Pacific Ocean between Alaska and California, and in the spring they travel to the Pribilof Islands, which are north of the Aleutian Islands, where the adult seals breed and new seals are born.
2. Elks live high in the mountains during the summer and lower down in the winter.

T. Some mammals, like the woodchuck and ground squirrel, are inactive, or **hibernate**, all winter.
1. During hibernation the animal's heartbeat slows down, the body temperature drops, breathing slows down to as little as once in 5 minutes, and the animal cannot be wakened.
2. Some mammals, like the bear, skunk, and raccoon, have a long winter sleep, where heartbeat and breathing slow down, and the mammal lives on stored food in its body.
3. This winter sleep is a little different from hibernation because mammals in winter sleep can wake up on mild days and then go back to sleep again, but animals in true hibernation cannot be wakened.

U. Mammals are classified into many smaller groups that have the same characteristics.

II. EGG-LAYING MAMMALS

A. The Australian duck-billed platypus and the spiny anteater are mammals that lay eggs instead of giving birth to their young alive.
B. The duck-billed platypus has fur like a beaver, webbed feet like a muskrat, and a horny bill like a duck.
1. It lays two or three eggs, which look very much like reptile eggs.
2. When the eggs hatch, the young lap up a kind of milk given off by mammary glands on the mother's abdomen.
C. The spiny anteater is covered with long spines that look like porcupine quills.
1. It has a tubelike bill and a long tongue, which it uses to catch ants.
2. It lays two eggs, which it places in a special pouch on its lower side.

III. POUCHED MAMMALS

A. This group includes such mammals as the kangaroo, opposum, the koala or "teddy bear," and the wallaby.
B. Their babies are helpless when they are born.
C. The newborn babies are immediately put into a special body pouch near the mother's mammary glands, which have nipples.
D. The babies feed on milk from the mammary glands until they are large and developed enough to leave the pouch.
E. Most pouched animals are found in Australia.

IV. TOOTHLESS MAMMALS

A. The sloth, armadillo, and great anteater are members of this group.
B. These animals are not completely toothless, but have no teeth at all in front.

C. The sloth is a bearlike animal that hangs upside down on trees and moves very slowly.

1. It feeds chiefly on leaves.
2. The hair of some kinds of sloths appears to be green because green algae grow in it.

D. The armadillo has a body that is covered with heavy, overlapping, bony scales.

1. It feeds chiefly on insects.
2. Its young are born either as identical twins or quadruplets.

V. INSECT-EATING MAMMALS

A. This group includes the mole, the shrew, and the hedgehog.
B. The mole and the shrew eat large numbers of grubs and worms.
C. The mole has soft, fine fur, which is used in making coats and capes.

1. It uses its sharp front legs to dig long burrows just underneath the surface of the ground, and lives underground.
2. It has a long, sharp nose, which it uses for digging grubs and worms out of the soil.
3. It has eyes that are blind.
4. Moles are pests in lawns and golf courses.

D. The tiny shrew looks both like a mouse and a mole.

1. It eats not only grubs and worms, but also mice and other shrews.

E. The hedgehog has long, quill-like hair, looks like a porcupine, and eats only insects.

VI. FLESH-EATING MAMMALS

A. All the members in this group have large, well-developed canine teeth, which are located near the corners of the mouth, and strong jaws for tearing flesh.
B. Their other teeth are pointed and help cut up the flesh.
C. Sea members of this group include the seal, walrus, and sea lion.

D. Land members of this group are divided into three subgroups, depending upon how they walk.

1. One subgroup includes the bear and raccoon, which walk flat-footed on the soles of their feet.
2. The second subgroup includes such mammals as the cat, dog, lion, tiger, wolf, and coyote, and these animals walk only on their toes.
3. The third subgroup includes the skunk, weasel, mink, and otter, which walk partly on their toes and partly on the soles of their feet.

VII. GNAWING MAMMALS

A. This group includes such mammals as the rat, mouse, squirrel, chipmunk, prairie dog, woodchuck, rabbit, hare, muskrat, and beaver.
B. All but the rabbit and hare have two large, chisellike front, or incisor, teeth on each jaw.

1. These teeth have very sharp edges, which stay sharp because the front edge is harder than the back edge so that the biting surface always wears out at an angle.
2. The teeth themselves do not wear out because they keep growing all the time.
3. The rabbit and hare have four of these teeth on each jaw.

C. They all have strong grinding teeth behind their sharp front teeth.
D. Most of the members of this group do a great deal of damage by eating grain and crops, and the rat spreads disease as well.

VIII. HOOFED MAMMALS

A. This group includes most of the tame animals that man uses for food, clothing, work, and transportation.
B. Biologists divide this group into two large subgroups: the odd-toed and the even-toed hoofed animals.
C. The odd-toed hoofed group includes such

animals as the horse and the rhinocerous.

D. The even-toed group is further divided into two smaller groups: the cud chewers and the noncud chewers.

E. The even-toed cud chewers include such animals as the cow, sheep, goat, camel, giraffe, and deer.
  1. They have four divisions to their stomach.
  2. They usually swallow large amounts of food quickly, and this food passes into the first stomach division, where it is stored for chewing.
  3. Later, the food is forced back into the mouth and chewed thoroughly as a cud.
  4. The cud then passes into the second stomach division, where it begins to be digested.

F. The even-toed noncud chewers include such animals as the pig and the hippopotamus.

G. Some hoofed mammals have horns.
  1. The cow, ox, and bison have hollow horns, which are never shed.
  2. The deer, elk, caribou, and moose have solid horns with many branches, and these horns are shed each year.

IX. TRUNK-NOSED MAMMALS

A. The elephant is the only trunk-nosed animal alive today.

B. It is the largest land mammal, and can weigh 6350 kilograms (7 tons).

C. Its trunk is really a stretched-out upper lip and nose.

X. FLYING MAMMALS

A. Bats are mammals that fly.
  1. The toe bones of their front legs are very long and have skin stretched over and between them.
  2. The skin is also attached to the side of the body, the back legs, and the tail.
  3. This gives the bat a large wingspread.

B. Because the skin covers both the bat's front and back legs, the bat cannot walk very well.

C. The bat flies by night, and during the day it stays in caves, hanging upside down by the claws of its back legs.

D. Most bats eat insects, but the vampire bat in the American tropics drinks the blood of large animals.

E. Bats can fly in complete darkness without bumping into things.
  1. Bats can hear very well, and listen to the echoes of their own very high-pitched voices as the echoes bounce back from objects around them.
  2. This listening helps the bats determine where the objects are, and the bats fly around the objects rather than into them.

XI. MARINE MAMMALS

A. The whale, dolphin, and porpoise are mammals that look like fish.

B. Although they have lungs and breathe air, they live all their lives in the ocean.

C. They use their tails for swimming and their finlike front limbs for balance.

D. They usually have one or two young, which are fed by their milk just like other mammals.

E. They eat fish and other sea animals.

XII. FLEXIBLE-FINGERED MAMMALS

A. Members of this group include the lemur, monkey, gibbon, orangutan, chimpanzee, and gorilla.

B. Scientists also include man in this group but place him in a special family by himself.

C. Most mammals in this group have well-developed brains and a high intelligence.

D. They have fingers and toes that are very flexible, and can be used for grasping.

E. They all have nails on their fingers and toes, instead of claws.

F. The lemur and monkey live mostly in trees.

G. The higher apes are built very much like man.
1. They have hairy bodies and no tails.
2. Their front feet are used as grasping hands, and their back feet can be used both for grasping and walking.
3. They can walk on two legs or move about on all four legs.

XIII. Mammals Can Be Helpful and Harmful

A. Some mammals are helpful to man, some are harmful, and others are neither helpful nor harmful.
B. Some mammals help man by eating pests.
1. The fox eats field mice and rats.
2. The mole and the shrew eat grubs and insects.
3. The anteater and the bat eat insects.
C. Some mammals help by doing work for us.
1. The horse and the ox are used for work in areas with temperate climates.
2. The reindeer and sled dog work in cold areas, the camel in desert areas, and the elephant in tropical areas.
D. Some mammals supply us with food.
1. We eat the food of such tame animals as the cow, sheep, goat, and pig.
2. We also eat the meat of such wild animals as the deer, bear, and seal.
3. We also get milk, cheese, butter, and lard from animals.
E. Some animals give us clothing.
1. Mammals like the cow, horse, pig, and alligator give us leather.
2. The sheep, camel, llama, alpaca, and vicuna give us wool.
3. Mammals like the seal, beaver, muskrat, racoon, skunk, fox, chinchilla, and mink give us fur.
4. Buttons and bone ornaments are made from the bones, hooves, and horns of such mammals as the cow, horse, and deer.
F. Mammals also supply us with tallow, lanolin, glue, and fertilizer.
G. Rats, mice, and guinea pigs are of great help in laboratories working on the causes and effects of diseases.
H. Some mammals are harmful to man.
1. The gnawing mammals, like the prairie dog, woodchuck, rabbit, mouse, and rat, eat grain and crops.
2. The rat and the mouse also eat or spoil our food, and spread disease.

XIV. The Conservation of Mammals

A. Many mammals have been killed without any thought being given to conserving them.
1. Fur-bearing animals have been slaughtered in very great numbers.
2. The bison of the Great Plains have almost been wiped out because of the demand for their fur and meat.
3. In the West the elk, antelope, and mule deer have been killed in large numbers for their meat and horns.
B. Both the states and the federal government have passed laws to protect and conserve some of our wildlife.
1. Some laws make it illegal to kill certain mammals at any time during the year.
2. Other laws allow certain mammals to be killed only at special periods of time, and place a limit on the number of animals a person can kill during this period.
C. The federal government has established more than 400 **game preserves** for the protection of both mammals and birds.
1. These preserves are the charge of the **Fish and Wildlife Bureau,** which is a wildlife conservation agency of the United States Department of the Interior.
2. Many of these game preserves are in national parks and monuments, such as the Yellowstone National Park in the state of Wyoming.
D. Fur farms, where such mammals as the mink, muskrat, chinchilla, and silver fox are raised, help reduce the number of similar wild mammals from being killed.

LEARNING ACTIVITIES FOR "ANIMALS"

COMPOSITION AND CLASSIFI-CATION OF ANIMALS

1. *Examine animal cells* • Obtain a toothpick with a blunt end. Gently scrape the inside of your cheek a few times with the blunt end of the toothpick. Spread the accumulated material on a microscope slide. Add a drop of water, stain with a drop of tincture of iodine, and then cover the material with a cover glass. Examine the material carefully under the microscope until you find a clearly defined cell. Look for and identify the different parts of the cell. Compare this animal cell with a plant cell, such as an onion cell, prepared as described in Learning Activity 1 of "Plants Are Living Things," Chapter 13A (p. 467). Note both the similarities and differences between the plant and animal cells.

2. *Examine different cells and tissues* • Repeat Learning Activity 1 above, using some dried skin scraped from the palm of your hand. From the butcher obtain small amounts of fresh animal tissue, such as steak (muscle tissue), nerves, and bones, for study. Examine tiny slivers of these tissues under the microscope and note any differences in the cells. Because blood is also a tissue, examine a drop of blood under the microscope. Note that all the cells in a tissue are alike.

3. *Examine body organs* • Obtain such animal organs as a cow's or pig's heart, liver, stomach, lungs, kidney, and brains from the butcher. Examine their appearance and discuss the basic function of each organ. If actual organs are unavailable or inconvenient to obtain and handle, show pictures instead. Point out that each organ is made up of a group of tissues working together.

4. *Discover how scientists classify animals* • Show how the cocker spaniel dog is classified, going step by step from the phylum to the variety itself. Such a classification would appear as shown in Table 14–1.

TABLE 14–1. Classification of the Cocker Spaniel Dog

KINGDOM: Animalia
PHYLUM: Chordata (have a notochord)
SUBPHYLUM: Vertebrata (have a backbone)
CLASS: Mammalia (are mammals)
ORDER: Carnivora (the flesh-eating mammals)
FAMILY: Canidae (including the foxes and the wolves)
GENUS: Canis (includes the wolf, coyote, and dog)
SPECIES: familiaris (domestic dog)
VARIETY: cocker spaniel

5. *Observe the major animal phyla* • Visit a natural history museum for animals that belong to different phyla. If a field trip is not feasible, show pictures of representative animals from each phylum. Discuss some of the differentiating characteristics of the animals in each phylum.

ANIMALS WITHOUT BACKBONES

1. *Examine a natural sponge* • Obtain a natural sponge. Have the children observe the many holes in the sponge. Let them feel the sponge, and then point out that this soft, flexible material is the skeleton of the sponge.

2. *Collect and observe hydras* • Hydras can be found attached to the submerged stems or the undersides of floating leaves of water plants in ponds. They are large enough to be seen with the naked eye. Tear off bits of plants to which the hydras are attached and place them in glass jars together with some of the pond water. In the classroom keep the jars in semidarkness and feed them a few tiny bits of lean meat once or twice a week.

Transfer one or two hydras to a saucer by using a medicine dropper with a wide tip. If necessary, break off part of the tip to make it wide enough to pick up the hydra without harming it. Place the tip of the medicine dropper directly over the hydra when sucking it up. After the hydra is in the saucer, add enough pond water to keep the hydra covered.

Wait until the hydra has relaxed and stretched, and then examine it with a magnifying glass. Note the movement of the tentacles. Tap the saucer with your finger. The frightened hydra will contract to a tiny ball. The hydra will also contract if you touch it with a pin. Place one or two tiny bits of lean meat near the hydra and observe how the tentacles take the meat and bring it to the hydra's mouth. The tentacles will sting live tiny animals, such as water fleas or mosquito wigglers, that are placed near them. Look to see if any of the hydras are reproducing by forming buds. Cut a hydra into two or more pieces with a razor blade and place the pieces and pond water in a glass jar. In 2 or 3 weeks each piece will have become a new hydra.

3. *Observe jellyfish and sea anemones* · If you live near the ocean, look for small jellyfish and sea anemones in shallow water just off the coast. Place them in glass jars containing seawater, and observe their parts and behavior.

4. *Examine coral* · If a sample of coral is available, have the children examine it and find where each coral animal lives. Note how the piece of coral is a solid mass of skeletons all joined together. Have the children read about and report how coral reefs are formed.

5. *Collect and observe planarians* · Planarians are often found in quiet ponds, either clinging to reeds or on the undersides of stones. You will have to look carefully because they are only 3 to 13 millimeters (⅛ to ½ in) long and they blend so well with their surroundings that they are difficult to see. Suck up the planarians with a medicine dropper and keep them in jars filled with pond water. Bring back an extra supply of pond water. Planarians may also be obtained

from scientific supply houses. Feed the planarians twice a week with a few tiny bits of lean beef or boiled egg yolk. It would be wise to change the water shortly after each feeding, using either the additional pond water you collected or tap water that has been allowed to stand for 2 or 3 days.

Observe the planarians with a magnifying glass or under the low power of a microscope. Note their spearlike heads and two dark "eyespots." See how planarians regenerate. Suck up three planarians with a medicine dropper and place them on a wet paper towel. By using a sharp razor blade, cut one planarian, horizontally in half, the second planarian horizontally into thirds, and the third planarian vertically in half (Figure 14–1). After each planarian is

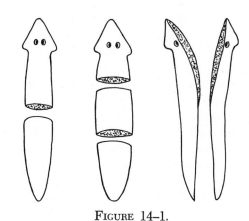

Figure 14–1.

WHEN PLANARIANS ARE CUT INTO SEGMENTS, THEY REGENERATE.

cut, wash the pieces in a saucer of pond water. Keep the saucers covered with glass squares to prevent evaporation. Feed and add water regularly. In about 2 weeks each piece will have become a new planarian.

6. *Explore parasitic flatworms and roundworms* · Have the children read about and discuss the life history of such flatworms and roundworms as the tapeworm, fluke, ascaris, hookworm, and trichinella.

[547

7. *Collect and observe earthworms* · The best place to find earthworms is in rich garden soil. Either dig them up or wait until after a heavy rain, when the worms come to the surface at night. Try to collect the large "night crawlers." Keep the worms in boxes containing equal parts of peat moss and rich garden soil. Cover the box with a damp piece of thick cloth towel. Keep the earth and towel damp, but not wet, at all times. About once a week feed the worms a quarter cup of oatmeal or bread that has been softened in water.

Place an earthworm on a damp paper towel and see how it crawls by lengthening and then contracting its body. Find the head of the earthworm by watching closely for the lip or pharynx that the worm pushes out as it moves along. Touch the head and note how the worm contracts the front part of its body; it may even crawl backward.

Pass your fingertips gently along the underside of the earthworm and feel the bristle feet or setae. Observe these feet through a magnifying glass. See what happens when you place the earthworm on a damp, smooth glass surface, where there is nothing for these bristle feet to grip.

Place an earthworm on a piece of damp paper towel and cover the earthworm with a saucer so the worm cannot escape. Keep the worm in a dark room for about an hour, and then shine a flashlight on the worm's head. Note how the worm quickly pulls its head away from the bright light.

8. *Observe a starfish* · If possible, obtain a preserved starfish. Feel the spines scattered all over the top part of its body. Look at the underside of the body and note the grooves that lead from each arm to the mouth in the center. Examine the tube feet with a magnifying glass. Have the children read about and report how the starfish opens up the shell of an oyster or clam.

9. *Observe a clam or oyster* · Obtain some clams or oysters from the fish store. Open the shellfish by inserting a knife on each side of the hinge and cutting the muscles that hold the shell together. Find the thin, fleshy mantle next to the surface of the shell. Look for the siphons and discuss their function. Find the muscular foot and note that it is attached to the body. Examine the shell and locate the mother-of-pearl layer. Show samples of materials that are either made of mother-of-pearl or else have mother-of-pearl in them.

10. *Collect and observe water snails* · Obtain some water snails from a pet shop or scientific supply house. Snails can be found among the water plants of a pond that has a muddy bottom. Place two or three snails in an aquarium or a large glass jar of tap water that has been allowed to stand for 2 or 3 days, making sure that there is a good supply of water plants in the container.

See how the snail uses its foot to move along the walls of the aquarium. Use a magnifying glass to watch the snail's rough "tongue" scrape the algae from the walls of the aquarium. Touch the snails and see how they withdraw into their shells and fall to the bottom of the aquarium. The snails may lay masses of transparent eggs on the walls of the aquarium. Examine these eggs periodically for 2 or 3 weeks and see them hatch.

11. *Collect and observe a land snail* · Land snails are often found early in the morning feeding on plants in the garden. They can be kept in an aquarium or in a large glass jar containing damp garden soil. If you use a glass jar, keep the mouth covered, either with a wire screen or with a screw top that has been perforated several times by a nail. Keep the snail well supplied with soft, green leaves or with lettuce.

Note how the snail's foot leaves a trail of slime, along which it travels. See how the snail quickly shreds the leaves and lettuce with its "tongue." Look for the eyes at the ends of the larger pair of feelers. Touch the feelers gently with a pencil and see how they retract. Touch the feelers more forcibly and make the snail withdraw into its shell.

12. *Observe squids and octopuses* · Have some children visit the natural history museum and observe specimens of squids and octopuses. Let them report on their observations and make a comparison of similarities and differences in form and structure. If possible, obtain and display pictures of these animals.

13. *Collect and observe crayfish* · The fresh-water crayfish and the ocean lobster are almost exactly alike, and either is highly suitable for the study of crustaceans. Crayfish are found in ponds and streams hiding under rocks and logs. They can be caught by tying one end of a string around a small piece of meat and dangling the meat near a rock at the bottom of the pond or stream. When the crayfish seizes the meat with its claws, pull up the string with a slow steady movement. If you are quick, you can also catch a crayfish by lifting up rocks and then grabbing it as it swims backward. Keep the crayfish you collect in large glass jars filled with pond water or tap water that has been allowed to stand for 2 or 3 days to allow any chlorine in the water to escape.

Observe the crayfish carefully. Note how the outside skeleton forms a hard, protective shield for the crayfish, especially over the head and chest area. Note the segments of the abdomen and the paddles of the tail. Count the number of jointed walking legs and examine the large pair of front claws. Feed the crayfish earthworms or small pieces of raw meat and see how the crayfish uses its claws and mouth parts. Locate the feelers and count how many there are. Observe the eyes and see how they move around on their stalks.

Put a crayfish on its back. Lift up the free, lower edge of the skeleton that covers the chest region and observe the gills. Find the mouth parts. Examine the swimmerets and see how the crayfish uses them. See how the crayfish uses its abdomen to swim backward quickly.

14. *Collect and observe water fleas* (*daphnia*) · Water fleas are tiny transparent crustaceans that can be found during the spring and summer in almost any quiet pool or stream. Because they eat algae, water fleas are easiest to find in ponds that are covered with green scum. A good way to catch them is to use a sieve or tea strainer that has been lined with cheesecloth. Use needle and thread to hold the cheesecloth against the sides of the sieve or strainer. Place the water fleas in glass jars containing pond water and a good supply of green algae, and keep the jars in sunlight. When you finish examining the water fleas, use them as food for fish, tadpoles, and hydra. They can also be placed in aquariums to remove excessive algae in the water.

Use a medicine dropper to suck up a water flea, and then place it on a microscope slide and examine it under the low power of a microscope. Because it is transparent, you will see not only the outer skeleton and the appendages, but also the inner organs. Notice the rapidly beating heart. Look for the intestine and trace it from the mouth to the anus.

15. *Collect insects* · To collect flying or jumping insects you will need a net, which you can either buy from a scientific supply house or make yourself. Untwist a wire coat hanger and shape the wire so that it forms a loop about 37½ centimeters (15 in) in diameter. Bend the ends of the wire so that they form two parallel straight pieces, and then cut off the ends to form a length of about 15 centimeters (6 in) (see Figure 14–2). Obtain a broomstick and use a file to make parallel grooves 15 centimeters (6 in) long on each side of one end of the broomstick. Put the ends of the wire into the grooves and wrap strong string tightly around the end of the broomstick until the wire is firmly attached to the stick. Make the net from cheesecloth, about 76 to 92 centimeters (30 to 36 in) long, and use strong thread to sew the net to the loop.

To collect water insects, a net with a straight edge will help catch insects found on or below the surface of the water. To make a straight-edge net, follow the same instructions as described in the preceding paragraph, but shape the coat hanger wire into an equilateral tri-

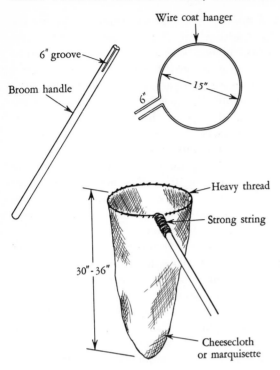

FIGURE 14–2.
A HOMEMADE NET FOR COLLECTING INSECTS.

angle instead of a circle. A kitchen strainer attached to a piece of wood or a broomstick is helpful in catching insects near the bottom of the pond or in dredging the bottom mud.

A variety of insects can be found feeding on or inside plants. Many of these, especially their larvae or caterpillars, can be picked by hand. Also, a large number of insects live in the ground, and are exposed when the soil is turned over with a shovel.

16. *Keep live insects* · Most land insects can be kept in wide-mouthed glass jars that have a few inches of soil on the bottom. Keep the soil moist, and feed the insects the kind of food they are accustomed to eat or were eating when you caught them. Always keep the mouth of the jar covered with cheesecloth or fine screen wire. Water insects should be kept either in balanced aquariums or in glass jars containing some of the water from which they were collected.

17. *Make an insect-killing bottle* · Place a large wad of absorbent cotton in the bottom of a wide-mouthed glass jar. Obtain carbon tetrachloride from a drugstore and pour it on the cotton until the cotton is saturated. Cover the cotton with a round piece of thick cardboard or blotting paper that has been perforated several times with a small nail (Figure 14–3). Keep the jar covered until you are ready to use it. When an insect is placed in the jar, the carbon tetrachloride fumes will kill it. For insects with delicate wings, like butterflies and moths, either put them into the killing bottle one at a time or else use separate jars. Keep hard-shelled insects, such as the beetle, in separate jars rather than together with the softer, more fragile insects. Add more carbon tetrachloride from time to time, as it evaporates from the cotton wad.

18. *Mount and display insects* · Insects should be mounted as quickly as possible. Otherwise they dry out and their bodies become brittle and break easily when handled.

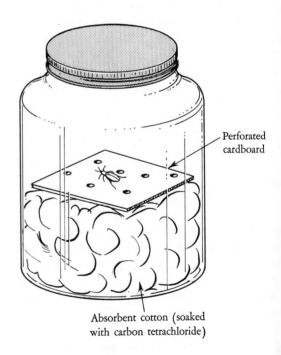

FIGURE 14–3.
AN INSECT-KILLING BOTTLE.

550]

If the insects also become dry before they can be mounted, place them in a jar containing moist blotting paper, and keep the jar covered for 24 hours. In this way the insects will be softened enough so that they can be handled easily.

Insects such as flies, grasshoppers, and beetles can be mounted directly from the killing bottle. Use either common pins or regular mounting pins purchased from a scientific supply house. To mount an insect, insert just one pin through the chest or thorax a little to the right of the center line of the body (see Figure 14–4). Straighten the legs, antennae, and wings as they dry.

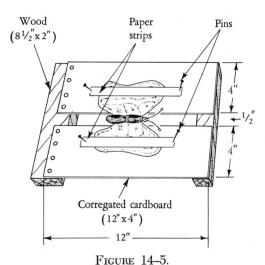

FIGURE 14–5.

A SPREADING BOARD FOR MOUNTING LARGE-WINGED INSECTS.

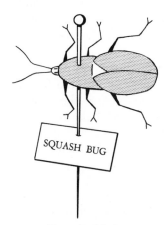

FIGURE 14–4.

A PROPERLY MOUNTED INSECT.

The large-winged insects, such a butterflies and moths, should be mounted on a spreading board. You can purchase such a board from a scientific supply house or make one yourself. Obtain two pieces of wood, each about 21½ centimeters (8½ in) long and 5 centimeters (2 in) wide. Cut out two pieces of corrugated cardboard, each about 30 centimeters (12 in) long and 10 centimeters (4 in) wide. Now glue the ends of the two pieces of cardboard to the two pieces of wood, as shown in Figure 14–5, so that there is a space of about 13 millimeters (½ in) between the two pieces of cardboard. Place the body of the butterfly in the space and

spread out the wings to show their colors and markings. Hold the wings down with strips of paper and pins, making sure to push the pins into the corrugated cardboard and not into the wings. If necessary, hold the antennae down the same way. Keep the butterfly on the spreading board for a week before mounting.

Some insects will be too small to be pinned. For such insects make a small pennant from stiff paper or thin cardboard, glue the insect to the tip of the pennant, and then push the pin through the broad end of the pennant (Figure 14–6).

Make a mounting box by gluing corrugated cardboard to the bottom of a cigar box or wood box. A thin layer of felt or absorbent cotton on the bottom will produce a more attractive appearance. Arrange the insects on their pins so that when they are mounted in the box they will all be about the same distance from the bottom of the box. A small, neat label should be placed below the insect (as shown in Figure 14–4). The label should contain the insect's common name and scientific name, the place collected, the date, and your name. If this label is too bulky, you may want to write just a code number and have the explanatory chart beside the mounting box. When the pinned insects

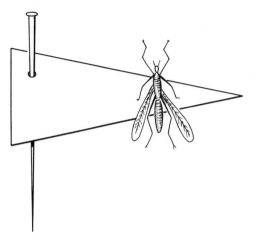

FIGURE 14–6.
MOUNTING A SMALL, DELICATE INSECT.

are in the desired position, push the pin firmly into the bottom of the box.

19. *Collect and observe grasshoppers* · Catch a live grasshopper and put it in a large glass jar together with some twigs, leaves, and blades of grass. Keep the jar covered with a lid that has several holes punched in it. Notice the division of the body into three regions. Locate and identify the parts attached to the head and the thorax. Point out the difference in size of the legs. Watch the grasshopper eat, and observe how it chews its food. Tap the side of the glass jar and note how the grasshopper jumps. See how the color of the grasshopper blends in with the color of the leaves and grass. When you hold the grasshopper between your finger and thumb, it will "spit molasses." This brown liquid is partially digested food from the grasshopper's crop.

Catch a live grasshopper and preserve it in a jar containing 70 percent alcohol. Examine the preserved grasshopper with a magnifying glass. Look at the eyes and the antennae. Find out how many mouth parts it has. Spread out and observe the outer and inner wings. Examine the sides of the abdomen and find the holes that are the openings of the grasshopper's breathing tubes.

Trace the life cycle of the grasshopper, using appropriate pictures or drawings. Note that the very young grasshopper has no wings, but develops them after it has molted a few times.

20. *Collect, observe, and compare butterflies and moths* · Collect a few specimens of butterflies and moths and examine them closely. Because many moths have colored wings, identify the moths and butterflies by comparing the size of their abdomens, the appearance of their antennae, and the position of their wings when at rest. Observe the bodies, legs, and wings of the moths and butterflies closely with a magnifying glass. Examine the scales of a butterfly's wing under the microscope and note the beautiful patterns and colors. Rub the scales off the wing with your fingers, and see how the wing begins to resemble that of a fly or bee. The vertical lines are the veins of the wing.

Place a toothpick or pin under the long, coiled, sucking tube of the butterfly or moth and gently pull the toothpick away from the insect's head, causing the tube to unroll. Point out that the butterfly and moth use this long tube to suck nectar from deep within the flower.

21. *Collect caterpillars, crysalids, and cocoons* · Collect caterpillars and place them in glass jars containing moist soil and some of the leaves upon which they were found. Each jar should also have a twig to support the crysalids or cocoons when they are formed. Cover the mouth of the jar with either fine screen wire or with the cover lid after it has been perforated several times with a small nail. Put only one caterpillar in a jar to determine whether the caterpillar is a butterfly or moth larva. Continue feeding the caterpillar until it passes into the pupa stage. If the caterpillar is a butterfly larva, it will form the hardened case called a crysalis. If the caterpillar is a moth, it will spin a cocoon.

Additional crysalids and cocoons may be collected in the garden and woods. You will have to look carefully because they often resemble dead leaves or twigs. Place each crysalid or cocoon in a glass jar with a perforated cover or fine screen wire over the mouth. The jars should contain some moist soil and a twig for the adult moths or butterflies to stand on when they come out of their containers. Keep the jars in a warm place and examine the crysalids and cocoons regularly until the adult moths and butterflies emerge.

22. *Observe ants* · Look for ants in the school yard or at home. Examine them closely. Note the three parts of their bodies and their six legs, all connected to the chest or thorax. Look at the antennae, eyes, and jaws of an ant under a magnifying glass. Note how the ant is always cleaning its antennae. If one ant meets another, watch and see if they touch antennae.

Follow the ants to their nest. If the nest is under a rock, lift up the rock and examine the tiny larvae and pupae. Try to find the queen ant. Observe the behavior of the disturbed ant workers.

If you find ants climbing up plants or bushes, watch them. They may lead you to the tiny plant lice called *aphids*. If they do, use a magnifying glass to watch an ant stroke an aphid with its antennae.

23. *Collect and observe fruit flies* · You can easily collect fruit flies most of the year. Peel a ripe banana and leave the skin, soft side up, on a saucer. The tiny fruit flies will soon gather on the skin. Collect some of the flies and put them in a glass or plastic jar. Put a small piece of banana peel on a thin slice of ripe banana in the jar to keep the fruit flies alive. Plug the mouth of the jar with a wad of cotton. The cotton will keep the fruit flies from escaping but still supply them with air.

Study the behavior of the flies, and observe them with a magnifying glass. If the flies mate and lay tiny eggs, observe the life cycle of the flies as larvae, pupae, and then adult flies appear. How long does it take for the rapid life cycle to occur? Try to distinguish the male from the female. The male fruit fly is a little smaller than the female, and its abdo-men tends to be more strongly colored than the female's.

24. *Observe and compare insects of different orders* · Look for and collect insects that represent insect orders other than those already mentioned in the learning activities above. Representative insects that could be collected would be the dragonfly, the water bug or bed bug, the aphid or cicada, the housefly or mosquito, and the ladybug, Japanese beetle or potato beetle.

Examine the different insects under a magnifying glass or the low power of a microscope. Describe and compare, wherever possible, their wings, antennae, mouth parts, and legs. Trace the kind of metamorphosis that each insect order undergoes. Discuss their food habits and decide whether they are helpful or harmful.

25. *Explore protective coloration of insects* · Have children read about and discuss protective coloration in insects. Try to collect pictures showing insects that look like their surroundings, insects that look like other more dangerous insects, and insects that look like the objects upon which they are resting.

26. *Investigate helpful and harmful insects* · Make a list of helpful and harmful insects found where you live. For the harmful insects, indicate whether they are harmful in the larval stage or in the adult stage. Have the children prepare a report about how the harmful insects can be controlled.

27. *Collect and observe spiders* · Collect some garden spiders, putting each in a separate, large glass jar. Put a few twigs or small branches in each jar for the spider to spin its web. Place a very small moist sponge in the jar because the spider needs water. Cover the mouth of the jar with a piece of fine mesh nylon stocking, and hold the nylon mesh firmly in place with rubber bands snapped around the neck of the jar. Feed the spider live insects only, such as flies, moths, or other flying insects. Keep the sponge moist at all times.

Examine the spider carefully, using a magnifying glass whenever necessary, and compare the parts of a spider with those of an insect. Note the spider's two body parts: the combined head and chest (thorax) and the abdomen. Count the eight legs of the spider, and also the eight simple eyes. Note the large poison fangs at the spider's mouth.

If the spider spins a web, note what part of the body the silk thread comes from. Put a live insect in the jar and observe how the insect becomes trapped in the web. The spider will then wrap the body of the insect completely with its silk thread. Note that the spider will not eat the insect, but will suck out all the insect's body juices, leaving the dried skeleton behind.

Collect and examine an outdoor spider web. Carefully place black paper against one side of the web, then gently spray the web with clear plastic spray or hair spray. The spray will attach the web to the paper.

ANIMALS WITH BACKBONES

1. *Set up a balanced classroom aquarium* · A rectangular tank that holds 23 liters (6 gal) is an excellent size for elementary classrooms. Clean the tank thoroughly with detergent and water, and rinse it several times. Obtain enough aquarium gravel from the pet shop to cover the bottom of the tank 5 centimeters (2 in) deep. Before adding the gravel to the tank, place the gravel in a large pan, tilt the pan to one side, and allow running water to flow in and overflow the pan. Continue running the water into the pan until the gravel is quite clean.

Place the gravel evenly in the tank, add one or two colored rocks, and put a few clam or oyster shells in the gravel. The shells will slowly dissolve in the water and provide the calcium that the growing snails will need for their shells.

Place a piece of paper over the gravel so that, when water is poured into the tank, the water will not become cloudy for a long time. Use either clear pond water or tap water that has been allowed to stand for 2 days so that the chlorine dissolved in it can escape. Pour water in the tank until it is almost to the top.

Place the tank in north or east light, but not in direct sunlight. From the pet shop obtain some rooted plants, such as sagittaria or vallisneria, and some floating plants, such as elodea or cabomba. Place the plants toward the back of the tank so you will have a clear view of the fish. The water plants will take in the carbon dioxide given off by the fish and give off oxygen that the fish will need. Do not put in too many plants because they will grow and spread. Remove any dead leaves. Allow the aquarium to stand for about a week until the water is clear and the plants are growing.

Now you are ready to add the fish. Do not overcrowd the aquarium. About 2½ centimeters (1 in) of fish to 3⅘ liters (1 gal) of water is recommended. The 23-liter (6-gal) tank will then hold either six 2½-centimeter (1-in) fish or three 5-centimeter (2-in) fish. Obtain small, active fish, such as guppies, rather than sluggish goldfish.

Add about 6 to 12 snails, also obtained from the pet shop, and then place a glass cover over the tank. Do not overfeed the fish because the water will become foul and the fish may be killed. Fish will eat prepared fish food, bread crumbs, bits of egg yolk, and oatmeal. Occasionally, give them small amounts of chopped earthworms or meal worms.

2. *Observe and compare fish* · Observe the fish in your aquarium. Compare shapes and sizes of the head, trunk, and tail regions. Identify the fins, and see which fins are paired. Observe how the fish use their fins and tail. Watch the eyes and see if they move. Note how the fish take in water through their mouths, and then force the water out through their gill covers. See how easily the fish can rise or sink in the water without using their fins very much. This movement is made possible by the inflation or deflation of the air bladder inside the fish.

Remove a small fish from the aquarium and wrap up the fish in wet absorbent cotton, leaving only the tail exposed. Place the fish on a lat, glass dish and observe the tail under the low power of the microscope. If the fish flaps its tail, place a microscope slide on the tail. You will see the arteries, veins, and capillaries. Note the blood corpuscles moving through the blood vessels, quickly through the arteries and slowly through the veins. In the small capillaries the corpuscles almost move in single file. Switch to the high power of the microscope and observe the corpuscles. Do not keep the fish out of water this way for more than 15 minutes.

Obtain a small dead fish from the fish market. Examine the gill covers, and then lift them up to see the gills and the slits through which the water passes. If possible, dissect the fish and examine all its internal organs. Remove some of the scales from the side of the fish and examine them under a magnifying glass or the low power of a microscope. Count the number of curved lines or rays on each scale. Each ray represents a year's growth so you will be able to tell the age of the fish.

3. *Make a terrarium* · Make a terrarium as described in Learning Activity 13 of "Plants Are Living Things," Chapter 13A (p. 469). The terrarium makes an excellent home for frogs, toads, salamanders, turtles, and lizards.

4. *Observe and compare frogs and toads* · Frogs and toads live very well in a terrarium. Put a frog and a toad in separate cartons and watch them closely. Compare their appearance, skin, and color. Touch their skin to see if it is wet or dry. Compare the way they hop. Count the number of toes on each foot and see if the frog and toad have the same amount of webbing between their toes. Bring your finger very near their eyes and see if they can wink. Locate their large ears, which correspond to a human's middle ear.

Place the frog and toad in separate, covered glass jars for a few minutes. Introduce some live house flies or fruit flies into each jar and see how the frog and toad use their tongues to catch and eat the flies. Note how the eyes move inward to help the frog and toad swallow

their food. Frogs and toads eat living insects only, such as flies, grasshoppers, caterpillars, June bugs, roaches, and meal worms. They can also be trained to eat bits of lean beef and liver if the meat is dangled in front of them with a string.

Place a frog in a large aquarium containing about 15 centimeters (6 in) of water. Watch how the frog swims. Note that when the frog is resting, it keeps its eyes and nostrils above the water. If you should hold the frog under water and gently rub its sides, it will usually croak. Replace the water in the aquarium with very cold water, and see how the frog becomes motionless, as if it is ready to go into hibernation.

5. *Raise tadpoles* · Frogs and toads lay their eggs in the spring. The eggs are found in shallow, quiet pond water, floating at or just beneath the surface near water plants. Frogs' eggs are found in clumps, whereas toads' eggs are found in strings. Both kinds of eggs are embedded in a jellylike material. Collect the eggs with a cup and pour them into a glass jar containing some of the pond water.

Place the eggs in an aquarium that has lots of water plants growing in it. If possible, add some of the green scum (algae) that is often found floating on top of ponds. Have the aquarium only partly full of water, and put a large rock in the aquarium that juts above the water. This rock will allow the tadpoles to leave the water and crawl around.

Watch the eggs each day with a magnifying glass. After a few days, tiny tadpoles will appear. Observe their growth and accompanying changes. Note that the toad's tadpole stage does not last as long as the frog's tadpole stage. Feed the tadpoles algae (green pond scum), small living insects, and dried fish food.

6. *Keep and observe salamanders* · The land salamanders can be kept very well in the woodland terrarium described in Learning Activity 3 above. Water salamanders can be kept in the balanced aquarium described in Learning Activity 1 above. They both can be fed earth-

worms, meal worms, ground lean beef, and liver cut into small pieces. It is better to feed the water salamander in a shallow pan of water outside the aquarium to avoid contamination of the water in the aquarium.

Observe the salamander closely. Although it may look like a reptile, it is really an amphibian and has all the characteristics of an amphibian. Touch the salamander's body gently with the palm of your hand and see how smooth and moist the skin is. Observe how small and weak the legs are. Count the number of toes on the front and hind legs, and see if the toes are webbed and have claws. Watch how the water salamander uses its tail for swimming. See how the salamander seizes and eats its food. Find out if the salamanders are attracted or repelled by strong light. Compare the salamander with other amphibians, such as the frog and toad, and note the similarities and differences. Contrast their living, feeding, and breeding habits as well.

7. *Keep and observe turtles* · The box turtle, which is mostly a land turtle, can be kept in the woodland terrarium described in Learning Activity 3 above. Water turtles can be kept in an aquarium tank that has about 7½ centimeters (3 in) of water, with a few flat stones jutting above the water. Feed the turtles earthworms, meal worms, tadpoles, snails, bits of raw hamburger, slices of apple and banana, berries, and small pieces of lettuce. Because water turtles eat only under water, be sure to throw the food directly into the water. Also, do not become alarmed if both water and land turtles refuse to eat for long periods of time and become sluggish. This inactivity is quite usual, so leave them alone.

Observe the turtle closely. Examine the top and bottom shells closely, and see how the shells form an excellent means of protecting the turtle from enemies and injury. Poke the turtle's head gently with a stick and watch the turtle pull its head, neck, legs, and tail inside its shell. Bring the stick near the turtle's eyes and see if they can blink. Observe how the turtle seizes and eats its food. Try to find out if the mouth contains any teeth. Also note how the

flexible neck can turn in all directions. Examine the short legs and count the number of toes on the front and hind legs. See if the toes are webbed and have claws. Observe how the water turtle swims. Review the characteristics of a reptile and see if the turtle meets all these characteristics. Have the children find out how to distinguish between a turtle, tortoise, and terrapin. Compare the turtle with other reptiles, such as the lizard and snake, and note the similarities and differences. Contrast their living, feeding, and breeding habits as well.

8. *Keep and observe snakes* · Garter snakes are easily found, and are very safe to keep and observe. When lifting the snake, hold it just behind the head with one hand and support the rest of the body with the other hand. When first captured, the frightened garter snake may give off a bad-smelling liquid. This liquid is not harmful and washes off easily. Bring the snake back to the classroom in a cloth bag or a pillow case with the mouth of the bag or pillow case tied securely.

Keep the snake in a large aquarium tank covered by zinc mesh (hardware cloth), which can be obtained from the hardware store. Get enough zinc mesh so that you can bend the edges down snugly against the sides of the tank (Figure 14–7). Then place at least two heavy bricks cater-cornered on the top frame of the tank. The mesh and the bricks will ensure that the snake does not escape. Place some rocks, one or two forked branches, and a pan of water in the aquarium. Clean the cage once a week by flushing the cage well with water. Wash the snake with water at the same time. Feed the snake small living animals, such as frogs, mice, lizards, tadpoles, earthworms, and other large insects. Snakes are especially hungry after they shed their skins so have plenty of food on hand at that time.

Observe the snake closely. Note how it moves. Locate the eyes and see if they blink. See if you can find any ears. Watch how and for what reason the snake uses its forked tongue. Observe how the snake seizes and eats its food. See if the snake has all the general

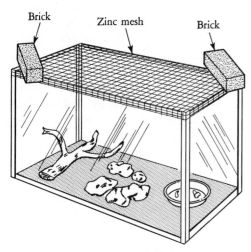

Brick   Zinc mesh   Brick

FIGURE 14–7.

PREPARING A CAGE FOR SNAKES.

characteristics of a reptile. Compare the snake with other reptiles, such as the lizard and turtle, and note the similarities and differences. Contrast their living, feeding, and breeding habits as well.

9. *Investigate poisonous snakes* · Learn the kinds of poisonous snakes, if any, in your region. Obtain pictures of them and have the children learn to recognize them on sight. Learn where these snakes are most likely to be found and caution the children about these places. Find out what the proper first-aid treatment would be for bites from these snakes.

10. *Keep and observe lizards* · Collect skinks, swifts, geckos, or desert lizards, depending upon the part of the country in which you live. Also, chameleons can be purchased at the pet shop. Lizards can be kept in the woodland or desert terrarium described in Learning Activity 3 above. They can also be kept in an aquarium with a cover of hardware cloth (zinc mesh), recommended for keeping snakes in Learning Activity 8 above. Place some rocks, forked sticks, one or two potted plants, and a pan of water in the aquarium. Feed lizards all kinds of living insects, especially meal worms, ants, small grasshoppers, and flies.

Observe the lizard closely. Touch the skin and see if it is moist or dry. See how it uses its tail when it runs. Count the number of toes on each foot and see if they have claws. Observe how the lizard seizes and eats its food. Review the characteristics of a reptile and see if the lizard meets all these characteristics. Compare the lizard with other reptiles, such as the turtle and snake, and note the similarities and differences. Contrast their living, feeding, and breeding habits as well.

11. *Observe a baby alligator* · Children often receive stuffed baby alligators as souvenirs or gifts. If one is available, have it brought to school. Note that the alligator has all the general characteristics of a reptile, and point out the strong physical similarity between the alligator and the lizard. Have the children read about and report on the living, feeding, and breeding habits of the alligator.

12. *Observe and compare birds* · Have some children bring in a parakeet, canary, or other pet bird. Do not keep the bird in the classroom over the weekend in the winter if the room temperature will change during that time. Observe the bird closely. How many toes does it have, and how are they arranged? What kind of a beak does it have? For what uses are the legs, toes, and beak adapted? Does the bird walk or hop? Examine the bird's eyes and see if they can blink. Describe the color of the feathers on the head, back, breast, and tail. What kinds of sounds does the bird make? Observe how the bird eats, drinks, bathes, and dusts or oils itself.

Try to obtain a feather from a bird's wing or tail. Note how light and flexible, yet strong, the feather is. Examine the feather under a magnifying glass or the low power of a microscope. See how the barbs are held together by interlocking hooks.

Bring in some of the bones from a roasted chicken. Saw the leg and wing bones in half, and note that the bones are hollow, which makes them light. Have some children study and report on a bird skeleton from the natural history museum.

[557

13. *Examine birds' nests* · Have the children bring in abandoned birds' nests. Let them consult reference books on birds, and try to find out what kind of bird built each nest. Pull the nest apart and sort out the materials. The children will learn not only the kinds but also the relative quantities of materials that were used to build the nest.

14. *Investigate bird migration* · Have the children read about and report on the migration habits of some birds. Find out which birds in your neighborhood do not migrate. Setting up a feeding station for birds would be very humane, especially when there is snow or ice on the ground. Have the children keep a record of the number of birds that visit the station.

15. *Compare adaptations and protective coloration of birds* · Post pictures or drawings of different birds' feet, beaks. wings, and tails. Include in each picture the names of the birds that have these kinds of body parts. Note how these parts are especially adapted for each bird's living and feeding habits. Look for pictures showing birds in their natural setting, which illustrate how the birds' coloring protects them by blending in with their surroundings.

16. *Keep and observe small mammals* · White mice, guinea pigs, gerbils, and hamsters are excellent small mammals to observe in the elementary classroom. Although different kinds of homemade animal cages can be built, it may be more expedient to purchase sturdy, well-built animal cages made of metal and of the proper size. The animals, together with suitable food and books on the care of these animals, can be obtained at a pet shop. There are also many reference books available on the care of pet mammals. When purchasing these animals, try to get young ones. They quickly become used to being around children and to being handled by them. Faithfully follow instructions for the care of these animals. Have the children note and compare the physical characteristics and the living and feeding habits of each animal.

17. *Investigate how animals care for their young* · Have children read about and report on different ways that animals feed, protect, and care for their young.

18. *Investigate conservation of wildlife* · Have children read about and report on conservation of fish, birds, and animals. Children can obtain a copy of the game laws for their area or state and find out what kinds of animals are protected by law. They can also find out what laws have been passed by the government of the United States to protect wildlife. Show pictures or films on the establishment of fish hatcheries, bird refuges, and game preserves. You can write to the following organizations or agencies for literature on conservation: (1) The Conservation Foundation, 30 East Fortieth Street, New York, N.Y.; (2) your particular state conservation department, usually located in the state capital; (3) The National Audubon Society, 1130 Fifth Avenue, New York, N.Y.; (4) The National Wildlife Federation, 232 Carroll Street, N.W., Washington, D.C.: (5) United States Department of the Interior, Fish and Wildlife Service, Washington, D.C.

BIBLIOGRAPHY FOR ''ANIMALS''

ABBOTT, R. TUCKER. *Seashells of North America.* New York: Golden Press, 1968. 280 pp.

———. *Seashells of the World.* New York: Golden Press, 1965. 160 pp.

ALLEN, THOMAS. *Vanishing Wildlife of North America.* Washington, D.C.: National Geographic Soc., 1974. 208 pp.

ANDERSON, JOHN. *The Changing World of Birds.* New York: Holt, Rinehart & Winston, 1973. 122 pp.

ANDERSON, MARGARET. *Exploring the Insect World.* New York: McGraw-Hill, 1974. 160 pp.

ARMOUR, RICHARD. *Sea Full of Whales.* New York: McGraw-Hill, 1974. 60 pp.

ASIMOV, ISAAC. *How Did We Find Out About Dinosaurs?* New York: Walker, 1973. 64 pp.

AUSTIN, OLIVER. *Families of Birds.* New York: Golden Press, 1971. 200 pp.

BEHRENS, JUNE. *Look at the Forest Animals.* Chicago: Childrens Press, 1974. 40 pp.

———. *Look at the Sea Animals.* Chicago: Childrens Press, 1975. 40 pp.

BENDICK, JEANNE. *How Animals Behave.* New York: Parents' Magazine, 1976. 64 pp.

———. *Why Things Change:— The Story of Evolution.* New York: Parents' Magazine, 1973. 64 pp.

BENTLEY, WILLIAM. *The Alligator Book—60 Questions and Answers.* New York: Walker, 1972. 64 pp.

BERGER, MELVIN. *Animal Hospital.* New York: John Day, 1973. 126 pp.

BRACEGIRDLE, CYRIL. *Zoos Are News.* New York: Thomas Y. Crowell, 1973. 176 pp.

BRAKER, WILLIAM P. *Exploring and Understanding Fish.* Westchester, Ill.: Benefic Press, 1971. 96 pp.

BURNETT, R. WILL, HARVEY I. FISHER, and HERBERT S. ZIM. *Zoology.* New York: Golden Press, 1969. 160 pp.

BURTON, MAURICE. *The Life of Birds.* New York: Western Pub., 1974. 64 pp.

———. *The Life of Fishes.* New York: Western Pub., 1974. 64 pp.

———. *The Life of Insects.* New York: Western Pub., 1974. 64 pp.

———. *The Life of Meat Eaters.* New York: Western Pub., 1974. 64 pp.

CALLAHAN, PHILIP. *The Evolution of Insects.* New York: Holiday House, 1972. 192 pp.

———. *Insects and How They Function.* New York: Holiday House, 1971. 192 pp.

———. *The Magnificent Birds of Prey.* New York: Holiday House, 1974. 192 pp.

CARTWRIGHT, SALLY. *Animal Homes.* New York: Coward, McCann & Geoghegan, 1973. 48 pp.

CHINERY, MICHAEL. *Animal Communities.* New York: Walker, 1973. 32 pp.

COHEN, DANIEL. *Animal Territories.* New York: Hastings House, 1975. 90 pp.

———. *Night Animals.* New York: Julian Messner, 1970. 96 pp.

COLLINS, BARBARA. *Exploring and Understanding Insects.* Westchester, Ill.: Benefic Press, 1970. 96 pp.

COPPS, DALE. *The Savage Survivor: 300 Million Years of the Shark.* Chicago: Follett, 1976. 64 pp.

COSGROVE, MARGARET. *Messages and Voices: The Communication of Animals.* New York: Dodd, Mead, 1974. 144 pp.

———. *Wintertime for Animals.* New York: Dodd, Mead, 1975. 30 pp.

DAVIDSON, ROSALIE. *When the Dinosaurs Disappeared.* Chicago: Childrens Press, 1973. 28 pp.

DEAN, ANABEL. *Animals That Fly.* New York: Julian Messner, 1975. 64 pp.

———. *How Animals Communicate.* New York: Julian Messner, 1977. 64 pp.

EARLE, OLIVE. *Scavengers.* New York: William Morrow, 1973. 64 pp.

FENTON, CARROLL, and HERMINIE KITCHEN. *Animals That Help Us.* New York: Thomas Y. Crowell, 1973. 128 pp.

FICHTER, GEORGE. *Insect Pests.* New York: Golden Press, 1966. 160 pp.

FLETCHER, ALAN. *Fishes and Their Young.* Reading, Mass.: Addison-Wesley, 1974. 46 pp.

FORD, BARBARA. *How Birds Learn to Sing.* New York: Julian Messner, 1975. 96 pp.

———. *Katydids: The Singing Insects.* New York: Julian Messner, 1976. 64 pp.

FREEDMAN, RUSSELL. *Animal Fathers.* New York: Holiday House, 1976. 32 pp.

———. *Animal Games.* New York: Holiday House, 1976. 32 pp.

———. *Growing Up Wild: How Animals Survive.* New York: Holiday House, 1975. 64 pp.

GANS, ROMA. *Bird Talk.* New York: Thomas Y. Crowell, 1973. 40 pp.

GRAHAM, ADA, and FRANK GRAHAM. *Let's Discover Birds in Our World.* New York: Western Pub., 1974. 48 pp.

HALMI, ROBERT. *Zoos of the World.* New York: Four Winds Press, 1975. 118 pp.

HARRIS, JOHN, and ALETA PAHL. *Endangered Predators.* New York: Doubleday, 1976. 84 pp.

HEADSTORM, RICHARD. *Your Insect Pet.* New York: Henry Z. Walck, 1973. 160 pp.

HOGNER, DOROTHY. *Good Bugs and Bad Bugs in Your Garden.* New York: Thomas Y. Crowell, 1974. 86 pp.

HUNTINGTON, HARRIET. *Let's Look at Reptiles.* New York: Doubleday, 1973. 108 pp.

HUTCHINS, ROSS. *The Bug Clan.* New York: Dodd, Mead, 1973. 128 pp.

———. *How Animals Survive.* New York: Parents' Magazine, 1974. 64 pp.

———. *Insects and Their Young.* New York: Dodd, Mead, 1975. 126 pp.

JACOBS, FRANCINE. *A Secret Language of Animals.* New York: William Morrow, 1976. 96 pp.

JACOBSON, MORRIS, and ROSEMARY PANG. *Wonders of Sponges.* New York: Dodd, Mead, 1976. 80 pp.

——— and ———. *Wonders of Starfish.* New York: Dodd, Mead, 1977. 80 pp.

JENKINS, MARIE. *The Curious Mollusks.* New York: Holiday House, 1972. 192 pp.

KAUFMANN, JOHN. *Flying Reptiles in the Age of Dinosaurs.* New York: William Morrow, 1976. 40 pp.

———. *Little Dinosaurs and Early Birds.* New York: Thomas Y. Crowell, 1977, 40 pp.

MAJOR, ALAN. *Collecting Fossils.* New York: St. Martin, 1974. 210 pp.

MARTIN, ALICE, and BERTHA PARKER. *Dinosaurs.* New York: Western Pub., 1973. 48 pp.

MCCLUNG, ROBERT. *How Animals Hide.* Washington, D.C.: National Geographic Soc., 1973. 40 pp.

MCGOVERN, ANN. *Sharks.* New York: Four Winds Press, 1976. 46 pp.

MCGOWAN, TOM. *Album of Prehistoric Animals.* Chicago: Rand McNally, 1974. 60 pp.

MORRIS, ROBERT. *Dolphin.* New York: Harper & Row, 1975. 62 pp.

MOSELEY, KATHERINE. *Only Birds Have Feathers.* Irvington-on-the-Hudson, N.Y.: Harvey House, 1973. 48 pp.

OHMART, EDNA, and OTTO OHMART. *Exploring and Understanding Birds.* Westchester, Ill.: Benefic Press, 1970. 96 pp.

OTTO, GEORGE R. *Exploring and Understanding Amphibians and Reptiles.* Westchester, Ill.: Benefic Press, 1968. 96 pp.

PAPE, DONNA. *A Gerbil for a Friend.* Englewood Cliffs, N.J.: Prentice-Hall, 1973. 30 pp.

PARISH, PEGGY. *Dinosaur Time.* New York: Harper & Row, 1974. 30 pp.

PATENT, DOROTHY. *Fish and How They Reproduce.* New York: Holiday House, 1976. 128 pp.

———. *Frogs, Toads, Salamanders, and How They Reproduce.* New York: Holiday House, 1975. 144 pp.

———. *How Insects Communicate.* New York: Holiday House, 1975. 128 pp.

PETTIT, TED. *Wildlife at Night.* New York: G. P. Putnam's Sons, 1976. 96 pp.

PRINCE, J. H. *Languages of the Animal World.* New York: Thomas Nelson, 1975. 160 pp.

PRINGLE, LAURENCE. *Cockroaches: Here, There, and Everywhere.* New York: Thomas Y. Crowell, 1973. 40 pp.

REEVES, MARTHA. *The Total Turtle.* New York: Thomas Y. Crowell, 1975. 128 pp.

RICCIUTI, EDWARD. *The American Alligator—Its Life in the Wild.* New York: Harper & Row, 1972. 72 pp.

———. *Do Toads Give You Warts? Strange Animal Myths Explained.* New York: Walker, 1975. 48 pp.

ROBBINS, CHANDLER S., BERTEL BRUUN, and HERBERT S. ZIM. *Birds of North America.* New York: Golden Press, 1966. 64 pp.

ROBERTS, HORTENSE. *You Can Make an Insect Zoo.* Chicago: Childrens Press, 1974. 64 pp.

ROEVER, J. M. and WILFRIED ROEVER. *The North American Eagles:* Austin, Texas: Steck-Vaugn, 1973. 30 pp.

ROWLAND-ENTWHISTLE, THEODORE. *Animal Worlds.* New York: Franklin Watts, 1976. 48 pp.

RUFFER, DAVID G. *Exploring and Understanding Mammals.* Westchester, Ill.: Benefic Press, 1971. 96 pp.

RUSSELL, SOLVEIG. *The Crusty Ones: A First Look at Crustaceans*. New York: Henry Z. Walck, 1974. 47 pp.

SCHISGALL, OSCAR. *That Remarkable Creature, the Snail*. New York: Julian Messner, 1970. 64 pp.

SELSAM, MILLICENT. *A First Look at Insects*. New York: Walker, 1975. 36 pp.

———. *A First Look at Mammals*. New York: Walker, 1973. 36 pp.

———. *Animals of the Sea*. New York: Four Winds Press, 1976. 40 pp.

———. *Is This a Baby Dinosaur?* New York: Harper & Row, 1971. 32 pp.

——— and JOYCE HUNT. *A First Look at Birds*. New York: Walker, 1973. 36 pp.

——— and ———. *A First Look at Fish*. New York: Walker, 1972. 36 pp.

——— and ———. *The Harlequin Moth: Its Life Story*. New York: William Morrow, 1975. 48 pp.

SHUTTLESWORTH, DOROTHY. *Animals That Frighten People*. New York: E. P. Dutton, 1973. 122 pp.

———. *How Wild Animals Fight*. New York: Doubleday, 1976. 96 pp.

———. *The Wildlife of South America*. New York: Hastings House, 1974. 120 pp.

SILVERSTEIN, ALVIN, and VIRGINA SILVERSTEIN. *Gerbils: All About Them*. Philadelphia: J. B. Lippincott, 1976. 160 pp.

——— and ———. *Hamsters: All About Them*. New York: Lothrop, Lee & Shepard, 1974. 126 pp.

——— and ———. *Rats and Mice: Friends and Foes of Man*. New York: Lothrop, Lee & Shepard, 1968. 96 pp.

SIMON, HILDA. *Frogs and Toads of the World*. Philadelphia: J. B. Lippincott, 1975. 128 pp.

SIMON, SEYMOUR. *Animals in Your Neighborhood*. New York: Walker, 1976. 48 pp.

———. *Birds on Your Street*. New York: Holiday House, 1974. 40 pp.

———. *Discovering What Garter Snakes Can Do*. New York: McGraw-Hill, 1975. 48 pp.

———. *Pets in a Jar: Collecting and Caring for Small Wild Animals*. New York: Viking Press, 1975. 96 pp.

SPRUNT, ALEXANDER, and HERBERT S. ZIM. *Gamebirds*. New York: Golden Press, 1965. 160 pp.

VEVERS, GWYNNE. *Fishes*. New York: McGraw-Hill. 1976. 48 pp.

VICTOR, JOAN. *Shells Are Skeletons*. New York: Thomas Y. Crowell, 1977. 40 pp.

VILLIARD, PAUL. *Birds As Pets*. New York: Doubleday, 1974. 178 pp.

WALKER, BRAZ. *Oddball Fishes and Other Strange Creatures of the Sea*. New York: Sterling, 1975. 192 pp.

WATERS, JOHN. *Camels: Ships of the Desert*. New York: Thomas Y. Crowell, 1974. 34 pp.

———. *Creatures of Darkness*. New York: Walker, 1975. 128 pp.

———. *Green Turtle Mysteries*. New York: Thomas Y. Crowell. 1974. 40 pp.

———. *Hungry Sharks*. New York: Thomas Y. Crowell, 1973. 34 pp.

———. *The Mysterious Eel*. New York: Hasting House, 1973. 64 pp.

WATSON, JANE. *Whales, Friendly Dolphins, and Mighty Giants of the Sea*. New York: Western Pub., 1975. 64 pp.

WATTS, CHRISTOPHER. *Prehistoric Life.* New York: Franklin Watts, 1976. 48 pp.

WEBSTER, DAVID. *Let's Find Out About Mosquitoes.* New York: Franklin Watts, 1974. 48 pp.

WILD, ROBERT, and JOCELYN WILD. *How Animals Work for Us.* New York: Parents' Magazine, 1973. 64 pp.

WISE, WILLIAM. *Monsters of the Deep.* New York: G. P. Putnam's Sons, 1975. 64 pp.

WOOD, LUCILLE. *The Amazing World of American Birds.* New York: G. P. Putnam's Sons, 1975. 128 pp.

ZIM, HERBERT S., and CLARENCE COTTAM. *Insects.* New York: Golden Press, 1966. 160 pp.

—— and IRA N. GABRIELSON. *Birds.* New York: Golden Press, 1966. 160 pp.

—— and DONALD F. HOFFMEISTER. *Mammals.* New York: Golden Press, 1965. 160 pp.

—— and LESTER INGLE. *Seashores.* New York: Golden Press, 1965. 160 pp.

—— and LUCRETIA KRANTZ. *Sea Stars and Their Kin.* New York: William Morrow, 1976. 64 pp.

—— and ——. *Snails.* New York: William Morrow, 1975. 64 pp.

—— and HOBART M. SMITH. *Reptiles and Amphibians: A Guide to Familiar American Species.* New York: Golden Press, 1966. 160 pp.

CHAPTER 15

THE HUMAN BODY

THE MAKEUP OF THE HUMAN BODY

I. THE HUMAN BODY IS MADE OF CELLS

A. The human body is made up of millions of tiny cells.
1. These cells are similar to the cells described in the chapter on "Animals."
2. Basically, they have the same parts and characteristics as animal cells.

B. These cells are not all alike.
1. Many cells have special work to do, and thus differ in size and shape, and they may even contain special materials.
2. This difference makes it possible for the cells to do their special kind of work.
3. Examples of special kinds of cells include blood, epithelial, muscle, nerve, and bone cells.

C. A group of the same kind of cells that carry on the same activity or work is called a tissue.

D. There are five main kinds of tissue in the human body.
1. **Muscle tissue** includes all the muscles in the body.
2. **Nerve tissue** makes up the nerves and the brain.
3. **Epithelial tissue** includes the outer skin and the linings of such parts as the mouth, nose, throat, heart, stomach, liver, and intestines.
4. **Connective tissue** helps hold the body parts together and includes such materials as tendons, ligaments, cartilage, and bone.
5. **Blood,** although a liquid, is also a tissue.

E. A group of different tissues, all working together, is called an **organ.**
1. An organ carries out a special activity or group of activities in the body.
2. Examples of organs include the heart, lungs, liver, stomach, eyes, and brain.

F. A group of organs working together on a special body activity is called a **system.**

G. There are ten large systems in the human body.
1. The **skin system** covers the body, and includes the skin, hair, and nails.
2. The **skeletal system** supports the body, and includes the bones.
3. The **muscular system** makes it possible for the body and its parts to move.
4. The **digestive system** digests the food we eat, and includes such organs as the mouth, stomach, intestines, and liver.
5. The **circulatory system,** or blood system, includes the heart, arteries, veins, and tiny blood vessels called the **capillaries.**
6. The **respiratory system,** or breathing system, includes such organs as the nose, windpipe, and lungs.
7. The **excretory system** gets rid of the waste products formed in the body, and

includes such organs as the kidneys and bladder.

8. The **nervous system** makes it possible for the body to respond to things around the body, and includes such organs as the nerves, brain, and spinal cord.
9. The **reproductive system** includes those organs that affect sex characteristics and produce offspring.
10. The **endocrine system,** or gland system, gives off special chemicals that control and regulate the action of the body.

II. THE REGIONS OF THE BODY

A. The human body is divided into three regions: the **head,** the **trunk,** and the **limbs** (arms and legs).
B. The trunk region is subdivided into two smaller regions: the **chest,** or **thorax,** and the **abdomen.**
C. There are three important cavities in the body.
1. The **head,** or **cranial, cavity,** which contains the brain.
2. The **chest,** or **thoracic, cavity,** which contains such organs as the heart, windpipe, and lungs.
3. The **abdominal cavity,** which contains such organs as the stomach, intestines, liver, pancreas, kidneys, bladder, and reproductive organs.

THE SKIN

I. PARTS OF THE SKIN

A. The skin is a tissue, about 3 millimeters (⅛ in) thick, that covers the body.
B. It has two layers: a thin outer layer, called the **epidermis,** and a thicker inner layer, called the **dermis.**
C. The outer layer (epidermis) is made up of many layers of cells.
1. The outer cells are flat, scaly, and horny.
2. These outer cells are dead and are constantly being rubbed off.
3. As these dead cells are rubbed off, new living cells from the underneath layers push up and take their place.
4. These new cells become flatter and harder as they come closer to the surface of the skin.
5. If a spot on the skin, such as the side of the large toe, is rubbed very much, a large number of living cells may push up very quickly and form an extra thick layer of dead cells, called a **callus,** at that spot.
6. The living cells of the epidermis have colored materials or pigments in them, which give the skin its characteristic color.
D. The thick inner layer (dermis) of the skin lies underneath the thin outer layer (epidermis).
1. It is made up of tough connective tissue.
2. In this connective tissue are blood vessels, nerves, oil glands, sweat glands, and cells that produce hair.
E. Beneath the dermis is a layer of fatty tissue that attaches the skin to the rest of the body.

II. HAIR AND NAILS

A. Hair is a thread of horny material that is produced in the skin.
1. This material is the same as the material found in the dead cells of the outer skin (epidermis).
2. The hair is formed by cells located in the dermis, or inner layer, of the skin.
3. The newly formed hair grows, passing up a tube through both the dermis and epidermis, and then moves out beyond the surface of the skin.

4. Although the root of the hair is alive, the rest of the hair is dead.
5. The hair grows until it reaches a certain length, and then falls out.
6. The length of a hair depends upon whether the hair is body, head, eyebrow, or eyelash hair.
7. When the hair falls out, a new one starts to grow in its place.
8. Oil glands in the skin produce an oil that flows into the tube where the hair is growing and helps keep the hair, as well as the surface of the skin, soft.
9. Inside the hair is a pigment that gives the hair its special color.
10. When persons become older, the hair pigment disappears and the hair becomes white.
11. Hair can be coarse, fine, straight, or curly.

B. Nails are also made of horny material that is produced in the skin.
  1. This material is the same material found in the dead cells of the outer skin (epidermis).
  2. The root of the nail is alive, but the rest of the nail is dead.
  3. Fingernails grow about three times as fast as toenails.

III. FUNCTIONS OF THE SKIN

A. The skin has many important functions.
B. It acts as a protective covering to prevent harmful bacteria from entering the body.
C. It forms a waterproof covering, preventing water and other liquids from leaving the inner tissues.
D. It protects the inner parts of the body from such injuries as scratches, bruises, bumps, and cuts.
  1. When the skin is injured, many of its cells are damaged or killed.
  2. However, the skin is able to repair itself and form new skin.
E. The pigment in the skin helps protect the skin from the sun's rays.

F. The skin has very many nerve endings, which make the skin sensitive to touch, pressure, pain, heat, and cold.
G. The sweat glands in the skin help the body get rid of some of its waste materials.
  1. Each sweat gland has a tiny tube leading from the surface of the skin to the lower part of the dermis, where the tube winds around and around to form a coil.
  2. Tiny blood vessels surround the cells of the sweat glands.
  3. The cells of the sweat glands take salt water, minerals, and other waste products from the blood, and the sweat then flows up the tube and out onto the skin, where the sweat evaporates.
  4. There are more than a million sweat glands in the skin, spread out over the entire body, but they are more numerous in the palm of the hand, the sole of the foot, and under the armpit.
H. The sweat glands help control or regulate body temperature.
  1. When it is warm outside, the sweat glands give off large amounts of sweat, which evaporates on the surface of the skin.
  2. Water needs heat to evaporate, and takes this heat from the surface of the skin, thus cooling the body.
  3. When it is cold outside, the sweat glands give off very little sweat, and only a small amount of evaporation and cooling of the body take place.
I. The blood vessels in the skin also help control or regulate body temperature.
  1. When the body becomes warm, the blood vessels expand and allow more of this heated blood to flow into the skin.
  2. The skin then becomes flushed with blood, making it possible for the heat to be conducted to the surface of the skin and then allowed to radiate off into the air.
  3. When the body is cold, the blood vessels contract and prevent the heat of the body from escaping.

THE SKELETAL SYSTEM

I. THE STRUCTURE OF THE SKELETON

A. There are more than 200 bones in the skeleton of the human body.
B. These bones are classified into four main groups: the **skull**, the **spinal column,** or backbone, the **ribs,** and the **limb** (arm and leg) bones.
C. In the skull there are the bones that form a case that surrounds the brain.
  1. In children the joints between these bones are movable, allowing the bones to grow.
  2. In adults the bones have grown together to form a solid case, and the joints cannot move.
D. The other important bones in the skull are the cheek, nose, and jaw bones.
E. The spinal column, or backbone, is made up of 33 blocklike bones, called **vertebrae,** one piled on top of the other.
  1. These vertebrae make it possible for the head and trunk of the body to turn and bend in different directions.
  2. They also form a strong support for the weight of the body and the head.
  3. The spinal column also protects a large nerve called the **spinal cord.**
F. The skeleton has 12 pairs of ribs, forming a rib cage that protects the heart and lungs.
  1. All 12 pairs are connected in back to the vertebrae of the spinal column.
  2. The upper seven pairs of ribs are connected in front to the breastbone.
G. The arm is made up of a long bone that runs from the shoulder to the elbow, the two bones of the forearm, the wrist bones, the hand bones, and the finger bones.
H. Two pairs of bones join each arm at the shoulder.
  1. The long, narrow collarbones connect the upper end of the breastbone with each shoulder.

2. The large, flat shoulder blades are at the back of each shoulder.
I. The leg is made up of a long bone that runs from the hip to the knee, a kneecap that protects the knee, the two bones that go from the knee to the ankle, the ankle bones, the foot bones, and the toe bones.
J. A number of hip bones together form the **pelvis,** and are connected to the vertebrae at the bottom of the spinal column.
  1. The pelvis provides a firm support for the body.
  2. It also allows the legs to move freely.

II. THE MATERIALS IN THE SKELETON

A. The skeleton is made of two kinds of material: **bone** and **cartilage.**
B. Both bone and cartilage are special kinds of connective tissue.
  1. In bone a large amount of hard mineral matter, especially calcium phosphate, has been deposited between the cells, making the bone quite hard.
  2. Cartilage has a soft and smooth material, which is tough and flexible, between its cells.
C. When a baby first begins to form inside its mother, its skeleton is mostly cartilage.
  1. Soon after, the bone cells begin to replace the cartilage cells.
  2. This change from cartilage to bone continues until the baby grows up and becomes an adult.
D. The adult skeleton still has some cartilage in it.
  1. The ears and the end of the nose are made of cartilage.
  2. There are discs of cartilage between the vertebrae of the spinal column.
  3. The ends of the long bones are covered with cartilage.
  4. The ribs are connected to the breastbone by strips of cartilage.

E. Many bones are hollow and have a soft tissue, called **marrow,** inside them.

F. There are two kinds of marrow: red and yellow marrow.

  1. The red marrow is found in the ends of long bones, in the vertebrae, and in flat bones like the ribs, breastbone, and shoulder bone.

  2. The yellow marrow is found in the center of the long bones.

III. THE SKELETAL JOINTS

A. The place where two bones meet is called a **joint.**

B. Some joints cannot move at all.

  1. This lack of mobility occurs because the bones have grown together to form one solid mass.

  2. Examples of immovable joints include the bones of the skull, breastbone, and hip bone.

C. Some joints, like the joint between the ribs and the backbone, are partially movable.

D. Some joints can move quite freely.

E. One type of movable joint is called the **hinge joint.**

  1. A hinge joint works just like the hinge on a door and allows a bone to move back and forth easily.

  2. The elbows, knees, fingers, and toes are examples of hinge joints.

F. Another type of movable joint is called the **ball-and-socket joint.**

  1. In this kind of joint the end of one bone forms a ball that fits into the hollow or socket of another bone.

  2. A ball-and-socket joint makes it possible for a bone to move in many directions.

  3. The shoulder and hip joints are examples of ball-and-socket joints.

G. Another type of movable joint is called the **pivot joint.**

  1. This joint works like a pivot to allow the bones to move around and back.

  2. The lower arm bones and the head on the spine move around on pivot joints.

H. The bones in movable joints are all held together by strong bands of connective tissue, called **ligaments.**

IV. FUNCTIONS OF THE SKELETON

A. The skeleton holds the body up and gives the body its shape.

B. It provides a place for the muscles to be attached, thus making it possible for the body to walk, breathe, and eat.

C. It protects delicate organs in the body.

  1. The skull protects the brain.

  2. The rib cage protects the heart and lungs.

  3. The spinal column, or backbone, protects the large nerve that is called the **spinal cord.**

THE MUSCULAR SYSTEM

I. KINDS OF MUSCLES

A. There are more than 400 different muscles in the human body.

B. The purpose of these muscles is to cause movement.

  1. The muscles move and make other parts of the body move.

  2. Every movement the body makes is done by muscles.

C. There are two kinds of muscles: **voluntary** and **involuntary** muscles.

D. Voluntary muscles are muscles we can control.

  1. These muscles move whenever we want them to move.

2. The muscles that move the bones of the skeleton are voluntary muscles.
3. Some voluntary muscles, like the arm muscles, are connected to the bones by tough, white cords of connective tissue, called **tendons,** which do not stretch.
4. Some voluntary muscles are connected directly to the bones.
5. Some voluntary muscles, like the lip muscles, are connected to other muscles.
6. The cells of voluntary muscles are long and round, and are bound together by connective tissue into small bundles.
7. These voluntary muscle cells have cross-stripes, and the muscles are called **striated** muscles.

E. Involuntary muscles are muscles that we cannot control.
1. The action of these muscles is controlled by the nervous system.
2. These muscles produce all the movements needed to keep us alive.
3. They move food through the digestive system, blood through the body, and control breathing.
4. The cells of involuntary muscles are spindle-shaped and are found in layers in the walls of the digestive system, blood vessels, and other organs.
5. The cells do not have any cross-stripes, and the involuntary muscles are called **smooth** muscles.

F. The heart muscles are a special kind of muscle found nowhere else in the body.
1. The heart muscle is an involuntary muscle.

2. The muscles have cells that are not only cross-striped (striated), but branched as well.

G. Some muscles are both voluntary and involuntary.
1. They operate automatically without our control, but we can also control them.
2. The muscles that operate the eyelid and the diaphragm (for breathing) are both voluntary and involuntary.

II. How Muscles Work

A. Muscles work in only one way, by tightening or contracting.
1. When muscles contract, they become shorter and thicker, and in this way exert a pull.
2. Muscles can only exert a pull, never a push.

B. The voluntary skeletal muscles that move joints always work in pairs.
1. When one muscle works, the other muscle rests.
2. The muscle that bends the joint is called a **flexor,** and the muscle that straightens the joint is called an **extensor.**
3. The flexor **biceps** muscle on top of your upper arm makes the forearm move up, and the extensor **triceps** muscle underneath your upper arm makes the forearm move down again.
4. When the biceps contracts and works, the triceps rests and relaxes.

C. Voluntary muscles usually work singly, and either contract or rest.

FOOD

I. The Body Needs Food

A. The body needs food to live and grow.
B. In the foods we eat there are materials that give the body energy, materials that repair and build tissues, and materials that

help regulate the activities of the body.
C. These necessary food materials can be divided into six main classes, **carbohydrates, fats, proteins, minerals, vitamins,** and **water.**
D. A person should eat different kinds of

foods to make sure that his body is getting all these necessary food materials.

II. CARBOHYDRATES

A. Carbohydrates are used in the body to supply energy.
B. They are digested in the body to produce heat for warmth and energy for movement.
C. Carbohydrates include sugars and starches.
1. Honey, sugar, candy, ice cream, and pastry are foods that are rich in sugars.
2. Bread, potatoes, rice, cereals, spaghetti, and macaroni are rich in starches.

III. FATS

A. Fats are also used in the body to supply energy.
B. Fats produce twice as much energy as carbohydrates.
C. Butter, shortening, oils, salad dressing, bacon, and nuts are rich in fats.
D. When a person eats more carbohydrates than his body needs, the extra carbohydrates are changed into fat and stored in the body.

IV. PROTEINS

A. Proteins are very important food materials because they repair and build muscles and other tissues.
B. Proteins have nitrogen, which the body needs to repair and grow cells, tissues, and organs.
C. Children especially need proteins for growing.
D. Lean meat, fish, eggs, milk, cheese, whole wheat, beans, peas, and nuts are rich in proteins.

V. MINERALS

A. The body needs small amounts of minerals for body growth, for the repair of body tissues, and for regulating some activities of the body.
B. Calcium and phosphorus are two important minerals the body needs.
1. Together with oxygen they make the hard material found in the bones and teeth.
2. Foods rich in calcium include milk, cheese, eggs, and leafy vegetables.
3. Foods rich in phosphorus include liver, nuts, peas, whole grain cereals, milk, cheese, eggs, and leafy vegetables.
C. Iron is an important mineral in the body.
1. Iron is present in the chemical that makes the blood red.
2. Foods rich in iron include liver, lean meats, eggs, green vegetables, and certain dried fruits such as prunes and raisins.
D. Iodine is important in regulating the activity of the body.
1. Iodine is present in a gland, called the **thyroid gland,** located in the neck.
2. This gland regulates the burning of the food in the body.
3. Iodine is found in seafood and in iodized salt.
E. Other important minerals include sodium, potassium, copper, and sulfur.

VI. VITAMINS

A. Vitamins are chemical compounds found in foods.
1. They control or regulate certain activities in the body, and are important for body growth.
2. Although the body needs only very small amounts of these vitamins, without them the body develops certain diseases, called **deficiency diseases.**
B. When vitamins were first discovered, their chemical names were not known so they were first given letters of the alphabet as names instead.
C. **Vitamin A** keeps the lining of the nose, throat, and eyelids healthy.
1. A lack of vitamin A makes it difficult for persons to see clearly in dim light or at night.

570]

2. A lack of vitamin A cuts down the body's resistance to colds and other infections.

3. A severe lack of vitamin A causes a serious eye disease that may result in blindness.

4. Vitamin A is found in the oils of fish livers and in milk, butter, eggs, tomatoes, and nearly all yellow and green vegetables.

D. **Vitamin B₁** (also called **thiamin**) helps control the digestion and use of carbohydrates in the body.

1. A mild lack of vitamin B₁ causes loss of appetite, poor digestion, headaches, tiredness, and irritability.

2. A severe lack of vitamin B₁ causes a serious nervous disease called **beriberi.**

3. Vitamin B₁ is found in whole grain foods and cereals, meat, milk, eggs, and green, leafy vegetables.

E. **Vitamin B₂** (also called **riboflavin**) is needed to help the cells in the body function properly, to keep the skin healthy, and to help control the digestion and use of carbohydrates in the body.

1. A lack of vitamin B₂ causes stunted growth, a disease of the mouth where the lips and tongue become cracked, and a scaly skin disease.

2. Vitamin B₂ is found in the same foods that have vitamin B₁.

F. **Vitamin P-P** (also called **niacin**) helps the digestive and nervous systems function properly, and is needed for the digestion and use of carbohydrates in the body.

1. A lack of vitamin P-P (niacin) causes a disease called **pellagra,** which produces skin rashes, a smooth tongue, digestive disturbances, mental disturbances, and paralysis.

2. Pellagra has been found in the South, where some farmers have been living mostly on molasses, corn, and salt or fat pork.

3. Vitamin P-P is found in lean meat, liver, milk, eggs, yeast, and green, leafy vegetables.

G. **Vitamin C** (also called **ascorbic acid**) regulates the use of calcium and phosphorus in the body and helps build and maintain healthy teeth and gums.

1. A mild lack of vitamin C produces sore gums, soft teeth, and weak blood vessels.

2. A severe lack of vitamin C causes a disease called **scurvy,** which produces bleeding gums, a swollen tongue, a tendency to bruise easily, bleeding around the bones, and sometimes teeth falling out.

3. Vitamin C is found in citrus fruits, tomatoes, green peppers, and green, leafy vegetables.

H. **Vitamin D** regulates the use of calcium and phosphorus in the body and helps build and maintain strong bones and teeth.

1. A lack of vitamin D produces soft bones and poor teeth.

2. Children who do not get enough vitamin D may develop a disease called **rickets,** where the bones grow out of shape and "bow legs" or "knock knees" are formed.

3. Vitamin D is found in fish liver oils, liver, eggs, and milk with vitamin D added to it.

4. The skin can make vitamin D when it is exposed to the ultraviolet rays of the sun.

I. **Vitamin K** (also called **menadione**) helps the blood clot.

1. It is used in blood injuries and in surgical operations to prevent loss of blood.

2. Vitamin K is found in tomatoes and green, leafy vegetables.

VII. WATER

A. Water is so important to the body that a person will die more quickly from lack of water than from lack of food.

B. All the cells in the body need water to function properly.

C. The body needs water to digest the food, absorb it, carry it to all parts of the body, and to get rid of the waste materials that are formed.

D. The body gets water in three ways.

1. Most of the foods have water in them.

2. Some water is formed when the food is burned in the body.

3. Water is taken into the body as drinking water or as milk and other liquids.

VIII. THE AMOUNT OF ENERGY THE BODY NEEDS

A. The human body uses food to produce energy.

B. The amount of energy a person needs depends upon many things.

1. Larger persons need more energy than smaller persons.

2. Active persons need more energy than quiet persons.

3. Younger persons use more energy than older persons.

4. Males usually use up more energy than females.

5. Some persons have bodies that use up energy more quickly than the bodies of other persons.

C. The amount of energy a food will produce when it is digested in the body is measured in units called **Calories.**

1. Every bit of food that you eat will produce a certain number of Calories.

2. Some foods are richer in Calories than other foods.

D. If a person takes in more food Calories a day than his body can use, the extra food material is stored in the body as fat, and the person gains weight.

E. If a person takes in less food Calories a day than his body needs, the body now uses the stored fat, and the person loses weight.

IX. THE FOUR BASIC FOOD GROUPS

A. A balanced diet is a diet that gives the body all the food materials it needs in the right amounts.

1. About four sixths of the diet should be carbohydrates, one sixth fats, and one sixth proteins.

2. The diet should also contain the proper minerals and vitamins that the body needs.

B. Food experts have divided all the foods we need to keep healthy into four basic food groups.

C. If a person eats the proper amounts of food from each food group every day, he will have a balanced diet.

D. The four basic food groups are the **milk group,** the **meat group,** the **bread-cereal group,** and the **vegetable-fruit group.**

E. The milk group includes milk, butter, cheese, and ice cream.

1. A child should drink at least four glasses of milk a day.

2. A serving of butter, cheese, or ice cream can take the place of one of the glasses of milk.

F. The meat group includes meat, chicken, fish, eggs, beans, peas, and nuts.

1. A child should have at least two servings of meat, chicken, fish, or eggs a day.

2. Beans, peas, or nuts can be substituted occasionally.

G. The bread-cereal group includes wholegrain or enriched bread and cereals, spaghetti, and macaroni, and a child should have four or more servings from this group each day.

H. A child should have four or more servings from the vegetable-fruit group each day, with at least one serving of a citrus fruit and one serving of a dark green or deep yellow vegetable.

I. A balanced diet is helpful in many ways.

1. It helps a person grow normally.

2. It helps keep the body free of excessive and harmful fat.

3. It gives the body the energy it needs.

THE DIGESTIVE SYSTEM

I. DIGESTION

A. For food to be used by the body, it must enter the bloodstream, where it is carried to all the cells in the body.

B. The food we eat is too large and too complicated to be sent directly into the bloodstream for use by the cells.

C. Also, some of the foods we eat do not dissolve in water and could not enter the cells even if the food reached the cells.

D. Therefore, the foods have to be broken down, simplified, and changed into dissolved forms that the cells can use.

E. The changing of foods into a simpler, dissolved form that can enter and be used by the cells is called **digestion.**

F. Digestion is carried on by special organs that make up the digestive system in the body.

G. There are two parts to the digestive system: the **alimentary canal** and the **digestive glands.**

H. The alimentary canal is the food tube or passageway through which the food moves in the body.

1. It includes all the organs that act on the food and digest it.

2. The alimentary canal includes the **mouth, throat** or **pharynx, gullet** or **esophagus, stomach, small intestine, large intestine, rectum,** and **anus.**

I. The digestive glands include the **salivary glands, liver, pancreas,** the **gastric glands** of the stomach, and the **intestinal glands** of the small intestine.

1. These glands give off juices that enter the alimentary canal through small tubes, called **ducts.**

2. These juices contain powerful chemicals, called **enzymes,** that act on the foods and break them up into simpler, dissolved forms.

3. These simpler, dissolved forms can now be digested very easily.

II. DIGESTION IN THE MOUTH

A. The purpose of the mouth is to prepare the food for digestion.

B. The teeth break up the food into smaller pieces.

C. There are different kinds of teeth in the mouth.

1. A child first gets a temporary set of 20 baby teeth, 10 on each jaw.

2. As the jaws grow larger, the child loses these baby teeth and grows a permanent set of 32 teeth, 16 on each jaw.

3. The four flat, sharp-edged front teeth on each jaw are called **incisors** and are used for biting and cutting.

4. The two long, pointed teeth, one on each side of the incisors, are called **canine** teeth and are used for tearing.

5. On each side of the canine teeth are two **premolars** and three **molars** (10 on each jaw), which have large surfaces and are used for grinding and chewing.

D. Most of the tooth is made of a hard, bone-like material, called **dentine.**

1. The part of the tooth above the gum is called the **crown,** and is covered with a very hard white material, called **enamel.**

2. The root of the tooth fits into a socket in the jawbone.

3. The incisor and canine teeth usually have one root, and the premolar and molar teeth have two, three, or even four roots.

4. Blood vessels and nerves run up from the root into the hollow center of the tooth.

E. While the food is being chewed, it is mixed with a liquid called **saliva.**

1. The saliva comes from three pairs of **salivary glands,** located in the sides of the face and under the jaw.

2. The saliva moistens and softens the food, making it easy to swallow.

3. Saliva also contains an enzyme (chemical substance) that digests starch, chang-

ing it into sugars that can dissolve in water.

F. The tongue helps in chewing the food by keeping the food between the teeth, and helps in swallowing by pushing the food to the back of the mouth.

G. The food stays in the mouth for only a short time, is swallowed, and then moves by muscles down the throat and esophagus into the stomach.

III. DIGESTION IN THE STOMACH

A. The stomach is a pear-shaped pouch located on the left side of the body under the lower ribs.

B. It is very elastic and can expand to hold large amounts of food.

C. The stomach's main function is to store the food and prepare it for digestion in the small intestine.

D. The food usually stays in the stomach for 2 to 3 hours.

E. The lining of the stomach has many glands, called **gastric glands.**
   1. These glands give off a juice, called **gastric juice,** that flows through tiny tubes (ducts) into the stomach and mixes with the food.
   2. The gastric juice contains an enzyme that breaks some proteins down into simpler materials.
   3. The gastric juice also contains a strong acid, called **hydrochloric acid,** that dissolves minerals in the food and kills many bacteria that enter the stomach with the food.

F. The stomach has powerful muscles that keep contracting and relaxing, and this action churns the food back and forth.

G. This churning action breaks the food up into very small pieces and mixes these tiny pieces very thoroughly with the gastric juice.

H. The food then passes into the small intestine, a little at a time, through a valve at the intestinal end, which opens and closes regularly.

IV. DIGESTION IN THE SMALL INTESTINE

A. The small intestine is the main organ for digesting food in the body.

B. It is about 7 meters (23 ft) long and 2½ centimeters (1 in) thick.
   1. Because it is so long, it coils back and forth many times inside the body.
   2. The food stays in the small intestine much longer than in the stomach.

C. While the food is in the small intestine, the juices from three digestive glands pour into the small intestine: **intestinal juice, pancreatic juice,** and **bile.**

D. The intestinal juice is produced by glands in the lining of the small intestine.

E. The pancreatic juice is produced by the pancreas, which is a long gland that lies just behind the stomach, and the juice flows through a duct (tube) into the upper end of the small intestine.

F. The bile is a brownish-green liquid that is produced in the liver, which is a very large gland located in the upper right-hand part of the abdomen.
   1. The bile flows into a sac, called the **gall bladder,** where it is stored until needed.
   2. When food leaves the stomach and enters the small intestine, the bile flows into the bile duct, which joins with the pancreatic duct just as they both reach the small intestine.
   3. The bile and the pancreatic juice enter the small intestine at the same time.

G. An enzyme in the bile breaks the fat up into simpler materials and at the same time the bile separates the fat into tiny droplets, which can be more easily attacked by enzymes from the pancreatic juice.

H. Both the pancreatic and intestinal juices have many enzymes that all together digest the carbohydrates, fats, and proteins, changing them into simple dissolved forms that can be used by the cells in the body.

I. After the food has been digested in the small intestine, it is then taken in or absorbed through the walls of the small intestine into the bloodstream.

1. The inside of the small intestine has many ridges and fingerlike projections or bulges, called **villi,** which absorb the simple dissolved forms of digested food.

2. The ridges and villi contain blood vessels that take in the food, and the bloodstream carries the food away to cells in all parts of the body.

3. Each cell takes the kind of food it needs and changes the food into living protoplasm.

V. THE FUNCTION OF THE LARGE INTESTINE

A. The large intestine is about 1½ meters (5 ft) long and 5 centimeters (2 in) thick, and starts below the small intestine.

B. Food that cannot be digested or used by the body passes from the small intestine into the large intestine as waste materials.

C. The waste materials also contain large amounts of bacteria that normally live in the small intestine.

D. The waste materials are quite watery at first.

1. They pass through the large intestine very slowly while the water is absorbed back into the bloodstream.

2. This removal of the water gives the waste material a more solid form, which is called **feces.**

E. The feces passes into the lower part of the large intestine, called the **rectum,** and then out through an opening, called the **anus.**

THE CIRCULATORY SYSTEM

I. THE FUNCTION OF THE CIRCULATORY SYSTEM

A. The circulatory system is made up of the heart, blood, and blood vessels.

B. The heart pumps the blood, which moves through blood vessels, to every part of the body and back again in about 30 seconds.

C. The circulatory system has three main functions.

1. It carries digested food to the cells in the body.

2. It brings oxygen to the cells for burning the food and producing heat and energy.

3. It takes away the waste materials produced by the cells and carries these materials to organs that remove them from the body.

II. THE BLOOD

A. Blood is a liquid tissue.

B. There are about 5¾ liters (6 qt) of blood in the human body.

C. The liquid part of blood is called **plasma.**

1. The plasma is mostly water.

2. It has salts such as table salt (sodium chloride) and calcium salts dissolved in it.

3. It contains a special protein, called **fibrinogen,** which helps the blood clot.

4. It contains special materials, called **antibodies,** which fight disease.

5. It contains special materials, called hormones, which are given off by ductless (tubeless) glands in the body, and which help control the activities of the body.

6. The plasma also brings food particles to the cells and carries away waste materials.

D. There are three kinds of solid materials in blood: **red cells, white cells,** and **platelets.**

E. The red cells are the most numerous cells in the body.

1. They are more commonly called **red corpuscles.**

2. They look like very small discs that have had both sides pushed in.
3. They contain an iron compound, called **hemoglobin**, which gives them their red color.
4. Red cells pick up oxygen from the lungs and carry it to the cells in the body.
5. The cells use the oxygen to burn food, and carbon dioxide is produced as a waste material.
6. The red cells pick up the carbon dioxide and carry it to the lungs, where the carbon dioxide is given off.

F. The white cells are larger than the red cells, but they are less numerous: there is about one white cell to every 600 red cells.
1. White cells are more commonly called **white corpuscles.**
2. They are clear, colorless, and have no special shape.
3. They can leave the walls of the blood vessels and move around among the cells in the body.
4. Their purpose is to destroy bacteria and other disease germs.

G. The platelets are much smaller than the red blood cells.
1. They are irregularly shaped and colorless.
2. They help blood clot when the body is injured and bleeds.
3. Clotting helps prevent the body from losing too much blood and thus bleeding to death.
4. When a blood vessel breaks and bleeds, the platelets stick to the edges of the wound and begin to dissolve.
5. The platelets give off a chemical that unites with the calcium salts and fibrinogen in the plasma to form threadlike fibers.
6. The fibers form a net that slows the flow of blood, traps the corpuscles, and forms a clot that prevents the blood from escaping.

H. The normal temperature of an adult's blood is about 37° Celsius (98.6° Fahrenheit).

1. Some persons have a normal temperature a little above or below this average.
2. When a person is ill, the body temperature usually becomes higher.

I. Harmful bacteria, disease germs, and worn-out blood cells in the blood are filtered and removed by the **liver** and the **spleen.**
1. The liver is quite large, and is located in the upper right-hand part of the abdomen.
2. The spleen is much smaller, and is located in the upper left-hand part of the abdomen in back of the stomach.
3. The spleen also stores blood and a reserve of red blood cells.

III. THE BLOOD VESSELS

A. The blood moves around the body in closed tubes called **blood vessels.**
B. There are three kinds of blood vessels in the body: **arteries, veins, and capillaries.**
C. Arteries are blood vessels that carry blood away from the heart.
1. A large artery leaves the heart and keeps branching into smaller and smaller arteries that spread throughout the body.
2. The smallest branches lead to every part of the body.
D. Veins are blood vessels that carry blood back to the heart.
1. There are tiny veins throughout the body.
2. These tiny veins keep coming together to form larger and larger veins until a large vein that enters the heart is formed.
E. Veins are wider than arteries, and their walls are thinner and less elastic so that the flow of blood in the veins is slower than the flow in the arteries.
F. The larger veins have cuplike valves that keep the blood from flowing backward.
G. Capillaries are very tiny blood vessels between the smallest arteries and veins.
1. Some are so small that the blood cells must go through them in single file.
2. The blood from the smallest arteries flows into the capillaries, travels through

the capillaries, and then flows into the smallest veins.

3. All the cells in the body are next to some capillary.

H. The capillaries are the blood vessels that actually supply the cells of the body with the materials they need.

1. The walls of the capillaries are so thin that molecules of materials in the blood can pass into the cells, and molecules of materials in the cells can pass into the blood.

2. The blood gives the cells food, oxygen, and minerals, whereas the cell gives the blood carbon dioxide and other waste materials.

IV. THE HEART

A. The heart is a strong muscle shaped like a pear and about as big as a fist.

B. It slants downward and is located to the left of the middle of the chest.

C. It acts as a pump by contracting and relaxing.

1. Whenever it contracts, blood is pumped out of it into the arteries.

2. Whenever it relaxes, blood flows into it from the veins.

D. The heart has two sides: a right side and a left side.

1. The two sides are completely separated by a wall called the **septum.**

2. Each side pumps blood separately from the other.

3. The blood in the two sides does not mix while it is in the heart.

E. The heart is also divided into four chambers or compartments.

1. The top two chambers are called **auricles.**

2. The bottom two chambers are called **ventricles.**

3. Thus we have a right auricle and a left auricle at the top, separated from each other by the septum, and a right ventricle and a left ventricle at the bottom, also separated by the septum.

4. The auricles receive blood from the veins in the body and pump it down into the ventricles.

5. The ventricles pump the blood into the arteries in the body.

6. Both auricles contract or pump at the same time, and both ventricles contract or pump at the same time.

F. The heart has valves that prevent the blood from flowing back into the auricles when the ventricles are contracting.

1. There is a flap of connective tissue between the opening of the right auricle and right ventricle, and also between the opening of the left auricle and left ventricle.

2. These flaps act like valves because they can only move one way.

3. When an auricle contracts, the flap is pushed aside, allowing the blood to move down into the ventricle.

4. But, when a ventricle contracts, the flap is pushed upward and closes the opening so that the blood cannot flow up into the auricle.

G. The large arteries also have valves, which are located just where the arteries leave the heart.

1. These valves are made of tissue, and are pushed aside when the blood leaves the heart and goes through the arteries.

2. When the blood tries to flow back into the heart, it pushes the valve shut, and this action stops the blood from flowing back.

H. Veins also have valves located all through the body, which prevent the blood from flowing back, and in this way force the blood to move toward the heart.

I. The sound of the heart beating is made by the closing of the valves between the auricles and ventricles of the heart and by the closing of the valves in the large arteries near the heart.

J. The contracting of the heart also makes the tip of the heart move back and forth so that you can feel the tip beating.

K. A **pulse** is the beat that can be felt in the

arteries every time the heart contracts, or beats.

1. The surge of blood through the arteries makes the artery walls expand and also produce a beat.
2. This pulse can be felt by placing the finger over an artery in the wrist or neck.
3. By counting the number of pulse beats in a minute, we can find out how fast the heart is beating, or contracting.

V. THE CIRCULATION OF THE BLOOD

A. There are really two large circulatory systems in the body.
  1. In one system the blood goes to the lungs and returns.
  2. In the other system the blood flows through the body and returns.
B. In the system that sends blood to the lungs, blood coming from all over the body enters the right auricle of the heart.
  1. The right auricle pumps the blood down to the right ventricle.
  2. The right ventricle then pumps the blood to the lungs.
  3. In this system the blood contains carbon dioxide, and, when the blood is sent to the lungs, it gives up the carbon dioxide and picks up oxygen.
C. In the system that sends blood to the body, blood coming from the lungs enters the left auricle of the heart.
  1. The left auricle pumps the blood down to the left ventricle.
  2. The left ventricle then pumps the blood to the parts of the body.
  3. In this system the blood brings fresh oxygen to the cells in the body, gives up the oxygen to the cells, and at the same time picks up carbon dioxide, which it brings back to the heart.
D. Each ventricle has only one artery leading from it.
  1. The artery leading to the lungs branches at about 1 inch above the heart, each branch going to one of the lungs.
  2. The other large artery passes down through the body and then branches at the legs, each branch going to one of the legs.
E. More than one vein comes back to the auricles.
  1. Four veins bring blood back from the lungs to the left auricle.
  2. Two veins bring blood back from the body, one vein coming from the head and arms, and the other vein coming from the lower part of the body.
F. In each system the large arteries keep branching again and again into smaller arteries and finally lead into capillaries; then the capillaries lead into small veins that keep coming together again and again to form the large veins.

VI. LYMPH

A. As the blood flows through the capillaries, some of the plasma passes through the thin capillary walls and fills the spaces between the cells of the body.
  1. This liquid is called **lymph.**
  2. Lymph is the clear liquid that fills blisters and appears when the skin is scraped and bruised.
B. The lymph contains digested food, water, salts, and other materials.
C. The lymph bathes the cells and gives them food, and the cells give the lymph the waste products that have been formed in the cells.
D. The lymph returns to the bloodstream through special lymph vessels.
  1. The lymph collects in tiny tubes that join again and again to form larger tubes.
  2. These lymph vessels have valves, just as veins do.
  3. Exercise moves the lymph through the lymph vessels.
  4. The lymph finally collects in two large vessels that open into two large veins just above the heart.
E. Occasionally, the lymph vessels enlarge to form swellings called **lymph nodes.**

1. In the lymph nodes the lymph tubes break up into many smaller tubes again.
2. The nodes contain large numbers of special white blood cells that kill bacteria and other disease germs that may have entered the lymph from the cells in the body.
3. The function of the lymph nodes, then, is to filter and purify the lymph before it returns to the blood.
4. There are many lymph nodes concentrated in the neck, armpit, and groin.
5. These lymph nodes may swell and become painful when there is an infection in the part of the body where the nodes are located.

THE RESPIRATORY SYSTEM

I. Parts of the Respiratory System

A. The action in the cells that produces energy is called respiration.
B. In respiration the cells of the body take in oxygen, use the oxygen to burn the digested food and produce heat and energy, and then give off carbon dioxide.
C. The function of the respiratory system is to bring oxygen into the body and to get rid of carbon dioxide.
D. The parts of the respiratory system include the **nose** and **nasal passages**, the **throat** or **pharynx**, the **windpipe** or **trachea**, the **voice box** or **larynx**, the **bronchi**, the **bronchial tubes**, and the **lungs**.
E. Air enters the nose through two **nostrils**, which are separated by a wall called the **septum**.
F. The air then passes through the nasal passages, which are spaces that lie above the mouth.
  1. In the nostrils and the front part of the nasal passages are hairs that trap dust and germs.
  2. In the rear part of the nasal passages are hairlike materials, called **cilia**, which are always moving.
  3. The cilia trap dust and other materials, and carry them toward the mouth, where they are either swallowed or coughed up.
  4. The nasal passages have a soft lining, which gives off a liquid that is called **mucus.**
  5. The mucus also helps trap dust and germs.
  6. As the air passes through the nasal passages, it becomes warm and moist.
G. The air passes from the nasal passages to the throat, or pharynx.
H. In the back of the throat are two tubes.
  1. The gullet, or esophagus, leads to the stomach.
  2. The windpipe, or trachea, which is in front of the esophagus, leads to the lungs.
I. At the top of the windpipe is a flap or lid of tissue called the **epiglottis.**
  1. The epiglottis covers and closes the windpipe when food and water are being swallowed because otherwise the food and water would go down the windpipe and cause choking.
  2. The epiglottis is raised during breathing, and allows air to enter the windpipe freely.
J. At the top of the windpipe is the voice box, or larynx.
  1. The voice box is really like a box, and is made of cartilage.
  2. The "Adam's apple" is a strip of cartilage that sticks out in front of the voice box.
  3. Inside the voice box are two strips of elastic tissue called the **vocal cords.**
  4. Tiny muscles can stretch these vocal cords and make them tight.
  5. When the vocal cords are tight and air

passes between them, the vocal cords move back and forth quickly, or vibrate.

6. This vibration produces sound.
7. The tighter the vocal cords, the faster the cords vibrate and the higher the sound produced.
8. The looser the vocal cords, the slower they vibrate, and the lower the sound produced.
9. Men have larger voice boxes than women and their vocal cords are longer and thicker, so their vocal cords vibrate more slowly and their voices are lower.

K. The bottom of the windpipe divides into two branches, called **bronchi,** and each branch enters one of the lungs.
L. The bronchi divides into smaller branches called **bronchial tubes.**
M. The bronchial tubes keep branching until the smallest tubes end in clusters of little air sacs called **alveoli.**
N. The air sacs look like tiny clusters of grapes, and each lung is one great mass of these clusters of air sacs.

II. How WE BREATHE

A. Breathing is different from respiration because breathing refers only to the process of getting air containing oxygen into the body and getting air containing carbon dioxide out of the body.
B. Many persons think that in breathing the lungs draw in air, expand, and make the chest bulge, but it is not true.
C. Air is breathed in because it is forced into the lungs because of changes in the size of the chest cavity and changes in the air pressure of the chest cavity.
  1. The **diaphragm,** a strong sheet of muscle between the chest and the abdomen, plays an important part in breathing.
  2. When muscles in the diaphragm contract, the diaphragm is pulled downward.
  3. At the same time the rib muscles contract and lift the ribs upward and outward.

4. The combined action of the diaphragm and ribs increases the size of the chest cavity, and the elastic lungs expand and become larger.
5. This increased lung size reduces the pressure of the air already in the lungs.
6. The air outside the body now has a greater pressure than the air inside the lungs, and so it is pushed into the nose, nasal passage, windpipe, and lungs.

D. Air is breathed out when the chest cavity becomes smaller.
  1. The muscles in the diaphragm relax, and the diaphragm moves up again.
  2. The muscles in the ribs relax, and the ribs move downward and inward.
  3. The chest cavity now becomes smaller, making the lungs smaller, so that air is forced out of the lungs and the body.
E. Breathing is one activity of the body that can take place involuntarily or voluntarily.
F. In involuntary breathing, nerves in the brain control the muscles of the diaphragm and the ribs so that breathing takes place automatically.

III. How RESPIRATION TAKES PLACE

A. The air sacs in the lungs are surrounded by millions of capillaries.
B. The oxygen that comes with the air into the lungs passes through the thin walls of the air sacs and through the thin walls of the capillaries into the blood.
C. Red blood cells pick up the oxygen, and the blood becomes bright red.
D. The blood passes from the lungs to the heart, which pumps it through the arteries and capillaries to every part of the body.
E. The cells in the body use the oxygen to burn the digested food, producing heat and energy and giving off carbon dioxide.
F. The red blood cells pick up the carbon dioxide, and the blood becomes dark red.
G. The blood passes through the capillaries and veins back to the heart.
H. The veins of the skin appear blue because skin has a yellow pigment that gives dark red blood a bluish appearance.

I. The heart sends the blood containing the carbon dioxide to the lungs.

J. In the lungs the carbon dioxide leaves the blood and passes out through the thin walls of the capillaries and through the thin walls of the air sacs into the lungs.

K. The air containing carbon dioxide is forced out of the lungs, and fresh air containing oxygen is forced in the lungs.

L. This action of getting oxygen into the body, using oxygen to produce heat and energy, and getting waste carbon dioxide out of the body goes on all the time.

IV. THE CELL ENERGY CYCLE

A. Cells get the energy to do work through a special energy process.

B. All cells—plant, animal, and human—contain high-energy **ATP** (adenosine triphosphate) molecules.

C. The cell breaks the ATP down into **ADP** (adenosine diphosphate) and **P** (phosphate), and energy is given off for the cell to do its work.

D. The ATP is replenished when the cell receives the sugar, glucose, from digested food.

1. The glucose combines with oxygen, giving off energy.

2. This energy changes ADP and P back into ATP again.

E. Thus, there is a continuous cycle, called the **cell energy cycle**, where ATP is broken down into ADP and P to provide energy, then energy obtained from glucose and oxygen changes the ADP and P back to ATP again.

THE EXCRETORY SYSTEM

I. EXCRETION

A. The removal of waste materials from the body is called **excretion.**

B. The human body produces many different kinds of waste materials.

1. Carbon dioxide, produced by the cells, is a waste material.

2. Excess water in the body is a waste material.

3. The used digestive juices left behind after digestion are waste materials.

4. When cells, tissues, and muscles wear out or break down, mineral salts and nitrogen compounds are formed as waste materials.

5. Undigested and unused food is waste material.

II. HOW WASTE MATERIALS ARE REMOVED

A. The body gets rid of waste materials in different ways.

B. The lungs give off carbon dioxide and some water in the form of water vapor.

C. The skin gives off perspiration, which contains water and dissolved mineral salts.

D. The **kidneys** play an important part in the removal of waste materials.

1. The kidneys are two dark red, bean-shaped organs located in the lower part of the back.

2. Each kidney is packed with millions of tiny tubes.

3. These kidney tubes remove from the blood such waste materials as mineral salts and protein compounds.

4. These wastes, together with excess water, form a liquid called **urine.**

5. The urine flows from the kidneys through two tubes, called **ureters,** to a storage organ called the **bladder.**

E. The undigested and unused food, together with used digestive juices, pass through the large intestine and out of the body as **feces.**

[581

THE NERVOUS SYSTEM

I. The Function and Parts of the Nervous System

A. The nervous system has many functions.
1. It controls the action of the muscles and other tissues.
2. It controls the action of the organs.
3. It controls sensations such as smell, taste, touch, pressure, sight, hearing, heat, cold, and pain.
4. It controls thinking, learning, and memory.
B. The central part of the nervous system is made up of the **brain** and **spinal cord.**
1. The brain is located in the skull.
2. The spinal cord lies along almost the whole length of the back.
C. The rest of the nervous system is made up of **nerves,** which spread out from the brain and spinal cord to every part of the body.

II. The Nerves

A. The cells of the nervous system are called **neurons.**
B. These nerve cells are different sizes and shapes, but they all are designed to carry messages, called **nerve impulses,** through the body.
C. Every nerve cell (neuron) has a cell body and many fine threads, called **nerve fibers,** which spread out from the body.
1. One of these nerve fibers, called an **axon,** is very long, and carries messages away from the cell body.
2. All the other nerve fibers, called **dendrites,** are much shorter, and carry messages to the cell body.
3. The axon and dendrites branch many times at their tips, making the tips look like tiny brushes.
D. The bodies of the nerve cells usually lie in the brain and spinal cord, and the nerve fibers run to the head, body, and feet.

E. There are three kinds of neurons (nerve cells): **sensory neurons, motor neurons,** and **associative neurons.**
F. Sensory neurons have to do with feelings or sensations.
1. Their cell bodies usually lie in the brain and spinal cord, and their nerve fibers spread out to sense organs all over the body.
2. The nerve fibers carry messages (nerve impulses) from the sense organs to the cell bodies.
G. Motor neurons have to do with producing motion in the body.
1. Their cell bodies also usually lie in the brain and spinal cord, and their nerve fibers spread out to the muscles, tissues, and organs of the body.
2. The nerve fibers carry messages from the cell bodies to the muscles, tissues, and organs.
H. Associative neurons, sometimes also called **central neurons,** are located between the cell bodies of the sensory and motor neurons.
1. Both the cell bodies and nerve fibers of associative neurons are usually located in the brain and spinal cord.
2. The associative neurons act as "go-betweens" in receiving and sending messages.
I. All three kinds of neurons (nerve cells) are involved in receiving and sending messages (nerve impulses).
1. Nerve fibers in the sense organs all over the body carry messages to the cell bodies of the sensory neurons.
2. The sensory neurons send these messages through nerve fibers to the cell bodies of the associative neurons, which immediately transfer these messages through nerve fibers to the cell bodies of the motor neurons.
3. The cell bodies of the motor neurons then send messages through nerve fibers

to the muscles, tissues, and organs of the body.

J. Bundles of nerve fibers are called **nerves.**
  1. In most nerves the fibers carry messages in one direction only.
  2. Nerves that only carry messages toward the brain and spinal cord are called **sensory nerves.**
  3. Nerves that only carry messages away from the brain and spinal cord are called **motor nerves.**
  4. A few nerves, called **mixed nerves,** can carry messages both toward and away from the brain and spinal cord.

III. THE BRAIN

A. The brain, located inside the skull, is perhaps the most highly specialized organ in the human body.
B. It has a wrinkled appearance because its surface is folded many times.
C. It is the control center of the body, receiving messages from all parts of the body and sending out orders in return.
D. There are three main parts to the brain: the **cerebrum,** the **cerebellum,** and the **medulla.**
E. The cerebrum is the largest part of the brain.
  1. It is made up of two halves that are firmly joined together.
  2. The cerebrum has many functions.
  3. It is the part of the brain that controls thinking, reasoning, learning, memory, and imagination.
  4. It receives messages from the sense organs and recognizes them as smell, taste, touch, pressure, sight, hearing, heat, cold, and pain.
  5. It also controls the voluntary movement of the muscles in the body.
  6. The left side of the cerebrum controls movement of the right side of the body, and the right side of the cerebrum controls movement of the left side of the body.

F. The much smaller cerebellum is located below and behind the cerebrum.
  1. It coordinates the movements of the muscles so that they operate together smoothly, as in walking.
  2. It also helps the body keep its sense of balance.
G. The medulla is located at the bottom of the brain, and joins the top of the spinal cord.
  1. It controls the operation of the involuntary muscles in the body.
  2. This operation means that it also controls such vital functions as heart action, breathing, digestion, coughing, and sneezing.

IV. THE SPINAL CORD

A. The spinal cord is a long rod of nerve tissue going down almost the whole length of the backbone.
B. It connects with the medulla of the brain through a large hole in the base of the skull.
C. Thirty-one pairs of nerves branch off the spinal cord and connect the brain with the rest of the body.
D. If the spinal cord should be cut, all the nerves below the point where the cut was made would not operate, and all the parts of the body controlled by these nerves would be paralyzed.

V. REFLEX ACTION

A. An action of the body that takes place automatically without thinking is called a **reflex action.**
B. The reflex action takes place before the brain has had time to learn about the action.
C. In most reflex actions the messages (nerve impulses) usually travel only to the spinal cord and back.
D. An example of a simple reflex action is the behavior that takes place when a per-

son touches something hot and burns his fingers.

1. The person pulls his fingers away almost immediately, even before he feels the pain.
2. This action occurs because the skin sends a message to sensory nerve cells in the spinal cord.
3. The sensory nerve cells transfer the message to nearby associative nerve cells, which then transfer the message to motor nerve cells.
4. The motor nerve cells now send a message to the muscles in the person's arm, and the muscles contract, pulling the arm and fingers away.

5. Meanwhile the spinal cord also sends a message to the brain, which then recognizes the sensations of both heat and pain.
6. The extra time saved by the reflex action, which takes place before the brain is able to learn what is happening, prevents the finger from becoming badly burned.

E. Other examples of reflex action include jumping when frightened, blinking the eyes when objects suddenly come near them, and laughing when tickled.
F. The medulla of the brain controls such reflex actions as swallowing, coughing, and sneezing.

THE SENSE ORGANS

I. THE SPECIAL SENSES OF MAN

A. The nervous system makes it possible for the human body to have many sensations.
B. Different sensory nerves located in special sense organs send nerve impulses (messages to the brain, which recognizes these impulses as sensations.
C. These sensations include touch, pressure, heat, cold, pain, smell, taste, sight, hearing, and balance.
D. All these sensations come from five sense organs: the **skin, nose, tongue, eyes,** and **ears.**

II. THE SKIN

A. The skin has five different kinds of sensory nerve endings, each responsible for a different kind of sensation.
B. These sensations are touch, pressure, heat, cold, and pain.
C. Each kind of nerve ending can produce only one special sensation.
D. The sensory nerves are not spread out evenly over the skin.

1. As a result, the skin is more sensitive in some parts than in others.
2. The fingertips and the forehead have a great many nerve endings that are sensitive to touch.

E. The nerve endings sensitive to touch are very near the surface of the skin, but the nerve endings sensitive to pressure are located deeper inside the skin.

III. THE NOSE

A. The sense of smell is located in the nose.
B. Nerve endings in the nose are sensitive to chemicals in the air that are breathed in.
C. These chemicals then dissolve in the liquid (mucus) that covers the lining of the nasal passages.
D. When the nose smells the same odor for a long time, the nerve endings become deadened to that particular odor, and then there is no more sensation of smell for that odor.
E. Man's sense of smell is poor compared to many animals, such as the deer and the dog.

IV. THE TONGUE

A. The sensation of taste is located in clusters of cells, called **taste buds,** that are spread unevenly over the tongue.
   1. Inside these cells are nerve endings that are sensitive to taste.
   2. The taste comes from chemicals in the food, which must first be dissolved in the saliva before the taste can be sensed.
B. The taste buds can recognize only four flavors: sweet, sour, salty, and bitter.
   1. The taste buds at the tip of the tongue are sensitive to sweet and salty flavors.
   2. The taste buds along the sides of the tongue are sensitive to sour flavors.
   3. The taste buds at the back of the tongue are sensitive to bitter flavors.
   4. Many foods have more than one flavor in them.
C. Much of what we think is taste is really smell.
   1. While the food is being chewed, odors are given off that enter the nasal passages and reach the nerve endings sensitive to smell.
   2. The combination of both taste and smell gives the food its complete flavor.

V. THE EYE

A. The sense of sight is located in the eye.
B. The bones of the skull protect the eyes on all sides except the front.
C. The **eyelids** have two main functions.
   1. They close, or blink, to protect the front of the eye.
   2. They help spread a watery liquid across the surface of the eye that keeps the eye surface moist, protects the eyes against germs, and washes out dirt.
   3. When drops of this watery liquid come out of the eye, they are called **tears.**
D. The complete eye is shaped like a ball, and is called the **eyeball.**
E. Most of the eyeball has a tight, white cover around it, and the part that we can see is called the **white of the eye.**

F. A small part of this cover, called the **cornea,** is transparent so that light can pass through it.
G. The cornea covers a dark opening in the eye, called the **pupil.**
   1. The pupil allows light to go into the eyeball.
   2. The pupil appears to be black because the inside of the eyeball is dark.
H. The colored circle around the pupil is called the **iris.**
   1. The iris protects the eye by controlling the amount of light that enters the eyeball.
   2. Muscles in the iris change the size of the pupil, depending upon how strong the light is that strikes the eye.
   3. When the light is bright, the iris becomes bigger, which makes the pupil smaller and cuts down the amount of light entering the eyeball.
   4. When the light is dim, the iris becomes narrower which makes the pupil larger and allows more light to enter the eyeball.
I. Inside the eyeball is a convex **lens,** which is thick in the middle and thin at the ends, and two liquids.
   1. The watery liquid in front of the lens is called the **aqueous humor.**
   2. The jellylike liquid behind the lens is called the **vitreous humor.**
   3. The lens, with the help of the two liquids, bends the rays of light as they enter the eyeball and makes the rays of light come together.
J. At the back of the eyeball is a sensitive lining, called the **retina.**
   1. The rays of light entering the eyeball are bent by the lens and come together, or focus, at the retina.
   2. The retina has tiny, sensitive nerve endings, leading to the **optic nerve.**
   3. When light strikes the retina, the tiny nerves send impulses (messages) through the optic nerve to the brain, where we experience the sensation of sight.

[585

K. There are two kinds of nerve cells in the retina: the **cones** and the **rods.**
1. The cones help us see objects that are in bright light, and help us recognize different colors.
2. The rods help us see objects that are in dim light.
3. Many animals see better than man at night because there are more rods in their retinas.
L. Muscles attached to the lens can make the lens thinner or thicker.
1. These muscles allow the rays of light reflected from objects to come together, or focus, at the retina.
2. When an object is far away, the lens becomes thinner because the rays of light from the distant object do not have to be bent very much to focus at the retina.
3. When an object is near, the lens becomes thicker because the rays of light from the close-by object must be bent very much to focus on the retina.
M. Because the lens of the eye is a convex lens, the image formed on the retina is upside down.
1. Yet, in some way that scientists do not know, the brain turns this message right side up.
2. Also, because we have two eyes, we get two images, which the brain is able to put together to get only one image.
N. The eye is able to see an object for a little while after the light from the object has stopped entering the eye.
1. This effect is called **persistence of vision.**
2. Motion pictures use persistence of vision to give still pictures the effect of motion.
3. A series of still pictures, each a little different from the other, is shown on a screen so quickly that we continue to see one picture while the next is being shown.
4. This persistence of vision makes the pictures blend together in the eye and gives the impression of movement.

VI. DEFECTS OF THE EYE

A. Many persons suffer from defects of the eye, and cannot see properly.
1. Four common defects of the eye are: **nearsightedness, farsightedness, astigmatism,** and **color blindness.**
2. All these defects except color blindness can be corrected with the help of eye glasses.
B. In nearsightedness, nearby objects can be seen clearly, but distant objects seem blurred and fuzzy.
1. Nearsightedness occurs if the eyeball is too long, or if the eye muscles make the lens too thick, so that the rays of light come together, or focus, in front of the retina.
2. Nearsightedness is corrected by glasses with concave lenses, which spread the rays of light before they enter the eye; in this way the rays come together farther back and form sharp, clear images on the retina.
C. In farsightedness, distant objects can be seen closely, but nearby objects seem blurred and fuzzy.
1. Farsightedness occurs if the eyeball is too short, or if the eye muscles do not make the lens thick enough, so that the rays of light still have not come together when they reach the retina.
2. Farsightedness is corrected by glasses with convex lenses, which bend the rays of light inward before they enter the eye, and in this way let the rays come together sooner and form sharp, clear images on the retina.
D. In astigmatism, lines running in one direction may seem clear, but lines running in another direction may seem blurred.
1. Astigmatism occurs if the cornea or the lens is not curved properly; this defect makes the lines curve either too much or too little in one direction.
2. Astigmatism is corrected by glasses with specially ground lenses, which have

exactly the opposite curve to the defect in the cornea or lens.

E. In color blindness, the eye is unable to recognize colors, especially red and green, so that they seem different.

1. Color blindness occurs if the retina does not have enough cones, or if the cones are defective.

2. Scientists do not know of any way to correct color blindness.

VII. THE EAR

A. The sense of hearing is located in the ear.

B. There are three parts to the ear: the **outer ear,** the **middle ear,** and the **inner ear.**

C. The outer ear collects the sound waves and sends them through a tube to the middle ear.

1. A thin piece of tissue (membrane), commonly called the **eardrum,** is stretched across the end of the tube.

2. When sound waves strike the eardrum, they make it move back and forth rapidly, or vibrate.

3. The higher the sounds, the faster the eardrum will vibrate.

4. The louder the sounds, the more strongly the eardrum will vibrate.

D. The middle ear passes the vibrations of the eardrum to the inner ear.

1. The middle ear has three small bones that are joined together, and are called the **hammer, anvil,** and **stirrup.**

2. The first bone, the hammer, is connected to the eardrum.

3. The third bone, the stirrup, is connected to the inner ear by another membrane, called the **oval window.**

4. When the three bones vibrate, they make the oval window vibrate.

E. The hearing part of the inner ear is a spiral passage, called the **cochlea,** shaped like a snail's shell and filled with a liquid.

1. Inside the liquid, attached to the spiral passage, are thousands of tiny nerve endings.

2. When the oval window of the inner ear vibrates, the liquid inside the spiral passage begins to vibrate.

3. The tiny nerve endings receive the vibrations of the liquid and send nerve impulses (messages) to the **auditory nerve.**

4. The auditory nerve carries these nerve impulses to the brain, where we get the sensation of sound.

F. The ear also helps control our sense of balance.

1. The inner ear also contains three tubes that curve around in half circles, and are called the **semicircular canals.**

2. The semicircular canals are laid out in the three different directions that the head can move: up and down, sideways, and turning.

3. The canals are filled with a watery liquid that moves every time the head moves.

4. Nerve endings line the walls of the canals, and, when the head moves, the liquid in one of the canals rushes to one end and presses on the nerve endings.

5. This pressure on the nerve endings causes nerve impulses (messages) to travel through a branch of the auditory nerve to the cerebellum of the brain.

6. The cerebellum then sends a message to the muscles which help us keep our balance.

7. Any whirling movement, or a steady up and down movement like that produced in a boat, makes the liquid in the canals move continuously from one side to the other, and causes dizziness and sometimes a feeling of nausea.

THE ENDOCRINE SYSTEM

I. THE DUCTLESS GLANDS

A. **Glands** are organs whose cells give off juices that have special uses in the body.

B. There are two kinds of glands: those with ducts (tubes) and those without.

C. Glands with ducts are called **duct glands,** and give off juices that travel through the ducts to the body parts they affect.
1. Examples of duct glands are the salivary glands in the mouth, and the sweat and oil glands in the skin.
2. The digestive juices that help digest food in the body are given off by duct glands in the stomach, the intestine, the pancreas, and the liver.

D. Glands without ducts are called **ductless glands,** and also **endocrine glands.**
1. These glands give off juices containing chemicals called **hormones.**
2. The hormones pass directly through the walls of the capillaries (tiny blood vessels) into the blood and travel to different parts of the body.
3. Their function is to regulate the body activities.
4. Some hormones affect every part of the body, but others affect only certain parts.

E. The six most common ductless or endocrine glands in the body are the **pituitary gland,** the **thyroid gland,** the **parathyroid glands,** the **Islands of Langerhans** in the **pancreas,** the **adrenal glands,** and the **reproductive glands.**

II. THE PITUITARY GLAND

A. The pituitary gland is a very tiny gland, about the size of a cherry, attached to the bottom of the brain.

B. It gives off at least 10 different hormones.
1. Some of these hormones affect or regulate the activity of almost all the other ductless glands.
2. Other hormones affect the activity of the kidneys and blood vessels.

C. One hormone, commonly called the **growth hormone,** regulates the growth of the skeleton and the body.
1. If the pituitary gland is overactive during childhood, the child will grow up to be a giant.
2. If the pituitary gland is overactive in an adult, the adult's jaws, nose, hands, and fingers will become very large.
3. If the pituitary gland is underactive during childhood, the child will become a **midget.**

D. Because the pituitary gland controls the activity of almost all the other ductless glands, it is often called the "master gland."

III. THE THYROID GLAND

A. The thyroid looks like a big butterfly with its wings spread out, and is located below the voice box on the windpipe.

B. It gives off a hormone, called **thyroxin,** which controls the speed or rate at which the body burns and uses food.
1. The thyroxin has iodine in it.
2. A lack of iodine in the diet will make the thyroid gland swell and the throat bulge out to form a **goiter.**
3. In those parts of the country where there is little iodine in the soil and in the food, specially prepared iodized salt is used.

C. If the thyroid gland is overactive, making the cells in the body speed up their activities, a person will become restless, nervous, and easily excited.
1. His heart will beat faster and his hands may shake.
2. Although he eats a lot, he will not get fat, and may even lose weight.
3. Doctors correct this overactivity by cutting out some of the thyroid gland.

D. If the thyroid gland is not active enough, a person will not have any energy.
1. The cells in the body slow down their activities.

2. The person may not eat much, but he will still gain weight.
3. Doctors correct this underactivity by giving the person thyroxin pills.

E. If a baby's thyroid gland is underactive, and the situation is not corrected in time, the child becomes a feebleminded dwarf.

IV. The Parathyroid Glands

A. The parathyroid glands are four small glands on the back of the thyroid gland.
B. They give off a hormone, called **para-thormone,** which controls the use of calcium in the body.
C. Too much parathormone takes calcium from the bones, making the bones soft.
D. Too little of this hormone in the body causes painful muscle cramps.

V. The Islands of Langerhans

A. The pancreas is both a duct gland and a ductless gland, and is located just behind the stomach.
B. As a duct gland it gives off pancreatic juice, which helps in the digestion of food in the small intestine.
C. Scattered throughout the pancreas are small groups of cells called the Islands of Langerhans, which are ductless glands and give off a hormone called **insulin.**
D. Insulin regulates the use and storage of sugar in the body.
   1. When the body digests food, the carbohydrates are broken down into simple sugars, especially one called **glucose.**
   2. The cells in the body use oxygen to burn some of this glucose, producing heat and energy.
   3. Whatever glucose the body does not use at the moment is stored in the liver until needed by the cells.
E. When the pancreas does not produce enough insulin, a person develops a sickness called **diabetes.**
   1. The liver cannot now store the sugar, and the cells cannot use it efficiently.
   2. The muscles and tissues cannot get the sugar they need, and the blood becomes flooded with sugar.
   3. The person loses weight, urinates very often, and is very thirsty.
   4. Some of the excess sugar in the blood passes out through the urine.
   5. Persons with diabetes are given insulin regularly by injection or by pill, and are also put on a controlled diet.

VI. The Adrenal Glands

A. The adrenal glands are two small glands located on top of the kidneys.
B. The outer layer of the adrenal glands gives off many hormones, which control the digestion of food and regulate the balance of salt and water in the body.
C. The inner layer gives off a hormone called **adrenalin.**
   1. When a person becomes angry or frightened, the adrenal glands pour adrenalin freely and quickly into the blood.
   2. The adrenalin makes the heart beat faster, blood pressure rise, digestion slow down, breathing becomes faster and deeper, and causes the liver to send more of its stored sugar to the blood.
   3. Adrenalin also makes blood clot more easily and quickly.
   4. When doctors are afraid the heart may stop beating, they give the patient adrenalin.
   5. Sometimes adrenalin is used in asthma attacks because it makes the small air tubes in the lungs open wider, and in this way breathing is helped.

VII. The Reproductive Glands

A. The male reproductive glands are called the **testes.**
   1. There are two testes, located below the pelvis and outside the body, in a pouch called the **scrotum.**
   2. The testes produce the male sex cells, which are called **sperm.**
   3. They also give off a hormone which pro-

duces the male sex characteristics that appear during puberty.

4. This hormone gives males their deep voices, broad shoulders and chests, narrow hips, beards, and body hair.

C. The female reproductive glands are called the **ovaries.**

1. There are two ovaries, located inside the lower abdomen, one on each side of the sex organ called the **uterus.**

2. The ovaries produce the female sex cells, which are called **eggs.**

3. They also give off hormones which produce the female sex characteristics that appear during puberty.

4. These hormones give females their high voices, rounded bodies due to more fat distributed under the skin, broad hips, sparse body hair, developed breasts, and menstruation.

LEARNING ACTIVITIES FOR "THE HUMAN BODY"

THE MAKEUP OF THE HUMAN BODY

1. *Examine body cells* · Repeat Learning Activity 1 of "Composition and Classification of Animals," Chapter 14 (p. 546) examining cells obtained from inside of your cheek.

2. *Compare different cells and tissues* · Repeat Learning Activity 2 of "Composition and Classification of Animals," Chapter 14 (p. 546), examining and comparing small amounts of steak, bones, nerves, blood, and other tissue under the microscope.

3. *Identify body organs* · Obtain a chart or model of the human body, and locate such key organs as the heart, liver, stomach, intestines, kidneys, lungs, eyes, ears, and brain. Discuss the basic functions of each organ, and point out that each organ is made up of a group of tissues working together.

4. *Identify the body systems* · By using a chart or model of the human body, identify the 10 large body systems and discuss the basic function of each. List the organs that make up each system.

THE SKIN

1. *Examine a cross section* · Obtain a chart or draw a diagram showing a cross-section of the skin. Distinguish between the dermis and epidermis. Note the presence of nerves and blood vessels, and locate the oil and sweat glands. Discuss the function of each constituent of the skin.

2. *Compare fingerprints* · Have the children make and compare fingerprints. Obtain an ink stamp pad. Let each child pick up ink on his right forefinger by pressing the right side of his finger tip against the pad and rolling the finger from right to left. Then have the child roll the inked finger tip from right to left on a small piece of white paper with the child's name on it. Let the children compare fingerprints, using a magnifying glass, and note that no two prints are the same.

3. *Examine human hair* · Study differently colored human hairs under the microscope. See if you can find three layers of cells. The middle layer is the one that contains the color. Note any difference in appearance and quality of the hairs.

4. *Measure the rate of growth of nails* · Place a tiny drop of dilute nitric acid close to the base of one fingernail and one toenail. The nitric acid will produce a permanent yellow stain on the nail. Measure the distance between the edge of each nail and the nitric acid spot. Repeat the measurement each week until the yellow spot is cut off. Determine and compare the rate of growth of each nail.

5. *Discover how skin helps regulate body temperature* · Wet your finger and blow on it. The finger feels cool as the moisture evaporates, heat energy being taken away from the finger to produce the evaporation. Point out that the evaporation of perspiration produces the same cooling effect.

Have the children recall how flushed their faces become when they are hot. Point out that this flushing occurs because the blood vessels expand and allow more of the heated blood to flow into the skin. Now have the children recall the "goose bumps" that formed on their arms when they became cold. These bumps occur because the blood vessels contract and the pores close tightly to prevent body heat from escaping. As a result, tiny bumps are formed all over the surface of the skin.

6. *Observe the action of oil glands* · Rub one finger along the side of the nose. Then rub this finger against the other fingers. You will feel the oil that the first finger picked up from the skin. Rub a cleansing tissue along the side of the nose and see the stain produced by the oil.

THE SKELETAL SYSTEM

1. *Observe the skeleton* · Obtain a model of the human skeleton. Examine the skull, spinal column, breastbone, ribs, pelvis, collarbones, arms, and legs. Observe how the bones of the skull have become firmly united, forming an immovable joint. Note the ball-and-socket joints in the shoulder and hip, and the hinge joints in the elbow and knee. There are also movable joints in the spinal column, the

fingers, and the toes. Point out that the bones of the joints are bound together by ligaments.

2. *Examine an animal bone* · If possible, obtain the leg bone of a lamb, calf, or pig from the meat market. Ask for a bone that has the end of a joint still on it, and have the bone split lengthwise in half. Examine the joint and distinguish between the cartilage and the bone. Identify the ligaments holding the joint together. Look for bits of tendon tissue that served to hold the muscles to the bone. Locate the yellow, fatty marrow in the center of the long part of the bone.

3. *Determine the composition of bone* · Put a chicken bone in a metal pie tin and heat over a Bunsen burner or in the oven until the bone is covered with a grayish-white ash. Let the bone cool, and then note how light and brittle the bone now is. Point out that the heat burned away all the animal matter in the bone, leaving the mineral matter behind. If you have an accurate balance, weigh the bone before and after heating, and determine the percentages of animal and mineral matter in the bone.

Soak the leg or thigh bone from a chicken in a jar of strong vinegar for 4 or 5 days. Remove the bone and wash it in water. Now bend the bone. The vinegar has dissolved and removed the mineral matter from the bone, leaving the soft, flexible animal matter behind. Although the bone still has its original shape and appearance, it will now be soft and flexible enough so that you can very easily tie it into a knot.

4. *Examine a ligament* · Obtain the joint from a calf, lamb, or pig shoulder from the meat market. Move the joint and examine the ligament that holds the ends of the bones together.

5. *Examine X-rays of broken bones* · Obtain X-rays of broken bones and point out the different kinds of breaks. Point out the need for a cast or splints in helping a broken bone to mend. Discuss what might happen if an un-

qualified person moves somebody who may have broken some bones in an accident.

THE MUSCULAR SYSTEM

1. *Investigate body muscles* · Obtain a chart of the muscular system and examine the arrangement of the muscles. Identify the large muscles that move the head, shoulders, torso, arms, and legs. Note that most of the muscles are connected to the bones either directly or by tendons.

2. *Examine a frog's muscles* · Obtain a freshly killed or preserved frog and carefully remove the skin. Examine the bands of muscles that make up the frog's muscular system. Observe the powerful hind leg muscles closely and see how they operate.

3. *Locate body tendons* · Move the fingers of both hands up and down rapidly, just as if you were playing the piano. Notice the movement of the tendons on the back of your hand. The tendons are being moved by muscles in your forearm. Continue the movement for a full minute or two, and you will feel the forearm muscles becoming tired.

Place the fingers of your left hand on the inside of the elbow of your right hand, just above the joint, and flex your right forearm a few times. You will feel the tendons moving. Grasp the back of one ankle and move your foot up and down. The large tendon that you feel moving is the Achilles tendon.

4. *Observe the tendons of a chicken's foot* · Obtain a chicken's foot from the meat market. Cut away some of the skin and flesh to expose the strong, white tendons. Pull the tendons one at a time. Some tendons will make the toes bend whereas others will straighten the toes. Because the tendons are attached to muscles, note that the muscles only pull, and never push, regardless of how the toes move.

5. *Observe how voluntary muscles work* ·

Double your arm and feel your "muscle." This "muscle" is the biceps muscle. Now grasp the outside of your upper arm near the elbow and straighten your arm. You will feel the pull of your triceps muscle. Note that muscles work in pairs. When you bend your arm, the biceps muscle contracts while the triceps muscle relaxes. When you straighten your arm, the biceps muscle relaxes and the triceps muscle contracts. Point out that when a muscle contracts, it becomes shorter and thicker, producing a pull on the bones.

Grip the back of your thigh and bend your leg at the knee, bringing your heel up toward the thigh. Note how the thigh muscle thickens as it contracts and pulls on the bone.

6. *See the action of involuntary muscles* · Look in a mirror. Watch your eyelid close automatically. This demonstration shows that involuntary muscles are working. Now use voluntary muscles to close the eyelid yourself. This condition is also true of the movement of your diaphragm. Note how involuntary muscles make the diaphragm move automatically as you breathe. Now use voluntary muscles to raise and lower the diaphragm muscles yourself.

7. *Observe action of the lip muscles* · Purse your lips tightly, just as if you were whistling, and feel the ring of muscles around the lips. Point out that these lip muscles are unusual in that they are attached to other muscles rather than to tendons or bones.

FOOD

1. *Test foods for the presence of simple sugars* · Obtain some Benedict's solution from the drugstore. Pour 1 teaspoon of corn syrup into a Pyrex test tube. Add a few drops of the Benedict's solution and heat the test tube gently over the flame of a Bunsen burner or an alcohol lamp, making sure to point the mouth of the test tube away from yourself and the children. The color of the blue solution will change first to a yellow-green and then to a

brick red color, showing the presence of simple sugars.

Repeat the test, using different fruit juices. Try using small amounts of solid foods, including soda crackers or saltines, raisins, and a bit of onion. The children will be surprised to learn that the onion is rich in simple sugars.

2. *Test foods for the presence of starch* · Place a small amount of corn starch in a test tube half-filled with water. Add one or two drops of tincture of iodine to the solution and stir. A blue-black color will form, showing the presence of starch. Place a drop or two of the iodine on a slice of raw potato and a slice of bread. The blue-black color will again show the presence of starch. Repeat the test, using a variety of both starchy and nonstarchy foods, such as soda crackers or saltines, boiled macaroni or spaghetti, boiled rice, a lump of table sugar, cooked egg white, cheese, bacon, and meat.

3. *Test foods for the presence of fats* · Rub a bit of butter on a piece of brown paper bag, and warm the paper gently over a hot plate. Put two or three drops of water on a second piece of brown paper. Now hold both pieces of paper up to sunlight or a bright light. Both spots will be translucent and allow light to pass through. However, the water spot will become dry and stop being translucent, but the "grease" spot will continue to be translucent.

Try this test for the presence of fats with such foods as bacon, nuts, the white and the yolk of a boiled egg, olive oil, mayonnaise, beef, bread, and leafy vegetables. Note which foods produce a permanent grease spot on the brown paper.

4. *Test foods for the presence of proteins* · Place a small piece of the white of a boiled egg in a test tube. Add enough nitric acid to cover the piece of egg white. Heat the test tube gently over the flame of a Bunsen burner or alcohol lamp, shaking the test tube to keep the egg white moving, *and at the same time*

keeping the mouth of the test tube pointed away from yourself and the children. Remove the test tube as soon as the nitric acid begins to boil. Pour off the nitric acid into the sink and let the cold water run for a little while to wash down all the acid. Note that the egg white has turned yellow. Now pour a little ammonia into the test tube. An orange color will form on the egg white, showing the presence of proteins. Repeat the test, using a variety of foods, such as bread, cheese, boiled spaghetti or macaroni, lean meat, and lima beans.

5. *Test foods for the presence of minerals* · Place a small piece of bread on an old spoon and, holding the spoon with an asbestos mitt, heat the spoon strongly over a Bunsen burner flame. The bread will burn, turn black, and finally become a small amount of grey-white ash. This ash shows the presence of minerals. Repeat the test, using a variety of foods.

6. *Test foods for the presence of water* · Place a few small pieces of bread in a dry test tube and heat the tube gently over the flame of a Bunsen burner or alcohol lamp. Tiny droplets of water will appear on the upper part of the test tube. The water was driven out of the heated bread in the form of steam, and then it condensed on the cool upper part of the test tube. Repeat the test, using a variety of foods.

7. *Investigate the vitamin content of foods* · Have the children make a chart listing foods that are good sources of vitamins. Let them check the foods in their daily diets to see if they appear on the chart. Have the children read and report on the diseases caused by vitamin deficiencies.

8. *Discover that foods release heat energy when digested* · Put a straightened paper clip through a peanut, brazil nut, or cashew. Apply a lighted match to the nut. The nut will burn, giving off heat energy. Pour some melted butter or cooking oil into a small saucer and place a piece of soft string in the butter or oil,

with one end of the string protruding above the liquid and hanging over the side of the saucer. After the string has become saturated with the butter or oil, apply a lighted match to the end of the string. The string will act as a wick, and the butter or oil will burn for some time. Point out that when foods are digested in the body, they give off heat energy.

9. *Investigate the calorie value of food* · Have children keep a record of what they have eaten each day for a week, being quite specific about the size of the portions and the number of helpings. Remind the children to include whatever they ate between meals. Have them consult a chart of the Calorie values for common foods, find out how many Calories they took in each day, and then take an average for the week. Let them compare their average daily Calorie intake with the value suggested in the Calorie chart. (Most large life insurance companies have booklets available including Calorie charts and other pertinent information.)

10. *Check diets for the four basic food groups* · Have the children keep a record of what they have eaten each day for a week, as described in Learning Activity 9 above. Then have the children check each day's diet to see if all four basic food groups were represented and if the recommended number of servings for each group has been consumed.

THE DIGESTIVE SYSTEM

1. *Identify the parts of the digestive system* · Obtain a chart or model of the body cavity with the digestive organs in place. Note how the gullet, stomach, small intestine, and large intestine form one long, continuous tube. Locate and identify the liver, pancreas, and gall bladder.

2. *Examine teeth* · Draw a diagram of the number of teeth that should be in the mouth, using a U-shape to represent the jaw (Figure

15–1). Have the children examine their teeth with a regular or magnifying mirror and note which of these permanent teeth they already have. They can also note which teeth are perfect, have fillings, have been extracted, or have not yet appeared.

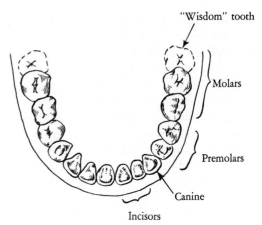

FIGURE 15–1.
DIAGRAM OF THE TEETH IN A JAW

Draw a diagram showing the parts and structure of a tooth, and discuss the proper method for brushing teeth.

3. *Discover that saliva changes starch to sugar* · The children have discovered in Learning Activities 1 and 2 of "Food" (p. 592) that starch, but little or no sugar, is present in most soda crackers. Have the children chew a soda cracker or saltine and note how the cracker tastes sweeter after it has been chewed for some time and the saliva has had a chance to act on the starch in the cracker. Place some of this chewed cracker-saliva mixture in a test tube and test with Benedict's solution for the presence of simple sugars, as described in Learning Activity 1 of "Food." As a control, test some saliva alone for the presence of simple sugars.

4. *Trace the digestion of food* · Obtain or draw a chart of all the organs of the digestive system. Have the children trace the digestion

of a ham sandwich (which contains carbohydrates, fats, and proteins) from the time it enters the mouth until the waste products leave the body. Describe the function of each organ in acting upon and digesting the contents of the sandwich.

THE CIRCULATORY SYSTEM

1. *Examine blood* · Wash your hands thoroughly and then rub a piece of cotton dipped in alcohol over one fingertip. Prick the fingertip with a sterilized needle and squeeze out a drop of blood. Press the blood against a clean microscope slide and cover with a cover glass. Observe the blood under the high power of a microscope. You will see many disc-shaped red blood cells and perhaps one or two of the larger white cells. Note that the red blood cells have no nucleus. Discuss the functions of the red cells, white cells, and platelets in the blood.

2. *Investigate blood clotting* · Discuss the role of the platelets in clotting. Have the children read about and report on hemophilia, including its inherited occurrence in the royal families of Russia and Spain.

3. *Investigate blood types* · Have children read about and report on the grouping of blood into four common types, and the grouping of blood according to whether or not it possesses the Rh factor. Let the children find out from their parents what type blood they have, and list on the chalkboard the prevalence of each type. Discuss the importance of giving the proper blood type for transfusions.

4. *Observe blood vessels* · Repeat that portion of Learning Activity 2 of "Animals with Backbones," Chapter 14 (p. 554) that deals with observing the arteries, veins, and capillaries in the tail of a fish. Note the movement of the corpuscles through the blood vessels.

5. *Observe the action of valves in the veins* ·

Let your arm hang down until the large veins on your hand become quite visible. Make a fist, place a fingertip on one vein, and push firmly downward toward the knuckles. While holding the finger in place, note how smooth the vein becomes as your finger presses on the valve and prevents blood from flowing into that portion of the vein. Now take away your finger. The vein will fill up with blood again.

6. *Examine an animal heart* · Obtain the heart of a calf, sheep, or pig from the meat market. Pare away any fatty material present, and note how muscular the heart walls are. Try to identify the ventricles and auricles before you begin to cut the heart open. Make incisions on either side of the lower narrow end of the wall. When you enter the ventricle, cut away more material so that you may see the cavities more clearly. Note how thick the walls are, especially those of the left ventricle.

Use a probe to find the main artery leading from the left ventricle to the body and the pulmonary artery leading from the right ventricle to the lungs. Also, probe for the flabbier veins entering the right and left auricles. Look for the valves between the auricles and ventricles. Also, slit the artery walls lengthwise and look for the valves that prevent blood from flowing back into the heart.

7. *Make a stethoscope* · Make a stethoscope from three funnels, a glass Y-tube or T-tube, and two long plus one short pieces of rubber or plastic tubing (Figure 15–2). Let the children take turns listening to heartbeats. Compare the heartbeats when they are quiet with their heartbeats after they have jumped up and down 15 to 20 times or exercised vigorously.

8. *Measure pulse beat* · By using the first two fingers of your right hand, feel for the pulse on your left hand at the base of the thumb where the left hand joins the wrist (Figure 15–3). Count the number of pulse beats in 1 minute. Now jump up and down 15 to 20 times, or exercise vigorously, and take your pulse beat for 1 minute again. Note how

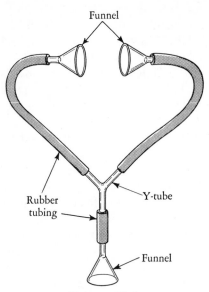

FIGURE 15–2.
A HOMEMADE STETHOSCOPE.

much stronger and faster the pulse beat becomes.

9. *Trace the circulation of blood* · Obtain a chart or draw a diagram of the human circulatory system. Trace the circulation of an imagi-

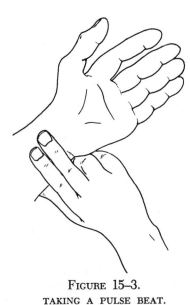

FIGURE 15–3.
TAKING A PULSE BEAT.

nary bubble of blood through the body. First have the blood leave the heart, travel through the body to the legs, and then return to the heart. Then have the blood go to the lungs and back. Follow the movement of the blood through the different auricles and ventricles of the heart.

10. *Discuss the function of lymph* · Recall the clear liquid that came out of blisters or oozed over the surface of a skinned knee or elbow. Point out that this clear liquid is lymph. Discuss the function of lymph and lymph nodes.

THE RESPIRATORY SYSTEM

1. *Locate the respiratory system organs* · Obtain a chart or draw a diagram of the respiratory system. Locate and identify the nose, nasal passages, pharynx, trachea, larynx, bronchi, bronchial tubes, and lungs. Discuss the function of each of these parts in the process of respiration.

2. *Examine animal lung tissue* · Obtain a portion of the lung of a calf, sheep, or pig from the meat market. Note how spongy the lung tissue is. Examine a section of this lung tissue under the low power of a microscope and locate a cluster of the many air sacs that are found throughout the tissue. Note that each air sac is surrounded by a fleshy wall. Change to the high power of the microscope, and you will be able to see capillaries in the wall.

3. *Discover how we breathe* · Obtain a lamp chimney and a one-hole rubber stopper to fit the top opening of the chimney. Insert a glass or plastic tube through the hole of the stopper. Use a rubber band to fasten a small rubber balloon to the bottom end of the glass tubing, and then insert the stopper into the top of the chimney (Figure 15–4). Cut a piece of rubber from a large rubber balloon and use a rubber band to fasten this piece of rubber firmly to the bottom opening of the chimney.

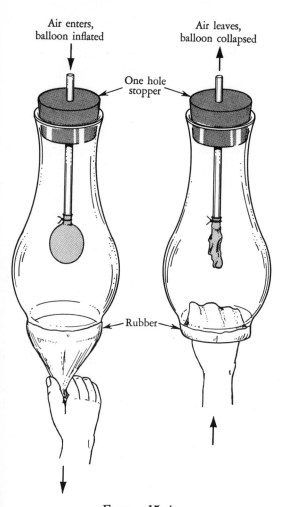

Air enters,
balloon inflated

Air leaves,
balloon collapsed

One hole
stopper

Rubber

FIGURE 15–4.
THE OPERATION OF THE DIAPHRAGM AND LUNGS
DURING BREATHING.

The chimney will represent the chest cavity, the balloon will represent one of your lungs, and the large piece of rubber will represent your diaphragm.

Pull the piece of rubber (diaphragm) downward. The air in the chimney (chest cavity) expands, reducing the air pressure in the chimney. Air from outside the chimney is forced in, inflating the balloon (lung). Now push the piece of rubber (diaphragm) upward. The air in the chimney (chest cavity) is compressed and contracts, increasing the air pressure in the chimney. Air will be forced out of the chimney through the glass tubing, causing the balloon (lung) to deflate. Repeat this procedure several times to simulate the steady action of inhaling and exhaling.

4. *Observe the effect of exercise on the rate of breathing* · Have one child place his hand on another child's chest and count the number of times the child is breathing in 1 minute. Let one inhalation and one exhalation together count as just one breath. Now have the second child jump up and down or exercise until he is breathing quite heavily, and then let the first child count the number of breaths in 1 minute again.

5. *Investigate artificial respiration* · Demonstrate and have the children learn the new methods of artificial respiration, such as the back pressure-arm lift method and the mouth-to-mouth method. Have the children read about and report on the function and use of the iron lung for persons who are unable to use their lungs normally.

THE EXCRETORY SYSTEM

1. *Observe the excretion of water* · Have the children recall the perspiration drops, containing water, that formed on their faces and bodies on a warm day after they had been running or playing actively. Let them recall how they could "see their breath" on a frosty day as the water vapor, present in the air expelled from their lungs, condensed into tiny droplets of water in the cold air. Have them breathe on a cold mirror and see the cloud or mist that forms as the water vapor from their breath condenses on the cool glass.

2. *Observe the excretion of carbon dioxide* · Get limewater from the drugstore and pour a little into a test tube. Have one of the children bubble the limewater with a soda straw until the limewater becomes milky, showing the presence of carbon dioxide. The carbon dioxide came from the air inside the child's lungs.

[597

3. *Observe the excretion of mineral salts* · Have the children lick their wrists after they return from a recess period where they have been playing actively. Point out that the salty taste is caused by the presence of mineral salts, which were dissolved in the perspiration and left behind after the perspiration evaporated.

4. *Examine an animal kidney* · Obtain the kidney of a calf, sheep, or pig from the meat market. Note the size and shape of the kidney. Observe where a large artery and a large vein enter the kidney. Cut the kidney lengthwise in half with a sharp knife. Note the many tubes in the tissue near the surface of the kidney and the large chamber where the urine collects. Point out that the urine leaves this chamber and travels through a duct that empties into the bladder.

THE NERVOUS SYSTEM

1. *Identify parts of the nervous system* · Obtain a chart of the human nervous system. Locate the central nervous system, which consists of the brain and spinal cord. Observe the major nerves that spread out from the brain and spinal cord to every part of the body.

2. *Examine an animal's brain* · Obtain a fresh, undamaged brain of a calf, sheep, or pig from the meat market. Locate and identify the cerebrum, cerebellum, and medulla. Note how large the cerebrum is and how its surface is folded in many places. Cut into the gray matter of the cerebrum and note the white matter underneath. See how the cerebellum is attached to the rest of the brain. Observe how the medulla connects with the other parts of the brain and with the spinal cord.

3. *Investigate nerves* · Draw a diagram of a nerve cell and label each part. Have the children stretch their arms with the fingers spread out wide. Their hands can represent the cell bodies, their fingers the dendrites, and

their arms the axons. Discuss the difference between sensory, motor, and associative nerve cells. Have the children distinguish between sensory, motor, and mixed nerves.

4. *Observe simple reflex action* · Have one child sit with his legs crossed so that one leg swings freely. Strike the leg just below the knee with the side of your hand. The leg will kick out immediately in a simple reflex action. Other simple reflex actions include blinking the eyes when an object suddenly comes near them, laughing when tickled, turning pale when frightened, blushing when embarrassed, coughing, yawning, sneezing, and shivering.

5. *Observe conditioned reflex* · Have children recall how mouths "water," as saliva flows, when tasty food is either mentioned or seen. Develop a conditioned reflex in the children by asking them to tap their pencils every time you say the word "tap." At first strike a ruler against your desk whenever you say "tap." After you have done this for some time, strike the ruler but do not say anything. Many children will still continue to tap their pencils even though you have not said the word "tap."

THE SENSE ORGANS

1. *Investigate sense of touch* · Touch the point of a thin, sharp nail to different spots, front and back, of a child's fingers. In some spots the child will feel only a sense of pressure. Other spots, which are more sensitive, will also produce a feeling of pain.

Spread a hairpin until the points are about 5 centimeters (2 in) apart. Blindfold a child and touch the palm of his hand with both ends of the hairpin. The child will feel both points. Repeat the procedure, bringing the points a little closer each time. Eventually the child will say that he feels just one point. At this stage both points of the hairpin are touching just one nerve cell. Repeat the experiment on the back of the hand, the forearm, and the back of the neck. Note the differences in frequency of distribution of the nerve cells in different parts of the body.

2. Investigate sense of smell · Have the pupils sit quietly in parts of the classroom. Pour some inexpensive strong perfume on a handkerchief and wave the handkerchief in the air. Ask the children to raise their hands as soon as they smell the perfume. Call their attention to the way that the odor diffuses progressively to all parts of the classroom.

3. Investigate the sense of taste · Blindfold a child and have him stick out his tongue. Dip an absorbent cotton stick into a solution of sugar and water. Touch the cotton to the tip, sides, and back of the tongue. Have the child identify the taste as sweet, sour, salty, or bitter in each case. Make sure the child's tongue is moist with saliva. Repeat, using salt solution, lemon juice, and a bitter solution of an aspirin tablet in a small amount of water, rinsing the mouth after each test. The child will detect sweet flavors mostly at the tip of his tongue, salt flavors at the tip and front sides, sour flavors along the sides, and bitter flavors at the back of the tongue.

Point out that smell has a lot to do with taste. Blindfold a child and have him hold his nose tightly. Give him raw mashed apple, pear, and potato to eat and have him try to identify what he is eating. Now let him eat a piece of apple while you hold a piece of pear under his nose. He will believe he is eating a pear. Reverse the procedure and he will now think he is eating an apple.

4. Investigate the human eye · Obtain a chart or model of the human eye. Locate and discuss the function of the main parts, including the cornea, pupil, iris, lens, vitreous and aqueous humors, retina, and optic nerve.

5. Examine an animal's eye · Obtain the eye of a cow, sheep, or pig from the meat market. Use a single edge razor to slice the eye in half lengthwise. The aqueous and vitreous humors will flow out. Examine the rest of the eye

closely and identify each of the parts. If you can obtain another eye, dissect it carefully and remove the lens. Note that the lens is convex.

6. Discover that a convex lens produces an image · Tape a sheet of paper on the wall opposite a window. Draw the shades on all the windows in the room except for the window facing the paper. Hold a magnifying glass close to the paper, and move the glass back and forth until you see a clear image on the paper (Figure 15–5). The convex lens of the magnify-

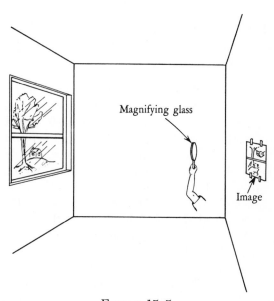

FIGURE 15–5.

A CONVEX LENS WILL PRODUCE A SMALL INVERTED IMAGE.

ing glass will form a smaller inverted image of the window, of whatever is on the window sill, and of objects that are outside the window at the time.

7. Observe the effect of light on the size of the pupil · Have a child sit in the dark part of the room for 5 minutes. Let the other children note how large the pupil of the eye has become to admit as much light as possible into the eye. Now shine a flashlight into the

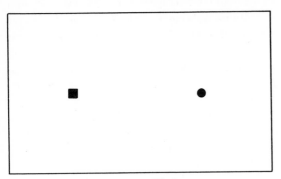

FIGURE 15–6.

FIND THE BLIND SPOT IN YOUR EYE.

child's eye. Note how quickly the pupil becomes smaller to cut down the amount of light entering the eye.

8. *Discover that the eye has a blind spot* · Make a square and a circle 10 centimeters (4 in) apart on a white card (Figure 15–6). Hold the card at arm's length. Close your left eye and look at the square with your right eye. Slowly bring the card toward you, staring at the square, and yet looking at the circle from the corner of your eye. At a certain position the circle will disappear. Point out that the image of the circle has fallen on that spot of the retina where all the nerves come together and go to the brain through the optic nerve. No image can form at this spot, making it a blind spot for the eye. When you continue to bring the card closer, the circle reappears.

9. *Discover that each eye produces a separate image* · Bring the forefinger of each hand together 30 centimeters (12 in) in front of you and at eye level (Figure 15–7). First look at

FIGURE 15–7.

IMAGES FROM EACH EYE OVERLAP TO PRODUCE A TINY THIRD FINGER.

both fingertips, and then look just over the fingertips at the wall across the room. You will see a third tiny finger appear between your two fingers. Point out that each eye sees both fingers, but the images from each eye overlap to produce the third finger.

10. *Discover that the retina holds an image for a short time* · Obtain a sturdy white cardboard about 7½ centimeters (3 in) long and 5 centimeters (2 in) wide. Draw a fish bowl on one side and a goldfish on the other side (Figure 15–8). Make four small holes at the

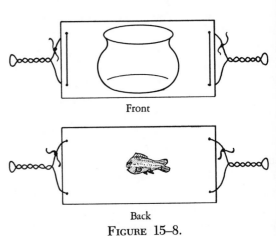

Front

Back

FIGURE 15–8.

PERSISTENCE OF VISION PUTS THE GOLDFISH INSIDE THE BOWL.

corners of the cardboard and thread a 30-centimeter (12-in) piece of fine, strong string through two holes on each side of the card, as shown in the diagram. Twist each string as much as you can, and then insert a finger in each of the loops and twirl the card rapidly by pulling the two loops hard sideways. When the card twirls, the goldfish will seem to be inside the bowl. Point out that the eye holds an image for a short time after the object has disappeared. When the card twirls, the pictures follow each other so rapidly that you see one picture before the image of the other picture has had time to disappear. As a result, you see both pictures at the same time.

11. *Investigate eye defects* · Draw diagrams on the board showing that the lens of the eye is unable to focus light on the retina in nearsightedness and farsightedness. Show how nearsightedness can be corrected with a concave lens and farsightedness with a convex lens.

Have the children test themselves for color blindness. Obtain a variety of colored threads and mix them together. Let the children take turns selecting specific colors and naming them.

12. *Investigate the ear* · Obtain a chart or model of the ear. Have children locate and discuss the function of the main parts of the outer, middle, and inner ear.

13. *Locate direction of sounds* · Blindfold a child and have him sit in the center of the room. Stand at different locations in the room and strike two pencils together. The child will be able to tell from what direction the sound is coming because the sound usually reaches one ear sooner than the other. Now have the child place one finger in his ear. Repeat the procedure. This time the child will have difficulty telling from what direction the sound is coming.

14. *Investigate sense of balance* · Have a child spin around for a short while. When the child stops, he will still have a spinning sensation because the liquid in the semicircular canals of the inner ear is still whirling around.

THE ENDOCRINE SYSTEM

1. *Identify endocrine glands* · Obtain a chart or draw a diagram of the endocrine system of the human body. Locate the pituitary gland, thyroid gland, and parathyroid glands in the head and neck region. Locate the pancreas and adrenal glands in the abdominal region. Discuss the function of each gland. Name the hormones secreted by these glands and describe the effect of these hormones on organs in other parts of the body.

2. *Investigate diseases of the endocrine glands* · Have children read about and report on effects on the body when the pituitary, thyroid, and parathyroid glands are either overactive or underactive. Let them also report on the cause of diabetes, its symptoms, and the current method of treating it.

BIBLIOGRAPHY FOR "THE HUMAN BODY"

AZIMOV, ISAAC. *How Did We Find Out About Vitamins?* New York: Walker, 1974. 64 pp.

BALESTRINO, PHILIP. *The Skeleton Inside You.* New York: Thomas Y. Crowell, 1971. 34 pp.

COBB, VICKI. *Cells: The Basic Structure of Life.* New York: Franklin Watts, 1970. 70 pp.

COLE, JOANNA, and MADELAINE MORROW. *Twins.* New York: William Morrow, 1972. 64 pp.

DOSS, HELEN, and RICHARD WELLS. *All the Better to Bite With.* New York: Julian Messner, 1976. 64 pp.

ELGIN, KATHLEEN. *The Fall Down, Break a Bone, Skin Your Knee Book.* New York: Walker, 1974. 64 pp.

———. *The Muscles.* New York: Franklin Watts, 1973. 72 pp.

————. *Read About the Ear.* New York: Franklin Watts, 1967. 50 pp.

————. *Read About the Eye.* New York: Franklin Watts, 1967. 50 pp.

JONES, HETTIE. *How to Eat Your ABC's: A Book About Vitamins.* New York: Four Winds Press, 1976. 84 pp.

KALINA, SIGMUND. *Your Blood and Its Cargo.* New York: Lothrop, Lee & Shepard, 1974. 48 pp.

MARR, JOHN. *The Food You Eat.* New York: M. Evans, 1973. 48 pp.

MAY, JULIAN. *How We Are Born.* Chicago: Follett, 1969. 48 pp.

————. *Man and Woman.* Chicago: Follett, 1969. 48 pp.

MCNAMARA, LOUISE, and ADA LITCHFIELD. *Your Busy Brain.* Boston: Little, Brown, 1973. 32 pp.

———— and ————. *Your Growing Cells.* Boston: Little, Brown, 1973. 32 pp.

———— and ————. *Your Living Bones.* Boston: Little, Brown, 1973. 32 pp.

MEEKS, ESTHER K., and ELIZABETH BAGWELL. *How New Life Begins.* Chicago: Follett, 1969. 47 pp.

———— and ————. *Families Live Together.* Chicago: Follett, 1969. 47 pp.

NAVARRA, JOHN, JOSEPH WEISBERG, and FRANK MELE. *From Generation to Generation: The Story of Reproduction.* New York: Doubleday, 1970. 116 pp.

SHOWERS, PAUL. *A Drop of Blood.* New York: Thomas Y. Crowell, 1970. 40 pp.

————. *What Happens to a Hamburger: The Process of Digestion.* New York: Thomas Y. Crowell, 1972. 40 pp.

————. *Use Your Brain.* New York: Thomas Y. Crowell, 1973. 40 pp.

SILVERSTEIN, ALVIN, and VIRGINIA SILVERSTEIN. *The Chemicals We Eat and Drink.* Chicago: Follett, 1973. 112 pp.

———— and ————. *The Endocrine System: Hormones in the Living World.* Englewood Cliffs, N.J.: Prentice-Hall, 1971. 68 pp.

———— and ————. *The Muscular System.* Englewood Cliffs, N.J.: Prentice-Hall, 1972. 74 pp.

———— and ————. *The Skeletal System.* Englewood Cliffs, N.J.: Prentice-Hall, 1972. 74 pp.

———— and ————. *Skin.* Englewood Cliffs, N.J.: Prentice-Hall, 1972. 90 pp.

WEISS, MALCOLM, and ANN WEISS. *The Vitamin Puzzle.* New York: Julian Messner, 1976. 96 pp.

ZIM, HERBERT S. *All About Bones.* New York: William Morrow, 1969. 64 pp.

————. *Your Stomach and Digestive Tract.* New York: William Morrow, 1973. 64 pp.

MATTER *and* ENERGY

CHAPTER 16

CHANGES *in* MATTER *and* ENERGY

THE STRUCTURE OF MATTER

I. MATTER

A. Matter is anything that takes up, or occupies, space and has weight.
   1. Air, water, wood, stones, and metals are examples of matter.
   2. Man, plants, animals, the sun, stars, and the planets are also examples of matter.

B. Some materials are made up of only one particular kind of matter, and other materials are made up of more than one kind of matter.
   1. A material that is made up of only one particular kind of matter is called a pure **substance.**
   2. Water, salt, sugar, silver, and oxygen are examples of substances.
   3. Air is an example of matter that is made up of many substances, such as oxygen, nitrogen, carbon dioxide, and others.

C. Matter is found in three forms, or **states,** and these states are called **solid, liquid,** and **gas.**

D. A solid has a definite size and shape.
   1. Wood, iron, glass, ice, rubber, wool, and butter are examples of solids.
   2. Solids can be hard or soft.

E. A liquid has a definite size, but it does not have a definite shape.

1. Water, milk, alcohol, oil, and gasoline are examples of liquids.
2. A liquid's shape depends upon the shape of the container into which it is poured.

F. A gas does not have either a definite size or a definite shape.
   1. Air, oxygen, carbon dioxide, and ammonia are examples of gases.
   2. When a gas is poured into a container, it spreads out until it has the same size of the container, and also takes the shape of the container.

G. Matter can be changed from one state to another by heating or cooling.
   1. When liquid water is cooled until it freezes, it becomes solid ice.
   2. When liquid water is heated until it boils, it becomes a gas called **steam.**

H. The science that deals with the different kinds of matter around us, of what they are made, and the changes that happen to them, is called chemistry.

II. GRAVITY, WEIGHT, AND MASS

A. Every body in the universe attracts, or pulls, on every other body.

B. This attraction or pull that each body has for another is called **gravity.**

1. The larger and heavier a body, the greater its pull of gravity will be.
2. The farther away two bodies are from each other, the smaller their pull of gravity on each other will be.
C. The earth's gravity pulls on every body at or near the earth's surface.
   1. This pull is always directed down toward the center, no matter where on the earth the body is located.
   2. This is the reason why we say that the earth's gravity has a downward pull.
   3. This downward pull of the earth's gravity keeps people from falling off the earth, and also holds the air and water on the earth.
D. The measure of the earth's pull of gravity on a body is called the **weight** of that body.
   1. The weight of a body will change, depending upon its distance from the center of the earth.
   2. The nearer a body is to the center of the earth, the greater the downward pull of the earth's gravity on the body will be, and the more the body will weigh.
   3. The farther a body is from the center of the earth, the smaller the downward pull of the earth's gravity on the body will be, and the less the body will weigh.
E. Every body has a **center of gravity**, which is the point where all of the weight of the body seems to be located.
F. The actual amount of matter in a body is called the mass of the body.
   1. Mass has nothing to do with the earth's pull of gravity.
   2. A body will have the same mass, whether it is on the earth's surface or far out into space.
G. The mass of a body is also a measure of the body's inertia.
   1. All objects have inertia.
   2. The tendency of a body to stay at rest if it is at rest or to stay in motion if it is in motion is called **inertia.**
   3. An outside force is needed to overcome or change the inertia of a body.
   4. The greater a body's mass, the more force is needed to overcome its inertia.

5. More force is needed to start moving an auto at rest than a bicycle at rest.
6. More force is needed to stop a rolling heavy ball than a rolling light ball.
7. Mass, then, is defined in terms of force needed to overcome or change a body's inertia.

III. PHYSICAL AND CHEMICAL PROPERTIES OF MATTER

A. All matter has certain qualities or characteristics, called **properties,** which help us tell one material from another, and also help us find out for what purposes the materials can be used.
B. These properties are divided into two main groups: **physical properties** and **chemical properties.**
C. The physical properties of a substance are those qualities or characteristics that we can readily observe with our five senses and that do not cause the substance to be changed into a different substance.
   1. Physical properties include such characteristics as color, odor, taste, heaviness, hardness, brittleness, elasticity, melting and boiling temperatures, solubility in water and other liquids, conductivity of heat and electricity, ductility and malleability.
   2. All substances differ in these physical properties.
D. The chemical properties of a substance are those qualities or characteristics that have to do with the activity of a substance with other substances.
   1. We observe chemical properties when we see air and moisture act on iron to make iron rust, vinegar act on baking soda to produce bubbles of carbon dioxide gas, and a fuel use the oxygen of air to burn.
   2. In each case a new substance is formed.
   3. A substance that acts readily with other substances is called **chemically active,** and a substance that does not act readily with other substances is called **chemically inert.**

[605

IV. PHYSICAL AND CHEMICAL.CHANGES

A. There are two kinds of changes that can happen to matter: **physical changes** and **chemical changes.**
   1. These changes in matter go on around us all the time.
   2. These two changes are very much different from one another.
B. In a physical change, only the physical properties or characteristics of the substance are changed, and it is still the same substance.
   1. A physical change takes place when a substance changes in size or shape, such as when wood is chopped, paper is torn, or glass is broken.
   2. A physical change takes place when a substance is heated and expands, or is cooled and contracts.
   3. A physical change takes place when a substance changes its form, or state, such as when a solid is changed into a liquid, or a liquid is changed into a gas.
   4. In most physical changes, the substance can be changed back into its original size, shape, or appearance.
C. In a chemical change, the chemical properties or characteristics of the substance are changed so that a new substance is formed, with properties that are different from the original substance.
   1. Examples of chemical change include the burning of wood, rusting of iron, tarnishing of silver, souring of milk, and digestion of food.
   2. For a chemical change to take place, energy—such as heat, light, or electricity—is either needed or given off.

V. MOLECULES

A. All substances are made up of tiny particles called **molecules.**
   1. These molecules are so small that only the largest of them can be seen by an electron microscope.
   2. One drop of water is made up of billions of molecules.

B. A molecule is the smallest particle of a substance that will still be that substance, and will still have all the properties of that substance.
   1. A lump of sugar can be crushed and broken up into many particles of sugar.
   2. These particles can be ground into a fine powder, but each tiny particle of powder will still be a particle of sugar.
   3. If we could keep breaking up a particle of sugar over and over again into smaller and smaller particles, we would finally end up with the smallest possible particle of sugar.
   4. This smallest possible particle of sugar would be one molecule of sugar.
C. All the molecules of a substance are alike, but the molecules of one substance are different from the molecules of another substance.
   1. For example, all the molecules of salt in a container are alike.
   2. But molecules of salt are different from molecules of sugar.
D. Molecules are always moving rapidly, striking other molecules and then bouncing off in different directions.
   1. In a gas, the molecules move very fast and are far apart.
   2. In a liquid, the molecules move more slowly and are closer together.
   3. In a solid, the molecules are very close together, and each molecule seems to be moving back and forth, or vibrating, in one fixed position rather than moving about freely.
E. All molecules attract each other.
   1. The attraction that molecules of the same substance have for each other is called **cohesion.**
   2. The attraction that molecules of different substances have for each other is called **adhesion.**
F. Cohesion makes it possible for molecules to come together and form the three physical states of matter.
   1. In a solid, the attraction between mole-

cules is very strong, so the solid holds its shape.

2. In a liquid, the attraction between molecules is much weaker, and, although the molecules still stick together, the liquid does not hold its shape but takes the shape of the container.

3. In a gas, there is practically no attraction between molecules, so the molecules move away from each other, and in this way the gas spreads throughout its container.

G. Adhesion makes it possible for two different substances to stick together.

1. Because of the attraction of molecules of different substances for each other, paint sticks to wood.

2. Because of adhesion, water sticks to other materials, making them wet.

3. The action of glue, cement, and paste also depends upon adhesion.

VI. ATOMS

A. Molecules are made up of even smaller particles called **atoms.**

B. In some cases a molecule is made up of just one atom.

1. This is why the word *molecule* is often confused with the word *atom.*

2. A molecule of neon is made up of just one atom of neon.

C. However, in most cases a molecule is made up of more than one atom.

1. A molecule of oxygen is made up of two atoms of oxygen that are close together.

2. A molecule of water is made up of two atoms of hydrogen and one atom of oxygen.

D. Scientists have discovered that all atoms are made up of three smaller kinds of particles: **electrons, protons,** and **neutrons.**

E. The electron is a particle with an electrical charge called negative (−).

1. Although it has a very small mass (the amount of matter in a body), it has a great deal of energy and moves around very quickly.

2. Because all electrons have the same negative charge, they repel each other.

F. The proton is a particle with an electrical charge called positive (+).

1. It is much heavier than the electron, having a mass about 1836 times as great as that of an electron.

2. A proton has about the same amount of energy as an electron, but, because it is heavier, it moves more slowly than the electron.

3. The positive (+) electrical charge of the proton is equal in strength to the negative (−) electrical charge of the electron, but both charges are exactly opposite to each other.

4. Because the electrical charges of the proton and the electron are unlike, or opposite, these two particles attract each other.

5. When an electron and a proton are brought together, their electrical charges neutralize each other, so that when put together the electron and proton are neither negatively nor positively charged.

G. The neutron is a particle that has a neutral charge.

1. The neutron has neither a positive nor a negative electrical charge.

2. As a result, the neutron does not attract or repel other neutrons.

3. The mass of a neutron is about equal to the combined masses of one electron and one proton.

4. It would appear, then that a neutron is made up of one electron and one proton combined together.

5. Also, the electrical charges of the electron and proton would neutralize each other to produce a neutral charge, just like the neutral charge of the neutron.

6. However, scientists have found that the energy of a neutron is just a little greater than the combined energies of one electron and one proton.

7. Scientists think that a neutron is made up of an electron and a proton held to-

gether by a small particle of energy, called a **neutrino,** which has no weight or electrical charge.

H. In an atom the protons and neutrons, which are heavier than electrons, are closely packed together in the center of the atom, which is called the **nucleus.**

 1. Because protons all have the same positive (+) charge, and because like charges always repel each other, the protons in the nucleus should also repel each other rather than stay close together.

 2. Scientists believe that there is a powerful form of energy that holds or binds the protons and neutrons closely together in the nucleus of an atom.

 3. This energy is called the **binding energy** of the nucleus.

I. The light electrons are spaced around the nucleus in rather definite regions or areas, called **shells** or **energy levels.**

 1. At first scientists thought that the electrons revolved around the nucleus in paths or orbits very much like the planets revolve around the sun.

 2. Now scientists believe that some electrons in any given energy level move about the nucleus more like bees swarming about their hive.

 3. In this way the electrons occupy the empty space around the nucleus, forming a sort of a hazy "electron cloud."

 4. Sometimes the electrons are near the nucleus and sometimes they are farther away, depending upon how much energy they have at the moment.

J. Because every atom is made up of electrons, protons, and neutrons, scientists believe that matter is really electrical in nature.

K. Every atom is electrically neutral because it has the same number of electrons and protons in it.

L. The difference between the atoms of different substances lies only in the number of electrons, protons, and neutrons the atoms of these substances have.

M. Although an atom may have many elec-

trons, protons, and neutrons, the atom is mostly empty space.

 1. The nucleus is small compared to the rest of the atom, and all the protons and neutrons in the nucleus are packed very tightly together.

 2. But the electrons, in their different shells or energy levels, are spread out so that there is a vast amount of space between the nucleus and the electrons.

VII. ELEMENTS

A. Although all atoms are made up of electrons, protons, and neutrons, all atoms are not alike.

B. Atoms differ in the number of electrons, protons, and neutrons they have, and, because of this difference, there are different kinds of atoms.

C. There are 92 different kinds of atoms found on earth.

 1. Each different kind of atom is called an **element.**

 2. Each element has its own particular number of protons and neutrons in the nucleus and electrons outside the nucleus.

 3. The atoms of each element are exactly the same, but the atoms of one element are different from the atoms of another element.

D. Chemists also define an element as a simple substance that cannot be broken up into anything simpler by ordinary chemical reactions.

E. Elements are often called the building blocks of matter.

 1. Elements can combine with each other to form new substances.

 2. All the substances on earth are made up of different combinations of these 92 natural elements.

F. In addition to the 92 natural elements, man has made 13 elements himself, bringing the total number to 105 elements.

G. Chemists divide the elements into two main groups because the elements in each group have many properties in common.

H. The elements in one group are called **metals.**
  1. Most metals have a special shiny surface, called a metallic luster.
  2. Most metals conduct electricity and heat very well.
  3. Many metals are **ductile,** which means they can be drawn out into wire.
  4. Many metals are also **malleable,** which means they can be hammered into thin sheets.
  5. Examples of metals are gold, silver, copper, iron, and aluminum.
I. The elements in the second group are called **nonmetals.**
  1. Most nonmetals conduct electricity and heat very poorly.
  2. Solid nonmetals cannot be drawn into wire or hammered into sheets because they are so brittle.
  3. Examples of nonmetals are sulfur, carbon, oxygen, hydrogen, and nitrogen.
J. Elements whose physical properties do not let them be classified as metals or nonmetals are called **metalloids.**

VIII. SYMBOLS

A. Chemists use a **symbol** for the name of an element instead of writing the whole word.
B. Sometimes the symbol is just one letter of the alphabet.
  1. In this case we use the first letter of the name of the element as the symbol.
  2. Examples of symbols with one letter are C for carbon, H for hydrogen, and O for oxygen.
C. Sometimes the symbol is two letters of the alphabet.
  1. Two letters are used when we have two or more elements whose names begin with the same first letter.
  2. In this case the symbol is made up of the first letter of the name of the element together with another letter that helps identify the element.
  3. Examples of symbols with two letters

are Ca for calcium, Co for cobalt, and Cr for chromium.
D. The first letter of a symbol is always a capital letter, but the second letter, if needed, is always a small letter.
E. For many of the elements the symbol is taken from the Latin name for the element.
  1. Most of these elements were well known long before English was spoken.
  2. For example, iron has the symbol Fe, from the Latin word *ferrum.*
F. Some common elements and their symbols are shown in Table 16–1.

TABLE 16–1. Some Common
Elements and Their Symbols

ELEMENT	SYMBOL	ELEMENT	SYMBOL
Aluminum	Al	Neon	Ne
Arsenic	As	Nickel	Ni
Calcium	Ca	Nitrogen	N
Carbon	C	Oxygen	O
Chlorine	Cl	Phosphorus	P
Copper	Cu	Platinum	Pt
Fluorine	F	Silicon	Si
Gold	Au	Silver	Ag
Helium	He	Sodium	Na
Hydrogen	H	Sulfur	S
Iodine	I	Tin	Sn
Iron	Fe	Tungsten	W
Lead	Pb	Radium	Ra
Magnesium	Mg	Uranium	U
Mercury	Hg	Zinc	Zn

IX. THE ATOMIC STRUCTURE OF THE ELEMENTS
A. The difference between the atoms of the different elements is in the number of electrons, protons, and neutrons that the atoms of these elements have.
B. There is also a definite arrangement of all the electrons, protons, and neutrons in the atoms of every single element.
C. In all atoms the protons and neutrons are located in the nucleus, and the electrons are located in shells or energy levels outside the nucleus.
D. The number of protons in the nucleus of an atom of an element is called the **atomic number** of the element.
  1. This number of protons in the nucleus

varies for the atoms of each element.

2. For example, an atom of the element oxygen has 8 protons in its nucleus and its atomic number is 8; and an atom of iron has 26 protons in its nucleus and its atomic number is 26.

E. The atomic number of an element definitely identifies the element, and determines its chemical properties as well.

1. For example, the element hydrogen is made up of atoms, all having one proton in their nucleus, so the atomic number is 1.

2. Therefore, any atom that has a nucleus with just one proton in it must have an atomic number of 1, and will be a hydrogen atom with all the chemical properties of the element hydrogen.

F. It is possible to arrange all 105 elements in a table of atomic numbers that range from 1 to 105.

1. In this table the first element has an atomic number of 1, the next element has an atomic number of 2, the third element an atomic number of 3, and so on until the last element, which has an atomic number of 105.

2. Each element in the table has an atomic number that is one number higher (one more proton) than the element before it, and one number lower (one less proton) than the element after it.

G. Because atoms are electrically neutral, there must be the same number of negatively charged (−) electrons outside the nucleus as there are positively charged (+) protons inside the nucleus.

1. Equal numbers of positive and negative charges balance each other to make the atom electrically neutral.

2. An atom of hydrogen, with an atomic number of 1, has one proton in its nucleus and one electron outside the nucleus.

3. An atom of uranium, with an atomic number of 92, has 92 protons in its nucleus and 92 electrons outside the nucleus.

H. The electrons are spaced around the nucleus in shells or energy levels.

1. Chemists have found that there are seven shells or energy levels that the electrons usually occupy.

2. There is a definite limit to the number of electrons that there can be in each shell or energy level.

3. For example, there can be no more than 2 electrons in the first shell or energy level nearest the nucleus, 8 electrons in the second shell or energy level, 18 electrons in the third shell or energy level, and 32 electrons in the fourth shell or energy level.

4. Generally, the farther away the shells or energy levels are from the nucleus, the more energy the electrons in these shells or energy levels will have.

5. When chemical changes take place, it is because of the action between the electrons in the outermost shells or energy levels of the atoms of two or more different elements.

I. The mass of an atom is called its **atomic mass.**

1. The atomic mass of an atom is usually called its **atomic weight.**

2. The atomic weight of an atom is the weight of all the electrons, protons, and neutrons in the atom.

3. Because the electrons have so little weight, for all practical purposes the weight of the atom can be said to be the weight of the protons and neutrons in the nucleus.

4. The neutron has a weight of one **atomic mass unit.**

5. The proton, which weighs about the same as the neutron, also has a weight of one atomic mass unit.

6. Because a proton and a neutron have just about the same weight, the number of neutrons in a nucleus can be found by subtracting the atomic number from the atomic weight.

7. For example, if the atomic number of

the element aluminum is 13 and its atomic weight is 27 mass units, this means that there are 13 protons and 27 minus 13, or 14, neutrons in the nucleus.

8. In general, as the atomic numbers of the different atoms increase, the atomic weights increase as well.

J. The atomic structure of the simplest element, hydrogen, is as follows.

1. The hydrogen atom has an atomic number of 1 and an atomic weight of 1.

2. The atomic number of 1 means that there is one proton in the nucleus and one electron in the first shell or energy level outside the nucleus.

3. The one proton in the nucleus makes up the atomic weight of 1.

K. The atomic structure of the next simplest element, helium, is as follows.

1. The helium atom has an atomic number of 2 and an atomic weight of 4.

2. The atomic number of 2 means that there are two protons in the nucleus and two electrons in the first shell or energy level outside the nucleus.

3. There are 4 minus 2, or two, neutrons in the nucleus, which together with the two protons make up the atomic weight of 4.

L. The atomic structure of the next element, lithium, is as follows.

1. The lithium atom has an atomic number of 3 and an atomic weight of 7.

2. This means that there are three protons in the nucleus and three electrons outside the nucleus.

3. Two of the three electrons are in the first shell or energy level outside the nucleus, and the other electron is in the second shell or energy level.

4. There are 7 minus 3, or four, neutrons in the nucleus, which together with the three protons make up the atomic weight of 7.

M. The atomic structure for the first 24 elements is given in Table 16–2.

TABLE 16–2. Atomic Structure of the First 24 Elements

ELEMENT	ATOMIC NUMBER	ATOMIC WEIGHT	NUMBER OF PROTONS	NUMBER OF NEUTRONS	ARRANGEMENT OF ELECTRONS BY ENERGY LEVELS
Hydrogen	1	1	1	0	1
Helium	2	4	2	2	2
Lithium	3	7	3	4	2,1
Beryllium	4	9	4	5	2,2
Boron	5	11	5	6	2,3
Carbon	6	12	6	6	2,4
Nitrogen	7	14	7	7	2,5
Oxygen	8	16	8	8	2,6
Fluorine	9	19	9	10	2,7
Neon	10	20	10	10	2,8
Sodium	11	23	11	12	2,8,1
Magnesium	12	24	12	12	2,8,2
Aluminum	13	27	13	14	2,8,3
Silicon	14	28	14	14	2,8,4
Phosphorus	15	31	15	16	2,8,5
Sulfur	16	32	16	16	2,8,6
Chlorine	17	35	17	18	2,8,7
Argon	18	40	18	22	2,8,8
Potassium	19	39	19	20	2,8,8,1
Calcium	20	40	20	20	2,8,8,2
Scandium	21	45	21	24	2,8,9,2
Titanium	22	48	22	26	2,8,10,2
Vanadium	23	51	23	28	2,8,11,2
Chromium	24	52	24	28	2,8,13,1

N. Not all the atoms of the same element have the same weight.
  1. Some atoms of an element have a slightly different number of neutrons from other atoms of the same element.
  2. Because of this difference in the number of neutrons, some atoms of an element have a different atomic weight from other atoms of the same element.
  3. This explains why atomic weights are not expressed as whole numbers only.
  4. However, even though these atoms of the same element differ in atomic weight, they all still have the same atomic number so they are all part of the same element and have the same chemical properties of that element.
  5. Atoms of an element that have the same atomic number but a different atomic weight are called **isotopes** of that element.
  6. Isotopes of the same element have the same number of protons and electrons but have a slightly different number of neutrons.
  7. Isotopes can occur naturally or they can be produced artificially by man.
O. The element hydrogen has three known isotopes.
  1. Hydrogen has an atomic number of 1, which means that all three isotopes have one proton in the nucleus and one electron outside the nucleus.
  2. The most common isotope has just the one proton in the nucleus, so its atomic weight is 1.
  3. A second isotope, called **deuterium,** has a neutron in the nucleus, as well as the one proton, so its atomic weight is 2.
  4. The third isotope, called **tritium,** has two neutrons in the nucleus, as well as the one proton, so its atomic weight is 3.
  5. Because all three isotopes have different weights, the average atomic weight of hydrogen is 1.0078.
P. A radioactive isotope of the element carbon is being used to estimate the age of rocks and minerals.

  1. Carbon has an atomic number of 6, which means that all isotopes of carbon have six protons in the nucleus and six electrons outside the nucleus.
  2. The common isotope of carbon has an atomic weight of 12, so there are 12 minus 6, or six, neutrons in the carbon-12 atom.
  3. The radioactive isotope of carbon has an atomic weight of 14, so there are 14 minus 6, or eight, neutrons in the carbon-14 atom.
Q. Two of the element uranium's many isotopes have atomic weights of 238 and 235.
  1. Both these isotopes have the same atomic number of 92 so there are 92 protons in the nucleus and 92 electrons outside the nucleus.
  2. In the uranium-238 isotope, there are 238 minus 92, or 146, neutrons in the nucleus.
  3. In the uranium-235 isotope there are 235 minus 92, or 143, neutrons in the nucleus.

X. COMPOUNDS AND MIXTURES

A. All the substances that make up matter can be divided into three main classes: **elements, compounds,** and **mixtures.**
B. Because there are only 92 natural elements on earth, most substances are either compounds or mixtures.
C. A compound is a substance that is made up of two or more elements that have combined in such a way that each element has lost its own special physical and chemical properties.
  1. As a result, the compound is a new substance with physical and chemical properties different from those of the elements that formed the compound.
  2. This means that a chemical change takes place when a compound is formed, with energy being either given off or required.
D. Every compound has its own special properties, and in this way it is possible for us to tell one compound from another.

E. A compound is always made up of the same elements, and the number of atoms of each element that combine to form one molecule of the compound is always the same.

  1. Water is a compound made from the elements hydrogen and oxygen, and there are always two atoms of hydrogen and one atom of oxygen in a molecule of water.

  2. Ammonia is a gaseous compound made from the elements nitrogen and hydrogen, and there always are one atom of nitrogen and three atoms of hydrogen in a molecule of ammonia.

F. The elements in a compound cannot be separated very easily, and some form of energy, such as electricity or heat, is needed to cause the separation to take place.

G. Because there are 92 natural elements, it is possible to make a vast number of compounds by using different combinations of elements.

  1. There are a few elements, like helium and neon, that rarely combine to form compounds.

  2. Also, some elements, like gold and platinum, do not combine very easily to form compounds.

  3. There are enough elements that do combine, however, to form hundreds of thousands of compounds.

H. A mixture is a substance made up of two or more elements or compounds that have combined in such a way that each element or compound has not lost its own special physical and chemical properties.

  1. As a result, no new substance has been formed.

  2. Energy, such as heat or electricity, is not given off or required when a mixture is formed.

I. The amounts of the different substances that make up a mixture are not fixed; in a mixture, any amount of one substance can be combined with any amount of other substances.

J. The air we breathe is a good example of a mixture.

  1. Air is made up of many gases, including oxygen, nitrogen, carbon dioxide, and water vapor.

  2. Each gas has not combined with the others, and each gas still retains its own special physical and chemical properties.

  3. The amounts of each gas in the air are not fixed, and they will change from time to time.

K. The substances in a mixture usually can be separated very simply.

  1. This separation is usually achieved by making use of the physical properties of the materials, such as their size, weight, color, and solubility in water or other liquids.

  2. For example, when a strong magnet is stirred in a mixture of iron powder and sulfur powder, the magnet picks up all the iron powder, separating the iron from the sulfur.

XI. FORMULAS

A. Chemists use a combination of symbols and, where necessary, small numbers beside the symbols to show the makeup of a compound.

B. This combination of symbols and small numbers is called a **formula.**

C. A chemical formula tells us two things.

  1. It tells us what elements are in the compound.

  2. It tells us how many atoms of each element are in a molecule of the compound.

D. The formula for water is H_2O.

  1. This formula shows that water is made up of the elements hydrogen and oxygen.

  2. It also shows that a molecule of water contains two atoms of hydrogen and one atom of water.

E. The formula for cane sugar is $C_{12}H_{22}O_{11}$.

  1. This formula shows that sugar is made

up of the elements carbon, hydrogen, and oxygen.

2. It also shows that a molecule of cane sugar contains 12 atoms of carbon, 22 atoms of hydrogen, and 11 atoms of oxygen.

F. A list of some common compounds and their formulas is shown in Table 16–3.

TABLE 16–3. Some Common Compounds and Their Formulas

COMPOUNDS	FORMULAS
Ammonia	NH_3
Baking soda (sodium bicarbonate)	$NaHCO_3$
Carbon dioxide	CO_2
Carbon monoxide	CO
Lime (calcium oxide)	CaO
Limestone (calcium carbonate)	$CaCO_3$
Salt (sodium chloride)	$NaCl$
Sand (silicon dioxide)	SiO_2
Sugar	$C_{12}H_{22}O_{11}$
Sulfuric acid	H_2SO_4
Vinegar (acetic acid)	$HC_2H_3O_2$
Water	H_2O

XII. TYPES OF CHEMICAL CHANGES OR REACTIONS

A. Chemical changes are also called **chemical reactions.**

B. All chemical changes or reactions can be grouped into the following four general kinds or types: **combination, decomposition, simple replacement,** and **double replacement** reactions.

C. In combination reactions, two or more elements or compounds combine to form a larger and more complicated compound.
1. For example, the elements carbon and oxygen combine to form carbon dioxide.
2. Also, the compounds water and carbon dioxide combine to form carbonic acid.

D. Chemists use **equations** to describe what happens during a chemical change or reaction.
1. These equations use formulas to tell us what materials took part in the chemical

change or reaction, and what new materials were formed.

2. For the two combination reactions described in C above, the equations are as follows:

$$C + O_2 \longrightarrow CO_2$$

$$H_2O + CO_2 \longrightarrow H_2CO_3$$

E. In decomposition reactions, a compound is broken up into the elements that formed it, or into simpler compounds.
1. For example, iron sulfide can be broken up into iron and sulfur, as follows:

$$FeS \longrightarrow Fe + S$$

2. Also, limestone (calcium carbonate) can be broken up into lime (calcium oxide) and carbon dioxide, as follows:

$$CaCO_3 \longrightarrow CaO + CO_2$$

F. In simple replacement reactions, a free element replaces another element from a compound.
1. For example, free iron will replace copper sulfate to form free copper and the compound iron sulfate, as follows:

$$Fe + CuSO_4 \longrightarrow Cu + FeSO_4$$

2. Also, free zinc will replace hydrogen from sulfuric acid to form free hydrogen gas and the compound zinc sulfate, as follows:

$$Zn + H_2SO_4 \longrightarrow H_2 + ZnSO_4$$

G. In double replacement reactions, the element in one compound trades places with the element in another compound to form two new compounds.
1. For example, the silver in silver nitrate trades places with the sodium in sodium chloride when both chemicals are first dissolved in water and then mixed together.
2. Two new compounds, silver chloride and sodium nitrate, are formed.

3. The equation for this reaction is as follows:

$$AgNO_3 + NaCl \longrightarrow AgCl + NaNO_3$$

XIII. SOLUTIONS

A. When a lump of sugar is added to a glass of water, the sugar gradually disappears.
   1. By tasting the water, we can tell there is sugar in the water.
   2. What has happened is that the molecules of sugar have spread out and moved between the molecules of water.
   3. The water has the same amount of sweetness all over because the molecules of sugar have spread out evenly and equally between all the molecules of water.
   4. We say that the sugar **dissolves** in the water.
B. This mixture of sugar in water is called **a solution.**
   1. Chemists call a solution any mixture of two substances or materials where the molecules of one substance are spread out evenly and equally between the molecules of the other substance.
   2. The substance that dissolves is called the **solute.**
   3. The solute can be either a solid, liquid, or gas.
   4. The substance that does the dissolving is called the **solvent.**
   5. The solvent is usually a liquid, such as water, although it can also be a gas or a solid.
   6. In a sugar solution, the sugar is the solute and the water is the solvent.
C. A **dilute** solution is one where only a small amount of solute is dissolved in the solvent.
D. A **concentrated** solution is one where a large amount of solute is dissolved in the solvent.
E. A **saturated** solution is one where as much solute as possible is dissolved in the solvent at a certain temperature and pressure.
F. The most common type of solution is one where a solid dissolves in a liquid.
G. Other common types of solutions are the following.
   1. A solution of a gas in a liquid, such as carbon dioxide gas dissolved under pressure in water to form soda water.
   2. A solution of a gas in a gas, such as air for example, where the several gases in the air are spread out evenly and equally among each other.
   3. A solution of a liquid in a liquid, such as a solution of alcohol and water.
H. Chemists use special words to tell whether a substance will or will not dissolve.
   1. For example, when a solid can dissolve in a liquid, we say that the solid is **soluble** in the liquid.
   2. A solid that does not dissolve in a liquid is said to be **insoluble.**
   3. When two liquids mix to form a solution, we say that the two liquids are **miscible.**
   4. Two liquids that will not mix to form a solution are said to be **immiscible** or **nonmiscible.**
I. Usually solids dissolve better in hot liquids than in cold liquids so that more of the solid will dissolve in the liquid when it is hot than when it is cold.
   1. More sugar can dissolve in hot water than in cold water.
   2. Some solids, such as salt, are almost as soluble in hot liquids as in cold liquids, so that almost as much salt will dissolve in hot water as in cold water.
   3. Some solids, such as calcium sulfate, are less soluble in hot liquids than in cold liquids, which means that less calcium sulfate will dissolve in hot water than in cold water.
J. Gases usually dissolve better in cold liquids than in hot liquids, which means that less of a gas will dissolve in a hot liquid than in a cold liquid.

[615

1. When a glass of cold water is allowed to stand in a warm room for a while, bubbles of air collect on the sides of the glass.
2. What happens is that, as the water becomes warmer, it cannot hold as much of the air dissolved in it, so some of the air comes out of the water.

K. An increase in pressure usually makes a gas more soluble in a liquid.
   1. Soda water is water in which much carbon dioxide has been made to dissolve by using great pressure.
   2. When the cap is removed from a bottle of soda water, the pressure is now lessened or reduced, and carbon dioxide escapes from the solution in the form of gas bubbles.

L. There are three ways to make solids dissolve more quickly in a liquid.
   1. **Stirring** will help the molecules of the solid spread quickly throughout the molecules of the liquid, and at the same time bring fresh parts of the liquid in contact with particles of the solid that have not yet dissolved.
   2. **Powdering** the solid will allow more of the liquid to come in contact with the solid at one time, and this increased contact will help the solid dissolve more quickly.
   3. **Heating** the liquid will make the molecules of liquid move more quickly so that the particles are spread more quickly throughout the molecules of the liquid, and at the same time fresh parts of the liquid will come more quickly in contact with particles of still undissolved solid.

XIV. THE LAW OF CONSERVATION OF MATTER

A. In many chemical changes, such as when hydrogen gas and oxygen gas combine to form water, it seems as if new matter has been created.
B. In other chemical changes, such as when a candle burns, matter seems to disappear, and we get the impression that matter has been destroyed.
C. However, the **law of conservation of matter** tells us that, in ordinary chemical reactions, matter is neither created nor destroyed, but only changed from one form to another.
   1. When wood is burned in air, gases are formed and ashes are left behind.
   2. We can show that the combined weight of the wood and the air that was used to burn the wood are exactly equal to the combined weight of the ashes and gases that are formed.
   3. So, in this chemical change, the matter changes from one form to another, but the amount of matter itself does not change.

ENERGY

I. WHAT ENERGY IS

A. **Energy** is the ability of matter to move other matter or to produce a chemical change in other matter.
   1. Scientists also define energy as the ability to do work, usually when they are talking about machines.
   2. According to scientists, work is done only when a force, which is a push or a pull, is moved through a distance.
B. There are two kinds of energy: **kinetic energy** and **potential energy**.
C. Kinetic energy is the energy that a body has because it is moving.
   1. Kinetic energy, therefore, is the energy of motion, and is an active energy.
   2. A moving automobile, falling water, a

strong wind, and expanding gas are all examples of kinetic energy.

D. Potential energy is the energy that a body has because of its position or condition.

1. Potential energy is stored-up energy.

2. It will not do any work until it is set free or released.

3. A rock held over a cliff has potential energy because it is in a position to do work when it is released.

4. Water at the top of a dam or waterfall also has potential energy because of its position.

5. A stretched rubber band and a wound-up spring both have potential energy because they are in a condition to do work when they are released.

6. A chemical, such as gunpowder, also has potential energy because it is in a condition to do work when it ignites and explodes.

7. The chemicals in a dry cell have potential energy because they are in a condition to do work when the dry cell is connected to an appliance.

E. When potential energy is set free, it is changed to kinetic energy.

1. When water at the top of a dam or waterfall falls down, it moves faster and faster, gaining more and more kinetic energy, and, when the water hits the bottom, its potential energy has been changed to kinetic energy.

2. The potential energy of a stretched rubber band and wound-up spring is changed to kinetic energy when the band and spring are released.

3. The potential energy of gunpowder is changed to kinetic energy when the gunpowder explodes.

II. FORMS OF ENERGY

A. There are many forms of energy.

B. Scientists divide these forms into six main groups as follows: **mechanical energy, heat energy, electrical energy, wave energy, chemical energy,** and **nuclear energy.**

C. Mechanical energy is the form we see most often around us.

1. All moving bodies produce mechanical energy.

2. The energy produced from all kinds of machines is mechanical energy.

D. Heat energy is the energy produced by the moving molecules in a substance.

1. The faster the molecules move, the more heat energy the substance has, and the hotter the substance becomes.

2. Heat energy heats our homes, dries our clothes, cooks our food, and runs power plants.

E. Electrical energy is the energy produced by electrons moving through a substance.

1. A stream of these electrons moving through a substance is called an electric current.

2. Electrical energy lights our homes, runs motors, and makes our telephones, radios, and television sets operate.

F. Wave energy is energy that travels in waves.

G. One kind of wave energy is **sound energy,** which is produced when matter moves back and forth, or vibrates, rapidly.

H. Another kind of wave energy is **radiant energy.**

1. There are many different forms of radiant energy.

2. These forms include light rays, X-rays, radio waves, infrared rays, ultraviolet rays, cosmic rays, and radiant heat.

I. Chemical energy is really a form of potential energy because the energy is stored in substances.

1. This chemical energy is released when a chemical reaction takes place and new substances are formed.

2. The new substances are formed because of the action between the electrons in the outermost shells or energy levels in atoms of the different substances.

J. Nuclear energy comes from the nucleus of the atom when the atom splits in two.

1. It also comes when the nuclei of atoms are fused together.

2. The amount of energy released in each case is very large.

III. THE TRANSFORMATION AND CONSERVATION OF ENERGY

A. Energy can be changed from one form into another.
B. The production of electricity in a power plant shows very well how energy can be changed from one form to another.
   1. When coal or another fuel is burned, the chemical energy in the fuel is released and changed into heat energy.
   2. The heat energy is used to change water into steam.
   3. The steam then turns a turbine to produce mechanical energy.
   4. The turbine runs an electric generator, or dynamo, that changes mechanical energy into electrical energy.
   5. The electrical energy may then be changed in a light bulb into light energy or it may be changed in the doorbell to sound energy.
C. In all these changes, the energy is not destroyed, but changed in form instead.
D. The **law of conservation of energy** tells us that energy is neither created nor destroyed, but only changed from one form to another.
E. When energy is changed from one form to another, other forms of energy are also produced.
   1. Usually these other forms of energy are not wanted, and are wasted because we have no use for them.
   2. For example, when we get light energy from an electric light bulb, unwanted and unused heat energy is also produced at the same time.
   3. When we get mechanical energy from a machine, unwanted and unused heat energy is also produced.
   4. When we get heat energy from an electric toaster, unwanted and unused light energy is also produced.

IV. HOW MATTER AND ENERGY ARE RELATED

A. For a long time scientists believed that matter and energy were completely different from one another.
   1. Matter took up space and had weight but energy did not.
   2. According to the law of conservation of matter, matter could be changed from one form to another, but could not be created or destroyed.
   3. Also, according to the law of conservation of energy, energy could be changed from one form to another, but could not be created or destroyed.
B. In 1905, however, Einstein proposed his famous theory, which said that matter and energy are related to each other.
   1. According to Einstein, matter could be changed into energy, and energy could be changed into matter.
   2. Matter could be destroyed, but it would reappear as newly created energy.
   3. Energy could be destroyed, but it would reappear as newly created matter.
C. Einstein's theory is usually expressed by the mathematical formula: $e = mc^2$.
   1. e stands for the amount of energy.
   2. m stands for the mass (the amount of matter in a body).
   3. c stands for the speed of light (300,000 kilometers or 186,000 miles a second).
   4. c^2 means that the value for the speed of light is multiplied by itself.
   5. Thus, the formula reads: energy equals mass times the speed of light times the speed of light.
D. Einstein's theory could not be proved until scientists began to study the atom.
E. They discovered that, when certain atoms break up into simpler atoms, the simpler atoms all together weigh less than the original atom from which they came.
   1. But, when the atoms do break up into simpler atoms, a tremendous amount of energy is also given off.
   2. Evidently some of the matter in the atom turns into energy.

F. The scientists also found that, when energy is used to make an electron move faster, the mass of the electron becomes greater.
   1. Giving the electron energy not only increased its speed, but its mass as well.
   2. Evidently some of the added energy turned into matter.
G. These two findings showed that the law of conservation of matter and the law of conservation of energy do not always hold true.

H. Today scientists combine both laws into a single law, called the **law of conservation of matter and energy.**
   1. According to this law, neither matter nor energy can be destroyed, but either can be changed into other forms of matter or energy.
   2. Matter can be changed into energy, and energy can be changed into matter.
   3. As a result, the total amount of matter and energy in the universe always stays the same.

NUCLEAR ENERGY

I. ATOMIC ENERGY

A. For a long time scientists believed that the atom had a tremendous amount of energy locked up in it.
B. They were able to prove this when they learned how to split the atom.
C. They found that this energy, which was released when the atom was split, came from the nucleus.
D. At first scientists called this energy **atomic energy,** but now it is more commonly and properly called **nuclear energy.**

II. NATURAL RADIOACTIVITY

A. Certain elements, such as radium and uranium, have been found to give off invisible radiations, or rays.
B. These radiations have very peculiar properties.
   1. They can penetrate solid materials, such as paper, wood, thin sheets of metal, and flesh.
   2. They affect a photographic negative in exactly the same way as visible light affects the negative when it is exposed to light.
   3. They can stop seeds from germinating, kill bacteria, and destroy small animals.

4. A person exposed to these rays for some time will receive severe burns, which take a long time to heal or may even kill the person.
C. When compounds of these elements are added to certain other compounds, the mixture will become **fluorescent,** or glow in the dark.
   1. For example, when a very small amount of radium bromide is mixed with zinc sulfide, the zinc sulfide will glow in the dark.
   2. This mixture is used to make luminous paint for coating the hands and dials of clocks, watches, and airplane instruments.
D. These elements and their compounds also give off heat and visible light, as well as invisible radiations.
E. Elements that give off these invisible radiations are said to be **radioactive,** and this highly unusual property is called **radioactivity.**

III. THE NATURE OF RADIOACTIVITY

A. Scientists have studied these radioactive elements and their invisible radiations very carefully.
B. They discovered that these radiations are

produced because the radioactive elements are breaking up.

1. In all cases it has been found that the breakup takes place in the nucleous.
2. While the breakup is going on, three different kinds of invisible radiations are given off.
3. Two of these radiations are really particles of matter, called **alpha particles** and **beta particles.**
4. The third radiation is an energy wave, called a **gamma ray.**

C. Alpha particles are the nuclei of helium atoms.

1. Each helium nucleus has two protons and two neutrons, and is about four times as heavy as a hydrogen atom.
2. Because of the positively charged protons in the helium nucleus, an alpha particle is positively charged.
3. When an alpha particle, or helium nucleus, gains two electrons, it becomes a helium atom.
4. Alpha particles have a speed of about 16,000 to 32,000 kilometers (10,000 to 20,000 mi) a second.
5. They have the smallest penetrating power of the three invisible radiations given off by radioactive elements, and can be stopped by a thin sheet of paper or aluminum foil.

D. Beta particles are electrons traveling at high speeds.

1. These electrons are given off by the neutrons in the nucleus of the radioactive element.
2. They are negatively charged, and travel 96,000 to 256,000 kilometers (60,000 to 160,000 mi) a second.
3. Because of their high speed, beta particles have a high penetrating power, and a good-sized sheet of aluminum metal is needed to stop them.

E. Gamma rays are high-energy X-rays.

1. They have more penetrating power than the other two radiations.
2. Very thick layers of lead or concrete are required to stop them.

F. Scientists believe that radioactive elements break up because the nuclei of their atoms are unstable.

1. These unstable nuclei give off either alpha or beta particles.
2. New nuclei are formed, which are a little lighter and are more stable than the original nuclei.
3. Scientists believe that gamma rays are produced because changes in energy levels take place in the nucleus when the new nuclei are formed.
4. At the same time, while the radioactive elements are breaking up, a small amount of their matter is changed into tremendous amounts of energy.

G. When the unstable nuclei of radioactive elements give off alpha particles, new elements are formed.

1. An alpha particle is a helium nucleus, with two protons and two neutrons in it.
2. When an atom of a radioactive element. loses an alpha particle from its nucleus, this means that the nucleus has lost two protons so the atomic number (number of protons in the nucleus) is now 2 less than it was before.
3. Because the atomic number has changed, an atom of a new element has now been formed.
4. Also, because the two protons and two neutrons in the alpha particle give it an atomic weight of 4, the loss of an alpha particle from the nucleus means that the atomic weight of the new element is 4 less than the atomic weight of the original element.
5. An example of how the loss of an alpha particle produces a change in atomic number and atomic weight is shown by the radioactive element radium, which has an atomic number of 86 and an atomic weight of 222.
6. When the nucleus of a radium atom loses an alpha particle, an atom of the element radon is formed, with an atomic number of 84 and an atomic weight of 218.

H. When the unstable nuclei of radioactive elements give off beta particles, new elements are also formed.

1. A beta particle is an electron given off by a neutron in the nucleus.

2. When a neutron gives off an electron, the neutron becomes a proton.

3. As a result, there is now one more proton in the nucleus than there was before so the atomic number has been increased by 1.

4. The new atomic number means that a new element has been formed.

5. Because an electron has little or no weight, the loss of a beta particle does not change the weight of the new element that has been formed.

6. An example of how the loss of a beta particle produces a change in atomic number but not in atomic weight is shown by the radioactive element thorium, which has an atomic number of 90 and an atomic weight of 234.

7. When an atom of thorium loses a beta particle, an atom of the element protoactinium is formed, with an atomic number of 91 and an atomic weight of 234.

I. The unstable nuclei of radioactive elements keep on giving off either alpha or beta particles, accompanied by gamma rays in each case, forming lighter and more stable nuclei until a nucleus is finally formed that is completely stable.

1. When this condition results, radioactivity stops and no more alpha or beta particles and gamma rays are given off.

2. For example, the radioactive element uranium goes through a series of breakups, giving off either alpha or beta particles and forming new radioactive elements with each breakup, until it finally becomes lead, which is nonradioactive and stable.

J. The stability of a nucleus seems to depend upon a comparison of the number of protons and neutrons in the nucleus.

1. The most stable nuclei have the same number of protons and neutrons.

2. The less stable nuclei have more neutrons than protons in the nucleus.

3. The greater the difference between the number of neutrons and protons in the nucleus, the more unstable the nucleus is likely to be.

4. Furthermore, nuclei with even numbers of both neutrons and protons are the most stable.

5. Nuclei with an even number of neutrons and an odd number of protons (or vice-versa) are less stable.

6. Nuclei with odd numbers of both neutrons and protons are the least stable.

IV. THE LIFE OF RADIOACTIVE ELEMENTS

A. Radioactivity is much different from ordinary chemical changes that take place around us.

1. Ordinary changes can be speeded up or slowed down by changes in heat, pressure, or other means.

2. However, radioactive elements break up at a steady rate of speed, which cannot be changed by any means at all.

B. The life of radioactive elements varies greatly.

1. Some elements take billions of years to break up into simpler elements.

2. Others take days, hours, minutes, or even seconds to break up.

C. The time required for one half of the atoms in a piece of radioactive element to break up into simpler atoms is called the **half-life** of that element.

D. Each radioactive element has its own half-life.

E. Radium has a half-life of 1600 years.

1. This half-life means that half of the atoms in a piece of radium will break up into simpler atoms in 1600 years.

2. One half of the radium atoms that remain, or one fourth of the original number, will break up in the next 1600 years.

3. One half of the remaining radium atoms, or one eighth of the original num-

[621

ber, will break up in the next 1600 years.

4. The radium atoms will keep on breaking up this way as long as there are radium atoms present.

F. The half-life of uranium-238 is about 5 billion years.

V. DETECTING AND MEASURING RADIOACTIVITY

A. Because the radiations from radioactive elements are invisible, special instruments are necessary to detect and measure these radiations.

B. It is important that these instruments be very sensitive and very accurate.

1. These radiations can be very harmful to the human body, and persons who work with or are exposed to radioactive elements use these instruments to learn if they are being affected by the radiations and, if so, the amount of radiation that their bodies have absorbed.

2. These instruments are used by scientists, by prospectors to locate new sources of radioactive materials, and by hospitals and industries that use radioactive materials.

C. One simple method of detecting radiations is to observe their action on special highly sensitive photographic film.

1. Radiations from radioactive materials affect photographic film even though the film has not been exposed to ordinary light.

2. When the film is developed, the negative becomes lighter. ·

3. The greater the amount of radiation, the lighter the negative will be.

4. Persons who work with or near radiations often wear **film badges** to detect the amount of radiation present.

5. These badges have inside them a small piece of special, highly sensitive photographic film, which is removed and developed to show the amount of radiation that has been absorbed by the person.

D. Another instrument used to detect and measure radiation is the **electroscope.**

1. An electroscope is an instrument that is commonly used to detect and measure small electrical charges.

2. When radiations from radioactive materials pass through air, they cause the particles of air to become electrically charged.

3. The electroscope detects and measures these electrically charged particles of air, and in this way also detects and measures radiations.

4. A type of electroscope, called a **dosimeter,** looks like a pencil, and is clipped to a person's lapel or breast pocket.

5. When the person looks at the dosimeter, he can tell readily whether or not he has been exposed to radiations.

E. The most common instrument used to detect and measure radiations is the **Geiger counter.**

1. This instrument is a cigar-shaped tube made of glass and metal, with a wire running through it, connected to a storage battery and a loudspeaker or amplifier.

2. When the Geiger counter is brought near a radioactive material, the radiations cause a small, pulselike flow of electricity to take place inside the tube.

3. This tiny electric current is amplified, and either produces a series of "clicks" or makes a neon lamp flash on and off.

4. Normally, a Geiger counter produces 25 to 50 clicks a minute even without being near a radioactive material.

5. These clicks come from cosmic rays passing through the air, and also from natural radioactivity in the ground.

6. But, when a radioactive material is present, the Geiger counter clicks very rapidly and produces a "machine gun" effect.

7. Geiger counters are used by prospectors when hunting uranium ore, and are also used in laboratories where radioactivity is being studied.

F. The particles that make up radiations are invisible, but their paths can be seen and photographed in a **cloud chamber.**
1. The cloud chamber is filled with air that is saturated with water vapor.
2. When the particles pass through the chamber, the water vapor condenses on them.
3. Although the particles themselves are still invisible, the paths of the condensed moisture, called **fog tracks,** are visible and can be photographed.
4. A fog track is very much like the vapor trail made by a jet plane flying so high that it is invisible.
5. You can see the path of the invisible plane by the vapor trail it leaves behind, just as you can see the path taken by the invisible particle in the cloud chamber.

VI. Nuclear Fission

A. After scientists learned how uranium, radium, and other radioactive elements break up naturally to form new lighter elements, they decided to try to break up atoms.
B. They began by bombarding atoms of simpler elements with all kinds of high-speed particles.
1. These particles included protons, electrons, alpha particles (the nuclei of helium atoms), and deuterons (the nuclei of hydrogen atoms with a proton and a neutron in them).
2. With the exception of the electrons, all these high-speed particles are positively charged.
3. The high speeds were given to these particles by instruments commonly called "atom smashers."
4. These "atom smashers" were able to give the particles speeds as high as 240,000 kilometers (150,000 mi) a second and tremendous amounts of energy.
5. In the "atom smasher" called the **cyclotron,** protons or deuterons are made to whirl around faster and faster in a spiral

path until they finally shoot out of the cyclotron at tremendous speed.
6. Other "atom smashers" used to give high speeds to positively charged particles include the **cosmotron,** the **synchroton,** and the **linear speed accelerator.**
7. The **betatron** is an "atom smasher" used to get high-speed electrons.
C. When scientists bombarded the nuclei of atoms of simple elements with the high-speed particles, new elements were formed.
1. A particle would enter the nucleus of an atom and make the nucleus unstable.
2. The unstable nucleus would then rearrange itself by giving off a proton or a neutron, forming a new element, and releasing much energy.
3. This nuclear energy is produced when a small amount of the element's matter is changed into large amounts of energy, in accordance with Einstein's formula of $e = mc^2$.
4. When scientists bombarded nitrogen with high-speed alpha particles (helium nuclei), oxygen and neutrons were formed.
5. When lithium was bombarded with high-speed protons, two alpha particles (helium nuclei) were formed.
6. When beryllium was bombarded with high-speed alpha particles, carbon and neutrons were formed.
7. The scientists had finally found a way to change one element into another.
D. However, scientists were dissatisfied with these high-speed particles.
1. The protons, deuterons, and alpha particles had to be given tremendous amounts of energy before they could enter the nucleus of an atom.
2. This high energy was necessary because these particles were all positively charged, and, when they came near the nucleus of an atom, they were repelled by the same kind of positive charges that the protons in the nucleus had.
3. On the other hand, although the electrons were negatively charged and were

[623

attracted to the positively charged protons in the nucleus, the electrons were so light that it was hard for them to break up the atom.

E. As a result, as soon as the scientists learned how to obtain neutrons by bombarding beryllium with high-speed alpha particles, they began to use neutrons to bombard the nuclei of atoms of the elements.

1. The neutrons were much better particles to use because they were neutral and would not be repelled by the positively charged nucleus of an atom.

2. At first the scientists used high-speed neutrons.

3. However, they soon learned that, because atoms were mostly empty space and because the nucleus is very small compared to the rest of the atom, too often these high-speed neutrons would go right through the atom without striking the tiny nucleus.

4. They discovered that when they slowed down the neutrons, the slowed-down neutrons were now more likely to hit and be captured by the nucleus.

5. In fact, the slowed-down neutrons seemed to behave as if they were attracted to the nucleus, and would go straight to the nucleus.

6. One of the ways commonly used to slow down the neutrons is to allow them to pass through graphite, which is a form of carbon.

7. The graphite is called a **moderator** because it slows down or moderates the speed of the neutrons.

F. When scientists began to bombard the atoms of heavy elements with neutrons, a strange thing happened.

1. When they bombarded uranium with slowed-down neutrons, it did not break up like the lighter elements, giving off a proton or a neutron and forming a new element.

2. Sometimes the uranium atom split into two parts, forming an atom of barium and an atom of krypton, both having medium atomic weights.

3. In addition, two or three slow-moving neutrons were given off, together with radiations in the form of gamma rays.

4. Also, more energy was given off than had ever been released before.

5. This energy was formed when a small amount of the matter in the nucleus of the uranium atom was changed into large amounts of energy.

6. Scientists called splitting of the nucleus of the atom **nuclear fission.**

G. The products of uranium fission are not always barium and krypton.

1. Sometimes they are strontium and xenon.

2. Other elements can also be produced.

H. Because the uranium atom released two or three slow-moving neutrons, scientists hoped that a continuous splitting up of uranium atoms would be produced.

1. These slow-moving neutrons could split more uranium atoms, which would release more neutrons, which could split even more uranium atoms.

2. In this way a continuous splitting, called a **chain reaction,** would take place, continuing until all the atoms split.

I. However, the scientists found that only a few uranium atoms would split.

J. One reason for the failure to produce a chain reaction was the uranium itself.

1. The uranium used had two isotopes: uranium-235 with 143 neutrons in its nucleus, and uranium-238 with 146 neutrons in its nucleus.

2. The uranium-235 isotope splits very easily, but the uranium-238 isotope does not.

3. More than 99 percent of the element uranium is made up of the uranium-238 isotope, and less than 1 percent is made up of the uranium-235 isotope.

4. So, for a chain reaction to take place, the uranium-235 isotope must be separated from the uranium-238 isotope, and only the uranium-235 isotope used.

K. A second reason for the failure of a chain reaction to take place had to do with the amount of uranium being used in the reaction.

1. If too small an amount of uranium is used, the released neutrons from the fission of one of the uranium atoms will go right through without striking any other uranium atoms, and the reaction stops.
2. Enough uranium must be present so that the neutrons will strike other uranium atoms and keep the chain reaction going.
3. The smallest amount of uranium needed to keep a chain reaction going is called the **critical size.**

L. Because so little uranium-235 is available, scientists began looking for other more easily available elements that could be split by neutrons.

1. They discovered that they could change the more common uranium-238 isotope into a new element that could be split by neutrons.
2. When uranium-238 atoms were bombarded with neutrons, each nucleus kept a neutron and became unstable, giving off a beta particle (an electron) and forming a new man-made element, called *neptunium*, with an atomic number of 93.
3. Neptunium is an unstable element, and gives off a beta particle too, forming a second man-made element, called *plutonium*, with an atomic number of 94.
4. Plutonium is comparatively stable, but when bombarded by neutrons it splits up just as easily as uranium-235 to produce a chain reaction.

VII. The Atomic Bomb

A. The first atomic bomb was tested at Alamogordo, New Mexico, on July 16, 1945.

1. The bomb had two separate pieces of uranium-235, each piece smaller than the critical size needed to produce a chain reaction.
2. At the exact moment when the explosion was scheduled to take place, the two pieces of uranium-235 were brought together, making just one piece of uranium equal to or larger than the critical size.
3. A chain reaction then took place, producing a tremendous explosion and releasing vast amounts of energy.

B. On August 6, 1945, an atomic bomb, also containing uranium-235, was dropped on Hiroshima, Japan.

C. Three days later an atomic bomb containing plutonium was dropped on Nagasaki, Japan.

D. There are four main effects produced by an atomic bomb.

E. One effect of an atomic bomb is the **shock wave,** or explosive effect.

1. An atomic bomb destroys everything within ⅘ kilometer (½ mi) in any direction from where it lands.
2. Severe damage can be found as far as 1⅗ kilometers (1 mi) away.
3. Some damage can be found as far as 3⅕ kilometers (2 mi) away.

F. A second effect of an atomic bomb is the **heat radiation, or flash effect.**

1. Where the bomb lands, the surface of materials will be heated as high as 3000° Celsius (5400° Fahrenheit).
2. Serious burns and fires can be found as far as 1⅗ kilometers (1 mi) from where the bomb lands.
3. Noticeable heat can be detected even 3⅕ kilometers (2 mi) away.
4. Persons looking at the explosion 48 to 64 kilometers (30 to 40 mi) away will be temporarily blinded.

G. A third effect of an atomic bomb is the **nuclear radiations** given off.

1. Nuclear radiations, such as gamma rays and neutrons, destroy living tissue.
2. This kind of damage is quite severe as far as ⅘ kilometer (½ mi) in all directions from where the bomb lands.
3. The damage is still severe, but much less so, as far as 1⅗ kilometers (1 mi) from where the bomb lands.

H. The fourth effect of an atomic bomb is the **radioactive fallout,** or radioactivity that remains after the explosion.

1. The nuclear explosion can blow radioactive particles into the stratosphere, more than 9150 meters (30,000 ft) above the earth's surface.
2. These particles may stay in the air for as long as 10 years.
3. During that time they will spread evenly throughout the stratosphere over all parts of the earth.
4. Eventually these particles will fall back to the earth's surface as a radioactive shower, or fallout.
5. The more nuclear explosions that take place, the greater the concentration of these radioactive particles throughout the stratosphere will be, and the more dangerous the radioactive fallout is likely to become.
6. A shower of highly radioactive particles can produce severe, or even fatal, burns.
7. If the particles fall on food and water, the tissues inside the body will be damaged when the food is eaten or the water is drunk.
8. Radiations may also cause changes in hereditary characteristics that are handed down from one generation to the next.
9. The radioactive isotope strontium-90, produced in some nuclear explosions, has a half-life of 22 years, and may affect humans quite harmfully in an indirect way.
10. Strontium is an element that is very similar to the element calcium and, like calcium, is deposited in the bones of our body.
11. Strontium-90 may fall to earth and be taken up from the soil by plants, which are then eaten by cows and other animals.
12. When a person drinks milk or eats meat, the strontium-90 may be deposited in his bones, giving off radiations that may eventually produce bone cancer or leukemia, both of which are usually fatal.

VIII. CONTROLLING AND USING NUCLEAR ENERGY

A. Man has learned how to control and use nuclear energy by using a device called a **nuclear reactor,** which is sometimes also called an **atomic pile.**
B. The nuclear reactor helps us keep a chain reaction under control, and makes use of the energy produced as a result of this reaction.
C. The reactor acts somewhat like a large oven or furnace.
   1. In the reactor there is a large block of graphite, which acts as a moderator to slow down the neutrons so that they can enter the nuclei of the uranium-235 and produce a chain reaction.
   2. Rods of uranium-235, sealed in aluminum cans for protection, are put into holes running horizontally through the graphite block from one end to the other.
   3. Boron-steel or cadmium-steel rods are inserted into holes at the top of the reactor and run vertically through the graphite block.
   4. These steel rods, called **control rods,** can be moved in and out of the reactor, and in this way control the speed of the chain reaction.
   5. The control rods absorb any neutrons that hit them.
   6. If the chain reaction is going too fast, the control rods are lowered further into the reactor so that they can absorb more neutrons and thus slow down the reaction.
   7. If the reaction is going too slow, the rods are lifted farther out of the reactor so that less neutrons are now absorbed, and the reaction can speed up.
   8. In some reactors the tremendous amount of heat that is produced is removed by blowing air through circulating tubes in the reactor.
   9. In other reactors the heat is removed by water or some other liquid passing

through the circulation tubes in the reactor.

10. The entire reactor is enclosed in a thick layer of solid concrete, which absorbs any dangerous radiations and therefore helps protect the persons operating the nuclear reactor.

D. The heat produced from the nuclear reaction is used to boil water and change the water into steam.

1. The steam then turns a turbine, which runs an electric generator that produces electricity.

2. After the steam passes through the turbines, it is condensed and returned to the boilers to be changed back into steam again.

E. Nuclear reactors are now being used to run submarines and ships.

1. Vessels driven by the power from nuclear reactors can sail for long distances without having to refuel.

2. The first nuclear submarine, the *Nautilus*, traveled almost 96,000 kilometers (60,000 mi) before it had to refuel.

IX. RADIOACTIVE ISOTOPES

A. Only a few of the 92 elements found on earth are naturally radioactive.

B. Most of the naturally radioactive elements are the heavy elements, like uranium and radium.

C. However, scientists discovered that, when they bombarded the other natural elements with neutrons or deuterons (the nuclei of hydrogen atoms with a proton and a neutron in them), radioactive isotopes of these elements are formed.

1. By using either the nuclear reactor or the cyclotron and other "atom smashers," radioactive isotopes of practically all the elements have now been prepared.

2. These man-made radioactive isotopes are more commonly called **radioisotopes.**

D. These radioisotopes have been most helpful in medicine, industry, agriculture, and research.

1. Because they all give off radiations that can be detected by such instruments as the Geiger counter, they can be used as tracers in many different ways.

2. They can be traced as they move through pipelines, to detect leaks in the pipes.

3. They can be used to study the wear of machine parts or automobile treads.

4. They can also be used to study refining processes in oil refineries, detect flaws in metal parts, and gauge the thickness of sheets of metal, rubber, plastic, cloth, and paper.

E. Radioactive carbon can be used to show how the leaves of green plants make food for the plant by photosynthesis.

1. The radioactive carbon is burned to form carbon dioxide gas.

2. This carbon dioxide is added to the air that the plant is using.

3. The atoms of radioactive carbon in the carbon dioxide gas are traced while the different steps in the process of photosynthesis take place in the leaves and the rest of the plant.

F. Radioisotopes are being used to tell how well the plant is making use of fertilizers that have been added to the soil.

1. For example, radioactive phosphorus is mixed with fertilizer that has phosphorus in it.

2. The Geiger counter traces the radioactive phosphorus that has gone from the soil into the plant, and measures the amount of phosphorus that the plant used.

G. The exposure of seeds and plants to radiations from radioisotopes is producing new and better varieties of plants.

H. Radioactive cobalt is now being used to treat cancer instead of radium because it is easily made, is cheaper, and is more satisfactory.

I. Radioactive phosphorus and arsenic are being used to detect brain tumors.

1. This detection is possible because the brain tumor picks up more of these ra-

dioactive elements than the normal brain tissue around the tumor.

2. These extra amounts of radioactive elements in the tumor are detected by the Geiger counter.

3. Another radioisotope, radioactive boron, is now being used to treat these brain tumors.

J. Radioactive iodine is used to detect diseases of the thyroid gland.

1. This detection is possible because most of the iodine taken in by the body goes to the thyroid gland.

2. When radioactive iodine is taken into the body, its path to the thyroid gland is traced by a Geiger counter.

3. If the Geiger counter shows that the gland has taken up very little of the radioactive iodine, doctors know that the gland is not working actively or normally.

4. On the other hand, if the gland takes up too much radioactive iodine, doctors know that the gland is overactive.

5. Radioactive iodine is also used to treat cancer of the thyroid gland.

K. Radioisotopes are used by chemists to discover how chemical changes take place, and to learn more about the structure and properties of matter.

X. NUCLEAR FUSION AND THE HYDROGEN BOMB

A. In nuclear fission, energy is obtained by getting the nucleus to break up or split in two.

1. The atomic bomb and the nuclear reactor, or atomic pile, get their energy this way.

2. The amount of energy we can get from nuclear fission is definitely limited because the size of each portion of radioactive material in the atomic bomb is limited.

3. Each portion must not be greater than the critical size needed to produce a continuous chain reaction.

B. Scientists have discovered that they can get even more energy by joining atoms together rather than by splitting them.

1. They found a way to combine lighter atoms to form heavier atoms.

2. They combined the nuclei of lighter atoms to form heavier, more stable nuclei.

3. In the process, vast amounts of energy were given off because some of the matter of the lighter atoms was changed into energy when the atoms were joined together.

4. This method of joining nuclei of atoms together is called **nuclear fusion.**

C. The **hydrogen bomb,** also called the **H-bomb** and the **thermonuclear bomb,** gets its energy from a nuclear fusion reaction.

D. One way to get a hydrogen bomb to explode is to begin with a compound of lithium and hydrogen, called lithium hydride.

1. The hydrogen used in this compound is deuterium, an isotope of hydrogen having a proton and neutron in its nucleus.

2. Ordinarily, in a molecule of lithium hydride, the lithium and hydrogen nuclei are slightly apart.

3. However, when the temperature becomes millions of degrees hot, and when there is very great pressure, the nuclei of the lithium and hydrogen atoms are fused together, forming two alpha particles (helium nuclei) and releasing tremendous amounts of energy.

4. An atomic bomb is used to get this very high temperature and pressure, which sets off the hydrogen bomb.

E. Another way to get a hydrogen bomb to explode is to use deuterium and tritium, both of which are isotopes of hydrogen.

1. Deuterium has a nucleus with a proton and a neutron in it, and tritium has a nucleus with a proton and two neutrons in it.

2. Under very high temperature and pressure, the deuterium and tritium combine to form a helium atom and a neutron, and vast amounts of energy are released.

3. An atomic bomb is also used in this reaction to get the temperature and pressure high enough to set off the hydrogen bomb.

F. A hydrogen bomb can be and is much more destructive than an atomic bomb.
1. First, more matter is changed into energy when there is a fusion reaction, so much more energy is released.
2. Second, there is no limit to the size of a hydrogen bomb, so the amounts of materials used in the hydrogen bomb are much greater and the explosive power is thousands of times more powerful.

XI. MAN-MADE ELEMENTS

A. By using the radiations from the nuclear reactor or from the cyclotron and other "atom smashers," scientists have been able to prepare radioactive isotopes of practically all of the 92 natural elements found on earth.
1. These radioactive isotopes may be new, but they are not new elements.
2. They are only new forms of already known elements.

B. However, scientists have also been able to use the nuclear reactor and the "atom smasher" to create entirely new elements as well.
1. All of these new elements have a higher atomic number than uranium, the ninety-second natural element.
2. They are all radioactive, and some of them have a long half-life, but others have a half-life that lasts for just a few seconds.

C. At present there are 12 new man-made elements.

TABLE 16–4. New Man-Made Elements

NAME	SYMBOL	ATOMIC NUMBER	SOURCE OF NAME
Neptunium	Np	93	The planet Neptune
Plutonium	Pu	94	The planet Pluto
Americum	Am	95	America
Curium	Cm	96	Marie Curie
Berkelium	Bk	97	University of California at Berkeley
Californium	Cf	98	University and State of California
Einsteinium	Es	99	Albert Einstein
Fermium	Fm	100	Enrico Fermi, Italian nuclear physicist
Mendelevium	Md	101	Dmitri Mendeleyev, Russian chemist
Nobelium	No	102	Alfred B. Nobel
Lawrencium	Lw	103	Ernest O. Lawrence, inventor of the cyclotron

LEARNING ACTIVITIES FOR "CHANGES IN MATTER AND ENERGY"

THE STRUCTURE OF MATTER

1. *Test the definition of matter* · Show that solids, liquids, and gases are matter because they occupy space and have weight. A book or block of wood is a solid that can be measured and weighed easily. Pouring water into a glass jar will show that a liquid occupies space, and weighing the jar before and after pouring will show the liquid has weight. Repeat Learning

Activities 11 and 12 of "Air," Chapter 12 (p. 417) to show that air, a gas, occupies space and has weight. Also, the children can make a list of different common materials that can be found in school or at home.

2. *Investigate states of matter* · Refer to Learning Activity 1 above to show a solid has a definite size and shape and a liquid has a definite size but not a definite shape. Pump air into a deflated bicycle tire to show that a gas does not have a definite size or shape, but spreads out until it has the same size and shape of its container.

Place some ice cubes in a Pyrex container and allow them to melt. Then heat the water until it boils. Point out the changes in state that have taken place. Have the children make a list of familiar changes in state that take place around them.

3. *Compare weight and mass* · Repeat Learning Activity 5 of "The Solar System," Chapter 9 (p. 274), on earth's pull of gravity. Relate the earth's pull of gravity to the concept of weight. Compare weights on earth with weights on the moon, where the moon's pull of gravity is only one sixth that of the earth. Point out that in all cases the mass does not change, but remains the same.

4. *Investigate center of gravity* · Have a child balance a uniform object, such as a meterstick or a yardstick, on the end of one finger. The point where the meterstick balances is where the center of gravity is located. Now make the meterstick unsymmetrical by putting some modeling clay at one end. Balance the meterstick again, and note that the center of gravity has shifted toward the thicker, and heavier, part of the meterstick.

5. *Describe properties of materials* · Have the children bring in materials from home, and ask them to describe some of their physical properties. Such properties could easily include size, shape, color, texture, density (heaviness or lightness), odor, taste, and solubility in water.

6. *Compare physical and chemical change* · Cut a piece of paper or wood into pieces, and then burn the paper or wood. Note that cutting the paper or wood is a physical change, but burning the material is a chemical change. Compare the basic differences between physical and chemical changes.

7. *Investigate the effect of molecular motion* · Place a spoon in a cup of hot water. That part above the water becomes hot because of molecular motion. The heat of the water makes the molecules in that part of the spoon below the water move faster, and so the spoon becomes hot. These faster moving molecules strike nearby molecules in that part of the spoon above the water, making them move faster too. Soon this faster molecular motion is transmitted throughout that part of the spoon above the water, and that part becomes hot too.

Allow a drop of food coloring to fall into a tumbler of cold water. The motion of the molecules of water disperses the coloring throughout the tumbler. Repeat the experiment, using hot water instead. Note how the faster moving molecules of hot water disperse the coloring more quickly.

Pour some inexpensive strong perfume on a piece of absorbent cotton. Place the cotton in a dish at one end of the room, and have the children raise their hands as soon as they smell the perfume. Point out that the perfume evaporates, and the molecules of perfume vapor then travel across the room.

8. *Compare cohesion and adhesion* · Allow a drop of water to fall on a mirror or glass. Point out that the drop of water remains intact because of the cohesion of the water molecules, whereas the water adheres to the glass because of adhesion.

9. *Make models of atoms* · Tape a sheet of paper on a piece of corrugated cardboard. Draw a small circle to represent the nucleus of an atom. Draw concentric circles to represent the shells or energy levels of the electrons outside the nucleus. Now use thumbtacks of three differ-

ent colors to represent the number of electrons, protons, and neutrons in an atom of aluminum (Figure 16–1). Place 13 protons and 14 neutrons in the nucleus, and position 13 electrons in the concentric circles as shown in the diagram. Try making similar representations for other common atoms. Point out that the atom is really three dimensional.

Have the children look at a table that provides the atomic numbers and atomic weights of several or all of the elements. Such a table can be found in any high school or college chemistry textbook. Let the children use these values to determine the number of electrons, protons, and neutrons in atoms of some of the well-known elements.

10. *Make models of isotopes* · Use diagrams or models to illustrate isotopes. Point out the complete similarity between isotopes of the same element except for the difference in number of neutrons.

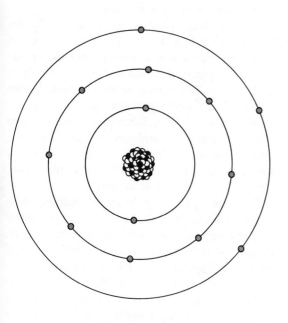

Electrons = ◎
Protons = ●
Neutrons = ○
FIGURE 16–1.
ATOMIC STRUCTURE OF AN ALUMINUM ATOM.

11. *Compare and classify elements* · Collect available elements like iron, copper, silver, gold, aluminum, magnesium, tin, zinc, carbon, and sulfur. (The evaporation of tincture of iodine will also provide the element iodine.) Point out that all the atoms of an element are the same, but the atoms of one element are different from atoms of other elements.

Divide the elements into two groups: metals and nonmetals. Make a list of all the properties that metals have in common. List some of the ways that metals differ from each other. Compare the differences between metals and nonmetals.

12. *Investigate symbols* · Have the children make a list of all well-known elements and their symbols. Such information can be found in a chemistry textbook or an encyclopedia. Note how the symbols in most cases provide a clue to the name of the element. Where the symbol does not correspond with the name of the element, have the children find out from the encyclopedia the element's name in another language, from which the symbol was derived.

13. *Investigate properties of mixtures* · Mix fine sand, sugar, iron filings, bits of cork filed from a stopper, and small marbles. Have the children think of and suggest ways and means of separating the components of the mixture. They should conclude that the marbles can be removed by hand or by pouring the mixture through a kitchen strainer. The iron filings can be removed with a strong magnet. Adding water to the remaining part of the mixture and then stirring causes the sugar to dissolve and the bits of cork to float on top of the solution. The bits of cork can be removed with a large spoon. Pour off the solution, leaving the sand behind. Now allow the solution to evaporate in a pie tin or other shallow container; this action causes the sugar to be left behind.

14. *Investigate properties of compounds* · Mix three parts sulfur powder and one part iron powder by weight. Stir until the mixture is uni-

form and the ingredients are undistinguishable. Place one half of the mixture in a shallow dish, and use a strong magnet to separate the iron from the sulfur, showing that the materials in a mixture retain their own special properties and can usually be separated by very simple means. Pass the magnet over the sulfur several times, to pick up all the iron powder.

Now pour the second half of this mixture of sulfur and iron powder into a Pyrex tube that is supported on a ring stand by a clamp (Figure 16–2). Heat the test tube with a Bunsen burner,

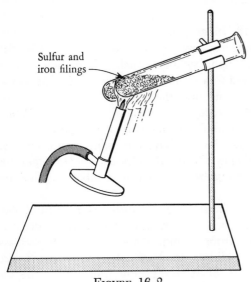

Sulfur and iron filings

FIGURE 16–2.

HEATING SULFUR AND IRON WILL PRODUCE A COMPOUND.

first gently and then strongly. Keep moving the flame up and down the lower half of the test tube to make sure the contents are being heated uniformly. Soon the contents will begin to glow, showing that a chemical change is taking place. Remove the flame and observe that the chemical change continues to take place, with the contents glowing strongly. Allow the test tube to cool to room temperature, wrap the tube in a piece of cloth or toweling, and break the end of the test tube gently with a hammer. Remove the contents with tweezers and place the material in a shallow

dish. Try to separate the iron powder with a magnet. Nothing will happen because a new substance, called iron sulfide, has been formed and it is not magnetic.

15. *Write chemical formulas* · Write on the board the names and chemical formulas of such common materials as salt, sugar, vinegar, rubbing alcohol, hydrogen peroxide, and sodium bicarbonate. Have the children name the elements in each formula and state how many atoms of each element are present.

16. *Show types of chemical changes* · To show combination, repeat Learning Activity 4 of "Air," Chapter 12 (p. 416). Remove the steel wool and examine the rust under a magnifying glass. Notice how the dark, metallic iron threads have been changed into the reddish-orange, powdery iron oxide. Soak another wad of steel wool in water and leave it exposed to the air for a few days until it has become quite rusty. Scrape off some of the rust and see if it can be attracted by a magnet.

To show decomposition, pour some 3% hydrogen peroxide into a glass jar. Add a piece of liver the size of a half dollar, then cover the jar with a piece of cardboard. (Keep the liver cool, but do not freeze, until one hour before using.) The bubbling shows that a liver enzyme, called catylase, decomposes the hydrogen peroxide into water and oxygen gas. When the bubbling subsides, insert a glowing wood splint into the jar. The splint will burst into flame, showing the presence of oxygen.

To show simple replacement, dissolve some copper sulfate crystals in a tumbler of water and stir until the crystals dissolve completely. Place one or two iron nails, which are free of grease coating, in the solution and allow them to stay overnight. Remove the nails and examine the coating of copper on them. Note that some iron from the nails replaced the copper from the solution of copper sulfate.

To show double replacement obtain a small amount of dilute silver nitrate solution from the drugstore. Dissolve some table salt (sodium chloride) in a glass tumbler or beaker half-filled with water. Pour the clear silver nitrate solution into the equally clear salt solution. A white solid, or precipitate, forms immediately. Point out that the silver nitrate and sodium chloride interact to form silver chloride and sodium nitrate. The sodium nitrate remains in solution whereas the silver chloride comes out of solution as the insoluble white solid.

17. *Investigate solutions* · Obtain three tumblers the same size. Fill each tumbler three-quarters full of tap water of the same temperature. To one tumbler add ¼ teaspoon of sugar and stir until all the sugar is dissolved. To the second tumbler add 2 teaspoons of sugar and stir until all the sugar is dissolved. Taste both solutions and note which is dilute and which is concentrated.

To the third tumbler add ½ teaspoon of sugar and stir until all the sugar is dissolved. Continue adding sugar, ½ teaspoon at a time and stirring after each addition, until no more sugar will dissolve and a small pile of undissolved sugar remains at the bottom of the tumbler. Total the number of teaspoons of sugar you added to obtain a saturated sugar solution.

18. *Observe that some substances are more soluble in water than others* · Add equal amounts of water at room temperature to three test tubes. Add a level teaspoon of sugar to one test tube, a level teaspoon of salt to the second test tube, and a level teaspoon of sodium bicarbonate to the third test tube. While placing your thumb over the mouth of the test tube, shake each test tube vigorously ten times, and then place the test tubes upright and allow any undissolved material to settle. Note the degree of solubility of the three different materials.

19. *Observe that some substances are insoluble in water* · Place a small stone in a test tube of water. Place your thumb over the mouth of the test tube and shake the tube vigorously. No dissolving will take place.

Add a few drops of oil to a test tube containing water. The oil will float on top of the water. Shake the test tube vigorously. Although the oil may break up into small drops, the drops will reassemble and the oil will continue to float undissolved on top of the water. Repeat the experiment, using carbon tetrachloride instead of water. This time the oil will be dissolved.

20. *Observe the effect of temperature on solubility of solids in liquids* · Pour a measured amount of water at room temperature into a tumbler. Add sugar, a teaspoon at a time and stirring after each addition, until no more will dissolve. Repeat the experiment, using an equal amount of hot water this time. Compare the number of teaspoons of sugar that dissolved in the cold and hot water, respectively.

21. *Observe the effect of pressure on the solubility of gases in liquids* · Obtain two identical bottles of soda. Put one in the refrigerator and allow it to stand overnight. Keep the other bottle at room temperature. The next day remove the caps from both bottles. Place the cold, open bottle back in the refrigerator, and let the warm, open bottle stand again at room temperature. At the end of an hour pour the contents of both bottles into each of two tumblers. The soda pop from the cold bottle will fizz fairly vigorously, showing the presence of dissolved gas. The soda pop from the warm bottle will fizz weakly, if at all, showing that most of the dissolved gas has been driven from the pop at the warmer temperature.

22. *Investigate ways of making solids dissolve more quickly in water* · Pour equal amounts of water at the same temperature in two tumblers. Obtain two cubes of sugar and crush one of the cubes into small crystals. Place the lump of sugar in one tumbler and the crushed sugar in the second tumbler. Stir the water in each tumbler vigorously. The crushed sugar will dissolve more quickly because more of the water can come in contact with the sugar at one time.

[633

Pour equal amounts of water at the same temperature into two tumblers. Add a level teaspoon of sugar to each of the tumblers. Stir the water in one of the tumblers. The sugar in the stirred water will dissolve more quickly because the stirring helps spread the sugar more quickly throughout the water and at the same time brings fresh parts of the water in contact with particles of sugar that have not yet dissolved.

Pour a measured amount of water at room temperature into a tumbler. Pour an equal amount of hot water into a second tumbler. Drop a sugar cube into each tumbler and note how much more quickly the sugar dissolves in the hot water.

ENERGY

1. *Find examples of kinetic energy* · Have the children look for common examples of kinetic energy in their everyday life. Wherever possible, let them show how these moving bodies can do work.

2. *Find examples of potential energy* · Holding a book in midair shows the potential energy a body has because of its position. Stretching a rubber band or squeezing together the ends of a spring coil will show the potential energy a body will have because of its condition. Have the children look for and list other everyday examples of potential energy.

3. *Convert potential energy into kinetic energy* · Drop the book and release the rubber band and spring coil described in Learning Activity 2 above. Note that the energy of position or condition (potential energy) has now been changed into energy of motion (kinetic energy).

Obtain or have one of the children bring in a paddle-ball toy, which consists of a wooden paddle connected in the center to a rubber ball with a long, single rubber band. Let the child work the toy. Point out that this is an example of a constant conversion of kinetic energy to potential energy and back again.

The paddle strikes the ball, making it move out and giving it kinetic energy. As the ball moves, the rubber band stretches. Kinetic energy is now being converted to potential energy. When the ball has moved out as far as it can, it stops for a fraction of a second before it begins its return to the paddle. At this moment the kinetic energy of the moving ball has been converted to the potential energy of the stretched rubber band. The ball travels back toward the paddle, and the potential energy is now being converted back to kinetic energy again. This same situation can be shown with a yo-yo as well.

4. *Find examples of energy transformation* · Write the six different forms of energy on the chalkboard and have the children list examples of how each form is used. Then have the children give examples of how energy can be changed from one form to another.

NUCLEAR ENERGY

1. *Investigate radioactivity* · Obtain a magnifying glass and watch or clock that has a luminous dial. Go into a completely darkened room and wait until your eyes become completely accustomed to the darkness. Hold the dial a few inches from one eye and adjust the distance until you see tiny bursts or flashes of light being given off from the numbers and hands of the dial. Now examine the phenomenon under the magnifying glass. Point out that the hands and numbers of the dial are coated with a paint that contains a material, such as zinc sulfide, and a tiny amount of radium compound. The radium compound breaks up, giving off invisible radiations that strike the zinc sulfide and make it give off these tiny bursts or flashes of light. Each burst of light represents the breaking up of one radioactive particle of the radium compound.

2. *Investigate the life of radioactive elements* · On the board trace the disintegration of a radioactive element, showing the particles

formed during each step of the disintegration, the changes in atomic weight and atomic number, the new elements formed, and their half-lives. Repeat, using other radioactive elements.

Have the children read about and report on the use of radioactivity to determine the age of rocks and of the earth. Show how a knowledge of the half-life of uranium and of radioactive carbon-14 plays an important role in determining this age.

3. *Detect radiations* · If possible, obtain a Geiger counter or an inexpensive radioactivity indicator. Bring a wrist watch or alarm clock with a luminous dial near the Geiger counter and note the increase in number of clicks. Some of the children's mineral collections or sets will have samples of uranium ore that can be tested with the Geiger counter. Have the children read about and report on other methods or instruments used to detect radiations.

4. *Discuss atom smashers* · Have the children read about and discuss such atom smashers as the cyclotron, cosmotron, synchroton, linear speed accelerator, and betatron.

5. *Investigate nuclear fission* · Contrast the slow rate of disintegration of naturally radioactive elements with the rapid rate of disintegration as a result of nuclear fission. Compare the products and amount of energy produced in each case.

Show the need for having the right amount, or critical size, of uranium to keep a chain reaction going. Shape a piece of modeling clay into a large circle about 13 millimeters (½ in) thick. Set wood matches upright in the clay, placing them so that each is about 5 centimeters (2 in) away from the other. Light one match at the edge of the circle. It will burn without setting the others on fire. Replace this burnt match and then insert more matches until each is only 13 millimeters (½ in) away from the other. Light one match, and it will produce a "chain reaction" by igniting all the others quickly.

6. *Discover how nuclear energy is controlled* · Draw diagrams or construct a model of a nuclear reactor. Discuss the parts of the reactor, their functions, and the method of controlling the rate of fission. Make a list of the actual and potential uses for nuclear reactors.

7. *Investigate man-made isotopes and elements* · Investigate radioisotopes. Have the children read about and report on their uses in research, medicine, industry, and agriculture. Have one group of children make up a list of the man-made elements, which includes the name of each element, its symbol, the atomic number, the atomic weight, and the person or object after which the element was named.

8. *Compare atom and hydrogen bombs* · Discuss and compare the difference between fission and fusion. List the materials used in each case and describe the products that are formed. Contrast the atom and hydrogen bombs, including the amounts of energy released and potential destructiveness. Have the children read about and report on radioactive fallout and its inherent dangers.

BIBLIOGRAPHY FOR "CHANGES IN MATTER AND ENERGY"

ADLER, IRVING. *Atomic Energy*. New York: Thomas Y. Crowell, 1973. 48 pp.

————. *Energy*. New York: Thomas Y. Crowell, 1972. 48 pp.

———— and RUTH ADLER. *Atoms and Molecules*. New York: John Day, 1966. 48 pp.

ASIMOV, ISAAC. *How Did We Find Out About Atoms?* New York: Walker, 1976. 64 pp.

————. *How Did We Find Out About Energy?* New York: Walker, 1975. 64 pp.

————. *How Did We Find Out About Nuclear Power?* New York: Walker, 1976. 64 pp.

BENDICK, JEANNE. *Solids, Liquids, and Gases*. New York: Franklin Watts, 1974. 72 pp.

————. *Why Things Work*. New York: Parents' Magazine, 1972. 64 pp.

BERGER, MELVIN. *Energy from the Sun*. New York: Thomas Y. Crowell, 1976. 40 pp.

BERRY, JAMES. *Exploring Crystals*. New York: Crowell-Collier, 1969. 104 pp.

BRANLEY, FRANKLIN M. *Energy for the Twenty-First Century*. New York: Thomas Y. Crowell, 1974. 128 pp.

————. *Weight and Weightlessness*. New York: Thomas Y. Crowell, 1971. 34 pp.

BROOKS, ANITA. *The Picture Book of Metals*. New York: John Day, 1972. 96 pp.

CARONA, PHILIP. *Crystals*. Chicago: Follett, 1971. 32 pp.

FUCHS, ERICH. *What Makes a Nuclear Plant Work*. New York: Dell, 1972. 24 pp.

GALLANT, ROY. *Explorers of the Atom*. New York: Doubleday, 1974. 96 pp.

GANS, ROMA. *Millions and Millions of Crystals*. New York: Thomas Y. Crowell, 1973. 34 pp.

————. *Oil: The Buried Treasure*. New York: Thomas Y. Crowell, 1975. 34 pp.

GUTNICK, MARTIN. *Energy: Its Past, Its Present, Its Future*. Chicago: Childrens Press, 1975. 48 pp.

HAINES, GAIL. *Explosives*. New York: William Morrow, 1976. 32 pp.

————. *What Makes a Lemon Sour?* New York: William Morrow, 1976. 32 pp.

HARRISON, GEORGE. *The First Book of Energy*. New York: Franklin Watts, 1965. 84 pp.

HELLMAN, HAL. *Energy and Inertia*. Philadelphia: J. B. Lippincott, 1970. 44 pp.

ISRAEL, ELAINE. *The Great Energy Search*. New York: Julian Messner, 1974. 64 pp.

KLEIN, AARON. *The Electron Microscope: A Tool of Discovery*. New York: McGraw-Hill, 1974. 86 pp.

KNIGHT, DAVID. *Harnessing the Sun: The Story of Solar Energy*. New York: William Morrow, 1976. 128 pp.

LEFKOWITZ, R. J. *Matter All Around You*. New York: Parents' Magazine, 1972. 64 pp.

————. *Push! Pull! Stop! Go!: A Book About Forces and Motion*. New York: Parents' Magazine, 1975. 64 pp.

NEAL, CHARLES, JAMES CUMMINS, and CHARLES HEINZ. *Exploring and Understanding Chemistry*. Westchester, Ill.: Benefic Press, 1970. 96 pp.

PALDER, EDWARD. *Magic With Chemistry*. New York: Grosset & Dunlap, 1966. 92 pp.

PEARL, RICHARD. *The Wonder World of Metals*. New York: Harper & Row, 1966. 116 pp.

PINE, TILLIE, and JOSEPH LEVINE. *Energy All Around Us*. New York: McGraw-Hill, 1975. 44 pp.

POLKING, KIRK. *Let's Go to an Atomic Energy Town*. New York: G. P. Putnam's Sons, 1968. 48 pp.

PRINGLE, LAURENCE. *Chains, Webs, and Pyramids: The Flow of Energy in Nature*. New York: Thomas Y. Crowell, 1975. 34 pp.

————. *Energy: Power for People*. New York: Macmillan, 1975. 146 pp.

SHUTTLESWORTH, DOROTHY. *Disappearing Energy: Can We End the Crisis?* New York: Doubleday, 1974. 96 pp.

STEPP, ANN. *The Story of Radioactivity*. Irvington-on-the-Hudson, N.Y.: Harvey House, 1971. 128 pp.

SZULC, TED. *The Energy Crisis*. New York: Franklin Watts, 1974. 128 pp.

CHAPTER 17

FRICTION *and* MACHINES

FRICTION

I. What Friction Is

A. Whenever the surfaces of two materials rub against each other, some **friction** is produced.

B. Friction is the force that resists the movement of one material over another material.

C. Friction is caused by the irregularities in the surfaces of materials.
1. Every surface has little bumps and hollows on it.
2. On rough surfaces these bumps and hollows can be seen or felt.
3. On smooth surfaces the bumps and hollows can be seen through a magnifying glass or microscope.
4. When two surfaces are rubbed together, the bumps and hollows catch and stick and resist the movement of the surfaces over each other.

D. Friction is also caused by the attraction of the molecules of one surface to the molecules of another surface as the surfaces rub against each other.

E. Whenever there is friction, heat is produced.

F. The greater the friction, the more heat will be produced.

G. Friction can make it hard to push one material across another material.

II. Factors Affecting Friction

A. The **nature of the materials** affects friction.
1. Firm, hard materials produce less friction than soft, sticky materials.

B. The **nature of the surfaces** affects friction.
1. Smooth surfaces produce less friction than rough surfaces.

C. The **amount of area** between two surfaces does not affect friction.
1. The friction between two narrow surfaces will be the same as the friction between two wide surfaces.

D. The **pressure of the two surfaces** against each other affects friction.
1. The greater the force pressing the surfaces against each other, the greater the friction will be.

E. **Sliding friction** is less than **starting friction.**
1. More force is needed to start an object sliding than to keep it sliding.

F. **Rolling friction** is less than **sliding friction.**
1. In sliding friction the bumps and hollows catch against each other.
2. In rolling friction, the roller or wheel lifts up over the bumps and hollows instead of sliding and catching against them.

III. Methods of Reducing Friction

A. Making the surfaces **smoother** levels out the bumps and hollows and reduces the friction between them.
B. A slippery material, called a **lubricant,** reduces friction.
1. The lubricant is placed between the two surfaces, filling up the hollows and covering the bumps.
2. In this way the lubricant prevents the two surfaces from rubbing directly against each other.
3. Oil is a lubricant used to reduce friction between parts of machines.
4. Grease is used to lubricate parts of an automobile.
5. Glycerine and water can also be used as lubricants to reduce the friction between rubber and glass.
6. Soap or candle wax are used as lubricants to reduce the friction between two pieces of wood, or between wood and metal.
7. Graphite (a form of carbon) can be used to reduce friction between two metals, or to reduce friction between wood and metal.
C. **Rollers, wheels,** or **ball bearings** reduce friction.
1. They change sliding friction to rolling friction.
2. The rollers, wheels, and ball bearings are placed between two materials, making it possible for the surfaces of these materials to roll over each other, and thus reduce friction.
D. **Streamlining** reduces the friction of the air rubbing against moving autos.
1. The air resists the forward motion of the auto and slows it down.
2. At high speeds the air resistance can be very great.
3. The shapes of fish, birds, and teardrops are used in streamlining.
4. The auto is designed in such a way that the air flows over the auto smoothly.
5. Planes and trains are also streamlined.

IV. Useful Effects of Friction

A. Friction can be very useful.
B. Without friction, we could not walk because our feet would slip.
C. Without friction we could not write with a pencil, pen, or chalk.
D. Sand or cinders are dropped in front of an automobile's rear wheels to increase friction and stop the wheels from spinning on icy roads.
E. Auto brakes use friction to slow down or stop a moving auto.
F. Friction helps hold nails and screws in wood.
G. Friction helps us unscrew the tops of bottles or jars, and helps us open cans.
H. Friction helps us hold a baseball and bat.
I. In industry, friction helps the conveyor belt move things along.
J. Friction is useful in making things smoother, like sanding wood or grinding lenses.
K. The heat caused by friction makes a match burst into flame.
L. The friction between the flint and the wheel of a cigarette lighter produces a spark that causes the wick to light up.

V. Harmful Effects of Friction

A. Friction wears away things.
1. Automobile tires, shoes, and clothing are worn away by friction.
2. The moving parts of machines rub against each other and wear away.
B. Friction makes work harder because extra force must be used to overcome friction.
C. Friction makes sliding parts stick.
D. Friction resists the movement of objects.
E. Friction between air and moving objects hinders the speed of these objects.
F. Friction produces heat, which may be harmful.
1. The heat may cause machine parts to melt and bend.
2. At high speed the friction between the air and a plane or rocket may cause

parts of the plane or rocket to become so hot that they will burn up, melt, or bend.

3. If we fall and slide across the gym- nasium floor, the heat produced by the friction between a part of the body and the floor may cause a very painful and easily infected burn.

MACHINES

I. WHAT MACHINES DO

A. Machines are devices that help make man's work easier.
B. A **force** must be used to make a machine work. A force is a push or a pull.
C. A force may be produced by the following:
 1. Electricity.
 2. Steam.
 3. Gasoline.
 4. Wind.
 5. Earth's gravity.
 6. Falling water.
 7. Sun's rays.
 8. Springs and weights.
 9. Muscles.
D. Machines can help us in four ways.
 1. All machines can transfer a force from one place to another.
 2. Some machines can increase the amount of a force so that we can lift heavier things or exert more force with the machine than we could alone.
 3. Some machines can change the direction of a force so that we can make things move in different directions.
 4. Some machines can increase the distance and speed of a force so that we can move things farther or faster.
E. No machine can increase both force and distance at the same time.
 1. If only a small force is needed to move or lift a heavy object, there is a gain in force.
 2. However, the heavy object will now move or be lifted through a shorter distance.

 3. So, although there is a gain in force, there is a loss in distance.

II. THE SIX SIMPLE MACHINES

A. All machines—no matter how many parts they have—are made up of one or more simple machines.
B. There are just six simple machines, as follows:
 1. Lever.
 2. Wheel-and-axle.
 3. Pulley.
 4. Inclined plane.
 5. Wedge.
 6. Screw.
C. Actually, the wheel-and-axle and the pulley are different forms of the lever, and the wedge and the screw are different forms of the inclined plane.

III. WORK

A. Machines help make work easier, but machines do not save work.
B. According to scientists, **work** is done only when an effort or a resistance moves through a distance.
 1. The force exerted on a machine is called the **effort.**
 2. The force that the machine exerts, or the object that the machine lifts or moves, is called the **resistance.**
C. No matter how much effort or resistance is exerted, if they have not moved through a distance, no work has been done.
D. To find out how much work has been

done, the force is multiplied by the distance through which the force moves.

1. Work can be stated as a formula:

Work = force used × distance moved

2. In the English system of measurement the force is usually stated in pounds, the distance in feet, and the work done is stated in **foot-pounds.**
3. To calculate the work that is put into a machine, multiply the effort times the distance the effort moves.
4. If you exert an effort of 2 pounds over a distance of 5 feet, you have done 2 × 5, or 10 foot-pounds of work.
5. To calculate the work that the machine does or puts out, multiply the resistance times the distance the resistance moves.
6. If a machine lifts an object weighing 5 pounds through a distance of 2 feet, the machine has done 2 × 5, or 10, foot-pounds of work.
7. In the metric system force is stated in **newtons,** distance in meters, and the work done is stated in **newton-meters** (more commonly called **joules**).
8. If you move a body 5 meters with a force of 2 newtons, you do 10 joules (or newton-meters) of work.

E. The speed with which the effort or resistance moves will make no difference in the amount of work done.
F. No machine can produce more work than the work that was put into the machine.
G. If there were no friction, the amount of work that a machine could do or put out would be exactly equal to the amount of work put into a machine.
1. This concept is the **principle of work.**
2. The principle of work helps explain why a small force must move through a longer distance to make a heavy object move through a shorter distance.

H. Because of friction, however, the amount of work put out by a machine is less than the work put into the machine.
1. Extra effort, which means more work, must be used to overcome friction.

2. The amount of extra effort involved in overcoming friction makes a difference in the efficiency of a machine.

IV. MECHANICAL ADVANTAGE

A. When we use a small force on a machine and the machine gives us more force, or lifts or moves a heavy object, we say we get a **mechanical advantage (M.A.)** of force.
B. If a machine produces a force that is five times as great as the force that is acting on the machine, the mechanical advantage of force is 5.
C. There are two ways of finding the mechanical advantage of a simple machine.
D. One way is to divide the resistance, or weight, by the effort that is exerted.
1. This expression can be stated as a formula:

$$\text{M.A.} = \frac{\text{Resistance}}{\text{Effort}}$$

2. If the effort is 2 pounds, and the resistance 8 pounds, the mechanical advantage is 8 ÷ 2, or 4.
3. This mechanical advantage is called the **actual mechanical advantage (A.M.A.)** because extra effort had to be exerted in overcoming friction, so this mechanical advantage is the advantage of force that you actually get when you use the machine.

E. The second way is to divide the distance the effort moves by the distance the resistance moves.
1. This expression can be stated as a formula, too:

$$\text{M.A.} = \frac{\text{Effort distance}}{\text{Resistance distance}}$$

2. If the effort moves 10 feet while the resistance moves 2 feet, the mechanical advantage is 10 ÷ 2, or 5.
3. This mechanical advantage is called the **ideal mechanical advantage (I.M.A.)**

because friction is not involved in this calculation.

4. For many of the simple machines there are also special, and usually easier, ways to find the ideal mechanical advantage (I.M.A.).

E. If extra effort were not needed to overcome friction, the actual mechanical advantage (A.M.A.) and ideal mechanical advantage (I.M.A.) would be exactly the same.

F. However, because extra effort is needed to overcome friction, the actual mechanical advantage (A.M.A.) is smaller than the ideal mechanical advantage (I.M.A.).

G. The ideal mechanical advantage (I.M.A.) then tells us the highest possible mechanical advantage we can get from a machine, whereas the actual mechanical advantage (A.M.A.) tells us the actual or real mechanical advantage we get when we use the machine.

H. A machine can also give us a mechanical advantage of speed.

1. When a machine makes an object move faster, we get a mechanical advantage of speed.

2. If the machine makes the object move five times as fast as the force that is acting on the machine, the mechanical advantage of speed is 5.

V. The Lever

A. A **lever** is a rigid bar, straight or curved, that rests on a fixed point called the **fulcrum.**

B. The force exerted on the lever is called the **effort.**

C. The force that the lever exerts, or the object that the lever lifts or moves, is called the **resistance.**

D. The distance from the fulcrum to the point where the effort is exerted is called the **effort arm.**

E. The distance from the fulcrum to the point where the resistance is exerted or lifted is called the **resistance arm.**

F. The closer the fulcrum is to the resistance, the less effort will be needed to move or lift the resistance, but the effort will move a longer distance, and the resistance will move a shorter distance.

1. There will be a gain in force, but a loss in distance and speed.

2. This action follows the principle of work.

G. The closer the fulcrum to the effort, the greater the force will be needed to move or lift the resistance, but now the effort will move a shorter distance, and the resistance will move a longer distance.

1. There will be a loss in force, but a gain in distance and speed.

2. This action also follows the principle of work.

H. The actual mechanical advantage (A.M.A.) of the lever can be found by dividing the resistance or weight by the effort.

I. The ideal mechanical advantage (I.M.A.) can be found in the following two ways:

1. Dividing the distance the effort moves by the distance the resistance moves.

2. Dividing the length of the effort arm by the length of the resistance arm.

J. Levers are divided into three classes, depending upon the positions of the effort, resistance, and fulcrum.

VI. First-Class Lever

A. A **first-class lever** is one in which the fulcrum is located anywhere between the effort (or force) and the resistance (or weight).

B. A first-class lever changes the direction of a force, so the effort pushes in one direction while the resistance moves in the opposite direction.

C. When the fulcrum is closer to the resistance than to the effort, we gain in force, but get less speed and distance.

D. When the fulcrum is closer to the effort than to the resistance, we get more speed and distance, but lose in force.

E. When the fulcrum is exactly between the effort and the resistance, there is no change in force, speed, or distance, but there is a change in direction.

F. Examples of first-class levers include the crowbar, scissors, pliers, tin snips, tack puller, and seesaw.

VII. SECOND-CLASS LEVER

A. A **second-class lever** is one in which the resistance is between the effort and the fulcrum.

B. A second-class lever does not change the direction of a force, so both the effort and resistance move in the same direction.

C. In a second-class lever the fulcrum is closer to the resistance, so there is a gain in force.

D. Examples of second-class levers include the wheel barrow, nut cracker, crowbar, bottle opener, and oar of a rowboat.

VIII. THIRD-CLASS LEVER

A. A **third-class lever** is one in which the effort is between the resistance and the fulcrum.

B. A third-class lever does not change the direction of the force.

C. In a third-class lever there is always a gain in speed and distance, and a loss in force.

D. Examples of third-class levers include the broom, shovel, sugar tongs, tweezers, and fishing pole.

IX. THE WHEEL-AND-AXLE

A. A simple **wheel-and-axle** machine is one where a large **wheel** is connected to a smaller wheel or shaft, called an **axle**.

  1. When either the wheel or the axle turns, the other part also turns.

  2. One complete turn of the wheel produces one complete turn of the axle.

  3. If the wheel turns but the axle does not, it is not a wheel-and-axle machine.

B. The wheel does not have to be a complete wheel.

  1. Instead there may be a crank that turns.

  2. When the crank is turned, it makes a complete circle, just as though it were a complete wheel.

C. A wheel-and-axle is really a form of the lever. It is a spinning lever.

  1. This spinning lever can be seen very clearly when a crank is used instead of a wheel.

  2. The fulcrum is at the center of the axle and the wheel or crank.

  3. The radius of the wheel is the effort arm, and the radius of the axle the resistance arm, of the lever.

D. A wheel-and-axle can change the direction of a force.

E. When the wheel turns the axle, there is a gain in force.

  1. A smaller force, or effort, at the wheel will move a larger weight, or resistance, at the axle.

  2. But the weight, or resistance, will not move as far or as fast as the force, or effort, because the wheel is larger than the axle.

  3. The larger the wheel, as compared to the axle, the greater the gain in force will be.

F. When the axle turns the wheel, there is a loss in force and a gain in distance and speed.

  1. A larger force must be exerted at the axle, but the resistance at the wheel will turn faster and farther.

  2. The smaller the axle, as compared to the wheel, the greater the gain in speed and distance.

G. The actual mechanical advantage (A.M.A.) of the wheel-and-axle can be found by dividing the weight or resistance lifted by the effort exerted.

H. The ideal mechanical advantage (I.M.A.) can be found in the following ways:

  1. Dividing the distance the effort moves by the distance the weight or resistance moves.

  2. Dividing the circumference of the wheel by the circumference of the axle.

3. Dividing the diameter of the wheel by the diameter of the axle.

4. Dividing the radius of the wheel by the radius of the axle.

I. Examples of wheel-and-axle machines containing complete wheels include the automobile steering wheel, gear wheels of the bicycle, door knob, and screw driver.

J. Examples of wheel-and-axle machines containing a crank instead of a complete wheel can be found in the pencil sharpener, meat grinder, and egg beater.

X. The Pulley

A. A **pulley** is a wheel that turns around a stationary axle.
1. Usually there is a groove in the rim of the pulley so that the rope around the pulley will not slip off.
2. Sometimes two or more wheels are placed side by side on the same axle.

B. There are two types of pulleys: the **fixed pulley** and the **movable pulley.**

C. The fixed pulley does not move.
1. It helps us only by changing the direction of the force.
2. It gives no gain in force, speed, or distance.
3. Fixed pulleys are used with flag poles, clothes lines, curtain rods, and Venetian blinds.
4. The fixed pulley acts like a turning first-class lever, with the fulcrum at the center of the axle, the effort at one rim of the pulley wheel, and the resistance at the other rim.

D. The movable pulley moves along the rope.
1. It helps us gain in force, but we lose in distance.
2. In a single movable pulley two sections of the rope support the pulley so that only half as much effort is needed to raise a resistance.
3. However, the effort must now move about twice as far as the resistance.
4. A movable pulley does not change the direction of the force.

5. A movable pulley acts like a turning second-class lever, with the fulcrum at one rim of the pulley wheel, the resistance at the center of the axle, and the effort at the other rim of the pulley wheel.

E. A single pulley may be combined with a movable pulley to change direction and gain force at the same time.
1. Such a combination is called a **block and tackle.**
2. Several fixed and movable pulleys can be used in a block and tackle.
3. Each fixed pulley changes the direction of the force, and each movable pulley changes the amount of the force.
4. The more movable pulleys used, the less force will be needed.
5. A block and tackle is used in scaffolds for painters and for billboard postermen.

F. The actual mechanical advantage (A.M.A.) of a pulley, or set of pulleys, can be found by dividing the resistance by the effort.

G. The ideal mechanical advantage (I.M.A.) can be found in the following ways:
1. Dividing the distance the effort moves by the distance the resistance moves.
2. Counting the number of sections of rope that support the **movable** pulleys.

XI. The Inclined Plane

A. An **inclined plane** is a slanting surface that connects one level to a higher level.

B. An inclined plane is a simple machine that gives us a gain in force.
1. By moving an object up an inclined plane we use less force in getting the object up to the higher level than if we had to lift the object directly from the lower to the higher level.
2. We gain in force at the expense of distance, so that now the object must be moved a longer distance as it travels up the inclined plane to reach the desired higher level.

C. The longer the inclined plane, the more gradual the slope becomes, and the less force will be needed to move the body·up the incline.

D. The shorter the inclined plane, the steeper the slope becomes, and the more force will be needed to move the body up the inclined plane.

E. The actual mechanical advantage (A.M.A.) of an inclined plane can be found by dividing the resistance by the effort.

F. The ideal mechanical advantage (I.M.A.) can be found by dividing the length of the inclined plane by the height.

G. Examples of the inclined plane include a plank, ramp, sloping floor of a theater or auditorium, straight road up a hill, escalator, and a stairway.

XII. THE WEDGE

A. A **wedge** is a simple machine that is used either to spread an object apart or to raise an object.

B. A wedge has a sloping or slanting side just like an inclined plane.

C. A **single** wedge looks just like an inclined plane, and has one sloping side.

D. A **double** wedge looks like two inclined planes that have been joined together with their sloping sides facing outward.

E. A wedge is a form of inclined plane with only one difference.
  1. With the inclined plane the object moves up the incline.
  2. With the wedge the incline moves into or under the object.

F. The wedge not only gives us a gain in force, but it also changes the direction of the force.
  1. The longer or thinner the wedge, the greater the gain in force.
  2. The gain in force is obtained at the expense of distance because the effort moves over a longer distance than the resistance.
  3. The farthest the resistance can be moved is the thickness of the big end of the wedge.

G. The actual mechanical advantage (A.M.A.)

of a wedge can be found by dividing the resistance by the effort.

H. The ideal mechanical advantage (I.M.A.) can be found by dividing the length of the wedge by the thickness of the big end.

I. The actual mechanical advantage of a wedge is always much less than the ideal mechanical advantage because there is much friction between the wedge and the object.

J. Friction is helpful in this case because it keeps the wedge from slipping out.

K. Examples of the wedge include the ax, knife blade, scissors blade, chisel, pin, nail, and plow.

XIII. THE SCREW

A. The **screw** is an inclined plane that winds around and around in a spiral.

B. The spiral ridge of the screw is called the **thread.**

C. One complete turn of the screw moves the screw into the object the distance from one thread to another.

D. The distance between two threads is called the **pitch** of the screw.

E. The screw gives us a gain in force, but at the expense of distance.
  1. The effort distance of one complete turn of the screw is larger than the resistance distance of one pitch.
  2. The closer the threads are together, the smaller the pitch becomes, and the greater the gain in force we get.

F. The actual mechanical advantage (A.M.A.) of the screw can be found by dividing the resistance by the effort.

G. The ideal mechanical advantage (I.M.A.) can be found by dividing the circumference of the screw (distance of one complete turn) by the pitch.

H. Because of friction the actual mechanical advantage is very much less than the ideal mechanical advantage.
  1. However, friction helps keep the screw from turning backward or pulling out.
  2. We can make up for the loss of force

caused by friction by using another machine, like the lever or wheel and axle, to turn the head of the screw.

   3. Using another machine to turn the head of the screw gives us a very large gain in force.

I. Examples of the screw are found in the wood screw, bolt, caps of jars and bottles, base of the electric light bulb, monkey wrench, clamp, vise, and piano stool.

XIV. EFFICIENCY OF MACHINES

A. There are two ways of finding out how efficient a machine is.

B. One way is to divide the actual mechanical advantage by the ideal mechanical advantage, and then multiplying by 100.

   1. This can be stated as a formula:

$$\text{Efficiency} = \frac{\text{A.M.A.}}{\text{I.M.A.}} \times 100$$

   2. We multiply by 100 so that we can describe the efficiency of a machine in percentages.

   3. If the A.M.A. of a machine is 4, and its I.M.A. is 5, the efficiency of the machine is $(4 \div 5) \times 100$, or 80 percent.

C. The second way to find the efficiency is to divide the amount of work put out by the machine by the amount of work put into the machine, and then multiply by 100.

   1. This can be stated as a formula:

$$\text{Efficiency} = \frac{\text{Work put out}}{\text{Work put in}} \times 100$$

   2. The work put out can be found by multiplying the resistance by the distance the resistance moves, and the work put in can be found by multiplying the effort by the distance the effort moves.

   3. If a machine puts out 30 foot-pounds of work while the work put into the machine is 50 foot-pounds, the efficiency of the machine is $(30 \div 50) \times 100$, or 60 percent.

D. Because extra force, or effort, is needed to overcome friction, the A.M.A. is always less than the I.M.A., and the work put out is always less than the work put in, so the efficiency of a machine is always less than 100 percent.

XV. POWER

A. When one machine can do the same or more work than another in a shorter time, we say that the first machine provides more power than the second machine.

B. **Power** is the rate of doing work.

C. The unit of power is the **horsepower,** which is 33,000 foot-pounds of work in one minute (or 550 foot-pounds of work in one second).

D. To find the horsepower of a machine, the foot-pounds of work done is divided by 33,000 times the number of minutes it took to do the work.

E. This can be stated as a formula:

$$\text{Horsepower} = \frac{\text{Work done}}{33{,}000 \times \text{minutes}}$$

XV. COMPOUND MACHINES

A. Most of the machines we use in daily life are made up of two or more simple machines.

B. A machine that is a combination of two or more simple machines is called a **compound machine.**

C. There are many examples of compound machines around us.

   1. The handle of an ax is a lever, and the blade is a wedge.

   2. A scissors has two levers with blades that are wedges.

   3. The handle of a pencil sharpener is part of a wheel-and-axle that turns two screws with sharp wedge-shaped edges that act like blades to sharpen the pencil.

   4. The meat grinder is just like the pencil sharpener except that it has just one screw with wedge-shaped edges that act like blades.

5. A rotary can opener is made up of a wheel-and-axle and a circular wedge.

XVI. GEARS

A. Sometimes, in compound machines, one wheel is used to turn another wheel.
B. Each wheel is connected to an axle that also turns, making a wheel-and-axle machine.
C. One way of making a wheel turn another wheel is by putting a tight belt around both wheels.
   1. When one wheel is turned, it makes the belt move and turn the other wheel.
   2. The second wheel moves in the same direction as the first wheel.
   3. If we want the second wheel to turn in the opposite direction to the first wheel, we cross the belt that goes around both wheels.
   4. When the first wheel, the **driving wheel,** is larger than the second wheel, the **driven wheel,** we get a gain in speed, but we lose in force.
   5. When the driving wheel is smaller than the driven wheel, we get a gain in force and a loss in speed.
D. A second way to make wheels turn is to put teeth on the wheels and slip a chain around both wheels.
   1. The teeth fit into the open places in the chain, and the cross-pieces of the chain fit into the notches between the teeth.
   2. The teeth and notches of the wheels stop the chain from slipping.
   3. Wheels with teeth and notches in them are called **gears** or **gear wheels.**
E. The bicycle is a machine that uses gears and a chain.
   1. The gears are part of a wheel-and-axle machine.
   2. The pedal turns a crank that turns a large gear.
   3. A chain connected from the large gear to the smaller gear on the rear wheel turns the smaller gear.
   4. The smaller gear then turns the rear

wheel, which drives the bicycle forward.
   5. Each time the pedals turn the larger gear around once, the smaller gear turns the rear wheel around many times.
   6. In this way the gears of a bicycle give up force but gain in speed and distance.
F. A third way to make wheels turn is to fit two gears together without a chain.
   1. The teeth of one gear fit into the notches of the second gear and make the second gear turn.
   2. Each gear is part of a wheel and axle.
   3. When one gear makes another gear move this way, the second gear moves in a direction opposite to the first gear.
   4. If a large gear turns a small gear, there is a gain in speed and distance and a loss in force.
   5. If a small gear turns a larger gear, there is a gain in force but a loss in speed and distance.
   6. To get two gears to move in the same direction, a third gear must be placed between them.
G. The actual mechanical advantage of two gears may be found by comparing the forces that both gears exert.
H. The ideal mechanical advantage can be found in the following ways:
   1. Comparing the number of teeth that each gear has.
   2. Comparing the speeds of both gears.

XVII. ENGINES

A. Although man had invented machines that multiplied the amount of force he could exert, he still had to supply the force needed to run the machines.
   1. At first man used the force of his muscles or the muscles of strong animals like the horse and the ox.
   2. Then man learned to use other more powerful forces, such as the movement of the wind, falling or moving water, and heat or gases produced from burning fuels.
   3. He invented devices and engines that

used these powerful forces to run his machines.

4. As these devices and engines became more improved and efficient, they were able to run larger and more complicated machines.

B. The **windmill** is a device for using the movement of the wind to run a machine and do work.

1. The windmill has blades, or propellers, connected to a shaft that runs through the center of the blades.

2. The blades are set at an angle and slope backward so that, when the wind hits the blades, it makes the blades turn around and around.

3. The turning blades make the shaft turn so that together they act like a wheel-and-axle machine.

4. The windmill can be used to pump water, grind grain, or run an electric generator to produce electricity.

5. The windmill runs only as long as the wind blows hard enough to turn the blades, so it works best in places where the wind blows much or most of the time.

C. The **water wheel** is a device that uses the force of falling or moving water to run machines.

1. It has many blades, which make the wheel turn quickly when the water strikes them.

2. A shaft in the center of the wheel turns as the wheel turns, forming a wheel-and-axle machine.

3. The first water wheels made use of the force of natural falling or moving water, and were used to grind grain or run machines in factories located beside rivers or waterfalls.

4. Today special water wheels, called **turbines**, use the tremendous force of falling or moving water from huge dams, such as the Grand Coulee Dam on the Columbia River or the Norris Dam on the Tennessee River.

5. Water turbines are used to run giant electric generators, which produce large amounts of electricity.

D. The **steam engine** uses the heat of burning fuels, such as coal, gas, and oil, to run machines.

1. The heat of the burning fuel changes water into steam.

2. When water changes into steam, it expands about 1700 times, and the expanding steam provides the energy to operate the engine.

3. The steam engine is called an **external combustion machine** because the fuel is burned outside the engine.

4. The steam is produced by making water boil in a boiler outside the engine.

5. The steam then passes through a pipe into a cylinder inside the engine.

6. In the cylinder the expanding steam pushes a sliding piston back and forth.

7. The piston is attached to a wheel with a lever called a **connecting rod**.

8. As the piston moves back and forth in the cylinder, the attached connecting rod makes the wheel turn.

9. Every movement of the piston is useful, producing power that makes the wheel turn.

10. The steam engine has been used to pull trains, push boats, saw wood, spin thread, and weave cloth.

E. The **steam turbine** also uses steam to run machines.

1. It is more powerful and runs more smoothly than the steam engine.

2. It works very much like the water turbine except that it is run by steam that comes from a boiler.

3. Most steam turbines have many curved blades arranged in rows so that a row of movable blades is followed by a row of fixed blades.

4. The expanding steam is shot through nozzles at a slant or angle against the movable blades, making the blades spin at a very high speed.

5. After the steam has passed a row of movable blades, it is then directed by a

row of fixed blades to the next row of movable blades.

6. Each row of movable blades is larger than the row before it because the steam expands as it travels through the turbine and can make good use of the larger space to get more power from the turbine.

7. The spinning movable blades turn a long rod that can run a large electric generator or turn the propellers of a big ship.

F. The **gasoline engine** uses the hot, expanding gases formed by burning gasoline to run machines.

1. It is called an **internal combustion engine** because the fuel is burned inside the cylinder of the engine.

2. Outside the engine a device called the **carburetor** changes the gasoline liquid into gasoline vapor and mixes this vapor with the right amount of air to make the gasoline burn properly.

3. Fitted into the top or head of the cylinder is a **spark plug**, which has a small space or gap between its two metal tips so that at the right moment a hot electric spark can jump across the gap and make the mixture of gasoline vapor and air in the cylinder burn.

4. A piston in the cylinder moves up and down when the gasoline engine is running.

5. In the most common gasoline engine, used by automobiles, the piston has to move four times, or make four strokes, inside the cylinder to get just one stroke that will produce power to run the machine.

6. In the first stroke or movement, called the **intake stroke**, the piston moves down, allowing a valve at the top of the cylinder to open and let the mixture of gasoline vapor and air enter the cylinder.

7. Then the piston moves up for its second stroke, called the **compression stroke**, compressing or squeezing the mixture of gasoline and air into a very small space.

8. Just when the mixture of gasoline and air is compressed the right amount, an electric spark from the spark plug sets the mixture on fire.

9. The mixture burns quickly, almost explosively, and produces very hot, expanding gases, which give the piston a tremendous downward push.

10. This third downward stroke is called the **power stroke,** and provides the power that runs the machine.

11. The piston then moves up again for its fourth stroke, called the **exhaust stroke,** pushing out the waste gases through another valve at the top of the cylinder.

12. Now the same series, or cycle, of four strokes starts all over again, and continues in this way as long as the engine is running.

13. The piston is attached to a **connecting rod,** which turns the **crankshaft** of the engine.

14. The crankshaft is connected to the **driveshaft,** which is then connected to the axle of a machine, like the automobile, and makes the machine run.

15. Because only one piston stroke in every four strokes is a power stroke, the more cylinders a gasoline engine has, the more smoothly it will run.

16. An automobile has at least four cylinders in its engine so that there will be one power stroke taking place all the time.

17. Compact automobiles usually have four-cylinder gasoline engines, but larger automobiles usually have six-cylinder or eight-cylinder engines.

18. Gasoline engines are also used to run small airplanes, motorcycles, motorbikes, outboard motors, lawn mowers, and power saws.

G. The **Diesel engine** also uses hot, expanding gases to run machines.

1. Machines that use Diesel engines do not use a carburetor or spark plugs.

2. They use a special fuel oil that is much cheaper than gasoline.

3. The most common Diesel engine uses a cycle of only two strokes to produce one power stroke.

4. The first stroke is a combination intake-compression-exhaust stroke.

5. During the first stroke, air is blown in at one side of the cylinder while waste gases are being forced out through two valves at the top of the cylinder.

6. Then the piston moves up, compressing the air very much more than in the cylinder of a gasoline engine, making the air very hot.

7. When the piston nears the top of the cylinder, the fuel oil is sprayed into the cylinder through a nozzle at the top, and the hot air makes the oil catch fire immediately and burn very quickly.

8. The hot, expanding gases push the piston down with great force for its second, or power, stroke.

9. When the piston nears the bottom of the cylinder, the waste gases are pushed out through the valves and more air enters the cylinder.

10. Because great pressure is produced in the cylinders, they must be made of thick metal, and the resulting weight makes it impractical to use Diesel engines in small machines and in automobiles.

11. Because the Diesel engine is so much more powerful and efficient than the gasoline engine, it is very commonly used to drive all kinds of trucks, buses, tractors, power shovels or bulldozers, locomotives, ships, submarines, and electric generators.

H. Man has also developed the electric motor (discussed in Chapter 21, "Magnetism and Electricity"), which uses electricity to run machines and do work.

LEARNING ACTIVITIES FOR "FRICTION AND MACHINES"

FRICTION

1. *Discover why uneven surfaces cause friction* · Rub two pieces of wood with rough surfaces together. Note the friction produced. Examine the surfaces under a magnifying glass and note the bumps and hollows.

Obtain a block of balsa wood about 15 centimeters (6 in) long, 7½ centimeters (3 in) wide, and 4 centimeters (1½ in) thick. Use a coping saw to cut out giant-sized bumps and hollows (Figure 17–1). Rub the two pieces of balsa wood together, reversing the position of one of the pieces, and see how the bumps and hollows catch and stick.

2. *Observe that friction produces heat* · Have the children rub the palms of their hands to-

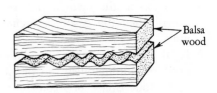

FIGURE 17–1.

BUMPS AND HOLLOWS CAUSE FRICTION.

gether briskly and note the heat produced by the resulting friction. The more briskly the hands are rubbed, the greater the friction, and the hotter the hands become.

3. *Observe the effect of nature of the materials on friction* · Rub two pieces of wood with smooth surfaces together. Then rub two pieces

of soft, white bread together. Note that firm, hard materials produce less friction than soft, clinging materials.

4. *Observe the effect of the nature of the surfaces on friction* · Rub some absorbent cotton first across the surface of some coarse sandpaper, and then across the surface of a mirror. Bits of cotton will catch and stick on the sandpaper, but not on the mirror.

5. *Observe the effect of the amount of area between surfaces on friction* · Obtain a rectangular block of wood and put a screw eye into one end. Place the block of wood, wide surface down, on a table and put a book on top of the block (Figure 17–2). Use a string to con-

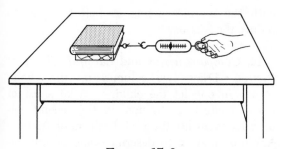

FIGURE 17–2.
THERE IS JUST AS MUCH FRICTION BETWEEN WIDE SURFACES AS NARROW SURFACES.

nect the screw eye to a spring balance. While holding the balance horizontally, pull the block of wood across the table and note how much force is needed to accomplish this. Repeat the experiment, using the narrower surface of the wooden block now. The forces will be the same. (A strong rubber band can be used instead of the spring balance, but the results will now be qualitative rather than quantitative.)

6. *Observe the effect of the pressure of surfaces against each other on friction* · Repeat Learning Activity 5 above, using first one book and then three books on the block. Note how the increase in pressure causes the friction between surfaces to become greater.

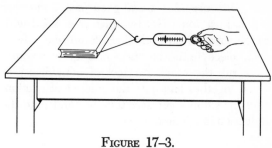

FIGURE 17–3.
SLIDING FRICTION IS LESS THAN STARTING FRICTION.

7. *Compare starting friction and sliding friction* · Slip a loop of string inside a large book and place the book on the table. Attach the string to a spring balance (Figure 17–3). Pull on the scale (making sure to hold it horizontally) until the book begins to move. Note the reading on the scale just before the book moves. Now pull the scale and book together along the table and note the reduced reading on the scale while the book is moving.

8. *Compare rolling friction and starting friction* · Slip a loop of string inside a large book and attach the string to a spring balance, as described in Learning Activity 7 above. Pull the scale and book together along the table and note the reading on the scale while the book is moving. Now place about a dozen round pencils underneath and beside the book, and pull the book along the table again (Figure 17–4). Note the reduced reading on the scale as the book moves along the rollers.

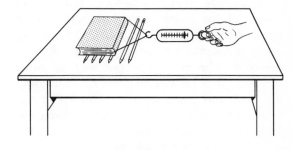

FIGURE 17–4.
ROLLERS WILL REDUCE FRICTION.

[651

9. *Discover that making surfaces smoother reduces friction* · Get two pieces of wood with rough surfaces on both sides. Sand one side of each piece until the surface is quite smooth. Now rub the rough surfaces of both pieces of wood together and note the amount of friction. Rub the smooth surfaces together and note the reduction in friction.

10. *Discover that lubricants reduce friction* · Rub two pieces of dry toast together. Note the amount of friction and also the wearing away of bits of toast. Now spread some jam thickly across each piece of toast and rub the pieces together again. The pieces will now slide smoothly over each other because the jam filled the hollows and covered the bumps, reducing the friction.

Have the children look for and make a list of examples of reducing friction with such lubricants as oil, grease, wax, soap, and graphite.

11. *Discover that rollers reduce friction* · Repeat Learning Activity 8 above, comparing rolling and sliding friction.

12. *Discover that wheels reduce friction* · Obtain a large cardboard carton the same size as the body of a child's play wagon. Place one child in the carton and have another child push the carton across the floor. Now have the child in the carton climb into a play wagon and have the second child push the wagon across the floor. Note the amount of force required to push the carton and the wagon.

13. *Discover that ball bearings reduce friction* · Put the metal screw cap from a large glass jar, lip down, on the table. Put a heavy book on the metal screw cap and try to spin the book. The book will spin once or twice and then stop because of friction. Take away the book and place some marbles under the screw cap (Figure 17–5). Make sure you use large enough marbles so that the lip of the screw cap does not touch the table. Now put the book back on the screw cap and try spinning the book again. The book spins easily,

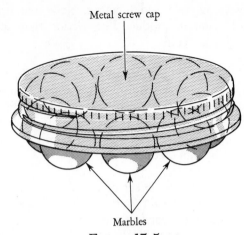

Metal screw cap

Marbles

FIGURE 17–5.
BALL BEARINGS WILL REDUCE FRICTION.

with the marbles acting as ball bearings to reduce the friction.

14. *Compare useful and harmful effects of friction* · Draw two columns on the chalkboard. In one let the children make a list of harmful effects of friction. In the second column let them list the useful effects of friction. Ask the children to describe some of the unusual situations that would happen if there were no friction on earth.

MACHINES

1. *Observe that machines transfer a force* · Operate hand tools and kitchen appliances. In each case show how a force is exerted on the machine at one place, and then how the machine transfers this force to another place where the work is done.

2. *Observe that machines can increase the amount of a force* · Drive a nail halfway into a board. Have the children try pulling the nail out of the board with their hands. Now let one of the children use a claw hammer to pull out the nail. Point out that the hammer changes a small force at the handle into a large force at the claws.

3. *Observe that machines can change the direction of a force* · Have the children observe the pulley of a school flagpole. The pulley changes the direction of a force because pulling down on one side of the rope slung over the pulley makes the flag fastened to the other side of the rope go up.

4. *Observe that machines can increase the distance and speed of a force* · Let a child sweep with a kitchen broom. As the child sweeps, point out that the upper part of the broom handle is moving just a short distance back and forth. However, the lower and bottom part of the broom are moving faster and farther.

5. *Observe that machines cannot increase both force and distance at the same time* · Repeat Learning Activities 2 and 4 above. When using the hammer, although there was an increase in force at the claws, the claws now moved a smaller distance than the handle. With the broom, the bottom part increased in speed and distance, but the force exerted at the bottom part was much less than the force being exerted on the upper part of the broom handle. As a result, the gain in speed and distance was accompanied by a loss in force.

6. *Investigate work* · Have a child try to pull open a bolted door. Point out that, although the child exerted a force, according to scientists he did not do any work because the force did not move through a distance. Let the children lift weighted objects to measured heights and calculate the number of foot-pounds of work done. Also, have the children pull objects with a spring balance across a surface, and then calculate the amount of work done.

7. *Discover how the first-class lever works* · Obtain a piece of wood 92 centimeters (36 in) long, 7½ centimeters (3 in) wide, and about 13 millimeters (½ in) thick. Use a triangular block of wood about 5 centimeters (2 in) wide and 2½ centimeters (1 in) high as a fulcrum.

Cut grooves on the underside of the board at each end and at the quarter, midway, and three-quarter marks. Rest the center of the board (at the midway groove) on the fulcrum. Put a weight or brick at one end of the board and push down at the other end (Figure 17–6).

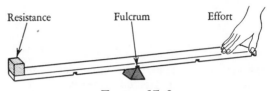

Resistance   Fulcrum   Effort

FIGURE 17–6.
A FIRST-CLASS LEVER.

Note the force you have to exert to lift the weight. Also, note that you push down while the weight moves up so that there is a change in direction, and your hand moves just as far down as the weight moves up.

Move the fulcrum nearer the weight and push down on the board again. This time less force will be needed to lift the weight, but now the weight moves up a little, while your hand moves down a lot. Now move the fulcrum so that it is near your hand. You will have to use a lot of force to lift the weight, but the weight will now move up a lot while your hand moves down just a little.

You may want to repeat this activity, this time using quantitative techniques. If so, insert a screw eye into one end of the board and have this end extend a little beyond the edge of the table (Figure 17–7). For the resistance use a known weight or a brick whose weight you have determined. Attach a spring balance to the screw eye to measure the effort needed to lift the weight. Now place the fulcrum at different positions under the board and measure the force necessary to lift the weight in each case.

Measure the length of the effort arm and the resistance arm. Also measure the distances that both the resistance and the effort move. Find the ideal and the actual mechanical advantage. Calculate the amount of work done, both input

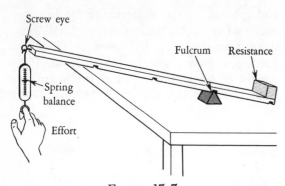

FIGURE 17–7.

LESS EFFORT IS NEEDED WHEN THE FULCRUM IS
NEARER THE RESISTANCE.

and output, and determine the efficiency of
the lever. Keep in mind that you will obtain
only approximate results because the weight of
the board will not have been taken into consideration in the calculations. Also, when the
spring balance is held upside down, this position affects the reading of the balance.

Have the children locate and identify other
examples of first-class levers. Let them repeat
this learning activity, using some of these
examples.

8. *Investigate the second-class lever* · Repeat Learning Activity 7 above, but now position the board as a second-class lever, with the
resistance between the effort and the fulcrum
(Figure 17–8). Conduct both qualitative and
quantitative measurements. Note that the
second-class lever does not change the direction of the force because both the effort and
the resistance move upward.

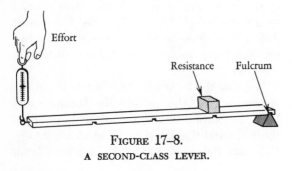

FIGURE 17–8.

A SECOND-CLASS LEVER.

Have the children locate and identify other
examples of second-class levers. Let them repeat this learning activity, using some of these
examples.

9. *Investigate the third-class lever* · Repeat
Learning Activity 7 above, now positioning the
board as a third-class lever, with the effort
between the resistance and the fulcrum (Figure 17–9). You will have to insert a second

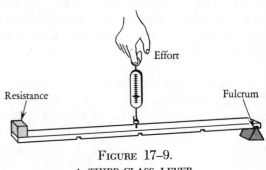

FIGURE 17–9.

A THIRD-CLASS LEVER.

screw eye into the board, this time into the top
surface. Also, you will have to press down on
the board just above the fulcrum to prevent
the board from being lifted up into the air
when you pull up on the spring balance. Conduct both qualitative and quantitative measurements. Note that the third-class lever does
not change the direction of the force because
both the effort and the resistance move upward.

Have the children locate and identify other
examples of third-class levers. Let them repeat
this learning activity, using some of these
examples.

10. *Discover how the wheel-and-axle works* ·
Clamp a pencil sharpener, with its cover removed, to the edge of the table, as shown in
Figure 17–10. Turn the handle of the sharpener
and point out that when the handle is turned,
it makes a complete circle, just as though it
were a complete wheel. The shaft of the
sharpener is the axle. When the handle

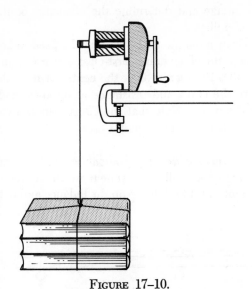

FIGURE 17–10.
THE PENCIL SHARPENER ACTS AS A WHEEL-AND-AXLE.

Draw a diagram to show that the wheel-and-axle is a form of spinning first-class lever (Figure 17–11). Its fulcrum is always at the

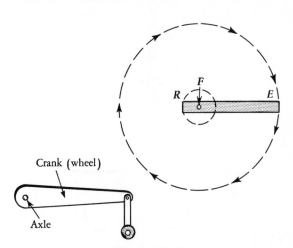

FIGURE 17–11.
THE WHEEL-AND-AXLE IS A SPINNING FIRST-CLASS LEVER.

(wheel) is turned, the shaft (axle) is turned.

Tie three books together with a string and have the children lift the books with the string, noting the force needed to do this. Tie the other end of the string firmly around the shaft of the sharpener, using cellophane tape, if necessary, to keep the string from slipping. Now turn the handle and lift the books. (Holding your forefinger lightly against the string while you turn the handle will help keep the string from slipping off the shaft.)

Note that much less force is needed to lift the books, using the handle. This gain in force is accompanied by a loss in distance and speed because the handle must move many times to raise the books a short distance. Find the ideal mechanical advantage of the pencil sharpener. (The radius of the wheel is the length of the handle, and the radius of the axle is one half the diameter of the shaft.)

Turn the handle of the pencil sharpener until the books are close to the shaft, and then let go of the handle and allow the books to move down. Now the axle is turning the wheel. Note the loss in force, but the large gain in distance and speed as the handle spins rapidly.

center of the axle and the wheel. The radius of the wheel and the radius of the axle are the two arms of the lever. Have the children locate and identify other examples of wheel-and-axle machines. Let them repeat the experiment described above, using some of these examples.

11. *Investigate the fixed pulley* · Screw 2 cup hooks about 10 centimeters (4 in) apart into a long rectangular wood board about 13 millimeters (½ in) thick. Rest the board on the backs of two chairs placed a short distance apart (Figure 17–12). Tie a string around a brick or book and weigh it with a spring balance. Attach a pulley to one cup hook and pass a string around the groove of the pulley. Connect one end of the string to the brick and the other end to a spring balance.

Pull down on the spring balance. Note that the force needed to raise the brick is just about equal to the weight of the brick, so all you have done is to change the direction of your force. Calculate the amount of work done, both input and output. Find the mechanical advantage and determine the efficiency of the fixed pulley.

Draw a diagram to show that the fixed pulley is a form of spinning first-class lever (Figure 17–13). Its fulcrum is at the center of the axle, with the effort and resistance at opposite ends of the wheel. Note that the effort arm and the resistance arm are equal.

12. *Investigate the movable pulley* · Rearrange the pulley as shown in the diagram (Figure 17–14). Pull up on the balance and note

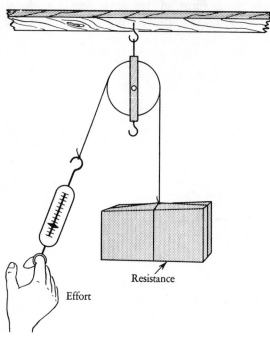

Resistance

Effort

FIGURE 17–12.
A FIXED PULLEY CHANGES DIRECTION.

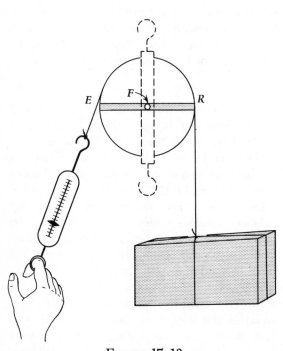

E   F   R

FIGURE 17–13.
A FIXED PULLEY IS A SPINNING FIRST-CLASS LEVER.

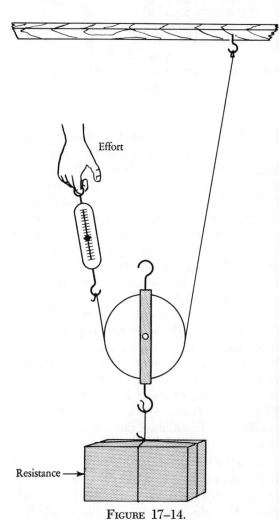

Effort

Resistance →

FIGURE 17–14.
A MOVABLE PULLEY REQUIRES HALF AS MUCH
FORCE AS A FIXED PULLEY.

that only half the force is needed as with the fixed pulley. However, your effort must move twice as far as the distance the brick was lifted. Note that there is now no change in the direction of your force. Calculate the amount of work done, both input and output. Find the ideal and actual mechanical advantage, and determine the efficiency of the movable pulley.

Draw a diagram to show that the movable pulley is a form of spinning second-class lever

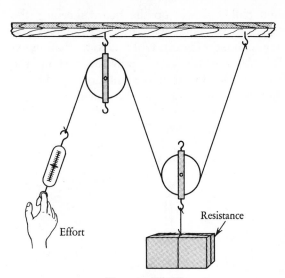

FIGURE 17–16.
A BLOCK AND TACKLE IS A COMBINATION OF A FIXED AND A MOVABLE PULLEY.

(Figure 17–15). Its fulcrum is at one end of the wheel, the effort at the opposite end, and the resistance at the center of the axle. The effort arm is twice as long as the resistance arm.

13. *Make a block and tackle* · Use two pulleys to form a combination fixed and movable pulley, as shown in the diagram (Figure 17–16). Note that there is no difference between this block and tackle and the movable pulley in Learning Activity 12 above as to increase in force, work done, mechanical advantage, and efficiency. The block and tackle gives you increasing force and changing direction at the same time. If possible, repeat, using a double fixed and a double movable pulley.

14. *Discover how the inclined plane works* · Rest one end of a long wood board at least 13 millimeters (½ in) thick on a pile of books so that the board makes an inclined plane. Obtain a toy cart and place some stones in it to give added weight. Tape the stones to the cart so they will not fall out, and then weigh the cart and stones with a spring balance.

Now attach the spring balance to the cart

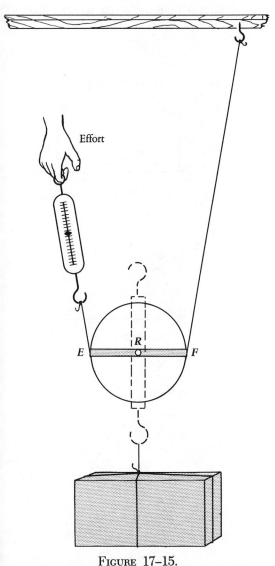

FIGURE 17–15.
A MOVABLE PULLEY IS A SPINNING SECOND-CLASS LEVER.

and pull it slowly up the board, keeping the balance horizontal with the board while you are pulling (Figure 17–17). Note that much less force is needed to pull the cart up the incline than to lift it straight up into the air, but the cart must now be moved a longer

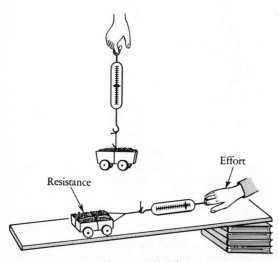

FIGURE 17–17.
LESS FORCE IS NEEDED WITH AN INCLINED PLANE.

distance to reach the same height. Find the height of the inclined plane by measuring the vertical distance from the higher end of the board to the surface upon which the books are resting. Calculate the amount of work done, both input and output. Find the ideal and actual mechanical advantage, and determine the efficiency of the inclined plane.

Make the slope of the inclined plane steeper, either by using a shorter board or by adding more books to the pile. Note the increase in force needed to pull the cart up the incline. Have the children locate and identify examples of inclined planes around them.

15. *Discover how the wedge works* · Make two wedges by sawing diagonally a block of wood 20 centimeters (8 in) long, 10 centimeters (4 in) wide, and 5 centimeters (2 in) thick (Figure 17–18). Hold up one wedge to show that it really is an inclined plane. Place both wedges back to back and form a double inclined plane. Measure the length of the wedge and the thickness of the big end, and then calculate the ideal mechanical advantage. Insert the sharp end of the wedge a short distance under a pile of books and tap the thick end with a hammer, driving the wedge into the books and lifting them. Have the children locate examples of wedges.

16. *Discover how the screw works* · Cut out a right triangle from a sheet of white paper.

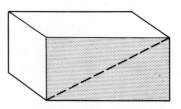

Block of wood

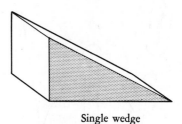

Single wedge

Double wedge
FIGURE 17–18.
MAKING A SINGLE AND A DOUBLE WEDGE.

Make the base of the triangle 20 centimeters (8 in) and the height 10 centimeters (4 in) in length. Hold up the triangle and show that the hypotenuse, or diagonal side, is an inclined plane. Make a heavy black line along the hypotenuse. Starting with the 10-centimeter (4-in) side, wrap the paper around a pencil so that the black line shows up clearly as a

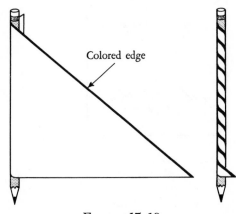

FIGURE 17–19.
A SCREW IS A SPIRAL INCLINED PLANE.

spiral (Figure 17–19). Hold up a large wood screw beside the pencil and show the similarity between the spiral and the screw. Point out the thread of the screw, and then find the pitch by measuring the distance between two threads. Locate and identify examples of screws.

17. *Analyze compound machines* · Have the children identify the simple machines in such everyday compound machines as the scissors, can opener, pencil sharpener, meat grinder, water faucet, and wrench.

18. *Investigate wheels and belts* · Obtain a thick rectangular block of wood and two spools the same size. Place the spools a short distance apart on the wood, insert loose-fitting nails into the holes of the spools, and drive the nails into the wood. Slip a wide rubber band over both spools (Figure 17–20). Have a child give one spool a complete turn. Note that

the other spool also makes a complete turn, moves at the same speed, and turns in the same direction.

Now cross the rubber band so that it makes a figure 8, and have the child give one spool a complete turn again. This time the driven spool will turn in the opposite direction.

Repeat both activities, using a smaller and a larger spool this time. When the larger spool drives the smaller spool and makes one complete turn, the smaller spool turns more than once and moves faster. When the smaller spool drives the larger spool and makes one complete turn, the larger spool turns less than once and moves more slowly. Point out that the fan belt in an automobile is one example of a belt turning a wheel.

19. *Investigate gears with chains* · Turn a bicycle upside down. Push the pedal with your hand and see how it turns the large gear wheel, which turns the chain, which turns the small gear wheel, which then turns the rear bicycle wheel. One turn of the large gear wheel makes the small gear wheel turn more than

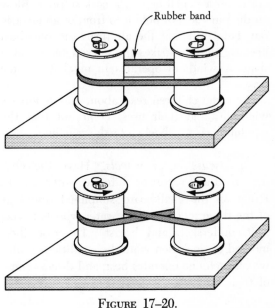

FIGURE 17–20.
A BELT MAKES IT POSSIBLE FOR ONE WHEEL TO TURN ANOTHER WHEEL.

[659

once and move faster. Compare the number of teeth in each gear and find the ideal mechanical advantage.

20. Investigate some gears without chains · Examine a hand-driven egg beater. Operate the beater slowly and see how the teeth of one gear fit into the notches of another gear and make the second gear turn. Note that when the large hand-driven gear makes one complete turn, the twin stirring gears make several turns and move faster. Also, note that the stirring gears move in opposite directions.

Use black crayon to place a mark on each gear. Make one complete turn of the large gear and see how many turns the smaller stirring gears make. Count the number of teeth on the large and small gears, and find the ideal mechanical advantage of the egg beater.

21. Make a pinwheel windmill · Cut out a paper sheet 15 centimeters (6 in) square and make lines and pin holes as shown in Figure 17–21. Cut each line, and then bend in the corners to bring the pin holes in line with the center hole of the paper. Run a pin through the pin holes, and then push the pin into the eraser on a pencil or into a cork stopper. Blow on the pinwheel or hold it in front of an electric fan. Point out that the air turns the pinwheel because the air strikes the curved blades at a slant. A windmill operates in much the same way.

Have the children read about and report on windmills and their uses. Point out that the windmill is a wheel-and-axle machine.

22. Discuss water wheels · Have the children read and report on different water wheels. Draw on the chalkboard simplified drawings of the three most common water wheels (overshot, undershot, and breast). Describe their method of operation, note the conditions under which each one operates best, and discuss some of their uses.

23. Investigate the water turbine · Repeat Activity 18 of "Water," Chapter 11 (p. 376),

on how a water turbine operates. Discuss the uses of the water turbine and compare it with the water wheel.

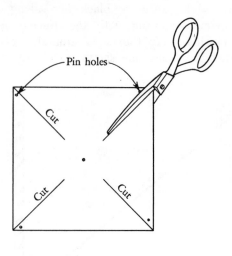

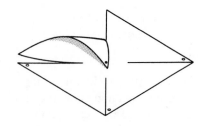

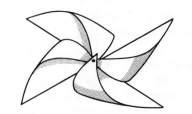

FIGURE 17–21.
MAKING A WINDMILL.

24. Discuss the steam engine · Have children read about and discuss the steam engine. Draw a diagram or construct a cardboard model of the engine and show how each part operates. Simple reproductions of the steam engine can be found in most general science textbooks. Discuss the uses of the steam engine and list its advantages and drawbacks.

25. Investigate the steam turbine · Repeat Activity 19 of "Water," Chapter 11 (p. 377), on how a steam turbine operates. Discuss the uses of the steam turbine and compare it with the water turbine.

26. Discover how the carburetor works · Place some alcohol or lighter fluid in an atomizer and spray the fluid into the air to show how quickly it becomes a vapor when it is broken up into tiny droplets. Now spray the fluid over a candle flame 15 centimeters (6 in) away, and note the vigorous almost explosive, flame produced by the rapid-burning fluid (Figure 17–22). (*Caution!* Keep the children well away from the candle!) Point out that the carburetor in an automobile also changes the gasoline into a vapor and mixes it with air to make a rapid-burning mixture.

27. Investigate gasoline engines · Draw models of gasoline engine cylinders. Include cylinders of both the older four-stroke cycle engine and the newer rotary engine. Excellent reproductions of the cycles of both kinds of engines can be found in most general science textbooks. Demonstrate the positions of the pistons and valves during a complete cycle in each engine. Discuss the advantages and the drawbacks of each engine.

28. Investigate the Diesel engine · Draw some models of Diesel engine cylinders. Demonstrate the strokes of both the older four-stroke cycle and the newer two-stroke cycle Diesel engines. Compare the cylinder operation of the Diesel engine with that of the gasoline engine. Discuss the advantages and drawbacks of the Diesel engine.

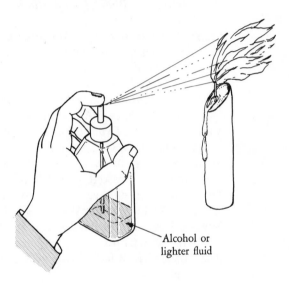

Alcohol or lighter fluid

FIGURE 17–22.
SPRAYED FUEL PRODUCES A VIGOROUS FLAME.

BIBLIOGRAPHY FOR "FRICTION AND MACHINES"

BUEHR, WALTER. *The First Book of Machines.* New York: Franklin Watts, 1965. 69 pp.

CORBETT, SCOTT. *What About the Wankel Engine?* New York: Four Winds Press, 1974. 72 pp.

DEVERE, NICHOLAS. *The Book of Fantastic Cars.* New York: Western Pub., 1975. 32 pp.

EPSTEIN, SAM, and BERYL EPSTEIN. *All About Engines and Power*. New York: Random House, 1965. 144 pp.

JAMES, ELIZABETH, and CAROL BARKIN. *The Simple Facts of Simple Machines*. New York: William Morrow, 1975. 64 pp.

KAUFMANN, JOHN. *Streamlined*. New York: Thomas Y. Crowell, 1974. 40 pp.

KNIGHT, DAVID. *From Log Roller to Lunar Rover*. New York: Parents' Magazine, 1971. 64 pp.

LEFKOWITZ, R. J. *Push! Pull! Stop! Go!: A Book About Forces and Motion*. New York: Parents' Magazine, 1975. 64 pp.

MEYER, JEROME. *Engines*. Cleveland: World Pub., 1965. 78 pp.

———. *Machines*. Cleveland: World Pub., 1965. 64 pp.

MITGUSCH, ALI. *World on Wheels*. New York: Western Pub., 1975. 48 pp.

ROCKWELL, ANNE, and HARLOW ROCKWELL. *Machines*. New York: Macmillan, 1972. 140 pp.

RUSH, JEAN. *The Book of Fantastic Machines*. New York: Western Pub., 1974. 32 pp.

SHARP, ELIZABETH. *Simple Machines and How They Work*. New York: Random House, 1966. 84 pp.

URQUART, DAVID. *The Bicycle and How It Works*. New York: Henry Z. Walck, 1972. 48 pp.

———. *The Internal Combustion Machine and How It Works*. New York: Henry Z. Walck, 1973. 48 pp.

VICTOR, EDWARD. *Exploring and Understanding Machines*. Westchester, Ill.: Benefic Press, 1969. 96 pp.

WEISS, HARVEY. *Motors and Engines and How They Work*. New York: Thomas Y. Crowell, 1969. 62 pp.

WIESENTHAL, ELEANOR, and TED WIESENTHAL. *Let's Find Out About Tools*. New York: Franklin Watts, 1969. 48 pp.

WYLER, ROSE, and GERALD AMES. *What Makes It Go?* New York: McGraw-Hill, 1965. 64 pp.

ZIM, HERBERT S. *What's Inside of Engines?* New York: William Morrow, 1966. 32 pp.

——— and JAMES R. SKELLY. *Machine Tools*. New York: William Morrow, 1969. 79 pp.

——— and ———. *Tractors*. New York: William Morrow, 1972. 64 pp.

ZINER, FEENIE. *About Wonderful Wheels*. Chicago: Childrens Press, 1966. 24 pp.

CHAPTER 18

HEAT, FIRE, *and* FUELS

THE NATURE OF HEAT

I. KINETIC THEORY OF HEAT

A. All materials, or substances, are made of tiny particles, called **molecules.**

B. These molecules are always moving.

C. The movement of these molecules is called **heat.**

D. The energy that these molecules have is called **kinetic energy (energy of motion).**
1. The faster the molecules of a material are made to move, the more kinetic energy they have, and the hotter the material becomes.
2. The slower the molecules of a material move, the less kinetic energy they have, and the cooler the material becomes.

E. Heat, then, is a form of energy. It is the energy of moving molecules.

II. SOURCES OF HEAT ENERGY

A. **Heat energy** can be produced from at least five other kinds of energy.

B. Heat energy can be produced from the **mechanical energy** of friction, compression, or percussion.
1. When two surfaces are rubbed together, friction makes the molecules move faster, and the materials become hotter.
2. When molecules of gas are crowded together, or compressed, heat is produced.

3. When a hammer pounds a piece of iron, the molecules of iron move faster and have more kinetic energy, so the iron becomes warmer.

C. Heat energy can be produced from **chemical energy.**
1. When two materials react chemically, often the chemical energy that is released is changed, or transformed, into heat.
2. The burning of fuels, such as oil, gas, coal, and wood, is a chemical action that produces heat.

D. Heat energy can be produced from **electrical energy.**
1. When an electric current flows through a thin wire of a light bulb or a toaster, heat is given off.
2. The resistance of the wire to the flow of electric current produces heat.

E. Heat energy can be produced from the **radiant energy** of the sun or other glowing materials.
1. The sun is our chief source of heat, either directly from the sun itself or indirectly as a result of the sun's energy stored up in fuels.
2. Radiant energy, then, is our chief source of heat energy on earth.

F. Heat energy can be produced from **atomic** or **nuclear energy.**
1. Scientists have discovered that the nu-

cleus of the atom is a tremendous store-house of energy.

2. When the nucleus of an atom is split, either naturally or artificially, this nuclear energy can be transformed into vast amounts of heat energy.

III. EFFECT OF HEAT UPON CHANGES IN THE STATE OF MATTER

A. All materials are found in any one of three forms, or **states**, of matter: solid, liquid, or gas.

1. In gases the molecules have very much energy. They move very fast and are very far apart.

2. In liquids the molecules have less energy. They move less quickly and are closer together.

3. In solids the molecules have much less energy. They are very close together, and each molecule seems to vibrate at one spot rather than move about.

B. Water is a material that we can usually find in all three forms, or states.

1. As ice it is in the form of a solid.

2. As water it is in the form of a liquid.

3. As water vapor it is in the form of a gas.

C. We can bring about a change in state of a material by heating or cooling the material.

D. If we add enough heat energy to a solid, the solid becomes a liquid.

1. The added heat energy makes the molecules in the solid vibrate more and more quickly until they finally break away and move about freely and are farther apart, as in a liquid.

2. When this condition occurs we say the solid melts, and the temperature at which melting takes place is called the **melting point.**

3. Every solid has its own melting point.

E. If we take enough heat energy away from a liquid, the liquid becomes a solid.

1. Taking away heat energy makes the molecules move more slowly and come closer together until they are very close

together, and each molecule vibrates at one spot rather than moves about.

2. When this condition occurs we say the liquid freezes, and the temperature at which freezing takes place is called the **freezing point.**

3. Every liquid has its own freezing point, but usually a material has the same melting and freezing points, depending upon whether heat is being added or taken away.

4. Butter is an exception to this rule, having a different melting and freezing point. It melts at a higher temperature and freezes at a lower temperature.

F. If we add enough heat energy to a liquid, the liquid becomes a gas.

1. The added heat energy makes the molecules in the liquid move more quickly and stay farther apart until they are moving very quickly and are very far apart, as in a gas.

2. When this condition occurs we say the liquid evaporates, or turns into a gas or vapor.

3. Evaporation takes place at all temperatures, but, if a liquid is heated hot enough, at a certain temperature bubbles of gas form, which rise to the surface of the liquid.

4. When bubbles form in this way, we say that the liquid boils, and the temperature at which boiling occurs is called the **boiling point.**

5. Every liquid has its own boiling point.

G. If we take enough heat energy away from a gas, the gas becomes a liquid.

1. Taking away heat energy makes the gas molecules move more slowly and come closer together until the gas condenses, or turns into a liquid.

2. Every gas has its own temperature at which it will become a liquid.

3. Usually a material boils or goes from a gas to a liquid at the same temperature, depending upon whether heat is being added or taken away.

IV. EXPANSION AND CONTRACTION

A. When materials are heated, the molecules move faster and spread farther apart so that the materials become bigger, or **expand.**
B. When materials are cooled, the molecules move more slowly and come closer together so that the materials become smaller, or **contract.**
C. The rate of expansion and contraction is different for solids, liquids, and gases.
   1. In solids the molecules are very close together and seem to vibrate rather than move, so solids expand and contract the least.
   2. In liquids the molecules move about quickly and are farther apart, so liquids can expand and contract more than solids.
   3. In gases the molecules move about very quickly and are very far apart, so gases expand and contract the most.
D. The rate of expansion and contraction differs between solids and between liquids.
   1. Because the molecules in all solids at the same temperature do not move at the same speed, some solids expand and contract more than other solids.
   2. The same is true of liquids.
   3. In gases the molecules are so far apart and move so fast that they all expand and contract about the same.

V. EXCEPTIONS TO THE RULE OF EXPANSION AND CONTRACTION

A. Almost all materials expand when heated and contract when cooled.
B. Water is an exception to this rule.
   1. When water is cooled, it contracts until its temperature reaches 4 degrees Celsius (39 degrees Fahrenheit).
   2. From 4 degrees Celsius (39 degrees Fahrenheit) down to the freezing point of water, 0 degrees Celsius (32 degrees Fahrenheit), water expands slightly.

   3. Because water also expands as it freezes, ice is lighter than water and floats on top of the water.
   4. This unusual form of expansion explains why the water in a lake freezes from the top down rather than from the bottom up.
   5. This unusual form of expansion also explains why water pipes burst when the temperature is below freezing.
C. Rubber is also an exception to the rule because it contracts when heated gently and expands when cooled.

VI. EXPANSION AND CONTRACTION IN OUR DAILY LIFE

A. When the metal lid of a glass jar is stuck tight, hot water makes the lid expand more than the jar, and the lid can unscrew easily.
B. When two glass tumblers are stuck, one inside the other, they can be loosened by pouring hot water on the outside tumbler while filling the inside tumbler with cold water.
C. When baking powder is used in baking a cake, carbon dioxide gas forms inside the dough and expands when heated, causing the cake to rise.
D. Telephone wires that are strung in summer are allowed to sag a little so that the wires can contract in winter.
E. Engineers place one end of a bridge on rollers to allow for expansion and contraction of the bridge in summer and winter.
F. Railroad tracks are laid with a small space between the end of one rail and the beginning of the next rail to allow the rails to expand and contract when the temperature changes.
G. Workmen leave small spaces between slabs of concrete road and sidewalk so that the concrete will not expand and bulge in the summer or contract and crack in the winter.

H. Metal rivets used in construction are hammered into place while red hot so that, when they cool, they will contract and pull the parts together with great force.

I. A blacksmith fits an iron rim on a wagon wheel when the rim is very hot so that, when the rim cools, it will contract and fit very tightly on the wheel.

J. Some thermometers have liquids inside them, which expand and rise up the thermometer tube when they are heated, and then contract and fall down the tube when they are cooled.

K. Thermostats and metallic thermometers contain a bar or coil made of strips of two different metals that expand at different rates, causing the bar or coil to turn when heated or cooled.

TEMPERATURE

I. TEMPERATURE

A. **Temperature** describes how hot or cold a material is.

B. Temperature has nothing to do with the amount of heat a material has; it only has to do with the degree of "hotness" or "coldness" of the material.

C. Temperature depends upon the speed that the molecules in a material are moving.
   1. The faster the molecules are moving, the hotter the material becomes, and the higher the temperature of the material will be.
   2. The slower the molecules move, the colder the material becomes, and the lower its temperature will be.

II. MEASUREMENT OF TEMPERATURE

A. A **thermometer** is used to measure temperature.

B. The operation of a thermometer depends upon the principle that materials expand when they are heated and contract when they are cooled.

C. The thermometer we commonly use to measure temperature is a sealed glass tube with a liquid such as mercury or colored alcohol in it.
   1. There is a very narrow, hollow passageway running up and down the tube. This passageway is called the **bore.**

   2. At the bottom of the bore is a bulb that contains the liquid.
   3. The liquid is also part of the way up the bore.
   4. When the liquid inside the bulb is heated, it expands and rises up the bore.
   5. When the liquid is cooled, it contracts and goes down the bore.

III. TEMPERATURE SCALES

A. A **scale** on the thermometer tells us just how high the liquid is in the thermometer, and gives us the temperature of whatever is around the bulb.

B. The scale on a thermometer is divided into many equal lines, or divisions, called **degrees.**

C. The degree (°) is the unit of measurement of temperature.

D. The two common temperature scales are the **Fahrenheit** scale and the **Celsius** scale.

E. In the Fahrenheit scale the freezing point of water registers at 32° and the boiling point of water registers at 212°.
   1. There are 180 lines, or divisions, between the freezing point and boiling point of water.
   2. Zero on the Fahrenheit scale is the lowest temperature the inventor (Fahrenheit) could get from a mixture of salt and ice in water.

3. The Fahrenheit scale is used by a few English-speaking countries.

F. In the Celsius scale, formerly called the Centigrade scale, the freezing point of water is at 0° and the boiling point of water is at 100°.

1. There are 100 lines, or divisions, between the freezing point and boiling point of water.

2. The rest of the world and all scientists use the Celsius scale.

G. It is possible to change from the Fahrenheit scale to the Celsius scale, and vice-versa.

1. Because there are 180 Fahrenheit degrees and 100 Celsius degrees between the freezing and boiling points of water, 1° F is equal to $^{100}/_{180}$, or $\frac{5}{9}$° C; and 1° C is equal to $^{180}/_{100}$, or $\frac{9}{5}$° F.

2. Also, because 0° on the Celsius scale is the same as 32° on the Fahrenheit scale, we must always *subtract* 32° when changing from the Fahrenheit to the Celsius scale, and always *add* 32° when changing from the Celsius to the Fahrenheit scale.

3. So, to change from °F to °C, subtract 32° from the Fahrenheit reading and multiply the result by $\frac{5}{9}$.

$$C = (F - 32) \times \frac{5}{9}$$

4. To change from °C to °F, multiply the Celsius reading by $\frac{9}{5}$ and add 32°.

$$F = \frac{9}{5}C + 32$$

IV. KINDS OF THERMOMETERS

A. *Mercury thermometer*

1. This thermometer has mercury, the only liquid metal at room temperature, in it.

2. Because mercury has a high boiling point (about 357° C or 675° F), the mercury thermometer is used to measure fairly high temperatures.

3. However, mercury freezes at −40° Celsius (−40° F), so it cannot be used to measure very low temperatures.

B. *Alcohol thermometer*

1. An alcohol thermometer looks and operates exactly like the mercury thermometer, except that alcohol—colored red or blue—is in the bulb and tube.

2. Because alcohol has a boiling point lower than water (about 78° C or 172° F), the alcohol thermometer cannot be used to measure high temperatures.

3. However, alcohol has a very low freezing point (about −130° C or −202° F), so the alcohol thermometer is used in arctic and polar regions.

4. Most indoor and outdoor household thermometers are alcohol thermometers.

C. *Clinical thermometer*

1. The clinical thermometer is a mercury thermometer, but is shorter than the regular mercury thermometer.

2. Its scale runs only from 33° C to 43° C (92° F to 110° F).

3. The bore, or hollow passageway, of this thermometer is very narrow so that even one tenth of a degree will make a big difference in the level of the mercury and can easily be read.

4. At one spot inside the bore there is a narrow bend or pinch.

5. When the clinical thermometer is placed inside a person's mouth, the mercury is heated and expands, pushing its way up and beyond this pinch to give the proper temperature reading.

6. When the thermometer is removed, however, the mercury cannot fall back through the pinch, so the level of the mercury stays at the temperature of the person's body.

7. This stationary position allows the doctor to get an accurate reading of the person's body temperature.

8. The only way to force the mercury down the tube again, past the pinch, is to shake the thermometer quite vigorously a few times.

[667

D. *Metal thermometer*
1. This thermometer does not have a glass tube, bulb, or liquid in it.
2. It has a small coil made of two strips of metal welded together along their lengths.
3. The inside strip of metal is usually brass, and the outside strip is steel.
4. When the coil is heated or cooled, the brass strip expands and contracts more than the steel strip, and makes the coil twist.
5. As the coil twists, a pointer connected to one end of the coil moves across a scale that is marked off in degrees.

V. Uses of Thermometers

A. Thermometers are used in the home to take the temperature indoors or outdoors, to take body temperature, and to test the temperature of cooking food.
B. Thermometers are used in industry by dairies, ice cream manufacturers, candy manufacturers, florists, and all organizations that use scientists.

VI. Measurement of the Amount of Heat

A. There are two units commonly used to measure the amount of heat: the **British thermal unit** (**Btu**) and the **calorie.**
B. The British thermal unit is the amount of heat needed to raise the temperature of 1 pound of water 1 degree on the Fahrenheit scale.
C. The calorie is the amount of heat needed to raise the temperature of 1 gram (about 3½ hundredths of an ounce by weight) of water 1 degree on the Celsius scale.
1. This calorie is called the **small calorie** and is spelled with a small "c."
2. The large **Calorie**, spelled with a capital "C," is equal to 1000 small calories.
3. We use large Calories to find out how much heat energy we get from different foods.

METHODS OF HEAT TRAVEL AND THEIR EFFECTS

I. Heat Can Travel by Conduction

A. When a material such as a metal rod is heated, the molecules next to the source of heat move faster.
B. The molecules bump into other molecules, making them move faster.
C. These molecules then bump into still other molecules, making them move faster too.
D. In this way all the molecules in the material are made to move faster and have more kinetic energy, so the material becomes hotter.
E. The heat energy has been passed, or conducted, from molecule to molecule within the material, yet the material itself does not move.
F. This method of heat travel, where energy is passed along from molecule to molecule by bumping, or collision, is called **conduction.**
G. Any material through which heat travels is called a **conductor.**
1. Metals are good heat conductors.
2. Good heat conductors are also good conductors of electricity.
3. In good heat conductors the molecules are very close together and conduct the heat energy from molecule to molecule very quickly and easily.
4. Some metals, such as silver and copper, are better heat conductors than other metals.
H. Materials that do not conduct heat very well are called **nonconductors,** or **poor conductors.**
1. Most nonmetals, liquids, and gases are poor conductors of heat.

2. In poor heat conductors the molecules are farther apart and do not conduct the heat energy from molecule to molecule quickly or easily.

I. A vacuum cannot conduct heat because there are no molecules to pass along the heat energy.

J. When a nonconductor is used to stop the conduction of heat, it is called an **insulator.**
   1. Pot and pan handles are covered with insulators made of wood or plastic.
   2. Rubber and cloth are also used as insulators.
   3. Because air is a very poor heat conductor, anything with air spaces in it, such as wool or cork, is a good insulator.

II. HEAT CAN TRAVEL BY CONVECTION

A. **Convection** is a method of heat travel that takes place only in gases and liquids, which are called fluids.

B. When a fluid such as air is heated, the molecules move faster and spread farther apart so that the air expands.
   1. When air expands, it becomes lighter.
   2. The colder air above it is heavier, and gravity pulls down harder on the colder, heavier air than on the warmer, lighter air.
   3. Because of this greater pull of gravity, the cold air moves down and pushes the warm air upward.
   4. This cold air in turn is heated, expands, becomes lighter, and is pushed upward by colder, heavier air above it.
   5. In this way continuous currents of rising and falling air are produced.
   6. The same currents are produced with a fluid such as water.

C. Convection, then, is a method of heat travel where the molecules of heated gas or liquid actually move from one place to another.
   1. The heat is carried from a place of higher temperature to a place of lower temperature by the molecules of moving gas or liquid.

2. The movement of the gas or liquid is called a **convection current.**
3. There can be no convection currents in a vacuum.

III. HEAT CAN TRAVEL BY RADIATION

A. **Radiation** as a method of heat travel is very different from conduction and convection because it has nothing to do with the passing of heat by moving molecules.

B. The sun and other glowing bodies give off, or radiate, energy in the form of invisible waves.
   1. These radiant energy waves travel out into space without the help of molecules.
   2. When the radiant energy strikes a solid, opaque material, the energy is absorbed and makes the molecules in the material move faster so the material becomes hotter.
   3. The radiant energy is not heat, but becomes heat when it is absorbed.
   4. The sun heats the earth 150 million kilometers (93 million mi) away this way.

C. This method of passing along heat by radiant energy waves is called **radiation.**

D. The kind of material decides how much radiant energy is changed into heat.
   1. Dark, rough materials are good absorbers of radiant energy and produce much heat.
   2. Light, smooth materials reflect most of the radiant energy that strikes them, and so do not produce much heat at all.
   3. Transparent materials, such as air and glass, allow almost all of the radiant energy to pass through them, so these materials produce little or no heat.

E. Radiant heat waves are part of a family of radiant energy waves called **electromagnetic waves.**
   1. This family includes radio waves, infrared rays or heat waves, light rays, ultraviolet rays, X-rays, gamma rays, and cosmic rays.
   2. All these waves travel at a speed of 300,000 kilomters (186,000 mi) a second,

but they all differ in the length of their waves and in the number of times a second these waves vibrate (their frequency).

IV. HEATING THE HOME

A. *The fireplace*
  1. When a fire is started in a fireplace, the heat of the fire warms the air in the fireplace and the air in the chimney.
  2. A convection current is produced, which moves through the fireplace and up the chimney.
  3. This convection current removes cold air from the floor, but the current also carries much of the heat of the fire up the chimney.
  4. The heat that warms the room is mostly radiant heat, where the radiant energy from the fire is absorbed by the walls, furniture, and other materials in the room.

B. *The stove*
  1. The heat from the fire in the stove passes through the metal walls by conduction, and also into the air next to the walls by conduction.
  2. The heated air sets up a convection current that heats the whole room.
  3. The hot walls of the stove radiate some heat as well.
  4. Gas, oil, kerosene, coal, and wood can be used as fuel for a stove.
  5. Today most stoves use gas or electricity, for cooking purposes only.

C. *Central heating systems*
  1. Most homes and buildings are heated by central heating systems.
  2. In central heating systems the stove, or furnace, is located in the basement or utility room.
  3. The heat is conducted from the furnace to the rooms by pipes or ducts.
  4. The most commonly used central heating systems today are: the **hot-air, hot-water, steam,** and **radiant heating** systems.

D. *The hot-air heating system*

1. In the hot-air heating system the furnace is surrounded by a brick or iron jacket filled with air.
2. The furnace heats the jacket by conduction, and the jacket heats the air by conduction.
3. The hot air inside the jacket is pushed up either by cold air entering at the bottom of the furnace or by a fan.
4. The hot air goes up the pipes into the different rooms in the house.
5. The hot air comes into each room through a metal grating, or register, in the floor or the walls.
6. The air circulates through the rooms and heats them by convection.
7. Then the air is either carried back to the furnace through a cold-air return so that it can be reheated, or the air is allowed to escape and is replaced by fresh air from outdoors.

E. *The hot-water heating system*
  1. In the hot-water heating system the furnace is surrounded by a boiler filled with water.
  2. When the water is heated, it is pushed up by cold water entering the bottom of a boiler.
  3. The hot water goes up the pipes into the different rooms in the house.
  4. The hot water goes into a metal radiator in each room.
  5. The radiator is divided into many sections of hollow pipe so that the radiator exposes a great deal of surface to the air.
  6. The hot water heats the walls of the radiator by conduction.
  7. The radiator walls heat the air next to them by conduction.
  8. The hot air then heats the room by convection.
  9. At the same time the radiator radiates some heat as well.
  10. After the hot water in the radiator gives up its heat and becomes cooler, it goes back to the boiler through return pipes and is reheated.

11. The same water is used over and over again.

F. *The steam heating system*
1. The steam heating system works very much like the hot-water heating system except that steam is used instead of hot water.
2. The boiler is only partly filled with water.
3. When the water is heated, it is changed into water vapor or "steam."
4. The steam has great pressure and is forced up the pipes into the radiators.
5. When the steam gives up its heat to the radiators, it condenses back into water, which goes down the pipes to the boiler, where it is reheated.

G. *The radiant heating system*
1. In this system hot water is circulated through copper pipes located in the floor or walls.
2. The hot water heats the pipes by conduction.
3. The pipes heat the floors and walls by conduction.
4. The floors and walls radiate much heat energy, and this radiant energy heats the people and furniture in the room.

H. *Solar heating*
1. In some parts of the country the sun is used to furnish part of the heat needed for the home.
2. The sides of the building facing the sun are mostly large glass windows.
3. Radiant energy from the sun passes through the windows into the rooms, where the radiant energy is absorbed and changed into heat.
4. Solar heating works well on clear days when it is not too cold or windy.
5. At night a regular heating system must be used.

I. *The heat pump system*
1. The heat pump system gets its heat from the earth.
2. A pump run by an electric motor makes water flow through long pipes in the earth outside the house.

3. The flowing water takes heat from the earth and brings it into the house.
4. In the summer the pump cools the house by having the flowing water take heat from the house and bring it to the earth outside.

V. INSULATING THE HOME

A. There are three ways in which heat is lost in the home.
1. Heat is conducted through the windows, walls, and roof.
2. Heat is radiated through the windows.
3. Heat escapes by convection through cracks around doors and windows.
B. This heat loss can be prevented in many ways.
C. Insulating materials can be used in the walls and under the roof.
1. These materials, such as rock wool or glass wool, have many air spaces in them, and are nonconductors, or **insulators.**
2. These materials stop heat from being conducted out through the walls and roof.
D. Storm windows, when fitted over regular windows, create an air space between the two windows.
1. Air is a poor conductor of heat and acts as an insulator.
2. This insulation prevents the windows from conducting heat out of the house.
E. Weather strips or special materials, when placed around windows and doors, stop heat from escaping through any cracks that might be present.
F. Insulation not only stops heat from leaving the house in the winter, but helps keep heat from getting into the house in the summer.

VI. COOLING IN THE HOME

A. *The refrigerator*
1. The refrigerator cools by taking heat away from materials.

2. The refrigerator has a pipe running through it.
3. Inside the pipe is a gas called **Freon,** which is changed into a liquid very easily when it is compressed.
4. In the electric refrigerator a motor runs a compressor, which compresses the Freon and takes heat away from it until the gas becomes a liquid.
5. The heat that is taken away from the gas passes out into the air of the room.
6. The liquid Freon then flows under pressure through the pipe in the refrigerator until it reaches the ice cube or freezer compartment.
7. Here the pressure is taken away from the liquid Freon so that the liquid evaporates into a gas again.
8. When a liquid evaporates, it needs heat, and takes this heat from the space surrounding the liquid.
9. Taking heat away will cool the materials in the space surrounding the liquid that is evaporating.
10. The Freon gas then continues to the motor and compressor, where it is turned into a liquid again.

B. *The deep freeze*
1. Special refrigeration machines freeze food quickly until the temperature of the food in the machines is 10 to 20 degrees below zero Fahrenheit.
2. The freezing must be quick, or else the food will lose much of its flavor and consistency.

3. When food is frozen, the water in the food freezes and forms ice crystals.
4. When food, especially fruits and vegetables, is frozen slowly, the ice crystals are large and break the cells of the food, killing their taste and flavor.
5. When the food is frozen quickly, the ice crystals are very small and do not break the food cells.

VII. Air Conditioning

A. An efficient air conditioner accomplishes four things.
1. It cools the air in the room.
2. It lowers the amount of water vapor (humidity) in the air.
3. It cleans the air.
4. It supplies fresh air and removes stale air.
B. The air conditioner has a cooling unit that acts just like a refrigerator.
1. The warm air passes through the cooling unit, and the heat is taken away from the air.
2. This heat is passed on to the air outdoors, which carries it away.
C. A special dehumidifying apparatus helps the excess water vapor in the air condense out as the air is cooled.
D. The air is blown by a fan through a filter, which removes dust and pollen.
E. The air conditioner usually has a fresh-air connection, which provides the conditioner with fresh outdoor air.

FIRE

I. The Nature of Fire

A. Fire is the burning of a material, and is also called **combustion.**
B. Fire is a chemical change that takes place when certain materials combine rapidly with oxygen to give off heat and light.

C. This chemical reaction, which takes place when a material combines with oxygen, is called **oxidation.**
D. Materials can also combine slowly with oxygen and produce some heat, but no light.
1. This combination is oxidation, too, but

it is a **slow** oxidation and is not called burning or combustion.

2. The rusting of iron is an example of slow oxidation.

3. To be called burning, the oxidation must be **fast** enough to produce both heat and light.

II. FACTORS NECESSARY TO PRODUCE FIRE

A. For burning to take place, three things are needed: **fuel, oxygen,** and **heat.**

B. A fire needs a material that will burn, which is called a **fuel.**

C. A fire needs **oxygen.**

1. Oxygen is one of the gases in the air.

2. The more oxygen a fuel gets, the faster the oxidation will take place, and the hotter the fire will become.

3. Supplying the fire with more air will give the fuel more oxygen.

4. Breaking the fuel into small pieces will expose more of the fuel's surface to the air, and in this way give the fuel more oxygen.

5. If a fuel is broken up into pieces so small that the pieces look like particles of dust, the fuel may combine with the oxygen so quickly that it will produce an explosion.

D. A fire needs enough heat to get the fuel hot enough to burn.

1. Some materials burn more easily than others.

2. We say that these materials have a lower kindling temperature.

3. The **kindling temperature** is the lowest temperature at which a material will catch fire and burn.

4. At this temperature the oxygen will combine quickly enough with the fuel to keep the chemical reaction going steadily.

5. Materials like phosphorus, sulfur, and paper have a low kindling temperature, and burst into flame easily.

6. Materials like wood and coal have a high kindling temperature and must be quite hot before they will burn.

III. THE PRODUCTS OF FIRE

A. Fire produces a **flame.**

1. A flame is a mass of **burning gas.**

2. Some fuels produce a flame directly, but other fuels must be partially changed into a gas before they can burn with a flame.

3. A gaseous fuel, such as natural gas, burns directly to produce a flame.

4. A liquid fuel, such as gasoline or kerosene, must be heated until it turns into a gas before it will burn.

5. Some solid fuels, like paraffin, first melt and then turn into a gas before they can burn.

6. Other solid fuels, like wood and coal, when heated will give off gases that burn.

B. The color of the flame depends upon how much oxygen the fuel is getting.

1. When a fuel gets all the oxygen it needs and burns completely, the flame is blue and is very hot.

2. When a fuel does not get enough oxygen to burn completely, the flame is yellow or orange and is not as hot as a blue flame.

3. The flame is yellow because the particles of unburned fuel are glowing.

C. A candle flame has three parts to it.

1. The center of the flame around the wick is dark, showing the presence of unburned gas.

2. Almost all the rest of the flame is yellow, which shows that the gas is burning but is not getting all the oxygen it needs.

3. Around the edges the flame is blue or colorless, which shows that here the gas is getting all the oxygen it needs and is burning completely.

D. Fire produces water vapor and carbon dioxide or carbon monoxide gas.

[673

1. Most common fuels contain the chemical elements carbon and hydrogen.
2. When the fuel burns, the hydrogen combines with the oxygen to form water vapor.
3. Water vapor forms instead of liquid water because so much heat is given off during the burning.
4. When the fuel has all the oxygen it needs and burns completely, the carbon combines with the oxygen to form carbon dioxide gas.
5. When the fuel does not get enough oxygen, the carbon combines with the oxygen to form carbon monoxide gas instead.
6. Carbon monoxide gas is made up of less oxygen than carbon dioxide gas.

E. **Smoke** is unburned fuel.
1. Smoke is made up of particles of carbon that did not receive enough oxygen to make them burn completely.
2. When smoke collects on walls or in chimneys, it is called **soot**.

F. Some fuels leave behind an **ash**, which is part of the fuel that does not ordinarily burn.

IV. Spontaneous Combustion

A. Sometimes materials burst into flame all by themselves.
1. This phenomenon is called **spontaneous combustion.**
2. Spontaneous combustion takes place when a slow oxidation is going on in a closed space where the air cannot circulate or escape.

B. An oily rag in a closed closet can often burst into flame by spontaneous combustion.
1. The oil combines with oxygen, or oxidizes, slowly and gives off a small amount of heat.
2. This heat cannot escape because the closet is closed and there is no movement of air to carry the heat away.
3. The heat makes the oil combine with oxygen more quickly, which produces more heat, which cannot escape and so makes the oil combine with oxygen even more quickly.
4. This process goes on and on, producing more and more heat, until the kindling point of the cloth rag is reached, and the rag bursts into flame.

C. If green or wet hay is stored in a barn, spontaneous combustion may take place because the damp hay ferments and gives off heat.

V. Factors Necessary to Put Out Fire

A. To put out a fire we must take away one or more of the three things needed to make a fire.
1. We can remove the fuel.
2. We can cut off the supply of oxygen.
3. We can cool the burning fuel, making its temperature lower than the kindling point.

B. The most common methods of putting out fires try to cut off the supply of oxygen and lower the temperature.

C. Removing the fuel is practical only with a small fire, such as a camp fire or a fire in a waste basket.

D. The supply of oxygen can be cut off by using sand, dirt, a heavy wool blanket or coat, water, carbon dioxide gas, and any other material that will not burn.

E. The temperature can be lowered by using water or any other cool material that will not burn.

VI. Fire Extinguishers

A. Fire extinguishers use chemicals to put out fires by cutting off the supply of oxygen and by cooling the burning fuel.

B. The **soda-acid** fire extinguisher, when turned upside down, mixes two chemicals together to form carbon dioxide gas.
1. The carbon dioxide gas smothers the fire by cutting off the supply of oxygen.
2. This type of extinguisher has water in

it, and cannot be used to put out oil fires because the water is heavier than oil and sinks to the bottom while the burning oil floats and even spreads out further on top of the water.

3. This type of extinguisher also cannot be used to put out electrical fires because the solution of chemicals in the extinguisher is a good conductor of electricity.

C. The **carbon dioxide** extinguisher is used for putting out oil and electrical fires.

1. The extinguisher has compressed liquid carbon dioxide in it.

2. When the liquid carbon dioxide goes out of the extinguisher, it turns into large amounts of very cold carbon dioxide gas.

3. The carbon dioxide gas puts out the fire by cutting off the supply of oxygen and by cooling the burning fuel.

D. The **carbon tetrachloride** extinguisher is also used to put out oil and electrical fires.

1. Liquid carbon tetrachloride is pumped out of the extinguisher.

2. The flames heat the liquid carbon tetrachloride and turn it into a heavy blanket of gas, which pushes the air away from the fire and smothers it.

E. The **foam-type** extinguisher is very effective against gasoline and large oil fires.

1. It works very much like the soda-acid extinguisher, but it also has a foam-making material, such as licorice extract, in it.

2. When the extinguisher is turned upside down, the chemicals mix together and produce a tough foamy mass of carbon dioxide bubbles.

3. This foamy mass of bubbles covers the burning gasoline or oil and shuts off the supply of oxygen.

VII. SOME SAFETY RULES FOR FIRES

A. Keep matches away from heat.

B. Keep matches away from small children.

C. If you have to strike a match, strike away from you and not toward you.

D. Be sure the flame is out when you throw the match away.

E. Surround a campfire with stones, bricks, or bare earth.

F. Be especially careful when making a campfire on a windy day.

G. Put out the campfire thoroughly when you do not want it any more.

H. Never use gasoline to start a fire.

I. Put a metal screen in front of the fireplace.

J. Put hot ashes in metal containers only.

K. Do not allow trash that will burn to pile up in the basement or attic.

L. Do not put oily rags in closets or other places where there is no circulation of air.

M. If a container has materials in it that will burn, keep it away from heat or an open flame.

N. Keep a pail of sand or a wool blanket nearby for putting out small fires.

O. Have a small carbon dioxide fire extinguisher in the home, where it can be quickly reached.

P. If your clothes catch on fire, do not run. Running supplies the fire with more air so the fire burns faster. Roll on the floor or wrap up in a rug, coat, or blanket.

Q. Learn how to telephone the fire department and turn in an alarm in the fire alarm box.

R. If a fire in a house is too big for you to put out, leave the house at once. Close the door to the room where the fire is, to cut down the supply of air in the room. Go to the nearest alarm box or telephone the fire department.

FUELS

I. Characteristics of a Good Fuel

A. A **fuel** is any material that is burned to produce heat for use in the home or in industry.

B. For a material to be considered a good fuel, it should have certain characteristics.
1. It should be inexpensive and easy to get.
2. It should be easy and safe to store, ship, and use.
3. It should burn fairly easily.
4. It should produce a large amount of heat.
5. It should produce very little smoke.

C. There are three classes of fuels: solid, liquid, and gas fuels.

II. Solid Fuels

A. Solid fuels include **wood, charcoal, coal, coke, peat,** and **lignite.**

B. Wood is still used very much as a fuel.
1. It has a low kindling temperature and gives a great amount of heat.
2. However, wood gives off much smoke and leaves behind a lot of ash.

C. Charcoal is wood that is heated in the absence of air. It is a man-made fuel.
1. The liquid and gas impurities in the wood are driven off, leaving mostly burnable carbon behind.
2. Charcoal burns with a great deal of heat, gives off no smoke, and leaves very little ash.

D. Coal is the remains of plants and ferns that were covered by the earth millions of years ago.
1. Because of the action of high temperatures, and tremendous pressures in the earth, the liquid and gas impurities were driven off, leaving mostly burnable carbon behind.
2. **Soft** coal has about 70 percent carbon in it and burns with a great deal of heat, but it gives off much smoke and leaves quite a bit of ash.
3. **Hard** coal has almost 90 percent carbon in it, burns with a great deal of heat, gives off much less smoke, and leaves little ash.

E. Peat and lignite are coal in its early stages of formation, and do not give very much heat.

F. Coke is soft coal that is heated in the absence of air. It also is a man-made fuel.
1. Gas impurities in the soft coal are driven off, leaving mostly burnable carbon behind.
2. It burns with a great deal of heat, gives off no smoke, and leaves very little ash.

III. Liquid Fuels

A. **Petroleum,** also known as "crude oil," was formed from the remains of small plants and animals that died millions of years ago.
1. These remains were buried in mud and rock beneath shallow seas.
2. Today most of the petroleum is found deep below the earth's surface in certain kinds of rock formations.
3. In some areas petroleum is also found below the earth's surface a short distance from the seashore.

B. The raw petroleum is not used as a fuel itself, but is broken up into different materials and refined.
1. From petroleum we get such fuels as **fuel oil, diesel oil, gasoline,** and **kerosene.**
2. From petroleum we also get such commercially important materials as **naphtha, benzine, lubricating oil, grease,** and **paraffin.**

C. Liquid fuels have replaced much of the solid fuels because they can be stored and shipped easily, burn cleaner and hotter, and leave no ash.

IV. GAS FUELS

A. Gas fuels include **natural** gas and **artificial,** or man-made, gases.
B. Natural gas is found together with petroleum deposits and also near coal fields.
C. Artificial gases are made from soft coal, coke, and petroleum.

D. All gas fuels have a large advantage over both solid and liquid fuels because they burn instantly.
1. At the same time gas fuels are clean and easy to handle, and they can be piped all over the country.
2. Gas fuels also give very much heat, produce no smoke, and leave no ash.

LEARNING ACTIVITIES FOR "HEAT, FIRE, AND FUELS"

THE NATURE OF HEAT

1. *Observe that heat is the energy of moving molecules* · Place tumblers of cold water and hot water side by side, and add two drops of red food coloring to each tumbler. Point out that the molecules of hot water have more kinetic energy and are moving more quickly than the molecules of cold water. These faster moving molecules of hot water disperse the food coloring more quickly than the slower moving molecules of cold water.

2. *Observe that friction is a source of heat* · Have the children rub the palms of their hands together briskly and note the heat produced by the resulting friction.

3. *Observe that compression is a source of heat* · Use a pump to inflate a tire or a football. Point out that the barrel of the pump becomes warm because the air inside has been compressed.

4. *Observe that percussion is a source of heat* · Pound a block of iron with a hammer. The continued percussion makes the molecules of iron move faster, and the block becomes warmer.

5. *Observe that chemical energy is a source of heat* · Strike a match and note that the friction of the match head rubbing against a rough surface produces enough heat to cause a chemical reaction to take place. The match head bursts into flame, and the chemical energy of the burning match is a source of heat.

6. *Observe that electrical energy is a source of heat* · Turn on a hot plate or electric toaster. Electrical energy is being converted to heat energy.

7. *Observe that radiant energy is a source of heat* · Put a match head on a pie tin. Use a magnifying glass to focus the sun's rays on the match head. The match head will burst into flame.

8. *Discuss nuclear energy as a source of heat* · Have the children read about and discuss the use of the nuclear reactor as a source of heat. Point out that one of the destructive effects of the atom bomb is the tremendous amount of heat produced.

9. *Observe the effect of heat upon the states of matter* · Put some ice cubes in a Pyrex container and heat the container on a hot plate until the ice cubes melt. Then heat the water until it boils. Explain the changes in state in terms of adding heat energy and making the

[677

molecules move faster. Make some ice cubes in the refrigerator and explain the change in state in terms of taking away heat energy and making the molecules move more slowly.

10. *Discover that solids expand when heated and contract when cooled* · Wrap one end of a wire around a nail and attach the other end to a clamp, covered with rubber or cloth, on a ringstand (Figure 18–1). Adjust the length of the wire so that the tip of the nail just clears the table and can swing freely. Now heat the wire with a Bunsen burner or alcohol lamp, moving the flame up and down the wire. The wire expands so that the tip of the nail touches the table and the nail can no longer swing freely. Remove the flame and let the wire cool. The wire will contract, letting the nail swing freely again.

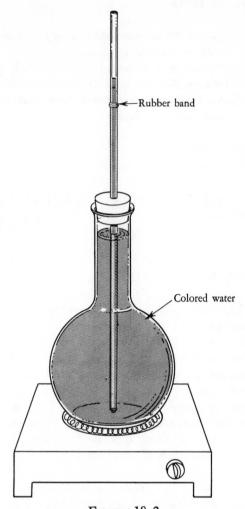

FIGURE 18–2.
THE WATER EXPANDS AND RISES WHEN HEATED AND CONTRACTS AND FALLS WHEN COOLED.

11. *Discover that liquids expand when heated and contract when cooled* · Pour water colored a dark red with food coloring into a Pyrex flask until the flask is almost full. Insert a long glass or plastic tube into a one-hole rubber stopper and fit the stopper tightly into the mouth of the flask. The amount of water in the flask will have to be adjusted so that, when the stopper is inserted, the colored water will rise about one half the distance of the part of the tube above the stopper (Figure 18–2). Place a small rubber band around the

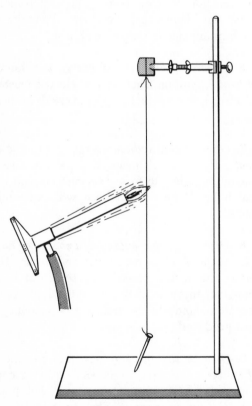

FIGURE 18–1.
THE WIRE EXPANDS WHEN HEATED AND CONTRACTS WHEN COOLED.

tube at the level of the liquid. Heat the flask on a hot plate just long enough to show the water expanding and rising up the tube. Transfer the flask to a pan of cold water and note that the water contracts and falls down the tube. Point out that both the rate and amount of expansion and contraction is greater for liquids than for solids.

12. *Discover that gases expand when heated and contract when cooled* · Repeat Activity 20 of "Air," Chapter 12 (p. 420). Note that the rate and amount of expansion and contraction is greatest for gases, as compared with liquids and solids.

13. *Discover that the rate of expansion and contraction differs between solids* · Obtain an inexpensive oven or desk thermometer and remove the back. Examine the metal coil. Point cut that two different metals (most likely brass and steel) have been welded together to form a single strip. Heat the coil with a lighted match and note how, as one metal (brass) expands more than the other, the coil twists and makes the pointer move across the scale. Allow the coil to cool, and watch the pointer return to its original position.

14. *Discover that water is an exception to the rule of expansion and contraction* · Fill a plastic bottle with water and screw the cap on tightly. Allow the bottle to stand overnight in the freezer of a refrigerator. Remove the bottle the next day and note how it bulges because the water expanded when it was cooled below 4° Celsius (39° Fahrenheit) and then froze.

15. *Discover that rubber is also an exception to the rule of expansion and contraction* · Cut a long rubber band. Tie one end of the band around the head of a nail and attach the other end to a ringstand, as described and pictured in Learning Activity 10 above. Now move a candle flame quickly up and down the rubber band several times, being careful not to hold the flame too close to the rubber band.

The rubber band will contract when heated and it will pull up the nail.

16. *Find some common examples of expansion and contraction* · Have the children make a list of examples of expansion and contraction that occur or are made use of in our daily life.

TEMPERATURE

1. *Show the principle underlying the operation of liquid thermometers* · Repeat Learning Activity 11 of "The Nature of Heat" (p. 678). Demonstrate a liquid thermometer for comparison, placing your fingers on the bulb to make the liquid in the thermometer rise.

2. *Make ribbon temperature scales* · Get some sturdy white cardboard about 76 centimeters (30 in) long and 25 centimeters (10 in) wide. Cut slits 2 centimeters (¾ in) wide in the center of the cardboard near the top and the bottom (Figure 18–3). Get some red ribbon and white ribbon, each about 13 millimeters (½ in) wide. Sew one end of the red ribbon neatly and firmly to one end of the white ribbon. Slip the loose ends of the red and white ribbon through the slits as shown in the diagram. Cut off any excess ribbon and sew the other two ribbon ends together. Now by pulling the ribbon at the back, you can make the red ribbon (which represents the mercury or alcohol in a thermometer) rise or fall. Use India ink to mark the distance between both slits into equal divisions to produce an accurate representation of the Fahrenheit scale.

Prepare a second ribbon thermometer illustrating the Celsius (Centigrade) scale. Then prepare a third thermometer showing the Fahrenheit scale on one side of the ribbon and the Celsius scale on the other side.

Have the children study each scale separately. Let them take readings with actual mercury thermometers of the temperature of the room, hot and cold liquids, etc. Find the boiling point and freezing point of water on each thermometer and scale (using a mixture

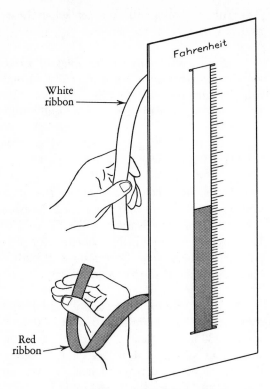

FIGURE 18–3.
A RED AND WHITE RIBBON THERMOMETER.

flask or bottle, a one-hole rubber stopper, and a narrow glass or plastic tube 45 centimeters (18 in) long. Insert the tube into the stopper and fit the stopper tightly into the neck of the flask. Support the flask with an iron ring attached to a ringstand, as shown in Figure 18–4. Place the end of the tube in a beaker or tumbler of water colored a very deep red with food coloring.

Heat the flask very gently with a small Bunsen burner flame or with an alcohol lamp, moving the flame back and forth along the flask. The heat will cause the air inside the flask to expand, and bubbles of air will leave the bottom of the tube. Drive out enough air so that, when the flame is removed and the air inside the flask cools and contracts, the colored water rises a sizable distance up the tube. Point out that the air pressure on the surface

of ice and water for the freezing point). Point out that the boiling point and freezing point vary, depending upon how much your city or town is above sea level.

After the children have mastered reading each scale separately, show them the ribbon thermometer containing both scales. Compare such fixed points as the boiling and freezing points of water on both scales. Show the children how to convert temperatures from one scale to another, checking the results on the ribbon thermometer.

3. *Discover how a clinical thermometer works* · Examine a clinical thermometer. Note the narrow bend that prevents the mercury from falling down the tube, and show how the mercury must be shaken down. Note that the scale is marked in tenths of a degree.

4. *Make an air thermometer* · Obtain a small

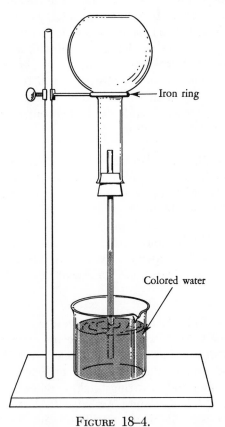

FIGURE 18–4.
AN AIR THERMOMETER WORKS DIFFERENTLY FROM A LIQUID THERMOMETER.

of the colored water forced the water up the tube, taking the place of the air that was driven out of the flask.

Now put your hands in hot water, dry them, and place them around the flask. The colored water will be driven down the tube as the air inside becomes warm and expands. Cool your hands and place them around the flask. This time the colored water will rise up the tube, as the air inside the flask cools and contracts. If you like, prepare a cardboard temperature scale behind the air thermometer and let the children take daily room temperature readings.

5. *Examine a metal thermometer* • Repeat Learning Activity 13 of "The Nature of Heat" (p. 679). Compare the accuracy of a metal thermometer with that of a mercury or alcohol thermometer.

6. *List the uses of thermometers* • Have the children list the uses of thermometers at home and by industry.

METHODS OF HEAT TRAVEL

1. *Discover that metals are good conductors of heat* • Place a metal spoon in a cup of very hot water. In a short time the part of the spoon above the hot water will become hot. Point out that the heat energy has been passed on, or conducted, from molecule to molecule.

2. *Observe that some metals conduct heat better than others* • Into a cup of hot water put a sterling silver spoon, a silverplated spoon, and a stainless steel spoon. Note which spoon handle becomes the hottest. Repeat the learning activity, using rods of different materials such a brass, iron, and copper.

3. *Observe that some solids are poor heat conductors* • Into a cup of hot water put rods of such materials as wood, glass, and plastic. Use rods of equal length and thickness.

Note that the parts above the surface of the water do not become hot, or even warm. Put a piece of rubber tubing in the hot water. The end outside the water will not become hot.

Wrap some cloth around one end of a metal rod and place the other end into the flame of a Bunsen burner or alcohol lamp. Because the cloth is a poor conductor of heat, you will not burn your hand even though the metal rod becomes very hot. Repeat this learning activity, using some thicknesses of paper wrapped around the metal rod.

4. *Discover that water is a poor conductor of heat* • Fill a test tube almost full of cold water and clamp the test tube to a ringstand (Figure 18–5). Have the clamp nearer to the bottom of the test tube. Now heat the top of the test tube with the flame of a Bunsen burner or alcohol lamp, moving the flame back and

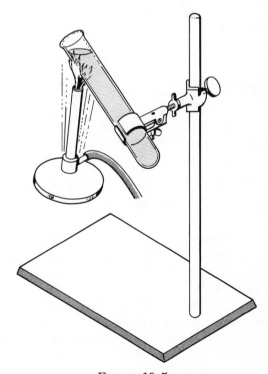

FIGURE 18–5.
THE WATER AT THE TOP OF THE TEST TUBE WILL BOIL WHILE THE WATER AT THE BOTTOM IS STILL COLD.

[681

forth, until the water boils. Feel the bottom of the test tube. The water will still be cold.

5. *Discover that air is a poor conductor of heat* · Hold one end of a short metal rod and place the other end in the flame of a Bunsen burner or alcohol lamp. In a very short time the end of the rod you are holding will become hot, as the heat travels along the rod by conduction.

Let the metal rod become cool and repeat the learning activity, this time holding the end of the rod with an asbestos mitt. At the same time hold with your bare hand one end of a second short rod about 2½ centimeters (1 in) away from the end of the first rod (Figure

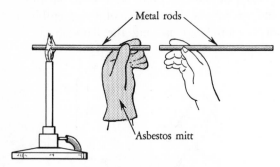

FIGURE 18–6.

BECAUSE AIR IS A POOR HEAT CONDUCTOR, THE SECOND ROD REMAINS COOL.

18–6). The second rod will remain cool because air is a poor conductor of heat.

6. *Discover that heat travels in water by convection* · Fill a Pyrex pot almost full of water. Shred a blotter with a food grater and place the fine particles in the water. Muddle the bits of blotting paper until they become thoroughly soaked and sink to the bottom of the beaker. Now place the beaker on one side of a hot plate and heat the beaker (Figure 18–7). The blotting paper will indicate the path of the convection current produced in the water. The bits of blotting paper will move up the side of the beaker resting on the hot

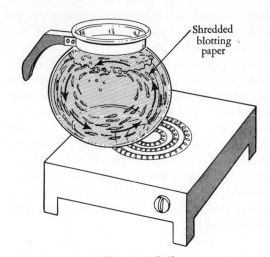

FIGURE 18–7.

A CONVECTION WATER CURRENT.

coils, and travel down on the cooler side of the beaker.

7. *Discover that heat travels in air by convection* · Repeat Learning Activity 3 of "Winds," Chapter 11 (p. 380). Trace the convection current moving from one lamp chimney through the box to the other chimney.

8. *Discover that heat can travel by radiation* · Hold the palm of your hand a short distance below a plugged-in hot electric clothes iron. The heat you feel is radiant energy that was absorbed by your hand and changed into heat. Note that the heat could not have reached your hand by conduction because the air between the iron and your hand is a poor heat conductor, Also, because your hand was below the iron, the heat could not have reached your hand by a rising convection current.

9. *Note the effect of radiant energy on materials* · Repeat Learning Activity 2 of "Winds," Chapter 11 (p. 380). Show that radiant energy passes through transparent materials without being changed into heat. Allow sunlight to pass through a glass window and fall on your face. Your face will absorb the sun's radiant energy

and feel warm, but the transparent glass will remain cool.'

10. *Investigate ways of heating the home* · Draw diagrams showing different kinds of heating systems in the home. Point out the methods of heat travel involved in each case. Discuss the advantages and disadvantages of each system. Have the children read about and report on such newer heating systems as solar heating and the heat pump system.

11. *Investigate insulating the home* · Have the children read about and discuss the ways that heat may be lost in the home and how this heat loss can be prevented. Obtain and examine samples of such insulating materials as rock wool and asbestos. Note how fluffy the material is, containing many air spaces which prevent heat from being conducted away. Wrap some of this insulating material around one end of a short metal rod and place the other end of the rod into the flame of a Bunsen burner or alcohol lamp. The insulating material will now prevent the heat from passing out of the metal rod and into your hand.

12. *Investigate refrigeration and deep freeze* · Have children read about and report on how refrigerators work. Show that evaporation is a cooling process by moistening a finger and blowing on it. When the water evaporates, it takes heat from the materials surrounding the water, and cools the materials.

Discuss the effects of slow freezing and quick freezing on foods. Find out the extent to which refrigeration and deep freezing slow down the spoiling of food. Compare the operation of a refrigerator and a freezer.

13. *Investigate air conditioning* · Have the children read about and discuss the functions of an air conditioner, and then describe how each function is accomplished. Ask the children to compare the operation of the cooling unit in an air conditioner with the cooling unit in a refrigerator.

FIRE

1. *Investigate oxidation* · Repeat Learning Activity 4 of "Air," Chapter 12 (p. 416). A simpler alternative would be to wet a wad of steel wool and leave it exposed to the air for a day or two. Point out that oxidation has taken place, whereby the iron combined with the oxygen in the air to form iron oxide (rust).

2. *Discover that slow oxidation produces heat* · Soak a wad of steel wool thoroughly in water, remove the wad, allow it to drain, and then stuff it in a Thermos bottle. Obtain a one-hole rubber stopper large enough to fit the mouth of the thermos bottle, and insert a thermometer into the hole. After the steel wool has been in the thermos for about 10 minutes, insert the stopper and the thermometer (Figure 18–8). The temperature will

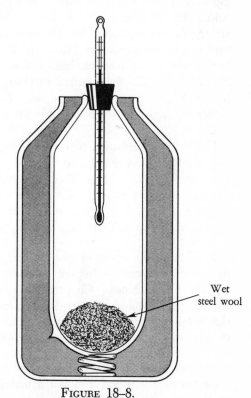

Wet steel wool

FIGURE 18–8.
WET STEEL WOOL OXIDIZES SLOWLY AND GIVES OFF HEAT.

[683

soon rise, showing that heat is being produced as oxidation takes place. The temperature will stop rising after about 20 minutes because all the oxygen present in the air inside the Thermos will be used up. When the temperature has stopped rising, remove the stopper, allow fresh air to enter, and then replace the stopper. The temperature will begin to rise again.

3. *Discover that rapid oxidation produces heat and light* · Show examples of rapid oxidation by lighting a match, burning paper or wood, and operating a cigarette lighter. In each case the rapid oxidation produced heat and light.

4. *Observe that fire needs oxygen* · Simultaneously invert different-sized glass jars over candles the same size. Compare the time it takes for the flame to go out in each jar.

5. *Observe the effect of the amount of oxygen on burning* · Prepare pure oxygen by pouring some 3% hydrogen peroxide into a glass jar. Add a piece of liver about the size of a half dollar, then cover the top of the jar with an index card or piece of cardboard. (Keep the liver cool, but do not freeze, until one hour before using.) An enzyme in the liver, called catylase, makes the hydrogen peroxide decompose, bubbling rather vigorously, to produce oxygen gas and water.

Untwist one end of a piece of picture wire and hold this untwisted end in a flame until the wire begins to glow. Then quickly insert the glowing wire into the jar of pure oxygen (Figure 18–9). The wire will burn like a Fourth of July sparkler in the pure oxygen.

6. *Observe the effect of the amount of surface area on burning* · Repeat Learning Activity 26 of "Machines," Chapter 17 (p. 661). Breaking the alcohol up into droplets increases the amount of surface area exposed to air, and thus greatly increases the rate of combustion.

7. *Investigate kindling temperature* · Invert a pie tin over a tripod and put a match head on the tin (Figure 18–10). Heat the tin with a Bunsen burner. When the tin reaches the

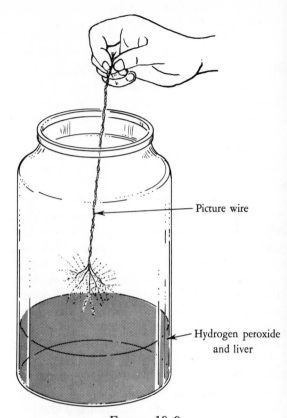

Picture wire

Hydrogen peroxide and liver

FIGURE 18–9.

PICTURE WIRE BURNS VIGOROUSLY IN PURE OXYGEN.

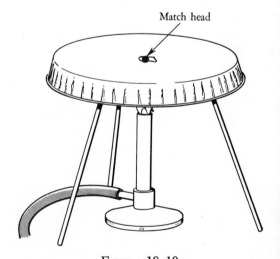

Match head

FIGURE 18–10.

A MATCH HEAD HAS A LOW KINDLING TEMPERATURE.

kindling temperature of the match head, the match head will burst into flame.

8. *Compare the kindling temperature of different materials* · Invert a pie tin over a tripod, as described in Learning Activity 7 above. Place around the tin a match head, a small amount of sulfur (if available), a piece of paper, a piece of match stick, and a piece of soft coal or charcoal. Have the materials all the same size, and space them equidistant from each other and from the center of the tin. Place a Bunsen burner or alcohol lamp under the center of the tin and light it. Note the order in which the materials reach their kindling temperatures. The match head will burst into flame, followed by the sulfur. The paper will char or burn, and the wood will just char slightly. The coal will not burn because its kindling temperature was not reached.

9. *Discover that flame is burning gas* · Light a candle and allow it to burn for a few minutes. Tilt the candle and note the liquid paraffin that drips down. Point out that when the wick first began to burn, it melted the paraffin, which rose up into the wick and was changed to a gas by the heat of the flame. The gas burns, giving off heat and light.

Snuff out the candle flame with a test tube, then immediately light a match and lower it toward the wick (Figure 18–11). You will light the candle before you touch the wick. Point out that when the candle was snuffed, the wick was still hot and continued to change the liquid paraffin to a gas for a short time. The burning match set fire to this gas, which then set fire to the wick.

10. *Observe that color of a flame depends upon the amount of oxygen available* · Light a Bunsen or a propane gas burner. Adjust the barrel so that the gas is getting all the air it needs, burning completely and making the flame blue. Now adjust the barrel so that the gas is getting little or no air, making the flame yellow. Point out that the yellow color is

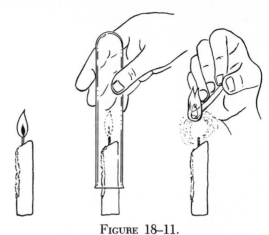

FIGURE 18–11.
A CANDLE IS A MASS OF BURNING GAS.

caused by glowing, unburned particles of fuel.

11. *Examine the parts of a flame* · Light a candle, and then partially darken the room. Examine the candle flame, using a magnifying glass for better observation. Note the dark inner part, the good-sized yellow part, and the small blue part around the edges of the flame. Repeat, using a Bunsen burner flame.

12. *Discover that burning produces carbon dioxide* · Wrap a wire around a burning candle, lower it into a glass jar, and cover the jar with an index card or cardboard (Figure 18–12). When the flame goes out, remove the candle, and pour in some limewater (obtained from the drugstore). Put your hand over the jar and shake it. The limewater will turn milky, showing the presence of carbon dioxide. You can first establish limewater as a test for the presence of carbon dioxide by bubbling your breath through a soda straw into a test tube containing some limewater.

13. *Discover that burning produces water* · Chill a glass tumbler in the refrigerator, then hold the beaker upside down over a candle flame. A film of dew or fine moisture will condense on the inside of the beaker.

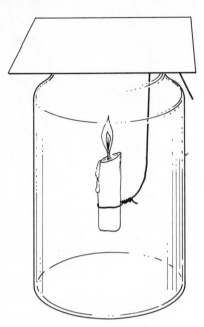

FIGURE 18–12.

A BURNING CANDLE PRODUCES CARBON DIOXIDE.

trough with three holes, each hole just large enough to fit snugly over the candles. Fit the trough over the candles so that it is just below the top of each candle (Figure 18–13), and then light the candles.

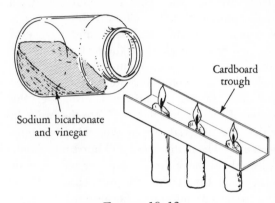

Sodium bicarbonate and vinegar

Cardboard trough

FIGURE 18–13.

CARBON DIOXIDE PUTS OUT THE CANDLE FLAMES.

14. *Investigate smoke and ash* · Burn damp paper towel and note the smoke produced. Burn a match, piece of paper, or strip of cotton cloth, and examine the ash that is left. Discuss the difference between smoke and ash.

15. *Investigate spontaneous combustion* · Repeat Learning Activity 2 above, using a wad of cotton soaked in boiled linseed oil instead. Point out that continued oxidation would soon produce enough heat to reach the kindling point of the cotton.

16. *Investigate factors necessary to put out fire* · Build a small campfire in a large pie tin. The fire can be put out by removing or scattering the fuel, by covering the fire with earth to cut off the supply of oxygen, and by adding water to cool the burning fuel below its kindling temperature.

17. *Discover that carbon dioxide puts out fire* · Place three candles of different sizes on a piece of cardboard. Prepare a cardboard

Obtain a large glass jar or beaker. Prepare carbon dioxide by pouring some baking soda (sodium bicarbonate) into the jar, adding vinegar, and then covering the jar with a piece of cardboard or an index card until the bubbling subsides. Remove the cardboard and tilt the jar over the higher end of the trough, allowing just the invisible carbon dioxide to flow into the trough and put out the candle flames.

18. *Make a foam fire extinguisher* · Put 2 tablespoons of baking soda into a tumbler of water, stir, and then pour into a quart-size glass jar. Break an egg and pour the contents into the jar. Cap the jar and shake the contents thoroughly. Obtain a large pie tin and place it on an asbestos mat. Pour some alcohol or lighter fluid into the tin and set fire to the alcohol with a lighted match (be very careful not to spread the fire). Place the jar in the center of the tin and immediately pour a cup of vinegar into the jar. A foam will form, which will overflow the jar, pour down the sides, and put out the fire. Point out that the egg made it possible for the bubbles of carbon dioxide to cling together and form a foamy mass.

19. *Investigate commercial fire extinguishers* · Have a representative of the fire department demonstrate different extinguishers. Let some children read about and report on how large forest, oil, factory, or home fires are put out.

20. *Discuss how fire helps man* · Have the children make a list of the different uses man has for fire.

21. *List safety rules for fires* · Determine fire hazards that may exist in the home. Follow with a list of safety rules for preventing fires.

FUELS

1. *Collect and classify kinds of fuels* · Have the children collect and exhibit different fuels available in the community. Let them describe for each fuel the characteristics that make it a good fuel. Divide the fuels into three groups: solids, liquids, and gases. (It would be wise to exclude gasoline from an exhibit.)

2. *Discover that most fuels contain carbon* · Lower a white china dish into a candle flame. Hold the dish in the flame until a good-sized black spot (soot) appears, and then remove the dish. The black spot consists of particles of unburned carbon.

3. *Discover that most fuels contain hydrogen* · Repeat Learning Activity 13 of "Fire" (p. 685). The hydrogen of the fuel combined with oxygen in the air to form water vapor, which condensed on the cool inside walls of the beaker.

4. *Make charcoal* · Punch a small hole in the cover of a coffee can with a nail. Obtain some soft pine wood and chop or cut it up into small strips or pieces. Place the wood in the coffee can and cover the can tightly with the cover. Heat the can on a hot plate. Smoke and gas will soon come through the nail hole. Wait a short while until all the air has been driven from the can, and then try to light the gas coming through the hole (Figure 18–14). After a few trials, the gas will burn with a flickering flame. Continue heating the can for at least ½ hour, and then remove the can from the hot plate and allow it to cool. Pull off the cover and examine the charcoal that has been formed. Repeat the learning activity, using either small pieces of soft coal or crumpled-up paper toweling.

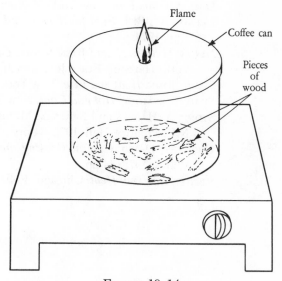

FIGURE 18–14.
HEATING WOOD IN THE ABSENCE OF AIR PRODUCES CHARCOAL.

BIBLIOGRAPHY FOR ''HEAT, FIRE, AND FUELS''

ADLER, IRVING. *Hot and Cold.* New York: John Day, 1965. 128 pp.

———. *Petroleum: Gas, Oil, and Asphalt.* New York: John Day, 1975. 48 pp.

——— and PEGGY ADLER. *Heat and Its Uses.* New York: Thomas Y. Crowell, 1973. 48 pp.

ANNO, MISUMASA. *Hot As an Ice Cube.* New York: Thomas Y. Crowell, 1973. 40 pp.

BENDICK, JEANNE. *Heat and Temperature.* New York: Franklin Watts, 1974. 72 pp.

BERRY, JAMES. *Why You Feel Hot, Why You Feel Cold: Your Body Temperature.* Boston: Little, Brown, 1973. 48 pp.

COBB, VICKI. *Heat.* New York: Franklin Watts, 1973. 60 pp.

DEAN, ANABEL. *Exploring and Understanding Heat.* Westchester, Ill.: Benefic Press, 1970. 96 pp.

HAINES, GAIL. *Fire.* New York: William Morrow, 1975. 32 pp.

LEFKOWITZ, R. J. *Fuel for Today and Tomorrow.* New York: Parents' Magazine, 1974. 64 pp.

NIXON, HERSHELL, and JOAN NIXON. *Oil and Gas: From Fossils to Fuels.* New York: Harcourt Brace Jovanovich, 1977. 64 pp.

SCOTT, JOHN. *Heat and Fire.* New York: Parents' Magazine, 1973. 64 pp.

SIMON, SEYMOUR. *Hot and Cold.* New York: McGraw-Hill, 1972. 40 pp.

STONE, A. HARRIS, and BERTRAM M. SIEGEL. *The Heat's On.* Englewood Cliffs, N.J.: Prentice-Hall, 1970. 64 pp.

URQUART, DAVID. *Central Heating and How It Works.* New York: Henry Z. Walck, 1972. 44 pp.

VICTOR, EDWARD. *Heat.* Chicago: Follett, 1967. 32 pp.

CHAPTER 19
SOUND

PRODUCING AND TRANSMITTING SOUND

I. How Sound Is Produced

A. Sound is a form of energy that is caused by an object that is moving back and forth, or **vibrating**, rapidly.
B. The vibrations can be produced by plucking, stroking, blowing, and hitting.
C. When the vibration stops, the sound stops.

II. How Sounds Travel

A. When an object, such as a violin string or a tuning fork, is made to vibrate, the sound travels out as waves in all directions.
  1. When the string vibrates, it moves back and forth very rapidly.
  2. As it moves forward, it pushes against the molecules of air in front of it and presses them closer together.
  3. The space where the molecules are pressed closer together is called a **compression.**
  4. As the string moves backward, it leaves behind a space with fewer molecules in it, and these molecules spread farther apart.
  5. The space where the molecules are spread farther apart is called a **rarefaction.**
  6. One compression and one rarefaction together make up one complete vibration, or **sound wave.**

7. As the object vibrates back and forth, it produces compressions and rarefactions, one after the other.
8. The presence of compressions and rarefactions means that the molecules of air have been made to move back and forth, or vibrate, too.
9. As the molecules of air vibrate, they bump into other molecules and make these molecules vibrate, which then make still other molecules vibrate.
10. No single molecule travels very far. Each moves back and forth, pushing against other molecules, as the sound waves travel out in all directions.

B. When sound waves, or vibrations, reach the ear, they are carried by the auditory nerve to the brain, which gives us the sensation of sound.

III. Sounds Travel Through Solids, Liquids, and Gases

A. Most sounds come to us through the air, which is a gas.
  1. High up on a mountain the air is not as heavy and does not contain as many molecules as the air in a valley, so sound does not travel as fast or as well high up in the air.
  2. Sounds travel faster and better in heavy gases, where the molecules are closer

together, than in light gases, where the molecules are farther apart.

3. The speed of sound in air is about 336 meters (1100 ft) a second or about 1 kilometer in 3 seconds (1 mile in 5 seconds).

4. The warmer the air, the faster the molecules move, and the greater the speed of sound will be.

5. The speed of sound in air increases about 30 centimeters (1 ft) a second for every degree rise in Fahrenheit temperature and about 60 centimeters (2 ft) a second for every degree rise in Celsius temperature.

B. Sound travels faster and better through liquids, like water, than through gases.

1. In liquids the molecules are closer together and carry the vibrations more easily and quickly.

2. Sound travels about 1464 meters (4800 ft) a second in water, or about four times as fast as in air.

C. Sound travels faster and better through hard solids than through liquids or gases.

1. In these solids the molecules are very close together and carry the vibrations very easily and quickly.

2. Sound travels more than 3000 meters (10,000 ft) a second in wood, or about nine times as fast as in air.

3. Sound travels more than 5000 meters (16,500 ft) a second in steel, or fifteen times as fast as in air.

D. Sound does not travel at all in a vacuum, where there are no molecules to carry the sound waves, or vibrations.

IV. CHARACTERISTICS OF SOUND

A. Sounds can differ in three ways: in **pitch**, in **intensity**, and in **quality.**

B. Pitch is the highness or lowness of a sound.

1. When a body is vibrating, it produces a certain number of vibrations, or sound waves a second.

2. The number of vibrations a body produces a second is called the **frequency.**

3. The faster a body vibrates, the more vibrations it produces a second, and the higher the sound, or pitch.

4. The slower a body vibrates, the less vibrations it produces a second, and the lower the sound, or pitch.

5. The normal human ear can hear sounds with a frequency that ranges between 20 and 20,000 vibrations a second.

6. Dogs are able to hear sounds with a frequency of more than 20,000 vibrations a second.

7. Very high frequency sound waves are called **ultrasonic** sound waves.

8. Ultrasonic sound waves can kill insects and pests, control and operate automatic garage doors, and clean clothes by shaking the dirt out of them.

C. Intensity is the loudness or softness of a sound.

1. The loudness or softness of a sound depends upon how strongly the object is vibrating.

2. The stronger the object vibrates, the more energy the sound wave has, and the greater the size of the sound wave.

3. The more energy we put into making a sound, the larger the sound wave, and the louder the sound wave will be.

4. Another way of making sounds louder is to make more air vibrate to produce larger sound waves.

5. Putting the base of a vibrating tuning fork against a table or chalkboard will make them vibrate also, which will then make the large amount of air around them vibrate as well.

6. The farther sound waves travel, the softer the sound becomes because, as the waves move away from the source of the sound, they become smaller and do not have as much energy.

7. The unit of measurement of the intensity of sound is called the **decibel**, and is measured by a machine called the **sound-level meter.**

8. Whispering produces 10 to 20 decibels of sound; talking rather loudly, 60

decibels; heavy traffic noises, 70 to 80 decibels; and thunder, 110 decibels.

D. The quality of a sound is what helps us tell the difference between different musical instruments, or between different persons that are producing the same sound.

1. Even though the sounds have the same pitch and intensity, they will sound differently.

2. This difference occurs because, when an object vibrates, it can vibrate as a whole and in parts at the same time.

3. When this multiple vibration takes place, sounds of different frequencies are heard at the same time.

4. Each frequency produces a sound of a different pitch.

5. The lowest sound the vibrating body produces is called the **fundamental tone.**

6. The other sounds, having different frequencies, that the vibrating body produces are called **overtones.**

7. The quality of a sound depends upon the number and strength of the different overtones that are produced.

8. The quality also depends upon the size, shape, and material of the vibrating object because these variations help decide how many overtones will be produced.

V. ECHOES

A. An **echo** is a sound wave that bounces back, or is reflected, from a large hard surface like a cliff or wall of a building.

B. To hear an echo we must be at least 17 meters (56 ft) away from the reflecting surface.

1. Less than 17 meters (56 ft) away, the sound wave bounces back fast enough to join or blend with the original sound and helps make the sound louder.

2. More than 17 meters (56 ft) away, the sound wave bounces back too late to join the original sound, and the echo now interferes with the new sounds that are being produced.

3. The farther away the reflecting surface is, the longer time it will take for us to hear the echo.

4. Sometimes the sound wave bounces off many surfaces and produces a series of echoes.

C. There are many ways that can be used to eliminate annoying echoes in a large room or auditorium.

1. Soft drapes on walls and window frames, and also rugs on the floor, will absorb the sound waves.

2. Covering the ceilings, and also the walls, with rough materials or materials that have many little holes in them will break up the sound waves so that very few are reflected back.

3. Even the persons in the auditorium will help absorb some of the sound waves.

VI. THE VOICE

A. At the top of the **windpipe,** or **trachea,** in your throat is the **voice box,** or **larynx.**

B. Stretched over the top of the voice box are two thin but strong bands of tissue called the **vocal cords.**

C. When air from the lungs is blown through a narrow slit (the **glottis**) between these two cords, the cords are made to vibrate by the moving air, and sound is produced.

1. Muscles attached to the vocal cords make the cords tight or loose, and in this way control the pitch of your voice.

2. The tighter the vocal cords, the faster they vibrate, and the higher the pitch will be.

3. The greater the force with which the air is blown between the vocal cords, the louder the sound that will be produced.

D. Men's vocal cords are longer and thicker than those of women, so they do not vibrate as fast.

1. This difference explains why men have lower or deeper voices than women.

2. A boy's vocal cords get longer and thicker as he gets older, so his voice changes from a high pitch to a low pitch.

E. The quality of your voice depends upon the kind of vocal cords you have.
  1. The air passages in your throat, mouth, and nose, as well as the sinuses in your head, affect the quality of your voice.
  2. The position of your lips, tongue, and teeth play an important part in the kind and quality of sounds you produce.

MUSIC AND MUSICAL INSTRUMENTS

I. MUSIC VERSUS NOISE

  A. Pleasant sounds that are produced by regular vibrations are called **music.**
  B. Harsh or unpleasant sounds that are produced by irregular vibrations are called **noise.**

II. MUSICAL INSTRUMENTS

  A. **Musical instruments** are devices used to produce pleasant sounds of different pitch, intensity, and quality.
  B. Musical instruments are divided into three classes: **stringed** instruments, **wind** instruments, and **percussion** instruments.

III. STRINGED INSTRUMENTS

  A. Stringed instruments contain one or more strings that are made to vibrate and produce musical sounds.
  B. The strings are made to vibrate in different ways.
    1. Some strings are stroked or rubbed with a bow, as in the violin, cello, and bass viol.
    2. Some strings are plucked, either with the fingers or with a pick, as in the ukulele, guitar, banjo, and harp.
    3. In the piano, which is also called a percussion instrument, the strings are struck by small hammers.
  C. The pitch, or frequency, of all the musical sounds that are produced by stringed instruments can be changed in three different ways.
    1. The looser the string, the lower the pitch; the tighter the string, the higher the pitch.
    2. The longer the string, the lower the pitch; the shorter the string, the higher the pitch.
    3. The thicker the string, the lower the pitch; the thinner the string, the higher the pitch.
  D. Stringed instruments like the violin, cello, bass viol, and banjo have just a few strings that are attached to pegs.
    1. The strings are of different thicknesses that produce sounds of higher or lower pitch.
    2. The pegs can be used to tighten or loosen the strings, and make the pitch higher or lower, too.
    3. When these instruments are played, the fingers move up and down the vibrating strings, making them longer and shorter, thus producing lower and higher musical sounds.
  E. Stringed instruments like the harp and piano have a great many strings.
    1. The strings all differ in length, thickness, and tightness so that they all produce sounds of different pitch.
    2. The harp also has pedals that can pull the strings tighter and make them produce sounds with a higher pitch.
  F. Sounds from stringed instruments can be made louder or softer.
    1. The harder a string is bowed or plucked, the more strongly it vibrates, and the louder the sound that is produced.
    2. The more gently a string is bowed or plucked, the weaker it vibrates, and the softer the sound that is produced.

3. Also, when a string vibrates, it makes the entire instrument vibrate at the same frequency, or pitch.

4. The vibrating instrument makes the air all around the instrument vibrate at the same frequency as well.

5. The large amount of vibrating air reinforces the original vibrations of the string and makes them stronger, which means the sound will be louder.

6. In the piano, a sounding board above the strings vibrates instead of the entire piano.

7. Some instruments, like the violin and the guitar, have holes in them.

8. Not only does the instrument vibrate, but also sound waves go inside the instrument and make the air inside it vibrate at the same pitch, or frequency.

9. The vibrating air joins and reinforces the original vibrations, making them stronger and producing a louder sound.

10. Reinforcement of the original vibrations to make the sound louder is called **resonance.**

G. The sounds from stringed instruments differ in quality.

1. When a string vibrates, the whole string vibrates.

2. The tone produced is called the **fundamental tone.**

3. A vibrating string can vibrate not only as a whole, but it can also vibrate in parts at the same time.

4. When a string vibrates in two parts, it is just as if two shorter strings were vibrating, with each part just half as long as the original string.

5. These shorter strings vibrate twice as fast, producing a tone one octave higher, called an **overtone.**

6. When a string vibrates in three parts, the parts vibrate three times as fast, producing overtones that are two octaves higher.

7. Vibrating as a whole, the string produces its fundamental tone, which is the lowest tone it can produce.

8. Vibrating in parts, the string produces overtones, which are higher than the fundamental tone.

9. The quality of the sound depends upon the number and strength of the overtones that are produced.

10. The quality also depends upon the size, shape, and material of the instrument because these factors help decide how many overtones will be produced.

IV. WIND INSTRUMENTS

A. Wind instruments contain a column of air that can be made to vibrate and produce musical sounds.

B. The air column can be made to vibrate by either blowing into it, as is done with the clarinet, saxophone, and trumpet, or by blowing across it, as is done with the flute and piccolo.

C. Wind instruments are divided into two main classes: **woodwind** and **brass** instruments.

D. In all woodwind instruments, except the flute and piccolo, a thin piece of wood or plastic, called a **reed,** is used to make the air column vibrate.

1. The reed is in the mouthpiece of the instrument.

2. Blowing into the mouthpiece makes the reed vibrate, which then makes the air column vibrate.

3. In the flute and piccolo, we blow across a hole and start the air column vibrating.

4. Examples of woodwind instruments include the flute, piccolo, clarinet, oboe, bassoon, and English horn.

5. The saxophone uses a reed, but is made of brass, so it belongs partly to the woodwind family and partly to the brass family.

E. All brass instruments are made of brass, and are played by vibrating the lips while they are pressed against the mouthpiece of the instrument.

1. The vibration of the lips starts the air column vibrating.

2. Examples of brass instruments include the trumpet, cornet, bugle, trombone, French horn, and tuba.

F. The pitch or frequency of the vibrating air column can be changed by making the air column longer or shorter.

1. The longer the air column, the lower the pitch; the shorter the air column, the higher the pitch.

2. Woodwind instruments have holes in them, usually covered by pads called keys.

3. Pressing or releasing the keys will open and close the holes, making the length of the air column inside the instrument longer or shorter.

4. Some brass instruments, like the trumpet and the tuba, have valves which are used to control the length of the air column.

5. The trombone has a slide that moves in and out to control the length of the air column.

6. There is no way to change the length of the air column in the bugle, so the different notes are produced by changing both the tightness of the lips and the force of the breath blowing into the instrument.

7. Many wind instruments, especially brass instruments with valves or a slide, also depend on the tightness of the lips and the force of the breath to produce notes of different pitch.

G. Sounds from wind instruments differ in quality.

1. An air column not only vibrates as a whole, but it also vibrates in parts at the same time.

2. Vibrating as a whole, the air column produces its fundamental tone, which is the lowest tone it can produce.

3. Vibrating in parts, the air column produces overtones, which are higher than the fundamental tone.

4. The quality of the sound depends upon the number and strength of overtones produced.

5. The quality also depends upon the size,

shape, and material of the instrument because these factors help decide how many overtones will be produced.

H. Blowing harder into the wind instrument will make the air column inside the instrument vibrate more strongly and produce a louder sound.

1. At the same time, the air column vibrates in parts.

2. These new vibrations join and reinforce the original vibrations produced by the air column vibrating as a whole.

3. This combination of vibrations makes the air column vibrate more strongly and produces a louder sound.

4. This reinforcement of the original vibrations to make the sound louder is called **resonance.**

5. In most wind instruments, blowing harder can make the sound not only louder but higher as well.

6. Blowing harder cuts out the fundamental tone so that only the higher overtones are heard.

V. PERCUSSION INSTRUMENTS

A. Percussion instruments are either made of solid materials, like wood and metal, or else they are made of materials stretched over a hollow container.

1. The solid or stretched materials are struck by mallets, hammers, or the hands, which make the materials vibrate and produce sounds.

2. Percussion instruments made of solid materials include the xylophone, glockenspiel, triangle, cymbals, chimes, bells, castanets, and wood block.

3. Percussion instruments made of materials stretched over a hollow container include the bongo drum, snare drum, bass drum, kettle drum, and tambourine.

B. For percussion instruments made of solid materials, the longer the material, the lower the pitch; the shorter the material, the higher the pitch.

C. For percussion instruments made of mate

rials stretched over a hollow container, the pitch can be changed in different ways.

1. The tighter the covering, the higher the pitch; the looser the covering, the lower the pitch.
2. The thinner the covering, the higher the pitch; the thicker the covering, the lower the pitch.
3. The smaller the covering, the higher the pitch; the larger the covering, the lower the pitch.

D. Striking the percussion instruments harder will make them vibrate more strongly and produce louder sounds.

1. At the same time the vibrating materials make the air around them vibrate at the same frequency.

2. The large amount of vibrating air reinforces the original vibrations and makes them stronger, producing louder sounds.
3. The hollow containers of percussion instruments like the drum, the marimba, and the chimes also help produce louder sounds.
4. The column of air inside the container is made to vibrate at the same frequency as the original sound, reinforcing the original vibrations and making them much stronger, thus producing a louder sound.
5. The vibrating column of air also affects the quality of the sound produced by the percussion instrument.

LEARNING ACTIVITIES FOR "SOUND"

PRODUCING AND TRANSMITTING SOUND

1. *Observe that sound is produced by a vibrating object* · Hold one end of a rubber band in your teeth and stretch the band. Pluck the band, noting the vibration and the sound produced. The vibration is so rapid that it produces a blur. Note that when the vibration stops, the sound stops./ Set a tuning fork vibrating by striking one prong sharply against your kneecap or the rubber heel of your shoe. (Never strike a tuning fork against a hard object.) To show that the tuning fork is vibrating, hold one end of a sheet of paper and touch one prong lightly to the other end of the paper. The vibrating prong will make the paper rattle.

Have the children feel the vibrations by touching the vibrating prongs lightly with their fingertips. Let them place tissue paper against the teeth of a comb and hum a tune. They will feel the vibrations as a ticklish sensation on their lips.

2. *Investigate how sound travels* · Pour some water into a tub or basin. Dip your finger quickly into the water and then pull it out, noting that waves are produced and spread out in concentric circles. Point out that sound waves themselves are not like water waves, but their method of travel is somewhat alike.

3. *Discover that sound travels in all directions* · Place children in four corners of the room, facing the wall. Have one child in the middle of the room produce a sound. Let the children raise their hands as soon as they hear the sound. Now place one child at the top of the stairs, a second child half-way down, and a third child at the foot of the stairs. Have the child half-way down the stairs make a sound. The sound will travel up and down, as well as in all horizontal directions.

Fill a large beaker or tumbler full of water. Strike the prongs of a tuning fork very sharply against your kneecap or the rubber heel of your shoe, and then quickly place the ends of the

[695

Compare this movement with the way sound travels by means of condensations and rarefactions of molecules. Point out that each coil (and molecule) moves back and forth just a little, yet the result is an extensive movement and travel of the impulse.

5. *Discover that sound travels through solids* · Put yourself and a child at opposite ends of a table. Scratch the table top so lightly with your fingernail that the child cannot hear the sound. Now have the child place one ear against the end of the table, and then scratch the table top again. The child will hear the scratching sound very clearly.

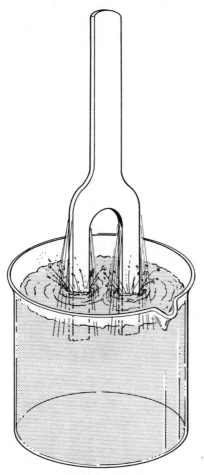

FIGURE 19–1.

THE VIBRATING TUNING FORK SCATTERS WATER IN ALL DIRECTIONS.

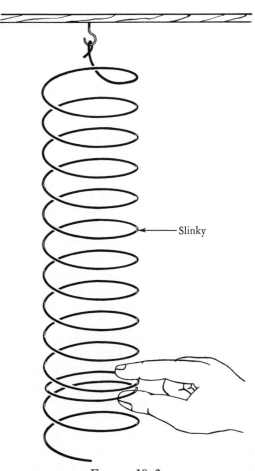

Slinky

FIGURE 19–2.

A "SLINKY" SHOWS HOW SOUND TRAVELS BY CONDENSATION AND RAREFACTION OF MOLECULES.

prongs in the center of the water (Figure 19–1). The vibrating prongs will make the water splash out of the beaker in all directions.

4. *Discover that sound travels by means of condensation and rarefaction of molecules* · Obtain a "Slinky" (a walking spring coil) from the toy store. Attach one end to a hook high off the floor and allow the rest of the Slinky to stretch to the floor (Figure 19–2). Now press together two of the stretched coils close to the floor, and then release these coils suddenly. An impulse, consisting of a series of condensations and rarefactions, will travel the length of the Slinky.

696]

Repeat Learning Activity 7 of "The Circulatory System," Chapter 15 (p. 595) to show how the use of the stethoscope illustrates that sounds travel through solids.

6. *Observe that sound will travel through liquids* · Fill a large aquarium with water. Click 2 spoons together about 15 centimeters (6 in) from a child's ear. Have the child put his ear against one end of the aquarium. Click the spoons again, this time under water in the aquarium. The child will hear the sound, but it will be much louder.

7. *Observe that sounds will travel through gases* · Send one child out of the room with one end of a garden hose, and have another child speak softly into the other end. The child outside will be able to hear the words very clearly. This activity also shows that sounds can be directed.

8. *Observe that sound does not travel through a vacuum* · Obtain a large Pyrex flask and a solid rubber stopper that fits the flask. Push a small hook into the underside of the stopper. From the hook suspend a string that is attached to a small jingle bell so that the bell will hang freely inside the flask when the stopper is inserted (Figure 19–3). Place a small amount of water in the flask, set the flask on a hot plate, and boil the water until almost all the air inside the flask has been driven off and there is mostly steam inside the flask. Remove the flask, insert the stopper, and allow the flask to cool. The steam will condense, leaving a partial vacuum in the flask.

Set up a second (control) flask exactly like the first, but do not boil the water so that this second flask is full of air. Now shake both flasks gently. Compare the loudness of the bell in the partial vacuum with that of the bell in air.

9. *Investigate the speed of sound* · Have the children read about and discuss the speed of sound in air, water, and solids like wood and steel. Discuss the effect of temperature on the

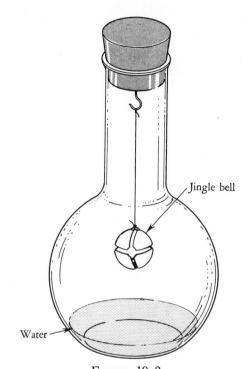

Jingle bell

Water

FIGURE 19–3.

THE SOUND OF THE BELL CANNOT BE HEARD IN A VACUUM.

speed of sound, pointing out that heat produces an increase in molecular motion.

Ask the children to watch a jet plane as it is traveling. The sound of the plane will seem to be coming from a point in the sky way behind the spot where they see the plane. Point out that light travels so much faster than sound that they see the plane immediately. It takes more time for the sound to reach their ears.

10. *Investigate pitch* · Draw the edge of an index card over a comb at different speeds. The faster the index card moves against the teeth, the faster it vibrates, and the higher the sound becomes.

11. *Investigate ultrasonic sound waves* · Blow a dog whistle. Note that we can only hear sounds within a definite frequency range. Have the children read about and report on the uses of ultrasonic sound waves.

[697

12. *Investigate intensity* · Repeat Learning Activity 1 above, producing soft and loud sounds by varying the intensity with which you pluck the rubber band, strike the tuning fork, and hum against the tissue paper. Place an alarm clock at one end of the room. Have the children listen to the ticking at different distances from the clock, and note that the intensity of the sound decreases as the distance from the source of the sound increases.

Have the children read about and report on measuring the intensity of sound, and have them find out the number of decibels produced by a variety of common sounds.

13. *Investigate quality* · Push a table against the wall. Attach an electric bell to a piece of wood and bend the clapper so that it will not strike the gong when it is moving back and forth. Connect the bell to two dry cells and a switch, as shown in Figure 19–4. Get 3 meters

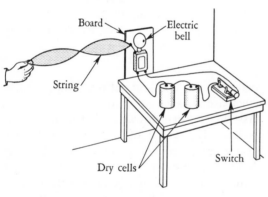

FIGURE 19–4.
FORMING LOOPS TO ILLUSTRATE FUNDAMENTAL TONE AND OVERTONES.

(10 ft) of thin, soft string and attach one end of the string to the clapper. Push down the switch to complete the electric circuit and set the clapper moving back and forth.

Stand some distance away and pull on the string as the clapper vibrates. By experimenting with the amount of pull on the string, you will be able to make the string vibrate as a whole to form just one loop, and then vibrate

in parts to form two, three, or even four loops. Compare this formation of loops with the formation of the fundamental tone and overtones in vibrating objects to produce sounds of different quality.

14. *Investigate echoes* · Take the children to the auditorium or gymnasium when it is empty. Stand at one end of the room and produce echoes. Have the children recall that these echoes are not heard when the auditorium is filled. The sounds are absorbed by the persons in the auditorium.

Discuss the use of such materials as drapes, curtains, carpeting, acoustical ceiling tiles, and foam rubber padding to absorb sound waves and eliminate echoes. Lower a ringing alarm clock about half-way down into a closed cardboard carton and note the loudness of the sound. Now tape the inside of the carton with foam rubber or thicknesses of cloth. Lower the ringing alarm clock again into the carton and note how much softer the sound becomes.

15. *Investigate the voice* · Have children feel their windpipes while humming or making low sounds. They will feel the vibrations of their vocal cords. Have them make loud and soft sounds, noting the greater force with which air is blown between the vocal cords to produce louder sounds. Let one child say something normally, and then repeat it while pinching his nostrils shut. Note the change in quality of the sounds produced.

Inflate a balloon and allow the air to escape while you pinch and stretch both sides of the neck of the balloon. The more you pinch and stretch the rubber, the higher the sound becomes. Compare this effect with the tightening of the vocal cords to produce higher sounds. Discuss the difference in length and thickness of men's and women's vocal cords, and the effect on the pitch of the sounds produced.

16. *Investigate hearing* · Repeat Learning Activities 13 and 14 of "The Sense Organs," Chapter 15 (p. 601) and trace the relationship between sounds, the ear, and hearing.

MUSIC AND MUSICAL INSTRUMENTS

1. *Compare music and noise* · Have the children list unpleasant noises they have heard. Relate noise with irregular vibrations and music with regular vibrations. Draw diagrams of both regular and irregular vibrations on the chalkboard (Figure 19–5).

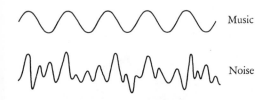

Music

Noise

FIGURE 19–5.
DIAGRAMS SHOWING THE DIFFERENCE BETWEEN MUSIC AND NOISE.

2. *Discover how sounds are produced in musical instruments* · Obtain or have children bring in a variety of instruments, making sure you have adequate representation of stringed, wind, and percussion instruments. For each instrument show how sounds are produced, made higher or lower, and louder or softer. Have the children produce sounds of the same pitch and intensity from different instruments, and note the difference in the quality of the sounds. Discuss the formation of overtones in each instrument and their relationship to the quality of the musical sounds produced.

3. *Observe that forced vibrations increase the intensity of sounds* · Strike a tuning fork, hold it up, and have the children listen to the sound produced. Strike the tuning fork again, but this time touch the handle of the tuning fork to a table top or the chalkboard. The vibrating tuning fork will force the table top to vibrate with the same frequency, and the vibrating table top will now force the air around it to vibrate with the same frequency too. This large amount of vibrating air reinforces the original vibrations of the tuning fork, making them stronger so that the sound becomes louder. Show how this same effect is produced with musical instruments.

4. *Discover how the pitch is changed in stringed instruments* · Obtain a cigar box, remove the cover, and cut three grooves on each edge of the box. Stretch three rubber bands of equal length but different thicknesses lengthwise around the box, placing them in the grooves to keep them in place (Figure 19–6).

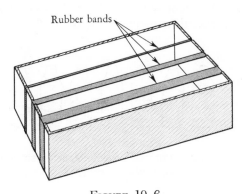

Rubber bands

FIGURE 19–6.
A STRINGED INSTRUMENT MADE FROM A CIGAR BOX.

Pluck each band and note that the thinner the band, the higher the sound will be.

Pluck one band and note the sound produced. Hold the middle of the band with your fingers and pluck either portion of the band that extends from your fingers to one edge of the box. Note that only half of the rubber band now vibrates and the sound is higher. In fact, the sound is now an octave higher than the original sound. Hold the band at different positions. The shorter the length of the vibrating band, the higher the sound will be.

Pluck one rubber band and listen to the note produced. Now pull the band at one end, making it tighter. Note that the tighter the band becomes, the higher the sound will be.

Use real stringed instruments to show how

[699

thickness, length, and tension are used to produce sounds of different pitch.

5. *Investigate changing the pitch in wind instruments* · Blow across an empty soda pop bottle. The sound is produced by the column of vibrating air inside the bottle. Repeat the activity, using bottles of different sizes. The smaller the bottle, the shorter the air column will be, and the higher the sound will become.

Obtain eight soda pop bottles all the same size and line them up in a row. Pour different amounts of water in them, adding or taking away water as needed, until you have produced the eight notes of the scale when you blow across their mouths (Figure 19–7). Note

FIGURE 19–7.
PRODUCING AIR COLUMNS OF DIFFERENT SIZES IN SODA POP BOTTLES.

the relationship between the length of the air column in each bottle and the pitch of the sound produced.

Use real wind instruments to show how changing the length of the vibrating air columns will produce sounds of different pitch.

6. *Investigate changing the pitch of percussion instruments* · Use a toy xylophone to show that the shorter the bar, the higher the

sound. Cut a piece of rubber from a large balloon or an old inner tube and place it over the mouth of a glass jar. Grasp the rubber with both hands and pull it downward while a child strikes the rubber repeatedly with the eraser part of a pencil (Figure 19–8). Note that the tighter the rubber drum head becomes as it is pulled further downward, the higher the sound will become. Repeat this activity with jars of the same size, but having mouths

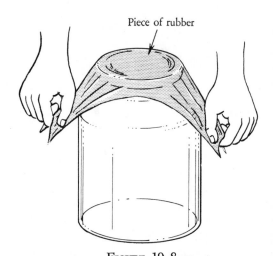

Piece of rubber

FIGURE 19–8.
THE TIGHTER THE DRUM HEAD, THE HIGHER THE SOUND WILL BECOME.

of different widths. The narrower the mouth of the jar, the higher the sound that is produced. Using rubber pieces of different thicknesses over the mouth of the jar will show that the thinner the rubber, the higher the sound that is produced.

BIBLIOGRAPHY FOR ''SOUND''

ANDERSON, DOROTHY. *Junior Science Book of Sound.* Champaign, Ill.: Garrard, 1964. 63 pp.

BERGER, MELVIN, and FRANK CLARK. *Science and Music.* New York: McGraw-Hill, 1964. 176 pp.

BRANLEY, FRANKLYN M. *High Sounds, Low Sounds.* New York: Thomas Y. Crowell, 1967. 33 pp.

FERAVOLO, ROCCO. *Wonders of Sound.* New York: Dodd, Mead, 1964. 54 pp.

FREEMAN, IRA M. *All About Sound and Ultrasonics.* New York: Random House, 1964. 138 pp.

GREY, JERRY. *Noise, Noise, Noise.* Philadelphia: Westminster, 1976. 104 pp.

HUTCHINS, CARLEEN M. *Who Will Drown the Sound?* New York: Coward, McCann & Geoghegan, 1972. 46 pp.

KNIGHT, DAVID. *Let's Find Out About Sound.* New York: Franklin Watts, 1975. 48 pp.

KOHN, BERNICE. *Echoes.* New York: Coward, McCann & Geoghegan, 1965. 52 pp.

MEADOWS, CHARLES. *Sounds and Signals: How We Communicate.* Philadelphia: Westminster, 1975. 92 pp.

OLNEY, ROSS. *Sound All-Around: How Hi-Fi and Stereo Work.* Englewood Cliffs, N.J.: Prentice-Hall, 1967. 60 pp.

NEAL, CHARLES. *Sound.* Chicago: Follett, 1964. 32 pp.

PERRERA, THOMAS, and GRETCHEN PERRERA. *Louder and Louder.* New York: Franklin Watts, 1973. 42 pp.

SCOTT, JOHN. *What Is Sound?* New York: Parents' Magazine, 1973. 64 pp.

VICTOR, EDWARD. *Exploring and Understanding Sound.* Westchester, Ill.: Benefic Press, 1969. 96 pp.

WINDLE, ERIC. *Sounds You Cannot Hear.* Englewood Cliffs, N.J.: Prentice-Hall, 1965. 69 pp.

CHAPTER 20

LIGHT

THE NATURE OF LIGHT

I. What Light Is

A. Light is a form of energy.
1. This energy is given out, or radiated, by the sun and other light-producing bodies in the form of waves.
2. Light energy is also called **radiant energy.**
B. Light is just one part of a group of radiant energy waves, called **electromagnetic waves.**
1. This group includes **Hertzian**, or **radio, waves, infrared rays, light rays, ultraviolet rays, X-rays, gamma rays**, and **cosmic rays.**
2. All of these electromagnetic waves are invisible to the human eye except light rays.
C. All electromagnetic waves, including light rays, travel at a speed of 300,000 kilometers (186,000 mi) a second.
1. These waves move in two directions at the same time: they move up and down as they travel forward.
2. Such waves are called **transverse** waves.
D. Although electromagnetic waves travel at the same speed, the waves differ in length and in frequency.
1. The length of the wave, called the **wavelength,** is the distance between corresponding parts of two of the waves.
2. The **frequency** of the waves is the number of waves that pass by a point in one second.
3. Electromagnetic waves with long wavelengths, such as radio waves, have a **low** frequency.
4. Electromagnetic waves with short wavelengths, such as X-rays, have a **high** frequency.
E. Although scientists know much about light and the other electromagnetic waves, they do not know the exact nature of these electromagnetic waves.
1. Scientists know that, although light travels in waves, it has certain behaviors that cannot be explained by this wave motion.
2. Scientists believe that light and other electromagnetic waves are made up of tiny bundles of energy called **quanta.**
3. These bundles of energy are given off, or radiated, and then travel in a wave-like motion.
4. The shorter the wavelength of the electromagnetic waves, the greater energy the waves will have, and the higher the frequency of the waves will be.

II. Light Travels in Straight Lines

A. Light waves travel in straight lines.
1. Light cannot travel around corners.
2. Even when light is made to change di-

rection, it continues to travel in straight lines.

3. A thin line of light is called a **ray.**
4. A **beam** of light is made up of many rays of light.

B. Light travels at a speed of about 300,000 kilometers (186,000 mi) a second, or more than 1060 million kilometers (660 million mi) an hour.

1. It takes about 8 minutes for light to travel from the sun to the earth.
2. This great speed explains why we see things happen at almost the exact moment they are happening.

C. Because the stars and planets are so far away from the earth, astronomers use the speed of light as a unit for measuring these great distances.

1. Until recently the astronomers used only the **light-year** as a unit for measuring long distances.
2. A light-year is the distance light will travel in 1 year, about 9½ trillion kilometers (6 trillion mi).
3. Proxima Centauri, the star nearest the earth (not counting the sun) is more than 4 light-years (42 trillion kilometers or 26 trillion miles) away.
4. Scientists now also use the **parsec** as a unit for measuring long distances.
5. One parsec is about 3¼ light-years or 30½ trillion kilometers (19 trillion mi).

III. TRANSPARENT, TRANSLUCENT, AND OPAQUE MATERIALS

A. Light can pass through some materials and is stopped by other materials.
B. Materials like air, water, and clear glass are called **transparent.**

1. When light strikes transparent materials, almost all of the light passes directly through them.
2. We can see clearly through transparent materials.

C. Materials like frosted glass and some plastics are called **translucent.**

1. When light strikes translucent materials, only some of the light passes through them.
2. The light does not pass directly through the materials, but changes directions many times, and is scattered.
3. Because light is scattered as it passes through translucent materials, we cannot see clearly through them.
4. Objects on the other side of mildly translucent materials are fuzzy and unclear.
5. With strongly translucent materials, we can see only lights and shadows.

D. Most materials are **opaque.**

1. When light strikes an opaque material, none of the light passes through the material.
2. We cannot see through opaque materials at all.
3. Most of the light is either reflected by the opaque material or else absorbed and converted into heat.
4. Even in transparent and translucent materials some of the light is absorbed and converted into heat.

IV. SHADOWS

A. **Shadows** are formed because light travels in straight lines.
B. Shadows are formed when an opaque material is placed in the path of rays of light.

1. The opaque material does not let the light pass through it.
2. A shadow is the dark space that is formed behind a material when the material stops rays of light.
3. The light rays that go past the edges of the material make an outline for the shadow.

C. Some parts of the shadow are darker than other parts.

1. The center part of the shadow, which gets no light at all, is the darkest part and is called the **umbra.**
2. The rest of the shadow is lighter because it gets light from some parts of the source of light, however, not from other parts, and is called the **penumbra.**

V. Sources of Light

A. Materials that give off light are called **luminous** materials.
B. Sources of light are classified either as **natural** or **artificial,** or man-made.
C. The sun is a natural source of light.
 1. It is our chief source of light.
 2. The light energy from the sun is believed to be produced by changes taking place in the nucleus of the atoms of materials in the sun.
D. Stars are also a natural source of light.
E. The moon and the planets do not produce their own light, but shine because sunlight strikes them and bounces off, or is reflected, from their surfaces.
F. Some living things, like the firefly, can produce their own light.
G. Common artificial sources of light include the **candle, kerosene lamp, gasoline lamp, electric light, fluorescent light,** and **neon light.**
H. The candle is a solid tube of wax, with a cotton or linen string, called the **wick,** inside the tube.
 1. When the wick is lighted, the heat melts the solid wax and a little cup of liquid wax is formed on top of the candle.
 2. The wick soaks up the liquid wax, and the heat of the burning wick then changes the liquid wax into a gas, which burns with a yellow flame.
I. The kerosene lamp works very much like the candle.
 1. The kerosene passes up the wick to the part that is burning, where the heat turns the kerosene into a gas that burns.
 2. A chimney protects the flame from drafts and helps keep the flame burning.
J. The gasoline lamp makes use of a fragile cone, called a **mantle,** that contains minerals that glow with a very white light when heated by the burning gasoline.
K. The electric light bulb contains a thin strip, or filament, of tungsten metal.
 1. When electricity flows through the fila-

ment, the filament becomes hot and glows brightly with a nearly white light.
 2. The light bulb is filled with an inactive gas, such as nitrogen and argon, instead of air.
 3. Air is not used because the oxygen in the air would make the tungsten filament burn away very quickly.
L. The fluorescent light tube has a small amount of mercury in it, and the inside of the tube is coated with certain chemicals called **phosphors.**
 1. When an electric current enters the tube, small filaments of tungsten metal at each end of the tube become hot and convert the liquid mercury into a vapor.
 2. The electric current then flows through the mercury vapor, giving off a bluish light together with many invisible ultraviolet rays.
 3. The ultraviolet rays then strike the phosphors, which produce visible light.
 4. The fluorescent lamp is cooler and gives more light for the money than the electric light bulb.
M. The neon light tube has a gas, called **neon,** in it.
 1. When a powerful electric current passes through the neon gas, the molecules of neon become excited and glow with a red color.
 2. Other gases, as well as different colored glass tubes, can be used to produce different colors.

VI. The Measurement of Light

A. Two different units of measurement have been used to measure light: the **candle power** and the **foot-candle.**
 1. The candle power is the unit used to measure the intensity, or strength, of the light that is given off by an object.
 2. The foot-candle is the unit used to measure the amount of light, or illumination, in a room or other place.
B. Because the candle was the principal source of light when scientists first began

to measure light, it was only natural to use the candle as a standard.

1. One **candle power** is the intensity of light that is produced by a standard candle.
2. A **standard candle** is one that has a certain size and quality.
3. Today, scientists use another unit of light power, called the **lumen.**

C. The amount of light, or illumination, that an object receives in a room or other places depends upon two things: the candle power of the light and the distance the object is from the source of light.

1. The stronger the source of light, and the nearer the object is to the source of light, the better the illumination will be.
2. One foot-candle is the amount of light a standard candle will give at a distance of 1 foot.

D. An instrument, called a **light meter,** is used to measure the amount of light falling upon a surface or object.

1. Some light meters contain a **photoelectric cell,** which converts light into electricity, and an **ammeter,** which measures the amount of electricity produced.
2. When light shines on the photoelectric cell, an electric current is generated.
3. The amount of electric current produced is shown by the movement of a pointer in the ammeter.
4. The brighter the light, the more current is produced, and the farther the pointer moves.
5. A **photoresistive cell** in other light meters contains cadmium sulfide, a chemical that is sensitive to light.
6. When light shines on the photoresistive cell, it affects the strength of an electric current flowing from a dry cell in the light meter.
7. This change in electric current makes a pointer move in the light meter.

THE REFLECTION OF LIGHT

I. Light Can Be Reflected

A. For us to see an object that does not produce its own light, three things must happen.

1. There must be a source of light.
2. The light must strike the object.
3. The light must bounce off, or be **reflected** from, the object and then travel to the eye.

B. When light is reflected, it changes direction, but it still travels in straight lines.

C. Transparent and translucent materials allow most of the light striking them to pass through, but some light is absorbed and some light is reflected.

D. Opaque materials do not allow any light to pass through them, but absorb and reflect the light instead.

1. Such materials differ greatly in how much light they absorb and reflect.
2. Dark, rough opaque materials absorb more light than they reflect.
3. Light, smooth opaque objects reflect more light than they absorb.

II. Law of Reflection

A. When a ray of light strikes a mirror straight down, up, or forward, the ray is reflected directly back.

1. In this case we say that the ray strikes the mirror in a perpendicular line.
2. A perpendicular line has an angle of 90 degrees.

B. When a ray of light strikes a mirror at a slant, or angle, the ray is reflected at a slant, or angle, in another direction.

1. The ray that strikes the mirror is called the **incident,** or striking, ray.
2. The ray that is reflected by the mirror is called the **reflected** ray.
3. The angle between the ray of light that strikes the surface at a point and the straight, or perpendicular, line at that point is called the **angle of incidence.**
4. The angle between the reflected ray and the perpendicular line is called the **angle of reflection.**

C. The law, or principle, of reflection states that the angle of incidence is equal to the angle of reflection.
D. The law of reflection holds true for all smooth, polished surfaces.
1. When a beam of light strikes a mirror, each ray in the beam is reflected regularly.
2. Each ray has the same angle of incidence and angle of reflection so that, although the rays change direction, they all do so the same amount, and in this way continue to form a beam.
E. The law of reflection does not hold true for rough surfaces.
1. When a beam of light strikes a rough surface, each ray is reflected irregularly.
2. The rays do not have the same angle of incidence and angle of reflection so that the beam of light is scattered, or spread out, in all directions.
3. When light strikes a sheet of very smooth paper, the light is reflected regularly to the eye, and we get a glare.
4. When light strikes a sheet of coarse paper, the uneven surface reflects the light irregularly and scatters it so that we get very little glare.

III. DIFFUSE REFLECTION IS BEST FOR LIGHTING IN THE HOME

A. **Direct** lighting is light that goes directly from the source of light to the surface to be lighted.
1. Almost all of the light strikes the surface directly.

2. This direct light produces much glare, which is caused either by light striking the eye directly or by light reflected to the eye from a smooth or shiny surface.
3. A frosted glass bulb is translucent and has an uneven surface so that it scatters the light and cuts down the glare a little.
B. With **semidirect** lighting a translucent bowl or shade directs some of the light to the ceiling.
1. The uneven surface of the ceiling reflects this light irregularly and scatters it all over the room.
2. The rest of the light goes directly from the source of light to the surface to be lighted.
3. Semidirect light has much less glare than direct light.
C. With **indirect lighting** most of the light is directed upward to the ceiling, which then scatters the light all over the room.
1. The light is directed to the ceiling either by using an opaque shade or by having the source of light close to the ceiling.
2. Any light that is directed downward is scattered by using a translucent globe or shade.
3. Indirect lighting provides the most irregular reflection and the least amount of glare.

IV. THE PLANE MIRROR

A. A **plane** mirror is usually made of a flat piece of clear glass, and the back of the glass has a thin coating of silver or some other shiny metal.
1. The light striking the mirror passes through the transparent glass, and then almost all the light is reflected back by the shiny, but opaque, silver.
2. Unbreakable mirrors can be made from highly polished steel, but these mirrors do not reflect light as well as glass ones do.
B. The objects that you see in a mirror seem to be behind the mirror, even though they are not.

1. What you really see is the reflection of objects in front of the mirror.
2. This reflection is called an **image.**
3. When you look into a mirror, you see an image of yourself.

C. The image in a mirror is reversed.
 1. The image in a mirror seems to face you so that everything is reversed.
 2. If you raise your right hand, your image will raise its left hand.
 3. If you wink your right eye, the image will wink its left eye.

D. The image in a mirror is just as large as the object in front of it.

E. The image in a mirror seems to be just as far behind the mirror as the object is in front of it.

V. CURVED MIRRORS

A. When mirrors are curved, we get different kinds of images.

B. Mirrors that curve inward are called **concave** mirrors.
 1. If a concave mirror curves inward just a little, the image is right-side up and larger, or magnified.
 2. If a concave mirror curves inward a lot, the image is upside down and smaller.

C. If a concave mirror is curved just the right way, it will reflect rays of light that strike its surface so that all the rays come together at one spot.
 1. This spot is called the **focus** of the mirror.

2. Concave mirrors are used in some astronomical telescopes to collect the light from a distant star and bring the light together so that the star may be examined.
3. Stars are too far away to be magnified, but the concave mirror in the astronomical telescope can make them very much brighter.
4. Such a telescope also helps astronomers look at stars that are too far away and faint to be seen with the naked eye.

D. Flashlights and automobile headlights also have concave mirrors made of shiny metal.
 1. These mirrors act just the opposite as the mirrors in the astronomical telescopes.
 2. The light bulb is placed at the focus of the mirror.
 3. The rays of light coming from the bulb are reflected by the mirror to throw a beam, instead of being scattered in all directions.

E. Mirrors that curve outward are called **convex** mirrors.
 1. A convex mirror does not bring rays of light together at one spot, but spreads them out in all directions.
 2. Images from a convex mirror are erect, smaller, and seem farther away, but the convex mirror gives you an image that covers a larger area.
 3. Some rear-view auto mirrors are convex mirrors.

THE REFRACTION OF LIGHT

I. THE NATURE OF REFRACTION

A. When light rays travel through a transparent material, they travel in a straight line and at the same speed.

B. But, when light rays pass at a slant, or angle, from one transparent material (such as air) into another transparent material (such as water), the light rays are bent, or **refracted,** so that they travel in a different direction.
 1. Although the rays are now traveling in a different direction, they still travel in a straight line.

2. The light rays must pass at a slant, or angle, from one transparent material into another; otherwise they will not be bent.
3. If light rays pass from one material into another in a perpendicular line (at an angle of 90 degrees), the rays will pass straight through without being bent.
C. The light is bent because there is a change in the speed of light as it passes from one transparent material into another.
 1. Light travels at different speeds through different kinds of transparent materials.
 2. The difference in speed depends upon the **density**, or heaviness, of the material.
 3. The greater the density of the material, the more slowly light will travel through it.
 4. Light travels more slowly in water than air because water is denser than air.
 5. Light travels more slowly in glass than water because glass is denser than water.
D. When light rays pass into a denser material at an angle, the light rays are slowed down and are bent inward.
E. When light rays pass into a less dense material at an angle, the light rays speed up and are bent outward.
F. The amount of refraction depends upon the density (heaviness) of the material.
 1. The greater the density of the material, the more the light rays will be bent inward.
 2. Glass is denser than water, so light rays passing from air into glass will be bent more than rays passing from air into water.

II. Lenses

A. A **lens** is a piece of curved glass or other transparent material.
B. The lens may be curved on one side and flat on the other side, or it may be curved on both sides.
C. Lenses are used to bend, or refract, light rays.
 1. The light rays strike the lens at a slant because the surface of the lens is curved.

2. This curvature of the lens makes the rays of light bend as they pass through the lens.
D. When light rays pass through a lens, they are always bent toward the thickest part of the lens.
E. There are two kinds of lenses: **convex** lenses and **concave** lenses.

III. Convex Lenses

A. A convex lens is thick in the middle and thin at the ends.
B. Light rays passing through a convex lens are bent toward the thicker middle of the lens.
 1. In this way, after passing through the lens, the rays come together and meet at a point.
 2. The point at which the rays meet is called the **focal point,** and we say that the convex lens brings the rays into **focus** at this point.
 3. The thicker the middle of the lens, the more the rays of light are bent and brought into focus.
C. By bending the rays of light and bringing them together, the convex lens can produce an image.
D. When a lens is placed between an object and a screen, an inverted, or upside down, image is formed on the screen.
 1. When the object is far away from the lens, the image is smaller than the object.
 2. The farther away the object is from the lens, the smaller the image is.
 3. The closer the object is brought to the lens, the larger the image becomes.
 4. When the object is close to the lens, the image becomes larger than the object.
E. When a convex lens is placed between your eyes and an object, the object appears larger, or is magnified.
 1. In this case, an image that is larger than the object is formed, and it is erect, or right side up.

2. The convex lens now acts as a magnifying glass.

IV. CONCAVE LENSES

A. A concave lens is thin in the middle and thick at the ends.
B. Light rays passing through a concave lens are bent toward the thicker ends of the lens.
  1. After passing through the lens, the rays are spread apart.
  2. The rays seem to be coming from an imaginary point behind the lens.
  3. The thicker the ends of the lens, the wider apart the rays are spread.
C. A concave lens produces only one kind of image: one that is smaller than the object, and is erect, or right side up.

V. USES OF LENSES IN INSTRUMENTS

A. The **camera.**
  1. The basic parts of a camera are a light-proof box, an opening in front of the camera, a shutter over the opening, a convex lens behind the opening, a film at the back of the camera, and a device to hold and turn the film.
  2. The shutter lets light enter the camera and strike the lens, which bends the light rays so that they come together, or are brought into focus, at the film.
  3. The film is coated with chemicals that are affected by light.
  4. When light rays are brought together at the film, a chemical change takes place.
  5. The film is then treated with chemicals and becomes a "negative," where the dark parts of the object appear light and the light part appear dark.
  6. When light is then passed through the "negative" to light-sensitive paper, a "positive" is produced where the dark parts of the "negative" now become light and the light parts become dark, just as they were in the original object.

7. In inexpensive cameras the lens is fixed so that it can only bring into sharp focus light rays coming from objects that are more than 2 meters (6½ ft) away from the camera.
8. In more expensive cameras the lens can be moved back and forth so that it can bring into sharp focus light rays coming from both near and far objects.

B. The **microscope.**
  1. A microscope has two convex lenses, which are placed at each end of a light-proof tube.
  2. The upper lens is called the **eyepiece,** and the lower lens the **objective.**
  3. Rays of light from an object pass through the lens of the objective and are bent, producing an enlarged image of the object inside the tube.
  4. The lens of the eyepiece acts like a magnifying glass and magnifies this image even more, making it many times larger than the object.
  5. To focus the microscope, one part of the tube is made to slide up or down inside another part.

C. The **telescope.**
  1. The **reflecting** telescope has a large concave mirror at one end, and at the other end there is a small convex lens that magnifies the image produced by the mirror.
  2. The **refracting** telescope works very much like the microscope, with an objective and an eyepiece.
  3. A very large convex lens in the objective collects all the light it can from a distant object and bends the light rays to produce an image, which is magnified by the smaller convex lens in the eyepiece.
  4. One part of the tube slides in and out of another part of the tube to bring objects located at different distances into focus.
  5. **Binoculars** and **opera glasses** are really two refracting telescopes connected side by side, one for each eye.
  6. Prisms in the binoculars and opera

glasses reflect the light rays so that the image is seen right side up.

D. **Projectors**
1. All projectors use one or more convex lenses to change a small film photograph into a large image on a screen.

2. A strong beam of light shines through the transparent film, and a convex lens bends the rays of light coming from the film to produce the large image on the screen.
3. Projectors are widely used in schools.

COLOR

I. THE SPECTRUM

A. When a narrow beam of sunlight passes at a slant into a triangular transparent material, called a **prism,** the sunlight is broken up into a band of colored lights, which can be seen on a white wall or screen.
1. This band of colored lights is called the **spectrum.**
2. There are seven colored lights in the spectrum: violet, indigo, blue, green, yellow, orange, and red.
3. Sometimes blue and indigo are treated as one color.

B. When a second prism (or a convex lens) is placed at just the right position in front of the rays of colored light coming from a prism, the rays of colored light combine to form white light again.

C. White light, then, is really a mixture of the seven colored lights of the spectrum.

D. These colored lights are called **pure** colored lights because each light cannot be broken up any further by another prism.

E. A prism breaks up white light into a spectrum because the colored lights that make up the spectrum all have different wavelengths.
1. Violet light has the shortest wavelength, red light the longest wavelength, and the wavelengths of the other colored lights are in between those of violet and red light.
2. When white light enters a prism at a

slant, the prism bends, or refracts, the different colored lights in different amounts.
3. The lights with the shorter waves are bent more than lights with the longer waves.
4. Violet light has the shortest waves and is bent the most, and red light has the longest wave and is bent the least.
5. The other colors are bent in different amounts so that all seven colored lights that make up white light are separated as they pass through the prism, and strike a screen at different places to form a band of colors.

II. RAINBOWS

A. A **rainbow** is a spectrum that is produced when the sun shines during or immediately after a rain shower.

B. The raindrops act as tiny prisms and break the sunlight up into a spectrum in the form of a large, beautiful arch.

C. An artificial rainbow can be made by spraying with a garden hose with your back to the sun, either early in the morning or late in the afternoon, when the sun is low.

III. PRIMARY AND COMPLEMENTARY COLORS

A. A colored light is only a part of white light.

B. To get a single colored light from white light, all the other colored lights except the one you want must be taken away, or absorbed.

1. When white light is passed through a transparent colored material, such as red cellophane, all the colors in white light are absorbed except the red light that is allowed to pass through the cellophane.
2. The colored light is always dimmer than white light because the rest of the colored lights have been absorbed.
3. The lights that have been absorbed are converted into heat.

C. Red, green, and blue colored lights are called **primary** colors.
1. Every shade of colored light can be made by mixing different combinations of these colored lights.
2. All three primary colors together produce white light.

D. Any two colors that, when mixed together, produce white light are called **complementary** colors.

E. The following pairs of colors are complementary colors.
1. Red and bluish-green.
2. Orange and greenish-blue.
3. Yellow and blue.
4. Green and purplish-red.
5. Violet and greenish-yellow.

IV. COLORED MATERIALS

A. A material is colored because, when white light strikes the material, all the colored lights have been absorbed except one, which is reflected to the eye.
1. A red dress looks red because the material absorbs all the colors of white light except red, which is reflected to the eye.
2. Grass appears green because it absorbs all the colors except green, which it reflects to the eye.
3. The colored lights that have been absorbed are converted into heat.

B. A white material appears white because all the colored lights are reflected to the eye.

C. A black material appears black because all the colored lights are absorbed so that not one light is reflected to the eye.

D. The color of a material also depends upon the kind of light shining on it.
1. When red light shines on a white material, the material appears red because the red light is the only color striking the white material, so red is the only color that can be reflected to the eye.
2. When blue light shines on a red material, the material appears black because the material can only reflect red light, and there is no red in the blue light shining on the material.

E. Colors may seem different in artificial light because this light has less blue and more red in it than sunlight.
1. In artificial light blue may seem to be almost black because there is so little blue to be reflected.
2. At the same time red seems to be much brighter because the artificial light has so much red that can be reflected.

F. Red, yellow, and blue are called the primary colors of paints.
1. Every other color can be produced by mixing different combinations of these colored paints.
2. Red and yellow paints make orange.
3. Red and blue paints make purple.
4. Yellow and blue paints make green.
5. Black and orange paints make brown.
6. Black and white paints make gray.

G. Mixing colored paints produces effects entirely different from those produced by mixing colored lights.
1. Most colored paints are not completely pure, so they also reflect small amounts of other colors.
2. Yellow paint usually reflects a little green light as well as yellow light.
3. Blue paint also reflects some green light as well as blue light.
4. When yellow paint and blue paint are mixed together, the mixture becomes green.
5. The yellow paint absorbs the blue light

and the blue paint absorbs the yellow light.
6. Neither paint absorbs the green light so that green is the only color reflected to the eye.
H. When red, yellow, and blue paints are mixed together, the mixture becomes black.
1. All the colors have been absorbed and none is reflected to the eye.
2. Black is not really a color, but rather the absence of all color.

V. THE COLOR OF THE SKY AND THE SUN

A. During the day the sky looks blue and the sun yellowish-white.
B. This effect is caused by the presence of dust in the air.
1. The sky looks blue because some of the blue color of sunlight is scattered by the dust and reflected to the eye.

2. The yellow and red colors of sunlight are not scattered, but rather pass straight through, so that the loss of some of the blue color of sunlight makes the sun look yellowish-white.
C. At sunrise and sunset the sunlight must travel at a greater slant, or angle, and it passes through more air and dust than before.
1. The blue color of sunlight is now scattered much more by the dust in the air, so that there is even less blue passing straight through.
2. The loss of more of the blue color of sunlight now makes the sun look reddish or orange.
3. The moisture in the clouds also absorbs green and blue from the sunlight, producing a still greater effect of reds, oranges, and yellows at sunrise and sunset.

ELECTROMAGNETIC RADIATIONS

I. THE ELECTROMAGNETIC SPECTRUM

A. Light rays are just one small part of a group of radiant energy waves, called **electromagnetic waves.**
1. This group includes **radio waves, infrared rays, light rays, ultraviolet rays, X-rays, gamma rays,** and **cosmic rays.**
2. All of these electromagnetic waves are invisible to the human eye, except light rays.
3. We recognize the other waves by the effects they produce.
B. All electromagnetic waves are transverse waves, which move in two directions at the very same time: up and down, and forward.
C. All travel at a speed of 300,000 kilometers (186,000 mi) a second.
D. Electromagnetic waves differ in length and in frequency, even though they all travel at the same speed.
1. The length of a wave, called the **wave-**

length, is the distance between corresponding parts of two of the waves.
2. The **frequency** of a wave is the number of waves that pass by a point in 1 second.
E. Some electromagnetic waves have very tiny wavelengths, whereas others have very long wavelengths.
F. Some electromagnetic waves have very low frequencies, whereas others have very high frequencies.
1. A **cycle** is one complete up and down movement of a wave.
2. The frequency of a wave, then, is also the number of cycles that take place in 1 second.
3. In a 60-cycle wave, the wave moves up and down 60 times in 1 second so that 60 complete waves pass by a point in 1 second.
4. Because electromagnetic waves have very high frequencies, the frequency is usually given in **kilocycles** (thousands

of cycles) or **megacycles** (millions of cycles).

5. We also use the terms **hertz, kilohertz,** and **megahertz** to express frequency.

G. Electromagnetic waves with long wavelengths have low frequencies, whereas those waves with short wavelengths have high frequencies.

H. Together all these different waves of radiant energy make up the electromagnetic spectrum.

1. At one end of this spectrum are those waves with long wavelengths and low frequencies.

2. At the other end are those waves with short wavelengths and high frequencies.

II. WAVES WITH LONG WAVELENGTHS AND LOW FREQUENCIES

A. Waves of this kind include **infrared rays** and **Hertzian, or radio, waves.**

B. Infrared rays are a band of invisible waves that can produce very much heat energy.

1. Infra means "below," and infrared rays are the first band of rays below visible red light rays.

2. Almost half of the sun's energy comes to us as infrared rays.

3. Infrared rays are used in taking pictures in the dark, in obtaining special photographic effects, in detecting fingerprints or changes in documents and paintings, and in medicine.

C. Hertzian or radio waves are a very wide band of invisible rays that are used in all kinds of communication.

1. This band of rays is found below the infrared rays.

2. The band is so wide that it is subdivided into smaller bands or channels.

3. Each channel is set aside and used for a different purpose.

4. The waves in each band or channel are often identified by their frequencies (kilocycles and megacycles) instead of their wavelengths.

5. Separate channels are used for AM radio,

FM radio, television, police calls, military communications, radar, amateur broadcasting, aviation, and distress signals.

III. WAVES WITH SHORT WAVELENGTHS AND HIGH FREQUENCIES

A. Waves of this kind include **ultraviolet rays, X-rays, gamma rays,** and **cosmic rays.**

B. Ultraviolet rays are a band of invisible waves found just beyond visible violet light rays.

1. Ultra means "beyond," and ultraviolet rays are the first band of rays beyond visible violet light rays.

2. Ultraviolet rays come from the sun and can produce severe, painful burns.

3. Ultraviolet rays can also be produced when an electric current flows through mercury vapor.

4. When the invisible ultraviolet rays strike certain chemicals, called **phosphors,** the chemicals glow and give off visible light.

5. This effect is used in fluorescent lamps and for identifying marks made on clothing by the laundry.

6. Ultraviolet light is also used for scientific research, in special lamps to kill germs, in advertising, and in safety-warning devices.

C. X-rays are a band of waves found beyond the ultraviolet rays.

1. They have a shorter wavelength and higher frequency than ultraviolet rays.

2. These rays can pass through nonmetals and through thin sheets of most metals.

3. The rays are stopped by thicker sheets of metals and by certain metallic salts, such as barium sulfate.

4. X-rays are used to take pictures of the bones and organs in the body, detect cracks in metals, and inspect fruits to see if they have been damaged by frost.

D. Gamma rays are very tiny electromagnetic waves.

1. They are found beyond the band of X-rays.

2. Radioactive materials give off gamma rays.

E. Cosmic rays are found beyond the band of gamma rays.

1. Cosmic rays are not true electromagnetic waves, but act as if they were tiny par-

ticles traveling at the speed of light.

2. These tiny particles that make up cosmic rays come from outer space and strike the earth and the atmosphere.

3. Scientists know very little about cosmic rays.

LEARNING ACTIVITIES FOR "LIGHT"

THE NATURE OF LIGHT

1. *Make transverse waves* · Obtain about 4 meters (13 ft) of clothes rope. Attach one end of the rope to a door knob. Shake the other end up and down to form transverse waves (Figure 20–1). Note that the waves move up

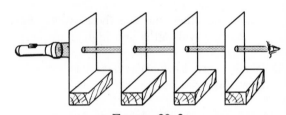

FIGURE 20–2.

LIGHT TRAVELS IN A STRAIGHT LINE THROUGH THE HOLES IN THE INDEX CARDS.

FIGURE 20–1.

MAKING A ROPE PRODUCE TRANSVERSE WAVES.

and down as they travel forward. Compare these waves with the longitudinal waves produced in Learning Activity 4 of "Sound," Chapter 17 (p. 696). Draw a series of transverse waves on the chalkboard. Mark off one wavelength. Note that the number of these waves passing by a fixed point in 1 second would be the frequency of these waves.

2. *Discover that light travels in straight lines* · Obtain four index cards and find their center by drawing diagonals on each card. Make a good-sized hole at this center, and then attach each card with thumb tacks to a small block of wood (Figure 20–2). Place the index cards one in front of the other, some distance apart, making sure that the holes are in a

straight line with each other. Rest a flashlight on some books set 1 meter (3 ft) from the first card, making sure that the height is just right for the flashlight to shine directly through the holes.

Turn on the flashlight and darken the room. Have a child look through the holes and see the light of the flashlight. Infer that the light can be seen only because it is passing through each hole in a straight line. (If you clap two chalkboard erasers repeatedly along the path of the light, the children can see a beam of light in a straight line). Now move one card so it is out of line. The child can not see the light because it travels in a straight line and is stopped by the card.

3. *Make a light-ray box* · Obtain a large rectangular cardboard carton and remove the flaps to create an open side. Put the carton down so that the open side is at the back. Remove most of the top and front side of the carton and replace with plastic wrap, pressing

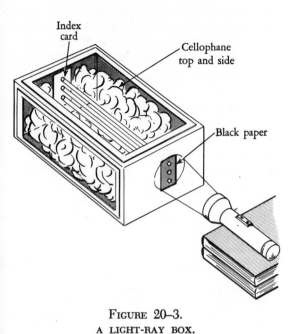

FIGURE 20–3.

A LIGHT-RAY BOX.

the plastic wrap firmly to the carton (Figure 20–3). Paint the inside cardboard of the carton with flat, black paint.

Obtain two pieces of black cloth, each slightly larger than half the length of the carton, and tack them to the open back in such a way that they overlap at the middle. You can now put your hand inside the carton without permitting any light to enter. Halfway down one end of the carton, cut a window 7½ centimeters (3 in) long and 5 centimeters (2 in) wide. Obtain a piece of black construction paper slightly larger than the window, punch out three holes, one underneath the other, and then tape the paper over the window. Tape a small white index card on the inside of the other end of the carton, directly opposite the black paper. The card will act as a screen.

Fill the carton with smoke by burning a cigarette, rope, damp paper, incense, or punk in an ash tray. Obtain a three-cell focusing flashlight and rest it on some books set 1 meter (3 ft) away from the carton, making sure the height is such that light from the flashlight will shine directly through the holes.

Turn on the flashlight, and then darken the room. Three parallel rays of light will be visible inside the carton. The rays are parallel, showing that light travels in straight lines.

4. *Investigate the speed of light* · Have the children read about and report on how the speed of light was determined. Let them calculate the time it takes for the sun's rays to reach the earth 150 million kilometers (93 million mi) away. Some children may be interested in calculating the distance traveled in one light-year. This distance can be found by multiplying 300,000 kilometers (186,000 mi) a second by 60 seconds, then by 60 minutes, then by 24 hours, and then by 365¼ days. Multiplying this answer by 3½ will give the distance traveled in a parasec.

5. *Compare transparent, translucent, and opaque materials* · Darken the room and aim a beam of light from a flashlight at a clear pane of glass. A distinct spot will be seen on the wall as the light passes directly through the transparent material. Now aim the beam at a pane of frosted glass or a piece of wax paper. Light will pass through, but it will be dispersed by the translucent material and there will not be a spot on the wall. Aim the beam of light at a square of cardboard. None of the light will pass through the opaque material.

Place a lighted candle behind the clear pane of glass. You will see the candle clearly through the transparent material. Repeat, using frosted glass or wax paper, and the candle will not be seen clearly through the translucent material. You will not be able to see the candle at all through opaque cardboard.

6. *Create shadows* · Place a screen at one end of the room. Remove the shade from a table lamp or gooseneck lamp and place it on a table about 5 meters (16½ ft) from the screen. Turn on the lamp and darken the room. Suspend a styrofoam ball between the lamp and the screen, and note the shadow cast on the screen. If the ball is quite close to the screen, only an umbra will be seen. If the ball is

nearer the lamp, both an umbra and penumbra will be seen.

7. *Investigate sources of light* · Have the children read and discuss sources of light as the sun, torch, candle, kerosene lamp, gas lamp, gasoline lamp, electric light, fluorescent light, and neon light. Let them describe how each source is produced. Make a display or exhibit of as many of these sources as are available.

8. *Measure illumination* · Obtain a light-meter to measure the illumination at different parts of the classroom and the school building. Have a child bring in a camera with a built-in lightmeter and explain its operation.

THE REFLECTION OF LIGHT

1. *Observe that light can be reflected* · Set up a light-ray box as described in Learning Activity 3 of "The Nature of Light" (p. 714). Hold a mirror at a 45-degree angle in the box. Note how the light is reflected (Figure 20–4). Hold

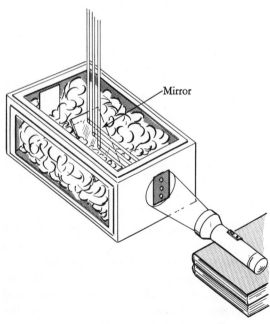

FIGURE 20–4.
LIGHT IS REFLECTED BY A PLANE MIRROR.

the mirror at different angles and observe the effect on the reflection of light. When you hold the mirror vertically (at an angle of 90 degrees), the rays will be reflected directly back to their source.

2. *Illustrate the law of reflection* · Place a mirror at the center of a table. Darken the room, and then turn on a focusing flashlight and aim it at an angle at the mirror. The light will be reflected and appear on the wall. Have a child clap two chalkboard erasers over the mirror and on each side of the mirror (Figure 20–5). Two rays of light, an incident and a

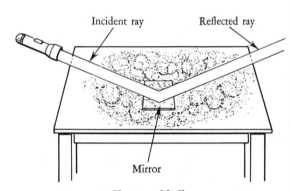

Incident ray   Reflected ray

Mirror

FIGURE 20–5.
ILLUSTRATING THE LAW OF REFLECTION.

reflected ray, will appear. Change the angle at which the ray strikes the mirror and note how the angle of the reflected ray changes accordingly. Point out that the angle of incidence and angle of reflection are always equal.

3. *Compare reflection from smooth and rough surfaces* · Repeat either Learning Activity 1 or 2 above, first using a mirror alone, then taping a piece of wax paper over the mirror. Note how the rays of light are reflected irregularly and scattered by the rougher surface of the wax paper.

4. *Compare reflection from light and dark surfaces* · Repeat Learning Activity 2 of "Winds," Chapter 11 (p. 380). Light surfaces reflect more of the sun's rays than dark surfaces.

5. *Discuss lighting in the home* · Have the children read about and discuss direct, semi-direct, and indirect lighting. Discuss which kind of lighting is best for use in the home.

6. *Investigate reflection in plane mirrors* · Stand before a mirror and raise your right hand. Your image will raise its left hand, showing that the image is reversed. Note that your image is the same size as you are. Step back two paces. Your image will be just as far behind the mirror as you are in front of it.

7. *Discover that light can be reflected again and again by mirrors* · Have a child sit or crouch next to a wall with a window. Give the child two mirrors and have him hold them in the position as shown in Figure 20–6. By tilting

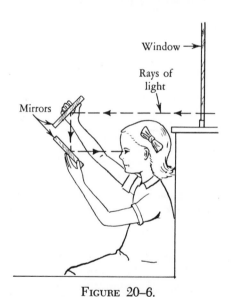

FIGURE 20–6.

A PERISCOPE WORKS BY REFLECTING LIGHT MORE THAN ONCE.

both mirrors at the proper angles, the child will be able to see objects outside the window. Draw a diagram on the chalkboard to show how the light from the window strikes the top mirror, is reflected to the lower mirror, and then reflected again to the child's eye. Point out that this is how a periscope works.

8. *Discover that plane glass can act as a mirror* · Obtain a pane of glass and tape a piece of white paper over one side. Turn on a table lamp and darken the room. Stand with your back to the lamp and hold up the glass and look at it, keeping the white paper behind the glass. You will see a very faint reflection because most of the light passing through the glass and striking the white paper is reflected irregularly and scattered. Now replace the white paper with a piece of black paper. You will see a very clear reflection because the black paper absorbed the light striking it, allowing a small amount of light to be reflected regularly from the surface of the glass.

9. *Investigate reflection in a concave mirror* · Have the children look into a magnifying mirror. Point out that the mirror is a concave mirror that curves inward just a little. This is the reason why the image is right side up and magnified.

Obtain a large, highly polished, silver tablespoon. Look at the concave (hollow) side of the bowl. This concave mirror curves inward a lot, and thus your image is upside down and smaller.

10. *Investigate reflection in a convex mirror* · Obtain a large, polished, silver tablespoon. Hold it vertically and look at the convex (bulging) side of the bowl. You will see a long, thin image of yourself that is smaller and right side up. Now hold the spoon horizontally and look again. The image becomes short and fat, but still is small and right side up.

THE REFRACTION OF LIGHT

1. *Observe that light can be refracted* · Fill a rectangular aquarium three-quarters full of water and add drops of milk until the water has a cloudy appearance. Darken the room, and then turn on a focusing flashlight and aim it at an angle at the aquarium (Figure 20–7). At the same time have a child clap two chalkboard erasers over the aquarium to outline the

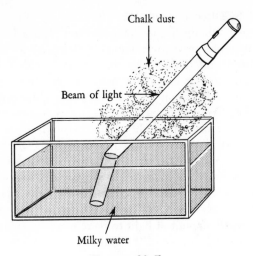

Chalk dust

Beam of light

Milky water

FIGURE 20–7.

THE LIGHT IS REFRACTED WHEN IT ENTERS THE WATER.

path of the beam of light coming from the flashlight. The beam of light will be bent inward as it passes from the air into the water. Now hold the flashlight so that the beam of light enters the water vertically (at an angle of 90 degrees). The beam will pass from the air into the water without being refracted.

2. *Discover that a convex lens causes light rays to converge* · Set up a light-ray box as described in Learning Activity 3 of "The Nature of Light" (p. 714). Hold a magnifying glass (convex lens) in the box and note how the light rays converge and meet (Figure 20–8).

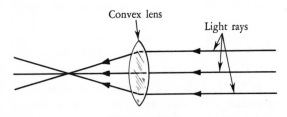

Convex lens

Light rays

FIGURE 20–8.

A CONVEX LENS CONVERGES RAYS OF LIGHT.

Move the magnifying glass back and forth until the rays of light meet at a point on the white

index card. Then move the magnifying glass so that the rays of light converge, and then spread out again. Note how the rays travel in straight lines, even after they are bent.

Repeat Learning Activity 7 of "The Nature of Heat," Chapter 18 (p. 677), showing how a convex lens converges the sun's rays so that they meet at a point on a match head, causing it to burst into flame.

3. *Investigate images formed by a convex lens* · Use a spring-type clothes pin to hold a large white cardboard vertically on a table. Place a lit candle about 1 meter (3 ft) away from the cardboard. Hold a magnifying glass near the cardboard and move the magnifying glass slowly toward the flame until a clear, inverted, smaller image of the candle appears on the cardboard (Figure 20–9).

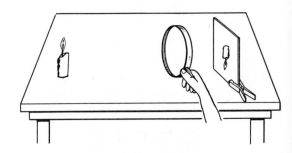

FIGURE 20–9.

A CONVEX LENS HELD FAR FROM AN OBJECT WILL PRODUCE AN INVERTED, SMALLER IMAGE.

Now hold the magnifying glass close to the candle and move the magnifying glass slowly toward the cardboard until a clear, inverted, larger image of the candle appears on the cardboard. You may have to push the cardboard farther back to obtain this image. Point out that when the object is close to the lens, you get a large image. When the object is far from the lens, you get a small image. Both images are upside down.

Now use the glass as a magnifying instrument by placing the glass between your eyes and an object. When used this way, the image produced is larger and right side up.

4. Discover that a concave lens causes light rays to diverge · Set up a light-ray box as described in Learning Activity 3 of "The Nature of Light" (p. 714). Get a concave lens from a scientific supply house or an optometrist. Hold the concave lens in the box and note how the rays of light spread out, or diverge (Figure 20–10).

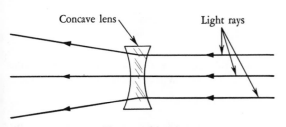

FIGURE 20–10.
A CONCAVE LENS DIVERGES RAYS OF LIGHT.

5. Investigate images formed by a concave lens · Hold a concave lens between your eyes and a page in a book. The picture and words will become smaller. Point out that a concave lens produces just one kind of image: an erect and smaller one.

6. Discover that water can act as a lens · Insert your thumb in a glass tumbler of water and look at it from the side. The water has assumed the curved shape of the tumbler and has become a convex (magnifying) lens. This change will explain why fish and food (such as olives) are magnified when placed in curved containers.

7. Investigate light and vision · Repeat Learning Activities 4 to 11 to "The Sense Organs," Chapter 15 (pp. 599–601), and show the relationship between light and vision.

8. Compare the eye and the camera · Display a camera and a model or diagram of the eye. List the key parts of each, describe their function, and then determine which parts of the eye correspond with those of the camera. Now show how the eye and the camera differ.

9. Investigate the use of lenses in instruments · Have the children read about and report on the part lenses play in such instruments as the camera, microscope, and telescope.

COLOR

1. Make a spectrum · On a sunny day, when the sun's rays are coming through the window into the classroom, hold a prism in the path of the sunlight. Roll the prism around until you are able to throw a rainbow on the wall (Figure 20–11). Have a child tape a white card-

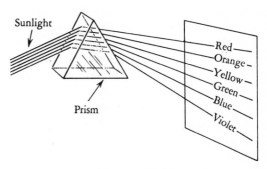

FIGURE 20–11.
A PRISM PRODUCES A BAND OF COLORED LIGHTS.

board to the wall so that the spectrum will show up more clearly. Ask the children to locate and identify the different colors of the spectrum.

2. Discover that the colored lights of a spectrum can be recombined · Repeat Learning Activity 1 above, but now place a magnifying glass between the prism and the cardboard (Figure 20–12). Move the magnifying glass back and forth until you make the spectrum disappear and there is only a spot of white light on the cardboard. Point out that the convex lens of the magnifying glass caused the colored lights of the spectrum to converge and combine, forming white light again.

3. Make a rainbow · Take the children out-

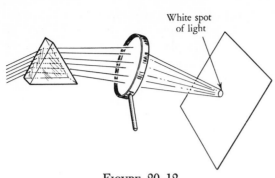

FIGURE 20–12.

A CONVEX LENS RECOMBINES THE SPECTRUM TO FORM WHITE LIGHT AGAIN.

the circle. Draw three equal sections on the cardboard and color them red, green, and blue with wax crayons. Make two small holes near the center of the circle and pass a loop of string through them (Figure 20–13). Now make the

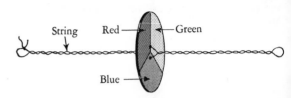

FIGURE 20–13.

COMBINING PRIMARY COLORED LIGHTS PRODUCES WHITE LIGHT.

side on the school lawn in the early morning or late afternoon. Stand with your back to the sun, facing a dark background if possible. Adjust the water from a garden hose so that a fine spray is produced. Now spray the water upward. A rainbow is produced as the water droplets, acting like tiny prisms, break up the sun's rays to form a spectrum.

Make a soap bubble pipe. Punch a hole in a styrofoam drinking cup and insert a soda straw slightly larger than the hole. Make a bubble solution by mixing thoroughly 2 cups of water, 1–2 tablespoons of liquid soap, and ¼ cup of pure glycerine. Hold the pipe upside down to make larger bubbles. The thin soap film breaks up the light rays to form rainbows.

4. *Produce colored lights* · Turn on a focusing flashlight and darken the room. Have a child clap two chalkboard erasers together in front of the flashlight. Note the beam of white light coming from the flashlight. Now wrap a piece of red cellophane smoothly around the glass of the flashlight. The beam of light is colored red because the cellophane absorbs all the colors of the spectrum except the red light, which is allowed to pass through. Produce other beams of colored light by using differently colored pieces of cellophane.

5. *Combine primary and complementary colors* · Draw a circle about 10 centimeters (4 in) in diameter on a white cardboard, then cut out

circle spin rapidly by twisting the string, stretching it, and then allowing it to rewind. Continue stretching and rewinding to keep the card spinning constantly. When the card is spinning, these primary colors will blend together to form a grayish white. (If one color shows up predominantly, scrape a little of it off and replace it with more of the other two colors. Usually more blue is needed.) To prevent the string from cutting through the holes and make them too big for effective spinning, glue the cardboard circle to a large button, lining up the holes of the cardboard with those of the button.

Repeat the activity, using another cardboard circle containing just two complementary colors, such as yellow and blue. The complementary colors will blend together when the circle is spinning, forming grayish white again.

6. *Observe colored materials* · Call the children's attention to the color of their clothes and objects such as pens, pencils, chalk, crayon, and book covers. Point out that each material has a certain color because, when white light strikes the material, all the colored lights have been absorbed except one, which is reflected to the eye.

7. *Observe the effect of colored lights on the color of materials* · Put a china saucer on a large

plate. Pour several tablespoons of alcohol into the saucer, add 2 teaspoons of table salt or borax, and stir thoroughly. Darken the room and set the alcohol on fire with a lighted match. The burning alcohol will heat the salt or borax and produce a pure yellow flame.

Hold a piece of white cloth near the flame. The cloth will appear yellow because only yellow light is striking the cloth and being reflected to the eye. Hold a piece of yellow cloth near the flame. The cloth will still appear yellow. Now hold a piece of red cloth near the flame. The cloth will appear black because it can only reflect red light, and there is no red light shining on the cloth. Hold other colored cloths near the flame, and note that they all appear black. Let the flame shine directly upon you. Your face will appear to be a mixture of yellow and black to the children.

8. *Combine colored pigments* · Draw some streaks of yellow and blue tempera paints separately on a piece of white cardboard. Now mix both colors and explain why the green color results. Repeat, using such combinations as red and yellow, red and blue, and black and orange. Mix the six spectrum colors together (or just red, yellow, and blue paints) and note that the mixture becomes black because it absorbs all the colors of the white light striking it and reflects none. Compare this effect with the mixing of colored lights in Learning Activities 2 and 5 above.

ELECTROMAGNETIC RADIATIONS

1. *Investigate the electromagnetic spectrum* · Draw a chalkboard diagram of the electromagnetic spectrum (Figure 20–14). Show the relationship between wavelength and frequency. Note that the visible light waves in the center are only a small portion of the entire electromagnetic spectrum.

2. *Investigate the nature of electromagnetic waves* · Repeat Learning Activity 1 of "The Nature of Light" (p. 714). Define the cycle, kilocycle, and megacycle.

3. *Investigate infrared waves* · Have the children explore the use of infrared waves on photography, medicine, and chemistry.

4. *Investigate Hertzian or radio waves* · Read about and discuss the use of Hertzian or radio waves in communication. Ask the children to designate the subdivision of this broad band of rays into smaller bands or channels, and state the special purpose for each channel.

5. *Discuss ultraviolet rays* · Have the children read and discuss where ultraviolet rays are found, the burns they can produce, their effect on phosphors to produce fluorescence, and their uses in science, medicine, and industry.

6. *Examine X-ray photographs* · Borrow

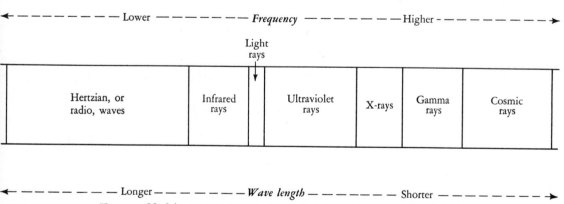

FIGURE 20–14. DIAGRAM OF THE ELECTROMAGNETIC SPECTRUM.

some X-ray photographs of bones and other body parts from your local doctor and let the children examine them. Have the children explore the uses of X-rays in medicine and in industry.

7. *Discuss gamma rays* · Have children read about and discuss the emission of gamma rays by radioactive materials. Let them describe the harmful effects these rays can produce.

BIBLIOGRAPHY FOR "LIGHT"

ASIMOV, ISAAC. *Light*. Chicago: Follett, 1970. 32 pp.

BRANLEY, FRANKLYN M. *Light and Darkness*. New York: Thomas Y. Crowell, 1975. 34 pp.

BREWER, A. C. *Exploring and Understanding Light*. Westchester, Ill.: Benefic Press, 1970. 96 pp.

BRINDZE, RUTH. *Look How People Wear Glasses: The Magic of Lenses*. New York: Atheneum Press, 1975. 102 pp.

CAMPBELL, ANN. *Let's Find Out About Color*. New York: Franklin Watts, 1975. 48 pp.

EPSTEIN, SAM, and BERYL EPSTEIN. *Look in the Mirror*. New York: Holiday House, 1973. 40 pp.

GARDNER, ROBERT, and DAVID WEBSTER. *Shadow Science*. New York: Doubleday, 1976. 124 pp.

HALACY, DANIEL. *X Rays and Gamma Rays*. New York: Holiday House, 1970. 160 pp.

HARRISON, GEORGE. *Lasers*. New York: Franklin Watts, 1971. 92 pp.

KETTLEKAMP, LARRY. *Tricks of Eye and Mind—The Story of Optical Illusion*. New York: William Morrow, 1974. 128 pp.

KLEIN, AARON. *The Electron Microscope: A Tool of Discovery*. New York: McGraw-Hill, 1974. 86 pp.

PASCHEL, HERBERT. *The First Book of Color*. New York: Franklin Watts, 1964. 45 pp.

PODENDORF, ILLA. *Shadows and More Shadows*. Chicago: Childrens Press, 1971. 48 pp.

RAINWATER, CLARENCE. *Light and Color*. New York: Golden Press, 1971. 160 pp.

SCHWALBERG, CAROL. *Light and Shadow*. New York: Parents' Magazine. 1972. 64 pp.

SCHNEIDER, HERMAN, and NINA SCHNEIDER. *Science Fun with a Flashlight*. New York: McGraw-Hill, 1975. 44 pp.

SIMON, SEYMOUR. *The Optical Illusion Book*. New York: Four Winds Press, 1976. 78 pp.

CHAPTER 21

MAGNETISM *and* ELECTRICITY

MAGNETISM

I. MAGNETS

A. Magnets are materials that will pick up or attract materials made of iron, steel, cobalt, and nickel.

B. Such materials are called **magnetic materials.**

C. There are two kinds of magnets: natural magnets and man-made magnets.

D. Natural magnets are found in the ground, and are called **lodestones.**
1. They contain an iron ore called **magnetite.**
2. They look like rocks and are irregular in shape.

E. Man-made magnets can be made only from iron, steel, cobalt, and nickel (magnetic materials).
1. Sometimes aluminum is added to these materials, making light but very strong magnets called **Alnico** magnets.
2. Man-made magnets are given the following names according to their shapes: **bar** magnets, **rod** magnets, **horseshoe** magnets, and **U-shaped** magnets.

II. THE LAW OF MAGNETIC ATTRACTION

A. The force (push or pull) of a magnet is strongest at its ends, which are called **poles.**

B. A man-made magnet always has two poles: a **north-seeking** pole and a **south-seeking** pole.
1. When a magnet is allowed to swing freely in space, its north-seeking pole points toward the north and its south-seeking pole points toward the south.
2. This is the reason why the poles are called north-seeking and south-seeking.

C. A natural magnet (lodestone) has many poles, but there are always just as many north-seeking poles as there are south-seeking poles.

D. When the poles of two magnets are brought near each other, they obey the **law of magnetic attraction,** which states that two unlike poles attract each other and two like poles repel each other.

III. THE MAGNETIC FIELD

A. The space around a magnet also can act like a magnet.

B. This space, around which the force of a magnet acts or is felt, is called the **magnetic field.**

C. If iron filings are sprinkled around a magnet, the filings arrange themselves into a pattern of lines.

D. These lines are called **lines of force,** and they show where the magnetic field is located and how it is arranged.

E. There are more lines of force, bunched

closely together, at the ends (poles) of the magnet, where the magnetic force is strongest, than at the middle of the magnet.

IV. THE FORCE OF A MAGNET CAN PASS THROUGH MANY MATERIALS

A. A magnet can attract magnetic materials (iron, steel, cobalt, nickel) without even touching them.
B. This attraction occurs because the force of a magnet can pass through any material that is not magnetic, such as air, paper, wood, glass, aluminum, and brass.
C. The nearer the magnetic material is to the magnet, the more strongly it will be attracted by the magnet.
D. The force of a magnet does not pass through magnetic materials because these materials hold or keep nearly all of the magnetic force so that practically none of the force can pass through.

V. THE NATURE OF MAGNETISM

A. At first scientists believed that magnetism in a magnetic material was due to the nature and arrangement of the molecules inside the magnetic material.
1. They believed that every molecule in a magnetic material behaved as if it were a tiny magnet, with a north-seeking and a south-seeking pole.
2. When the magnetic material was not magnetized, the molecules were arranged in a haphazard way so that the poles neutralized (or acted against) each other.
3. But, when the magnetic material was magnetized, all the molecules had been lined up so that all the north-seeking poles were facing one direction and all the south-seeking poles were facing the opposite direction.
4. This arrangement left free north-seeking poles at one end of the magnet and free south-seeking poles at the other end of the magnet.

B. This molecular theory of magnetism explained why the force of the magnet was strongest at the ends (where there were free poles) and weakest in the middle (where north-seeking and south-seeking poles were next to each other).
1. The theory also explained why a magnetized bar or rod, when cut in half, produced two new magnets even though the middle of the magnetized bar originally had little or no magnetic force.
2. Each of the two new magnets now had free north-seeking poles at one end and free south-seeking poles at the other end.
C. Today scientists believe that the magnetism of magnetic materials is due to the spinning movement of the electrons as they revolve or travel around the nucleus in the atom.
1. Each spinning electron acts as a tiny magnet.
2. In atoms of non-magnetic materials half their electrons spin in one direction and half spin in the opposite direction, which cancels their magnetic effects.
3. In atoms of magnetic materials more electrons spin in one direction than the other, making each atom a tiny magnet.
D. These magnetized atoms group together in large clusters, called **domains,** which line up the same way as the molecules in the older theory do.

VI. HOW MAGNETS ARE MADE

A. Only magnetic materials (iron, steel, cobalt, nickel) can be made into magnets.
B. It is possible to make temporary or permanent magnets.
C. Temporary magnets are made from soft iron.
1. Materials like soft iron are easy to magnetize, but they lose their magnetism just as easily.
2. Their domains (or molecules)are easy to line up, but they lose their arrangement just as easily.

3. Nails, tacks, screws and bolts are made of soft iron.

D. One way of making a temporary magnet is to bring a magnetic material near a permanent magnet or have the magnetic material touch the permanent magnet.

1. The magnetic material now becomes a magnet, but only temporarily, because, as soon as the material is taken away from the permanent magnet and its magnetic field, the material loses its magnetism.

2. This way of making magnets is called **induction** or **induced magnetism.**

E. A second way of making a temporary magnet is to stroke a piece of soft iron (such as a nail) many times with a permanent magnet, but only in one direction.

1. Stroking only in one direction helps line up the domains (or molecules) in the soft iron so that all the north-seeking poles are facing one direction and all the south-seeking poles are facing the opposite direction.

2. The soft iron is only a temporary magnet because the domains (or molecules) soon lose their arrangement.

F. A third way of making a temporary magnet is to wrap an insulated wire many times around a piece of soft iron, and then connect the bare ends of the wire to the posts of a dry cell.

1. This kind of temporary magnet is called an **electromagnet.**

2. An electromagnet will stay a magnet only as long as the electric current flows from the dry cell through the wire.

G. Permanent magnets are made from steel.

1. Materials like hard steel are hard to magnetize, but their magnetism is more permanent because they do not lose their magnetism easily.

2. Their molecules (or electrons) are harder to line up, but once the lining up is done, it is just as hard to throw them out of line.

3. Needles, knives, scissors, and screw drivers are made of steel.

H. One way of making a permanent magnet is to stroke a piece of steel (such as a knitting needle) many times with a permanent magnet in one direction only.

I. A second way of making a permanent magnet is to use a piece of steel instead of soft iron in an electromagnet.

VII. How Magnets Can Lose Their Magnetism

A. There are three common ways in which magnets can be made to lose their magnetism.

1. By dropping or striking them.

2. By heating them.

3. By placing the north-seeking poles of two magnets side by side or on top of each other.

B. In each case the domains (or molecules) will be disarranged and thrown out of line, and in this way neutralize each other.

C. There are two common ways of keeping magnets strong.

1. One way is to put a piece of soft iron, commonly called a **keeper,** across the poles of a horseshoe magnet or U-shaped magnet.

2. A second way is to store two bar magnets so that the north-seeking pole of one magnet is beside or on top of the south-seeking pole of the other magnet, and then place a keeper across the poles of both magnets.

VIII. The Earth Behaves as a Magnet

A. If a magnet is suspended so that it can swing freely, the magnet will move until it is in a north-south position, with the north-seeking pole of the magnet pointing to the north.

B. This movement occurs because the earth behaves as if it were a huge magnet, with a north magnetic pole, a south magnetic pole, and a magnetic field.

C. The north and south magnetic poles are not located at the same points as the north and south geographic poles, but are slightly to one side.

D. A compass tells us where the direction north is because it contains a magnetized needle whose north-seeking pole is affected by the earth's magnetic field and points in the direction of the north magnetic pole.

E. A compass needle will always point to the north unless it is brought near magnetic materials or a magnet, which then affect its position.

F. Many persons are often confused because the pole of a free-swinging magnet marked "north" points to the north.

1. This attraction of apparently like poles occurs because the poles of a magnet were named north and south poles long before we knew that the earth acted as a huge magnet.

2. If we had known about the earth's mag- netic field first, then most likely the pole of a magnet that points to the north would originally have been called the south pole, as it should have been.

3. To make this change now would be most confusing, so instead we use the term "north-seeking" and "south-seeking" for the poles of a magnet.

IX. The Uses of Magnets

A. Magnets can be used to pick up pins and needles, to keep cabinet and refrigerator doors closed, to hold the lids of cans after the can opener has removed them, and to hold pieces of paper and other objects to bulletin boards.

B. Magnets are also used in electric motors and generators, in compasses, and in many toys and games.

ELECTROMAGNETS

I. Magnetism Can Be Obtained from Electricity

A. When an electric current passes through a wire, there is a magnetic field around the wire.

B. When the wire carrying the electric current is placed over a compass, the compass needle turns away from its north-seeking position.

C. If the wire carrying the electric current is wound into a coil, the coil will act just like a magnet, with north- and south-seeking poles.

D. Placing a bar of soft iron in the center of the coil will increase the strength of this magnet greatly.

E. A magnet of this kind, made from electricity passing through a wire, is called an **electromagnet.**

II. How an Electromagnet Is Made

A. Three things are needed to make a strong electromagnet.

1. A bar of **soft iron,** such as a large iron nail, which is called the core.

2. A coil of **insulated wire** wrapped around the core.

3. A source of **electric current,** like that from a dry cell.

B. When the ends of the coil of wire are connected to the dry cell, the core and coil act like a magnet.

C. The magnetism will continue as long as an electric current passes through the coil.

D. When the ends of the coil are disconnected from the dry cell, the coil and core lose their magnetism.

E. Soft iron is almost always used as the core of an electromagnet because it magnetizes easily and loses its magnetism easily.

F. The poles of an electromagnet can be determined very easily by bringing a compass near it.

1. If the north-seeking part of the compass needle swings toward one end of the electromagnet, this end is the south-seeking pole of the electromagnet.

2. If the north-seeking part of the compass needle swings away from one end of the electromagnet, this end is the north-seeking pole of the electromagnet.

G. When the connections of the wire to the dry cell or other source of electric current are reversed, the poles of the electromagnet are also reversed.

H. Commercial electromagnets use yards and yards of wire, one or more large cores, and a much stronger electric current.

III. Making Electromagnets Stronger

A. Increasing the number of turns of wire around the core will make an electromagnet stronger.

B. Increasing the strength of the electric current (using more dry cells) will make the electromagnet stronger.

C. If the number of turns of wire is doubled, or the strength of the current is doubled, the electromagnet will become twice as strong.

D. Using a U-shaped core will also make the electromagnet stronger.

IV. How an Electromagnet Is Like a Permanent Magnet

A. An electromagnet has two poles: a north-seeking and a south-seeking pole.

B. An electromagnet has a magnetic field around it.

C. An electromagnet will attract magnetic materials like iron, steel, cobalt, and nickel.

D. The force of an electromagnet can pass through nonmagnetic materials, like glass and wood.

V. How an Electromagnet Differs from a Permanent Magnet

A. An electromagnet is a temporary magnet so that its magnetism can be turned on or off at will.

B. The poles of an electromagnet can be reversed.

C. The electromagnet can be made stronger or weaker.

D. An electromagnet usually has a soft iron core, but the permanent magnet is usually made of hard steel.

VI. Uses of Electromagnets

A. One of the early commercial uses of electromagnets was in the telegraph.

B. A simple telegraph circuit has four parts.

1. A source of **electric current**, such as one or two dry cells.

2. A **key**, which acts like a switch to turn the current on and off.

3. A **wire**, which connects the parts of the telegraph circuit together.

4. A **sounder**, which receives the electrical energy and converts it to sound.

C. The sounder has two parts.

1. A **U-shaped electromagnet**, placed so that its poles are up in the air.

2. A metal bar, called an **armature**, which is located above the poles of the electromagnet.

D. The telegraph operates as follows.

1. When the key is pressed down, a current flows through the circuit and the electromagnet becomes magnetized.

2. The electromagnet attracts the armature, which hits a metal screw below it and makes a clicking noise.

3. When the key is released, the electric current stops flowing and the electromagnet loses its magnetism.

4. The armature is no longer attracted, and a spring pulls it back into position again above the poles of the electromagnet.

5. When the armature springs back, it hits

another metal screw above it and makes a second clicking noise.

6. By pressing the key down for a longer or shorter time, we can control the time between the clicks that are produced.

7. If the time between the clicks is short so that we get two clicks close together, we call the two clicks, a **dot.**

8. Two clicks farther apart are called a **dash.**

9. A code of dots and dashes, called the **Morse code,** is used to send messages by telegraph.

10. Combinations of dots and dashes are used to stand for letters of the alphabet and for numbers.

E. Electromagnets are used in other forms of communication, such as the telephone, radio, and television.

F. Electromagnets are used in industry in such devices as the motor, generator, transformer, and crane.

G. Electromagnets are found in the home in bells, buzzers, chimes, circuit breakers, some electric appliances, and in many electric toys.

STATIC ELECTRICITY

I. How Static Electricity Is Produced

A. Static electricity is produced by friction.

1. When two different materials, especially nonmetals, are rubbed together, they each attract light objects, such as small bits of paper and cotton thread, to them.

2. We say that these materials have become **electrically charged.**

B. The kind of electricity that has been produced in these materials does not move, and is called **static,** or stationary, electricity.

C. When electricity does move, it is now called **current** electricity.

II. The Nature of Static Electricity

A. All matter is made up of tiny particles called **atoms.**

B. Inside the atom are three even tinier particles: **protons, neutrons,** and **electrons.**

1. The protons and neutrons are much heavier than the electrons and are located in the center, or **nucleus,** of the atom.

2. The much lighter electrons are outside the nucleus and move rapidly around the nucleus.

3. The electrons move freely around the nucleus while the protons are packed closely together with the neutrons in the nucleus.

4. Each proton has a **positive** (+) electrical charge, and each electron has a **negative** (−) electrical charge.

5. The neutron is neither positively nor negatively charged. It is said to be **neutral.**

C. Ordinarily there are the same number of positively charged protons and negatively charged electrons in the atom.

1. As a result, the atom is electrically neutral.

2. The atom is neither positively nor negatively charged.

D. However, it is possible to remove electrons from the atoms in a material by rubbing the material with another material.

1. When two materials are rubbed together, electrons pass from one material to another.

2. The material that loses electrons now has more positively charged (+) protons than negatively charged (−) electrons, so this material becomes positively charged.

3. The material that gains electrons now has more negatively charged (−) elec-

trons than positively charged (+) protons, so it becomes negatively charged.

E. Protons cannot be removed from the atom by rubbing.

F. When a hard rubber rod is rubbed with wool or fur, some electrons are rubbed off the wool or fur and onto the rubber.

1. The rubber has gained negative electrons and now has more negative electrons than positive protons, so it becomes negatively charged.

2. The wool or fur has lost negative electrons and now has more positive protons than negative electrons, so it becomes positively charged.

G. But when the rubber rod is rubbed with a plastic bag, electrons are rubbed off the rubber and onto the plastic.

1. The rubber has lost electrons, so it is now positively charged.

2. The plastic has gained electrons, so it is now negatively charged.

H. When a glass rod is rubbed with a piece of nylon, some of the electrons are rubbed off the glass and onto the nylon.

1. The glass has lost negative electrons and becomes positively charged because it now has more positive protons than negative electrons.

2. The nylon has gained negative electrons and becomes negatively charged because it now has more negative electrons than positive protons.

I. Materials will stay charged only as long as electrons have no way of entering or leaving the materials.

III. LAW OF ELECTROSTATIC ATTRACTION AND REPULSION

A. When two negatively charged materials are brought close to each other, they will repel, or move away from, each other.

B. The same thing will happen when two positively charged materials are brought close together.

C. But when a positively charged material is brought close to a negatively charged ma-

terial, they will both be attracted and move closer to each other.

D. These behaviors can be stated as a law of electrostatic attraction and repulsion: the same kind of electrical charges will repel each other, but different kinds of electrical charges will attract each other.

IV. WHY ELECTRICALLY CHARGED MATERIALS ATTRACT MATERIALS THAT ARE NOT CHARGED

A. Materials that are either positively or negatively charged will attract materials that are not charged.

1. Materials that are not electrically charged are said to be **neutral.**

2. Neutral materials have neither lost nor gained electrons.

B. When a negatively charged hard rubber rod is brought close to a small piece of paper, the paper is attracted to the rod.

1. The negatively charged rubber rod repels electrons from the side of the paper nearest the rod.

2. These electrons move to the other side of the paper, as far away from the rod as possible.

3. The side of the paper nearest the rod is now positively charged because it has more positive protons than negative electrons, so it is attracted to the negatively charged rod.

4. When the paper touches the rod, some of the excess electrons from the rod flow into the paper, and the paper becomes negatively charged, too.

5. The paper then drops off the rod because it now has the same electrical charge (negative) as the rod and is repelled.

C. When a positively charged glass rod is brought close to a small piece of paper, the paper is attracted to the rod.

1. The positively charged rod attracts electrons, and they accumulate on the side of the paper nearest the rod.

2. The side of the paper nearest the glass rod is now negatively charged because

it has more negative electrons than positive protons, so it is attracted to the positively charged rod.

3. When the paper touches the rod, some of the electrons from the paper flow into the rod, leaving the entire piece of paper positively charged, too.

4. The paper then drops off the rod because it now has the same electrical charge (positive) as the rod and is repelled.

V. CONDUCTORS AND NONCONDUCTORS

A. Some materials allow electrons to move or flow easily through them.
  1. These materials are called **conductors**.
  2. Current electricity is the rapid flow of electrons through a good conductor.
  3. Most metals are good conductors of electricity.
  4. Carbon, a nonmetal, can also conduct electricity.
B. Other materials will not let electrons flow easily through them.
  1. These materials are called **nonconductors, or insulators**.
  2. Some insulators are rubber, glass, wool, fur, plastics, wood, and dry air.
C. Static electricity works best with insulators because the electric charges that are produced remain on the insulators and do not leak away.
D. Static electricity is most easily produced in the winter, when it is very cold outside, and warm and dry inside.
  1. In the summer there is more water in the air, making air a better conductor.
  2. As a result, the electric charges leak away almost as soon as they are formed, so it is very hard to give the materials an electric charge that will last.

VI. ELECTRIC SPARKS

A. Ordinarily electrons do not flow very easily through the air because the air is an insulator.

B. Under certain conditions, however, electrons can be made to flow through the air.
  1. This flow may occur when a highly charged material is brought near an oppositely charged material, or even a neutral material.
  2. The electrostatic force of attraction between the positively and negatively charged materials is very great.
  3. If the force of attraction becomes great enough, the resistance of the air to a flow of electrons breaks down, and a flow of electrons takes place between the two materials.
C. This rapid movement of electrons through the air appears as a **spark,** and is actually a flow of **current electricity**.

VII. LIGHTNING AND THUNDER

A. **Lightning** is a huge electric spark produced by static electricity.
B. During thunderstorms rapidly rising or falling air currents may rub against the rain clouds.
  1. This rubbing will produce very large and strong electrical charges in the clouds.
  2. Sometimes one part of the cloud will become positively charged and the other part will become negatively charged.
  3. Sometimes a cloud will be ripped into two parts by the rapidly moving air, producing two new clouds, each with a different electrical charge.
C. When a negatively charged cloud comes close to the earth's surface, the electrons in the earth's surface will be repelled into the earth, leaving the surface positively charged.
D. When a positively charged cloud comes close to the earth's surface, the electrons in the earth will be attracted to the surface, leaving the surface negatively charged.
E. Lightning is the huge spark produced when electrons leap suddenly from the following places:
  1. One charged part of a cloud to another.

2. One charged cloud to another of opposite charge.

3. A charged cloud to the earth.

4. The earth to a charged cloud.

F. When lightning strikes the earth, it usually strikes an object, such as a tall tree, that is the highest point on the earth's surface.

1. Lightning strikes this object because electrons flow more easily through solid objects than through a gas like air.

2. Therefore, it is a good idea to keep away from trees or other tall objects during a thunderstorm.

G. **Lightning rods** are used to protect buildings from damage by lightning.

1. The lightning rod is made of a metal such as copper, which is a good conductor of electricity.

2. The lightning rod's highest point is kept higher than the building so that the lightning will be attracted to the rod and not the building.

3. The lowest point of the rod goes deeply into the ground so that the lightning can be conducted quickly and harmlessly to the ground.

H. As the lightning passes through the air, the air becomes very hot and expands suddenly.

1. This expansion of the heated air sets up giant vibrations and produces the sound we know as **thunder.**

2. We see the lightning first and then hear the thunder because light travels much faster than sound.

3. Because it takes longer for the sound to travel from the farther end of the lightning than from the nearest end, we hear the thunder as a long rolling sound.

4. Many flashes of lightning at one time will also produce thunder with a long rolling sound.

VIII. OTHER COMMON OCCURRENCES OF STATIC ELECTRICITY

A. Scuffing, or even just walking across a rug on a very cold day, when it is warm and dry inside, will produce a shock or a spark when your finger touches a metal object.

1. The body picks up negative electrons through the shoes and releases these electrons upon contact with the metal object.

2. The same thing happens when you slide your body across the nylon seat of a car and touch the door handle.

B. Combing your dry hair with a rubber comb will charge the hair and make it stand on end.

1. The comb removes electrons from the hair, leaving the hair positively charged.

2. Because each strand of hair has the same positive charge, they all repel one another and your hair tends to stand on end.

3. The same thing happens when you stroke a cat's fur.

C. Nylon sweaters and undergarments will become charged as they rub against your body, and will crackle and spark when they are removed.

D. Trucks containing gasoline and other flammable liquids can build up a large electric charge as the liquid sloshes inside the tank.

1. If there were no way to stop the charge from building up, a spark might be produced that would make the gasoline explode.

2. This building up of an electric charge is prevented by attaching a metal chain to the tank and letting the chain dangle to the ground.

3. As soon as an electric charge is formed in the tank, the charge is allowed to escape through the chain and into the ground.

E. Even the tires of trucks and passenger cars will produce an electric charge in the car as the tires rub against the road when they are moving.

1. Some cars have strips containing metal running from the body of the car to the ground so that the charge may escape.

2. At toll booths a flexible upright metal rod touches the car first and lets the charge escape so that both the attend- ant and the person paying the toll will not receive a shock when their hands touch.

CURRENT ELECTRICITY

I. THE NATURE OF CURRENT ELECTRICITY

A. Scientists do not know exactly what electricity is.
B. The word *electricity* is used to describe a flow of electrons.
   1. All matter is made up of tiny particles called **atoms.**
   2. Inside the atom are three even tinier particles: **protons, neutrons,** and **electrons.**
   3. The protons and neutrons are much heavier than the electrons and are located in the center, or **nucleus,** of the atom.
   4. The much lighter electrons are outside the nucleus and move rapidly around the nucleus.
   5. The electrons move freely around the nucleus while the protons are packed closely together with the neutrons in the nucleus.
   6. Each electron is **negatively charged** and is thought to be a particle of negative electricity.
   7. Each proton is **positively charged** and is thought to be a particle of positive electricity.
   8. The neutron is a **neutral** particle. It is neither positively charged nor negatively charged.
   9. Ordinarily an atom has the same number of electrons and protons, so it is electrically neutral.
C. Scientists think that when an electric current is flowing through a material the electrons move from atom to atom inside the material.

II. THE SIMPLE ELECTRIC CIRCUIT

A. There are three parts to a simple electric circuit.
   1. A source of electricity, such as a dry cell or electric generator.
   2. A path along which the electric current can travel, such as a copper wire.
   3. An appliance that uses the electricity, such as a bell or a light bulb.
B. In an electric circuit the electric current flows from the source of electricity along one path to the appliance, passes through the appliance, and then returns through a second path to the source of electricity.
C. When all three parts of the circuit are connected so that an electric current is flowing, the circuit is said to be **completed or closed.**
D. When any of the three parts of the circuit are disconnected so that an electric current is not flowing, the circuit is said to be **incomplete** or **open.**

III. CONDUCTORS AND NONCONDUCTORS

A. Some materials allow an electric current to flow through them easily.
   1. Such materials are called **conductors.**
   2. The atoms in a good conductor of electricity do not have a very tight hold on some of their electrons so that these electrons can flow freely through the material.
   3. Most metals are good conductors of electricity. Examples of metals that are good conductors include copper, silver, aluminum, iron, and zinc.

4. Carbon, although a nonmetal, can also conduct electricity.
5. When certain chemicals, known as acids, bases, and salts, are dissolved in water, the solutions will conduct an electric current.

B. Materials that do not allow an electric current to flow through them easily, if at all, are called **nonconductors** or **insulators.**
1. The atoms in a nonconductor of electricity have such a tight hold on their electrons that few if any, flow through the material.
2. Examples of insulators (nonconductors) are paper, wood, glass, porcelain, cloth, dry air, rubber, and many plastics.

C. Whenever it is necessary, conductors are covered with or supported by insulators.
1. The insulators protect you from receiving an electric shock if you should happen to touch the conductor.
2. Insulators also prevent the electric current from leaving the conductor and taking an unwanted path.

D. Pure water itself is a nonconductor of electricity.
1. But water will make many insulators become good conductors when they are wet.
2. Thus, it is a good and safe practice not to touch electric appliances or wires when your hands are wet or if you are standing on a wet bathroom floor.

IV. SWITCHES

A. Electricity is turned on or off by **switches.**
B. Switches are devices that make it easy and convenient to close or open an electric circuit.
1. When the switch is turned or pushed one way, it will complete the electric circuit and the electric current will flow.
2. When the switch is turned or pushed the opposite way, it will open or "break" the circuit and the electric current stops flowing.

C. Three common kinds of switches are the **knife, pushbutton,** and **snap** switch.
1. The knife switch has a metallic, movable blade that moves in and out of metallic "jaws" to close or open an electric circuit.
2. The pushbutton switch, which is used with door bells, has a flat, coillike spring that pushes forward to close the circuit and flies back to open the circuit.
3. The snap switch, which is used on walls, moves one way to close the circuit and the opposite way to open the circuit.

V. SERIES AND PARALLEL CIRCUITS

A. If more than one dry cell is used in an electric circuit, the dry cells are usually connected in series.
1. When dry cells are connected in **series,** the wires run from the outside, or negative, terminal of one cell to the center, or positive, terminal of another cell.
2. Connecting dry cells in series will increase the amount of electrical force produced.

B. Appliances in an electric circuit may be connected either in series or in parallel.

C. When appliances in an electric circuit are connected in **series,** all the electric current flows **through** each appliance, one after the other, when the circuit is closed.
1. If one appliance fails to function, or is turned off, the other appliances stop functioning because the circuit has been broken.
2. A good example of appliances connected in series is the single strand set of Christmas tree lights.
3. If one light goes out in this set of lights, the circuit is broken and all the lights go out.
4. Because all the electricity flows through each light, the more lights that are added, the more resistance the electricity meets, and the less current there is to flow through the lamps.

5. Because the brightness of the lights depends upon the amount of current flowing through them, the lights will become dimmer.

D. When appliances in an electric circuit are connected in **parallel**, the electric current flows **across** each appliance.

1. The appliances are connected in such a way that the electric current **branches off**, and only part of the current goes through each appliance.
2. Now each appliance can operate independently of the other so that, if one appliance fails to function, the circuit is not broken and the other appliances continue to function.
3. The electric current flowing through each appliance is completely separate from the current flowing through the other appliances.
4. A good example of appliances connected in parallel is the double strand set of Christmas tree lights.
5. If one light goes out in this set of lights, there is still a complete circuit through the rest of the lights and they all stay on.
6. Since the electricity flowing through each light is separate from the electricity flowing through all the other lights, the addition of more lights to the set will not affect their brightness.

E. All house circuits are wired in parallel so that the lights and other appliances can all be turned on and off separately, without breaking the circuit.

F. In most houses the main circuit has at least two branches, connected in parallel, which carry electricity to appliances in different parts of the house.

VI. OVERLOADING AN ELECTRIC CIRCUIT

A. Whenever there is a flow of electrons (electric current) in a wire, heat is produced.

B. This heat is formed because the metal of the wire opposes the flow of electrons through the wire.

C. The more current there is flowing through a wire, the hotter the wire will become.

D. In a house each branch circuit is designed to carry only so much current.

E. As appliances are connected into the circuit, each uses a certain amount of current.

F. If too many appliances are connected into a circuit at one time, the circuit will become overloaded.

1. The combined current needed by all the appliances may be more than what the circuit can carry.
2. This large amount of current may make the wires so hot that they will burn away the insulation and even start a fire.

G. Another way of overloading a circuit is to have a **short circuit** happen.

1. Electricity will always take the shortest and easiest path back to its source.
2. When the insulation on the wires of an electric circuit wears off and exposes the bare wires, a short circuit will take place if the bare wires touch.
3. When the bare wires touch, the electric current will take a short cut, or circuit, back to its source without first flowing through an appliance that will use the electrical energy.
4. A large amount of electricity will now flow quickly through the wires, making them very hot.

H. **Fuses** and **circuit breakers** are safety devices used to prevent the wires from becoming too hot when an overload takes place.

1. They are connected in series with the circuit so that the current must pass through them on its way to the appliances.
2. They act like emergency switches to open the circuit if too much current is flowing through it.

I. A fuse contains a strip of metal that will melt easily when heated.

1. The metal melts more easily than the wires in a circuit.
2. When a circuit becomes overloaded, either because of too many appliances in

the circuit or because of a short circuit, the wires become very hot.

3. But the metal strip in the fuse also becomes hot and melts, or "blows," before the wires do, thus breaking the circuit before any damage can be done.

4. The fuse is usually enclosed in a tube or socket to prevent the melted metal from spattering and causing a fire.

5. No current will flow through the circuit until the blown fuse is replaced.

J. A circuit breaker has a bar, made up of two strips of metal connected together.

1. One metal strip will expand more than the other strip, when heated, causing the bar to curve.

2. When a normal amount of electric current flows through the circuit and the circuit breaker, the bar remains flat and keeps the circuit closed.

3. When there is an overload, the bar becomes hot and begins to curve, and opens the circuit.

4. The circuit breaker does not need to be replaced, but can be pushed back into place after the cause of the overloading is removed.

VII. ELECTRICAL UNITS OF MEASURE

A. The **volt** is the unit of electrical pressure. It is a measure of the force pushing the electrons through a conductor and overcoming the resistance of the conductor.

B. The **ampere** is the unit of the rate of flow of the electric current. It is a measure of the number of electrons flowing per second, or the intensity of the current.

C. The **ohm** is the unit of electrical resistance. It is a measure of the resistance a conductor offers to the flow of electric current.

D. There is a relationship between electrical pressure, rate of flow of current, and electrical resistance.

1. The greater the electrical pressure (number of volts), the greater the current (number of amperes) will be, and vice-versa.

2. The greater the electrical resistance (number of ohms), the smaller the current (number of amperes) will be, and vice-versa.

3. This relationship, called **Ohm's law,** can be expressed as follows:

$$\text{Amount of Current} = \frac{\text{Electrical pressure}}{\text{Electrical resistance}}$$

4. Ohm's law is more commonly stated in electrical units, as follows:

$$\text{Amperes} = \frac{\text{Volts}}{\text{Ohms}}$$

E. The **watt** is the unit of electrical power.

1. It is the measure of the rate, or how fast, electrical energy is being used.

2. Watts can be found by multiplying the number of volts by the number of amperes.

F. The **watt-hour** is the unit of electrical energy.

1. It is the amount of energy used at the rate of one watt for one hour.

2. When we pay for electrical energy we pay by the **kilowatt-hour.**

3. A kilowatt is 1000 watts.

VIII. SOURCES OF ELECTRICITY

A. Electricity can be obtained in several different ways.

B. Electricity is a form of energy and therefore can be produced from other forms of energy.

C. The following forms of energy can be changed, or transformed, into electrical energy.

1. **Chemical** energy, using the wet cell, dry cell, and storage battery.

2. **Mechanical** energy, using the generator and the piezoelectric cell.

3. **Light** energy, using the photoelectric cell and the solar battery.

4. **Heat** energy, using the thermocouple.

[735

IX. THE WET CELL

A. The **wet cell**, also known as the **voltaic cell**, consists of two different metals placed in a chemical solution that will conduct an electric current.
   1. The metals that are selected must be such that one will react faster with the solution than the other.
   2. When the metals are in the solution they must be kept apart.
   3. A solution of an acid, a base, or a salt in water will be able to conduct an electric current.
B. A commonly used wet cell is made by inserting a strip of zinc and a strip of copper partially in a glass of water containing a little sulfuric acid.
C. The sulfuric acid acts chemically on the atoms of zinc, leaving many electrons behind on the zinc that remains.
   1. As the negative electrons accumulate on the zinc, the strip becomes negatively charged.
   2. The zinc strip is called the **negative pole** of the cell.
D. At the same time the copper strip loses electrons to the sulfuric acid.
   1. The copper strip now becomes positively charged because it has lost negative electrons.
   2. The copper strip is called the **positive pole** of the cell.
E. In this way an **electrical pressure** is built up between the two strips.
F. When a wire is connected to the dry ends of the strips, there is a flow of electrons from the negatively charged zinc to the positively charged copper, and an electric current has been produced.
G. The electric current flows in one direction only, from the zinc to the copper, and is called **direct current** (**DC**).

X. THE DRY CELL

A. The **dry cell** is a more convenient form of wet cell.

B. The materials are placed in a sealed container so that nothing can spill when the dry cell is carried or tipped.
C. A dry cell is not really dry.
   1. The chemicals inside must be kept moist.
   2. If the inside of the dry cell becomes dry, the cell will no longer operate.
D. The older and more commonly used dry cell is the carbon-zinc cell.
   1. There is a zinc can, which serves as the negative pole and also as a container for the rest of the chemicals in the cell.
   2. A carbon rod in the middle of the can serves as the positive pole.
   3. The can is then filled with a wet paste of ammonium chloride and zinc chloride, mixed with particles of manganese dioxide and powdered carbon.
   4. Blotting paper soaked in ammonium chloride solution lines the inside of the zinc can to help keep the chemicals moist longer.
   5. Metal posts, or terminals, are on top of the can: one attached to the carbon rod, the other to one end of the can.
E. The chemical action in carbon-zinc cells is much like that of the wet cell.
   1. The zinc reacts with the moist ammonium chloride and accumulates electrons, becoming negatively charged.
   2. The carbon rod loses electrons and becomes positively charged.
   3. An electrical pressure is built up between the zinc and the carbon.
   4. When a wire is connected to the two terminals on top of the dry cell, an electric current flows from the zinc to the carbon terminal.
F. The newer **alkaline-manganese** cell lasts longer than the carbon-zinc cell.
   1. It has a steel can filled with moist potassium hydroxide.
   2. The positive pole is manganese dioxide; the negative pole is granulated zinc.
G. All dry cells, large or small, have an electrical pressure of about 1½ volts.
H. Dry cells cannot give a large steady electric current for a long time.

I. Dry cells are used in flashlights, portable radios, and doorbell circuits.

XI. THE STORAGE BATTERY

A. The common **storage battery** produces electricity, just as the wet and dry cells do, from chemical energy.
B. A storage battery has lead as the negative pole, lead dioxide as the positive pole, and a solution of sulfuric acid.
C. When the two terminals are connected, an electric current will flow.
D. As the battery is used, both the lead and lead dioxide poles become covered with a chemical called lead sulfate.
E. When enough lead sulfate covers the poles, the storage battery will not operate, and we say that it has lost its charge.
F. But the storage battery is different from the wet and dry cell because it can be recharged and used again and again.
  1. Its terminals can be connected to a source of direct electric current, which changes the lead sulfate on the poles back into lead and lead dioxide.
  2. In this way electrical energy is used to give back the storage battery its chemical energy.
G. Most storage batteries now contain six cells, connected in series.
  1. Each cell has an electrical pressure of 2 volts.
  2. Each cell adds its voltage to the others, so we get a 12-volt battery.
H. The most common use of the storage battery is in the automobile to start the motor and to run many small electrical appliances in the car.
I. A storage battery can also be recharged while the car is running.
  1. Every car has a **generator,** which is a machine for producing electricity.
  2. The generator is driven by the motor of the car.
  3. When the car is running, the electricity produced by the generator flows into the storage battery and recharges it.

4. In this way the generator gives the battery back the electrical energy that was used to start the car and run the appliances.

XII. THE NICKEL-CADMIUM BATTERY

A. The **nickel-cadmium** battery is a small, efficient battery that performs like the storage battery.
B. A nickel-cadmium cell has a positive pole of nickel oxide, a negative pole of cadmium, and a solution of potassium hydroxide.
C. Like the storage battery, the nickel-cadmium battery can be recharged repeatedly.
D. It uses a recharger that plugs into an electrical outlet and changes alternating current (AC) into direct current (DC).
E. The nickel-cadmium battery is used in cordless electrical appliances.

XIII. THE GENERATOR

A. The **generator** produces electricity from mechanical energy.
B. When a wire is moved up and down between the poles of a horseshoe or U-shaped magnet so that the wire cuts across the lines of force in the magnetic field, an electric current is produced.
  1. The electric current can be detected by connecting the ends of the wire to the terminals of a sensitive instrument, called a **galvanometer,** which is used to measure or detect weak electric currents.
  2. When the wire is moved down, the needle of the galvanometer moves in one direction; when the wire is moved up, the needle moves in the opposite direction.
  3. The movement of the needle shows that the electric current that is produced changes direction.
C. This kind of current is called **alternating current (AC)** because it alternates by first

flowing in one direction, then in the opposite direction.

D. An alternating electric current will also be produced if the wire is held stationary and the magnet is moved.

E. If the wire or the magnet do not move, no current is produced.

F. Thus the mechanical energy of motion that is needed to move the wire or the magnet is changed to electrical energy by means of magnetism.

G. A generator is just a machine used to make wires cut lines of force very quickly.

H. A simple alternating current generator has four necessary parts.

1. A **coil** of many turns of wire, called an **armature.**

2. A **U-shaped magnet,** with the armature placed between the poles of the magnet.

3. Two **metal rings,** called **slip rings,** each connected to an end of the coil to collect the current produced in the armature.

4. **Brushes,** made of metal or carbon, to lead the current out of the generator.

I. With small generators and many large generators, the coil moves and the magnet remains stationary.

J. With some large generators, the magnet moves and the coil remains stationary.

K. The amount of current produced by a generator depends upon how many lines of force are cut and on how quickly they are cut.

L. There are several ways of increasing the number of lines of force to be cut:

1. Using more magnets.

2. Making the magnets stronger by using electromagnets instead of permanent magnets.

3. Using more turns of wire in the coil of wire.

4. Inserting an iron core inside the coil.

M. Increasing the speed with which the lines of force are cut can be done by moving either the coil or the magnet faster.

N. At large electric power stations falling

water or steam is used to turn large wheels, called **turbines,** which turn the coils or magnets of the generator and produce electric current.

O. Trains and ships burn fuel to run engines or turbines, which operate generators that supply the electricity needed to drive the wheels or propellers.

P. The alternating electric current produced at power plants has a high electrical pressure or voltage.

1. This high electrical pressure is necessary to send the electricity over long distances and overcome the resistance of miles and miles of wire.

2. Sometimes the electrical pressure in the wires amounts to several thousand volts.

3. But appliances in the home use only 110 volts, and several thousand volts in the home would be dangerous.

4. Just before the wires that branch off the main wires enter the home, the high voltage is stepped down to 110 volts by a device called a **transformer.**

5. Transformers are voltage changers. They can either step down or step up the voltage, as needed.

Q. Alternating current changes its direction many times each second.

1. Two changes in direction are called a **cycle.**

2. In the home a 60-cycle alternating current is used.

3. This means that in 1 second the current flows 60 times in one direction and 60 times in the opposite direction.

R. Sometimes generators are needed that will produce direct current instead of alternating current.

1. Direct current is needed for long periods of time to charge storage batteries and put metal plate on materials.

2. To produce direct current a generator uses a **commutator** instead of slip rings.

3. The commutator is a single ring that is split in half.

4. The commutator automatically reverses

the flow of alternating current just as the current changes direction.

5. As a result, the current flows only in one direction and so becomes a direct current.

XIV. THE PIEZOELECTRIC CELL

A. The **piezoelectric cell** is another way of producing electrical energy from mechanical energy.

B. When certain crystals like quartz and Rochelle salt are squeezed mechanically, an electric current is produced.

C. Piezoelectric cells containing such crystals are used in the arms of some record players to "pick up" the sound as the needle moves along the groove of the record.

XV. THE PHOTOELECTRIC AND PHOTORESISTIVE CELL

A. Certain metals, like potassium, selenium, and cadmium, are sensitive to light.

B. When light strikes such a metal, electrons flow from the metal and produce a weak electric current.

C. The stronger the light, the stronger the electric current.

D. Both the **photoelectric cell** and the **photoresistive cell** contain a light-sensitive metal and are able to change light energy into electrical energy.

E. Both these cells are used in camera light meters to control the amount of light that enters the camera.

1. When the light is strong, the cell makes the shutter cut down the amount of light that is entering the camera.

2. When the light is weak, the cell makes the shutter open wider, so more light can enter the camera.

F. The electricity produced by photoresistive cells is also used to open doors and operate burglar alarms.

XVI. THE SOLAR BATTERY

A. The **solar battery** is a recent invention of scientists to produce electricity from sunlight.

B. The solar battery has in it many plates made from pure silicon.

C. When the plates are exposed to sunlight, an electric current is produced.

D. The solar battery is still being tested and promises to be valuable because it needs no chemical other than the silicon and there are no parts to wear out.

XVII. THE THERMOCOUPLE

A. The **thermocouple** makes it possible to change heat energy into electrical energy.

B. A thermocouple can be made by twisting together one end of two wires of different metals and heating the twisted ends.

C. When the free ends of the metal wires are connected to a galvanometer, the needle of the galvanometer moves, showing that a weak electric current has been produced.

D. Thermocouples are being used as delicate thermometers to measure very small differences in temperature.

XVIII. USES OF ELECTRICITY

A. Electricity can be used to produce heat.

1. Every electrical heating appliance has a conductor that gets hot when an electric current flows through it.

2. The conductor can be a coil of wire or a solid rod.

3. The heat is produced by the resistance that the conductor offers to the flow of electricity through it.

4. The greater the resistance, the hotter the conductor becomes.

5. The resistance can be increased either by making the wires thin or by using a material, such as nichrome metal, that

has a high resistance to the flow of electric current.

6. Also, the larger the electric current, the hotter the conductor becomes.

7. Electrical appliances that produce heat include toasters, irons, coffee percolators, hot plates, roasters, stoves, water heaters, and blankets.

B. Electricity can be used to produce light.

1. If a conductor becomes hot enough, it will give off light.

2. The filament of wire in a light bulb is long and thin.

3. The filament offers so much resistance to the flow of electric current that the filament becomes hot enough to give off a bright light.

4. Neon lights do not have a filament, but are filled with neon gas instead.

5. When an electric current of high voltage is sent through the neon gas in the tube, the gas glows with a red color.

6. Other gases and colored glass can be used to produce different colors.

7. In the fluorescent bulb, or tube, the light is produced by minerals that glow when invisible ultraviolet light strikes them.

8. The ultraviolet light is produced by sending an electric current of high voltage through a small amount of mercury vapor (gas) that is in the tube.

9. The ultraviolet light strikes the coating of minerals on the inside of the glass tube and makes them glow.

C. Electricity can be used to produce motion and power.

1. Electricity is used to run **motors.**

2. The parts of a motor are exactly the same as the parts of a direct current (DC) generator.

3. Most motors have an armature, magnet, a commutator, and brushes.

4. The generator changes mechanical energy to electrical energy; the motor changes electrical energy to mechanical energy.

5. The generator uses magnetism to pro-

duce electricity; the motor uses electricity to produce magnetism.

6. The motor makes use of the law of attraction between unlike poles and of repulsion between like poles of magnets to make the armature move.

7. When an electric current passes from the brushes and commutator into the armature of a motor, the armature becomes an electromagnet.

8. The north-seeking pole of the electromagnetic armature is attracted by the south-seeking pole of the permanent magnet, and the south-seeking pole of the electromagnet is attracted by the north-seeking pole of the permanent magnet, so the electromagnetic armature moves.

9. As the armature turns, it reaches a position where the unlike poles of the armature and the permanent magnet face each other.

10. At this point the commutator reverses the direction of the current flowing into the electromagnetic armature, which automatically reverses the poles of the electromagnetic armature.

11. Now we have like poles of the armature and the permanent magnet facing each other.

12. These like poles repel each other and the armature moves again.

13. As a result, we get continuous motion of the armature, due to first the attraction of unlike poles and then the repulsion of like poles.

14. The commutator keeps reversing the current regularly to change the poles of the electromagnetic armature.

15. The power of a motor can be increased by making the magnetic fields of the armature and the permanent magnets stronger.

16. The magnetic field of the armature can be increased by using more turns of wire around the core and by sending more current through the armature.

17. The magnetic field of the permanent

magnet can be increased by using more magnets and by converting the permanent magnets to electromagnets.

18. Some motors are built to run on alternating current only.
19. Others run on direct current only.
20. Still others can run on either alternating or direct current, and are called universal motors.
21. There are so many uses for motors that it would be impossible to keep our present way of living without them.

D. Electricity can be used to plate metals.
1. Using electricity, metals can be coated, or plated, with other metals.
2. This process is called **electroplating**.
3. Only direct current can be used for electroplating.
4. To copper plate an object, the object to be plated and a bar of copper are placed in a solution containing a chemical called copper sulfate.
5. This arrangement is very much like the wet cell, except that in the wet cell a chemical action produces electricity, whereas in electroplating electricity produces a chemical action.
6. The object and the bar of copper are connected to a source of direct current.
7. The object to be plated acts as the negative pole, and is connected to the negative terminal, or connection, of the source of direct current.
8. The copper bar acts as the positive pole, and is connected to the positive terminal, or connection, of the source of direct current.
9. When a direct current flows, the copper in the solution is plated on the object.
10. At the same time, copper from the bar replaces the copper in the solution.
11. The longer the current flows, and the stronger the electric current used, the thicker the plate becomes.
12. Electroplating is used to plate silverware

and to put chromium on automobile bumpers, grills, and other trimmings.

E. Electricity is used in many forms of communication, such as the telegraph, telephone, radio, television, and motion pictures.

XIX. SAFETY RULES FOR ELECTRICITY

A. Disconnect all electrical appliances, especially heating appliances, when they are not being used.
B. Never touch a switch or electrical appliance when your hands are wet.
C. Never touch a switch, electrical appliance, radio, or telephone set when you are in the bathtub.
D. Make sure the switch is turned off whenever you disconnect or connect an electrical appliance.
E. Do not overload your home circuit by plugging too many appliances in one wall plug.
F. Never touch a bare wire that is carrying an electric current.
G. Never poke around the back of a radio or television set when these appliances are turned on.
H. Never put your finger into an open electric socket.
I. Replace electric cords where the insulation is cracked or worn thin.
J. Never touch an electric cord with wet hands.
K. Do not touch an electric cord with one hand and a water pipe, faucet, or radiator with the other hand.
L. When a fuse "blows," always replace the fuse with a new one that will carry the same amount of current.
M. When a fuse "blows," first find out what made it "blow" and correct the condition before putting in a new fuse.
N. Never put a penny in the fuse box instead of a new fuse.

LEARNING ACTIVITIES FOR "MAGNETISM AND ELECTRICITY"

MAGNETISM

1. *Determine what materials a magnet will attract* · Have the children collect a variety of materials, such as tacks, nails, paper clips, pins, needles, coins, rubber bands, pebbles, sand, and small pieces of chalk, crayon, wood, paper, glass, cloth, leather, and aluminum foil. Let the children try to pick up or attract each object with a magnet. Put to one side all those objects that are attracted by the magnet, and note that these objects are all made of iron or steel.

Point out that cobalt and nickel are also attracted by magnets. If the children comment that the American coin, the nickel, was not attracted by the magnet, explain that American nickels have mostly copper in them. Canadian nickels have much more nickel metal in them and will be attracted by the magnet.

2. *Discover that the attraction of a magnet is strongest at its poles* · Make a pile of tacks or iron filings. Iron filings can be obtained from a scientific supply house, or you can make your own filings by cutting up fine steel wool into very small pieces with a scissors. Now try picking up the tacks or filings with a bar magnet, using different parts of the magnet each time. The tacks or filings will be attracted most strongly to the poles of the magnet. Repeat the activity, using a horseshoe and a U-shaped magnet.

3. *Observe that a lodestone is a natural magnet* · Get a lodestone and some iron filings from a scientific supply house. You can make your own iron filings by cutting up fine steel wool into very small pieces with a scissors. Dip the lodestone into a pile of iron filings. The filings will cling in bunches at the various poles of the lodestone. Count the number of poles in

the lodestone. There should be an even number, with just as many north-seeking as south-seeking poles.

4. *Discover the law of magnetic attraction* · Let a magnet swing freely by cradling it in a piece of copper wire and connecting the wire with string to a ruler inserted into a pile of books (Figure 21–1). Bring the north-seeking

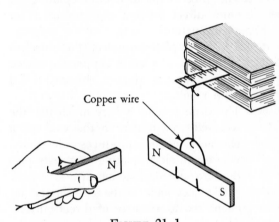

FIGURE 21–1.
LIKE POLES REPEL EACH OTHER, AND UNLIKE POLES ATTRACT EACH OTHER.

pole of another magnet near the north-seeking pole of the suspended magnet. Bring the two south-seeking poles together. Now bring the north-seeking pole of the magnet in your hand near the south-seeking pole of the suspended magnet. Note that like poles repel each other and unlike poles attract each other.

5. *Show magnetic fields and lines of force* · Place a sheet of cardboard or window glass over a bar magnet. Sprinkle iron filings or tiny bits of cut-up steel wool all over the cardboard, and then tap the cardboard gently a few times (Figure 21–2). The filings will rearrange them-

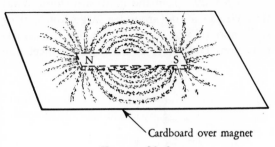

FIGURE 21-2.
LINES OF FORCE IN A MAGNETIC FIELD.

selves to form a definite pattern, showing the magnetic field and the lines of force located within the field. Note how the lines of force are concentrated at the poles.

Repeat the activity, using two bar magnets with the north-seeking pole of one bar magnet 5 centimeters (2 in) from the south-seeking pole of the other bar magnet (Figure 21-3). Note how the lines of force seem to attract each other. Repeat the activity, this time placing two like poles near each other. The lines of force show the repulsion between like poles.

6. *Discover that magnets can attract through nonmagnetic materials* · Place a cardboard on two piles of books set a short distance apart.

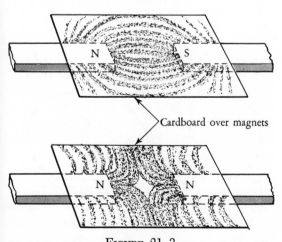

FIGURE 21-3.
LINES OF FORCE BETWEEN UNLIKE AND LIKE POLES.

Put some thumb tacks on the cardboard, and then slide a magnet along the underside of the cardboard (Figure 21-4). The magnet will attract the tacks and make them move. Repeat the activity, using sheets of glass, wood, aluminum foil, and cloth. Now use a sheet of iron, cut from a large "tin" can with tin snips. The tacks will not move because the force of the magnet passes into the iron, making it a magnet that attracts the tacks and holds them fast.

7. *Discover that a compass needle is a magnet* · Examine a compass. The end of the

FIGURE 21-4.
THE FORCE OF A MAGNET PASSES THROUGH NON-MAGNETIC MATERIALS.

needle that points to the north is usually colored blue or black and is called the north-seeking pole. Bring the north-seeking pole of a bar magnet near the compass. The north-seeking pole of the compass needle will be repelled while the south-seeking pole of the needle will be attracted. Point out that a compass needle can be used to determine the poles of an unmarked magnet.

8. *Investigate the nature of magnetism* · Fill a test tube half full of iron filings and stopper it. Stroke the test tube from end to end with one pole of a strong bar magnet about 20 times. Stroke slowly and gently **in one direction only**, being sure to lift your hand up in the air before coming down for another stroke. The test tube

[743

will now act like a magnet because you have lined up all the filings so that they behave just as the molecules in them would behave, with their north-seeking poles pointing in one direction and their south-seeking poles pointing in the opposite direction. Bring a compass near the test tube and determine the poles of this test-tube magnet (see Learning Activity 7 above).

Now shake the test tube vigorously for some time, and then test with the compass again. Mixing up the filings causes the test tube to lose its behavior as a magnet.

9. *Make a temporary magnet by induction* · Plunge one pole of a bar magnet into a pile of small tacks, and then lift up the magnet. There will be a cluster of tacks around the pole. Each tack becomes a magnet by induction and attracts other tacks. Note that this induced magnetism is temporary because as soon as the bar magnet is taken away, the tacks do not attract each other any more.

Hold a large iron nail or spike quite close to one pole of a strong bar magnet. Keeping the nail and magnet in this position, dip the nail into a pile of small tacks, and then lift up the nail (Figure 21–5). The nail has been magnetized by induction, without even touching the magnet, and attracts the tacks. The tacks in turn are also magnetized by induction. When the bar magnet is removed, the nail loses its magnetism and the tacks fall off.

10. *Make a temporary magnet by stroking* · Stroke a large iron nail or spike from end to end with one pole of a strong bar magnet about 20 times. Stroke slowly and gently **in one direction only**, being sure to lift your hand up in the air before coming down for another stroke (Figure 21–6). The nail will become a magnet and pick up iron filings or tacks. Set the nail aside for 3 to 4 days. Because the nail is made of soft iron, it will have lost most of its magnetism and it will pick up very few filings or tacks.

11. *Make a temporary magnet with electricity* · Obtain some insulated copper bell

wire (No. 20) from the hardware store. Wind this wire in a coil around a large iron nail or spike about 15 to 20 times. Remove the insulation from both ends of the wire, connect one

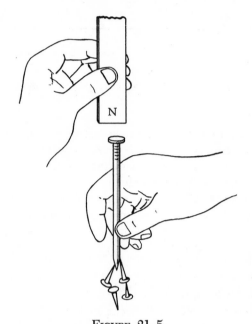

FIGURE 21–5.

THE NAIL ATTRACTS THE TACKS BECAUSE OF INDUCED MAGNETISM.

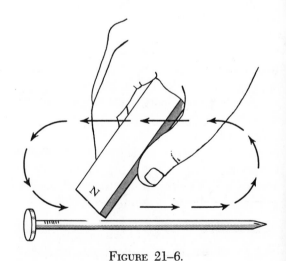

FIGURE 21–6.

THE NAIL BECOMES A TEMPORARY MAGNET WHEN STROKED WITH ONE POLE OF A BAR MAGNET.

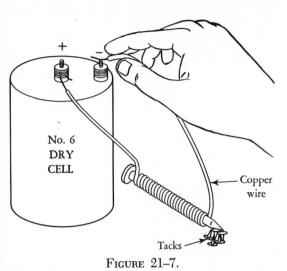

FIGURE 21–7.
AN ELECTROMAGNET IS A TEMPORARY MAGNET.

end to a terminal of a dry cell, and touch the other end to the second terminal for a few seconds (Figure 21–7). The nail will now pick up tacks and other objects made of iron or steel, and is called an electromagnet. When you remove the wire from one of the terminals, the electric current stops flowing and the nail loses its magnetism. (*Note:* Keep the wires connected to the dry cell for as short a time as possible. Otherwise the dry cell will be used up very quickly.)

12. *Make a permanent magnet by stroking* · Repeat Learning Activity 10 above, using a steel knitting needle instead of an iron nail. Note that the needle retains most of its magnetism after it has been set aside for 3 to 4 days.

Determine the poles of this magnetized needle by bringing a compass near it (see Learning Activity 7 above). Then cut the needle in half with cutting pliers. Each half will become a new magnet, with poles.

13. *Make a permanent magnet with electricity* · Obtain a cardboard tube, such as a mailing tube, about 25 centimeters (10 in) long and 2½ centimeters (1 in) in diameter. Obtain some insulated thin copper wire (No. 26 or 28)

from the hardware store. Wind the wire around the tube, covering almost all of the tube, leaving about 45 centimeters (18 in) of wire free at each end. Connect two dry cells in series, as shown in Figure 21–8. Place a steel knitting needle all the way into the cardboard tube. Now touch the two end wires to the terminals of the dry cells, as shown in the diagram, for 2 to 3 seconds only. Remove the needle and test it for magnetism on tacks and other iron or steel objects.

14. *Discover how magnets lose their magnetism* · Magnetize two large steel sewing needles by stroking them with one pole of a strong bar magnet, as described in Learning Activities 10 and 12 above. See how many iron filings or small tacks each needle will attract. Now hold one needle with forceps or pliers in the flame of a Bunsen burner or alcohol lamp for about 3 minutes. At the same time have one of the children pound the other needle repeatedly with a hammer. Now test both needles again to see how many iron filings each needle will attract. Point out that heating and striking or jarring a magnet will disarrange the molecules, causing the magnet to lose its magnetism.

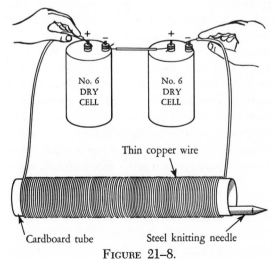

Thin copper wire

Cardboard tube   Steel knitting needle

FIGURE 21–8.
MAKING A STEEL KNITTING NEEDLE BECOME A
PERMANENT MAGNET.

[745

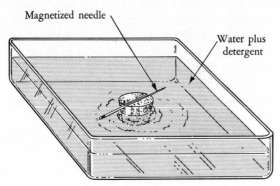

FIGURE 21–9.

A FLOATING, MAGNETIZED NEEDLE COMPASS.

15. *Observe that a freely moving magnet points north and south* · Set up a free-swinging bar magnet, as described in Learning Activity 4 above. Keep the magnet away from any objects made of iron or steel. The magnet will eventually come to rest with its north-seeking pole pointing to the north. Point out that this behavior is exactly like that of a compass needle.

16. *Make a floating compass* · Magnetize a steel sewing needle by stroking it with one pole of a strong bar magnet, as described in Learning Activities 10 and 12 above. Slice a round piece 13 millimeters (½ in) thick from a stopper. Cut a groove across the center of the top of the cork. Put the needle into the groove and place the cork into a glass, china, or aluminum dish filled with water (Figure 21–9). A teaspoon of detergent in the water will lower the surface tension of the water and prevent the cork from moving to one side of the dish and staying there. The needle will soon behave like a compass needle by assuming a north-south position because of the earth's magnetic field.

ELECTROMAGNETS

Note: Electromagnets draw a lot of current and can use up dry cells very quickly. When working with electromagnets, keep the wires connected to the dry cells for as short a time as possible.

1. *Observe that a wire carrying an electric current is magnetic* · Get some copper bell wire (No. 20) from the hardware store. Remove the insulation from both ends of the wire and connect one end to a terminal of a dry cell. Now touch the other bare end of the wire to the second terminal of the dry cell for a few seconds and try to pick up some iron filings or finely cut-up steel wool with the middle part of the wire (Figure 21–10). The wire will attract the filings, showing that a wire carrying an electric current has a magnetic field around. Place a compass beside the wire, and then touch the bare end of the wire to the terminal of the dry cell again. The compass needle will move, showing that the magnetic field around the wire affects the magnetized needle.

2. *Discover that a coil of wire carrying an electric current acts like a magnet* · Wrap bell wire (No. 20) about 15 to 20 times around a pencil to form a coil, and then remove the pencil. Remove the insulation from both ends

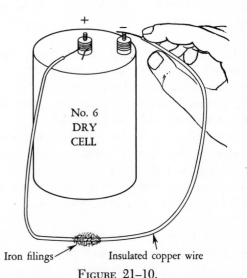

Iron filings   Insulated copper wire

FIGURE 21–10.

WIRE CARRYING ELECTRIC CURRENT ACTS LIKE A MAGNET.

of the wire, connect one end to a terminal of a dry cell, and touch the other end to the second terminal for a few seconds (Figure 21–11). The coil will act like a magnet, picking up tacks and other objects made of iron or steel.

Determine the poles of this coil magnet by bringing a compass near it. The blue or black end of the magnetized compass needle is a north-seeking pole, so it will be attracted to the coil magnet's south-seeking pole and repelled by the north-seeking pole. Repeat Learning Activity 5 of "magnetism" (p. 742) to show the magnetic field around the coil of wire.

3. *Make a simple electromagnet* · Repeat Learning Activity 11 of "Magnetism" (p. 744). Note that the coil of wire and nail together make a stronger magnet than just the coil of wire alone, which is described in Learning Activity 2 above. Determine the poles of the electromagnet by bringing a compass near it, also as described in Learning Activity 2 above. Now reverse the connections of the wires to the terminals of the dry cells. Note that this reverses the direction of the current flowing through the wire, which causes the poles of the electromagnet to reverse as well.

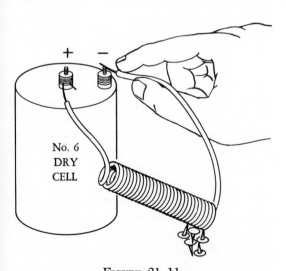

FIGURE 21–11.

A WIRE COIL CARRYING ELECTRIC CURRENT ACTS LIKE A MAGNET.

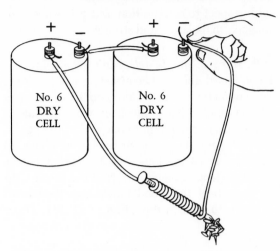

FIGURE 21–12.

INCREASING THE STRENGTH OF THE ELECTRIC CURRENT MAKES THE ELECTROMAGNET STRONGER.

4. *Making an electromagnet stronger* · Make an electromagnet as described in Learning Activity 3 above, winding the wire around the nail exactly 20 times. Count the number of tacks the electromagnet will attract. Now wind 20 more turns of wire around the same nail and again count the number of tacks the electromagnet will pick up. Doubling the number of turns will double the strength of the electromagnet.

Make another electromagnet with just 20 turns of wire and count the number of tacks it will pick up. Now connect the electromagnet to two dry cells aranged in series (Figure 21–12) and again count the number of tacks that will be attracted. Doubling the strength of the electric current will double the strength of the electromagnet. Have the children predict (and test) what will happen when both the number of turns and the strength of the electric current are doubled.

5. *Compare the electromagnet and the regular magnet* · Discuss the ways in which electromagnets are similar to and different from regular magnets. Compare their similarities with respect to polarity, magnetic field, and kinds of materials they will attract. Compare their differences

with respect to composition and permanence of magnetism, polarity, and strength.

6. *Make a simple telegraph set* · Obtain a wood board about 30 centimeters (12 in) long, 20 centimeters (8 in) wide, and 13 millimeters (½ in) thick. Nail a block of wood about 7½ centimeters (3 in) high to one end of the board. Use tin snips to cut a strip of iron about 10 centimeters (4 in) long and 2½ centimeters (1 in) wide from a metal can. Nail the metal strip to the top of the wood block, and then bend it down to form a dip (Figure 21–13). Drive

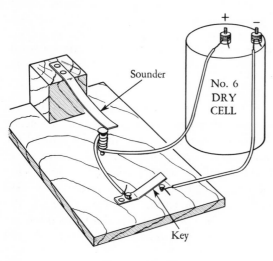

FIGURE 21–13.
A SIMPLE TELEGRAPH SET.

a long nail with a large head (roofing nail) into the board so that its head is just below the metal strip. This part of the set is called the sounder.

Now make a telegraph key. Nail one end of a second metal strip to the board, using two nails but driving one only partially into the board. Bend the strip back so that it angles away from the board. Drive a smaller roofing nail partially into the board so that its head is under the metal strip. Now wire the key and sounder, as shown in the diagram, using about 50 turns of wire around the nail. When you press the key, the sounder will click. (You may

have to adjust the distance between the bent metal strip and the nail head of the sounder. If the click is faint, use two dry cells connected in series, as shown in Figure 21–12.)

Detailed instructions for making a variety of single and two-way telegraph sets may be found in the reference and source books listed at the end of this chapter and in Chapter 7, "Materials for Teaching Science."

7. *Investigate uses of electromagnets* · Have the children read and discuss uses of electromagnets in industry and the home.

STATIC ELECTRICITY

Note: Learning Activities in static electricity should be conducted in the winter when the days are dry and cold.

1. *Discover that friction produces static electricity* · Rub a hard rubber comb briskly with wool cloth. The comb will pick up small bits of paper. Rub a blown-up balloon with the wool and put the balloon against the wall. It will stick to the wall. In each case electrons are rubbed off the wool onto the objects, charging the objects negatively and the wool positively. Hold the balloon over very fine sand. You will hear and see the sand being attracted to the balloon.

2. *Investigate the nature of static electricity* · Repeat Learning Activity 9 of "The Structure of Matter," Chapter 16 (p. 630) on the structure of the atom. Show how electrons can be added or removed to make an atom negatively or positively charged.

3. *Discover the law of electrostatic attraction and repulsion* · Blow up two balloons to the same size and suspend each balloon from a string so that they are 2½ centimeters (1 in) apart. Rub each balloon briskly with a wool cloth. The balloons will become negatively charged and repel each other (Figure 21–14).

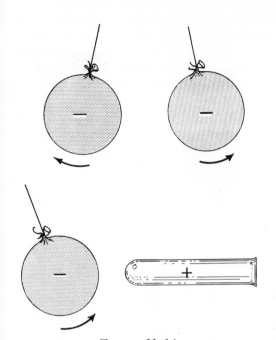

FIGURE 21–14.
LIKE CHARGES REPEL EACH OTHER; UNLIKE CHARGES ATTRACT EACH OTHER.

Now rub a narrow glass jar or a test tube with nylon or a plastic bag and bring the jar near each of the balloons. The jar, having become positively charged, will attract the negatively charged balloons.

4. *Investigate some effects of static electricity* · Charge a comb by rubbing it briskly with a wool cloth. Allow a thin stream of water to flow from the faucet, and then hold the comb near the water. The stream will be attracted by the comb and bend towards it.

Charge a balloon by rubbing it briskly with wool cloth. Pass the balloon over a child's head and cause the hair to stand on end.

Rub a fluorescent light tube briskly with a piece of nylon or silk in a completely darkened room or closet. The fluorescent tube will glow faintly.

5. *Observe the effect of charged materials upon uncharged materials* · Cut out a piece 6 millimeters (¼ in) thick from a styrofoam ball.

(A pith ball of the same size can be obtained from a scientific supply house.) Suspend the styrofoam from a silk or nylon thread. Charge a comb negatively by rubbing it briskly with a wool cloth, and then bring the comb near the styrofoam (Figure 21–15). The styrofoam will be attracted to the comb because the negatively charged comb repels electrons from the side of the styrofoam nearest the comb, leaving this side positively charged. Now touch the styrofoam with the negatively charged comb. Electrons will flow into the styrofoam, making the styrofoam negatively charged, and the styrofoam will be repelled by the comb.

Charge a glass test tube positively by rubbing it with a plastic bag or nylon. Make the

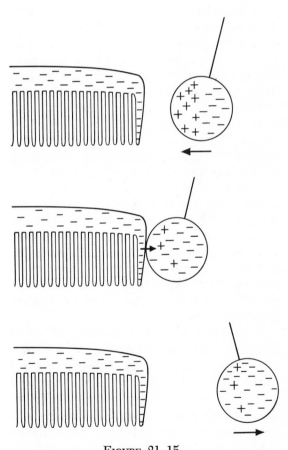

FIGURE 21–15.
A CHARGED BODY FIRST ATTRACTS, THEN REPELS, AN UNCHARGED BODY.

styrofoam neutral again by touching it with your fingers. Bring the positively charged test tube near the neutral styrofoam. The styrofoam will be attracted to the test tube because the positively charged test tube attracts electrons to the side of the styrofoam nearest the test tube, making this side negatively charged. Now touch the styrofoam with the positively charged test tube. Electrons will flow from the styrofoam into the test tube, leaving the styrofoam positively charged, and the styrofoam will be repelled by the test tube.

6. *Make an electroscope (electrical-charge detector)* · Obtain a bottle with a narrow neck and a cork stopper to fit. Obtain some insulated copper bell wire (No. 20) from the hardware store. Use an ice pick to make a small hole through the stopper. Force a piece of the bell wire, with all its insulation removed, through the stopper. Make an angular bend at the lower end of the wire and wind the upper end into a close circular coil (Figure 21–16). Hang a strip of thin aluminum foil about 7½ centimeters (3 in) long and 5 millimeters (¼ in) thick over the angular bend of wire. The foil can be obtained from a chewing gum wrapper by soaking the wrapper in rubbing alcohol and then working the foil loose. Press the cork firmly into the neck of the bottle.

Now charge a comb negatively by rubbing it briskly with a wool cloth. Touch the comb to the wire coil on top, rubbing it back and forth a few times. Electrons will leave the comb and flow down the wire into the aluminum halves, charging them negatively and causing them to spread apart because they repel each other. Remove the comb.

The electroscope is now charged and can be used to direct and determine the unknown charges on other objects. Bring a charged object near (but not touching) the wire coil at the top. If the charged object is negative, more electrons will be repelled from the coil down into the aluminum halves. The aluminum halves will become more negatively charged and will spread farther apart. On the other hand, if the charged object is positive, some

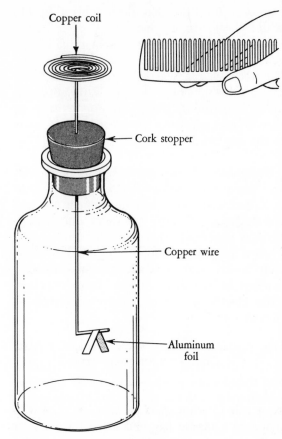

FIGURE 21–16.

AN ELECTRICAL CHARGE DETECTOR (ELECTROSCOPE).

electrons from the aluminum halves will be attracted up to the coil on top. The aluminum halves will now become less negatively charged and will come closer together.

To discharge the electroscope, touch the wire coil at the top with your fingers. Touching the coil allows electrons to leave the aluminum halves and travel through the wire, into your body, and then to the ground. The aluminum halves become neutral and collapse together.

7. *Discover that only nonconductors build up electrostatic charges* · Charge a blown-up balloon by rubbing it with wool and determine its charge with an electroscope, as described in Learning Activity 6 above. Repeat, using a

glass test tube that has been rubbed briskly with a plastic bag or nylon.

Now rub metal objects, such as nails and coins, and bring them near the electroscope. No static charge will be detected. Point out that good conductors, like metals, do not build up an electrostatic charge because, as soon as they acquire electrons, they conduct electrons to the ground.

8. *Produce electric sparks by static electricity* · Have the children shuffle across the rug in a darkened room, and then touch a metal object. In addition to the shock, an electric spark is produced. The same effect is created when a blown-up balloon is charged by rubbing briskly with a wool cloth and then is touched to the metal object. Point out that static electricity has now been converted to current electricity.

9. *Explore lightning and thunder* · Have the children read and discuss how lightning and thunder are produced. Compare lightning and thunder with the electric spark and crackle produced in Learning Activity 8 above. Draw diagrams to show how lightning is produced within a cloud, from cloud to cloud, from cloud to ground, and from ground to cloud.

10. *List some common occurrences of static electricity* · Have the children describe and list common static electricity phenomena they have seen or that can occur at home or school and in an automobile.

CURRENT ELECTRICITY

1. *Investigate the nature of current electricity* · Repeat Learning Activity 9 of "The Structure of Matter," Chapter 16 (p. 630) on the structure of the atom. Show how the flow of electrons from atom to atom within a material constitutes an electric current.

2. *Make a simple electric circuit* · Obtain a No. 6 dry cell, insulated copper bell wire (No.

20), a one-cell flashlight bulb, and a small porcelain socket to hold the bulb from a scientific supply house or a hardware store. Set up a simple electric circuit, as shown in Figure 21–17, being sure to remove the insulation from the ends of the wires. Trace the flow of current through the completed circuit. Now

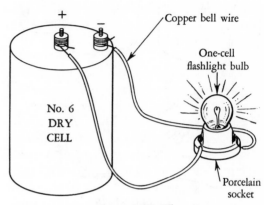

FIGURE 21–17.
A SIMPLE ELECTRIC CIRCUIT.

break the circuit by disconnecting one of the wires attached to the dry cell or porcelain socket.

3. *Compare conductors and nonconductors* · Connect a dry cell, copper bell wire (No. 20), one-cell flashlight bulb, and porcelain socket as shown in Figure 21–18, being sure to remove the insulation from the ends of the wires. Touch the bare ends of the two wires to a nail, the metal part of a pen or pencil, various coins, aluminum foil, and pieces of wood, rubber, cloth, and glass. Note which kinds of materials do and do not conduct electricity. Establish the relationship between electrical conductivity and how tightly or loosely the atoms hold some of their electrons.

4. *Investigate the switch* · Get a knife switch from the hardware store or scientific supply house. Insert the switch into the simple electric circuit described in Learning Activity 2 above (Figure 21–19). Operate the switch and show

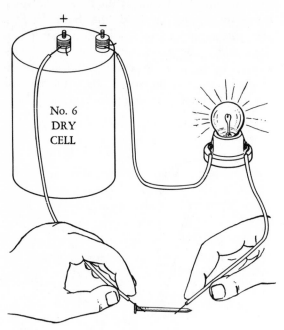

FIGURE 21–18.

A NAIL IS A GOOD CONDUCTOR OF ELECTRICITY.

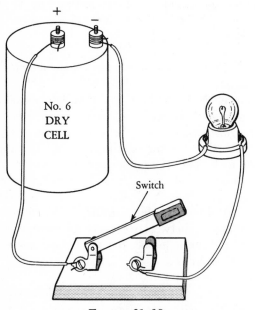

FIGURE 21–19.

A KNIFE SWITCH CAN OPEN AND CLOSE AN ELEC-
TRIC CIRCUIT.

how it closes and opens the circuit. Replace the knife switch with a pushbutton switch and a snap switch.

Make your own switch by cutting a strip of metal, 10 centimeters (4 in) long and 2½ centimeters (1 in) wide, with tin snips from a can. Nail one end to a small board. Use two nails, but drive one only partially into the board. Bend the strip back so that it angles away from the board. Drive a small roofing nail partially into the board so that its head is under the metal strip. Now insert this homemade switch into your simple circuit, as shown in Figure 21–20.

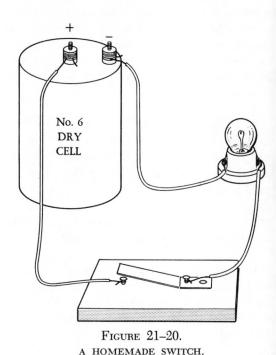

FIGURE 21–20.

A HOMEMADE SWITCH.

Operate the switch to open and close the circuit.

5. *Compare appliances in series and in parallel* · Connect three porcelain sockets and one-cell flashlight bulbs in series, as shown in Figure 21–21. Note that the electric current flows through each bulb, one after the other, and the bulbs light up dimly. Unscrewing one

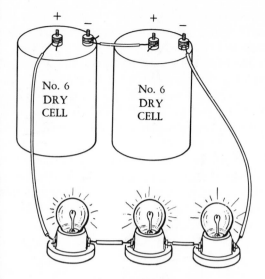

FIGURE 21–21.
FLASHLIGHT BULBS CONNECTED IN SERIES.

that the current branches off so that part of the current goes through one socket and part goes on to the next socket. Note how brightly lighted all the bulbs are. Unscrewing one of the bulbs will break only that part of the circuit that flows through the bulb so that the remaining two bulbs continue to stay lighted. If you unscrew a second bulb, the third bulb will still continue to burn.

6. *Produce a short circuit* · Make a simple circuit as described in Learning Activity 2 above. However, remove some insulation from the middle of each wire so that the bare wires are exposed. Place the blade of a screw driver across both bare wires, **only for a second or two,** and the bulb will go out (Figure 21–23).

of the bulbs will break the complete circuit so that the other bulbs go out.

Now connect the sockets and bulbs in parallel as shown in Figure 21–22. Point out

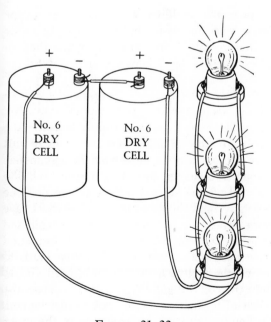

FIGURE 21–22.
FLASHLIGHT BULBS CONNECTED IN PARALLEL.

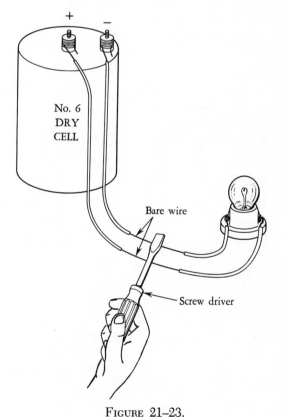

FIGURE 21–23.
THE BLADE OF THE SCREWDRIVER PRODUCES A SHORT CIRCUIT.

Trace the shorter path (or circuit) that the electric current now travels. Produce a short circuit again by pressing the bare wires together with your fingers, and feel how hot the wires become.

7. *Show how a fuse works* · Make a short circuit setup as described in Learning Activity 6 above. However, use two dry cells in series, place a two-cell flashlight bulb in the socket, and insert a homemade fuse (Figure 21–24). To make the homemade fuse, obtain two thumb tacks and two paper clips, and press them into one end of a small wood board so the clips are upright and 2½ centimeters (1 in) apart. Cut a narrow strip of aluminum foil and insert it between the paper clips. When you produce a short circuit by placing the blade of a screw driver across the bare wires, the aluminum foil will melt and break the circuit. (If the room is darkened, you may see the aluminum glow as it becomes hot and melts.)

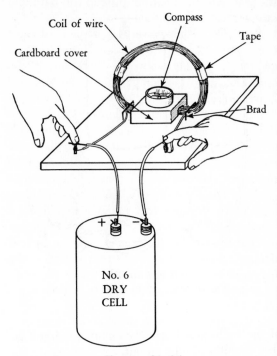

FIGURE 21–25.

A CURRENT DETECTOR (GALVANOMETER).

Have the children examine a screw-type house fuse and note the short strip of easily melted metal in the fuse. Compare the appearance of a fresh and a burned-out fuse.

8. *Make a galvanometer (current detector)* · Obtain some insulated thin copper wire (No. 26 or 28) from a scientific supply house or the hardware store. Wind about 100 turns of this wire around a glass jar, about 7½ centimeters (3 in) in diameter, to form a narrow coil. Slip the coil off the jar and tape it at two or three points to hold the wires neatly in place. Leave some wire free at each end of the coil and remove 2½ centimeters (1 in) of insulation from each end of the wire. Use two brads to attach the coil to a small wood board and to hold the coil upright (Figure 21–25). Place the cover of a small cardboard box inside the coil, first cutting grooves on each side of the cover so that it will rest in a stable and even position on the board. Drive two small nails almost all

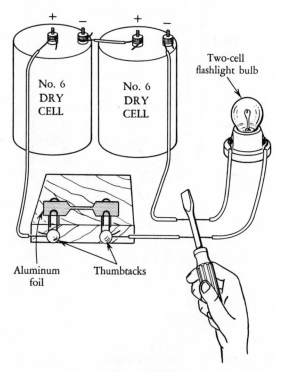

FIGURE 21–24.

A HOMEMADE FUSE.

the way into the board and wrap the bare end of each wire around a nail.

Now rest a compass on top of the cardboard cover, and turn the board until the compass needle is parallel with the direction of the coil. Then turn the compass until the N and S letters are under the needle. Your galvanometer is now ready to operate. Connect a dry cell to the galvanometer by touching the bare ends of the wires from the dry cell to the nails of the galvanometer. The compass needle will be deflected, showing the presence of an electric current. Point out that, when an electric current flows through the galvanometer coil, a magnetic field is formed that affects the magnetized compass needle. The greater the current flowing through the coil, the stronger the magnetic field will be, and the more the compass needle will be deflected.

9. *Investigate electrical units of measure* · Have the children examine electrical appliances in the home (such as light bulbs, toasters, heaters, and motors) and list the number of watts printed on each appliance. Have the children calculate the current each appliance will draw, assuming that 120 volts is being used. Then let them find the resistance of each appliance.

Have the children observe an electric meter when electricity is passing through it. Study the units on each dial and develop an understanding of the watt, kilowatt, and kilowatt-hour.

10. *Make a simple electric cell* · Dissolve a tablespoon of common table salt in a glass tumbler of warm water. Obtain a metal washer, a penny, and two lengths of insulated copper bell wire (No. 20). Strip 7½ centimeters (3 in) of insulation from one end of each wire and 2½ centimeters (1 in) from the other end. Wrap the penny and the washer separately with the longer bare end of the wire and suspend them in the salt water by bending the wires tightly over the edge of the tumbler (Figure 21–26). Make sure that the coin and the washer are not touching each other. Now touch the other ends of the wires to the nails of the galvanometer

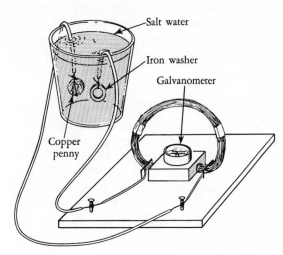

FIGURE 21–26.
A SIMPLE ELECTRIC WET CELL.

described in Learning Activity 8 above. The compass needle will be deflected, showing the presence of an electric current. Repeat the activity, using other combinations of two different metals. Point out that chemical energy has been changed into electrical energy.

11. *Examine a dry cell* · Cut a used-up dry cell lengthwise in half with a hack saw. Examine each part and discuss its function.

12. *Examine a storage and a nickel-cadmium battery* · Examine a 12-volt auto storage battery and a nickel-cadmium battery. Draw a diagram of their parts, and compare their function. Note that these batteries, unlike dry cells, can be recharged.

13. *Generate electricity with a magnet and a coil of wire* · Wind about 50 turns of insulated copper bell wire (No. 20) around a glass jar, about 5–7½ centimeters (2–3 in) in diameter, to form a coil. Slip the coil off the jar and tape it at a few points to hold the wires neatly in place. Leave 1 meter (3 ft) of wire free at each end of the coil and remove the insulation from the end of each wire. Connect the coil to a galvanometer (described in Learning Activity 8 above) as shown in Figure

21–27. Hold the coil as far away from the galvanometer as possible and move the center of the coil across a bar magnet. The compass needle of the galvanometer will be deflected,

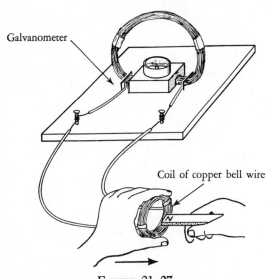

FIGURE 21–27.

GENERATING ELECTRICITY WITH A MAGNET AND COIL OF WIRE.

showing the presence of an electric current. When you move the coil in the opposite direction, the needle is also deflected in the opposite direction. When you hold the coil stationary, there is no deflection because no lines of force in the magnetic field are being cut. When you move the coil continuously back and forth across the magnet, a continuous alternating current is produced. Repeat the learning activity, this time holding the coil stationary and moving the magnet. Point out that mechanical energy is being changed into electrical energy.

14. *Make a model generator* · Detailed instructions for making a variety of simple generators may be found in the reference and source books listed at the end of this chapter and in Chapter 7, "Materials for Teaching Science."

15. *Investigate the photoelectric and photoresistive cell* · Bring in a camera with a built-in

light meter and explain the operation of both the photoelectric and photoresistive cell. Use a light meter to measure the illumination at different parts of the classroom and the school building.

16. *Make a thermocouple* · Cut off a piece of wire from a coat hanger and scrape the paint away from both ends. Obtain two pieces of copper bell wire (No. 20) and remove the insulation from the ends of both wires. Tightly twist together one end of a copper wire to each end of the coat hanger wire and connect the other free ends of each copper wire to a galvanometer (described in Learning Activity 8 above). Now place one of the twisted ends into a glass tumbler containing cold water and ice cubes, and heat the other twisted end with the flame of an alcohol lamp or Bunsen burner (Figure 21–28). The compass needle of the galvanometer will be deflected, showing the presence of an electric current. Heat energy has been changed into electrical energy.

17. *Make a model electric motor* · Detailed instructions for making a variety of simple

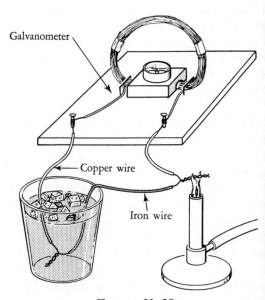

FIGURE 21–28.

GENERATING ELECTRICITY WITH A THERMOCOUPLE.

Model motors may be found in the reference and source books listed at the end of this chapter and in Chapter 7.

18. *Discover that electricity can plate materials* · Get some copper sulfate crystals, some dilute sulfuric acid, and a copper strip from your high school chemistry teacher. Put a heaping tablespoon of copper sulfate into a glass tumbler of warm water and stir vigorously until the copper sulfate dissolves. Then add a few drops of the sulfuric acid. Obtain two pieces of copper bell wire (No. 20), each piece ⅔ meter (26 in) long. Remove quite a bit of the insulation from the end of one piece of wire and wrap a few turns of bare wire around one end of the copper strip, making sure you have a good contact between the strip and the wire. Bend the copper strip so it will hang over a pencil placed across the rim of the tumbler (Figure 21–29).

Wrap the bare end of the second piece of wire around a house key and suspend the key in the copper sulfate solution by wrapping the wire around the pencil. Now connect the other bare ends of both wires to two dry cells connected in series, as shown in the diagram, making sure that the key is connected to a negative terminal and the copper strip is connected to a positive terminal. Allow the current to flow for 15 minutes, and then disconnect the wires and remove the key. The key will be coated with copper.

19. *Discuss uses of electricity* · Have the children read and discuss how electricity is converted to motion, heat, light, and sound in the home, school, and in industry. Let them make a list of all the appliances they can think of that make use of electricity.

20. *List safety rules* · Have the children make either one composite or several individual lists of safety rules for using and handling electric appliances, wires, switches, and fuses.

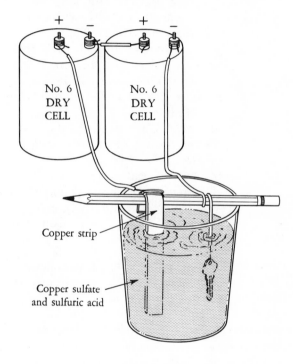

FIGURE 21–29.

COATING A KEY WITH COPPER.

BIBLIOGRAPHY FOR "MAGNETISM AND ELECTRICITY"

ADLER, IRVING. *Electricity in Your Life.* New York: John Day, 1965. 128 pp.

——, and RUTH ADLER. *Magnets.* New York: John Day, 1966. 48 pp.

ASIMOV, ISAAC. *How Did We Find Out About Electricity?* New York: Walker, 1973. 64 pp.

HALL, JAMES P. *Exploring and Understanding Electricity.* Westchester, Ill.: Benefic Press, 1971. 96 pp.

HOLDEN, RAYMOND. *Magnetism.* New York: Golden Press, 1963. 64 pp.

KNIGHT, DAVID C. *Let's Find Out About Magnets.* New York: Franklin Watts, 1967. 55 pp.

LIEBERG, OWEN S. *Wonders of Magnets and Magnetism.* New York: Dodd, Mead, 1967. 64 pp.

MARCUS, ABRAHAM, and REBECCA B. MARCUS. *Power Unlimited!* Englewood Cliffs, N.J.: Prentice-Hall, 1962. 152 pp.

PAGE, ROBERT MORRIS. *The Origin of Radar.* Garden City, N.Y.: Doubleday, 1962. 196 pp.

PINE, TILLIE S., and JOSEPH LEVINE. *Electricity and How We Use It.* New York: McGraw-Hill, 1962. 48 pp.

PODENDORF, ILLA. *The True Book of Magnets and Electricity.* Chicago: Childrens Press, 1961. 47 pp.

SACHS, RAYMOND. *Magnets.* New York: Coward-McCann, 1967. 48 pp.

SCHNEIDER, HERMAN, and NINA SCHNEIDER. *More Power to You.* Chicago: Scott, Foresman, 1961. 128 pp.

SEEMAN, BERNARD. *The Story of Electricity and Magnetism.* Irvington-on-Hudson, N.Y.: Harvey House, 1967. 124 pp.

SHEPHERD, WALTER. *Electricity.* New York: John Day, 1964. 48 pp.

SOOTIN, HARRY. *Experiments with Electric Currents.* New York: W. W. Norton, 1970. 88 pp.

STONE, A. HARRIS, and BERTRAM M. SIEGEL. *Turned On: A Look at Electricity.* Englewood Cliffs, N.J.: Prentice-Hall, 1970. 64 pp.

VEGLAHN, NANCY. *Coils, Magnets, and Rings: Michael Faraday's World.* New York: Coward, McCann, & Geoghegan, 1976. 64 pp.

VICTOR, EDWARD. *Electricity.* Chicago: Follett, 1967. 32 pp.

——. *Exploring and Understanding Magnets and Electromagnets.* Westchester, Ill.: Benefic Press, 1967. 96 pp.

——. *Magnets.* Chicago: Follett, 1962. 32 pp.

APPENDIX
COMMON LABORATORY EQUIPMENT

GRADUATED
CYLINDER

ROUND BOTTOM
FLASK

FLAT BOTTOM
FLASK

ERLENMEYER
FLASK

FUNNEL

BEAKER

TEST
TUBE

THISTLE
TUBE

TEST TUBE
BRUSH

CRUCIBLE
AND COVER

PLAIN
MICROSCOPE SLIDE

SQUARE & ROUND
COVER GLASS

WATCH
GLASS

1-HOLE
RUBBER STOPPER

FROSTED END
MICROSCOPE SLIDE

PETRI
DISH

PORCELAIN
EVAPORATING DISH

2-HOLE
RUBBER STOPPER

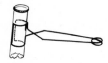
TEST TUBE
CLAMP (METAL)

PIPE-STEM
TRIANGLE

WIRE GAUZE
(ASBESTOS CENTER)

ELECTRIC
KNIFE SWITCH

TEST TUBE
CLAMP (WOOD)

TEST TUBE
RACK

DRY CELL
NO. 6

ELECTRIC LIGHT
RECEPTACLE

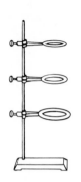

RING STAND
AND RINGS

BURET CLAMP

RIGHT ANGLE
CLAMP

SPRING
TUBING CLAMP

SCREW
TUBING CLAMP

TRIPOD

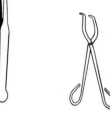

FORCEPS

TONGS

TIN SNIPS

SPATULA

ROUND FILE

TRIANGULAR FILE

FLAT FILE

GOOSENECK
LAMP

SPRING
BALANCE

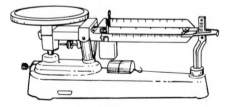

TRIPLE-BEAM BALANCE

ALCOHOL
LAMP

BURNER
WING TOP

BUNSEN
BURNER

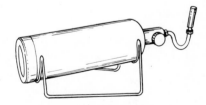

LIQUEFIED PETROLEUM
GAS (PROPANE) BURNER

INDEX

D

TABLES OF WEIGHTS AND MEASURES

METRIC UNITS	ENGLISH UNITS

LENGTH

10 millimeters (mm) = 1 centimeter (cm)	12 inches (in) = 1 foot (ft)
100 centimeters (cm) = 1 meter (m)	3 feet (ft) = 1 yard (yd)
1,000 millimeters (mm) = 1 meter (m)	1,760 yards (yd) = 1 mile (mi)
1,000 meters (m) = 1 kilometer (km)	5,280 feet (ft) = 1 mile (mi)

LIQUID VOLUME

1,000 milliliters (ml) = 1 liter (l)	16 ounces (oz) = 1 pint (pt)
1,000 liters (l) = 1 kiloliter (kl)	2 pints (pt) = 1 quart (qt)
	4 quarts (qt) = 1 gallon (gal)
	128 ounces (oz) = 1 gallon (gal)
	8 pints (pt) = 1 gallon (gal)

DRY VOLUME

1,000 cubic millimeters (mm³) = 1 cubic centimeter (cm³)	1,728 cubic inches (cu in) = 1 cubic foot (cu
1,000,000 cubic centimeters (cm³) = 1 cubic meter (m³)	27 cubic feet (cu ft) = 1 cubic yard (cu
	46,656 cubic inches (cu in) = 1 cubic yard (cu

WEIGHT

1,000 milligrams (mg) = 1 gram (g)	16 ounces (oz) = 1 pound (lb)
1,000 grams (g) = 1 kilogram (kg)	2,000 pounds (lb) = 1 ton
1,000 kilograms (kg) = 1 metric ton	

METRIC PREFIX MEANINGS

kilo- = one thousand

deci- = one tenth

centi- = one hundredth

milli- = one thousandth

micro- = one millionth